International GAAP® 2012

Generally Accepted Accounting Practice
under International Financial Reporting Standards

Elizer Baltazar   Emily Moll
Martin Beyersdorff   Richard Moore
Mike Bonham   Victoria O'Leary
Angela Covic   Margaret Pankhurst
Matthew Curtis   Inayatullah Qureshi
Tai Danmola   Hedy Richards
Mike Davies   Tim Rogerson
Tim Denton   Anna Sirocka
Joanna Frykowska   Tracey Waring

ERNST &
Quality In Eve

WILEY
ley and Sons, Ltd, Publication

About this book

International GAAP® 2012 has been fully revised and updated in order to:

- Deal with all new and amended authoritative pronouncements, including the new standards on Consolidated Financial Statements (IFRS 10), Joint Arrangements (IFRS 11), Disclosure of Interests in Other Entities (IFRS 12) and Fair Value Measurement (IFRS 13) and revisions to standards including Financial Instruments (IFRS 9), Presentation of Financial Statements (IAS 1), Income Taxes (IAS 12), Employee Benefits (IAS 19), Separate Financial Statements (IAS 27) and Investments in Associates and Joint Ventures (IAS 28).

- Explain the many initiatives that are currently being pursued by the IASB and IFRS Interpretations Committee and that will lead to changes in accounting requirements. In particular, projects on Revenue Recognition, Leases, Financial Statement Presentation, Financial Instruments and Insurance Contracts may all significantly change current accounting practices.

- Provide insight and guidance on the interpretation and practical application of IFRS from a truly global perspective, based on the experience of the book's authors in dealing with recent day-to-day practical issues.

In this edition we have, for the first time, included the chapters on financial instruments and insurance contracts in a separate volume.

The book is published in three volumes, comprising 53 chapters, three indexes and detailed lists of contents and examples for each chapter. These are split between the three volumes as follows:

Volume 1

- Chapters 1 to 21, each preceded by a detailed list of contents and examples
- Index of extracts from financial statements
- Index of standards
- Index

Volume 2

- Chapters 22 to 41, each preceded by a detailed list of contents and examples
- Index of extracts from financial statements
- Index of standards
- Index

Volume 3

- Chapters 42 to 53, each preceded by a detailed list of contents and examples
- Index of extracts from financial statements
- Index of standards
- Index.

Preface

2011 was a milestone year for the International Accounting Standards Board (IASB). The end of June saw the retirement of Sir David Tweedie, the IASB's chairman for the ten years since its inception. During that decade, IFRS has become the predominant globally recognised accounting language in most major capital markets.

This represents a considerable achievement by all concerned: the European Union, whose leaders had the vision to set the agenda for a common financial reporting regime across the EU; the former Board of the International Accounting Standards Committee (IASC), who undertook the core standards programme that laid the groundwork for global acceptance of international standards; the many countries throughout the world whose standard-setters have contributed to the work of the IASC and the IASB; the members of the IASB; and the large number of governments that have recognised the value of a common financial reporting regime and adopted IFRS. We must in particular recognise the enormous contribution made by Sir David Tweedie.

Yet the past year has been difficult for standard-setters. There has been slow progress on key accounting standards (those relating to financial instruments, revenue and leasing) and there is still uncertainty about the adoption of IFRS by the United States. The US Securities and Exchange Commission (SEC) is still expected in 2011 to set out its views on the role of IFRS in the US. As part of its fact-gathering and analysis, the SEC staff has put forward a potential mechanism for incorporating IFRS into US GAAP, suggesting that the FASB could incorporate newly issued or amended IFRSs into US GAAP without any 'first-time adoption'. Although this is only one of a number of possible methods of incorporation, it indicates a willingness by the SEC to consider approaches that, at best, could extend for many years the period until there is a single set of global standards.

Sir David has been succeeded by Hans Hoogervorst as chairman, with Ian Mackintosh as vice-chairman. Hopefully the combination of political and technical skills held by this new leadership team will enable it to navigate the choppy waters ahead. In his first speech in the US since his appointment, Hans Hoogervorst made an appeal to the SEC to come to a positive decision on adopting IFRS. He noted that it was difficult to imagine that the United States would intentionally choose to discard international leadership in something as fundamental as financial reporting. We continue to await the SEC's decision with much interest. Constituents still recognise the benefits that would accrue from a single set of global accounting standards and continue to press the IASB and FASB ('the Boards') to move forward. Looking ahead, though, it seems less clear in 2011 that the goal of the single global accounting language will come about in the form that was originally envisaged.

Meanwhile, hopes that the global economy would recover have not been fulfilled. Economic growth in many of those countries that have experienced recession is weak at best and there remain fears that some will succumb to a 'double dip' recession. In Europe, the banking crisis of 2008/2009 has been followed by a sovereign debt crisis as some governments have been unable to reduce debts to levels that are considered sustainable. This, in turn, has resulted in a crisis of confidence that spreads far beyond the countries directly affected to other economies and businesses and has put further pressure on the banking system. Unsurprisingly, there has been debate over the part that financial reporting requirements may have played in the recent turbulent times. The continuing crisis draws attention to the slow progress by the Boards in developing accounting standards for financial instruments that are simpler to apply and to understand but, at the same time, better reflect the risks undertaken by entities. The delay is not surprising; these are difficult matters for which there are no easy solutions and there has been a commendable level of consultation with users, regulators, accountants and affected entities.

2011 has also seen the launch of the IASB's first formal agenda consultation. This acknowledges that preparers and users of financial statements have had to deal with many changes during the last ten years and that new standards already in progress will involve major effort. Moreover, there are now many more users of IFRS financial statements and these users may have views about the priorities that should be set for the future. We support the agenda consultation process as it allows the IASB to receive views from a wide range of constituents, in addition to creating further transparency around the IASB's agenda-setting process and it is to be hoped that there is a positive response. We believe that the agenda should focus on the following key strategic areas:

- The IASB should step back and focus on the long-term goals of IFRS. The IASB has the opportunity to re-assess the strategic direction of IFRS as a valuable tool for financial reporting. The most important project would be a long-term analysis of the future of performance reporting which would consider IFRS financial statements as a whole and their usefulness to decision-makers. This will help to enhance confidence in the relevance of IFRS financial statements for both users and preparers.

- A period of calm is needed. Preparers and users of financial statements need time to implement and digest the new standards that will have been completed by the end of 2012.

- There is an opportunity to focus on post-implementation reviews and ensuring that standards are consistently applied and interpreted. However, further efforts are needed in addition to post-implementation reviews to ensure the continued value, usefulness and consistency of IFRS into the future. These key steps include providing interpretations (or application guidance where needed) at a global level through greater use of the IFRS Interpretations Committee and engaging regulators in the standard-setting process.

With a new chairman and vice-chairman and much of its existing work program near completion, there is a momentous opportunity for the IASB to reshape the IFRS brand for the future. Now is the time to take big strategic decisions rather than simply prioritising a list of separate projects. We encourage the IASB to be bold.

****

We are deeply indebted to many of our colleagues within the global organisation of Ernst & Young for their selfless assistance and support in the publication of this book. It has been a truly international effort, with valuable contributions from Ernst & Young people around the globe.

Our thanks go particularly to those who reviewed, edited and assisted in the preparation of drafts, most notably: Justine Belton, Doug Cameron, Sonja Carshagen, Tony Clifford, Garth Coppin, Michael Elliot, Charlie Feeney, Ann Gillan, Peter Gittens, John Guess, Paul Hebditch, Danial Jabbar, Parbin Khatun, Kevin Kispert, Michiel van der Lof, Robert McCracken, Lan Ming, John O'Grady, Eric Ohlund, Shannon O'Mahony, Robert Overend, Ruth Picker, Christoph Piesbergen, Gerard van Santen, Jeffrey Schaeffer, Ken Smith, Alison Spivey, Leo van der Tas, Lynda Tomkins, Hans van der Veen, Paul Wallek and Allister Wilson.

Within the Financial Reporting Group itself, our thanks go to everyone who directly and indirectly contributed to the book's creation: Denise Brand, Robin Chatterjee, Larissa Connor, Julie Dempers, Sharon Johal, Bernd Kremp, Amanda Marrion, Claire Taylor, Sarah Vinall and Lawrence Wong.

We also thank Jeremy Gugenheim for his assistance with the production technology throughout the period of writing.

London,
October 2011

Elizer Baltazar	Joanna Frykowska	Inayatullah Qureshi
Martin Beyersdorff	Kevin Guckian	Hedy Richards
Mike Bonham	Meredith Lloyd	Tim Rogerson
Angela Covic	James Luke	Anna Sirocka
Matthew Curtis	Emily Moll	Tracey Waring
Tai Danmola	Richard Moore	Matt Williams
Mike Davies	Victoria O'Leary	Srividya Vaidison
Tim Denton	Margaret Pankhurst	

List of chapters

Volume 1

The lists of chapters in volumes 2 and 3 follow overleaf.

Volume 2

Volume 3

Abbreviations

The following abbreviations are used in this book:

Professional and regulatory bodies:

AASB	Australian Accounting Standards Board
AcSB	Accounting Standards Board of Canada
AICPA	American Institute of Certified Public Accountants
AOSSG	Asian-Oceanian Standard-Setters Group
APB	Accounting Principles Board (of the AICPA, predecessor of the FASB)
ARC	Accounting Regulatory Committee of representatives of EU Member States
ASB	Accounting Standards Board in the UK
ASBJ	Accounting Standards Board of Japan
CASC	China Accounting Standards Committee
CESR	Committee of European Securities Regulators, an independent committee whose members comprise senior representatives from EU securities regulators (now replaced by ESMA)
CICA	Canadian Institute of Chartered Accountants
EC	European Commission
ECB	European Central Bank
EFRAG	European Financial Reporting Advisory Group
EITF	Emerging Issues Task Force in the US
ESMA	European Securities and Markets Authority (see CESR)
EU	European Union
FAF	Financial Accounting Foundation
FASB	Financial Accounting Standards Board in the US
FCAG	Financial Crisis Advisory Group
FEE	Federation of European Accountants
G4+1	The (now disbanded) group of four plus 1, actually with six members, that comprised an informal 'think tank' of staff from the standard setters from Australia, Canada, New Zealand, UK, and USA, plus the IASC
G20	The Group of Twenty Finance Ministers and Central Bank Governors
HKICPA	Hong Kong Institute of Certified Public Accountants

ICAI	Institute of Chartered Accountants of India
IASB	International Accounting Standards Board
IASC	International Accounting Standards Committee. The former Board of the IASC was the predecessor of the IASB
IASCF	International Accounting Standards Committee Foundation (predecessor of the IFRS Foundation)
ICAEW	Institute of Chartered Accountants in England and Wales
ICAS	Institute of Chartered Accountants of Scotland
IFRIC	International Financial Reporting Interpretations Committee of the IASB (now simply termed the IFRS Interpretations Committee)
IGC	Implementation Guidance Committee on IAS 39 (now disbanded)
IOSCO	International Organisation of Securities Commissions
IPTF	International Practices Task Force (a task force of the SEC Regulations Committee)
JWG	Joint Working Group of Standard-setters that comprised representatives from the IASC, the FASB, and eight other international bodies. The purpose of the (now disbanded) group was to develop an integrated and harmonised standard on financial instruments – a task they were unable to complete
SAC	Standards Advisory Council, predecessor of the IFRS Advisory Council which provides advice to the IASB on a wide range of issues
SEC	Securities and Exchange Commission (the US securities regulator)
SIC	Standing Interpretations Committee of the IASC (replaced by IFRIC)
TEG	Technical Expert Group, an advisor to the European Commission

Accounting related terms:

ADS	American Depositary Shares
AFS	Available-for-sale investment
ARB	Accounting Research Bulletins (issued by the AICPA)
ARS	Accounting Research Studies (issued by the APB)
ASC	Accounting Standards Codification. US GAAP accounting standards are now organised by a comprehensive Accounting Standards Codification scheme, which is now the single source of authoritative US GAAP
CGU	Cash Generating Unit
CIS	Comprehensive Income Statement, as developed by the G4+1 group of accounting standard-setters, and published in June 1999 in the ASB Discussion Paper *Reporting Financial Performance: Proposals for Change*
CU	Currency Unit
CULS	Convertible Unsecured Loan Stock

DD&A	Depreciation, Depletion and Amortisation
DPF	Discretionary Participation Feature
EBIT	Earnings Before Interest and Taxes
EBITDA	Earnings Before Interest, Taxes, Depreciation and Amortisation
EPS	Earnings per Share
FAS	Financial Accounting Standards (issued by the FASB)
FC	Foreign currency
FIFO	First-In, First-Out basis of valuation
FRS	Financial Reporting Standard (issued by the ASB)
FTA	First-time Adoption
FVLCS	Fair value less costs to sell
GAAP	Generally accepted accounting practice (as it applies under IFRS), or generally accepted accounting principles (as it applies to the US)
HTM	Held-to-maturity investment
IAS	International Accounting Standard (issued by the former board of the IASC)
IBNR	Incurred but not reported claims
IFAC	International Federation of Accountants
IFRS	International Financial Reporting Standard (issued by the IASB)
IPO	Initial Public Offering
IPR&D	In-process Research and Development
IRR	Internal Rate of Return
JA	Joint Arrangement
JCA	Jointly Controlled Asset
JCE	Jointly Controlled Entity
JCO	Jointly Controlled Operation
JO	Joint Operation
JV	Joint Venture
LAT	Liability Adequacy Test
LC	Local Currency
LIBOR	London Inter Bank Offered Rate
LIFO	Last-In, First-Out basis of valuation
NCI	Non-controlling Interest
NBV	Net Book Value
NRV	Net Realisable Value
OCI	Other Comprehensive Income

PP&E	Property, Plant and Equipment
R&D	Research and development
SFAC	Statement of Financial Accounting Concepts (issued by the FASB as part of its conceptual framework project)
SFAS	Statement of Financial Accounting Standards (issued by the FASB)
SPE	Special Purpose Entity
SV	Separate Vehicle
TSR	Total Shareholder Return
VIU	Value In Use
WACC	Weighted Average Cost of Capital

References to IFRSs, IASs, Interpretations and supporting documentation:

AG	Application Guidance
AV	Alternative View
B, BCZ	Basis for Conclusions on IASs
BC	Basis for Conclusions on IFRSs and IASs
DO	Dissenting Opinion
DP	Discussion Paper
ED	Exposure Draft
IE	Illustrative Examples on IFRSs and IASs
IG	Implementation Guidance
IN	Introduction to IFRSs and IASs

Authoritative literature

The content of this book takes into account all accounting standards and other relevant rules issued up to September 2011. Consequently, it covers the IASB's *Conceptual Framework for Financial Reporting* and authoritative literature listed below.

Unless otherwise indicated therein, all references in the main text of each chapter to the extant pronouncements below are to the versions of those pronouncements as approved and expected to be included in the Blue Book edition of the Bound Volume 2012 International Financial Reporting Standards IFRS – Consolidated without early application – Official pronouncements applicable on 1 January 2012 published by the IASB. References to those extant pronouncements below which have an effective date after 1 January 2012 (such as IFRS 9: *Financial Instruments*) are to the versions of those pronouncements as denoted by the ISBN references noted below. These are expected to be included in the Red Book edition of the Bound Volume 2012 International Financial Reporting Standards IFRS – Official pronouncements issued at 1 January 2012 that will be published by the IASB.

With effect from 1 July 2009 US GAAP accounting standards issued by various standard-setters have been organised within a comprehensive Accounting Standards Codification scheme, which is now the single source of authoritative US GAAP and has been applied in this publication.

† The standards and interpretations marked with a dagger have been withdrawn or superseded.

IASB Framework
The Conceptual Framework for Financial Reporting

International Financial Reporting Standards (2012 Bound Volume)	
IFRS 1	First-time Adoption of International Financial Reporting Standards
IFRS 2	Share-based Payment
IFRS 3	Business Combinations
IFRS 4	Insurance Contracts
IFRS 5	Non-current Assets Held for Sale and Discontinued Operations
IFRS 6	Exploration for and Evaluation of Mineral Resources
IFRS 7	Financial Instruments: Disclosures
IFRS 8	Operating Segments

IFRS Interpretations Committee Interpretations

Standing Interpretations Committee Interpretations

Other IASB publications

Presentation of Items of Other Comprehensive Income (Amendments to IAS 1)

International Financial Reporting Standard (IFRS) for Small and Medium-sized Entities (SMEs)

IFRS Practice Statement: Management Commentary – A Framework for Presentation

Request for Views: Agenda Consultation 2011

IASB Exposure Drafts

	Amendments to IAS 37 Provisions, Contingent Liabilities and Contingent Assets and IAS 19 Employee Benefits
ED/2009/2	Income Tax
ED/2009/8	Rate-regulated Activities
ED/2009/12	Financial Instruments: Amortised Cost and Impairment
	Financial Instruments: Impairment (Supplement to ED/2009/12 - Financial Instruments: Amortised Cost and Impairment)
ED/2010/1	Measurement of Liabilities in IAS 37 (proposed amendments to IAS 37)
ED/2010/2	Conceptual Framework for Financial Reporting – The Reporting Entity
ED/2010/6	Revenue from Contracts with Customers
ED/2010/7	Measurement Uncertainty Analysis Disclosure of Fair Value Measurements (Limited re-exposure of proposed disclosure)
ED/2010/8	Insurance Contracts
ED/2010/9	Leases
ED/2010/13	Hedge Accounting
ED/2011/1	Offsetting Financial Assets and Financial Liabilities
ED/2011/2	Improvements to IFRSs
ED/2011/3	Mandatory Effective Date of IFRS 9
ED/2011/4	Investment Entities

IFRS Interpretations Committee Exposure Drafts

DI/2010/1	Stripping Costs in the Production Phase of a Surface Mine

Chapter 22   Impairment of fixed assets and goodwill

Chapter 22

List of examples

Chapter 22   Impairment of fixed assets and goodwill

1   THE THEORY BEHIND THE IMPAIRMENT REVIEW

In principle an asset is impaired when an entity will not be able to recover that asset's balance sheet carrying value, either through using it or selling it. If circumstances arise which indicate assets might be impaired, a review should be undertaken of their cash generating abilities either through use or sale. This review will produce an amount which should be compared with the assets' carrying value, and if the carrying value is higher, the difference must be written off as an impairment adjustment in the income statement. The provisions within IAS 36 – *Impairment of Assets* – that set out exactly how this is to be done, and how the figures involved are to be calculated, are detailed and quite complex.

The purpose of the review is to ensure that intangible and tangible assets, and goodwill are not carried at a figure greater than their *recoverable amount*. This recoverable amount is compared with the carrying value of the asset to determine if the asset is impaired.

Recoverable amount is defined as the higher of *fair value less costs to sell* (FVLCS) and *value in use* (VIU); the underlying concept being that an asset should not be carried at more than the amount it will raise, either from selling it now or from using it.

Fair value less costs to sell essentially means what the asset could be sold for, having deducted *costs of disposal* (incrementally incurred direct selling costs). *Value in use* is defined in terms of discounted future cash flows, as the present value of the cash flows expected from the future use and eventual sale of the asset at the end of its useful life. As the recoverable amount is to be expressed as a present value, not in actual terms, discounting is a central feature of the impairment test.

Diagrammatically, this comparison between carrying value and recoverable amount, and the definition of recoverable amount, can be portrayed as follows:

It may not always be necessary to identify both VIU and FVLCS, as if either of VIU or FVLCS is higher than the carrying amount then there is no impairment and no write-down is necessary. Thus, if FVLCS is greater than the carrying amount then no further consideration need be given to VIU, or to the need for an impairment write down. The more complex issues arise when the FVLCS is not greater than the carrying value, and so a VIU calculation is necessary.

Although an impairment review might theoretically be conducted by looking at individual assets, this is likely to be a rare occurrence. It may not be possible to obtain reliable FVLCS estimates for all assets and some, such as goodwill or certain intangible assets, may not have a separate FVLCS at all. Even if FVLCSs can be obtained for individual items of property plant and equipment, estimates of VIUs usually cannot be. This is because the cash flows necessary for the VIU calculation are not usually generated by single assets, but by groups of assets being used together.

Often, therefore, the impairment review cannot be done at the level of the individual asset and it must be applied to a group of assets. IAS 36 uses the term *cash generating unit* (CGU) for the smallest identifiable group of assets that together have cash inflows that are largely independent of the cash inflows from other assets and that therefore can be the subject of a VIU calculation. This focus on the CGU is fundamental, as it has the effect of making the review essentially a business-value test, in as much as the assets of a business unit cannot usually be carried at an amount greater than the value of that business unit.

As it might be unduly onerous for all fixed assets and goodwill to be reviewed for impairment every year, IAS 36 in the main requires property, plant and equipment to be reviewed only if there is an indication that impairment may have occurred. If there are indications that the carrying amount of an asset may not be recoverable, a review for impairment should be carried out. The 'indications' of impairment may relate to either the assets themselves or to the economic environment in which they are operated. IAS 36 gives examples of indications of impairment, but makes it clear this is not an exhaustive list, and states explicitly that the entity may identify other indications that an asset is impaired, that would equally trigger an impairment review. *[IAS 36.13].*

2 THE REQUIREMENTS OF IAS 36

IAS 36 was originally published in April 1998. It has recently been amended, principally to take account of the following:

- The revised IFRS 3 – *Business Combinations* – which came into force for accounting periods beginning on or after 1 July 2009 but may be applied early to accounting periods beginning on or after 30 June 2007. This changed the way in which non-controlling interests are calculated, with consequential effects on impairment testing in IAS 36 (see 5.5 below). Changes include a new Appendix C that describes the revised processes and replaces the paragraphs dealing with impairment and non-controlling interests;

- The IASB simultaneously revised IAS 27 – *Consolidated and Separate Financial Statements*; changes affect the manner in which acquisitions of non-controlling interests are accounted for. It has also revised the 'cost' method that defined the carrying value of investments. The distinction between pre- and post-acquisition dividends has been removed. Instead there are circumstances in which receipt of a dividend from subsidiaries and jointly controlled entity triggers an impairment review. *[IAS 27.30, 31]*. See further details in Chapter 9 at 2.4.1.

2.1 Scope

The standard is a general impairment standard and its provisions are referred to in other standards, for example IAS 16 – *Property, Plant and Equipment*, IAS 38 – *Intangible Assets* – and IFRS 3, where impairment is to be considered.

The standard has a general application to all assets, but the following are outside its scope: inventories, assets arising from construction contracts, deferred tax assets, assets arising from employee benefits, financial assets that are included in the scope of IAS 39 – *Financial Instruments: Recognition and Measurement,* investment property that is measured at fair value, biological assets under IAS 41 – *Agriculture* – deferred acquisition costs and intangible assets arising from an insurer's contractual rights under insurance contracts within the scope of IFRS 4 – *Insurance Contracts*, and non-current assets (or disposal groups) classified as held for sale in accordance with IFRS 5 – *Non-current Assets Held for Sale and Discontinued Operations*. *[IAS 36.2]*. This, the standard states, is because these assets are subject to specific recognition and measurement rules. *[IAS 36.3]*. The effect of these exclusions is to reduce the scope of IAS 36; however, it does not exempt investment properties not carried at fair value, oil and mineral exploration and evaluation assets or an entity's own shares held by a share trust. Investments in subsidiaries, jointly controlled entities and associates in the separate financial statements of the parent are within its scope. *[IAS 36.4]*. Interests in jointly controlled entities and associates included in the consolidated accounts by way of the equity method are brought into scope by IAS 28 – *Investments in Associates*. *[IAS 28.33]*.

The standard applies to assets carried at revalued amounts, e.g. under IAS 16 (or rarely IAS 38) for two reasons. First, the only difference between fair value based on market value and FVLCS is the costs of disposal. Therefore, if these are not negligible, the entity may have to consider the asset's value in use. Second, in the absence of market values, the entity may have constructed a fair value using a technique acceptable under IAS 16 (see Chapter 20), in which case it would be quite possible for the asset to be impaired. *[IAS 36.5]*. A specific example of a situation in which this might happen is if the asset is valued using depreciated replacement cost, a valuation method that may not correspond to FVLCS and that often gives a higher valuation than one using market-based evidence.

2.2   When an impairment test is required

There is an important distinction in IAS 36 between assessing whether there are indications of impairment and actually carrying out an impairment test. The standard has two different general requirements governing when an impairment test should be carried out:

- For goodwill and all intangible assets with an indefinite life the standard requires an annual impairment test. The impairment test may be performed at any time in the annual reporting period, but it must be performed at the same time every year; *[IAS 36.10]*

  In addition, the carrying amount of an intangible asset that has not yet been brought into use must be tested at least annually. This, the standard argues, is because intangible assets are intrinsically subject to greater uncertainty before they are brought into use. *[IAS 36.11]*.

- For all other classes of assets within the scope of IAS 36, the entity is required to assess at each balance sheet date whether there are any indications of impairment. The impairment test itself only has to be carried out if there are such indications. *[IAS 36.8-9]*.

The particular requirements of IAS 36 concerning the impairment testing goodwill and of intangible assets with an indefinite life are discussed separately at 5 below, however the methodology used is identical for all types of assets.

If indications of impairment exist, then an impairment test, i.e. a formal estimate of the asset's recoverable amount as set out in the standard, must be performed. *[IAS 36.9]*. The only exception is where there was sufficient headroom in a previous impairment calculation that would not have been eroded by subsequent events or the asset or CGU is not sensitive to a particular indicator; these exceptions are discussed further below. *[IAS 36.15]*.

2.2.1   *Indicators of impairment*

Identifying indications of impairment is a crucial stage in the process. IAS 36 lists examples of indicators but stresses that they represent the minimum indications that should be considered by the entity and that the list is not exhaustive. *[IAS 36.13]*. They are divided into external and internal indications.

External sources of information:

(a)   a decline in an asset's market value during the period that is significantly more than would be expected from normal use;

(b)   significant adverse changes that have taken place during the period, or will take place in the near future, in the technological, market, economic or legal environment in which the entity operates or in the market to which an asset is dedicated;

(c)   an increase in the period in market interest rates or other market rates of return on investments if these increases are likely to affect the discount rate used in calculating an asset's value in use and decrease the asset's recoverable amount materially;

(d)   the carrying amount of the net assets of the entity exceeds its market capitalisation.

Internal sources of information:

(e)   evidence of obsolescence or physical damage of an asset;

(f)   significant changes in the extent to which, or manner in which, an asset is used or is expected to be used, that have taken place in the period or soon thereafter and that will have an adverse effect on it. These changes include the asset becoming idle, plans to dispose of an asset sooner than expected, reassessing its useful life as finite rather than indefinite or plans to restructure the operation to which the asset belongs;

(g)   internal reports that indicates that the economic performance of an asset is, or will be, worse than expected. *[IAS 36.12]*.

The standard amplifies and explains relevant evidence from internal reporting that indicates that an asset may be impaired:

(a)   cash flows for acquiring the asset, or subsequent cash needs for operating or maintaining it, are significantly higher than originally budgeted;

(b)   operating profit or loss or actual net cash flows are significantly worse than those budgeted;

(c)   a significant decline in budgeted net cash flows or operating profit, or a significant increase in budgeted loss; or

(d)   operating losses or net cash outflows for the asset, if current period amounts are aggregated with budgeted amounts for the future. *[IAS 36.14]*.

The presence of indicators of impairment will not necessarily mean that the entity has to calculate the recoverable amount of the asset in accordance with IAS 36. A previous calculation may have shown that an asset's recoverable amount was significantly greater than its carrying amount and it may be clear that subsequent events have been insufficient to eliminate this headroom. Similarly, previous analysis may show that an asset's recoverable amount is not sensitive to one or more of these indicators. *[IAS 36.15]*.

2.2.1.A   Market capitalisation

Market capitalisation is, potentially, a powerful indicator as, if it shows a lower figure than the book value of equity, it suggests the market considers that the business is overvalued. However, the market may have taken account of factors other than the return that the entity is generating on its assets. An individual entity may have a high level of debt that it is unable to service fully or a financial crisis may have led to a general collapse in market prices; a market capitalisation below equity will not necessarily be reflected in an equivalent impairment loss. An entity's response to this indicator depends very much on facts and circumstances. Most entities cannot avoid examining their CGUs in these circumstances. They may have to test goodwill for impairment unless there was sufficient headroom in a previous impairment calculation that would not have been eroded by subsequent events or none of the assets or CGUs is sensitive to market capitalisation as an indicator. IAS 36 does not require a formal reconciliation between market capitalisation of the entity, FVLCS and VIU. However, entities need to be able to understand the reason for the shortfall. If recoverable amount exceeds market capitalisation, entities need to consider whether they have made sufficient disclosures to indicate why this is so as well as describing those factors that could result in impairment in the next periods.

2.2.1.B   Future performance

Another significant element is an explicit reference in (b), (c) and (d) above to internal evidence that *future* performance will be worse than expected. Thus IAS 36 requires an impairment review to be undertaken if performance is or will be significantly below that previously budgeted. In particular, there may be indicators of impairment even if the asset is profitable in the current period if budgeted results for the future indicate that there will be losses or net cash outflows when these are aggregated with the current period results.

2.2.1.C   Individual assets or part of CGU?

Some of the indicators are aimed at individual fixed assets rather than the CGU of which they are a part, for example a decline in the market value of an asset or evidence that it is obsolete or damaged. However, they may also imply that a wider review of the business or CGU is required. For example, if there is a property slump and the market value of the entity's new head office falls below its carrying value this would constitute an indicator of impairment and trigger a review. At the level of the individual asset, as FVLCS is below carrying amount, this might indicate that a write-down is necessary. However, the building's recoverable amount may have to be considered in the context of a CGU of which it is a part and if it is, the recoverable amount will most likely be based on VIU, not FVLCS. This is an example of a situation where it may not be necessary to re-estimate an asset's recoverable amount because it may be obvious that the CGU has suffered no impairment. In short, it may be irrelevant to the recoverable amount of the CGU that it contains a head office whose market value has fallen.

2.2.1.D   Interest rates

Including interest rates as indicators of impairment could imply that assets are judged to be impaired if they are no longer expected to earn a market rate of return, even though they may generate the same cash flows as before. However, it may well be that an upward movement in general interest rates will not give rise to a write-down in assets because they may not affect the rate of return expected from the asset or CGU itself. The standard indicates that this may be an example where the asset's recoverable amount is not sensitive to a particular indicator.

An entity is not required to make a formal estimate of an asset's recoverable amount if the discount rate used in calculating the asset's VIU is unlikely to be affected by the increase in market rates. The discount rate used in a VIU calculation should be based on the rate specific for the asset, and if the asset has a long remaining useful life this may not be materially affected by increases in short-term rates. Previous sensitivity analyses of the recoverable amount may show that it is unlikely that there will be a material decrease because future cash flows are also likely to increase to compensate. Consequently, the potential decrease in recoverable amount may simply be unlikely to be material. *[IAS 36.16]*.

Events in the financial crisis of 2008/2009 demonstrated that the reverse may also be true. A substantial decline in short-term market interest rates did not lead to an equivalent decline in the (long term) market rates specific to the assets.

If there are indications that the asset is impaired, it may also be necessary to examine the remaining useful life of the asset, its residual value and the depreciation method used, as these may also need to be adjusted even if no impairment loss is recognised. *[IAS 36.17]*.

2.3 The impairment test

IAS 36 defines VIU as the present value of the future cash flows expected to be derived from an asset or CGU and FVLCS as the amount obtainable from the sale of an asset or CGU in an arm's length transaction between knowledgeable, willing parties, less the costs of disposal. *[IAS 36.6]*. The standard requires the carrying amount to be compared with the recoverable amount, which is the higher of VIU and FVLCS. *[IAS 36.18]*. If either the FVLCS or the VIU is higher than the carrying amount, no further action is necessary as the asset is not impaired. *[IAS 36.19]*. Recoverable amount is calculated for an individual asset, unless that asset does not generate cash inflows that are largely independent of those from other assets or groups of assets. *[IAS 36.22]*.

Estimating the VIU of an asset involves estimating the future cash inflows and outflows that will be derived from the use of the asset and from its ultimate disposal, and discounting them at an appropriate rate. *[IAS 36.31]*. There are complex issues involved in determining the cash flows and choosing a discount rate and often there is no agreed methodology to follow (refer to 4.4 below for a discussion of some of these difficulties).

It may be possible to estimate FVLCS even in the absence of an active market but if it cannot be estimated satisfactorily then the value of an asset must be based on its VIU. *[IAS 36.20]*. There are two practical points to emphasise. First, IAS 36 allows the use of estimates, averages and computational shortcuts to provide a reasonable approximation of FVLCS or VIU. *[IAS 36.23]*. Second, if the FVLCS is greater than the asset's carrying value, no VIU calculation is necessary. However, it is not uncommon for the FVLCS of an asset to be readily obtainable while the asset itself does not generate largely independent cash inflows, as is the case with many property assets held by entities. If the FVLCS of the asset is lower than its carrying value then the recoverable amount will have to be calculated by reference to the CGU of which the asset is a part.

2.3.1   Impairment of assets held for sale

The standard describes circumstances in which it may be appropriate to use an asset or CGU's FVLCS without calculating its VIU, as the measure of its recoverable amount. There may be no significant difference between FVLCS and VIU, in which case the asset's FVLCS may be used as its recoverable amount. This is the case, for example, if management is intending to dispose of the asset or CGU, as apart from its disposal proceeds there will be few if any cash flows from further use. *[IAS 36.21]*.

The asset may also be held for sale as defined by IFRS 5, by which stage it will be outside the scope of IAS 36, although IFRS 5 requires such assets to be measured immediately before their initial classification as held for sale 'in accordance with applicable IFRSs'. *[IFRS 5.18]*. A decision to sell is a triggering event for an impairment review, which means that any existing impairment will be recognised at the point of classification and not be rolled into the gain or loss on disposal of the asset. See Chapter 4 for a description of the subsequent measurement of the carrying amounts of the assets.

Clearly IFRS 5's requirement to test for impairment prior to redesignation is intended to avoid impairment losses being recognised as losses on disposal. However, one effect is that this rule may require the recognition of impairment losses on individual assets that form part of a single disposal group subsequently sold at a profit, as in the following example.

Example 22.1:   Impairment of assets held for sale

Entity A decided to sell a group of three assets in one transaction to the same acquirer. Each asset had been part of a different CGU. The decision to sell was made on 20 December 2010, just prior to Entity A's year end of 31 December. The assets met IFRS 5's requirements for classification as a disposal group on 10 January 2011.

The information about the carrying amounts and fair values less cost to sell of individual assets at 20 December 2010 and the disposal group on 10 January 2011 is summarised below. There was no change in the fair values of these assets between the two dates.

Asset	Carrying amount	FVLCS of separate assets	Aggregate of the lower of the carrying amount and FVLCS	Fair value of the group
	€	€	€	€
X	4,600	4,300	4,300	
Y	5,700	5,800	5,700	
Z	2,400	2,500	2,400	
Total	12,700	12,600	12,400	12,600

Although these assets were classified as held for sale subsequent to the year end, the decision to sell them was an indicator of impairment. Accordingly, it is necessary to determine whether the three assets together comprise a new CGU. If so, impairment would be assessed on the three assets together, prior to reclassification and remeasurement under IFRS 5.

If the three assets together do not comprise a CGU, they would have to be tested for impairment individually at the year end, which would result in an impairment loss on Asset X of €300. As there is no change in the recoverable amount between the year end and immediately before the classification under IFRS 5, the aggregate value of these assets prior to classification under IFRS 5 would be €12,400 (4,300 + 5,700 + 2,400). The FVLCS of the disposal group at the date of the first application of IFRS 5 (10 January 2011) is €12,600. Therefore according to the measurement criteria under IFRS 5 the carrying amount of the disposal group remains at €12,400 and the impairment loss previously recognised on Asset A would only be reversed, should the FVLCS of the disposal group exceed €12,600.

An entity might, however, sell a CGU for less than the apparent aggregate FVLCS of individual assets. IAS 36 does not allow an asset to be written down below the higher of its VIU or FVLCS. *[IAS 36.105]*. If this happens, the carrying amount of the disposal group is capped at the total sales proceeds so the impairment loss is allocated to all non-current assets, even if their carrying amounts are reduced below their fair value less cost to sell. See Chapter 4.

In different circumstances the requirement to take an impairment write down on reclassification may be far less clear-cut. Assets no longer form part of their original CGU once they have been designated for disposal. It is possible that a group of assets could comprise a new CGU if they are to be sold to a single purchaser as part of an arrangement. Their individual FVLCSs may be uncertain if they are sold as a parcel, as the seller receives aggregate proceeds for the group of assets (this could be the case whether the sale is of a CGU or a group of assets). There may be little separation in time between the decision to sell and designation as held for sale.

3   FAIR VALUE LESS COSTS TO SELL

The best evidence of an asset's FVLCS is the sales price of the asset in question, based on a binding sale agreement negotiated at arm's length, less incremental costs directly attributable to the sale. *[IAS 36.25]*. If there is a binding sale agreement, the asset is either already classified as held for sale, in which case IFRS 5's measurement rules apply (see Chapter 4), or it is about to be reclassified and must be tested for impairment as described above.

If there is no binding sale agreement for the asset in question, but there is an active market for assets of this type, FVLCS may be estimated from current or recent bid prices. If there are no current bid prices, the price may be estimated from the most recent transaction provided there has been no significant change in economic circumstances in the intervening period. *[IAS 36.26]*.

In reality there are few active markets for most tangible and intangible assets, given that IFRSs define an active market as one in which all of the items traded are homogeneous, that has a constant supply of willing buyers and sellers and prices that are available to the public. Consequently, most estimates of fair value will be based on estimates of the market price of the asset in an arm's length transaction. This will involve consideration of the outcome of recent transactions for similar assets in the same industry. The entity will use the best information it has available at the balance sheet date to construct the price payable in an arm's length transaction between knowledgeable, willing parties. *[IAS 36.27]*.

FVLCS does not reflect a forced sale unless the management is compelled to sell immediately. *[IAS 36.27]*. In all cases, FVLCS should take account of estimated disposal costs. These include legal costs, stamp duty and other transaction taxes, costs of moving the asset and other direct incremental costs. Business reorganisation costs and employee termination costs (as defined in IAS 19 – *Employee Benefits* – see Chapter 33) may not be treated as costs of disposal. *[IAS 36.28]*.

Although the approach to determining FVLCS is similar to that in IFRS 13 – *Fair Value Measurement* – issued by the IASB in May 2011, it is not identical. IFRS 13 applies to financial statements for annual periods beginning on or after 1 January 2013, although earlier application is permitted subject to the usual requirement to disclose this fact. Until the new standard is applied, entities will continue to apply IAS 36.

IFRS 13 as it applies to testing for impairment is discussed briefly at 3.1.2 below.

If the disposal of an asset would entail the buyer assuming a liability, then this liability should be deducted from the FVLCS in arriving at the relevant amount for determining the recoverable amount. *[IAS 36.29]*. The obligation must also be taken into account in calculating the carrying value of the asset to enable a meaningful comparison.

3.1   Using FVLCS for the purposes of impairment testing

IAS 36 allows an entity to estimate FVLCS less costs to sell of an asset even if there is no active market for assets of this type *[IAS 36.20]* and there is no binding sale agreement for the asset in question. *[IAS 36.27]*. Some of the issues that need to be taken into account are discussed below. IFRS 13 is discussed in Chapter 16 but some of its consequences for impairment testing are discussed at 3.1.2 below.

3.1.1   *Estimating FVLCS without an active market*

Few assets are traded on an active market and there are no obvious examples of traded CGUs. However, it may be possible to determine fair value provided there is a basis for making a reliable estimate of the amount obtainable from the sale of the asset in an arm's length transaction between knowledgeable and willing parties.

IAS 36 permits entities to consider 'the outcome of recent transactions for similar assets within the same industry.' *[IAS 36.27]*. If the entity has only recently acquired the asset or CGU in question then it may be able to demonstrate that its purchase price remains an appropriate measure of FVLCS, although it would have to make adjustments for material costs to sell. *[IAS 36.28]*.

To rely on the outcome of a recent transaction for a similar asset by a third party, the following conditions must be met:

a)   the transaction should be in the same industry, unless the asset is generic and its fair value would not be affected by the industry in which the purchaser operates;

b)   the assets must be shown to be substantially the same as to their nature and condition;

c)   the economic environment of the entity must be similar to the environment in which the previous sale occurred (e.g. no circumstances have arisen since the earlier transaction that affect the value of the asset). This means that previous transactions are particularly unreliable if markets are falling.

It would be unusual to be able to estimate FVLCS reliably from a single market transaction. As discussed below, if reliable market assumptions are known, it is much more likely that a recent market transaction would be one of the factors taken into account in the calculation of FVLCS and used in conjunction with other valuation techniques.

If the entity cannot demonstrate that a recent transaction alone provides a reliable estimate of FVLCS, the transaction may be one of the sources of evidence used to validate an estimate of FVLCS using other valuation techniques. This is particularly likely to be the case if the impairment review is of a CGU or CGU group rather than an individual asset, as market transactions for CGUs may less relevant.

IAS 36 allows the use of cash flow valuation techniques such as discounted cash flows or other valuation techniques such as earnings multiples. However, the use of these techniques and assumptions is only acceptable if it can be demonstrated that they would be used by the relevant 'market participants' i.e. other businesses in the same industry. When using a valuation technique to estimate FVLCS, all of the following conditions must be met:

a)   a relevant model must be selected – this requires consideration of industry practice, for example, a multiple of EBITDA is often used in the hotel industry to estimate fair value, while discounted cash flows are used by many manufacturing entities;

b)   assumptions used in the model must only be those that other market participants would use. They cannot be based on management's uncorroborated views or information that would not be known or considered by other market participants; and

c)   there must be reliable evidence showing that these assumptions would be taken into account by market participants. For this purpose, it may be necessary for the entity to obtain external advice.

It is particularly important when markets are unstable to ensure that multiples remain valid. Entities cannot assume that the basis underlying the multiples remains unchanged.

IAS 36 notes that sometimes it is not possible to obtain reliable evidence regarding the assumptions and techniques that market participants would use (IAS 36 uses the phrase 'no basis for making a reliable estimate'); if so, the recoverable amount of the asset must be based on its value in use. *[IAS 36.20]*. Interestingly, although the wording of paragraph 20 is to be updated by IFRS 13 to apply the revised terminology, the requirements will remain unchanged.[1] Therefore, the IASB still accepts that there are some circumstances in which it will not be possible to calculate a reliable fair value.

Therefore a discounted cash flow technique may be used if this is commonly used in that industry to estimate fair value. Cash flows used when applying the model may only reflect cash flows that market participants would take into account when assessing fair value. This includes the type of cash flows, for example future capital expenditure, as well as the estimated amount of cash flows. For example, an entity may wish to take into account cash flows relating to future capital expenditure, which would not be permitted for a VIU calculation (see 4.3.1 below). These cash flows can be included if, but only if, other market participants would consider them when evaluating the asset. It is not permissible to include assumptions about cash flows or benefits from the asset that would not be available to or considered by a typical market participant.

Obtaining reliable evidence of market assumptions is not straightforward, and may not be available to many entities wishing to apply valuation techniques. However, if the information is available then entities ought to take it into account in calculating FVLCS. This is consistent with the approach taken in IFRS 13, described briefly in 3.1.2 below; while an entity may base its fair value on its own internal data, it must take into account all information about market participant assumptions that is reasonably available and make adjustments where necessary.

Deutsche Telekom calculated the FVLCS of one of its CGUs and took a third party transaction in the same sector and geographical area into account in its valuation model, as can be seen in the following extract:

Extract 22.1: Deutsche Telekom AG (2007)

Notes to the consolidated income statement [extract]

16.   Depreciation, amortization and impairment losses [extract]

In the 2005 financial year, Deutsche Telekom recognized an impairment loss of EUR 1.9 billion at the T-Mobile UK cash-generating unit. Telefónica announced its offer to acquire the UK group O2 at a price of 200 pence per share (approximately GBP 17.7 billion) on October 31, 2005. When determining the fair value less costs to sell, the purchase prices paid in comparable transactions must generally be given preference over internal DCF calculations. The fair value of the cash-generating unit T-Mobile UK was derived from the Telefónica offer in accordance with a valuation model based on multipliers.

3.1.2   IFRS 13 – Fair Value Measurement – and IAS 36

The IASB issued IFRS 13 – *Fair Value Measurement* – in May 2011. The IFRS provides guidance on how to measure fair value, but does not change when fair value is required or permitted under IFRS. The IFRS must be applied in annual periods beginning on or after 1 January 2013. As usual, earlier application is permitted as long as the entity discloses that fact. IFRS 13 is discussed in detail in Chapter 16.

The standard defines 'fair value' as the price that would be received to sell an asset or paid to transfer a liability in an orderly transaction between market participants at the measurement date under current market conditions. It is explicitly an exit price. [IFRS 13.2]. Consequential changes will be made to IAS 36. Most of these are simply changes of terminology so the main effect is that references to 'fair value' in FVLCS will be replaced by references to fair value, which will have the meaning in IFRS 13.

Costs to sell, now referred to as costs of disposal, will continue to be calculated in accordance with IAS 36.

IAS 36 has its own hierarchy for establishing FVLCS, described above, which will be superseded; while not the same as that in IFRS 13, it is similar in approach. FVLCS in IAS 36 is already an exit value but the requirements of the new standard may in some instances result in a fair value that differs from FVLCS under the current standard. Similarly, FVLCS, like fair value is not an entity-specific measurement but is focused on market participants' assumptions for a particular asset or liability. *[IFRS 13.11]*.

Entities calculating fair value will have to take account of the highest and best use (by the entity or another market participant) to which the asset could be put. *[IFRS 13.27]*. In some circumstances this could result in a fair value that is different to FVLCS. However, an entity's current use of a non-financial asset is presumed to be its highest and best use unless market or other factors suggest that a different use by market participants would maximise the value of the asset. *[IFRS 13.29]*.

Using the IFRS's approach, estimating fair value will use Level 2 inputs that are directly or indirectly observable other than quoted prices and Level 3 inputs that are not based on observable market data but reflect assumptions used by market participants, including risk.

IFRS 13 allows entities to use unobservable inputs, which can include the entity's own data, to calculate fair value. This does not mean that the entity can ignore external evidence. It must use the best information that is available to it and adjust its own data if 'reasonably available information indicates that other market participants would use different data or there is something particular to the entity that is not available to other market participants such as an entity-specific synergy'. An entity need not undertake exhaustive efforts to obtain information about market participant assumptions. 'However, an entity shall take into account all information about market participant assumptions that is reasonably available. Unobservable inputs developed in the manner described above are considered market participant assumptions and meet the objective of a fair value measurement'. *[IFRS 13.89]*. This process is already undertaken by entities calculating FVLCS under IAS 36; see for example, Extract 22.1 above in which Deutsche Telekom explains that it has taken external transactions into account in calculating FVLCS.

IFRS 13 specifically excludes VIU from its scope. *[IFRS 13.6]*.

Entities will not have to make the disclosures required by IFRS 13 when recoverable amount is fair value less costs of disposal. *[IFRS 13.7(c)]*. However, consequential changes to IAS 36 paragraph 134 will require disclosures of the level of the fair value hierarchy without giving regard to the observability of 'costs of disposal' and, if there has been a change in valuation technique, the change and the reason(s) for making it. *[IFRS 13.D86]*.

Chapter 22

4   DETERMINING VALUE IN USE (VIU)

IAS 36 requires the following elements to be reflected in the VIU calculation:

'(a)   an estimate of the future cash flows the entity expects to derive from the asset;

(b)   expectations about possible variations in the amount or timing of those future cash flows;

(c)   the time value of money, represented by the current market risk-free rate of interest;

(d)   the price for bearing the uncertainty inherent in the asset; and

(e)   other factors, such as illiquidity, that market participants would reflect in pricing the future cash flows the entity expects to derive from the asset.' *[IAS 36.30].*

The calculation requires the entity to estimate the future cash flows and discount them at an appropriate rate. *[IAS 36.31].* It also requires uncertainty as to the timing of cash flows or the market's assessment of risk in those assets ((d) and (e) above) to be taken into account either by adjusting the cash flows or the discount rate. The intention is that the VIU should be the expected present value of those future cash flows.

If possible, recoverable amount is calculated for individual assets. *[IAS 36.66].*

If an impairment review has to be carried out then it will frequently be necessary to calculate the VIU of the CGU of which it is a part. This is because:

* the single asset may not generate sufficiently independent cash inflows *[IAS 36.67],* as is often the case; and

* in the case of the possible impairment of a single asset, FVLCS will frequently be lower than the carrying amount.

Where a CGU is being reviewed for impairment, this will involve calculation of the VIU of the CGU as a whole unless a reliable estimate of the CGU's FVLCS can be made. If no such FVLCS is identifiable, or if it is below the total of the CGU's net assets, VIU will have to be calculated.

VIU calculations at the level of the CGU will thus be required when no satisfactory FVLCS is available or FVLCS is below the CGU's carrying amount and:

* goodwill is suspected of being impaired;

* a CGU itself is suspected of being impaired; or

* intangible assets or other fixed assets are suspected of being impaired and individual future cash flows cannot be identified for them.

Goodwill may be tested at the level of a CGU group rather than an individual CGU (see 5.1 below). The standard contains detailed requirements concerning the data to be assembled to calculate VIU that can best be explained and set out as a series of steps. These are set out in 4.1 to 4.5 below. The steps also contain a discussion of the practicalities and difficulties in determining the VIU of an asset. The steps in the process are:

Step 1: Dividing the entity into CGUs (4.1 below);

Step 2: Identifying the carrying amount of CGU assets (4.2 below);

Step 3: Estimating the future pre-tax cash flows of the CGU under review (4.3 below);

Step 4: Identifying an appropriate discount rate and discounting the future cash flows (4.4 below);

Step 5: Comparing carrying value with VIU and recognising impairment losses (4.5 below).

Although this process describes the determination of the VIU of a CGU, steps 2 to 5 are the same as those that would be applied to an individual asset if it generated cash inflows independently of other assets.

4.1 Dividing the entity into cash-generating units (CGUs)

If a calculation of VIU is required, one of the first tasks will be to identify the individual assets affected and if those assets do not have individually identifiable cash flows, divide the entity into CGUs. The group of assets that is considered together should be as small as is reasonably practicable, i.e. the entity should be divided into as many CGUs as possible – an entity must identify the lowest aggregation of assets that generate largely independent cash inflows. *[IAS 36.6, 68].*

Example 22.2:   Identification of cash-generating units and largely independent cash flows

An entity obtains a contract to deliver mail to all users within a region, for a price that depends solely on the weight of the item, regardless of the distance between sender and recipient. It makes a significant loss in deliveries to outlying regions. Because of the entity's service obligations, the CGU is the whole region covered by its mail services.

The division should not go beyond the level at which each income stream is *capable* of being separately monitored. For example, it may be difficult to identify a level below an individual factory as a CGU but of course an individual factory may or may not be a CGU.

A practical approach to identifying CGUs involves two stages, the first being to work down to the smallest group of assets for which a stream of cash inflows can be identified. These groups of assets will be CGUs unless the performance of their cash inflow-generating assets is dependent on those generated by other assets, or *vice versa* their cash inflows are affected by those of other assets. If the cash inflows generated by the group of assets are not largely independent of those generated by other assets, the second stage is to add other assets to the group to form the smallest collection of assets that generates largely independent cash inflows. This approach might be characterised as a 'bottom-up' approach to identifying CGUs and is illustrated in Example 22.3 below. The existence of a degree of flexibility over what constitutes a CGU is obvious. Indeed, the standard acknowledges that the identification of CGUs involves judgement. *[IAS 36.68].* The key guidance offered by the standard is that CGU selection will be influenced by 'how management monitors the entity's operations (such as by product lines, businesses, individual locations, districts or regional areas) or how management makes decisions about continuing or disposing of the entity's assets and operations'. *[IAS 36.69]*. While monitoring by management may help identify CGUs, it does not override the requirement that the identification of CGUs is based on largely independent cash *inflows*.

Example 22.3: Identification of cash-generating units

Example A – newspapers

An entity publishes 10 suburban newspapers, each with a different mast-head, across 4 distinct regions within a major city. The price paid for a purchased mast-head is recognised as an intangible asset. The newspapers are distributed to residents free of charge. No newspaper is distributed outside its region. All of the revenue generated by each newspaper comes from advertising sales. An analysis of advertising sales shows that for each mast-head:

- Approximately 90% of sales come from advertisers purchasing 'bundled' advertisements that appear in all those newspapers published in one particular region of the city;
- Approximately 6% of sales come from advertisers purchasing 'bundled' advertisements that appear in all 10 newspapers in the major city; and
- Approximately 4% of sales come from advertisers purchasing advertisements that appear in one newspaper only.

What is the cash-generating unit for an individual mast-head?

Stage 1: Identify the smallest aggregation of assets for which a stream of cash inflows can be identified.

The fact that it is possible to use a pro-rata allocation basis to determine the cash inflows attributable to each newspaper means that each mast-head is likely to represent the smallest aggregation of assets for which a stream of cash inflows can be identified.

Stage 2: Are the cash inflows generated by an individual mast-head largely independent of those of other mast-heads and, conversely, is that individual mast-head affecting the cash inflows generated by other mast-heads?

As approximately 96% of cash inflows for each mast-head arise from 'bundled' advertising sales across multiple mast-heads, the cash inflows generated by an individual mast-head are not largely independent.

Therefore, the individual mast-heads would most likely need to be aggregated to form the smallest collection of assets that generates largely independent cash inflows. On the basis that approximately 90% of cash inflows for each mast-head arise from 'bundled' advertising sales across all of the newspapers published in a particular region, it is likely that those mast-heads published in one region will together form a cash-generating unit.

Example B – retail outlets

An entity has a chain of retail outlets located in the same country. The business model of the entity is highly integrated and the majority of the entity's revenue generating decisions, such as decisions about investments and monitoring of performance, are carried out at an entity level by the executive committee, with some decisions (such as product range and marketing) delegated to the regional or store levels. The majority of the operations, such as purchasing, are centralised. Management operates its business on a regional basis; but sales are monitored at the individual store level.

The outlets are usually bought and sold in packages of outlets that are subject to common economic characteristics e.g. outlets of similar size or location such as a shopping centre or city or region. Only in rare situations has the entity sold or closed down an individual outlet.

The determining factor for CGUs is the level at which largely independent cash inflows are generated, and not the manner in which the entity's operations are organised and monitored. The fact that operations and costs are managed centrally does not of itself affect the source and independence of the cash inflows. The interdependence of cash outflows is unlikely to be relevant to the identification of CGUs.

The key issue in deciding whether CGUs should be identified at the level of the individual store as opposed to a group of stores is whether, if a store is closed down, all the customers of that store would seek out another of the entity's stores such that there is no overall 'leakage' of custom from the store closure. In the highly likely event that all the customers would not do this, the individual stores are separate CGUs.

Example B above illustrates a very important point. Management may consider that the primary way in which they monitor their business is on a regional or segmental basis, but crucially, cash inflows are monitored at the level of an individual store and closure decisions are made at this level. In other cases it may be that the entity is capable of monitoring individual cash inflows from assets but this may not be the most relevant feature in determining the composition of its CGUs.

Example 22.4:   Identification of cash-generating units – grouping of assets

Example A – A tour operator's hotels

A tour operator owns three hotels of a similar class near the beach at a large holiday resort. These hotels are advertised as alternatives in the operator's brochure, at the same price. Holidaymakers are frequently transferred from one to another and there is a central booking system for independent travellers. In this case, it may be that the hotels can be regarded as offering genuinely substitutable products by a sufficiently high proportion of potential guests and can be grouped together as a single cash-generating unit. Effectively, the hotels are being run as a single hotel on three sites. The entity will have to bear in mind that disposal decisions may still be made on a hotel-by-hotel basis and have to weight this appropriately in its determination of its CGUs.

Example B – Flagship stores

Store Z is a flagship store located in a prime site location in a capital city. Although store Z is loss making, its commercial performance is in line with expectations and with budgets. How should the impairment issues of the flagship store Z be considered?

It is difficult to conclude that a flagship store is a corporate asset, discussed at 4.2.2 below. It may be possible to argue for the aggregation of a flagship store with others in the vicinity into a single CGU as flagship stores are usually designed to enhance the image of the brand and hence other stores as well. They may be budgeted to run with negative cash flows; perhaps in substance the losses are not an impairment. However, this argument for not recognising an impairment would generally only be acceptable during a start-up phase and it must be borne in mind that the added function of the flagship store is largely marketing. As marketing expenditures are expensed, it would not necessarily be inconsistent to take an impairment loss and the entity may have to consider whether it should have capitalised these costs in the first place.

The standard allows reasonable approximations and one way in which entities may apply this in practice is to group together assets that are separate CGUs, but which if considered individually for impairment would not be material. Retail outlets may be grouped on a geographical basis (e.g. all of the retail outlets in a city centre owned by a branded clothes retailer) because they are all subject to the same economic circumstances and individually will have an immaterial effect. However, the entity will still have to scrutinise the individual CGUs to ensure that those that it intends to sell or that have significantly underperformed the others with which they are grouped are identified and dealt with individually.

In practice different entities will inevitably have varying approaches to determining their CGUs. There is judgement to be exercised in determining an income stream and in determining whether it is largely independent of other streams. Given this, therefore, entities may tend towards larger rather than smaller CGUs, to keep the complexity of the process within reasonable bounds.

4.1.1 Active markets and identifying CGUs

The standard stresses the significance of an active market for the output of an asset in identifying a CGU. An active market is a market in which the items traded within the market are homogeneous, willing buyers and sellers can normally be found at any time and prices are available to the public. *[IAS 36.6]*. If there is an active market for the output produced by an asset or group of assets, the assets concerned are identified as a cash-generating unit, even if some or all of the output is used internally. If the cash inflows generated by the asset or CGU are based on internal transfer pricing, the best estimate of an external arm's length transaction price should be used in estimating the future cash flows to determine the asset's or CGU's VIU. *[IAS 36.70]*. The reason given for this rule is that the existence of an active market means that the assets or CGU could generate cash inflows independently from the rest of the business by selling on the active market. *[IAS 36.71]*. There are active markets for many metals, energy products (various grades of oil product, natural gas) and other commodities that are freely traded.

Example A below, based on Example 1B in IAS 36's accompanying section of illustrative examples, illustrates the point. Example B describes circumstances in which the existence of an active market does not necessarily lead to the identification of a separate CGU.

Example 22.5:   Identification of cash-generating units – internally-used products

Example A – Plant for an Intermediate Step in a Production Process

A significant raw material used for plant Y's final production is an intermediate product bought from plant X of the same entity. X's products are sold to Y at a transfer price that passes all margins to X. 60 per cent of X's final production is sold to Y and the remaining 40 per cent is sold to customers outside of the entity. Y sells 80 per cent of its products to customers outside of the entity

If X can sell its products in an active market and generate cash inflows that are largely independent of the cash inflows from Y, it is likely that X is a CGU even though part of its production is used by Y. Therefore, its cash inflows can be regarded as being largely independent. It is likely that Y is also a separate CGU. However, internal transfer prices do not reflect market prices for X's output. Therefore, in determining value in use of both X and Y, the entity adjusts financial budgets/forecasts to reflect management's best estimate of future prices that could be achieved in arm's length transactions for those of X's products that are used internally.

If, on the other hand, there is no active market, it is likely that the recoverable amount of each plant cannot be assessed independently of the recoverable amount of the other plant. The majority of X's production is used internally and could not be sold in an active market. Cash inflows of X depend on demand for Y's products. Therefore, X cannot be considered to generate cash inflows that are largely independent of those of Y. In addition, the two plants are managed together. As a consequence, it is likely that X and Y together are the smallest group of assets that generates cash inflows that are largely independent. *[IAS 36.IE5-10]*.

Example B – 'Market' for intermediate product not relevant to identification of a separate CGU

A vertically integrated operation located in Australia produces an intermediate product that is fully used internally to manufacture the end product. There is no active market for the intermediate product in Australia. The entity has only one other competitor in Australia, which is also vertically integrated and, likewise, uses the intermediate product internally. Both entities are, and have always been, very profitable when looking at their vertically integrated manufacturing processes to the end-stage product.

There is an active market for the intermediate product in China, but the prices at which the product can be sold are so low that a company based in Australia whose sole activity is to sell the intermediate product into China would never be profitable and a company would never set up manufacturing operations in Australia in order to sell into China.

Each of the Australian companies will occasionally sell small surpluses of their intermediate products into the active market in China, rather than make that product available to their competitor in Australia.

The existence of an active market for the intermediate product in China might suggest that the operations involved in it should be treated as a separate CGU. However, the mere existence of an active market somewhere in the world does not mean that the asset or CGU could realistically generate cash inflows independently from the rest of the business by selling on that active market. If such sales are a genuine incidental activity (i.e. if it is genuinely a case of obtaining some proceeds from excess product that would otherwise be scrapped), it may be appropriate not to regard that market as an active market for the intermediate product for IAS 36 purposes.

If the market is not regarded as an active market for IAS 36 purposes, the assets/operations involved in producing the intermediate product will not be treated as a separate CGU.

IAS 36 also requires that identification of cash generating units to be consistent from period to period unless the change is justified; if changes are made and the entity makes or reverses an impairment, disclosures are required. *[IAS 36.72-73].*

Assets held for resale cannot be subsumed within a larger CGU and their impairment should be judged solely by the cash flows expected to be generated by sale. Once they are classified as held for sale they will be accounted for in accordance with IFRS 5 and carried at an amount that may not exceed their FVLCS (see 2.3.1 above and Chapter 4 for a further discussion of IFRS 5's requirements).

4.2   Identifying the carrying amount of CGU assets

The recoverable amount of a CGU is determined in the same way as for an individual asset and its carrying amount must be determined on a basis that is consistent with the way in which its recoverable amount is determined. *[IAS 36.74-75].*

The carrying amount of a CGU includes only those assets that can be attributed directly, or allocated on a reasonable and consistent basis. These must be the assets that will generate the future cash inflows used in determining the CGU's value in use. It does not include the carrying amount of any recognised liability, unless the recoverable amount of the cash-generating unit cannot be determined without taking it into account. Both FVLCS and VIU of a CGU are determined excluding cash flows that relate to assets that are not part of the cash-generating unit and liabilities that have been recognised. *[IAS 36.76].*

The standard emphasises the importance of completeness in the allocation of assets to CGUs. Every asset used in generating the cash flow being tested must be included in the CGU; otherwise an impaired CGU might appear to be unimpaired, as its carrying value would be understated by having missed out assets. *[IAS 36.77].*

There are exceptions allowed to the rule that recognised liabilities are not included in arriving at the CGU's carrying value or VIU. If the buyer would have to assume a liability if it acquired an asset, then this liability should be deducted from the CGU's carrying amount and VIU. This will enable a meaningful comparison between carrying amount and recoverable amount, whether the latter is based on FVLCS or VIU. *[IAS 36.78].*

For practical reasons the entity may determine the recoverable amount of a CGU after taking into account assets and liabilities such as receivables or other financial assets, trade payables, pensions and other provisions that are outside the scope of IAS 36. *[IAS 36.79].* If the cash flows of a CGU or its FVLCS are determined taking into account these sorts of items, then it is essential that cash flows and assets and liabilities within CGUs are prepared on a consistent basis. However, this frequently causes confusion in practice.

Other assets such as goodwill and corporate assets may not be able to be attributed on a reasonable and consistent basis and the standard has separate rules regarding their treatment. Goodwill is dealt with separately at 5 below.

4.2.1   Consistency and the impairment test

Consistency is a very important principle underlying IAS 36. In testing for impairment entities must ensure that the carrying amount of the CGU is consistent for VIU and FVLCS; in calculating VIU, or using a discounted cash flow methodology for FVLCS, entities must ensure that there is consistency between the assets and liabilities of the CGU and the cash flows taken into account, as there must also be between the cash flows and discount rate.

In determining VIU, 4.2 above describes the exceptions to the rule that recognised liabilities are not included in arriving at the CGU's carrying value or VIU. The first exception is straightforward. If the buyer would have to assume a liability if it acquired an asset or CGU, then this liability should be deducted from the CGU's carrying amount and recoverable amount in order to perform a meaningful comparison between VIU and FVLCS.

It is also accepted in IAS 36 that an entity might for practical reasons determine the recoverable amount of a CGU after taking into account assets and liabilities such as receivables or other financial assets, trade payables, pensions and other provisions that are outside the scope of IAS 36.

In all cases:

- the carrying amount of the CGU must be calculated on the same basis for VIU and FVLCS, i.e. including the same assets and liabilities; and

- it is essential that cash flows are prepared on a consistent basis to the assets and liabilities within CGUs.

In addition, some of these assets and liabilities have themselves been calculated using discounting techniques. There is a danger of distortion as the cash flows for impairment purposes will be discounted using a different rate to the rate used to calculate the item itself.

4.2.1.A   Environmental provisions and similar provisions and liabilities

IAS 36 illustrates liabilities that must be deducted from the carrying amount using an example of a mine in a country in which there is a legal obligation to restore the site by replacing the overburden. The restoration provision, which is the present value of the restoration costs, has been provided for and included as part of the carrying value of the asset. It will be taken into account in the estimation of FVLCS but must also be deducted in arriving at VIU so that both methods of estimating recoverable amount are calculated on a comparable basis. To calculate VIU, the cash flows essential to replace the overburden must be included whenever the restoration takes place. If the outflow does not take place within the period covered by budgets and forecasts then the costs must be built into the calculation of the terminal value.

There are other provisions for liabilities that would be taken over by the purchaser of a CGU, e.g. property dilapidations or similar contractual restoration provisions. These may relate to an off-balance sheet leasehold interest in property or equipment rather than a fixed asset. The provision will be accrued as the 'damage' is incurred and hence expensed over time rather than capitalised. If the provision is deducted from the assets of the CGU then the cash outflows must reflect the amount that will be paid to settle the contractual obligation.

Indeed, any provision made in accordance with IAS 37 – *Provisions, Contingent Liabilities and Contingent Assets* – may be reflected in the CGU's carrying amount as long as the relevant cash flows are reflected both as to their amount and timing. However, this class of liability will reflect a discount rate suitable for provisions, based on the time value of money and the risks relating to the provision. This is likely to be considerably lower than a suitable discount rate for an asset and the distortion caused by this will have to be considered. A simple illustration is that the present value of a cash outflow of €100 in 10 years' time is €39 discounted at 10% but €68 if a discount rate of 4% is used. Deducting the respective cash flows discounted at the asset discount rate could result in an overstatement of the CGU's recoverable amount.

4.2.1.B   Finance leases

A CGU may include assets held under finance leases. IAS 17 – *Leases* – requires an entity to apply IAS 36 in determining whether leased assets have become impaired in value. An entity may exclude the finance lease liability from the carrying amount but then it must also exclude the rental payments under the lease. Alternatively, it can deduct the related liabilities from the assets of the CGU and include the rental payments in the cash outflows, even though finance lease costs are charged to profit or loss as depreciation and finance costs. The entity will have to ensure consistent treatment of the carrying value for FVLCS purposes as an acquirer of the CGU will take account of all payments under finance and operating leases.

4.2.1.C   Trade debtors and creditors

Whether an entity either includes or excludes trade debtors and creditors in the assets of the CGU, it must avoid double counting the cash flows that will repay the receivable or pay those liabilities. This may be tricky because cash flows do not normally distinguish between cash flows that relate to working capital items and others. A practical solution often applied is to include working capital items in the carrying amount of the CGU and include the effect of changes in the working capital balances in the cash flow forecast, The same applies to the inclusion of any financial asset or financial liability: including the asset or deducting the liability has no significant effect as long as the relevant cash flows are included for the relevant period of time.

4.2.1.D   Pensions

Pensions are mentioned by IAS 36 as items that might be included in the recoverable amount of a CGU. In practice this could be fraught with difficulty, especially if it is a defined benefit scheme, as there can be so much difference between the measurement basis of the pension asset or (more likely) liability and the cash flows that relate to pensions. This can make it extremely difficult to distinguish between repayment of the liability and cash flows that are employee costs of the CGU. Nevertheless, entities will have to reflect the costs of providing pensions to employees and may need to make a pragmatic allocation to estimate an appropriate pension cost as part of the employee cost cash flows.

4.2.1.E   Cash flow hedges

In the examples considered until now, the basis for including or excluding various items has more to do with ease of preparation than any underlying principle. Indeed, in the case of a cash flow hedge, it makes no significant difference if the hedging asset or liability and the hedging cash flows are included in the calculation of recoverable amount. The result is to gross up or net down the assets of the CGU and the relevant cash flows by an equivalent amount, after taking account of the distorting effects of differing discount rates. However, some entities argue that they ought to be able to take into account cash flows from instruments hedging their sales that are designated as cash flow hedges under IAS 39 because not to do so misrepresents their economic position. In order to do this, they wish to include the cash flows but either exclude the derivative asset or liability from the CGU or alternatively reflect the related cash flow hedge reserve in the CGU as well (this latter treatment would not be a perfect offset to the extent of ineffectiveness). They argue that the cash flow hedges protect the fair value of assets through their effect on price risk. They also note that this introduces a profit or loss mismatch by comparison with instruments that meet the 'normal purchase/normal sale' exemption under which the derivative remains off balance sheet until exercised.

Although logical from an income perspective, IAS 36 does not support these arguments. The derivative asset or liability can only be included in the CGU as a practical expediency and the hedge reserve is neither an asset nor liability to be reflected in the CGU. IAS 39 would not permit an entity to mitigate the effects of impairment by recycling the appropriate amount from the hedging reserve. Finally, entities must be aware that cash flow hedges may have negative values as well as positive ones.

4.2.2   Corporate assets

An entity may have assets that are inherently incapable of generating cash inflows independently, such as headquarters buildings or central IT facilities that contribute to more than one CGU. The characteristics that distinguish these corporate assets are that they do not generate cash inflows independently of other assets or groups of assets and their carrying amount cannot be fully attributed to the CGU under review. *[IAS 36.100].*

This presents a problem in the event of those assets showing indications of impairment. It also raises a question of what those indications might actually be, in the absence of cash inflows directly relating to this type of asset. Some, but not all, of these assets may have relatively easily determinable FVLCSs but while this is usually true of a headquarters building, it could not be said for a central IT facility. We have already noted in 2.2.1.C above that a decline in market value of itself may not trigger a need for an impairment review if it is obvious that the CGUs of which corporate assets are a part are not showing any indications of impairment – unless, of course, management has decided to dispose of the asset. It is most likely that a corporate asset will show indications of impairment if the CGU or group of CGUs to which it relates are showing indications and this is reflected in the methodology by which corporate assets are tested.

Therefore the corporate asset's carrying value has to be allocated to CGUs. This allocation allows the recoverable amount of all of the assets involved, both CGU and corporate ones, to be considered. *[IAS 36.101].*

If possible, the corporate assets are to be allocated to individual CGUs on a 'reasonable and consistent basis'. *[IAS 36.102].* This is not expanded upon and affords some flexibility, although plainly consistency is vital; the same criteria must be applied at all times. If the carrying value of a corporate asset can be allocated on a reasonable and consistent basis between individual CGUs, each CGU has its impairment test done separately and its carrying value includes its share of the corporate asset.

If the corporate asset's carrying value cannot be allocated to an individual CGU, there are three steps. As noted above, indicators of impairment for corporate assets that cannot be allocated to individual CGUs are likely to relate to the CGUs that use the corporate asset as well. First the CGU is tested for impairment and any impairment written off. Then a group of CGUs is identified to which, as a group, all or part of the carrying value of the corporate asset can be allocated. This group must include the CGU that was the subject of the first test. Finally, all CGUs in this group have to be tested to determine if the group's carrying value (including the allocation of the corporate asset's carrying value) is in excess of the group's VIU. *[IAS 36.102].* If it is not sufficient, the impairment loss will be allocated pro-rata to all assets in the group of CGUs and the allocated portion of the corporate asset, as described under 4.5 below.

In IAS 36's accompanying section of illustrative examples, Example 8 has a fully worked example of the allocation and calculation of a VIU involving corporate assets. *[IAS 36.IE69-IE79].* The table below is included in it, and serves to illustrate the allocation of the corporate asset to CGUs:

Example 22.6: Allocation of corporate assets

An entity comprises three CGUs and a headquarters building. The carrying amount of the headquarters building of 150 is allocated to the carrying amount of each individual cash-generating unit. A weighted allocation basis is used because the estimated remaining useful life of A's cash-generating unit is 10 years, whereas the estimated remaining useful lives of B and C's cash-generating units are 20 years.

Schedule 1. Calculation of a weighted allocation of the carrying amount of the headquarter building

End of 20X0	A	B	C	Total
Carrying amount	100	150	200	450
Remaining useful life	10 years	20 years	20 years	
Weighting based on useful life	1	2	2	
Carrying amount after weighting	100	300	400	800
Pro-rata allocation of the building	(100/800)= 12%	(300/800)= 38%	(400/800)= 50%	100%
Allocation of the carrying amount of the building (based on pro-rata above)	19	56	75	(150)
Carrying amount (after allocation of the building)	119	206	275	600

The allocation need not be made on carrying value or financial measures such as turnover – employee numbers or a time basis might be a valid basis in certain circumstances.

One effect of this pro-rata process is that the amount of the head office allocated to each CGU will change as the useful lives and carrying values change. In the above example, the allocation of the head office to CGU A will be redistributed to CGUs B and C as A's remaining life shortens. The entity will have to ensure that B and C can support an increased head office allocation. Similar effects will be observed if the sizes of any other factor on which the allocation to the CGUs is made change relative to one another.

4.3   Estimating the future pre-tax cash flows of the CGU under review

This step needs to be performed only if the CGU concerned either has no identifiable FVLCS or a FVLCS that is lower than its carrying value.

In order to calculate the VIU the entity needs to estimate the future cash flows that it will derive from its use and consider possible variations in their amount or timing. *[IAS 36.30].* In estimating future cash flows the entity must:

(a)   base its cash flow projections on reasonable and supportable assumptions that represent management's best estimate of the range of economic conditions that will exist over the remaining useful life of the asset. Greater weight must be given to external evidence;

(b)   base cash flow projections on the most recent financial budgets/forecasts approved by management, excluding any estimated future cash inflows or outflows expected to arise from future restructurings or from improving or enhancing the asset's performance. These projections can only cover a maximum period of five years, unless a longer period can be justified;

(c)   estimate cash flow projections beyond the period covered by the most recent budgets/forecasts by extrapolating them using a steady or declining growth rate for subsequent years, unless an increasing rate can be justified. This growth rate must not exceed the long-term average growth rate for the products, industries, or country or countries in which the entity operates, or for the market in which the asset is used, unless a higher rate can be justified. *[IAS 36.33].*

4.3.1   *Budgets and cash flows*

The standard describes in some detail the responsibilities of management towards the estimation of cash flows. Management are required to ensure that the assumptions on which its current cash flow projections are based are consistent with past actual outcomes by examining the causes of differences between past cash flow projections and actual cash flows. They can, of course, take account of the effects of subsequent events or circumstances that did not exist when those actual cash flows were generated. *[IAS 36.34]*.

IAS 36 states that the cash flows should be based on the most recent budgets and forecasts for a maximum of five years because reliable forecasts are rarely available for a longer period. If management is confident that its projections are reliable and can demonstrate this from past experience, it may use a longer period. *[IAS 36.35]*. In using budgets and forecasts, management is required to consider whether these really are the best estimate of economic conditions that will exist over the remaining useful life of the asset. *[IAS 36.38]*. Cash flows for the period beyond that covered by the forecasts or budgets assume a steady, declining or even negative rate of growth. An increase in the rate may be used if it is supported by objective information. *[IAS 36.36]*.

Therefore only in exceptional circumstances should an increasing growth rate be used, or should the period before a steady or declining growth rate is assumed extend to more than five years. This five year rule is based on general economic theory that postulates above-average growth rates will only be achievable in the short-term, because such above-average growth will lead to competitors entering the market. This increased competition will, over a period of time, lead to a reduction of the growth rate, towards the average for the economy as a whole. IAS 36 suggests that entities will find it difficult to exceed the average historical growth rate for the products, countries or markets over the long term, say twenty years. *[IAS 36.37]*.

This stage of the impairment review illustrates the point that it is not only fixed assets that are being assessed. The future cash flow to be forecast is *all* cash flows – receipts from sales, purchases, administrative expenses, etc. It is akin to a free cash flow valuation of a business with the resulting valuation then being compared to the carrying value of the assets in the CGU.

The cash flow forecast should include three elements:

* cash inflows from the continuing use of the asset;
* the cash outflows necessary to generate these cash inflows, including cash outflows to prepare the asset for use, that can either be directly attributed, or allocated on a reasonable and consistent basis; and
* the net cash flows, if any, that the entity may receive or pay for the disposal of the asset at the end of its useful life. *[IAS 36.39]*.

Cash flows can be estimated by taking into account general price changes caused by inflation, or on the basis of stable prices. If inflation is excluded from the cash flow then the discount rate selected must also be adjusted to remove the inflationary effect. *[IAS 36.40]*. Generally entities will use whichever method is most convenient to them that is consistent with the method they use in their budgets and forecasts and it is, of course, fundamental that cash flows and discount rate are both estimated on a consistent basis.

To avoid the danger of double counting, the future cash flows exclude those relating to financial assets, including receivables and liabilities such as payables, pensions and provisions. *[IAS 36.43]*. However, see 4.2 above: paragraph 79 allows the inclusion of such assets and liabilities for practical reasons, in which case the cash flows must be reflected as well, and a discussion of some of the assets and liabilities that may or may not be reflected together with the implications of so doing.

The expected future cash flows of the CGU being assessed for impairment should not include cash inflows or outflows from financing activities or tax receipts or payments. This is because the discount rate used and the future cash flows are themselves determined on a pre-tax basis. *[IAS 36.50-51]*.

4.3.1.A   Cash inflows and outflows from improvements and enhancements

Projections in the cash flow should include costs of day-to-day servicing as well as overheads that can be reasonably attributed to the use of the asset. *[IAS 36.41]*. Whilst a part-completed asset must have the costs to complete it included in the cash flow, *[IAS 36.42]*, the general rule is that future cash flows should be forecast for CGUs or assets in their current condition. Forecasts should not include estimated future cash inflows or outflows that are expected to arise from improving or enhancing the asset's performance. *[IAS 36.44]*.

While the restriction on enhanced performance may be understandable, it adds an element of unreality that is hard to reconcile with other assumptions made in the VIU process. For example, the underlying forecast cash flows that the standard makes the foundation of the procedure will obviously be based on the business as it is actually expected to develop in the future, growth, improvements and all. Producing a special forecast based on unrealistic assumptions, even for this limited purpose, may be difficult.

Nevertheless, paragraph 48 explicitly states that improvements to the current performance of an asset may not be included in the estimates of future cash flows until the expenditure that provides those improvements is incurred. The treatment of such expenditure is illustrated in Example 6 in the standard's accompanying section of illustrative examples. *[IAS 36.48]*. The implication of this requirement is that if an asset is impaired, and even if the entity is going to make the future expenditure to reverse that impairment, the asset will still have to be written down. Subsequently, the asset's impairment can be reversed, to the degree appropriate, after the expenditure has taken place. Reversal of asset impairment is discussed at 6 below.

An assumption of new capital investment is in practice intrinsic to the VIU test. What has to be assessed are the future cash flows of a productive unit such as a factory or hotel. The cash flows, out into the far future, will include the sales of product, cost of sales, administrative expenses, etc. They must necessarily include capital expenditure as well, at least to the extent required to keep the CGU functioning as forecast. This is explicitly acknowledged as follows:

'Estimates of future cash flows include future cash outflows necessary to maintain the level of economic benefits expected to arise from the asset in its current condition. When a cash-generating unit consists of assets with different estimated useful lives, all of which are essential to the ongoing operation of the unit, the replacement of assets with shorter lives is considered to be part of the day-to-day servicing of the unit when estimating the future cash flows associated with the unit. Similarly, when a single asset consists of components with different estimated useful lives, the replacement of components with shorter lives is considered to be part of the day-to-day servicing of the asset when estimating the future cash flows generated by the asset.' *[IAS 36.49]*.

Accordingly, *some* capital expenditure cash flows must be built into the forecast cash flows. Whilst improving capital expenditure may not be recognised, routine or replacement capital expenditure necessary to maintain the function of the asset or assets in the CGU has to be included. This distinction may not be easy to draw in practice.

Entities must therefore distinguish between maintenance, completion and enhancement expenditure. This is not always straightforward, as shown in the following example.

Example 22.7:   Distinguishing enhancement and maintenance expenditure

A telecommunications company provides fixed line, telephone, television and internet services. It must develop its basic transmission infrastructure (by overhead wires or cables along streets or railway lines etc) and in order to service a new customer it will have to connect the customer's home via cable and other equipment. It will extend its network to adjoining areas and perhaps acquire an entity with its own network. It will also reflect changes in technology, e.g. fibre optic cables replacing copper ones.

Obviously, when preparing the budgets which form the basis for testing the network for impairment, it will make assumptions regarding future revenue growth and will include the costs of connecting those customers. However, its infrastructure maintenance spend will inevitably include replacing equipment with the current technology. There is no option of continuing to replace equipment with something that has been technologically superseded. Once this technology exists it will be reflected in the entity's budgets and taken into account in its cash flows when carrying out impairment tests, even though this new equipment will enhance the performance of the transmission infrastructure.

This maintenance and replacement expenditure must be distinguished from step changes in services and the technology used to provide them. BT Group plc noted the following in its 2008 Operating and financial review.

Extract 22.2: BT Group plc (2008)

Operating and financial review
Technological advances

Our continued success depends on our ability to exploit new technology rapidly.

We operate in an industry with a recent history of rapid technological changes and we expect this to continue – new technologies and products will emerge, and existing technologies and products will develop further.

> We need continually to exploit next-generation technologies in order to develop our existing and future services and products. However, we cannot predict the actual impact of these future technological changes on our business or our ability to provide competitive services. For example, there is evidence of substitution by customers using mobile phones for day-to-day voice calls in place of making such calls over the fixed network and of calls being routed over the internet in place of the traditional switched network. If these trends accelerate, our fixed-network assets may be used uneconomically and our investment in these assets may not be recovered through profits on fixed-line calls and line rentals.
>
> The complexity of the 21CN programme, and the risk that our major suppliers fail to meet their obligations may result in delays to the delivery of expected benefits. Impairment write-downs may be incurred and margins may decline if fixed costs cannot be reduced in line with falling revenue.

Further examples indicate another problem area – the effects of future expenditure that the entity has identified but to which the entity is not yet committed. An entity may have acquired an asset with the intention of enhancing it in future and may, therefore, have paid for future synergies which will be reflected in the calculation of goodwill. Another entity may have plans for an asset that involve expenditure that will enhance its future performance and without which the asset may be impaired.

Examples could include:

- a TV transmission company that, in acquiring another, would expect to pay for the future right to migrate customers from analogue to digital services; or
- an aircraft manufacturer that expects to be able to use one of the acquired plants for a new model at a future point, a process that will involve replacing much of the current equipment.

In both cases the long-term plans reflect both the capital spent and the cash flows that will flow from it. There is no obvious alternative to recognising an impairment when calculating the CGU or CGU group's VIU as IAS 36 insists that the impairment test has to be performed for the asset in its current condition. This means that it is not permitted to include the benefit of improving or enhancing the asset's performance in calculating its VIU.

In the TV example above, it does not appear to matter whether the entity recognises goodwill or has a separable intangible right that it has not yet brought into use.

An entity in this situation may attempt to avoid an impairment write down by calculating the appropriate FVLCS, as this is not constrained by rules regarding future capital expenditure. As discussed above, these cash flows can be included only to the extent that other market participants would consider them when evaluating the asset. It is not permissible to include assumptions about cash flows or benefits from the asset that would not be available to or considered by a typical market participant.

4.3.1.B   Restructuring

The standard contains similar rules with regard to any future restructuring that may affect the VIU of the asset or CGU. The prohibition on including the results of restructuring applies only to those plans to which the entity is not committed. Again, this is because of the general rule that the cash flows must be based on the asset in its current condition so future events that may change that condition are not to be taken into account. *[IAS 36.44-45]*. When an entity becomes committed to a restructuring (as set out in IAS 37 - see Chapter 29), IAS 36 then allows an entity's estimates of future cash inflows and outflows to reflect the cost savings and other benefits from the restructuring, based on the most recent financial budgets/forecasts approved by management. *[IAS 36.46-47]*. Treatment of such a future restructuring is illustrated by Example 5 in the standard's accompanying section of illustrative examples. The standard specifically points out that the increase in cash inflows as a result of such a restructuring may not be taken into account until after the entity is committed to the restructuring. *[IAS 36.47]*.

Entities will sometimes be required to recognise impairment losses that will be reversed once the expenditure has been incurred and the restructuring completed.

4.3.1.C Terminal values

In the case of long-lived assets, a large component of value attributable to an asset or CGU arises from its terminal value, which is the net present value of all of the forecast free cash flows that are expected to be generated by the asset or CGU after the explicit forecast period. IAS 36 includes specific requirements if the asset is to be sold at the end of its useful life. The disposal proceeds and costs should be based on current prices and costs for similar assets, adjusted if necessary for price level changes if the entity has chosen to include this factor in its forecasts and selection of a discount rate. The entity must take care that its estimate is based on a proper assessment of the amount that would be received in an arm's length transaction. *[IAS 36.52-53]*. However, CGUs usually have indefinite lives, as have some assets, and the terminal value is calculated by having regard to the forecast maintainable cash flows that are expected to be generated by the asset or CGU in the final year of the explicit forecast period ('the terminal year').

It is essential that the terminal year cash flows reflect maintainable cash flows as otherwise any material one-off or abnormal cash flows that are forecast for the terminal year will inappropriately increase or decrease the valuation.

The maintainable cash flow expected to be generated by the asset or CGU is then capitalised by a perpetuity factor based on either:

- the discount rate if cash flows are forecast to remain relatively constant; or
- the discount rate less the long term growth rate if cash flows are forecast to grow.

Care is required in assessing the growth rate to ensure consistency between the long term growth rate used and the assumptions used by the entity generally in its business planning.

4.3.1.D Foreign currency cash flows

Foreign currency cash flows should first be estimated in the currency in which they will be generated and then discounted using a discount rate appropriate for that currency. An entity should translate the present value calculated in the foreign currency using the spot exchange rate at the date of the value in use calculation. *[IAS 36.54]*. This is to avoid the problems inherent in using forward exchange rates, which are based on differential interest rates. Using such a rate would result in double-counting the time value of money, first in the discount rate and then in the forward rate. *[IAS 36.BCZ49]*. However, the method requires an entity to perform, in effect, separate impairment tests for cash flows generated in different currencies but make them consistent with one another so that the combined effect is meaningful, an extremely difficult exercise. Many different factors need to be taken into account including relative inflation rates and relative interest rates as well as appropriate discount rates for the currencies in question. Because of this, the possibility for error is great and the greatest danger is understating the present value of cash outflows by using too high a discount rate. In practice, valuers may assist entities to obtain a good enough result by assuming that cash flows are generated in a single currency even though they may be received or paid in another.

Significantly, the rate used to translate the cash flows could well be different from that used to translate the foreign currency assets, goodwill and liabilities of a subsidiary at the period end. For example, a non-monetary asset such as an item of property, plant and equipment may be carried at an amount based on exchange rates on the date on which it was acquired but generates foreign currency cash flows. In order to determine its carrying amount if there are indicators of impairment, IAS 21 – *The Effects of Changes in Foreign Exchange Rates* – states that the recoverable amount will be calculated in accordance with IAS 36 and the present value of the cash flows translated at the exchange rate at the date when that value was determined. *[IAS 21.25]*. IAS 21 notes that this may be the rate at the balance sheet date. The VIU is then compared to the carrying value and the item is then carried forward at the lower of these two values. Similarly, different rates may be used if the impairment review is of goodwill or an intangible asset with indefinite life, where the review need not be carried out at the year-end.

4.4   Identifying an appropriate discount rate and discounting the future cash flows

Finally, although probably inherent in their identification, the forecast cash flows of the CGU have to be allocated to different periods for the purpose of the discounting step. The present value of these cash flows should then be calculated by discounting them. The discount rate is to be a pre-tax rate that reflects current market assessments of the time value of money and the risks specific to the asset for which the future cash flow estimates have not been adjusted. *[IAS 36.55]*.

This means the discount rate to be applied should be an estimate of the rate that the market would expect on an equally risky investment. The standard states:

> 'A rate that reflects current market assessments of the time value of money and the risks specific to the asset is the return that investors would require if they were to choose an investment that would generate cash flows of amounts, timing and risk profile equivalent to those that the entity expects to derive from the asset.' *[IAS 36.56]*.

Therefore, if at all possible, the rate is to be obtained from market transactions or market rates. It should be the rate implicit in current market transactions for similar assets or the weighted average cost of capital (WACC) of a listed entity that has a single asset (or a portfolio of assets) with similar service potential and risks to the asset under review. *[IAS 36.56]*. If such a listed entity could be found, care would have to be taken in using its WACC as the standard specifies that the discount rate is independent of the entity's capital structure and the way it financed the purchase of the asset (see below). The effect of gearing and its effect on calculating an appropriate WACC are discussed further in Example 22.8 and there is more discussion on the use of the WACC in 4.4.1 below.

Only in rare cases (e.g. property assets) can such market rates can be obtained. If an asset-specific rate is not available from the market, surrogates should be used as set out in Appendix A of IAS 36. The discount rate that investors would require if they were to choose an investment that would generate cash flows of amounts, timing and risk profile equivalent to those that the entity expects to derive from the asset will not be easy to determine. IAS 36 suggests that, as a starting point, the entity may take into account the following rates:

(a)   the entity's weighted average cost of capital determined using techniques such as the Capital Asset Pricing Model;

(b)   the entity's incremental borrowing rate; and

(c)   other market borrowing rates. *[IAS 36.A17]*.

Appendix A also gives the following guidelines for selecting the appropriate discount rate:

• it should be adjusted to reflect the specific risks associated with the projected cash flows (such as country, currency, price and cash flow risks) and to exclude risks that are not relevant; *[IAS 36.A18]*

• to avoid double counting, the discount rate does not reflect risks for which future cash flow estimates have been adjusted; *[IAS 36.A18]*

• the discount rate is independent of the entity's capital structure and the way it financed the purchase of the asset; *[IAS 36.A19]*

• if the basis for the rate is post-tax (such as a weighted average cost of capital), it is adjusted to reflect a pre-tax rate; *[IAS 36.A20]* and

• normally the entity uses a single discount rate but it should use separate discount rates for different future periods if the VIU is sensitive to different risks for different periods or to the term structure of interest rates. *[IAS 36.A21]*.

The discount rate specific for the asset or CGU will take account of the period over which the asset or CGU is expected to generate cash inflows and it may not be sensitive to changes in short-term rates – this is discussed in 2.2.1.D above. *[IAS 36.16]*.

It is suggested that the incremental borrowing rate of the business is relevant to the selection of a discount rate. This could only be a starting point as the appropriate discount rate should be independent of the entity's capital structure or the way in which it financed the purchase of the asset. The incremental borrowing rate must be used with extreme caution as it might, for example, include an element of default risk for the entity as a whole, which is not relevant in assessing the return expected from the assets.

In practice many entities use the WACC to estimate the appropriate discount rate. The appropriate way to calculate WACC is an extremely technical subject, and one about which there is much academic literature and no general agreement. The selection of the rate is obviously a crucial part of the impairment testing process and in practice it will probably not be possible to obtain a theoretically perfect rate. The objective, therefore, must be to obtain a rate which is sensible and justifiable. There are probably a number of acceptable methods of arriving at the appropriate rate and one method is set out below. While this illustration may appear to be quite complex, it has been written at a fairly general level as the calculation of the appropriate discount rate may be difficult and specialist advice may be needed.[2]

Example 22.8:   Calculating a discount rate

This example is based on determining the WACC for a listed company with a similar risk profile to the CGU in question. Because it is highly unlikely that such a company will exist, it will usually have to be simulated by looking at a hypothetical company with a similar risk profile.

The following three elements need to be estimated for the hypothetical listed company with a similar risk profile:

- gearing, i.e. the ratio of market value of debt to market value of equity
- cost of debt; and
- cost of equity.

Gearing can best be obtained by reviewing quoted companies operating predominantly in the same industry as the CGU and identifying an average level of gearing for such companies. The companies need to be quoted so that the market value of equity can be readily determined.

Where companies in the sector typically have quoted debt, the cost of such debt can be determined directly. In order to calculate the cost of debt for bank loans and borrowings more generally, one method is to take the rate implicit in fixed interest government bonds – with a period to maturity similar to the expected life of the assets being reviewed for impairment – and to add to this rate a bank's margin, i.e. the commercial premium that would be added to the bond rate by a bank lending to the hypothetical listed company. In some cases, the margin being charged on existing borrowings to the company in question will provide evidence to help with establishing the bank's margin. Obviously, the appropriateness of this will depend upon the extent to which the risks facing the CGU being tested are similar to the risks facing the company or group as a whole.

If goodwill or intangible assets with an indefinite life were being included in a CGU reviewed for impairment (see 5 below) the appropriate Government bond rate to use might have to be adjusted towards that for irredeemable bonds. The additional bank's margin to add would be a matter for judgement but would vary according to the ease with which the sector under review was generally able to obtain bank finance and, as noted above, there might be evidence from the borrowings actually in place of the likely margin that would be chargeable. Sectors that invest significantly in tangible assets such as properties that are readily available as security for borrowings, would require a lower margin than other sectors where such security could not be found so easily.

Cost of equity is the hardest component of the cost of capital to determine. One technique referred to in the standard, frequently used in practice and written up in numerous textbooks is the 'Capital Asset Pricing Model' (CAPM). The theory underlying this model is that the cost of equity is equal to the risk-free rate plus a multiple, known as the beta, of the market risk premium. The risk-free rate is the same as that used to determine the nominal cost of debt and described above as being obtainable from government bond yields with an appropriate period to redemption. The market risk premium is the premium that investors require for investing in equities rather than government bonds. There are also reasons why this rate may be loaded in certain cases, for instance to take account of specific risks in the CGU in question that are not reflected in its market sector generally. Loadings are typically made when determining the cost of equity for a small company. The beta for a quoted company is a number that is greater or less than one according to whether market movements generally are reflected in a proportionately greater (beta more than one) or smaller (beta less than one) movement in the particular stock in question. Most betas fall into the range 0.4 to 1.5.

Various bodies, such as The London Business School, publish betas on a regular basis both for individual stocks and for industry sectors in general. Published betas are levered, i.e. they reflect the level of gearing in the company or sector concerned (although unlevered betas (based on risk as if financed with 100% equity) are also available and care must be taken not to confuse the two).

The cost of equity for the hypothetical company having a similar risk profile to the CGU is:

Cost of equity = risk-free rate + (levered beta × market risk premium)

Having determined the component costs of debt and equity and the appropriate level of gearing, the WACC for the hypothetical company having a similar risk profile to the CGU in question is:

$$\text{WACC} = (1 - t) \times D \times \frac{g}{(1 + g)} + E \times \left[1 - \frac{g}{(1 + g)} \right]$$

where:
D is the cost of debt;
E is the cost of equity
g is the gearing level (i.e. the ratio of debt to equity) for the sector; and
t is the rate of tax relief available on the debt servicing payments.

IAS 36 requires that the forecast cash flows are before tax and finance costs, though it is more common in discounted cash flow valuations to use cash flows after tax. However, as pre-tax cash flows are being used, the standard requires a pre-tax discount rate to be used. *[IAS 36.55].* This will theoretically involve discounting higher future cash flows (before deduction of tax) with a higher discount rate. This higher discount rate is the post-tax rate adjusted to reflect the specific amount and timing of the future tax flows. In other words, the pre-tax discount rate is the rate that gives the same present value when discounting the pre-tax cash flows as the post-tax cash flows discounted at the post-tax rate of return. *[IAS 36.BCZ85].*

Once the WACC has been calculated, the pre-tax WACC can be calculated. If a simple gross up is appropriate, it can be calculated by applying the fraction 1/(1–t). Thus, if the WACC comes out at, say, 10% the pre-tax WACC will be 10% divided by 0.7, if the relevant tax rate for the reporting entity is 30%, which will give a pre-tax rate of 14.3%. However, the standard warns that in many circumstances a gross up will not give a good enough answer as the pre-tax discount rate also depends on the timing of future tax cash flows and the useful life of the asset; these tax flows can be scheduled and an iterative process used to calculate the pre-tax discount rate. *[IAS 36.BCZ85].* The relationship between pre- and post-tax rates is discussed further below.

The selection of discount rates leaves considerable room for judgement in the absence of more specific guidance, and it is likely that many very different approaches will be applied in practice, even though this may not always be evident from the financial statements. However, once the discount rate has been chosen, the future cash flows are discounted in order to produce a present value figure representing the VIU of the CGU or individual asset that is the subject of the impairment test. The final step in the impairment review can now be taken.

4.4.1   Discount rates and the weighted average cost of capital

The WACC is often used in practice. It is usually acceptable to auditors as it is supported by valuation experts and is an accepted methodology based on a well-known formula and widely available information. In addition, many entities already know their own WACC. However, it can only be used as a starting point for determining an appropriate discount rate and some of the issues that must be taken into account are as follows:

a) the WACC is a post-tax rate and IAS 36 requires VIU to be calculated using pre-tax cash flows and a pre-tax rate. Converting the former into the latter is not simply a question of grossing up the post-tax rate by the effective tax rate;

b) other tax factors may need to be considered, whether or not these will result in tax cash flows in the period covered by budgets and cash flows;

c) an entity's own WACC may not be suitable as a discount rate if there is anything atypical about the entity's capital structure compared with 'typical' market participants;

d) the WACC must reflect the risks specific to the asset and not the risks relating to the entity as a whole, such as default risk; and

e) the entity's WACC is an average rate derived from its existing business, yet entities frequently operate in more than one sector. Within a sector, different types of projects may have different levels of risk (e.g. a start-up as against an established product).

These are discussed further below.

One of the most difficult areas in practice is the effect of taxation on the WACC. In order to determine an appropriate pre-tax discount rate it is likely to be necessary to adjust the entity's actual tax cash flows.

Ultimately, the appropriate discount rate to select is one that reflects current market assessments of the time value of money and the risks specific to the asset in question, including taxation. Such a rate is one that reflects 'the return that investors would require if they were to choose an investment that would generate cash flows of amounts, timing and risk profile equivalent to those that the entity expects to derive from the asset.' *[IAS 36.56].*

4.4.2   Calculating a pre-tax discount rate

VIU is primarily an accounting concept rather than a business valuation of the asset or CGU. One fundamental difference is that IAS 36 requires pre-tax cash flows to be discounted using a pre-tax discount rate. Why not calculate VIU on a post-tax basis? The reason is the complexities created by tax losses carried forward, temporary tax differences and deferred taxes.

The standard explains in the basis for conclusions that, 'Future income tax cash flows may affect recoverable amount. It is convenient to analyse future tax cash flows into two components:

(a)   the future tax cash flows that would result from any difference between the tax base of an asset (the amount attributed to it for tax purposes) and its carrying amount, after recognition of any impairment loss. Such differences are described in IAS 12 – *Income Taxes* – as 'temporary differences'.

(b)   the future tax cash flows that would result if the tax base of the asset were equal to its recoverable amount.' *[IAS 36.BCZ81].*

The language is complex but it refers to the following issues.

An impairment test, say at the end of 2012, takes account of estimated future cash flows. The tax that an entity will pay in future years that will be reflected in the actual tax cash flows that it expects may depend on tax depreciation that the entity has already received (or, less often, that it yet to receive) in respect of the asset or CGU being tested for impairment. The value of the asset to the business on a post-tax basis must take account of all tax effects and not only those that will only arise in future.

Although these 'temporary differences' are accounted for as deferred taxation, IAS 12 does not allow entities to recognise all deferred tax liabilities or deferred tax assets, deferred tax assets are not recognised using the same criteria as deferred tax liabilities and the amounts are not discounted. Therefore, deferred taxation as provided in the income statement and balance sheet is not sufficient to take account of the actual temporary differences relating to the asset or CGU.

At the same time, an asset valuation implicitly assumes that the carrying amount of the asset is deductible for tax. For example, if the tax rate is 25%, an entity must receive pre-tax cash flows with a present value of 400 in order to recover a carrying amount of 300. *[IAS 36.BCZ88].* In principle, therefore, VIU on a post-tax basis would include the present value of the future tax cash flows that would result if the tax base of the asset were equal to its value in use.

To calculate VIU on a post-tax basis is not straightforward because:

(i)   to avoid double-counting, it is necessary to exclude the effect of temporary differences, as described above; and

(ii)   VIU would need to be determined by 'an iterative and possibly complex computation so that value in use itself reflects a tax base equal to that value in use.' *[IAS 36.BCZ84].*

For these reasons, the (then) IASC decided to require an enterprise to determine value in use by using pre-tax future cash flows and a pre-tax discount rate.

This means that there is a different problem, calculating an appropriate pre-tax discount rate because there are no observable pre-tax discount rates. Two important points must be taken into account:

- *The pre-tax discount rate is not always the post-tax discount rate grossed up by a standard rate of tax.* There are some circumstances in which a gross-up will give a reasonable approximation, discussed further at 4.4.3.A below.

- *The pre-tax discount rate is not the post-tax rate grossed up by the entity's actual tax cash flows.* As discussed above, a post-tax discount rate such as the WACC is based on certain assumptions about the tax-deductibility of the asset and not the actual tax cash flows experienced by the entity,

IAS 36.BCZ85, recognising this, states that 'in theory, discounting post-tax cash flows at a post-tax discount rate and discounting pre-tax cash flows at a pre-tax discount rate should give the same result, as long as the pre-tax discount rate is the post-tax discount rate adjusted to reflect the specific amount and timing of the future tax cash flows'.

Therefore, the only accurate way to calculate a pre-tax WACC is to calculate the VIU by applying a post-tax rate to post-tax cash flows, tax cash flows being based on the allowances and charges available to the asset and to which the revenue is subject (see discussion below at 4.4.3). The effective pre-tax rate is calculated by removing the tax cash flows and, by iteration, one can identify the pre-tax rate that makes the present value of the adjusted cash flows equal the VIU calculated using post tax cash flows.

Paragraph BCZ85 includes an example of how to calculate a pre-tax discount rate where the tax cash flows are irregular because of the availability of tax deductions for the asset's capital cost. See also the calculations in Example 22.9 below. This is a relatively straightforward calculation for a single asset at the inception of the relevant project.

It may be far more complex at a later date. This is because entities may be attempting to calculate a discount rate starting with post-tax cash flows and a post-tax discount rate at a point in time when there are already temporary differences relating to the asset. A discount rate based on an entity's prospective tax cash flows may under- or overstate IAS 36's impairment charge unless it reflects these previous allowances or disallowances. This is the same problem that will be encountered if an entity attempts to test VIU using post-tax cash flows that are described below.

A notional adjustment will have to be made if the entity is not paying tax because it is making, or has made, tax losses. It is unwarranted to assume that the post- and pre-tax discount rates will be the same if the entity pays no tax because of its own tax losses as this will be double counting. It is taking advantage of the losses in the cash flows but excluding that value from the assets of the CGU.

Entities may attempt to deal with the complexity of determining a pre-tax rate by trying to calculate VIU on a post-tax basis but this approach means addressing all of the many difficulties that have been identified by the IASB and the reasons why it mandated a pre-tax approach in testing for impairment in the first place.

Some approximations and short cuts that may give an acceptable answer in practice are dealt with at 4.4.4 below.

4.4.3   Calculating VIU using post-tax cash flows

Because of the challenges in calculating an appropriate pre-tax discount rate and because it aligns more closely with their normal business valuation approach, some entities attempt to perform a VIU calculation based on a post-tax discount rate and post-tax cash flows. In support of the post-tax approach, the example in IAS 36.BC85 which explains how to calculate a pre-tax discount rate, is erroneously misunderstood as a methodology for a post-tax VIU calculation using an entity's actual tax cash flows.

Entities that try a post-tax approach generally use the year-end WACC and estimated post-tax cash flows for future years that reflect the actual tax that they expect to pay in those years.

A calculation on this basis will only by chance correspond to an impairment test in accordance with IAS 36 because it is based on inappropriate assumptions, i.e. it does not take account of the temporary differences that affect the entity's future tax charges. Some include in the post-tax calculation the benefit of tax deductions or tax losses by bringing them into the cash flows in the years in which the tax benefit is expected to be received. In these cases the calculation will not correctly take account of the timing differences reflected in the tax cash flows.

In order to calculate a post-tax VIU that is the equivalent to the VIU required by IAS 36, an entity will usually have to make adjustments to the actual tax cash flows or otherwise adjust its actual post-tax cash flows.

There are two approaches that can give a post-tax VIU that is equivalent to IAS 36's pre-tax calculation.

(a)   Post-tax cash flows based on notional tax cash flows. The assumptions that need to be made are the same as those used in calculating a pre-tax discount rate as described in paragraph BCZ85. Therefore, there must be no timing differences associated with the asset which means including only the future cash flows that would result if the tax base of the asset were equal to its VIU. In addition, no account is taken of tax losses, which may mean making appropriate notional adjustments if there is no tax charge.

(b)   Post-tax cash flows reflecting actual tax cash flows as adjusted for deferred tax. The relevant deferred tax asset or liability, discounted as appropriate, should be treated as part of the net assets of the relevant CGU.

It is very important to note that these are methodologies to determine IAS 36's required VIU and they will only be acceptable if the result can be shown to be materially the same as a pre-tax impairment calculation as required by IAS 36.

Example 22.9:   Impairment calculations using pre- and post-tax cash flows and discount rates

The following examples illustrate impairment calculations using pre- and post-tax cash flows and discount rates.

(a)   Comparing pre- and post-tax rates

An entity has invested €2,139 in a facility with a 10 year life. Revenue and operating costs are expected to grow by 5% annually. The cost of the plant is equal to the net present value of the post-tax future cash flows, discounted at the WACC of 8.1%.

The budgeted pre-tax cash flows are as follows:

Year	1	2	3	4	5	6	7	8	9	10
	€	€	€	€	€	€	€	€	€	€
Revenues	500	525	551	579	608	638	670	703	739	776
Operating expenses	200	210	220	232	243	255	268	281	296	310
Pre-tax cash flow	300	315	331	347	365	383	402	422	443	465

The following tax amortisation and tax rate apply to the business:

Tax and accounting depreciation	straight line
Tax rate	30%

These apply to the budgeted cash flows as follows:

Depreciation and tax amortisation	214	214	214	214	214	214	214	214	214	214
Taxation	26	30	35	40	45	51	56	62	69	75
Post-tax cash flow	274	285	296	307	319	332	346	360	374	390

The pre-tax rate can be calculated using an iterative calculation and this can be compared to a gross up using the standard rate of tax. The NPV using these two rates is as follows:

Pre-tax rate (day 1) – iterative calculation	10.92%
Cost of investment at NPV future cash flows	€2,139
Standard gross up (day 1) (8.1% ÷ 70%).	11.57%
NPV at standard gross up	€2,077

The NPV of the pre-tax cash flows at 11.57% is €2.077. This is only 2.9% lower than the number calculated using the true pre-tax rate. In many circumstances this difference would not have a material effect.

If the tax and depreciation are straight line then the distortion introduced by a standard gross-up can be relatively small and could be of less significance to an impairment test than, for example the potential variability in cash flows. See also 4.4.4 below.

(b)   Comparing pre- and post-tax rates when the asset is impaired

Assume that the facility is much less successful than had previously been assumed and that the revenues are 20% lower than the original estimates. The pre- and post-tax cash flows are as follows.

Year	1	2	3	4	5	6	7	8	9	10
	€	€	€	€	€	€	€	€	€	€
Revenues	400	420	441	463	486	511	536	563	591	621
Operating expenses	200	210	221	232	243	255	268	281	295	310
Pre-tax cash flow	200	210	221	232	243	255	268	281	295	310
Depreciation and tax allowances	214	214	214	214	214	214	214	214	214	214
Taxation	(4)	(1)	2	5	9	12	16	20	24	29
Post-tax cash flows	204	211	219	226	234	243	252	261	271	281

The asset is clearly impaired as the previous cash flows were just sufficient to recover the carrying amount of the investment. If these revised cash flows are discounted using the pre- and post-tax discount rates discussed above, the resulting impairment is as follows:

		NPV	Impairment	Deferred tax	Net loss
Original investment		2,139			
Pre-tax cash flows, discounted at pre-tax discount rate	10.92%	1,426	713	214	499
Post-tax cash flows discounted at post-tax discount rate	8.1%	1,569	570	171	399

Unless adjustments are made to the post-tax calculation, it will understate the impairment loss by 143 (pre-tax) and 100 (post-tax, assuming full provision for the deferred tax asset). This difference is the present value of the deferred tax on the actual impairment loss, a point explored in more detail in (d) below.

(c)   *Impairment and variable tax cash flows*

The assumption of straight-line amortisation for taxation and accounting purposes does not reflect the circumstances of certain sectors, particularly where there are significant deductions for tax for the cost of the asset being tested for impairment, e.g. in the extractive sector. Impairment tests have to be calculated on finite life assets and variable tax cash flows. In many jurisdictions there are, or have been, substantial tax allowances for the construction of the asset but high rates of tax in the production phase.

The following example assumes that the entity gets a tax deduction for the cost of the asset in year 1. Once again, this assumes that in year 1 the cost of the investment is equal to the NPV of the cash flows.

Year	1	2	3	4	5	6	7	8	9	10
	€	€	€	€	€	€	€	€	€	€
Revenues	500	525	551	579	608	638	670	704	739	776
Operating expenses	200	210	221	232	243	255	268	281	295	310
Pre-tax cash flow	300	315	331	347	365	383	402	422	443	465
Tax amortisation	2367									
Taxation	(620)	95	99	104	109	115	121	127	133	140
Post-tax cash flows	920	221	232	243	255	268	281	295	310	326

Assuming the same post-tax WACC of 8.1%, the pre-tax WACC is now considerably lower owing to the effect of the tax deduction in the first year. It can be calculated using an iterative process at 8.76%, rather than 10.92%, which is the pre-tax rate in (a) and (b) above. Therefore, the NPV of the pre- and post-tax cash inflows is €2,367 rather than €2,139 – the first year tax allowances enhance the VIU of the project. If the entity discounted the pre-tax cash flows at 11.57%, the post-tax rate grossed up at the standard rate of taxation, these cash flows would have a NPV of €2,077, which is approximately 12% lower than the actual NPV. It is clear that a standardised gross up will not give a reasonable approximation in these circumstances.

(d)   *correctly measuring impairment using post-tax information*

If an entity applies a post-tax rate to post-tax cash flows, what can it do to ensure that impairment is correctly measured in accordance with IAS 36?

Assume, in example (c) above, that cash flows decline by 20% commencing at the beginning of year 2. The net cash inflows will be the same as those in (2) above. The net present value of the pre-tax cash flows at 8.75% is €1,360.

Year	2	3	4	5	6	7	8	9	10
	€	€	€	€	€	€	€	€	€
Pre-tax cash flow	210	221	232	243	255	268	281	295	310
Taxation	63	66	69	73	77	80	84	89	93
Post-tax cash flows	147	154	162	170	179	188	197	207	217

The asset's book value, assuming straight line depreciation over 10 years, is €2,130. Impairment calculated using pre-tax cash flows and discount rates is as follows:

		€
Original investment		2,367
Net book value (end of year 1)		2,130
Pre-tax cash flows, discounted at pre-tax discount rate	8.76%	1,516
Impairment		614
Deferred tax asset (reduction deferred tax liability)		(184)
Net impairment loss		430

A post-tax calculation overstates the impairment, as follows:

		€
Original investment		2,367
Net book value (end of year 1)		2,130
Post-tax cash flows, discounted at post-tax discount rate	8.1%	1,092
Impairment – overstated by 424		1,038
Deferred tax asset (reduction deferred tax liability)		(311)
Net impairment loss – overstated by 297		727

There are two ways in which the post-tax calculation can be adjusted so as to give the right impairment charge.

Method (a): Post-tax cash flows based on notional tax cash flows. The assumptions that need to be made are the same as those used in calculating a pre-tax discount rate. Therefore, there must be no timing differences associated with the asset which means including only the future cash flows that would result if the tax base of the asset were equal to its VIU.

This means assuming that the VIU of the asset (1,516) is deductible for tax purposes in year 2. This would usually be calculated iteratively

Year	2	3	4	5	6	7	8	9	10
	€	€	€	€	€	€	€	€	€
Pre-tax cash flow	210	221	232	243	255	268	281	295	310
Deemed tax amortisation	1,516								
Taxation	(392)	66	69	73	77	80	84	89	93
Post-tax cash flows	602	155	163	170	178	188	197	206	217

The present value of the notional post-tax cash flows at the post-tax discount rate of 8.1% is now, of course, €1,516, i.e. the VIU of the asset is fully deductible for tax purposes, so the impairment charge, before taxation, is €614.

Method (b): Post-tax cash flows reflecting actual tax cash flows as adjusted for deferred tax. The relevant deferred tax asset or liability, discounted as appropriate, should be treated as part of the net assets of the relevant CGU.

The net present value of the post-tax cash flows at the post-tax discount rate is €1,092. The gross deferred tax liability relating to the asset is 1,516 at 30%, i.e. €455. The NPV of €455, discounted for one year at the post-tax discount rate of 8.1%, is €424. Revised, the post-tax calculation is a follows:

		€
Original investment		2,367
Net book value (end of year 1)		2,130
Post-tax cash flows, discounted at post-tax discount rate	8.1%	1,092
Discounted deferred tax		424
Impairment (2,130 – (1,092 + 424))		614

It will rarely be practicable to apply this methodology to calculate a discount rate for a CGU, as so many factors need to be taken into account. Even if all assets within the CGU are individually acquired or self-constructed, they may have a range of lives for depreciation and tax amortisation purposes, up to and including indefinite lives. There are additional issues if the CGU comprises or includes assets acquired in a business combination; the fair value may or may not reflect tax benefits and there may be complications caused by deferred tax If goodwill is being tested it has an indefinite life whilst the underlying assets in the CGU or CGU group to which it has been allocated will usually have finite lives. It is likely that a reasonable approximation to the 'true' discount rate is the best that can be achieved and this is discussed further below.

4.4.4 Approximations and short cuts

The illustrations in Example 22.9 are of course simplified, and in reality it is unlikely that entities will need to schedule all of the tax cash flows and tax consequences in order to calculate a pre-tax discount rate every time they perform an impairment review. In practice it will probably not be possible to obtain a rate that is theoretically perfect – the task is just too intractable for that. The objective, therefore, must be to obtain a rate which is sensible and justifiable. Some of the following may make the exercise somewhat easier.

An entity may calculate a pre-tax rate using adjusted tax cash flows based on the assumptions that we have described and apply that rate to discount pre-tax cash flows. This pre-tax rate will only need to be reassessed when there is an external factor that affects risks, relevant market rates or the taxation basis of the asset or CGU.

The market may conclude that the risks relating to a particular asset are higher or lower than had previously been assumed. The market might consider risks to have reduced if, for example, a new project, process or product proves to be successful; the converse would also be true if there were previously unforeseen problems with an activity. Relevant changes in market rates are those for instruments with a period to maturity similar to the expected life of the assets being reviewed for impairment, so these will not necessarily need to be recalculated every time an impairment review is carried out. Short-term market rates may increase or decrease without affecting the rate of return that the market would require on long-term assets. Significant changes in the basis of taxation could also affect the discount rate, e.g. if tax deductions are applied or removed for all of a class of asset or activity. The discount rate will not necessarily be affected if the entity ceases to make taxable profits.

Valuation practitioners often use approximations when computing tax cash flows that may also make the task more straightforward. It may often be a valid approximation to assume that the tax amortisation of assets equals their accounting depreciation. Tax cash flows will be based on the relevant corporate tax rate and the forecast earnings before interest and taxation to give post-tax 'cash flows' that can then be discounted using a post-tax discount rate. The circumstances in which this could lead to a material distortion (perhaps in the case of an impairment test for an individual asset) will probably be obvious. This approach is consistent with the overall requirement of IAS 36, which is that the appropriate discount rate to select is one that reflects current market assessments of the risks specific to the asset in question.

The circumstances in which a standardised gross up at the corporation tax rate will give the relevant discount rate are:

- no growth in cash flows;
- a perpetuity calculation; and
- tax cash flows that are a constant percentage of total cash flows.

As long as these conditions remain unchanged, it will be straightforward to determine the discount rate for an impairment review at either the pre- or post-tax level.

If these criteria are met (or there is a close approximation, which may be the case for some CGUs) a simple gross up may be materially correct. The criteria are unlikely to apply to the VIU of individual assets, not least because these are rarely perpetuity calculations. If it is inappropriate to make such a gross up, an iterative calculation may be necessary to compute the appropriate pre-tax discount rate.

4.4.5   Disclosing pre-tax discount rates when using a post-tax methodology

If an entity calculates impairment using a post-tax methodology, it must still disclose the appropriate pre-tax discount rate. *[IAS 36.134(d)(iv)]*. There is a widely-held view that the relevant pre-tax discount rate is the rate that will discount the pre-tax cash flows to the same VIU as the post-tax cash flows discounted using the post-tax discount rate. This will not necessarily give an answer that is consistent with IAS 36 if the post-tax cash flows in question are based on the entity's actual tax. IAS 36 makes it clear that pre- and post-tax discount rates will only give the same answer if 'the pre-tax discount rate is the post-tax discount rate adjusted to reflect the specific amount and timing of the future tax cash flows'. *[IAS 36.BCZ84]*. It is no different in principle whether grossing up for a pre-tax rate or grossing up for disclosure purposes.

As well as not being consistent with IAS 36, it can be demonstrated that the apparent pre-tax discount rate calculated as described above will show a rising trend over the life of the asset as the ratio of pre- to post-tax cash flows changes and the effect of discounting becomes smaller. A rate based on actual post-tax cash flows will also vary from year to year depending on the tax situation. These effects can be very marked. Neither of these distortions is consistent with the principle that the pre-tax discount rate is the rate that reflects current market assessments of the time value of money and the risks specific to the asset. *[IAS 36.55]*.

4.4.6   Determining pre-tax rates taking account of tax losses

A common problem relates to the effect of tax losses on the impairment calculation, as they may reduce the total tax paid in the period under review or even eliminate it altogether. As noted above, however, a post-tax discount rate is based on certain assumptions about the tax-deductibility of the asset and not the actual tax cash flows. It is therefore unwarranted to assume that the post- and pre-tax discount rates will be the same if the entity pays no tax because of its own tax losses. The pre-tax rate should not include the benefit of available tax benefits and any deferred tax asset arising from tax losses carried forward at the reporting date must be excluded from the assets of the CGU if the impairment review is based on VIU. Similarly, if the entity calculates a post-tax VIU (see 4.4.3 above), it will also make assumptions about taxation and not base the calculation on the actual tax cash flows.

In many circumstances the past history of tax losses affects the level of risk in the cash flows in the period under review, but one must take care not to increase the discount rate to reflect risks for which the estimated cash flows have been adjusted. *[IAS 36.A15]*. To do so would be to double count.

4.4.7   Entity-specific WACCs and different project risks within the entity

The entity's WACC is an average rate derived from its existing business, yet entities frequently operate in more than one sector. Within a sector, different types of projects may have different levels of risk, e.g. a start-up as against an established product.

Therefore, entities must ensure that the different business risks of different CGUs are properly taken into account when determining the appropriate discount rates.

It must be noted that these areas of different risk will not always coincide with the assets or CGUs that are being tested for impairment as this is a test for impairment and not necessarily a determination of business value.

Example 22.10: Different project risks and CGUs

An aircraft manufacturer makes both civilian and military aircraft. The risks for both sectors are markedly different as they are much lower for defence contractors than for the civilian market. The assembly plants for civilian and military aircraft are separate CGUs. In this sector there are entities that are based solely in one or other of these markets, i.e. they are purely defence or civilian contractors, so there will be a basis for identifying the different discount rates for the different activities. If the entity makes its own components then the defence CGU or CGUs could include the manufacturing activity if defence is vertically integrated and components are made solely for military aircraft. Manufacturing could be a separate CGU if components are used for both activities and there is an external market for the products.

A manufacturer of soft drinks uses the same plant to produce various flavours of carbonated and uncarbonated drinks. Because the market for traditional carbonated drinks is declining, it develops and markets a new uncarbonated 'health' drink, which is still produced using the same plant. The risks of the product are higher than those of the existing products but it is not a separate CGU.

Many sectors generate many new products but have a high attrition rate as most of their new products fail (pharmaceuticals and biotechnology, for example) and this is likely built into industry WACCs. If the risk of failure is not reflected in the WACC because the entity is not typical of the industry then either the discount rate or the cash flows ought to be adjusted to reflect the risk (but not so as to double count).

4.4.8 Entity-specific WACCs and capital structure

The discount rate is a pre-tax rate that reflects current market assessments of the time value of money and the risks specific *to the asset* for which the future cash flow estimates have not been adjusted. *[IAS 36.55].* An entity's own WACC may not be suitable as a discount rate if there is anything atypical about the entity's capital structure compared with 'typical' market participants. In other words, would the market assess the cash flows from the asset or unit as being riskier or less risky than the entity-wide risks reflected in the entity-wide WACC? Some of the risks that need to be thought about are country risk, currency risks and price risk.

Country risk will reflect the area in which the assets are located. In some areas assets are frequently nationalised by governments or the area may be politically unstable and prone to violence. In addition, the potential impact of physical instability such as weather or earthquakes, and the effects of currency volatility on the expected return from the asset, must be considered.

Two elements of price risk are the gearing ratio of the entity in question (if, for example, it is much more or less geared than average) and any default risk built into its cost of debt. However, IAS 36 explicitly notes that the discount rate is independent of the entity's capital structure and the way the entity financed the purchase of the asset, because the future cash flows expected to arise from an asset do not depend on these features. *[IAS 36.A19].*

Example 22.11:   Effect of entity default risk on its WACC

The formula for calculating the (post tax) WACC, as given in Example 22.8 above, is

$$\text{WACC} = (1 - t) \times D \times \frac{g}{(1 + g)} + E \times \left[1 - \frac{g}{(1 + g)} \right]$$

where:

t is the rate of tax relief available on the debt servicing payments

D is the pre-tax cost of debt;

E is the cost of equity;

g is the gearing level (i.e. the ratio of debt to equity) for the sector.

The cost of equity is calculated as follows:

Cost of equity = risk-free rate + (levered beta (β*) × market risk premium)

Assume that the WACC of a typical sector participant is as follows:

Cost of equity	
risk free rate	4%
levered beta (β)	1.1
market risk premium	6%
cost of equity after tax (market risk	10.6%
premium × β + risk-free rate)	
Cost of debt	
risk free rate	4%
credit spread	3%
cost of debt (pre-tax)	7%
cost of debt (post-tax)	5.25%
Capital structure	
debt / (debt + equity)	25%
equity / (debt + equity)	75%
tax rate	25%
post-tax cost of equity (10.6 × 75%)	8%
post-tax cost of debt (5.25 × 25%)	1.3%
WACC (Post tax, nominal)	9.3%

* The beta is explained in Example 22.8 above.

However, the company has borrowed heavily and is in some financial difficulties. Its gearing ratio is 75% and its actual cost of debt, based on the market price of its listed bonds, is 18% (13.5% after taking account of tax at 25%). This makes its individual post-tax WACC 12.8% (10.6×25% + 13.5×75%). This is not an appropriate WACC for impairment purposes because it does not represent a market rate of return *on the assets*. Its entity WACC has been increased by default risk.

Ultimately it might be acceptable to use the entity's own WACC, but an entity cannot conclude on this without going through the exercise of assessing for risk each of the assets or units and concluding on whether or not they contain additional risks that are not reflected in the WACC.

4.4.9   *Use of discount rates other than the WACC*

IAS 36 allows an entity to use rates other than the WACC as a starting point in calculating the discount rate. These include:

(a)   the entity's incremental borrowing rate; and

(b)   other market borrowing rates. *[IAS 36.A17].*

If borrowing rates (which are, of course, pre-tax) were used as a starting point, could this avoid some of the problems associated with adjusting the WACC for the effects of taxation? Unfortunately, this is unlikely. Debt rates reflect the entity's capital structure and do not reflect the risk inherent in the asset. A pure asset/business risk would be obtained from an entity funded solely by equity and equity risk premiums are always observed on a post-tax basis. Therefore the risk premium that must be added to reflect the required increased return required over and above a risk free rate by an investor will always have to be adjusted for the effects of taxation.

It must be stressed that the appropriate discount rate, which is the one that reflects current market assessments of the time value of money and the risks specific to the asset in question, ought to be the same whatever the starting point for the calculation of the rate.

Vodafone in its description of its pre-tax discount rate starts from the relevant bond (i.e. debt) rate (Extract 22.4 below). However, this note also describes many of the elements of the WACC calculation and how Vodafone has obtained these; it does not suggest that Vodafone has used anything other than an adjusted WACC as a discount rate for the purposes of the impairment test.

4.5   Recognition of impairment losses

If the carrying value of an individual asset or of a CGU is equal to or less than its calculated VIU, there is no impairment. On the other hand, if the carrying value of the CGU is greater than its VIU and FVLCS, or the FVLCS cannot be calculated, an impairment write-down should be recognised.

There are three scenarios, an impairment loss on an individual asset, an impairment loss on an individual CGU and an impairment loss on a group of CGUs. The last of these may occur where there are corporate assets (see 4.2.2 above) or goodwill (see 5 below) that have been allocated to a group of CGUs rather than to individual ones.

4.5.1   *Impairment losses on individual assets*

For individual assets IAS 36 states:

'If, and only if, the recoverable amount of an asset is less than its carrying amount, the carrying amount of the asset shall be reduced to its recoverable amount. That reduction is an impairment loss. *[IAS 36.59].*

An impairment loss shall be recognised immediately in profit or loss, unless the asset is carried at revalued amount in accordance with another Standard (for example, in accordance with the revaluation model in IAS 16). Any impairment loss of a revalued asset shall be treated as a revaluation decrease in accordance with that other Standard'. *[IAS 36.60].*

If there is an impairment loss on an asset that has not been revalued, it is recognised in profit or loss. However, an impairment loss on a revalued asset is first used to reduce the revaluation surplus for that asset. Only when the impairment loss exceeds the amount in the revaluation surplus for that same asset is any further impairment loss recognised in profit or loss. In our view, asset revaluation reserves arising from a business combination achieved in stages in accordance with paragraphs 58 to 60 of IFRS 3(2007) (see Chapter 10 at 9) can also be used to offset a future impairment loss applicable to that same asset.

However, as the asset revaluation reserve only arises as a result of the business combination, it only exists in the consolidated financial statements and can only be utilised in those consolidated financial statements.

IAS 36 does not require impairment losses to be shown in any particular position in the income statement.. Nor does it address whether any amounts written off a fixed asset should be treated as a deduction from the gross amount (cost or valuation) or as an increase in cumulative depreciation, in the reconciliation required by IAS 16 between the carrying amounts at the beginning and end of the year. *[IAS 16.73(d)]*. If the asset is carried at cost, we consider that it is more appropriate to carry an impairment write down within cumulative depreciation. If the asset is held at revalued amount then there is less of an issue and the impairment will be reflected in the revalued carrying amount.

An impairment loss greater than the carrying value of the asset does not give rise to a liability unless another standard requires it, presumably as this would be tantamount to providing for future losses. *[IAS 36.62]*. An impairment loss will reduce the depreciable amount of an asset and the revised amount will be depreciated or amortised prospectively over the remaining life. *[IAS 36.63]*. However, an entity ought also to review the useful life and residual value of its impaired asset, as both of these may need to be revised. The circumstances that give rise to impairments frequently affect these as well.

Finally, an impairment loss will have implications for any deferred tax calculation involving the asset and in the standard's accompanying section of illustrative examples Example 3, on which the following is based, illustrates the possible effects.

Example 22.12: Recognition of an impairment loss creates a deferred tax asset

An entity has an asset with a carrying amount of €2,000 whose recoverable amount is €1300. The tax rate is 30% and the tax base of the asset is €1,500. Impairment losses are not deductible for tax purposes. The effect of the impairment loss is as follows:

	Before impairment €	Effect of impairment €	After impairment €
Carrying amount	2,000	(700)	1,300
Tax base	1,500	–	1,500
Taxable (deductible) temporary difference	500	(700)	(200)
Deferred tax liability (asset) at 30%	150	(210)	(60)

The entity will recognise the deferred tax asset to the extent that it is probable that there will be available taxable profits against which the deductible temporary difference can be utilised.

4.5.2 *Impairment losses and CGUs*

Impairment losses in a CGU can occur in two ways:

(i)   an impairment loss is incurred in a CGU on its own, and that CGU may or may not have corporate assets or goodwill included in its carrying value;

(ii)   an impairment loss is identified that must be allocated across a group of CGUs because a corporate asset or goodwill is involved whose carrying value could only be allocated to a group of CGUs as a whole, rather than to individual CGUs (the allocation of corporate assets to CGUs is discussed in 4.2.2 above, and goodwill is discussed at 5 below).

The relevant paragraphs from the standard deal with both instances but are readily understandable only if the above distinction is appreciated. The standard lays down that impairment losses in CGUs should be recognised to reduce the carrying amount of the assets of the unit (group of units) in the following order:

(a)   first, to reduce the carrying amount of any goodwill allocated to the CGU or group of units; and

(b)   if the goodwill has been written off, to reduce the other assets of the CGU (or group of CGUs) pro rata to their carrying amount. *[IAS 36.104].*

If there are indicators of impairment in connection with a CGU with which goodwill is associated, i.e. the CGU is part of a CGU group to which the goodwill is allocated, this CGU should be tested and any necessary impairment loss taken, before goodwill is tested for impairment (see 5.3.2 below). *[IAS 36.88].* These impairment losses and consequent reductions in carrying values are treated in exactly the same way as those for individual assets, in accordance with paragraph 60 of IAS 36, as explained above.

The important point is to be clear about the order set out above. Goodwill must be written down first, and if an impairment loss remains, the other assets in the CGU or group of CGUs are written down pro-rata to their carrying values.

This pro-rating is in two stages if a group of CGUs is involved:

(i)   the loss is eliminated against goodwill (which by definition in this instance is unallocated to individual CGUs in the group);

(ii)   any remaining loss is pro-rated between the carrying values of the individual CGUs in the group; and

(iii)   within each individual CGU the loss is again pro-rated between the individual assets' carrying values.

Unless it is possible to estimate the recoverable amount of each individual asset within a CGU, it is necessary to allocate impairment losses to individual assets in such a way that the revised carrying amounts of these assets correspond with the requirements of the standard. Therefore, the entity does not reduce the carrying amount of an individual asset below the highest of its FVLCS or VIU (if these can be established), or zero. The amount of the impairment loss that would otherwise have been allocated to the asset is then allocated pro-rata to the other assets of the CGU or CGU group. *[IAS 36.105].* The standard argues that this arbitrary allocation to individual assets when their recoverable amount cannot be individually assessed is appropriate because all assets of a CGU 'work together'. *[IAS 36.106].*

If corporate assets are allocated to a CGU or group of CGUs, then any remaining loss at (ii) above (i.e. after allocation to goodwill) is pro-rated against the allocated share of the corporate asset and the other assets in the CGU.

This process, then, writes down the carrying value attributed or allocated to a CGU until the carrying value of the net assets is equal to the computed VIU. It is logically possible, after all assets and goodwill are either written off or down to their FVLCS, for the carrying value of the CGU to be higher than the computed VIU. There is no suggestion that the net assets should be reduced any further because at this point the FVLCS would be the relevant impairment figure. The remaining amount will only be recognised as a liability if that is a requirement of another standard. *[IAS 36.108]*.

IAS 36 includes in the standard's accompanying section of illustrative examples Example 2 which illustrates the calculation, recognition and allocation of an impairment loss across CGUs.

However, the standard stresses that no impairment loss should be reflected against an individual asset if the CGU to which it belongs has not been impaired, even if its carrying value exceeds its FVLCS. This is expanded in the following example, based on that in paragraph 107 of the standard:

Example 22.13:   Individually impaired assets within CGUs

A machine has suffered physical damage but is still working, although not as well as before it was damaged. The machine's FVLCS less costs to sell is less than its carrying amount. The machine does not generate independent cash inflows. The smallest identifiable group of assets that includes the machine and generates cash inflows that are largely independent of the cash inflows from other assets is the production line to which the machine belongs. The recoverable amount of the production line shows that the production line taken as a whole is not impaired.

Assumption 1: budgets/forecasts approved by management reflect no commitment of management to replace the machine.

The recoverable amount of the machine alone cannot be estimated because its VIU may be different from its FVLCS less costs to sell (because the entity is going to continue to use it) and can be determined only for the CGU to which it belongs (the production line).

As the production line is not impaired, no impairment loss is recognised for the machine. Nevertheless, the entity may need to reassess the depreciation period or the depreciation method for the machine. Perhaps a shorter depreciation period or a faster depreciation method is required to reflect the expected remaining useful life of the machine or the pattern in which economic benefits are expected to be consumed by the entity.

Assumption 2: budgets/forecasts approved by management reflect a commitment of management to replace the machine and sell it in the near future.

Cash flows from continuing use of the machine until its disposal are estimated to be negligible. The machine's VIU can be estimated to be close to its FVLCS less costs to sell. Therefore, the recoverable amount of the machine can be determined and no consideration is given to the CGU (the production line) to which it belongs. As the machine's carrying amount exceeds its FVLCS less costs to sell, an impairment loss is recognised to write it down to FVLCS less costs to sell. *[IAS 36.107]*.

Note that it is assumed that the asset is still useable (otherwise it would not be contributing to the cash flows of the CGU and would have to be written off) and that it is not held for sale as defined by IFRS 5. The impairment implications when an asset is held for sale are discussed further at 2.3.1 above.

5   IMPAIRMENT OF GOODWILL

Goodwill is subject to an annual impairment test instead of being systematically depreciated. IAS 38 exempts from amortisation intangible assets that have indefinite useful lives. These are, like goodwill, subject to an annual impairment test. *[IAS 38.89, 107-108]*. Intangible assets with finite useful lives must be depreciated systematically over their useful lives and are subject to impairment reviews when there are indications of impairment in the same way as any other asset within scope of IAS 36.

The impairment tests for goodwill and intangible assets with an indefinite life must be performed at least annually, but not necessarily at the end of the reporting period although an impairment test must be performed at the reporting date as well if there are indicators of impairment. This is in contrast to the impairment tests for other assets described in 2.2 above that are required only if there are indications of impairment, but which must be performed at the reporting date. The detailed requirements of IAS 36 concerning intangible assets with an indefinite life are discussed at 5.7 below.

5.1   Goodwill and its allocation to cash-generating units

The initial recognition and measurement of the goodwill acquired in a business combination is discussed in Chapter 10 at 6.

Since it was revised in 2008, IFRS 3 defines 'goodwill' in terms of its nature, rather than in terms of its measurement as 'an asset representing the future economic benefits arising from other assets acquired in a business combination that are not individually identified and separately recognised.' *[IFRS 3 Appendix A]*. The acquirer must recognise goodwill as an asset but as the direct measurement of goodwill is not possible, the standard requires that goodwill is measured as a residual. *[IFRS 3.BC328]*. IFRS 3 states that the acquirer measures goodwill acquired in a business combination at the amount recognised at the acquisition date less any accumulated impairment losses and refers to IAS 36. *[IFRS 3.B63]*.

An impairment test cannot be carried out on goodwill alone, as it does not generate cash flows independently of other assets. Testing goodwill for impairment necessitates its allocation to a cash-generating unit (CGU) of the acquirer or to a group of CGUs.

From the acquisition date, acquired goodwill is to be allocated to each of the acquirer's CGUs, or to a group of CGUs, that are expected to benefit from the synergies of the combination. This is irrespective of whether other assets or liabilities of the acquiree are assigned to those CGUs or group of CGUs. The standard recognises that goodwill sometimes cannot be allocated on a non-arbitrary basis to an individual CGU, so permits it to be allocated to a group of CGUs. However, each CGU or group of CGUs to which the goodwill is so allocated must:

(a)   represent the lowest level within the entity at which the goodwill is monitored for internal management purposes; and

(b)   not be larger than an operating segment determined in accordance with IFRS 8 – *Operating Segments*. *[IAS 36.80-81]*.

All CGUs or groups of CGUs to which goodwill has been allocated have to be tested for impairment on an annual basis.

The standard takes the view that applying these requirements results in goodwill being tested for impairment at a level that reflects the way an entity manages its operations and with which the goodwill would naturally be associated. Therefore, the development of additional reporting systems is typically not necessary. *[IAS 36.82]*. Only if an entity did not monitor goodwill at or below the segment level would it be necessary to develop new or additional reporting systems in order to comply with the standard. *[IAS 36.BC140]*.

IAS 36 emphasises that a CGU to which goodwill is allocated for the purpose of impairment testing may not coincide with the level at which goodwill is allocated in accordance with IAS 21 for the purpose of measuring foreign currency gains and losses (see Chapter 17). *[IAS 36.83]*. In many cases the allocation under IAS 21 will be at a lower level. This will apply not only on the acquisition of a multinational operation but could also apply on the acquisition of a single operation where the goodwill is allocated to a larger cash generating unit under IAS 36 that is made up of businesses with different functional currencies. However, IAS 36 clarifies that the entity is not required to test the goodwill for impairment at that same level unless it also monitors the goodwill at that level for internal management purposes. *[IAS 36.83]*.

Groups that do not have publicly traded equity or debt instruments are not required to apply IFRS 8. In our view, these entities must still meet the requirements of paragraph 80 of IAS 36 as described below. The group of cash-generating units to which goodwill is allocated must represent the lowest level within the entity at which goodwill is monitored for internal management purposes and, in addition, the group of cash-generating units cannot be larger than an operating segment would have been had the entity been required to apply IFRS 8.

5.1.1   The effect of IFRS 8 – Operating Segments – on impairment tests

Goodwill to be tested for impairment cannot be allocated to a CGU or CGU group larger than an *operating* segment as defined by that standard. *[IAS 36.80-81]*. IFRS 8 is discussed in Chapter 34.

Organisations managed on a matrix basis cannot test goodwill for impairment at the level of internal reporting, if this level crosses more than one operating segment as defined in IFRS 8 paragraph 5. In addition, the operating segments selected by the entities may not correspond with their CGUs.

These are entities that manage their businesses simultaneously on two different bases; for example, some managers may be responsible for different product and service lines while others are responsible for specific geographical areas. IFRS 8 notes that the characteristics that define an operating segment may apply to two or more overlapping sets of components for which managers are held responsible. Financial information is available for both and the chief operating decision maker may regularly review both sets of operating results of components. In spite of this, IFRS 8 requires the entity to characterise one of these bases as determining its operating segments. *[IFRS 8.10]*. Similarly, the entity will have to allocate its goodwill to CGUs or groups of CGUs no larger than operating segments even if this means an allocation of goodwill between segments on a basis that does not correspond with the way it is monitored it for internal management purposes.

The designation of business segments as IFRS 8 operating segments may have the effect that a single CGU contains more than one operating segment. The classification as a CGU (the smallest identifiable group of assets that generates largely independent cash inflows) is unaffected by the IFRS 8 operating segment analysis. Therefore, the CGU may contain operating segments to which goodwill relates. For example, a telecommunications business may designate its network in a particular country as its CGU but its operating segments may be identified by the type of service or type of clients (e.g. telephone, internet and television; individual clients, business clients, other operators, etc).

The network CGU will be tested for impairment in the same way as before. However, when the goodwill is tested for impairment, it is possible for an impairment charge to exceed the goodwill relating to that segment. IAS 36 requires an entity to allocate the remaining impairment charge to the other non-current assets of the CGU until they are reduced to zero or, if determinable, their individual recoverable amount. The assets in a CGU that crosses more than one operating segment cannot be written down to a value lower than their own recoverable amount. *[IAS 36.105]*. Pro-rata allocation of impairment to all CGU non-current assets, including assets in a CGU that crosses more than one operating segment, is not appropriate if the carrying value of such assets is lower than the recoverable amount determined in a separate test.

5.1.2 Aggregation of operating segments for disclosure purposes

IFRS 8 allows an entity to aggregate two or more operating segments into a single operating segment if this is 'consistent with the core principles' and, in particular, that the segments have similar economic characteristics. *[IFRS 8.12]*. Whilst this is specifically in the context of segmental reporting, it might also, in isolation, have suggested that individual operating segments could also be aggregated to form one operating segment that would also apply for impairment purposes. The IASB in its Annual Improvements project has clarified that the 'unit of accounting' for goodwill impairment is before any aggregation allowed by paragraph 12 of IFRS 8 and paragraph 80(b) has been amended accordingly. The required unit for goodwill impairment is not larger than the operating segment level as defined in paragraph 5 of IFRS 8 before any aggregation. This is because IAS 36 requires allocation of goodwill at the level monitored by management for internal purposes. *[IAS 36.80]*. An operating segment under IFRS 8 is the component monitored by the chief operating decision maker to assess performance and allocate resources. *[IFRS 8.5]*. The monitoring will be at the same level in both standards.

5.2 Goodwill initially unallocated to cash-generating units

IFRS 3 (as revised in 2008) allows a 'measurement period' after a business combination to provide the acquirer with a reasonable time to obtain the information necessary to identify and measure all of the various components of the business combination as of the acquisition date in accordance with the standard. *[IFRS 3.46]*.

The measurement period ends as soon as the acquirer receives the information it is seeking and cannot exceed one year from the acquisition date. *[IFRS 3.45].*

IAS 36 recognises that in such circumstances, it might also not be possible to complete the initial allocation of the goodwill to a CGU or group of CGUs for impairment purposes before the end of the annual period in which the combination is effected. *[IAS 36.85].* Where this is the case, IAS 36 does not require a provisional allocation to be made, but the goodwill (or part of it) is left unallocated for that period. Goodwill must then be allocated before the end of the first annual period beginning after the acquisition date. *[IAS 36.84].* The standard requires disclosure of the amount of the unallocated goodwill together with an explanation as to why that is the case (see 7.2 below).

However, so much time may have elapsed since the acquisition that there could be indicators of impairment, e.g. because of a general fall in market prices. The question arises as to whether the entity ought, in some circumstances, to test for impairment of goodwill acquired during the current annual period because it may be able to make an allocation of goodwill on a provisional basis.

Although an entity might not be able to complete the initial allocation of goodwill before the end of the annual period in which the combination is effected, it is quite possible that in some circumstances it may be able to do so.

If the entity is able to quantify goodwill with sufficient accuracy, a provisional allocation of goodwill could be made in the following circumstances:

(a)   The entity might know that all goodwill relates to a single CGU or to a group of CGUs no larger than a single operating segment.

(b)   The entity may know that the initial accounting for the combination is complete in all material respects, although some details remain to be finalised.

In our view, an entity that did not finalise the goodwill allocation to CGUs must carry out an impairment test where there are indicators that the provisional goodwill could be impaired. In other words, if a provisional allocation can be make, that provisional goodwill is tested for impairment in accordance with IAS 36, even if the fair values have not been finalised or goodwill has not necessarily been allocated to the relevant CGUs or CGU groups and the test is therefore carried out at a higher level.

The entity must then consider the appropriate actions in a subsequent period. In some circumstances the acquirer ought to test the final allocated goodwill for impairment retrospectively, on the basis that the test on provisional goodwill was in fact the first impairment test applying IAS 36:

• If the entity did not allocate provisional goodwill to the related CGUs and therefore tested at a different level to the ultimate allocation (scenario (a) above), there were indicators that the provisional goodwill may have been impaired and the impairment test resulted in an impairment;

• If the entity allocated provisional goodwill to CGUs, although it had not completed its fair value exercise, and tested provisional goodwill for impairment in accordance with IAS 36 (scenario (b) above).

If the entity did not allocate provisional goodwill to CGUs, there were indicators that the provisional goodwill may have been impaired and the impairment test did not result in an impairment, the entity can choose whether to update the prior year's impairment test retrospectively, but is not required to do so.

In all other scenarios, the acquirer performs only a current year impairment test (i.e. after the allocation has been completed) on a prospective basis.

If the acquirer updates the prior year's impairment test as outlined above, this update could decrease the original goodwill impairment recognised. Such a decrease is an adjustment to the original goodwill impairment. This will not qualify as a reversal and does not violate the prohibition on reversing any goodwill impairments. *[IAS 36.124]*. See 6.1 below.

If an entity were to change its annual reporting date, it could mean that it has a shorter period in which to allocate goodwill.

Example 22.14: Impact of shortened accounting period

Entity A prepares its financial statements for annual periods ending on 31 December. It acquired Entity B on 30 September 2010. In accounting for this business combination in its financial statements for the year ended 31 December 2010, Entity A has only been able to determine the fair values to be assigned to Entity B's assets, liabilities and contingent liabilities on a provisional basis and has not allocated the resulting provisional amount of goodwill arising on the acquisition to any CGU (or group of CGUs). During 2011, Entity A changes its annual reporting date to June and is preparing its financial statements as at its new period end of 30 June 2011. IFRS 3 does not require the fair values assigned to Entity B's net assets (and therefore the initial amount of goodwill) to be finalised by that period end, since Entity A has until 30 September 2011 to finalise the values. However, IAS 36 would appear to require the allocation of the goodwill to CGUs for impairment purposes be completed by the date of those financial statements since these are for the first annual period beginning after the acquisition date, despite the fact that the initial accounting under IFRS 3 is not yet complete.

5.3 Testing cash-generating units with goodwill for impairment

IAS 36 requires a CGU or group of CGUs to which goodwill has been allocated to be tested for impairment annually by comparing the carrying amount of the CGU or group of CGUs, including the goodwill, with its recoverable amount. *[IAS 36.90]*. The requirements of the standard in relation to the timing of such an annual impairment test (which need not be at the period end) are discussed below. This annual impairment test is not a substitute for management being aware of events occurring or circumstances changing between annual tests that might suggest that goodwill is impaired. *[IAS 36.BC162]*. IAS 36 requires an entity to assess at each reporting date whether there is an indication that a CGU may be impaired. *[IAS 36.9]*. So, whenever there is an indication that a CGU or group of CGUs to which goodwill has been allocated may be impaired it is to be tested for impairment by comparing the carrying amount, including the goodwill, with its recoverable amount. *[IAS 36.90]*.

If the carrying amount of the CGU (or group of CGUs), including the goodwill, exceeds the recoverable amount of the CGU (or group of CGUs), then an impairment loss has to be recognised in accordance with paragraph 104 of the standard (see 4.5.2 above). *[IAS 36.90]*.

5.3.1   *Timing of impairment tests*

IAS 36 requires an annual impairment test of CGUs or groups of CGUs to which goodwill has been allocated. The impairment test does not have to be carried out at the end of the reporting period. The standard permits the annual impairment test to be performed at any time during an annual period, provided the test is performed at the same time every year. Different CGUs may be tested for impairment at different times.

However, if some or all of the goodwill allocated to a CGU or group of CGUs was acquired in a business combination during the current annual period, that unit must be tested for impairment before the end of the current annual period. *[IAS 36.96]*.

The IASB observed that acquirers can sometimes 'overpay' for an acquiree, so that the amount initially recognised for the business combination and the resulting goodwill exceeds the recoverable amount of the investment. The Board was concerned that without this requirement it might be possible for entities to delay recognising such an impairment loss until the annual period after the business combination. *[IAS 36.BC173]*.

It has to be said that the wording of the requirement may not achieve that result, as the goodwill may not have been allocated to a CGU in the period in which the business combination occurs (see 5.2 above). Consider also the following example.

Example 22.15:   Testing for impairment of goodwill allocated in the period after acquisition after the annual impairment testing date

Entity A prepares its financial statements for annual reporting periods ending on 31 December. It performs its annual impairment test for all cash-generating units (CGUs) to which it has allocated goodwill at 30 September.

On 31 October 2010, Entity A acquires Entity B. Entity A completes the initial allocation of goodwill to CGUs at 31 October 2011, before the end of the annual reporting period on 31 December 2011. Therefore, Entity A does not allocate the goodwill until after its annual date for testing goodwill, 30 September 2011.

There are no indicators of impairment of goodwill at 31 December 2011. If there is any such indicator, Entity A is required to test goodwill for impairment at that date, regardless of the date of its impairment test. At 31 December 2010, the entity had not yet allocated its goodwill and did not test it for impairment, because there were no impairment indications at that time). During 2011, as permitted by IFRS 3, Entity A does not finalise the fair values assigned to Entity B's net assets (and therefore the initial amount of goodwill) until 30 October 2011. Also, IAS 36 only requires Entity A to allocate the goodwill to CGUs by the end of the financial year. It does this in December.

In this case, at the time of carrying out its annual impairment tests at 30 September 2011, Entity A has not yet allocated the goodwill relating to Entity B, therefore no impairment test of that goodwill should be carried out at that time. When it does allocate the goodwill in December, the requirement to perform an impairment test for the CGUs to which this goodwill is allocated does not seem to be applicable since the goodwill does not relate to a business combination during the current annual period. It actually relates to a business combination in the previous period; it is just that it has only been allocated for impairment purposes in the current period. Nevertheless Entity A should perform an updated impairment test for the CGUs to which this goodwill is allocated for the purposes of its financial statements for the year ended 31 December 2011 since this would seem to be the intention of the IASB. Not to do so, would mean that the impairment of this goodwill would not be tested until September 2012, nearly 2 years after the business combination.

5.3.2   Sequence of impairment tests for goodwill and other assets

When a CGU to which goodwill has been allocated is tested for impairment, there may also be an indication of impairment of an asset within the unit. IAS 36 requires the entity to test the asset for impairment first and recognise any impairment loss on it before carrying out the impairment test for the goodwill, although this is unlikely to have any practical impact as the assets within the CGU by definition will not generate separate cash flows. An entity will have to go through the same process if there is an indication of an impairment of a CGU within a group of CGUs containing the goodwill. The entity must test the CGU for impairment first, and recognise any impairment loss for that CGU, before testing the group of CGUs to which the goodwill is allocated. *[IAS 36.97-98].*

5.3.3   Carry forward of a previous impairment test calculation

IAS 36 permits the most recent detailed calculation of the recoverable amount of a CGU or group of CGUs to which goodwill has been allocated to be carried forward from a preceding period provided all of the following criteria are met:

(a)   the assets and liabilities making up the CGU or group of CGUs have not changed significantly since the most recent recoverable amount calculation;

(b)   the most recent recoverable amount calculation resulted in an amount that exceeded the carrying amount of the CGU or group of CGUs by a substantial margin; and

(c)   based on an analysis of events that have occurred and circumstances that have changed since the most recent recoverable amount calculation, the likelihood that a current recoverable amount determination would be less than the current carrying amount of the CGU or group of CGUs is remote. *[IAS 36.99].*

The Basis for Conclusions indicates that the reason for this dispensation is to reduce the costs of applying the impairment test, without compromising its integrity. *[IAS 36.BC177].* However, clearly it is a matter of judgement as to whether each of the criteria is actually met.

5.3.4   Reversal of impairment loss for goodwill prohibited

Once an impairment loss has been recognised for goodwill, IAS 36 prohibits its reversal in a subsequent period. *[IAS 36.124].* The standard justifies this on the grounds that any reversal 'is likely to be an increase in internally generated goodwill, rather than a reversal of the impairment loss recognised for the acquired goodwill', and IAS 38 prohibits the recognition of internally generated goodwill. *[IAS 36.125].* The impairment test does not distinguish between purchased and internally generated goodwill.

5.4   Impairment of assets and goodwill recognised on acquisition

There are a number of circumstances in which the fair value of assets or goodwill acquired as part of a business combination and as recorded in the consolidated accounts, may be measured at a higher amount through recognition of deferred tax or notional tax benefits. This raises the question of how to test for impairment and even whether there is, in fact, a 'day one' impairment in value. In other circumstances, deferred tax assets may or may not be recognised as part of the fair value exercise and this, too, may affect subsequent impairment tests of the assets and goodwill acquired as part of the business combination.

5.4.1   *Testing goodwill 'created' by deferred tax for impairment*

As described in Chapter 31 at 12, the requirement of IAS 12 to recognise deferred tax on all temporary differences arising on net assets acquired in a business combination may well lead to the recognition of goodwill and an increase in the net assets recognised in the consolidated accounts. This then begs the question of how to perform an impairment test on that goodwill. This is illustrated in the following example (see also Chapter 31 at 12.3):

Example 22.16:   Apparent 'day one' impairment arising from recognition of deferred tax in a business combination

Entity A, which is taxed at 40%, acquires Entity B for €100m in a transaction that is a business combination. The fair values and tax bases of the identifiable net assets of Entity B are as follows:

	Fair value	Tax base
	€m	€m
Brand name	60	nil
Other net assets	20	15

This will give rise to the following consolidation journal:

	€m	€m
Goodwill (balance)	46	
Brand name	60	
Other net assets	20	
Deferred tax[1]		26
Cost of investment		100

[1] 40% of (€[60m + 20m] – €15m)

The fair value of the consolidated assets of the subsidiary (excluding deferred tax) and goodwill is now €126m, but the cost of the subsidiary is only €100m. Clearly €26m of the goodwill arises solely from the recognition of deferred tax. However, IAS 36, paragraph 50, explicitly requires tax to be excluded from the estimate of future cash flows used to calculate any impairment. This raises the question of whether there should not be an immediate impairment write-down of the assets to €100m.

We think that this is unlikely to have been the intention of IAS 36 because certain assumptions about taxation have been incorporated into the carrying amount of goodwill that are represented by the deferred tax liability. Adjustments need to be made to the post-tax discount rate in order to determine the appropriate pre-tax discount rate. This means, in effect, that as at the point of acquisition, the deferred tax liability can be offset against the CGU or CGU group in order to test that goodwill for impairment as this will reflect those taxation assumptions. As a result, the entity does not have to recognise an immediate loss.

This conclusion is consistent with the fact that the goodwill that is being recognised as part of this acquisition is a result of a measurement mismatch between two standards. IFRS 3 only addresses impairment due to overpayment, *[IFRS 3.BC382].* and does not address impairment created by measurement issues in accordance with an accounting standard. However, this was clearly addressed in the previous version of the standard. In the Basis for Conclusions to IFRS 3(2007), it is noted that goodwill, measured as a residual, could include 'errors in measuring and recognising the fair value of either the cost of the business combination or the acquiree's identifiable assets, liabilities or contingent liabilities, or *a requirement in an accounting standard to measure those identifiable items at an amount that is not fair value*' (our emphasis). *[IFRS 3(2007).BC130]*. IFRS 3, of course, continues to have exceptions to the basic principle that assets and liabilities be measured at fair value and goodwill continues to reflect measurement differences (see Chapter 10 at 5.6).

This example assumes that the entity cannot get a deduction for tax purposes for the goodwill and brand name, as is often the case for assets that arise only on consolidation. It also assumes that the fair value of the brand name does not reflect the benefits of any tax deductions had the asset been tax deductible (valuations that do reflect such assumptions are considered further below). Deferred tax is measured at its full and undiscounted value and not at fair value; had it been so, it is plausible that in this case its fair value would be negligible or zero. Note that despite this 'mismatch', goodwill still has to be recognised in the financial statements and is subject to all of IAS 36's requirements.

If it is assumed that the brand name is amortised over a finite useful life then the deferred tax relating to that asset (€24m in this example) will be released over that life with the effect that the net amount charged to the income statement of €36m (€60m – €24m) will be the same as if the amortisation charge were tax deductible. Although the deferred tax liability is diminishing in line with the amortisation of the brand, the total amount of goodwill is not amortised. This does not necessarily mean that the 'mismatch' goodwill will be impaired in line with the release of the deferred tax liability as this will depend on the individual circumstances of the entity and the manner in which purchased goodwill has been allocated to CGUs or CGU groups and their post-acquisition performance.

Only deferred tax that has arisen as described in Example 22.16 above may be taken into account in considering the impairment of the related goodwill; other unrelated deferred tax, whether it arises at the same time or subsequently, will be disregarded. Entities may, of course, find it difficult to track the relevant deferred tax an ongoing basis.

Xstrata plc discloses separately the amount of goodwill that has resulted from the recognition of deferred tax liabilities.

Extract 22.3: Xstrata plc (2008)

Notes to the Financial Statements [extract]

15.   Impairment

Goodwill

Goodwill has been allocated to a cash-generating unit (CGU) or groups of cash-generating units no larger than the reportable segment which are expected to benefit from the related acquisitions. The carrying values of goodwill by cash-generating unit are as follows:

US$m	2008	2007
Chrome – Africa	35	47
Copper – Americas	1,185	1,185
Zinc Lead	1,546	1,546
Zinc Lead – Europe	212	222
	2,978	3,000

The following goodwill balances result from the requirement to recognise a deferred tax liability, calculated as the difference between the tax effect of the fair value of the acquired assets and liabilities and their tax bases. For the purpose of testing this goodwill for impairment, any of the related deferred tax liabilities recognised on acquisition that remain at balance date are treated as part of the relevant CGU or group of CGUs.

US$m	2008	2007
Coal – Australia	233	125
Coal – Americas South	464	464
Copper – Americas South*	1,500	1,537
Copper – Australasia	151	151
Nickel – Americas North	856	856
Nickel – Americas South*	119	295
Nickel – Africa	78	78
Nickel – Australasia	79	34
Platinum – Africa	284	384
Zinc Lead – Americas North	244	244
Zinc Lead – Americas South	160	160
Zinc Lead – Australasia	–	8
	4,168	4,336
	7,146	7,336

* Net of 2008 impairment loss discussed below.

The Group performs goodwill impairment testing on an annual basis and at the reporting date if there are indicators of impairment. The most recent test was undertaken at 31 December 2008.

[...]

For the purpose of goodwill impairment testing, recoverable amounts have been determined based on 'fair value less costs to sell' (FVLCS) calculations, with the exception of Coal – Australia goodwill, Coal – Colombia goodwill, Chrome – Africa goodwill and partially as Copper Australasia which have been based on 'value-in-use' (VIU) calculations.

If the brand name is deemed to have an indefinite life it will not be amortised. It may be possible to continue to apply the short cut method of deducting the deferred tax liability from the CGU or CGU group of which the goodwill and brand name are part, unless the intangible asset is impaired or sold. It is still a requirement for the entity to be able to track the relevant deferred tax liability. The goodwill still has to be tested annually for impairment, even though in this case the goodwill itself ought to have no net effect on the net assets of the CGU or group of CGUs to which it is allocated. The standard's disclosure requirements including the pre-tax discount rate, principally described at 7.3 below, will apply.

5.4.2 *Assets whose fair value reflects tax benefits*

This is a related area to the one described in 5.4.1 that may also affect the post-acquisition impairment test. In order to determine the fair value in an acquisition of an asset (typically an intangible asset), its value on a post-tax basis may be grossed up to take account of the tax benefits (sometimes called 'tax amortisation benefits') that the owner might have obtained if the asset had been bought separately, i.e. not as part of a business combination. Yet the asset may be one that is wholly or in part not tax-deductible by the entity. This is demonstrated in the following example:

Example 22.17: *Impairment testing assets whose fair value reflects tax amortisation benefits*

Assume that the entity in Example 22.16 above has acquired a brand that would be tax deductible if separately acquired but that also has a tax base of zero. The entity concludes that the fair value will reflect the tax benefit, whose gross amount is €40 (€60m × 40% / 60%) but in calculating the fair value this will be discounted to its present value – say €30m. The consolidation journal is now as follows:

	€m	€m
Goodwill (balance)	28	
Brand name (€(60 + 30))	90	
Other net assets	20	
Deferred tax[1]		38
Cost of investment		100

[1] 40% of (€[90m + 20m] – €15m)

Overall, the gross assets that cost €100m will now be recorded at €138m, as against the total of €126m in Example 22.16. This increase has come about because of recognition of deferred tax of €12m, which is 40% of €30m, the assumed tax amortisation benefit.

In this example, only €8m goodwill results from the recognition of deferred tax [€28m – (€100 – (€60m + €20m))] and its treatment is discussed above at 5.4.1.

Unlike goodwill, the intangible asset will only have to be tested for impairment if there are indicators of impairment, if it has an indefinite useful life or if it has not yet been brought into use. *[IAS 36.10].* Because its 'fair value' of €90m is much in excess of the amount that the entity considers that it paid to acquire the asset could this be considered an indicator of impairment? Not necessarily, and should it be necessary to test it for impairment, the asset has been valued on the assumption that it will generate future tax inflows and it is only consistent that the impairment test takes account of the same assumptions. A discount rate is calculated using the assumptions about taxation described in 4.4.2 above (i.e. that VIU equals tax base). Whatever rate is selected, it will be one that reflects market assumptions about the availability of tax relief and the level of taxation. The implications are similar to those discussed in 4.4.2 above.

5.4.3 *Deferred tax assets and losses of acquired businesses*

Deferred tax assets arising from tax losses carried forward at the reporting date must be excluded from the assets of the CGU for the purpose of calculating its VIU. However, tax losses may not meet the criteria for recognition as deferred tax assets in a business combination, which means that their value is initially subsumed within goodwill. Under IFRS 3 as revised in 2008 and an amended IAS 12, only acquired deferred tax assets recognised within the 12 month measurement period are to reduce goodwill, with any excess once goodwill has been reduced to zero being taken to profit or loss. *[IFRS 3.67, IAS 12.95].* Unlike other changes in IFRS 3, this applies to acquisitions originally accounted for under IFRS 3(2007). See also Chapter 31 at 12.1.2B. Under the previous version of IFRS 3, deferred tax assets recognised at a later date reduced the amount of goodwill which was written down to the extent of the deferred tax asset at the date of acquisition.

Unless and until the deferred tax asset is recognised (and this will be less likely to happen under the amended IFRS 3), this raises the same problems as in 5.4.1 and 5.4.2 above. Certain assumptions regarding future taxation are built into the carrying value of goodwill. In such situations it may be appropriate to recognise the benefits of this 'contingent asset' in the VIU calculation for the CGU or CGU group.

5.5 Non-controlling interests

The amount of goodwill recorded by an entity when it acquires a controlling stake that is less than 100% of the equity in a subsidiary depends on whether the entity has accounted for the acquisition under IFRS 3 as it has applied for accounting periods beginning on or after 1 July 2009 or in its earlier form ('IFRS 3 (2007)').

Under the original standard, such goodwill represented only the goodwill acquired by a parent based on the parent's ownership interest, rather than the amount of goodwill controlled by the parent as a result of the business combination. Goodwill attributable to a minority interest is not recognised in the parent's consolidated financial statements as the minority interest is stated at its proportion of the net fair value of the acquiree. Accordingly, the carrying amount of that CGU comprises:

(a) both the parent's interest and the minority interest in the identifiable net assets of the CGU; and

(b) the parent's interest in goodwill.

However, part of the recoverable amount of the CGU determined in accordance with IAS 36 is attributable to the minority interest in goodwill.

IFRS 3 now requires any non-controlling interest (as minority interests have been renamed) in an acquiree to be recognised, *[IFRS 3.10],* but provides a choice of measurement methods; these are described in more detail in Chapter 10 at 8. The previous treatment is retained but an entity may also choose to measure the non-controlling interest at its acquisition-date fair value, which means that its share of goodwill will also be recognised. *[IFRS 3.19, IAS 36.C1].*

The choice of method is to be made for each business combination, rather than being a policy choice, and could have a significant effect on the amount recognised for goodwill.

The IASB itself noted that there are likely to be differences arising from measuring the non-controlling interest at its proportionate share of the acquiree's net identifiable assets, rather than at fair value. First, the amounts recognised in a business combination for the non-controlling interest and goodwill are likely to be lower (as illustrated in the example given in Chapter 10 at 8).

Second, if a CGU to which the goodwill has been allocated is subsequently impaired, any impairment of goodwill recognised through income is likely to be lower than it would have been if the non-controlling interest had been measured at fair value.

The IASB has amended IAS 36 to reflect these different treatments. It has also clarified the existing requirements of IAS 36 to reflect the fact that not all of the goodwill arising will necessarily be allocated to a CGU or group of CGUs which includes the subsidiary with the non-controlling interest. *[IAS 36.C2, IFRS 3.C10, IGA3].*

Guidance is given on the allocation of impairment losses:

(a) If a subsidiary, or part of a subsidiary, with a non-controlling interest is itself a CGU, the impairment loss is allocated between the parent and the non-controlling interest on the same basis as that on which profit or loss is allocated; *[IAS 36.C6]*

(b)   If it is part of a larger CGU, goodwill impairment losses are allocated to the parts of the CGU that have a non-controlling interest and the parts that do not on the following basis: *[IAS 36.C7]*

   (a)   to the extent that the impairment relates to goodwill in the CGU, the relative carrying values of the goodwill of the parts before the impairment; and

   (b)   to the extent that the impairment relates to identifiable assets in the CGU, the relative carrying values of these assets before the impairment. Any such impairment is allocated to the assets of the parts of each unit pro-rata on the basis of the carrying amount of each asset in the part.

5.5.1   Testing for impairment in entities with non-controlling interests measured at the proportionate share of net assets

The same method applies whether the entity applies IFRS 3 in its original or modified form. To enable a like-for-like comparison, IAS 36 requires the carrying amount of a non-wholly-owned CGU to be notionally adjusted by grossing up the carrying amount of goodwill allocated to the CGU to include the amount attributable to the non-controlling interest. This notionally adjusted carrying amount is then compared with the recoverable amount. If there is an impairment, the entity allocates the impairment loss as usual, first reducing the carrying amount of goodwill allocated to the CGU (see 4.5.2 above). *[IAS 36.C3, C4]*. However, because only the parent's goodwill is recognised, the impairment loss is apportioned between that attributable to the parent and that attributable to the non-controlling interest, with only the former being recognised. *[IAS 36.C6]*.

If any impairment loss remains, it is allocated in the usual way to the other assets of the CGU pro rata on the basis of the carrying amount of each asset in the CGU. *[IAS 36.104]*.

These requirements are illustrated in the following example. *[IAS 36.IE62-68]*.

Example 22.18:   A CGU with goodwill and non-controlling interest

Entity X acquires an 80 per cent ownership interest in Entity Y for €1,600 on 1 January 2012. At that date, Entity Y's identifiable net assets have a fair value of €1,500. Entity X recognises in its consolidated financial statements:

(a)   goodwill of €400, being the difference between the cost of the business combination of €1,600 and the non-controlling interest of €300 (20% of €1,500) and the identifiable net assets of Entity y of €1,500;

(b)   Entity Y's identifiable net assets at their fair value of €1,500; and

(c)   a non-controlling interest of €300.

At the end of 2012, the carrying amount of Entity Y's identifiable assets has reduced to €1,350 and Entity X determines that the recoverable amount of CGU Y is €1,000.

The carrying amount of CGU Y must be notionally adjusted to include goodwill attributable to the non-controlling interest, before being compared with the recoverable amount of €1,000. Goodwill attributable to Entity X's 80% interest in Entity Y at the acquisition date is €400. Therefore, goodwill notionally attributable to the 20% non-controlling interest in Entity Y at the acquisition date is €100, being €400 × 20 ÷ 80.

Testing CGU Y for impairment at the end of 2012 gives rise to an impairment loss of €850 calculated as follows:

	Goodwill €	Identifiable net assets €	Total €
Carrying amount	400	1,350	1,750
Unrecognised non-controlling interest	100	–	100
Notionally adjusted carrying amount	500	1,350	1,850
Recoverable amount			1,000
Impairment loss			850

The impairment loss of €850 is allocated to the assets in the CGU by first reducing the carrying amount of goodwill to zero. Therefore, €500 of the €850 impairment loss for the CGU is allocated to the goodwill. However, because Entity X only recognises its 80% ownership interest in Entity Y, it recognises only 80 per cent of that goodwill impairment loss (i.e. €400). The remaining impairment loss of €350 is recognised by reducing the carrying amounts of Entity Y's identifiable assets, as follows:

	Goodwill €	Identifiable net assets €	Total €
Carrying amount	400	1,350	1,750
Impairment loss	(400)	(350)	(750)
Carrying amount after impairment loss	–	1,000	1,000

Of the impairment loss of €350 relating to Entity Y's identifiable assets, €70 (i.e. 20% thereof) would be attributed to the minority interest.

In this example the same result would have been achieved by just comparing the recoverable amount of €1,000 with the carrying amount of €1,750. However, what if the recoverable amount of the CGU had been greater than the carrying amount of the identifiable net assets prior to recognising the impairment loss?

Assume the same facts as above, except that at the end of 2012, Entity X determines that the recoverable amount of CGU Y is €1,400. In this case, testing CGU Y for impairment at the end of 2012 gives rise to an impairment loss of €450 calculated as follows:

	Goodwill €	Identifiable net assets €	Total €
Carrying amount	400	1,350	1,750
Unrecognised minority interest	100	–	100
Notionally adjusted carrying amount	500	1,350	1,850
Recoverable amount			1,400
Impairment loss			450

All of the impairment loss of €450 is allocated to the goodwill. However, Entity X recognises only 80 per cent of that goodwill impairment loss (i.e. €360). This allocation of the impairment loss results in the following carrying amounts for CGU Y in the financial statements of Entity X at the end of 2012.

	Goodwill €	Identifiable net assets €	Total €
Carrying amount	400	1,350	1,750
Impairment loss	(360)	–	(360)
Carrying amount after impairment loss	40	1,350	1,390

Of the impairment loss of €360, none of it is attributable to the non-controlling interest since it all relates to the majority shareholder's goodwill.

In this case the total carrying amount of the identifiable net assets and the goodwill has not been reduced to the recoverable amount of €1,400, but is actually less than the recoverable amount. This is because the recoverable amount of goodwill relating to the non-controlling interest (20% of [€500 – €450]) is not recognised in the consolidated financial statements.

5.5.1.A   Acquisitions of non-controlling interests measured at the proportionate share of net assets,

As described above, in order to enable a like-for-like comparison, IAS 36 requires the carrying amount of a non-wholly-owned CGU to be notionally adjusted by grossing up the carrying amount of goodwill allocated to the CGU to include the amount attributable to the non-controlling interest.

What happens if the non-controlling interest is acquired by the entity so that it is now wholly owned? IFRS 3 now requires these purchases to be reflected as equity transactions, which means that there is no change to goodwill. *[IAS 27.30]*. Other methods have been used in the past that may still be reflected in the carrying amounts of goodwill. These could have partially or wholly reflected the fair value of the additional interest acquired. See Chapter 8.

No notional adjustment seems to be required when the remaining non-controlling interest is acquired and the carrying amount of the unit, including the recognised goodwill i.e. the goodwill paid in the acquisition where control was obtained should be tested against 100% of the recoverable amount of the unit.

5.5.2   Testing for impairment in entities with non-controlling interests initially measured at fair value

The following examples in which the non-controlling interest is initially measured at fair value, is based on the Examples 7B and 7C in IAS 36's Illustrative Examples and illustrate the revised requirements.

Example 22.19:   Non-controlling interests measured initially at fair value

Entity X acquires an 80 per cent ownership interest in Entity Y for €2,100 on 1 January 2012. At that date, Entity Y's identifiable net assets have a fair value of €1,500. Entity X chooses to measure the non-controlling interests at its fair value of €350. Goodwill is €950, which is the aggregate of the consideration transferred and the amount of the non-controlling interests (€2,100 + €350) and the net identifiable assets (€1,500).

(a)   the acquired subsidiary is a stand-alone CGU

Entity Y is a CGU but part of the goodwill is allocated to other of Entity X's CGUs that are expected to benefit from the synergies of the combination. Goodwill of €450 is allocated to the Entity Y CGU and €500 to the other CGUs.

At the end of 2012, the carrying amount of Entity Y's identifiable assets excluding goodwill has reduced to €1,350 and Entity X determines that the recoverable amount of CGU Y is €1,650.

	Goodwill €	Identifiable net assets €	Total €
Carrying amount	450	1,350	1,800
Recoverable amount			1,650
Impairment loss			150

Of the goodwill impairment loss of €150, €30 (20%) will be allocated to the non-controlling interest because the goodwill is allocated to the controlling interest and non-controlling interest on the same basis as profit or loss.

(b)   the acquired subsidiary is part of a larger CGU

Entity Y becomes part of a larger CGU, Z. As before, €500 of the goodwill is allocated to other of Entity X's CGUs that are expected to benefit from the synergies of the combination. Goodwill of €450 is allocated to Z. Z's goodwill related to previous business combinations is €800.

At the end of 2012, Parent determines that the recoverable amount of the Z CGU is €3,300. The carrying amount of its net assets excluding goodwill is €2,250.

	Goodwill €	Identifiable net assets €	Total €
Carrying amount	1,250	2,250	3,500
Recoverable amount			3,300
Impairment loss			200

All of the impairment loss of €200 is allocated to the goodwill. As the partially-owned subsidiary forms part of a larger CGU, the goodwill impairment loss must be allocated first to the parts of the cash-generating unit, Z, and then to the controlling and non-controlling interests of Entity Y.

The impairment loss is allocated on the basis of the relative carrying values of the goodwill of the parts before the impairment. Entity Y is allocated 36% of the impairment (450 ÷ 1,250), in this case €72, of which €14.40 (20%) will be allocated to the non-controlling interest.

5.5.3   *Issues in testing for impairment when there is NCI*

It is not always clear how an entity should test for impairment when there is a NCI. The issues include:

- calculating the 'gross up' of the carrying amount of goodwill when partial goodwill is recognised because NCI is measured on a proportionate share basis;

- allocation of impairment losses between the parent and NCI; and

- reallocation of goodwill between NCI and controlling interests after a change in a parent's ownership interest in a subsidiary that does not result in a loss of control.

Each of these issues arises in one or more of the following situations:

(a)   NCI is measured on a proportionate share, rather than fair value basis (see 5.5 above), and there are non-present (i.e. future) ownership interests such as options ('NPOI'). Accounting for these interests is discussed in Chapter 8 at 4.2 and Chapter 10 at 8.

IAS 36 requires the grossing up of the carrying amount of goodwill allocated to the unit to include the goodwill attributable to the NCI if the proportionate share approach is used to value NCI that comprises present ownership interests. The adjusted carrying amount is then compared with the recoverable amount of the unit to determine whether the CGU is impaired. *[IAS 36.C4]*.

If the entity has NPOI, how does this affect the allocation of the impairment loss between the parent and the NCI? The impairment loss is generally allocated to the parent and the NCI on the same basis as that on which profit or loss is allocated, *[IAS 36.C6]* which generally follows ownership interests. This means any impairment loss would not be allocated to NPOI because they do not represent present ownership interests. Accordingly, their balances will remain until the NPOI either expire or are exercised.

(b)   goodwill is allocated between the parent and NCI on a basis that is disproportionate to the percentage of equity owned by the parent and the NCI shareholders (e.g. because of the existence of a control premium).

This may have two effects. First, the 'gross' goodwill amount to be tested under the partial goodwill method may be higher than under the full goodwill method.

Second, the impairment loss allocation following IAS 36 is generally based on ownership percentages rather than the goodwill allocation percentages. This mismatch could even cause goodwill attributable to NCI to become negative when the parent has a control premium because the loss allocated to NCI is higher than its allocated goodwill.

(c)   there are subsequent changes in ownership between the parent and NCI shareholders, but the parent maintains control.

There are a number of different methods to calculate the apportionments in (a) and (c) above, while the treatment required by the standard in scenario (b) is not self-evidently the most appropriate answer and raises questions as to whether this was the intended outcome.

The Interpretations Committee considered these issues but declined to propose an amendment to IAS 36 as part of the Annual Improvements. They were concerned that there could be possible unintended consequences of making any changes, and recommended that the Board should consider the implication of these issues as part of the IFRS 3 post-implementation review.[3]

Until the review or unless a consensus develops, entities will have to determine an appropriate treatment based on their circumstances and there may well be diversity in practice.

5.6   Disposal of operation within a cash-generating unit to which goodwill has been allocated

If goodwill has been allocated to a CGU (or a group of CGUs) and the entity disposes of an operation within that CGU, IAS 36 requires that the goodwill associated with the operation disposed of is included in the carrying amount of the operation when determining the gain or loss on disposal. For that purpose, the standard requires that the amount to be included is measured on the basis of the relative values of the operation disposed of and the portion of the CGU retained, unless the entity can demonstrate that some other method better reflects the goodwill associated with the operation disposed of. *[IAS 36.86]*.

Example 22.20:   Goodwill attributable to the disposal of an operation based on relative values

An entity sells for €100 an operation that was part of a CGU to which goodwill of €60 has been allocated. The goodwill allocated to the CGU cannot be identified or associated with an asset group at a level lower than that CGU, except arbitrarily. The recoverable amount of the portion of the CGU retained is €300. Because the goodwill allocated to the CGU cannot be non-arbitrarily identified or associated with an asset group at a level lower than that CGU, the goodwill associated with the operation disposed of is measured on the basis of the relative values of the operation disposed of and the portion of the CGU retained. Therefore, 25 per cent of the goodwill allocated to the CGU, i.e. €15 is included in the carrying amount of the operation that is sold.

The standard refers to the 'relative values' of the parts without specifying how these are to be calculated. The recoverable amount of the part that it has retained will be based on the principles of IAS 36, i.e. at the higher of FVLCS and VIU. This means that the VIU or FVLCS of the part retained may have to be calculated as part of the allocation exercise on disposal.

In addition, the VIU and FVLCS of the part disposed of will be materially the same. This is because the VIU will consist mainly of the net disposal proceeds; it cannot be based on the assumption that the sale would not take place.

It will not necessarily follow, for example, that the business disposed of generated 25% of the net cash flows of the combined CGU. Therefore, the method advocated by the standard to be applied in most circumstances may be based on a mismatch in the valuation bases used on the different parts of the business, reflecting the purchaser's assessment of the value of the part disposed of at the point of sale rather than that of the vendor at purchase.

The standard allows the use of some other method if it better reflects the goodwill associated with the part disposed of. The IASB had in mind a scenario in which an entity buys a business, integrates it with an existing CGU that does not include any goodwill in its carrying amount and immediately sells a loss-making part of the combined CGU. It is accepted that in these circumstances it may be reasonable to conclude that no part of the carrying amount of the goodwill has been disposed of. *[IAS 36.BC156]*. The loss-making business being disposed of could, of course, have been owned by the entity before the acquisition or it could be part of the acquired business.

Where the operation disposed of is a foreign operation for the purposes of IAS 21, another possibility might be to use the goodwill allocated to that foreign operation for the purpose of measuring foreign currency gains and losses, particularly as the exchange gains and losses on that amount of goodwill will also be taken to profit or loss on disposal of that foreign operation (see Chapter 17). Even then, this might only be a better method if there has been no previous impairments recognised in respect of goodwill allocated to the CGU including that foreign operation since it was acquired.

One has to bear in mind that any basis of allocation of goodwill on disposal other than that recommended by the standard could be an indication that goodwill should have been allocated on a different basis on acquisition. It could suggest that there may have been some reasonable basis of allocating goodwill to the CGUs within a CGU group.

5.6.1 Changes in composition of cash-generating units

If an entity reorganises its reporting structure in a way that changes the composition of one or more CGUs to which goodwill has been allocated, IAS 36 requires that the goodwill be reallocated to the units affected. For this purpose, the standard requires the reallocation to be performed using a relative value approach similar to that discussed above when an entity disposes of an operation within a CGU, unless the entity can demonstrate that some other method better reflects the goodwill associated with the reorganised units. *[IAS 36.87].*

Example 22.21: Reallocation of goodwill to CGUs based on relative values

Goodwill of €160 had previously been allocated to CGU A. A is to be divided and integrated into three other CGUs, B, C and D. Because the goodwill allocated to A cannot be non-arbitrarily identified or associated with an asset group at a level lower than A, it is reallocated to CGUs B, C and D on the basis of the relative values of the three portions of A before those portions are integrated with B, C and D. The recoverable amounts of these portions of A before integration with the other CGUs are €200, €300 and €500 respectively. Accordingly, the amounts of goodwill reallocated to CGUs B, C and D are €32, €48 and €80 respectively.

Again, the standard gives no indication as to what other methods might better reflect the goodwill associated with the reorganised units.

As in the case of a disposal, the recoverable amount of the CGUs will be based on the principles of IAS 36, so it will often be necessary to assess the VIU or FVLCS of all of the CGUs to which the goodwill is to be allocated.

In practice, situations may be considerably more complex than Examples 18.19 and 18.20 above. Elements of both may arise following an acquisition whereby there are disposals of acquired businesses, reorganisations and integrations. The entity may sell some parts of its acquired business immediately but may also use the acquisition in order to replace part of its existing capacity, disposing of existing elements. In addition, groups frequently undertake reorganisations of their statutory entities. It is often the case that CGUs do not correspond to these individual entities and the reorganisations may be undertaken for taxation reasons so the ownership structure within a group may not correspond to its CGUs. This makes it clear how important it is that entities identify their CGUs and the allocation of goodwill to them, so that they already have a basis for making any necessary allocations when an impairment issue arises or there is a disposal.

5.7   Impairment of intangible assets with an indefinite useful life

IAS 38 makes the point that 'indefinite' does not mean 'infinite', and unforeseeable factors may affect the entity's ability and intention to maintain the asset at its standard of performance assessed at the time of estimating the asset's useful life. *[IAS 38.91]*. The requirements of IAS 36 for this type of asset can be summarised as follows:

1.   All intangible assets with indefinite useful lives must be tested for impairment at least once per year and at the same time each year; *[IAS 36.10]*

2.   Any intangible asset with an indefinite useful life recognised during the reporting period must be tested for impairment before the end of the period; *[IAS 36.10]*

3.   Any intangible asset (regardless of whether it has an indefinite useful life or not) *that is not yet available for use* recognised during the reporting period must be tested for impairment before the end of the period; *[IAS 36.10-11]*

4.   If an intangible asset that has an indefinite useful life or is not yet available for use can only be tested for impairment as part of a CGU, then that CGU must be tested for impairment at least annually; *[IAS 36.89]*

5.   If there are indicators of impairment a period end test must also be performed; *[IAS 36.9]* and

6.   For an intangible asset that has an indefinite useful life that is part of a CGU, there are specific concessions, discussed below, allowing an impairment test in a previous period to be used if that test showed sufficient headroom. *[IAS 36.24]*.

Any intangible asset not yet ready for use must be tested annually because its ability to generate sufficient future economic benefits to recover its carrying amount is usually subject to greater uncertainty before the asset is available for use than after it is available for use. *[IAS 36.11]*.

This will obviously affect any entity that capitalises development expenditure in accordance with IAS 38 where the period of development may straddle more than one accounting period. The requirement will also apply to in-process research and development costs recognised in a business combination (see Chapter 10 at 5.5.2).

An intangible asset with an indefinite useful life may generate independent cash inflows as an individual asset, in which case the impairment testing procedure for a single asset as set out in 4 above applies. Most intangible assets form part of the assets within a CGU, in which case the procedures relevant to testing a CGU as set out above apply. In particular IAS 36 makes it clear that if an intangible asset with an indefinite useful life, or any intangible asset not yet ready for use, is included in the assets of a CGU, then that CGU has to be tested for impairment annually. *[IAS 36.89]*. As with other assets, it may be that the FVCLCS of the intangible asset with an indefinite useful life can be ascertained but the asset itself does not generate largely independent cash flows. If its individual FVLCS is lower than the carrying amount then the recoverable amount will have to be based on the CGU of which the asset is a part.

IAS 36 allows a concession that only applies to those intangible assets with an indefinite useful life that form part of a CGU. It allows the most recent detailed calculation of such an asset's recoverable amount made in a preceding period to be used in the impairment test in the current period if all of the following criteria are met:

(a)   if the intangible asset is part of a CGU and the assets and liabilities making up that unit have not changed significantly since the most recent recoverable amount calculation;

(b)   that calculation of the asset's recoverable amount exceeded its carrying amount by a substantial margin; and

(c)   the likelihood that an updated calculation of the recoverable amount would be less than the asset's carrying amount is remote, based on an analysis of events and circumstances since the most recent calculation of the recoverable amount. *[IAS 36.24]*.

Thus if there was sufficient headroom on the last calculation and little has changed in the CGU to which the asset belongs, it can be revisited and re-used rather than having to be entirely restarted from scratch, which considerably reduces the work involved in the annual test. The impairment test cannot be rolled forward forever, of course, and an entity will have to take a cautious approach to estimating when circumstances have changed sufficiently to require a new test.

Impairment losses experienced on intangible assets with an indefinite useful life are recognised exactly as set out above in 4.5, either as an individual asset or as part of a CGU, depending upon whether the intangible concerned is part of a CGU or not. Note that there is an important distinction concerning the allocation of losses in a CGU between the treatment of goodwill and that of intangible assets with an indefinite useful life. As set out above in 4.5.2, if goodwill forms part of the assets of a CGU, any impairment loss first reduces the goodwill and thereafter the remaining assets are reduced pro-rata. However, if an intangible asset is part of a CGU that is impaired, there is no requirement to write down the intangible before the other assets in the CGU, rather all assets are written down pro-rata.

6   REVERSING IMPAIRMENT LOSSES

6.1   Reversal of impairment loss relating to goodwill prohibited

IAS 36 does not permit an impairment loss on goodwill to be reversed under any circumstances. *[IAS 36.124]*. The standard justifies this on the grounds that such a reversal would probably be an increase in internally generated goodwill, rather than a reversal of the impairment loss recognised for the acquired goodwill, and that recognition of internally generated goodwill is prohibited by IAS 38. *[IAS 36.125]*.

Example 22.22: Impairment of goodwill

Company A has a CGU that has a carrying value of $2,000,000 at 31 December 2010. This carrying value comprises $500,000 relating to goodwill and $1,500,000 relating to net tangible assets.

In 2011, as a result of losses, net tangible assets have decreased to $1,400,000 reducing the total carrying value of the unit to $1,900,000. Changes in the regulatory framework surrounding its business mean that the income-generating unit has a recoverable amount of $1,600,000 and has thus suffered an impairment loss of $300,000. This is charged to the profit and loss account. The carrying value of goodwill is reduced to $200,000.

In 2012 the company develops a new product with the result that the recoverable amount of the income-generating unit rises to $1,700,000. Net tangible assets have remained at $1,400,000. Despite the recoverable amount of the business unit now being $1,700,000 compared to its carrying value of $1,600,000, it is not possible to reverse $100,000 of the prior year's impairment loss of $300,000.

6.2   Reversal of impairment losses relating to assets other than goodwill

For all other assets, including intangible assets with an indefinite life, IAS 36 requires entities to assess at each reporting date whether there is any indication that an impairment loss may no longer exist or may have decreased. If there is any such indication, the entity has to recalculate the recoverable amount of the asset. *[IAS 36.110].*

Therefore if there are indications that a previously recognised impairment loss has disappeared or reduced, it is necessary to determine again the recoverable amount (i.e. the higher of FVLCS or VIU) so that the reversal can be quantified. The standard sets out examples of what it notes are in effect 'reverse indications' of impairment. *[IAS 36.111].* These are the reverse of those set out in paragraph 12 of the standard as indications of impairment (see 2.2 above) and are, as in paragraph 12, in two categories:

External sources of information:

(a)   a significant increase in the asset's market value;

(b)   significant changes during the period or expected in the near future in the entity's technological, market, economic or legal environment that will have a favourable effect;

(c)   decreases in market interest rates or other market rates of return on investments and those decreases are likely to affect the discount rate used in calculating the asset's value in use and increase the asset's recoverable amount materially.

Internal sources of information:

(d)   significant changes during the period or expected in the near future that will affect the extent to which, or manner in which, the asset is used. These changes include costs incurred during the period to improve or enhance the asset's performance or restructure the operation to which the asset belongs;

(e)   evidence from internal reporting that the economic performance of the asset is, or will be, better than expected. *[IAS 36.111].*

Compared with paragraph 12, there are two notable omissions from this list of 'reverse indicators', one external and one internal.

The external indication not included is the mirror of the impairment indicator 'the carrying amount of the net assets of the reporting entity is more than its market capitalisation'. No explanation is provided as to why, if a market capitalisation below shareholders' funds is an indication of impairment, its reversal should not automatically be an indication of a reversal. However, the most likely reason is that all of the facts and circumstances need to be considered before assuming that an impairment has reversed. In any event, deficits below market capitalisation may affect goodwill so the impairment charge cannot be reversed.

The internal omission from the list of 'reverse indicators' is that evidence of obsolescence or physical deterioration has been reversed. Once again no reason is given. It may be that the standard-setters have assumed that no such reversal could take place without the entity incurring costs to improve or enhance the performance of the asset or the CGU so that this is, in effect, covered by indicator (d) above.

The standard also reminds preparers that a reversal, like an impairment, is evidence that the depreciation method or residual value of the asset should be reviewed and may need to be adjusted, whether or not the impairment loss is reversed. *[IAS 36.113]*.

A further restriction is that impairment losses should be reversed only if there has been a change in the estimates used to determine the impairment loss, e.g. a change in cash flows or discount rate (for VIU) or a change in FVLCS. The 'unwinding' of the discount will increase the present value of future cash flows as they become closer but IAS 36 does not allow the mere passage of time to trigger the reversal of an impairment. In other words the 'service potential' of the asset must genuinely improve if a reversal is to be recognised. *[IAS 36.114-116]*. However, this inability to recognise the rise in value can give rise to what is in effect a double recognition of losses, which may seem illogical, as demonstrated by the following example:

Example 22.23: Double counted losses

At the end of 2012, an entity with a single CGU is carrying out an impairment review. The discounted forecast cash flows for years 2014 and onwards would be just enough to support the carrying value of the firm's assets. However, 2013 is forecast to produce a loss and net cash outflow. The discounted value of this amount is accordingly written off the carrying value of the fixed assets in 2012 as an impairment loss. It is then suffered again in 2013 (at a slightly higher amount being now undiscounted) as the actual loss. Once that loss is past, the future cash flows are sufficient to support the original unimpaired value of the fixed assets. Nevertheless, the assets cannot be written back up through the profit and loss account to counter the double counting effect as the increase in value does not derive from a change in economic conditions or in the expected use of an asset.

In this type of scenario, which is common in practice, the entity will only 'benefit' as the assets are depreciated or amortised at a lower amount.

If, on the other hand, the revival in cash flows is the result of expenditure by the entity to improve or enhance the performance of the asset or the CGU or on a restructuring of the CGU, there may be an obvious improvement in the service potential and the entity may be able to reverse some or all of the impairment write down.

In the event of an individual asset's impairment being reversed, the reversal may not raise the carrying value above the figure it would have stood at taking into account depreciation, if no impairment had originally been recognised. *[IAS 36.117]*. Any increase above this figure would really be a revaluation, which would have to be accounted for in accordance with the standard relevant to the asset concerned. *[IAS 36.118]*.

Example 22.24: Reversal of impairment losses

At the beginning of 2008 an entity acquires an asset with a useful life of 10 years for $1000. The asset generates net cash inflows that are largely independent of the cash inflows of other assets or groups of assets. At the end of 2010, when the carrying amount after depreciation is $700, the entity recognises that there has been an impairment loss of $210. The entity writes the asset down to $490. As the useful life is not affected, the entity commences amortisation at $70 per annum which, if applied in each of the years 2011 – 2017, would amortise the carrying value over the remaining useful life, as follows:

Table 1	2008	2009	2010	2011	2012	2013	2014	2015	2016	2017
	$	$	$	$	$	$	$	$	$	$
NBV – beginning of the year	1000	900	800	490	420	350	280	210	140	70
Depreciation	100	100	100	70	70	70	70	70	70	70
Impairment			210							
NBV – end of the year	900	800	490	420	350	280	210	140	70	–
NBV without impairment	900	800	700	600	500	400	300	200	100	–

At the beginning of 2012, before depreciation for the year, the asset's carrying value is $420. Thanks to improvements in technology, the entity is able to increase the asset's VIU to $550 by spending $120 on parts that improve and enhance its performance.

However, this has taken no account of the previous impairment of $210 in 2010 or of the revised VIU at the end of 2012 of $550. Therefore, at the end of 2012, the asset can be written up to the *lower* of:

- $600, which the net book value of the asset after the additional expenditure, assuming that there had never been any impairment This is the balance brought forward at the beginning of 2012 of $600 (Table 1 bottom row) plus expenditure of $120 less depreciation for the year of (720/6) = $120; and

- $550, which is the VIU.

i.e. it can write the asset's net book value back up to $550. Therefore, the entity can reverse $100 of the impairment write down and amortise the remaining net book value of the asset of $550 to zero over the remaining five years, 2013 – 2017, at $110 per annum.

Table 2	2012	2013	2014	2015	2016	2017
	$	$	$	$	$	$
Cost	1000	1120	1120	1120	1120	1120
Expenditure in the year	120					
Cost carried forward	1120	1120	1120	1120	1120	1120
Accumulated depreciation brought forward	580	570	680	790	900	1010
Charge for the year (on opening balance – Table 2)	90	110	110	110	110	110
Reversal of impairment	(100)					
Accumulated depreciation carried forward	570	680	790	900	1010	1120
NBV	550	440	330	220	110	–

The Standard includes an illustration of the reversal of an impairment loss in the standard's accompanying section of illustrative examples, in Example 4.

All reversals are to be recognised in the income statement immediately, except for revalued assets which are dealt with below. *[IAS 36.119].*

If an impairment loss is reversed against an asset, its depreciation or amortisation is adjusted to allocate its revised carrying amount less residual value over its remaining useful life. *[IAS 36.121].*

6.2.1 *Reversals of impairments – cash-generating units*

Where an entity recognises a reversal of an impairment loss on a CGU, the increase in the carrying amount of the assets of the unit should be allocated by increasing the carrying amount of the assets, other than goodwill, in the unit on a pro-rata basis. However, the carrying amount of an individual asset should not be increased above the lower of its recoverable amount and the carrying amount that would have resulted had no impairment loss been recognised in prior years. Any 'surplus' reversal is to be allocated to the remaining assets pro-rata, always remembering that goodwill, if allocated to an individual CGU, may not be increased under any circumstances. *[IAS 36.122, 123].*

6.2.2 *Reversals of impairments – revalued assets*

If an asset is recognised at a revalued amount under another standard any reversal of an impairment loss should be treated as a revaluation increase under that other standard. Thus a reversal of an impairment loss on a revalued asset is credited directly to equity under the heading revaluation surplus. However, to the extent that an impairment loss on the same revalued asset was previously recognised as an expense in the income statement, a reversal of that impairment loss is recognised as income in the income statement. *[IAS 36.119, 120].*

As with assets carried at cost, after a reversal of an impairment loss is recognised on a revalued asset, the depreciation charge should be adjusted in future periods to allocate the asset's revised carrying amount, less any residual value, on a systematic basis over its remaining useful life. *[IAS 36.121].*

7 DISCLOSURES REQUIRED BY IAS 36

7.1 Introduction

This section sets out the principal disclosures for impairment required in financial statements as set out in IAS 36. Any disclosures required relating to impairment by other standards are dealt with in the chapter concerned. Disclosures that may be required by other authorities such as national statutes or listing authorities are not included.

7.2 IAS 36 disclosures

The disclosures required fall into two broad categories:

(i)   disclosures concerning any actual impairment losses or reversals made in the period, that are obviously only required if such a loss or reversal has occurred, regardless of the type of asset involved; and

(ii) yearly disclosures concerning the annual impairment tests required for goodwill and intangible assets with an indefinite useful life, that are required regardless of whether an impairment adjustment to these types of assets has occurred or not.

7.2.1   *Disclosures required for impairment losses or reversals*

IAS 36 defines a class of assets as 'a grouping of assets of similar nature and use in the entity's operations'. *[IAS 36.126].* For each class of assets the entity must disclose:

'(a)   the amount of impairment losses recognised in profit or loss during the period and the line item(s) in profit or loss in which those impairment losses are included;

(b)   the amount of reversals of impairment losses recognised in profit or loss during the period and the line item(s) in profit or loss in which those impairment losses are reversed;

(c)   the amount of impairment losses on revalued assets recognised directly in other comprehensive income during the period;

(d)   the amount of reversals of impairment losses on revalued assets recognised directly in other comprehensive income during the period.' *[IAS 36.126].*

These disclosures can be made as an integral part of the other disclosures, for example the property plant and equipment note reconciling the opening and closing values (as set out in Chapter 20) may contain the required information. *[IAS 36.128].*

Additionally, IAS 36 links disclosure of impairments with segment disclosures. Thus, if a business is subject to IFRS 8 after the implementation of that standard then any impairments or reversals must be disclosed by operating segment as follows:

(a)   the amount of impairment losses recognised in profit or loss and directly in other comprehensive income during the period;

(b)   the amount of reversals of impairment losses recognised in profit or loss and directly in other comprehensive income during the period. *[IAS 36.129].*

7.2.2   *Material impairments*

If an impairment loss for an individual asset or an individual cash-generating unit is recognised or reversed during the period and is material to the financial statements of the reporting entity as a whole, the following disclosures are required:

(a)   the events and circumstances that led to the recognition or reversal of the impairment loss;

(b)   the amount of the impairment loss recognised or reversed;

(c)   for an individual asset:

(i)   the nature of the asset; and

(ii)   if the entity reports segmental information in accordance with IFRS 8, the reportable segment to which the asset belongs.

(d)   for a cash-generating unit:

(i)   a description of the cash-generating unit (such as whether it is a product line, a plant, a business operation, a geographical area, or a reportable segment as defined in IFRS 8;

(ii)   the amount of the impairment loss recognised or reversed by class of assets and if the entity reports segmental information in accordance with IFRS 8, by reportable segment; and

(iii)   if the aggregation of assets for identifying the cash-generating unit has changed since the previous estimate of the cash-generating unit's recoverable amount (if any), a description of the current and former way of aggregating assets and the reasons for changing the way the cash-generating unit is identified.

(e)   whether the recoverable amount of the asset or cash-generating unit is its fair value less costs to sell (FVLCS) or its value in use (VIU);

(f)   if recoverable amount is FVLCS, the basis used to determine FVLCS (such as whether FVLCS was determined by reference to an active market); and

(g)   if recoverable amount is VIU, the discount rate used in the current estimate and previous estimate (if any) of VIU. *[IAS 36.130].*

It is logically possible for impairment adjustments *in aggregate* to be material, yet no single one material in itself, in which case the previous requirement that relates to individual assets or CGUs could theoretically be circumvented. Therefore the following 'catch all' requirement is added:

'An entity shall disclose the following information for the aggregate impairment losses and the aggregate reversals of impairment losses recognised during the period for which no information is disclosed in accordance with paragraph 130:

(a)   the main classes of assets affected by impairment losses and the main classes of assets affected by reversals of impairment losses;

(b)   the main events and circumstances that led to the recognition of these impairment losses and reversals of impairment losses.' *[IAS 36.131].*

If there are any cases of impairment adjustments where intangible assets with indefinite useful life and goodwill are not involved, IAS 36 encourages the disclosure of key assumptions made in the recoverable amount calculations used to determine any impairments recognised in the period. *[IAS 36.132].* However, as set out below, if there is any impairment of a CGU containing intangible assets with an indefinite useful life or goodwill, this type of disclosure is required.

7.3   Annual impairment disclosures required for goodwill and intangible assets with an indefinite useful life.

Paragraph 84 of IAS 36 accepts that following a business combination it may not have been possible to allocate all the goodwill to individual CGUs or groups of CGUs by the end of the period in which the acquisition has been made (see 5.2 above). In these circumstances the standard requires that the amount of any such unallocated goodwill be disclosed, together with the reasons why it has not been allocated. *[IAS 36.133].*

The annual disclosures are intended to provide the user with information about the types of estimates that have been used in arriving at the recoverable amounts of goodwill and intangible assets with an indefinite useful life, that are included in the assets of the entity at the period end. They are divided into two broad categories:

(i)   those concerning individual CGUs or group of CGUs in which the carrying amount of goodwill or of intangible assets with an indefinite useful life is 'significant' in comparison with the entity's total carrying amount of these items. In this category disclosures are to be made separately for each significant CGU or group of CGUs; and

(ii) those concerning CGUs or groups of CGUs in which the carrying amount of goodwill or of intangible assets with an indefinite useful life is *not* 'significant' individually in comparison with the entity's total carrying amount of these items. In this case the disclosures can be made in aggregate.

No definition of 'significant' is given; but it must be taken to mean significant in relation to any or all of asset values, shareholders funds, and to profit for the year if a write off were to be required.

For each cash-generating unit or group of units for which the carrying amount of goodwill or intangible assets with indefinite useful lives allocated to that unit or group of units is significant, the following disclosures are required every year:

(a)   the carrying amount of goodwill allocated to the CGU (group of CGUs);

(b)   the carrying amount of intangible assets with indefinite useful lives allocated to the CGU (group of CGUs);

(c)   the basis on which the CGU's or group of CGUs' recoverable amount has been determined (i.e. VIU or FVLCS);

(d)   if the CGU's or group of CGUs' recoverable amount is based on VIU:

  (i)   a description of each key assumption on which management has based its cash flow projections for the period covered by the most recent budgets/forecasts. Key assumptions are those to which the unit's (group of units') recoverable amount is most sensitive;

  (ii)   a description of management's approach to determining the value(s) assigned to each key assumption, whether those value(s) reflect past experience or, if appropriate, are consistent with external sources of information, and, if not, how and why they differ from past experience or external sources of information;

  (iii) the period over which management has projected cash flows based on financial budgets/forecasts approved by management and, when a period greater than five years is used for a cash-generating unit (group of units), an explanation of why that longer period is justified;

  (iv)   the growth rate used to extrapolate cash flow projections beyond the period covered by the most recent budgets/forecasts, and the justification for using any growth rate that exceeds the long-term average growth rate for the products, industries, or country or countries in which the entity operates, or for the market to which the unit (group of units) is dedicated;

(v)   the discount rate(s) applied to the cash flow projections.

(e)   if the CGU's or group of CGUs' recoverable amount is based on FVLCS, the methodology used to determine FVLCS. If FVLCS is not determined using an observable market price for the unit (group of units), the following information shall also be disclosed:

     (i)   a description of each key assumption on which management has based its determination of FVLCS. Key assumptions are those to which the unit's (group of units') recoverable amount is most sensitive;

     (ii)   a description of management's approach to determining the value(s) assigned to each key assumption, whether those value(s) reflect past experience or, if appropriate, are consistent with external sources of information, and, if not, how and why they differ from past experience or external sources of information.

If FVLCS is determined using discounted cash flow projections, the following information shall also be disclosed:

     (iii)   the period over which management has projected cash flows;

     (iv)   the growth rate used to extrapolate cash flow projections;

     (v)   the discount rate(s) applied to the cash flow projections.

(f)   if a reasonably possible change in a key assumption on which management has based its determination of the CGU's or group of CGUs' recoverable amount would cause the CGU's or group of CGUs' carrying amount to exceed its recoverable amount:

     (i)   the amount by which the CGU's or group of CGUs' recoverable amount exceeds its carrying amount;

     (ii)   the value assigned to the key assumption;

     (iii)   the amount by which the value assigned to the key assumption must change, after incorporating any consequential effects of that change on the other variables used to measure recoverable amount, in order for the CGU's or group of CGUs' recoverable amount to be equal to its carrying amount. *[IAS 36.134].*

As set out above, there are separate disclosure requirements for those CGUs or groups of CGUs that taken individually do not have significant amounts of goodwill in comparison with the total carrying value of goodwill or of intangible assets with an indefinite useful life within their carrying values. *[IAS 36.135].*

- First, an aggregate disclosure has to be made of the 'not significant' amounts of goodwill or of intangible assets with an indefinite useful life. If some or all of the carrying amount of goodwill or intangible assets with indefinite useful lives is allocated across multiple CGUs or group of CGUs, and the amount so allocated to each CGU or group of CGUs is not significant in comparison with the entity's total carrying amount of goodwill or intangible assets with indefinite useful lives, that fact shall be disclosed, together with the aggregate carrying amount of goodwill or intangible assets with indefinite useful lives allocated to those CGUs or group of CGUs.

- Second, if in aggregate these amounts are significant in relation to the entirety of the carrying amount of the entity's goodwill or intangible assets with an indefinite useful life, the following is required to be disclosed. If the recoverable amounts of any of those CGUs or group of CGUs are based on the same key assumption(s) and the aggregate carrying amount of goodwill or intangible assets with indefinite useful lives allocated to them is significant in comparison with the entity's total carrying amount of goodwill or intangible assets with indefinite useful lives, an entity shall disclose that fact, together with:

  (a) the aggregate carrying amount of goodwill allocated to those CGUs or group of CGUs);

  (b) the aggregate carrying amount of intangible assets with indefinite useful lives allocated to those CGUs or group of CGUs;

  (c) a description of the key assumption(s);

  (d) a description of management's approach to determining the value(s) assigned to the key assumption(s), whether those value(s) reflect past experience or, if appropriate, are consistent with external sources of information, and, if not, how and why they differ from past experience or external sources of information;

  (e) if a reasonably possible change in the key assumption(s) would cause the aggregate of the CGU's or group of CGUs' carrying amounts to exceed the aggregate of their recoverable amounts:

    (i) the amount by which the aggregate of the CGU's or group of CGUs' recoverable amounts exceeds the aggregate of their carrying amounts;

    (ii) the value(s) assigned to the key assumption(s);

    (iii) the amount by which the value(s) assigned to the key assumption(s) must change, after incorporating any consequential effects of the change on the other variables used to measure recoverable amount, in order for the aggregate of the CGU's or group of CGUs' recoverable amounts to be equal to the aggregate of their carrying amounts. *[IAS 36.135].*

Example 9 in IAS 36's Illustrative Examples gives an indication of the types of assumptions and other relevant information the IASB envisages being disclosed under this requirement. The IASB expects disclosure of: budgeted gross margins, average gross margins, expected efficiency improvements., whether values assigned to key assumptions reflect past experience, what improvements management believes are reasonably achievable each year, forecast exchange rates during the budget period, forecast consumer price indices during the budget period for raw materials, market share and anticipated growth in market share.

An example of disclosures including key assumptions and sensitivities is given by Vodafone Group Plc.

Extract 22.4: Vodafone Group Plc (2011)

Notes to the consolidated financial statements [extract]

10.   Impairment [extract]

Impairment losses

The net impairment losses recognised in the consolidated income statement, as a separate line item within operating profit, in respect of goodwill and licences and spectrum fees are as follows:

Cash generating unit:	Reportable segment:	2011[1] £m	2010 £m	2009 £m
Italy	Italy	1,050	–	–
Spain	Spain	2,950	–	3,400
Greece	Other Europe [2]	800	–	–
Ireland	Other Europe [2]	1,000	–	–
Portugal	Other Europe [2]	350	–	–
Turkey	Other Europe	–	(200)	2,250
India	India	–	2,300	–
Ghana	Other Africa, Middle East and Asia Pacific	–	–	250
		6,150	2,100	5,900

Notes:
[1]   Impairment charges for the year ended 31 March 2011 relate solely to goodwill.
[2]   Total impairment losses in the Other Europe segment were £2,150 million in the year ended 31 March 2011.

Year ended 31 March 2011

The impairment losses were based on value in use calculations. The pre-tax adjusted discount rates used in the most recent value in use calculation in the year ended 31 March 2011 are as follows:

	Pre-tax adjusted discount rate
Italy	11.9%
Spain	11.5%
Greece	14.0%
Ireland	14.5%
Portugal	14.0%

During the year ended 31 March 2011, the goodwill in relation to the Group's investments in Italy, Spain, Greece, Ireland and Portugal was impaired by £1,050 million, £2,950 million, £800 million, £1,000 million and £350 million, respectively. The impairment charges were primarily driven by increased discount rates as a result of increases in government bond rates. In addition, business valuations were negatively impacted by lower cash flows within business plans, reflecting weaker country-level macro economic environments.

The pre-tax risk adjusted discount rates used in the previous value in use calculations at 31 March 2010 are disclosed below.

Year ended 31 March 2010

The net impairment losses were based on value in use calculations. The pre-tax adjusted discount rates used in the value in use calculation in the year ended 31 March 2010 were as follows:

	Pre-tax adjusted discount rate
India	13.8%
Turkey	17.6%

During the year ended 31 March 2010 the goodwill in relation to the Group's operations in India was impaired by £2,300 million primarily due to intense price competition following the entry of a number of new operators into the market. The pre-tax risk adjusted discount rate used in the previous value in use calculation at 31 March 2009 was 12.3%.

In addition, impairment losses of £200 million, previously recognised in respect of intangible assets in relation to the Group's operations in Turkey, were reversed. The reversal was in relation to licences and spectrum and was as a result of favourable changes in the discount rate. The cash flow projections within the business plans used for impairment testing were substantially unchanged from those used at 31 March 2009. The pre-tax risk adjusted discount rate used in the previous value in use calculation at 31 March 2009 was 19.5%.

Year ended 31 March 2009

The impairment losses were based on value in use calculations. The pre-tax adjusted discount rates used in the value in use calculation in the year ended 31 March 2009 were as follows:

	Pre-tax adjusted discount rate
Spain	10.3%
Turkey	19.5%
Ghana	26.9%

During the year ended 31 March 2009 the goodwill in relation to the Group's operations in Spain was impaired by £3,400 million following a fall in long-term cash flow forecasts resulting from the economic downturn.

In addition, the goodwill and other intangible assets in relation to the Group's operations in Turkey was impaired by £2,250 million. At 30 September 2008 the goodwill was impaired by £1,700 million following adverse movements in the discount rate and adverse performance against previous plans. During the second half of the 2009 financial year, impairment losses of £300 million in relation to goodwill and £250 million in relation to licences and spectrum resulted from adverse changes in both the discount rate and a fall in the long-term GDP growth rate. The cash flow projections within the business plans used for impairment testing were substantially unchanged from those used at 30 September 2008.

The goodwill in relation to the Group's operations in Ghana was also impaired by £250 million following an increase in the discount rate.

Goodwill

The carrying value of goodwill at 31 March was as follows:

	2011 £m	2010 £m
Germany	12,200	12,301
Italy	13,615	14,786
Spain	7,133	10,167
	32,948	37,254
Other	12,288	14,584
	45,236	51,838

Key assumptions used in the value in use calculations

The key assumptions used in determining the value in use are:

Assumption	How determined
Budgeted EBITDA	Budgeted EBITDA has been based on past experience adjusted for the following: • voice and messaging revenue is expected to benefit from increased usage from new customers, the introduction of new services and traffic moving from fixed networks to mobile networks, though these factors will be offset by increased competitor activity, which may result in price declines, and the trend of falling termination rates; • non-messaging data revenue is expected to continue to grow strongly as the penetration of 3G enabled devices and smartphones rises and new products and services are introduced; and • margins are expected to be impacted by negative factors such as an increase in the cost of acquiring and retaining customers in increasingly competitive markets and the expectation of further termination rate cuts by regulators and by positive factors such as the efficiencies expected from the implementation of Group initiatives.
Budgeted capital expenditure	The cash flow forecasts for capital expenditure are based on past experience and include the ongoing capital expenditure required to roll out networks in emerging markets, to provide enhanced voice and data products and services and to meet the population coverage requirements of certain of the Group's licences. Capital expenditure includes cash outflows for the purchase of property, plant and equipment and computer software.
Long-term growth rate	For businesses where the five year management plans are used for the Group's value in use calculations, a long-term growth rate into perpetuity has been determined as the lower of: • the nominal GDP rates for the country of operation; and • the long-term compound annual growth rate in EBITDA in years six to ten estimated by management. For businesses where the plan data is extended for an additional five years for the Group's value in use calculations, a long-term growth rate into perpetuity has been determined as the lower of: • the nominal GDP rates for the country of operation; and • the compound annual growth rate in EBITDA in years nine to ten years of the management plan.
Pre-tax risk adjusted discount rate	The discount rate applied to the cash flows of each of the Group's operations is generally based on the risk free rate for ten year bonds issued by the government in the respective market. Where government bond rates contain a material component of credit risk, high quality local corporate bond rates may be used. There rates are adjusted for a risk premium to reflect both the increased risk of investing in equities and the systematic risk of the specific Group operating company. In making this adjustment, inputs required are the equity market risk premium (that is the required increased return required over and above a risk free rate by an investor who is investing in the market as a whole) and the risk adjustment, beta, applied to reflect the risk of the specific Group operating company relative to the market as a whole. In determining the risk adjusted discount rate, management has applied an adjustment for the systematic risk to each of the Group's operations determined using an average of the betas of comparable listed mobile telecommunications companies and, where available and appropriate, across a specific territory. Management has used a forward-looking equity market risk premium that takes into consideration both studies by independent economists, the average equity market risk premium over the past ten years and the market risk premiums typically used by investment banks in evaluating acquisition proposals.

Sensitivity to changes in assumptions [extract]

Other than as disclosed below, management believes that no reasonably possible change in any of the above key assumptions would cause the carrying value of any cash generating unit to exceed its recoverable amount.

31 March 2011

The estimated recoverable amount of the Group's operations in Italy, Spain, Greece, Ireland and Portugal equalled their respective carrying value and, consequently, any adverse change in key assumption would, in isolation, cause a further impairment loss to be recognised. The estimated recoverable amount of the Group's operations in Turkey, India and Ghana exceeded their carrying value by approximately £1,481 million, £977 million and £138 million, respectively.

The table below shows the key assumptions used in the value in use calculations.

| | Assumptions used in value in use calculation | | | | | | | |
	Italy %	Spain %	Greece %	Ireland %	Portugal %	Turkey %	India %	Ghana %
Pre-tax adjusted discount rate	11.9	11.5	14.0	14.5	14.0	14.1	14.2	20.8
Long term growth rate	0.8	1.6	2.0	2.0	1.5	6.1	6.3	6.3
Budgeted EBITDA[1]	(1.0)	–	1.2	2.4	(1.2)	16.8	16.5	41.4
Budgeted capital expenditure[2]	9.6-11.3	7.8-10.6	10.7-12.3	9.4-11.6	12.4-14.1	10.0-16.6	12.9-22.7	7.3-41.3

Notes:
[1] Budgeted EBITDA is expressed as the compound annual growth rates in the initial ten years for Turkey and Ghana and the initial five years for all other cash generating units of the plans used for impairment testing.
[2] Budgeted capital expenditure is expressed as the range of capital expenditure as a percentage of revenue in the initial ten years for Turkey and Ghana and the initial five years for all other cash generating units of the plans used for impairment testing.

The table below shows, for Turkey, India and Ghana, the amount by which each key assumption must change in isolation in order for the estimated recoverable amount to be equal to its carrying value.

| | Change required for the carrying value to equal the recoverable amount[1] | | |
	Turkey pps	India pps	Ghana pps
Pre-tax adjusted discount rate	5.6	1.1	6.9
Long term growth rate	(19.6)	(1.0)	n/a
Budgeted EBITDA[2]	(4.7)	(2.2)	(8.7)
Budgeted capital expenditure[3]	7.0	2.5	8.9

Notes:

(1)   The recoverable amount for Greece, which was impaired at 30 September 2010, equals the carrying value at 31 March 2011.

(2)   Budgeted EBITDA is expressed as the compound annual growth rates in the initial ten years for Turkey and Ghana and the initial five years for all other cash generating units of the plans used for impairment testing.

(3)   Budgeted capital expenditure is expressed as the range of capital expenditure as a percentage of revenue in the initial ten years for Turkey and Ghana and the initial five years for all other cash generating units of the plans used for impairment testing.

8   TESTING FOR IMPAIRMENT: GROUP ISSUES

There are some challenging problems in testing for impairment when looking at part of a group. This section looks at a series of such issues.

There are issues that relate to testing for impairment in the ultimate parent's consolidated financial statements. These include:

- Testing goodwill that relates to associates and jointly-controlled entities, dealt with at 8.1.1 below.

- Acquisitions by subsidiaries and determining the level at which the group tests goodwill for impairment (8.1.2 below).

Other issues relate to the financial statements of individual subsidiaries or to consolidated financial statements prepared by group companies other than the ultimate parent.

- Testing for impairment at the level of an individual group company, whether it prepares separate financial statements in accordance with IAS 27 or individual financial statements (see Chapter 9 at 1 for an explanation of the difference). The separate or individual financial statements can be those of any group company including the ultimate parent. Although IAS 36 explicitly applies to separate financial statements, actually applying the standard is fraught with difficulty, as described in 8.2 below.

- A group entity other than the ultimate parent may prepare consolidated financial statements. Applying IAS 36 in the consolidated financial statements of a (sub)group headed by a subsidiary raises difficult issues, considered at 8.3 below, about the definition of the reporting entity and the CGU and how to apply the concepts to complex groups that may have (re)organised their businesses to obtain fiscal or regulatory advantages.

Finally, in many groups the amount that is paid or received for transactions and arrangements is not based on market values. The consequences of non-arm's length transfers between group companies are considered at 8.4 below.

The specific issue of dividends and their effect on investments in subsidiaries is dealt with in Chapter 9 at 2.4.

8.1 Issues affecting the group's consolidated financial statements

8.1.1 Associates and jointly controlled entities and testing goodwill for impairment

When calculating its share of an equity accounted investee's results, an investor makes adjustments to the associate's profit or loss to reflect depreciation and impairments of the associate's identifiable assets based on their fair values at the date the investor acquired its investment. This is covered in paragraph 23 of IAS 28 which states that:

> 'Appropriate adjustments to the investor's share of the associate's profits or losses after acquisition are also made to account, for example, for depreciation of the depreciable assets, based on their fair values at the acquisition date. Similarly, appropriate adjustments to the investor's share of the associate's profits or losses after acquisition are made for impairment losses recognised by the associate, such as for goodwill or property, plant and equipment.'

Although this refers to 'appropriate adjustments' for goodwill impairment losses, this should not be interpreted as requiring the investor to recalculate the goodwill impairment on a similar basis to depreciation and impairment of tangible and intangible assets. The 'appropriate adjustment' is to reverse that goodwill impairment before calculating the investor's share of the investee's profit. After application of the equity method the entire equity-accounted carrying amount of the investor's investment, including the goodwill included in that carrying amount, is tested for impairment in accordance with paragraphs 31-34 of IAS 28. Note that there is no requirement to test investments in associates for impairment annually but only when there are indicators that the amount may not be recoverable. These requirements are described in detail in Chapter 12 at 4.

With jointly controlled entities, the treatment varies depending on whether the interest is included by way of proportionate consolidation or by equity accounting. If the investor uses proportionate consolidation then it accounts for its share of the underlying assets, including goodwill, and liabilities of the investee. Therefore, the investor's share of goodwill is tested for impairment annually as described in 5.3 above.

If, on the other hand, the investor uses the equity method then it applies the requirements of IAS 28 as described above.

Impairment write-offs made against investments in associates or jointly controlled entities included by way of the equity method may be reversed if an impairment loss no longer exists or has decreased (see 6.2 above). IAS 36 does not allow impairments of goodwill to be reversed [IAS 36.124] but this is not a write-off against goodwill so this prohibition does not apply. This was confirmed when IAS 28 was amended in 2008's Annual Improvements, applicable to accounting periods beginning on or after 1 January 2009; paragraph 33 now states that 'an impairment loss recognised in those circumstances is not allocated to any asset, including goodwill, that forms part of the carrying amount of the investment in the associate. Accordingly, any reversal of that impairment loss is recognised in accordance with IAS 36 to the extent that the recoverable amount of the investment subsequently increases'.

Similarly, although IAS 39 restricts the circumstances in which impairments in investments in certain financial assets may be reversed (see Chapter 49 at 6) these do not apply to interests included in consolidated accounts using the equity method (or included in individual financial accounts if the entity applies the equity method).

8.1.2 Acquisitions by subsidiaries and determining the level at which the group tests goodwill for impairment

IAS 36 requires goodwill to be allocated to the lowest level within the entity at which the goodwill is monitored for internal management purposes. If a subsidiary undertakes acquisitions and recognises goodwill in its own financial statements, the level at which the subsidiary's management monitors the goodwill may differ from the level at which the parent's or group's management monitors goodwill from the group's perspective.

If a subsidiary's management monitors its goodwill at a lower level than the level at which the parent's or group's management monitors its goodwill, a key issue is whether that lower level should, from the group's perspective, be regarded as the 'lowest level within the entity at which the goodwill is monitored for internal management purposes'? The answer is no, as is demonstrated in the following example.

Example 22.25: Monitoring goodwill arising from acquisitions by subsidiaries

A parent acquired 100% of the issued shares of a company that operates autonomously and is required to prepare IFRS-compliant financial statements. The subsidiary has acquired various businesses both before and after becoming part of the group. Those business combinations have included significant amounts of goodwill.

The subsidiary's management monitors its acquired goodwill at the level of the subsidiary's operating segments. However, management of the parent/group monitors its acquired goodwill at the level of the group's operating segments, which is a higher level than the subsidiary's operating segments. The subsidiary's operations form part of two of the group's six operating segments.

The subsidiary's goodwill comprises goodwill arising on its acquisitions, some of which took place *before*, and some *after*, the subsidiary became part of the group.

In contrast, the goodwill recognised by the group comprises:

- Goodwill acquired by the parent in the acquisition of the subsidiary (some of which represents goodwill acquired and therefore recognised by the subsidiary and some of which was internally generated goodwill from the subsidiary's perspective and therefore not recognised by the subsidiary);
- Goodwill acquired by the subsidiary since becoming part of the group;
- Goodwill acquired by the parent in other operating combinations (i.e. goodwill that relates to other subsidiaries and businesses that make up the group).

The goodwill acquired in the acquisition of the subsidiary that is recognised by the parent in its consolidated financial statements is therefore different from the goodwill recognised by the subsidiary (which relates only to the acquisitions made by the subsidiary and was measured at the date of the acquisition concerned).

In such circumstances the actions of the subsidiary's management in deciding the level at which it tests its goodwill for impairment will *not* cause the group to be 'locked in' to testing goodwill at the same level in the consolidated financial statements.

Rather, the group should test its goodwill for impairment at the level at which management of the parent or group monitors its various investments in goodwill, namely, in this example, at the group's or operating segment level.

8.2   Testing investments in subsidiaries, jointly controlled entities and associates for impairment in separate financial statements

Many entities within a group prepare separate financial statements in accordance with IAS 27 either through choice or legal obligation. Of these, most probably choose to carry their investments in subsidiaries, jointly controlled entities and associates at cost, which means that they are within scope of IAS 36 *[IAS 27.38, IAS 36.4].* Alternatively they may carry investments 'in accordance with IAS 39', *[IAS 27.38],* which means applying one of the classifications allowed by that standard (most likely at fair value through profit or loss or available for sale – see Chapter 46).

The IASB has not finalised a proposal made in the *Improvements to IFRSs* issued by the IASB in August 2009 to 'clarify' that in its separate financial statements the investor is to carry these investments at cost or at fair value through profit or loss, both in accordance with IAS 39 and to use that standard to test these investments for impairment.[4] Therefore, investments in subsidiaries, jointly controlled entities and associates carried at cost must be tested for impairment using IAS 36. This is a challenge as it is not entirely clear how IAS 36's requirements are to be applied. The meaning of VIU is particularly opaque when applied to an investment in shares.

A variety of methods are used in practice, including methods that value the individual investments and those that test for impairment by considering the recoverable amount of the underlying assets of the investment, as discussed further below.

8.2.1   Applying an IAS 36 methodology based on underlying assets

If an entity can demonstrate that a subsidiary contains one or more CGUs in their entirety then it will be able to use impairment tests of the underlying CGUs to test the investment for impairment. If the aggregate VIU or FVLCS of the CGU or CGUs is not less than the carrying value of the investment, then the investment will not be impaired.

However, it may not be so straightforward in practice. There are particular problems if the asset (the investment) and the underlying CGU are not the same. CGUs may overlap individual subsidiaries so, for example, a single CGU may contain more than one such subsidiary. There may be apparent indicators of impairment of the investment: the individual subsidiary may be loss-making or there may be little or no history of distributions. Even if the CGU and investment coincide, the shares may have been acquired in a business combination. It is quite possible that the synergies that gave rise to goodwill on acquisition are in another part of the group not controlled by the intermediate parent in question. Views on how to take these matters into consideration vary. Some consider that the individual investments can be valued only on the basis of the cash flows directly generated by the underlying assets while others take into consideration the manner in which the group has organised its activities and make notional adjustments. Some of the matters that may be taken into account in testing subsidiaries for impairment are discussed at 8.3 below.

8.2.2 IAS 28's approach to impairment

IAS 28 includes guidance on establishing the VIU of an equity interest in an associate. It states that:

'In determining the value in use of the investment, an entity estimates:

(a) its share of the present value of the estimated future cash flows expected to be generated by the associate, including the cash flows from the operations of the associate and the proceeds on the ultimate disposal of the investment; or

(b) the present value of the estimated future cash flows expected to arise from dividends to be received from the investment and from its ultimate disposal.

Under appropriate assumptions, both methods give the same result. *[IAS 28.33].*

The recoverable amount of an investment in an associate is assessed for each associate, unless the associate does not generate cash inflows from continuing use that are largely independent of those from other assets of the entity.' *[IAS 28.34].*

Testing an investment in an associate or jointly controlled entity carried under the equity method in consolidated accounts using this method cannot always provide assurance about the cost of shares in the investor's separate financial statements. Accounting for the group's share of losses may take the equity interest below cost and an impairment test could reveal no need for an impairment loss. This might not provide any assurance about the (higher) carrying value of shares in the separate financial statements.

Some have taken the view that this approach can be applied to an investment in the shares of an associate carried at cost in the investor's accounts and, by analogy, to an investment in a subsidiary or jointly controlled entity.

Applying the IAS 28 methodology may also run into problems if there have been group reorganisations. Entities may have reorganised the businesses within their subsidiaries in such a way that value and future cash flows have been transferred from one to another. One common example is discussed at 8.2.4 below.

8.2.3 Dividend discount models

Dividend discount models (DDMs) are financial models frequently used by financial institutions that value shares at the discounted value of future dividend payments. Such models value a company on the basis of future cash flows that may be distributed to the shareholders in compliance with the capital requirements provided by law, discounted at a rate expressing the cost of risk capital.

The Interpretations Committee considered the use of DDMs in testing for impairment under IAS 36. It was of the view that calculations using DDMs may be appropriate when calculating the VIU of a single asset, for example when determining whether an investment is impaired in the separate financial statements of an entity.

However, the Interpretations Committee had been asked whether DDMs were an appropriate basis for calculating the VIU of a CGU in consolidated financial statements. The Committee concluded that calculations using DDMs would rarely be appropriate for this purpose. The cash flows used to calculate the VIU of a CGU in the consolidated financial statements may be different to those used to calculate the VIU of an investment in the separate financial statements. Dividends are paid from the net profits of entities, after finance charges and taxation and relate to the net assets of the subsidiary. Assets are tested for impairment without deduction of liabilities. The cash flows associated with liabilities are excluded when testing the value in use of a CGU but are reflected in dividends paid by the subsidiary.[5]

8.2.4   Group reorganisations and the carrying value of investments in subsidiaries

A common form of group reorganisation involves the transfer to another group company of the tangible assets and trade of a subsidiary. These transactions often take place at the book value of the transferor's assets rather than at fair value. If the original carrying value was a purchase price that included an element of goodwill, the remaining 'shell', i.e. an entity that no longer has any trade or activities, may have a carrying value in the parent company's balance sheet in excess of its net worth. It could be argued that as the subsidiary is now a shell with no possibility in its current state of generating sufficient profits to support its value, a loss should be recognised by the parent to reduce its investment in the shell company to its net worth. However, the transfer of part of the group's business from one controlled entity to another has no substance from the perspective of the group and will have no effect in the consolidated accounts. There has also been no loss overall to the parent as a result of this reorganisation.

This is, of course, a transaction between companies under common control as all of the combining entities or businesses are ultimately controlled by the same party or parties both before and after the business combination, and that control is not transitory. *[IFRS 3.10]*. This means that the treatment by the acquirer (the transferee) is out of the scope of IFRS 3.

From the transferor entity's perspective, the transaction combines a sale of its assets at an undervalue to the transferee, by reference to the fair value of the transferor's net assets, and a distribution of the shortfall in value to its parent. The fair value of those assets to the parent may well not be reflected in the transferor's own balance sheet because there is no push-down accounting under IFRS. The transferor is not obliged to record the 'distribution' to its parent at fair value. IFRIC 17 – *Distributions of Non-cash Assets to Owners* – issued in November 2008, will require gains or losses measured by reference to fair value of the assets distributed to be taken to profit or loss but, amongst other restrictions, excludes from its scope non-cash distributions made by wholly-owned group companies (see Chapter 9 at 2.4.2).

This interpretation of the transferor's transaction (as a sale at an undervalue and a deemed distribution to the parent) is wholly consistent with a legal analysis in some jurisdictions, for example the United Kingdom, where a company that does not have zero or positive distributable reserves is unable to sell its assets at an undervalue because it cannot make any sort of distribution.

The parent, in turn, could be seen as having made a capital contribution of the shortfall in value to the transferee. The parent may choose to record the distribution from the transferor (and consequent impairment in its carrying value) and the contribution to the transferee (and consequent increase in its carrying value). This is consistent with our analysis in Chapter 9 at 4.2 regarding intra-group transactions and the extent to which the arrangement affects the individual financial statements of the parent.

The transferee will not necessarily record the capital contribution even if this is an option available to it.

However, the underlying principles are not affected by whether or not the transferee makes this choice – there has been a transfer of value from one subsidiary to another. This demonstrates why the business transfer alone does not necessarily result in an impairment charge in the parent entity.

If the above analysis is not supportable in a particular jurisdiction then an impairment write down may have to be taken.

Actual circumstances may be less straightforward. In particular, the transferor and transferee entities may not be held directly by the same parent. This may make it necessary to record an impairment loss against the carrying value of the transferor ('shell') company in its intermediate parent to reflect its loss in value, which will be treated as an expense or as a distribution, depending on the policy adopted by the entity and the relevant facts and circumstances. See Chapter 9 at 4.4.1 for a discussion of the policy choices available to the entity. There may be another, higher level within the group at which the above arguments against impairment will apply.

Example 22.26: Group reorganisations and impairment

Topco has two directly held subsidiaries, Tradeco and Shellco. It acquired Shellco for £30 million and immediately thereafter transferred all of its trade and assets to its fellow subsidiary Tradeco for book value of £10 million with the proceeds being left outstanding on intercompany account. Shellco now has net assets of £10 million (its intercompany receivable) but a carrying value in Topco of £30 million. On the other hand, the value of Tradeco has been enhanced by its purchase of the business at an undervalue.

In our view, there are two acceptable ways in which Tradeco may account for this. The cost of the business combination may be the fair value of the cash given as consideration, i.e. £10 million and Tradeco will recognise no goodwill. Alternatively, it is the fair value of the cash given as consideration (£10 million), together with a deemed capital contribution received from Topco for the difference up to the fair value of the business of Shellco of £20 million, which will be recognised in equity, giving a total consideration of £30 million. Tradeco will recognise goodwill of £20 million.

The capital contribution measured under the second method represents the value distributed by Shellco to its parent Topco and thence to Tradeco.

If there is an intermediate holding company between Topco and Shellco but all other facts remain the same, then it would appear that an impairment ought to be made against the carrying value of Shellco in its immediate parent. The argument against impairment would still apply in Topco.

8.3 Testing assets for impairment in separate and individual financial statements

In many jurisdictions, subsidiary entities are not exempt from preparing financial statements and these may be required to comply with IFRSs. These may be accounts for the subsidiary on a stand-alone basis or may be consolidated accounts for the subgroup that it heads. Either way, there may be problems in testing its own assets or CGUs, or the assets or CGUs in its consolidated accounts, for impairment.

Although the following discussion refers to a subsidiary, the same issues apply to a subgroup's consolidated financial statements.

The first issue is whether CGUs are different from the perspective of the subsidiary entity compared with that of the parent's consolidated accounts. Some consider that the answer is no; once CGUs have been properly established for the group as a whole, they cannot be subdivided or differently assessed. They are defined as the smallest identifiable group of assets that generates cash inflows that are largely independent of the cash inflows from other assets or groups of assets. Therefore, the first challenge is to ensure that the group has set its CGUs at an appropriate level and there are no smaller identifiable groups of assets that meet the definition. However, even if one assumes that CGUs are set at the level of the consolidated accounts, it may still not be possible to use a test of a CGU under IAS 36 to provide sufficient assurance of the value of assets in an individual subsidiary. The issue that may have to be faced is how to test part of a CGU for impairment, if that is what is represented by the subsidiary's net assets and operations.

Not all accept this analysis and consider that the CGU must be considered from the perspective of the individual subsidiary, irrespective of the CGU in the consolidated accounts. Some that take this view may take into account only those cash flows arising in the individual entity although others accept the substitution of fair values for internal pricing. Indeed, in many situations, applying arm's length values for the internal transactions may mean that there is no difference between the first view (that the consolidated CGUS are, in effect, immutable) and this subsidiary-based position. In essence, the problems may be the same as whether one assumes that the CGU is set for the consolidated accounts or for the subsidiary. This is considered further below.

Regardless of which view is taken, it is necessary first of all to determine if there is any impairment in the CGUs in the consolidated financial statements, no matter how those CGUs relate to individual entities within the group. Only then is it possible to see whether a reasonable allocation of the CGU's value can be made to the interests in subsidiaries in question. If any of the CGUs in the consolidated financial statements is impaired then it would be surprising if this were not reflected in some manner in the individual entities.

It is necessary to establish whether there is an identifiable feature that has caused the apparent impairment as that will have an impact on how impairment is tested in the subsidiary. Issues relating to transfer pricing, on what basis intra-group charges are made or whether, indeed, they are made at all, may need to be considered.

The above analysis may be different for goodwill impairment analysis, as goodwill is not necessarily tested at the lowest level of CGUs, but at the level of a CGU group in accordance with IAS 36.80 (see also 8.1.2 above).

8.3.1   Transfer pricing

A subsidiary's assets may appear to be impaired because internal transfer pricing is not based on fair values for the products or services in question. As discussed in Chapter 9 at 4.3, entities can choose to recognise transactions at fair value, irrespective of the actual consideration, unless recognition and measurement is mandated by an IFRS. Any difference between the fair value and the agreed consideration may reflect additional goods or services but once all of these have been identified and accounted for, any remaining difference is a contribution or distribution of equity for a subsidiary, or an increase in the investment held or a distribution received by the parent. In this section, it is assumed that the transactions have been recorded at the agreed consideration and notional adjustments can be made on this basis.

There are a number of different ways in which fair values could be substituted in order to test the assets of individual subsidiaries or consolidated financial statements for a subgroup.

- *apportionment of consolidated CGUs to individual subsidiaries*

  The VIU of the consolidated CGU of which the loss making subsidiary is a part could be apportioned between the various subsidiaries, substituting the fair values of inputs and outputs of the subsidiaries in question for the internal transfer prices. This is similar to the requirement to substitute the value on an active market for the internal transfer price when determining the VIU of a CGU, as described in 4.1.1 above. *[IAS 36.70]*. Calculating the VIU of the whole CGU and apportioning it in this manner will avoid the potential pitfall of taking account of a notional increase in income to one subsidiary but neglecting to reflect the notional increase in costs to another.

- *substituting fair values in the financial statements of individual subsidiaries*

  This is a similar approach to above except that the test does not start with the VIU of the CGU in the consolidated financial statements. In principle, however, the answer ought to be very similar. Care would need to be taken to ensure that the consequences for other group companies were taken into account as an increase in notional cash flows for one group company will obviously result in a decrease for another.

- *Group companies fulfilling corporate function*

  Individual subsidiaries may be related to a number of fellow subsidiary companies, for example group finance, property holding or service companies, in which case the value could be considered by reference to a larger group of CGUs, in a manner analogous with corporate assets (see 4.2.2 above).

All of these approaches rest, at least notionally, on the assumption that the group has allocated its activities between its various subsidiaries for its own benefit. Group companies may make transactions at off-market values at the behest of the parent but at least in principle there would be a basis for charging the fair value.

In some circumstances it is not clear that there could be cash flows between the subsidiaries in question. For example, if goodwill is being tested in consolidated subgroup financial statements, it may be that the synergies that gave rise to the goodwill are in another part of the larger group because the subgroup is part of a CGU containing other subsidiary companies. It may not be possible to translate some synergies such as economies of scale into cash flows to the subgroup in question. Although there is no impairment at the level of the CGU in the group consolidated financial statements, the entity may not be able to avoid making an impairment charge in the subgroup statements, possibly to be accounted for as an equity distribution. The impact of an impairment may be limited, depending on the uses to which the subgroup financial statements are put.

In the absence of any consensus about how to test subsidiary and subgroup assets for impairment, there will be differences in practice.

Few subsidiaries can be allowed to carry on making losses in the longer term. In particular, unless they return to profitability they will eventually need financial support in order to be able to pay their creditors. The requirement for support represents a crucial difference when compared with the 'shell company' situation described above, because a parent does not need to do anything if it wishes to support indefinitely a non-trading subsidiary. This reinforces the need to understand why the subsidiary is loss-making. Only a subsidiary that is genuinely part of a larger CGU can have its value supported in this manner. If the parent is unprepared to make such a commitment, this is evidence that the investment in the subsidiary is in fact impaired.

References

1 IFRS 13 *Fair Value Measurement*, IASB, May 2011, para. D82 has revised IAS 36 para 20 as follows: 'However, sometimes it will not be possible to measure fair value less costs of disposal because there is no basis for making a reliable estimate of the price at which an orderly transaction to sell the asset would take place between market participants at the measurement date under current market conditions. In this case, the entity may use the asset's value in use as its recoverable amount.'

2 One source of reference which may prove useful is a Digest issued by the Corporate Finance Faculty of the ICAEW – *The Cost of Capital*, Simon Pallett, ICAEW, 1999.

3 *IFRIC Update,* September 2010

4 *Improvements to IFRSs*, August 2009, IASB, IAS 27, para. 38.

5 *IFRIC Update,* September 2010

Chapter 23

Capitalisation of borrowing costs

List of examples

Chapter 23   Capitalisation of borrowing costs

1   INTRODUCTION

A point of contention in determining the initial measurement of an asset is whether or not finance costs incurred during the period of its construction should be capitalised. There have always been a number of strong arguments in favour of the capitalisation of directly attributable finance costs. It is argued that they are just as much a cost as any other directly attributable cost, that expensing finance costs distorts the choice between purchasing and constructing an asset, that capitalising the costs leads to a carrying value that is far more akin to the market value of the asset and that the accounts are more likely to represent the true success or failure of the project.

In accounting periods commencing prior to 1 January 2009, entities were permitted to capitalise borrowing costs as an alternative to expensing them in the period they were incurred. However, in March 2007, in order to eliminate some (but not all) of the differences between IFRS and US GAAP in this area, the IASB issued a revised version of IAS 23 – *Borrowing Costs* – mandating capitalisation of borrowing costs directly attributable to the acquisition, construction or production of a qualifying asset.

The new standard applies to accounting periods commencing on or after 1 January 2009 although early implementation was permitted. It is this new standard that is the subject of this chapter.

The IASB noted that this new IAS 23 eliminates the main differences with FASB Statement No. 34 – *Capitalization of Interest Cost* (SFAS 34) although there remain many differences of detail that have not been addressed. The IASB justified its change in stance by arguing that 'this will result in an improvement in financial reporting as well as achieving convergence in principle with US GAAP'. *[IAS 23.BC3].*

2   THE REQUIREMENTS OF IAS 23

2.1   Core principle

IAS 23 requires that borrowing costs must be capitalised if they are directly attributable to the acquisition, construction or production of a qualifying asset. These borrowing costs are included in the cost of the asset; all other borrowing costs are recognised as an expense in the period in which they are incurred.

2.2   Scope and definitions

2.2.1   Scope

IAS 23 deals with the treatment of borrowing costs in general, rather than solely focusing on capitalising borrowing costs as part of the carrying value of assets.

The standard does not deal with the actual or imputed costs of equity. *[IAS 23.3]*. This means that any distributions or other payments made in respect of equity instruments, as defined by IAS 32 – *Financial Instruments: Presentation* – are not within the scope of IAS 23; conversely, interest and dividends payable on instruments classified as financial liabilities would appear to be within the scope of the standard.

2.2.2   Qualifying assets

IAS 23 defines a qualifying asset as 'an asset that necessarily takes a substantial period of time to get ready for its intended use or sale'. *[IAS 23.5]*.

Assets that are ready for their intended use or sale when acquired are not qualifying assets. *[IAS 23.7]*.

Examples of qualifying assets in the standard are manufacturing plants, power generation facilities, investment properties and intangible assets. *[IAS 23.7]*.

2.2.2.A   Inventories

Inventories are within scope of IAS 23 as long as they meet the definition of a qualifying asset and require a substantial period of time to bring them to a saleable condition. However, an entity is not required to apply the standard to inventories that are routinely manufactured or otherwise produced in large quantities on a repetitive basis. *[IAS 23.4]*. There is no requirement that this production be only over a short period of time.

This scope exemption has been allowed because of the difficulty of calculating and monitoring the amount to be capitalised. There are many examples of such inventories, including large manufactured or constructed items that take some time to complete but are basically sold as standard items, such as aircraft and large items of equipment or food and drink that takes a long time to mature, such as cheeses or alcohol that matures in bottle or cask.

2.2.2.B   Assets measured at fair value

IAS 23 does not require entities to capitalise interest in respect of assets that are measured at fair value that would otherwise be qualifying assets. If the assets are held under a full fair value model with all changes going to profit or loss then capitalisation does not affect measurement in the balance sheet and would be no more than a reallocation between finance costs and the fair value movement in profit or loss. However, IAS 23 does not restrict the exemption to assets where the fair value movement is taken to profit or loss. Assets measured at fair value that fall under the revaluation model of IAS 16 – *Property, Plant and Equipment* – are also eligible for this scope exemption even though the revaluation goes to other comprehensive income, not profit. *[IAS 16.31].*

2.2.2.C   Construction contracts

IAS 11 – *Construction Contracts* – permits borrowing costs to be capitalised when they can be attributable to contract activity and allocated to specific contracts. *[IAS 11.18].*

Although the reference to IAS 23 in that paragraph was deleted, borrowing costs will need to be capitalised when they otherwise meet the criteria under IAS 23. The IASB argued that it is unnecessary to refer to IAS 23 as attributing borrowing costs to contracts is really a matter of identifying the contract costs and does not affect the recognition of borrowing costs as specified in IAS 23. *[IAS 23.BC27].*

2.2.2.D   Financial assets

IAS 23 excludes all financial assets (including equity accounted investments) from the definition of qualifying assets. *[IAS 23.7].*

2.2.3   Borrowing costs

Borrowing costs are interest and other costs incurred by an entity in connection with the borrowing of funds. *[IAS 23.5].*

Borrowing costs are defined to include:

*   interest expense calculated using the effective interest method as described in IAS 39 – *Financial Instruments: Recognition and Measurement*;

*   finance charges in respect of finance leases recognised in accordance with IAS 17 – *Leases*; and

*   exchange differences arising from foreign currency borrowings to the extent that they are regarded as an adjustment to interest costs. *[IAS 23.6].*

The identification and measurement of finance costs is not a matter for IAS 23 (see 3.2 below).

2.3   Capitalisation of borrowing costs

2.3.1   Directly attributable borrowing costs

In determining which borrowing costs satisfy the 'directly attributable' criterion, the standard starts from the premise that directly attributable borrowing costs are those that would have been avoided if the expenditure on the qualifying asset had not been made. *[IAS 23.10].*

The standard notes that the borrowing costs that are directly related can be readily identified if an entity borrows funds specifically for the purpose. *[IAS 23.10]*. In this case, the borrowing costs eligible for capitalisation are the actual borrowing costs incurred during the period. *[IAS 23.12]*.

However, entities frequently borrow funds in advance of expenditure on qualifying assets and may temporarily invest the borrowings. Any investment income on the temporary investment of those borrowings should be deducted and only the net amount capitalised (see Example 23.5). *[IAS 23.12-13]*. There is no restriction in IAS 23 as to the type of investments in which the funds can be invested, but in our view, to maintain the conclusion that the funds are specific borrowings, the investment must be of a nature that does not expose the principal amount to the risk of not being recovered. The more risky the investment, the greater is the likelihood that the borrowing is not specific to obtain the qualifying asset. If the investment returns a loss rather than income, such losses are not added to the borrowing costs to be capitalised.

In addition, as described in the next section, an entity that does not borrow specifically for the purpose may still be able to consider some of the borrowing costs on its general borrowings as directly attributable.

2.3.2   General borrowings

IAS 23 concedes that there may be practical difficulties in identifying a direct relationship between particular borrowings and a qualifying asset and in determining the borrowings that could otherwise have been avoided. As such, the determination of attributable borrowing costs may be difficult and require the exercise of judgement. *[IAS 23.11]*.

This situation could arise if the financing activity of an entity is co-ordinated centrally, by which the standard presumably means that the entity borrows to meet its requirements as a whole and the construction is being financed out of general borrowings. Other circumstances that may cause difficulties are identified by the standard as follows:

- an entity has a group treasury function that uses a range of debt instruments to borrow funds at varying rates of interest and lends those funds on various bases to other entities in the group; or
- loans are denominated in, or linked to, foreign currency, or the group operates in highly inflationary economies.

If funds are borrowed generally and used for the purpose of obtaining a qualifying asset, the amount of borrowing costs eligible for capitalisation should be determined by applying a capitalisation rate to the expenditures on that asset. The capitalisation rate should be the weighted average of the borrowing costs applicable to the borrowings of the entity that are outstanding during the period, other than borrowings made specifically for the purpose of obtaining a qualifying asset.

The amount of borrowing costs capitalised during a period should not exceed the amount of borrowing costs incurred during that period. *[IAS 23.14]*. Where funds are borrowed generally, the amount of borrowing costs capitalised cannot be reduced by interest income earned on those general funds. The standard accepts that the average carrying amount of the asset during a period, including borrowing costs previously capitalised, is normally a reasonable approximation of the expenditures to which the capitalisation rate is applied in that period. *[IAS 23.18]*.

2.3.2.A   Group considerations

In some circumstances all borrowings made by the group can be taken into account in determining the weighted average of the borrowing costs. In other circumstances only those borrowings made by individual subsidiaries may be taken into account. *[IAS 23.15]*. It is likely that this will be largely determined by the extent to which borrowings are made centrally (and, perhaps, expenses met in the same way) and passed through to individual group companies via intercompany accounts and intra-group loans.

The capitalisation rate is discussed further at 3.3 below.

2.3.3   Impairment considerations

An entity continues to capitalise borrowing costs that are directly attributable to the acquisition, construction or production of a qualifying asset as part of the carrying amount of the asset, even if the capitalisation causes the carrying amount of the asset to exceed its recoverable amount.

If the carrying amount of the qualifying asset exceeds its recoverable amount or net realisable value, the asset must be written down in accordance with the relevant international standard. If the asset is incomplete, this assessment is performed by considering the assets expected ultimate cost. *[IAS 23.16]*. The expected ultimate cost must include costs to complete and the estimated capitalised interest thereon.

IAS 36 – *Impairment of Assets* – will apply if the qualifying asset is property, plant and equipment accounted for in accordance with IAS 16 – *Property, Plant and Equipment* – or if the asset is otherwise within the scope of IAS 36. The following assets that could potentially be qualifying assets are outside the scope of IAS 36: inventories, assets arising from construction contracts and non-current assets (or disposal groups) classified as held for sale in accordance with IFRS 5 – *Non-current Assets Held for Sale and Discontinued Operations.* *[IAS 36.2]*. Impairment is discussed in Chapter 22.

2.3.4   Capitalisation of borrowing costs in hyperinflationary economies

Paragraph 21 of IAS 29 – *Financial Reporting in Hyperinflationary Economies* – states that 'the impact of inflation is usually recognised in borrowing costs. It is not appropriate both to restate the capital expenditure financed by borrowing and to capitalise that part of the borrowing costs that compensates for the inflation during the same period. This part of the borrowing costs is recognised as an expense in the period in which the costs are incurred'. *[IAS 29.21]*.

IAS 23 specifies that when an entity applies IAS 29, the borrowing costs that can be capitalised should be restricted and the entity must expense the part of borrowing costs that compensate for inflation during the same period.

Issues relating to exchange differences that do not arise in hyperinflationary situations and their eligibility for capitalisation are dealt with at 3.1 below.

2.4   Commencement, suspension and cessation of capitalisation

2.4.1   *Commencement of capitalisation*

IAS 23 requires that capitalisation should commence when:

(a)   expenditures for the asset are being incurred;

(b)   borrowing costs are being incurred; and

(c)   activities that are necessary to prepare the asset for its intended use or sale are in progress. *[IAS 23.17].*

The standard makes it explicit that only those expenditures on a qualifying asset that have resulted in payments of cash, transfers of other assets or the assumption of interest-bearing liabilities, may be included in determining borrowing costs. Such expenditures must be reduced by any progress payments and grants received in connection with the asset. *[IAS 23.18].*

The activities necessary to prepare an asset for its intended use or sale extend to more than the physical construction of the asset. Necessary activities can start before the commencement of physical construction and include, for example, technical and administrative work such as obtaining permits. This does not mean that borrowing costs can be capitalised if it is not certain that permits that are necessary for the construction will be obtained. No cost could be considered 'directly attributable' prior to this point.

Interest may not be capitalised during a period in which there are no activities that change the asset's condition. For example a house-builder or property developer may not capitalise borrowing costs on its 'land bank' i.e. that land which is held for future development. Borrowing costs incurred while land is under development are capitalised during the period in which activities related to the development are being undertaken. However, borrowing costs incurred while land acquired for building purposes is held without any associated development activity represent a holding cost of the land and hence would be considered a period cost. *[IAS 23.21].*

An entity may make a payment to third party contractor before that contractor commences construction activities. It is unlikely to be appropriate that capitalisation of borrowing costs should commence in the event of such a prepayment until that contractor commences activities that are necessary to prepare the asset for its intended use or sale.

Kazakhmys's policy describes the period during which borrowing costs are capitalised, as well as noting that it uses either an actual rate or a weighted average cost of borrowings.

Extract 23.1: Kazakhmys PLC (2010)

Notes to the consolidated financial statements [extract]

3. Summary of significant accounting policies [extract]

(v)   Borrowing costs

Borrowing costs directly relating to the acquisition, construction or production of a qualifying capital project under construction are capitalised and added to the project cost during construction until such time as the assets are considered substantially ready for their intended use i.e. when they are capable of commercial production. Where funds are borrowed specifically to finance a project, the amount capitalised represents the actual borrowing costs incurred. Where surplus funds are available for a short term from money borrowed specifically to finance a project, the income generated from the temporary investment of such amounts is also capitalised and deducted from the total capitalised borrowing cost. Where the funds used to finance a project form part of general borrowings, the amount capitalised is calculated using a weighted average of rates applicable to relevant general borrowings of the Group during the year. All other borrowing costs are recognised in the income statement in the period in which they are incurred using the effective interest rate method.

2.4.2   Suspension of capitalisation

IAS 23 states that capitalisation should be suspended during extended periods in which active development is interrupted. However, the standard distinguishes between extended periods of interruption (when capitalisation would be suspended) and periods of temporary delay that are a necessary part of preparing the asset for its intended purpose (when capitalisation is not normally suspended).

Capitalisation continues during periods when inventory is undergoing slow transformation – the example is given of inventories taking an extended time to mature (presumably such products as Scotch whisky or Cognac, although the relevance of this may be limited as these products are likely to meet the exemption for 'routinely manufactured' products – see 2.2.2.A above). A bridge construction delayed by temporary adverse weather conditions, where such conditions are common in the region, would also not be a cause for suspension of capitalisation. *[IAS 23.21]*.

2.4.3   Cessation of capitalisation

The standard requires capitalisation to cease when substantially all the activities necessary to prepare the qualifying asset for its intended use or sale are complete. *[IAS 23.22]*.

An asset is normally ready for its intended use or sale when the physical construction of the asset is complete even though routine administrative work might still continue. If minor modifications, such as the decoration of a property to the purchaser's specification, are all that are outstanding, this indicates that substantially all the activities are complete. *[IAS 23.23]*. In some cases there may be a requirement for inspection (e.g. to ensure that the asset meets safety requirements) before the asset can be used. 'Substantially all the activities' must have been completed before this point is reached so capitalisation will cease prior to the inspection.

When the construction of a qualifying asset is completed in parts and each part is capable of being used while construction continues on other parts, capitalisation should cease when substantially all the activities necessary to prepare that part for its intended use or sale are completed. *[IAS 23.24]*. An example of this might be a business park comprising several buildings, each of which is capable of being fully utilised while construction continues on other parts. *[IAS 23.25]*. This principle also applies to single buildings where one part is capable of being fully utilised even if the building as a whole is incomplete.

2.5   Disclosure requirements

2.5.1   The requirements of IAS 23

An entity shall disclose:

- the amount of borrowing costs capitalised during the period; and
- the capitalisation rate used to determine the amount of borrowing costs eligible for capitalisation. *[IAS 23.25]*.

AngloGold Ashanti discloses in its 'tangible assets' note its capitalisation rate used to determine its borrowing costs. The amount of borrowing costs capitalised during the period is disclosed within the table of movements in property, plant and equipment that precedes this narrative disclosure.

Extract 23.2: *AngloGold Ashanti (2009)*

Notes to the Group Financial Statements [extract]
16.   Tangible assets [extract]

The weighted average capitalisation rate used to determine the amount of borrowing costs eligible for capitalisation is 4.10% (2008: 8.17%).

2.5.2   Other requirements

As noted in 3.1 below, the Interpretations Committee has considered a request for guidance on the treatment of foreign exchange gains and losses and on the treatment of any derivatives used to hedge such foreign exchange exposures.

The Interpretations Committee decided not to add the issue to their agenda but concluded both that (i) how an entity applies IAS 23 to foreign currency borrowings is a matter of accounting policy requiring the exercise of judgement and (ii) that IAS 1 – *Presentation of Financial Statements* – requires disclosure of significant accounting policies and judgements that are relevant to an understanding of the financial statements.

3   PRACTICAL ISSUES

3.1   Exchange differences as a borrowing cost

Borrowings in one currency may have been used to finance a development the costs of which are incurred primarily in another currency, e.g. a US dollar loan financing a Russian rouble development. This may have been done on the basis that, over the period of the development, the cost, after allowing for exchange differences, was expected to be less than the interest cost of an equivalent rouble loan.

IAS 23 defines borrowing costs as including exchange differences arising from foreign currency borrowings to the extent that they are regarded as an adjustment to interest costs. *[IAS 23.6(e)]*. The standard does not expand on this point. In 2008, the Interpretations Committee considered a request for guidance on the treatment of foreign exchange gains and losses and on the treatment of any derivatives used to hedge such foreign exchange exposures. The Interpretations Committee decided not to add the issue to their agenda because:

- the standard acknowledges that judgement will be required in its application; and

- The IASB had considered this issue when developing the new IAS 23 and had decided not to provide any guidance.

We, however, consider that, as exchange rate movements are largely a function of differential interest rates, in most circumstances the foreign exchange differences on directly attributable borrowings will be an adjustment to interest costs that can meet the definition of borrowing costs. Care will have to be taken if there is a sudden fluctuation in exchange rates that cannot be attributed to changes in interest rates. In such cases we believe that a practical approach is to cap the exchange differences taken as borrowing costs at the amount of borrowing costs on functional currency equivalent borrowings.

If this approach is used and the construction of the qualifying asset takes more than one accounting period, there could be situations, where in one period, only a portion of foreign exchange differences could be capitalised. However, in subsequent years if the borrowings were assessed on a cumulative basis, the losses capitalised may meet the recognition criteria. The two methods of dealing with this are illustrated in Example 23.1 below:

Example 23.1:   Foreign exchange differences in more than one period

Method A – The discrete period approach

The amount of foreign exchange differences eligible for capitalisation is determined for each period separately. Foreign exchange losses that did not meet the criteria for capitalisation in previous years are not capitalised in subsequent years.

Method B – The cumulative approach

The borrowing costs to be capitalised are assessed on a cumulative basis based on the cumulative amount of interest expense that would have been incurred had the entity borrowed in its functional currency. The amount of foreign exchange differences capitalised cannot exceed the amount of foreign exchange losses incurred on a cumulative basis at the end of the reporting period. The cumulative approach looks at the construction project as a whole as the unit of account ignoring the occurrence of reporting dates. Consequently, the amount of the foreign exchange differences eligible for capitalisation as an adjustment to the borrowing cost in the period is an estimate, which can change as the exchange rates changes over the construction period.

An illustrative calculation of the amount of foreign exchange differences that may be capitalised under Method A and Method B is set out below.

	Year 1 CU	Year 2 CU	Total CU
Interest expense in foreign currency (A)	25,000	25,000	50,000
Hypothetical interest expense in functional currency (B)	30,000	30,000	60,000
Foreign exchange loss (C)	6,000	3,000	9,000
Method A – Discrete Approach			
Foreign exchange loss capitalised – lower of C and (B minus A)	5,000	3,000	8,000
Foreign exchange loss expensed	1,000	–	1,000
Method B – Cumulative Approach			
Foreign exchange loss capitalised	5,000 *	4,000 **	9,000
Foreign exchange loss expensed	1,000	(1,000)	–

* Lower of C and (B minus A) in Year 1

** Lower of C and (B minus A) in total across the two years. In this example this represents the sum of the foreign exchange loss of CU3,000 capitalised using the discrete approach plus the CU1,000 not capitalised in year 1.

In our view, it is a matter of accounting policy, which must be consistently applied, as to whether foreign exchange gains and losses are assessed on a discrete period basis or cumulatively over the construction period.

3.2   Other finance costs

IAS 23 does not address many of the ways in which an entity may finance its operations or other finance costs that it may incur. For example, the standard does not address any of the following:

- the many derivative financial instruments such as interest rate swaps, floors, caps and collars that are commonly used to manage interest rate risk on borrowings;

- gains and losses on derecognition of borrowings, for example early settlement of directly attributable borrowings that have been renegotiated prior to completion of an asset in the course of construction;

- dividends payable on shares classified as financial liabilities (such as certain redeemable preference shares) that have been recognised as an expense in profit or loss; and

- the unwinding of discounts that may be included within the caption 'finance costs' in an entity's income statement.

We consider that IAS 23 does not preclude the classification of costs other than those that it identifies as borrowing costs that may be eligible for capitalisation. However, they must meet the basic criterion in the standard, i.e. that they are costs that are directly attributable to the acquisition, construction or production of a qualifying asset, which would, therefore, preclude the classification of unwinding discounts as borrowing costs. In addition, as in the case of exchange differences, capitalisation of such costs should be permitted only 'to the extent that they are regarded as an adjustment to interest costs'.

3.2.1 Derivative financial instruments

The most straightforward and commonly encountered derivative financial instrument used to manage interest rate risk is a floating to fixed interest rate swap, as in the following example.

Example 23.2:   Floating to fixed interest rate swaps

Entity A has borrowed CU4 million for five years at a floating interest rate to fund the construction of a building. In order to hedge the cash flow interest rate risk arising from these borrowings, A has entered into a matching pay-fixed receive-floating interest rate swap, based on the same underlying nominal sum and duration as the original borrowing, that effectively converts the interest on the borrowings to fixed rate. The net effect of the periodic cash settlements resulting from the hedged and hedging instruments is as if A had borrowed CU4 million at a fixed rate of interest. Prior to IAS 39, entities simply recognised, on an accruals basis, each periodic net cash settlement in profit or loss.

These instruments are not addressed in IAS 23.

IAS 39 sets out the basis on which such instruments are recognised and measured. See Chapter 51 regarding how to account for effective hedges and the conditions that these instruments must meet.

An entity may consider that a derivative financial instrument it has taken out, such as an interest rate swap, is directly attributable to the acquisition, construction or production of a qualifying asset. If the instrument does not meet the conditions for hedge accounting then the effects on income will be different from those if it does, and they will also be dissimilar from year to year. The question arises as to the impact of the derivative on borrowing costs eligible for capitalisation. In particular, does the accounting treatment of the derivative financial instrument affect the amount available for capitalisation? If hedge accounting is not adopted, does this affect the amount available for capitalisation?

The following examples illustrate the potential differences.

Example 23.3:   Cash flow hedge of variable-rate debt using an interest rate swap

Entity A is constructing a building and expects it to take 18 months to complete. To finance the construction, on 1 January 2011, the entity issues an eighteen month, CU20,000,000 variable-rate note payable, due on 30 June 2012 at a floating rate of interest plus a margin of 1%. At that date the market rate of interest is 8%. Interest payment dates and interest rate reset dates occur on 1 January and 1 July until maturity. The principal is due at maturity. Also on 1 January 2011, the entity enters into an eighteen month interest rate swap with a notional amount of CU10,000,000 from which it will receive periodic payments at the floating rate and make periodic payments at a fixed rate of 9%, with settlement and rate reset dates every 30 June and 31 December. The fair value of the swap is zero at inception.

On 1 January 2011, the debt is recorded at CU20,000,000. No entry is required for the swap on that date because its fair value was zero at inception.

During the eighteen month period, floating interest rates change as follows:

	Cash payments Floating rate on principal	Rate paid by Entity A
Period to 30 June 2011	8%	9%
Period to 31 Dec 2011	8.5%	9.5%
Period to 30 June 2012	9.75%	10.75%

Under the interest rate swap, Entity A receives interest at the market floating rate as above and pays at 9% on the nominal amount of CU10,000,000 throughout the period.

At 31 December 2011 the swap has a fair value of CU37,500, reflecting the fact that it is now in the money as Entity A is expected to receive a net cash inflow of this amount in the period until the instrument is terminated. There are no further changes in interest rates prior to the maturity of the swap and the fair value of the swap declines to zero at 30 June 2012. Note that this example excludes the effect of issue costs and discounting. In addition, it is assumed that, if Entity A is entitled to, and applies, hedge accounting, there will be no ineffectiveness.

The cash flows incurred by the entity on its borrowing and interest rate swap are as follows:

	Cash payments		
	Interest on principal	Interest rate swap (net)	Total
	CU	CU	CU
30 June 2011	900,000	50,000	950,000
31 Dec 2011	950,000	25,000	975,000
30 June 2012	1,075,000	(37,500)	1,037,500
Total	2,925,000	37,500	2,962,500

There are a number of different ways in which Entity A could calculate the borrowing costs eligible for capitalisation, including the following.

(i)   The interest rate swap meets the conditions for, and entity A applies, hedge accounting. The finance costs eligible for capitalisation as borrowing costs will be CU1,925,000 in the year to 31 December 2011 and CU1,037,500 in the period ended 30 June 2012.

(ii) Entity A does not apply hedge accounting. Therefore, it will reflect the fair value of the swap in income in the year ended 31 December 2011, reducing the net finance costs by CU37,500 to CU1,887,500 and increasing the finance costs by an equivalent amount in 2012 to CU1,075,000. However, it considers that it is inappropriate to reflect the fair value of the swap in borrowing costs eligible for capitalisation so it capitalises costs based on the net cash cost on an accruals accounting basis. In this case this will give the same result as in (i) above.

(iii) Entity A does not apply hedge accounting and considers only the costs incurred on the borrowing, not the interest rate swap, as eligible for capitalisation. The borrowing costs eligible for capitalisation would be CU1,850,000 in 2011 and CU1,075,000 in 2012.

We consider that all these methods are valid interpretations of IAS 23, although the preparer will need to consider what method is more appropriate in the circumstances.

In particular, if using method (ii) it is necessary to demonstrate that the derivative financial instrument is directly attributable to the construction of a qualifying asset. In making this assessment it is clearly necessary to consider the term of the derivative and this method may not be practicable if the derivative has a different term to the underlying directly attributable borrowing.

Based on the facts in this example, method (iii) appears to be inconsistent with the underlying principles of IAS 23 – which is that the costs eligible for capitalisation are those costs that could have been avoided if the expenditure on the qualifying asset had not been made – and is not therefore appropriate. *[IAS 23.10]*. However, it may not be possible to demonstrate that specific derivative financial instruments are directly attributable to particular qualifying assets, rather than being used by the entity to manage its interest rate exposure on a more general basis. In such a case method (iii) may be a preferable treatment.

Note that these methods would not be permitted under US GAAP which prohibits the capitalisation of the gain or loss on the hedging instrument in a cash flow hedge. Instead, ASC 815 states that 'the amounts in accumulated other comprehensive income related to a cash flow hedge of the variability of that interest shall be reclassified into earnings over the depreciable life of the constructed asset, because that depreciable life coincides with the amortization period for the capitalized interest cost on the debt.'[1]

Whatever policy is chosen by the entity, it needs to be consistently applied in similar situations.

3.2.2 Gains and losses on derecognition of borrowings

If an entity repays borrowings early, in whole or in part, then it may recognise a gain or loss on the early settlement. This gain or loss includes amounts attributable to expected future interest rates; in other words it includes an estimated prepayment of the future cash flows under the instrument. The gain or loss is a function of relative interest rates and how the interest rate of the instrument differs from current and anticipated future interest rates. There may be circumstances in which a loan is repaid while the qualifying asset is still under construction. IAS 23 does not address the issue.

We consider that, generally, gains and losses on derecognition of borrowings are not eligible for capitalisation. It would be extremely difficult to determine an appropriate amount to capitalise and it would be inappropriate thereafter to capitalise any interest amounts (on specific or general borrowings) if to do so would amount to double counting. Decisions to repay borrowings are not usually directly attributable to the qualifying asset but to other circumstances of the entity.

3.2.3 Gains or losses on termination of derivative financial instruments

If an entity terminates a derivative financial instrument, for example, an interest rate swap, before the end of the term of the instrument, it will usually either have to make or receive a payment, depending on the fair value of the instrument at that time. This fair value is based on expected future interest rates; in other words it is an estimated prepayment of the future cash flows under the instrument.

The treatment of the gain or loss for the purposes of capitalisation will depend on the following:

- the basis on which the entity capitalises the gains and losses associated with derivative financial instruments; and
- whether the derivative is associated with a borrowing that has also been terminated.

Entities must adopt a treatment that is consistent with their policy for capitalising the gains and losses of derivative financial instruments.

The accounting under IAS 39 will differ depending on whether the instrument has been designated as a hedge or not; in the former case, and assuming that the borrowing has not also been repaid, the entity will usually continue to account for the cumulative gain or loss on the instrument as if the hedge were still in place. In such a case, the amounts that are reclassified from other comprehensive income will be eligible for capitalisation for the remainder of the period of construction.

If the entity is not hedge accounting for the derivative financial instrument but considers it to be directly attributable to the construction of the qualifying asset then it will have to consider whether part of the gain or loss relates to a period after construction is complete.

If the underlying borrowing is also terminated then the gain or loss will not be capitalised and the treatment will mirror that applied to the borrowing, as described in 3.2.2 above.

3.2.4   *Dividends payable on shares classified as financial liabilities*

An entity might finance its operations in whole or in part by the issue of preference shares and in some circumstances these will be classified as financial liabilities (see Chapter 45). In some circumstances these dividends would meet the definition of borrowing costs. For example, it is possible that an entity has issued redeemable preference shares that are redeemable at the option of the holder (and are classified as financial liabilities with the interest charge calculated using the effective interest method in IAS 39) to fund the development of a qualifying asset. In this case the dividends would meet the definition of borrowing costs. However, this would not apply to irredeemable shares as these would not be borrowings that could be avoided and hence could never be directly attributable to a qualifying asset.

3.2.5   *Unwinding discounts on provisions classified as finance costs in profit or loss*

Many unwinding discounts are treated as finance costs in profit or loss. These include discounts relating to various provisions such as those for onerous leases and decommissioning costs. These finance costs will not be borrowing costs under IAS 23 because they do not arise in respect of funds borrowed by the entity that can be attributed to a qualifying asset. Therefore, they cannot be capitalised.

3.3   Borrowings and capitalisation rate

IAS 23 requires that the borrowing costs capitalised are those costs that would have been avoided if the expenditure on the qualifying asset had not been made. If a project has been financed from the entity's general borrowings, the standard imposes a detailed calculation method as indicated at 2.3.2 above.

3.3.1   *Definition of general borrowings*

As noted at 2.3.2 above, determining general borrowings will not always be straightforward and as a result, the determination of the amount of borrowing costs that are directly attributable to the acquisition of a qualifying asset is difficult and the exercise of judgement is required.

In July 2009 the Interpretations Committee received a request for guidance on what borrowings comprise 'general borrowings' for purposes of capitalising borrowing costs in accordance with IAS 23. The request asked for guidance on the treatment of general borrowings used to purchase a specific asset other than a qualifying asset.

The Interpretations Committee noted that paragraph 14 of IAS 23 states that 'To the extent that an entity borrows funds generally and uses them for the purpose of obtaining a qualifying asset, the entity shall determine the amount of borrowing costs eligible for capitalisation by applying a capitalisation rate to the expenditures on that asset. The capitalisation rate shall be the weighted average of the borrowing costs applicable to the borrowings of the entity that are outstanding during the period, other than borrowings made specifically for the purpose of obtaining a qualifying asset.'

The Interpretations Committee also noted that because paragraph 14 refers only to qualifying assets:

- Some conclude that borrowings related to specific assets other than qualifying assets cannot be excluded from determining the capitalisation rate for general borrowings.

- Others note the general principle in paragraph 10 that the borrowing costs that are directly attributable to the acquisition, construction or production of a qualifying asset are borrowing costs that would have been avoided if the expenditure on the qualifying asset had not been made.

Consequently, the Interpretations Committee concluded that any guidance it could provide would be in the nature of application guidance rather than an interpretation and, because the IASB was due to consider whether to add this issue to the annual improvements project, decided not to add the issue to its agenda.

The IASB did subsequently consider the issue of whether debt incurred specifically to acquire a non-qualifying asset could be excluded from general borrowings but as IAS 23 excludes only debt used to acquire qualifying assets from the determination of the capitalisation rate, decided not to include this issue in its annual improvements process.

Another question that arises is whether a specific borrowing undertaken to obtain a qualifying asset ever changes its nature into a general borrowing. Differing views exist as to whether or not borrowings change their nature throughout the period they are outstanding. Some consider that once the asset for which the borrowing was incurred has been completed, and the entity chooses to use its funds on constructing other assets rather than repaying the loan, this changes the nature of the loan into a general borrowing. However, to the extent that the contract linked the repayment of the loan to specific proceeds generated by the entity, its nature as a specific borrowing would be preserved. Others take the view that once the borrowing has been classified as specific, its nature does not change while it remains outstanding. Management will therefore need to exercise judgment in determining its policy and assessing the nature of the loans when construction activity is completed.

3.3.2 Calculation of capitalisation

As the standard acknowledges that determining general borrowings will not always be straightforward, it will be necessary to exercise judgement to meet the main objective – a reasonable measure of the directly attributable finance costs.

The following example illustrates the practical application of the method of calculating the amount of finance costs to be capitalised:

Example 23.4:   Calculation of capitalisation rate (no investment income)

On 1 April 2011 a company engages in the development of a property, which is expected to take five years to complete, at a cost of CU6,000,000. The balance sheets at 31 December 2010 and 31 December 2011, prior to capitalisation of interest, are as follows:

	31 December 2010 CU	31 December 2011 CU
Development property	–	1,200,000
Other assets	6,000,000	6,000,000
	6,000,000	7,200,000
Loans		
5.5% debenture stock	2,500,000	2,500,000
Bank loan at 6% p.a.	–	1,200,000
Bank loan at 7% p.a.	1,000,000	1,000,000
	3,500,000	4,700,000
Shareholders' equity	2,500,000	2,500,000

The bank loan with an effective interest rate at 6% was drawn down to match the development expenditure on 1 April 2011, 1 July 2011 and 1 October 2011.

Expenditure was incurred on the development as follows:

	CU
1 April 2011	600,000
1 July 2011	400,000
1 October 2011	200,000
	1,200,000

If the bank loan at 6% p.a. is a new borrowing specifically to finance the development then the amount of interest to be capitalised would be the amount of interest charged by the bank of CU42,000 (i.e. principal × 6%).

However, if all the borrowings were general (i.e. the bank loan at 6% was not specific to the development) and would have been avoided but for the development then the amount of interest to be capitalised is:

$$\frac{\text{Total interest expense for period}}{\text{Weighted average total borrowings}} \times \text{Development expenditure}$$

Total interest expense for the period

	CU
CU2,500,000 × 5.5%	137,500
CU1,200,000 (as above)	42,000
CU1,000,000 × 7%	70,000
	249,500

Therefore the capitalisation rate is calculated as:

$$\frac{249,500}{3,500,000 + 700,000} = 5.94\%$$

The capitalisation rate is then applied to the expenditure on the qualifying asset, resulting in an amount to be capitalised of CU41,580 as follows:

	CU
CU600,000 × 5.94% × 9/12	26,730
CU400,000 × 5.94% × 6/12	11,880
CU200,000 × 5.94% × 3/12	2,970
	41,580

If the 5.5% debenture stock were irredeemable then it would be excluded from the above calculation as it could no longer be a borrowing that could have been avoided. The calculation would be done using the figures for the bank loans and their related interest costs only.

In this example, all borrowings are at fixed rates of interest and the period of construction extends beyond the end of the period. If borrowings are at floating rates then only the interest costs incurred during that period, and the weighted average borrowings for that period, will be taken into account.

Note that the company's share capital will not be taken into account and outstanding borrowings are presumed to finance the acquisition or construction of qualifying assets.

Example 23.4 also assumes that loans are drawn down to match expenditure on the qualifying asset. If, however, a loan is drawn down immediately and investment income is received on the unapplied funds, then the calculation is different than set out in (a). This is illustrated in Example 23.5.

Example 23.5:   *Calculation of amount to be capitalised – specific borrowings with investment income*

On 1 April 2011 a company engages in the development of a property, which is expected to take five years to complete, at a cost of CU6,000,000. In this example, however, a bank loan of CU6,000,000 with an effective interest rate at 6% was taken out on 31 March 2011 and fully drawn. The total interest charge for the year ended 31 December 2011 was consequently CU270,000.

However, investment income was also earned at 3% on the unapplied funds during the period as follows:

	CU
CU5,400,000 × 3% × 3/12	40,500
CU5,000,000 × 3% × 3/12	37,500
CU4,800,000 × 3% × 3/12	36,000
	114,000

Consequently, the amount of interest to be capitalised is:

	CU
Total interest charge	270,000
Less: investment income	(114,000)
	156,000

3.4   Accrued costs

IAS 23 states that expenditures on qualifying assets include only those that have resulted in the payments of cash, transfers of other assets or the assumption of interest-bearing liabilities. *[IAS 23.18]*. Therefore, costs of a qualifying asset that have only been accrued but have not yet been paid in cash should be excluded from the amount on which interest is capitalised, as by definition no interest can have been incurred on an accrued payment.

The effect of applying this principle is often merely to delay the commencement of the capitalisation of interest since the capital expenditures will be included once they have been paid in cash. In most cases it is unlikely that the effect will be material as the time between accrual and payment of the cost will not be that great. However, the effect is potentially material where a significant part of the amount capitalised relates to costs that have been financed interest-free by third parties for a long period. An example of this is retention money that is not generally payable until the asset is completed.

3.5   Assets carried in the balance sheet below cost

An asset may be recognised in the financial statements during the period of production on a basis other than cost, i.e. it may have been written down below cost as a result of being impaired. As discussed in 2.3.3 above, an asset may be impaired when its expected ultimate cost, including costs to complete and the estimated capitalised interest thereon, exceed its estimated recoverable amount or net realisable value.

The question then arises whether the calculation of interest to be capitalised should be based on the asset's cost or its carrying amount. In this case, cost should be used, as this is the amount that the company or group has had to finance. In the case of an impaired asset, the continued capitalisation based on the asset's cost, may well necessitate a further impairment.

3.6   Group financial statements

3.6.1   Borrowings in one company and development in another

A question which often arises in practice is whether it is appropriate to capitalise interest in the group financial statements on borrowings that appear in the financial statements of a different group company from that carrying out the development. Based on the underlying philosophy of IAS 23, capitalisation in such circumstances would only be appropriate if the amount capitalised fairly reflected the interest cost of the group on borrowings from third parties which could have been avoided if the expenditure on the qualifying asset were not made.

Although it may be appropriate to capitalise interest in the group financial statements, the company carrying out the development should not capitalise any interest in its own financial statements as it has no borrowings. If, however, the company has intra-group borrowings then interest on such borrowings may be capitalised.

3.6.2   *Qualifying assets held by joint ventures*

A number of sectors carry out developments through the medium of joint ventures – this is particularly common with property developments. In such cases, the joint venture may be financed principally by equity and the joint venture partners may have financed their participating interests by borrowings.

It is not appropriate to capitalise interest in the joint venture on the borrowings of the partners as the interest charge is not a cost of the joint venture. Neither would it be appropriate to capitalise interest in the individual (as opposed to group) financial statements of the venturers because the qualifying asset does not belong to them. The investing entities have an investment as an asset, which is excluded by IAS 23 from being a qualifying asset (see 2.2.2 above). If, however, the venturer is using proportionate consolidation and the jointly controlled entity itself does not incur borrowing costs, then the venturer should capitalise borrowing costs that relate to its share of the qualifying asset in its consolidated accounts.

References

1 ASC 815-30-35-45   (formerly   EITF 99-9),
*Effect of derivative gains and losses on the
capitalisation of interest*, FASB, July 1999,
para. 6.

Chapter 23

Chapter 24   Inventories

Chapter 24   Inventories

1   INTRODUCTION

Under IFRS the relevant standard for inventories is IAS 2 – *Inventories*. The term 'inventories' includes raw materials, work-in-progress, finished goods and goods for resale, although the standard does not include all instances of these categories; some are covered by other standards, for example growing crops are covered by IAS 41 – *Agriculture*. This chapter deals only with the inventories within the scope of IAS 2. Long-term contracts and the associated work in progress are the subject of a separate standard, IAS 11 – *Construction Contracts* – which is dealt with in Chapter 25.

1.1   Objectives of inventory measurement

Historically, the principal objective of inventory measurement within the historical cost accounting system has been the proper determination of income through the process of matching costs with related revenues. Under this system, costs of inventories comprise expenditure which has been incurred in the normal course of business in bringing the product or service to its present location and condition. All costs incurred in respect of inventories are charged as period costs, except for those which relate to those unconsumed inventories which are expected to be of future benefit to the entity. These are carried forward, to be matched with the revenues that they will generate in the future. A secondary objective of inventory measurement has been to provide a balance sheet entry. Under the historical cost system, inventories in the balance sheet have characteristics similar to those of prepaid expenses or property, plant and equipment – they are effectively deferred costs.

When IAS 2 was revised in 2003 all references to matching and to the historical cost system were deleted, even though historical cost was retained as the main measurement method for IAS 2 inventories. However, there have been no recent developments suggesting a move away from this widely accepted and traditional cost-based inventory measurement model to one based on fair value. The Exposure Draft – *Revenue from Contracts with Customers* – only applies when there is a contract with a customer.[1] It therefore will have an impact on accounting for construction contracts currently accounted for under IAS 11 (see Chapter 25) but will not apply to inventory in the absence of a contract.

2   THE SCOPE OF IAS 2

IAS 2 applies to inventories in all financial statements except work-in-progress arising under construction contracts including directly related service contracts (both of which are dealt with by IAS 11, see Chapter 25), financial instruments (see Chapters 42 to 52), and biological assets related to agricultural activity and agricultural produce at the point of harvest (see Chapter 40). *[IAS 2.2]*.

Agricultural produce that has been harvested by the entity from its biological assets, is initially recognised at its fair value, less costs to sell at the point of harvest, as set out in IAS 41 (see Chapter 40). This figure becomes the cost of inventories at that date for the purposes of IAS 2. *[IAS 2.20]*.

The measurement provisions of IAS 2 do not apply to the measurement of inventories held by:

(a)   producers of agricultural and forest products, agricultural produce after harvest, and minerals and mineral products, to the extent that they are measured at net realisable value in accordance with well-established practices in those industries. When such inventories are measured at net realisable value, changes are recognised in profit or loss in the period of the change *[IAS 2.3]*. This occurs, for example, when agricultural crops have been harvested or minerals have been extracted and sale is assured under a forward contract or a government guarantee, or when an active market exists and there is a negligible risk of failure to sell; *[IAS 2.4]*

(b)   commodity broker-traders who measure their inventories at fair value less costs to sell. If these inventories are measured at fair value less costs to sell, the changes are recognised in profit or loss in the period of the change. *[IAS 2.3]*. Broker-traders are those who buy or sell commodities for others or on their own account and these inventories are principally acquired with the purpose of selling in the near future and generating a profit from fluctuations in price or broker traders' margin. *[IAS 2.5]*.

In both cases, the standard stresses that these inventories are only scoped out from the measurement requirements of IAS 2; the standard's other requirements, such as disclosure, continue to apply.

Inventories are defined by IAS 2 as:

(a)   assets held for sale in the ordinary course of business;

(b)   assets in the process of production for such sale; or

(c)   materials or supplies to be consumed in the production process or in the rendering of services. *[IAS 2.6]*.

Inventories can include all types of goods purchased and held for resale including, for example, merchandise purchased by a retailer and other tangible assets such as land and other property held for resale, although investment property accounted for under IAS 40 – *Investment Property* – is not treated as an inventory item. The term also encompasses finished goods produced, or work in progress being produced by the entity, and includes materials and supplies awaiting use in the production process. If the entity is a service provider, its inventories may be intangible (e.g. the costs of the service for which the entity has not yet recognised the related revenue). *[IAS 2.8]*. The inventory of service providers will probably consist mainly of the labour costs of the people providing the service. There is a separate standard, IFRS 5 – *Non-current Assets Held for Sale and Discontinued Operations* – that governs the accounting treatment of non-current assets held for sale, for example a group of assets held for sale such as a business being disposed of. IFRS 5 is discussed in Chapter 4.

2.1 Scope issues: IAS 2 or another IFRS

2.1.1 Core inventories – IAS 2 or IAS 16

In certain industries, for example the petrochemical industry, certain processes or storage arrangements require a core of inventory to be present in the system at all times. For example in order for a crude oil refining process to take place, the plant must contain a certain minimum quantity of oil. This can only be taken out once the plant is abandoned and could then only be sold as sludge. Similarly, underground gas storage caves are filled with gas; but a substantial part (perhaps say 25%) of that gas can never be sold as its function is to pressurise the cave, thereby allowing the remaining 75% to be extracted. Even though the gas will be turned around on a continuing basis, at any one time 25% of it will never be available to sell and cannot be recouped from the cave.

It is our view that if an item of inventory is not held for sale or consumed in a production process, but is necessary to the operation of a facility during more than one operating cycle, and its cost cannot be recouped through sale (or is significantly impaired), this item of inventory should be accounted for as an item of property, plant and equipment (PP&E) under IAS 16 – *Property, Plant and Equipment*. This applies even if the part of inventory that is deemed to be an item of PP&E cannot be separated physically from the rest of inventory.

These matters will always involve the exercise of judgement, however, in the above instances, we consider that:

(i)   the deemed PP&E items do not meet the definition of inventories;

(ii)   although it is not possible to physically separate the chemicals involved into inventory and PP&E categories, there is no accounting reason why one cannot distinguish between identical assets with different uses and therefore account for them differently. Indeed, IAS 2 does envisage such a possibility in paragraph 25 when discussing different cost formulas;

(iii) the deemed PP&E items are necessary to bring another item of PP&E to the condition necessary for it to be capable of operating in the manner intended by management. This meets the definition of the costs of PP&E in IAS 16.16(b) upon initial recognition;

(iv)   recognising these items as inventories would lead to an immediate loss because these items cannot be sold or consumed in a production process, or during the process of rendering services. This does not properly reflect the fact that the items are necessary to operate another asset over more than one operating cycle.

Chapter 24

2.1.2 Broadcast rights – IAS 2 or IAS 38

Broadcasters purchase programs under a variety of different arrangements. Often they commit to purchasing programs that are at a very early stage of development, perhaps merely being concepts. The broadcaster may have exclusive rights over the program or perhaps only have the rights to broadcast for a set period of time or on a set number of occasions. IFRS is not clear on how these rights should be classified and when they should recognised.

We believe that an entity can either treat these rights as intangible assets and classify them under IAS 38 – *Intangible Assets*, see Chapter 19 at 13.6, or alternatively classify them as inventory under IAS 2. Such rights would certainly seem to meet the definition of inventory under IAS 2; i.e. given that the acquisition of these rights are a part of the cost of the broadcaster's programming schedule they meet the general IAS 2 definition in that they are:

(a)   held for sale in the ordinary course of business;

(b)   in the process of production for such sale; or

(c)   in the form of materials or supplies to be consumed in the production process or in the rendering of services. *[IAS 2.6]*.

When classified as inventory the rights will need to be disclosed within current assets, even if the intention is not to consume them within 12 months. *[IAS 1.68]*. As with costs of other inventory the cash outflow from acquisition will be classified as an operating cash flow and the expense will be presented within cost of sales when the right is consumed.

There is also the issue of the timing of recognition of these rights. In accordance with paragraph 4.4 of the *Conceptual Framework for Financial Reporting* an asset is a resource controlled by an entity from which future economic benefits are expected to flow to the entity. Hence it is necessary to determine when control is obtained. Under IFRS, executory contracts where both parties are still to perform (such as purchase orders where neither payment nor delivery has yet been made) are generally not recognised. When a broadcaster initially contracts to purchase a program it will not generally result in immediate recognition of that program. At this point there will not normally be an asset under the control of the broadcaster. Factors that may be relevant in determining when the entity controls an asset include whether:

• the underlying resource is sufficiently developed to be identifiable (e.g. whether the manuscript or screenplay has been written, and whether directors and actors have been hired),

• the entity has legal, exclusive rights to broadcast (which may be in respect of a defined period or geographic area),

• there is a penalty to the licensor for non-delivery of the content,

• it is probable that content will be delivered, and

• it is probable that economic benefits will flow to the entity.

Where there is difficulty in determining when control of the asset is obtained it may be helpful to assess at what point any liability arises, since a liability will generally indicate that an asset has been acquired. In practice an entity might recognise an asset and liability for a specific broadcast right on the following trigger dates:

- when a screening certificate is obtained,
- when programming is available for exhibition,
- at the beginning of season,
- at the beginning of license period, or
- on the date the event occurs (e.g. game-by-game basis).

The issue of when a licensor recognises revenue on the sale of such broadcast rights is covered in the revenue recognition chapter (see Chapter 30 at 6.10).

3   MEASUREMENT

The standard's basic rule is that inventories, apart from those inventories scoped out of its measurement requirements as explained above, are measured at the lower of cost and net realisable value. *[IAS 2.9]*. Net realisable value is 'the estimated selling price in the ordinary course of business less the estimated costs of completion and the estimated costs necessary to make the sale.' *[IAS 2.6]*. Fair value is 'the amount for which an asset could be exchanged, or a liability settled, between knowledgeable, willing parties in an arm's length transaction.' *[IAS 2.6]*. The standard points out that net realisable value is an entity-specific value – the amount that the entity actually expects to make from selling that particular inventory – while fair value is not. Therefore, net realisable value may not be the same as fair value less costs to sell. *[IAS 2.7]*.

This basic measurement rule inevitably raises the question of what may be included in an inventory's cost.

3.1   What may be included in cost?

The costs attributed to inventories under IAS 2 comprise all costs of purchase, costs of conversion and other costs incurred in bringing the inventories to their present location and condition. *[IAS 2.10]*. These costs include import duties and other unrecoverable taxes, transport and other costs directly attributable to the inventories. Trade discounts and similar rebates should be deducted from the costs attributed to inventories. *[IAS 2.11]*. For example a supplier may pay to its customer an upfront cash incentive when entering into a contract. This is a form of rebate and the incentive should be accounted for as a liability by the customer until it receives the related inventory, which is then shown at cost net of this incentive.

Costs of conversion include direct costs such as direct labour and materials, and also overheads. It must be remembered that the inclusion of overheads is not voluntary. Overheads may comprise indirect labour and materials or other indirect costs of production. For the most part there are few problems over the inclusion of direct costs in inventories although problems may arise over the inclusion of certain types of overheads and over the allocation of overheads into the inventory valuation. Overhead costs must be apportioned using a 'systematic allocation of fixed and variable production overheads that are incurred in converting materials into finished goods'. *[IAS 2.12]*. Overheads should be allocated to the cost of inventory on a consistent basis from year to year, and should not be omitted in anticipation of a net realisable value difficulty.

Variable production overheads are indirect costs that vary with the volume of production such as indirect material and indirect labour. *[IAS 2.12]*. Fixed production overheads are indirect costs that remain relatively constant over a wide range of production, such as building and equipment maintenance and depreciation, and factory management expenses. The allocation of fixed production overheads is to be based on the normal capacity of the facilities. Normal capacity is defined as 'the production expected to be achieved on average over a number of periods or seasons under normal circumstances, taking into account the loss of capacity resulting from planned maintenance.' *[IAS 2.13]*. While actual capacity may be used if it approximates to normal capacity, increased overheads may not be allocated to production as a result of low output or idle capacity. In these cases the unrecovered overheads must be expensed. The contrary situation is also considered; in periods of abnormally high production, the fixed overhead absorption must be reduced, as otherwise inventories would be recorded at an amount in excess of cost. *[IAS 2.13]*.

In computing the costs to be allocated via the overhead recovery rate, costs such as distribution and selling must be excluded, together with cost of storing raw materials and work in progress, unless it is necessary that these latter costs be incurred prior to further processing, which may occasionally be the case.

The assumptions about normal levels of activity relates to all costs including direct costs. Although determining the normal level of activity when allocating overheads is a judgemental area, it is relatively straightforward when dealing with the manufacturing and processing of physical inventory. It is far harder to establish what this can mean in the context of service industries where the 'inventory' is intangible and based on work performed for customers that has not yet been recognised as income. There really is no equivalent to the normal capacity of production facilities in these cases. However, the standard still requires the inclusion of attributable overheads, and entities must take care to establish an appropriate benchmark to avoid the distortions that could occur if overheads were attributed on the basis of actual 'output'.

Extract 24.1 below shows how Syngenta AG describes its inventory valuation policies.

Extract 24.1: Syngenta AG (2008)

Notes to the Syngenta Group Consolidated Financial Statements [extract]
2.   Accounting policies [extract]
Inventories

Purchased products are recorded at acquisition cost while own-manufactured products are recorded at manufacturing cost including related production expenses. In the balance sheet, inventory is valued at historical cost determined on a first-in-first-out basis, and this value is used for the cost of goods sold in the income statement. Allowances are made for inventories with a net realizable value less than cost, or which are slow moving. Unsalable inventory is fully written off. Inventories of biological assets, principally young plants and cuttings in the Seeds flowers business, are recorded at fair value less estimated point of sale costs.

IAS 2 mentions the treatment to be adopted when a production process results in the output of more than one product, for example a main product and a by-product. If the costs of converting each product are not separately identifiable, they should be allocated between the products on a rational and consistent basis; for example this might be the relative sales value of each of the products. If the value of the by-product is immaterial, it may be measured at net realisable value and this value deducted from the cost of the main product. *[IAS 2.14].*

Other costs are to be included in inventories only to the extent that they bring them into their present location and condition. An example is given in IAS 2 of design costs for a special order for a particular customer as being allowable, *[IAS 2.15],* and as a result other non-production overheads may possibly be appropriately included. However a number of examples are given of costs that are specifically disallowed. These include:

(a)   abnormal amounts of wasted materials, labour, or other production costs;

(b)   storage costs, unless those costs are necessary in the production process prior to a further production stage;

(c)   administrative overheads that do not contribute to bringing inventories to their present location and condition; and

(d)   selling costs. *[IAS 2.16].*

3.1.1   *Storage and distribution costs*

Storage costs are not permitted as part of the cost of inventory unless they are necessary in the production process. This appears to prohibit including the costs of the warehouse and the overheads of a retail outlet as part of inventory, as neither of these is a prelude to a further production stage.

Where it is necessary to store raw materials or work in progress prior to a further processing or manufacturing stage, the costs of such storage should be included in production overheads. In addition, it would appear reasonable to allow the costs of storing maturing stocks, such as cheese, wine or whisky, in the cost of production.

Although distribution costs are obviously a cost of bringing an item to its present location, the question arises as to whether costs of transporting inventory from one location to another are eligible.

Costs of distribution to the customer are not allowed; they are selling costs and the standard prohibits their inclusion in the carrying value of inventory. It therefore seems probable that distribution costs of inventory whose production process is complete should not normally be included in its carrying value.

If the inventory is transferred from one of the entity's storage facilities to another and the condition of the inventory is not changed at either location, none of the warehousing costs may be included in inventory costs.

Unless they are an essential part of the production process, it is not clear on what sensible basis transportation costs between two such locations could be included in inventory costs A question arises about the meaning of 'production' in the context of large retailers, for example supermarkets. As the transport and logistics involved are essential to their ability to put goods on sale at a particular location in an appropriate condition, it seems reasonable to conclude that such costs are an essential part of the production process and can be included in the cost of inventory.

Chapter 24

3.1.2   General and administrative overheads

IAS 2 specifically disallows administrative overheads that do not contribute to bringing inventories to their present location and condition. *[IAS 2.16]*. Other costs and overheads that do contribute are allowable as costs of production. There is a judgement to be made about such matters, as on a very wide interpretation any department could be considered to make a contribution. For example, the accounts department will normally support the following functions:

(a) production – by paying direct and indirect production wages and salaries, by controlling purchases and related payments, and by preparing periodic financial statements for the production units;

(b) marketing and distribution – by analysing sales and by controlling the sales ledger; and

(c) general administration – by preparing management accounts and annual financial statements and budgets, by controlling cash resources and by planning investments.

Only those costs of the accounts department that can be allocated to the production function fall to be included in the cost of conversion. Part of the management and overhead costs of a large retailer's logistical department may be included in cost if it can be related to bringing the inventory to its present location and condition. These types of cost are unlikely to be material in the context of the inventory total held by organisations. In our view, an entity wishing to include a material amount of overhead of a borderline nature must ensure it can sensibly justify its inclusion under the provisions of IAS 2 by presenting an analysis of the function and its contribution to the production process similar to the above.

3.1.3   Borrowing costs

IAS 2 states that, in limited circumstances, borrowing costs are to be included in the costs of inventories. *[IAS 2.17]*. IAS 23 – *Borrowing Costs* – requires that borrowing costs be capitalised on qualifying assets but the scope of that standard exempts inventories that are manufactured in large quantities on a repetitive basis. *[IAS 23.4, 8]*. In addition the standard clarifies that inventories manufactured over a short period of time are not qualifying assets. *[IAS 23.7]*. However, any manufacturer that is producing small quantities over a long time period has to capitalise borrowing costs. This is further discussed in Chapter 23.

The standard also states that on some occasions, an entity might purchase inventories on deferred settlement terms, accompanied by a price increase that effectively makes the arrangement a combined purchase and financing. Under these circumstances the price difference is to be recognised as an interest expense over the period of the financing. *[IAS 2.18]*.

3.1.4   Service providers

IAS 2 deals specifically with the inventories of service providers – effectively their work-in-progress. For this type of business, IAS 2 allows the labour and other costs of personnel directly engaged in providing the service, including supervisory personnel and attributable overheads, to be included in the cost of inventories. However, labour and other costs relating to sales and general administrative personnel must be expensed as incurred and inventories should not include profit margins or non-attributable overheads. *[IAS 2.19]*.

3.1.5   Forward contracts to purchase inventory

The standard scopes out commodity broker-traders that measure inventory at fair value less costs to sell from its measurement requirements (see 2 above). If a broker-trader had a forward contract for purchase of inventory this contract would be accounted for as a derivative under IAS 39 – *Financial Instruments: Recognition and Measurement* – since it would not meet the normal purchase or sale exemption (see Chapter 43 at 4.2) and when the contract was physically settled the inventory would likewise be shown at fair value less costs to sell. *[IAS 2.3(b)]*. However, if such an entity were not measuring inventory at fair value less costs to sell it would be subject to the measurement requirements of IAS 2 and would therefore have to record the inventory at the lower of cost and net realisable value. This raises the question: what is cost when such an entity takes delivery of inventory that has been purchased with a forward contract? Upon delivery, the cash paid (i.e. the fixed price agreed in the forward contract) is in substance made up of two elements:

(i)   an amount that settles the forward contract; and

(ii) an amount that represents the 'cost of purchase', being the market price at the date of purchase.

This 'cost of purchase' represents the forward contract price adjusted for the derivative asset or liability. For example, assume that the broker-trader was purchasing oil and the forward contracted price was $140 per barrel of oil, but at the time of delivery the spot price of oil was $150 and the forward contract had a fair value of $10 at that date. The oil would be recorded at the fair value on what is deemed to be the purchase date of $150. The $140 cash payment would in substance consist of $150 payment for the inventory offset by a $10 receipt upon settlement of the derivative contract. This is exactly the same result as if the entity had been required to settle the derivative immediately prior to, and separate from, the physical delivery of the oil.

3.1.6   Drug production costs within the pharmaceutical industry

Pharmaceutical companies often commence production of drugs prior to obtaining the necessary regulatory approval to sell them. As long as the regulatory approval has been applied for and it is believed highly likely that this will be successfully obtained then it is appropriate to be recognising an asset and classifying this as inventory. Prior to this application for regulatory approval being made any costs would need to be classified as research and development costs rather than inventory and the criteria within IAS 38 assessed to determine if capitalisation was appropriate (see Chapter 19).

3.2   Cost measurement methods

IAS 2 specifically allows the use of standard costing methods or of the retail method provided that the method gives a result which approximates to cost. Standard costs should take into account normal levels of materials and supplies, labour, efficiency and capacity utilisation. They must be regularly reviewed and revised where necessary. *[IAS 2.21]*. Normal levels of activity are discussed in 3.1 above.

The retail method is typically used in businesses with high volumes of various line items of inventory, where similar mark-ups are applied to ranges of inventory items or groups of items. In such a situation, it may be unnecessarily time-consuming to determine the cost of the period-end inventory on a conventional basis. Consequently, the most practical method of determining period-end inventory may be to record inventory on hand at selling prices, and then convert it to cost by removing the normal mark-up.

A complication in applying the retail method is in determining the margin to be applied to the inventory at selling price to convert it back to cost. The percentage has to take account of circumstances in which inventories have been marked down to below original selling price. Adjustments have to be made to eliminate the effect of these markdowns so as to prevent any item of inventory being valued at less than both its cost and its net realisable value. In practice, however, entities that use the retail method apply a gross profit margin computed on an average basis appropriate for departments and/or ranges, rather than applying specific mark-up percentages. This practice is, in fact, acknowledged by IAS 2 that states: 'an average percentage for each retail department is often used'. *[IAS 2.22]*.

Items that are not interchangeable and goods or services produced for specific projects should have their costs specifically identified, *[IAS 2.23]*, and these costs will be matched with the goods physically sold. In practice this is a relatively unusual method of valuation, as the clerical effort required does not make it feasible unless there are relatively few high value items being bought or produced. Consequently, it would normally be used where the inventory comprised items such as antiques, jewellery and automobiles in the hands of dealers. However, this method is inappropriate where there are large numbers of items that are interchangeable, as specific identification of costs could distort the profit or loss arising from these inventories. *[IAS 2.24]*.

Where it is necessary to use a cost-flow assumption (i.e. when there are large numbers of ordinarily interchangeable items) IAS 2 allows either a FIFO (first-in, first-out) or a weighted average cost formula to be used. *[IAS 2.25]*.

(a) *FIFO* – In the vast majority of businesses it will not be practicable to keep track of the cost of identical items of inventory on an individual unit basis; nevertheless, it is desirable to approximate to the actual physical flows as far as possible. The FIFO method probably gives the closest approximation to actual cost flows, since it is assumed that when inventories are sold or used in a production process, the oldest are sold or used first. Consequently the balance of inventory on hand at any point represents the most recent purchases or production. *[IAS 2.27]*. This can best be illustrated in the context of a business which deals in perishable goods (e.g. food retailers) since clearly such a business will use the first goods received earliest. The FIFO method, by allocating the earliest costs incurred against revenue, matches actual cost flows with the physical flow of goods reasonably accurately. In any event, even in the case of businesses which do not deal in perishable goods, this would reflect what would probably be a sound management policy. Therefore, in practice where it is not possible to value inventory on an actual cost basis, the FIFO method is generally used since it is most likely to approximate the physical flow of goods sold, resulting in the most accurate measurement of cost flows;

(b) *Weighted average* – This method, which like FIFO is suitable where inventory units are identical or nearly identical, involves the computation of an average unit cost by dividing the total cost of units by the number of units. The average unit cost then has to be revised with every receipt of inventory, or alternatively at the end of predetermined periods. *[IAS 2.27]*. In practice, weighted average systems are widely used in packaged inventory systems that are computer controlled, although its results are not very different from FIFO in times of relatively low inflation, or where inventory turnover is relatively quick.

LIFO (last-in, first-out), as its name suggests, is the opposite of FIFO and assumes that the most recent purchases or production are used first. In certain cases this could represent the physical flow of inventory (e.g. if a store is filled and emptied from the top). However it is not an acceptable method under IAS 2. LIFO is an attempt to match current costs with current revenues so that the profit and loss account excludes the effects of holding gains. Essentially, therefore, LIFO is an attempt to achieve something closer to replacement cost accounting for the profit and loss account, whilst disregarding the balance sheet. Consequently, the period-end balance of inventory on hand represents the earliest purchases of the item, resulting in inventories being stated in the balance sheet at amounts which may bear little relationship to recent cost levels. LIFO is allowable under US GAAP, and is popular in the US as the Internal Revenue Service officially recognises LIFO as an acceptable method for the computation of tax provided that it is used consistently for tax and financial reporting purposes.

The standard makes it clear that the same cost formula should be used for all inventories having a similar nature and use to the entity, although items with a different nature and use may justify the use of a different cost formula. *[IAS 2.25]*. For example the standard allows that inventories used in one business segment may have a use to the entity different from the same type of inventories used in another business segment. However, a difference in geographical location of inventories (or in their respective tax rules) is not sufficient, by itself, to justify the use of different cost formulas. *[IAS 2.26]*.

3.3   Transfers of rental assets to inventory

It is sometimes the case that an entity, in the course of its ordinary activities, routinely sells items that had previously been held for rental and classified as property, plant and equipment. For example, car rental companies may acquire vehicles with the intention of holding them as rental cars for a limited period and then selling them. IAS 16 requires that when such items become held for sale rather than rental they be transferred to inventory at their carrying value. *[IAS 16.68A]*. Revenue from the subsequent sale is then recognised gross rather than net as discussed in Chapter 20 at 7.2.

Chapter 24

3.4   Net realisable value

IAS 2 in paragraphs 28 to 33 carries substantial guidance on the identification of net realisable value, where this is below cost and therefore inventory must be written down.

The cost of inventory may have to be reduced to its net realisable value if it has become damaged, is wholly or partly obsolete, or if its selling price has declined. Additionally, the costs to complete, or the estimated selling costs, may have increased to levels such that the costs of inventory may not be recovered from sale. *[IAS 2.28].* However the costs to consider in making this assessment should only comprise direct and incremental costs to complete and sell the inventory and will not include any profit margin on these activities. They will also not include overheads or the costs of the distribution channel, such as shops, since these costs will be incurred regardless of whether or not any sale of this inventory actually takes place. The only situation in which the costs of a shop might be considered to be included in these selling costs is the exceptional case where one shop is entirely dedicated to selling impaired goods.

Writing inventory down to net realisable value should normally be done on an item-by-item basis. IAS 2 specifically states that it is not appropriate to write down an entire class of inventory, such as finished goods, or all the inventory of a particular industry. However, it may be necessary to write down an entire product line or group of inventories in a given geographical area that cannot be practicably evaluated separately. Service contracts usually accumulate costs on a contract-by-contract basis and net realisable value must be considered on this basis. *[IAS 2.29].*

Estimates of net realisable value must be based on the most reliable evidence available and take into account fluctuations of price or cost after the end of the period if this is evidence of conditions at the end of the period. *[IAS 2.30].* A loss realised on a sale of a product after the end of the period may well provide evidence of the net realisable value of that product at the end of the period. However if this product is, for example, an exchange traded commodity and the loss realised can be attributed to a fall in prices on the exchange after the period end date then this loss would not, in itself, provide evidence of the net realisable value at the period end date.

Estimates of net realisable value must also take into account the purpose for which the inventory is held. Therefore inventory held for a particular contract has its net realisable value based on the contract price, and only any excess inventory held would be based on general selling prices. If there is a firm contract to sell and this is in excess of inventory quantities that the entity holds or is able to obtain under a firm purchase contract, this may give rise to a provision that should be recognised in accordance with IAS 37 – *Provisions, Contingent Liabilities and Contingent Assets* (see Chapter 29). *[IAS 2.31].*

IAS 2 explains that materials and other supplies held for use in the production of inventories are not written down below cost if the final product in which they are to be used is expected to be sold at or above cost. *[IAS 2.32].* This is the case even if these materials in their present condition have a net realisable value that is below cost and therefore would otherwise require write down. Thus, a whisky distiller would not write down an inventory of grain because of a fall in the grain price, so long as it expected to sell the whisky at a price which is sufficient to recover cost. However the standard does also explain that where a decline in the price of materials indicates that the cost of the final product will exceed net realisable value then write down of these materials is necessary and that their replacement cost may be the best measure of their net realisable value. *[IAS 2.32]*. In addition, where a write down is required in respect of finished goods, the carrying value of any related raw materials must also be reviewed to see if they too need to be written down.

Often raw materials are used to make a number of different products. In these cases it is normally not possible to arrive at a particular net realisable value for each item of raw material based on the selling price of any one type of finished item. If the current replacement cost of raw materials is less than their historical cost, a provision is only required to be made if the finished goods into which they will be made are expected to be sold at a loss. No provision should be made just because the anticipated profit will be less than normal.

When the circumstances that previously caused inventories to be written down below cost no longer exist, or when there is clear evidence of an increase in net realisable value because of changed economic circumstances, the amount of the write-down is reversed. The reversal cannot be greater than the amount of the original write-down, so that the new carrying amount will always be the lower of the cost and the revised net realisable value. *[IAS 2.33]*.

4   REAL ESTATE INVENTORY

4.1   Classification of real estate as inventory

Quite often real estate businesses develop and construct residential properties for sale, often consisting of several units. The strategy is to make a profit from the development and construction of the property rather than to make a profit in the long term from general price increases in the property market. The intention is to sell the property units as soon as possible following their construction, and is therefore in the ordinary course of the entity's business. When construction is complete it is not uncommon for individual property units to be leased at market rates to earn revenues to partly cover expenses such as interest, management fees, and real estate taxes. In practice, the leasing of properties prior to sale is common in the real estate industry. Large-scale buyers of property, such as insurance companies, are often reluctant to buy unless tenants are *in situ*, as this assures immediate cash flows from the investment.

It is our view that if it is in the entity's ordinary course of business (supported by its strategy) to hold property for short-term sale rather than for long-term capital appreciation, the entire property (including the leased units) should be accounted for and presented as inventory. This will continue to be the case as long as it remains the intention to sell the property in the short term. Rent received should be included in other income as it does not represent a reduction in the cost of inventory.

Investment property is defined in paragraph 5 of IAS 40 as 'property ... held ... to earn rentals or for capital appreciation or both, rather than for ... use in the production or supply of goods or services or for administrative purposes; or ... for sale in the ordinary course of business.' Therefore in the case outlined above, the property does not meet the definition in IAS 40 of investment property. Properties intended for sale in the ordinary course of business – no matter whether leased out or not – are outside the scope of IAS 40. However, if a property is not intended for sale, IAS 40 requires it to be transferred from inventory to investment property when there is a change in use. Such change can be evidenced by the commencement of an operating lease to another party (see Chapter 21 at 9).

4.2   Costs of real estate inventory

4.2.1   *Allocation of costs to individual units in multi-unit developments*

A real estate developer of a multi-unit complex will be able to track and record various costs that are specific to individual units, such as individual fit out costs. However there will also be various costs that are incurred which are not specific to any individual unit, such as the costs of land and any shared facilities, and a methodology will be required to allocate these costs to the individual units. This will of course impact the profit that is recognised on the sale of each individual unit.

There are two general approaches to this, both of which we believe are acceptable under IAS 2. Our preferred approach is to allocate these non-unit specific costs based on some relative cost basis. A reasonable proxy of relative cost is likely to be the size of each unit and hence an appropriate methodology would be to calculate a non-unit specific cost per square metre and allocate to the individual units based upon the floor area of each unit. Another proxy of (total) relative cost may be the specific cost of each unit and hence marking up the specific cost that is attributable to each unit by a fixed percentage so as to cover and account for the non-unit specific costs would also seem reasonable. This relative cost approach is consistent with the guidance under IAS 2 in respect of allocation of overheads which requires a 'systematic allocation of variable and production overheads'. *[IAS 2.12].*

The alternative approach would be to allocate these non-unit specific costs based on the relative sales value of each unit. This methodology is specifically referred to by the standard in the context of where a production process results in more than one product being produced simultaneously. *[IAS 2.14].* This latter approach will lead to a more consistent profit margin being achieved on the sale of each unit.

Whichever approach is adopted it must be used consistently. In addition the developer should initially, as far as is practicable, segregate the non-unit specific costs between any commercial, retail and residential components before applying these methodologies.

4.2.2 *Property demolition and operating lease costs*

During the course of a property redevelopment project, an existing building may need to be demolished in order for the new development to take place. The question arises, therefore, of how the cost of the existing building that will be demolished should be treated. Should it be capitalised as part of the construction cost for the new building to be erected on the same piece of land, or should the cost of the original building be derecognised and charged to profit or loss?

In all such cases judgement must be made on the basis of the particular facts involved, as the exact circumstances of the entity will bear upon the decision. There are three distinct scenarios to consider:

(a) the entity is the owner-occupier, in which case the matter falls under IAS 16;

(b) the entity holds the property to earn rentals, in which case the matter falls under IAS 40;

(c) the entity sells such properties in its normal course of business.

If it is the strategy of the developer to sell the developed property after construction, the cost of the old building as well as demolition costs and costs of developing the new one would be treated as inventory, but must still be subjected to the normal 'lower of cost and net realisable value' requirements.

Paragraph 6 of IAS 2 defines inventories as assets (a) held for sale in the ordinary course of business; or (b) in the process of production for such sale; or (c) in the form of materials or supplies to be consumed in the production process or in the rendering of services. Paragraph 10 states that 'the cost of inventories shall comprise all costs of purchase, costs of conversion and other costs incurred in bringing the inventories to their present location and condition.' As the new development is to be held for sale in the normal course of business by the developer, it falls within the scope of IAS 2.

In our view a similar argument can be applied to operating lease costs for the land upon which a building is being constructed. If, for example, an entity enters into a 50 year operating lease for land on which it intends to construct a building for sale as part of its ordinary business activities then the operating lease expense during the time taken to construct the building may be regarded as part of the 'costs incurred in bringing the inventories to their present location and condition' referred to in paragraph 10 of the standard. However an alternative view could also be taken, that is that these operating lease costs are for the right to control the land during the 50 year period rather than costs in bringing this inventory to any particular condition, in which case expensing may be appropriate.

5 RECOGNITION IN PROFIT OR LOSS

IAS 2 specifies that when inventory is sold, the carrying amount of the inventory must be recognised as an expense in the period in which the revenue is recognised. *[IAS 2.34]*. It is also clear that a failure to recognise revenue would not justify the non-recognition as an expense of inventory over which the entity no longer had control.

Any write-downs or losses of inventory must be recognised as an expense when the write-down or loss occurs. Reversals of previous write-downs are recognised as a reduction in the inventory expense recognised in the period in which the reversal occurs. *[IAS 2.34]*.

Judging when to recognise revenue (and therefore to charge the inventory expense) is one of the more complex accounting issues that can arise, particularly in the context of extended payment arrangements and manufacturer financing of sales to customers. In some industries, for example automobile manufacturing and retailing, aircraft manufacturing, railway carriage manufacturing and maintenance, and mobile phone handset retailing, it is customary for the goods concerned to be subject to extended and complex delivery, sales and settlement arrangements. For these types of transactions, the accounting problem that arises principally concerns when to recognise revenue, the consequent derecognition of inventory being driven by the revenue recognition judgement, not vice-versa.

Revenue recognition is dealt with in Chapter 30, to which reference should be made in considering such issues.

Inventory that goes into the creation of another asset, for instance into a self constructed item of property, plant or equipment, is expensed through the depreciation of that item during its useful life. *[IAS 2.35]*.

6 DISCLOSURE REQUIREMENTS OF IAS 2

The financial statements should disclose:

(a) the accounting policies adopted in measuring inventories, including the cost formula used;

(b) the total carrying amount of inventories and the carrying amount in classifications appropriate to the entity;

(c) the carrying amount of inventories carried at fair value less costs to sell;

(d) the amount of inventories recognised as an expense during the period;

(e) the amount of any write-down of inventories recognised as an expense in the period;

(f) the amount of any reversal of any write-down that is recognised as a reduction in the amount of inventories recognised as expense in the period;

(g) the circumstances or events that led to the reversal of a write-down of inventories; and

(h) the carrying amount of inventories pledged as security for liabilities. *[IAS 2.36]*.

IAS 2 does not specify the precise classifications that must be used to comply with (b) above. However it states that 'information about the carrying amounts held in different classifications of inventories and the extent of the changes in these assets is useful to financial statement users', and suggests suitable examples of common classifications such as merchandise, production supplies, materials, work-in-progress, and finished goods. *[IAS 2.37]*.

Extract 24.2 below shows how the Unilever Group disclosed the relevant information.

Extract 24.2: Unilever N.V. (2010)

Notes to the consolidated financial statements [extract]
12   Inventories

Inventories	€million 2010	€million 2009
Raw materials and consumables	1,554	1,298
Finished goods and goods for resale	2,755	2,280
	4,309	3,578

Inventories with a value of €132 million (2009: €91 million) are carried at net realisable value, this being lower than cost. During 2010, €135 million (2009: €200 million) was charged to the income statement for damaged, obsolete and lost inventories. In 2010, €42 million (2009: €19 million) was utilised or released to the income statement from inventory provisions taken in earlier years.

In 2010, inventories with a carrying amount of €3 million were pledged as security for certain of the Group's borrowings (2009: €10 million).

The amount of inventory recognised as an expense in the period is normally included in cost of sales; this category includes unallocated production overheads and abnormal costs as well as the costs of inventory that has been sold. However, the circumstances of the entity may warrant the inclusion of distribution costs into cost of sales. *[IAS 2.38]*. Hence when a company presents its profit or loss based upon this function of expense or 'cost of sales' method it will normally be disclosing costs that are greater than those that have been previously classified as inventory, but this appears to be explicitly allowable by the standard.

Extract 24.3 below shows how Stora Enso Oyj classified its inventories in its 2008 financial statements.

Extract 24.3: Stora Enso Oyj (2008)

Notes to the consolidated financial statements [extract]
Note 18   Inventories

	As at 31 December		
EUR million	**2008**	**2007**	**2006**
Materials and supplies	496.9	474.8	424.1
Work in progress	87.5	90.7	72.0
Finished goods	737.7	980.3	1,064.0
Spare parts and consumables	274.5	298.8	369.8
Other inventories	9.7	10.5	5.0
Advance payments & cutting rights	181.3	226.1	135.7
Obsolescence provision – spare parts	−68.2	−66.2	−28.1
Obsolescence provision – finished goods	−14.1	−16.4	−14.6
Net realisable value provision	−11.7	−6.0	−8.4
Total	**1,693.6**	**1,992.6**	**2,019.5**

Some entities adopt a format for profit or loss that results in amounts other than the cost of inventories being disclosed as an expense during the period. This will happen if an entity presents an analysis of expenses using a classification based on the nature of expenses. The entity then discloses the costs recognised as an expense for raw materials and consumables, labour costs and other costs together with the amount of the net change in inventories for the period. *[IAS 2.39].*

Formats for the presentation of profit or loss are discussed in Chapter 3.

References

1 Exposure Draft – *Revenue from Contracts with Customers,* para. 1, June 2010.

Chapter 25   Construction contracts

Chapter 25

List of examples

Chapter 25   Construction contracts

1   INTRODUCTION

IAS 11 – *Construction Contracts* – is a standard designed under the historical cost system to deal with the accounting issues raised by its subject. Like a number of other older standards that have not yet been revised significantly by the IASB (IAS 11 was originally approved in 1978 and last revised in 1993), the focus is on the income statement and the basis on which income and expenditure should be recognised. IAS 11 identifies its principal purpose as the allocation of contract revenue and contract costs to the accounting periods in which contract work is performed, not on the identification of assets and liabilities as defined in paragraph 4.4 of the IASB's *Conceptual Framework for Financial Reporting ('Framework')*.

The IASB, in conjunction with the FASB, is developing a new revenue recognition standard. The Boards, in June 2010, issued an Exposure Draft entitled *Revenue from Contracts with Customers*. This joint project and Exposure Draft are discussed in Chapter 30 and, as highlighted in that Chapter, the proposals could significantly affect the manner in which revenue is recognised under construction contracts. The IASB's intention is that any standard that results from this project will replace both IAS 18 – *Revenue* – and IAS 11, as well as those Interpretations that address revenue related matters (e.g. IFRIC 15 – *Agreements for the Construction of Real Estate*).

1.1   Scope and definitions of IAS 11

IAS 11 applies to accounting for construction contracts in the financial statements of the contractor. *[IAS 11.1]*.

A construction contract is defined as follows:

> 'a contract specifically negotiated for the construction of an asset or a combination of assets that are closely interrelated or interdependent in terms of their design, technology and function or their ultimate purpose or use.' *[IAS 11.3]*.

The meaning of 'specifically negotiated for the construction of an asset' has been considered by the Interpretations Committee. In July 2008 Interpretation 15 – *Agreements for the Construction of Real Estate* (IFRIC 15) was issued. Although IFRIC 15 has been written in the specific context of its title, it includes an analysis of the distinguishing features of construction contracts and it is, therefore, more generally relevant in determining whether any contract that involves the construction of an asset is within the scope of IAS 11 or is a sale of goods. See 1.2 below.

Something that may be accounted for as a single construction contract can comprise a number of different elements. Single constructions could include a bridge, a building, a dam, a pipeline, a road, a ship or a tunnel. Other single contracts include groups of inter-related assets such as an oil refinery or complex pieces of plant and equipment. *[IAS 11.4]*. Whether a contract is, in fact a single construction contract or one that should be separated into components, each of which is dealt with individually, is one of the more difficult and subjective areas of contract accounting and one that has also been considered by the Interpretations Committee (see 2 below).

Contracts for services directly related to construction contracts are covered by IAS 11 and not by IAS 18. These include contracts for the services of project managers and architects. Contracts for the demolition and restoration of assets and restoration of the environment after an asset is demolished are also construction contracts. *[IAS 11.5]*.

IAS 11 does not specify any minimum period of duration for a construction contract. This means that any such contract which starts and ends in two different reporting periods will need to be accounted for under this standard. The standard identifies two specific types of construction contract:

> 'A *fixed price contract* is a construction contract in which the contractor agrees to a fixed contract price, or a fixed rate per unit of output, which in some cases is subject to cost escalation clauses;
>
> A *cost plus contract* is a construction contract in which the contractor is reimbursed for allowable or otherwise defined costs, plus a percentage of these costs or a fixed fee.' *[IAS 11.3]*.

These types determine the basis on which income is recognised, as is discussed in 3.3.1 below.

Contracts that contain elements of both types, e.g. a cost plus contract that has an agreed maximum price, will have to be analysed in order to determine when to recognise contract revenue and expenses. *[IAS 11.6]*.

1.2   Whether an arrangement is a construction contract

The debate that led to the publication of IFRIC 15 was precipitated by the inconsistent accounting treatment of certain real estate sales. At issue was whether, or in what circumstances, residential or commercial real estate developments could be treated as construction contracts. This would require revenue to be recognised using the percentage of completion method under IAS 11. Otherwise these would be governed by IAS 18, and revenue would not be recognised until the risks and rewards of ownership and control had passed. In developing the Interpretation, the meaning of the term 'construction contract' as defined in IAS 11 has been addressed; this helps clarify the scope of this standard.

IAS 11 defines a construction contract as 'a contract specifically negotiated for the construction of an asset or a combination of assets ...'. *[IAS 11.3]*.

Although IFRIC 15 provides guidance in the particular context of real estate, as described below, it can be applied by analogy to other arrangements that do not include real estate. IFRIC 15 is discussed further in Chapter 30 at 6.11.2.

Under the Interpretation:

- an agreement for the construction of real estate meets the definition of a construction contract when the buyer is able to specify the major structural elements of the design of the real estate before construction begins and/or specify major structural changes once construction is in progress (whether or not it exercises that ability). When IAS 11 applies, the construction contract also includes any contracts or components for the rendering of services that are directly related to the construction of the real estate. *[IFRIC 15.11]*;

- an agreement for the construction of real estate in which buyers have only limited ability to influence the design of the real estate, for example to select a design from a range of options specified by the entity, or to specify only minor variations to the basic design, is an agreement for the sale of goods and therefore within the scope of IAS 18. *[IFRIC 15.12]*.

The Interpretation notes that within a single agreement, an entity may contract to deliver goods or services in addition to the construction of real estate (for example a sale of land or provision of property management services – see 3.3.8 below). Such an agreement may need to be split into separately identifiable components, which may include one for the construction of real estate. The fair value of the total consideration received or receivable for the agreement must be allocated to each component. *[IFRIC 15.8]*. The Basis for Conclusions to the Interpretation points to IFRIC 12 – *Service Concession Arrangements* – and IFRIC 13 – *Customer Loyalty Programmes* – for guidance on allocating the fair value *[IFRIC 15.BC11]*; in these Interpretations it is based on the fair values of the separate components. Segmenting of contracts is discussed below at 2.

The Interpretation assumes that there is revenue to be recognised, i.e. it assumes that the entity retains neither continuing managerial involvement to the degree usually associated with ownership nor effective control over the constructed real estate to an extent that would preclude recognition of some or all of the consideration as revenue. *[IFRIC 15.7]*.

It can be seen that, with these types of contracts in general, there is a range of contractual arrangements for similar products from, at one end, sales of 'off the shelf' items through to large projects where a similar type of asset is constructed to a purchaser's specification. Whether an arrangement is a construction contract, which should be accounted for under IAS 11 or a sale of goods, which should be accounted for under IAS 18, is relatively simple in arrangements at either end of this spectrum but can be less clear in other cases.

Chapter 25

An example of an entity whose activities cover this range is Vestas Wind Systems A/S whose revenue recognition policy is as follows:

Extract 25.1: Vestas Wind Systems A/S (2010)

Notes to the Consolidated Accounts
1. Group accounting policies [extract]
Income statement [extract]
Revenue [extract]

Revenue comprises sale of wind turbines and wind power systems, aftersales service and sale of spare parts.

Sale of individual wind turbines and small wind power systems based on standard solutions (supply-only and supply-and-installation projects) as well as spare parts sales are recognised in the income statement provided that the risk has been transferred to the buyer prior to the year end, and provided that the income can be measured reliably and is expected to be received. Contracts to deliver large wind power systems with a high degree of customisation are recognised in revenue as the systems are constructed based on the stage of completion of the individual contract (turnkey projects). Where the profit from a contract cannot be estimated reliably, revenue is only recognised equalling the expenses incurred to the extent that it is probable that the expenses will be recovered.

Although IFRIC 15 has been considered further by the Interpretations Committee during 2011, it has decided to defer further discussion until the criteria for the determination of the transfer of goods and services are finalised as part of the revenue recognition project.[1]

1.3   Service concession agreements

Service concession agreements commonly include the construction of an asset followed by a period in which the constructor maintains and services that asset; this secondary period may include asset replacement and refurbishment as well as service elements. Alternatively, the contract might provide for the refurbishment of an existing infrastructure asset together with related services. These agreements provide particular accounting difficulties because they combine contract accounting issues and issues arising from a number of other accounting standards including IAS 11, IAS 17 and IAS 18. The accounting issues raised by IFRIC 12 are discussed further in Chapter 28.

2   COMBINATION AND SEGMENTATION OF CONTRACTS

IAS 11 should be applied separately to each construction contract. *[IAS 11.7]*. However, in order to reflect the substance of the transaction it may be necessary for a contract to be sub-divided and the standard to be applied individually to each component, or for a group of contracts to be treated as one.

IAS 11 provides guidance in three separate cases. The first is where a single contract covers the construction of a number of separate assets, each of which is in substance a separate contract, i.e.

(a)   separate proposals have been submitted for each asset;

(b)   the contractor and customer have negotiated separately for each asset and can accept or reject that part of the contract relating to each asset; and

(c)   the costs and revenues relating to each asset can be identified. *[IAS 11.8]*.

The second case is effectively the reverse of the first and deals with situations where in substance there is only a single contract with a customer, or a group of customers. This group of contracts should be treated as a single contract where:

(a)   the group of contracts is negotiated as a single package;

(b)   the contracts are so closely interrelated that they are, in effect, part of a single project with an overall profit margin; and

(c)   the contracts are performed concurrently or in a continuous sequence. *[IAS 11.9].*

The third case is where a contract anticipates the construction of a further asset at the customer's discretion. Whether these options should be accounted for in combination with, or separately from, the original contract is discussed at 2.1 below.

One clear weakness of IAS 11 is that it contains little guidance on the combining and segmenting of contracts. It really only considers the issues in very clear-cut circumstances, i.e. where a number of contracts that purport to be separate have been negotiated as a single package or where a series of separate contracts have been subsumed within a single contract document but where the individual contracts should be dealt with separately. However, there is no further guidance in the standard on whether or how individual contracts or groups of contracts should be segmented or combined and contract revenue and costs recognised on the basis of the individual segments or combined contracts. These treatments can have a major effect on the recognition of income. Segmenting a contract can affect the profile of income recognition, perhaps allowing earlier recognition of revenue. If a series of contracts is negotiated as a package with the objective of achieving an overall profit margin, this will not be reflected if the individual contracts are accounted for separately, while inappropriate combining of the segments of a contract could result in the timing of profits or losses not being recognised on the basis required by the standard.

The Interpretations Committee has discussed whether some of the detailed guidance under US GAAP for combining and segmenting contracts (ASC 605-35) should be incorporated into IAS 11 but concluded that it was not appropriate to do so. The Interpretations Committee members were not aware of any significant divergence in practice. They also concluded that, because of differences between the two standards, full convergence of the conditions for combining and segmenting construction contracts could not be achieved simply through interpretation.[2] Therefore these differences will remain until the proposed new revenue recognition model that is being jointly developed by the IASB and the FASB comes into effect.

In the meantime segmentation and combination of construction contracts should be assessed in accordance with paragraphs 8 and 9 of IAS 11, as described above.

2.1   Options for the construction of an additional asset

Another area where it is necessary to consider whether contracts should be combined is in contract options and additions. Once again, combining of contracts is important because of its potential impact on the recognition of revenue and profits on transactions. If the optional asset is treated as part of the original contract, contract revenue will be recognised using the percentage of completion method over the combined contract.

IAS 11 considers the circumstances in which a contract gives a customer an option for an additional asset (or is amended in this manner) and concludes that this should be treated as a new contract if:

(a)   the asset differs significantly in design, technology or function from the asset or assets covered by the original contract; or

(b)   the price of the asset is negotiated without regard to the original contract price. *[IAS 11.10]*.

This means, for example, that the contract for an additional, identical asset would be treated as a separate contract if its price was negotiated separately from the original contract price. Costs often decline with additional production, not only because of the effects of initial costs but also because of the 'learning curve' (the time taken by the workforce to perform activities decreases with practice and repetition). This could result in a much higher profit margin on the additional contract. If, for example, a government department takes up its option with a defence contractor for five more aircraft, in addition to the original twenty-five that had been contracted for, but the option was unpriced and the new contract is priced afresh, then it cannot be combined with the original contract regardless of the difference in profit margins. Note that this conclusion appears consistent with US GAAP, which would only allow contracts not executed at the same time to be combined if they were negotiated as a package in the same economic environment. This means that the time period between the commitments of the parties to the individual contracts must be reasonably short.[3] Although 'short' is not defined, it is unlikely to cover a period of several years, as could happen in defence contracting.

The combining of contracts may also have unexpected results. If, for example, an entity has a contract with a government to build two satellites and a priced option to build a third, it may be obliged to combine the contracts as at the point at which the option is exercised. This could well be in a different accounting period to the commencement of the contract. Using the rules outlined in 3.3.3 below, there will be a cumulative catch-up of revenue, and probably also of profits. In subsequent periods results will be based on the combined contracts.

3   CONTRACT REVENUE, COSTS AND EXPENSES

3.1   Contract revenue

Contract revenue comprises the amount of revenue initially agreed by the parties together with any variations, claims and incentive payments as long as it is probable that they will result in revenue and can be measured reliably. *[IAS 11.11]*. The standard states that such revenue is to be measured at the fair value of the consideration received and receivable. In this context, 'fair value' appears to refer to the process whereby the consideration is to be revised as events occur and uncertainties are resolved. These may include contractual matters such as increases in revenue in a fixed price contract as a result of cost escalation clauses or, when a contract involves a fixed price per unit of output, contract revenue may increase as the number of units is increased. Penalties for delays may reduce revenue. In addition, variations and claims must be taken into account. *[IAS 11.12]*. If deferred payments are due after completion of the contract, for example retention payments, such payments will be brought into account at their present value. Similarly if advance payments are received, and these constitute financing transactions, it may be appropriate to accrue interest on them (see Chapter 30 at 6.1.4).

Variations are instructions by the customer to change the scope of the work to be performed under the contract, including changes to the specification or design of the asset or to the duration of the contract. Variations may only be included in contract revenue when it is probable that the customer will approve the variation and the amount to be charged for it, and the amount can be measured reliably. *[IAS 11.13].*

Given the extended periods over which contracts are carried out and changes in circumstances prevailing whilst the work is in progress, it is quite normal for a contractor to submit claims for additional sums to a customer. Claims may be made for costs not included in the original contract or arising as an indirect consequence of approved variations, such as customer caused delays, errors in specifications or design and disputed variations. Because their settlement is by negotiation (which can in practice be very protracted), they are subject to a high level of uncertainty; consequently, no credit should be taken for them unless negotiations have reached an advanced stage such that:

- it is probable that the customer will accept the claim; and
- the amount that it is probable will be accepted by the customer can be measured reliably. *[IAS 11.14].*

This means that, as a minimum, the claims must have been agreed in principle and, in the absence of an agreed sum, the amount to be accrued must have been prudently assessed.

Contracts may provide for incentive payments, for example, for early completion or superior performance. They may only be included in contract revenue when the contract is at such a stage that it is probable the required performance will be achieved and the amount can be measured reliably. *[IAS 11.15].*

Where contract revenue is denominated in a foreign currency it will be necessary to apply an appropriate exchange rate to record that revenue in the functional currency of the entity concerned. IAS 21 – *The Effects of Changes in Foreign Exchange Rates* – requires that foreign currency transactions be recorded at the spot exchange rate at the date of a transaction. *[IAS 21.21].* Where work is performed on a steady basis over a period of time it may be appropriate to use an average exchange rate for that period.

3.2 Contract costs

Contract costs are those that relate directly to the specific contract and to those that are attributable to contract activity in general that can be allocated to the contract. In addition, they include costs that are specifically chargeable to the customer under the terms of the contract. *[IAS 11.16].*

Directly related costs include:

(a) direct labour costs, including site supervision;

(b) costs of materials used in construction;

(c) depreciation of plant and equipment used on the contract;

(d)   costs of moving plant, equipment and materials to and from the contract site;

(e)   costs of hiring plant and equipment;

(f)   costs of design and technical assistance that is directly related to the contract;

(g)   the estimated costs of rectification and guarantee work, including expected warranty costs; and

(h)   claims from third parties. *[IAS 11.17]*.

If the contractor generates incidental income from any directly related cost, e.g. by selling surplus materials and disposing of equipment at the end of the contract, this is treated as a reduction in contract costs. *[IAS 11.17]*.

The second category of costs comprises those attributable to contract activity in general that can be allocated to a particular contract. These include design and technical assistance not directly related to an individual contract, insurance, and construction overheads such as the costs of preparing and processing the payroll for the personnel actually working on the contract. These must be allocated using a systematic and rational method, consistently applied to all costs having similar characteristics. Allocation must be based on the normal level of construction activity. *[IAS 11.18]*.

There are various costs that, in most circumstances, are specifically precluded by IAS 11 from being attributed to contract activity or allocated to a contract. These include general administration costs, selling costs, research and development costs and the depreciation of idle plant and equipment that is not used on a particular contract. *[IAS 11.20]*. However, the entity is allowed to classify general administration costs and research and development as contract costs if they are specifically reimbursable under the terms of the contract. *[IAS 11.19-20]*. An example is given by EADS, which discloses the following:

Extract 25.2: EADS N.V. (2010)

Notes to the Consolidated Financial Statements [extract]

2. Summary of significant accounting policies

Research and development expenses [extract]

Research and development expenses – Research and development activities can be (i) contracted or (ii) self-initiated.

i)   Costs for contracted research and development activities, carried out in the scope of externally financed research and development contracts, are expensed when the related revenues are recorded.

Costs may be attributed to a contract from the date on which it is secured until its final completion. Additionally, costs relating directly to the contract, which have been incurred in gaining the business, may be included in contract costs if they have been incurred once it is probable the contract will be obtained. These costs must be separately identified and measured reliably. *[IAS 11.21]*. This is not dissimilar to the general rules for recognition of an asset. An asset is defined in the Framework as 'a resource controlled by the entity as a result of past events and from which future economic benefits are expected to flow to the entity'. *[Framework.4.4]*. Therefore, we believe that this should be read restrictively and that these costs should not be recognised until they can themselves be seen as an asset of the entity through its control of the future economic benefits from the contract.

One entity that takes a prudent view of pre-contract costs is Balfour Beatty plc, which sets out that such costs are expensed until it is *virtually certain* that a contract will be awarded.

Extract 25.3: Balfour Beatty plc (2010)

Notes to the accounts [extract]

1.7   Construction and service contracts [extract]

Pre-contract costs are expensed as incurred until it is virtually certain that a contract will be awarded, from which time further pre-contract costs are recognised as an asset and charged as an expense over the period of the contract. Amounts recovered in respect of pre-contract costs that have been written off are deferred and amortised over the life of the contract.

Costs that have been written off cannot be reinstated if the contract is obtained in a subsequent period. *[IAS 11.21]*.

Costs incurred in securing a contract include such things as the building of models (including computer modelling exercises) for tender purposes, travelling costs of technicians to survey sites, technical tendering costs, and similar expenses relating specifically to a given contract.

3.2.1   Borrowing costs

Borrowing costs may be specific to individual contracts or attributable to contract activity in general. IAS 23 – *Borrowing Costs* – requires capitalisation of borrowing costs that are directly attributable to the acquisition, construction or production of qualifying assets. *[IAS 23.8]*. A specific reference to IAS 23 that was previously included in paragraph 18 of IAS 11 has been deleted. The IASB argued that it was unnecessary, stating 'attributing borrowing costs to contracts is not a matter of capitalisation. Rather, it is a matter of identifying the contract costs'. *[IAS 23.BC27]*. In other words, the inclusion of borrowing costs into construction contract costs means that the borrowing costs concerned will be expensed when the contract costs are expensed.

While it may appear initially that this change to the standard will require all companies to commence capitalising borrowing costs into their construction contracts, another decision, this time from the Interpretations Committee, may have exactly the opposite effect and reduce capitalisation to an insignificant amount. During its debates on accounting for service concessions the Interpretations Committee concluded that the 'amount due from customers' asset is a financial asset within the scope of IAS 32 – *Financial Instruments: Presentation*. This asset is not a qualifying asset for the purposes of capitalisation of borrowing costs because the treatment requires interest income to be imputed (see Chapter 28 at 4). *[IFRIC 12.BC58]*. Therefore, once revenue is recognised on work that has been performed, capitalisation of borrowing costs will cease. Only contract costs that related to future activity could be a qualifying asset and this will usually be an insignificant amount. In June 2005, the Interpretations Committee decided not to prepare an Interpretation to this effect, stating that it 'was not aware of any evidence that the conclusion was of major importance outside the service concession sector'. The Interpretations Committee noted that it would reconsider this decision if the responses to the draft Interpretations on service concession arrangements indicated otherwise.[4] It did not reconsider. IFRIC 12 – *Service Concession Arrangements* – was issued in November 2006; the position taken with regard to amounts due from customers, i.e. that they are financial assets, remains unchanged and there has been no other comment on the matter.

The Interpretations Committee's conclusion is significant for all entities engaged in construction contracts if these are deemed to fall under IFRIC 12 and if, under this Interpretation, the operator has a financial asset rather than an intangible asset. Borrowing costs will only be capitalised under IFRIC 12 if the operator has an intangible asset. *[IFRIC 12.22]*. Where the operator has a financial asset the borrowing costs will need to be expensed and, in addition, part of the contract revenue will be taken as finance income, as income is accreted on the carrying value of the financial asset. *[IFRIC 12.BC58]*. This changes the profile of income recognition. The implications of this conclusion outside service concessions remain unclear.

3.3   The recognition of contract revenue and expenses

If the basic rule of accounting for inventories were applied to contracts, it would result in an annual income statement that reflected only the outcome of contracts completed during the year. In a contracting company this might bear no relation to the company's actual level of activity for that year. IAS 11 therefore requires revenue and expenses to be recognised on uncompleted contracts in order to present a consistent view of the results of the company's activities during the period and from one period to the next. The underlying principle in IAS 11 is that, once the outcome of a construction contract can be estimated reliably, revenue associated with the construction contract should be recognised by reference to the stage of completion of the contract activity at the end of the reporting period. *[IAS 11.22]*. The standard does not define the attributable profit in a contract, which will therefore be the balancing figure once revenue and expenses are known.

If it is anticipated that the contract will be loss-making, the expected loss must be recognised immediately. This is described further in 3.3.6 below.

3.3.1   *Types of construction contract*

IAS 11 identifies two types of construction contract, fixed price and cost plus contracts.

3.3.1.A   *Fixed price contracts*

In the case of a fixed price contract, the standard states that the outcome of a construction contract can be estimated reliably when all the conditions discussed below are satisfied.

*   First, it must be probable that the economic benefits associated with the contract will flow to the entity, which must be able to measure total contract revenue reliably. As discussed further below, these conditions will usually be satisfied when there are adequate contractual arrangements between the parties;
*   Second, both the contract costs to complete the contract and the stage of contract completion at the end of the reporting period must be able to be measured reliably; and

- Third, the entity must be able to identify and measure reliably the contract costs attributable to the contract so that actual contract costs incurred can be compared with prior estimates. *[IAS 11.23]*. This means that it must have adequate reporting and budgeting systems.

3.3.1.B   Cost plus contracts

Cost plus contracts are not subject to all of the same uncertainties as fixed price contracts. As with any transaction, it must be probable that the economic benefits associated with the contract will flow to the entity in order to recognise income at all. In most contracts this will be evidenced by the contract documentation. The fundamental criterion for a cost plus contract is the proper measurement of contract costs. Therefore, the contract costs attributable to the contract, whether or not specifically reimbursable, must be clearly identified and measured reliably. *[IAS 11.24]*.

3.3.2   The stage of completion method

There are certain general principles that apply whether the contract is classified as fixed cost or as cost plus. Recognition of revenue is by reference to the 'stage of completion method', also known as the 'percentage of completion method'. Contract revenue and costs are recognised as revenue and expenses in profit or loss in the period in which the work is performed. Any anticipated excess of contract costs over contract income (i.e. a loss on the contract) is recognised as soon as it is anticipated. *[IAS 11.25-26]*.

This does not mean that contract activity is necessarily based on the total costs that have been incurred by the entity. Contract costs that relate to future contract activity (i.e. that activity for which revenue has not yet been recognised) may be deferred and recognised as an asset as long as it is probable that they will be recovered. This point is made explicitly by Royal BAM Group nv in Extract 25.5 below. These costs are usually called contract work in progress. *[IAS 11.27]*. An example of this may be materials purchased and stored for future use on a contract. Otherwise, contract costs are recognised in the profit or loss as they are incurred.

Importantly, neither does it mean that an entity can determine what it considers to be an appropriate profit margin for the whole contract and spread costs over the contract so as to achieve this margin, thereby classifying deferred costs as work in progress. As noted at 3.3 above, IAS 11 defines revenue and contract costs and not attributable profit. The standard does not seek to achieve a uniform profit margin throughout the contract, unless, of course, it is a cost plus contract.

An entity does not adjust the cumulative revenue it has recognised if it transpires in a subsequent period that there are doubts about the recoverability of an amount it has recognised as revenue and it consequently has to make provision against its debtor. Instead the amount that is no longer considered recoverable is written off as an expense. *[IAS 11.28]*.

In order to be able to recognise revenue, the construction entity must be able to make reliable estimates of its income and costs. It is usually possible to do so once the parties have agreed to a contract that establishes both parties' enforceable rights, the contract consideration and the manner and terms of settlement. However, the entity must also be able to review and, where necessary, revise, the estimates of contract revenue and contract costs as the contract progresses. This means that the entity must have an effective system of internal financial budgets and reporting systems. *[IAS 11.29]*.

The standard allows the stage of completion of a contract to be determined in a number of ways, including:

- the proportion that contract costs incurred for work performed to date bear to the estimated total contract costs;
- surveys of work performed; or
- completion of a physical proportion of the contract work. *[IAS 11.30]*.

These could, of course, give different answers regarding the stage of completion of a contract as demonstrated in the following example.

Example 25.1:   *Determination of revenue*

A company is engaged in a construction contract with an expected sales value of £10,000. It is the end of the accounting period during which the company commenced work on this contract and it needs to compute the amount of revenue to be reflected in the profit and loss account for this contract.

Scenario (i)   **Stage of completion is measured by the proportion that contract costs incurred for work performed to date bear to the estimated total contract costs**

The company has incurred and applied costs of £4,000. £3,000 is the best estimate of costs to complete. The company should therefore recognise revenue of £5,714, being the appropriate proportion of total contract value, and computed thus:

$$\frac{4,000}{7,000} \times 10,000 = 5,714$$

Scenario (ii)   **Stage of completion is measured by surveys of work performed**

An independent surveyor has certified that at the period-end the contract is 55% complete and that the company is entitled to apply for cumulative progress payments of £5,225 (after a 5% retention). In this case the company would record revenue of £5,500 being the sales value of the work done. (If it is anticipated that rectification work will have to be carried out to secure the release of the retention money then this should be taken into account in computing the stage of completion – but the fact that there is retention of an amount does not, in itself, directly impact the amount of revenue to be recorded.)

Scenario (iii)   **Stage of completion is measured by completion of a physical proportion of the contract work**

The company's best estimate of the physical proportion of the work it has completed is that it is 60% complete. The value of the work done and, therefore, the revenue to be recognised is £6,000.

Note that in each of the above scenarios the computation of the amount of revenue is quite independent of the question of how much (if any) profit should be taken. This is as it should be, because even if a contract is loss-making the sales price will be earned and this should be reflected by recording revenue as the contract progresses. In the final analysis, any loss arises because costs are greater than revenue, and costs should be reflected through cost of sales. Different methods of determining revenue will, as disclosed above, produce different results, which highlights the importance of disclosing the method adopted by the entity.

An entity that discloses that it uses a variety of methods to determine revenue is EADS, as shown in the following extract.

Extract 25.4: EADS N.V. (2010)

Notes to the Consolidated Financial Statements [extract]
2. Summary of significant accounting policies
Revenue recognition [extract]

For construction contracts, when the outcome can be estimated reliably, revenues are recognised by reference to the percentage of completion ("PoC") of the contract activity by applying the estimate at completion method. The stage of completion of a contract may be determined by a variety of ways. Depending on the nature of the contract, revenue is recognised as contractually agreed technical milestones are reached, as units are delivered or as the work progresses. Whenever the outcome of a construction contract cannot be estimated reliably – for example during the early stages of a contract or when this outcome can no longer be estimated reliably during the course of a contract's completion – all related contract costs that are incurred are immediately expensed and revenues are recognised only to the extent of those costs being recoverable ("early stage method of accounting"). In such specific situations, as soon as the outcome can (again) be estimated reliably, revenue is from that point in time onwards accounted for according to the estimate at completion method, without restating the revenues previously recorded under the early stage method of accounting. Changes in profit rates are reflected in current earnings as identified. Contracts are reviewed regularly and in case of probable losses, loss-at-completion provisions are recorded. These loss-at-completion provisions in connection with construction contracts are not discounted.

By contrast, many entities use just one principal method to calculate the percentage of completion.

The Royal BAM Group considers contract costs incurred as a proportion of total costs.

Extract 25.5: Royal BAM Group nv (2010)

3.   Summary of significant accounting policies [extract]
3.10   Construction contracts [extract]

The Group uses the 'percentage of completion method' to determine the appropriate amount to be recognised in a given period. The stage of completion is measured by reference to the contract cost incurred as percentage of total actual or estimated project cost. Revenues and result are recognised in the income statement based on this progress.

Projects are presented in the balance sheet as receivables from or payables to customers on behalf of the contract. If the costs incurred (including the result recognised) exceed the invoiced instalments, the contract will be presented as a receivable. If the invoiced instalments exceed the costs incurred (including the result recognised) the contract will be presented as a liability.

Contracts containing the construction of a project and the possibility of subsequent long-term maintenance of that project as separate components, or for which these components could be negotiated individually in the market, are accounted for as two separate contracts. Revenue and results are recognised accordingly in the income statement as construction contracts for third parties or the rendering of services respectively.

Chapter 25

The Vitec Group relies on surveys of work completed.

Extract 25.6: The Vitec Group plc (2010)

Notes to the Consolidated Accounts [extract]

2   Accounting Policies [extract]

Long term contracts [extract]

Contract revenue and expenses are recognised in the Income Statement in proportion to the stage of completion of the contract, to the extent that the contract outcome can be estimated reliably. The stage of completion is assessed by reference to surveys of work performed. When the outcome of a long term contract cannot be estimated reliably then contract revenue is only recognised to the value of contract costs incurred to date that are likely to be recoverable. An expected loss on a contract is recognised immediately in the Income Statement.

There are, of course, other ways of measuring work done, e.g. labour hours, which depending upon the exact circumstances might lead to a more appropriate basis for computing revenue.

The above examples apply only to fixed-price contracts. Where a contract is on a cost-plus basis, it is necessary to examine the costs incurred to ensure they are of the type and size envisaged in the terms of the contract. Only once this is done and the recoverable costs identified can the figure be grossed up to arrive at the appropriate revenue figure.

If the stage of completion is determined by reference to the contract costs incurred to date, it is fundamental that this figure includes only those contract costs that reflect work actually performed so far. Any contract costs that relate to future activity on the contract must be excluded. This includes the costs of materials that have been delivered to a contract site or set aside for use in a contract but not yet installed, used or applied during contract performance, unless the materials have been made especially for the contract. Payments made to subcontractors in advance of work performed under the subcontract would similarly not relate to work performed to date and have to be excluded. *[IAS 11.31]*.

Example 25.2:   Determination of revenue – exclusion of unapplied costs

The circumstances are as in Scenario (i) of Example 25.1 above. The entity has incurred and applied costs of £4,000. £3,000 is the best estimate of costs to complete. If the costs incurred to date included, say, £500 in respect of unapplied raw materials, then the revenue to be recognised falls to £5,000 being:

$$\frac{\text{costs incurred and applied}}{\text{total costs}} = \frac{(4,000 - 500)}{7,000} \times 10,000 = 5,000$$

3.3.3   Changes in estimates

The percentage of completion method is applied on a cumulative basis in each accounting period to the current estimates of contract revenues and costs. The effect of any changes in estimates of revenue and costs, or the effect of any change in the estimate of the outcome of a contract, must be treated as a change in accounting estimate, in accordance with IAS 8 – *Accounting Policies, Changes in Accounting Estimates and Errors*. The revised estimates must be used in determining the amount of revenue and expenses recognised in profit or loss in the period in which the change is made, and in subsequent periods. *[IAS 11.38].*

3.3.4 The determination of contract revenue and expenses

It is now possible to see how these features of accounting for construction contracts are put together to calculate the timing and measurement of contract revenue and expenses throughout the term of a construction contract, as in the following example, based on that in the Appendix to IAS 11:

Example 25.3:   *Cumulative example – the determination of contract revenue and expenses*

The following example illustrates the determination of the stage of completion of a contract and the timing of the recognition of contract revenue and expenses, measured by the proportion that contract costs incurred for work performed to date bear to the estimated total contract costs.

A construction contractor has a fixed price contract to build a bridge. The initial amount of revenue agreed in the contract is €9,000. The contractor's initial estimate of contract costs is €8,000. It will take 3 years to build the bridge.

By the end of year 1, the contractor's estimate of contract costs has increased to €8,050.

In year 2, the customer approves a variation resulting in an increase in contract revenue of €200 and estimated additional contract costs of €150. At the end of year 2, costs incurred include €100 for standard materials stored at the site to be used in year 3 to complete the project.

The contractor determines the stage of completion of the contract by calculating the proportion that contract costs incurred for work performed to date bear to the latest estimated total contract costs. A summary of the financial data during the construction period is as follows:

	Year 1 €	Year 2 €	Year 3 €
Initial amount of revenue agreed in contract	9,000	9,000	9,000
Variation	–	200	200
Total contract revenue	9,000	9,200	9,200
Contract costs incurred to date	2,093	6,168	8,200
Contract costs to complete	5,957	2,023	–
Total estimated contract costs	8,050	8,200	8,200
Estimated profit	950	1,000	1,000
Stage of completion	26%	74%	100%

The constructor uses the percentages calculated as above to calculate the revenue, contract costs and profits over the term of the contract. The stage of completion for year 2 (74%) is determined by excluding from contract costs incurred for work performed to date the €100 of standard materials stored at the site for use in year 3.

The amounts of revenue, expenses and profit recognised in profit or loss in the three years are as follows:

	To date	Recognised in prior years	Recognised in current years
Year 1			
Revenue (9,000 × 26%)	2,340	–	2,340
Expenses	2,093	–	2,093
Profit	247	–	247

Year 2

Revenue (9,200 × 74%)	6,808	2,340	4,468
Expenses (6,168 incurred less 100 of materials in storage)	6,068	2,093	3,975
Profit	740	247	493

Year 3

Revenue (9,200 × 100%)	9,200	6,808	2,392
Expenses	8,200	6,068	2,132
Profit	1,000	740	260

3.3.5 *Inability to estimate the outcome of a contract reliably*

When the outcome of a construction contract cannot be estimated reliably, an entity will first of all have to determine whether it has incurred costs that it is probable will be recovered under the contract. It can then recognise revenue to the extent of these costs. Contract costs should be recognised as an expense in the period in which they are incurred, *[IAS 11.32]*, unless, of course, they relate to future contract activity, such as materials purchased for future use on the contract as explained at 3.3.2 above.

It is often difficult to estimate the outcome of a contract reliably during its early stages. This means that it is not possible to recognise contract profit. However, the entity may be satisfied that some, at least, of the contract costs it has incurred will be recovered and it will be able to recognise revenue to this extent.

If it is probable that total costs will exceed total revenues, even if the outcome of the contract cannot be estimated reliably, any expected excess of contract costs must be expensed immediately. *[IAS 11.33]*. The standard also identifies a number of situations that may give rise to irrecoverable contract costs that must be recognised as expenses immediately. There may be deficiencies in the contract, which means that it is not fully enforceable. Other problems may be caused by the operation of law, such as the outcome of pending litigation or legislation or the expropriation of property. The customer or the contractor may no longer be able to meet their obligations or the contractor may be unable for some reason to complete the contract. *[IAS 11.34]*.

If these uncertainties that prevent the outcome of the contract being estimated reliably are resolved, revenue and expenses are recognised by the stage of completion method. *[IAS 11.35]*.

3.3.6 *Loss-making contracts*

As soon as the entity considers that it is probable that the contract costs will exceed contract revenue it must recognise immediately the expected loss as an expense. It is irrelevant whether work has commenced on the contract or the stage of completion of contract activity. In addition, the entity may not take into account any anticipated profits on other contracts with the same customer unless all of these contracts are treated as a single construction contract. *[IAS 11.36-37]*.

3.3.7 *Contract inefficiencies*

IAS 2 – *Inventories* – explicitly excludes from the costs of inventories 'abnormal amounts of wasted materials, labour or other production costs'. *[IAS 2.16(a)]*. There is no such requirement in IAS 11 and this is reflected in a degree of uncertainty about how to account for inefficiencies and 'abnormal costs' incurred during the course of a construction contract. If such costs are simply added to the total contract costs, this may affect the stage of completion if contract activity is estimated based on the total costs that have been incurred (see 3.3.2 above).

It is clear in principle that abnormal costs and inefficiencies that relate solely to a particular period ought to be expensed in that period as they are not 'costs that relate directly to the specific contract'. *[IAS 11.16(a)]*. The issue is often a practical one of how to distinguish such costs from revisions of estimates that can more reasonably be treated as contract costs.

Usually inefficiencies that result from an observable event can be identified and expensed. If a major supplier collapses and the materials from another source are more expensive, this may be an inefficiency that ought to be expensed, as well as being one where the costs ought to be identifiable without undue difficulty. By contrast, an unexpected increase in costs of materials unrelated to such an event may be a revision to the estimate of costs. There are more marginal situations. A load of bricks may develop an off colour and not be suitable for their designated purpose. This is a natural, but intermittent defect that builders must face and here it is much less clear whether it is an inefficiency or change in estimate. In any particular case an assessment may have to be based on the significance to the project. It is relatively easy to distinguish cases at either extreme but much less so when the issues are marginal, where judgement will have to be exercised.

Note that this must be distinguished from cost increases that will result in the contract becoming loss-making, as these must be expensed immediately (see above).

3.3.8 Contracts that contain sales of assets and construction contracts

In some real estate markets an entity may enter into a contract to construct a building on land that the entity owns and then – after construction is complete – to deliver the entire property to a customer.

If the contract can be segmented into a construction contract and the sale of the land, the delivery of land follows the revenue recognition guidance of IAS 18 for sale of land. The construction of the building follows the revenue recognition guidance of IAS 11 or IAS 18 as appropriate, as it may be necessary to apply IFRIC 15's guidance to the construction of the building; see 1.2 above. The effect of this can be seen below:

Example 25.4: Segmented construction contract

On 1 January 2011, entity A entered into a contract to construct a building on a piece of land it has acquired and, when construction is complete, to deliver the entire property to a customer. A applies the percentage of completion method to account for contract revenues and expenses. The relative percentage of cost incurred is considered a reliable method for measuring the progress of the contract.

- Total cost of land: €2m
- Estimated total cost of construction: €8m
- Estimated total cost of contract: €10m
- Agreed sales price of the completed building: €11m

Construction has commenced and at the end of the reporting period (31 December 2011) total construction costs incurred amount to €2m.

Entity A considers that the amount of revenue in the contract attributable to the construction is €8.5m and the amount to the sale of land is €2.5m.

The percentage completion of the construction contract is 25% – calculated as €2m costs incurred as a proportion of the €8m estimated total cost of construction.

Accordingly, as at 31 December 2010 the following amounts are recorded:

Revenue	(€8.5m × 25%)	€2.13m
Contract expense	(Actual incurred on construction)	€2.00m
Gross amount due from customer	(Revenue of €2.13m)	€2.13m
Inventory	(Cost of the land)	€2.00m

The revenue and cost relating to the land will be recognised when the revenue recognition criteria of IAS 18 are met – this is often when legal title passes.

4   DISCLOSURE REQUIREMENTS OF IAS 11

IAS 11 has detailed and onerous disclosure requirements. The following disclosures must be given by entities in respect of construction contracts:

(a)   the amount of contract revenue recognised as revenue in the period;

(b)   the methods used to determine the contract revenue recognised in the period; and

(c)   the methods used to determine the stage of completion of contracts in progress. [IAS 11.39].

The standard includes in its Appendix an example of accounting policy disclosures, shown below.

Example 25.5:   Disclosure of accounting policies

Revenue from fixed price construction contracts is recognised on the percentage of completion method, measured by reference to the percentage of labour hours incurred to date to estimated total labour hours for each contract.

Revenue from cost plus contracts is recognised by reference to the recoverable costs incurred during the period plus the fee earned, measured by the proportion that costs incurred to date bear to the estimated total costs of the contract.

The following is the accounting policy of Thales, which also refers to the treatment of the related balances in the balance sheet.

Chapter 25

Extract 25.7: Thales (2010)
Notes to the Consolidated Financial Statements [extract]
Revenues [extract]
i)   Construction contracts

A construction contract is a contract specifically negotiated for the construction of an asset or of a group of assets, which are interrelated in terms of their design, technology, function, purpose or use.

According to its characteristics, a notified construction contract can either be accounted for separately, be segmented into several components which are each accounted for separately, or be combined with another construction contract in progress in order to form a single construction contract for accounting purposes in respect of which revenues and expenses will be recognised.

Revenues and expenses on construction contracts are recognised in accordance with the technical percentage of completion method. However, when there is no significant timing difference between technical percentage of completion and contractual dates of transfer of ownership, the percentage of completion is determined according to the contractual transfer of ownership.

Penalties for late payment or relating to improper performance of a contract are recognised as a deduction from revenues. In the balance sheet, provisions for penalties are deducted from assets related to the contract.

Expected losses on contracts are fully recognised as soon as they are identified.

Selling, administrative and interest expenses are directly charged to the profit and loss account in the financial year in which they are incurred.

Estimates of work remaining to be completed on loss-making contracts do not include revenues from claims made by the Group, except when it is highly probable that such claims will be accepted by the customer.

Progress payments received on construction contracts are deducted from contract assets as the contract is completed. Progress payments received before the corresponding work has been performed are classified in "advances received from customers on contracts" in balance sheet liabilities.

The cumulative amount of costs incurred and profit recognised, reduced by recognised losses and progress billings, is determined on a contract-by-contract basis. If this amount is positive it is classified as "construction contracts: assets" in balance sheet assets. If it is negative it is classified as "construction contracts: liabilities" in balance sheet liabilities.

EADS identifies different features by which its contract revenue is recognised, as is disclosed in Extract 25.4 above.

In the case of contracts in progress at the end of the reporting period, an entity should disclose each of the following:

(a)   the aggregate amount of costs incurred and recognised profits (less recognised losses) to date;

(b)   the amount of advances received; and

(c)   the amount of retentions. *[IAS 11.40]*.

Retentions, progress billings and advances are defined as follows:

'Retentions are amounts of progress billings which are not paid until the satisfaction of conditions specified in the contract for the payment of such amounts or until defects have been rectified. Progress billings are amounts billed for work performed on a contract whether or not they have been paid by the customer. Advances are amounts received by the contractor before the related work is performed.' *[IAS 11.41]*.

In addition, an entity should present:

(a)   the gross amount due from customers for contract work as an asset for all contracts in progress for which costs incurred plus recognised profits (less recognised losses) exceed progress billings (i.e. the net amount of costs incurred plus recognised profits, less the sum of recognised losses and progress billings); and

(b)   the gross amount due to customers for contract work as a liability for all contracts in progress for which progress billings exceed costs incurred plus recognised profits (i.e. the net amount of costs incurred plus recognised profits, less the sum of recognised losses and progress billings). *[IAS 11.42-44].*

The following example is based on the Appendix to IAS 11, and serves to illustrate the financial statement disclosure requirements of the standard as they apply to the various circumstances that might arise concerning construction contracts. It is followed by an example of the disclosures in practice from the financial statements of Thales.

Example 25.6:   Disclosure of numerical information regarding construction contracts

A contractor has reached the end of its first year of operations. All its contract costs incurred have been paid for in cash and all its progress billings and advances have been received in cash. Contract costs incurred for contracts B, C and E include the cost of materials that have been purchased for the contract but which have not been used in contract performance to date.

For contracts B, C and E, the customers have made advances to the contractor for work not yet performed.

The status of the entity's five contracts in progress at the end of year 1 is as follows:

Contract	A	B	C	D	E	Total
Contract revenue recognised in accordance with IAS 11.22 (see 3.3 above)	145	520	380	200	55	1,300
Contract expenses recognised in accordance with IAS 11.22 (see 3.3 above)	110	450	350	250	55	1,215
Expected losses recognised in accordance with IAS 11.36 (see 3.3.6 above)	–	–	–	40	30	70
Recognised profits less recognised losses	35	70	30	(90)	(30)	15
Contract costs incurred in the period	110	510	450	250	100	1,420
Contract costs incurred recognised as contract expenses in the period in accordance with IAS 11.22	110	450	350	250	55	1,215
Contract costs that relate to future activity recognised as an asset in accordance with IAS 11.27	–	60	100	–	45	205
Contract revenue	145	520	380	200	55	1,300
Progress billings (IAS 11.41: see above)	100	520	380	180	55	1,235
Unbilled contract revenue	45	–	–	20	–	65
Advances (IAS 11.41: see above)	–	80	20	–	25	125

The amounts to be disclosed in accordance with IAS 11 are as follows:

Contract revenue recognised as revenue in the period	1,300
Contract costs incurred and recognised profits (less recognised losses) to date	1,435
Advances received	125
Gross amount due from customers for contract work (presented as an asset)	220
Gross amount due to customers for contract work (presented as a liability)	(20)

These amounts are calculated as follows:

Contract	A	B	C	D	E	Total
Contract costs incurred	110	510	450	250	100	1,420
Recognised profits less recognised losses	35	70	30	(90)	(30)	15
	145	580	480	160	70	1,435
Progress billings	100	520	380	180	55	1,235
Due from customers	45	60	100	–	15	220
Due to customers	–	–	–	(20)	–	(20)

The amount disclosed in accordance with IAS 11.40(a) (the aggregate amount of costs incurred and recognised profits (less recognised losses) to date) is the same as the amount for the current period because the disclosures relate to the first year of operation.

Thales discloses its contracts in progress at the year end as follows:

Extract 25.8: Thales (2010)

Notes to the Consolidated Financial Statements [extract]

16.   Construction contracts [extract]

	31/12/10	31/12/09
Construction contracts: assets	**2,057.7**	2,243.2
Construction contracts: liabilities	**(1,365.7)**	(882.7)
Total	692.0	1,360.5
Work in progress on construction contracts	**1,097.5**	1,305.8
Unbilled receivables on construction contracts	**1,033.5**	1,080.4
Reserves for losses at completion	**(944.7)**	(614.1)
Other reserves on construction contracts	**(494.3)**	(411.6)
Total	**692.0**	1,360.5
Advances received from customers on construction contracts	**2,282.8**	2,708.3

References

1 *IFRIC Update*, May 2011, p.5.
2 *IFRIC Update*, February 2005, p.5.
3 FASB ASC 605-35-25-8.
4 *IFRIC Update*, June 2005, p.6.

Chapter 26   Leases

List of Examples

Chapter 26   Leases

1   INTRODUCTION

IAS 17 – *Accounting for Leases* – having been originally issued in September 1982, has been in place for many years. So have its equivalent standards around the world, SFAS 13 – *Accounting for Leases*, (1976) in the US and SSAP 21 – *Accounting for leases and hire purchase contracts*, (1984) in the UK. These standards, all dealing with accounting for leases, were the first to apply the concept of 'substance over form' and the first to incorporate the present value basis of measurement into the historical cost model. In prescribed circumstances they required companies to capitalise assets in their balance sheets, together with the corresponding obligations, irrespective of the fact that legal title to those assets vested in another party.

The substance over form approach is based on the view that a lease that transfers substantially all of the risks and rewards of ownership to the lessee should be accounted for as an acquisition of an asset and the assumption of an obligation by the lessee and as a sale by the lessor. Such leases are termed 'finance leases'. By contrast, operating leases are not capitalised in the lessee's balance sheet. Instead, operating lease rentals are charged to the profit and loss account of the lessee over the lease term, usually on a straight-line basis.

The IASB's requirements for lease accounting have remained essentially unchanged for more than twenty five years. Consequently, the accounting requirements are generally well understood and the distinction between finance and operating leases, and the related accounting consequences, are widely accepted internationally and applied in practice, even though much debate still takes place as to whether individual leases are financing or operating in nature. At the same time, though, conventional accounting in this area has been challenged. Lease accounting has always been a convergence project and the IASB and the FASB have developed proposals under which the finance/operating distinction will be removed and rights and obligations arising under lease contracts will, with few exceptions, be recognised in the balance sheets of lessees and many lessors. Although the IASB and FASB issued an Exposure Draft in August 2010, there have been so many revisions that it is to be re-exposed later in 2011. The original exposure draft and the Boards' redeliberations are discussed at 10 below.

2   WHAT IS A LEASE?

IAS 17 defines a lease as 'an agreement whereby the lessor conveys to the lessee in return for a payment or series of payments the right to use an asset for an agreed period of time.' *[IAS 17.4]*. The standard applies to agreements that transfer the right to use assets even though substantial services by the lessor may be called for in connection with the operation or maintenance of such assets. It does not apply to agreements that are contracts for services that do not transfer the right to use assets from one contracting party to the other. The definition of a lease includes contracts for the hire of an asset that contain a provision giving the hirer an option to acquire title to the asset when agreed conditions have been complied with (sometimes known as hire purchase contacts). *[IAS 17.6]*.

In recent years new types of arrangements have arisen that do not take the legal form of leases. They take many forms, but essentially combine rights to use assets, and possibly the provision of services or outputs, for agreed periods of time in return for a payment or series of payments. As it was uncertain whether IAS 17 applied to such arrangements, the issues have been considered by The Interpretations Committee and are dealt with in IFRIC 4 – *Determining whether an Arrangement contains a Lease* – which is considered further in 2.1 below. Some of the arrangements under service concession arrangements give rise to further accounting issues that have been separately addressed by the Interpretations Committee; service concessions have been ruled out of scope of lease accounting and are discussed in Chapter 28.

The SIC had previously considered whether all transactions in the legal form of a lease should be considered under IAS 17. The results of these deliberations, SIC-27 – *Evaluating the Substance of Transactions Involving the Legal Form of a Lease,* are covered in 2.2 below.

2.1   Determining whether an arrangement contains a lease

IFRIC 4 notes that arrangements have been developed in recent years that do not take the legal form of a lease but that nevertheless convey rights to use items for agreed periods of time in return for a payment or series of payments. *[IFRIC 4.1]*. The Interpretation not only addresses this type of arrangement but also some more traditional forms of arrangement that are also within its scope.

The Interpretation focuses on the accounting implications of the following, in all of which an entity (the supplier) conveys a right to use an asset to another entity (the purchaser), together with related services or outputs:

- outsourcing arrangements, including outsourcing of the data processing functions of an entity;
- arrangements in the telecommunications industry, where suppliers of network capacity enter into contracts to provide purchasers with rights to capacity; and
- take-or-pay and similar contracts, in which purchasers must make specified payments regardless of whether they take delivery of the contracted products or services (e.g. where purchasers are committed to acquiring substantially all of the output of a supplier's power generator). *[IFRIC 4.1]*.

The Interpretations Committee concluded that an arrangement of one of these types could be within the scope of IAS 17 if it met the definition of a lease, e.g. if it conveyed to the lessee the right to use an asset for an agreed period of time in return for a payment or series of payments. *[IFRIC 4.BC2].* IAS 17 applies to the lease element of the arrangement notwithstanding the related services or outputs because IAS 17 applies to 'agreements that transfer the right to use assets even though substantial services by the lessor may be called for in connection with the operation or maintenance of such assets.' *[IAS 17.3].* This is regardless of the fact that the arrangement is not described as a lease and is likely to grant rights that are significantly different from those in a formal lease agreement. The Interpretations Committee therefore concluded that it should provide guidance to assist in determining whether an arrangement is, or contains, a lease. *[IFRIC 4.BC2].*

An example of an entity that applied IFRIC 4 and as a result identified an arrangement within scope of IAS 17 was Gaz de France, now GDF Suez, which, in its 2006 financial statements, identified a finance lease with the Group as lessor, as shown in the following extract.

Extract 26.1: Gaz de France (2006)

FINANCIAL INFORMATION FOR THE YEAR ENDED DECEMBER 31, 2006 [extract]
NOTES TO THE CONSOLIDATED FINANCIAL STATEMENTS [extract]
B –   **Comparability between financial years** [extract]
2 –   **Changes in accounting policies and presentation** [extract]
2.1.2   **IFRIC 4 –Determining whether an Arrangement Contains a Lease** [extract]

This interpretation deals with the method of identifying and recognizing service, purchase and sale contracts that do not take the legal form of a lease but convey a right to use an asset in return for a payment or series of payments. The lease element may constitute an operating lease or a finance lease. If a contract is assessed as containing a finance lease where the Group is lessor, a finance receivable should be recorded to reflect the financing provided to the customer.

IFRIC 4 applies to one of Gaz de France's contracts with an industrial customer, which provides for the operation by the Group of dedicated assets.

Application of IFRIC 4 led to the reclassification from "Property, plant and equipment" to "Other non-current assets" (long-term receivables) of 196 million euros at December 31, 2006, 233 million euros at December 31, 2005 and 200 million euros at December 31, 2004. The impact on equity and profit was not material.

IFRIC 4 has the objective only of dealing with the practical issues that arise when applying IAS 17 to arrangements that are not leases in form: how to identify an arrangement that is in substance a lease, when to make the assessment and how to measure the lease element. *[IFRIC 4.5].* The Interpretation does not provide any guidance for determining lease classification under IAS 17 *[IFRIC 4.2]* (in other words, it could be a finance lease or an operating lease under IAS 17), nor does it expect the guidance to extend the scope of that standard. If an arrangement turns out to contain a lease or licence of a type excluded from the scope of IAS 17 (see 3.1.1 below), the Interpretation does not apply. Service concession arrangements to which IFRIC 12 – *Service Concession Arrangements* – applies are also out of scope (see Chapter 28). *[IFRIC 4.4].*

Chapter 26

2.1.1   *Identification of an asset*

The first condition that must be met to determine whether an arrangement is, or contains a lease is that fulfilment of the arrangement depends on a specific asset or assets. *[IFRIC 4.6].*

IAS 17 applies only to an arrangement in which there is a 'right to use an asset', so an arrangement will not contain a lease unless it depends on a specific asset or assets. It provides the following additional guidance.

A specific asset that is explicitly identified by the arrangement will not be the subject of a lease if the arrangement is not dependent on the asset. If the seller is required under the arrangement to deliver a specified quantity of goods or services and has the right or ability to provide those goods using other assets not specified in the agreement, the arrangement will not contain a lease. *[IFRIC 4.7].*

However, an arrangement may still contain a lease if a specific asset is not explicitly identified but it would not be economically feasible or practical for the supplier to provide the use of alternative items. For example, the supplier may only own one suitable asset. *[IFRIC 4.8].*

Some arrangements may allow the supplier to replace the specified asset with a similar asset if the original asset is unavailable (e.g. because it is unexpectedly inoperable). The Interpretations Committee takes the view as that such a requirement is in effect a warranty obligation it does not preclude lease treatment. *[IFRIC 4.7].*

To take a relatively simple example, an arrangement in which an entity (the purchaser) outsources its product delivery department to another organisation (the supplier) will not contain a lease if the supplier is obliged to make available a certain number of delivery vehicles of a certain standard specification and the supplier is a delivery organisation with many other vehicles available. However, if the supplier has to supply and maintain a specified number of specialist vehicles in the purchaser's livery, then this arrangement is more likely to contain a lease. The latter arrangement may be commercially more akin to outsourcing the purchaser's acquisitions of delivery vehicles rather than its delivery functions. Similar issues would have to be taken into account if data processing functions are outsourced as these may require substantial investment by the supplier in computer hardware dedicated to the use of a single customer.

It is important to note that where the above examples are likely to contain leases (delivery vehicles in livery, dedicated hardware), the purchaser cannot be unaware that there are specific assets underlying the service. There would have been negotiations between supplier and purchaser that would probably be reflected in the contract documentation. By contrast, if the purchaser does not know what assets are used to provide the service (beyond the fact that they are trucks and computers, of course), and in the circumstances it is reasonable not to know, it is plausible that there is no underlying lease in the arrangement. This remains true even if the supplier has dedicated specific assets to the service being provided and expects their cost to be recouped during the course of the contractual relationship.

2.1.2   *Parts of assets and the unit of account*

IFRIC 4 notes that some arrangements transfer the right to use an asset that is a component of a larger asset but the issue of whether and when such rights should be accounted for as leases is not dealt with in the Interpretation. It states merely that 'arrangements in which the underlying asset would represent a unit of account in either IAS 16 or IAS 38' are within the scope of the Interpretation. *[IFRIC 4.3]*. 'Unit of account' presumably means an asset whose cost, replacement, impairment and depreciation are separately accounted for under one of these standards (see Chapters 19 and 20). However, the opposite is not necessarily the case. It does not mean that a component of one of these assets cannot be the underlying asset.

There are many arrangements in practice that demonstrate this issue. For example, a plant may contain more than one production unit or line that might be regarded as a single 'component' (because each makes the same product) or alternatively each of its units or lines might be regarded as separate 'components'. Depending on other aspects of the arrangement, a particular production line may be the asset that is the subject of a lease, if the supplier cannot transfer production to a different line to supply the goods. Similar examples from the telecommunications industry include communication satellites that contain dozens of identical transponders or fibre optical cables that contain many hundreds of fibres. Arrangements may vary from those that allow use of the whole cable, through those that specify a certain number of fibres (where the purchaser is restricted to those fibres) to the most common arrangements which are essentially for capacity and the operator is enabled to use any part of the whole cable to provide the service. As a result, arrangements have to be examined carefully to see if they do specify an asset. The Interpretation does not attempt to address whether there is any conceptual difference between, say, using a quarter of the capacity of a whole pipeline and all of the capacity of a pipeline a quarter of the size. Generally, a capacity portion of a larger asset that is not physically distinct is not considered to be a specified asset.

2.1.3   *The arrangement conveys a right to use the item*

In order to contain a lease, the arrangement must convey a right to use the asset. *[IFRIC 4.6]*. An arrangement does not convey the right to use an asset unless the purchaser has the right to control the use of the underlying item, which depends on any one of the following conditions being met: *[IFRIC 4.9]*

(a)   The purchaser has the ability or right to operate the asset or direct others to operate the asset in a manner it determines while obtaining or controlling more than an insignificant amount of the output or other utility of the asset;

(b)   The purchaser has the ability or right to control physical access to the underlying asset while obtaining or controlling more than an insignificant amount of the output or other utility of the asset; or

(c)   Facts and circumstances indicate:

    (i)   it is remote that one or more parties other than the purchaser will take more than an insignificant amount of the output or other utility that will be produced or generated by the asset during the term of the arrangement: and

    (ii)   the price that the purchaser will pay for the output is neither contractually fixed per unit of output; nor equal to the current market price per unit of output as of the time of delivery of the output.

Therefore, control of the asset may be obtained in circumstances in which an entity obtains 'more than an insignificant amount of the output' but *only* if it has the ability or right to operate (or direct others to operate) in a manner that it determines or can control physical access to the asset.

By contrast, a purchaser that pays market price at the date of transfer will not control the asset just because it takes almost all of the output. It would also have to be demonstrated that it controlled the asset by virtue of (a) or (b) above. The same applies if the price is contractually fixed, typically the case in take-or-pay contracts. Just because the price is fixed, it does not necessarily follow that the arrangement contains a lease. Control of the underlying asset must be demonstrated under (a) or (b).

When the arrangement involves a single purchaser in taking substantially all of the output from a specific asset other than at market price and the price varies other than in response to market price changes, the variability ('off-market' nature) is regarded by IFRIC 4 as indicating that payment is being made for the right to use the asset rather than for the actual use of or output from the asset.

The effects of this are demonstrated by the following examples.

The following examples of arrangements that may or may not contain a lease explain the identification of an asset and the application of the control criteria described above. Example 26.1 is based on an illustrative example in IFRIC 4. *[IFRIC 4.IE3-4].*

Example 26.1:   An arrangement that contains a lease

A production company (the purchaser) enters into an arrangement with a third party (the supplier) to supply a minimum quantity of gas needed in its production process for a specified period of time. The supplier designs and builds a facility near to the purchaser's plant to produce the needed gas and maintains ownership and control over all significant aspects of operating the facility. The agreement provides for the following:

- The facility is explicitly identified in the arrangement, and the supplier has the contractual right to supply gas from other sources. However, supplying gas from other sources is not economically feasible or practicable;

- The supplier has the right to provide gas to other customers and to remove and replace the facility's equipment and modify or expand the facility to enable the supplier to do so. However, at inception of the arrangement, the supplier has no plans to modify or expand the facility. The facility is designed to meet only the purchaser's needs;

- The supplier is responsible for repairs, maintenance and capital expenditures;

- The supplier must stand ready to deliver a minimum quantity of gas each month;

- On a monthly basis, the purchaser will pay a fixed capacity charge and a variable charge based on actual production taken. The purchaser must pay the fixed capacity charge irrespective of whether it takes any of the facility's production. The variable charge includes the facility's actual energy costs, which comprise approximately 90 per cent of the facility's total variable costs. The supplier is subject to increased costs resulting from the facility's inefficient operations;
- If the facility does not produce the stated minimum quantity, the supplier must return all or a portion of the fixed capacity charge.

The arrangement contains a lease within the scope of IAS 17. An asset (the facility) is explicitly identified in the arrangement and fulfilment of the arrangement is dependent on the facility. While the supplier has the right to supply gas from other sources, its ability to do so is not substantive. The purchaser has obtained the right to use the facility because, on the facts presented – in particular, that the facility is designed to meet only the purchaser's needs and the supplier has no plans to expand or modify the facility – it is remote that one or more parties other than the purchaser will take more than an insignificant amount of the facility's output and the price the purchaser will pay is neither contractually fixed per unit of output nor equal to the current market price per unit of output as of the time of delivery of the output.

Having concluded that the arrangement contains a lease, it is then necessary to classify it as an operating or a finance lease. Identifying the relevant lease payments is dealt with below.

The next two examples illustrate arrangements that do not contain a lease. The first, Example 26.2, illustrates two of the concepts in IFRIC 4. The first describes circumstances in which an arrangement does not contain a lease because no specific asset has been identified. The significance of the control concept is shown in the second example based on the second illustrative example in IFRIC 4. *[IFRIC 4.IE4-5].*

Example 26.2:   *Arrangements that do not contain leases*

(a)   Take-or-pay contract that does not depend on a specific asset

A purchaser enters into a take-or-pay contract to buy industrial gases from a supplier. The supplier is a large company operating similar plants at various locations. The amount of gas that the purchaser is committed to buy is roughly equivalent to the total output of one of the plants. Because a good distribution network is available, the supplier is able to provide gas from various locations to fulfil its supply obligation.

In this example, the arrangement does not depend upon a specific asset. This is because it is economically feasible and practical for the supplier to fulfil the arrangement by providing use of more than one plant. A specific asset has therefore not been identified either explicitly or implicitly.

Payments under the contract may be unavoidable (because it is a take-or-pay arrangement) and the purchaser may in fact take all of the output of a single plant but the arrangement does not convey a right to use the asset. The purchaser does not have the right to control the use of the underlying asset. It does not have the ability or right to operate the asset in a manner it determines (or to direct others to do so on its behalf), and it does not control physical access. The arrangement does not contain a lease.

(b)   The right to control the use of an underlying asset is not conveyed

A manufacturing company (the purchaser) enters into an arrangement with a third party (the supplier) to supply a specific component part of its manufactured product for a specified period of time. The supplier designs and constructs a plant next to the purchaser's factory to produce the component part. The designed capacity of the plant exceeds the purchaser's current needs, and the supplier maintains ownership and control over all significant aspects of operating the plant.

The supplier's plant is explicitly identified in the arrangement, but the supplier has the right to fulfil the arrangement by shipping the component parts from another plant owned by the supplier. However, to do so for any extended period of time would be uneconomical. The supplier must stand ready to deliver a minimum quantity. The purchaser is required to pay a fixed price per unit for the actual quantity taken. Even if the purchaser's needs are such that they do not need the stated minimum quantity, they still pay only for the actual quantity taken.

The supplier has the right to sell the component parts to other customers and has a history of doing so (by selling in the replacement parts market) so it is expected that parties other than the purchaser will take more than an insignificant amount of the component parts produced at the supplier's plant.

The supplier is responsible for repairs, maintenance, and capital expenditures of the plant.

This arrangement does not contain a lease. An asset (the plant) is explicitly identified in the arrangement and fulfilment of the arrangement is dependent on the facility. While the supplier has the right to supply component parts from other sources, the supplier would not have the ability to do so because it would be uneconomical. However, the purchaser has not obtained the right to use the plant because it does not control it, for the following reasons:

(a) the purchaser does not have the ability or right to operate or direct others to operate the plant or control physical access to the plant; and

(b) the likelihood that parties other than the purchaser will take more than an insignificant amount of the component parts produced at the plant is more than remote, based on the facts presented.

(c) the price paid by the purchaser is fixed per unit of output taken is also mentioned in IFRIC 4 as a consideration.

2.1.4   Fixed or current market prices and control of the asset

The third control condition noted above states that an arrangement will not contain a lease notwithstanding that a purchaser takes all but an insignificant amount of the output or other utility if the price is contractually fixed per unit of output. We consider that by this the Interpretation means absolutely fixed, with no variance per unit based on underlying costs or volumes, whether discounts or stepped pricing.

In the manufacturing industry 'lifetime' agreements with step pricing between the supplier and the purchaser are not uncommon. The parties to the agreement agree in advance on progressive unit price reductions on achievement of specified production volume levels, reflecting the supplier's increasing efficiencies and economies of scale. These types of contracts should be closely analysed, especially to see whether one of the other two conditions, the 'right to operate the asset' or the 'right to control the physical access to the asset', is also met before concluding that the arrangement contains a lease.

'Current market price per unit of output' means that the cost is solely a market price for the output of the asset without any other pricing factors. A 'market price per KWH plus x per cent change in the price of natural gas' would not be the current market price per unit of the output of the asset. Price increases based on a general index such as a retail and prices index are unlikely to result in a current market price for the output in question.

Example 26.3:   Fixed prices per unit

Purchaser P and supplier S enter in a parts supply agreement for the lifetime of the finished product concerned. S uses tooling equipment that is specific to the needs of P. The tooling is explicitly identified in the agreement and S could not use an alternative asset. The estimated capacity of the tooling equipment is 500,000 units which corresponds to the total production of the finished product units over its life cycle. P takes substantially all of the output produced by S using the specific tooling.

Purchaser P and supplier S agree upon the following unit price reductions in the parts supply agreement to reflect S's increasing efficiencies and economies of scale:

- from 0 to 100,000 units, price per each unit €150;
- from 100,001 to 200,000, price per each unit €140;
- from 200,001 to 300,000, price per each unit €135;
- from 300,001 to 400,000, price per each unit €132;
- above 400,000 price per each unit €130.

The fulfilment of the arrangement depends on the use of a specific asset, the tooling. P has obtained the right to use the tooling because, on the facts presented, the likelihood is remote that one or more parties other than the P will take more than an insignificant amount of the tooling's output. As the estimated capacity of the tooling equipment corresponds to the total production of the finished product units produced by P, P takes substantially all of the output produced using that tooling.

However, stepped pricing does not mean price 'fixed per unit of output' and, particularly as the stepped pricing is agreed in advance, it is not equal to the current market price per unit as of the time of delivery of the output. The arrangement contains a lease within the scope of IAS 17.

2.1.5 When to assess the arrangements

IFRIC 4 states that assessing whether an arrangement contains a lease should be made at the inception of the arrangement, which is the earlier of the date of the arrangement and the date of commitment by the parties to the principal terms of the arrangement, on the basis of all the facts and circumstances. A reassessment of whether the arrangement contains a lease should be made only if: *[IFRIC 4.10]*

(a) there is a change in the terms of the contract, except for a renewal or extension of the arrangement;

(b) a renewal option is exercised or an extension is agreed, unless these had been taken into account in the original assessment of the lease term in accordance with IAS 17; *[IAS 17.4]*

(c) there is a change in whether or not the arrangement depends on specified item; or

(d) there is a substantial physical change to the specified assets.

Changes to estimates, for example of the amount of output that would be taken by the purchaser, would not trigger a reassessment. *[IFRIC 4.11]*.

If the arrangement is reassessed and found to contain a lease or vice versa then lease accounting will be applied or discontinued as from the time that the arrangement is reassessed, or renewal option exercised when this was not previously anticipated, as described in (b) above. *[IFRIC 4.11]*.

2.1.6 Separation of leases from other payments within the arrangement

If an arrangement contains a lease, both parties to the arrangement are to apply IAS 17 to the lease element of the arrangement unless it is an arrangement that is not within IAS 17's scope. Other elements of the arrangement must be accounted for in accordance with the appropriate standards. *[IFRIC 4.12]*.

It must be stressed that this means that the lease element of the arrangement may be classified as an operating or finance lease. Therefore, having identified the lease payments, the entity may still classify the arrangement as an operating lease if it does

Chapter 26

not transfer substantially all the risks and rewards incidental to ownership of an asset (see 3.2 below). *[IAS 17.4, 8].*

In order to apply IAS 17, the payments and other consideration under the arrangement must be separated at inception or on reassessment between those for the lease of the asset (that will meet the definition of minimum lease payments, see 3.4.3) and those for other services and outputs. IFRIC 4 requires this to be done on the basis of their relative fair values. *[IFRIC 4.13].* This may require the purchaser to use estimation techniques – this appears to be somewhat of an understatement as, unless the price to be paid for both elements is clear and they have both been negotiated at market value, it will always be necessary to use some form of estimation. The Interpretation suggests that it may be possible to estimate either the lease payments (by comparison with similar leases that do not contain other elements) or the other elements (using comparable arrangements) and then deduct the estimated amount from the total under the arrangement. *[IFRIC 4.14].*

This is not a straightforward exercise and the Interpretation does not go into any further detail as to how it would be carried out. There may be no market-based evidence of fair value of the underlying assets because of their specialised nature or because they are rarely sold, in which case it will be necessary to use valuation techniques. Discounted cash flow projections based on estimated future cash flows that will be generated by specialised assets may be difficult to obtain, although it should be possible to make some form of estimate, if need be with the assistance of valuation experts. The service elements within these agreements are by no means standardised and it may not be easy to identify comparable arrangements. The exercise will be complicated by the fact that the fair value of a bundle of services is not necessarily the same as the aggregation of their individual fair values and making such an assumption could lead to an overstatement of the service element and consequent understatement of the fair value of the lease element or *vice versa*. The discount rates should reflect current market assessments of the uncertainty and timing of the cash flows, i.e. the risk inherent in the separate elements of the transaction. There are usually very different risk profiles for the provision of services and for leasing assets. If, as suggested by the Interpretation, the entity estimates one of the elements under the arrangement and derives the other by deduction, it will always be necessary to carry out a 'sense check' on the derived payments.

IFRIC 4 suggests also that only in rare cases will a purchaser conclude that it is impracticable to separate the payments reliably. In the case of a finance lease, the entity should recognise an asset at an amount equal to the fair value of the underlying asset that it has identified as the subject of the lease, as described in 2.1.1 above. A liability should be set up at the same amount as the asset. The entity would impute a finance charge based on the purchaser's incremental borrowing rate of interest and, from this, compute the reduction in the liability as payments are made. *[IFRIC 4.15].* Presumably the Interpretations Committee considers that the entity's incremental borrowing rate would have to be used because, if it were possible to determine the interest rate implicit in the lease, the arrangement would not be one in which it was impracticable to separate the payments reliably.

What this means, of course, is that an entity may be required to account for an asset held under a finance lease when it is, in fact, unable to identify the lease payments. It is to be hoped that the application of the control model means that this will not often happen in practice as control is more likely to result in an entity being able to identify the underlying payment streams.

If the lease is assessed as an operating lease, applying the Interpretation might affect the recognition of revenue over the term of the arrangement. IAS 17 requires lessors and lessees to recognise operating lease payments on a straight-line basis over the lease term (unless another systematic basis is more representative) and this may not be in line with the payments for the lease element so some adjustments might be required. *[IFRIC 4.BC39].*

There are disclosure implications if the arrangement is deemed to contain an operating lease and the purchaser concludes that it is impracticable to separate the payments reliably. These are discussed further below.

2.1.7 Disclosure requirements

IAS 17 required a general description of the lessee's material leasing arrangements, *[IAS 17.31(e)],* which will require disclosure of the details of major transactions that have fallen within IFRIC 4.

There are no specific disclosure requirements if the arrangements are assessed as containing finance leases as these arrangements are deemed to be within the scope of IAS 17 and therefore within its disclosure requirements.

However, if it were considered to be an operating lease, the Interpretation may result in additional disclosures, because IAS 17 specifies that the lessor and lessee should disclose the future minimum lease payments. Although the arrangements discussed in the Interpretation typically represent significant future commitments, purchasers are not required to disclose them in the financial statements unless they fall within IAS 17. The Interpretations Committee argues that bringing such arrangements within the scope of IAS 17 will provide users of financial statements with relevant information that is useful for assessing the purchaser's solvency, liquidity and adaptability. *[IFRIC 4.BC39].*

As long as the entity is able to distinguish the lease payments from other elements of the lease, then the disclosed information will relate only to the lease element of the arrangement. There appears to be no intention to require entities to disclose the service (executory) element of arrangements; The Interpretations Committee agreed that it would consider addressing the disclosure of executory contracts more generally in a separate project. *[IFRIC 4.BC39].* However, if the arrangement is one of those in which it is impracticable to separate the payments reliably, the Interpretation requires disclosure of all payments under the arrangement separately from other minimum lease payments, together with a statement that the disclosed payments also include payments for non-lease elements in the arrangement. *[IFRIC 4.15].*

2.2   Transactions that are not, in substance, leases

While there are some arrangements that contain leases that are not formally lease contracts, the reverse is also true: there are some 'lease agreements' that are not, in substance leases. These issues are addressed by SIC-27.

Essentially, SIC-27 deals with the issue of how to evaluate the substance of transactions, or a series of linked transactions, in the legal form of a lease. The main purpose of the Interpretation is to reinforce the principle of substance over form, and to ensure that, where appropriate, a series of linked transactions should be accounted for as one transaction. If the transaction does not meet the definition of a lease under IAS 17, SIC-27 deals with the extent to which the arrangement gives rise to other assets and liabilities of the reporting entity, the reporting of any other obligations and the recognition of fee income. *[SIC-27.2]*.

An entity may enter into a transaction or a series of structured transactions (an arrangement) with an unrelated party or parties (an investor) that involves the legal form of a lease. Although the details may vary considerably, a typical example involves an entity leasing or selling assets to an investor and leasing the same assets back. The lease and leaseback transactions are often entered into so that the investor may achieve a tax advantage. *[SIC-27.1]*. The following example illustrates an arrangement that does not, in substance, involve a lease under IAS 17:

Example 26.4:   Substance of an arrangement

An entity (Company A) leases a specialised asset that it requires to conduct its business to an Investor and leases the same asset back for a shorter period of time under a sublease. At the end of the sublease period, Company A has the right to buy back the rights of the Investor under a purchase option. If Company A does not exercise its purchase option, the Investor has options available to it under each of which it receives a minimum return on its investment in the headlease – the Investor may put the underlying asset back to Company A, or require it to provide a return on the Investor's investment in the headlease.

The arrangement achieves a tax advantage for the Investor who pays a fee to Company A and prepays the lease payment obligations under the headlease. The agreement requires the amount prepaid to be invested in risk-free assets and, as a requirement of finalising the execution of the legally binding arrangement, placed into a separate investment account held by a Trustee outside of the control of the entity.

Over the term of the sublease, the sublease payment obligations are satisfied with funds of an equal amount withdrawn from the separate investment account. Company A guarantees the sublease payment obligations, and will be required to satisfy the guarantee should the separate investment account have insufficient funds. Company A, but not the Investor, has the right to terminate the sublease early under certain circumstances (e.g. a change in local or international tax law causes the Investor to lose part or all of the tax benefits, or Company A decides to dispose of (e.g. replace, sell or deplete) the underlying asset) and upon payment of a termination value to the Investor. If Company A chooses early termination, then it would pay the termination value from funds withdrawn from the separate investment account, and if the amount remaining in the separate investment account is insufficient, the difference would be paid by Company A. *[SIC-27 Appendix A]*.

SIC-27 argues that a series of transactions that involve the legal form of a lease should be accounted for as one transaction when the overall economic effect cannot be understood without reference to the series of transactions as a whole. All aspects and implications of an arrangement should be evaluated to determine the substance of the arrangement, with greater weight given to those aspects and implications that will have an economic effect in practice. The accounting should reflect the substance of the arrangement. *[SIC-27.3-4]*.

First, it must be part of a single 'arrangement'; a series of transactions may be closely interrelated, negotiated as a single transaction, and take place concurrently or in a continuous sequence. *[SIC-27.3]*.

Second, there must be indicators that individually demonstrate that an arrangement may not, in substance, involve a lease under IAS 17. SIC-27 states that in the example above, these indicators are as follows:

(a)   the entity retains all the risks and rewards of ownership and there is no significant change in its rights to use the asset;

(b)   the primary reason for the arrangement is to achieve a particular tax result, and not to convey the right to use an asset; and

(c)   the options on which the arrangement depends are included on terms that make their exercise almost certain (e.g. a put option that is exercisable at a price sufficiently higher than the expected fair value when it becomes exercisable). *[SIC-27.5]*.

In other words, the entity retains more rights than it would in a straightforward sale and finance leaseback. In the example, for instance, it retains all of the residual interests in the asset. The investor has no interest at all in the underlying asset while a lessor under a finance lease will often retain title and some residual value in the asset. The investor has only entered into the transaction to obtain a tax benefit.

Third, the balances arising under the arrangement (in the example these comprise the separate investment account and the lease payment obligations under the sublease) must be assessed to see whether they represent assets and liabilities of the entity. SIC-27 refers to definitions of assets and liabilities and guidance in paragraphs 4.4 to 4.19 of the *Conceptual Framework for Financial Reporting ('Framework')*. It argues that:

(a)   the investment account is not an asset of the entity because it cannot control it;

(b)   there is only a remote risk that the entity will have to pay out under the guarantee or reimburse the entire amount of any fee received; and

(c)   once the arrangement has been set up and the initial payments have been made, no further cash flows will be made by Company A.

Company A cannot use the cash in the investment account for its own benefit, nor can it prevent it being used to make lease payments to the investor. The lease payments will be satisfied solely from funds withdrawn from the separate investment account established with the initial cash flows. In the example, the terms of the arrangement require that a prepaid amount is invested in risk-free assets that are expected to generate sufficient cash flows to satisfy the lease payment obligations. *[SIC-27.6]*. This also demonstrates, *inter alia*, that Company A is not, in substance, entering into a financing arrangement, as it has no need of the funds.

However, other obligations of the entity, including any guarantees provided and obligations incurred upon early termination, should be accounted for under IFRS 4 – *Insurance Contracts*, IAS 37 – *Provisions, Contingent Liabilities and Contingent*

Assets – or IAS 39 – *Financial Instruments: Recognition and Measurement* – depending on the terms of the arrangement. *[SIC-27.7]*. Therefore, if Company A were to elect to terminate the arrangement, it would have to provide for its exposure in excess of the available funds in the investment account.

Fourth, SIC-27 addresses the recognition of fee income. There are many factors that could affect the economic substance and nature of the fee and it may not be appropriate to recognise it in its entirety at the inception of the agreement if the entity has significant future performance obligations, retained risks or a significant risk of repayment. Factors to be taken into account include:

(a)   obligations that are conditions of earning the fee so that entering into the agreement is not the most significant act required by the arrangement;

(b)   limitations are put on the use of the underlying asset that lead to significant changes in the entity's rights to use the asset, e.g. the entity's right to deplete or sell it or pledge it as collateral;

(c)   the possibility of reimbursing any amount of the fee and possibly paying some additional amount is not remote. This occurs when, for example:

  (i)   the underlying asset is essential for the entity's business, in which case there is a possibility that the entity may be prepared to pay to terminate the arrangement early (and thereby be required to repay all or part of the fee); or

  (ii)   the possibility that there are insufficient assets in the investment account to meet the lease payment obligations is not remote, and therefore it is possible that the entity may be required to pay some additional amount. This may occur if the entity is required, or has some or total discretion, to invest in assets carrying more than an insignificant amount of risk (e.g. currency, interest rate or credit risk). *[SIC-27.8]*.

Finally there are some specific presentation and disclosure requirements. The fee must be presented in the income statement based on its economic substance and nature. *[SIC-27.9]*. The entity must disclose the following in each period that an arrangement exists:

An entity has to make the disclosures that are necessary to understand the arrangement and the accounting treatment adopted, including the following:

(a)   a description of the arrangement including:

  (i)   the underlying asset and any restrictions on its use;

  (ii)   the life and other significant terms of the arrangement;

  (iii) the transactions that are linked together, including any options; and

(b)   the accounting treatment of any fee received, the amount that has been recognised as income in the period, and the line item of the income statement in which it is included.

These disclosures should be provided individually for each arrangement or in aggregate for each class of arrangement. A class is a grouping of arrangements with underlying assets of a similar nature. *[SIC-27.10, 11]*. The following extract illustrates the disclosures.

Extract 26.2: Swisscom AG (2007)

Notes to the Consolidated Financial Statements [extract]
25   Financial liabilities [extract]
Financial liabilities from cross-border tax lease arrangements

Between 1996 and 2002, Swisscom entered into cross-border tax lease arrangements, under the terms of which parties of its fixed and mobile networks were to be sold or leased long-term to US Trusts and leased back with terms of up to 99 years. Swisscom has an early buyout option on these assets after a contractually agreed period.

The financial liabilities are based on lease and leaseback transactions from the years 1999, 2000, and 2002. The sale and leaseback from the year 1997 are presented as finance lease obligations.

Swisscom defeased a major part of the lease obligations through highly rated financial assets and payment undertaking agreements. The financial assets were irrevocably placed with trusts. The payment undertaking agreements were signed with financial institutions with a high credit standing. In accordance with Interpretation SIC-27 "Evaluating the substance of transactions involving the legal form of a lease", these financial assets or payment undertaking agreements and the liabilities in the same amount are offset and not presented in the balance sheet. One of the transactions entered into in 2000 does not meet the conditions of SIC-27 and is consequently reported in the balance sheet as a long-term financial asset and the corresponding lease obligation presented as a long-term financial liability.

As of December 31, 2007, the financial assets and liabilities resulting from these transactions including interest totalled USD 4,124 million (CHF 4,679 million) and USD 3,751 million (CHF 4,250 million), respectively. Of this amount USD 2,990 million (CHF 3,387 million) are not reported in the balance sheet in accordance with SIC-27. Of the liabilities reported in the amount of CHF 1,177 million (previous year CHF 1,459 million), CHF 862 million (previous year: CHF 1,125 million) are covered by financial assets.

The gains from the transactions were recorded as financial income in the period the transactions were closed.

Swisscom is exposed to market-related risks in connection with cross-border lease agreements. One particular risk lies in the credit standing of the counterparties in which investments were made. Swisscom must fulfill the agreed rating requirements for financial assets with a nominal value of USD 559 million (CHF 634 million) including interest incurred up to December 31, 2007. All the rating requirements are fulfilled. It is possible that the contractual rating requirements will no longer be fulfilled until the agreements expire. In such case the financial assets are to be replaced by assets with the required minimum rating. Swisscom would then incur costs amounting to the difference between the market value of the existing and the new financial assets.

Other market risks in connection with cross-border lease agreements are interest rate and foreign exchange risks, although most of these risks have been hedged through interest rate and currency swaps.

Future minimum lease payments resulting from cross-border lease arrangements are due as follows:

CHF in millions	31.12.2007	31.12.2006
Within 1 year	106	303
Within 1 to 2 years	16	116
Within 2 to 3 years	118	18
Within 3 to 4 years	107	129
Within 4 to 5 years	59	117
After 5 years	2,608	2,920
Total minimum lease payments	**3,014**	**3,603**
Less future finance costs	(1,841)	(2,234)
Total present value of financial liabilities from cross-border lease agreements	**1,173**	**1,369**
Fair value adjustments	4	2
Accrued interest	–	88
Total financial liabilities from cross-border lease agreements	**1,177**	**1,459**
Less current portion	(18)	–
Total non-current financial liabilities from cross-border lease agreements	**1,159**	**1,459**

Chapter 26

3   SCOPE AND DEFINITIONS OF IAS 17

3.1   Scope of IAS 17

The standard applies in accounting for all leases other than:

- lease agreements to explore for or use minerals, oil, natural gas and similar non-regenerative resources; and
- licensing agreements for such items as motion picture films, video recordings, plays, manuscripts, patents and copyrights.

Furthermore, the standard should not be applied to the measurement by:

- lessees of investment property held under finance leases;
- lessors of investment property leased out under operating leases, as in these cases IAS 40 – *Investment Property* – applies; (see Chapter 21);
- lessees of biological assets held under finance leases; or
- lessors of biological assets leased out under operating leases, as in these cases IAS 41 – *Agriculture* – applies (see Chapter 40). *[IAS 17.2]*.

3.1.1   Leases and licences – IAS 17 and arrangements over intangible assets

IAS 17 does not define a licensing agreement so the distinction between 'leases' and 'licensing agreements' is not clear. This is not helped by the fact that the agreements may be economically similar. Further, while the examples of licensing agreements excluded from the scope of IAS 17 (motion picture films, video recordings, plays, manuscripts, patents and copyrights) are specific intangible assets, IAS 17 does not exclude leases of intangible assets from its scope. IAS 38 – *Intangible Assets* – by contrast, excludes from its scope 'lease agreements', stating 'this standard shall be applied in accounting for intangible assets, except intangible assets that are within the scope of another Standard.' *[IAS 38.2]*. It emphasises that 'if another Standard prescribes the accounting for a specific type of intangible asset, an entity applies that Standard instead of this Standard. For example, this Standard does not apply to... leases that are within the scope of IAS 17, Leases.' *[IAS 38.3]*.

IAS 17 does not apply to agreements that are contracts for services that do not transfer the right to use assets from one contracting party to the other. A conventional licence over an intangible asset (such as a film or video) commonly gives a non-exclusive right of 'access' to show or view the video simultaneously with many others but not a 'right of use' of the original film or video itself because the licensee does not control that asset. Arguably, this puts such a conventional licence outside the scope of IAS 17. There is a similar argument underlying IFRIC 4 that is considered further in 2.1 above. Many licences of these intangible assets are paid for by way of royalties on some sort of 'per use' basis. Again, the relationship between these rights and the underlying asset is explored further by IFRIC 4.

On the other hand, there are arrangements involving intangible assets that could fall within IAS 17. Examples include the transfer of exclusive rights for a finite period (which may be a finance or operating lease over the right in question) and sale and leaseback transactions involving assets to which one party has legal title.

There are further issues to be considered because of some of the characteristics of intangible assets which mean that there can be a variety of co-existing rights relating to the same underlying asset as well as different methods of paying for the rights. Many intangible rights can be purchased for an upfront sum, which will be accounted for as the acquisition of an intangible asset and capitalised at cost. *[IAS 38.24]*. The right itself may have a finite life, e.g. a radio station may acquire a licence that gives it a right to broadcast over specified frequencies for a period of seven years. Yet the underlying asset on which the right depends exists both before and after the 'right' has been purchased. If, as an alternative to up-front purchase, an entity pays for the same right in a series of instalments over a period of time, does it become an operating lease (because it is only a short period out of the life of the underlying asset) or is it a finance lease over the *right* in question? Alternatively, is it the purchase of an intangible asset by instalments?

Whether it is a finance lease or an acquisition in instalments can be very significant because the arrangement may include contingent payments. IAS 17 excludes these from the measurement at inception of the asset and liability (see 3.4.3 below). IAS 38 requires an intangible asset to be measured initially at cost. *[IAS 38.24]*. If the arrangement is seen as the acquisition of an asset on deferred payment terms, IAS 39 principles would apply. The effective interest rate method as defined in IAS 39 paragraph 9 is mandated. This will take account of estimated future cash payments or receipts through the expected life of the financial instrument that may include some of the 'contingent' payments (see 3.5 below).

Therefore, there are arguments as to whether there are assets and liabilities to be recognised and, even if recognition is accepted, measurement depends on the view that is taken of the applicable standard. In the absence of a clear principle, there is bound to be diversity in practice.

The new approach to lease accounting described at 10 below proposes that leases of intangible assets would be excluded from mandatory scope but it is assumed that entities will be allowed as an accounting policy election to apply the new standard to them. Although this means that these arrangements would be accounted for as acquisitions of assets, should they meet the definition in IAS 38, it might also create issues where assets include tangible and intangible elements.

3.2 Lease classification

3.2.1 Finance and operating leases

A finance lease is a 'lease that transfers substantially all the risks and rewards incidental to ownership of an asset', and an operating lease is 'a lease other than a finance lease', *[IAS 17.4]*, i.e. a lease that does not transfer substantially all the risks and rewards incidental to ownership.

However, the individual circumstances of a lessor and lessee may differ in respect of a single lease contract. As a result, it is perfectly possible that the application of the definitions to the different circumstances of the lessor and lessee may result in the same lease being classified differently by them. For example, a lease may be classified as an operating lease by the lessee and as a finance lease receivable by the

Chapter 26

lessor if it includes a residual value guarantee provided by a third party. *[IAS 17.9]*. These are discussed further under 3.4.6 below.

3.2.2   *Determining the substance of transactions*

The classification of leases adopted in the standard is based on the extent to which the risks and rewards incidental to ownership of a leased asset lie with the lessor or the lessee. Risks include the possibilities of losses from idle capacity or technological obsolescence and of variations in return due to changing economic conditions. Rewards may be represented by the expectation of profitable operation over the asset's economic life and of gain from appreciation in value or realisation of a residual value. *[IAS 17.7]*. However, unlike some national standards which include the rebuttable presumption that the transfer of substantially all of the risks and rewards occurs if, at the inception of the lease, the present value of the minimum lease payments amounts to substantially all (normally 90% or more) of the fair value of the leased asset, IAS 17 provides no numerical guidelines to be applied in classifying a lease as either finance or operating. It seems that it was a conscious decision of the (then) IASC Board not to refer to a percentage such as 90% in the standard, as it wanted to avoid the possibility of lease classification being reduced to a single pass or fail test.

Instead, the standard takes a more principles-based substance over form approach. It makes the statement that the classification of a lease depends on the substance of the transaction rather than the form of the contract, and lists a number of examples of situations that individually or in combination would normally lead to a lease being classified as a finance lease: *[IAS 17.10]*

(a)   the lease transfers ownership of the asset to the lessee by the end of the lease term;

(b)   the lessee has the option to purchase the asset at a price which is expected to be sufficiently lower than the fair value at the date the option becomes exercisable such that, at the inception of the lease, it is reasonably certain that the option will be exercised (frequently called a 'bargain purchase' option);

(c)   the lease term is for the major part of the economic life of the asset even if title is not transferred;

(d)   at the inception of the lease the present value of the minimum lease payments amounts to at least substantially all of the fair value of the leased asset; and

(e)   the leased assets are of a specialised nature such that only the lessee can use them without major modifications being made.

All of these are indicators that the lessor will only look to the lessee to obtain a return from the leasing transaction, so it can be presumed that the lessee will, in fact, pay for the asset.

Although the first criterion refers to title being transferred, it is clear from the standard that title does not have to be transferred to the lessee for a lease to be classified as a finance lease. *[IAS 17.4]*. The point is that the lease will almost certainly be classified as a finance lease if title does transfer.

'Fair value' is defined as the amount for which an asset could be exchanged or a liability settled, between knowledgeable, willing parties in an arm's length transaction (see 3.4.2 below). *[IAS 17.4]*. Options such as those referred to under (b) are common in lease agreements. The bargain purchase option is designed to give the lessor its expected lender's return but no more (comprising interest on its investment perhaps together with a relatively small fee), over the life of the agreement.

Criteria (c) and (d) above also include the unquantified expressions 'major part of' and 'substantially all', which means that judgement must be used in determining their effect on the risks and rewards of ownership. By contrast, in US GAAP the equivalent to (c) above in ASC 840 (formerly SFAS 13) does quantify when a lease will be a capital lease, (the equivalent of a finance lease). In ASC 840, if the lease term is equal to 75% or more of the estimated economic life of the leased asset, the lease will normally be a capital lease (there is an exception if the beginning of the lease term falls within the last 25% of the total estimated economic life of the leased property, including earlier years of use, where this criterion is not used for purposes of classifying the lease).[1] However in practice, if the lease is for the major part of the economic life of the asset then it is unlikely that the lessor will rely on any party other than the lessee to obtain its return from the lease.

Similarly, whilst (d) above refers to the present value of the minimum lease payments being at least 'substantially all of the fair value of the asset', it does so without putting a percentage to it. We have already speculated as to why this may be; nevertheless, we see no harm in practice in at least applying the '90% test' described above as a rule of thumb benchmark as part of the overall process in reaching a judgement as to the classification of a lease. Clearly, though, it cannot be applied as a hard and fast rule.

For an example of the 90% test, see Example 26.7 at 3.4.9 below. In that example, the present value of the minimum lease payments is calculated to be 92.74% of the asset's fair value; as this exceeds 90%, this would normally indicate that the lease is a finance lease. Nevertheless, the other criteria discussed above would need to be considered as well.

Consequently, we would stress that the 90% test is not an explicit requirement of the standard and should not be applied as a rule or in isolation, but it may be a useful tool to use in practice in attempting to determine the economic substance of a lease arrangement.

The standard then goes on to list the following indicators of situations that, individually or in combination, could also lead to a lease being classified as a finance lease: *[IAS 17.11]*.

(a)   if the lessee can cancel the lease, the lessor's losses associated with the cancellation are borne by the lessee;

(b)   gains or losses from the fluctuation in the fair value of the residual fall to the lessee (for example, in the form of a rent rebate equalling most of the sale proceeds at the end of the lease); and

(c)   the lessee has the ability to continue the lease for a secondary period at a rent which is substantially lower than market rent.

In our view, other considerations that could be made in determining the economic substance of the lease arrangement include the following:

- are the lease rentals based on a market rate for use of the asset (which would indicate an operating lease) or a financing rate for use of the funds, which would be indicative of a finance lease?

- is the existence of put and call options a feature of the lease? If so, are they exercisable at a predetermined price or formula (indicating a finance lease) or are they exercisable at the market price at the time the option is exercised (indicating an operating lease)?

And finally, we have found the following to be a useful 'acid test' question to consider:

- does the lessor intend to earn his total return on this transaction alone or does he intend to rely on subsequent sales or lease revenue? Clearly, if the lessor is looking to a return from a single lessee, then this would indicate that the lease is a finance lease.

3.2.3   *Changes to lease provisions*

Lease classification is made at the inception of the lease, *[IAS 17.13]*, which is the earlier of the date of the lease agreement or of a commitment by the parties to the principal provisions of the lease. *[IAS 17.4]*. Lease classification is only changed if, at any time during the lease, the lessee and the lessor agree to change the provisions of the lease (without renewing it) in such a way that it would have been classified differently at inception had the changed terms been in effect at that time. The revised agreement is considered as a new agreement and should be accounted for appropriately, prospectively over the remaining term of the lease.

Changes in circumstances or intentions do not give rise to a new classification of a lease for accounting purposes, provided that the circumstances or intentions concerned do not indicate that the initial lease classification was not based on the substance of the lease arrangement at the time it was entered into, in which case the initial lease classification would be an error. The renewal of a lease or the execution of a purchase option, if these were not considered probable at the inception of the lease, does not require re-assessment of the classification of a lease.

By contrast, changes in estimates (for example, changes in estimates of the economic life or of the residual value of the leased item) or changes in circumstances (for example, default by the lessee) do not result in the lease being reclassified for accounting purposes. *[IAS 17.13]*. This is of particular relevance given the requirement in IAS 16 – *Property, Plant and Equipment* – that the residual value and useful life of an asset must be reviewed at least at each financial year end. *[IAS 16.51]*.

Example 26.5:   Lease classification

Consider the following two scenarios:

- Entity A leases a motor vehicle from Entity B for a non-cancellable three-year period. At the inception of the lease, the lease was assessed as an operating lease. The lease did not contain any explicit option in the lease contract to extend the term of the lease. After 2 years, Entity A applies to Entity B to extend the lease for a further two years after the initial three-year period is complete. This extension is granted by the leasing company on an arm's length basis.

- Entity C leases an asset from Entity D for 10 years. The lease includes a purchase option under which Entity C may purchase the asset from Entity D at the end of the lease. The exercise price is fair value. Entity C is required to give notice of its intention to purchase no later than the end of the eighth year of the lease (since this arrangement allows Entity D time to market the leased asset for sale). On inception, Entity C classifies the lease as an operating lease, believing there was a reasonable commercial possibility that it would not exercise the option. Near the end of the eighth year of the lease, Entity C serves notice that it will purchase the asset, thereby creating a binding purchase commitment.

In neither of these cases will Entity A and Entity C reclassify the original lease as a finance lease, even though that would likely have been the assessment had the exercise of these options been assumed at inception. There may be accounting consequences of the exercise of the options; see section 6.

IAS 17 does not, however, give any guidance on how to assess whether modified lease terms give rise to a new classification or on how to measure modifications of leases if changes affect the value of the assets and liabilities for both lessor and lessee. These issues are discussed at 6 below.

3.3 Leases of land – finance or operating leases?

Land normally has an indefinite economic life and, until IAS 17 was amended in 2009 as part of the Improvements Project, all leases over land were classified as operating leases unless title was expected to pass to the lessee by the end of the lease term. The special rules that related only to leases of land have now been significantly reduced in an amendment that came into force on 1 January 2010. The standard now s an entity to assess the classification of leases over land as finance or operating leases in accordance with the general rules in paragraphs 7-13 that are described above. Many leases include elements for both land and buildings and both parts must be considered separately as discussed in 3.3.4 below. Although entities would normally apply the amendment retrospectively, the IASB was aware that entities might not have fair value information of the respective elements as at the inception of the lease. In these circumstances, the lease assets and liabilities relating to a land lease that has been newly classified as a finance lease will have been recognised at their fair values on the date that the revision was adopted, with any difference between those fair values being recognised in retained earnings. *[IAS 17.68A].*

The revised standard includes a reminder that 'in determining whether the land element is an operating or a finance lease, an important consideration is that land normally has an indefinite economic life'. *[IAS 17.15A].* A lease term for the major part of the economic life of the asset can indicate that a lease is a finance lease, even if title is not transferred, *[IAS 17.10],* and by repeating this in the amendment the IASB is stressing that this particular feature of finance leases is not likely to be met.

It is not clear exactly how the IASB expects the revised requirement to be applied in practice. It does appear that the Board expects the amendment to affect current lease classification, noting that it will be an improvement in accounting for leases and the significance of this issue in countries in which property rights are obtained under long-term leases. *[IAS 17.BC8E].* In these jurisdictions these interests are frequently purchased for single lease premiums in a manner comparable to the purchase of a freehold, although there may also be a small annual rent payable (a 'ground rent' in the UK). The Basis for Conclusions suggests that the lessee in leases of this type 'will typically be in a position economically similar to an entity that purchased the land and buildings. The present value of the residual value of the property in a lease with a term of several decades would be negligible. The Board concluded that accounting for the land element as a finance lease in such circumstances would be consistent with the economic position of the lessee.' *[IAS 17.BC8C]*. Therefore, the fact that land has an indefinite life will be assessed alongside other features that distinguish finance leases from operating leases. As well as considering whether the minimum lease payments amount to substantially all of the fair value, it is necessary to consider whether the lease includes other features that indicate that the significant risks and rewards of ownership rest with the lessor rather than the lessee. These include significant contingent rentals, rentals that are reset to market rates and fair value purchase options, all of which could indicate that the lease is an operating lease.

An advantage of classifying certain land leases as finance leases is that they can then be presented in the financial statements as property, plant and equipment. Under the previous standard, unless title to the land transfers to the lessee, premiums paid for a leasehold interest in land always represented pre-paid lease payments to be amortised over the lease term in accordance with the pattern of benefits provided. *[IAS 17.14 (2008)]*. This treatment is now reserved for pre-paid land rentals that are not classified as finance leases. An example would be a lease premium that comprises ten year's prepaid rentals, which is most unlikely to be classified as a finance lease.

A company that has reclassified land leases as finance leases as a result of the change to IAS 17 is Wm Morrison Supermarkets PLC.

Extract 26.3: Wm Morrison Supermarkets PLC (2011)

Consolidated financial statements under International Financial Reporting Standards [extract]
Group accounting policies [extract]
Long-leasehold land

The amendment to IAS 17 Leases is effective for annual periods beginning on or after 1 January 2010. During the period, the Group has reassessed the classification of unexpired land leases between operating and finance leases. Leases newly classified as finance leases have been accounted for retrospectively in accordance with IAS 8 Accounting policies, changes in accounting estimates and errors, and the required disclosures have been made.

The adoption of the amendment to IAS 17 Leases has resulted in a) derecognising long-lease land premiums previously classified within non-current asset lease prepayments, and the current element classified within debtors; and b) recognising a corresponding increase in the closing net book value of leasehold land and buildings to reflect the carrying value of the leased assets. The impact on previously disclosed costs and net book value for each of the balance sheet dates of 30 January 2011, 31 January 2010 and 1 February 2009 is detailed in notes 11 and 15.

The Group has assessed the present value of future minimum lease payments and considers these obligations to be immaterial for disclosure.

The depreciation rate on the newly classified leases is consistent with the annual amortisation charge incurred on the previous lease prepayments. Therefore there is no impact on profit for the period for the year ended 30 January 2011, or reserves of comparative periods.

There is no impact on earnings per share previously disclosed.

Notes to the Group financial statements [extract]
11 Property, plant and equipment [extract]

Leasehold land and buildings have been restated for the comparative periods as a result of an amendment to IAS 17 Leases. At 30 January 2011, the effect is a decrease of £271m (2010: £257m; 2009: £250m) to non-current asset lease prepayments and an increase to closing net book value of leasehold land and buildings of £273m (2010: £259m; 2009: £251m).

3.3.1 Lessors and land leases

The requirement to treat all leases over land as operating leases probably had a more profound effect on lessors than lessees. The lessee could not classify its prepaid lease premium as 'property, plant and equipment' and could not revalue it, unless the interest met the definition of investment property (see 3.3.5 below) but it indubitably had acquired an asset that would be amortised over its useful life. Lessors selling a leasehold interest, no matter how long its term, were apparently unable to treat the element of the proceeds that related to the land as anything other than prepaid rent to be spread on a straight-line basis over the lease term. After applying the amendment, lessors ought to be able to treat leases over land as finance leases and recognise a profit on disposal when they conclude that the land lease element is a finance lease.

3.3.2 Measurement of operating leases over land

Prepayments that are classified as operating leases over land and buildings will continue to be disclosed as current or non-current assets, as appropriate, in the entity's balance sheet. If certain costs arise at the inception of the lease that are necessary to consummate the agreement and enable a lessee to exercise its rights under the lease agreement, these costs are incurred as a direct result of the lease. Therefore, it is appropriate to consider these as lease-related costs that should be subject to the same accounting treatment as prepaid lease payments.

3.3.3 Presentation of operating leases over land

The following is an example of presentation of pre-paid operating leases in the balance sheet, together with the supporting note.

Extract 26.4: VTech Holdings Ltd. (2008)
Consolidated Financial Statements [extract]
Consolidated Balance Sheet [extract]
As at 31st March 2008

	Note	2008 US$ million	2007 US$ million
Non-current assets			
Tangible assets	7	**101.3**	78.4
Leasehold land payments	8	**3.8**	3.7
Deferred tax assets	9	**6.9**	5.5
Investments	10	**0.2**	0.2
		112.2	87.8

Notes to the Financial Statements [extract]

Principal Accounting Policies [extract]
J   Leases [extract]

Leasehold land payments are up-front payments to acquire long-term leasehold interests in land. These payments are stated at cost and are amortised on a straight-line basis over the respective period of the leases.

8   Leasehold Land Payments

	Note	2008 US$ million	2007 US$ million
Net book value at 1st April		3.7	3.7
Amortisation	2	(0.1)	(0.1)
Effect of changes in exchange rates		0.2	0.1
Net book value at 31st March		3.8	3.7
Leasehold land payments in respect of:			
Owner-occupied properties		3.8	3.7

3.3.4   Separating land and buildings

A characteristic of property leases in some jurisdictions (such as the UK) is that it is not possible to lease a building without leasing the land on which it stands – under UK property law all such leases are leases of land. There is no separate fair value for the land and buildings elements as they cannot be disposed of separately and in substance such leases may differ little from buying a property. *[IAS 17.BC5]*. The standard states explicitly that the land and buildings elements of leases are considered separately for the purposes of lease classification. *[IAS 17.15A]*. Each part must be classified as an operating or finance lease in the same way as leases of other assets This does not apply to leases of investment properties where there is no requirement to separate the land and buildings elements; see 3.3.5 below.

Before the amendment to IAS 17 allowing land leases to be accounted for as finance leases, initial classification was based on whether or not title passed. Where title to the land did not pass and it had an indefinite economic life, the land was normally classified as an operating lease while the buildings element was be an operating lease or finance lease according to the classification in the standard. *[IAS 17.15 (2008)]*. The initial classification now depends on the individual assessment of both land and buildings parts of the lease.

Entities may need to make the allocation between the land and buildings elements even if both are clearly finance leases as there could be a difference in amortisation methods, although this would be very unusual. *[IAS 17.BC8F]*. Much more common is a difference in useful economic life, where an entity takes out a lease for land and buildings where the term is longer than the useful life of any building on the land, e.g. a lease of 75 years over land on which there is a building that has a remaining useful life of 30 years.

If either or both parts of the lease might comprise a finance lease, the minimum lease payments need to be allocated between the land and buildings elements in proportion to the respective fair values of the leasehold interest in the land and buildings elements at the inception of the lease. The minimum lease payments must, of course, include any up-front payments, such as the payment for a lease premium. *[IAS 17.16]*.

The allocation of the minimum lease payments should be weighted to reflect the fair value of the land and buildings components to the extent they are the subject of the lease. This means that the amount that is being allocated is the lessee's leasehold interest in the land and buildings and the compensation received by the lessor, not the relative fair values of the land and buildings. The amount for which the land could be purchased at the inception of the lease is not the same as the value of that interest to the lessee. As land has an indefinite life, the value to the lessor may not be significantly affected by the grant of the lease. *[IAS 17.BC9-11]*.

The standard addresses the fact that it may not be possible to determine the fair values of the elements at inception and allows the following:

- if it is difficult or impossible to allocate the payments between the two elements, then the entire lease may be classified as a finance lease unless it is obvious that both the land and buildings elements are operating leases; *[IAS 17.16]*

- if the land element is immaterial, the lease may be treated as a single unit and classified as a finance or operating lease. The economic life of the entire leased asset will be the economic life of the buildings. *[IAS 17.17]*.

Some examples of the ways in which these exemptions may operate in practice are as follows:

Example 26.6:   Leases of land and buildings

Consider the following scenarios:

- Company A leases a building (and the underlying land) for 10 years. The remaining economic life of the building when the lease is entered into is 30 years. The lease is for considerably less than the economic life of the building so it is clear that both the land and buildings elements are operating leases and no separation is necessary.

- Company B takes on a 30-year lease of a new building and the underlying land. It is on a retail park and almost all of the value is ascribed to the building as land values are low. Although the building has a fabric life of 60 years, its economic life is estimated to be 30 years, after which it is expected to be technologically obsolete. The lease is for most of the economic life of the buildings and the present value of the minimum lease payments amounts to substantially all of the fair value of the building. It is not legally possible to lease the building without leasing the underlying land or, therefore, to estimate the relative fair values reliably. In any event, the lessor retains the residual value in the land and the lessee's interest in the land alone must be insignificant. The entire lease is accounted for as a finance lease with an economic life of 30 years.

- Company C takes out a 25 year non-cancellable lease of premises in the centre of a major town where land values are high. There are upward-only rent reviews every 5 years. It is a modern building that may have a remaining economic life of 35 years (or perhaps more, as the building has a fabric life of 60 years) and the land is clearly valuable to the lessor, who will want a reasonable return from it over the lease term. In this case the interest in the building may or may not be a finance lease and the lessee's leasehold interest in the land is not insignificant. Company C will have to undertake a valuation exercise to determine the allocation of minimum lease payments between the land and building elements of the lease in order to determine whether or not it has finance or operating leases over the land and buildings.

There will be many circumstances in which it is unclear whether the lessee has a finance or operating lease over land and buildings. In such cases it will probably be necessary to obtain the help of a valuation expert.

Chapter 26

In the UK, The Royal Institution of Chartered Surveyors has produced an information paper analysing the apportionments for lease classification under IFRSs.[2] This notes that there are four elements that need to be taken into account in the valuation (the value within the lease of the buildings and the land but also the residual value of both buildings and land) and proposes a method for apportioning the lease rentals based on these elements. The principal steps are as follows:

(a)   assess the freehold value of the land and buildings;

(b)   apportion the freehold value between the value within the lease and the residual (reversionary) value;

(c)   apportion the freehold value between land and buildings by calculating the value of one or other interest (usually, in practice, the building element) and deducting this from the value obtained in (b) to obtain the other;

(d)   apportion the value of the buildings element calculated at (c) between the residual and the value within the lease;

(e)   the value within the lease (b) can now be allocated between the buildings element (calculated at (d)) and the land element ((b) less (d)); and

(f)   apportion minimum lease payment between land and buildings in the ratio in (e) above.

This methodology makes it possible to calculate the implicit interest rate separately for the building as all elements needed for the calculation are known (fair value of the building, value of its residual and an appropriate proportion of the rentals paid).[3]

3.3.5   *Leases and investment properties*

Until both IAS 17 and IAS 40 were amended in 2003, it was not possible under IFRS for an interest in property held under an operating lease to be classified as an investment property. This was of great significance to the property industry in places such as the UK, where long leasehold interests in property are common, and to other jurisdictions such as Hong Kong where there are no freehold interests. In the UK these leasehold interests are normally acquired for an up-front premium that, if not recognised as an investment property asset, would have to be treated as a prepayment and gradually amortised. The amortisation of the prepayment would have effectively forced these entities to depreciate assets that would not otherwise have been depreciated (investment properties are not depreciated under IAS 40). Under IAS 17 and IAS 40, entities are allowed to treat interests under operating leases as investment properties as long as they apply the fair value model (see Chapter 21).

IAS 17 requires leases to be separated into land and building components, subject to this being possible or the land element being material. If the interest is an investment property carried at fair value in accordance with IAS 40, there is no requirement to separate the land and buildings elements of the lease. *[IAS 17.18]*.

Once the lessee has classified an operating lease property interest as if it were held under a finance lease, it must apply the fair value model and it must continue to do so even if subsequent changes in circumstances mean that the property interest is no longer an investment property to the lessee. IAS 17 gives two examples:

(a)   the lessee occupies the property, in which case it is transferred to owner-occupied property at fair value at the date of change of use; or

(b)   the lessee grants a sublease over substantially all of its property interest to an unrelated third party. It will treat the sublease as a finance lease to the third party even though the interest may well be accounted for as an operating lease by that party. *[IAS 17.19].*

In some arrangements, a developer may acquire a headlease over land and sell its rights under that same headlease. In these circumstances the developer may apply an IAS 40 analysis and treat the transaction as a purchase and sale of the same investment property. However, this does depend on the disposal in substance of the same asset as the one that has been acquired.

3.4   Defined terms

3.4.1   *Inception and commencement of the lease*

The standard distinguishes between the inception of the lease (when leases are classified) and the commencement of the lease term (when recognition takes place). The *inception* of the lease is the earlier of the date of the lease agreement and the date of commitment of the parties to the principal terms of the lease. This is the date on which a lease is classified as a finance or operating lease and, for finance leases, the date at which the amounts to be recognised at commencement are recognised. *[IAS 17.4].* The *commencement* of the lease term is the date on which the lessee is entitled to exercise its right to use the leased asset and is the date of initial recognition of the assets, liabilities, income and expenses of the lease in the financial statements. *[IAS 17.4].* This means that the entity makes an initial calculation of the assets and liabilities under a finance lease at inception of the lease but does not recognise these in the financial statements until the commencement date, if this is later. These amounts may in some circumstances be revised; this is discussed below.

It is not uncommon for these two dates to be different, especially if the asset is under construction. Lease payments may be adjusted for changes in the lessor's costs during the period between inception and commencement. The lease may allow for changes in respect of costs of construction, acquisition costs, changes in the lessor's financing costs and any other factor, such as changes in general price levels, during the construction period. Changes to the lease payments as a result of such events are deemed to take place at inception of the lease, i.e. are taken into account in establishing, at inception, whether it is a finance or operating lease. *[IAS 17.5].* In other words, if the final cost of the asset, and hence its fair value, is not known until after the date of inception, hindsight is used to establish that fair value.

The fair value may be known at inception but payment delayed until commencement, which may happen with large but routinely constructed assets such as aircraft or railway locomotives. The lease liability will increase between the date of inception and the date of commencement, taking account of payments made and the interest rate implicit in the lease (see 3.4.5 below). Although IAS 17 does not address this, the lessee will add the increase in the liability until the commencement date to the asset. It is not a finance cost on the liability (no liability is recognised prior to commencement) and nor need it be an expense. It is not appropriate to recognise at commencement the liability that was calculated at inception as that would change the interest rate implicit in the lease.

The standard also considers what will happen if the lease terms are changed so radically (but without entering into a new lease agreement) that it would have been classified in a different way, e.g. it would have been a finance lease instead of an operating lease. Such changes could happen at any stage during the lease (see 3.2.3 above) but if they happen in the period between inception and commencement, the lease will be classified at inception in accordance with the revised terms as if they had existed as at that date. Modifications are discussed at 6 below.

3.4.2   Fair value

Fair value is defined, as elsewhere in IFRSs, as the amount for which an asset could be exchanged or a liability settled, between knowledgeable, willing parties in an arm's length transaction. *[IAS 17.4]*. In practice, the transaction price, i.e. the purchase price of the asset that is the subject of the lease, will be its fair value, unless there is evidence to the contrary. This definition will be superseded by that in IFRS 13 – *Fair Value Measurement* – which applies to annual periods beginning on or after 1 January 2013 (early application permitted) and is discussed in Chapter 16.

3.4.3   Minimum lease payments

The minimum lease payments are the payments over the lease term that the lessee is or can be required to make, excluding contingent rent, costs for services and taxes to be paid by and reimbursed to the lessor, together with:

(a)   for a lessee, any amounts guaranteed by the lessee or by a party related to the lessee;

(b)   for a lessor, any residual guaranteed to the lessor by:

　　(i)   the lessee or by a party related to the lessee; or

　　(ii)   a third party unrelated to the lessor who is financially capable of discharging the obligations under the guarantee.

The lessee may have an option to purchase the asset at a price that is expected to be sufficiently lower than the fair value at the date the option becomes exercisable so that, at the inception of the lease, it is reasonably certain to be exercised. In this case the minimum lease payments comprise the minimum payments payable over the lease term to the expected date of exercise of this purchase option and the payment required to exercise it. *[IAS 17.4]*.

3.4.4   Lease term and non-cancellable period

The lease term is the non-cancellable period for which the lessee has contracted to lease the asset, together with any further terms for which the lessee has the option to continue to lease the asset, with or without further payment, if it is reasonably certain at the inception of the lease that the lessee will exercise the option. *[IAS 17.4]*. A non-cancellable lease is either a lease that has no cancellation terms or one that has terms that effectively force the lessee to continue to use the asset for the period of the agreement. Therefore, a lease is considered to be non-cancellable if it can be cancelled only:

(a) on the occurrence of a remote contingency;

(b) with the permission of the lessor;

(c) if the lessee enters into a new lease with the same lessor for the same or an equivalent asset; or

(d) if the lessee is required to pay additional amounts that make it reasonably certain at inception that the lessee will continue the lease. *[IAS 17.4]*.

An example of (d) is a requirement that the lessee pays a termination payment equivalent to the present value of the remaining lease payments.

3.4.5 *Interest rate implicit in the lease and incremental borrowing rate*

The interest rate implicit in the lease is the discount rate that, at the inception of the lease, causes the aggregate present value of

(a) the minimum lease payments; and

(b) the unguaranteed residual value

to be equal to the sum of the fair value of the leased asset and any initial direct costs of the lessor.

If it is not practicable to determine this then the lessee may use its incremental borrowing rate of interest, which it is the rate of interest the lessee would have to pay on a similar lease or, if that is not determinable, the rate that, at the inception of the lease, the lessee would have to pay to borrow over a similar term, and with a similar security, the funds necessary to purchase the asset. *[IAS 17.4]*.

3.4.6 *Residual value*

The guaranteed residual value is:

(a) for a lessee, the part of the residual value that is guaranteed by itself or by one of its related parties. The amount of the guarantee is the maximum amount that could, in any event, become payable; and

(b) for a lessor, it is the part of the residual value that is guaranteed by the lessee or by a third party unrelated to the lessor who is financially capable of discharging the obligations under the guarantee.

The lessor's unguaranteed residual value is any part of the residual value of the leased asset, the realisation of which is not assured or is guaranteed solely by a party related to it. *[IAS 17.4]*.

If the net present value of the residual value of an asset is significant and is not guaranteed by the lessee or a party related to it, then the lease is likely to be classified as an operating lease. This is explained by the fact that the risks of recovering the significant residual value will be the lessor's, consequently it is unlikely that 'substantially all' of the risks and rewards of ownership will have passed to the lessee. There are frequently problems of interpretation regarding the significance of residual values in lease classification. Lessees may find it difficult to obtain information in order to calculate the unguaranteed residual values. However,

Chapter 26

lessees may guarantee all or part of the residual value of the asset and this has to be taken into account in the lease classification.

3.4.6.A   Residual value guarantors

A lessee and lessor may legitimately classify the same lease differently if the lessor has received a residual value guarantee provided by a third party. *[IAS 17.9].* Residual value guarantors undertake to acquire the assets from the lessor at an agreed amount at the end of the lease term because they can dispose of the assets on a ready and reliable market. As a result, the lease is an operating lease for the lessee and a finance lease for the lessor. This is particularly common with vehicle leases where there is an efficient second-hand market, including price guides, many car dealers and car auctions. Residual value guarantors may be prepared to take the residual risk with many types of assets as long as there is a second-hand market.

3.4.7   Contingent rents

Contingent rents (which are excluded from minimum lease payments) are defined in the standard as that portion of the lease payments that are not fixed in amount, but are based on a factor other than just the passage of time (for example, percentage of sales, amount of usage, price indices, market rates of interest). *[IAS 17.4].*

Contingent rents are embedded derivatives, as defined by IAS 39, and in principle within scope of that standard. An embedded derivative is a component of a hybrid or combined instrument that also includes a non-derivative host contract; it has the effect that some of the cash flows of the combined instrument vary in a similar way to a stand-alone derivative. In other words, it causes some or all of the cash flows that otherwise would be required by the contract to be modified according to a specified underlying. *[IAS 39.10].* Embedded derivatives have to be separated from the host contract and recognised separately in the financial statements of the entity unless they are closely related to the economic characteristics and risks of the host contract. *[IAS 39.11].*

IAS 39 specifically identifies the specific examples of contingent rents referred to above as being 'closely related' to the lease contract and hence not separately accounted for. *[IAS 39.11, IAS 39.AG33(f)].* This means that lessees continue to expense such contingent payments as they arise.

However, other types of contingent rent could be embedded derivatives, e.g. an index that relates to inflation in another economic environment. *[IAS 39.AG33(f)].* In the case of more complex lease terms, reference should be made to IAS 39 paragraphs 10 to 13 and Section 5 of Chapter 49.

3.4.7.A Contingent rents and operating leases

IAS 17 specifies that lessees expense contingent rents relating to finance leases in the period in which they are incurred. *[IAS 17.25]*. However, the Standard is not explicit in the treatment of contingent elements of operating lease rentals.

In its May 2006 meeting, The Interpretations Committee considered whether an estimate of contingent rents should be included in the total operating lease payments or lease income to be recognised on a straight line basis over the lease term. It concluded that current practice was to exclude such amounts (which is consistent with our view of the issue) and did not, therefore, add the matter to its agenda for further consideration. Accordingly, lease payments or receipts under operating leases will exclude contingent amounts.

Although the IASB has proposed a clarification that would have achieved consistency in the treatment of contingent rent for finance and operating leases, nothing has in fact appeared in any of the Annual Improvements. It may be that any change has been deferred because of the proposals to change the method of accounting for leases described at 10 below.

3.4.8 Initial direct costs

Initial direct costs are incremental costs that are directly attributable to negotiating and arranging a lease, except for such costs incurred by manufacturer or dealer lessors. *[IAS 17.4]*.

If the lessee incurs costs that are directly attributable to activities it has performed to obtain a finance lease, these are added to the amount recognised as an asset. *[IAS 17.24]*.

Initial direct costs of lessors include amounts such as commissions, legal fees and internal costs that are incremental and directly attributable to negotiating and arranging a lease. Internal costs must exclude general overheads such as those incurred by a sales or marketing team. *[IAS 17.38]*. Lessors must add internal direct costs to the carrying value of leased assets under both finance and operating leases – see 4.2 and 5.2 below – unless they are manufacturer and dealer lessors, in which case they must be expensed – see 4.4 below.

3.4.9 Calculation of the implicit interest rate and present value of minimum lease payments

The following example illustrates the calculation of the implicit interest rate and present value of minimum lease payments:

Example 26.7: Calculation of the implicit interest rate and present value of minimum lease payments

Details of a non-cancellable lease are as follows:

(i)   Fair value = €10,000

(ii) Five annual rentals payable in advance of €2,100

(iii) Lessor's unguaranteed estimated residual value at end of five years = €1,000

Chapter 26

The implicit interest rate in the lease is that which gives a present value of €10,000 for the five rentals plus the total estimated residual value at the end of year 5. This rate can be calculated as 6.62%, as follows:

Year	Capital sum at start of period €	Rental paid €	Capital sum during period €	Finance charge (6.62% per annum) €	Capital sum at end of period €
1	10,000	2,100	7,900	523	8,423
2	8,423	2,100	6,323	419	6,742
3	6,742	2,100	4,642	307	4,949
4	4,949	2,100	2,849	189	3,038
5	3,038	2,100	938	62	1,000
		10,500		1,500	

In other words, 6.62% is the implicit interest rate that, at the inception of the lease, causes the aggregate present value of the minimum lease payments (€10,500) and the unguaranteed residual value (€1,000) to be equal to the fair value of the leased asset. Lessor's initial direct costs have been excluded for simplicity.

This implicit interest rate is then used to calculate the present value of the minimum lease payments, i.e. €10,500 discounted at 6.62%. This can be calculated at €9,274, which is 92.74% of the asset's fair value, indicating that the present value of the minimum lease payments is substantially all of the fair value of the leased asset and a finance lease is therefore indicated.

It would be appropriate for the lessee to record the asset at €9,274 as the present value of the minimum lease payments is lower than the fair value and this would take account of the lessor's residual interest in the asset.

The lessor will know all of the information in the above example, as it will have been used in the pricing decision for the lease. However, the lessee may not know either the fair value or the unguaranteed residual value and, therefore, not know the implicit interest rate. In such circumstances the lessee will substitute a rate from a similar lease or its incremental borrowing rate. The lessee is also unlikely to know the lessor's initial direct costs even if the other information is known, but this is unlikely to have more than a marginal effect on the implicit interest rate.

3.5   Leases as financial instruments

In accordance with the accounting model in IAS 17, a finance lease is essentially regarded as an entitlement to receive, and an obligation to make, a stream of payments that are substantially the same as blended payments of principal and interest under a loan agreement. Consequently the lessor accounts for its investment in the amount receivable under the lease contract rather than for the leased asset itself. An operating lease, on the other hand, is regarded primarily as an uncompleted contract committing the lessor to provide the use of an asset in future periods in exchange for consideration similar to a fee for a service. The lessor continues to account for the leased asset itself rather than any amount receivable in the future under the contract.

Accordingly, a finance lease is regarded as a financial instrument and an operating lease is not regarded as a financial instrument (except as regards individual payments currently due and payable). [IAS 32.AG9].

In general the lease rights and obligations that come about as a result of IAS 17's recognition and measurement rules are not included within the scope of IAS 39. Finance lease assets and liabilities are not necessarily stated at the same amount as they would be if they were measured under IAS 39. The most obvious differences are those between the implicit interest rate (IIR) and the effective interest rate. The IIR (as described in 3.4.5 above) is the discount rate that, at the inception of the lease, causes the aggregate present value of the minimum lease payments (receivable during the non-cancellable lease term and any option periods that it is reasonably certain at inception the lessee will exercise) and the unguaranteed residual value to be equal to the sum of the fair value of the leased asset and any initial direct costs of the lessor. *[IAS 17.4]*. The effective interest rate, by contrast, is the rate that exactly discounts estimated future cash payments or receipts through the expected life of the financial instrument (see Chapter 49 at 5). *[IAS 39.9]*. The latter may include payments that would be considered contingent rentals, and hence excluded, from the calculation of the IIR and may take account of cash flows over a different period.

However, the following aspects of accounting for leases are within IAS 39's scope *[IAS 39.2(b)]*:

(a)   finance lease payables recognised by a lessee are subject to the derecognition provisions (see 4.3.1 below);

(b)   lease receivables recognised by a lessor, which are subject to the derecognition and impairment provisions of IAS 39 (see 4.3.2 and 4.3.3 below); and

(c)   derivatives that are embedded in leases are subject to IAS 39's embedded derivatives provisions (see 3.4.7 above). *[IAS 39.2(b)]*.

IAS 39 has little impact on traditional, straightforward leases. However, its requirements will have to be considered in many more complex situations and in relation to sub-leases and back-to-back leases, as described in 8 below.

4   ACCOUNTING FOR FINANCE LEASES

Lessees recognise finance leases as assets and liabilities in their balance sheets at the commencement of the lease term at amounts equal at the inception of the lease to the fair value of the leased item or, if lower, at the present value of the minimum lease payments. In calculating the present value of the minimum lease payments the discount factor is the interest rate implicit in the lease, if this is practicable to determine; if not, the lessee's incremental borrowing rate should be used. Any initial direct costs of the lessee are added to the asset. *[IAS 17.20]*. 'Fair value' and 'minimum lease payments' are defined in 3.4.2 and 3.4.3 above.

The fair value and the present value of the lease payments are both determined as at the inception of the lease. At commencement, the asset and liability for the future lease payments are recognised in the balance sheet at the same amount. *[IAS 17.22]*. The terms and calculations of initial recognition by lessees are discussed further in 4.1 below.

Chapter 26

Lease payments made by the lessee are apportioned between the finance charge and the reduction of the outstanding liability. The finance charge should be allocated to periods during the lease term so as to produce a constant periodic rate of interest on the remaining balance of the liability for each period. *[IAS 17.25]*. This is covered in 4.1.2 below.

Lessors recognise assets held under a finance lease as receivables in their balance sheets and present them as a receivable at an amount equal to the net investment in the lease. *[IAS 17.36]*. Lessors who are not manufacturers or dealers include costs that they have incurred in connection with arranging and negotiating a lease as part of the initial measurement of the finance lease receivable. Initial recognition by lessors, which is in many respects a mirror image of lessee recognition, follows at 4.2 below. The recognition of finance income and other issues in connection with subsequent measurement of the lessor's assets arising from finance leases is dealt with in 4.2.1 to 4.2.4 below.

Manufacturer or dealer lessors have specific issues with regard to recognition of selling profit and finance income. These are dealt with at 4.4 below.

4.1 Accounting by lessees

4.1.1 *Initial recognition*

At commencement of the lease, the asset and liability for the future lease payments are recorded in the balance sheet at the same amount, which is an amount equal to the fair value of the leased asset or the present value of the minimum lease payments, if lower, with initial direct costs of the lessee being added to the asset. *[IAS 17.22]*. An example of the calculation is given in Example 26.7 above.

4.1.2 *Allocation of finance costs*

The standard requires that lease payments should be apportioned between the finance charge and the reduction of the outstanding liability. The finance charge should be allocated to periods during the lease term so as to produce a constant periodic rate of interest on the remaining balance of the liability for each period. *[IAS 17.25]*.

Example 26.8: Allocation of finance costs

In Example 26.7 above, the present value of the lessee's minimum lease payments was calculated at €9,274 by using the implicit interest rate of 6.62%. The total finance charges of €1,226 (total rentals paid of €10,500 less their present value of €9,274) are allocated over the lease term as follows:

Year	Liability at start of period €	Rental paid €	Liability during period €	Finance charge (6.62% per annum) €	Liability at end of period €
1	9,274	2,100	7,174	475	7,649
2	7,649	2,100	5,549	368	5,917
3	5,917	2,100	3,817	253	4,070
4	4,070	2,100	1,970	130	2,100
5	2,100	2,100	–	–	–
		10,500		1,226	

The standard notes that, in practice, when allocating the finance charge to periods during the lease term some form of approximation may be used to simplify the calculation. *[IAS 17.26]*. However, it provides no guidance as to the methodology that should be applied in allocating finance charges to accounting periods.

Two methods that are used as approximations are the 'sum of the digits' ('rule of 78') or simply taking the finance costs on a straight line basis over the lease term. These are progressively easier to apply but also give progressively less accurate answers. There is, therefore, a trade-off to be made between the costs versus benefits of achieving complete accuracy, but in making this trade-off, the question of materiality is important. If differences between allocated finance charges under each method are immaterial, the simplest method may be used for convenience. The converse also applies and, of course, a number of individually immaterial differences may in aggregate be material. The following example illustrates the implicit interest rate and sum of the digits methods of allocating finance charges to accounting periods.

Example 26.9: *Sum-of-digits allocation as compared to implicit interest rate*

Continuing the lease example from Example 26.7 above, the sum of the digits method calculation is as follows:

Year	Number of rentals not yet due	×	$\dfrac{\text{total finance charge}}{\text{sum of number of rentals}}$	=	Finance charge per annum €
1	4	×	€1,226 ÷ 10	=	490
2	3	×	€1,226 ÷ 10	=	368
3	2	×	€1,226 ÷ 10	=	245
4	1	×	€1,226 ÷ 10	=	123
5	–	×	€1,226 ÷ 10	=	
	10				1,226

We can now compare the finance charges in each of the five years under the implicit interest rate (IIR) as calculated in Example 26.7 and sum of the digits methods:

	Annual finance charge		Annual finance charge as % of total rentals	
Year	IIR €	Sum of the digits €	IIR %	Sum of the digits %
1	475	490	39	40
2	368	368	30	30
3	253	245	20	20
4	130	123	11	10
5	–	–	–	–
	1,226	1,226	100	100

As can be seen above, in situations where the lease term is not very long (typically not more than seven years) and interest rates are not very high, the sum of the digits method gives an allocation of finance charges that is close enough to that under the implicit interest rate method to allow the simpler approach to be used.

4.1.3 *Recording the liability*

The carrying amount of the liability will always be calculated in the same way, by adding the finance charge (however calculated) to the outstanding balance and deducting cash paid. The finance charge depends on the method used to apportion the finance costs. The liability in each of the years, as apportioned between the current and non-current liability, if the IIR method is used, is as follows:

Example 26.10: Lessee's liabilities and interest expense

The entity entering into the lease in Example 26.7 will record the following liabilities and interest expense in its balance sheet:

Year	Liability at end of period €	Current liability at end of period €	Non-current liability at end of period €	Interest expense (at 6.62%) for the period €
1	7,649	1,732	5,917	475
2	5,917	1,847	4,070	368
3	4,070	1,970	2,100	253
4	2,100	2,100	–	130
5	–	–	–	–
				1,226

4.1.4 *Accounting for the leased asset*

At commencement of the lease, the asset and liability for the future lease payments are recorded in the balance sheet at the same amount, with initial direct costs of the lessee being added to the asset. *[IAS 17.22]*. These are costs that are directly attributable to the lease in question and are added to the carrying value *[IAS 17.24]* in an analogous way to the treatment of the acquisition costs of property, plant and equipment.

Accounting for the leased asset follows the general rules for accounting for property, plant and equipment or intangible assets. A finance lease gives rise to a depreciation expense for depreciable assets as well as a finance expense for each accounting period. The depreciation policy for depreciable leased assets should be consistent with that for depreciable assets that are owned, and the depreciation recognised should be calculated in accordance with IAS 16 and IAS 38. If there is reasonable certainty that the lessee will obtain ownership by the end of the lease term, the period of expected use is the useful life of the asset. If there is no reasonable certainty, the asset is be depreciated fully over the shorter of the lease term or its useful life. *[IAS 17.27-28]*. The useful life is the estimated remaining period, from the commencement of the lease term, over which the entity expects to consume the economic benefits embodied in the asset. This is different to the economic life which takes account of the period of time for which the asset is economically usable by one or more users and would therefore include additional lease terms with the same or different lessees. *[IAS 17.4]*.

Because the interest expense and depreciation must be calculated separately and are unlikely to be the same it is not appropriate simply to treat the lease payments as an expense for the period. *[IAS 17.29]*. This is demonstrated in the following example.

Example 26.11: Lessee's depreciation and interest expense

The entity that has entered into the lease agreement described in Example 26.7 will depreciate the asset (whose initial carrying value, disregarding initial direct costs, is €9,274) on a straight-line basis over five years in accordance with its depreciation policy for owned assets, i.e. an amount of €1,855 per annum. The balances for asset and liability in the financial statements in each of the years 1-5 will be as follows:

Year	Carrying value of asset at end of period €	Total liability at end of period €	Total charged to income statement* €	Lease payments €
1	7,419	7,649	2,330	2,100
2	5,564	5,917	2,222	2,100
3	3,709	4,070	2,108	2,100
4	1,854	2,100	1,985	2,100
5	–	–	1,855	2,100
			10,500	10,500

* The total charge combines the annual depreciation of €1,855 and the interest calculated according to the IIR method in Example 26.8, which is in aggregate the initial carrying value of the asset of €9,274 and the total finance charge of €1,226, i.e. the total rent paid of €10,500. Note that this example assumes that the asset is being depreciated to a residual value of zero over the lease term, which is shorter than its useful life, so IAS 16's requirement to reconsider the residual value and useful life at least at each financial year end is unlikely to have an effect. *[IAS 16.51]*.

An entity applies IAS 36 – *Impairment of Assets* – to determine whether the leased asset has become impaired in value (see Chapter 22). *[IAS 17.30]*.

4.2 Accounting by lessors

Under a finance lease, a lessor retains legal title to an asset but passes substantially all the risks and rewards of ownership to the lessee in return for a stream of rentals. In substance, therefore, the lessor provides finance and expects a return thereon.

The standard requires lessors to recognise assets held under a finance lease in their balance sheets as a receivable at an amount equal to the net investment in the lease. *[IAS 17.36]*. The lease payments received from the lessee are treated as repayments of principal and finance income. *[IAS 17.37]*. Initial direct costs may include commissions, legal fees and internal costs that are incremental and directly attributable to negotiating and arranging the lease. They are included in the measurement of the net investment in the lease at inception and reflected in the calculation of the implicit interest rate. *[IAS 17.38]*.

The recognition of finance income should be based on a pattern reflecting a constant periodic rate of return on the lessor's net investment outstanding in respect of the finance lease. *[IAS 17.39]*.

4.2.1　*The lessor's net investment in the lease*

The lessor's gross investment in the lease is the aggregate of the minimum lease payments receivable by the lessor under a finance lease and any guaranteed and unguaranteed residual value to which the lessor is entitled. The net investment in the lease is the gross investment discounted at the interest rate implicit in the lease, *[IAS 17.4]*, i.e. at any point in time it comprises the gross investment after deducting gross earnings allocated to future periods.

The lessor's gross investment is, therefore, the same as the aggregate figures used to calculate the implicit interest rate and the net investment is the present value of those same figures – see 3.4.9 and Example 26.7 above.

Therefore, at inception, the lessor's net investment in the lease is the cost of the asset as increased by its initial direct costs. The difference between the net and gross investments is the gross finance income to be allocated over the lease term. Example 26.12 below illustrates this point.

4.2.2　*Allocation of finance income*

As noted above the lessor recognises finance income based on a pattern reflecting a constant periodic rate of return on the lessor's net investment outstanding in respect of the finance lease. *[IAS 17.39]*. Lease payments, excluding costs for services, are applied against the gross investment in the lease to reduce both the principal and the unearned finance income. *[IAS 17.40]*. The standard does not refer to the use of approximations by lessors and, accordingly, the methods noted at 4.1.2 should not be used unless the differences are clearly immaterial. Example 26.7 at 3.4.9 can be examined from the lessor's perspective:

Example 26.12:　The lessor's gross and net investment in the lease

The lease has the same facts as described in Example 26.7, i.e. the asset has a fair value of €10,000, the lessee is making five annual rentals payable in advance of €2,100 and the total unguaranteed estimated residual value at the end of five years is estimated to be €1,000. The lessor's direct costs have been excluded for simplicity.

The lessor's gross investment in the lease is the total rents receivable of €10,500 and the unguaranteed residual value of €1,000. The gross earnings are therefore €1,500. The initial carrying value of the receivable is its fair value of €10,000, which is also the present value of the gross investment discounted at the interest rate implicit in the lease of 6.62%.

Year	Receivable at start of period €	Rental received €	Finance income (6.62% per annum) €	Gross investment at end of period €	Gross earnings allocated to future periods €	Receivable at end of period €
1	10,000	2,100	523	9,400	977	8,423
2	8,423	2,100	419	7,300	558	6,742
3	6,742	2,100	307	5,200	251	4,949
4	4,949	2,100	189	3,100	62	3,038
5	3,038	2,100	62	1,000	–	1,000
		10,500	1,500			

The gross investment in the lease at any point in time comprises the aggregate of the rentals receivable in future periods and the unguaranteed residual value, e.g. at the end of year 2,, the gross investment of €7,300 is three years' rental of €2,100 plus the unguaranteed residual of €1,000. The net investment, which is the amount at which the debtor will be recorded in the balance sheet, is €7,300 less the earnings allocated to future periods of €558 = €6,742.

4.2.3 Residual values

Residual values have to be taken into account in assessing whether a lease is a finance or operating lease as well as affecting the calculation of the IRR and finance income.

- Unguaranteed residual values have to be estimated in order to calculate the IIR and finance income receivable under a finance lease. Any impairment in the residual must be taken into account; this is illustrated in A below.

- Residual values can be guaranteed by the lessee or by a third party. The effects of third party guarantees on risks and rewards are described in 3.4.6A above.

- The terms of a lease guarantee can affect the assessment of the risks and rewards in the arrangement as in the example in B below.

- A common form of lease requires the asset to be sold at the end of the lease term. The disposition of the proceeds has to be taken into account in assessing who bears residual risk, as described in C below.

4.2.3.A Unguaranteed residual values

Income recognition by lessors can be extremely sensitive to the amount recognised as the asset's residual value. This is because the amount of the residual directly affects the computation of the amount of finance income earned over the lease term – this is illustrated in Example 26.13 below. The standard gives no guidance regarding the estimation of unguaranteed residual values but it does require them to be reviewed regularly. If there has been a reduction in the estimated value, the income allocation over the lease term is revised and any reduction in respect of amounts accrued is recognised immediately. *[IAS 17.41].*

Example 26.13: Reduction in residual value

Taking the same facts as used in Example 26.12 above, the lessor concludes at the end of year 2 that the residual value of the asset is only €500 and revises the income allocation over the lease term accordingly. It continues to apply the same implicit interest rate, 6.62%, as before.

Year	Receivable at start of period €	Rental received €	Finance income (6.62% per annum) €	Gross investment at end of period* €	Gross earnings allocated to future periods €	Receivable at end of period €
2	8,423	2,100	419	6,800	471	6,329
3	6,329	2,100	280	4,700	191	4,509
4	4,509	2,100	160	2,600	31	2,569
5	2,569	2,100	31	500	–	500

* The gross investment in the lease now takes account of the revised unguaranteed residual of €500, rather than the original €1,000.

The lessor will have to write off €413, being the difference between the carrying amount of the receivable as previously calculated and the revised balance above (€6,742 – €6,329). This is the present value as at the end of year 2 of €500 and represents the part of the unguaranteed residual written off.

Impairment of lease receivables is within the scope of IAS 39 *[IAS 39.2(b)]* and this methodology is required by IAS 39 paragraph 63, described in 4.3.3 below.

4.2.3.B   *Residual values guaranteed by the lessee*

Although a lessee may give a residual value guarantee in a lease, the lease itself may be structured so that the most likely outcome of events relating to the residual value indicates that no significant risk will attach to the lessee.

Example 26.14:   *A lease structured such that the most likely outcome is that the lessee has no significant residual risk*

Brief details of a motor vehicle lease are:

Fair value   –   €10,000
Rentals   –   20 monthly payments @ €300, followed by a final rental of €2,000

At the end of the lease, the lessee sells vehicle as agent for the lessor and if sold for:

(i)   more than €3,000, 99% of the excess is repaid to the lessee; or

(ii)   less than €3,000, lessee pays the deficit to the lessor up to a maximum of 0.4 pence per mile above 25,000 miles p.a. on average that the leased vehicle has done.

The net present value of the minimum lease payments excluding the guarantee amounts to €7,365.

This lease involves a guarantee by the lessee of the residual value of the leased vehicle of €3,000, as a result of (ii) above. However, the guarantee will only be called upon if both:

(a)   the vehicle's actual residual value is less than €3,000; and

(b)   the vehicle has travelled more than 25,000 miles per year on average over the lease term.

Further, the lessee is only liable to pay a certain level of the residual; namely, €100 for each 2,500 miles above 25,000 miles that the vehicle has done.

One could argue that the guarantee should be assumed to apply only to the extent that experience or expectations of the sales price and/or the mileage that vehicles have done (and the inter-relationship between these) indicate that a residual payment by the lessee will be made and if this best estimate is that a zero or minimal payment will be made, this should be used for the purposes of lease classification. This would be applying the principles in IAS 37 to the calculation of the liability. However, IAS 17 states that the amount of the guarantee is 'the maximum amount that could, in any event, become payable'. Therefore, the standard appears to require the maximum guarantee of €3,000 to be taken into account.

By taking the maximum guarantee into account, the present value of the minimum lease payments might equal the fair value of the asset. This does not necessarily mean that the lease will be automatically fall to be treated as a finance lease. This depends on the substance of the arrangement and the entity might take account of the residual it estimates it will actually pay in making this assessment. Another interpretation is given in Example 26.16 below, in which the entity capitalises the full residual guarantee and factors the amount that it expects to recover into the residual value of the asset.

4.2.3.C   *Rental rebates*

IAS 17 suggests that an indicator that the lease is a finance lease is that 'the gains or losses from the fluctuation in the fair value of the residual fall to the lessee (for example, in the form of a rent rebate equalling most of the sales proceeds at the end of the lease)'. *[IAS 17.11]*. This is because a lessee that obtains most of the sales proceeds has received most of the risks and rewards of the residual value in the asset. This would indicate that the lessor has already been compensated for the transaction and hence that it is a finance lease.

Other leases require the asset to be sold at the end of the lease but the lessor receives the first tranche of proceeds and only those proceeds above a certain level are remitted to the lessee. These arrangements may have a different significance as the lessor may be taking the proceeds to meet its unguaranteed residual value. Lessors are prepared to take risks on residual values of such assets if there is an established and reliable market in which to sell them. This could mean that the gains or losses from the fluctuation in the fair value of the residual do not fall predominantly to the lessee and, in the absence of other factors, could indicate that it is an operating lease.

Example 26.15:   *Rental rebates*

The lease arrangements are as in Example 26.14, except that at end of the lease, the lessee sells the vehicle as agent for the lessor, and if it is sold for

(i)   up to £3,000, all of the proceeds are received by the lessor; or

(ii) more than £3,000, 99% of excess is repaid to the lessee. The lessee does not have to make good any deficit, should one arise.

In this example, it appears that the lessor is using the sale proceeds to meet its unguaranteed residual value but it is also taking the first loss provision. Only thereafter does the lessee gain or lose from the fluctuations in the fair value. The lessee's minimum lease payments have a net present value of €7,365, it has not guaranteed the residual value at all and is not exposed to any risk of any fall in value, although it may benefit from increases in the fair value in excess of €3,000. On balance this indicates that the arrangement is an operating lease.

4.2.4   *Disposals by lessors of assets held under finance leases*

If a lessor is to dispose of an asset under a finance lease that is classified as held for sale, or is included in a disposal group that is so classified, it is to apply the requirements of IFRS 5 – *Non-current Assets Held for Sale and Discontinued Operations* – to the disposal. *[IAS 17.41A]*. The 'asset under a finance lease' is the receivable from the lessee, which is not a financial asset under IAS 39; see 3.5 above for an analysis of the extent to which assets and liabilities under leases are within scope of that standard. This means that measurement as well as classification of the asset under the finance lease is within scope of IFRS 5, unlike financial assets within scope of IAS 39 that are subject only to its classification rules. Once classified as held for sale, it must be measured at the lower of carrying amount and fair value less costs to sell. Any residual interest in the leased asset, which is accounted for under IAS 16 or IAS 38, is clearly within scope of IFRS 5. IFRS 5's requirements are dealt with in Chapter 4.

4.3   Termination of finance leases

The expectations of lessors and lessees regarding the timing of termination of a lease may affect the classification of a lease as either operating or finance. This is because it will affect the expected lease term, level of payments under the lease and expected residual value of the lease assets.

Termination during the primary lease term will generally not be anticipated at the lease inception because the lessee can be assumed to be using the asset for at least that period. In addition, such an early termination will be unlikely because most leases are non-cancellable. A termination payment is usually required which will give the lessor an amount equivalent to most or all of the rental receipts which would have been received if no termination had taken place, which means that it is reasonably certain at inception that the lease will continue to expiry.

However, there are consequences if the lease is terminated. The issues for finance lessees and lessors are discussed in the following sections.

4.3.1   *Termination of finance leases by lessees*

Finance lease payables recognised by a lessee are subject to the derecognition provisions of IAS 39. *[IAS 39.2(b)]*.

IAS 39 requires an entity to derecognise (i.e. remove from its balance sheet) a financial liability (or a part of a financial liability) when, and only when, it is 'extinguished', that is, when the obligation specified in the contract is discharged, cancelled, or expires. *[IAS 39.39]*. This will be achieved when the debtor either:

- discharges the liability (or part of it) by paying the creditor, normally with cash, other financial assets, goods or services; or
- is legally released from primary responsibility for the liability (or part of it) either by process of law or by the creditor. *[IAS 39.AG57]*.

The difference between the carrying amount of a financial liability (or part of a financial liability) extinguished or transferred to another party and the consideration paid, including any non-cash assets transferred or liabilities assumed, is to be recognised in profit or loss.

In order to identify the part of a liability derecognised, an entity allocates the previous carrying amount of the financial liability between the part that continues to be recognised and the part that is derecognised based on the relative fair values of those parts on the date of the repurchase. *[IAS 39.41-42]*. Derecognition of part of a lease liability will most likely come about in the context of a lease renegotiation, discussed at 6 below.

The derecognition of financial liabilities is dealt with in Chapter 40.

4.3.1.A   *Early termination by lessees*

Except as part of a renegotiation or business combination or similar larger arrangement, early termination of a finance lease results in derecognition of the capitalised asset by the lessee, with any remaining balance of the capitalised asset being written off as a loss on disposal. Any payment made by the lessee will reduce the lease obligation that is being carried in the balance sheet. If either a part of this obligation is not eliminated or the termination payment exceeds the previously existing obligation, then the remainder or excess will be included as a gain or loss respectively on derecognition of a financial liability.

A similar accounting treatment is required where the lease terminates at the expected date and there is a residual at least partly guaranteed by the lessee. For the lessee, a payment made under such a guarantee will reduce the obligation to the lessor as the guaranteed residual would obviously be included in the lessee's finance lease obligation. If any part of the guaranteed residual is not called upon, then the lessee would treat this as a profit on derecognition of a financial liability.

The effect on the derecognition of the capitalised asset will depend on the extent to which the lessee expected to make the residual payment as this will have affected the level to which the capitalised asset has been depreciated. For example, if the total guaranteed residual was not expected to become payable by the lessee, then the depreciation charge may have been calculated to give a net book value at the end of the lease term equal to the residual element not expected to become payable. If this estimate was correct then the remaining obligation will equal the net book value of the relevant asset, so that the gain on derecognition of the liability will be equal to the loss on derecognition of the asset.

Example 26.16: Early termination of finance leases by lessees

In Example 26.15 in 4.2.3C above there is effectively a guarantee of a residual of €3,000 dependent on the mileage done by the leased vehicle. Assuming that the lease is capitalised as a finance lease, if the lessee considers at the lease inception that the guarantee will not be called upon, then he will depreciate the vehicle to an estimated residual value of €3,000 over the lease term. In the event that his estimate is found to be correct, then the loss on disposal of the asset at its written down value will be equal and opposite to the gain on derecognition of the lease obligation of €3,000. However, if, for example, €1,000 of the guarantee was called upon, whereas the lessee had estimated that it would not be, then the net book value of €3,000 and the unused guarantee of €2,000 will both be derecognised and a loss of €1,000 will be shown on disposal of the vehicle.

4.3.2   Termination and impairment of finance leases by lessors

Although lease receivables are not financial instruments, the carrying amounts recognised by a lessor are subject to the derecognition and impairment provisions of IAS 39. Generally, a financial asset is derecognised when the contractual rights to the cash flows from that asset have expired. *[IAS 39.17]*. This will apply to most leases at the end of the term when the lessor has no more right to cash flows from the lessee.

If the cash flows from the financial asset have not expired, it is derecognised when, and only when, the entity 'transfers' the asset within the specified meaning of the term in IAS 39, and the transfer has the effect that the entity has either:

(a)   transferred substantially all the risks and rewards of the asset; or

(b)   neither transferred nor retained substantially all the risks and rewards of the asset and has not retained control of the asset. *[IAS 39.20]*. If the rights to the cash are retained then there are other tests that must be met. *[IAS 39.19]*.

These requirements are relevant to common lease situations such as sub-leases and back-to-back leases, dealt with in 8 below. Derecognition of financial assets is a complex area discussed in particular in Chapter 50.

4.3.2.A Impairment of lease receivables

If a lease receivable is impaired, for example, because the lessee is in default of lease payments, the amount of the impairment is measured as the difference between the carrying value of the receivable and the present value of the estimated future cash flows, discounted at the implicit interest rate used on initial recognition. Therefore, if the lessor makes an arrangement with the lessee and reschedules and/or reduces amounts due under the lease, the loss is by reference to the new carrying amount of the receivable, calculated by discounting the estimated future cash flows at the original implicit interest rate. *[IAS 39.63]*. This methodology has been used in Example 26.13 at 4.2.3.A above.

4.3.2.B Early termination of finance leases by lessors

Any termination payment received by a lessor upon an early termination will reduce the lessor's net investment in the lease shown as a receivable. If the termination payment is greater than the carrying amount of the net investment, the lessor will account for a gain on derecognition of the lease; conversely, if the termination payment is smaller than the net investment, a loss will be shown.

Losses on termination in the ordinary course of business are less likely to arise because a finance lease usually has termination terms so that the lessor is compensated fully for early termination and the lessor has legal title to the asset. The lessor can continue to include the asset in current assets as a receivable to the extent that sales proceeds or new finance lease receivables are expected to arise. If the asset is then re-leased under an operating lease, the asset may be transferred to property, plant and equipment and depreciated over its remaining useful life. There is no guidance about the amount at which the asset is recognised in PP&E. Although the net investment is not a financial instrument within scope of IAS 39, *[IAS 39.2(b)]*, in general we expect that entities would use the carrying amount of the net investment as the cost of the reacquired item of PP&E. However, in the absence of authoritative guidance we would expect there to be divergence in practice. If the asset is designated as held for sale then the requirements of IFRS 5 will apply (see Chapter 4). The aspects of lease assets and liabilities that are within scope of IAS 39 are described at 3.5 above.

4.4 Manufacturer or dealer lessors

Manufacturers or dealers often offer customers the choice of either buying or leasing an asset. While there is no selling profit on entering into an operating lease because it is not the equivalent of a sale, *[IAS 17.55]*, a finance lease of an asset by a manufacturer or dealer lessor gives rise to two types of income:

(a) the profit or loss equivalent to the profit or loss resulting from an outright sale of the asset being leased, at normal selling prices, reflecting any applicable volume or trade discounts; and

(b) the finance income over the lease term. *[IAS 17.43]*.

If the customer is offered the choice of paying the cash price for the asset immediately or paying for it on deferred credit terms then, as long as the credit terms are the manufacturer or dealer's normal terms, the cash price (after taking account of applicable or volume discounts) can be used to determine the selling profit. *[IAS 17.42]*. However, in many cases such an approach should not be followed as the manufacturer or dealer's marketing considerations often influence the terms of the lease. For example, a car dealer may offer 0% finance deals instead of reducing the normal selling price of his cars. It would be wrong in this instance for the dealer to record a profit on the sale of the car and no finance income under the lease.

The standard, therefore, requires sales revenue to be based on the fair value of the asset (i.e. the cash price) or, if lower, the present value of the minimum lease payments computed at a market rate of interest. As a result, if artificially low rates of interest are quoted, selling profit is restricted to that which would apply if a commercial rate of interest were charged. *[IAS 17.44-45]*. The cost of sales is reduced to the extent that the lessor retains an unguaranteed residual interest in the asset. *[IAS 17.44]*.

Initial direct costs should be recognised as an expense in the income statement at the inception of the lease. This is not the same as the treatment when a lessor arranges a finance lease, where the costs are added to the finance lease receivable; the standard argues that this is because the costs are related mainly to earning the selling profit. *[IAS 17.46]*. If the manufacturer or dealer is in the (relatively unlikely) position of incurring an overall loss because the total rentals receivable under the finance lease are less than the cost to it of the asset then this loss should be taken to the profit and loss account at the inception of the lease. IAS 17 assumes that the manufacturer or dealer will have a normal implicit interest rate based on its other leasing activity. However, in other situations where the manufacturer or dealer does not conduct other leasing business, an estimate will have to be made of the implicit rate for the leasing activity.

5 ACCOUNTING FOR OPERATING LEASES

5.1 Operating leases in the financial statements of lessees

IAS 17 requires that lease payments under an operating lease, excluding costs for services such as insurance and maintenance, should be recognised as an expense on a straight-line basis over the lease term unless another systematic basis is representative of the time pattern of the user's benefit, even if the payments are not on that basis. *[IAS 17.33-34]*. Generally, the only other acceptable bases are where rentals are based on a unit of use or unit of production.

IAS 17 requires a straight line recognition of the lease expenses even when amounts are not payable on this basis. This does not require anticipation of contingent rental increases, such as those that will result from a periodic re-pricing to market rates or those that are based on some other index (see 3.4.7 above). However, lease payments may vary over time for other reasons that will have to be taken into account in calculating the annual charge. Described in more detail below are some examples: leases that are inclusive of services, leases with increments intended to substitute for inflation and security deposits made with lessors that attract low or no interest. Lease incentives are another feature that may affect the cash flows under a lease; they are dealt with in more detail in 5.1.4 (for lessees) and 5.2.2 (for lessors).

5.1.1 Leases that include payments for services

There is a wide range of services that can be subsumed into a single 'lease' payment. For a vehicle, the payment may include maintenance and servicing. Property leases could include cleaning, security, reception services, gardening, utilities and local and property taxes. Single payments for operating facilities may include lease payments for the plant and the costs of operating them, as discussed in the context of IFRIC 4; see example 26.2 above. IAS 17 says that the costs of services should be excluded to arrive at the lease payments. This is straightforward enough if the payments are made by the lessor and quantified in the payments made by the lessee. It will be somewhat less so if, for example, the lessor makes all maintenance payments but does not specify the amounts; instead, payments are increased periodically to take account of changes in such costs. In such a case the lessee will have to estimate the amount paid for services and deduct them from the total. The remaining payments, which relate solely to the right to use the asset, will then be spread on a straight line basis over the non-cancellable term of the lease.

5.1.2 Straight-line recognition over the lease term

Operating lease payments must be recognised on a straight line basis over the lease term, unless another systematic basis is more representative of the time pattern of the user's benefit. *[IAS 17.33]*. There are some leases that increase annually by fixed increments intended to compensate for expected annual inflation over the lease period. There has been debate as to whether such increases must also be taken on a straight-line basis over the non-cancellable lease term.

In considering the issue, the Interpretations Committee noted that IAS 17 does not incorporate adjustments to operating lease payments to reflect the time value of money. Except in those cases where another basis is more appropriate, it requires all operating leases to be taken on a straight-line basis. They concluded that to allow recognition of these increases on an annual basis would be inconsistent with the treatment of other operating leases.[4]

Some leases allow for an annual increase in line with an index but with a fixed minimum increment. As discussed in 3.4.7 above, contingent rents are excluded from the lease payments but the fixed minimum increment will have to be spread so as to take the payments on a straight line basis over the lease term.

Example 26.17: Operating lease expenses with fixed annual increment

Entity A leases a property at an initial rent of €1,000,000 per annum. The lease has a non-cancellable term of 30 years and rent increases annually in line with the Retail Prices Index (RPI) of the country in which the property is situated but with a minimum increase of 2.5% (the estimated long-term rate of inflation in the country in question) and a maximum of 5% per annum.

The annual increase of 2.5% must be taken into account in calculating the operating lease payment charged to profit or loss. On a straight-line basis this will be €1,463,000 per annum. Therefore, by the end of year 15 (at which point the amounts payable under the lease will exceed the straight-lined amount) the entity will have paid rentals of €15 million, charged €22 million to income and will be recording an accrual of €7 million.

If the increase in the RPI exceeds 2.5% these additional amounts will be charged to income as contingent rents.

5.1.3 Notional or actual interest paid to lessors

Lessees are sometimes required to place security deposits with lessors on which they will receive either no or a reduced rate of interest. In accordance with IAS 39, the lessee initially measures the deposit at fair value and subsequently at amortised cost (assuming that the deposit is classified as a loan and receivable *[IAS 39.46]*) using the effective interest method; accordingly interest income is recognised through profit and loss over the useful life of the deposit. *[IAS 39.9]*. At inception of an operating lease, the difference between the nominal value of the deposit and its fair value should be considered additional rent payable to the lessor. This will be expensed on a straight-line basis over the lease term.

Example 26.18: Operating lease expenses reflecting interest payments to the lessor

A lessee makes an interest-free security deposit of €1,000 on entering into a five year lease. It assesses an appropriate rate of interest for the deposit to be 4% and accordingly the fair value of the deposit at inception is €822. On making the deposit, it will record it as follows:

Year		€	€
1	Security deposit	822	
	Advance rentals	178	
	Cash		1,000

During the five years of the lease, it will record interest income and additional rental expense as follows:

Year	Interest income	Rental expense	Difference
1	33	(36)	(3)
2	34	(35)	(1)
3	36	(36)	–
4	37	(36)	1
5	38	(35)	3
	178	(178)	

5.1.4 Lease incentives – accounting by lessees

Incentives that may be given by a lessor to a lessee as an incentive to enter into a new or renewed operating lease agreement include an up-front cash payment to the lessee or the reimbursement or assumption by the lessor of costs of the lessee, such as relocation costs, leasehold improvements and costs associated with a pre-existing lease commitment of the lessee. Alternatively, the lessor may grant the lessee rent-free or reduced rent initial lease periods. *[SIC-15.1]*.

The consensus reached by the SIC in Interpretation SIC-15 – *Operating Leases – Incentives* – was that all incentives for the agreement of a new or renewed operating lease should be recognised as an integral part of the net consideration agreed for the use of the leased asset, irrespective of the incentive's nature or form or the timing of payments. *[SIC-15.3]*. The lessee should recognise the aggregate benefit of incentives as a reduction of rental expense over the lease term, on a straight-line basis unless another systematic basis is representative of the time pattern of the lessee's benefit from the use of the leased asset. *[SIC-15.5]*. Finally, SIC-15 requires that costs incurred by the lessee, including costs in connection with a pre-existing lease (for example, costs for termination, relocation or leasehold improvements), to be accounted for by the lessee in accordance with the IAS applicable to those costs, including costs which are effectively reimbursed through an incentive arrangement. *[SIC-15.6]*. In an Appendix to SIC-15, the SIC has set out the following two examples that illustrate how to apply the Interpretation:

Example 26.19:   Application of SIC-15

Example 1

An entity agrees to enter into a new lease arrangement with a new lessor. The lessor agrees to pay the lessee's relocation costs as an incentive to the lessee for entering into the new lease. The lessee's moving costs are 1,000. The new lease has a term of 10 years, at a fixed rate of 2,000 per year.

The accounting is:

The lessee recognises relocation costs of 1,000 as an expense in Year 1. Net consideration of 19,000 consists of 2,000 for each of the 10 years in the lease term, less a 1,000 incentive for relocation costs. Both the lessor and lessee would recognise the net rental consideration of 19,000 over the 10 year lease term using a single amortisation method in accordance with paragraphs 4 and 5 of SIC-15.

Example 2

An entity agrees to enter into a new lease arrangement with a new lessor. The lessor agrees to a rent-free period for the first three years as incentive to the lessee for entering into the new lease. The new lease has a term of 20 years, at a fixed rate of 5,000 per annum for years 4 through 20.

The accounting is:

Net consideration of 85,000 consists of 5,000 for each of 17 years in the lease term. Both the lessor and lessee would recognise the net consideration of 85,000 over the 20-year lease term using a single amortisation method in accordance with paragraphs 4 and 5 of SIC-15.

One point about SIC 15 that has attracted considerable debate is its requirement to spread incentives over the lease term. The validity of this has been questioned if rentals are re-priced to market rates at periodic intervals – it is argued that in these circumstances the rent-free period is being given solely to compensate for an above-market rental in the primary period.

In its April 2005 meeting the Interpretations Committee decided not undertake a project to modify SIC-15. It did not accept that the lease expense of a lessee after an operating lease is re-priced to market ought to be comparable with the lease expense of an entity entering into a new lease at that same time at market rates. Nor did it believe that the re-pricing itself would be reflective of a change in the time patterns of the lessee's benefit from the use of the leased asset.[5] In other words, incentives are seen in the context of the total cash flows under the lease and, except where the benefit of the lease is not directly related to the time during which the entity has the right to use the asset, IAS 17 requires these to be taken on a straight line basis.

There is a similar argument when lessees contend (as they often do) that they should not be obliged to spread rentals over a void period as they are not actually benefiting from the property during this time – it is a fit-out period or a start-up so activities are yet to increase to anticipated levels. However, the argument against this is really no different to the above: the lessee's period of benefit from the use of the asset is the lease term, so the incentive cannot be taken over the initial period. This was reinforced by the Interpretations Committee in July 2008, when it noted that IAS 16 and IAS 38 require an entity to recognise the use of productive assets using the method that best reflects 'the pattern in which the asset's future economic benefits are expected to be consumed by the entity' *[IAS 16.60, IAS 38.97]* but IAS 17 refers to the time pattern of the user's benefit. *[IAS 17.33]*. Therefore, any alternative to the straight-line recognition of lease expense under an operating lease must reflect the time pattern of the use of the leased property rather than the amount of use or other factor related to economic benefits.[6] The Interpretations Committee has not shown any indication that it is prepared to accept economic arguments for other than straight-line treatment.

5.1.5 Onerous contracts

IAS 37 prohibits the recognition of provisions for future operating losses *[IAS 37.63]* but the standard specifically addresses the issue of onerous contracts. It requires that if an entity has a contract that is onerous, the present obligation under the contract should be recognised and measured as a provision. *[IAS 37.66]*.

The standard defines an onerous contract as 'a contract in which the unavoidable costs of meeting the obligations under it exceed the economic benefits expected to be received under it'. *[IAS 37.10]*. This is taken to mean that the contract itself is onerous to the point of being directly loss-making, not simply uneconomic by reference to current prices. A common example of an onerous contract seen in practice relates to operating leases for the rent of property, and the standard includes the following example in Appendix C:

Chapter 26

Example 26.20:   An onerous contract

An entity operates profitably from a factory that it has leased under an operating lease. During December 20X0 the entity relocates its operations to a new factory. The lease on the old factory continues for the next four years, it cannot be cancelled and the factory cannot be re-let to another user.

Present obligation as a result of a past obligating event	The obligating event is the signing of the lease contract, which gives rise to a legal obligation.
Transfer of economic benefits in settlement	When the lease becomes onerous, a transfer of economic benefits is probable. (Until the lease becomes onerous, the entity accounts for the lease by applying IAS 17, Leases.)
Conclusion	A provision is recognised for the best estimate of the unavoidable lease payments (see IAS 37, paragraphs 5(c), 14 and 66).

Care must be taken to ensure that the lease itself is onerous. If an entity has a number of retail outlets and one of these is loss-making, this is not sufficient to make the lease onerous. However, if the entity vacates the premises and sub-lets them at an amount less than the rent it is paying, then the lease becomes onerous and the entity should provide for its best estimate of the unavoidable lease payments. This will include the difference between the lease and sub-lease payments, together with provision as appropriate for any period where there is no sub-tenant.

The accounting for onerous contracts is discussed in more detail in Chapter 29 at 5.3.

5.2   Operating leases in the financial statements of lessors

5.2.1   Accounting for assets subject to operating leases

Lessors should present assets subject to operating leases in their balance sheets according to the nature of the asset, i.e. usually as PP&E or as an intangible asset. Lease income from operating leases should be recognised in income on a straight-line basis over the lease term, unless another systematic basis is more representative of the time pattern in which, the standard states, 'use benefit derived from the leased asset is diminished'. *[IAS 17.49-50]*. Generally, the only other basis that is encountered is based on unit-of-production or service.

Lease income excludes receipts for services provided such as insurance and maintenance. IAS 18 – *Revenue* – provides guidance on how to recognise service revenue – see Chapter 30. Costs, including depreciation, incurred in earning the lease income are recognised as an expense. *[IAS 17.51]*. Initial direct costs incurred specifically to earn revenues from an operating lease are added to the carrying amount of the leased asset and allocated to income over the lease term in proportion to the recognition of lease income. *[IAS 17.52]*. This means that the costs will be depreciated on a straight-line basis if this is the method of recognising the lease income, regardless of the depreciation basis of the asset.

The depreciation policy for depreciable leased assets is to be consistent with the entity's policy for similar assets that are not subject to leasing arrangements and calculated in accordance with IAS 16 or IAS 38, as appropriate. *[IAS 17.53]*. If the lessor does not use similar assets in its business then the depreciation policy must be set solely by reference to IASs 16 and 38. This also means that the lessor is obliged in accordance with IAS 16 to consider the residual value and economic life of the assets at least at each financial year-end. *[IAS 16.51]*. There are similar requirements in the case of intangible assets, although IAS 38 notes that they rarely have a residual value. *[IAS 38.100]*. These matters are discussed in Chapters 19 and 20. These assets are also tested for impairment in a manner consistent with other tangible and intangible fixed assets; IAS 17 refers to IAS 36 (discussed in Chapter 22) in providing guidance on the need to assess the possibility of an impairment of assets. *[IAS 17.54]*.

5.2.2 Lease incentives – accounting by lessors

In negotiating a new or renewed operating lease, a lessor may provide incentives for the lessee to enter into the arrangement. In the case of a property lease, the tenant may be given a rent-free period but other types of incentive may include up-front cash payments to the lessee or the reimbursement or assumption by the lessor of lessee costs such as relocation costs, leasehold improvements and costs associated with a pre-existing lease commitment of the lessee. This issue was addressed by the SIC in Interpretation SIC-15, which states that the lessor should recognise the aggregate cost of incentives as a reduction of rental income over the lease term, on a straight-line basis unless another systematic basis is representative of the time pattern over which the benefit of the leased asset is diminished. *[SIC-15.4]*. The SIC rejected the argument that lease incentives for lessors are part of the initial direct costs of negotiating or arranging the contract; instead concluding that they are in substance, related to the amount of consideration received by the lessor for the use of the asset. This view was confirmed in the IASB's 2003 revision of IAS 17, which requires initial direct costs to be capitalised as part of the carrying value of the asset – see 3.4.8 above). Lessor accounting is, therefore, the mirror image of lessee accounting for the incentives, as described in 5.1.4 above.

5.3 Payments made in connection with the termination of operating leases

Payments for terminating operating leases or payments between a lessee and a third party regarding a lease are extremely common but not all are directly addressed by either IAS 17 or SIC-15. In addition, neither statement addresses payments made between a lessee and a third party in connection with a lease. The following example addresses a variety of payments that might arise in connection with an operating lease over a property:

Chapter 26

Example 26.21:   Payments made in connection with terminating an operating lease

| | *Treatment in the financial statements of* | | |
Transaction	*Lessor*	*Old tenant*	*New tenant*
Lessor pays			
Old lessee – lessor intends to renovate the building.	Expense unless it meets the definition of an asset under IAS 16 (note 1)	Recognise income immediately (note 1)	
New tenant – an incentive to occupy	Prepayment amortised over the lease term on a straight line basis under SIC-15 (see 5.2.2 above)		Deferred lease incentive amortised over the lease term on a straight line basis under SIC-15 (see 5.1.4 above).
Building alterations specific to the lessee with no further value to the lessor after completion of the lease period.	Prepayment amortised over the lease term on a straight line basis under SIC-15 (see 5.2.2 above)		Leasehold improvements capitalised and depreciated or expensed as maintenance expenditure. Deferred lease incentive amortised over the lease term on a straight line basis under SIC-15 (see 5.1.4 above).
Old tenant pays			
Lessor, to vacate the leased premises early	Recognised as income immediately to the extent not already recognised (note 2)	Recognised as expense immediately to the extent not already recognised (note 2)	
New tenant to take over the lease		Recognise as an expense immediately (note 3)	Recognise as income immediately, unless compensation for above market rentals, in which case amortise over expected lease term (note 3)

Transaction	Lessor	Old tenant	New tenant
New tenant pays			
Lessor to secure the right to obtain a lease agreement	Recognise as deferred revenue under IAS 17 and amortise over the lease term on a straight line basis (see 5.2.1 above)		Recognise as a prepayment under IAS 17 and amortise over the lease term on a straight line basis (see 5.1.3 above).
Old tenant to buy out the lease agreement		Recognise as a gain immediately (note 4)	Recognised as an intangible asset with a finite economic life (note 4)

Note 1   A payment by a lessor to a lessee to terminate the lease is not dealt with under IAS 17 or SIC-15. If the lessor's payment meets the definition of a cost of an item of property, plant and equipment it must be capitalised. *[IAS 16.7]*. If not, the payment will be expensed, as it does not meet the definition of an intangible asset in IAS 38. *[IAS 38.8]*. As the lessee has no further performance obligation the receipt should be income.

Note 2   A payment made by the lessee to the lessor to get out of a lease agreement does not meet the appropriate definitions of an asset in IAS 16 or IAS 38 and does not fall within IAS 17 as there is no longer a lease – the payments are not for the use of the asset. Therefore it should be expensed. Similarly, from the lessor's perspective, income should be recorded.

Note 3   A payment made by an existing tenant to a new tenant to take over the lease would also not meet the definition of an asset under IAS 16 or IAS 38 (see notes above) and falls outside IAS 17 as the lease no longer exists. The old tenant must expense the cost. The new tenant will recognise the payment as income except to the extent that it is compensation for an above-market rental, in which case the treatment required by SIC-15 for a lease incentive must be applied and it will be amortised over the lease term (see 5.1.4 above)

Note 4   The new tenant has made a payment to an old tenant, and while it is in connection with the lease arrangements, it is not directly related to the actual lease as it was made to a party outside the lease contract. Therefore it cannot be accounted for under IAS 17. The old tenant will treat the receipt as a gain immediately. Any remaining balances of the lease will be removed and a net gain (or loss) recorded. The payment by the lessee will generally meet the definition of an intangible asset in IAS 38 and therefore will be amortised over the useful life, being the term of the lease. However, if other conditions and circumstances in the arrangement mean that this definition is not met, the payment will be expensed in the period in which it is incurred.

Compensation amounts paid by lessors to lessees are sometimes described as 'compensation for loss of profits' or some similar term. This is a method of calculation and the receipt is not a substitute for the revenue or profits that the lessee would otherwise have earned. The description will not affect the treatment described above.

Chapter 26

6   MODIFYING THE TERMS OF LEASES

Lessees may renegotiate lease terms for a variety of reasons. They may wish to extend the term over which they have a right to use the asset or to alter the number of assets that they have a right to use. They may consider that the lease is too expensive by comparison with current market terms. The renegotiations may deal with several such issues simultaneously. Lessors may also renegotiate leases, for example one lessor may sell the lease to another that offers to provide the lease service more cheaply to the lessee, usually because the new lessor's transactions have different tax consequences. Lease contracts may allow for changes in payments if specified contingencies occur, for example a change in taxation or interest rates.

6.1   IAS 17 and accounting for renegotiations

The standard has little to say on the consequences of such renegotiations. It states:

> 'If at any time the lessee and the lessor agree to change the provisions of the lease, other than by renewing the lease, in a manner that would have resulted in a different classification of the lease ... if the changed terms had been in effect at the inception of the lease, the revised agreement is regarded as a new agreement over its term.' *[IAS 17.13]*.

As described at 3.2.3 above, the consequences of a different classification are clear. A revised agreement that is reclassified (e.g. an operating lease is reassessed as a finance lease or *vice versa*) is accounted for prospectively in accordance with the revised terms. However, IAS 17 leaves many questions of application unanswered. It provides no practical guidance on what to take into account to determine whether there would have been a different classification. It does not explain how to account for the consequences of modifications, whether or not they would lead to a different classification. These matters are described below.

Other changes to lease terms that do not lead to reclassification but that nevertheless need to be accounted for, for example variations due to changes in rates of taxation or interest rates, are discussed in 6.1.4 below.

Changes in estimates, for example changes in estimates of the economic life or of the residual value of the leased item, or changes in circumstances, for example default by the lessee, do not result in a different classification (see 3.2.2 above). *[IAS 17.13]*. Changes in estimates also include the renewal of a lease or the execution of a purchase option, if these were not considered probable at the inception of the lease.

6.1.1   *Determining whether there is a different classification*

Paragraph 13 of IAS 17 states that, if the terms of a lease are modified so that the revised terms would have resulted in a different classification of the lease had they been in effect at inception, the revised agreement is regarded as a new agreement over its term.

The modification must, therefore, be one that affects the risks and rewards incidental to ownership of the asset by changing the terms and cash flows of the existing lease, for example a renegotiation that changes the duration and/or the payments due under the lease.

One of the indicators used in practice is an assessment of the net present value of the minimum lease payments and whether or not these amount to substantially all of the fair value of the leased asset. An entity might use this test to help assess whether the revised lease is a finance or operating lease, in conjunction with a reassessment of the other factors described at 3.2.2 above. Therefore, the entity might use one of the following methods to calculate the net present value:

(a)   recalculate the net present value based on the revised lease term and cash flows (and revised residual value, if relevant), which will result in a different implicit interest rate to that used in the original calculation;

(b)   take into consideration the changes in the agreement but calculate the present value of the asset and liability using the interest rate implicit in the original lease. This approach, which is consistent with the remeasurement of the carrying value of financial instruments applying the effective interest rate method, as required by IAS 39, *[IAS 39.AG8]*, will result in a 'catch up' adjustment as at the date of the reassessment; or

(c)   consider the revised agreement to be a new lease and assess the classification based on the terms of the new agreement and the fair value and useful life of the asset at the date of the revision. The inference of this method, unlike (a) and (b), is that the entity already considers that there is likely to be a new classification to the lease, based on an assessment of other factors.

A lessee under an operating lease will be able to apply methods (a) and (c) but (b) will not be available to it unless it has sufficient information to be able to calculate the IIR at the inception of the original lease. Lessees that are party to more complex leases or sale and leaseback arrangements are more likely to have the necessary information available to them.

Each of these three approaches is likely to lead to a different net present value for the minimum lease payments. They are compared in the following example.

Example 26.22:   Modifying the terms of leases

Details of a non-cancellable lease taken out on the first day of the year are as follows:

(i)   Fair value = €25,000

(ii)   Estimated useful life of asset = 8 years

(iii)   Five annual rentals payable in advance of €4,200

(iv)   At the end of year 5, the asset must be sold and all proceeds up to €8,292 taken by the lessor. If any amount in excess of €8,292 is received, 99% of the excess is repaid to the lessee.

The lease does not contain any renewal options.

The lessee assesses this as an operating lease because the terms suggest that substantially all of the risks and rewards of ownership have not been transferred to it – the lease term is only 62.5% of the useful life of the asset and there is clearly significant residual value.

At the end of year 2, the parties renegotiate the lease, with the changes coming into effect on the first day of year 3. The lease term is to be extended for a further two years, making the term seven years in total. Payments for the four years 3-6 have been reduced to €4,000 and €1,850 is payable for year 7. At the time of the renegotiation the estimated fair value of the asset is €17,500 and its residual value at the end of year 7 is €1,850.

The implicit interest rate in the original lease can be calculated because the maximum amount receivable by the lessor on the sale of the asset at the end of the lease term is the residual value (on the assumption that the lessor disregards any potential upside in its contingent 1%); the IIR is 5.92%, as follows:

Year	Capital sum at start of period €	Rental paid €	Capital sum during period €	Finance charge (5.92% per annum) €	Capital sum at end of period €
1	25,000	4,200	20,800	1,231	22,031
2	22,031	4,200	17,831	1,056	18,887
3	18,887	4,200	14,687	869	15,556
4	15,556	4,200	11,356	672	12,028
5	12,028	4,200	7,828	464	8,292
		21,000		4,292	

This supports the lessee's assessment that this is an operating lease as the present value of the minimum lease payments is €18,588, which is 74.35% of the fair value of the asset.

If these revised terms had been in existence at inception then the implicit interest rate and NPV calculation would have been as follows. This corresponds to (a) above.

Year	Capital sum at start of period €	Rental paid €	Capital sum during period €	Finance charge (4.10% per annum) €	Capital sum at end of period €
1	25,000	4,200	20,800	853	21,653
2	21,653	4,200	17,453	715	18,168
3	18,168	4,000	14,168	581	14,749
4	14,749	4,000	10,749	441	11,190
5	11,190	4,000	7,190	294	7,484
6	7,484	4,000	3,484	143	3,627
7	3,627	1,850	1,777	73	1,850
		26,250		3,100	

The NPV of the lessee's minimum lease payments is €23,603 which is 94.41% of the fair value of the asset. The lease would be classified as a finance lease.

Method (b) results in the following calculation:

Year	Capital sum at start of period €	Rental paid €	Capital sum during period €	Finance charge (5.92% per annum) €	Capital sum at end of period €
1	25,000	4,200	20,800	1,231	22,031
2	22,031	4,200	17,831	1,056	18,887
3	17,566	4,000	13,566	803	14,369
4	14,369	4,000	10,369	613	10,982
5	10,982	4,000	6,982	414	7,396
6	7,396	4,000	3,396	201	3,597
7	3,597	1,850	1,747	103	1,850
		26,250		4,421	

The present value of the total payments over the revised lease term at the original discount rate is €22,585, which is 90.34% of the fair value of the asset at commencement of the lease. In order to make the computation, an adjustment is made to the capital amount as at the date that the lease is renegotiated. The outstanding amount is recomputed from €18,887 (the balance at the end of year 2 calculated using the original assumptions) to €17,566, the amount that corresponds to the new assumptions.

If method (c) is applied, the modified lease is considered as if it were a new five year lease. The IIR calculated prospectively over the remaining term is now 6.13%

Year	Capital sum at start of period	Rental paid	Capital sum during period	Finance charge (6.13% per annum)	Capital sum at end of period
	€	€	€	€	€
3	17,500	4,000	13,500	827	14,327
4	14,327	4,000	10,327	633	10,960
5	10,960	4,000	6,960	426	7,386
6	7,386	4,000	3,386	207	3,593
7	3,593	1,850	1,743	107	1,850
		17,850		2,200	

The present value of the remaining payments is €16,126, which is 92.15% of the fair value of the asset (€17,500) at the date of entering into the new lease.

In this example, all three methods result in a present value of the minimum lease payments that exceeds 90% but this would not, of course, always be the case. It must be stressed that all features of the arrangement must be considered in order to assess whether or not the lease transfers substantially all of the risks and rewards of ownership.

6.1.2 Accounting for reclassified leases

IAS 17 states that the revised agreement is treated as a new agreement over its term.

If the original lease was a finance lease and the revised lease is an operating lease, then the balances relating to the finance lease must be derecognised. For the lessee, this involves derecognising both the asset (which will have been depreciated up to the point of derecognition over the shorter of the useful life or the lease term) and the finance lease liability. Finance lease derecognition is discussed further at 4.3 above.

If the original lease was an operating lease and the revised lease is a finance lease, then any balances resulting from recognising the lease cost on a straight line basis will be expensed and the balances relating to the finance lease must be recognised for the first time.

Although the standard says that 'the revised agreement is regarded as a new agreement over its term,' *[IAS 17.13]*, this refers to classification; there is no consensus regarding the measurement of assets and liabilities as at this point.

The most obvious interpretation is that the revised lease is accounted for as a new lease as from the date on which the terms were changed, based on the fair value of the assets as at the date of revision. This is consistent with using either method (a) or method (c) in 6.1.1 above to help determine the revised classification. An example of the calculation is in Example 26.22 above – method (c) calculates the assets and liabilities as if the revised agreement were a new lease as from the date of reassessment.

However, some consider that the new lease can be accounted for using method (b) above, by taking into consideration the changes in the agreement but calculating the present value of the asset and liability by using the interest rate implicit in the

Chapter 26

original lease. This uses an accepted methodology and is consistent with the fact that there has, in fact, only been a change to the original terms and not a completely new lease; it also has the advantage that the revised fair value of the assets does not have to be known.

If the original lease agreement and the revised lease agreement are both finance leases, then the modification will have accounting consequences that are discussed in the following section.

6.1.3 Accounting for modifications to finance leases

If the rights under a finance lease have changed without a change in the classification, these changes to lease term and cash flows must be accounted for. Once again, the accounting consequences are not dealt with by IAS 17.

The two most obvious methods of calculating the impact of the changes are as follows:

(a)   Even though the classification has not changed, the revised agreement is accounted for as if it were a new lease. The calculation will be based on the fair value and useful life of the asset at the date of the revision.

(b)   Use the original IIR to discount the revised minimum lease payments and (for a lessee) adjust any change in lease liability to the carrying amount of the asset. Lessors will adjust the carrying value of the asset, taking gains or losses to income. As noted before, this approach is consistent with the requirements of IAS 39 when the effective interest rate method is applied and the cash flows change. [IAS 39.AG8].

These are described in 6.1.1 and example 26.22 above (method (c) and method (b)). For lessees, both of these methods will affect the carrying value of the asset and hence its future amortisation.

Another method that might be considered is to reflect changes prospectively over the remaining term of the lease; this is only likely to be appropriate if the cash flows are modified but all other rights remain unchanged. Some of the circumstances in which such changes can arise are considered at 6.1.4 below.

Example 26.23:   Accounting for lease modifications

The details of a lease are as in Example 26.22 above, except that the lease has an original duration of six years with an annual rent of €4,200, rather than five years. The present value of the minimum lease payments is €21,931, which is 87.72% of the fair value of the leased asset, calculated as follows:

Year	Capital sum at start of period €	Rental paid €	Capital sum during period €	Finance charge (5.92% per annum) €	Capital sum at end of period €
1	21,931	4,200	17,731	1,050	18,780
2	18,780	4,200	14,580	863	15,443
3	15,443	4,200	11,243	666	11,909
4	11,909	4,200	7,709	456	8,165
5	8,165	4,200	3,965	235	4,200
6	4,200	4,200	0	0	0
		25,200		3,270	

The directors of the entity assess this as a finance lease, taking account of all of the circumstances surrounding the agreement. The entity capitalise the asset at €21,931 at commencement of the lease and recognise an equivalent liability.

At the end of year 2, the lease term is extended for a further year, making the term seven years in total. Payments for the four years 3-6 are reduced to €4,000 and €1,850 is payable for year 7.

The asset (which has a useful life to the lessee of six years) has been depreciated on a straight line basis for two years and its carrying amount is €14,620, while the lessee's lease liability (as calculated above) is €15,443:

(a) If the modification is treated as a new lease, it will be accounted for as follows, using the revised fair value of €16,126and IIR of 6.13% calculated at Example 26.22(c) above:

Year	Capital sum at start of period €	Rental paid €	Capital sum during period €	Finance charge (6.13% per annum) €	Capital sum at end of period €
3	16,126	4,000	12,126	743	12,868
4	12,868	4,000	8,868	543	9,412
5	9,412	4,000	5,412	331	5,743
6	5,743	4,000	1,743	107	1,850
7	1,850	1,850	0	0	0
		17,850		1,724	

Therefore, the entity will derecognise both the leased asset of €14,620 and liability of €15,443, recognising a net gain of €823. The new asset of €16,126 will be depreciated prospectively over the remaining life of 5 years.

(b) If the modification is accounted for by restating the liability using the original IIR of 5.92%, the liability will be €16,178 calculated as follows:

Year	Capital sum at start of period €	Rental paid €	Capital sum during period €	Finance charge (5.92% per annum) €	Capital sum at end of period €
3	16,178	4,000	12,178	721	12,899
4	12,899	4,000	8,899	526	9,425
5	9,425	4,000	5,425	322	5,747
6	5,747	4,000	1,747	103	1,850
7	1,850	1,850	0	0	0
		17,850		1,672	

The entity will increase the lease liability by €735 (from €15,443 to €16,178) but it will increase the asset's carrying mount by the same amount from €14,620 to €15,355 which will be depreciated prospectively over the asset's remaining life of 5 years.

6.1.4 Tax and interest variation clauses and similar modifications

The relationship between leasing and taxation is frequently complex. It depends on whether tax deductions or taxable income are based on amounts receivable or payable in accordance with the lease or on the amounts that are taken to the income statement. It further depends on the availability of tax deductions for the cost of leased assets and who is able to claim these deductions. Some lessors draw up leases that are based on a post-tax return that takes account of these factors. These leases include tax variation clauses that enable lessors to change the amounts receivable

Chapter 26

from the lessee so that their post-tax return remains constant. The rental could be adjusted in a number of different ways, e.g. a new fixed payment, an up-front sum or an adjustment on a rental-by-rental basis.

The variations are unlikely of themselves to change the lease classification because their potential impact will have been taken into account in making that original assessment. Nor are they likely to lead to an impairment of the lessor's finance lease asset (assuming that it is a finance lease) as the profitability of the lease (on a post-tax basis) is unaffected.

IAS 17 does not refer to variation clauses so the question is whether the change is a variety of contingent rent, defined by the standard as that portion of the lease payments that is not fixed in amount but is based on a factor that varies other than with the passage of time, such as percentage of sales, amount of usage, price indices or market rates of interest, *[IAS 17.4]*, or another type of event. Contingent rent is recognised when it is incurred. This means that a reduction in rentals because of a reduction in rates of taxation would be a negative contingent rent.

However, it is also argued that the effect of the change in tax rates is far more like the lease modifications described at 6.1.3 above and there is some merit in this argument. As a result, some lessors take the view that the most relevant method of accounting for the changes is to use the original IIR to discount the revised minimum lease payments, taking the change in value of the finance lease asset to income (this is method (b) as described in 6.1.3). If rental payments decrease because the revised rate of taxation is lower, lessors applying this approach will recognise a loss on remeasuring the asset.

Leases may also contain interest variation clauses which adjust the rental by reference to movements in bank base rates or similar. As market rates of interest are specific examples of contingent rent in the standard, they must be accounted for as such. These movements could be positive or negative over the lease term.

6.1.5   *Accounting for modifications to operating leases*

Lessees may renegotiate terms with lessors, e.g. in circumstances in which the lessee has financial difficulties or where there is evidence that the lease terms are at higher than market rates.

Operating leases may include explicit or implicit options to extend the lease and the extension may have different payment terms. If there is a formal option, the lessee might be required to give notice to the lessor of its intention to extend at a set date before the lease expires. There may be similar arrangements with purchase options.

If the lessee renews a lease or exercises a purchase option, it does not have to re-assess the classification of a lease if the renewal and exercise were not considered probable at the inception of the lease (see 3.2.3 above). There may still be accounting consequences in connection with spreading the lease costs because of IAS 17's requirement to take lease costs on a straight line over the lease term, save in unusual circumstances (see 5.1 above).

The revised terms should be taken into account prospectively from the date of the agreement. There are good arguments against any alternative treatment.

A catch-up adjustment as if the new terms had always existed is not consistent with the fact that the modification is a change in estimate and these are normally accounted for prospectively.

Accounting for the original lease until its expiry and then treating the modification (e.g. the extended term) as if it were a new lease may be an attractive option as it avoids any change if there are straight line prepayments or accruals; these will reduce to zero at the end of the original lease term. However, it is inconsistent with the fact that there has been a contractual modification to the existing lease.

The lessee now has a contractual obligation to continue the lease and the effect on any existing straight line prepayment or accrual should be taken into account. Both previously recognised amounts and aggregate future minimum lease payments should be recognised on a straight-line basis prospectively over the remaining revised lease term, whether or not the original lease contract contained a renewal option.

Because these modifications are given to tenants in financial difficulties, any asset that is being spread forward may need to be assessed for impairment.

7 SALE AND LEASEBACK TRANSACTIONS

These transactions involve the original owner of an asset selling it to a provider of finance and immediately leasing it back. These parties will be termed the seller/lessee (the original owner) and buyer/lessor (the finance provider) respectively. Sometimes, instead of selling the asset outright, the original owner will lease the asset to the other party under a finance lease and then lease it back. Such a transaction is known as a 'lease and leaseback' and has similar effects so for these purposes is included within the term 'sale and leaseback'.

Sale and leaseback transactions are a fairly common feature of a number of industries, such as the retail and hotel industries, where it is as accepted a form of financing as taking out a mortgage or a bank overdraft. Many parties are involved as buyer/lessors, not only finance houses and banks but also pension funds and property groups. From a commercial point of view, the important point of difference lies between an entity that decides that it is cheaper to rent than to own – and is willing to pass on the property risk to the landlord – and an entity which decides to use the property as a means of raising finance – and will therefore retain the property risk. However from the accounting point of view, a major consideration is whether a profit can be reported on such transactions.

The buyer/lessor will treat the lease in the same way as it would any other lease that was not part of a sale and leaseback transaction. The accounting treatment of the transaction by the seller/lessee depends on the type of lease involved, i.e. whether the leaseback is under a finance or an operating lease. *[IAS 17.58]*.

7.1 Sale and finance leaseback

In order to assess whether the leaseback is under a finance lease, the seller/lessee will apply the qualitative tests in IAS 17 that are described at 3.2.2 above. If a sale and leaseback transaction results in a finance lease, any excess of sales proceeds over the carrying amount should not be recognised immediately as income by a seller/lessee. Instead, the excess is deferred and amortised over the lease term. *[IAS 17.59].* It is inappropriate to show a profit on disposal of an asset which has then, in substance, been reacquired by the entity under a finance lease as the lessor is providing finance to the lessee with the asset as security. *[IAS 17.60].* The asset will be restated to its fair value (or the present value of the minimum lease payments, if lower) in exactly the same way as any other asset acquired under a finance lease.

Example 26.24:   Sale and finance leaseback – accounting for the excess sale proceeds

An asset that has a carrying value of €700 and a remaining useful life of 7 years is sold for €1,200 and leased back on a finance lease. This is accounted for as a disposal of the original asset and the acquisition of an asset under a finance lease for €1,200. The excess of sales proceeds of €500 over the original carrying value should be deferred and amortised (i.e. credited to profit or loss) over the lease term.

The net impact on income of the charge for depreciation based on the carrying value of the asset held under the finance lease of €171 and the amortisation of the deferred income of €71 is the same as the annual depreciation of €100 based on the original carrying amount.

In 2007 the Interpretations Committee considered the related area of sale and repurchase options, concluding that IAS 17 itself contains 'the more specific guidance with respect to sale and leaseback transactions'.[7] However, many still consider that there is an alternative treatment which is more consistent with the substance of the arrangement and with the approach in SIC-27 described at 2.2 above, which deals with transactions that have the form but not the substance of leases. It follows the standard's description of the transaction as 'a means whereby the lessor provides finance to the lessee, with the asset as security'. *[IAS 17.60].* The previous carrying value is left unchanged, with the sales proceeds being shown as a liability to be accounted for under IAS 39. The creditor balance represents the finance lease liability under the leaseback. This is consistent with IAS 18 which states that a transaction is not a sale and revenue is not recognised if the entity retains significant risks of ownership. *[IAS 18.16].* By definition the entity will have retained the significant risks and rewards, because it now holds the asset under a finance lease.

Both methods of accounting for sale and leaseback transactions are seen in practice. Therefore, an entity should select a treatment as a matter of accounting policy and apply it consistently.

If the sales value is less than the carrying amount then the apparent 'loss' need not be taken to income unless there has been an impairment under IAS 36. *[IAS 17.64].* There may be an obvious reason why the sales proceeds are less than the carrying value; for example, the fair value of a second-hand vehicle or item of plant and machinery is frequently lower than its book value, especially soon after the asset has been acquired by the entity. This fall in fair value after sale has no effect on the asset's value in use. What this means, of course, is that in the absence of impairment, a deficit (sales proceeds lower than carrying value) will be deferred in the same manner as a profit and spread over the lease term.

7.2   Operating leaseback

If a sale and leaseback transaction results in an operating lease, and it is clear that the transaction is established at fair value, any profit or loss should be recognised immediately. If the sale price is below fair value, any profit or loss should be recognised immediately unless the loss is compensated by future lease payments at below market price, in which case it should be deferred and amortised in proportion to the lease payments over the period for which the asset is expected to be used. If the sale price is above fair value, the excess over fair value should be deferred and amortised over the period for which the asset is expected to be used. *[IAS 17.61-62].*

The rationale behind the above treatments is that if the sales value is not based on fair values then it is likely that the normal market rents will have been adjusted to compensate. For example, a sale at above fair value followed by above-market rentals is similar to a loan of the excess proceeds by the lessor that is being repaid out of the rentals. Accordingly, the transaction should be recorded as if it had been based on fair value.

However, this will not always be the case. Where the sales value is less than fair value there may be legitimate reasons for this to be so, for example where the seller has had to raise cash quickly. In such situations, as the rentals under the lease have not been reduced to compensate, the profit or loss should be based on the sales value.

The standard includes an Appendix, which comprises the following table of the standard's requirements concerning sale and leaseback transactions, and is aimed at providing guidance in interpreting the various permutations of facts and circumstances that are set out in the requirements.

Sale price established at fair value (paragraph 61)	Carrying amount equal to fair value	Carrying amount less than fair value	Carrying amount above fair value
Profit	no profit	recognise profit immediately	not applicable
Loss	no loss	not applicable	recognise loss immediately

Sale price below fair value (paragraph 61)			
Profit	no profit	recognise profit immediately	no profit (note 1)
Loss *not* compensated by future lease payments at below market price	recognise loss immediately	recognise loss immediately	(note 1)
Loss compensated by future lease payments at below market price	defer and amortise loss	defer and amortise loss	(note 1)

Sale price above fair value (paragraph 61)			
Profit	defer and amortise profit	defer and amortise profit	defer and amortise profit (note 2)
Loss	no loss	no loss	(note 1)

Note 1   These parts of the table represent circumstances that would have been dealt with under paragraph 63 of the Standard. Paragraph 63 requires the carrying amount of an asset to be written down to fair value where it is subject to a sale and leaseback.

Note 2   The profit would be the difference between fair value and sale price as the carrying amount would have been written down to fair value in accordance with paragraph 63.

IAS 17's disclosure requirements for lessees and lessors apply equally to sale and leaseback transactions. The requirement in paragraph 35(d) of the standard for lessees to give a general description of their significant leasing arrangements will lead to the disclosure of unique or unusual provisions of the agreement or terms of the sale and leaseback transactions. *[IAS 17.65]*. Furthermore, sale and leaseback transactions may meet the separate disclosure criteria for 'exceptional items' set out in IAS 1 – *Presentation of Financial Statements* (see Chapter 3). *[IAS 17.66]*.

Sale and leaseback arrangements may also include features such as repurchase options. These are not addressed by IAS 17 and are discussed below.

7.3   Sale and leaseback arrangements including repurchase agreements and options

IAS 17 identifies a particular condition that may result in a lease being classified as a finance lease: where the lessee has a 'bargain purchase' option to acquire the asset. However, the standard does not deal explicitly with the function of options in the context of sale and leaseback arrangements, where circumstances are more complex and there may be a variety of options that may affect the overall assessment of the lease.

The Interpretations Committee considered whether these arrangements would have to meet the derecognition criteria in IAS 18 in order to recognise the sale of the asset. If this were the case then it would be unlikely that the seller/lessee would ever achieve derecognition. Arguably the vendor would retain effective control through continuing managerial involvement to the degree usually associated with ownership. It might also retain the significant risks and rewards of ownership, e.g. through fixed price repurchase terms that allowed it to retain the rewards but not the risks of ownership. *[IAS 18.14]*.

The Interpretations Committee concluded that there was no such requirement as IAS 17 itself contained 'the more specific guidance with respect to sale and leaseback transactions'. However, these transactions may be outside the scope IAS 17 because they do not 'convey a right to use an asset' as defined by SIC-27 and IFRIC 4, whose requirements are described at 2.1 above. If the purchaser/lessor does not have a right of use, the transaction is outside the scope of IAS 17 and the sale and leaseback accounting in IAS 17 should not be applied.

The Interpretations Committee considered that 'significantly divergent interpretations do not exist in practice on this issue and that it would not expect such divergent interpretations to emerge'. Consequently, The Interpretations Committee decided not to take the issue onto its agenda.[8]

The Interpretations Committee considers, therefore, that entities should use IFRIC 4 and SIC-27 to analyse whether or not the arrangement contains a lease and then apply IAS 18 to determine whether or not there is revenue relating to the transaction. SIC-27 is helpful in the analysis; it includes the following indicators that an arrangement is not in substance a lease:

(a)   the entity retains all the risks and rewards of ownership and there is no significant change in its rights to use the asset; and

(b)   the options on which the arrangement depends are included on terms that make their exercise almost certain (e.g. a put option that is exercisable at a price sufficiently higher than the expected fair value when it becomes exercisable). *[SIC-27.5].*

In practice entities may well have obtained the same answer by moving straight to IAS 18 and applying a 'risks and rewards' analysis, rather than considering whether the arrangement contains a lease, which could explain the lack of divergence in practice.

7.3.1   Sale and leaseback arrangements with put and call options

If a lease arrangement includes an option that can only be exercised by the seller/lessee at the then fair value of the asset in question, the risks and rewards inherent in the residual value of the asset have passed to the buyer/lessor. The option amounts to a right of first refusal to the seller/lessee.

Where there is both a put and a call option in force on equivalent terms at a determinable amount other than the fair value, it is clear that the asset will revert to the seller/lessee. It must be in the interests of one or other of the parties to exercise the option so as to secure a profit or avoid a loss, and therefore the likelihood of the asset remaining the property of the buyer/lessor rather than reverting to the seller must be remote. In such a case, this is a bargain purchase option and the seller/lessee has entered into a finance leaseback.

However, the position is less clear where there is only a put option or only a call option in force, rather than a combination of the two. Where there is only a put option by the buyer/lessor, the effect will be (in the absence of other factors) that the seller/lessee has disposed of the rewards of ownership to the buyer/lessor but retained the risks. This is because the buyer/lessor will only exercise his option to put the asset back to the seller/lessee if its value at the time is less than the repurchase price payable under the option. This means that if the asset continues to rise in value the buyer/lessor will keep it and reap the benefits of that enhanced value; conversely if the value of the asset falls, the option will be exercised and the downside on the asset will be borne by the seller/lessee.

This analysis does not of itself answer the question whether the deal should be treated as an operating or financing leaseback. The overall commercial effect will still have to be evaluated, taking account of all the terms of the arrangement and by considering the motivations of both of the parties in agreeing to the various terms of the deal; in particular it will need to be considered why they have each agreed to have this one-sided option.

Where there is only a call option exercisable by the seller/lessee, the position will be reversed. In this case, the seller/lessee has disposed of the risks, but retained the rewards to be attained if the value of the asset exceeds the repurchase price specified in the option. Once again, though, the overall commercial effect of the arrangement has to be evaluated in deciding how to account for the deal. Emphasis has to be given to what is likely to happen in practice, and it is instructive to look at the arrangement from the point of view of both parties to see what their expectations are and what has induced them to accept the deal on the terms that have been agreed. It may be obvious from the overall terms of the arrangement that the call option will be exercised, in which case the deal will again be a financing arrangement and should be accounted for as such. For example, the exercise price of the call option may be set at a significant discount to expected market value, the seller/lessee may need the asset to use on an ongoing basis in its business, or the asset may provide in effect the only source of the seller/lessee's future income. Equally, the financial effects of *not* exercising the option, such as continued exposure to escalating costs, may make it obvious that the option will have to be exercised (so-called 'economic compulsion').

The following is an example of a sale and leaseback deal where the seller has a call option to repurchase the asset but has no commitment to do so:

Example 26.25:   Sale and leaseback transaction involving escalating rentals and call options

Company S sells a property to Company B for £100,000,000 and leases it back on the following terms:

Rental for years 1 to 5	£3,900,000 per annum
Rental for years 6 to 10	£5,875,000 per annum
Rental for years 11 to 15	£8,830,000 per annum
Rental for years 16 to 20	£13,280,000 per annum
Rental for years 21 to 25	£19,970,000 per annum
Rental for years 26 to 30	£30,025,000 per annum
Rental for years 31 to 35	£45,150,000 per annum
Rental thereafter	open market rent

Rentals are payable annually in advance.

Company S has a call option to buy back the property at the following dates and prices:

At the end of year 5	£125,000,000
At the end of year 10	£150,000,000
At the end of year 15	£168,000,000
At the end of year 20	£160,000,000
At the end of year 25	£100,000,000

Company B has no right to put the property back to Company S.

An analysis of the economics of this deal suggests that whilst Company S has no legal obligation to repurchase the property, there is no genuine commercial possibility that the option will not be exercised. This is because the rentals and option prices are structured in such a way as to give the buyer of the property a lender's return whilst, at the same time, there is no commercial logic for the seller not to exercise the option at year 25, if not earlier. Exercising the option at the end of year 25 will mean that Company S will regain ownership of the property and will have had the use of the £100,000,000 at an effective rate of approximately 8.2% per annum; failure to exercise the option will mean additional lease obligations of £375,875,000 over the ten years from years 25 to 35, followed by the obligation to pay market rents thereafter.

8   SUB-LEASES AND BACK-TO-BACK LEASES

8.1   Introduction

Situations arise where there are more parties to a lease arrangement than simply one lessor and one lessee. The discussion below relates to situations involving an original lessor, an intermediate party and an ultimate lessee. The intermediate party is unrelated to both lessor and lessee and may be acting either as both a lessee and lessor of the asset concerned or, alternatively, as an agent of the lessor in the transaction.

Both sub-leases and back-to-back leases involve the intermediate party acting as both lessor and lessee of the asset. The difference between the two arrangements is that, for a back-to-back lease, the terms of the two lease agreements match to a greater extent than would be the case for a sub-lease arrangement. This difference is really only one of degree, and the important decision to be made concerns whether the intermediate party is acting as both lessee and lessor in two related but independent transactions or whether the nature of the interest is such that it need not recognise the rights and obligations under the leases in its financial statements.

8.1.1   The original lessor and the ultimate lessee

The accounting treatment adopted by these parties will not be affected by the existence of sub-leases or back-to-back leases. The original lessor has an agreement with the intermediate party, which is not affected by any further leasing of the assets by the intermediate party unless the original lease agreement is thereby replaced.

Similarly, the ultimate lessee has a lease agreement with the intermediate party. The lessee will have use of the asset under that agreement and must make a decision, in the usual way, as to whether the lease is of a finance or operating type under the requirements of IAS 17.

8.1.2   The intermediate party

It is common for entities whose business is the leasing of assets to third parties to finance these assets themselves through leasing arrangements. There are also arrangements in which a party on-leases assets as an intermediary between a lessor and a lessee while taking a variable degree of risk in the transaction. The appropriate accounting treatment by the intermediate party depends on the substance of the series of transactions. Either the intermediate party will act as lessee to the original lessor and lessor to the ultimate lessee or, if in substance it has transferred the risks and rewards of ownership, it may be able to derecognise the assets and liabilities under its two lease arrangements and recognise only its own commission or fee income.

In order to analyse the issues that may arise, it is worth considering the various combinations of leases between lessor/intermediate and intermediate/lessee, which are summarised in the following table:

	Lessor	Intermediate party		Lessee
	Lease to Intermediate	Lease from Lessor	Lease to Lessee	Lease from Intermediate
(1)	Operating lease	Operating lease	Operating lease	Operating lease
(2)	Finance lease	Finance lease	Operating lease	Operating lease
(3)	Finance lease	Finance lease	Finance lease	Finance lease

Only in unusual circumstances could there be an operating lease from the lessor to the intermediate and a finance lease from the intermediate to the lessee. The intermediate would have to acquire an additional interest in the asset from a party other than the lessor in order to be in a position to transfer substantially all of the risks and rewards incidental to ownership of that asset to the lessee.

There are no significant accounting difficulties for the intermediate party regarding (1), an operating lease from the lessor to the intermediate and from the intermediate to the lessee. The intermediate may be liable to the lessor if the lessee defaults, in which case it would have to make an appropriate provision, but otherwise both contracts are executory and will be accounted for in the usual way.

In situation (2), the intermediate will record at commencement of the lease term an asset acquired under a finance lease and an obligation to the lessor of an equal and opposite amount. As it has granted an operating lease to the lessee, its risks and rewards incidental to ownership of the asset exceed those assumed by the lessee under the lease. It is appropriate for the intermediate party to record a fixed asset, which it will have to depreciate as set out in 4.1.4 above.

However, under scenario (3), the intermediate is the lessee under a finance lease with the lessor and lessor under a finance lease with the lessee. Its balance sheet, *prima facie*, records a finance lease receivable from the lessee and a finance lease obligation to the lessor. Both of these are treated as if they are financial instruments for derecognition purposes (see 4.3 above for the circumstances in which lease assets and liabilities are within scope of IAS 39).

The intermediate may be in a position to derecognise its financial asset and liability if it transfers to the lessor the contractual right to receive the cash flows of the lessee and thereby extinguishes its liability under the lease. *[IAS 39.18]*. However, it is more likely that it retains the contractual right to receive the cash flow under the lease and takes on a contractual obligation to pay the cash flows to the lessor. In accordance with the derecognition rules in IAS 39 it can derecognise its asset and liability if, and only if, it meets certain criteria, which are summarised below and described in detail in Chapter 50.

In the context of leases, the most important of these conditions is that the intermediate has no obligation to pay amounts to the lessor unless in collects equivalent amounts from the lessee. *[IAS 39.18-19]*. If the ultimate lessee defaults on its lease obligations (for whatever reason), the original lessor must have no recourse against the intermediate party for the outstanding payments under the lease if derecognition is to be appropriate. Another important factor is what happens if the original lessor defaults, for example through insolvency. The analysis will also have to take account of the following conditions for derecognition of a financial asset in IAS 39:

(a)   the entity (i.e. the intermediate party) is prohibited by the terms of the transfer contract from selling or pledging the original asset; and

(b)   the entity has an obligation to remit any cash flows it collects without material delay. Investment in cash or cash equivalents is permitted, but interest earned must be passed to the eventual recipients. *[IAS 39.19]*.

If these factors indicate that the intermediate party has derecognised its interest in the two leases, i.e. commercially it is acting merely as a broker or agent for the original lessor, it should not include any asset or obligation relating to the leased asset in its balance sheet. The income received by such an intermediary should be taken to profit and loss account on a systematic and rational basis – the discussion of the recognition of fee income in SIC-27, as discussed in 2.2 above, may be helpful. If, on the other hand, the intermediate party is taken to be acting as both lessee and lessor in two independent although related transactions, the assets and obligations under finance leases should be recognised in the normal way.

It should not be inferred from the above discussion that all situations encountered can be relatively easily analysed. In practice this is unlikely to be the case, as the risks and rewards will probably be spread between the parties involved. This is especially likely where more than the three parties discussed above are involved. Therefore, even if the arrangements meet the definition of a 'transfer' under IAS 39, the intermediate may have retained some of the risks and rewards of ownership or control of the asset and it may be necessary to recognise other assets and liabilities in this respect. The complex area concerning derecognition of financial assets is dealt with in Chapter 50.

9   DISCLOSURES REQUIRED BY IAS 17

This section deals only with the disclosure requirements of IAS 17 and those of other accounting standards to which it specifically refers. Disclosures required by SIC-27 are dealt with in 2.2 above.

9.1   Disclosures relating to financial assets and liabilities

Because finance lease assets and obligations and individual payments currently due and payable under operating leases are financial assets and liabilities, lessees and lessors have to meet the requirements of IFRS 7 – *Financial Instruments: Disclosures,* which came into effect for accounting periods beginning on or after 1 January 2007. This principally applies to the general requirements regarding classification and disclosure of financial assets and liabilities in the balance sheet and disclosure of interest income and expense, together with other gains and losses arising from financial instruments, whether reflected in profit or loss or other comprehensive income. IFRS 7's disclosure requirements are covered in Chapter 52. However, if the lease arrangements contain more complex terms then there may be additional disclosure requirements, which are also summarised in Chapter 52.

Chapter 26

9.2   Disclosure by lessees

9.2.1   *Disclosure of finance leases*

As well as meeting the IFRS7 disclosure requirements, IAS 17 requires lessees to make the following disclosures for finance leases: *[IAS 17.31]*

(a)   for each class of asset, the net carrying amount at the balance sheet date. Assets that are recognised under a finance lease will generally be considered to be the same class of assets with a similar nature that are owned, so there is no need to provide separate reconciliations of movements in owned assets from assets under finance leases;

(b)   a reconciliation between the total of future minimum lease payments at the balance sheet date, and their present value. The minimum lease payments will include adjustments that have been made following a rent review. In addition, an entity shall disclose the total of future minimum lease payments at the balance sheet date, and their present value, for each of the following periods:

   (i)   not later than one year;

   (ii)   later than one year and not later than five years;

   (iii)   later than five years.

(c)   contingent rents recognised as an expense in the period;

(d)   the total of future minimum sublease payments expected to be received under non-cancellable subleases at the balance sheet date;

(e)   a general description of the lessee's material leasing arrangements including, but not limited to, the following:

   (i)   the basis on which contingent rent payable is determined;

   (ii)   the existence and terms of renewal or purchase options and escalation clauses; and

   (iii)   restrictions imposed by lease arrangements, such as those concerning dividends, additional debt, and further leasing.

The following is an example of disclosures made in practice:

Extract 26.5: Deutsche Telekom AG (2010)

Notes to the Consolidated Financial Statements [extract]
34   Disclosures on leases [extract]
Deutsche Telekom as lessee [extract]

Finance leases. When a lease transfers substantially all risks and rewards to Deutsche Telekom as lessee, Deutsche Telekom initially recognizes the leased assets in the statement of financial position at the lower of fair value or present value of the future minimum lease payments. Most of the leased assets carried in the statement of financial position as part of a finance lease relate to long-term rental and lease agreements for office buildings with a typical lease term of up to 25 years. The agreements include extension and purchase options. The table [...] shows the net carrying amounts of leased assets capitalized in connection with a finance lease as of the reporting date:

	Dec. 31, 2010	Of which: sale and leaseback transactions	Dec. 31, 2009	Of which: sale and leaseback transactions
	millions of €	millions of €	millions of €	millions of €
Land and buildings	954	539	1,035	591
Technical equipment and machinery	91	3	35	9
Other	15	1	21	0
Net carrying amounts of leased assets capitalized	1,060	543	1,091	600

At the inception of the lease term, Deutsche Telekom recognizes a lease liability equal to the carrying amount of the leased asset. In subsequent periods, the liability decreases by the amount of lease payments made to the lessors using the effective interest method. The interest component of the lease payments is recognized in the income statement.

The following table provides a breakdown of these amounts:

	Minimum lease payments		Interest component		Present values	
	Total	Of which: sale and leaseback	Total	Of which: sale and leaseback	Total	Of which: sale and leaseback
	millions of €	millions of €	millions of €	millions of €	millions of €	millions of €
Dec. 31, 2010						
Maturity						
Within 1 year	235	106	93	63	142	43
In 1 to 3 years	405	213	185	114	220	99
In 3 to 5 years	360	211	154	96	206	115
After 5 years	1,279	758	447	290	832	468
	2,279	1,288	879	563	1,400	725
Dec. 31, 2009						
Maturity						
Within 1 year	231	114	110	66	121	48
In 1 to 3 years	387	211	202	120	185	91
In 3 to 5 years	358	213	154	104	204	109
After 5 years	1,415	860	502	334	913	526
	2,391	1,398	968	624	1,423	774

In addition, the leased asset is accounted for as property, plant and equipment of the reporting entity and the requirements for disclosure in accordance with IAS 16 (Chapter 20), IAS 36 (Chapter 22), IAS 38 (Chapter 19), IAS 40 (Chapter 21) and IAS 41 (Chapter 40) are applicable as appropriate. *[IAS 17.32]*.

9.2.2 *Disclosure of operating leases*

In addition to meeting the requirements of IFRS 7, lessees must make the following disclosures for operating leases: *[IAS 17.35]*

(a) the total of future minimum lease payments under non-cancellable operating leases for each of the following periods:

(i) not later than one year;

(ii) later than one year and not later than five years;

(iii) later than five years.

(b)   the total of future minimum sublease payments expected to be received under non-cancellable subleases at the balance sheet date;

(c)   lease and sublease payments recognised as an expense in the period, with separate amounts for minimum lease payments, contingent rents, and sublease payments;

(d)   a general description of the lessee's significant leasing arrangements including, but not limited to, the following:

(i)   the basis on which contingent rent payable is determined;

(ii)   the existence and terms of renewal or purchase options and escalation clauses; and

(iii)   restrictions imposed by lease arrangements, such as those concerning dividends, additional debt and further leasing.

An example of the disclosures made by a lessee in respect of their obligations under operating leases is as follows.

Extract 26.6: Deutsche Telekom AG (2010)

Notes to the Consolidated Financial Statements [extract]
34   Disclosures on leases [extract]

Deutsche Telekom as lessee [extract]

Operating leases. Beneficial ownership of a lease is attributed to the lessor if this is the party to which all the substantial risks and rewards incidental to ownership of the asset are transferred. The lessor recognizes the leased asset in its statement of financial position. Deutsche Telekom recognizes the lease payments made during the term of the operating lease in profit or loss. Deutsche Telekom's obligations arising from operating leases are mainly related to long-term rental or lease agreements for network infrastructure, radio towers and real estate.

Some leases include extension options and provide for stepped rents. Most of these leases relate to radio towers in the United States. In the 2010 financial year (as of June 30, 2010), Deutsche Telekom revised its assessment of lease terms for existing U.S. operating leases with regard to the exercise of extension options. Contrary to the original assessment, the exercising of extension options is only reasonably certain up to a total term of 15 years against the background of the altered market situation and new technical framework. This is shorter than the original assessment, where a total term of between 20 and 25 years was expected. As a result of this change in assessment, the expected future minimum lease payments from operating leases decreased by USD 11.4 billion (December 31, 2010: EUR 8.5 billion; December 31 2009: EUR 7.9 billion) in the United States operating segment.

The operating lease expenses recognized in profit or loss amounted to EUR 2.2 billion as of the end of 2010 (2009: EUR 2.1 billion; 2008: EUR 2.0 billion). The following table provides a breakdown of future obligations arising from operating leases:

	Dec. 31, 2010	Dec. 31, 2009
	millions of €	millions of €
Maturity		
Within 1 year	**2,627**	2,553
In 1 to 3 years	**4,502**	4,195
In 3 to 5 years	**3,767**	3,325
After 5 years	**6,767**	14,475
	17,663	24,548

The obligations from operating leases as of December 31, 2009 did not include the obligations of T-Mobile UK which was classified as held for sale.

9.3   Disclosure by lessors

9.3.1   *Disclosure of finance leases*

In addition to meeting the requirements in IFRS 7 (see 9.1 above), lessors must disclose the following for finance leases:

(a)   a reconciliation between the gross investment in the lease at the balance sheet date, and the present value of minimum lease payments receivable at the balance sheet date. In addition, an entity shall disclose the gross investment in the lease and the present value of minimum lease payments receivable at the balance sheet date, for each of the following periods:

    (i)   not later than one year;

    (ii)   later than one year and not later than five years;

    (iii) later than five years;

(b)   unearned finance income;

(c)   the unguaranteed residual values accruing to the benefit of the lessor;

(d)   the accumulated allowance for uncollectible minimum lease payments receivable;

(e)   contingent rents recognised as income in the period;

(f)   a general description of the lessor's material leasing arrangements. *[IAS 17.47].*

IAS 17 also recommends but does not require disclosure of the gross investment less unearned income in new business added during the period, after deducting the relevant amounts for cancelled leases as a useful indicator of growth. *[IAS 17.48].*

Deutsche Telekom discloses its activities as a finance lessor as follows:

Extract 26.7: Deutsche Telekom AG (2010)

Notes to the Consolidated Financial Statements [extract]

34   Disclosures on leases [extract]

Deutsche Telekom as lessor [extract]

Finance Leases. Deutsche Telekom acts as lessor in connection with finance leases. Essentially, these relate to the leasing of routers which Deutsche Telekom provides to its customers for data and telephone network solutions. Deutsche Telekom recognizes a receivable in the amount of the net investment in the lease. The lease payments made by the lessees are split into an interest component and a principal component using the effective interest method. The lease receivable is reduced by the principal received. The interest component of the payments is recognized as finance income in the income statement. The amount of the net investment in a finance lease is determined as shown in the following table:

	Dec. 31, 2010 millions of €	Dec. 31, 2009 millions of €
Minimum lease payments	328	307
Unguaranteed residual value	–	–
Gross investment	328	307
Unearned finance income	(39)	(43)
Net investment **(present value of the minimum lease payments)**	289	264

Chapter 26

The gross investment amount and the present value of payable minimum lease payments are shown in the following table:

	Dec. 31, 2010		Dec. 31, 2009	
	Gross investment millions of €	Present value of minimum lease payments millions of €	Gross investment millions of €	Present value of minimum lease payments millions of €
Maturity				
Within 1 year	126	110	98	83
In 1 to 3 years	142	124	131	112
In 3 to 5 years	55	50	57	49
After 5 years	5	5	21	20
	328	**289**	**307**	**264**

9.3.2 *Disclosure of operating leases*

Lessors must, in addition to meeting the requirements of IFRS 7, disclose the following for operating leases:

(a)   the future minimum lease payments under non-cancellable operating leases in the aggregate and for each of the following periods:

    (i)   not later than one year;

    (ii)   later than one year and not later than five years;

    (iii)   later than five years;

(b)   total contingent rents recognised as income in the period;

(c)   a general description of the lessor's leasing arrangements. *[IAS 17.56]*.

Deutsche Telekom's lessor interests in operating leases are disclosed as follows.

Extract 26.8: Deutsche Telekom AG (2010)

Notes to the Consolidated Financial Statements [extract]
34   Disclosures on leases [extract]

Deutsche Telekom as lessor [extract]

Operating leases: Deutsche Telekom acts as a lessor in connection with operating leases and continues to recognize the leased assets in its statement of financial position. The lease payments received are recognized in profit or loss. The leases mainly relate to the rental of building space and radio towers and have an average term of ten years. The future minimum lease payments arising from non-cancelable operating leases are shown in the following table:

	Dec. 31, 2010 millions of €	Dec. 31, 2009 millions of €
Maturity		
Within 1 year	359	338
In 1 to 3 years	456	406
In 3 to 5 years	346	318
After 5 years	756	624
	1,917	**1,686**

In addition, the leased asset is accounted for as a fixed asset of the reporting entity and the requirements for disclosure in accordance with IAS 16 (Chapter 20), IAS 36 (Chapter 22), IAS 38 (Chapter 19), IAS 40 (Chapter 21) and IAS 41 (Chapter 40) as appropriate. *[IAS 17.57]*.

10 UPDATING LEASE ACCOUNTING: EXPOSURE DRAFT – LEASES

10.1 Introduction

Chapter 2 of this book discusses the IASB policy to move towards an asset/liability fair value approach to financial reporting. This approach could fundamentally change the way in which financial contracts such as leases are accounted for.

The IASB's *Framework* defines assets and liabilities as follows: an asset is 'a resource controlled by the entity as a result of past events and from which future economic benefits are expected to flow to the entity'; whilst a liability is 'a present obligation of the entity arising from past events, the settlement of which is expected to result in an outflow from the entity of resources embodying economic benefits'. *[Framework.4.4]*.

A consequence of these two definitions is that most leases, irrespective of whether finance or operating in nature, contain an unavoidable legal obligation to transfer economic benefits to the lessor, i.e. contain a liability. The Boards argue that the lessee is likely both to control and enjoy the future economic benefits embodied in the leased asset, and should therefore recognise these rights as an asset (the 'right-of-use asset').

Lease accounting has always been a convergence project and it became a priority under the revised Memorandum of Understanding in 2008. In August 2010 the Boards issued their exposure drafts, IASB: ED/2010/9 – *Leases* – and FASB: Proposed Accounting Standards Update – *Leases*. The Boards have made significant revisions to their original proposals, primarily to address constituents' concerns. The description of the lease approach that follows summarises the revised leases proposal for topics that the Boards redeliberated through June 2011. All of the decisions made by the Boards to date are tentative and will not be finalised until the Boards approve a final standard. What is being proposed is not a comprehensive fair value approach. The model measures lease obligations and right-of-use assets at the present value of expected lease payments, not at their fair value. Unlike earlier approaches, the Boards have not required separate measurement and accounting for renewal or purchase options and residual value guarantees.

Under the new approach, a lessee will recognise an asset representing its right to use the leased asset for the lease term (the 'right-of-use' asset) and a liability for its obligation to make lease payments.

The following discussion of the main features of the new approach is based on the Boards' redeliberations in 2011, except where the original proposals are unchanged. All of these decisions are tentative and may not be carried forward into the revised exposure draft.

10.2   The new lease model – definitions and scope

Neither definition nor scope is expected to differ much in practice from IAS 17. A lease will be defined as a contract in which the right to use an asset is conveyed, for a period of time, in exchange for consideration. To be a lease, an arrangement will have to meet two criteria:[9]

(1)   fulfilment of the contract depends on a 'specified asset'; and

(2)   the contract conveys the 'right to control the use' of the specified asset. Consistent with current standards, a 'specified asset' will be an asset that is implicitly or explicitly identifiable.

Although a physically distinct portion of a larger asset (e.g. a floor in a multi-storey building) could be a specified asset, a non-physically distinguishable portion of an asset (e.g. 50% of the capacity of a pipeline) would not qualify as a specified asset and would not be the subject of a lease.

Contracts that provide the supplier with substantive substitution rights (i.e. that allow the supplier to use any one of a number of different assets to fulfil the contract) will not be considered leases because they do not depend on the use of a specified asset. It is likely that they would be accounted for as executory arrangements. A substitution right would be considered substantive if substitution of the asset is both practical and economically feasible and the asset could be substituted without the customer's consent.[10]

An entity will have the 'right to control the use' of a specified asset if it has the ability to both direct the use of the asset and receive the benefit from its use. An arrangement under which a customer obtains all of the benefit from the use of an asset, but does not direct its use, would not be considered a lease. The ability to direct the use of the asset would be demonstrated by the ability to make decisions about the use of the specified asset (e.g. determining how, when and in what manner the specified asset is used) that significantly affect the benefits received by the customer from the asset.[11] For example, the customer specifying the quantity and timing of the delivery of goods would not, by itself, indicate the customer's ability to direct the use of the asset used to produce or deliver those goods. In contrast, if the vendor operates the asset according to the specific instructions of the customer, the customer has the ability to direct the use of the asset.

The revised right-to-control-the-use condition is intended to align with control concepts the Boards have developed in their joint revenue recognition project. This means that the customer must meet both requirements (direct the use and receive the benefits). Pricing terms would not be considered in evaluating the right-to-control-the-use criterion. This contrasts with the analysis of leases in IFRIC 4. When the arrangement involves a single purchaser in taking substantially all of the output from a specific asset other than at market price and the price varies other than in response to market price changes, the variability ('off-market' nature) is regarded by IFRIC 4 as indicating that payment is being made for the right to use the asset rather than for the actual use of or output from the asset (see 2.1.3 above).

The following arrangements would not be in scope:[12]

(i)   leases for the right to explore for or use natural resources (such as minerals, oil, natural gas and similar non-regenerative resources)

(ii)   leases of biological assets

(iii)   leases of service concession arrangements within the scope of IFRIC 12

(iv)   for lessors, leases of investment property measured at fair value

The Boards also stated that leases of intangible assets would not be required to be accounted for in accordance with the leases standard but it is assumed that entities will be allowed as an accounting policy election to account for them under the leases standard.[13]

10.3   The new lease model – accounting by lessees

The major inputs into lessee accounting, including the lease term and determining lease payments and the treatment of contingent rentals, have all been reconsidered as a result of comments on the original ED. The current proposals are described below.

Many constituents sought exemptions for some arrangements classified as operating leases under IAS 17 and the Boards are actively considering allowing some short-term leases to be accounted for in the same way as they are at present – see below. However, it appears that other suggestions made during the consultation process, such as a regime that would allow a modified treatment for property rentals, will not be carried forward into the re-exposed ED.

Short-term leases: the revised ED is expected to include exemptions for short-term leases. Lessees will be allowed to recognise lease expenses on a straight-line basis over the lease term (unless another systematic and rational basis better represents the pattern of use) for leases with a maximum possible lease term, including any options to renew, of 12 months. The lessee will not recognise any lease-related assets and lease liabilities. Lease will be defined as short-term based solely on the maximum possible lease term in the contract. The entity's intentions, expectations or lease term for accounting purposes will not be considered. Entities will have to make a policy election to use the simplified accounting.[14]

Separation of lease and non-lease components: non-lease components, including services and executory costs, will be separated from the lease components. Executory costs have not been defined, but are likely to include insurance, maintenance and taxes. Payments are to be allocated on a relative purchase price basis (if the purchase price of each component can be observed) or using a residual method (if the purchase price of one or more but not all of the components can be observed). If there are no observable purchase prices, lessees will account for all of the payments required by the contract as a lease (i.e. not separate payments between lease and non-lease components). The Boards agreed to include application guidance in the standard on how a lessee should determine an observable price.[15]

Lease term: this will be defined as the non-cancellable period, plus any options where there is a significant economic incentive to extend or not terminate the lease.[16] Factors that might create an economic incentive include:

- renewal rates priced at a bargain;
- penalty payments for cancellation or non-renewal;
- economic penalties, such as significant customisation or installation costs (e.g. leasehold improvements); and
- a sublease term that extends beyond the non-cancellable period of the head lease (e.g. the head lease has a non-cancellable term of five years and a five-year renewal option and the sublease term is 10 years)

Purchase options: will be accounted for consistently with options to extend a lease. If the lessee has a significant economic incentive to exercise a purchase option, as described above, the exercise price will be included in the lease payments and the right-of-use asset will be amortised over the life of the underlying asset as opposed to the term of the lease.[17]

Lease payments: these will include:

- fixed lease payments and payments that are in substance fixed;[18]
- the exercise price of purchase options if there is a significant economic incentive to exercise;
- residual value guarantees;
- termination option penalties; and
- lease payments that depend on an index or rate.[19]

Residual value guarantees will be included in the lease-related assets and liabilities at the amounts expected to be payable (e.g. gross guaranteed amount minus the expected value of the underlying asset).[20]

Contingent rent: based on performance (e.g. a percentage of sales) or usage (e.g. number of miles flown) of the underlying asset will be recognised as an expense when incurred. For example, a contingent rent based on annual sales of a leased store will not be included in the right-of-use asset and liability to make lease payments recognised by the lessee. Instead, these payments will be recognised as expenses as the sales at the store occur. There will be specific disclosure requirements but they have not yet been addressed in the redeliberations. Payments must be truly variable to be excluded from the amounts recognised on the balance sheet. Payments that are contractually described as variable, but in substance are fixed, would be treated as fixed lease payments.[21]

Discount rate: this will be determined on a lease-by-lease basis. The discount rate would be the rate that the lessor charges the lessee if available; otherwise, the lessee would use its incremental borrowing rate. Practically speaking, lessees will rarely know the rate they are charged by the lessor. The rate the lessor charges the lessee could be based on:

- the implicit rate in the lease
- the lessee's incremental borrowing rate;
- for leases of property, the yield on the property.

The lessee's incremental borrowing rate would be the rate of interest that the lessee would have to pay to borrow over a similar term (i.e. the lease term), and with a similar security, the funds necessary to purchase a similar underlying asset.

The Boards agreed to provide application guidance for determining the yield on property and whether to use a rate that reflects a parent's or subsidiary's incremental borrowing rate.[22]

Initial recognition and measurement: the liability to make lease payments will be based on the present value of the lease payments to be made over the lease term. The right-of-use asset will be measured initially at cost and will include the amount of the liability to make lease payments plus any initial direct costs incurred by the lessee. Initial direct costs are direct and incremental to the lease transaction (e.g. commissions, legal fees).[23]

Subsequent measurement: if the lessee adopts the amortised cost approach, after the date of commencement of the lease, it will:

- amortise the right-of-use asset on a systematic basis that reflects the pattern of consumption of the expected future economic benefits (generally straight-line);
- recognise interest expense using the interest method (i.e. a level effective rate throughout the lease term); and
- reduce the liability for lease payments made.[24]

The amortisation period for most right-of-use assets will be the shorter of the lease term or the life of the underlying asset. If title transfers at the end of the lease term or the lessee has a significant economic incentive to exercise a purchase option, the amortisation period will be the remaining life of the underlying asset.

Because of the consistent interest rate and decreasing liability over the lease term, lessees will recognise higher total periodic expense (i.e. total interest and amortisation expense) in the earlier periods of a lease and lower total periodic expense in later periods. This expense recognition pattern is consistent with the treatment of finance leases under current lease accounting, but would accelerate lease expense for current operating leases.

Chapter 26

Reassessment: lessees must reassess certain key considerations throughout the life of the lease. Reassessment requirements vary, as follows:[25]

	Reassessment indicator	Accounting treatment
Lease term and purchase options	A significant change in factors that may indicate a significant economic incentive to exercise(excluding market factors)	Adjust right-of-use asset
Discount rate	Change in lease payments due to a change in lease term	Adjust right-of-use asset
Residual value guarantees	Events or circumstances indicate that there has been a significant change in the amounts expected to be payable	Amounts relating to current or prior periods – net income Amounts relating to future periods – adjust right-of-use asset

Lease payments that depend on an index or rate are yet to be redeliberated. The lessee will determine the revised inputs and remeasure the liability to make lease payments as at the reassessment date. The lessee will adjust the liability to make lease payments to reflect the change in the calculation with the offset either to the right-of-use asset or net income. Reassessing key considerations is a significant change from current standards.

Sale and leaseback transactions: Sale and leasebacks will no longer provide off-balance sheet financing as all leases (other than short-term leases) will be recognised on the balance sheet. Whether these transactions are accounted for as a sale and a lease, or as a financing transaction, will be based on control criteria developed in the joint revenue recognition project (see Chapter 30). If the arrangement qualifies as a sale and leaseback and the consideration exchanged (i.e. sales price for the sale of the asset and rental rate for the lease) is at fair value, the seller-lessee will recognise a gain or loss. If the consideration is not at fair value, the assets, liabilities, gain or loss will be adjusted to reflect current market rentals.[26] Under current accounting, the seller-lessee may be required to defer and amortise some or all of the profit or loss on a sale based on the specific terms of the particular transaction. A transaction that is not a sale will be accounted for as a financing transaction.

10.4   The new lease model – accounting by lessors

In a significant change from current lease accounting and the proposals in last year's ED, the Boards tentatively decided in their July meeting, that lessors should apply a single 'receivable and residual' approach to leases, with a few exceptions.[27] The Boards still need to discuss other lessor-specific issues, including the interaction with the financial instruments project, changes in lease agreements, residual value guarantees, impairment, financial statement presentation, disclosure and transition.

All of the decisions made by the Boards to date are tentative and will not be finalised until the Boards approve a final standard. The following are expected to be exceptions to the approach:

- Investment properties: leases of investment properties that are measured at fair value
- Short-term leases: an accounting policy election to apply current operating lease accounting to short-term leases, defined as in 10.3 above.

Under the *receivable and residual approach,* the lessor will, on commencement of the lease:

- recognise a lease receivable for the lessor's right to receive lease payments;
- allocate the carrying value of the underlying asset being leased between the portion related to the right of use granted to the lessee and the portion retained by the lessor (i.e. the residual asset); and
- recognise profit, if this is reasonably assured, or any loss on the arrangement.

The lease receivable will be initially measured at the present value of the lease payments over the lease term discounted using the rate the lessor charges the lessee. The lessor will determine the lease term and lease payments using the same principles applied by the lessee, described in 10.3 above.

The carrying amount of the underlying asset is allocated in the ratio of the lease receivable at recognition (the portion allocated to the right of use asset) to the fair value of the underlying asset being leased. If the profit under the lease is reasonably assured, the portion allocated to the right of use granted to the lessee is derecognised. Profit is the difference between the lease receivable recognised and the portion of the underlying asset derecognised.

Over the term of the lease, the lessor will recognise interest income from the right to receive payments, using the rate the lessor charges the lessee. It will also accrete the residual asset using the same rate. The carrying amount of the residual asset at the end of the lease term will not represent either the expected value or the amortised cost of the underlying asset at the end of the lease.

This approach would generally result in lower initial profits being recognised for this type of lease. Under current finance lease accounting, initial profit recognised reflects the profit on the sale of the entire asset, not just the portion relating to the lease receivable that is derecognised.

Profit is only recognised at commencement if it is reasonably assured. This is intended to make lessor accounting consistent with principles in the revenue recognition project, described in Chapter 30 at 5, although exactly how this will be applied in practice is yet to be clarified. There may be instances in which the residual value at the end of the lease term or the day one fair value of the underlying asset cannot be estimated.

If the profit is not reasonably assured, the residual asset will be measured initially as the difference between the lease receivable and the carrying value of the underlying asset. The residual asset will be accreted over the lease term to an amount equal to the underlying asset's carrying amount at the end of the lease term if it had been subject to depreciation using its original depreciable life and salvage value. That is, the lessor would recognise income, using a constant rate of return, over the lease term to accrete the residual asset to the amount that the underlying asset would have been measured at if it had remained on the balance sheet of the lessor and been subject to depreciation. Interest income on the lease receivable will be recognised over the lease term using the interest rate the lessor charges the lessee.

References

1 ASC 840-10-25-1.
2 Valuation Information Paper No. 9, The Royal Institution of Chartered Surveyors, May 2006.
3 RICS Valuation Information Paper No. 9, paras. 4.7 and 4.8.
4 *IFRIC Update*, September 2005.
5 *IFRIC Update*, April 2005.
6 *IFRIC Update*, July 2008.
7 *IFRIC Update*, March 2007.
8 *IFRIC Update*, March 2007.
9 *IASB Update*, April 2011.
10 ED/2010/9, para. B2.
11 *IASB Update*, April 2011.
12 ED/2010/9, para. 5.
13 *IASB Update*, 2 March 2011.
14 *IASB Update*, 14 March 2011.
15 *IASB Update*, 21-22 March 2011.
16 *IASB Update*, February 2011.
17 *IASB Update*, 21-22 March 2011.
18 *IASB Update*, April 2011.
19 *IASB Update*, April 2011.
20 *IASB Update*, 31 May-1 June 2011.
21 *IASB Update*, April 2011.
22 *IASB Update*, 21-22 March 2011.
23 *IASB Update*, May 2011. At this meeting, the Boards decided to revert to the method in ED/2010/9, para. 10. The definition of initial direct costs was clarified in *IASB Update*, 21-22 May 2011.
24 *IASB Update*, May 2011; the Boards broadly reaffirmed ED/2010/9, para. 16.
25 *IASB Update*, May and June 2011.
26 *IASB Update*, 21-22 March 2011.
27 *IASB Update*, July 2011.

Chapter 27   Government grants

List of examples

Chapter 27   Government grants

1   INTRODUCTION

IAS 20 – *Accounting for Government Grants and Disclosure of Government Assistance* – applied for the first time more than twenty-five years ago. *[IAS 20.41]*. After such a period of time it is perhaps not surprising that the standard is showing its age. The standard, in fact, pre-dates the IASB's *Framework* and the IASB itself notes that it is inconsistent with it,[1] resulting in the recognition in the balance sheet of deferred debits and credits that do not meet the Framework's definitions of assets and liabilities and allowing a method of presentation that could result in an understatement of assets controlled by an entity. In due course it will undergo fundamental revision but this has not been a priority issue for the IASB.

In presenting its proposals for the standard setting agenda going forward, the status of Government Grants as a potential project is unclear at best. The IASB notes that work on this project was deferred pending progress on the revenue recognition and emission trading schemes project (the latter of which was itself identified as 'important but less urgent' and suspended in November 2010).[2] The project is simply classified in the IASB's Agenda Consultation within 'Projects for which little or no work performed', with no suggestion that it is being put forward by the IASB as a new project suggestion.[3]

1.1   Government grants

Government grants are defined in IAS 20 as assistance by government in the form of transfers of resources to an entity in return for past or future compliance with certain conditions relating to the operating activities of the entity. *[IAS 20.3]*. Such assistance has been available to commercial businesses for many years, although its form and extent will often have undergone changes depending on the priorities of governments over time and from country to country. The purpose of government grants, which may be called subsidies, subventions or premiums, *[IAS 20.6]* and other forms of government assistance is often to encourage a private sector entity to take a course of action that it would not normally have taken if the assistance had not been provided. *[IAS 20.4]*. As the standard notes, the receipt of government assistance by an entity may be significant for the preparation of the financial statements for two reasons: *[IAS 20.5]*

- if resources have been transferred, an appropriate method of accounting for the transfer must be found; and

- it is desirable to give an indication of the extent to which an entity has benefited from such assistance during the reporting period, because this facilitates comparison of its financial statements with those of prior periods and with those of other entities.

The main accounting issue that arises from government grants is how to deal with the income that the grant represents. IAS 20 adopts a matching approach as its guiding principle, whereby grants are recognised in profit or loss in the same period as the costs that the grants are intended to compensate.

The standard recognises that an entity may receive other forms of government assistance, such as free technical or marketing advice and the provision of guarantees. Rather than prescribe how these should be accounted for, it requires disclosure about such assistance.

2   REQUIREMENTS OF IAS 20

The principal international accounting standard that deals with government grants is IAS 20, issued in 1983. Government grants related to biological assets are excluded from the scope of IAS 20 and are dealt with in IAS 41 – *Agriculture* (see Chapter 40 at 3.3). *[IAS 20.2(d)]*.

2.1   Nature of government grants and government assistance

IAS 20 is applied in accounting for, and in the disclosure of, government grants and in the disclosure of other forms of government assistance. *[IAS 20.1]*. The distinction between government grants and other forms of government assistance is important because the standard's accounting requirements only apply to the former.

The standard regards the term 'government' to include governmental agencies and similar bodies whether local, national or international. *[IAS 20.3]*.

2.1.1   *Government assistance*

Government assistance is defined as action by government designed to provide an economic benefit to an entity or range of entities qualifying under certain criteria (see 2.6 below). *[IAS 20.3]*. Government assistance takes many forms 'varying both in the nature of the assistance given and in the conditions which are usually attached to it'. *[IAS 20.4]*. However, such assistance does not include benefits provided indirectly through action affecting general trading conditions, such as the provision of infrastructure in development areas or the imposition of trading constraints on competitors. *[IAS 20.3]*.

2.1.2   *Government grants*

Government grants are a specific form of government assistance. Under IAS 20, *government grants* represent assistance by government in the form of transfers of resources to an entity in return for past or future compliance with certain conditions relating to the operating activities of the entity. *[IAS 20.3]*. The standard identifies the following types of government grants: *[IAS 20.3]*

- *grants related to assets* are government grants whose primary condition is that an entity qualifying for them should purchase, construct or otherwise acquire long-term assets. Subsidiary conditions may also be attached restricting the type or location of the assets or the periods during which they are to be acquired or held; and

- *grants related to income* are government grants other than those related to assets.

Government grants exclude *[IAS 20.3, 35]*:

(a) assistance to which no value can reasonably be assigned, e.g. free technical or marketing advice and the provision of guarantees; and

(b) transactions with government that cannot be distinguished from the normal trading transactions of the entity, e.g. where the entity is being favoured by a government's procurement policy.

Such excluded items are to be treated as falling within the standard's disclosure requirements for government assistance (see 2.1.1 above and 2.6 below).

Loans at below market interest rates were also deemed to be a form of government assistance and the benefit was not quantified by the imputation of interest. However, the standard now requires entities to measure the benefit of the below-market rate of interest in accordance with IAS 39 – *Financial Instruments: Recognition and Measurement* – or IFRS 9 – *Financial Instruments* – as appropriate. *[IAS 20.10A]*. The accounting consequences are discussed at 2.3.1 below.

2.2   Scope

IAS 20 applies in accounting for, and the disclosure of, government grants and the disclosure of other forms of government assistance, *[IAS 20.1]*. The standard does not deal with:

(a) accounting for government grants if the entity prepares financial information that reflect the effects of changing prices, whether as financial statements or in supplementary information;

(b) government assistance in the form of benefits that are available in determining taxable profit or loss or are determined or limited on the basis of income tax liability, i.e. income tax holidays, investment tax credits, accelerated depreciation allowances and reduced income tax rates;

(c) government participation in the ownership of the entity; and

(d) government grants covered by IAS 41. *[IAS 20.2]*.

The reason for exclusion (d) above is that the presentation permitted by IAS 20 of deducting government grants from the carrying amount of the asset (see 3.1 below) was considered inconsistent with a fair value model in which an asset is measured at its fair value. *[IAS 41.B66]*. The requirements of IAS 41 in relation to government grants are dealt with in Chapter 40 at 3.3.

There are no requirements for government grants in IAS 40 – *Investment Property* – which includes a similar fair value model (see Chapter 21), nor was IAS 20 revised to deal with the matter. This is probably because government grants in the investment property sector are relatively rare compared to the agricultural sector. However, governments do on occasion provide grants and subsidised loans to finance the acquisition of social housing that meets the definition of investment property. The discount on these subsidised loans is now considered to be a government grant, as described in 2.3.1 below.

IAS 20 rejects a 'capital approach', under which a grant is credited directly to equity, *[IAS 20.13]* in favour of the 'income approach', under which grants are taken to income over one or more periods, because: *[IAS 20.15]*

(a)   government grants are receipts from a source other than shareholders, they should not be credited directly to shareholders' interests but should be recognised as income in appropriate periods;

(b)   government grants are rarely gratuitous. An entity earns them through compliance with their conditions and meeting the envisaged obligations. They should therefore be recognised as income and matched with the associated costs which the grant is intended to compensate; and

(c)   as income and other taxes are charges against income, it is logical to deal also with government grants, which are an extension of fiscal policies, in the income statement.

The SIC considered the situation in some countries where government assistance is aimed at entities in certain regions or industry sectors, but without there being any conditions specifically relating to the operating activities of the entity concerned. It determined that such forms of government assistance are to be treated as government grants. *[SIC-10.3]*. This ruling was made to avoid any suggestion that such forms of assistance were not governed by the standard and could be credited directly to equity.

In public-to-private service concession arrangements a government may give certain assets to the operator of the service concession. If the entire arrangement is to be accounted for under IFRIC 12 – *Service Concession Arrangements* – the assets are not a government grant. *[IFRIC 12.27]*. Service concessions are discussed in Chapter 28.

While grants of emission rights and renewable energy certificates typically meet the definition of government grants under IAS 20, the rights and certificates themselves are intangible assets. Accounting for emission rights and renewable energy certificates is discussed in Chapter 19 at 13.3 and 13.4.

2.3   Recognition and initial measurement

IAS 20 requires that government grants should be recognised only when there is reasonable assurance that:

(a)   the entity will comply with the conditions attaching to them; and

(b)   the grants will be received. *[IAS 20.7]*.

The standard does not define 'reasonable assurance', which raises the question whether or not it means the same as 'probable'. When developing IAS 41 the Board believed that recognition of government grants when there is 'reasonable assurance' was different from recognition when 'it is probable that the entity will meet the conditions attaching to the government grant' and from 'the entity meets the conditions attaching to the government grant'. *[IAS 41.B70]*. The Board also noted that 'it would inevitably be a subjective decision as to when there is reasonable assurance that the conditions are met and that this subjectivity could lead to inconsistent income recognition.' *[IAS 41.B69]*. Nevertheless, we would not expect an entity to recognise government grants before it was at least probable that the entity would comply with the conditions attached to them, even though these conditions may relate to future performance and other future events, and the grants would be received. The standard notes that receiving a grant does not of itself provide conclusive evidence that the conditions attaching to the grant have been or will be fulfilled. *[IAS 20.8]*.

After an entity has recognised a government grant, any related contingent liability or contingent asset should be accounted for under IAS 37 – *Provisions, Contingent Liabilities and Contingent Assets. [IAS 20.11]*.

Accounting for government grants is not affected by the manner in which they are received, i.e. grants received in cash, as a non-monetary amount, or forgiveness of a government loan, are all accounted for in the same manner. *[IAS 20.9]*. A forgivable loan from government, the repayment of which will be waived under certain prescribed conditions *[IAS 20.3]*, is to be treated as a government grant when there is reasonable assurance that the entity will meet the terms for forgiveness of the loan. *[IAS 20.10]*.

Example 27.1:   Government grant by way of forgivable loan

An entity participates in a government sponsored research and development programme under which it is entitled to receive a government grant of up to 50% of the costs incurred for a particular project. The government grant is interest-bearing and fully repayable based on a percentage ('royalty') of the sales revenue of any products developed. Although the repayment period is not limited, no repayment is required if there are no sales of the products.

The entity should account for this type of government grant as follows:

– initially recognise the government grant as a forgivable loan;

– apply the principles underlying the effective interest rate method in subsequent periods, which would involve estimating the amount and timing of future cash flows;

– review at each balance sheet date whether there is reasonable assurance that the entity will meet the terms for forgiveness of the loan, i.e. the entity assesses that the product will not achieve sales. If this is the case then derecognise part or all of the liability initially recorded with a corresponding profit in the income statement; and

– if the entity subsequently revises its estimates of future sales upwards, it recognises a liability for any amounts previously included in profit and recognises a corresponding loss in the income statement.

A government grant in the form of a transfer of a non-monetary asset, such as land or other resources, which is intended for use by the entity, is usually recognised at the fair value of that asset. *[IAS 20.23]*. Fair value is 'the amount for which an asset could be exchanged between a knowledgeable, willing buyer and a knowledgeable, willing seller in an arm's length transactions.' *[IAS 20.3]*. In May 2011, the IASB issued IFRS 13 – *Fair Value Measurement*, which clarifies the definition of fair value, establishes a single framework for measuring fair value and requires disclosures about fair value measurements. *[IFRS 13.1]*. The standard is mandatory for annual periods beginning on or after 1 January 2013 and will apply when another IFRS requires or permits fair value measurement, including in IAS 20. *[IFRS 13.5, D64]*. The requirements of IFRS 13 are discussed in Chapter 16.

The alternative of recognising such assets, and the related grant, at a nominal amount is permitted. *[IAS 20.23]*. Under IAS 8 – *Accounting Policies, Changes in Accounting Estimates and Errors* – an entity should select an accounting policy and apply it consistently to all non-monetary government grants. *[IAS 8.13]*.

2.3.1   Loans at less than market rates of interest

IAS 20 requires government loans that have a below-market rate of interest to be recognised and measured in accordance with IAS 39 or IFRS 9 as appropriate, i.e. at their fair value. *[IAS 20.10A, IAS 39.43, IFRS 9.5.1.1]*. The loans could be interest-free. The difference between the initial carrying value of the loan (its fair value), and the proceeds received is treated as a government grant. Subsequently, interest will be imputed to the loan using the effective interest method (see Chapter 49 at 5). Crucially, the grant will not necessarily be released on a basis that is consistent with the interest expense. The standard stresses that the entity has to consider the conditions and obligations that have been, or must be, met when 'identifying the costs for which the benefit of the loan is intended to compensate'. *[IAS 20.10A]*. This process of matching the benefit to costs is discussed at 2.4 below.

As well as routine subsidised lending to meet specific objectives, loans made as part of government rescue plans may now be within scope of IAS 20 if they are at a lower than market rates of interest. PSA Peugeot Citroën describes the treatment of one such loan in Extract 27.1 below.

Extract 27.1: PSA Peugeot Citroën (2009)

Half-Year Financial Report 2009 [extract]

17.2. REFINANCING TRANSACTIONS [extract]

– EIB loan

In April 2009, Peugeot Citroën Automobiles S.A. obtained a €400 million 4-year bullet loan from the European Investment Bank (EIB). Interest on the loan is based on the 3-month Euribor plus 179 bps. At June 30, 2009 the government bonds (OATs) given by Peugeot S.A. as collateral for all EIB loans to Group companies had a market value of €160 million. In addition, 4,695,000 Faurecia shares held by Peugeot S.A. were pledged to the EIB as security for the loans. The interest rate risk on the new EIB loan has not been specifically hedged.

This new loan is at a reduced rate of interest. The difference between the market rate of interest for an equivalent loan at the inception date and the rate granted by the EIB has been recognised as a government grant in accordance with IAS 20. The grant was originally valued at €38 million and was recorded as a deduction from the capitalized development costs financed by the loan. It is being amortised on a straight-line basis over the life of the underlying projects. The loan is measured at amortised cost, in the amount of €362 million at June 30, 2009. The effective interest rate is estimated at 5.90%.

This will also affect the manner in which arrangements that are similar in substance to loans are accounted for. Governments sometimes allow entities to retain sums that they collect on behalf of the government (e.g. value added taxes) to be retained until a future event, as in the following example:

Example 27.2: Loan at less than market rates of interest

The local government of an underdeveloped region is trying to stimulate investment by allowing local companies to retain the value added tax (VAT) on their sales. An entity participating in this scheme is entitled to retain an amount up to 40% of its investment in fixed assets. The retained VAT must be paid to the local government after 5 years. The deferred VAT liability is comparable in nature to an interest free loan. The entity can reasonably place a value on the government assistance using the principles in IAS 39 and the benefit will be accounted for as government grants.

2.4   Matching grants against costs

Grants should be recognised in the income statement on a systematic basis that matches them with the related costs that they are intended to compensate. *[IAS 20.12].* They should not be credited directly to shareholders' funds. Income recognition on a receipts basis, which is not in accordance with the accruals accounting assumption, is only acceptable if no basis existed for allocating a grant to periods other than the one in which it was received. *[IAS 20.16].*

IAS 20 envisages that in most cases, the periods over which an entity recognises the costs or expenses related to the government grant are readily ascertainable and thus grants in recognition of specific expenses are recognised as income in the same period as the relevant expense. *[IAS 20.17].*

Grants related to depreciable assets are usually recognised as income over the periods, and in the proportions, in which depreciation on those assets is charged. *[IAS 20.17].* Grants related to non-depreciable assets may also require the fulfilment of certain obligations, in which case they would be recognised as income over the periods in which the costs of meeting the obligations are incurred. For example, a grant of land may be conditional upon the erection of a building on the site and it may be appropriate to recognise it as income over the life of the building. *[IAS 20.18].*

IAS 20 acknowledges that grants may be received as part of a package of financial or fiscal aids to which a number of conditions are attached. In such cases, the standard indicates that care is needed in identifying the conditions giving rise to the costs and expenses which determine the periods over which the grant will be earned. It may also be appropriate to allocate part of the grant on one basis and part on another. *[IAS 20.19].*

Where a grant relates to expenses or losses already incurred, or for the purpose of giving immediate financial support to the entity with no future related costs, the grant should be recognised in income when it becomes receivable. If such a grant is recognised as income of the period in which it becomes receivable, the entity should disclose its effects to ensure that these are clearly understood. *[IAS 20.20-22].*

Many of the problems in accounting for government grants relate to that of interpreting the requirement to match the grant with the related costs, particularly because of the international context in which IAS 20 is written. It does not address specific questions that relate to particular types of grant that are available in individual countries.

Chapter 27

2.4.1 Achieving the most appropriate matching

Most problems of accounting for grants fall into a single category: interpreting the requirement to match the grant against the costs that it is intended to compensate. This apparently simple principle can be extremely difficult to apply in practice, because it is sometimes far from clear what the essence of the grant was. Moreover, grants are sometimes given for a particular kind of expenditure that forms an element of a larger project, making the allocation a highly subjective matter. For example, government assistance that is in the form of a training grant might be:

(a)   matched against direct training costs;

(b)   taken over a period of time against the salary costs of the employees being trained, for example over the estimated duration of the project;

(c)   taken over the estimated period for which the company or the employees are expected to benefit from the training;

(d)   not distinguished from other project grants received and therefore matched against total project costs;

(e)   taken to income systematically over the life of the project, for example the total grant receivable may be allocated to revenue on a straight-line basis;

(f)   as in (d) or (e) above, but using, instead of project life, the period over which the grant is paid; or

(g)   taken to income when received in cash.

Depending on the circumstances, any of these approaches might produce an acceptable result. However, our observations on these alternative methods are as follows:

Under method (a), the grant could be recognised as income considerably in advance of its receipt, since often the major part of the direct training costs will be incurred at the beginning of a project and payment is usually made retrospectively. As the total grant receivable may be subject to adjustment, this may not be prudent or may lead to a mismatch of costs and revenues.

Methods (b) to (e) all rely on different interpretations of the expenditure to which the grant is expected to contribute, and could all represent an appropriate form of matching.

Method (f) has less to commend it, but the period of payment of the grant might in fact give an indication (in the absence of better evidence) of the duration of the project for which the expenditure is to be subsidised.

Similarly, method (g) is unlikely to be the most appropriate method *per se*, but may approximate to one of the other methods, or may, in the absence of any conclusive indication as to the expenditure intended to be subsidised by the grant, be the only practicable method that can be adopted.

In some jurisdictions grants are taxed as income on receipt; consequently, this is often the argument advanced for taking grants to income when received in cash. However, it is clear that the treatment of an item for tax purposes does not necessarily determine its treatment for accounting purposes, and immediate recognition in the income statement may result in an unacceptable departure from the principle that government grants should be matched with the costs that they are intended to compensate. *[IAS 20.16]*. Consequently, the recognition of a grant in the income statement in a different period from that in which it is taxed, gives rise to a temporary difference that should be accounted for in accordance with IAS 12 – *Income Taxes* (see Chapter 31).

In the face of the problems described above of attributing a grant to related costs, it is difficult to offer definitive guidance; entities will have to make their own judgements as to how the matching principle is to be applied. The only overriding considerations are that the method should be systematically and consistently applied, and that the policy adopted in respect of both capital and revenue grants, if material, should be adequately disclosed.

The example below illustrates that the interpretation of the matching requirement in the standard is not always straightforward.

Example 27.3:   Grant associated with investment property

The government provides a grant to an entity that owns an investment property. The grant is intended to compensate the entity for the lower rent it will receive when the property is let as social housing at below market rates. That means that future rental income will be lower over the period of the lease which, at the same time, reduces the fair value of the investment property.

If the entity accounts for the investment property under the IAS 40 cost model then it could be argued that the government grant should be recognised over the term of the lease to offset the lower rental income.

Alternatively, if the entity applied the IAS 40 fair value model then the cost being compensated is the reduction in fair value of the investment property. In that case it is more appropriate to recognise the benefit of the government grant immediately.

If, instead of a grant, the government subsidises a loan used by the entity to acquire the property, then the loan will be brought in at its fair value. The difference between the face value and fair value will be a government grant and the arguments above will apply to its treatment.

If the government imposes conditions, e.g. that the building must be used for social housing for ten years, this does not necessarily mean that the grant should be taken to income over that period. Rather, it should apply a process similar to that in Example 27.1 above. The entity estimate whether there is reasonable assurance that it will meet the terms of the grant and, to that extent, treat an appropriate amount as a grant as above. This should be reviewed at each balance sheet date and adjustments made if it appears that the conditions will not be met (see 2.5 below).

2.4.2   The period to be benefited by the grant

IAS 20 cautions that care is needed in identifying the conditions giving rise to the costs and expenses, which determine the periods over which the grant will be earned. *[IAS 20.19]*. The qualifying conditions that have to be satisfied are not necessarily conclusive evidence of the period to be benefited by the grant. For example, certain grants may become repayable if assets cease to be used for a qualifying purpose within a certain period; notwithstanding this condition, the grant should be recognised over the whole life of the asset, not over the qualifying period.

Chapter 27

2.4.3   *Separating grants into elements*

The grant received may be part of a package, the elements of which have different costs and conditions. In such cases, it is common that the elements for which the grant is given are not specifically identified or quantified. It will often be appropriate to treat these different elements on different bases rather than accounting for the entire grant in one way. For example, a grant may be given on the basis that an entity makes approved capital expenditure in a particular area and employs a specified number of local people for an agreed period of time. The amount of grant may be based on the approved capital expenditure but this does not mean that the grant is necessarily treated wholly as a capital grant. It will be necessary to examine the full circumstances of the grant in order to determine its purpose.

In general, the most straightforward way of recognising a grant is by linking it to long-term assets where this is a possible interpretation, particularly where the payment of the grant depends on the cost of acquisition of long-term assets. However, this approach can only be taken if there is no clear indication to the contrary.

Allocation of a grant between the elements will always be a matter of judgement and entities may place more stress on some features than on others. We believe that the most important consideration where there are significant questions over how the grant is to be recognised, and where the effect is material, is that the financial statements should explicitly state what treatment has been chosen and disclose the financial effect of adopting that treatment.

2.5   Repayment of government grants

A government grant that becomes repayable should be accounted for as a revision of an accounting estimate. Repayment of a grant related to income should be charged against the related unamortised deferred credit and any excess should be recognised as an expense immediately. *[IAS 20.32]*.

Repayment of a grant related to an asset should be recognised by increasing the carrying amount of the related asset or reducing the related unamortised deferred credit. The cumulative additional depreciation that would have been recognised to date as an expense in the absence of the grant should be charged immediately to profit or loss. *[IAS 20.32]*.

IAS 20 emphasises that the circumstances giving rise to the repayment of a grant related to an asset may require that consideration be given to the possible impairment of the asset. *[IAS 20.33]*.

2.6   Government assistance

As indicated above, IAS 20 excludes from the definition of government grants 'certain forms of government assistance which cannot reasonably have a value placed upon them and transactions with government which cannot be distinguished from the normal trading transactions of the entity'. *[IAS 20.34]*. In many cases the 'existence of the benefit might be unquestioned but any attempt to segregate the trading activities from government assistance could well be arbitrary'. *[IAS 20.35]*. The standard therefore requires disclosure of significant government assistance (see 4.1 below).

Under IAS 20, 'government assistance does not include the provision of infrastructure by improvement to the general transport and communication network and the supply of improved facilities such as irrigation or water reticulation that is available on an ongoing indeterminate basis for the benefit of an entire local community.' *[IAS 20.38]*.

3   PRESENTATION OF GRANTS

3.1   Presentation of grants related to assets

Grants that are related to assets (i.e. those whose primary condition is that an entity qualifying for them should purchase, construct or otherwise acquire long-term assets) should be presented in the balance sheet either: *[IAS 20.24]*

(a)   by setting up the grant as deferred income, which is recognised as income on a systematic and rational basis over the useful life of the asset; *[IAS 20.26]* or

(b)   by deducting the grant in arriving at the carrying amount of the asset, in which case the grant is recognised in income as a reduction of depreciation. *[IAS 20.27]*.

IAS 20 regards both these methods of presenting grants in financial statements as acceptable alternatives. *[IAS 20.25]*.

A company that adopted the former treatment is Greencore Group, as shown below:

Extract 27.2: Greencore Group plc (2010)

Group Statement of Accounting Policies year ended 24 September 2010 [extract]

Government Grants

Government grants for the acquisition of assets are recognised at their fair value when there is reasonable assurance that the grant will be received and any conditions attached to them have been fulfilled. The grant is held on the Balance Sheet as a deferred credit and released to the Income Statement over the periods necessary to match the related depreciation charges, or other expenses of the asset, as they are incurred.

An example of a company adopting a policy of deducting grants related to assets from the cost of the assets is shown below:

Extract 27.3: AkzoNobel N.V. (2010)

Notes to the consolidated financial statements [extract]

Note 1 Summary of significant accounting policies [extract]

Government grants

Government grants related to costs are deducted from the relevant cost to be compensated in the same period. Emission rights granted by the government are recorded at cost. A provision is recorded if the actual emission is higher than the emission rights granted. Government grants to compensate for the cost of an asset are deducted from the cost of the related asset.

3.1.1   Cash flows

The purchase of assets and the receipt of related grants can cause major movements in the cash flow of an entity. Therefore, such movements are often disclosed as separate items in the cash flow statement whether or not the grant is deducted from the related asset for the purpose of balance sheet presentation. *[IAS 20.28]*.

3.2   Presentation of grants related to income

Grants related to income should be presented either as: *[IAS 20.29]*

(a)   a credit in the income statement, either separately or under a general heading such as 'other income'; or

(b)   a deduction in reporting the related expense.

The standard points out that supporters of method (a) consider it inappropriate to present income and expense items on a net basis and that 'separation of the grant from the expense facilitates comparison with other expenses not affected by a grant'. *[IAS 20.30]*. Furthermore, method (a) is consistent with the general prohibition of offsetting in IAS 1 – *Presentation of Financial Statements*. *[IAS 1.32-33]*. However, supporters of method (b) would argue that 'the expenses might well not have been incurred by the entity if the grant had not been available and presentation of the expense without offsetting the grant may therefore be misleading'. *[IAS 20.30]*. Although the arguments in favour of method (b) are not that convincing (it compares the accounting for the actual facts with that for a scenario that did not take place), the standard regards both methods as acceptable for the presentation of grants related to income. *[IAS 20.31]*. In any case, the standard considers that disclosure of the grant may be necessary for a proper understanding of the financial statements. Furthermore, disclosure of the effect of grants on any item of income or expense, which should be disclosed separately, is usually appropriate. *[IAS 20.31]*.

As illustrated below, InBev has adopted a policy of presenting grants within other operating income, although not separately on the face of the income statement, rather than as a deduction from the related expense.

Extract 27.4: AB InBev NV (2010)

3. Summary of significant accounting policies [extract]

(X) Income recognition [extract]

Government grants

A government grant is recognized in the balance sheet initially as deferred income when there is reasonable assurance that it will be received and that the company will comply with the conditions attached to it. Grants that compensate the company for expenses incurred are recognized as other operating income on a systematic basis in the same periods in which the expenses are incurred. Grants that compensate the company for the acquisition of an asset are presented by deducting them from the acquisition cost of the related asset in accordance with IAS 20 *Accounting for Government Grants and Disclosure of Government Assistance*.

AkzoNobel N.V. is an example of a company presenting the grant as a deduction from the related expense in the income statement, as illustrated in Extract 27.3 above.

4   DISCLOSURES

IAS 20 requires that entities should disclose the following information regarding government grants: *[IAS 20.39]*

(a)   the accounting policy, including the method of presentation adopted in the financial statements;

(b)   a description of the nature and extent of the grants recognised and an indication of other forms of government assistance from which the entity has directly benefited; and

(c)   unfulfilled conditions or contingencies attaching to government assistance that has been recognised.

The extract below illustrates how companies typically disclose government grants under IFRS. It should be noted that disclosures concerning the nature and conditions of government grants are sometimes relatively minimal, possibly because the amounts involved are immaterial.

Extract 27.5: Danisco A/S (2010)

Note 38 – Accounting policies [extract]

Government grants

Government grants, which are disclosed in a note, include grants for research and development, CO2 allowances and investments. Grants for research and development and CO2 allowances are recognised as income on a systematic basis to match the related cost. Investment grants are set off against the cost of the subsidised assets.

33 Government grants

During the financial year ended, Danisco received government grants for research and development of DKK 2 million (2008/09 DKK 3 million) DKK 1 million (2008/09 DKK 9 million) for investments and DKK 6 million (2008/09 DKK 14 million) for other purposes.

Further Danisco was granted quotas of 49,551 tonnes of CO2 allowances (2008/09 610,277 tonnes). The value at grant date was DKK 5 million (2008/09 DKK 88 million), and the quotas match the expected emission tax.

Additional examples of accounting policies for government grants can be found in Extracts 27.2, 23.3 and 23.4 above.

4.1   Government assistance

In addition to the disclosures noted above, for those forms of government assistance that are excluded from the definition of government grants, the significance of such benefits may be such that the disclosure of the nature, extent and duration of the assistance is necessary to prevent the financial statements from being misleading. *[IAS 20.36]*.

References

1 IASB website, *www.iasb.org*, June 2011.
2 *IASB Work Plan – projected timetable as at 26 July 2011*, IASB.
3 Request for Views *Agenda Consultation 2011*, IASB, June 2011, Appendix C.

Chapter 28   Service concession arrangements

List of examples

Chapter 28   Service concession arrangements

1   INTRODUCTION

Service concession arrangements are of great complexity, often devised to meet political as well as purely commercial ends. The issues cross the boundaries of a number of accounting standards, and this has made it extremely difficult to devise an adequate accounting model. IFRIC Interpretation 12 – *Service Concession Arrangements* – which took more than three years to develop, was finally approved by the IASB in November 2006.

Service concession arrangements have been developed as a mechanism for procuring public services. Under a service concession arrangement ('SCA'), private capital is used to provide major economic and social facilities for public use. The initial idea was that, rather than having bodies in the public sector taking on the entire responsibility for funding and building infrastructure assets such as roads, bridges, railways, hospitals, prisons and schools, some of these should be contracted out to private sector entities from which the public sector bodies would buy services. As time has passed, the types of services covered by such arrangements have changed and they no longer necessarily include the construction of a major asset. Many service concessions now require the private sector to bring an existing facility or service up to an agreed standard and continue to maintain it for a contracted period; this type of arrangement has covered a range of projects from the refurbishment of social housing and street lighting to major civil engineering projects to restore a city's underground rail system. In addition, similar arrangements have been developed between private sector bodies, thereby creating an indistinct boundary between service concessions and outsourcing arrangements.

The accounting challenge is to reflect the substance of these arrangements fairly in the accounts of both of the contracting parties. It would be possible simply to take the contracts at fair value and account for the amounts received as revenue when due under the contract; however, closer analysis may sometimes reveal that this is, in reality, a composite transaction whereby the public sector body is paying for an asset to be constructed and operated at its direction as well as for services. There is the issue of how to account for the operations period of the contract, which may also include asset replacement and refurbishment as well as more obvious services.

The issues raised by service concessions range across a number of accounting standards and interpretations, including IAS 11 – *Construction Contracts*, IAS 16 – *Property, Plant and Equipment*, IAS 17 – *Leases*, IFRIC Interpretation 4 – *Determining whether an Arrangement contains a Lease*, IAS 18 – *Revenue*, IAS 20 – *Accounting for Government Grants and Disclosure of Government Assistance*, IAS 23 – *Borrowing Costs*, IAS 32 – *Financial Instruments: Presentation*, IAS 37 – *Provisions, Contingent Liabilities and Contingent Assets*, IAS 38 – *Intangible Assets* – and IAS 39 – *Financial Instruments: Recognition and Measurement* (or IFRS 9 – *Financial Instruments,* as appropriate), which makes it extremely difficult to develop a coherent accounting model that deals with all of the features of service concessions simultaneously, and from the position of both the private sector (i.e. the 'operator') and public sector (i.e. the 'grantor'). Moreover, entrenched national positions had developed and differing accounting treatments had been widely adopted in various jurisdictions, with or without a basis in specific local accounting standards. For example, in the UK, where there is formal accounting guidance under UK GAAP, operators are required to analyse assets constructed for the concession as property, plant and equipment or as financial assets (receivables due from the public sector body).[1] Indeed, some jurisdictions accepted more than one treatment of broadly similar arrangements, some of which are associated with a taxation basis that has been agreed with the jurisdictional revenue authorities.

In May 2001, SIC-29 – *Disclosure – Service Concession Arrangements* – was issued. This did not attempt to address the accounting issues but considered the information that should be disclosed in the notes to the financial statements of an 'operator' and 'grantor' under a service concession arrangement. Its requirements are described further at 6 below.

Since then, the complex accounting issues raised by service concessions have been subject to prolonged debate. The IFRIC (now the Interpretations Committee) began its formal discussions in 2003 but it took until November 2006 to issue IFRIC Interpretation 12 – *Service Concession Arrangements*. The Interpretations Committee discussions clearly demonstrate the complexity of the issues and the difficulty in fitting them into the existing accounting framework.

1.1   The Interpretations Committee's approach to accounting for service concessions

The Interpretations Committee views the primary accounting decision for the operator as being between:

- infrastructure assets where the grantor cedes control to the operator, or assets (whether constructed for the concession or otherwise) that remain within the operator's control; and
- infrastructure assets constructed for the concession or acquired from a third party that become those of the grantor because it controls them, or existing assets that remain under its control.

The Interpretations Committee suggests that the first category (where the asset is either derecognised by the grantor or is an asset constructed for the concession that the grantor never controls) can be dealt with adequately by other accounting standards or interpretations. The interrelationship with other accounting standards is discussed further at 2 below.

The second category (infrastructure assets constructed for the concession that become those of the grantor because it controls them or existing assets that remain under its control) is the subject of IFRIC 12 relating to service concessions. *[IFRIC 12.7].*

'Control' is a central concept and its definition and consequences are discussed further at 3 below.

Thus any infrastructure that remains under the control of the grantor will be accounted for using these two service concession models – the 'financial asset' model or the 'intangible asset' model. These are considered further at 4 below.

2   SCOPE OF IFRIC 12

The Interpretations Committee concluded that the scope should be limited to the accounting by the operator in a public-to-private service concession that meets its control criteria. *[IFRIC 12.4, 5].*

The grantor, including parties related to it, will be considered to control the property if the arrangement meets two conditions:

(a)   the grantor controls or regulates the services that the operator must provide using the infrastructure, to whom it must provide them, and at what price; and

(b)   the grantor controls any significant residual interest in the property at the end of the concession term through ownership, beneficial entitlement or otherwise. Infrastructure used for its entire useful life is within the scope if the arrangement meets the conditions in (a). *[IFRIC 12.5, 6].*

The Interpretations Committee was deliberately restrictive in setting the scope of IFRC 12, on the basis that the above conditions were likely to be met in most of the public-to-private arrangements for which guidance had been sought. The Committee concluded that other standards apply when these conditions are not a feature of the arrangement, *[IFRIC 12.BC 11-13],* for example arrangements where infrastructure is leased by the operator of the service or where an activity previously undertaken by government is privatised and the infrastructure becomes the operator's property.

Infrastructure assets within scope are those constructed or acquired for the purpose of the concession or existing infrastructure to which the operator is given access for these purposes (see 3.3 below). *[IFRIC 12.7].* Accounting is based on who controls the right to use the infrastructure. Crucially, control may be separated from ownership. Therefore, if the grantor controls the infrastructure assets, they should be accounted for according to one of the service concession models (see 4 below).

Arrangements within scope will be those that meet the following criteria:

1   the arrangement is a public-to-private service concession (2.1 below);

2   the grantor controls or regulates the services (3.1 below);

3   the grantor controls any significant residual interest (3.2 below);

4   infrastructure is constructed or acquired for the purpose of the service concession (3.3 below); and

5   The operator has either a contractual right to receive cash from or at the direction of the grantor; or a contractual right to charge users of the service.

If the answer to all of these is 'yes', then the arrangement is in scope of IFRIC 12. The last question also determines which of IFRIC 12's accounting models, financial asset or intangible asset, described at 4 below, should be applied.

While the Interpretations Committee expects IFRIC 12 to be applied to transactions that share the features of the public service obligation, it does not rule out the application of the principles to private-to-private arrangements. The Basis for Conclusions notes that this could be appropriate under the hierarchy in IAS 8 – *Accounting Policies, Changes in Accounting Estimates and Errors* – if the arrangement were of a similar type and met the control criteria quoted above. *[IFRIC 12.BC14].* The Interpretation does not expand on the features that could make a private-to-private arrangement 'similar' to a transaction that is within scope.

The Interpretation applies only to accounting by the operator, not the grantor. *[IFRIC 12.9].* This seems reasonable as most grantors are governments who may have their own views about accounting and do not necessarily apply IFRS, to the extent that they prepare publicly available financial information at all.

The Interpretations Committee's accounting framework for public-to-private arrangements is summarised in the following diagram from Information Note 1 in IFRIC 12. The diagram starts with the presumption that the arrangement has already been determined to be a service concession:

In an attempt to clarify the scope, the Interpretations Committee has produced a table on which the following is based (included as Information Note 2 to IFRIC 12) and which shows the range of arrangements between the public and private sectors. The Interpretations Committee's view is that it is interpreting IFRSs for the transactions in the middle of this range, where the application of standards is unclear. These are described in the table below as 'Rehabilitate-operate-transfer' and 'Build-operate-transfer' arrangements.

Chapter 28

Category	Lessee	Service Provider			Owner	
Typical Arrangement Types	Lease, e.g. Operator leases asset from grantor	Service and/or maintenance contract, e.g. specific tasks e.g. debt collection	Rehabilitate-operate-transfer	Build-operate-transfer	Build-own-operate	100% Divestment, privatisation, Corporation
Asset Ownership	Grantor				Operator	
Capital Investment	Grantor		Operator			
Demand Risk	Shared	Grantor	Operator and/or Grantor		Operator	
Typical Duration	8-20 years	1-5 years	25-30 years			Indefinite (or may be limited by license)
Residual Interest	Grantor				Operator	
Examples of IFRSs that may apply	IAS 17	IAS 18	IFRIC 12		IAS 16	

2.1   Public-to-private service concession arrangements within scope

One of the first problems faced by the Interpretations Committee was defining the scope of any Interpretation on service concession accounting. The Committee has applied a narrow interpretation to the scope of IFRIC 12, restricting it to guidance on public-to-private service concession arrangements. *[IFRIC 12.4].* A broader interpretation based solely on the control criteria could have applied to many existing outsourcing and similar arrangements.

Therefore, to be within scope, an arrangement has to involve a private sector entity (the operator), a public sector body (the grantor), and a service concession. None of these terms is entirely self-explanatory.

2.1.1   Private sector entity (the operator)

An arrangement may be within scope even if the operator is ultimately controlled by the state.

Generally, a private sector entity would be expected to be one that was entirely independent of the state. However, there may be circumstances in which an entity is partially or wholly state-owned but allowed autonomy to conduct its own affairs. Entities such as these are common, not only in jurisdictions where there is state ownership of all economic activity. Some governments allow utilities to control most of their own affairs while retaining ownership of the utility. Governments may take total or partial ownership of entities as a means of encouraging economic development but allow the entity control over its contractual arrangements.

If there is an arrangement that in all other respects appears to be the same as a service concession arrangement between a private entity and the state, the state-owned entity may be considered as if it were a private sector entity and IFRIC 12 will apply. If the activity of the 'service concession' is regulated only by law rather than in a contractual arrangement between the operator and the grantor, then the arrangement is not within scope (see 2.1.5 below).

2.1.2 Public sector body

IFRIC 12 notes that control over services and prices in paragraph 5(a), described at 2 above:

> '... includes circumstances in which the grantor buys all of the output as well as those in which some or all of the output is bought by other users. In applying this condition, the grantor and any related parties shall be considered together. If the grantor is a public sector entity, the public sector as a whole, together with any regulators acting in the public interest, shall be regarded as related to the grantor for the purposes of this Interpretation.' *[IFRIC 12.AG2]*.

This means that the entire public may be considered as part of the 'public sector' if the grantor purchases all of the output and provides services for free, e.g. health services.

Not every related party of the grantor (as defined in paragraph 9 of IAS 24 – *Related Party Disclosures* – see Chapter 37) need be taken into account in determining whether the grantor controls the service concession. Some services may be provided simultaneously to more than one public sector body but they will only be taken into account together if they operate in concert to control the 'output'. For instance, an entity may provide similar information technology services to several government departments and local government bodies but each contract is negotiated separately; the departments and bodies are not necessarily 'related parties'.

Regulators must be taken into account although they may not be related parties of the grantor as defined by IAS 24 as they may be required to be independent to act in the public interest.

The Interpretation states that a governmental body or a private sector entity to which the responsibility for the service has been devolved will be regarded as the grantor of the service arrangement. *[IFRIC 12.3(a)]*.

Control of prices is discussed further at 3.1 below.

2.1.3 Service concession arrangement ('SCA')

IFRIC 12 does not describe the features of a service concession agreement in the scope paragraphs; instead they are included in 'background' information where they help explain what is, and what is not, a public-to-private service arrangement. The main characteristic of a service concession is the public service nature of the obligation undertaken by the operator. The services related to the infrastructure are to be provided to the public as a matter of policy, irrespective of the identity of the party that operates the services. The service concession arrangement contractually obliges the operator to provide the services to the public on behalf of the public sector entity. IFRIC 12 states that 'other common features are:

(a)   the party that grants the service arrangement (the grantor) is a public sector entity, including a governmental body, or a private sector entity to which the responsibility for the service has been devolved.

(b)   the operator is responsible for at least some of the management of the infrastructure and related services and does not merely act as an agent on behalf of the grantor.

(c)   the contract sets the initial prices to be levied by the operator and regulates price revisions over the period of the service arrangement.

(d)   the operator is obliged to hand over the infrastructure to the grantor in a specified condition at the end of the period of the arrangement, for little or no incremental consideration, irrespective of which party initially financed it.' *[IFRIC 12.3]*.

The meaning of the public service obligation remains somewhat elusive. SCAs fall into two broad categories where the public service obligation can be identified:

1   SCAs that provide services directly to the public (e.g. transport, water supply, sewage, landfills).

2   SCAs where the services 'related to the infrastructure' continue to be provided by the grantor, e.g. the services provided by hospitals, prisons or schools, all of which would usually be considered to be examples of service concession arrangements. However, the infrastructure that is the subject of the contractual arrangement is used to provide services directly to the public, or to a significant part of it.

In other cases, it is far less clear that there is a public service obligation. Some arrangements are controlled by government bodies that may only comprise a few municipal authorities within that jurisdiction. Some European city authorities, for example, control car parking but in the vast majority of cities car parking *per se* is not considered a public service. In these cases the entity simply has to provide services to the grantor through an asset it has constructed and the arrangement may well be the same as those with local supermarkets and cinemas. The arrangement with the city authority may meet the control criteria in paragraph 5 of IFRIC 12, described at 3.2 below but so, too, may the contract with the cinema.

The services may be those that need to be provided to the public as a matter of policy (e.g. the provision of electricity) but the contractual arrangement itself is unrelated to any public service obligation. There are no services in addition to the provision of power (a combination of assets and services is often thought as typical of SCAs) and the grantor pays for the fixed and variable costs of the power produced, as do many private purchasers of power.

These outsourcing-type arrangements are examples of perhaps the most problematic boundary, that between IFRIC 12 and IFRIC 4 – *Determining whether an Arrangement contains a Lease*. The Interpretations Committee has attempted to deal with this, not wholly successfully, by introducing an amendment to IFRIC 4 specifically to exclude arrangements falling within the scope of IFRIC 12 from its scope. *[IFRIC 4.4]*. This is discussed at 2.2 below.

2.1.4 Agent type arrangements

A feature of SCAs is that the operator is responsible for at least some of the management of the infrastructure and related services and does not merely act as an agent on behalf of the grantor. *[IFRIC 12.3]*.

For example, an operator constructs and maintains for 25 years a building that will be used for administrative purposes by the Defence Ministry in a particular country. The building does not have any parts dedicated to services provided directly to the public although the service that is provided within the building (national security) may be considered a matter of policy. At the end of the concession term, the building reverts to the Ministry for a nominal sum. In the interests of national security, all details of the services to be provided are predetermined. In this type of arrangement there may be virtually no scope for the operator to make any management decisions.

This will always be a question of degree and is unlikely to be the crucial feature in making a decision but it may help distinguish SCAs within scope of IFRIC 12 from some of the 'outsourcing' type arrangements discussed at 2.2 below.

2.1.5 A contract with the grantor

An arrangement can only be a SCA if there is a contract with the grantor 'that sets out performance standards, mechanisms for adjusting prices, and arrangements for arbitrating disputes'. *[IFRIC 12.2]*.

If the operator of an asset obtains a licence to provide services but has no contractual obligation to the grantor (including parties 'related' to the grantor in the sense in which the term is used in IFRIC 12, see 3.1 below) then the arrangement will not be within scope. There are many activities that require a formal licence; in some jurisdictions these include licences to operate pharmacies, provide childcare or carry out certain waste disposal activities, any of which could be considered public service obligations in some countries. Obtaining the licence does not bring the activity into scope of IFRIC 12 unless there is a separate contractual arrangement that governs the provision of the service.

Information Note 2 to IFRIC 12, reproduced at 2 above, indicates that there are certain contractual arrangements between grantor and operator that are not within scope of the Interpretation. These include arrangements in which there is a service and/or maintenance contract, i.e. to perform specific tasks, where IAS 18 is the relevant standard. Another example is where the operator leases assets from the grantor, in which case IAS 17 would provide relevant guidance, unless, for example, the lease payments are made as part of a wider service concession, in which case the costs may have to be accrued as part of the costs of an infrastructure asset (see 3.3 below).

However, the contractual arrangement does not need to be for construction services in respect of any infrastructure. The arrangement may be within scope of IFRIC 12 in respect of post-construction services alone. Accounting for the post-construction period is described at 5 below.

2.2   IFRIC 4 and IFRIC 12: outsourcing arrangements and SCAs

The Interpretations Committee amended IFRIC 4 specifically to exclude arrangements falling within the scope of IFRIC 12 from its scope. *[IFRIC 4.4]*. However, while this clarifies the treatment of arrangements that are clearly within scope of IFRIC 12, in which case that Interpretation takes priority, it does not help in the type of case where it is not clear that the arrangement ought to fall within scope of IFRIC 12 in the first place.

The Interpretations Committee was unable to come up with a robust definition of public service obligation. The description of the features of SCAs (discussed at 2.1.3 above), is included in a 'background' section preceding the body of the Interpretation itself. In the period since IFRIC 12 was issued, it has still not proved possible to come up with a workable definition of public service obligation. To some extent this is because the public policy component of its meaning comes from a political or ideological determination of what activities should be provided by the state. This means that there will always be a certain amount of confusion over whether an arrangement that meets the control criteria but that does not appear to contain any obvious public service obligation ought, as a matter of course, to be accounted for under IFRIC 12.

It is arguable whether all outsourcing-type arrangements were intended to be within scope of IFRIC 12. The Interpretations Committee noted in September 2005 that it would not expect an information technology outsourcing arrangement for a government department to be dealt with under the Interpretation.[2] The Interpretations Committee presumably concluded that, as an outsourcing arrangement, this more properly fell within IFRIC 4; the infrastructure is used by the grantor in order that it can provide a public service but it is not used itself to provide the service.

The control test alone does not seem to be adequate to distinguish SCAs from other arrangements. There are numerous examples of arrangements in which the grantor controls the services in their entirety and controls the residual interest in the infrastructure asset but that would have been seen as containing leases under IAS 17 by applying an IFRIC 4 analysis. In other words, a grantor may have a 'right to control the use' of an infrastructure asset, under an IFRIC 4 analysis, *[IFRIC 4.9]*, see Chapter 26 at 2.1, or an operator may have a 'right of access' of that same asset, if it is within the scope of IFRIC 12. This could make a significant difference to the manner in which the arrangement is accounted for. IFRIC 12's control model and IAS 17's risks and rewards tests could result in different assets being recognised in the financial statements of operator and grantor. An arrangement could be accounted for under the financial asset model under IFRIC 12, so the asset would be accounted for as a receivable by the operator, yet considered an operating lease under IAS 17, in which case the operator would consider the asset to be PP&E. The operator may have arrangements on the same terms with private sector bodies and with the public sector. One example is power supply. In many parts of the world, governments have chosen to expand power generation by entering into contracts with operators. Some of these arrangements have the same features as power supply contracts to private sector purchasers to which IFRIC 4 applies. Commonly, the contract allows for a fixed charge that is payable irrespective of deliveries, which may or may not cover all of the capital expenditure, a variable charge related to the variable costs of generating power and a penalty regime under which part of the fixed cost is refundable. These are the features that are described in Chapter 26, Example 26.1, as 'An arrangement that contains a lease'. Providing power is a public service yet the public service element may be irrelevant to the structure of the contract. The use to which the grantor puts the power need not affect the arrangement; for example, the power could be used solely by Government department buildings, by a government-owned industry, for naval dockyards or it could be put directly into the national electricity distribution network.

In such a case there may be no services in addition to those necessary to maintain the power supply, unlike the much more extensive services that are supplied as part of what are usually considered typical SCAs such as hospitals or prisons. By contrast, other 'typical' SCAs such as toll roads and bridges have few associated services but are clearly used directly by the public. The existence or otherwise of services is not sufficient to distinguish SCAs from other contractual arrangements with grantors.

In the end, it is always likely to be a matter of judgement and there will be different views in practice. IFRIC 12 was developed because there are transactions that are so complex that it is very difficult to fit them into an existing accounting model and it is important not to lose sight of this. It appears that it was not the intention of the Interpretations Committee to change the manner in which outsourcing arrangements were accounted for solely because the contracting party is a government body but the control criteria in paragraph 5 of IFRIC 12 may apply to these arrangements.

3   THE CONTROL MODEL

IFRIC 12 includes the following guidance that expands and explains its control criteria:

(a)   the grantor controls or regulates the services that the operator must provide using the infrastructure, to whom it must provide them, and at what price; and

(b)   the grantor controls any significant residual interest in the property at the end of the concession term through ownership, beneficial entitlement or otherwise. *[IFRIC 12.5]*.

The Interpretations Committee considers that, taken together, these conditions identify when the infrastructure is controlled by the grantor for the whole of its economic life, in which case an operator is only managing the infrastructure on the grantor's behalf. *[IFRIC 12.AG4, AG5]*. Crucially, it has concluded from this that an infrastructure asset controlled by the grantor cannot be the property, plant and equipment of the operator. *[IFRIC 12.BC21, BC22]*.

3.1   Regulation of services

The control or regulation of services does not have to be by contract – it could include control via an industry regulator. Control also extends to circumstances in which the grantor buys all of the output as well as those in which it is bought by other users. The grantor and any related parties must be considered together. If the grantor is a public sector entity, the public sector as a whole, together with any independent regulators acting in the public interest, are to be regarded as related to the grantor. *[IFRIC 12.AG2]*.

Chapter 28

'Price' can mean the amount at which the grantor buys the service or the amount that the operator charges members of the public or a combination of both.

This means that many regulated public utilities (water, sewage, electricity supply etc.) will fall within (a). Other arrangements that fall within (a) include public health facilities that are free to users and subsidised transport facilities (rail, some toll roads and bridges) that are partly paid by public sector grant and partly by passenger fares. Of course, all of these will only be within scope of IFRIC 12 if any significant residual interest is also 'controlled' by the grantor under (b).

The Interpretations Committee stresses that the grantor does not need to have complete control of the price. It is sufficient for the price to be regulated, which could be by way of a capping mechanism (regulated utilities are usually free to charge *lower* prices). Other 'caps' may not be so apparent. A contract may give the operator freedom to set its prices but any excess is clawed back by the grantor (e.g. through setting a maximum return on an agreed investment in the infrastructure). In such a case, the operator's return is capped and the price element of the control test is substantively met. [IFRIC 12.AG3].

Obviously, it is a requirement to look to the substance of the agreements so a cap that only applies in remote circumstances will be ignored.

Some arrangements only allow the grantor to control prices for part of the life of the infrastructure, particularly if it is a lease-type arrangement. For example, an operator may construct clinical facilities that are used by a government health care provider (the grantor) for a five year contract term. At the end of the term, the grantor may extend the contract by renegotiation. If it does not do so, the operator can run the facilities for private health care. Although the prices are controlled for the first five years, this arrangement is unlikely to meet the control condition in (a) above.

Alternatively, the contract might allow regulation of the prices of some but not all of the services provided with the infrastructure. Judgement is required in determining whether arrangements involving partially regulated assets fall within the scope of IFRIC 12 (see 3.4 below).

3.2   Control of the residual interest

In order for an arrangement to be within scope of IFRIC 12, the grantor must control any significant residual interest in the property at the end of the concession term through ownership, beneficial entitlement or otherwise. [IFRIC 12.5(b)]. The grantor's control over any significant residual interest should restrict the operator's ability to sell or pledge the infrastructure. The grantor must have a right of use of the infrastructure throughout the concession term. [IFRIC 12.AG4].

Many infrastructure assets are partially replaced during the course of the concession and the impact of this on condition (b) has been considered. If the operator has to replace part of an item of infrastructure during the life of the concession (for example, the top layer of a road or the roof of a building), the item of infrastructure is to be considered as a whole, so that condition (b) will be met for the whole of the infrastructure, including the part that is replaced, if the grantor has the residual interest in the final replacement of that part. [IFRIC 12.AG6].

IFRIC 12 pays little attention to the residual interest. Its application guidance states that 'the residual interest in the infrastructure is the estimated current value of the infrastructure as if it were already of the age and in the condition expected at the end of the period of the arrangement'. *[IFRIC 12.AG4]*. This echoes the definition of 'residual value' in IAS 16, but excludes any deduction for the estimated costs of disposal *[IAS 16.6]* (see Chapter 20). However, the Interpretation does not expand on what is regarded as 'significant'. Some infrastructure assets such as toll roads and bridges generate cash flows directly and it may be possible to use estimated future cash flows to calculate the significance of the residual value, whether or not the grantor will charge tolls after reversion of the asset. It may not be possible to base the assessment of 'significance' on the cash flows received by the operator on handing back the asset to the grantor as these may be nominal amounts; indeed, the grantor may pay nothing. In such a case, the remaining useful life of the asset when it reverts may give a good indication, e.g. if a hospital is handed back to the public sector with a remaining useful life of twenty years, this residual interest is likely to be significant.

There are a number of features that indicate whether the grantor controls the residual interest. There are usually several contractual alternatives: the operator is granted a second concession term, a new operator is allowed to acquire the assets or the grantor acquires the assets and brings the arrangement 'in house'. The grantor still controls the residual as it will determine which of these alternatives applies and the option exercise price (if it or a new operator acquires the infrastructure) is irrelevant.

In some arrangements the grantor only has an option to reacquire the asset at the end of the concession term. The operator cannot control the infrastructure until the grantor decides what to do with the option. An option at fair value at the date of exercise may by itself be enough to give the grantor control over the residual under IFRIC 12 if it is sufficient to restrict the operator's ability to sell or pledge the infrastructure. This is a clear difference between a 'risks and rewards' and a 'control' model as under the former, the operator would be seen as keeping the risks and rewards of ownership if another party had the right to acquire the asset at fair value.

Example 28.1:   *Residual arrangements*

A gas transmission system is being operated under a concession arrangement with the State Gas Authority. At the end of the term, the grantor will either acquire the infrastructure assets at their net book value, determined on the basis of the contract, or it may decide to grant a new SCA on the basis of a competitive tender, which will exclude the current operator. If the grantor elects to do the latter, the operator will be entitled to the lower of the following two amounts:

(a)   the net book value of the infrastructure, determined on the basis of the contract; and

(b)   the proceeds of a new competitive bidding process to acquire a new contract.

Although the operator cannot enter the competitive tender, it also has the right to enter into a new concession term but in order to do so, it must match the best tender offer made. It has to pay to the grantor the excess of the best offer (b) above the amount in (a); should the tender offer be lower than (a), it will receive an equivalent refund.

In this arrangement, the grantor will control the residual. It can choose to take over the activities of the concession itself or it can allow potential operators, including the incumbent, to bid for a second term. The price that might be received by the operator, or paid by the grantor, is not relevant.

Chapter 28

What if the arrangement is for the whole life of the infrastructure? Assets in service concession arrangements may revert to the grantor at the end of the concession term but they may not have much, if any, remaining useful life. Many modern buildings, for example, only have a useful life of thirty years or so and this is a common concession term. Consequently, infrastructure used in a service concession arrangement for the whole of its useful life ('whole of life infrastructure') is included within the scope of IFRIC 12. *[IFRIC 12.6].*

The Interpretations Committee noted that one reason for including the 'significant residual interest' requirement was to differentiate between regulated industries and service concession arrangements, thereby seeming to confirm that it had not intended regulated industries to be in scope.[3] We assume that the Interpretations Committee considers that privatised regulated industries should generally be out of scope, because they are divestitures or privatisations where it is more appropriate to treat the infrastructure as the property, plant and equipment of the operator. It is usually the case in a privatisation that the infrastructure only reverts to the grantor in the event of a major breach of the conditions of the regulatory framework as otherwise the right of the operator to provide the regulated services may roll over indefinitely into a new term. In other cases it may require legislative change to bring the assets back into the control of the grantor. This may well mean that the grantor does not control the residual interest in the property as required by IFRIC 12.

GDF Suez discloses that some of its concessions are not considered to be within scope of IFRIC 12 as the infrastructure is not returned to the grantor at the end of the contract. These assets (for water and gas distribution) are likely to have a life in excess of the contract term.

Extract 28.1: GDF Suez SA (2010)

Notes to the Consolidated Financial Statements [extract]

Note 22   Service concession arrangements [extract]

The Group manages a large number of concessions as defined by SIC-29 covering drinking water distribution, water treatment, waste collection and treatment, and gas and electricity distribution.

These concession arrangements set out rights and obligations relative to the infrastructure and to the public service, in particular the obligation to provide users with access to the public service. In certain concessions, a schedule is defined specifying the period over which users should be provided access to the public service. The terms of the concession arrangements vary between 10 and 65 years, depending mainly on the level of capital expenditure to be made by the concession operator.

In consideration of these obligations, GDF SUEZ is entitled to bill either the local authority granting the concession (mainly incineration and BOT water treatment contracts) or the users (contracts for the distribution of drinking water or gas and electricity) for the services provided. This right to bill gives rise to an intangible asset, a tangible asset, or a financial asset, depending on the applicable accounting model (see note 1.4.7).

The tangible asset model is used when the concession grantor does not control the infrastructure. For example, this is the case with water distribution concessions in the United States, which do not provide for the return of the infrastructure to the grantor of the concession at the end of the contract (and the infrastructure therefore remains the property of GDF SUEZ), and also natural gas distribution concessions in France, which fall within the scope of law no. 46-628 of April 8, 1946.

3.3 Assets within scope

There are two groups of assets within scope of IFRIC 12:

(a) the infrastructure that the operator constructs or acquires from a third party for the purpose of the concession; and

(b) existing infrastructure to which the grantor gives the operator access for the purpose of the concession. *[IFRIC 12.7].*

It is usually relatively straightforward to apply (a) above, infrastructure that the operator constructs or acquires from a third party for the purpose of the concession. However, there are some issues of interpretation relating to infrastructure acquired under lease arrangements. Infrastructure under (b) above could include other arrangements in the form of leases over assets. As part of a SCA, an operator may make lease payments to a grantor, e.g. it may lease the land on which a facility is to be built. These issues are discussed at 3.3.1 below.

The Interpretations Committee's view is that accounting for assets is already covered by existing accounting standards, principally IAS 16, and therefore it will not specify how the operator should account for its previously existing assets that now form part of the infrastructure. *[IFRIC 12.8].* The treatment of existing assets is discussed further at 3.3.2 below.

3.3.1 Leases relating to assets used in concessions

Assets within scope of IFRIC 12 include infrastructure that the operator constructs or acquires from a third party for the purpose of the service arrangement and existing infrastructure to which the grantor gives the operator access for the purpose of the service arrangement. *[IFRIC 12.7].* IFRIC 12 contains no explicit guidance regarding assets leased from the grantor or leased on terms in which the leased asset is controlled by the grantor. These arrangements may include leases over assets used to provide the services or leases over assets that will form part of the infrastructure.

Some public transport arrangements, for example, involve the operator leasing rolling stock or buses from a third party in order to provide the services required by the contract. Generally, 'infrastructure' is interpreted broadly and, on this basis, it is accepted that 'the infrastructure' used to provide services can include moveable assets. Although IFRIC 12 uses the word 'infrastructure', the Interpretation is based on the definition of an asset under IFRS ('An asset is a resource controlled by the entity as a result of past events and from which future economic benefits are expected to flow to the entity', *[Framework.4.4]*), and is therefore considered to apply to all assets, including rolling stock, not solely to assets such as tunnels and bridges.

There are arrangements in which the assets (e.g. new rolling stock) are constructed for a service concession arrangement and financed via a lease contract with a third party. The operator makes payments to the lessor over the arrangement term. Ownership of the assets (i.e. the beneficial residual interest) passes from the lessor to the grantor at the end of the arrangement. The concession term is such that the lease assessed on a stand-alone basis would be an operating lease.

Arguably, payments to the lessor should be treated as the cost of acquiring part of the infrastructure asset, measured at the present value of the 'lease' payments, with the recognition of a corresponding financial liability. The operator does not have any 'right of use' or control of the assets and has a right of access no different to that over assets that it has constructed or acquired for the contract. The substance of the arrangement is similar to that in which the operator pays the grantor and the grantor, in turn, pays the lessor.

It is not relevant that the arrangement might have been classified as an operating lease. Infrastructure accounted for under IFRIC 12 is distinct from the physical underlying assets and the measurement rules are those that apply in the interpretation.

The situation would be different if the lessor retained control of the leased assets at the end of the concession term, in which case the grantor would not control the residual and IAS 17 would apply.

It is common as part of service concession arrangements for the operator to lease from the grantor the land on which infrastructure is constructed and make separate payments to the grantor for the lease. In these cases the land is not 'the infrastructure' but this raises similar issues with respect to accounting for the costs. On the assumption that the lease costs of land are a cost of gaining access to the infrastructure, they are one of the costs to be taken into account in calculating the fair value of services provided to the grantor under the service concession agreement. On this basis, the present value of the rentals should be calculated at inception of the agreement and a liability recognised for the obligation to make payments.

There is more dispute as to whether the corresponding debit in either case, should be considered as part of the costs of providing the services under the concession or whether they ought to be accounted for as a separate intangible asset, regardless of whether the financial or intangible asset model applies (see 4 below regarding choice of accounting model), Given the absence of guidance in the Interpretation it is likely that there will be divergence in practice.

3.3.2   *Previously held assets used for the concession*

IFRIC 12 states that the service concession arrangement may convey a right of use of existing assets of the operator to the grantor, in which case the operator would apply the derecognition requirements of IAS 16 to determine whether it should derecognise them. *[IFRIC 12.8]*. The Interpretations Committee's view is that accounting for assets is already covered by existing accounting standards, principally IAS 16, and therefore it will not specify how the operator should account for its previously existing assets that now form part of the infrastructure.

The implication is that losing control of the infrastructure asset by contractually giving control of its use to the grantor may in some circumstances be a deemed disposal of the asset under IAS 16. The existing asset would be derecognised and any consideration received on the disposal recognised at its fair value. *[IAS 16.72]*. This means that the total consideration received under the contract would be disaggregated to calculate the relevant amount receivable for the transfer of the asset to the control of the grantor. See 4.1.1 below for a discussion of the allocation of the consideration, which depends on the accounting model appropriate to the particular SCA. Gains and losses must be calculated as the difference between any net disposal proceeds and the carrying value of the item of PP&E *[IAS 16.71]* and recognised in profit or loss. Derecognition of assets within scope of IAS 16 in general is discussed in Chapter 20 at 7.

The operator may use some of its existing assets for the purpose of the concession without transferring control to the grantor. These are out of scope.

Therefore, an entity may already control infrastructure that it has constructed and used for its operations before it enters into a concession arrangement. Unless the contract transfers the residual interest in these pre-existing assets to the grantor, these assets are out of scope of IFRIC 12. The SCA might include, for example, extensions to that asset, upgrades to it and a contractual period of using the infrastructure asset to provide services. In this case, the total consideration payable under the concession will be allocated between the extension, upgrade and operating services within scope of IFRIC 12.

3.4   Partially regulated assets

IFRIC 12 notes that it is not uncommon for the use of infrastructure to be partly regulated and partly unregulated and gives examples while noting that these activities take a variety of forms:

'(a)   any infrastructure that is physically separable and capable of being operated independently and meets the definition of a cash generating unit as defined in IAS 36 shall be analysed separately if it is used wholly for unregulated purposes. For example this might apply to a private wing of a hospital, where the remainder of the hospital is used by the grantor to treat public patients.

(b)   where purely ancillary activities (such as a hospital shop) are unregulated, the control tests shall be applied as if those services did not exist, because in cases in which the grantor controls the services described in paragraph 5, the existence of ancillary activities does not detract from the grantor's control of the relevant infrastructure.' *[IFRIC 12.AG7].*

In both of these cases, the operator may have a lease from the grantor that gives it a right to use the asset in question; if so, this is to be accounted for in accordance with IAS 17. *[IFRIC 12.AG8].* This would be likely to involve using IFRIC 4's principles to distinguish the lease payments from other parts of the service concession arrangement (see Chapter 26 at 2.1).

The Interpretation gives no further guidance on how an entity might interpret the term 'purely ancillary' in evaluating whether an unregulated activity is ignored for the purposes of determining if the control criteria are met or considered to detract from the grantor's control of the asset. The example of a hospital shop is clearly insignificant by virtue of its size relative to the whole hospital, the proportion of cash flows attributable to it and the fact that the existence of a shop has no direct impact on the function of the infrastructure in the provision of regulated services. However, it is not clear at what point a secondary activity would become or cease to be 'purely ancillary'.

In addition, there may be unregulated services that are neither purely ancillary nor delivered by using a physically separable portion of the total infrastructure, a situation not addressed by AG 7. For example, a grantor may control prices charged to children, pensioners and the unemployed who use a sports facility but the

Chapter 28

amounts charged to other adults are not controlled. The same swimming pool is being used by all, regardless of the amount that they pay. Alternatively, price regulation could apply only to services provided at certain times of the day rather than to different classes of user. In such cases it will be a matter of judgement whether enough of the service is unregulated in order to demonstrate that the grantor is not considered to control the asset.

4   ACCOUNTING FOR THE INFRASTRUCTURE ASSET: THE FINANCIAL ASSET AND INTANGIBLE ASSET MODELS

The two models in the analysis utilise several decisions of principle:

- the control model applies as described at 3 above, which means that the operator will not recognise infrastructure assets as its property, plant and equipment; *[IFRIC 12.11]* and

- the operator is providing 'construction services' and not, for example, constructing an item of property, plant and equipment for sale. Construction services are to be accounted for separately from 'operation services' in the operations phase of the contract. *[IFRIC 12.BC31]*.

There is a third important point of principle: the 'amounts due from customers' asset that arises from the application of the stage of completion method of revenue recognition required by IAS 11 (whose principles are used during the period of construction of the asset) is a financial asset as defined in IAS 32 (see 4.2 below).

4.1   Consideration for services provided and the choice between the two models

Operators almost always negotiate a single contract with the grantor and, although the Interpretation does not refer to this, this will usually include a single payment mechanism throughout the concession term (sometimes called a 'unitary payment'). The operator is unlikely to be remunerated separately for its different activities. The payment mechanism often falls into one or other of the following models:

Example 28.2:   Payment mechanisms for service concessions

(a)   a hospital where the payment is based on the availability of the whole hospital

The unitary payment is based on the full provision of an overall accommodation requirement which is divided into different units, such as hospital wards, consulting rooms, operating theatres, common parts and reception. Availability is defined in terms of being usable and accessible and, includes some associated core services such as heating, power and (in the case of operating theatres) appropriate cleanliness. There is a payment deduction for failure to provide an available unit according to a contractual scale. There are no separate payment streams for any of the non-core services but substandard performance can result in payment deductions.

$P = (F \times I) - (D + E)$
P = unitary payment per day
F = price per day for overall accommodation requirement
I = Indexation increase based on the retail prices index
D = deductions for unavailability
E = performance deductions

The payments for both schemes are not immediately separable between amounts attributable to the construction or other services.

b)   a prison where payment is made based on the number of occupied places

The unitary payment is based on the number of occupied places. Occupied means not only that a prisoner is allocated a physical space but the associated core services and minimum requirements must be met in relation to services such as heating, mail delivery and food. No payment is made for unoccupied places. There are no separate payment streams for any of the non-core services (i.e. not associated with the definition of an occupied place) but deductions from the unitary payment can be made for substandard performance of these services.

The unitary payment is based on the following formula:

$P = (F \times I) - Z$
P = unitary payment per place
F = Fixed amount per occupied place per day
I = Indexation increase based on the retail prices index
Z = Performance deductions

Payments usually start only when the infrastructure asset has been completed and accepted as suitable for purpose by the grantor. Operators usually seek payment during the construction phase but whether or not they receive any is inevitably a result of negotiation between the parties.

IFRIC 12 clarifies the basis on which revenue is recognised in accordance with IAS 11 and IAS 18. It argues that if the operator provides separate services as part of its overall contractual arrangement it will allocate the consideration receivable by reference to their relative fair values. *[IFRIC 12.13].* The exercise to separate the consideration receivable for the separate services (e.g. construction, upgrading or operating services) provided by the operator is expanded at 4.1.1 below. The nature of the consideration determines the accounting model, as described at 4.1.2 below.

4.1.1   Allocating the consideration

The Interpretation Committee argues that it is a requirement of IAS 18, to separate the construction services that will be accounted for under IAS 11 from the remainder of the contract. Thereafter the separate services within this contract (for example 'upgrade services' or 'operations services') may also be disaggregated on the basis of their 'distinct skills, requirements and risks'. *[IFRIC 12.BC31].* IFRIC 12 argues that the operator might report different profit margins for its construction services within IAS 11 and the other services that are within IAS 18. The inference is that these different margins may also help allocate the total consideration. *[IFRIC 12.BC31].* One must be very cautious here as IAS 11 does not permit an entity to determine what it considers to be an appropriate profit margin for the contract and use this as the basis of recognising revenue and attributable contract costs (unless, of course, it is a cost plus contract, see Chapter 25 at 3.3.1). The profit margin must be a consequence of the different fair values of the separate elements of the contract rather than driving the allocation of the consideration.

Chapter 28

Although there is a single contract and a single payment mechanism, it is often straightforward in practice to identify the underlying revenue streams that relate to different activities. This may be on the basis of the original contract negotiations or because the contract contains terms allowing for subsequent price adjustments by 'market testing' or benchmarking. However, the revenue streams may not reflect the fair value of the underlying services so care will have to be taken. There will always be practical problems when it comes to apportioning the total contract consideration between the elements of the contract and the allocation will always be a matter of judgement.

4.1.2   *Determining the accounting model*

IFRIC 12 states that the operator may receive a financial asset or an intangible asset as consideration for its construction services and the asset that it receives determines the subsequent treatment. *[IFRIC 12.15].*

The operator will recognise a financial asset to the extent that it has a contractual right to receive cash or other financial assets from the grantor for the construction services, where the grantor has little, if any, discretion to avoid payment. This is usually because the agreement is legally enforceable. *[IFRIC 12.16].* The operator will recognise an intangible asset to the extent that it receives a licence to charge users of the public service. *[IFRIC 12.17].*

As described at 4.2 and 4.3 below, IAS 11 will apply to the operator's activities ('construction or upgrade services') during the construction period. *[IFRIC 12.14].*

The Interpretations Committee decided that the boundary between the financial and the intangible asset models should be based on the operator's contractual right to receive cash from, or at the direction of, the grantor. The grantor does not need to pay the cash to the operator directly. Fees or tolls received directly from users are viewed as essentially no more than collections on behalf of the grantor if they are part of an overall arrangement under which the grantor bears ultimate responsibility. If the grantor pays but the amounts are wholly based on usage of the infrastructure and there is no minimum guaranteed payment, the entity has no contractual right to receive cash. Therefore the intangible asset model will apply.

Sometimes it is necessary to 'bifurcate' the operator's right to cash flows for construction services into a financial asset and an intangible asset and account separately for each component of the operator's consideration. This, the Interpretations Committee argues, is because the operator is paid for its services partly by a financial asset and partly by an intangible asset. *[IFRIC 12.18].*

The analysis between the different models can be seen in the following table:

	Arrangement	*Applicable model*
1	Grantor pays – fixed payments	Financial asset
2	Grantor pays – payments vary with demand	Intangible asset
3	Grantor retains demand risk – users pay but grantor guarantees amounts	Financial asset or bifurcated (part financial, part intangible)
4	Grantor retains demand risk – operator collects revenues from users until it achieves specified return	Intangible asset
5	Users pay – no grantor guarantees	Intangible asset

Of the two arrangements in Example 28.2 above, the hospital is an example of (1) above: the payments are contractually fixed if all obligations and services are provided. The prison, as described in Example 28.2 above, would fall within (2) and be accounted for as an intangible asset. However, the prison operator might be paid on a different basis, e.g. it might be paid for 1000 'available places' and receive this as long as heating and food were capable of being provided. In this case it would be no different to the hospital and be a financial asset. There are, of course, many potential variations and a combination of fixed and variable demand could lead to bifurcation.

Common examples of arrangements that fall within (3) above are transport concessions where the operator collects revenue from users but is entitled to an agreed return on capital invested in the infrastructure. The fees or tolls are considered to be collections on behalf of the grantor. There will be a financial asset to the extent of the guaranteed return. There may be an intangible asset as well if the operator retains a right to collect tolls in excess of the guaranteed amount.

However, arrangements of the type in (4) above remain to be treated as intangible assets even if the overall risk to the operator of not obtaining a specified result is very low. An arrangement that effectively caps revenue collected from users once an agreed level of return is reached, it is argued, is not a contractual right to cash but a right to collect revenues from users and it is not relevant that the risk is low or that the operator will, in effect, get a fixed return.

The following are examples of arrangements that will be accounted for using the intangible asset model:

(a)   A municipality grants the operator a contract to treat all of its waste collections for which it will be paid per unit processed. The arrangement does not provide for any guaranteed volume of waste to be treated by the operator (so it does not contain a take-or-pay arrangement) or any form of guarantee by the grantor. Historically, however, the annual volume of waste has never been less than 40,000 tons and the average annual volume over the last 20 years has been 75,000 tons.

(b)   An operator enters into a toll bridge concession. The operator is permitted to collect revenues from users or the grantor until it achieves a 6% return on its agreed infrastructure spend, at which point the arrangement comes to an end.

The crucial difference is the grantor's guarantee. The toll bridge concession may be virtually commercially identical to a transaction that falls within (3), e.g. where the users pay tolls but the grantor guarantees a minimum 6% return. Somewhat ironically, this arrangement, which will contain a financial asset, is likely to leave more of the rewards of ownership with the operator than the intangible arrangement in (b) as the operator will be entitled to benefits in excess of the 6% return.

There are jurisdictions where public-to-private contract laws or the concession arrangements themselves allow an operator to ask the grantor for a revision of the tariffs for the public service when the operator's actual return is below initial expectations. Although this feature in the concession arrangement is included to reduce the operator's risk, it only gives the operator a right to re-negotiate and the outcome of that is not certain. As a result, the operator does not have an unconditional right to receive cash and, therefore, the operator may not apply the financial asset model.

Chapter 28

Many payment mechanisms include deductions for substandard performance of services. These do not affect the analysis of the contract as a financial asset or intangible asset and are discussed further below.

4.2   The financial asset model

Under the financial asset model, which applies if the entity has a contractual right to receive cash or another financial asset, *[IFRIC 12.16]*, the service element that relates to the construction of the infrastructure asset ('construction services') is accounted for in accordance with IAS 11. The consideration received by the operator for other services is addressed at 5 below.

As noted above, the Interpretations Committee has argued that the 'amounts due from customers', i.e. those amounts recognised as revenue under IAS 11 from the point of initial recognition of the service concession, net of cash received, are deemed to be financial assets under IAS 32 because they represent contractual rights to receive cash or another financial asset from another entity. *[IAS 32.11]*. This analysis is not affected by the fact that this contractual right may be contingent on performance standards, as in the example of a unitary charge for a hospital in Example 28.2 above. The Interpretations Committee points out that this is no different from other circumstances and other financial assets where the payment depends on the subsequent performance of the asset. *[IFRIC 12.BC44]*.

The financial asset will fall into one of the following three categories under IAS 32:

- a loan or receivable;
- an available-for-sale financial asset; or
- at fair value through profit or loss, if so designated on initial recognition. *[IFRIC 12.24]*.

In the first two cases, interest income will be recognised, calculated using the effective interest method. *[IFRIC 12.25]*.

The financial asset will not be classified as held-to-maturity. *[IFRIC 12.BC61]*.

It is argued that under IAS 39, amounts may only be classified as loans and receivables if the holder will receive 'substantially all of its initial investment, other than through credit deterioration'. *[IAS 39.9]*. In this regard, the potential for variation that exists in any service concession arrangement does not comprise an embedded derivative because it is specific to the parties in the contract. *[IFRIC 12.BC62]*. When the amount to be received by the operator could vary with the quality of services it provided or according to performance or efficiency targets, the arrangement does not contain an embedded derivative. These are non-financial measures and the remainder of the arrangement may still meet the definition of a loan and receivable. Non-compliance with this contractual requirement is a breach of contract and the resulting adjustment of future payments would be considered a penalty which causes forfeiture of some or the entire financial asset but it does not need to be considered part of the original financial asset.

This approach is consistent with general practice for accounting for receivables arising from the sale of goods and services with performance conditions under IASs 11 and 18. The Basis for Conclusions notes that the operator's position is the same as that of any other entity in which payment for goods or services is contingent on subsequent performance of the goods or service sold. *[IFRIC 12.BC44]*. Following this argument, the financial asset is recognised as consideration for delivering construction services and is no different from any other such receivable.

In practice many entities classify IFRIC 12 financial assets as loans and receivables.

Extract 28.2: Vinci (2010)

Consolidated financial statements
3   **Measurement rules and methods** [extract]
3.5   **Concession contracts** [extract]

In return for its activities, the operator receives consideration from ...

• **the grantor: the financial asset model** applies. The operator has an unconditional contractual right to receive payments from the grantor, irrespective of the amount of use made of the infrastructure. Under this model, the operator recognises a financial asset, attracting interest, in its balance sheet, in consideration for the services it provides (designing, building, operation or maintenance). Such financial assets are recognised in the balance sheet under Loans and receivables, for the amount of the fair value of the infrastructure on first recognition and subsequently at amortised cost. The receivable is settled by means of the grantor's payments received. The financial income calculated on the basis of the effective interest rate, equivalent to the project's internal rate of return, is recognised under operating income.

3.20   **Other non-current financial assets**[extract]
3.20.2   **Loans and receivables at amortised cost** [extract]

Loans and receivables at amortised cost mainly comprise receivables connected with shareholdings, current account advances to equity-accounted companies or unconsolidated entities, guarantee deposits, collateralised loans and receivables and other loans and financial receivables. It also includes the financial receivables relating to concession contracts and Public-Private Partnerships whenever the concession operator has an unconditional right to receive remuneration (generally in the form of "scheduled construction payments") from the grantor. When first recognised, these loans and receivables are recognised at their fair value plus the directly attributable transaction costs. At each balance sheet date, these assets are measured at their amortised cost using the effective interest method. In the particular case of receivables coming under the scope of IFRIC 12, the effective interest rate used corresponds to the project's internal rate of return.

If the contract is not classified as a loan and receivable it will most likely be classified as available-for-sale and be accounted for at fair value with changes in value taken to equity. These definitions are further described in Chapter 46.

Whichever of these classifications apply, the financial asset will be measured on initial recognition at its fair value, and interest will be calculated on the balance using the effective interest rate method. *[IAS 39.43]*. Revenue will be recognised in accordance with IAS 11 when the contract work is performed using the percentage of completion method. *[IAS 11.26]*. This means that the financial asset will be recognised from the beginning of contract activity.

How to measure this could represent a conundrum: it is necessary to recognise interest (using the effective interest rate method) on the financial asset simultaneously with recognising revenue using the percentage of completion method. Part of what would otherwise have been recognised as construction revenue is now finance income. The Illustrative Example 1 in IFRIC 12, on which Example 28.3 below is based, demonstrates how to avoid this problem by deeming the fair value of the consideration for construction services to be based on construction costs plus a margin. Potential issues with the use of a profit margin have previously been discussed at 4.11 above.

Borrowing costs cannot be capitalised under the financial asset model. *[IFRIC 12.22]*.

Example 28.3:   The Financial Asset Model – recording the construction asset

Table 1 Concession terms

The terms of the arrangement require an operator to construct a road – completing construction within two years – and maintain and operate the road to a specified standard for eight years (i.e. years 3-10). The terms of the concession also require the operator to resurface the road at the end of year 8. At the end of year 10, the arrangement will end. The operator estimates that the costs it will incur to fulfil its obligations will be:

	Year	€
Construction Services	1	500
	2	500
Operation Services (per year)	3-10	10
Road resurfacing	8	100

The terms of the concession require the grantor to pay the operator €200 per year in years 3-10 for making the road available to the public.

For the purpose of this illustration, it is assumed that all cash flows take place at the end of the year.

Table 2 Contract revenue

The operator recognises contract revenue and costs in accordance with IAS 11 – *Construction Contracts*. The costs of each activity – construction, operation, maintenance and resurfacing – are recognised as expenses by reference to the stage of completion of that activity. Contract revenue – the fair value of the amount due from the grantor for the activity undertaken – is recognised at the same time.

The total consideration (€200 in each of years 3-8) reflects the fair values for each of the services, which are:

	Fair value		
Construction	Forecast cost	+	5%
Operation and maintenance	" "	+	20%
Road resurfacing	" "	+	10%
Lending rate to grantor	6.18% per year		

In year 1, for example, construction costs of €500, construction revenue of €525 (cost plus 5 per cent), and hence construction profit of €25 are recognised in the income statement.

Financial asset

The amount due from the grantor meets the definition of a receivable in IAS 39. The receivable is measured initially at fair value. It is subsequently measured at amortised cost, i.e. the amount initially recognised plus the cumulative interest on that amount calculated using the effective interest method minus repayments.

Table 3 Measurement of receivable

	€
Amount due for construction in year 1	525
Receivable at end of year 1*	525
Effective interest in year 2 on receivable at the end of year 1 (6.18% × €525)	32
Amount due for construction in year 2	525
Receivable at end of year 2	1,082
Effective interest in year 3 on receivable at the end of year 2 (6.18% × €1,082)	67
Amount due for operation in year 3 (€10 × (1 + 20%))	12
Cash receipts in year 3	(200)
Receivable at end of year 3	961

* No effective interest arises in year 1 because the cash flows are assumed to take place at the end of the year.

4.3 The intangible asset model

If the financial asset model does not apply (i.e. there is no contractual right to cash or other financial assets), the operator's consideration for its construction services will be an intangible asset. *[IFRIC 12.15]*. As with the financial asset model, the operator cannot have an item of property, plant and equipment because the physical infrastructure is an asset of the grantor (see 3 above). Therefore, the Interpretations Committee has concluded that the right of an operator to charge users of the public service, for example the right to collect tolls from a road or a bridge, meets the definition of an intangible asset, that should be accounted for in accordance with IAS 38. It is, in effect, a licence 'bought' in exchange for construction services. *[IFRIC 12.17]*.

The Interpretations Committee has concluded that an intangible asset will be recorded during the construction phase as activity progresses, representing the operator's right to receive the licence. On this assumption, the entity will account for the construction of the infrastructure asset as follows:

(i)   revenue will be measured at the fair value of the intangible asset received. *[IFRIC 12.15]*

(ii) it will record this contract revenue in accordance with IAS 11 as it provides 'construction services' by constructing the asset. *[IFRIC 12.14]*.

The intangible asset under the concession (the licence received in return for construction services) meets the definition of a qualifying asset because it will not be ready for use until the infrastructure is constructed. Therefore borrowing costs must be capitalised during the period of construction. *[IFRIC 12.22]*. This contrasts with the treatment of borrowing costs under the financial asset model, where capitalisation is forbidden but financial income (the accretion of interest on the financial asset) is recognised.

Chapter 28

Furthermore, it is argued that an inevitable consequence of applying the intangible model is that there must be an exchange transaction in which the operator receives the intangible right in exchange for its construction services. As this is an exchange of dissimilar assets, revenue must be recognised in accordance with IAS 18, which requires the recognition of revenue and a profit (or loss) based on the fair value of the assets received (unless the fair value of the assets given up can be measured more reliably). *[IFRIC 12.BC32-BC35]*. This means that the operator must establish the fair value of either the intangible asset it receives or the fair value of the services it has provided. The following example, based on Illustrative Example 2 in IFRIC 12, indicates how the Interpretations Committee expects this to apply in practice. It assumes that the fair value can be based on the cost of the construction services plus a margin – a similar methodology to that applied for the financial asset model above.

Example 28.4:   The Intangible Asset Model – recording the construction asset

Arrangement terms

The terms of a service arrangement require an operator to construct a road – completing construction within two years – and maintain and operate the road to a specified standard for eight years (i.e. years 3-10). The terms of the arrangement also require the operator to resurface the road when the original surface has deteriorated below a specified condition. The operator estimates that it will have to undertake the resurfacing at the end of the year 8. At the end of year 10, the service arrangement will end. The operator estimates that the costs it will incur to fulfil its obligations will be:

Table 1 Contract costs

	Year	€
Construction Services	1	500
	2	500
Operation services (per year)	3-10	10
Road resurfacing	8	100

The terms of the arrangement allow the operator to collect tolls from drivers using the road. The operator forecasts that vehicle numbers will remain constant over the duration of the contract and that it will receive tolls of €200 in each of years 3-10.

For the purpose of this illustration, it is assumed that all cash flows take place at the end of the year.

Intangible asset

The operator provides construction services to the grantor in exchange for an intangible asset, i.e. a right to collect tolls from road users in years 3-10. In accordance with IAS 38, the operator recognises the intangible asset at cost, i.e. the fair value of consideration received or receivable.

During the construction phase of the arrangement the operator's asset (representing its accumulating right to be paid for providing construction services) is classified as an intangible asset (licence to charge users of the infrastructure). The operator estimates the fair value of its consideration received to be equal to the forecast construction costs plus 5 per cent margin. It is also assumed that the operator adopts the allowed alternative treatment in IAS 23 – *Borrowing Costs* – and therefore capitalises the borrowing costs, estimated at 6.7 per cent, during the construction phase:

Table 2 Initial measurement of Intangible asset

	€
Construction services in year 1 (€500 × (1 + 5%))	525
Capitalisation of borrowing costs	34
Construction services in year 2 (€500 × (1 + 5%))	525
Intangible asset at end of year 2	1,084

The intangible asset is amortised over the period in which it is expected to be available for use by the operator, i.e. years 3-10. In this case, the directors determine that it is appropriate to amortise using a straight-line method. The annual amortisation charge is therefore €1,084 divided by 8 years, i.e. €135 per year.

Construction costs and revenue

The operator recognises the revenue and costs in accordance with IAS 11 i.e. by reference to the stage of completion of the construction. It measures contract revenue at the fair value of the consideration received or receivable. Thus in each of years 1 and 2 it recognises in its income statement construction costs of €500, construction revenue of €525 (cost plus 5 per cent) and, hence, construction profit of €25.

Toll revenue

The road users pay for the public services at the same time as they receive them, i.e. when they use the road. The operator therefore recognises toll revenue when it collects the tolls.

4.3.1 Amortisation

The intangible asset will subsequently be accounted for in accordance with IAS 38 *[IFRIC 12.26]*, which means that the amount at which it is measured initially, i.e. after the exchange transaction, is its cost. *[IAS 38.45]*. It will be amortised on a systematic basis over its useful life, using a method that reflects 'the pattern in which the asset's future economic benefits are expected to be consumed by the entity'. *[IAS 38.97]*. This means that the methods permitted by IAS 38 are available (straight line, diminishing balance or unit-of-production). *[IAS 38.98]*. The requirements of IAS 38 are discussed in detail in Chapter 19. Interest methods of amortisation are forbidden. *[IFRIC 12.BC65]*.

The Interpretations Committee expressly considered unit-of-production methods to be appropriate in some circumstances; in March 2006, it was noted in *IFRIC Update* that the Basis of Conclusions had been redrafted to avoid the impression that these methods were not allowed.[4] There were still concerns as a unit-of-production method could result in lower amortisation in the early years of the asset's operation so IAS 38 itself was amended to remove a statement discouraging methods that might have such a result.[5] This clarifies that there is no prohibition when the method is the most appropriate, whatever the resulting profile of amortisation.

Unit-of-production methods are typically considered in the context of toll roads and bridges. Obviously the method might apply if there is a right to charge a specified number of users. Questions still remained as to whether it might also be used if the basis was the estimated number of users, e.g. the number of vehicles that might use a particular road during the concession term. Could the amortisation be based on revenue?

Whether or not a method is appropriate depends on the meaning of 'consumption of economic benefits' in the context of intangible assets with finite lives. In November 2009 and January 2010 the Interpretations Committee considered whether they should bring this onto their Agenda but decided against this because of the diversity of views.[6]

The debate, however inconclusive, clarified the distinction between the *consumption* of the asset's economic benefits and the *generation* of economic benefits through the asset's use in generating revenues and profits. In principle, methods based on usage appear to be consistent with the requirements of IAS 38. However, revenue-based methods can also be used if it can be demonstrated that they are a reasonable approximation to a usage method based on consumption of the asset.

The IFRIC reiterated that the choice of amortisation method is a matter of judgement. One of the most fundamental issues, therefore, is whether reasonable estimates can be made, especially in circumstances in which the entity has little or no past experience on which to base its decision about the most appropriate method of amortisation. In the following extract from its accounting policies, GDF Suez indicates that it amortises its intangible assets on a straight line basis over the concession term if the pattern of consumption cannot be determined reliably.

Extract 28.3: GDF Suez SA (2010)

Notes to the Consolidated Financial Statements [extract]

1.4.4.2   Other intangible assets [extract]

Other internally-generated or acquired intangible assets

Other intangible assets include mainly:

- amounts paid or payable as consideration for rights relating to concession contracts or public service contracts;
- customer portfolios acquired on business combinations;
- power station capacity rights: the Group helped finance the construction of certain nuclear power stations operated by third parties and in consideration received the right to purchase a share of the production over the useful life of the assets. These rights are amortized over the useful life of the underlying assets, not to exceed 40 years;
- surface and underground water drawing rights, which are not amortized as they are granted indefinitely;
- concession assets;
- the GDF Gaz de France brand and gas supply contracts acquired as part of the business combination with Gaz de France in 2008.

Intangible assets are amortized on the basis of the expected pattern of consumption of the estimated future economic benefits embodied in the asset. Amortization is calculated mainly on a straight-line basis over the following useful lives (in years):

	Useful life	
	Minimum	Maximum
Concession rights	10	65
Customer portfolios	10	40
Other intangible assets	1	40

Some intangible assets with an indefinite useful life such as trademarks and water drawing rights are not amortized.

4.3.2 Impairment during the construction phase

The operator will recognise an intangible right during the construction phase of the arrangement, which is before the asset has been brought into use. There may be other circumstances in which the operator will continue to recognise an intangible asset prior to the service being provided to users. IAS 36 – *Impairment of Assets* – requires any intangible asset that has not yet been brought into use to be tested for impairment annually, irrespective of whether there are any indications of impairment. *[IAS 36.10]*. See Chapter 22 at 2.2.

4.4 Revenue recognition implications of the two models

There are major differences in the way in which revenue is measured under the two models. Under the financial asset model, total revenue over the concession term will be the same as the total cash inflows under the contract. By contrast, the fair value of the intangible asset is recognised as revenue under the intangible asset model, so total revenue measured using this model will be higher by this amount. The consequences of the two models can be demonstrated by the following simple example:

Example 28.5:   Revenue under the financial asset and intangible models

An operator builds a road at a cost of 100. The construction profit is 10 and total cash inflows over the life of the concession are 200.

Under the financial asset model, the operator will recognise construction revenue of 110 and a receivable of 110. Of the future cash inflows of 200, 110 will be treated as repaying the receivable, with the remaining 90 being recognised as revenue over the life of the concession. Total revenue will be 200.

Under the intangible asset model, the operator will recognise construction revenue of 110, an intangible of 110, and a construction profit of 10. Over the life of the concession, the intangible asset of 110 would be amortised against revenues (which in this case would be from users) of 200. The net position is the same as in the financial asset case, but total revenues will be 310 rather than 200.

It is fair to say that this has proved highly controversial. In fact, the September 2004 *IFRIC Update* stated that 'the majority of the Interpretations Committee strongly disliked this outcome.'[7] However, the Interpretations Committee maintains that this is the appropriate application of accounting standards to the arrangements and is consistent with the treatment generally accorded to barter transactions, *[IFRIC 12.BC35]*, although, of course, there are no other sectors where barter transactions are fundamental to the arrangement. The possible implications for many other transactions with governmental grantors where licences are granted have not been considered.

4.5 'Bifurcation' – single arrangements that contain both financial and intangible assets

As part of its redeliberations, the Interpretations Committee agreed that it may be necessary in certain circumstances to divide the operator's right to cash flows into a financial asset and an intangible asset. *[IFRIC 12.18]*. The *IFRIC Update* (March 2006) reported that 'With this change, the proposed amendment would better reflect the economic reality of concession arrangements: to the extent that the operator is remunerated for its construction services by obtaining a contractual right to receive cash from, or at the direction of, the grantor, the operator would recognise a financial asset and, to the extent that the operator receives only a licence to charge users, it would recognise an intangible asset.'

The Basis for Conclusions to IFRIC 12 explains more of the reasoning and potential impact. In some arrangements both parties to the contract share the risk (demand risk) that the cash flows generated by the project will not be sufficient to recover the operator's capital investment. A common mechanism for achieving this is where the grantor pays partly by a financial asset (i.e. the grantor will pay cash for the services provided) but gives the operator the right to charge for services (i.e. the operator has an intangible asset). The operator's infrastructure asset is to be split into a financial asset component for any guaranteed amount of cash and an intangible asset for the remainder. *[IFRIC 12.BC53].*

These are common in transport concessions, e.g. a rail system paid for partly by grantor subsidy and partly by the payment of fares. There are clearly going to be difficult matters of interpretation. It may not be clear how much of the arrangement is a financial asset and, therefore, where to draw the boundary between the two assets. There may be minor amounts within a contract that fall within another model and entities may conclude that these are *de minimis.*

4.6   Accounting for residual interests

Unless the infrastructure is used in a service concession arrangement for the whole of its useful life (within scope of IFRIC 12 – see 3.2 above), there will be a residual interest at the end of the contract that will be controlled by the grantor. The way in which the grantor controls the residual interest will affect the way in which the operator accounts for it. If the operator has a contractual right to cash (or another financial asset) for the residual interest in the infrastructure, this right will be a financial asset. It will be recognised as part of the consideration for the construction services. *[IFRIC 12.16].* This is unaffected by the basis on which the consideration is calculated.

There are many different arrangements over residual interests in the infrastructure at the end of the concession term but broadly they depend on whether the grantor has a right or an option to acquire the residual interest and on the rights or options of the operator:

(a)   The grantor may control the residual via a right to purchase the infrastructure from the operator but this could be at fair value, net book value, a notional amount or zero.

(b)   It may only have an option to acquire the assets, on similar bases to (a), but it also has a right to put in place other arrangements, e.g. granting the operator a new term or selecting a new party to take on the assets. Payment might be made by the grantor or by the new operator but always at the direction of the grantor.

(c)   The grantor has an option to acquire the assets but if this is not exercised then the operator may retain them.

The implications of grantor options and control of the residual interest have been discussed at 3.2 above.

If the terminal arrangements fall within (a) or (b), the operator will have a contractual right to cash. It will recognise a financial asset, initially at fair value, which will then be accounted for according to the relevant classification under IAS 39 or IFRS 9, as appropriate (see 4.2 above). If the financial asset is classified as a loan and receivable or as available for sale then interest will be calculated using the effective interest rate method. At the end of the contract the residual interest will be stated at the operator's best estimate of the amount receivable.

If the arrangement is of the type described in (c), then the operator's residual interest is not a financial asset. Nor does it have a residual interest in the underlying property, plant and equipment because this is an arrangement within scope of IFRIC 12 and the entity cannot recognise the underlying assets, in whole or in part. *[IFRIC 12.11].* The only option is to recognise an intangible right to receive cash or the residual interest in the assets. By contrast to the residual financial asset, it is most unlikely that the operator would be able to restate the value of this right over the term to its best estimate of the amount receivable at the end of the contract. IAS 38 only allows intangible assets to be revalued in very restricted circumstances; see Chapter 19 at 10.2.

The operator will have to account for its residual interests as described above based on the contractual rights, whatever model is being applied to its construction services. This is similar to the explicit requirements for upgrade services described at 5.1 below: IFRIC 12 recognises that upgrade services have to be recognised on the basis of their individual contract terms regardless of the model applied. *[IFRIC 12.14].* The result is that an entity that has recognised an intangible asset for the major part of its construction services might have to recognise a financial asset for the residual interests – or *vice versa* if its construction services have been accounted for as a financial asset. This treatment is a variation of the bifurcation described at 4.5 above except that the financial asset relates only to the residual interest in the infrastructure rather than to a portion of the consideration receivable for the infrastructure as a whole. The residual rights will be taken into account in calculating the revenue receivable under the contract, as described at 4.2 and 4.3 above.

As the termination arrangements can be complex, care will have to be taken to ensure that the effects are fully analysed.

Example 28.6: Contractual rights to cash in termination arrangements

The facts of the SCA are as in Example 28.1 above. At the end of the term, the grantor will either pay for the infrastructure assets at their net book value, determined on the basis of the contract, or it may decide to grant a new SCA on the basis of a competitive tender, which will exclude the current operator. If the grantor elects to do the latter, the operator will be entitled to the lower of the following two amounts:

(a)   the net book value of the infrastructure, determined on the basis of the contract; and

(b)   the proceeds of a new competitive bidding process to acquire a new contract.

Although the operator cannot enter the competitive tender, it also has the right to enter into a new concession term but in order to do so, it must match the best tender offer made. It has to pay to the grantor the excess of the best offer (b) above the amount in (a); should the tender offer be lower than (a), it will receive an equivalent refund.

In this arrangement, the operator has a contractual right to cash that should be recognised as a financial asset. It has a right to receive the lower of (a) and (b). It may *choose* to use its right to cash to settle part or all of the price of a new concession agreement but this does not affect the fact that it has a right to cash. This example also illustrates that calculating the fair value of the contractual right to cash may be complex as it has to take account of a number of different estimates, including the net book value of the infrastructure at the end of the contract, as well as the options available to the parties to the contract.

5   REVENUE AND EXPENDITURE DURING THE OPERATIONS PHASE OF THE CONCESSION AGREEMENT

So far, we have described the recognition and measurement of the infrastructure asset in the accounts of the operator under the two models. A significant issue in practice is that service concession arrangements are composite transactions. They usually have a long duration (twenty-five to thirty years is not uncommon) during which time the operator has a variety of obligations. These may be in connection with the infrastructure asset itself and include:

- enhancement of the infrastructure or construction of new infrastructure;
- infrastructure components that must be replaced in their entirety;
- infrastructure subject to major cyclical repairs; and
- regular repairs and maintenance.

In addition, many service concession arrangements involve the provision of services. In the case of a hospital, for example, this could include utilities (such as water and electricity) and a wide range of 'soft' services such as cleaning, laundry, meals, portering, security and grounds maintenance, amongst others. All of these might be paid for as a single unitary charge that would probably be adjusted according to performance as in Example 28.2 above. The accounting models for service concessions must be able to deal with all of these issues.

5.1   Additional construction and upgrade services

The concession may include obligations to construct new infrastructure (construction services) or to enhance either new or existing infrastructure to a condition better than at the start of the concession (upgrade services). IFRIC 12 does not deal in detail with the treatment to be adopted other than to say that revenue and costs relating to construction or upgrade services are recognised in accordance with IAS 11. *[IFRIC 12.14].* This means that all construction or upgrade services are accounted for in accordance with the appropriate model, regardless of when they take place. Contractual obligations to maintain or restore infrastructure may also include an upgrade element. *[IFRIC 12.21].*

Upgrade or construction services are separate revenue-generating activities. This means that the contract has to require the particular service to be carried out at a specified time. It is not sufficient for there to be a general requirement to maintain the asset in a specified condition.

It would be unusual for a toll road concession, for example, to require resurfacing to take place according to a predetermined schedule as road surfaces degrade with usage (based on both the number of vehicles and weight per axle) as well as weather conditions. However, the contract might require a new bridge or access road after a specified period of time and either of these could be separate upgrade services.

Upgrade services must be recognised in accordance with IAS 11, using the percentage of completion method and recognising revenue during the construction period, as described at 4.2 and 4.3 above.

If the financial asset model applies to the upgrade, the entity has to determine the fair value of consideration received for the upgrade services. This may be part of the allocation at inception of the contract, as shown in Example 28.3 above where part of the contract revenue is attributed to road resurfacing, or the contract may specify a separate payment. In the latter case the entity would account for the upgrade service as a separate financial asset once it started to provide the services (e.g. started to build the bridge) which means recognising revenue during construction. If the infrastructure is being accounted for as a financial asset, the entity cannot simply add upgrade-related maintenance costs as incurred to an existing financial asset.

Similar issues for intangible assets are discussed in further detail below. Are the construction services part of the original asset or should they be accounted for as a new asset? If it is a new asset, when should it be recognised?

5.1.1 Subsequent construction services that are part of the initial infrastructure asset

In some circumstances, the 'enhancement' spend is part of the original intangible asset and should be recognised as part of the exchange transaction described at 4.3 above. An example of this is the common requirement in concession contracts that the operator replace certain items at the operator's cost, whether or not the items concerned have become unserviceable. For example, a water supply operator may be contractually required to replace all lead pipes for environmental and health reasons; similarly, a gas supply operator may be required to replace all cast-iron pipes for safety reasons.

Assuming that the intangible asset model is the relevant one, the first issue is whether these expenditures should be treated as operating costs (obligations to maintain or to restore the infrastructure) and treated as described at 5.2 below or as an additional cost of the intangible asset. They do not directly increase the future economic benefits of any particular infrastructure asset when the costs are incurred. IAS 16 explicitly allows such expenditure to be capitalised as part of an item of property, plant and equipment *[IAS 16.10]* and here the upgrade is a requirement of the contract so there seems little doubt that capitalisation is the appropriate treatment.

However, these features indicate that these expenditures should be included in the consideration given for the intangible asset and therefore recognised as part of its carrying value on initial recognition. This would require the recognition of a liability for the present value of the best estimate of the amount required to replace the underlying asset, such as the pipes. Note that the revenue earned in the construction phase is based on the fair value of the intangible asset on initial recognition, which in turn is based on the revenue that will be generated. In other words, the fair value of the 'construction services' may remain unchanged although the entity has accrued additional costs.

The Interpretations Committee did not address the accounting treatment of subsequent variations in the amount of the liability for the operator's unfulfilled obligations that is recognised as part of the cost of the intangible asset (the licence) e.g. when the estimated amount of the expenditures to be incurred is revised. The situation may be regarded as analogous to the situation addressed by IFRIC 1 – *Changes in Existing Decommissioning, Restoration and Similar Liabilities* – where the obligation is recognised as a liability in accordance with IAS 37 and as part of the cost of an asset. *[IFRIC 1.1]*. Therefore, the principles set out in IFRIC 1 should be applied, i.e. a change in the measurement of the liability should be added to, or deducted from the cost of the intangible asset, subject to impairment testing and to the extent that the amount deducted from the cost of the asset does not exceed the carrying amount of the intangible asset. The periodic unwinding of the discount must be recognised in income.

5.1.2   *Subsequent construction services that comprise a new infrastructure asset*

An operator may be contractually entitled to add to or upgrade the infrastructure and from this generate additional revenues. The operator may have a right to extend a distribution network and, under its right to charge for the services, it will obtain revenues from newly connected users. There is an example of such a right in Extract 28.4 below, in which Telenor ASA discloses that it has a right 'to arrange, expand, operate and provide the cellular system radio communication services in various areas in Thailand'.

Extract 28.4: Telenor ASA (2010)

Notes to the financial statements /Telenor Group [extract]

19.   Intangible assets [extract]

DTAC operates under a concession right to operate and deliver mobile services in Thailand granted by the Communication Authority of Thailand ("CAT"). CAT allows DTAC to arrange, expand, operate and provide the cellular system radio communication services in various areas in Thailand. The concession originally covered a 15-year period but the agreement was amended on 23 July 1993 and 22 November 1996, with the concession period being extended to 22 and 27 years, respectively. Accordingly, the concession period under the existing agreement expires in 2018.

Revenues generated by the new infrastructure will be determined under the terms of the *original* licence granted to the operator. However, in this case there is no pre-existing obligation to incur the cost of the extension work, meaning that it will only be recognised when the expenditure is made. Accordingly, that new cost is not an additional component of the cost of the original intangible asset but will be a new intangible asset in its own right, recognised at cost using the same principles as the original as described at 4.3 above.

5.2   Accounting for the operations phase

Both the financial and intangible asset models apply the same accounting in the operations phase of the SCA. According to the September 2006 *IFRIC Update*, 'the nature of the asset recognised by the operator as consideration for providing construction services (a financial asset or an intangible asset) does not determine the accounting for the operation phase of the arrangement'.[8]

Revenue and costs for the operation services will be recognised in accordance with IAS 18. *[IFRIC 12.20]*. This means that most operating and maintenance costs are likely to be executory and will be accounted for as incurred. Contractual obligations, including obligations to maintain, replace or restore infrastructure, are to be recognised and measured in accordance with IAS 37, i.e. once there is a present obligation as a result of a past event, and measured at the best estimate of the expenditure required to settle the present obligation at the balance sheet date, as shown in Example 28.7 below. These include obligations to restore infrastructure to a specified condition before it is returned to the grantor at the end of the concession. *[IFRIC 12.21]*. These do not include any upgrade element which is treated as an additional construction service (see 5.1 above).

Distinguishing between executory maintenance spend and contractual obligations is not always straightforward. A concession arrangement may provide for a specified total amount of expenditure to be incurred by the operator throughout the contract. Sometimes, the contract provides for mechanisms whereby at the end of the contract, any shortfall in the agreed amount is paid in cash to the grantor by the operator. Particularly in the case of older contracts, it is common for the maintenance and repair obligation to be expressed in very general terms such as keeping the infrastructure in 'good working condition' or 'state of the art' working condition. The obligation may include the requirement that the asset be handed over with a certain number of years' useful life remaining.

Local regulations or laws also change over time. Some operators are obliged to report annually to the grantor on the level of maintenance and renewal expenditure incurred during the year and on a cumulative basis from inception of the contract. Sometimes, the operator must report on expected expenditures over some future period of time (e.g. over the next 12 months or two years) as well. In these situations, more often than not the grantor compares the cumulative expenditure at any point in time with either the operator's prior estimates of expenditures or with the level of expenditure that had been anticipated at the outset of the arrangement and was factored into the level of usage charges. In such circumstances, judgment is required in deciding whether expenditure on renewals is an obligation or an executory contract.

Example 28.7:   Executory and contractual obligations to maintain and restore the infrastructure

The operator under a water supply service concession is required as part of the overall contractual arrangement to replace four water pumps as soon as their performance drops below certain quality levels. The operator expects this to be the case after 15 years of service. The expected cost of replacing the pumps is CU 1,000. The operator's best estimate is that the service potential of the pumps is consumed evenly over time and provision for the costs is made on this basis from inception of the service concession arrangement until the date of expected replacement. The provision is measured at the net present value of the amounts expected to be paid, using the operator's discount rate of 5%. The amount provided in the first year can be calculated as CU 33.67. Assuming no changes to estimates, in 15 years CU 1,000 would have been provided and would be utilised in replacing the pumps. The provision would be adjusted on a cumulative basis to take account of changes in estimates to the cost of replacement pumps, the manner in which they are wearing out or changes to the operator's discount rate.

The Interpretations Committee has also provided an example in Illustrative Example 2, the intangible asset model, of how operational expenditure might be accounted for in accordance with IAS 37. Although this illustration is in the context of an intangible asset, IAS 37 can apply to obligations whatever model applies. Major maintenance, in this case the requirement to resurface the road, will be recognised as the best estimate of the expenditure required to settle the present obligation at the balance sheet date and it is suggested that this might 'arise as a consequence of use of the road', therefore increasing in measurable annual increments. *[IFRIC 12.IE19]*. The basis for accounting for such obligations is discussed further in Chapter 29.

Example 28.8:   The Intangible Asset Model – recording the operations phase

The terms of the arrangement are the same as in Example 28.4 above. The contract costs and initial measurement of the intangible asset are set out in Table 1 and Table 2 in that example.

Resurfacing obligations

The operator's resurfacing obligation arises as a consequence of use of the road during the operating phase. It is recognised and measured in accordance with IAS 37, i.e. at the best estimate of the expenditure required to settle the present obligation at the balance sheet date.

For the purpose of this illustration, it is assumed that the terms of the operator's contractual obligation are such that the best estimate of the expenditure required to settle the obligation at any date is proportional to the number of vehicles that have used the road by that date and increases by €17 (discounted to a current value) each year. The operator discounts the provision to its present value in accordance with IAS 37. The income statement charge each period is:

Table 3 Resurfacing obligation

Year	3 €	4 €	5 €	6 €	7 €	8 €	Total €
Obligation arising in year (€17 discounted at 6%)	12	13	14	15	16	17	87
Increase in earlier years' provision arising from passage of time	0	1	1	2	4	5	13
Total expense recognised in income statement	12	14	15	17	20	22	100

Overview of cash flows, income statement and balance sheet

For the purpose of this illustration, it is assumed that the operator finances the arrangement wholly with debt and retained profits. It pays interest at 6.7% a year on outstanding debt. If the cash flows and fair values remain the same as those forecast, the operator's cash flows, income statement and balance sheet over the duration of the arrangement will be:

Table 4 Cash flows

Year	1 €	2 €	3 €	4 €	5 €	6 €	7 €	8 €	9 €	10 €	Total €
Receipts	–	–	200	200	200	200	200	200	200	200	1,600
Contract costs	(500)	(500)	(10)	(10)	(10)	(10)	(10)	(110)	(10)	(10)	(1,180)
Borrowing costs†	–	(34)	(69)	(61)	(53)	(43)	(33)	(23)	(19)	(7)	(342)
Net inflow/ (outflow)	(500)	(534)	121	129	137	147	157	67	171	183	78

† Debt at start of year (table 6) × 6.7%

Table 5 Income statement

Year	1 €	2 €	3 €	4 €	5 €	6 €	7 €	8 €	9 €	10 €	Total €
Revenue	525	525	200	200	200	200	200	200	200	200	2,650
Amortisation	–	–	(135)	(135)	(136)	(136)	(136)	(136)	(135)	(135)	(1,084)
Resurfacing expense	–	–	(12)	(14)	(15)	(17)	(20)	(22)	–	–	(100)
Other operating costs†	(500)	(500)	(10)	(10)	(10)	(10)	(10)	(10)	(10)	(10)	(1,080)
Borrowing costs* (table 4)	–	–	(69)	(61)	(53)	(43)	(33)	(23)	(19)	(7)	(308)
Net profits	25	25	(26)	(20)	(14)	(6)	1	9	36	48	78

* Borrowing costs are capitalised during the construction phase

† Table 1

Table 6 Balance sheet

End of Year	1 €	2 €	3 €	4 €	5 €	6 €	7 €	8 €	9 €	10 €
Intangible asset	525	1,084	949	814	678	542	406	270	135	–
Cash/ (debt)*	(500)	(1,034)	(913)	(784)	(647)	(500)	(343)	(276)	(105)	78
Resurfacing obligation	–	–	(12)	(26)	(41)	(58)	(78)	–	–	–
Net assets	25	50	24	4	(10)	(16)	(15)	(6)	30	78

* Debt at start of year plus net cash flow in year (table 4)

To make this illustration as clear as possible, it has been assumed that the arrangement period is only ten years and that the operator's annual receipts are constant over the period. In practice, arrangement periods may be much longer and annual revenue may increase with time. In such circumstances, the changes in net profit from year to year could be greater.

Chapter 28

5.3   Items provided to the operator by the grantor

Following the basic principles underlying the proposed accounting treatment and under both models, infrastructure items to which the operator is given access by the grantor for the purpose of the service concession are not recognised as its property, plant and equipment. *[IFRIC 12.27]*. This is because they remain under the control of the grantor.

There is a different treatment for assets that are given to the operator as part of the consideration for the concession that can be kept or dealt with as the operator wishes. These assets are not to be treated as government grants as defined in IAS 20. Instead, they are brought into account by the operator at fair value, together with a liability in respect of any unfulfilled obligations assumed in exchange for the assets. *[IFRIC 12.27]*.

What this means is that an operator that has been given a licence or similar arrangement over a piece of land on which a hospital is to be built does not recognise the land as an asset. If, on the other hand, the operator has been given a piece of surplus land on which it can build private housing for sale, it will recognise an asset. The consideration, which is the fair value of that land, will be aggregated with the remainder of the consideration for the transaction and accounted for according to the model being used.

6   CURRENT DISCLOSURE REQUIREMENTS: SIC-29

IFRIC 12 has no specific disclosure requirements although the disclosure requirements of the various applicable standards (such as IFRS 7 – *Financial Instruments: Disclosures* – and IAS 38) will have to be made as appropriate. SIC-29, which pre-dates IFRIC 12 by several years, includes additional disclosure requirements. It is important to note that the scope of SIC-29 is not defined in terms of IFRIC 12 and is potentially broader than IFRIC 12's scope as described above. It applies to a type of transaction that is described although not really defined and which does not depend on the control criteria described at 3 above. It also applies to both sides of the transaction, whereas IFRIC 12 applies only to the operator under the concession agreement.

SIC-29 describes service concessions as arrangements in which an entity (the operator) provides services on behalf of another entity (the grantor, which may be a public or private sector entity, including a governmental body) that give the public access to major economic and social facilities. The examples of service concession arrangements given by SIC-29 include water treatment and supply facilities, motorways, car parks, tunnels, bridges, airports and telecommunication networks. *[SIC-29.1]*.

SIC-29 states that the common characteristic of all service concession arrangements is that the operator both receives a right and incurs an obligation to provide public services. *[SIC-29.3]*. It excludes from its scope an entity outsourcing the operation of its internal services (e.g. employee cafeteria, building maintenance, and accounting or information technology functions). *[SIC-29.1]*. This means that some of the arrangements that do not include the construction of a major capital asset, as discussed above, may not be caught by the requirements of the SIC, although there is no hard-and-fast dividing line between service concessions and outsourcing arrangements. For example, a contract between a government department and an operator to maintain the existing computer system, including replacement of hardware and software as appropriate, may be outside the scope of SIC-29.

SIC-29 summarises the rights and obligations as follows:

For the period of the concession, the operator has received from the grantor:

(a)   the right to provide services that give the public access to major economic and social facilities; and

(b)   in some cases, the right to use specified tangible assets, intangible assets, and/or financial assets,

in exchange for the operator:

(a)   committing to provide the services according to certain terms and conditions during the concession period; and

(b)   when applicable, committing to return at the end of the concession period the rights received at the beginning of the concession period and/or acquired during the concession period. *[SIC-29.2]*.

The disclosure requirements in respect of such projects are as follows:

SIC-29 requires disclosure in addition to that required by other standards that may cover part of the transaction, such as IAS 16 (see Chapter 20), IAS 17 (see Chapter 26) and IAS 38 (see Chapter 19). *[SIC-29.5]*. All aspects of a service concession arrangement should be considered in determining the appropriate disclosures in the notes to the financial statements. *[SIC-29.6]*.

An operator and a grantor should disclose the following in each period:

(a)   a description of the arrangement;

(b)   significant terms of the arrangement that may affect the amount, timing and certainty of future cash flows (e.g. the period of the concession, re-pricing dates and the basis upon which re-pricing or re-negotiation is determined);

(c)   the nature and extent (e.g. quantity, time period or amount as appropriate) of:

   (i)   rights to use specified assets;

   (ii)   obligations to provide or rights to expect provision of services;

   (iii) obligations to acquire or build items of property, plant and equipment;

   (iv) obligations to deliver or rights to receive specified assets at the end of the concession period;

   (v)   renewal and termination options; and

   (vi) other rights and obligations (e.g. major overhauls);

(d)   changes in the arrangement occurring during the period; and

(e)   how the service arrangement has been classified.

These disclosures should be provided individually for each service concession arrangement or in aggregate for each class of service concession arrangements. A class is a grouping of service concession arrangements involving services of a similar nature (e.g. toll collections, telecommunications and water treatment services). *[SIC-29.6-7]*.

Chapter 28

IFRIC 12 has added a requirement to disclose 'the amount of revenue and profits or losses recognised in the period on exchanging construction services for a financial asset and an intangible asset'. *[SIC-29.6A]*.

Vinci has made aggregate disclosures for the principal terms of its arrangements. The following extract is part only of the extensive disclosures that separately address concession arrangements under the financial asset model and mixed model.

Extract 28.5: VINCI S.A. (2010)

Notes to the consolidated financial statements [extract]

G.   Notes on the main features of concession and PPP contracts

26.   Controlled subsidiaries' concession contracts – intangible asset model [extract]

26.1   Main features of concession contracts [extract]

The main features of the contracts for the concessions accounted for using the intangible asset model and operated by controlled subsidiaries are as follows:

	Control and regulation of prices by concession grantor	Remuneration paid by	Grant or guarantee from concession grantor	Residual value	Concession end date or average duration	Accounting model
Highway infrastructure (including bridges and tunnels)						
ASF Group						
ASF (2,714 km of toll motorway of which 22 km at project stage and 53 km under construction)	Pricing law as defined in the concession contract. Price increases subject to agreement by grantor.	Users	Nil	Infrastructure returned to grantor for no consideration at the end of the contract, unless purchased before term by the grantor on the basis of the economic value.	End of contract in 2033	Intangible asset
Escota (459 km toll motorway in France)	Pricing law as defined in the concession contract. Price increases subject to agreement by grantor.	Users	Nil	Infrastructure returned to grantor for no consideration at the end of the contract, unless purchased before term by the grantor on the basis of the economic value.	End of contract in 2027	Intangible asset

Cofiroute						
Intercity toll motorway network in France (1,100 km toll motorways)	Pricing law as defined in the concession contract. Price increases subject to agreement by grantor.	Users	Nil	Infrastructure returned to grantor for no consideration at the end of the contract, unless purchased before term by the grantor on the basis of the economic value.	End of contract in 2031	Intangible asset
A86 Duplex (11 km toll tunnel)	Pricing law as defined in the concession contract. Price increases subject to agreement by grantor.	Users	Grant of €120 million to offset extra construction costs resulting from application of new safety standards in the tunnels	Infrastructure returned to grantor for no consideration at the end of the contract, unless purchased before term by the grantor on the basis of the economic value.	End of contract in 2086	Intangible asset

26.2   Commitments made under concession contracts – intangible asset model [extract]
Contractual investment, renewal and financing obligations

(in € millions)	31/12/2010	31/12/2009[*]
ASF Group	**3,199.3**[**]	**3,270.2**
of which, Lyons to Balbigny	963.1	1,217.6
Cofiroute	**686.7**[**]	**609.6**
of which, intercity network	252.0	263.0
of which, A86 Duplex	68.6	126.4
Arcour	**39.8**	**52.9**
Other	**91.4**	**73.8**
Total	**4,017.3**	**4,006.5**

[*] Restated following the change of method described in Note A.1.2 "Change of method: equity accounting of jointly controlled entities".
[**] Including the "green motorway" package for €444.4 million for ASF Group and €167.1 million for Cofiroute.

The above amounts do not include maintenance expenditure on infrastructure under concession.
The investments by ASF, Escota, Cofiroute and Arcour are financed by drawings on their available credit facilities, by taking out new loans from the European Investment Bank (EIB) and by issuing bonds on the market.
On 25 January 2010, ASF Group and Cofiroute signed the green motorway package with the French government, under which the motorway operating companies have undertaken to carry out an environmental upgrading programme on their networks in exchange for a one-year extension of their concession contracts.

Chapter 28

Collateral security connected with the financing of concessions

Some concession operating companies have given collateral securities to guarantee the financing of their investments in concession infrastructure. These break down as follows:

(in € millions)	**State date**	**End date**	**Amount**
Arcour	2008	2045	600.0
VINCI Park	2006	2026	421.5[*]
Gefyra (Rion-Antirion bridge)	2001	2029	329.0
Other concession operating companies			151.0

[*]   *Shares in subsidiaries pledged to guarantee a loan of €500 million taken out at the end of June 2006.*

Vinci also disclosed the revenue and profit earned from its concession arrangements. The following extract discloses revenue from concessions as a component of revenue by business line.

Extract 28.6: VINCI S.A. (2010)

Notes to the consolidated financial statements [extract]
D.   Segment information [extract]
1.   Revenue [extract]
1.1   Breakdown of revenue by business line

(in € millions)	2010	2009[*]	Change 2010/2009
Concessions	**5,097.1**	**4,889.1**	**4.3%**
VINCI Autoroutes	4,258.7	4,095.0	4.0%
VINCI Park and other concessions	838.4	794.0	5.6%
Contracting	**28,150.4**	**25.728.8**	**9.4%**
Energy	7,102.0	4,861.7	46.1%
Eurovia	7.930.2	7,851.1	1.0%
VINCI Construction	13,118.2	13,016.0	0.8%
Eliminations and miscellaneous	**128.4**	**123.0**	**4.3%**
Revenue[**]	**33,375.8**	**30,740.9**	**8.6%**
Concession subsidiaries' revenue derived from works carried out by non-Group companies[***]	627.0	436.7	43.6%
Total revenue	34,002.8	31,177.7	9.1%

[*]   Restated following the change of method described in Note A.1.2 "Change of method: equity accounting of jointly controlled entities" and the internal reorganisation of the facilities management activity (in France and Germany) reclassified from the Construction business line to the Energy business line.

[**]   Excluding Concession subsidiaries' revenue derived from works carried out by non-Group companies.

[***]   Including intragroup revenue of Contracting business lines from work for concession operating companies (€285.9 million at 31 December 2010 and €376.1 million at 31 December 2009).

References

1 FRS 5, *Reporting the substance of transactions*, ASB, April 1994 (with subsequent amendments), Application Note F, *Private finance initiative and similar contracts*.
2 *IFRIC Update*, September 2005.
3 *IFRIC Update*, September 2005.
4 *IFRIC Update*, March 2006.
5 IAS 38 (2007), *Intangible Assets*, IASB, 2007 Bound Volume, para. 98 stated that 'there is rarely, if ever, persuasive evidence to support an amortisation method for intangible assets with finite useful lives that results in a lower amount of accumulated amortisation than under the straight-line method.' This was removed by *Improvements to IFRSs*, May 2008.
6 *IFRIC Update*, January 2010.
7 *IFRIC Update*, September 2004.
8 *IFRIC Update*, September 2006.

Chapter 28

Chapter 29

Provisions, contingent liabilities and contingent assets

Chapter 29

List of examples

Chapter 29

Chapter 29

Provisions, contingent liabilities and contingent assets

1 INTRODUCTION

1.1 Background

This chapter focuses only on those provisions that are the subject of IAS 37 – *Provisions, Contingent Liabilities and Contingent Assets*. Thus it only deals with provisions that are shown as liabilities in a balance sheet, since the definition of a provision in IAS 37 is 'a liability of uncertain timing or amount'. *[IAS 37.10]*. Like IAS 37, the chapter does not deal with items termed 'provisions' that reduce the carrying amount of assets such as depreciation, impairment of assets and doubtful debts. *[IAS 37.7]*.

IAS 37 was developed in parallel with the equivalent UK standard, FRS 12 – *Provisions, Contingent Liabilities and Contingent Assets* – under a joint project between the IASC and the ASB. As a result, the two standards were published on the same day in September 1998. There were no differences of substance between the requirements of the two standards – indeed the text is still mostly identical (apart from consequential amendments made to IAS 37 as a result of later standards issued by the IASB) – but FRS 12 includes slightly more guidance on two areas:

- recognition of an asset when a provision is recognised (see 3.3 below), and
- the discount rate to be used in the net present value calculation (see 4.3 below).

1.2 Interpretations related to the application of IAS 37

The Interpretations Committee has issued a number of pronouncements relating to the application of IAS 37 (although one of them was subsequently withdrawn).

1.2.1   IFRIC 1

In May 2004, the IASB issued IFRIC 1 – *Changes in Existing Decommissioning, Restoration and Similar Liabilities*. This interpretation provides guidance on how to account for the effect of changes in the measurement of existing provisions for obligations to dismantle, remove or restore items of property, plant and equipment. This is discussed at 5.5.1 below.

1.2.2   IFRIC 3

Another issue considered by the Interpretations Committee was how to account for a 'cap and trade' emission rights scheme. In December 2004, the IASB issued IFRIC 3 – *Emission Rights* – but this was later withdrawn in June 2005 with immediate effect. This interpretation, *inter alia*, required that as emissions are made, a liability was to be recognised for the obligation to deliver allowances equal to the emissions that had been made by the entity. Such liability was a provision within the scope of IAS 37, and was to be measured at the present market value of the number of allowances required to cover emissions made up to the end of the reporting period. This is discussed at 5.6 below.

1.2.3   IFRIC 5

In December 2004, the IASB issued IFRIC 5 – *Rights to Interests arising from Decommissioning, Restoration and Environmental Rehabilitation Funds*. This deals with the accounting by an entity when it participates in a 'decommissioning fund', the purpose of which is to segregate assets to fund some or all of the costs of its decommissioning or environmental liabilities for which it has to make a provision under IAS 37. This is discussed at 5.5.3 below.

1.2.4   IFRIC 6

In September 2005, the IASB issued IFRIC 6 – *Liabilities arising from Participating in a Specific Market – Waste Electrical and Electronic Equipment* – giving guidance on the accounting for liabilities for waste management costs. This clarifies when certain producers of electrical goods will need to recognise a liability for the cost of waste management relating to the decommissioning of waste electrical and electronic equipment (historical waste) supplied to private households. This is discussed at 5.8 below.

The number of other Interpretations that refer to IAS 37 demonstrates just how pervasive the consideration of non-financial liabilities is in developing accounting practice. For example, IAS 37 is also referred to in IFRIC 12 – *Service Concessions* (see Chapter 28); IFRIC 13 – *Customer Loyalty Programmes* (see Chapter 30); IFRIC 14 – *IAS 19 – The Limit on a Defined Benefit Asset, Minimum Funding Requirements and their Interaction* (see Chapter 33); and IFRIC 15 – *Agreements for the Construction of Real Estate* (see Chapter 25).

1.3   Definitions used in IAS 37

The following terms are used in IAS 37 with the meanings specified: *[IAS 37.10]*

Term	Definition
Provision	A liability of uncertain timing or amount.
Liability	A present obligation of the entity arising from past events, the settlement of which is expected to result in an outflow from the entity of resources embodying economic benefits.
Obligating event	An event that creates a legal or constructive obligation that results in an entity having no realistic alternative to settling that obligation.
Legal obligation	An obligation that derives from a contract (through its explicit or implicit terms); legislation; or other operation of law.
Constructive obligation	An obligation that derives from an entity's actions where: (a) by an established pattern of past practice, published policies or a sufficiently specific current statement, the entity has indicated to other parties that it will accept certain responsibilities; and (b) as a result, the entity has created a valid expectation on the part of those other parties that it will discharge those responsibilities.
Contingent liability	(a) a possible obligation that arises from past events and whose existence will be confirmed only by the occurrence or non-occurrence of one or more uncertain future events not wholly within the control of the entity; or (b) a present obligation that arises from past events but is not recognised because: (i) it is not probable that an outflow of resources embodying economic benefits will be required to settle the obligation; or (ii) the amount of the obligation cannot be measured with sufficient reliability.
Contingent asset	A possible asset that arises from past events and whose existence will be confirmed only by the occurrence or non-occurrence of one or more uncertain future events not wholly within the control of the entity.
Onerous contract	An contract in which the unavoidable costs of meeting the obligations under the contract exceed the economic benefits expected to be received under it.
Restructuring	A programme that is planned and controlled by management, and materially changes either: (a) the scope of a business undertaken by an entity; or (b) the manner in which that business is conducted.

Chapter 29

2   OBJECTIVE AND SCOPE OF IAS 37

2.1   Objective

The objective of IAS 37 'is to ensure that appropriate recognition criteria and measurement bases are applied to provisions, contingent liabilities and contingent assets and that sufficient information is disclosed in the notes to enable users to understand their nature, timing and amount'. *[IAS 37, Objective]*.

2.2   Scope of IAS 37

The standard is required to be applied by all entities in accounting for provisions, contingent liabilities and contingent assets, except those arising from executory contracts (unless the contract is onerous) and those covered by another standard. *[IAS 37.1]*.

The following table lists the specific types of transaction or circumstances referred to in the standard that might give rise to a provision, contingent liability or contingent asset. In some cases, the transaction is identified in IAS 37 only to prohibit recognition of any liability, such as for future operating losses and repairs and maintenance of owned assets. This chapter does not address those items identified below as falling outside the scope of the standard.

Types of transaction or circumstances referred to	*In scope*	*Out of scope*	*Another standard*
Restructuring costs	•		
Environmental penalties or clean-up costs	•		
Decommissioning costs	•		
Product warranties / refunds	•		
Legal claims	•		
Reimbursement rights	•		
Future operating costs (training, relocation, etc.)	•		
Future operating losses	•		
Onerous contracts	•		
Repairs and maintenance costs	•		
Provisions for depreciation, impairment or doubtful debts		•	
Executory contracts (unless onerous)		•	
Construction contracts		•	IAS 11
Income taxes		•	IAS 12
Leases (unless onerous)		•	IAS 17
Employee benefits		•	IAS 19

Insurance contracts with policyholders	•	IFRS 4
Contingent liabilities in a business combination	•	IFRS 3
Financial instruments in the scope of IAS 39 and IFRS 9	•	IAS 39 / IFRS 9
Financial guarantees in the scope of IAS 39 and IFRS 9	•	IAS 39 / IFRS 9
Trade payables or accruals	•	

The standard defines a provision as 'a liability of uncertain timing or amount'. *[IAS 37.10]*. Thus it only deals with provisions that are shown as liabilities in a balance sheet. The term 'provision' is also used widely in the context of items such as depreciation, impairment of assets and doubtful debts. Such 'provisions' are not addressed in IAS 37, since these are adjustments to the carrying amounts of assets. *[IAS 37.7]*.

2.2.1 Items outside the scope of IAS 37

2.2.1.A Executory contracts, except where the contract is onerous

The standard uses the term executory contracts to mean 'contracts under which neither party has performed any of its obligations, or both parties have partially performed their obligations to an equal extent'. *[IAS 37.3]*. This means that contracts such as supplier purchase contracts and capital commitments, which would otherwise fall within the scope of the standard, are exempt.

This exemption prevents the balance sheet from being grossed up for all sorts of commitments that an entity has entered into, and is to be welcomed as a pragmatic measure. However, there is little theoretical justification for it, in that such items meet the definition of liabilities used by the standard, and of course give rise to corresponding assets. The need for this exemption arises because the liability framework on which this standard is based includes the concept of a constructive obligation (see 3.1.1 below) which, when applied to executory contracts would otherwise give rise to all sorts of contingent promises requiring recognition or disclosure.

An executory contract will still require recognition as a provision if the contract becomes onerous. *[IAS 37.3]*. Onerous contracts are dealt with at 5.3 below.

2.2.1.B   Items covered by another standard

Where another standard deals with a specific type of provision, contingent liability or contingent asset, it should be applied instead of IAS 37. Examples given in the standard are: [IAS 37.5]

- construction contracts (dealt with in IAS 11 – *Construction Contracts*);
- income taxes (dealt with in IAS 12 – *Income Taxes*);
- leases (dealt with in IAS 17 – *Leases*). However, the standard argues that if operating leases become onerous, there are no specific requirements within IAS 17 to address the issue and thus IAS 37 applies to such leases;
- employee benefits (dealt with in IAS 19 – *Employee Benefits*); and
- insurance contracts (dealt with in IFRS 4 – *Insurance Contracts*). However, IAS 37 requires an insurer to apply the standard to provisions, contingent liabilities and contingent assets, other than those arising from its contractual obligations and rights under insurance contracts within the scope of IFRS 4.

Before its amendment by IFRS 3 (as revised in 2008), IAS 37 also referred to the specific requirements in IFRS 3 (2007) – *Business Combinations* – relating to the recognition and measurement of contingent liabilities assumed in a business combination as superseding those in IAS 37.[1] Following its amendment, whilst IAS 37 contains no similar reference, the revised IFRS 3 states that the requirements in IAS 37 do not apply in determining which contingent liabilities to recognise as of the acquisition date [IFRS 3.23] (see Chapter 10 at 5.6.1).

In addition, the standard does not apply to financial instruments (including guarantees) that are within the scope of IAS 39 and IFRS 9 – *Financial Instruments* [IAS 37.2] (see Chapter 42). This means that guarantees of third party borrowings (including those of subsidiaries, associates and joint ventures) are not covered by IAS 37 (see 3.2.1 below).

IAS 37 also notes that some amounts treated as provisions may relate to the recognition of revenue, for example where an entity gives guarantees in exchange for a fee, and states that the standard does not address the recognition of revenue. This is dealt with by IAS 18 – *Revenue* (see Chapter 30), and IAS 37 does not change the requirements of that standard. [IAS 37.6].

The standard applies to provisions for restructurings, including discontinued operations. However, it emphasises that when a restructuring meets the definition of a discontinued operation under IFRS 5 – *Non-current Assets Held for Sale and Discontinued Operations*, additional disclosures may be required under that standard (see Chapter 4 at 3). [IAS 37.9].

2.2.2   Provisions and other liabilities

IAS 37 states that the feature distinguishing provisions from other liabilities, such as trade payables and accruals, is the existence of 'uncertainty about the timing or amount of the future expenditure required in settlement. By contrast:

(a)   trade payables are liabilities to pay for goods or services that have been received or supplied and have been invoiced or formally agreed with the supplier; and

(b)   accruals are liabilities to pay for goods or services that have been received or supplied but have not been paid, invoiced or formally agreed with the supplier, including amounts due to employees (for example, amounts relating to accrued vacation pay). Although it is sometimes necessary to estimate the amount or timing of accruals, the uncertainty is generally much less than for provisions.

Accruals are often reported as part of trade and other payables whereas provisions are reported separately'. *[IAS 37.11]*.

This is true, but the contrast with trade payables and their associated accruals is only the most straightforward case. In practice the difference between provisions and other liabilities is often far from clear-cut.

One reason why this distinction matters is that provisions are subject to disclosure requirements that do not apply to other payables, as discussed at 6.1 below. In fact, although questions of recognition and measurement are important, transparency of disclosure is also a very significant matter in relation to accounting for provisions. The issue is that, once a provision has been established, expenditure that is charged to it bypasses the income statement and to some extent therefore disappears from view. The original charge may well have been dealt with as an exceptional item in the income statement and glossed over by management in any discussion of their performance, and the subsequent application of the provision has no further impact on earnings – giving rise to a kind of 'off income statement' treatment.

2.2.3   *Provisions and contingent liabilities*

There is an area of overlap between provisions and contingent liabilities. Although contingent liabilities are clearly not as likely to give rise to outflows, similar judgments are made in assessing the nature of the uncertainties, the need for disclosures and ultimately the recognition of a liability in the financial statements. The standard notes that in a general sense, all provisions are contingent because they are uncertain in timing or amount. However, in IAS 37 the term 'contingent' is used for liabilities and assets that are not recognised because their existence will be confirmed only by the occurrence of one or more uncertain future events not wholly within the entity's control. In addition, the term 'contingent liability' is used for liabilities that do not meet the recognition criteria for provisions. *[IAS 37.12]*.

Accordingly, the standard distinguishes between: *[IAS 37.13]*

(a)   provisions – which are recognised as liabilities (assuming that a reliable estimate can be made) because they are present obligations and it is probable that an outflow of resources embodying economic benefits will be required to settle the obligations; and

(b)   contingent liabilities – which are not recognised as liabilities because they are either:

   (i)   possible obligations, as it has yet to be confirmed whether the entity has a present obligation that could lead to an outflow of resources embodying economic benefits; or

   (ii)   present obligations that do not meet the recognition criteria in the standard because either it is not probable that an outflow of resources embodying economic benefits will be required to settle the obligation, or a sufficiently reliable estimate of the amount of the obligation cannot be made.

3   RECOGNITION

3.1   Determining when a provision should be recognised

IAS 37 requires that a provision should be recognised when: *[IAS 37.14]*

(a)   an entity has a present obligation (legal or constructive) as a result of a past event;

(b)   it is probable that an outflow of resources embodying economic benefits will be required to settle the obligation; and

(c)   a reliable estimate can be made of the amount of the obligation.

No provision should be recognised unless all of these conditions are met.

Each of these three conditions is discussed separately below.

3.1.1   'An entity has a present obligation (legal or constructive) as a result of a past event'

The standard defines both legal and constructive obligations. The definition of a legal obligation is fairly straightforward and uncontroversial; it refers to an obligation that derives from a contract (through its explicit or implicit terms), legislation or other operation of law. *[IAS 37.10]*.

The definition of a constructive obligation, on the other hand, may give rise to more problems of interpretation. A constructive obligation is defined as an obligation that derives from an entity's actions where: *[IAS 37.10]*

(a)   by an established pattern of past practice, published policies or a sufficiently specific current statement, the entity has indicated to other parties that it will accept certain responsibilities; and

(b)   as a result, the entity has created a valid expectation on the part of those other parties that it will discharge those responsibilities.

The following examples in IAS 37 illustrate how a constructive obligation is created.

Example 29.1:   Recognising a provision because of a constructive obligation

Scenario 1;   Environmental policy – contaminated land [IAS 37 Appendix C, Example 2B]

An entity in the oil industry operates in a country with no environmental legislation. However, it has a widely published environmental policy in which it undertakes to clean up all contamination that it causes and it has a record of honouring this published policy. During the period the entity causes contamination to some land in this country.

In these circumstances, the contamination of the land gives rise to a constructive obligation because the entity (through its published policy and record of honouring it) has created a valid expectation on the part of those affected by it that the entity will clean up the site.

Scenario 2;   Refunds policy – product returns [IAS 37 Appendix C, Example 4]

A retail store has a generally known policy of refunding purchases by dissatisfied customers, even though it is under no legal obligation to do so.

In these circumstances, the sale of its products gives rise to a constructive obligation because the entity (through its reputation for providing refunds) has created a valid expectation on the part of customers that a refund will be given if they are dissatisfied with their purchase.

These examples demonstrate that the essence of a constructive obligation is the creation of a valid expectation that the entity is irrevocably committed to accepting and discharging its responsibilities.

The standard states that in almost all cases it will be clear whether a past event has given rise to a present obligation. However, it acknowledges that there will be some rare cases, such as a lawsuit against an entity, where this will not be so because the occurrence of certain events or the consequences of those events are disputed. *[IAS 37.16]*. When it is not clear whether there is a present obligation, a 'more likely than not' evaluation (taking into account all available evidence) is deemed to be sufficient to require recognition of a provision at the end of the reporting period. *[IAS 37.15]*.

The evidence to be considered includes, for example, the opinion of experts together with any additional evidence provided by events after the reporting period. If on the basis of such evidence it is concluded that a present obligation is more likely than not to exist at the end of the reporting period, a provision will be required (assuming that the other recognition criteria are met). *[IAS 37.16]*. This is an apparent relaxation of the standard's first criterion for the recognition of a provision as set out at 3.1 above, which requires there to be a definite obligation, not just a probable one. However, this interpretation is confirmed in IAS 10 – *Events after the Reporting Period*, which includes 'the settlement after the reporting period of a court case that confirms that the entity had a present obligation at the end of the reporting period' as an example of an adjusting event. *[IAS 10.9]*.

The second half of this condition uses the phrase 'as a result of a past event'. This is based on the concept of an obligating event, which the standard defines as 'an event that creates a legal or constructive obligation and that results in an entity having no realistic alternative to settling that obligation'. *[IAS 37.10]*. The standard says that this will be the case only: *[IAS 37.17]*

(a)   where the settlement of the obligation can be enforced by law; or

(b)   in the case of a constructive obligation, where the event (which may be an action of the entity) creates valid expectations in other parties that the entity will discharge the obligation.

This concept of obligating event is used in the standard when discussing specific examples of recognition, which we discuss further at 5 below. However, it is worth mentioning here that this concept, like that of a constructive obligation, is open to interpretation and requires the exercise of judgement, as the obligating event is not always easy to identify.

Chapter 29

The standard emphasises that the financial statements deal with the financial position of an entity at the end of its reporting period, not its possible position in the future. Accordingly, no provision should be recognised for costs that need to be incurred to operate in the future. The only liabilities to be recognised are those that exist at the end of the reporting period. *[IAS 37.18]*. Care should be taken to ensure that provisions are not recognised for liabilities that arise from events after the reporting period (see Chapter 36 at 2).

Example 29.2:   No provision without a past obligating event
                          [IAS 37 Appendix C, Example 7]

The government introduces a number of changes to the income tax system. As a result of these changes, an entity in the financial services sector will need to retrain a large proportion of its administrative and sales staff in order to ensure continued compliance with financial services regulation. At the end of the reporting period, no training has taken place.

In these circumstances, no event has taken place at the reporting date to create an obligation. Only once the training has taken place will there be a present obligation as a result of a past event.

IAS 37 disallows certain provisions that might otherwise qualify to be recognised by stating that it 'is only those obligations arising from past events existing independently of an entity's future actions (i.e. the future conduct of its business) that are recognised as provisions'. In contrast to situations where the entity's past conduct has created an obligation to incur expenditure (such as to rectify environmental damage already caused), a commercial or legal requirement to incur expenditure in order to operate in a particular way in the future, will not of itself justify the recognition of a provision. It argues that because the entity can avoid the expenditure by its future actions, for example by changing its method of operation, there is no present obligation for the future expenditure. *[IAS 37.19]*.

Example 29.3:   Obligations must exist independently of an entity's future actions
                          [IAS 37 Appendix C, Example 6]

Under legislation passed in 2011, an entity is required to fix smoke filters in its factories by 30 June 2013. The entity has not fitted the smoke filters.

At 31 December 2012, the end of the reporting period, no event has taken place to create an obligation. Only once the smoke filters are fitted or the legislation takes effect, will there be a present obligation as a result of a past event, either for the cost of fitting smoke filters or for fines under the legislation.

At 31 December 2013, there is still no obligating event to justify provision for the cost of fitting the smoke filters required under the legislation because the filters have not been fitted. However, an obligation may exist as at the reporting date to pay fines or penalties under the legislation because the entity is operating its factory in a non-compliant way. However, a provision would only be recognised for the best estimate of any fines and penalties if, as at 31 December 2013, it is determined to be more likely than not that such fines and penalties will be imposed.

The standard expects strict application of the requirement that, to qualify for recognition, an obligation must exist independently of an entity's future actions. Even if a failure to incur certain costs would result in a legal requirement to discontinue an entity's operations, this example states that no provision can be recognised. As discussed at 5.9 below, IAS 37 considers the example of an airline required by law to overhaul its aircraft once every three years. It concludes that no provision is recognised because the entity can avoid the requirement to perform the overhaul, for example by replacing the aircraft before the three year period has expired. *[IAS 37 Appendix C, Example 11B]*. Significantly, however, such considerations do not apply in the case of obligations to dismantle or remove an asset at the end of its useful life, where an obligation is recognised despite the entity's ability to dispose of the asset before its useful life has expired. This might be the case because such costs are required to be included by IAS 16 – *Property, Plant and Equipment* – as part of the measure of an asset's initial cost. *[IAS 16.16]*. Decommissioning provisions are discussed at 5.5 below. A further distinction can be drawn where the requirement to maintain the asset is a contractual obligation, such as when the asset in question is held under an operating lease (see 5.10 below). Accordingly, the determination of whether an obligation exists independently of an entity's future actions can be a matter of judgement that depends on the particular facts and circumstances of the case.

There is no requirement for an entity to know to whom an obligation is owed. The obligation may be to the public at large. It follows that the obligation could be to one party, but the amount ultimately payable will be to another party. For example, in the case of a constructive obligation for an environmental clean-up, the obligation is to the public, but the liability will be settled by making payment to the contractors engaged to carry out the clean-up. However, the principle is that there must be another party for the obligation to exist. It follows from this that a management or board decision will not give rise to a constructive obligation unless it is communicated in sufficient detail to those affected by it before the end of the reporting period. *[IAS 37.20]*. The most significant application of this requirement relates to restructuring provisions, which is discussed further at 5.2 below.

The standard discusses the possibility that an event that does not give rise to an obligation immediately may do so at a later date, because of changes in the law or an act by the entity (such as a sufficiently specific public statement) which gives rise to a constructive obligation. *[IAS 37.21]*. Changes in the law will be relatively straightforward to identify. The only issue that arises will be exactly when that change in the law should be recognised. IAS 37 states that an obligation arises only when the legislation is virtually certain to be enacted as drafted and suggests that in many cases, this will not be until it is enacted. *[IAS 37.22]*.

The more subjective area is the possibility that an act by the entity will give rise to a constructive obligation. The example given is of an entity publicly accepting responsibility for rectification of previous environmental damage in a way that creates a constructive obligation. *[IAS 37.21]*. This seems to introduce a certain amount of flexibility to management when reporting results. By bringing forward or delaying a public announcement of a commitment that management had always intended to honour, it can affect the reporting period in which a provision is recognised. Nevertheless, the existence of a public announcement provides a more transparent basis for recognising a provision than, say, a decision made behind the closed doors of a boardroom.

Chapter 29

3.1.2   'It is probable that an outflow of resources embodying economic benefits will be required to settle the obligation'

This requirement has been included as a result of the standard's attempt to incorporate contingent liabilities within the definition of provisions. This is discussed in detail at 3.2 below.

The interpretation of *probable* in these circumstances is that the outflow of resources is more likely than not to occur; that is, it has a probability greater than 50%. *[IAS 37.23].* The standard also makes it clear that where there are a number of similar obligations, the probability that an outflow will occur is based on the class of obligations as a whole. This is because in the case of certain obligations such as warranties, the possibility of an outflow for an individual item may be small (likely to be much less than 50%) whereas the possibility of at least some outflow of resources for the population as a whole will be much greater (almost certainly greater than 50%). *[IAS 37.24].*

3.1.3   'A reliable estimate can be made of the amount of the obligation'

The standard takes the view that a sufficiently reliable estimate can almost always be made for a provision where an entity can determine a range of possible outcomes. Hence, the standard contends that it will only be in extremely rare cases that a range of outcomes cannot be determined and so no provision is recognised. *[IAS 37.25].* In these circumstances, the liability should be disclosed as a contingent liability (see disclosure requirements at 6.2 below). *[IAS 37.26].* Whether such a situation is as rare as the standard asserts is open to question, especially for entities trying to determine estimates relating to potential obligations that arise from litigation and other legal claims (see 5.12 below).

3.2   Contingencies

IAS 37 says that contingent liabilities and contingent assets should not be recognised, but only disclosed. *[IAS 37.27-28, 31, 34].*

Contingent liabilities that are recognised separately as part of allocating the cost of a business combination are covered by the requirements of IFRS 3. *[IFRS 3.23].* Such liabilities continue to be measured after the business combination at the higher of: *[IFRS 3.56]*

(a)   the amount that would be recognised in accordance with IAS 37, and

(b)   the amount initially recognised less, if appropriate, cumulative amortisation recognised in accordance with IAS 18.

The requirements in respect of contingent liabilities identified in a business combination are discussed in Chapter 10 at 5.6.1.

3.2.1   Contingent liabilities

A contingent liability has been defined in the standard as: *[IAS 37.10]*

(a)   a possible obligation that arises from past events and whose existence will be confirmed only by the occurrence or non-occurrence of one or more uncertain future events not wholly within the control of the entity; or

(b)   a present obligation that arises from past events but is not recognised because:

  (i)   it is not probable that an outflow of resources embodying economic benefits will be required to settle the obligation; or

  (ii)   the amount of the obligation cannot be measured with sufficient reliability.

This definition is not easy to understand because a natural meaning of 'contingent' would include any event whose outcome depends on future circumstances. The meaning is perhaps clearer when considering those obligations that the then IASC decided did not merit recognition as a provision. On that basis a contingent liability under IAS 37 means one of the following obligations that arise from past events:

(a)   an obligation that is estimated to be less than 50+% likely to exist. Where it is more likely than not that a present obligation exists at the end of the reporting period, a provision is recognised. *[IAS 37.16(a)]*. Where it is more likely that no present obligation exists, a contingent liability is disclosed (unless the possibility is remote); *[IAS 37.16(b)]* or

(b)   a present obligation that has a less than 50+% chance of requiring an outflow of economic benefits. Where it is not probable that a present obligation exists, an entity discloses a contingent liability (unless the possibility is remote); *[IAS 37.23]* or

(c)   a present obligation for which a sufficiently reliable estimate cannot be made. In these rare circumstances, a liability cannot be recognised and it is disclosed as a contingent liability. *[IAS 37.26]*.

The term 'possible' is not defined, but literally it could mean any probability greater than 0% and less than 100%. However, the standard effectively divides this range into four components, namely 'remote', 'possible but not probable', 'probable' and 'virtually certain'. The standard requires a provision to be recognised if 'it is more likely than not that a present obligation exists at the end of the reporting period'. *[IAS 37.16(a)]*. Therefore, IAS 37 distinguishes between a 'probable' obligation (which is more likely than not to exist and, therefore requires recognition as a provision) and a 'possible' obligation (for which either the existence of a present obligation is yet to be confirmed or where the probability of an outflow of resources is 50% or less). *[IAS 37.13]*. Appendix A to IAS 37, in summarising the main requirements of the standard, uses the phrase 'a possible obligation ... that may, but probably will not, require an outflow of resources'. Accordingly, the definition restricts contingent liabilities to those where either the existence of the liability or the transfer of economic benefits arising is less than 50+% probable (or where the obligation cannot be measured at all, but as noted at 3.1.3 above, this would be relatively rare).

The standard's definition of a contingent liability is therefore tortuous and counter-intuitive. To say that a contingent liability is no longer contingent if it becomes more than 50% probable can cause a great deal of confusion. However, this interpretation is a corollary to the criteria for recognition of a provision, which are the (more likely than not) existence of a present obligation; the probable outflow of economic benefits; and the ability to reliably estimate the amount of the obligation. *[IAS 37.14]*.

Chapter 29

The standard requires that contingent liabilities are assessed continually to determine whether an outflow of resources embodying economic benefits has become probable. Where this becomes the case, then provision should be made in the period in which the change in probability occurs (except in the rare circumstances where no reliable estimate can be made). *[IAS 37.30].*

Example 29.4:   When the likelihood of an outflow of benefits becomes probable

After a wedding in 2011, ten people died, possibly as a result of food poisoning from products sold by the entity. Legal proceedings are started seeking damages from the entity. The entity disputes any liability and, up to the date on which its financial statements for the year ended 31 December 2011 are authorised for issue, its lawyers have advised that is probable that the entity will not be found liable. However, when the entity prepares its financial statements for the year ended 31 December 2012, its lawyers advise that, owing to developments in the case, it is probable that the entity will be found liable.

At 31 December 2011, no provision is recognised and the matter is disclosed as a contingent liability unless the probability of any outflow is regarded as remote. On the basis of the evidence available when the financial statements were approved, there is no obligation as a result of a past event.

At 31 December 2012, a provision is recognised for the best estimate of the amount required to settle the obligation. The fact that an outflow of economic benefits is now believed to be probable means that there is a present obligation. *[IAS 37 Appendix C, Example 10].*

3.2.2   Contingent assets

A contingent asset is defined in a more intuitive way. It is 'a possible asset that arises from past events and whose existence will be confirmed only by the occurrence or non-occurrence of one or more uncertain future events not wholly within the control of the entity'. *[IAS 37.10].* In this case, the word 'possible' is *not* confined to a level of probability of 50% or less, which may further increase the confusion over the different meaning of the term in the definition of contingent liabilities.

Contingent assets usually arise from unplanned or other unexpected events that give rise to the possibility of an inflow of economic benefits to the entity. An example is a claim that an entity is pursuing through legal process, where the outcome is uncertain. *[IAS 37.32].*

The standard states that a contingent asset should not be recognised, as this could give rise to recognition of income that may never be realised. However, when the realisation of income is virtually certain, then the related asset is no longer regarded as contingent and recognition is appropriate. *[IAS 37.33].*

Virtual certainty is not defined in the standard, but it is certainly a much higher hurdle than 'probable' and arguably more challenging than the term 'highly probable', defined in IAS 39 – *Financial Instruments: Recognition and Measurement* – as indicating a much greater likelihood of happening than the term 'more likely than not' *[IAS 39.F.3.7]* and in IFRS 5 as 'significantly more likely than probable'. *[IFRS 5 Appendix A].* In practice, virtual certainty is interpreted as being at least 95% likely to occur.

The standard requires disclosure of the contingent asset when the inflow of economic benefits is probable. *[IAS 37.34].* For the purposes of the standard 'probable' means that the event is more likely than not to occur; that is, it has a probability greater than 50%. *[IAS 37.23].* The disclosure requirements are detailed at 6.3 below.

As with contingent liabilities, any contingent assets should be assessed continually to ensure that developments are appropriately reflected in the financial statements. If it has become virtually certain that an inflow of economic benefits will arise, the asset and the related income should be recognised in the period in which the change occurs. If a previously unlikely inflow becomes probable, then the contingent asset should be disclosed. *[IAS 37.35]*.

The requirement to recognise the effect of changing circumstances in the period in which the change occurs extends to the analysis of information available after the end of the reporting period and before the date of approval of the financial statements. In our view, such information would not give rise to an adjusting event after the reporting period. In contrast to contingent liabilities (in respect of which IAS 10 includes as a specific example of an adjusting event 'the settlement after the reporting period of a court case that confirms that the entity had a present obligation at the end of the reporting period' *[IAS 10.9]*), no adjustment should be made to reflect the subsequent settlement of a legal claim in favour of the entity. In this instance, the period in which the change occurs is subsequent to the reporting period. There is also no suggestion that the example in IAS 10 is referring to anything but liabilities. An asset could only be recognised if, at the end of the reporting period, the entity could show that it was virtually certain that its claim would succeed.

3.2.3 Summary

The following matrix summarises the treatment of contingencies under IAS 37:

Likelihood of outcome	Accounting treatment: contingent liability	Accounting treatment: contingent asset
Virtually certain (say, >95% probable)	Not a contingent liability, therefore recognise	Not a contingent asset, therefore recognise
Probable (say, 50-95% probable)	Not a contingent liability, therefore recognise	Disclose
Possible but not probable (say, 5-50% probable)	Disclose	No disclosure permitted
Remote (say, <5% probable)	No disclosure required	No disclosure permitted

The standard does not put a numerical measure of probability on either 'virtually certain' or 'remote', which lie at the outer ends of the range, but we think it reasonable to regard them as falling above the 95th percentile and below the fifth percentile respectively. However, these are not definitive guides and each case must be decided on its merits. In any event, it is usually possible to assess the probability of the outcome of a particular event only very approximately.

Chapter 29

3.3   Recognising an asset when recognising a provision

In most cases, the recognition of a provision results in an immediate expense in profit or loss. Nevertheless, in some cases it may be appropriate to recognise an asset. These issues are not discussed in IAS 37, which neither prohibits nor requires capitalisation of the costs recognised when a provision is made. It states that other standards specify whether expenditures are treated as assets or expenses. *[IAS 37.8].*

This issue was dealt with explicitly in FRS 12, the UK equivalent standard. FRS 12 establishes a principle that when a provision is recognised or changed, an asset is also recognised when, and only when, the incurring of the present obligation recognised as a provision gives access to future economic benefits; otherwise the setting up of the provision should be charged immediately to the profit and loss account.[2]

FRS 12 contains a specific reference to the recognition of an asset at the same time as a provision for decommissioning costs.[3] Whilst the main body of IAS 37 is silent on the matter, the standard contains the following example that arrives at the same conclusion that an asset should be recognised when a decommissioning provision is established. *[IAS 37 Appendix C, Example 3].*

Example 29.5:   When the recognition of a provision gives rise to an asset

An entity operates an offshore oilfield where its licensing agreement requires it to remove the oil rig at the end of production and restore the seabed. 90% of the eventual costs relate to the removal of the oil rig and restoration of damage caused by building it, with 10% expected to arise through the extraction of oil. At the end of the reporting period, the rig has been constructed but no oil has been extracted.

A provision is recognised in respect of the probable costs relating to the removal of the rig and restoring damage caused by building it. This is because the construction of the rig, combined with the requirement under the licence to remove the rig and restore the seabed, creates an obligating event as at the end of the reporting period. These costs are included as part of the cost of the oil rig.

However, there is no obligation to rectify any damage that will be caused by the future extraction of oil.

This conclusion is supported by IAS 16, which requires the cost of an item of property, plant and equipment to include the initial estimate of the costs of dismantling and removing an asset and restoring the site on which it is located, the obligation for which an entity incurs either when the item is acquired or as a consequence of having used the item during a particular period for purposes other than to produce inventories during that period. *[IAS 16.16(c), 18].* The treatment of decommissioning costs is discussed further at 5.5 below.

4   MEASUREMENT

4.1   Best estimate of provision

IAS 37 requires the amount to be recognised as a provision to be the best estimate of the expenditure required to settle the present obligation at the end of the reporting period. *[IAS 37.36].* This measure is determined before tax, as the tax consequences of the provision, and changes to it, are dealt with under IAS 12. *[IAS 37.41].*

The standard equates this 'best estimate' with 'the amount that an entity would rationally pay to settle the obligation at the end of the reporting period or to transfer it to a third party at that time'. *[IAS 37.37]*. It is interesting that a hypothetical transaction of this kind should be proposed as the conceptual basis of the measurement required, rather than putting the main emphasis upon the actual expenditure that is expected to be incurred in the future.

The standard does acknowledge that it would often be impossible or prohibitively expensive to settle or transfer the obligation at the end of the reporting period. However, it goes on to state that 'the estimate of the amount that an entity would rationally pay to settle or transfer the obligation gives the best estimate of the expenditure required to settle the present obligation at the end of the reporting period'. *[IAS 37.37]*.

The estimates of outcome and financial effect are determined by the judgement of the entity's management, supplemented by experience of similar transactions and, in some cases, reports from independent experts. The evidence considered will include any additional evidence provided by events after the reporting period. *[IAS 37.38]*.

The standard suggests that there are various ways of dealing with the uncertainties surrounding the amount to be recognised as a provision. It mentions three, an expected value (or probability-weighted) method; the mid-point of the range of possible outcomes; and an estimate of the individual most likely outcome. An expected value approach would be appropriate when a large population of items is being measured, such as warranty costs. This is a statistical computation which weights the cost of all the various possible outcomes according to their probabilities, as illustrated in the following example taken from IAS 37. *[IAS 37.39, 40]*.

Example 29.6:   Calculation of expected value

An entity sells goods with a warranty under which customers are covered for the cost of repairs of any manufacturing defects that become apparent within the first six months after purchase. If minor defects were detected in all products sold, repair costs of £1 million would result. If major defects were detected in all products sold, repair costs of £4 million would result. The entity's past experience and future expectations indicate that, for the coming year, 75 per cent of the goods sold will have no defects, 20 per cent of the goods sold will have minor defects and 5 per cent of the goods sold will have major defects. In accordance with paragraph 24 of IAS 37 (see 3.1.2 above) an entity assesses the probability of a transfer for the warranty obligations as a whole.

The expected value of the cost of repairs is:

(75% of nil) + (20% of £1m) + (5% of £4m) = £400,000.

In a situation where there is a continuous range of possible outcomes and each point in that range is as likely as any other, IAS 37 requires that the mid-point of the range is used. *[IAS 37.39]*. This is not a particularly helpful example. It does not make it clear what the principle is meant to be, since the mid-point in this case represents the median as well as the expected value. The latter may have been what the IASC had in mind, but the median could be equally well justified on the basis that it is 50% probable that at least this amount will be payable, while anything in excess of that constitutes a possible but not a probable liability, that should be disclosed rather than accrued. Interestingly, US GAAP has a different approach to this issue in relation to contingencies. FASB ASC Topic 450 – *Contingencies* – states that where a contingent loss could fall within a range of amounts then, if there is a best estimate within the range, it should be accrued, with the remainder noted as a contingent liability. However, if there is no best estimate then the *lowest* figure within the range should be accrued, with the remainder up to the maximum potential loss noted as a contingent liability.[4]

Where the obligation being measured relates to a single item, the standard suggests that the best estimate of the liability may be the individual most likely outcome. However, even in such a case, it notes that consideration should be given to other possible outcomes. It gives an example of an entity that has to rectify a fault in a major plant that it has constructed for a customer. The most likely outcome is that the repair will succeed at the first attempt. However, a provision should be made for a larger amount if there is a significant chance that further attempts will be necessary. *[IAS 37.40]*. This again sounds like a vague leaning towards an expected value approach.

4.2   Dealing with risk and uncertainty in measuring a provision

It is clear from the definition of a provision as a liability of uncertain timing or amount that entities will have to deal with risk and uncertainty in estimating an appropriate measure of the obligation at the end of the reporting period. It is therefore interesting to consider how the measurement rules detailed in IAS 37 help entities achieve a faithful representation of the obligation in these circumstances. A faithful representation requires estimates that are neutral, that is, free from any bias. *[Framework.QC12, QC14]*. The *Framework* warns against the use of undue conservatism or prudence in estimates because this is 'likely to lead to a bias'. It adds that the exercise of prudence can be counterproductive, in that the overstatement of liabilities in one period frequently leads to overstated financial performance in later periods, 'a result that cannot be described as prudent or neutral'. *[Framework.BC3.28]*.

The standard does not refer to neutrality as such; however it does discuss the concept of risk and the need for exercising caution and care in making judgements under conditions of uncertainty. It states that 'the risks and uncertainties that inevitably surround many events and circumstances shall be taken into account in reaching the best estimate of a provision'. *[IAS 37.42]*. It refers to risk as being variability of outcome and suggests that a risk adjustment may increase the amount at which a liability is measured, but gives no indication of how this may be done. At the same time it warns that caution is needed in making judgements under conditions of uncertainty, so that expenses or liabilities are not understated. However, it says that uncertainty does not justify the creation of excessive provisions or a deliberate overstatement of liabilities. Accordingly, care is needed to avoid duplicating adjustments for risk and uncertainty, for example by estimating the costs of a particularly adverse outcome and then overestimating its probability. *[IAS 37.43]*. Any uncertainties surrounding the amount of the expenditure are to be disclosed (see 6.1 below). *[IAS 37.44]*.

The overall result of all this is somewhat confusing. Whilst a best estimate based solely on the expected value approach or the mid-point of a range addresses the uncertainties relating to there being a variety of possible outcomes, it does not fully reflect risk, because the actual outcome could still be higher or lower than the estimate. Therefore, the discussion on risk suggests that an additional adjustment should be made. However, apart from indicating that the result may be to increase the recognised liability and pointing out the need to avoid duplicating the effect of risk in estimates of cash flows and probability, *[IAS 37.43]*, it is not clear quite how this might be achieved. This rather vague drafting leaves a certain amount of scope for variation in the estimation of provisions and is further complicated when the concept of risk is combined with considerations relating to the time value of money (see 4.3.2 below).

4.3 Discounting the estimated cash flows to a present value

The standard requires that where the effect of the time value of money is material, the amount of a provision should be the present value of the expenditures expected to be required to settle the obligation. *[IAS 37.45]*. The discount rate (or rates) to be used in arriving at the present value should be 'a pre-tax rate (or rates) that reflect(s) current market assessments of the time value of money and the risks specific to the liability. The discount rate(s) shall not reflect risks for which the future cash flow estimates have been adjusted.' *[IAS 37.47]*. However, it is worth noting that for many provisions, no discounting will be required as the cash flows will not be sufficiently far into the future for discounting to have a material impact. *[IAS 37.46]*.

IAS 37 gives no guidance as to how these requirements are to be applied. On the other hand, FRS 12 in the UK gives some guidance on the discount rate to be used in the net present value calculation. The main types of provision where the impact of discounting will be significant are those relating to decommissioning and other environmental restoration liabilities. IFRIC 1 addresses some of the issues relating to the use of discounting (in the context of provisions for obligations to dismantle, remove or restore items of property, plant and equipment, referred to as 'decommissioning, restoration and similar liabilities') which are discussed at 5.5.1 below.

4.3.1 Real v. nominal rate

IAS 37 does not indicate whether the discount rate should be a real discount rate or a nominal discount rate (although a real discount rate is referred to in Example 2 in Appendix D which illustrates the narrative disclosure for decommissioning costs). FRS 12 in the UK notes that the discount rate used depends on whether:[5]

(a)   the future cash flows are expressed in current prices, in which case a real discount rate (which excludes the effects of general inflation) should be used; or

(b)   the future cash flows are expressed in expected future prices, in which case a nominal discount rate (which includes a return to cover expected inflation) should be used.

FRS 12 then allows either method to be used, and both these methods may produce the same figure for the initial present value of the provision. However, the effect of the unwinding of the discount will be different in each case (see 4.3.5 below). In Extract 29.7 at 5.4 below, BP plc discloses how its provision for the costs of decommissioning production facilities and pipelines is estimated using current prices and discounted using a real rate.

4.3.2 Adjusting for risk

IAS 37 also requires that risk is taken into account in the calculation of a provision, but gives little guidance as to how this should be done. Where discounting is concerned, it merely says that the discount rate should not reflect risks for which the future cash flow estimates have been adjusted. *[IAS 37.47]*. FRS 12 in the UK suggests that using a discount rate that reflects the risk associated with the liability (a risk-adjusted rate) may be easier than trying to adjust the future cash flows for risk.[6] It gives no indication of how to calculate such a risk adjusted rate, but a little more information can be obtained from the ASB's earlier Working Paper – *Discounting in Financial Reporting*[7] – on which the following example is based.

Example 29.7:   Calculation of a risk-adjusted rate[8]

A company has a provision for which the expected value of the cash outflow in three years' time is £150, and the risk-free rate (i.e. the nominal rate unadjusted for risk) is 5%. However, the possible outcomes from which the expected value has been determined lie within a range between £100 and £200. The company is risk averse and would settle instead for a certain payment of, say, £160 in three years' time rather than be exposed to the risk of the actual outcome being as high as £200. The effect of risk in calculating the present value can be expressed as either:

(a)   discounting the risk-adjusted cash flow of £160 at the risk-free (unadjusted) rate of 5%, giving a present value of £138; or

(b)   discounting the expected cash flow (which is unadjusted for risk) of £150 at a risk-adjusted rate that will give the present value of £138, i.e. a rate of 2.8%.

As can be seen from this example, the risk-adjusted discount rate is a *lower* rate than the unadjusted (risk-free) discount rate. This may seem counter-intuitive initially, because the experience of most borrowers is that banks and other lenders will charge a higher rate of interest on loans that are assessed to be higher risk to the lender. However, in the case of a provision a risk premium is being suffered to eliminate the possibility of the actual cost being higher (thereby capping a liability), whereas in the case of a loan a premium is required to compensate the lender for taking on the risk of not recovering its full value (setting a floor for the value of the lender's financial asset). In both cases the actual cash flows incurred by the paying entity are higher to reflect a premium for risk. In other words, the discount rate for an asset is increased to reflect the risk of recovering less and the discount rate for a liability is reduced to reflect the risk of paying more.

A problem with changing the discount rate to account for risk is that this adjusted rate is a theoretical rate and has no obvious meaning in real life. However a lower discount rate is consistent with the premise that a risk-adjusted liability should be higher than a liability without risk. *[IAS 37.43]*. It is also possible for the adjusted rate to be negative, although in practice the maximum amount a liability could increase to is the nominal amount of the expected future cash flow. It is also difficult to see how a risk-adjusted rate could be obtained in practice. In the above example, it was obtained only by reverse-engineering; it was already known that the net present value of a risk-adjusted liability was £138, so the risk-adjusted rate was just the discount rate applied to unadjusted cash flow of £150 to give that result.

FRS 12 does offer an alternative approach – instead of using a risk-adjusted discount rate, the cash flows themselves can be adjusted for risk and then discounted using a risk-free (unadjusted) rate.[9] This does of course present the problem of how to adjust the cash flows for risk. However, this may be easier than attempting to risk-adjust the discount rate.

FRS 12 suggests that an example of a risk-free rate would be a government bond rate.[10] Presumably, this government bond rate should strictly have a similar remaining term to the liability, although this is not specified in FRS 12. For the purposes of discounting post-employment benefit obligations, IAS 19 requires the discount rate to be determined by reference to market yields at the end of the reporting period on high quality corporate bonds (although in countries where there is no deep market in such bonds, the market yields on government bonds should be used). *[IAS 19.78]*. Although IAS 19 indicates that this discount rate reflects the time value of money (but not the actuarial or investment risk), *[IAS 19.79]*, we do not believe it is appropriate to use the yield on a high quality corporate bond for determining a risk-free rate to be used in discounting provisions under IAS 37. Accordingly, in our view, where an entity is using a risk-free discount rate for the purposes of calculating a provision under IAS 37, that rate should be based on a government bond rate with a similar currency and remaining term as the provision. It follows that because a risk-adjusted rate is always lower than the risk-free rate, an entity cannot justify the discounting of a provision at a rate that is higher than a government bond rate with a similar currency and term to the provision.

Whichever method of reflecting risk is adopted, IAS 37 emphasises that care must be taken that the effect of risk is not double-counted by inclusion in both the cash flows and the discount rate. *[IAS 37.47]*.

4.3.3 Own credit risk

In considering the risk factors that might give rise to a difference between the actual cash flows required to settle a liability and their previously estimated amounts, an entity would not take into account its own credit risk; that is, the risk that the entity could be unable to settle the amount finally determined to be payable. This is because IAS 37 requires the discount rate to reflect 'the risks specific to the liability'. *[IAS 37.47]*. Credit risk usually relates to the entity subject to the obligation rather than to the liability itself.

In deciding not to take to its agenda a request for guidance on this matter, the Interpretations Committee acknowledged that IAS 37 is not explicit on the question of own credit risk; but understood that the predominant practice was to exclude it for this reason.[11]

4.3.4 Pre-tax discount rate

Since IAS 37 requires provisions to be measured before tax, it follows that cash flows should be discounted at a pre-tax discount rate. *[IAS 37.47]*. No further explanation of this is given in the standard. On the other hand, FRS 12 in the UK does have some discussion about pre- and post-tax rates in an appendix.[12]

However, it is unlikely that entities will need to compute a pre-tax rate from post-tax information. This is because, in reality, the discount rate will be calculated directly as a pre-tax discount rate. Supposing, for example, that the risk-free rate of return is being used, then the discount rate used will be a government bond rate. This rate will be obtained gross. Thus, the idea of obtaining a required post-tax rate of return and adjusting it for the tax consequences of different cash flows will seldom be relevant.

Chapter 29

The calculation is illustrated in the following example.

Example 29.8:   Use of discounting and tax effect

It is estimated that the settlement of an environmental provision will give rise to a gross cash outflow of £500,000 in three years time. The gross interest rate on a government bond maturing in three years time is 6%. The tax rate is 30%.

The net present value of the provision is £419,810 (£500,000 × 1 ÷ $(1.06)^3$). Hence, a provision of £419,810 should be booked in the balance sheet. A corresponding deferred tax asset of £125,943 (30% of £419,810) would be set up if it met the criteria for recognition in IAS 12. (See Chapter 31 at 7.4).

4.3.5   Unwinding of the discount

IAS 37 indicates that where discounting is used, the carrying amount of a provision increases in each period to reflect the passage of time, and that this increase is recognised as a borrowing cost. *[IAS 37.60]*. This is the only guidance that the standard gives on the unwinding of the discount. IFRIC 1 in relation to provisions for decommissioning, restoration and similar liabilities requires that the periodic unwinding of the discount is recognised in profit or loss as a finance cost as it occurs. The Interpretations Committee concluded that the unwinding of the discount is not a borrowing cost as defined in IAS 23 – *Borrowing Costs* – and thus cannot be capitalised under that standard. *[IFRIC 1.8]*.

However, there is no discussion of the impact that the original selection of discount rate can have on its unwinding, that is the selection of real versus nominal rates, and risk-free versus risk-adjusted rates. The IASB (and the ASB for its part) appear to have overlooked the fact that these different discount rates will unwind differently. This is best illustrated by way of an example.

Example 29.9:   Effect on future profits of choosing a real or nominal discount rate

A provision is required to be set up for an expected cash outflow of €100,000 (estimated at current prices), payable in three years' time. The appropriate nominal discount rate is 7.5%, and inflation is estimated at 5%. If the provision is discounted using the nominal rate, the expected cash outflow has to reflect future prices. Accordingly, if prices increase at the rate of inflation, the cash outflow will be €115,762 (€100,000 × 1.05^3). The net present value of €115,762, discounted at 7.5%, is €93,184 (€115,762 × 1 ÷ $(1.075)^3$). If all assumptions remain valid throughout the three-year period, the movement in the provision would be as follows:

	Undiscounted cash flows	Provision
	€	€
Year 0	115,762	93,184
Unwinding of discount (€93,184 × 0.075)		6,989
Revision to estimate		–
Year 1	115,762	100,173
Unwinding of discount (€100,173 × 0.075)		7,513
Revision to estimate		–
Year 2	115,762	107,686
Unwinding of discount (€107,686 × 0.075)		8,076
Revision to estimate		–
Year 3	115,762	115,762

If the provision is calculated based on the expected cash outflow of €100,000 (estimated at current prices), then it needs to be discounted using a real discount rate. This may be thought to be 2.5%, being the difference between the nominal rate of 7.5% and the inflation rate of 5%. However, it is more accurately calculated using the Fisher relation or formula as 2.381%, being $(1.075 \div 1.05) - 1$. Accordingly, the net present value of €100,000, discounted at 2.381%, is €93,184 ($€100,000 \times 1 \div (1.02381)^3$), the same as the calculation using future prices discounted at the nominal rate.

If all assumptions remain valid throughout the three-year period, the movement in the provision would be as follows:

	Undiscounted cash flows	Provision
	€	€
Year 0	100,000	93,184
Unwinding of discount (€93,184 × 0.02381)		2,219
Revision to estimate (€100,000 × 0.05)	5,000	4,770
Year 1	105,000	100,173
Unwinding of discount (€100,173 × 0.02381)		2,385
Revision to estimate (€105,000 × 0.05)	5,250	5,128
Year 2	110,250	107,686
Unwinding of discount (€107,686 × 0.02381)		2,564
Revision to estimate (€110,250 × 0.05)	5,512	5,512
Year 3	115,762	115,762

It can be seen from the second table in the above example that using the real discount rate will give rise to a much lower finance charge each year. However, this does not lead to a lower provision in the balance sheet at the end of each year. Provisions have to be revised annually to reflect the current best estimate of the obligation. *[IAS 37.59]*. Thus, the provision in the above example at the end of each year needs to be adjusted to reflect current prices at that time (and any other adjustments that arise from changes in estimate of the provision), as well as being adjusted for the unwinding of the discount. For example, the revised provision at the end of Year 1 is €100,173, being €105,000 discounted for two years at 2.381%. After allowing for the unwinding of the discount, this required an additional provision of €4,770. Although the total expense in each year is the same under either method, what will be different under the two methods is the allocation of the change in provision between operating costs (assuming the original provision was treated as an operating expense) and finance charges. If the real discount rate is used, the finance charge each year will be lower and the operating costs higher than if the nominal rate is used.

A more significant difference will arise where the recognition of the original provision is included as part of the cost of property, plant or equipment, rather than an expense, such as when a decommissioning provision is recognised. In that case, using a real discount rate will result initially in a lower charge to the income statement, since under IFRIC 1 any revision to the estimate of the provision is not taken to the income statement but is treated as an adjustment to the carrying value of the related asset, which is then depreciated prospectively over the remaining life of the asset (see 5.5.1 below).

A similar issue arises with the option of using the risk-free or the risk-adjusted discount rate. However, this is a more complex problem, because it is not clear what to do with the risk-adjustment built into the provision. This is illustrated in the following example, using the same facts as in Example 29.7 at 4.3.2 above:

Example 29.10:   Effect on future profits of choosing a risk-free or risk-adjusted rate

As before, a company is required to make a provision for which the expected value of the cash outflow in three years' time is £150, when the risk-free rate (i.e. the rate unadjusted for risk) is 5%. However, the possible outcomes from which the expected value has been determined lie within a range between £100 and £200. The reporting entity is risk averse and would settle instead for a certain payment of, say, £160 in three years' time rather than be exposed to the risk of the actual outcome being as high as £200. The measurement options to account for risk can be expressed as either:

(a)   discounting the risk-adjusted cash flow of £160 is discounted at the risk-free (unadjusted) rate of 5%, giving a present value of £138; or

(b)   discounting the expected cash flow (which is unadjusted for risk) of £150 at a risk-adjusted rate that will give the present value of £138, i.e. a rate of 2.8%.

Assuming that there are no changes in estimate required to be made to the provision during the three-year period, alternative (a) will unwind to give an overall finance charge of £22 and a final provision of £160. Alternative (b) will unwind to give an overall finance charge of £12 and a final provision of £150.

In this example, the unwinding of different discount rates gives rise to different provisions. The difference of £10 relates to the risk adjustment that has been made to the provision. The standard gives no guidance as to how to treat this £10 if the provision is unwound at the risk-free rate. Given that the expected cash outflow is only £150, this additional £10 is likely to have to be released at some point, but it is unclear how to do this. Two alternatives are that it could be done gradually over the period in which the provision is unwound (perhaps as a reassessment of the required provision as it becomes less risky), or it could be taken in total once the provision has been settled. The lack of explicit guidance in the standard appears to give entities flexibility on this point. However, in reality the estimates of the range of possible outcomes (and accordingly the expected value of the outflow) and the premium the entity would accept for certainty will change over time. As such, the effect of any anomaly related to the decision to apply a risk-free or risk-adjusted rate will be lost in the other estimation adjustments that would be made over time.

4.3.6   The effect of changes in interest rates on the discount rate applied

The standard requires the discount rate to reflect current market assessments of the time value of money. *[IAS 37.47]*. This appears to mean that where interest rates change, the provision should be recalculated on the basis of revised interest rates. This interpretation is reinforced by the disclosure requirement in the standard that entities should disclose the effect of any change in discount rate. *[IAS 37.84(e)]*.

This will give rise to an adjustment to the carrying value of the provision, but the standard does not explicitly say how this should be classified in the income statement. Arguably, it could be treated in the same way as the unwinding of the discount and therefore included as a borrowing or finance cost in the year of change, which may be either a debit or a credit depending on which way interest rates move. However, we believe that the adjustment to the provision is a change in accounting estimate, as defined in IAS 8 – *Accounting Policies, Changes in Accounting Estimates and Errors* (see Chapter 3 at 4.5). Accordingly, it should be reflected in the line item of the income statement in which the expense establishing the provision was originally recorded. Indeed, this latter approach is the one required by IFRIC 1 in relation to provisions for decommissioning, restoration and similar liabilities in relation to assets measured using the cost model (see 5.5.1 below). However, in that case the original provision gives rise to an asset rather than an expense, so any subsequent adjustment is not included in profit or loss *[IAS 8.36]*, but added to or deducted from the cost of the asset to which it relates *[IFRIC 1.5]*. The adjusted depreciable amount of the asset is then depreciated prospectively over its remaining useful life. *[IFRIC 1.7]*.

Calculating this adjustment is not straightforward either, because the standard gives no specific guidance on how it should be done. For example, it is unclear whether the new discount rate should be applied during the year or just at the year-end, and whether the rate should be applied to the new estimate of the provision or the old estimate. IFRIC 1 implies that the finance cost is adjusted after the date on which the liability is remeasured. Example 1 to IFRIC 1 states that if the change in the liability had resulted from a change in discount rate, instead of a change in the estimated cash flows, the change would still have been reflected in the carrying value of the related asset, but next year's finance cost would have reflected the new discount rate. *[IFRIC 1.IE5]*. Because IAS 37 requires the value of a provision to reflect the best estimate of the expenditure required to settle the obligation to be assessed as at the end of the reporting period, *[IAS 37.36]*, it would appear that the effect of a change in the estimated discount rate is accounted for prospectively from the end of the reporting period, as illustrated in the following example.

Example 29.11: Accounting for the effect of changes in the discount rate

A provision is required to be set up for an expected cash outflow of €100,000 (estimated at current prices), payable in three years' time. The appropriate nominal discount rate is 7.5%, and inflation is estimated at 5%. At future prices the cash outflow will be €115,762 (€100,000 × 1.05³). The net present value of €115,762, discounted at 7.5%, is €93,184 (€115,762 × 1 ÷ (1.075)³).

At the end of Year 2, all assumptions remain valid, except it is determined that a current market assessment of the time value of money and the risks specific to the liability would require a decrease in the discount rate to 6.5%. Accordingly, at the end of Year 2, the revised net present value of €115,762, discounted at 6.5%, is €108,697 (€115,762 ÷ 1.065).

The movement in the provision would be reflected as follows:

	Undiscounted cash flows	Provision
	€	€
Year 0	115,762	93,184
Unwinding of discount (€93,184 × 0.075)		6,989
Revision to estimate		–
Year 1	115,762	100,173
Unwinding of discount (€100,173 × 0.075)		7,513
	115,762	107,686
Revision to estimate (€108,697 – €107,686)		1,011
Year 2	115,762	108,697
Unwinding of discount (€108,697 × 0.065)		7,065
Revision to estimate		–
Year 3	115,762	115,762

Chapter 29

In Year 2, the finance charge is based on the previous estimate of the discount rate and the revision to the estimate of the provision would be charged to the same line item in the income statement that was used to establish the provision of €93,184 at the start of Year 1.

4.4   Anticipating future events that may affect the estimate of cash flows

The standard states that 'future events that may affect the amount required to settle an obligation shall be reflected in the amount of a provision where there is sufficient objective evidence that they will occur'. *[IAS 37.48]*. The types of future events that the standard has in mind are advances in technology and changes in legislation.

The requirement for objective evidence means that it is not appropriate to reduce the best estimate of future cash flows simply by assuming that an unspecified new technology will be developed before the liability is required to be settled. There will need to be sufficient objective evidence that such future developments are likely. For example, an entity may believe that the cost of cleaning up a site at the end of its life will be reduced by future changes in technology. The amount recognised has to reflect a reasonable expectation of technically qualified, objective observers, taking account of all available evidence as to the technology that will be available at the time of the clean-up. Thus it is appropriate to include, for example, expected cost reductions associated with increased experience in applying existing technology or the expected cost of applying existing technology to a larger or more complex clean-up operation than has previously been carried out. However, an entity does not anticipate the development of a completely new technology for cleaning up unless it is supported by sufficient objective evidence. *[IAS 37.49]*.

Similarly, if new legislation is to be anticipated, there will need to be evidence both of what the legislation will demand and whether it is virtually certain to be enacted and implemented. In many cases sufficient objective evidence will not exist until the new legislation is enacted. *[IAS 37.50]*.

These requirements are most likely to impact provisions for liabilities that will be settled some distance in the future, such as decommissioning costs (see 5.5 below).

4.5   Reimbursements and other recoveries from third parties

In some circumstances an entity is able to look to a third party to reimburse part of the costs required to settle a provision or to pay the amounts directly. Examples are insurance contracts, indemnity clauses and suppliers' warranties. *[IAS 37.55]*. A reimbursement asset is recognised only when it is virtually certain to be received if the entity settles the obligation. The asset cannot be greater than the amount of the provision. No 'netting off' is allowed in the balance sheet, with any asset classified separately from any provision. *[IAS 37.53]*. However, the expense relating to a provision can be shown in the income statement net of reimbursement. *[IAS 37.54]*.

The main area of concern with these requirements is whether the 'virtually certain' criterion that needs to be applied to the corresponding asset might mean that some reimbursements will not be capable of recognition at all. For items such as insurance contracts, this may not be an issue, as entities will probably be able to confirm the existence of cover for the obligation in question and accordingly be able to demonstrate that a recovery on an insurance contract is virtually certain if the entity is required to settle the obligation. Of course, it may be more difficult in complex situations for an entity to confirm it has cover against any loss. For other types of reimbursement, it may be more difficult to establish that recovery is virtually certain.

In the majority of cases where a recovery is expected, a net presentation in the balance sheet is prohibited. This is because the entity would remain liable for the whole cost if the third party failed to pay for any reason, for example as a result of the third party's insolvency. In such situations, the provision should be made gross and any reimbursement should be treated as a separate asset (but only when it is virtually certain that the reimbursement will be received if the entity settles the obligation). *[IAS 37.56]*.

If the entity has no liability in the event that the third party cannot pay, then these costs are excluded from the estimate of the provision altogether because, by its very nature, there is no liability. *[IAS 37.57]*.

Extract 29.1 at 4.6 illustrates how Syngenta classifies amounts recoverable from third parties as separate assets.

A generally accepted exception to gross presentation for an expected recovery is a vacant leasehold property provision, where the amount of the provision is determined net of the cash flows that may be expected to arise from sub-letting the property. This is discussed further at 5.3.

4.6 Joint and several liability

It is interesting to contrast the approach of IAS 37 to reimbursements with the case where an entity is jointly and severally liable for an obligation. In that case, the entity recognises only its own share of the obligation, based on the amount it is probable that the entity will pay. The remainder that is expected to be met by other parties is treated only as a contingent liability. *[IAS 37.29, 58]*.

The fact that the other third parties in this situation have a direct (albeit shared) obligation for the past event itself, rather than only a contractual relationship with the entity, is enough of a difference in circumstances to allow a form of net determination of the amount to recognise. Arguably, however, the economic position is similar, whereby the entity is exposed to further loss in the event that the third parties are unable or unwilling to pay. If joint and several liability was treated in the same way as reimbursement, then a liability would have to be set up for the whole amount for which the entity is jointly and severally liable, with a corresponding asset being recognised for the amount expected to be met by other parties.

Chapter 29

The extract below illustrates how Syngenta describes its policy for the classification of amounts recoverable from third parties and measurement where liability is joint and several.

Extract 29.1: Syngenta AG (2010)

2.   Accounting policies [extract]
Provisions

A provision is recognized in the balance sheet when Syngenta has a legal or constructive obligation to a third party or parties as a result of a past event the amount of which can be reliably estimated and it is probable that an outflow of economic benefits will be required to settle the obligation. The amount recognized as a provision is the best estimate of the expenditure required to settle the obligation at the balance sheet date. If the effect of discounting is material, provisions are discounted to the expected present value of the future cash flows using a pre-tax rate that reflects current market assessments of the time value of money and, where appropriate, the risks specific to the liability. Where some or all of the expenditures required to settle a provision are expected to be reimbursed by another party, the expected reimbursement is recognized as a separate asset only when virtually certain. Where Syngenta has a joint and several liability for a matter with one or more other parties, no provision is recognized by Syngenta for those parts of the obligation expected to be settled by another party. Syngenta self-insures or uses a combination of insurance and self-insurance for certain risks. Provisions for these risks are estimated in part by considering historical claims experience and other actuarial assumptions and, where necessary, counterparty risk.

4.7   Provisions are not reduced for gains on disposal of related assets

IAS 37 states that gains from the expected disposal of assets should not be taken into account in measuring a provision, even if the expected disposal is closely linked to the event giving rise to the provision. Such gains should be recognised at the time specified by the Standard dealing with the assets concerned. *[IAS 37.51-52].* This is likely to be of particular relevance in relation to restructuring provisions (see 5.2.4 below). However, it may also apply in other situations. Extract 29.8 at 5.5 below illustrates an example of a company excluding gains from the expected disposal of assets in determining its provision for decommissioning costs.

The introduction of the equivalent requirement in FRS 12 in the UK led British Aerospace to write off the sum of £267 million, as shown in this extract:

Extract 29.2: British Aerospace Public Limited Company (1998)

24 Reserves [extract]
FRS 12 – Provisions, contingent liabilities and contingent assets

In previous years, expenditure on rationalisation schemes initiated before 1991 was included within development properties to the extent that it was recoverable from the estimated disposal proceeds. FRS 12 does not permit such expected gains to be taken into account when assessing the level of provision relating to such schemes. These rationalisation costs which amounted to £267 million at 31 December 1997 are now no longer included.

4.8 Changes and uses of provisions

After recognition, a provision will be re-estimated, used and released over the period up to the eventual determination of a settlement amount for the obligation. IAS 37 requires that provisions should be reviewed at the end of each reporting period and adjusted to reflect the current best estimate. If it is no longer probable that an outflow of resources embodying economic benefits will be required to settle the obligation, the provision should be reversed. *[IAS 37.59]*. Where discounting is applied, the carrying amount of a provision increases in each period to reflect the passage of time. This increase is recognised as a borrowing cost. *[IAS 37.60]*. As discussed at 4.3.5 above, the periodic unwinding of the discount is recognised as a finance cost in the income statement, and it is not a borrowing cost capable of being capitalised under IAS 23. *[IFRIC 1.8]*.

The standard does not allow provisions to be redesignated or otherwise used for expenditures for which the provision was not originally recognised. *[IAS 37.61]*. In such circumstances, a new provision is created and the amount no longer needed is reversed, as to do otherwise would conceal the impact of two different events. *[IAS 37.62]*. This means that the questionable practice of charging costs against a provision that was set up for a different purpose is specifically prohibited.

4.9 Changes in contingent liabilities recognised in a business combination

In a business combination, the usual requirements of IAS 37 do not apply and the acquirer recognises a liability at the acquisition date for those contingent liabilities of the acquiree that represent a present obligation arising as a result of a past event and in respect of which the fair value can be measured reliably. *[IFRS 3.23]*. After initial recognition, and until the liability is settled, cancelled or expires, the acquirer measures the contingent liability recognised in a business combination at the higher of: *[IFRS 3.56]*

(a) the amount that would be recognised in accordance with IAS 37; and

(b) the amount initially recognised less, if appropriate, cumulative amortisation recognised in accordance with IAS 18.

This requirement does not apply to contracts accounted for in accordance with IAS 39 and IFRS 9. See Chapter 10 at 5.6.1.B.

This requirement prevents the immediate release to post acquisition profit of any contingency recognised in a business combination.

5 SPECIFIC EXAMPLES OF PROVISIONS AND CONTINGENCIES

IAS 37 expands on its general recognition and measurement by including more specific requirements for particular situations, i.e. future operating losses, future restructuring costs and onerous contracts. This section discusses those situations; looks at other examples, including those addressed in an appendix to the Standard and other areas where the Interpretations Committee has considered how the principles of IAS 37 should be applied.

Chapter 29

5.1   Entities should not provide for future operating losses

IAS 37 explicitly states that 'provisions shall not be recognised for future operating losses'. *[IAS 37.63]*. This is because such losses do not meet the definition of a liability and the general recognition criteria of the standard. *[IAS 37.64]*. In particular there is no present obligation as a result of a past event. Such costs should be left to be recognised as they occur in the future in the same way as future profits.

However, it would be wrong to assume that this requirement has effectively prevented the effect of future operating losses from being anticipated, because they are sometimes recognised as a result of requirements in another standard, either in the measurement of an asset of the entity or to prevent inappropriate recognition of revenue. For example:

- under IAS 2 – *Inventories* – inventories are written down to the extent that they will not be recovered from future revenues, rather than leaving the non-recovery to show up as future operating losses (see Chapter 24 at 3.4);

- under IAS 11 provision is made for losses expected on construction contracts (see Chapter 25 at 3.3.6); and

- under IAS 36 – *Impairment of Assets*, impairment of assets is measured on the basis of the present value of future operating cash flows, meaning that the effect of not only future operating losses but also sub-standard operating profits will be recognised (see Chapter 22). IAS 37 specifically makes reference to the fact that an expectation of future operating losses may be an indication that certain assets are impaired. *[IAS 37.65]*.

This is therefore a rather more complex issue than IAS 37 acknowledges. Indeed, IAS 37 itself has to navigate closely the dividing line between the general prohibition of the recognition of future losses and the recognition of contractual or constructive obligations that are expected to give rise to losses in future periods.

5.2   Restructuring provisions

IAS 37 restricts both the freedom of entities to recognise restructuring provisions and the types of cost that are eligible for inclusion in such provisions, as discussed below.

5.2.1   Definition

IAS 37 defines a restructuring as 'a programme that is planned and controlled by management, and materially changes either: *[IAS 37.10]*

(a)   the scope of a business undertaken by an entity; or

(b)   the manner in which that business is conducted'.

This is said to include: *[IAS 37.70]*

(a)   the sale or termination of a line of business;

(b)   the closure of business locations in a country or region or the relocation of business activities from one country or region to another;

(c)   changes in management structure, for example, eliminating a layer of management; and

(d)   fundamental reorganisations that have a material effect on the nature and focus of the entity's operations.

This definition is very wide and whilst it may be relatively straightforward to establish whether an operation has been sold, closed or relocated, the determination of whether an organisational change is fundamental, material or just part of a process of continuous improvement is a subjective judgment. Whilst organisational change is a perennial feature in most business sectors, entities could be tempted to classify all kinds of operating costs as restructuring costs and thereby invite the user of the financial statements to perceive them in a different light from the 'normal' costs of operating in a dynamic business environment. Even though the requirements in IAS 37 prevent such costs being recognised too early, the standard still leaves the question of classification open to judgment. As such there can be a tension between the permitted recognition of expected restructuring costs, subject to meeting the criteria set out at 5.2.2 below, and the general prohibition in IAS 37 against provision for future operating losses, which is discussed above at 5.1.

IAS 37 emphasises that when a restructuring meets the definition of a discontinued operation under IFRS 5, additional disclosures may be required under that standard (see Chapter 4 at 3). *[IAS 37.9]*.

5.2.2   *Recognition of a restructuring provision*

IAS 37 requires that restructuring costs are recognised only when the general recognition criteria in the standard are met, i.e. there is a present obligation (legal or constructive) as a result of a past event, in respect of which a reliable estimate can be made of the probable cost. *[IAS 37.71]*. The standard's specific requirements for the recognition of a provision for restructuring costs seeks to define the circumstances that give rise to a constructive obligation and thereby restrict the recognition of a provision to cases when an entity: *[IAS 37.72]*

(a)   has a detailed formal plan for the restructuring identifying at least:

    (i)   the business or part of a business concerned;

    (ii)   the principal locations affected;

    (iii)   the location, function, and approximate number of employees who will be compensated for terminating their services;

    (iv)   the expenditures that will be undertaken; and

    (v)   when the plan will be implemented; and

(b)   has raised a valid expectation in those affected that it will carry out the restructuring by starting to implement that plan or announcing its main features to those affected by it.

The standard gives examples of the entity's actions that may provide evidence that the entity has started to implement a plan, quoting the dismantling of plant or selling of assets, or the public announcement of the main features of the plan. However, it also emphasises that the public announcement of a detailed plan to restructure will not automatically create an obligation; the important principle is that the announcement is made in such a way and in sufficient detail to give rise to valid expectations in other parties such as customers, suppliers and employees that the restructuring will be carried out. *[IAS 37.73]*.

The standard also suggests that for an announced plan to give rise to a constructive obligation, its implementation needs to be planned to begin as soon as possible and to be completed in a timeframe that makes significant changes to the plan unlikely. Any extended period before commencement of implementation, or if the restructuring will take an unreasonably long time, will mean that recognition of a provision is premature, because the entity is still likely to have a chance of changing the plan. *[IAS 37.74]*.

In summary, these conditions require the plan to be detailed and specific, to have gone beyond the directors' powers of recall and to be put into operation without delay or significant alteration.

The criteria set out above for the recognition of provisions mean that a board decision, if it is the only relevant event arising before the end of the reporting period, is not sufficient. This message is reinforced specifically in the standard, the argument being made that a constructive obligation is not created by a management decision. There will only be a constructive obligation where the entity has, before the end of the reporting period: *[IAS 37.75]*

(a)   started to implement the restructuring plan; or

(b)   announced the main features of the restructuring plan to those affected by it in a sufficiently specific manner to raise a valid expectation in them that the entity will carry out the restructuring.

If the restructuring is not started or announced in detail until after the end of the reporting period, no provision is recognised. Instead, the entity discloses a non-adjusting event after the reporting period. *[IAS 37.75, IAS 10.22(e)]*.

The following examples in IAS 37 illustrate how a constructive obligation for a restructuring may or may not be created.

Example 29.12:   The effect of timing of the creation of a constructive obligation on the recognition of a restructuring provision

Scenario 1:   Closure of a division – no implementation before end of the reporting period [IAS 37 Appendix C, Example 5A].

On 12 December 2012, the board of Entity A decided to close down a division. No announcement was made before the end of the reporting period (31 December 2012) and no other steps were taken to implement the decision before that date.

In these circumstances, no provision is recognised because management's actions are insufficient to create a constructive obligation before the end of the reporting period.

Scenario 2:   Closure of a division – communication/implementation before end of the reporting period [IAS 37 Appendix C, Example 5B].

In another case, the board of Entity B decides on 12 December 2012 to close down one of its manufacturing divisions. On 20 December 2012 a detailed plan for closure was agreed by the board; letters were sent to customers warning them to seek an alternative source of supply and redundancy notices were sent to the staff of the division.

The communication of management's decision to customers and employees on 20 December 2012 creates a valid expectation that the division will be closed, thereby giving rise to a constructive obligation from that date. Accordingly a provision is recognised at 31 December 2012 for the best estimate of the costs of closing the division.

The standard acknowledges that there will be circumstances where a board decision could trigger recognition, but not on its own. Only if earlier events, such as negotiations with employee representatives for termination payments or with purchasers for the sale of an operation, have been concluded subject only to board approval would the decision of the board create an obligation. In such circumstances, it is reasoned that when board approval has been obtained and communicated to the other parties, the entity is committed to restructure, assuming all other conditions are met. *[IAS 37.76]*.

There is also discussion in the standard of the situation that may arise in some countries where, for example, employee representatives may sit on the board, so that a board decision effectively communicates the decision to them, which may result in a constructive obligation to restructure. *[IAS 37.77]*.

In practice it can be very difficult to determine whether it is appropriate to recognise a provision for the future costs of a restructuring programme. The determination of whether an organisational change is fundamental, material or just part of a process of continuous improvement is a subjective judgment. Once it has been established that the activities in question constitute a restructuring rather than an ongoing operating cost, it can be difficult to determine whether management's actions before the reporting date have been sufficient to have 'raised a valid expectation in those affected'. *[IAS 37.72]*. Even if a trigger point is easily identifiable, such as the date of an appropriately detailed public announcement, it might not necessarily commit management to the *whole* restructuring, but only to specific items of expenditure such as redundancy costs. When the announcement is less clear, referring for example to consultations, negotiations or voluntary arrangements, particularly with employees, judgment is required. Furthermore, taken on its own, the 'valid expectation' test is at least as open to manipulation as one based on the timing of a board decision. Entities anxious to accelerate or postpone recognition of a liability could do so by advancing or deferring an event that signals such a commitment, such as a public announcement, without any change to the substance of their position.

In these situations it is important to consider all the related facts and circumstances and not to 'home in' on a single recognition criterion. The objective of the analysis is to determine whether there is a past obligating event at the reporting date. The guidance in the standard about restructuring, referring as it does to constructive obligations and valid expectations is ultimately aimed at properly applying the principle in IAS 37 that only those obligations arising from past events and existing independently of an entity's future actions are recognised as provisions. *[IAS 37.19]*. In essence, a restructuring provision qualifies for recognition if, as at the reporting date, it relates to a detailed plan of action from which management cannot realistically withdraw.

5.2.3 *Recognition of obligations arising from the sale of an operation*

IAS 37 has some further specific rules governing when to recognise an obligation arising on the sale of an operation, stating that no obligation arises for the sale of an operation until the entity is committed to the sale, i.e. there is a binding sale agreement. *[IAS 37.78]*. Thus a provision cannot be made for a loss on sale unless there is a binding sale agreement by the end of the reporting period. The standard says

Chapter 29

that this applies even when an entity has taken a decision to sell an operation and announced that decision publicly, it cannot be committed to the sale until a purchaser has been identified and there is a binding sale agreement. Until there is such an agreement, the entity will be able to change its mind and indeed will have to take another course of action if a purchaser cannot be found on acceptable terms. *[IAS 37.79].*

Even in cases where it is part of a larger restructuring that qualifies for recognition under IAS 37, an obligation arising from the sale is not recognised until there is a binding sale agreement. Instead, the assets of the operation must be reviewed for impairment under IAS 36. This may therefore mean that an expense is recorded in the income statement; it is just that the expense gives rise to a reduction of the carrying amount of assets rather than the recognition of a liability. The standard also recognises that where a sale is only part of a restructuring, the entity could be committed to the other parts of restructuring before a binding sale agreement is in place. *[IAS 37.79].* Hence, the costs of the restructuring will be recognised over different reporting periods.

5.2.4   Costs that can (and cannot) be included in a restructuring provision

Having met the specific tests in the standard for the recognition of a restructuring provision at the end of the reporting period, IAS 37 imposes further criteria to restrict the types of cost that can be provided for. Presumably these additional restrictions are intended to ensure that the entity does not contravene the general prohibition in IAS 37 against provision for future operating losses. *[IAS 37.63].*

A restructuring provision should include only the direct expenditures arising from the restructuring, which are those that are both: *[IAS 37.80]*

(a)   necessarily entailed by the restructuring; and

(b)   not associated with the ongoing activities of the entity.

The standard gives specific examples of costs that may not be included within the provision, because they relate to the future conduct of the business. Such costs include: *[IAS 37.81]*

(a)   retraining or relocating continuing staff;

(b)   marketing; or

(c)   investment in new systems and distribution networks.

Because these costs relate to the future conduct of the business, they are recognised on the same basis as if they arose independently of a restructuring. *[IAS 37.81].* In most cases, this means that the costs are recognised as the related services are provided.

Example 29.13:   Distinguishing restructuring costs from ongoing expenses

On 15 November 2012, management announced its intention to close down its operation in the North of the country and relocate to a new site in the South, primarily to be closer to its key customers. Before the end of the reporting period (31 December 2012) the principal elements of the plan were agreed with employee representatives; a lease signed for a building at the new location; and a notice to vacate the existing facility given to the landlord, all on the basis that production would start at the new location on 31 March 2013 and the existing site would be vacated on 30 April 2013. Production would cease at the existing site on 28 February 2013 to allow plant and equipment to be relocated. Inventory levels would be increased up to that date so that customers could be supplied with goods sent from the Northern facility until 31 March.

Whilst the majority of the 600 existing staff was expected to take redundancy on 28 February 2013, 50 had agreed to accept the entity's offer of relocation, including an incentive of €3,000 each towards relocation costs. Of those employees taking redundancy, 20 had agreed to continue to work for the entity until 30 June 2013, to dismantle plant and equipment at the Northern site; install it at the new facility in the South; and train new staff on its operation. A bonus of €4,500 per employee would be payable if they remained until 30 June. A further 60 had agreed to stay with the entity until 31 March 2013, to ensure that inventory was sent out to customers before the new site was operational, of which 10 would remain until 30 April 2013 to complete the decommissioning of the Northern facility. These employees would also receive a bonus for staying until the promised date.

The announcement of management's decision on 15 November 2012 and the fact that the key elements of the plan were understood by employees, customers and the landlord of the Northern site before the end of the reporting period give rise to a constructive obligation that requires a provision to be recognised at 31 December 2012 for the best estimate of the costs of the reorganisation.

However, only those direct costs of the restructuring not associated with ongoing activities can be included in the provision. For example, as follows:

Type of expense	*Direct cost of restructuring*	*Associated with ongoing activities*
Redundancy payments to 550 staff	•	
Payroll costs to 28 February 2013 (all 600 staff)		•
Relocation incentive of €3,000 per employee (50 staff)		•
Payroll costs – to 31 March 2013 (60 staff dispatching goods)		•
Payroll costs – March to June 2013 (20 staff relocating plant)[Note 1]	•	•
Payroll costs – April 2013 (10 staff decommissioning site)	•	
Costs of dismantling plant and equipment [Note 1]	•	•
Cost of transporting PP&E and inventory to the new site		•
Costs of recruiting and training staff for the Southern site		•
Rent of Northern site to 31 March 2013		•
Rent of Northern site for April 2013	•	
Cost of terminating lease of Northern site	•	
Rent of new site to 31 March 2013 (pre-production)		•
Cost of invoices, forms and stationery showing new address		•

Note 1: Costs relating to dismantling plant and equipment that is no longer intended for use in the business could be regarded as a direct cost of restructuring. However, costs relating to the dismantling and installation of equipment at the new site and training staff to operate it are costs associated with ongoing operations and, therefore, ineligible for inclusion in the restructuring provision.

This example shows that individual classes of expenditure should be disaggregated into components that distinguish those elements associated with ongoing activities. Even if expenditure would not have been incurred without the restructuring activity, its association with ongoing activities means that it is ineligible for inclusion in a provision. IAS 37 requires the cost to be *both* necessarily entailed by the restructuring *and* not associated with the ongoing activities of the entity. *[IAS 37.80].*

For that reason, whilst the cost of making employees redundant is an eligible restructuring cost, amounts paid to retain staff to ensure a smooth transition of operations from one location to another are not eligible because they are incurred to facilitate ongoing activities. Similarly, whilst the costs of dismantling plant and equipment intended to be scrapped is an eligible restructuring cost, the costs of dismantling plant and equipment intended to be relocated and installed at the new site is ineligible, because it is associated with ongoing activities.

A further rule in IAS 37 is that the provision should not include identifiable future operating losses up to the date of the restructuring, unless they relate to an onerous contract. *[IAS 37.82].* This means that even if the operation being reorganised is loss-making, its ongoing costs are not provided for. This is consistent with the general prohibition against the recognition of provisions for future operating losses. *[IAS 37.63].*

The general requirement in the standard that gains from the expected disposal of assets cannot be taken into account in the measurement of provisions *[IAS 37.51]* is also relevant to the measurement of restructuring provisions, even if the sale of the asset is envisaged as part of the restructuring. *[IAS 37.83].* Whilst the expected disposal proceeds from asset sales might have been a significant element of the economic case for a restructuring, the income from disposal is not anticipated just because it is part of a restructuring plan.

5.3   Onerous contracts

Although future operating losses in general cannot be provided for, IAS 37 requires that 'if an entity has a contract that is onerous, the present obligation under the contract shall be recognised and measured as a provision'. *[IAS 37.66].*

The standard notes that many contracts (for example, some routine purchase orders) can be cancelled without paying compensation to the other party, and therefore there is no obligation. However, other contracts establish both rights and obligations for each of the contracting parties. Where events make such a contract onerous, the contract falls within the scope of the standard and a liability exists which is recognised. Executory contracts that are not onerous fall outside the scope of the standard. *[IAS 37.67].*

IAS 37 defines an onerous contract as 'a contract in which the unavoidable costs of meeting the obligations under the contract exceed the economic benefits expected to be received under it'. *[IAS 37.10].* This seems to require that the contract is onerous to the point of being directly loss-making, not simply uneconomic by reference to current prices.

IAS 37 considers that 'the unavoidable costs under a contract reflect the least net cost of exiting from the contract, which is the lower of the cost of fulfilling it and any compensation or penalties arising from failure to fulfil it'. *[IAS 37.68].* An example of such a provision is BG Group's capacity contract provisions, which are described in this extract.

Extract 29.3: BG Group plc (2010)

22 PROVISIONS FOR OTHER LIABILITIES AND CHARGES [extract]

OTHER [extract]

A provision for onerous contracts was recognised in 2007 in respect of capacity contracts in the Interconnector pipeline, retained following disposal of the Group's 25% equity interest in Interconnector (UK) Limited. The obligation associated with these contracts extends to 2018.

The balance as at 31 December 2010 includes provisions for onerous contracts $191m (2009 $218m) ...

5.3.1   Recognition of provisions for vacant leasehold property

The most common example of an onerous contract in practice relates to leasehold property. From time to time entities may hold vacant leasehold property (or property which is only partly occupied) which they have substantially ceased to use for the purpose of their business and where sub-letting is either unlikely, or would be at a significantly reduced rental from that being paid by the entity. In these circumstances, the obligating event is the signing of the lease contract (a legal obligation) and when the lease becomes onerous, an outflow of resources embodying economic benefits is probable. Accordingly, a provision is recognised for the best estimate of the unavoidable lease payments. *[IAS 37 Appendix C, Example 8].*

Entities have to make systematic provision when such properties become vacant, and on a discounted basis where the effect is sufficiently material. Indeed, it could be argued that it is not just when the properties become vacant that provision would be required, but that provision should be made at the time the expected economic benefits of using the property fall short of the unavoidable costs under the lease. Although the Interpretations Committee had a preliminary discussion in December 2003 about the timing of recognition and the measurement of a provision for an onerous lease, including its application to other types of executory contracts such as a take or pay contract, it agreed that the issue should not be taken onto its agenda at that time.[13] However, it is sometimes the case in practice that entities interpret the requirements of IAS 37 as meaning that they should only recognise a provision when the properties are vacated.

Nevertheless, where a provision is to be recognised a number of difficulties remain. The first is how the provision should be calculated. It is unlikely that the provision will simply be the net present value of the future rental obligation, because if a substantial period of the lease remains, the entity will probably be able either to agree a negotiated sum with the landlord to terminate the lease early, or to sub-lease the building at some point in the future. Hence, the entity will have to make a best estimate of its future cash flows taking all these factors into account.

Another issue that arises from this is whether the provision should be shown net of any cash flows that may arise from sub-leasing the property, or whether the provision must be shown gross, with a corresponding asset set up for expected cash flows from sub-leasing only if they meet the recognition criteria of being 'virtually certain' to be received. The strict offset criteria in the standard (see 4.5 above) would suggest the latter to be required, as the entity would normally retain liability for the full lease payments if the sub-lessee defaulted. However, the standard makes no explicit

Chapter 29

reference to this issue. It is common for entities to apply a net approach for such onerous contracts under IAS 37. Indeed, it could be argued that because an onerous contract provision relates to the excess of the unavoidable costs over the expected economic benefits, *[IAS 37.68]*, there is no corresponding asset to be recognised. In its 2005 exposure draft, the IASB confirms that if an onerous contract is an operating lease, the unavoidable cost of the contract is the remaining lease commitment reduced by the estimated rentals that the entity could reasonably obtain, regardless of whether or not the entity intends to enter into a sublease.[14]

In the past, some entities may have maintained that no provision is required for vacant properties, because if the property leases are looked at on a portfolio basis, the overall economic benefits from properties exceed the overall costs. However, this argument is not sustainable under IAS 37, as the definition of an onerous contract refers specifically to costs and economic benefits *under the contract. [IAS 37.10].*

It is more difficult to apply the definition of onerous contracts to the lease on a head office which is not generating revenue specifically. If the definition were applied too literally, one might end up concluding that all head office leases should be provided against because no specific economic benefits are expected under them. It would be more sensible to conclude that the entity as a whole obtains economic benefits from its head office, which was presumably the reason for entering in to the lease to start with. However, this does not alter the fact that if circumstances change and the head office becomes vacant, a provision should then be made in respect of the lease.

IAS 37 requires that any impairment loss that has occurred in respect of assets dedicated to an onerous contract is recognised before establishing a provision for the onerous contract. *[IAS 37.69].* For example, any leasehold improvements that have been capitalised should be written off before provision is made for excess future rental costs.

One company which has provided for onerous leases under IAS 37 is Jardine Matheson as indicated by the following extract.

Extract 29.4: Jardine Matheson Holdings Limited (2010)

35   Provisions

	Motor vehicle warranties US$m	Closure cost provisions US$m	Obligations under onerous leases US$m	Reinstatement and restoration costs US$m	Statutory employee entitlements US$m	Others US$m	Total US$m
2010							
At 1st January	20	8	4	31	50	12	**125**
Exchange differences	2	–	–	2	2	–	**6**
New subsidiary undertakings	–	–	–	2	–	–	**2**
Additional provisions	3	4	–	4	19	1	**31**
Unused amounts reversed	–	(1)	–	(1)	–	–	**(2)**
Utilized	(4)	(1)	(1)	(1)	(3)	(3)	**(13)**
At 31st December	**21**	**10**	**3**	**37**	**68**	**10**	**149**
Non-current	–	–	2	34	55	3	**94**
Current	21	10	1	3	13	7	**55**
	21	**10**	**3**	**37**	**68**	**10**	**149**

2009						
At 1st January	18	9	4	28	33	20	112
Exchange differences	1	–	–	1	6	3	11
Additional provisions	5	1	1	3	12	3	25
Unused amounts reversed	–	(1)	–	–	–	(9)	(10)
Utilized	(4)	(1)	(1)	(1)	(1)	(5)	(13)
At 31st December	20	8	4	31	50	12	125
Non-current	–	–	3	28	38	3	72
Current	20	8	1	3	12	9	53
	20	8	4	31	50	12	125

Motor vehicle warranties are estimated liabilities that fall due under the warranty terms offered on sale of new and used vehicles beyond that which is reimbursed by the manufacturers.

Closure cost provisions are established when legal or constructive obligations arise on closure or disposal of businesses.

Provisions are made for obligations under onerous operating leases when the properties are not used by the Group and the net costs of exiting from the leases exceed the economic benefits expected to be received.

Other provisions comprise provisions in respect of indemnities on disposal of businesses and legal claims.

5.3.2 Recognition of provisions for occupied leasehold property

The discussion above deals with situations where the leasehold property becomes vacant (or only partly occupied). However, what if the rentals payable by an entity increase due to market rates or are in excess of market rates. Does this mean that an entity has an onerous contract for which it should make a provision? Not necessarily. As noted above, IAS 37 defines an onerous contract as 'a contract in which the unavoidable costs of meeting the obligations under the contract exceed the economic benefits expected to be received under it'. *[IAS 37.10]*. This seems to require that the contract is onerous to the point of being directly loss-making, not simply uneconomic by reference to current prices. Thus, if the entity still expects to operate profitably from the leased property over the remaining period of its use, despite these higher rental payments, no provision should be made. If the business operated out of the leased property has become loss-making, and the entity does not expect to be able to improve its operating results to recover the higher rental payments over the remaining period of its use, then a provision may be necessary. However, before a separate provision for an onerous contract is established, IAS 37 requires that an entity should first recognise any impairment loss that has occurred on assets dedicated to the contract. *[IAS 37.69]*.

Tesco PLC includes in its property provisions an amount for the excess of future rents over market value on its loss-making stores.

> *Extract 29.5: Tesco PLC (2010)*
> **Note 26 Provisions** [extract]
> Property provisions comprise future rents payable net of rents receivable on onerous and vacant property leases, provisions for terminal dilapidations and provisions for future rents above market value on unprofitable stores. The majority of the provision is expected to be utilised of the period to 2020.

Tesco also provides for dilapidation costs relating to leasehold properties, which are discussed at 5.10 below.

Chapter 29

5.4   Environmental provisions

The standard illustrates its recognition requirements in two examples relating to environmental provisions. The first deals with the situation where it is virtually certain that legislation will be enacted which will require the clean up of land already contaminated. In these circumstances, the virtual certainty of new legislation being enacted means that the entity has a present legal obligation as a result of the past contamination of the land, requiring a provision to be recognised. *[IAS 37 Appendix C, Example 2A]*. However, in its discussion about what constitutes an obligating event, the standard notes that 'differences in circumstances surrounding enactment make it impossible to specify a single event that would make the enactment of a law virtually certain. In many cases, it will be impossible to be virtually certain of the enactment of a law until it is enacted.' *[IAS 37.22]*. The second example deals with a similar situation, except that the entity is not expected to be legally required to clean it up. Nevertheless, the entity has a widely publicised environmental policy undertaking to clean up all contamination that it causes, and has a record of honouring this policy. In these circumstances a provision is still required because the entity has created a valid expectation that it will clean up the land, meaning that the entity has a present constructive obligation as a result of past contamination. *[IAS 37 Appendix C, Example 2B]*. It is therefore clear that where an entity has a present legal or constructive obligation to make good any environmental damage; it is probable that an outflow of resources will be required to settle the obligation; and a reliable estimate can be made of the amount, a provision will be required. *[IAS 37.14]*.

One company making provision for environmental costs is Syngenta, which describes some of the practical difficulties and uncertainties relating to its measurement in the extract below.

Extract 29.6: Syngenta AG (2010)

2.   Accounting policies [extract]

Environmental provisions [extract]

Provisions for remediation costs are made when there is a present obligation, it is probable that expenditures for remediation work will be required within ten years (or a longer period if specified by a legal obligation) and the cost can be estimated within a reasonable range of possible outcomes. The costs are based on currently available facts; technology expected to be available at the time of the clean up, laws and regulations presently or virtually certain to be enacted and prior experience in remediation of contaminated sites. Environmental liabilities are recorded at the estimated amount at which the liability could be settled at the balance sheet date and are discounted if the impact is material and if cost estimates and timing are considered reasonably certain.

19.   Provisions [extract]

Movements in provisions during the year ended December 31, 2010 are as follows: [extract]

(US$ million)	January 1	Charged to income	Release of provisions credited to income	Payments	Reclassi-fications	Currency translation effects	December 31
Environmental provisions	405	36	(30)	(38)	–	20	393

25.   Commitments and contingencies [extract]
Environmental Matters

Syngenta has recorded provisions for environmental liabilities at some currently or formerly owned, leased and third party sites throughout the world. These provisions are estimates of amounts payable or expected to become payable and take into consideration the number of other potentially responsible parties ("PRP") at each site and the identity and financial positions of such parties in light of the joint and several nature of certain of the liabilities.

In the USA, Syngenta and/or its indemnitors or its indemnities, have been named under federal legislation (the Comprehensive Environment Response, Compensation and Liability Act of 1980, as amended) as a PRP in respect of several sites. Syngenta expects to be indemnified against a proportion of the liabilities associated with a number of these sites by the sellers of the businesses associated with such sites and, where appropriate, actively participates in or monitors the clean-up activities at the sites in respect of which it is a PRP.

The material components of Syngenta's environmental provisions consist of a risk assessment based on investigation of the various sites. The nature and timing of future remediation expenditures are affected by a number of uncertainties which include, but are not limited to, the method and extent of remediation, the percentage of material attributable to Syngenta at the remediation sites relative to that attributable to other parties, and the financial capabilities of the other PRPs. As a result, it is inherently difficult to estimate the amount of environmental liabilities that will ultimately become payable. It is also often not possible to estimate the amounts expected to be recovered via reimbursement, indemnification or insurance due to the uncertainty inherent in this area.

Syngenta believes that its provisions are adequate based upon currently available information. However, given the inherent difficulties in estimating liabilities in this area, due to uncertainty concerning both the amount and the timing of future expenditures and the results of future operations, it cannot be guaranteed that additional costs will not be incurred beyond the amounts accrued.

If the expenditure relating to an environmental obligation is not expected to be incurred for some time, a significant effect of the standard is its requirement that provisions should be discounted, which can have a material impact. For example, as a result of implementing FRS12 in the UK, BP changed its policy to reflect this, reducing its environmental provision by £350 million because of discounting. Its current policy is as shown in the following extract.

Extract 29.7: BP p.l.c. (2010)

1   Significant accounting policies [extract]

Environmental expenditures and liabilities

Environmental expenditures that relate to current or future revenues are expensed or capitalized as appropriate. Expenditures that relate to an existing condition caused by past operations and do not contribute to current or future earnings are expensed.

Liabilities for environmental costs are recognized when a clean-up is probable and the associated costs can be reasonably estimated. Generally, the timing of recognition of these provisions coincides with the commitment to a formal plan of action or, if earlier, on divestment or on closure of inactive sites.

The amount recognized is the best estimate of the expenditure required. Where the liability will not be settled for a number of years, the amount recognized is the present value of the estimated future expenditure.

Chapter 29

Decommissioning [extract]

Liabilities for decommissioning costs are recognized when the group has an obligation to dismantle and remove a facility or an item of plant and to restore the site on which it is located, and when a reliable estimate of that liability can be made. Where an obligation exists for a new facility, such as oil and natural gas production or transportation facilities, this will be on construction or installation. An obligation for decommissioning may also crystallize during the period of operation of a facility through a change in legislation or through a decision to terminate operations. The amount recognized is the present value of the estimated future expenditure determined in accordance with local conditions and requirements.

A corresponding item of property, plant and equipment of an amount equivalent to the provision is also recognized. This is subsequently depreciated as part of the asset.

Other than the unwinding discount on the provision, any change in the present value of the estimated expenditure is reflected as an adjustment to the provision and the corresponding item of property, plant and equipment.

37   Provisions [extract]

	Decom-missioning	Environ-mental
		$ million
At 1 January 2010	9,020	1,719
Exchange adjustments	(114)	–
Acquisitions	188	–
New or increased provisions	1,800	1,290
Write-back of unused provisions	(12)	(120)
Unwinding of discount	168	29
Change in discount rate	444	22
Utilization	(164)	(460)
Reclassified as liabilities directly associated with assets held for sale	(381)	(1)
Deletions	(405)	(14)
At 31 December 2010	10,544	2,465
Of which – current	432	635
– non-current	10,112	1,830

	Decom-missioning	Environ-mental
		$ million
At 1 January 2009	8,418	1,691
Exchange adjustments	398	15
New or increased provisions	169	588
Write-back of unused provisions	–	(259)
Unwinding of discount	184	32
Change in discount rate	324	18
Utilization	(383)	(308)
Deletions	(90)	(58)
At 31 December 2009	9,020	1,719
Of which – current	287	368
– non-current	8,733	1,351

The group makes full provision for the future cost of decommissioning oil and natural gas production facilities and related pipelines on a discounted basis on the installation of those facilities. The provision for the costs of decommissioning these production facilities and pipelines at the end of their economic lives has been estimated using existing technology, at current prices or future assumptions, depending on the expected timing of the activity, and discounted using a real discount rate of 1.5% (2009 1.75%). These costs are generally expected to be incurred over the next 30 years. While the provision is based on the best estimate of future costs and the economic lives of the facilities and pipelines, there is uncertainty regarding both the amount and timing of incurring costs.

Provisions for environmental remediation are made when a clean-up is probable and the amount of the obligation can be estimated reliably. Generally, this coincides with commitment to a formal plan of action or, if earlier, on divestment or closure of inactive sites. The provision for environmental liabilities has been estimated using existing technology, at current prices and discounted using a real discount rate of 1.5% (2009 1.75%). The majority of these costs are expected to be incurred over the next 10 years. The extent and cost of future remediation programmes are inherently difficult to estimate. They depend on the scale of any possible contamination, the timing and extent of corrective actions, and also the group's share of liability.

5.5 Decommissioning provisions

Decommissioning costs arise when an entity is required to dismantle or remove an asset at the end of its useful life and to restore the site on which it has been located, for example, when an oil rig or nuclear power station reaches the end of its economic life.

Rather than allowing an entity to build up a provision for the required costs over the life of the facility, IAS 37 requires that the liability is recognised as soon as the obligation arises, which will normally be at commencement of operations.

The accounting for decommissioning costs is dealt with in IAS 37 by way of an example relating to an oil rig in an offshore oilfield (see Example 29.5 at 3.3 above). A provision is recognised at the time of constructing the oil rig in relation to the eventual costs that relate to its removal and the restoration of damage caused by building it. Additional provisions are recognised over the life of the oil field to reflect the need to reverse damage caused during the extraction of oil. *[IAS 37 Appendix C, Example 3]*. The total decommissioning cost is estimated, discounted to its present value and it is this amount which forms the initial provision. This 'initial estimate of the costs of dismantling and removing the item and restoring the site' is added to the corresponding asset's cost. *[IAS 16.16]*. Thereafter, the asset is depreciated over its useful life, while the discounted provision is progressively unwound, with the unwinding charge shown as a finance cost.

The effect of discounting on the statement of comprehensive income is to split the cost of the eventual decommissioning into two components: an operating cost based on the present value of the provision; and a finance element representing the unwinding of the discount. The overall effect is to produce a rising pattern of cost over the life of the facility, often with much of the total cost of the decommissioning classified as a finance cost.

Chapter 29

AngloGold Ashanti's accounting policies and provisions note in respect of decommissioning obligations and restoration obligations are shown in the following extract.

Extract 29.8: AngloGold Ashanti Limited (2010)

1.3   Summary of significant accounting policies [extract]

Environmental expenditure

The group has long-term remediation obligations comprising decommissioning and restoration liabilities relating to its past operations which are based on the group's environmental management plans, in compliance with the current environmental and regulatory requirements. Provisions for non-recurring remediation costs are made when there is a present obligation, it is probable that expense on remediation work will be required and the cost can be estimated within a reasonable range of possible outcomes. The costs are based on currently available facts, technology expected to be available at the time of the clean up, laws and regulations presently or virtually certain to be enacted and prior experience in remediation of contaminated sites.

Contributions for the South African operations are made to Environmental Rehabilitation Trust Funds, created in accordance with local statutory requirements where applicable, to fund the estimated cost of rehabilitation during and at the end of the life of a mine. The amounts contributed to the trust funds are accounted for as non-current assets in the company. Interest earned on monies paid to rehabilitation trust funds is accrued on a time proportion basis and is recorded as interest income. For group purposes the trusts are consolidated.

Decommissioning costs

The provision for decommissioning represents the cost that will arise from rectifying damage caused before production commenced. Accordingly an asset is recognised and included within mine infrastructure.

Decommissioning costs are provided at the present value of the expenditures expected to settle the obligation, using estimated cash flows based on current prices. The unwinding of the decommissioning obligation is included in the income statement. Estimated future costs of decommissioning obligations are reviewed regularly and adjusted as appropriate for new circumstances or changes in law or technology. Changes in estimates are capitalised or reversed against the relevant asset. Estimates are discounted at a pre-tax rate that reflects current market assessments of the time value of money.

Gains or losses from the expected disposal of assets are not taken into account when determining the provision.

Restoration costs

The provision for restoration represents the costs of restoring site damage after the start of production. Increases in the provision are charged to the income statement as a cost of production.

Restoration costs are estimated at the present value of the expenditures expected to settle the obligation, using estimated cash flows based on current prices and adjusted for the risks specific to the liability. The estimates are discounted at a pre-tax rate that reflects current market assessments of the time value of money.

Figures in million	**2010**	2009
	US Dollars	
27 Environmental rehabilitation and other provisions [extract]		
Environmental rehabilitation obligations		
Provision for decommissioning		
Balance at beginning of year	**181**	161
Change in estimates[(1)]	**11**	6
Transfer to assets held for sale	**–**	(2)
Unwinding of decommissioning obligation (note 7)	**9**	7
Translation	**12**	21
Balance at end of year	**213**	181

Provision for restoration		
Balance at beginning of year	237	215
Charge to income statement	36	3
Change in estimates(1)	47	1
Transfer to assets held for sale	–	(2)
Unwinding of restoration obligation (note 7) (2)	11	7
Utilised during the year	(6)	(8)
Translation	13	21
Balance at end of year	338	237

(1)   The change in estimates relates to changes in laws and regulations governing the protection of the environment and factors relative to rehabilitation estimates and a change in the quantities of material in reserves and a corresponding change in the life of mine plan. These provisions are anticipated to unwind beyond the end of the life of mine.

(2)   Included in the unwinding of the restoration obligation is $2m, R13m (2009: nil) which is recoverable from a third party. The asset is included in non-current debtors.

5.5.1   Changes in estimated decommissioning costs (IFRIC 1)

IAS 37 requires provisions to be revised annually to reflect the current best estimate of the provision. *[IAS 37.59]*. However, the standard gives no guidance on accounting for changes in the decommissioning provision. Similarly, IAS 16 is unclear about the extent to which an item's carrying amount should be affected by changes in the estimated amount of dismantling and site restoration costs that occur *after* the estimate made upon initial measurement. This was addressed by the IASB with the publication of IFRIC 1 in May 2004.

IFRIC 1 applies to any decommissioning, restoration or similar liability that has been both included as part of the cost of an asset measured in accordance with IAS 16 and recognised as a liability in accordance with IAS 37. *[IFRIC 1.2]*. It addresses how the effect of the following events that change the measurement of an existing decommissioning, restoration or similar liability should be accounted for: *[IFRIC 1.3]*

(a)   a change in the estimated outflow of resources embodying economic benefits (e.g. cash flows) required to settle the obligation;

(b)   a change in the current market-based discount rate (this includes changes in the time value of money and the risks specific to the liability); and

(c)   an increase that reflects the passage of time (also referred to as the unwinding of the discount).

IFRIC 1 requires that (c) above, the periodic unwinding of the discount, is recognised in profit or loss as a finance cost as it occurs. *[IFRIC 1.8]*. The Interpretations Committee concluded that the unwinding of the discount is not a borrowing cost as defined in IAS 23, and thus cannot be capitalised under that standard. *[IFRIC 1.BC26-27]*.

For a change caused by (a) or (b) above, however, the adjustment is not taken to the income statement as it occurs, but is recognised in the carrying value of the related asset or in other comprehensive income, depending on whether the asset is measured at cost or using the revaluation model. *[IFRIC 1.4-7]*.

Chapter 29

If the related asset is measured using the cost model, the change in the liability should be added to or deducted from the cost of the asset to which it relates. Where the change gives rise to an addition to cost, the entity should consider the need to test the new carrying value for impairment. Reductions over and above the remaining carrying value of the asset are recognised immediately in profit or loss. *[IFRIC 1.5]*. The adjusted depreciable amount of the asset is then depreciated prospectively over its remaining useful life. *[IFRIC 1.7]*. IFRIC 1 includes the following illustrative example. *[IFRIC 1.IE1-4]*.

Example 29.14:   Changes in decommissioning costs – related asset measured at cost

An entity has a nuclear power plant and a related decommissioning liability. The nuclear power plant started operating on 1 January 2000. The plant has a useful life of 40 years. Its initial cost was $120,000; this included an amount for decommissioning costs of $10,000, which represented $70,400 in estimated cash flows payable in 40 years discounted at a risk-adjusted rate of 5%. The entity's financial year ends on 31 December.

On 31 December 2009, the plant is 10 years old. Accumulated depreciation is $30,000. Because of the unwinding of discount over the 10 years, the decommissioning liability has grown from $10,000 to $16,300.

On 31 December 2009, the discount rate has not changed. However, the entity estimates that, as a result of technological advances, the net present value of the expected cash flows has decreased by $8,000. Accordingly, the entity reduces the decommissioning liability from $16,300 to $8,300 and reduces the carrying amount of the asset by the same amount.

Following this adjustment, the carrying amount of the asset is $82,000 ($120,000 – $8,000 – $30,000), which will be depreciated over the remaining 30 years of the asset's life to give a depreciation expense for 2010 of $2,733 ($82,000 ÷ 30). The next year's finance cost for the unwinding of the discount will be $415 ($8,300 × 5%).

In illustrating the requirements of the Interpretation, the example in IFRIC 1 reduces the carrying value of the whole asset (comprising its construction cost and decommissioning cost) by the reduction in the present value of the decommissioning provision. The solution set out in the example does not treat the decommissioning element as a separate component of the asset. Had this been the case, the component would have had accumulated depreciation as at 31 December 2009 of $2,500 ($10,000 × 10/40), giving a carrying amount of $7,500 at that date and a gain of $500 when reduced by the decrease in the provision of $8,000. Accordingly, we believe that it would not be appropriate to recognise any gain until the carrying value of the whole asset is extinguished.

If the related asset is measured using the revaluation model, changes in the liability alter the revaluation surplus or deficit previously recognised for that asset. Changes to the provision are recognised in other comprehensive income and increase or decrease the value of the revaluation surplus in respect of the asset, except to the extent that:

(a)   a decrease in the provision reverses a previous revaluation deficit that was recognised in profit or loss;

(b)   a decrease in the provision exceeds the carrying amount of the asset that would have been recognised under the cost model; or

(c)   an increase in the provision exceeds the previous revaluation surplus relating to that asset,

in which case the change is recognised in profit or loss. Changes in the provision might also indicate the need for the asset (and therefore all assets in the same class) to be revalued. *[IFRIC 1.6].*

The illustrative examples in **IFRIC 1** address this alternative. *[IFRIC 1.IE6-12].*

Example 29.15:   Changes in decommissioning costs – related asset carried at valuation

Assume that the entity in Example 29.14 above instead adopts the revaluation model in IAS 16, and its policy is to eliminate accumulated depreciation at the revaluation date against the gross carrying amount of the asset.

The entity first revalues the asset as at 31 December 2002 when the nuclear power plant is 3 years old. The valuation of $115,000 comprises a gross valuation of $126,600 and an allowance of $11,600 for decommissioning costs, which represents no change to the original estimate, after the unwinding of three years' discount. The amounts included in the statement of financial position at 31 December 2002 and the related revaluation reserve movements are therefore:

	Net book value	Valuation	Revaluation reserve
	$	$	$
Cost or valuation	120,000	126,600	6,600
Accumulated depreciation (3/40)	(9,000)	–	9,000
Carrying amount of asset	111,000	126,600	15,600
Original provision	10,000		
Unwinding of discount (3 years @ 5%)	1,600		
	11,600	11,600	
Carrying amount less provision	99,400	115,000	15,600

The depreciation expense for 2003 is therefore $3,420 ($126,600 ÷ 37) and the discount expense for 2003 is $580 (5% of $11,600). On 31 December 2003, the decommissioning liability (before any adjustment) is $12,180 and the discount rate has not changed. However, on that date, the entity estimates that, as a result of technological advances, the present value of the decommissioning liability has decreased by $5,000. Accordingly, the entity adjusts the decommissioning liability to $7,180. To determine the extent to which any of the change to the provision is recognised in profit or loss, the entity has to keep a record of revaluations previously recognised in profit or loss; the carrying amount of the asset that would have been recognised under the cost model; and the previous revaluation surplus relating to that asset. *[IFRIC 1.6].* In this example, the whole of the adjustment is taken to revaluation surplus, because it does not exceed the carrying amount that would have been recognised for the asset under the cost model of $103,000 (see below).

In addition, the entity decides that a full valuation of the asset is needed at 31 December 2003, in order to ensure that the carrying amount does not differ materially from fair value. Suppose that the asset is now valued at $107,000, which is net of an allowance of $7,180 for the reduced decommissioning obligation. The valuation of the asset for financial reporting purposes, before deducting this allowance, is therefore $114,180. The effect on the revaluation reserve of the revision to the estimate of the decommissioning provision and the new valuation can be illustrated in the table below.

Chapter 29

	Cost model	Revaluation	Revaluation reserve
	$	$	$
Carrying amount as at 31 December 2002	111,000	126,600	15,600
Depreciation charge for 2003	(3,000)	(3,420)	
Carrying amount as at 31 December 2003	108,000	123,180	
Revision to estimate of provision	(5,000)		
Revaluation adjustment in 2003		(9,000)	(9,000)
	103,000	114,180	
Provision as at 31 December 2002	11,600	11,600	
Unwinding of discount @ 5%	580	580	
Revision to estimate	(5,000)	(5,000)	5,000
Provision as at 31 December 2003	7,180	7,180	
Carrying amount less provision	95,820	107,000	11,600

These requirements are discussed further in Chapter 20 at 4.3.

As indicated at 4.3.6 above, IAS 37 is unclear whether a new discount rate should be applied during the year or just at the year-end, and whether the rate should be applied to the new estimate of the provision or the old estimate. Although IFRIC 1 requires that changes in the provision resulting from a change in the discount rate is added to, or deducted from, the cost of the related asset in the current period, it does not deal specifically with these points. However, Example 1 in the illustrative examples to IFRIC 1 indicates that a change in discount rate would be accounted for in the same way as other changes affecting the estimate of a provision for decommissioning, restoration and similar liabilities. That is, it is reflected as a change in the liability at the time the revised estimate is made and the new estimate is discounted at the revised discount rate from that point on. *[IFRIC 1.IE5].*

When accounting for revalued assets to which decommissioning liabilities attach, the illustrative example in IFRIC 1 states that it is important to understand the basis of the valuation obtained. For example: *[IFRIC 1.IE7].*

(a)   if an asset is valued on a discounted cash flow basis, some valuers may value the asset without deducting any allowance for decommissioning costs (a 'gross' valuation), whereas others may value the asset after deducting an allowance for decommissioning costs (a 'net' valuation), because an entity acquiring the asset will generally also assume the decommissioning obligation. For financial reporting purposes, the decommissioning obligation is recognised as a separate liability, and is not deducted from the asset. Accordingly, if the asset is valued on a net basis, it is necessary to adjust the valuation obtained by adding back the allowance for the liability, so that the liability is not counted twice. This is the case in Example 29.15 above.

(b)   if an asset is valued on a depreciated replacement cost basis, the valuation obtained may not include an amount for the decommissioning component of the asset. If it does not, an appropriate amount will need to be added to the valuation to reflect the depreciated replacement cost of that component.

5.5.2   Changes in legislation after construction of the asset

The scope of IFRIC 1 is set out in terms of any existing decommissioning, restoration or similar liability that is both recognised as part of the cost of the asset under IAS 16; and recognised as a liability in accordance with IAS 37. *[IFRIC 1.2]*. The Interpretation does not address the treatment of obligations arising after the asset has been constructed, for example as a result of changes in legislation. *[IFRIC 1.BC23]*. Nevertheless, in our opinion the cost of the related asset should be measured in accordance with the principles set out in IFRIC 1 regardless of whether the obligation exists at the time of constructing the asset or arises later in its life.

As discussed at 3.2 in Chapter 20, IAS 16 makes no distinction in principle between the initial costs of acquiring an asset and any subsequent expenditure upon it. In both cases any and all expenditure has to meet the recognition rules, and be expensed in profit or loss if it does not. IAS 16 states that the cost of an item of property, plant and equipment includes 'the initial estimate of the costs of dismantling and removing the item and restoring the site on which it is located, the obligation for which an entity incurs either when the item is acquired or as a consequence of having used the item during a particular period for purposes other than to produce inventories during that period.' *[IAS 16.16(c)]*.

When changes in legislation give rise to a new decommissioning, restoration or similar liability that is added to the carrying amount of the related asset, it would be appropriate to perform an impairment review in accordance with IAS 36 (see Chapter 22).

5.5.3   Funds established to meet an obligation (IFRIC 5)

Some entities may participate in a decommissioning, restoration or environmental rehabilitation fund, the purpose of which is to segregate assets to fund some or all of the costs of decommissioning for which the entity has to make a provision under IAS 37. IFRIC 5 was issued in December 2004 to address this issue, referring to 'decommissioning to mean not only the dismantling of plant and equipment but also the costs of undertaking environmental rehabilitation, such as rectifying pollution of water or restoring mined land. *[IFRIC 5.1]*.

Contributions to these funds may be voluntary or required by regulation or law, and the funds may have one of the following common structures: *[IFRIC 5.2]*

- funds that are established by a single contributor to fund its own decommissioning obligations, whether for a particular site, or for a number of geographically dispersed sites;

- funds that are established with multiple contributors to fund their individual or joint decommissioning obligations, where contributors are entitled to reimbursement for decommissioning expenses to the extent of their fund contributions plus any actual earnings on those contributions less their share of the costs of administering the fund. In addition, contributors may have an obligation to make potential additional contributions, for example, in the event of the bankruptcy of another contributor;

- funds that are established with multiple contributors to fund their individual or joint decommissioning obligations when the required level of contributions is based on the current activity of a contributor, but the benefit obtained by that contributor is based on its past activity. Thus, there is a potential mismatch in the amount of contributions made by a contributor (based on current activity) and the value realisable from the fund (based on past activity).

Such funds generally have the following features: *[IFRIC 5.3]*

- the fund is separately administered by independent trustees;
- entities (contributors) make contributions to the fund, which are invested in a range of assets that may include both debt and equity investments, and are available to help pay the contributors' decommissioning costs. The trustees determine how contributions are invested, within the constraints set by the fund's governing documents and any applicable legislation or other regulations;
- the contributors retain the obligation to pay decommissioning costs. However, contributors are able to obtain reimbursement of decommissioning costs from the fund up to the lower of the decommissioning costs incurred and the entity's share of assets of the fund; and
- the contributors may have restricted or no access to any surplus of assets of the fund over those used to meet eligible decommissioning costs.

IFRIC 5 applies to accounting in the financial statements of a contributor for interests arising from decommissioning funds that have both the following features: *[IFRIC 5.4]*

- the assets are administered separately (either by being held in a separate legal entity or as segregated assets within another entity); and
- a contributor's right to access the assets is restricted.

A residual interest in a fund that extends beyond a right to reimbursement, such as a contractual right to distributions once all the decommissioning has been completed or on winding up the fund, may be an equity instrument within the scope of IAS 39 or IFRS 9, as appropriate, and is not within the scope of IFRIC 5. *[IFRIC 5.5]*.

The issues addressed by IFRIC 5 are: *[IFRIC 5.6]*

(a)   How should a contributor account for its interest in a fund?

(b)   When a contributor has an obligation to make additional contributions, for example, in the event of the bankruptcy of another contributor, how should that obligation be accounted for?

5.5.3.A   Accounting for an interest in a fund

As far as issue (a) is concerned, IFRIC 5 requires the contributor to recognise its obligations to pay decommissioning costs as a liability and recognise its interest in the fund separately, unless the contributor is not liable to pay decommissioning costs even if the fund fails to pay. *[IFRIC 5.7]*.

The contributor determines whether it has control, joint control or significant influence over the fund by reference to IAS 27 – *Consolidated and Separate Financial Statements*, IAS 31 – *Interests in Joint Ventures*, IAS 28 – *Investments in Associates* – and SIC-12 – *Consolidation – Special Purpose Entities*. If the contributor determines that it has such control, joint control or significant influence, it should account for its interest in the fund in accordance with the relevant standards (see Chapters 6, 12 and 13 respectively). *[IFRIC 5.8].*

One company that started to consolidate its interest in a decommissioning fund following the issue of IFRIC 5 is Anglo Platinum as shown below:

Extract 29.9: Anglo Platinum Limited (2005)

Principal Accounting Policies [extract]

IFRIC 5 – Rights to interests arising from Decommissioning, Restoration and Environmental Restoration Funds

On 1 January 2005, the Group adopted the requirements of IFRIC 5. The objective of the interpretation is to determine the accounting in the financial statements of a contributor for interests arising from decommissioning funds that have the following features:

(a)   the assets are administered separately (either by being held in a separate legal entity or as segregated assets within another entity).

(b)   A contributor's right to access the assets in restricted.

Adoption has the effect that the Platinum Producers' Environmental Trust is consolidated. The effect is that the balance previously included in originated loans is now reflected in non-current cash deposits held by Platinum Producers' Environmental Trust.

Otherwise, the contributor should recognise the right to receive reimbursement from the fund as a reimbursement in accordance with IAS 37 (see 4.5 above). This reimbursement should be measured at the lower of: *[IFRIC 5.9]*

- the amount of the decommissioning obligation recognised; and
- the contributor's share of the fair value of the net assets of the fund attributable to contributors.

This 'asset cap' means that the asset recognised in respect of the reimbursement rights can never exceed the recognised liability. Accordingly, rights to receive reimbursement to meet decommissioning liabilities that have yet to be recognised as a provision are not recognised. *[IFRIC 5.BC14].* Although many respondents expressed concern about this asset cap and argued that rights to benefit in excess of this amount give rise to an additional asset, separate from the reimbursement asset, the Interpretations Committee, despite having sympathy with the concerns, concluded that to recognise such an asset would be inconsistent with the requirement in IAS 37 that 'the amount recognised for the reimbursement should not exceed the amount of the provision'. *[IFRIC 5.BC19-20].*

Changes in the carrying value of the right to receive reimbursement other than contributions to and payments from the fund should be recognised in profit or loss in the period in which these changes occur. *[IFRIC 5.9].*

The effect of this requirement is that the amount recognised in the statement of comprehensive income relating to the reimbursement bears no relation to the expense recognised in respect of the provision, particularly for decommissioning liabilities where most changes in the measurement of the provision are not taken to the profit or loss immediately, but are recognised prospectively over the remaining useful life of the related asset (see 5.5.1 above).

One company that has been affected by the 'asset cap' is Fortum Corporation as shown below.

Extract 29.10: Fortum Corporation (2010)

1.   Accounting Policies [extract]

1.25   Assets and liabilities related to decommissioning of nuclear power plants and the disposal of spent fuel [extract]

Fortum owns Loviisa nuclear power plant in Finland. Fortum's nuclear related provisions and the related part of the State Nuclear Waste Management Fund and the related nuclear provisions are both presented separately on the balance sheet. Fortum's share in the State Nuclear Waste Management Fund has been accounted for according to IFRIC 5, *Rights to interests arising from decommissioning, restoration and environmental rehabilitation funds* which states that the fund assets are measured at the lower of fair value or the value of the related liabilities since Fortum does not have control or joint control over the State Nuclear Waste Management Fund. The related provisions are the provision for decommissioning and the provision for disposal of spent fuel...

... Fortum's actual share of the State Nuclear Waste Management Fund, related to Loviisa nuclear power plant, is higher than the carrying value of the Fund in the balance sheet. The legal nuclear liability should, according to the Finnish Nuclear Energy Act, be fully covered by payments and guarantees to the State Nuclear Waste Management Fund. The legal liability is not discounted while the provisions are, and since the future cash-flow is spread over 100 years, the difference between the legal liability and the provisions are material...

34.   Nuclear Related Assets and Liabilities [extract]

Fortum owns the Loviisa nuclear power plant in Finland. Based on the Nuclear Energy Act in Finland Fortum has a legal obligation to fully fund the legal liability, decided by the governmental authorities, for decommissioning of the power plant and disposal of spent fuel through the State Nuclear Waste Management Fund. The text below should be read in conjunction with information in Note 1 Accounting policies on page 67.

EUR million	2010	2009
Amounts recognised in the balance sheet		
Nuclear provisions	625	570
Share in the State Nuclear Waste Management Fund	625	570
Legal liability and actual share of the State Nuclear Waste Management Fund		
Liability for nuclear waste management according to the Nuclear Energy Act	944	913
Funding obligation target	886	830
Fortum's share in the State Nuclear Waste Management Fund	843	786

34.1 Nuclear related provisions [extract]

... The legal liability by the end of 2010, decided by the Ministry of Employment and the Economy and calculated according to the Nuclear Energy Act is EUR 944 million (2009: 913). The carrying value of the nuclear provisions in the balance sheet, calculated according to IAS 37, have increased by EUR 55 million compared to 31 December 2009, totalling EUR 625 million on 31 December 2010. The main reason for the difference between the carrying value of the provision and the legal liability is the fact that the legal liability is not discounted to net present value.

The increase of the provision for spent fuel caused a negative one-time effect in 2010 of EUR –8 million in comparable operating profit (2009: 7) due to higher nuclear waste management costs related to already spent fuel. The increase of the provision for spent fuel also caused a negative one-time effect in interest costs, due to unwinding of the provision for the period during which the spent fuel provision has been accumulated and present point in time, which are recognised immediately in the income statement.

The increase of the provision for decommissioning is added to the nuclear decommissioning cost and depreciated over the remaining estimated operating time of the nuclear power plant. See Note 22 Property, plant and equipment.

Nuclear provisions **EUR million**	**2010**	**2009**
1 January	570	566
Additional provisions	35	–4
Used during the year	–20	–18
Unwinding of discount	40	26
31 December	625	570
Fortum's share in the State Nuclear Waste Management Fund	625	570

34.2 Fortum's share in the State Nuclear Waste Management Fund [extract]

Fortum contributes funds to the State Nuclear Waste Management Fund in Finland to cover future obligations based on the legal liability calculated according to the Finnish Nuclear Energy Act. The fund is managed by governmental authorities. The carrying value of the Fund in Fortum's balance sheet is calculated according to IFRIC 5 *Rights to interests arising from Decommissioning, Restoration and Environmental Rehabilitation Funds*.

According to the Nuclear Energy Act, Fortum is obligated to contribute the funds in full to the State Nuclear Waste Management Fund to cover the legal liability. Based on the law, Fortum applied for periodising of the payments to the Fund over six years, due to the proposed increase in the legal liability. The application was approved by Council of State in December 2007.

The periodisation of the payments to the State Nuclear Waste Management Fund has an impact on cash-flow, but also on operating profit since the carrying value of the Fund in the balance sheet cannot exceed the carrying value of the nuclear provisions according to IFRIC Interpretation 5. The Fund is from an IFRS perspective overfunded with EUR 218 million (2009: 216), since Fortum's share of the Fund on 31 December 2010 is EUR 843 million (2009: 786) and the carrying value in the balance sheet is EUR 625 million (2009: 570).

Operating profit for 2010 includes a negative total adjustment of EUR –2 million (2009: –59), since the value of the Fund has increased more than the carrying value of the provision...

34.2.1 The funding obligation target [extract]

The funding obligation target for the each year is decided by the Ministry of Employment and the Economy in December each year after the legal liability has been decided. The difference between the funding obligation target for Fortum and Fortum's actual share of the State Nuclear Waste Fund is paid in Q1 each year.

The funding obligation target, corresponding to both the new legal liability and the new decision for periodisation to the Fund, amounts EUR 886 million (2009: 830)...

5.5.3.B   Accounting for obligations to make additional contributions

As far as issue (b) is concerned, IFRIC 5 requires that when a contributor has an obligation to make potential additional contributions, for example, in the event of the bankruptcy of another contributor or if the value of the investments held by the fund decreases to an extent that they are insufficient to fulfil the fund's reimbursement obligations, this obligation is a contingent liability that is within the scope of IAS 37. The contributor shall recognise a liability only if it is probable that additional contributions will be made. *[IFRIC 5.10]*.

5.5.3.C   Gross presentation of interest in the fund and the decommissioning liability

IFRIC 5 requires the contributor to a fund to recognise its obligations to pay decommissioning costs as a liability and recognise its interest in the fund separately, unless the contributor is not liable to pay decommissioning costs even if the fund fails to pay. *[IFRIC 5.7]*. Accordingly, in most cases it would not be appropriate to offset the decommissioning liability and the interest in the fund.

The Interpretations Committee reached this conclusion because IAS 37 requires an entity that remains liable for expenditure to recognise a provision even where reimbursement is available and to recognise a separate reimbursement asset only when the entity is virtually certain of its receipt. *[IFRIC 5.BC7]*. The Interpretations Committee also noted that the conditions in IAS 32 – *Financial Instruments: Presentation* – for offsetting a financial asset and a financial liability would rarely be met because of the absence of a legal right of set off and the likelihood that settlement will not be net or simultaneous. *[IAS 32.42]*. Arguments that the existence of a fund allows derecognition of the liability by analogy to IAS 39; or a net presentation similar to a pension fund, were also rejected. *[IFRIC 5.BC8]*.

5.6   Emission rights

A number of countries around the world either have, or are developing, schemes to encourage reduced emissions of pollutants, in particular of greenhouse gases. These schemes comprise tradable emissions allowances or permits, an example of which is a 'cap and trade' model whereby participants are allocated emission rights or allowances equal to a cap (i.e. a maximum level of allowable emissions) and are permitted to trade those allowances. A cap and trade emission rights scheme typically has the following features:[15]

- an entity participating in the scheme (participant) is set a target to reduce its emissions to a specified level (the cap). The participant is issued allowances equal in number to its cap by a government or government agency. Allowances may be issued free of charge, or participants may pay the government for them;

- the scheme operates for defined compliance periods;

- participants are free to buy and sell allowances;

- if at the end of the compliance period a participant's actual emissions exceeded its emission rights, the participant will incur a penalty;

- in some schemes emission rights may be carried forward to future periods; and

- the scheme may provide for brokers – who are not themselves participants – to buy and sell emission rights.

As there was no guidance on the accounting for cap and trade emission rights schemes and no consensus had emerged among market participants on what the accounting treatment should be, the Interpretations Committee concluded that it would explain how IFRS should be applied to such schemes. Accordingly, in December 2004 the IASB issued IFRIC 3 – *Emission Rights* – to address the accounting for emission allowances that arise from cap and trade emission rights schemes.

IFRIC 3 took the view that a cap and trade scheme did not give rise to a net asset or liability, but that it gave rise to various items that were to be accounted for separately:[16]

(a) *an asset for allowances held* – Allowances, whether allocated by government or purchased, were to be regarded as intangible assets and accounted for under IAS 38 – *Intangible Assets*. Allowances issued for less than fair value were to be measured initially at their fair value;[17]

(b) *a government grant* – When allowances are issued for less than fair value, the difference between the amount paid and fair value was a government grant that should be accounted for under IAS 20 – *Accounting for Government Grants and Disclosure of Government Assistance*. Initially the grant was to be recognised as deferred income in the balance sheet and subsequently recognised as income on a systematic basis over the compliance period for which the allowances were issued, regardless of whether the allowances were held or sold;[18]

(c) *a liability for the obligation to deliver allowances equal to emissions that have been made* – As emissions are made, a liability was to be recognised as a provision that falls within the scope of IAS 37. The liability was to be measured at the best estimate of the expenditure required to settle the present obligation at the end of the reporting period. This would usually be the present market price of the number of allowances required to cover emissions made up to the end of the reporting period.[19]

However, the interpretation met with significant resistance because application of IFRIC 3 would result in a number of accounting mismatches:[20]

- a measurement mismatch between the assets and liabilities recognised in accordance with IFRIC 3;
- a mismatch in the location in which the gains and losses on those assets are reported; and
- a possible timing mismatch because allowances would be recognised when they are obtained – typically at the start of the year – whereas the emission liability would be recognised during the year as it is incurred.

Consequently, the IASB decided in June 2005 to withdraw IFRIC 3 despite the fact that it considered it to be 'an appropriate interpretation of existing IFRSs'.[21] The IASB also decided to reconsider the accounting for cap and trade emission right schemes itself rather than ask the IFRIC to continue its work, because developing an approach that eliminates the mismatches will require the amendment of one or more standards. Work on emission rights and government grants had been deferred pending conclusion of work on other relevant projects, in particular the project to amend IAS 37.[22] However, in December 2007, the IASB decided that the continuing proliferation of such schemes, diversity in practice and requests to act by national standard setters required it to bring the issue back onto the IASB agenda. The Board decided to limit the scope of the project to accounting issues relating to emissions trading schemes, rather than to consider more general issues regarding the accounting for government grants[23] (see 7.3 below).

Chapter 29

Given that IFRIC 3 has been withdrawn, and pending any substantive output from the IASB project on emission trading schemes, what can or should entities do in the absence of any precise guidance? As can be seen above, the topic cuts across a number of different areas of accounting, not just that of provisions. A fuller discussion of the issues and methods applied in practice are covered in Chapter 19 at 13.3.

5.7   Green certificates

Some countries have launched schemes to promote the production of power from renewable sources based on green certificates – also known as renewable energy certificates (RECs), green tags, or tradable renewable certificates.

In a green certificates system, a producer of electricity from renewable sources is granted certificates by the government based on the power output (kWh) of green electricity produced. These certificates may be used in the current and future compliance periods as defined by the particular scheme. The certificates can be sold separately. Generally the cost to produce green electricity is higher than the cost of producing an equivalent amount of electricity generated from non-renewable sources, although this is not always the case. Distributors of electricity sell green electricity at the same price as other electricity.

In a typical green certificates scheme, distributors of electricity to consumers (businesses, households etc.) are required to remit a number of green certificates based on the kWh of electricity sold on an annual basis. Distributors must therefore purchase green certificates in the market (such certificates having been sold by producers). If a distribution company does not have the number of required certificates, it is required to pay a penalty to the environmental agency. Once the penalty is paid, the entity is discharged of its obligations to remit certificates.

It is this requirement to remit certificates that creates a market in and gives value to green certificates (the value depends on many variables but primarily on the required number of certificates that have to be delivered relative to the amount of power that is produced from renewable sources, and the level of penalty payable if the required number of certificates are not remitted).

There are similarities between green certificates and emission rights. However, whereas emission rights are granted to producers as a means of settling future obligations, green certificates are granted on the basis of 'good' production achieved rather than 'bad' emissions in the future, irrespective of whether or not there is a subsequent sale of energy to an end consumer.

For a distributor of energy under a green certificate regime, a green certificate is similar in nature to an emission right except that a distributor of energy under a green certificate regime must acquire the certificates from the market (i.e. they are not granted to the distributor by the government). As with emission rights, the topic of green certificates cuts across a number of different areas of accounting, not just that of provisions. A fuller discussion of the issues and methods applied in practice are covered in Chapter 19 at 13.4.

5.8   EU Directive on 'Waste Electrical and Electronic Equipment'[24] (IFRIC 6)

This Directive, regulates the collection, treatment, recovery and environmentally sound disposal of waste electrical or electronic equipment (WE&EE). It applies to entities involved in the manufacture and resale of electrical or electronic equipment, including entities (both European and Non-European) that import such equipment into the EU. As member states in the EU began to implement this directive into their national laws, it has given rise to questions about when the liability for the decommissioning of WE&EE should be recognised. The Directive distinguishes between 'new' and 'historical' waste and between waste from private households and waste from sources other than private households. New waste relates to products sold after 13 August 2005. All household equipment sold before that date is deemed to give rise to historical waste for the purposes of the Directive. *[IFRIC 6.3]*.

The Directive states that the cost of waste management for historical household equipment should be borne by producers of that type of equipment that are in the market during a period to be specified in the applicable legislation of each Member State (the measurement period). The Directive states that each Member State shall establish a mechanism to have producers contribute to costs proportionately 'e.g. in proportion to their respective share of the market by type of equipment.' *[IFRIC 6.4]*.

The Interpretations Committee was asked to determine in the context of the decommissioning of WE&EE what constitutes the obligating event in accordance with paragraph 14(a) of IAS 37 for the recognition of a provision for waste management costs: *[IFRIC 6.8]*

- the manufacture or sale of the historical household equipment?
- participation in the market during the measurement period?
- the incurrence of costs in the performance of waste management activities?

IFRIC 6 was issued in September 2005 and provides guidance on the recognition, in the financial statements of producers, of liabilities for waste management under the EU Directive on WE&EE in respect of sales of historical household equipment. *[IFRIC 6.6]*. The interpretation addresses neither new waste nor historical waste from sources other than private households. The Interpretations Committee considers that the liability for such waste management is adequately covered in IAS 37. However, if, in national legislation, new waste from private households is treated in a similar manner to historical waste from private households, the principles of IFRIC 6 are to apply by reference to the hierarchy set out in IAS 8 (see Chapter 3 at 4.3). The IAS 8 hierarchy is also stated to be relevant for other regulations that impose obligations in a way that is similar to the cost attribution model specified in the EU Directive. *[IFRIC 6.7]*.

IFRIC 6 regards participation in the market during the measurement period as the obligating event in accordance with paragraph 14(a) of IAS 37. Consequently, a liability for waste management costs for historical household equipment does not arise as the products are manufactured or sold. Because the obligation for historical household equipment is linked to participation in the market during the measurement period, rather than to production or sale of the items to be disposed of, there is no obligation unless and until a market share exists during the measurement

Chapter 29

period. It is also noted that the timing of the obligating event may also be independent of the particular period in which the activities to perform the waste management are undertaken and the related costs incurred. *[IFRIC 6.9].*

The following example, which is based on one within the accompanying Basis for Conclusions on IFRIC 6, illustrates its requirements. *[IFRIC 6.BC5].*

Example 29.16:   Illustration of IFRIC 6 requirements

An entity selling electrical equipment in 2008 has a market share of 4 per cent for that calendar year. It subsequently discontinues operations and is thus no longer in the market when the waste management costs for its products are allocated to those entities with market share in 2012. With a market share of 0 per cent in 2012, the entity's obligation is zero. However, if another entity enters the market for electronic products in 2012 and achieves a market share of 3 per cent in that period, then that entity's obligation for the costs of waste management from earlier periods will be 3 per cent of the total costs of waste management allocated to 2012, even though the entity was not in the market in those earlier periods and has not produced any of the products for which waste management costs are allocated to 2012.

The Interpretations Committee concluded that the effect of the cost attribution model specified in the Directive is that the making of sales during the measurement period is the 'past event' that requires recognition of a provision under IAS 37 over the measurement period. Aggregate sales for the period determine the entity's obligation for a proportion of the costs of waste management allocated to that period. The measurement period is independent of the period when the cost allocation is notified to market participants. *[IFRIC 6.BC6].*

Some constituents asked the Interpretations Committee to consider the effect of the following possible national legislation: the waste management costs for which a producer is responsible because of its participation in the market during a specified period (for example 2012) are not based on the market share of the producer during that period but on the producer's participation in the market during a previous period (for example 2011). The Interpretations Committee noted that this affects only the measurement of the liability and that the obligating event is still participation in the market during 2012. *[IFRIC 6.BC7].*

IFRIC 6 notes that terms used in the interpretation such as 'market share' and 'measurement period' may be defined very differently in the applicable legislation of individual Member States. For example, the length of the measurement period might be a year or only one month. Similarly, the measurement of market share and the formulae for computing the obligation may differ in the various national legislations. However, all of these examples affect only the measurement of the liability, which is not within the scope of the interpretation. *[IFRIC 6.5].*

5.9   Entities should not provide for repairs and maintenance of owned assets

Repairs and maintenance provisions in respect of owned assets are generally prohibited under IAS 37. Under the standard, the following principles apply:

(a)   provisions are recognised only for obligations existing independently of the entity's future actions (i.e. the future conduct of its business) and in cases where an entity can avoid future expenditure by its future actions, for example by changing its method of operation, it has no present obligation; *[IAS 37.19]*

(b)   financial statements deal with an entity's position at the end of the reporting period and not its possible position in the future. Therefore, no provision is recognised for costs that need to be incurred to operate in the future; *[IAS 37.18]* and

(c)   for an event to be an obligating event, the entity can have no realistic alternative to settling the obligation created by the event. *[IAS 37.17]*.

These principles are applied strictly in the case of an obligation to incur repairs and maintenance costs in the future, even when this expenditure is substantial, distinct from what may be regarded as routine maintenance and essential to the continuing operations of the entity, such as a major refit or refurbishment of the asset. This is illustrated by two examples in an appendix to the standard. *[IAS 37 Appendix C, Examples 11A, 11B]*.

Example 29.17:   Prohibition on maintenance provisions relating to owned assets

Scenario 1;   Re-lining costs of a furnace

An entity operates a furnace, the lining of which needs to be replaced every five years for technical reasons. At the end of the reporting period, the lining has been in use for three years. In these circumstances, a provision for the cost of replacing the lining is not recognised because, at the end of the reporting period, no obligation to replace the lining exists independently of the entity's future actions. Even the intention to incur the expenditure depends upon the entity deciding to continue operating the furnace or to replace the lining. Instead of a provision being recognised, the initial cost of the lining is treated as a significant part of the furnace asset and depreciated over a period of five years. [IAS 16.43]. The re-lining costs are then capitalised when incurred and depreciated over the next five years.

Scenario 2;   Overhaul costs of an aircraft

An airline is required by law to overhaul its aircraft once every three years. Even with the legal requirement to perform the overhaul, there is no obligating event until the three year period has elapsed. As with Scenario 1, no obligation exists independently of the entity's future actions. The entity could avoid the cost of the overhaul by selling the aircraft before the three year period has elapsed. Instead of a provision being recognised, the overhaul cost is identified as a separate part of the aircraft asset under IAS 16 and is depreciated over three years.

Entities might try to argue that a repairs and maintenance provision should be recognised on the basis that there is a clear intention to incur the expenditure at the appointed time and that this means it is more likely than not, as at the end of the reporting period, that an outflow of resources will occur. However, the application of the three principles noted above, particularly that an entity should not provide for future operating costs, make such an argument irrelevant. In the example above, recognition was not allowed because the entity could do all manner of things to avoid the obligation, including selling the asset, however unlikely that might be in the context of the entity's business or in terms of the relative cost of replacement as compared to repair. The existence of a legal requirement, probably resulting in the aircraft being grounded, was still not enough.

It is interesting, however, that a similar argument had not been used in respect of the recognition of decommissioning costs, where presumably an entity could also avoid such obligations by selling, for example, its oil and gas assets.

Chapter 29

The effect of the prohibition on setting up provisions for repairs obviously has an impact on balance sheet presentation. It may not always, however, have as much impact on the statement of comprehensive income. This is because it is suggested in the examples that depreciation would be adjusted to take account of the repairs. For example, in the case of the furnace lining, the lining should be depreciated over five years in advance of its expected repair. Similarly, in the case of the aircraft overhaul, the example in the standard suggests that an amount equivalent to the expected maintenance costs is depreciated over three years. The result of this is that the depreciation charge recognised in profit or loss over the life of the component of the asset requiring regular repair may be equivalent to that which would previously have arisen from the combination of depreciation and a provision for repair.

5.10   Dilapidation and other provisions relating to leased assets

Whilst it is not appropriate to recognise provisions that relate to repairs and maintenance of owned assets (including assets held under finance leases) the position can be different in the case of obligations relating to assets held under operating leases. Nevertheless, the same principles under IAS 37 apply:

(a)   provisions are recognised only for obligations existing independently of the entity's future actions (i.e. the future conduct of its business) and in cases where an entity can avoid future expenditure by its future actions, for example by changing its method of operation, it has no present obligation; *[IAS 37.19]*

(b)   financial statements deal with an entity's position at the end of the reporting period and not its possible position in the future. Therefore, no provision is recognised for costs that need to be incurred to operate in the future; *[IAS 37.18]* and

(c)   for an event to be an obligating event, the entity can have no realistic alternative to settling the obligation created by the event. *[IAS 37.17]*.

Operating leases often contain clauses which specify that the lessee should incur periodic charges for maintenance, make good dilapidations or other damage occurring during the rental period or return the asset to the configuration that existed as at inception of the lease. These contractual provisions may restrict the entity's ability to change its future conduct to avoid the expenditure. For example, the entity might not be able to transfer the asset in its existing condition. Alternatively, the entity could return the asset to avoid the risk of incurring costs relating to any future damage, but would have to make a payment in relation of dilapidations incurred to date. So the contractual obligations in a lease could create an environment in which a present obligation could exist as at the reporting date from which the entity cannot realistically withdraw.

Whilst IAS 37 is not clear as to whether provision for such obligations under operating leases meet the standard's recognition criteria, this issue is mentioned briefly in the appendix to FRS 12 in the UK in discussing the development of that standard. This notes that 'the principle illustrated in [the example on repairs] does not preclude the recognition of such liabilities once the event giving rise to the obligation under the lease has occurred'.[25] Since the repair examples in IAS 37 are the same as those in FRS 12, then we believe that the same comment is relevant in interpreting IAS 37.

Under principle (b) above, any provision should reflect only the conditions as at the reporting date. This means that a provision for specific damage done to the leased asset would merit recognition, as the event giving rise to the obligation under the lease has certainly occurred. For example, if an entity has erected partitioning or internal walls in a leasehold property and under the lease these have to be removed at the end of the term, then provision should be made for this cost (on a discounted basis, if material) at the time of putting up the partitioning or the walls. In this case, an equivalent asset would be recognised and depreciated over the term of the lease. This is similar to a decommissioning provision discussed at 5.5 above. Another example would be where an airline company leases aircraft under an operating lease, and upon delivery of the aircraft has made changes to the interior fittings and layout, but under the leasing arrangements has to return the asset to the configuration that existed as at inception of the lease.

What is less clear is whether a more general provision can be built up over time for maintenance charges and dilapidation costs in relation to a leased asset. It might be argued that in this case, the event giving rise to the obligation under the lease is simply the passage of time, and so a provision can be built up over time. However, a stricter interpretation of the phrase 'the event giving rise to the obligation under the lease' may lead one to conclude that a more specific event has to occur; there has to be specific evidence of dilapidation etc. before any provision can be made.

Example 29.17 at 5.9 above dealt with an owned aircraft that by law needs overhauling every three years, but no provision could be recognised for such costs. Instead, IAS 37 suggests that an amount equivalent to the expected maintenance costs is treated as a separate part of the asset and depreciated over three years. Airworthiness requirements for the airline industry are the same irrespective of whether the aircraft is owned or leased. So, if an airline company leases the aircraft under an operating lease, should a provision be made for the overhaul costs? The answer will depend on the terms of the lease.

If the lease requires the lessee to maintain the airworthiness of the aircraft and to return the aircraft at the end of the lease in the same condition as it was taken at inception of the lease, i.e. the aircraft has to be overhauled prior to its return, then the lessee should make provision. In this case the overhaul of the aircraft is a contractual obligation under the lease. The specific event that gives rise to the obligation is each flown hour or cycle completed by the aircraft as these determine the timing and nature of the overhaul that must be carried out. Provision should therefore be made for the costs of overhaul as the obligation towards the lessor arises (typically based upon the specific requirements of each aircraft type such as each flown hour or cycle), with a corresponding expense recognised in the statement of comprehensive income. For certain aircraft types and aircraft leases it is likely that the provision for the costs will be built up and then released, as the expenditure is incurred, a number of times during the term of the operating lease.

However, if the lease does not require the overhaul to be undertaken prior to the return of the aircraft (or require the lessee to make a contribution towards the next overhaul), then no provision should be made as the lessee does not have a contractual obligation to incur these costs that is independent of its own future actions.

Chapter 29

The fact that a provision for repairs can be made at all in these circumstances might appear inconsistent with the case where the asset is owned by the entity. In that case, as discussed at 5.9 above, no provision for repairs could be made. There is, however, a difference between the two situations. Where the entity owns the asset, it has the choice of selling it rather than repairing it, and so the obligation is not independent of the entity's future actions. However, in the case of an entity leasing the asset, it can have a contractual obligation to repair any damage from which it cannot walk away.

Extract 29.4 at 5.3.1 above, shows an example of a company that has provided for dilapidation costs.

5.11   Warranty provisions

Warranty provisions are specifically addressed in one of the examples appended to IAS 37. However, it is worth noting that the IASB decided to exclude warranty costs from the scope of any new standard on liabilities.[26] Warranty costs are addressed instead in its Exposure Draft on Revenue from Contracts with Customers, which is expected to be re-exposed in late 2011.[27] The revenue recognition project is discussed in Chapter 30.

Example 29.18:   Recognition of a provision for warranty costs

A manufacturer gives warranties at the time of sale to purchasers of its product. Under the terms of the contract for sale, the manufacturer undertakes to make good, by repair or replacement, manufacturing defects that become apparent within three years from the date of sale. On past experience, it is probable (i.e. more likely than not) that there will be some claims under the warranties.

In these circumstances the obligating event is the sale of the product with a warranty, which gives rise to a legal obligation. Because it is more likely than not that there will be an outflow of resources for some claims under the warranties as a whole, a provision is recognised for the best estimate of the costs of making good under the warranty for those products sold before the end of the reporting period. *[IAS 37 Appendix C, Example 1].*

The assessment of the probability of an outflow of resources is made across the population as a whole, and not using each potential claim as the unit of account. *[IAS 37.24].* On past experience, it is probable that there will be some claims under the warranties, so a provision is recognised.

The assessment over the class of obligations as a whole makes it more likely that a provision will be recognised, because the probability criterion is considered in terms of whether at least one item in the population will give rise to a payment. Recognition then becomes a matter of reliable measurement and entities calculate an expected value of the estimated warranty costs. IAS 37 discusses this method of 'expected value' and illustrates how it is calculated in an example of a warranty provision. *[IAS 37.39].* See Example 29.6 at 4.1 above.

An example of a company that makes a warranty provision is Nokia as shown below:

Extract 29.11: Nokia Oyj (2010)

1.   Accounting principles [extract]

Provisions [extract]

Provisions are recognized when the Group has a present legal or constructive obligation as a result of past events, it is probable that an outflow of resources will be required to settle the obligation and a reliable estimate of the amount can be made. Where the Group expects a provision to be reimbursed, the reimbursement would be recognized as an asset only when the reimbursement is virtually certain. At each balance sheet date, the Group assesses the adequacy of its pre-existing provisions and adjusts the amounts as necessary based on actual experience and changes in future estimates.

Warranty provisions

The Group provides for the estimated liability to repair or replace products under warranty at the time revenue is recognized. The provision is an estimate calculated based on historical experience of the level of volumes, product mix, repair and replacement cost.

Use of estimates and critical accounting judgements [extract]

Warranty provisions

The Group provides for the estimated cost of product warranties at the time revenue is recognized. The Group's warranty provision is established based upon best estimates of the amounts necessary to settle future and existing claims on products sold as of each balance sheet date. As new products incorporating complex technologies are continuously introduced, and as local laws, regulations and practices may change, changes in these estimates could result in additional allowances or changes to recorded allowances being required in future periods.

5.12   Litigation and other legal claims

IAS 37 includes an example of a court case in its appendix to illustrate how its principles distinguish between a contingent liability and a provision in such situations. See Example 29.4 at 3.2.1 above. However, the assessment of the particular case in the example is clear-cut. In most situations, assessing the need to provide for legal claims is one of the most difficult tasks in the field of provisioning. This is due mainly to the inherent uncertainty in the judicial process itself, which may be very long and drawn out. Furthermore, this is an area where either provision or disclosure might risk prejudicing the outcome of the case, because they give an insight into the entity's own view on the strength of its defence that can assist the claimant. Similar considerations apply in other related areas, such as tax disputes.

In principle, whether a provision should be made will depend on whether the 3 conditions for recognising a provision are met, i.e.

(a)   there is a present obligation as a result of a past event;

(b)   it is probable that an outflow of resources embodying economic benefits will be required to settle the obligation; and

(c)   a reliable estimate can be made of the amount of the obligation. *[IAS 37.14]*.

In situations such as these, a past event is deemed to give rise to a present obligation if, taking account of all available evidence (including, for example, the opinion of experts), it is more likely than not that a present obligation exists at the end of the reporting period. *[IAS 37.15]*. The evidence to be considered includes any additional

Chapter 29

evidence occurring after the end of the reporting period. Accordingly, if on the basis of the evidence it is concluded that a present obligation is more likely than not to exist, a provision will be required, assuming the other conditions are met. *[IAS 37.16]*.

Condition (b) will be met if the transfer of economic benefits is more likely than not to occur, that is, it has a probability greater than 50%. In making this assessment, it is likely that account should be taken of any expert advice.

As far as condition (c) is concerned, the standard takes the view that a reasonable estimate can generally be made and it is only in extremely rare cases that this will not be the case. *[IAS 37.25]*.

Clearly, whether an entity should make provision for the costs of settling a case or to meet any award given by a court will depend on a reasoned assessment of the particular circumstances, based on appropriate legal advice.

5.13   Refunds policy

Example 29.1 at 3.1.1 above reflects an example given in the appendix of IAS 37 of a retail store that has a policy of refunding goods returned by dissatisfied customers. There is no legal obligation to do so, but the company's policy of making refunds is generally known. The example argues that the conduct of the store has created a valid expectation on the part of its customers that it will refund purchases. The obligating event is the original sale of the item, and the probability of some economic outflow is greater than 50%, as there will nearly always be some customers demanding refunds. Hence, a provision should be made, *[IAS 37 Appendix C, Example 4]*, presumably calculated on the 'expected value' basis.

This example is straightforward when the store has a very specific and highly publicised policy on refunds. However, some stores' policies on refunds might not be so clear cut. A store may offer refunds under certain conditions, but not widely publicise its policy. In these circumstances, there might be doubt as to whether the store has created a valid expectation on the part of its customers that it will honour all requests for a refund. As with warranty costs (discussed at 5.11 above), the accounting treatment of refunds impinges into the area of revenue recognition and is therefore an element of the project to develop a new standard on Revenue from Contracts with Customers (see Chapter 30).

5.14   Staff training costs

In the normal course of business it is unlikely that provisions for staff training costs would be permissible, because it would normally contravene the general prohibition in the standard on the recognition of provisions for future operating costs. *[IAS 37.18]*. In the context of a restructuring, IAS 37 identifies staff retraining as an ineligible cost because it relates to the future conduct of the business. *[IAS 37.81]*. Example 29.2 at 3.1.1 above reproduces an example in the standard where the government introduces changes to the income tax system, such that an entity in the financial services sector needs to retrain a large proportion of its administrative and sales workforce in order to ensure continued compliance with financial services regulation. The standard argues that there is no present obligation until the actual training has taken place and so no provision should be recognised. We agree with this outcome, and note that in many cases the need to incur training costs is not only future operating expenditure but also fails the 'existing independently of an entity's future actions' criterion, *[IAS 37.19]*, in that the cost could be avoided by the entity, for example, if it withdrew from that market or hired new staff who were already appropriately qualified.

This example again illustrates how important it is to properly understand the nature of any potential 'constructive obligation' or 'obligating event' and to determine separately its financial effect in relation to past transactions and events on the one hand and in relation to the future operation of the business on the other. Otherwise, it can be easy to mistakenly argue that a provision is required, such as for training costs to ensure that staff comply with new legal requirements, when in fact the related expense is a cost of operating in the future and therefore ineligible for recognition. An alternative interpretation of the fact pattern in the above example could be that the entity has a constructive obligation to retrain its sales force, as it has built up a valid expectation in its employees and customers that the sales force will be up to date on changes to the income tax system which affect the products it sells, to enable it to adequately meet the needs of its customers. If the entity had published some sort of policy statement reassuring employees and customers that the sales force would receive adequate training on the income tax changes, then is the existence of a constructive obligation not unquestionable? However, the obligation, constructive or not, declared or not, relates to the entity's future conduct; is a future cost of operation and is therefore ineligible for recognition under the standard until the training takes place.

However, in other situations an obligating event could arise before the training has taken place, for example where a regulator has required staff retraining as part of the remedy for a breach of its regulations.

This all goes to show how sometimes it appears the standard is inconsistent. For example, the argument that no provision is made for future operating costs does not help in distinguishing staff training costs from provisions for refunds, which are required to be made. After all, the customer in the Example 29.1 at 3.1.1 has no legal right to a refund. The entity could refuse, but presumably would not because of the bad publicity and loss of goodwill that would be suffered. Similarly, in this example, the sales force could cease selling certain financial products, but would be reluctant to do so because it would lose customers.

In reality, the distinction between these two examples comes down to when the benefits are obtained in each case, not whether the entity has a liability at the end of the reporting period. In the case of the refund policy, the revenue from the sale has already been booked, so any reversal of it should be recognised. However, in the case of staff training, the benefits of the training will be the impact on future sales, so it is not appropriate to provide for the costs of training in advance. This dimension of revenue and expense recognition is not acknowledged in the standard, presumably because it does not sit well within a framework centred on the balance sheet, but it does seem to underlie a number of the conclusions that are reached.

5.15   Self insurance

Another situation where entities sometimes make provisions is self insurance which arises when an entity decides not to take out external insurance in respect of a certain category of risk because it would be uneconomic to do so. The same position may arise when a group insures its risks with a captive insurance subsidiary, the effects of which have to be eliminated on consolidation. In fact, the term 'self insurance' is potentially misleading, since it really means that the entity is not insured at all and will settle claims from third parties from its own resources in the event that it is found to be liable. Accordingly, the recognition criteria in IAS 37 should be applied, with a provision being justified only if there is a present obligation as a result of a past event; if it is probable that an outflow of resources will occur; and a reliable estimate can be determined. *[IAS 37.14]*.

Therefore, losses are recognised based on their actual incidence and any provisions that appear in the balance sheet should reflect only the amounts expected to be paid in respect of those incidents that have occurred by the end of the reporting period.

This is the conclusion of an example in FRS 12 in the UK for which there is no equivalent example in IAS 37.[28] Entities in the UK had previously sought to build up a provision from period to period by reference to a simulated insurance premium that it had not in fact paid.

In certain circumstances, a provision will often be needed not simply for known incidents, but also for those which insurance companies call IBNR – Incurred But Not Reported – representing an estimate of the latent liabilities at the end of the reporting period that experience shows will come to the surface only gradually. We believe that it is entirely appropriate that provision for such expected claims is made.

5.16   Regulatory liabilities

Under certain national GAAPs, an entity can defer benefits that would otherwise be included in profit for the period (for example, revenues) as regulatory liabilities on the basis that the regulator requires it to reduce its tariffs so as to return the amounts concerned to customers. Under IFRS, should an entity recognise a liability (or a provision) when a regulator requires the entity to reduce its future prices/revenues so as to return to customers what the regulator regards as the excess amounts collected in the current period?

No reference is made within IAS 37, or any of its examples, to this type of situation. However, we believe that under IFRS no such liabilities can be recognised since there is no present obligation relating to a past transaction or event. A liability is defined in IAS 37 as 'a present obligation of the entity arising from past events, the settlement of which is expected to result in an outflow from the entity of resources embodying economic benefits'. *[IAS 37.10]*.

The return to customers of amounts mandated by a regulator depends on future events including:

- future rendering of services;
- future volumes of output (generally consisting of utilities such as water or electricity) consumed by users; and
- the continuation of regulation.

Consequently, items described as 'regulatory liabilities' do not meet the definition of a liability cited above since there needs to be a present obligation at the end of the reporting period before a liability can be recognised. Entities, in general, would recognise a liability for those items only if an obligation to refund exists as a result of past events or transactions, and regardless of future events.

This conclusion is consistent with the position in Appendix VII to FRS 12, which discusses the development of the UK standard, noting that by basing the recognition of a provision on the existence of a present obligation, FRS 12 rules out the recognition of any provision made simply to allocate results over more than one period or otherwise to smooth the results reported. To illustrate this, it goes on to say 'For example, in a regulated industry the results achieved in the current period may cause the pricing structure in the next period to be adjusted, e.g. the higher the profits in this year the lower the prices permitted for next year. There is no justification under the FRS for a provision to be recognised in such circumstances. The purpose of such a provision would be to transfer some of the current year's profit to the following year, which would suffer from lower prices because of the current year's profits. However, there is no present obligation that requires the transfer of economic benefits to settle it and nothing to justify recognition of a provision.'[29]

As discussed in more detail at 13.1 in Chapter 19, the Interpretations Committee has been asked a number of times to consider whether such regulatory liabilities should be recognised and on each occasion, the most recent being in November 2008, decided not to add the issue to its agenda, noting in particular that whilst rate regulation is widespread and significantly affects the economic environment of regulated entities, divergence did not seem to be significant in practice for entities that were already applying IFRS.[30] The current consensus among existing IFRS reporters is that no regulatory liabilities are recognised, unless in those rare cases where they meet the definition of a financial liability.[31]

However, in response to a request made to the November 2008 meeting of the IFRS Advisory Council and discussions at its December 2008 meeting, the IASB decided to add a project on rate-regulated activities to its agenda. The Board acknowledged that while divergence in practice did not currently exist, this was a matter of significant interest in a number of countries that would be adopting IFRS in the near future and where recognition of regulatory liabilities (and assets) was either permitted or required. The approaching conversion of these jurisdictions to IFRS would increase pressure for a definitive conclusion on the question.[32] In July 2009, the IASB issued an exposure draft on rate-regulated activities (see 7.2 below).

Chapter 29

5.17   Obligations to make donations to non-profit organisations

When an entity promises to make donations to a non-profit organisation it can be difficult to determine whether a past obligating event exists that requires a provision to be recognised or whether it is appropriate instead to account for the gift as payments are made.

Example 29.19:   Accounting for donations to non-profit organisations

An entity decides to enter into an arrangement to 'donate' €1m in cash to a university. A number of different options are available for the arrangement and the entity's management want to determine whether the terms of these options make any difference to the timing, measurement or presentation of the €1m expenditure, as follows:

Option 1:
The entity enters into an unenforceable contract to contribute €1m for general purposes. News of the donation will be published in a press release. The benefits to the entity are deemed only to relate to its reputation as a 'good corporate citizen'; the entity does not receive any consideration or significant benefit from the university in return for the donation.

Option 2:
As per Option 1 except the university publishes a press release in relation to the donation and payment is to be made in equal instalments of €200,000 over 5 years.

Option 3:
As per Option 2, except that the contract is legally enforceable in the event that the entity does not pay all the instalments under the contract.

Option 4:
As per Option 2, except that the entity is only required to make the donation if the university raises €4m from other sources.

Option 5:
As per Option 2, except that the contract is legally enforceable and the funds will be used for research and development activities specified by the entity. The entity will retain proprietary rights over the results of the research.

The following principles are relevant in determining when a promise to make a donation should be recognised as an obligation:

- to the extent that there is an enforceable contract, the donor should recognise an expense and a liability upon entry into that contract;

- where the agreement is not enforceable, the donor recognises an expense and a liability when a constructive obligation arises. The timing of recognition depends on whether the donation is conditional, whether it is probable that those conditions are substantially met and whether a past event has occurred; and

- if the donor expects to receive benefits commensurate with the value of the donation, the arrangement should be treated as an exchange transaction. Such transactions are in some cases executory contracts and may also give rise to the recognition of an asset rather than an expense.

In cases where the 'donation' is made under an enforceable contract, a present obligation is created when the entity enters into that contract. When payment is required in cash, the signing of an enforceable contract gives rise to a financial liability *[IAS 32.11]* which is measured initially at fair value. *[IAS 39.43]*.

Where there is no legal obligation to make the payments, a liability is recognised when a constructive obligation arises. It is a matter of judgement whether and when a constructive obligation exists. In many unenforceable contracts, there is no constructive obligation simply because the contract has been signed; hence the donor would recognise the expenditure when the cash or other assets are transferred.

By contrast, an exchange transaction is a reciprocal transfer in which each party receives and sacrifices approximately equal value. Assets and liabilities are not recognised until each party performs their obligations under the arrangement.

Applying these principles to the options listed in Example 29.19 above:

- In Option 1, the contract is unenforceable, there is no announcement or conditions preceding payment and there is no exchange of benefits. Accordingly, an expense would be recognised when the entity transfers cash to the university.

- For Option 2, it would be appropriate for the entity to conclude that the university's announcement of the donation to be paid by instalments creates a constructive obligation. Alternatively, it could determine that once the first instalment is paid, the entity has created a valid expectation that it will make the remaining payments. This is a matter of judgement. In this case the entity would recognise an expense and a liability, measured at the net present value of the 5 instalments of €200,000, at the point when it is determined that a constructive obligation exists.

- Option 3 involves an enforceable contract with no exchange of benefits. Therefore a liability and an expense is recognised on signing the enforceable contract, measured at the present value of the 5 instalments of €200,000.

- Under Option 4, the contract is unenforceable and the donation is subject to a condition. In these circumstances, management come to the judgement that no constructive obligation exists until it is probable that the condition is met (which might not be until the additional funds have been collected). Only then would a liability and expense be recognised, measured at the net present value of the €1m promised.

- Option 5 involves an enforceable contract. Therefore a liability is recognised when the contract is signed. In addition, there is an exchange of benefits relating to the research and development activities performed on behalf of the entity. Whether these benefits have a value close to the present value of the 5 instalments of €200,000 is a matter of judgment. If it determined that this is an exchange transaction, an asset or expense would be recognised for the research and development costs in accordance with IAS 38.

Where the arrangement gives rise to an exchange transaction rather than a donation, the expenditure is recorded in accordance with the relevant IFRS.

Chapter 29

6   DISCLOSURE REQUIREMENTS

The real distinction between the accounting treatment of provisions and other liabilities is the level of disclosure required.

6.1   Provisions

For each class of provision an entity should provide a reconciliation of the carrying amount of the provision at the beginning and end of the period showing:

(a)   additional provisions made in the period, including increases to existing provisions;

(b)   amounts used, i.e. incurred and charged against the provision, during the period;

(c)   unused amounts reversed during the period; and

(d)   the increase during the period in the discounted amount arising from the passage of time and the effect of any change in the discount rate.

Comparative information is not required. *[IAS 37.84]*.

Disclosure (d) effectively requires the charge for discounting that is recognised in profit or loss to be split between the element that relates to the straightforward unwinding of the discount, and any further charge or credit that arises if discount rates have changed during the period. It is interesting that there is no specific requirement to disclose the discount rate used.

One of the important disclosures which is reinforced here is the requirement to disclose the release of provisions found to be unnecessary. This disclosure, along with the requirement in the standard that provisions should be used only for the purpose for which the provision was originally recognised, *[IAS 37.61]*, is designed to prevent entities from concealing expenditure by charging it against a provision that was set up for another purpose.

In addition, for each class of provision an entity should disclose the following:

(a)   a brief description of the nature of the obligation and the expected timing of any resulting outflows of economic benefits;

(b)   an indication of the uncertainties about the amount or timing of those outflows. Where necessary to provide adequate information, an entity should disclose the major assumptions made concerning future events, as addressed in paragraph 48 of the standard (discussed at 4.4 above). This refers to future developments in technology and legislation and is of particular relevance to environmental liabilities; and

(c)   the amount of any expected reimbursement, stating the amount of any asset that has been recognised for that expected reimbursement. *[IAS 37.85]*.

Appendix D to the standard provides examples of suitable disclosures in relation to warranties and decommissioning costs.

Most of the above disclosures are illustrated in the extract below.

Extract 29.12: Roche Group (2010)

25.   Provisions and contingent liabilities [extract]

Provisions: movements in recognised liabilities *in millions of CHF*

	Legal provisions	Environ- mental provisions	Restruct- uring provisions	Employee provisions	Other provisions	Total
Year ended 31 December 2009						
At 1 January 2009	223	161	264	279	531	1,458
Additional provisions created	513	101	457	131	582	1,784
Unused amounts reversed	(113)	(3)	(22)	(12)	(62)	(212)
Utilised during the year	(64)	(20)	(157)	(126)	(342)	(709)
Unwinding of discount	5	13	1	2	–	21
Business combinations	–	–	2	–	2	4
Currency translation effects	(15)	(5)	(13)	4	1	(28)
At 31 December 2009	549	247	532	278	712	2,318
Of which						
– Current portion	514	17	421	60	606	1,618
– Non-current portion	35	230	111	218	106	700
Total provisions	549	247	532	278	712	2,318
Year ended 31 December 2010						
At 1 January 2010	549	247	532	278	712	2,318
Additional provisions created	444	42	897	118	430	1,931
Unused amounts reversed	(54)	(13)	(80)	(6)	(153)	(306)
Utilised during the year	(76)	(17)	(299)	(100)	(237)	(729)
Unwinding of discount	5	12	2	1	–	20
Business combinations						
– Acquired companies	–	–	–	–	–	–
– Contingent consideration	–	–	–	–	118	118
Currency translation effects	(87)	(10)	(82)	(38)	(55)	(272)
At 31 December 2010	781	261	970	253	815	3,080
Of which						
– Current portion	716	10	761	61	598	2,146
– Non-current portion	65	251	209	192	217	934
Total provisions	781	261	970	253	815	3,080

	Legal provisions	Environ- mental provisions	Restruct- uring provisions	Employee provisions	Other provisions	Total
Expected outflow of resources						
– within one year	716	10	761	61	598	2,146
– between one to two years	42	8	138	31	16	235
– between two to three years	7	33	63	21	104	228
– more than three years	16	210	8	140	97	471
Total provisions	781	261	970	253	815	3,080

Legal provisions

Legal provisions consist of a number of other separate legal matters, including claims arising from trade, in various Group companies. The majority of any cash outflows for these other matters are expected to occur within the next one to three years, although these are dependent on the development of the various litigations. Significant provisions are discounted by between 4% and 5% where as the time value of money is material.

Environmental provisions

Provisions for environmental matters include various separate environmental issues in a number of countries. By their nature the amounts and timing of any outflows are difficult to predict. The estimated timings of these cash outflows are shown in the table above. Significant provisions are discounted by between 5% and 6% where the time value of money is material.

Restructuring provisions

These arise from planned programmes that materially change the scope of business undertaken by the Group or the manner in which business is conducted. Such provisions include only the costs necessarily entailed by the restructuring which are not associated with the recurring activities of the Group. The timings of these cash outflows are reasonably certain on a global basis and are shown in the table above. These provisions are not discounted as the time value of money is not material in these matters.

Employee provisions

These mostly relate to certain employee benefit obligations, such as sabbatical leave and long-service benefits. The timings of these cash outflows can be reasonable estimated based on past performance and are shown in the table above. These provisions are not discounted as the time value of money is not material in these matters.

Other provisions

Other provisions mostly relate to sales returns and various other provisions from Group companies that do not fit into the above categories. The timings of cash outflows are by their nature uncertain and the best estimates are shown in the table above. These provisions are not discounted as the time value of money is not material in these matters.

Contingent liabilities

The operations and earnings of the Group continue, from time to time and in varying degrees, to be affected by political, legislative, fiscal and regulatory developments, including those relating to environmental protection, in the countries in which it operates. The industries in which the Group operates are also subject to other risks of various kinds. The nature and frequency of these developments and events, not all of which are covered by insurance, as well as their effect on future operations and earnings, are not predictable.

The Group has entered into strategic alliances with various companies in order to gain access to potential new products or to utilise other companies to help develop the Group's own potential new products. Potential future payments may become due to certain collaboration partners achieving certain milestones as defined in the collaboration agreements. The Group's best estimates of future commitments for such payments are given in Note 14.

The standard states that in determining which provisions may be aggregated to form a class, it is necessary to consider whether the nature of the items is sufficiently similar for a single statement about them to fulfil the requirements of (a) and (b) above. An example is given of warranties: it is suggested that, while it may be appropriate to treat warranties of different products as a single class of provision, it would not be appropriate to aggregate normal warranties with amounts that are subject to legal proceedings. *[IAS 37.87]*. This requirement could be interpreted to mean that in disclosing restructuring costs, the different components of the costs, such as redundancies, termination of leases, etc, should be disclosed separately. However, materiality will be an important consideration in judging how much analysis is required.

As indicated at 5.2.1 above, IAS 37 emphasises that when a restructuring meets the definition of a discontinued operation under IFRS 5, additional disclosures may be required under that standard (see Chapter 4 at 3). *[IAS 37.9]*.

6.2   Contingent liabilities

Unless the possibility of any outflow in settlement is remote, IAS 37 requires the disclosure for each class of contingent liability at the end of the reporting period to include a brief description of the nature of the contingent liability, and where practicable:

(a)   an estimate of its financial effect, measured in accordance with paragraphs 36-52 of IAS 37 (discussed at 4 above);

(b)   an indication of the uncertainties relating to the amount or timing of any outflow; and

(c)   the possibility of any reimbursement. *[IAS 37.86].*

Where any of the information above is not disclosed because it is not practicable to do so, that fact should be stated. *[IAS 37.91].*

The guidance given in the standard on determining which provisions may be aggregated to form a class referred to at 6.1 above also applies to contingent liabilities.

A further point noted in the standard is that where a provision and a contingent liability arise from the same circumstances, an entity should ensure that the link between the provision and the contingent liability is clear. *[IAS 37.88].* This may arise, for instance, where there is a range of possible losses under a claim, for which part of the potential maximum has been provided. A further example of when this may arise would be where an entity is jointly and severally liable for an obligation. As noted at 4.6 above, in these circumstances the part that is expected to be met by other parties is treated as a contingent liability.

It is not absolutely clear what is meant by 'financial effect' in (a) above. Is it the *potential* amount of the loss or is it the *expected* amount of the loss? The explicit cross-reference to the measurement principles in paragraphs 36-52 might imply the latter, but in our view the former would be preferable.

6.3   Contingent assets

IAS 37 requires disclosure of contingent assets where an inflow of economic benefits is probable. The disclosures required are:

(a)   a brief description of the nature of the contingent assets at the end of the reporting period; and

(b)   where practicable, an estimate of their financial effect, measured using the principles set out for provisions in paragraphs 36-52 of IAS 37. *[IAS 37.89].*

Where any of the information above is not disclosed because it is not practicable to do so, that fact should be stated. *[IAS 37.91].* The standard goes on to emphasise that the disclosure must avoid giving misleading indications of the likelihood of income arising. *[IAS 37.90].*

One problem that arises with IAS 37 is that it requires the disclosure of an estimate of the potential financial effect for contingent assets to be measured in accordance with measurement principles in the standard. Unfortunately, the measurement principles in

Chapter 29

the standard are all set out in terms of the settlement of obligations, and these principles cannot readily be applied to the measurement of contingent assets. Hence, judgement will have to be used as to how rigorously these principles should be applied.

6.4   Exemption from disclosure when seriously prejudicial

IAS 37 contains an exemption from disclosure of information in the following circumstances. It says that, 'in extremely rare cases, disclosure of some or all of the information required by [the disclosure requirements at 6.1 to 6.3 above] can be expected to prejudice seriously the position of the entity in a dispute with other parties on the subject matter of the provision, contingent liability or contingent asset'. *[IAS 37.92].*

In such circumstances, the information need not be disclosed. However, disclosure will still need to be made of the general nature of the dispute, together with the fact that, and the reason why, the required information has not been disclosed. *[IAS 37.92].*

In the following extract, Virgin Atlantic Airways Limited applied this exemption in its 2007 financial statements in relation to investigations into various aspects of pricing in the airline industry. Whilst these disclosures are made under FRS 12 in the UK, its requirements are identical with those of IAS 37 in this respect.

Extract 29.13: *Virgin Atlantic Airways Limited (2007)*

23 Contingent liabilities [extract]

The competition authorities in a number of jurisdictions in which the Company operates are in the process of investigating various aspects of pricing in the airline industry. The Company is co-operating in full with such investigations and has carried out certain internal investigations into its compliance with competition laws. In addition, civil claims for damages have been filed against the Company in the US in relation to aspects of its pricing and the Company has engaged legal advisers to act for it in relation to these claims. No further disclosures regarding contingent liabilities arising from any of these investigations and damages actions are being made by the Company at this time since the directors of the Company believe that such disclosures might be expected to be seriously prejudicial to the position of the Company.

As it can be seen in the above example, an entity applying the 'seriously prejudicial' exemption is still required to describe the general nature of the dispute, resulting in a level of disclosure that many entities might still find uncomfortable in the circumstances.

7   FUTURE DEVELOPMENTS

In November 2010, the IASB and FASB decided to amend the timetable for projects determined to be 'important but less urgent'. The projects affected include the Liabilities Project, to revise IAS 37, and the project of Emissions Trading Schemes.[33] These projects, together with the question of accounting for rate-regulated activities, have been identified by the IASB as candidates for its Agenda Consultation which was issued in June 2011.[34]

In addition, the IASB decided to exclude warranty costs from the scope of any new standard on liabilities.[35] Warranty costs are addressed instead in its Exposure Draft on Revenue from Contracts with Customers, issued on 24 June 2010 and expected to be re-exposed in late 2011.[36] The revenue recognition project is discussed in Chapter 30.

7.1 Liabilities (amendments to IAS 37)

The IASB originally issued an exposure draft proposing amendments to IAS 37 in June 2005. Following a long period of deliberation, including round-table meetings held with constituents to discuss their views, the Board revised its proposals for the measurement of liabilities, issuing a second exposure draft in January 2010. In the months that followed, other documents were issued:

- a working draft of the proposed new IFRS, combining the original proposals with the exposure draft on measurement and incorporating other amendments identified by the Board during its deliberations; and

- an IASB Staff Paper on recognising liabilities arising from lawsuits.

Under the Board's proposals, the terms 'provision', 'contingent liability' and 'contingent asset' would be eliminated. Instead, a new standard would refer simply to 'liabilities'. The only assets addressed by the exposure draft were reimbursement rights. For these, the current recognition requirement of 'virtual certainty' would be removed; such rights being recognised unless they cannot be measured reliably.[37] Items previously meeting the definition of contingent assets (and hence currently within the scope of IAS 37) are intended to be brought within the scope of IAS 38.

An important objective for the IASB is alignment of the requirements for recording costs of restructuring activities with those in US GAAP, and alignment of the criteria for recording liabilities with the criteria of other IFRSs. The project also aims to provide more specific requirements on the measurement of liabilities within the new standard's scope. Following discussion of the results of outreach activities by IASB staff later in 2011, the IASB would expect to issue a further exposure draft of the revised standard.[38]

7.2 Rate-regulated activities

Rate regulation refers to the way a regulator restricts the level of or movement in prices charged by an entity to its customers for its services or products. Whilst such regulation is common all over the world, the price control strategies applied can vary considerably. Where the price established by the regulator is, at least in part, derived from an objective to give an entity a fair return on its costs, the question arises as to whether an imposed price reduction in recognition of a past over recovery of costs should be recognised as a liability; and whether a future price increase in recognition of past costs incurred gives rise to an asset. As discussed at 5.16 above, the current consensus among existing IFRS reporters is that regulatory liabilities should be recognised only in those rare cases where they meet the definition of a financial liability.[39]

The IASB issued an exposure draft on rate-regulated activities in July 2009. The Board acknowledged that while divergence in practice did not currently exist, this was a matter of significant interest in a number of countries that would be adopting IFRS in the near future and where recognition of regulatory assets and liabilities was either permitted or required. The approaching conversion of these jurisdictions to IFRS would increase pressure for what the Board describes as 'a definitive conclusion on the question'.[40]

Chapter 29

The scope of the proposals was intended to be restrictive, applying only to entities subject to price regulation where that price is designed to recover the specific costs the entity incurs in providing the regulated goods or services and to earn a specified return (cost-of-service regulation).[41] Regulatory mechanisms applying targeted or assumed costs, such as industry averages, rather than an entity's specific costs, were outside the scope of the proposals.[42]

The main proposal in the Exposure Draft was that when an entity falling within its scope has the right to increase or the obligation to decrease prices in future periods as a result of the actual or expected actions of the regulator, it shall recognise:[43]

(a)   a regulatory asset for its right to recover specific previously incurred costs and to earn a specified return; or

(b)   a regulatory liability for its obligation to refund previously collected amounts and to pay a specified return.

Any regulatory liability would reflect amounts that would otherwise be recorded in those future periods in the statement of comprehensive income as revenue[44] and would be measured at its expected present value.[45] Regulatory assets and liabilities would be presented separately from other assets and liabilities on the face of the balance sheet, and classified as current and non-current items.[46] Offsetting would only be allowed for each category of asset or liability subject to the same regulator.[47]

In July 2010, the IASB noted that it was divided on whether to amend IFRS to require the recognition of regulatory assets and liabilities and, if so, how to measure those regulatory assets and liabilities. It noted that the issues raised in the project could have broader implications than originally anticipated, for example on the accounting for intangible assets.[48] The IASB discontinued the project in September 2011, citing resource constraints, but it identified the following options which have now been presented in its 2011 agenda consultation document:[49]

• a disclosure-only standard;

• an interim standard, similar to IFRS 4 or IFRS 6 – *Exploration for and Evaluation of Mineral Resources*, to grandfather previous GAAP with some limited improvements, pending a longer-term project;

• a medium-term project focused on the effects of rate regulation; or

• addressing it as part of a comprehensive project on intangible assets.

Until any project is completed and a new standard becomes effective, regulatory liabilities and assets are not eligible for recognition under IFRS, as discussed at 5.16 above and in Chapter 19 at 13.1.

7.3   Emissions trading schemes

As noted at 5.6 above, the IASB resumed its project on emissions trading schemes in December 2007, deciding to limit the scope of the project to accounting issues relating to emissions trading schemes, rather than to consider more general issues regarding the accounting for government grants.[50] It was then suspended in November 2010 as noted above.[51]

In presenting the project for inclusion in its agenda going forward, the IASB states that the main financial reporting issues are how the assets and liabilities in emissions trading schemes should be recognised and measured. In particular the project considers how allowances received from the scheme administrator should be recognised and what liabilities, if any, relating to the receipt of allowances should be recognised and measured.[52]

References

1 IAS 37.5 (2007).
2 FRS 12, *Provisions, Contingent Liabilities and Contingent Assets*, ASB, September 1998, para. 66.
3 FRS 12. 67.
4 FASB ASC Topic 450, Contingencies, para. 450-20-30-1.
5 FRS 12.50.
6 FRS 12.49.
7 *Discounting in Financial Reporting*, ASB, April 1997.
8 *Discounting in Financial Reporting*, ASB, April 1997, para. 2.10.
9 FRS 12.49.
10 FRS 12.49.
11 *IFRIC Update*, March 2011, p. 4.
12 Paragraph 27 in Appendix VII to FRS 12 on the *Development of the FRS* states that 'the discount rate should be the rate of return that will, after tax has been deducted, give the required post-tax rate of return'. The paragraph goes on to explain that because the tax consequence of different cash flows may be different, the pre-tax rate of return is not always the post-tax rate of return grossed up by the standard rate of tax.
13 *IFRIC Update*, December 2003, pp. 4-5.
14 *Exposure Draft of Proposed Amendments to IAS 37 Provisions, Contingent Liabilities and Contingent Assets* (IAS 37 ED) *and IAS 19 Employee Benefits* (IAS 19 ED), IASB, June 2005, para 58.
15 IFRIC 3, *Emission Rights*, IASB, December 2004, para. 6.
16 IFRIC 3.5.
17 IFRIC 3.6.
18 IFRIC 3.7.
19 IFRIC 3.8.
20 *IASB Update*, June 2005, p. 1.
21 *IASB Update*, June 2005, p. 1.
22 *IASB Insight*, May 2006, p. 13.
23 *IASB Update*, December 2007, p. 1.
24 Directive 2002/96/EC of the European Parliament and of the Council of 27 January 2003 on waste electrical and electronic equipment and Directive 2003/108/EC of the European Parliament and of the Council of 8 December 2003 amending Directive 2002/96/EC on waste electrical and electronic equipment.
25 FRS 12, Appendix VII, para. 39.
26 IAS 37 ED.7.
27 *IASB Work Plan – projected timetable as at 26 July 2011*, IASB.
28 FRS 12, Appendix III, Example 12.
29 FRS 12, Appendix VII, para. 16.
30 *IFRIC Update*, November 2008, p. 4.
31 Information for Observers (December 2008 IASB Meeting), *Agenda proposal: rate-regulated activities (Agenda Paper 12)*, para. 14.
32 Exposure Draft (ED 2009/8), *Rate-regulated Activities*, IASB, July 2009, para. BC8.
33 *IASB Work Plan – projected timetable as at 26 July 2011*, IASB.
34 Request for Views *Agenda Consultation 2011*, IASB, July 2011, Appendix C.
35 IAS 37 ED.7.
36 *IASB Work Plan – projected timetable as at 26 July 2011*, IASB.
37 IAS 37 ED.46.
38 Request for Views *Agenda Consultation 2011*, IASB, July 2011, Appendix C.
39 Information for Observers (December 2008 IASB Meeting), *Agenda proposal: rate-regulated activities (Agenda Paper 12)*, para. 14.
40 *Exposure Draft ED/2009/8, Rate-regulated Activities,* IASB, July 2009, ED/2009/8 BC8.
41 ED/2009/8.3.
42 ED/2009/8.6.
43 ED/2009/8.8.
44 ED/2009/8.10.
45 ED/2009/8.12.

Chapter 29

46 ED/2009/8.22.
47 ED/2009/8.23.
48 *IASB Update*, July 2010, p. 11.
49 Request for Views *Agenda Consultation 2011*, IASB, July 2011, Appendix C.
50 *IASB Update*, December 2007, p. 1.
51 *IASB Work Plan – projected timetable as at 26 July 2011*, IASB.
52 Request for Views *Agenda Consultation 2011*, IASB, July 2011, Appendix C.

Chapter 30   Revenue recognition

List of examples

Chapter 30

Chapter 30   Revenue recognition

1   THE NATURE OF REVENUE

Until relatively recently, the revenue recognition debate has taken place in the context of the historical cost system. The accounting principles that evolved focused on determining when transactions should be recognised in the financial statements, what amounts were involved in each transaction, how these amounts should be classified and how they should be allocated between accounting periods. These principles were reflected in the original version of IAS 18 – *Revenue* – which was issued in 1982, in which revenue was defined as the 'gross inflow of cash, receivables or other consideration arising in the course of the ordinary activities of an entity from the sale of goods, from the rendering of services, and from the use by others of entity resources yielding interest, royalties and dividends'.[1]

Historical cost accounting in its pure form avoids having to take a valuation approach to financial reporting by virtue of the fact that it is transactions-based; in other words, it relies on transactions to determine the recognition and measurement of assets, liabilities, revenues and expenses. Over the life of an entity, its total income will be represented by net cash flows generated; however, because of the requirement to prepare periodic financial statements, it is necessary to break up the entity's operating cycle into reporting periods. The effect of this is that at each reporting date the entity will have entered into a number of transactions that are incomplete; for example, it might have delivered a product or service to a customer for which payment has not been received, or it might have received payment in respect of a product or service yet to be delivered. Alternatively, it might have expended cash on costs that relate to future sales transactions, or it might have received goods and services that it has not yet paid for in cash.

Consequently, the most important accounting questions that have to be answered revolve around how to allocate the effects of these incomplete transactions between periods for reporting purposes, as opposed to simply letting them fall into the periods in which cash is either received or paid. Under historical cost accounting this allocation process is based on two, sometimes conflicting, fundamental accounting concepts: accruals (or matching), which attempts to allocate the costs associated with earning revenues to the periods in which the related revenues will be reported; and prudence (or conservatism), under which revenue and profits are not anticipated, whilst anticipated losses are provided for as soon as they are foreseen, with the result that costs are not deferred to the future if there is doubt as to their recoverability.

As a result, the pure historical cost balance sheet contains items of two types: cash (and similar monetary items), and debits and credits that arise as a result of allocating the effects of transactions between reporting periods by applying the accruals and prudence concepts; in other words, the balance sheet simply reflects the balances that result from the entity preparing an accruals-based profit and loss account rather than a receipts and payments account. A non-monetary asset under the historical cost system is purely a deferred cost that has been incurred before the balance sheet date and, by applying the accruals concept, is expected (provided it passes the prudence test) to give rise to economic benefits in periods beyond the balance sheet date, so as to justify it being carried forward. Similarly, the balance sheet incorporates non-monetary credit balances that are awaiting recognition in the profit and loss account but, as a result of the application of the prudence and/or matching concepts, have been deferred to future reporting periods.

The IASB's accounting model has been based on fair values, meaning that gains and losses are determined by reference to the change in fair value that has occurred over the financial reporting period. This approach is evident in a number of standards, including IAS 39 – *Financial Instruments: Recognition and Measurement* – and the IFRS that will replace it, *IFRS 9 – Financial Instruments*, IAS 40 – *Investment Property*, IAS 41 – *Agriculture* – and IFRS 2 – *Share-based Payment*. Because so many standards incorporate the concept of fair value, the IASB in conjunction with the FASB has issued IFRS 13 – *Fair Value Measurement*. It is clear also that as new standards are developed, greater emphasis will be placed on the balance sheet, with fair value as the relevant measurement attribute.

However, financial reporting under IFRS is still not a pure historical cost system; it incorporates a mixed model that embraces both historical costs and fair values. IAS 18 was issued in its original form in 1982 and received its last major revision in 1993. Consequently, it is a standard that is based on historical cost principles, not fair value. Thus, it is a standard that focuses on profit or loss, not assets and liabilities and therefore relies heavily on the concepts of prudence and matching. The current standard is therefore based upon concepts that, at least in their strictest sense, are not viewed with much importance by the IASB. In addition the standard does not address many of the complex transactions undertaken by modern business, such as those involving multiple deliverables.

It is therefore not surprising that the IASB and FASB have been working on a joint project to develop a new approach to revenue recognition which resulted in them issuing, in June 2010, an Exposure Draft entitled *Revenue from Contracts with Customers*. However, comments on the Exposure Draft revealed complex implementation issues and a series of amendments were made. The Boards have decided to re-expose the proposals in the latter part of 2011. The new model is discussed at 5 below.

Until the new model comes into effect, the traditional historical cost approach to revenue recognition remains in place for most practical purposes and companies and their auditors will have to continue to live with the inherent weaknesses of IAS 18.

The chapter discusses the subject drawing on both IASB and US pronouncements. For companies reporting under IFRS, IAS 18 is the main source of authoritative guidance on revenue recognition, but several other standards also address revenue recognition issues. These include IAS 11 – *Construction Contracts*, IAS 17 – *Leases*, IFRS 4 – *Insurance Contracts*, SIC-13 – *Jointly Controlled Entities – Non-Monetary Contributions by Venturers*, SIC-31 – *Revenue – Barter Transactions Involving Advertising Services*, IFRIC 13 – *Customer Loyalty Programmes*, IFRIC 15 – *Agreements for the Construction of Real Estate* – and IFRIC 18 – *Transfers of Assets from Customers*. In most cases, this revenue recognition guidance was developed in order to deal with specific issues on a piecemeal basis, rather than to follow any form of conceptual approach to revenue recognition.

The US in particular has a substantial body of literature on revenue recognition that can, on occasion, prove useful when there is no IFRS guidance available (see 4 below). Historically this was particularly relevant for IFRS-reporting companies registered with the US SEC, who wished to avoid as far as possible having IFRS/US GAAP differences. This is now less significant as reconciliation to US GAAP is no longer required. However, such differences are sometimes unavoidable, and it is not always the case that a revenue recognition policy under US GAAP is acceptable under IFRS, and vice versa.

2   THE TIMING OF REVENUE RECOGNITION

Under the historical cost system revenues are the inflows of assets to an entity as a result of the transfer of products and services by the entity to its customers during a period of time, and are recorded at the cash amount received or expected to be received (or, in the case of non-monetary exchanges, at their cash equivalent) as the result of these exchange transactions. However, because of the system of periodic financial reporting, it is necessary to determine the point (or points) in time when revenue should be measured and reported. This has traditionally been governed by what is known as the 'realisation principle', which acknowledges the fact that for revenue to be recognised it is not sufficient merely for a sale to have been made – there has to be a certain degree of performance by the vendor as well. Whilst there are many different (and sometime inconsistent) rules for different circumstances, the rules underlying revenue recognition have been developed from two broad approaches to the recognition of revenue: the critical event and the accretion approaches, each of which is appropriate under particular circumstances. These are discussed below.

2.1   The critical event approach

The fundamental approach to revenue recognition under both IFRS and US GAAP has been built on the foundation of critical event theory. The new approach to revenue recognition discussed in 5 below still essentially follows a critical event

Chapter 30

approach but it is a control-based model rather than one that depends on the transfer of risks and rewards.

The critical event approach is based on the belief that revenue is earned at the point in the operating cycle when the most critical decision is made or the most critical act is performed.[2] In theory, the critical event could occur at various stages during the operating cycle; for example, at the completion of production, at the time of sale, at the time of delivery or at the time of cash collection.

Revenue recognition is subject to a number of measurement uncertainties which could occur at any of these points. However, since these uncertainties fall away at various stages throughout the operating cycle, it is necessary to identify a point in the cycle at which the remaining uncertainties can be estimated with sufficient accuracy to enable revenue to be recognised. As discussed later in this chapter, the decision is often not straightforward; further complications arise in the case of transactions that involve multiple elements and/or significant post-delivery obligations.

2.1.1   *The recognition of revenue at the completion of production*

An entity may enter into a firm contract for the production and delivery of a product, where the sales price will have been determined and the selling costs will have already been incurred. Consequently, provided that both the delivery expenses and the bad debt risk can reasonably be assessed, it may be appropriate to report revenue on the completion of production, unless it is a transaction for which the percentage of completion method is mandated by IAS 11 or IAS 18. The completed contract method of recognising revenue on construction contracts is not common and is not permitted under IFRS (see Chapter 25).

It has also become accepted practice in a limited number of industries to recognise revenue at the completion of production, even though a sales contract may not have been entered into. This practice has been adopted, for example, in the case of the some agricultural and minerals and mineral products. IAS 2 – *Inventories* – allows such entities to carry inventory at net realisable value if it is a 'well-established' practice, as long as changes in net realisable value are recognised in profit or loss in the period of the change. *[IAS 2.3(a)].* IAS 2 specifies that the treatment might be appropriate if, for example, the minerals have been extracted, the sale is assured under a forward contract or a government guarantee, there is an active market and there is a negligible risk of failure to sell. *[IAS 2.4].* Note that this is different to recognising biological products at fair value throughout the period of growth, which is an example of the accretion approach described at 2.2 below that is mandated by IAS 41.

The US FASB's Concepts Statement 5 – *Recognition and Measurement in Financial Statements of Business Enterprises* – allows a similar treatment. It acknowledges that revenue may be recognised on the completion of production of such assets, provided that they consist of interchangeable units and quoted prices are available in an active market that can rapidly absorb the quantity held by the entity without significantly affecting the price.[3]

2.1.2 The recognition of revenue at the time of sale

The point of sale is probably the most widely used basis of recognising revenue from transactions involving the sale of goods. The sale is usually the critical point in the earning process when most of the significant uncertainties are eliminated; the only uncertainties that are likely to remain are those of possible return of the goods (where the customer has the right to do so, thereby cancelling the sale), the failure to collect the sales price (in the case of a credit sale), and any future liabilities in terms of any express or implied customer warranties. Under normal circumstances, these uncertainties will be both minimal and estimable to a reasonable degree of accuracy, based, *inter alia*, on past experience.

However, should revenues be recognised at the time of sale if the sale takes place before production, or if delivery only takes place at some significantly distant time in the future? In practice, the time of sale is generally taken to be the point of delivery; among other reasons, this reflects the law in a large number of jurisdictions, under which title passes to the buyer upon delivery, whether or not payment has been made.

See 3.7 below for a discussion of the principles laid down in IAS 18 for determining when to recognise revenue from a transaction involving the sale of goods.

2.1.3 The recognition of revenue subsequent to delivery

The uncertainties that exist after delivery may be of such significance that recognition should be delayed beyond the normal recognition point.

If the principal uncertainty concerns collectability, it might be appropriate to defer recognition of the whole sale (and not just the profit) until collection is reasonably assured – as is the requirement under US GAAP.

The entity may sell its product but give the customer the right to return the goods (for example, in the case of a mail order business where the customer is given an approval period of, say, 14 days). Revenue may be recognised on delivery if future returns can be predicted reasonably accurately; otherwise it should be recognised on receipt of payment for the goods, or on customer acceptance of the goods and express or implied acknowledgement of the liability for payment, or after the 14 days have elapsed – whichever is considered to be the most appropriate under the circumstances.

In fact, this is an area where practice has been somewhat inconsistent. A transaction with a right of return is usually accounted for as a sale, whereas revenue from a transaction with a 14-day acceptance period is usually deferred – despite the fact that the transactions are virtually identical in terms of the legal rights and obligations of the parties.

Chapter 30

This area of uncertainty is dealt with in US GAAP under ASC 605-15 (previously SFAS 48) which states that if an entity sells its product but gives the buyer the right to return the product, revenue from the sales transaction is recognised at time of sale only if *all* of the following conditions are met:[4]

(a)   the seller's price to the buyer is substantially fixed or determinable at the date of sale;

(b)   the buyer has paid the seller, or the buyer is obligated to pay the seller and the obligation is not contingent on resale of the product;

(c)   the buyer's obligation to the seller would not be changed in the event of theft or physical destruction or damage of the product;

(d)   the buyer acquiring the product for resale has economic substance apart from that provided by the seller (i.e. the buyer does not merely exist 'on paper' with little or no physical facilities, having been established by the seller primarily for the purpose of recognising revenue);

(e)   the seller does not have significant obligations for future performance to directly bring about resale of the product by the buyer; and

(f)   the amount of future returns can be reasonably estimated.

Revenue that was not recognised at the time of sale because these conditions were not met should be recognised either when the return privilege has 'substantially expired', or when all the above conditions are met, whichever occurs first.[5]

The ability to make a reasonable estimate of future returns depends on many factors and will vary from one case to the next. US GAAP lists the following factors as being those that might impair a seller's ability to make such an estimate:[6]

(a)   the susceptibility of the product to significant external factors, such as technological obsolescence or changes in demand;

(b)   relatively long periods in which a particular product may be returned;

(c)   absence of historical experience with similar types of sales of similar products, or inability to apply such experience because of changing circumstances; for example, changes in the selling entity's marketing policies or its relationships with its customers; and

(d)   absence of a large volume of relatively homogeneous transactions.

The right of return is, therefore, viewed as a significant uncertainty that would preclude recognition under circumstances when the level of returns cannot be estimated. This means, for example, that a 14-day acceptance period would not require deferral of a sale, provided that the 14-day period is normal and routine.

2.2   The accretion approach

The accretion approach involves the recognition of revenue during the process of production, rather than at the end of a contract or when production is complete. There are four broad areas of entity activity where the application of the accretion approach might be appropriate.

(a) The use by others of entity resources

The traditional accrual basis of accounting recognises revenue as entity resources are used by others; this approach is followed, for example, in the case of rental or interest income. Uncertainty of collection should always be considered, in which case it might be appropriate to delay recognition until cash is received or ultimate collection is assured beyond all reasonable doubt.

(b) Long-term contracts

The second accepted application of the accretion approach may be found in the accounting practice for long-term construction contracts. For example, under IAS 11 the amount of revenue to be recognised on construction contracts is determined according to the 'percentage-of-completion method', whereby contract revenue is matched with the contract costs incurred in reaching the stage of completion, resulting in the reporting of revenue, expenses and profit that can be attributed to the proportion of work completed at each balance sheet date. *[IAS 11.25]*. Normally, the main uncertainties in the application of this approach are the estimation of the total costs and the degree of completion attained at the balance sheet date, particularly in the early stages of the contract. However, the selling price is sometimes uncertain as well, owing to contract modifications that give rise to revenue from 'extras'. Accounting for construction contracts is dealt with in detail in Chapter 25.

(c) The rendering of services

This is probably the most widespread example of the application of the accretion approach. For example, IAS 18 requires that when the outcome of a transaction involving the rendering of services can be estimated reliably, revenue is recognised 'by reference to the stage of completion of the transaction at the end of the reporting period' *[IAS 18.20]*, (in other words, using the percentage-of-completion method). This is discussed further at 3.8 below.

(d) Natural growth and 'biological transformation'

Where an entity's activity involves production through natural growth or ageing, the accretion approach suggests that revenue should be recognised at identifiable stages during this process. For example, in the case of livestock, there could be market prices available at the various stages of growth; revenue could, therefore, be recognised throughout the production process by making comparative stock valuations and reporting the accretions at each accounting date.

This is dealt with by IAS 41. The standard requires application of fair value accounting to all 'biological assets' (which are defined as being living animals and plants), *[IAS 41.5]*, throughout their period of growth. Entities that undertake agricultural activity are required to measure all biological assets at fair value less costs to sell, *[IAS 41.12]*, whilst all agricultural produce should be measured at fair value less costs to sell at the point of harvest, and thereafter inventory accounting (IAS 2 – *Inventories*) should be applied. Fair value at harvest becomes 'cost' for IAS 2 purposes at the date at which that standard first applies. *[IAS 41.13]*.

Chapter 30

The change in fair value of biological assets during a period is reported in net profit or loss for the period. *[IAS 41.26]*. However, IAS 41 contains no guidance on revenue recognition. In fact, the term 'revenue' is not mentioned in the entire standard and in the illustration of the statement of comprehensive income set out in the Appendix to IAS 41, there is no revenue line. IAS 41 amended IAS 18 to exclude from the scope of IAS 18 changes in fair value and initial recognition at fair value of agricultural assets and produce before harvest. Fair value gains and revenue from the sale of biological assets and agricultural produce should not be aggregated as this may result in double counting.

IAS 41 is dealt with in detail in Chapter 40 and it includes a discussion of the treatment of fair value movements in the statement of comprehensive income at 5.1.2.

3   THE REQUIREMENTS OF IAS 18

3.1   Scope

Income is defined in the IASB's *Conceptual Framework for Financial Reporting ('Framework')* as increases in economic benefits during the accounting period in the form of inflows or enhancements of assets or decreases of liabilities that result in increases in equity, other than those relating to contributions from equity participants. *[Framework.4.25(a)]*. The revised IAS 18 – *Revenue* – embraces in its objective the definition of income from the *Framework,* adding that 'revenue is income that arises in the course of ordinary activities of an entity and is referred to by a variety of different names including sales, fees, interest, dividends and royalties'. *[IAS 18, Objective]*. However, having established the link between the *Framework's* definition of income and IAS 18's definition of revenue, IAS 18 reverts to the transactions-based critical event approach for the recognition of revenues derived from the sale of goods.

The standard explains that its objective is to prescribe the accounting treatment of revenue arising from the following types of transactions and events:

(a)   the sale of goods;

(b)   the rendering of services; and

(c)   the use by others of entity assets yielding interest, royalties and dividends. *[IAS 18.1]*.

The term 'goods' includes goods produced by the entity for the purpose of sale and goods purchased for resale, such as merchandise purchased by a retailer or land and other property held for resale. *[IAS 18.3]*.

The rendering of services typically involves the performance by the entity of a contractually agreed task over an agreed period of time. The services may be rendered within a single period or over more than one period. However, some contracts for the rendering of services are directly related to construction contracts, for example, those for the services of project managers and architects. Consequently, revenue arising from these contracts is not specified by IAS 18, but is dealt with in accordance with the requirements for construction contracts in IAS 11 (see Chapter 25). *[IAS 18.4]*.

The use by others of entity assets gives rise to revenue in the form of:

(a)   interest – charges for the use of cash or cash equivalents or amounts due to the entity;

(b)   royalties – charges for the use of long-term assets of the entity, for example, patents, trademarks, copyrights and computer software; and

(c)   dividends – distributions of profits to holders of equity investments in proportion to their holdings of a particular class of capital. *[IAS 18.5].*

It is important to note that there are a number of matters that the standard expressly states that it does not deal with, because they are all dealt with in other standards. These are: *[IAS 18.6]*

(a)   lease agreements (see IAS 17). However, IAS 17 itself does not apply to licensing agreements for such items as motion picture films, video recordings, plays, manuscripts, patents and copyrights, *[IAS 17.2],* thus leaving a substantial gap in the revenue recognition literature (see Chapter 26 at 3.1);

(b)   dividends arising from investments that are accounted for under the equity method (see Chapter 12);

(c)   insurance contracts within the scope of IFRS 4 (see Chapter 53);

(d)   the changes in the fair value of financial assets and financial liabilities or their disposal (see Chapters 48 and 49);

(e)   the changes in the value of other current assets;

(f)   revenue arising from the initial recognition and from changes in the fair value of biological assets related to agricultural activity (see Chapter 40);

(g)   the initial recognition of agricultural produce (see Chapter 40); and

(h)   the extraction of mineral ores (see Chapter 41).

3.2   The distinction between income, revenue and gains

The *Framework* explains that its definition of income encompasses both 'revenue' and 'gains'. Revenue arises in the course of the ordinary activities of an entity; as we have seen above it can include sales, fees, interest, dividends, royalties and rent. Gains represent other items that meet the definition of income and may, or may not, arise in the course of the ordinary activities of an entity. Gains include, for example, those arising on the disposal of non-current assets. The definition of income also includes unrealised gains; for example, those arising on the revaluation of marketable securities and those resulting from increases in the carrying amount of long-term assets. *[Framework.4.31].*

The rules on offset in IAS 1 – *Presentation of Financial Statements* – distinguish between revenue and gains. The standard states that an entity undertakes, in the course of its ordinary activities, other transactions that do not generate revenue but are incidental to the main revenue-generating activities. When this presentation reflects the substance of the transaction or other event, the results of such transactions are presented by netting any income with related expenses arising on the same transaction. For example, gains and losses on the disposal of non-current assets, including investments and operating assets, are reported by deducting from the proceeds on disposal the carrying amount of the asset and related selling expenses. *[IAS 1.34]*. IAS 16 – *Property, Plant and Equipment* – has a general rule that 'gains shall not be classified as revenue'. *[IAS 16.68]*. The only exception to this rule is where an entity routinely sells property, plant and equipment (PP&E) that it has held for rental to others. This results from a recent amendment to IAS 16 which is discussed further at 6.11.1 below.

IAS 18 explains that revenue includes only the gross inflows of economic benefits received and receivable by the entity on its own account. In practice, the distinction between gross and net revenues is not always straightforward but there is now guidance regarding revenue and agency relationships that is discussed below.

Amounts collected on behalf of third parties such as sales taxes, goods and services taxes and value added taxes are not economic benefits that flow to the entity and do not result in increases in equity. Therefore, they are excluded from revenue. See 6.8 below for a discussion of some of the factors that need to be considered in determining whether gross or net revenue presentation is appropriate in relation to excise taxes and goods and services taxes.

3.3   Revenue and agency relationships

In an agency relationship, the gross inflows of economic benefits include amounts collected on behalf of the principal and which do not result in increases in equity for the entity. The amounts collected on behalf of the principal are not revenue; instead, revenue is the amount of commission. *[IAS 18.8]*.

The IASB, in April 2009, added guidance to the Appendix of IAS 18 to help determine whether an entity is acting as a principal or as an agent. *[IAS 18.IE21]*. An entity is acting as a principal when it has exposure to the significant risks and rewards associated with the sale of goods or rendering of services. There are four criteria that, individually or in combination, indicate that an entity is acting as principal: *[IAS 18.IE21]*

- the entity has the primary responsibility for providing the goods or services to the customer or for fulfilling the order, for example by being responsible for the acceptability of the products or services ordered or purchased by the customer;

- the entity has inventory risk before or after the customer order, during shipping or on return;

- the entity has latitude in establishing prices, either directly or indirectly, for example by providing additional goods or services; and

- the entity bears the customer's credit risk on the receivable due from the customer.

Conversely an entity is acting as agent when it does not have exposure to the significant risks and rewards associated with the sale of goods or rendering of services and this may be evidenced by the entity earning a predetermined amount, perhaps a fixed fee per transaction or a stated percentage of customer billings. *[IAS 18.IE21]*.

This amendment is closely related to the more detailed US GAAP guidance now codified in ASC 605-45 (previously EITF 99-19) which had been widely used as guidance on agency and gross versus net accounting.

An entity may make sales to parties that are acting as agents. In order to recognise revenue on the sale of goods the seller must have transferred the significant risks and rewards of ownership to the buyer and must not retain either continuing managerial involvement to the degree usually associated with ownership or effective control over the goods sold. *[IAS 18.14(a)-(b)].* This may not be the case if the buyer is an agent of the seller. For example, revenue from sales to intermediate parties, such as distributors, dealers or others for resale is generally recognised when the risks and rewards of ownership have passed. When the buyer is acting, in substance, as an agent, the sale is treated as a consignment sale, i.e. no revenue is recognised until the goods are sold to a third party. *[IAS 18.IE6, IE2(c)].*

3.4 Income and distributable profits

IFRS generally and IAS 18 specifically do not address the issue of the distribution of profit. Whether or not revenue and gains recognised in accordance with IFRS are distributable to shareholders of an entity will depend entirely on the national laws and regulations with which the entity needs to comply. Thus, income reported in accordance with IFRS does not necessarily imply that such income would either be realised or distributable under a reporting entity's applicable national legislation.

3.5 Measurement of revenue

Revenue should be measured at the fair value of the consideration received or receivable. *[IAS 18.9].* IAS 18 states that the amount of revenue arising on a transaction is usually determined by agreement between the entity and the buyer or user of the asset. This means that it is measured at the fair value of the consideration received or receivable taking into account the amount of any trade discounts and volume rebates allowed by the entity. *[IAS 18.10].* The standard defines fair value as 'the amount for which an asset could be exchanged, or a liability settled, between knowledgeable, willing parties in an arm's length transaction'. *[IAS 18.7].*

Usually, this will present little difficulty, as the consideration will normally be in the form of cash or cash equivalents and the amount of revenue will be the amount of cash or cash equivalents received or receivable. However, if the inflow is deferred, the fair value of the consideration will then be less than the nominal amount of cash received or receivable. IAS 18 introduces a discounting requirement. When an arrangement effectively constitutes a financing arrangement, the fair value of the consideration is determined by discounting all future receipts using an imputed rate of interest. The imputed rate of interest is the more clearly determinable of either:

(a) the prevailing rate for a similar instrument of an issuer with a similar credit rating; or

(b) a rate of interest that discounts the nominal amount of the instrument to the current cash sales price of the goods or services. *[IAS 18.11].*

Chapter 30

The difference between the fair value and the nominal amount of the consideration is recognised as interest revenue using the effective interest method as set out in IAS 39, paragraphs 9 and AG5 to AG8. *[IAS 18.11, 30(a)]*. The application of the effective interest rate method is discussed in Chapter 49 at 5.

A further issue arises if a company offers prompt settlement discounts to its customers. An example of a prompt settlement discount is a reduction of 5% of the selling price for paying an invoice within 7 days instead of the usual 60 days. In such cases, in order to comply with IAS 18's requirement that revenue should be measured at the fair value of the consideration received or receivable, *[IAS 18.9]*, prompt settlement discounts should be estimated at the time of sale and deducted from revenues.

3.6   Identification of the transaction

IAS 18 states that the recognition criteria of the standard are usually applied separately to each transaction. However, it goes on to say that, in certain circumstances, it is necessary to apply the recognition criteria to the separately identifiable components of a single transaction in order to reflect the substance of the transaction. *[IAS 18.13]*. This means that transactions have to be analysed in accordance with their economic substance in order to determine whether they should be combined or segmented for revenue recognition purposes. For example, when the selling price of a product includes an identifiable amount for subsequent servicing, that amount is deferred and recognised as revenue over the period during which the service is performed.

Conversely, the recognition criteria are applied to two or more transactions together when they are linked in such a way that the commercial effect cannot be understood without reference to the series of transactions as a whole – as is the case, for example, with the sale of mobile phones combined with related service contracts (the issue of bundled offers in the telecommunications sector is discussed below at 6.7). A further example might be where an entity sells goods and, at the same time, enters into a separate agreement to repurchase the goods at a later date, thus negating the substantive effect of the transaction; in such a case, the two transactions are dealt with together. *[IAS 18.13]*. The following extracts from the revenue recognition policies of Sandvik and Renault illustrate this point:

Extract 30.1: Sandvik AB (2008)

Accounting policies [extract]
REVENUE [extract]
Revenue from sales and services [extract]

Buy-back commitments may entail that sales revenue cannot be recognized if the agreement with the customer in reality implies that the customer has only rented the product for a certain period of time.

Extract 30.2: Renault SA (2007)

7.2.6.1 Accounting policies and scope of consolidation [extract]

2 – ACCOUNTING POLICIES [extract]

G – Revenues and margin [extract]

Sales of goods and services and margin recognition [extract]

Sales and margin recognition

Sales of goods are recognised when vehicles are made available to the distribution network in the case of non-Group dealers, or upon delivery to the end-user in the case of direct sales. The margin on sales is recognised immediately for normal sales by the Automobile division, including sales with associated financing contracts that can be considered as finance leases (long-term or with a purchase option). However, no sale is recognised when the vehicle is covered by an operating lease from a Group finance company or the Group has made a buy-back commitment, when the term of the contract covers an insufficient portion of the vehicle's useful life.

In such cases, the transactions are recorded as operating leases and included in sales of services. The difference between the price paid by the customer and the buy-back price is treated as rental income, and spread over the period the vehicle is at the customer's disposal. The production cost for the new vehicle concerned is recorded in inventories for contracts of less than one year, or included in property, plant and equipment under vehicles leased to customers when the contracts exceed one year. The sale of the vehicle as second-hand at the end of the lease gives rise to recognition of sales revenue and the related margin. As soon as a loss is expected on the resale, a provision (if the vehicle is in inventories) or additional depreciation (if the vehicle is included in property, plant and equipment) is recognised to cover the loss.

IAS 18 does not establish criteria for segmenting and combining revenue transactions. However, IAS 11 includes a requirement similar to that of IAS 18 in that it requires companies to apply the standard to separately identifiable components of a single construction contract, or to a group of contracts together, in order to reflect the substance of a contract or a group of contracts. *[IAS 11.7]*. IAS 11 also sets down the following criteria to help determine whether construction contracts should be combined or segmented: *[IAS 11.8-10]*

When a contract covers a number of assets, the construction of each asset should be treated as a separate construction contract when:

(a)   separate proposals have been submitted for each asset;

(b)   each asset has been subject to separate negotiation and the contractor and customer have been able to accept or reject that part of the contract relating to each asset; and

(c)   the costs and revenues of each asset can be identified.

A group of contracts, whether with a single customer or with several customers, should be treated as a single construction contract when:

(a)   the group of contracts is negotiated as a single package;

(b)   the contracts are so closely interrelated that they are, in effect, part of a single project with an overall profit margin; and

(c)   the contracts are performed concurrently or in a continuous sequence.

A contract may provide for the construction of an additional asset at the option of the customer or may be amended to include the construction of an additional asset.

Chapter 30

The construction of the additional asset should be treated as a separate construction contract when:

(a)   the asset differs significantly in design, technology or function from the asset or assets covered by the original contract; or

(b)   the price of the asset is negotiated without regard to the original contract price.

In the absence of any equivalent practical guidance in IAS 18, the above criteria set out in IAS 11 may be helpful in determining whether revenue transactions should be combined or segmented. However the underlying principle in paragraph 13 of IAS 18, which focuses on whether combination or segmentation is necessary to reflect the substance and understand the commercial effect, should remain the primary consideration in making this assessment. The practical issues in connection with combining and segmenting contracts (including the Interpretations Committee's discussion thereof) are considered further in Chapter 25 at 2.

In the case of certain arrangements with multiple deliverables, it may also be helpful (but not required), under the hierarchy in IAS 8 – *Accounting Policies, Changes in Accounting Estimates and Errors*, [IAS 8.12], to refer to the US GAAP guidance codified in ASC 605-25 – *Multiple-Element Arrangements* (previously EITF 00-21), which deals with the issue of separating elements of revenue. See 6.7.1 below for a discussion of how this US GAAP guidance has been applied to recognising revenue on bundled offers in the telecommunications sector.

3.7   The sale of goods

IAS 18 lays down the following five criteria that must be satisfied in order to recognise revenue from the sale of goods: [IAS 18.14]

(a)   the entity has transferred to the buyer the significant risks and rewards of ownership of the goods;

(b)   the entity retains neither continuing managerial involvement to the degree usually associated with ownership nor effective control over the goods sold;

(c)   the amount of revenue can be measured reliably;

(d)   it is probable that the economic benefits associated with the transaction will flow to the entity; and

(e)   the costs incurred or to be incurred in respect of the transaction can be measured reliably.

If the costs incurred cannot be measured reliably, the standard requires that 'any consideration already received for the sale of the goods is recognised as a liability.' [IAS 18.19].

IAS 18 views the passing of risks and rewards as the most crucial of the five criteria, giving the following four examples of situations in which an entity may retain the significant risks and rewards of ownership: [IAS 18.16]

(a)   when the entity retains an obligation for unsatisfactory performance not covered by normal warranty provisions;

(b)   when the receipt of the revenue from a particular sale is contingent on the derivation of revenue by the buyer from its sale of the goods;

(c)   when the goods are shipped subject to installation and the installation is a significant part of the contract which has not yet been completed by the entity; and

(d)   when the buyer has the right to rescind the purchase for a reason specified in the sales contract and the entity is uncertain about the probability of return.

It is clear that the standard still advocates an earnings process-driven critical event approach to revenue recognition. It is, therefore, necessary to establish at which point in the earnings process both the significant risks and rewards of ownership are transferred from the seller to the buyer and any significant uncertainties (which would otherwise delay recognition) are removed. For example, the responsibilities of each party during the period between sale and delivery should be established, possibly by examination of the customer agreements. If the goods have merely to be uplifted by the buyer, and the seller has performed all his associated responsibilities, then the sale may be recognised immediately. However, if the substance of the sale is merely that an order has been placed, and the goods have still to be acquired or manufactured by the seller, then the sale should not be recognised. The following extract from the accounting policies of Atlas Copco illustrates the deferral of revenue recognition until installation is completed in those cases where installation is a significant part of the contract:

Extract 30.3: Atlas Copco AB (2008)

Notes to the Consolidated Financial Statements [extract]

1.   Significant accounting principles [extract]

Revenue recognition [extract]

Goods sold [extract]

Revenue from sale of goods is recognized when the significant risks and rewards of ownership have been transferred to the buyer, which in most cases occurs in connection with delivery. When the product requires installation and installation is a significant part of the contract, revenue is recognized when the installation is completed.

The terms of delivery, and the associated legal implications, may also be relevant in determining the timing of revenue recognition. If the seller is responsible for transport costs and insuring the goods during this period (CIF – cost, insurance and freight), this indicates that the risks and rewards do not pass to the customer until delivery, and hence this generally precludes recognition of revenue prior to that point. Where the customer becomes responsible for the goods as soon as they are delivered to the agreed shipping point (Free on Board or FOB shipping point), it may be clear that any risk of loss or damage from that time is wholly borne by the customer, justifying revenue recognition at this earlier date.

IAS 18 recognises also that, under certain circumstances, goods are sold subject to reservation of title in order to protect the collectability of the amount due; in such circumstances, provided that the seller has transferred the significant risks and rewards of ownership, the transaction can be treated as a sale and revenue can be recognised. *[IAS 18.17]*. The standard assumes that 'in most cases, the transfer of risks

Chapter 30

and rewards of ownership coincides with the transfer of legal title or the passing of possession to the buyer', *[IAS 18.15]*, but acknowledges that this may not always be the case. Transfer of legal title is, therefore, not a condition for revenue recognition under IAS 18, *[IAS 18.14]*, as the standard recognises that transactions occur where the transfer of risks and rewards of ownership occurs at a different time from the transfer of legal title or the passing of possession. *[IAS 18.15]*.

This point is reinforced in the Appendix to IAS 18, which notes that laws in different countries may mean that the recognition criteria in the standard are met at different times. In particular, the law may determine the point in time at which an entity transfers the significant risks and rewards of ownership. Therefore, the examples in the Appendix need to be read in the context of the laws relating to the sale of goods in the country in which the transaction takes place.[7]

The following extracts from the financial statements of Smith & Nephew and Roche illustrate both the measurement principles of IAS 18 and the application of the critical event approach in determining the timing of revenue recognition:

Extract 30.4: Smith & Nephew plc (2007)

Notes to the Group Accounts [extract]

2.   Accounting policies [extract]

Revenue [extract]

Revenue comprises sales of products and services to third parties at amounts invoiced net of trade discounts and rebates, excluding taxes on revenue. Revenue from the sale of products is recognised upon transfer to the customer of the significant risks and rewards of ownership. This is generally when goods are despatched to customers except that sales of inventory located at customer premises and available for customers' immediate use are recognised when notification is received that the product has been implanted or used. Appropriate provisions for returns, trade discounts and rebates are deducted from revenue. Rebates comprise retrospective volume discounts granted to certain customers on attainment of certain levels of purchases from the Group. These are accrued over the course of the arrangement based on estimates of the level of business expected and adjusted at the end of the arrangement to reflect actual volumes.

Extract 30.5: Roche Holding Ltd (2008)

Notes to the Roche Group Consolidated Financial Statements [extract]

1.   Summary of significant accounting policies [extract]

Revenues

Sales represent amounts received and receivable for goods supplied to customers after deducting trade discounts, cash discounts and volume rebates, and exclude value added taxes and other taxes directly linked to sales. Revenues from the sale of products are recognised upon transfer to the customer of significant risks and rewards. Trade discounts, cash discounts and volume rebates are recorded on an accrual basis consistent with the recognition of the related sales. Estimates of expected sales returns, charge-backs and other rebates, including Medicaid in the United States and similar rebates in other countries, are also deducted from sales and recorded as accrued liabilities or provisions or as a deduction from accounts receivable. Such estimates are based on analyses of existing contractual or legislatively-mandated obligations, historical trends and the Group's experience. Other revenues are recorded as earned or as the services are performed. Where necessary, single transactions are split into separately identifiable components to reflect the substance of the transaction. Conversely, two or more transactions may be considered together for revenue recognition purposes, where the commercial effect cannot be understood without reference to the series of transactions as a whole.

3.8   The rendering of services

IAS 18 requires that when the outcome of a transaction involving the rendering of services can be estimated reliably, revenue is recognised 'by reference to the stage of completion of the transaction at the end of the reporting period' *[IAS 18.20]* (in other words, using the percentage-of-completion method). In applying the percentage-of-completion method, the requirements of IAS 11 are 'generally applicable to the recognition of revenue and the associated expenses for a transaction involving the rendering of services.' *[IAS 18.21]*.

According to IAS 18, the outcome of a transaction can be estimated reliably when all the following conditions are satisfied: *[IAS 18.20]*

(a)   the amount of revenue can be measured reliably;

(b)   it is probable that the economic benefits associated with the transaction will flow to the entity;

(c)   the stage of completion of the transaction at the end of the reporting period can be measured reliably; and

(d)   the costs incurred for the transaction and the costs to complete the transaction can be measured reliably.

When the outcome cannot be estimated reliably, revenue is recognised only to the extent of the expenses recognised that are recoverable. *[IAS 18.26]*. During the early stages of a transaction, it is often the case that the outcome of the transaction cannot be estimated reliably. Nevertheless, it may be probable that the enterprise will recover the transaction costs incurred. Therefore, revenue is recognised only to the extent of costs incurred that are expected to be recoverable. As the outcome of the transaction cannot be estimated reliably, no profit is recognised. *[IAS 18.27]*. For an example of this see the Nokia Corporation revenue recognition policy in Extract 30.7 below.

When the outcome of a transaction cannot be estimated reliably and it is not probable that the costs incurred will be recovered, revenue is not recognised and the costs incurred are recognised as an expense. When the uncertainties that prevented the outcome of the contract being estimated reliably no longer exist, revenue is recognised by reference to the stage of completion of the transaction at the balance sheet date. *[IAS 18.28]*.

The Appendix to IAS 18 provides several illustrative examples of transactions involving the rendering of services. It is clear from these examples that the performance of the service is the critical event for revenue recognition. *[IAS 18.IE10-19]*.

The standard claims that an entity is generally able to make reliable estimates after it has agreed to the following with the other parties to the transaction: *[IAS 18.23]*

(a)   each party's enforceable rights regarding the service to be provided and received by the parties;

(b)   the consideration to be exchanged; and

(c)   the manner and terms of settlement.

Chapter 30

The standard suggests further that it is usually necessary for the entity to have an effective internal financial budgeting and reporting system. The entity reviews and, when necessary, revises the estimates of revenue as the service is performed. The need for such revisions does not necessarily indicate that the outcome of the transaction cannot be estimated reliably. *[IAS 18.23]*.

When it comes to determining the stage of completion of a transaction, IAS 18 suggests three methods that may be used: *[IAS 18.24]*

(a)   surveys of work performed;

(b)   services performed to date as a percentage of total services to be performed; or

(c)   the proportion that costs incurred to date bear to the estimated total costs of the transaction. Only costs that reflect services performed to date are included in costs incurred to date. Only costs that reflect services performed or to be performed are included in the estimated total costs of the transaction.

For practical purposes, when services are performed by an indeterminate number of acts over a specified period, the standard states that revenue should be recognised on a straight-line basis over the specified period unless there is evidence that some other method better represents the stage of completion. However, when a specific act is much more significant than any other acts, the standard requires that the recognition of revenue be postponed until the significant act is executed. *[IAS 18.25]*.

What this means in practice can be seen by considering outsourcing arrangements. These are contracts that require services to be provided on an ongoing basis, often for a number of years, rather than the provision of a single service or a number of services that constitute a single project. These arrangements are common across a wide range of services including processing, provision of telecommunications services, general professional advice, help desk support, accounting advice, maintenance or cleaning, The 'service' to which IAS 18's method applies is the individual act, whether it be the individual process, answering the telephone help line or cleaning the office each night. Clearly in most cases it would not be feasible to identify the costs and revenue for each of these acts so revenue is taken on a straight line over the contract term and costs are expensed as incurred.

The entities that provide outsourcing services frequently provide single services as well. The following revenue recognition policy for Cap Gemini illustrates both the treatment of revenue for outsourcing contracts and for its long-term contracts.

Extract 30.6: Cap Gemini S.A. (2007)

Notes to the consolidated financial statements [extract]

Note 1.   Accounting policies [extract]

F) Recognition of revenues and the cost of services rendered

The method for recognizing revenues and costs depends on the nature of the services rendered:

A. TIME AND MATERIALS CONTRACTS:

Revenues and costs relating to time and materials contracts are recognized as services are rendered.

B. LONG-TERM FIXED-PRICE CONTRACTS:

Revenues from long-term fixed-price contracts, including systems development and integration contracts, are recognized under the "percentage-of-completion" method. Costs related to long-term fixed price contracts are recognized as they are incurred.

C. OUTSOURCING CONTRACTS:

Revenues from outsourcing agreements are recognized over the life of the contract as the services are rendered. When the services are made up of different components which are not separately identifiable, the related revenues are recognized on a straight-line basis over the life of the contract.

Nokia provides an illustration of an accounting policy whereby revenue from contracts involving the modification of complex telecommunications equipment is recognised using the percentage-of-completion method:

Extract 30.7: Nokia Corporation (2008)

Notes to the consolidated financial statements [extract]

1.   Accounting principles [extract]

Revenue recognition [extract]

In addition, sales and cost of sales from contracts involving solutions achieved through modification of complex telecommunications equipment are recognized using the percentage of completion method when the outcome of the contract can be estimated reliably. A contract's outcome can be estimated reliably when total contract revenue and the costs to complete the contract can be estimated reliably, it is probable that the economic benefits associated with the contract will flow to the Group and the stage of contract completion can be measured reliably. When the Group is not able to meet those conditions, the policy is to recognize revenues only equal to costs incurred to date, to the extent that such costs are expected to be recovered.

Progress towards completion is measured by reference to cost incurred to date as a percentage of estimated total project costs, the cost-to-cost method.

3.9   Exchanges of goods and services

Under IAS 18, when goods or services are exchanged or swapped for goods or services that are of a similar nature and value, the exchange is not regarded as a transaction that generates revenue. The standard notes exchanges of commodities like oil or milk, where suppliers exchange or swap inventories in various locations to fulfil demand on a timely basis in a particular location as examples of this. There are similar reasons behind exchanges of capacity in the telecommunications sector.

When goods are sold or services are rendered in exchange for dissimilar goods or services, the exchange is regarded as a transaction that generates revenue. The revenue is measured at the fair value of the goods or services received, adjusted by the amount of any cash or cash equivalents transferred. When the fair value of the goods or services received cannot be measured reliably, the revenue is measured at the fair value of the goods or services given up, adjusted by the amount of any cash or cash equivalents transferred. *[IAS 18.12].*

IFRIC 18 – *Transfers of Assets from Customers* – provides guidance in situations where an entity receives an item of PP&E from a customer (or cash for the acquisition or construction of such items) that must then be used by the entity either to connect the customer to a network or to provide the customer ongoing

Chapter 30

access to a supply of goods or services. *[IFRIC 18.4-6]*. These arrangements are relatively common in the utilities and automobile industries. The Interpretation is discussed at 6.13 below.

3.10   Exchanges of property plant and equipment

Accounting for exchanges of PP&E is dealt with in IAS 16, which takes a different approach to IAS 18's treatment of exchanges of goods and services. IAS 16 does not contain the distinction between similar and dissimilar assets that still remains in IAS 18 in respect of exchanges of goods and services. Instead, IAS 16 requires PP&E acquired in exchange for a non-monetary asset or assets, or a combination of monetary and non-monetary assets, to be accounted for at fair value, unless:

(a)   the exchange transaction lacks commercial substance, or

(b)   the fair value of neither the asset received nor the asset given up is reliably measurable. *[IAS 16.24]*.

The acquired item is measured in this way even if an entity cannot immediately derecognise the asset given up. *[IAS 16.24]*.

The fair value of an asset for which there are no comparable market transactions is reliably measurable if:

(a)   the variability in the range of reasonable fair value estimates is not significant for that asset, or

(b)   the probabilities of the various estimates within the range can be reasonably assessed and used in estimating fair value. *[IAS 16.26]*.

If an entity is able to determine reliably the fair value of either the asset received or the asset given up, then the fair value of the asset given up is used to measure the cost of the asset received unless the fair value of the asset received is more clearly evident. *[IAS 16.26]*. If the acquired item is not measured at fair value, its cost is measured at the carrying amount of the asset given up. *[IAS 16.24]*. Exchanges of assets are discussed in Chapter 20 at 4.4.

BP p.l.c. is an example of an entity that discloses an accounting policy for asset exchanges:

Extract 30.8: BP p.l.c. (2008)

Notes on financial statements [extract]

1   Significant accounting policies [extract]

Property, plant and equipment [extract]

Exchanges of assets are measured at fair value unless the exchange transaction lacks commercial substance or the fair value of neither the asset received nor the asset given up is reliably measurable. The cost of the acquired asset is measured at the fair value of the asset given up, unless the fair value of the asset received is more clearly evident. Where fair value is not used, the cost of the acquired asset is measured at the carrying amount of the asset given up. The gain or loss on derecognition of the asset given up is recognized in profit or loss.

IAS 16 stipulates that gains arising from the derecognition of PP&E may not be classified as revenue *[IAS 16.68]* and it is clear that this applies equally to derecognition by way of an exchange, sale and abandonment; this means that an exchange of PP&E does not result in the recognition of revenue.

IAS 38 – *Intangible Assets* – deals with exchanges of intangible assets, and includes the same requirements with respect to intangible assets as IAS 16 for exchanges of property, plant and equipment. *[IAS 38.45-47]*.

IFRS 5 – *Non-current Assets Held for Sale and Discontinued Operations* – lays down additional requirements for assets held for disposal; these requirements include measurement rules that affect the measurement of the amount of the gain on disposal to be recognised. These are discussed in Chapter 4 at 2.2.

3.11 Barter transactions involving advertising services

This is an issue that arose during the dotcom boom of the late 1990s and early 2000s, and is addressed in SIC-31. The issue arises where an entity (the seller) enters into a barter transaction to provide advertising services in exchange for receiving advertising services from its customer. Advertisements may be displayed on the Internet or poster sites, broadcast on television or radio, published in magazines or journals, or presented in another medium. In some cases, no cash or other consideration is exchanged between the entities although equal or approximately equal amounts of cash or other consideration may pass between them.

IAS 18 specifically addresses the recognition of revenue from advertising commissions, discussed at 6.5 below. It is clear that, under IAS 18, a seller that provides advertising services in the course of its ordinary activities recognises revenue from a barter transaction involving advertising when, amongst other criteria, the services exchanged are dissimilar, *[IAS 18.12]*, and the amount of revenue can be measured reliably. *[IAS 18.20(a)]*. However, an exchange of similar advertising services is not a transaction that generates revenue under IAS 18.

The Standing Interpretations Committee (SIC) concluded that revenue cannot be measured reliably at the fair value of advertising services received. A seller can only measure revenue reliably at the fair value of the advertising services it provides by reference to non-barter transactions that:

(a) involve advertising similar to the advertising in the barter transaction;

(b) occur frequently;

(c) represent a predominant number of transactions and amount when compared to all transactions to provide advertising that is similar to the advertising in the barter transaction;

(d) involve cash and/or another form of consideration (e.g. marketable securities, non-monetary assets, and other services) that has a reliably measurable fair value; and

(e) do not involve the same counterparty as in the barter transaction. *[SIC-31.5]*.

The conditions represent a relatively high hurdle for companies to overcome, and it would seem that in most instances they would find it difficult to be able to recognise any revenue. For example, a swap of cheques for equal or substantially equal amounts between the same entities that provide and receive advertising services does not provide reliable evidence of fair value. An exchange of advertising services that also includes only partial cash payment provides reliable evidence of the fair value of the transaction to the extent of the cash component (except when partial cash payments of equal or substantially equal amounts are swapped), but does not provide reliable evidence of the fair value of the entire transaction. *[SIC-31.9]*.

Barter transaction involving services occur mainly in the media industry. German television corporation, ProSiebenSat.1 discloses the following accounting policy for barter transactions involving advertising:

Extract 30.9: ProSiebenSat.1 Media AG (2008)

Notes to the consolidated financial statements [extract]

[6]   ACCOUNTING POLICIES [extract]

Recognition of revenues [extract]

Revenues from barter transactions are considered realized when goods or services that are not of the same kind are exchanged, and the amount of the proceeds and costs, as well as the economic benefit, can be clearly measured. Revenues are recognized at the market value of the received bartered item or service, and may be adjusted with an additional cash payment. Barter transactions at the ProSiebenSat.1 Group are primarily trade-off transactions relating to the sale of advertising time.

In our view, SIC-31 was issued as a specific anti-abuse rule that does not have wider implications and should not be applied to other situations by analogy.

3.12   Interest, royalties and dividends

When it is probable that the economic benefits associated with the transaction will flow to the entity and that the amount of revenue can be measured reliably, IAS 18 requires that the revenue arising from the use by others of entity assets yielding interest, royalties and dividends should be recognised as follows: *[IAS 18.29-30]*

(a)   *interest:* using the effective interest method as set out in IAS 39, paragraphs 9 and AG5-AG8;

(b)   *royalties:* on an accrual basis in accordance with the substance of the relevant agreement; and

(c)   *dividends:* when the shareholder's right to receive payment is established.

When unpaid interest has accrued before the acquisition of an interest-bearing investment, the subsequent receipt of interest is allocated between pre-acquisition and post-acquisition periods; only the post-acquisition portion is recognised as revenue.

Until May 2008, IAS 18 required an entity to assess whether dividends on equity securities had been declared from pre-acquisition net income and, if so, those dividends were deducted from the cost of the securities. *[IAS 18.32]*. This was consistent with the 'cost method' in IAS 27 – *Consolidated and Separate Financial Statements.* IAS 27 has been revised to remove all references to the cost method and instead states that an entity is to recognise dividends from subsidiaries, jointly controlled entities or associates in profit or loss in its separate financial statements when its right to receive the dividend is established. *[IAS 27.38A]*. Entities now determine as a separate exercise whether or not the investment has been impaired as a result of the dividend. IAS 36 – *Impairment of Assets* – has been expanded to include specific triggers for impairment reviews on receipt of dividends. IAS 18 has been modified in line with this; references to dividends from pre-acquisition profits being removed from paragraph 32. The treatment of dividends received is discussed in Chapter 9 at 2.3.

Scrip dividends, whereby new shares are issued to investors in lieu of a cash dividend, are popular in certain jurisdictions. Where the investor has the option to receive cash or the equivalent value in new shares this arrangement is in substance a cash dividend with an immediate reinvestment in shares. If the investment is either an associate or joint venture held at cost under IAS 27, or an investment classified as available for sale under IAS 39, the scrip dividend will be recorded as revenue in the normal manner when the right to receive payment is established. The debit entry will be recognised as an addition to the investment. However where the scrip dividend is compulsory with no cash alternative, or where the cash alternative is priced at such an unfavourable rate that an investor would be unlikely to take that option, the arrangement cannot be considered to be in substance a cash dividend with immediate reinvestment. The transaction will not result in economic benefits to the investor and therefore revenue will not be recognised.

Royalties accrue in accordance with the terms of the relevant agreement and are usually recognised on that basis unless, having regard to the substance of the agreement, it is more appropriate to recognise revenue on some other systematic and rational basis. *[IAS 18.33]*.

Anglo Platinum provides a straightforward example of accounting policies for dividends, interest and royalties:

Extract 30.10: Anglo Platinum Limited (2007)

PRINCIPAL ACCOUNTING POLICIES [extract]

Revenue recognition [extract]

- Dividends are recognised when the right to receive payment is established.
- Interest is recognised on a time proportional basis, which takes into account the effective yield on the asset over the period it is expected to be held.
- Royalties are recognised when the right to receive payment is established.

3.13 Uncollectible revenue

Revenue is recognised only when it is probable that the economic benefits associated with the transaction will flow to the entity. Because it is recognised at fair value, the revenue may be lower than the contracted amount, to take account of expected non-recoveries. In some cases, part or all of the revenue may not be probable until the consideration is received or until an uncertainty is removed. However, when an uncertainty arises about the collectability of an amount already included in revenue, the uncollectible amount or the amount in respect of which recovery has ceased to be probable is recognised as an expense, rather than as an adjustment of the amount of revenue originally recognised. *[IAS 18.18, 22, 34]*.

3.14 Disclosure

IAS 18's disclosure requirements relate to both revenue recognition policies and amounts included in the financial statements under the different categories of revenue. They are set down in the standard as follows: *[IAS 18.35]*

(a) the accounting policies adopted for the recognition of revenue including the methods adopted to determine the stage of completion of transactions involving the rendering of services;

(b) the amount of each significant category of revenue recognised during the period including revenue arising from:
   (i) the sale of goods;
   (ii) the rendering of services;
   (iii) interest;
   (iv) royalties;
   (v) dividends; and

(c) the amount of revenue arising from exchanges of goods or services included in each significant category of revenue.

The disclosures required under (b) and (c) above may be provided in the notes to the financial statements, rather than on the face of the statement of comprehensive income or separate income statement (if presented).

3.15 Revenue in the statement of comprehensive income

IAS 1 contains minimum requirements for the contents of the statement of comprehensive income. This states that an entity is to present all items of income and expense recognised in a period either in a single 'statement of comprehensive income', or in two statements:

• a statement displaying components of profit or loss (separate income statement); and

• a second statement beginning with profit or loss and displaying components of other comprehensive income (the statement of comprehensive income).

If the second approach applies, the separate income statement will correspond to the income statement required by the previous version of the standard. There are minimum requirements for what must be disclosed on the face of the statement of comprehensive income or separate income statement (if presented). The formats and their requirements are described in Chapter 3. The following must be shown on the face of the statement of comprehensive income or separate income statement (if presented): *[IAS 1.81-82]*

(a) revenue;

(b) finance costs; and

(c) share of the profit or loss of associates and joint ventures accounted for using the equity method.

IAS 1 goes on to state that additional line items, headings and subtotals are to be presented in the statement of comprehensive income and the separate income statement (if presented) when such presentation is relevant to an understanding of the entity's financial performance. Additional line items are included, and the descriptions used and the ordering of items are amended, when this is necessary to explain the elements of financial performance. Factors to be considered include materiality and the nature and function of the components of income and expenses. *[IAS 1.85-86]*.

These requirements provide a company with a substantial amount of flexibility with regard to the presentation of its statement of comprehensive income and separate income statement (if presented). However, they also raise a number of practical questions about the presentation of revenue, such as:

• can the amount for 'finance costs' be shown net of interest and other finance income? and

• can gains on disposal of PP&E be shown within revenue?

3.15.1 Interest and other finance income

IAS 18 requires interest income to be disclosed as one of the categories of revenue. *[IAS 18.35(b)]*. It used to be a fairly widespread practice under a number of national GAAPs for companies to show finance costs net of interest and other finance income. However IAS 1 paragraph 32 states that income and expenses should not be offset unless required or permitted by a Standard or an Interpretation. *[IAS 1.32]*. IAS 1 paragraph 82 lists 'finance costs' as one of the line items that must be included on the face of the statement of comprehensive income or separate income statement (if presented). *[IAS 1.82(b)]*. Taken together, these paragraphs preclude an entity presenting 'net finance costs' on the face of the statement of comprehensive income and separate income statement (if presented) without showing separately the finance costs and finance revenue included in the net amount, e.g. by presenting gross interest income and gross interest expense and then striking a sub-total that shows net interest.

The IASB has removed a reference in IFRS 7 – *Financial Instruments: Disclosures* – paragraph IG13 to 'total interest income' as a component of finance costs. This amendment confirmed the IASB's intention that finance income and finance expense be separately disclosed on the face of profit or loss.

IAS 1 permits some gains and losses arising from a group of similar transactions to be reported on a net basis, for example, foreign exchange gains and losses or gains and losses arising on financial instruments held for trading. Such gains and losses are, however, reported separately if they are material. *[IAS 1.35]*.

Although there is no Standard or Interpretation that permits interest income to be offset against interest expense, we believe that net presentation is appropriate in the case of trading activities; in our view, the interest income on financial instruments (e.g. bonds) that are held as trading assets (e.g. by a financial institution) could be included within net trading income.

Chapter 30

UBS provide shows interest income and expense gross in the income statement but provides note disclosure on a net basis by business activity.

Extract 30.11: UBS AG (2007)

Notes to the Financial Statements [extract]

Income Statement

		For the year ended			% change from
CHF million, except per share data	Note	**31.12.07**	31.12.06	31.12.05	31.12.06
Continuing operations					
Interest income	3	**109,112**	87,401	59,286	25
Interest expense	3	**(103,775)**	(80,880)	(49,758)	28
Net interest income	3	**5,337**	6,521	9,528	(18)
Credit loss (expense)/recovery		**(238)**	156	375	
Net interest income after credit loss expense		**5,099**	6,677	9,903	(24)
Net fee and commission income	4	**30,634**	25,456	21,184	20
Net trading income	3	**(8,353)**	13,743	8,248	
Other income	5	**4,332**	1,598	1,127	171
Revenues from industrial holdings		**268**	262	229	2
Total operating income		**31,980**	47,736	40,691	(33)

Note 3   Net Interest and Trading Income

Accounting standards require separate disclosure of net interest income and net trading income (see the tables on this and the next page). This required disclosure, however, does not take into account that net interest and trading income are generated by a range of different businesses. In many cases, a particular business can generate both net interest and trading income. Fixed income trading activity, for example, generates both trading profits and coupon income. UBS management therefore analyzes net interest and trading income according to the businesses that drive it.

The second table below (labeled Breakdown by businesses) provides information that corresponds to this management view. Net income from trading businesses includes both interest and trading income generated by the Group's trading businesses and the Investment Bank's lending activities. Net income from interest margin businesses comprises interest income from the Group's loan portfolio. Net income from treasury and other activities reflects all income from the Group's centralized treasury function.

Net interest and trading income

	For the year ended			% change from
CHF million	**31.12.07**	31.12.06	31.12.05	31.12.06
Net interest income	**5,337**	6,521	9,528	(18)
Net trading income	**(8,353)**	13,743	8,248	
Total net interest and trading income	**(3,016)**	20,264	17,776	

Breakdown by businesses

	For the year ended			% change from
CHF million	**31.12.07**	31.12.06	31.12.05	31.12.06
Net income from trading businesses[1]	**(10,658)**	13,730	11,795	
Net income from interest margin businesses	**6,230**	5,718	5,292	9
Net income from treasury activities and other	**1,412**	816	689	73
Total net interest and trading income	**(3,016)**	20,264	17,776	

1   Includes lending activities of the Investment Bank.

Net interest income[1]

CHF million	For the year ended 31.12.07	31.12.06	31.12.05	% change from 31.12.06
Interest income				
Interest earned on loans and advances[2]	21,263	15,266	11,678	39
Interest earned on securities borrowed and reverse repurchase agreements	48,274	39,771	23,362	21
Interest and dividend income from trading portfolio	39,101	32,211	24,134	21
Interest income on financial asses designated at fair value	298	25	26	
Interest and dividend income from financial investments available-for-sale	176	128	86	38
Total	109,112	87,401	59,286	25
Interest expense				
Interest on amounts due to banks and customers	29,318	20,024	11,226	46
Interest on securities lent and repurchase agreements	40,581	34,021	20,480	19
Interest and dividend expense from trading portfolio	15,812	14,533	10,736	9
Interest on financial liabilities designated at fair value	7,659	4,757	2,390	61
Interest on debt issued	10,405	7,545	4,926	38
Total	103,775	80,880	49,758	28
Net interest income	5,337	6,521	9,528	(18)

1   Interest includes forward points on foreign exchange swaps used to manage short-term interest rate risk on foreign currency loans and deposits.
2   Includes interest income on impaired loans and advances of CHF 110 million for 2007, CHF 158 million for 2006 and CHF 123 million for 2005.

Net trading income[1]

CHF million	For the year ended 31.12.07	31.12.06	31.12.05	% change from 31.12.06
Equities	9,048	7,064	3,900	28
Fixed income	(20,949)	2,755	1,240	
Foreign exchange and other[2]	3,548	3,924	3,108	(10)
Net trading income	(8,353)	13,743	8,248	
thereof net gains/(losses) from financial assets designated at fair value	(30)	(397)	70	
thereof net gains/(losses) from financial liabilities designated at fair value	(3,779)	(3,659)	(4,024)	

1   Please refer to the table "Net Interest and Trading Income" on the previous page for the Net income from trading businesses (for an explanation, read the corresponding introductory comment).
2   Includes cash & collateral trading and commodities.

3.15.2 Gains on disposal of property, plant and equipment

As discussed at 3.2 above, the IASB's *Framework* explains that income includes both 'revenue' and 'gains'. Gains include, for example, those arising on the disposal of non-current assets. IAS 16 also makes it clear that 'gains shall not be classified as revenue'. *[IAS 16.68]*.

Therefore, gains arising on the disposal of PP&E do not form part of revenue (aside from where an entity routinely sells PP&E that it has held for rental to others as discussed at 6.11.1 below). However, in our view, it is acceptable to show such gains net of any losses on disposal as part of income, whilst net losses on disposal should be shown within expenses.

Chapter 30

4   REVENUE RECOGNITION UNDER US GAAP

4.1   Applicability of US literature

Although IAS 18 lays down general principles of revenue recognition, there is a lack of specific guidance in relation to matters such as multiple-element revenue arrangements and industry-specific issues – for example, those relating to the software industry. The underlying approach to revenue recognition under US GAAP is closely aligned with that of IAS 18, in that it is based clearly on the earnings process and realisation principle. Therefore US revenue recognition guidance will in many instances be compatible with IAS 18. Consequently, whilst the US literature does not override the specific requirements of IFRS, some companies might choose to avail themselves of the hierarchy set out in paragraph 11 of IAS 8 in order to use US GAAP as guidance to formulate appropriate accounting policies with respect to specific transactions. However, whilst US GAAP might provide useful guidance in certain instances, the IAS 8 hierarchy does not require companies to refer either to US GAAP or, indeed, any other national GAAP. It is crucial to bear in mind that not all industry practices under US GAAP are permissible under IFRS; for example, utility companies should not adopt a revenue recognition policy that gives rise to regulatory assets/liabilities (although the IASB is currently conducting a project on rate-regulated activities – see below at 6.12). It may also be the case that the application of the principles in IAS 18 could result in different accounting from that which would be achieved if the detailed rules in US GAAP were applied. Care always needs to be taken to ensure that the adoption of the more detailed US GAAP requirements results in IFRS compliance.

4.2   The general approach to revenue recognition under US GAAP

The accounting literature of US GAAP on revenue recognition includes both broad conceptual discussions and certain industry-specific guidance. If a transaction is within the scope of specific authoritative literature that provides revenue recognition guidance, that literature should be applied. However, in the absence of authoritative literature addressing a specific arrangement or a specific industry, the SEC staff will consider the existing authoritative accounting standards as well as the broad revenue recognition criteria specified in the FASB's conceptual framework that contain basic guidelines for revenue recognition.[8]

The FASB's Concepts Statement No. 5 – *Recognition and Measurement in Financial Statements of Business Enterprises* – deals with recognition issues primarily from the angle of providing reliability of measurement. However, the broad principle for revenue recognition laid down by Concepts Statement 5 is that revenues are not recognised until they are (a) realised or realisable and (b) earned.[9] Concepts Statement 5 states that 'an entity's revenue-earning activities involve delivering or producing goods, rendering services, or other activities that constitute its ongoing major or central operations, and revenues are considered to have been earned when the entity has substantially accomplished what it must do to be entitled to the benefits represented by the revenues'.[10] It goes on to state that 'the two conditions (being realized or realizable and being earned) are usually met by the time product or merchandise is delivered or services are rendered to customers, and revenues from manufacturing and selling activities and gains and losses from sales of other assets are commonly recognized at time of sale (usually meaning delivery).'[11] In addition, it states 'if services are rendered or rights to use assets extend continuously over time (for example, interest or rent), reliable measures based on contractual prices established in advance are commonly available, and revenues may be recognized as earned as time passes.'[12]

The SEC staff believes that revenue generally is realised or realisable and earned when all of the following criteria are met:

- persuasive evidence of an arrangement exists;
- delivery has occurred or services have been rendered;
- the seller's price to the buyer is fixed or determinable; and
- collectability is reasonably assured.[13]

Generally, a sales price is not fixed or determinable when a customer has the unilateral right to terminate or cancel the contract and receive a cash refund. A sales price or fee that is variable until the occurrence of future events (other than short-term rights of return that are not considered to be cancellation privileges and fall under the guidance provided within ASC 605-15) generally is not fixed or determinable until the future event occurs. The revenue from such transactions should not be recognised in earnings until the sales price or fee becomes fixed or determinable.[14]

IAS 18 states that revenue can be recognised at the time of sale if only an insignificant risk of ownership is retained, the seller can estimate returns and it provides for them. *[IAS 18.17]*. This means that a retailer who offers refunds if the customer is not satisfied can generally recognise revenue for those sales.

4.3   US GAAP requirements for multiple-element transactions

One area of US GAAP guidance that is often referred to by IFRS reporters is that relating to transactions that comprise multiple components. The guidance under IFRS is extremely limited, simply pointing out that it may be necessary to apply the requirements of IAS 18 to separately identifiable components of a single transaction in order to reflect the substance of a transaction, *[IAS 18.13]*, along with an example illustrating the need to defer an amount relating to subsequent servicing when this servicing fee is included in the price of a product. *[IAS 18.IE11]*. Given this lack of guidance it is not surprising that IFRS reporters have looked to US GAAP which has significant detail on accounting for what it terms 'multiple-element' arrangements.

The key issues relate to how the components within these multiple-element transactions should be broken down (i.e. what is the unit of account?) and when revenue on each element should be recognised.

The primary US GAAP guidance is included within ASC 605-25 although this does not apply to software arrangements which is included within industry specific guidance and briefly explained at 6.6 below.

Chapter 30

ASC 605-25 requires that in multiple-element arrangements, the delivered item or items is considered a separate unit of accounting if:[15]

- the delivered item or items have stand-alone value; and
- when a general right of return exists for the delivered item, the delivery or performance of the undelivered item is probable and is substantially under the control of the seller.

The consideration is allocated to components based on their relative selling prices. These selling prices are calculated based upon vendor-specific objective evidence (VSOE) where available or third party evidence where not available. If neither VSOE nor third-party evidence of selling price exists for a component, the entity should use its best estimate of the selling price for that component, i.e. the price at which the entity would transact if the component were sold by the entity regularly on a stand-alone basis.[16]

Amendments made by EITF 08-01 removed the requirement for VSOE of a delivered component in order that it be treated as a separate unit of account,[17] and no longer allows the residual method in allocating consideration[18] (i.e. where VSOE was available for the undelivered element but not the delivered element the 'residual' was allocated to the delivered element). These changes only become effective for US GAAP reporters from 2010,[19] but these detailed requirements were never included within IFRS. Rather, IFRS reporters have always had to comply with the general principles of IAS 18.

5   THE IASB/FASB JOINT REVENUE RECOGNITION PROJECT

5.1   Project background

The IASB and FASB have been working since 2002 on a joint project on revenue recognition. In June 2010, the Boards issued an Exposure Draft entitled *Revenue from Contracts with Customers*. However, comments on the Exposure Draft revealed complex implementation issues and a series of amendments were made. The Boards have decided to re-expose the proposals in the latter part of 2011.

The Exposure Draft explains the principles that entities should apply in determining the amount, timing and uncertainty of revenue recognition arising from contracts to provide goods and services to their customers.[20] It is intended that this new model will replace all of the main pronouncements that presently address the recognition of revenue comprising IAS 11 – *Construction Contracts*, IAS 18 – *Revenue*, IFRIC 13 – *Customer Loyalty Programmes*, IFRIC 15 – *Agreements for the Construction of Real Estate*, IFRIC 18 – *Transfers of Assets from Customers* and SIC 31 – *Revenue – Barter Transactions Involving Advertising Services*.[21]

Although the accounting for some transactions may not be significantly changed, it is likely that all entities will be affected by the new guidance. The proposals will also introduce more detailed guidance on accounting for certain transactions, such as multiple-element arrangements, than is currently contained in IAS 18. IFRS reporters that have looked to US GAAP for guidance on these transactions will also need to consider these changes. This is because the proposed model brings the two frameworks together, and reduces the amount of industry-specific guidance that currently exists under US GAAP.

The proposed guidance will apply to all contracts with customers except financial instruments within scope of IAS 39 or IFRS 9, insurance contracts within scope of IFRS 4, leasing contracts within scope of IAS 17 and certain non-monetary transactions.[22]

The Boards are proposing that entities apply the new guidance retrospectively for all periods presented in the period of adoption[23], although some limited reliefs, e.g. allowing estimations and reducing disclosures, are expected to be offered in the revised exposure draft.[24]

5.2   Summary of the proposed model

Under the proposed model the individual performance obligations under a contract with a customer are identified, revenue allocated to these obligations at the outset, and then revenue recognised when control of the related good or service is passed to the customer i.e. it is a control-based model rather than one primarily focused on risks and rewards as presently is the case under IAS 18.

The model includes the following five steps that entities would apply to determine the appropriate timing and amount of revenue recognition. This summary reflects the tentative decisions taken by the Boards in their meetings during 2011, as reported periodically in *IASB Update.* These decisions are all subject to revision before the revised Exposure Draft is issued.

Step 1: Identify the contract(s) with the customer

In order to apply the proposed revenue recognition model, an entity must first identify the contract(s). The proposed guidance indicates that contracts may be written, verbal or implied, and that the entity's business practices may influence its determination of whether or not a contract exists.[25]

Step 2: Identify the separate performance obligations in the contract

Under the model, the entity evaluates the terms of the contract as well as the entity's normal business practices to identify all promised goods and services within the contract, and to determine whether each needs to be treated as a separate performance obligation.[26]

The model in the ED requires promised goods and services to be treated as separate performance obligations only if the good or service is 'distinct'; the Boards intend to retain this overall approach but they have decided to simplify it.[27] A bundle of promised goods or services will be accounted for as one performance obligation if the entity provides a service of integrating those goods or services into a single item that it provides to the customer.

If the good or service has a different pattern of transfer to the customer from other goods and services in the contract and has a distinct function, then each promised good or service (or a bundle of goods or services, as above) will be accounted for as a separate performance obligation.

A 'distinct function' is where either:

- the entity regularly sells the good or service separately; or
- the customer can use the good or service either on its own or together with resources that are readily available to the customer (including resources obtained in previous transfers of goods or services or that the customer could purchase separately).

The separate performance obligations need not be individually legally enforceable. Some had interpreted this as a requirement in the original ED but the Boards have indicated that this was not their intention and this is to be clarified in the re-exposed document.[28]

Step 3: Determine the transaction price

In changes from its original proposals, the transaction price is to exclude the effects of a customer's credit risk, so revenue will be based on the amount in the contract. Entities will present revenue without deducting amounts that may not be collectible and will present an allowance for expected impairment losses on a separate line immediately below gross revenue. The line item will include recognition of the initial allowance as well as the effects of subsequent changes in collectability.[29]

For some transactions, portions of the transaction price may be variable, i.e. contingent on future events. In another significant change from the original ED, it is now proposed that the entity should estimate either of the following amounts, depending on which is best predicts the amount of consideration to which the entity will be entitled:[30]

a)   the probability-weighted amount: or

b)   the most likely amount.

An entity need only reduce the transaction price for the time value of money if the effect would be significant. The Boards tentatively decided that, as a practical expedient, an entity would not be required to assess whether a contract has a significant financing component if the period between payment by the customer and the transfer of the promised goods or services to the customer is one year or less.[31]

Step 4: Allocate the transaction price to the separate performance obligations

Once the performance obligations are identified and the transaction price determined, the proposed model requires an entity to allocate the transaction price to the performance obligations, usually in proportion to their stand-alone selling prices, that is, on a relative stand-alone selling price basis.

When available, the observable price of a good or service sold separately provides the best evidence of stand-alone selling price. In many situations, stand-alone selling prices will not be readily observable, in which case the entity should estimate the amount for which it would sell each performance obligation on a stand-alone basis.[32] The proposed model gives two examples of possible approaches to estimating a stand-alone selling price, including an 'expected cost plus a margin approach' or an 'adjusted market assessment approach' (e.g.

estimating what a customer would be willing to pay for the good or service).[33] These approaches have not been revisited in their subsequent redeliberations. However, the Boards have moved towards allowing a type of residual technique if the standalone selling price of a good or service underlying a separate performance obligation is highly variable. An entity would determine a standalone selling price by reference to the total transaction price less the standalone selling prices of other goods or services in the contract.[34]

The Boards have modified their approach to subsequent changes in the total estimated transaction price. Any change is allocated to all performance obligations based upon measurement at contract inception, i.e. they are not updated to reflect changes in relative stand-alone selling prices after contract inception.[35] However, the Boards now consider that an entity should allocate a portion of (or a change in) the transaction price entirely to one (or more) performance obligation in the following circumstances:

a)   the contingent payment terms relate specifically to the entity's efforts to satisfy that performance obligation or a specific outcome from satisfying it; and

b)   the amount allocated to that particular performance obligation, including the change in the transaction price, is reasonable relative to all of the performance obligations and payment terms (including other potential contingent payments) in the contract.[36]

Step 5: Recognise revenue when each performance obligation is satisfied

The model states that revenue allocated to a particular performance obligation should be recognised at the point the customer obtains control of the underlying good or service. A customer 'obtains control of a good or service when the customer has the present ability to direct the use of, and receive the benefit from, the good or service.'[37]

In many situations, the determination of when the customer obtains control is relatively straightforward. However, in other scenarios this determination is more complex. In an effort to help entities determine when a customer has obtained control of a particular good or service, the proposed model includes the following indicators that the customer has obtained control:[38]

- the customer has an unconditional obligation to pay;
- the customer has legal title; or
- the customer has physical possession

These indicators should be assessed together rather than any single one being the sole determinant of whether or not the customer has gained control of the good or service.[39]

A particular area of concern about the ED was how to apply the control model to services. The revised ED is now expected to provide additional guidance for arrangements in which performance obligations are satisfied over time; the Boards consider any performance obligation that is satisfied continuously will include services. A performance obligation is satisfied continuously if:

Chapter 30

(i)   the entity's performance creates or enhances an asset that the customer controls as the asset is being created; or

(ii)   the entity's performance does not create an asset with alternative use to the entity and at least one of the following conditions is met:

- the customer receives a benefit as each task is being performed;
- another entity would not need to re-perform all of the task(s) performed to date if that other entity were to fulfil the remaining obligation; and
- the entity has a right to payment for performance to date even if the customer or the entity could cancel the contract for convenience.[40]

The Exposure Draft also addresses whether a customer has obtained control of an asset in contracts containing repurchase agreements. If the customer has the ability to require the entity to repurchase the asset, then the buyer has obtained control of the asset and a sale should be recorded. The entity would also recognise a liability for the right of return. Conversely, if the entity has an unconditional obligation (forward) or right (call option) to repurchase the asset, the customer has not obtained control of the asset and such transaction likely represents a lease or a financing transaction rather than a sale.[41] Other than clarifying when arrangements are to be treated as leases, this guidance is expected to be broadly unchanged. [42]

Other features of the model

Performance obligations may have to be treated as onerous if the direct costs of fulfilling them exceed the consideration allocated to them. If it is onerous, the entity must recognise a liability and a corresponding expense to the extent the direct costs exceed the allocated transaction price. The liability for onerous contracts is remeasured at each reporting date using the most current estimates.[43] The requirements may be more limited than in the original ED; the Boards have suggested that companies need to assess whether a performance obligation is onerous only for performance obligations satisfied over time (e.g. long-term service contracts).[44]

The model indicates that costs incurred in connection with fulfilling the performance obligations of a contract that are not eligible for capitalisation under another standard (i.e. IAS 2 – *Inventories*, IAS 16 – *Property, Plant and Equipment* or IAS 38 – *Intangible Assets*) may give rise to a separate asset if the cost:[45]

- relate directly to the contract or a specific contract under negotiation;
- generate or enhance resources of the entity that will be used in satisfying performance obligations in the future; and
- are expected to be recovered.

The Exposure Draft also includes a number of new disclosure requirements. The overall disclosure objective is to provide quantitative and qualitative disclosures to 'help users of financial statements understand the amount, timing and uncertainty of revenue and cash flows arising from contracts with customers'.[46] Based on that objective, the Exposure Draft requires much greater disclosure than presently required under IAS 18. Although there has been some relaxation of the detailed disclosures as a result of the redeliberations, the amount of disclosure is still expected to increase.[47]

5.3   Changes to current practice that would result from the proposed model

There are a number of areas that may be affected by this new model:

- revenue on construction contracts under IAS 11 is recognised in the period the work is performed. *[IAS 11.26]*. The new model will only allow revenue to be recognised when a performance obligation is satisfied which will be when control of the asset has been transferred to the customer. Many construction contracts involve the continual transfer of such rights and work in progress to the customer but there are some that do not, which would lead to later revenue recognition on these;

- an entity will be required to separate contracts into different performance obligations for goods or services that are deemed to be 'distinct', as explained above, and this may well differ to the components that are treated as separate units of account under current practice. However, the revised approach using a 'bundle' of goods and services might mitigate the effect;

- the model requires an entity to estimate the stand-alone selling prices for separate performance obligations in multiple-element contracts;

- greater estimation will be required under the new model, especially where there is an element of variable consideration, and in calculating the relative stand-alone selling prices of each of the performance obligations which is the basis by which the transaction price is allocated;

- the disclosures required under the Exposure Draft and expected under the revised ED are more detailed than under IAS 18 and will be more onerous to prepare.

6   PRACTICAL ISSUES

IAS 18 could be said to be one of the few truly principles-based standards in the IFRS literature. However, the broader the principles the more that judgement is required to apply them in practice, with the inevitable result that consistency is not always achieved. Nevertheless, consistency has tended to be achieved over time within specific industries on the basis of principles-based consensuses between the preparer, regulator and auditor communities.

The following table summarises the broad approaches to revenue reporting that would appear to have achieved general acceptance through existing reporting practice. The table indicates the circumstances under which it might be appropriate to apply each of the approaches; nevertheless, it is essential that each situation is considered on its individual merits, with particular attention being paid to the risks and uncertainties that remain at each stage of the earnings process and the extent to which the amount of revenue can be measured reliably.

Chapter 30

The timing of recognition	*Criteria*	*Examples of practical application*
During production (accretion)	Revenues accrue over time, and no significant uncertainty exists as to measurability or collectability. A contract of sale has been entered into and future costs can be estimated with reasonable accuracy.	Most services. The accrual of interest and dividend income. Accounting for construction contracts using the percentage-of-completion method.
At the completion of production	There is a ready market for the commodity that can rapidly absorb the quantity held by the entity; the commodity comprises interchangeable units; the market price should be determinable and stable; there should be insignificant marketing costs involved.	Certain precious metals and commodities.
At the time of sale (but before delivery)	Goods must have already been acquired or manufactured; goods must be capable of immediate delivery to the customer; selling price has been established; all material related expenses (including delivery) have been ascertained; no significant uncertainties remain (e.g. ultimate cash collection, returns).	Certain sales of goods (e.g. 'bill and hold' sales). Property sales where there is an irrevocable contract.
On delivery	Criteria for recognition before delivery were not satisfied and no significant uncertainties remain.	Most sales of goods and some services. Property sales where it is not certain that the sale will be completed.
Subsequent to delivery	Significant uncertainty regarding collectability existed at the time of delivery; at the time of sale it was not possible to value the consideration with sufficient accuracy.	Certain sales of goods and services (e.g. where the right of return exists). Goods shipped subject to conditions (e.g. installation and inspection/performance).
On an apportionment basis (the revenue allocation approach)	Where revenue represents the supply of initial and subsequent goods/services.	Franchise fees. Sale of goods with after sales service.

All the same, because minimal implementation guidance is given in IFRS about the timing of revenue recognition, we have devoted the remainder of this Chapter to the examination of specific areas of revenue recognition in practice that might be open to inconsistent, controversial or varied accounting practices. Some of this comprises a discussion of the issues addressed in Appendix A to IAS 18, which expands on the principles in the standard. The IFRIC Interpretations that have a particular impact on revenue recognition (IFRIC 13 – *Customer Loyalty Programmes*, IFRIC 15 – *Agreements for the Construction of Real Estate* – and IFRIC 18 – *Transfers of Assets from Customers*) are also discussed below. Many of the issues discussed below relate to specific industries that pose particular revenue recognition problems.

6.1 Sale of goods

Appendix A of IAS 18 identifies a number of different arrangements that may affect the point at which the risks and rewards of ownership pass to the buyer. The law governing the sale of goods in any particular jurisdiction must be taken into account.

6.1.1 'Bill and hold' sales

The term 'bill and hold' sale is used to describe a transaction where delivery is delayed at the buyer's request, but the buyer takes title and accepts billing.

Under the guidance provided in the Appendix to IAS 18, revenue is recognised when the buyer takes title, provided:

(a)   it is probable that delivery will be made;

(b)   the item is on hand, identified and ready for delivery to the buyer at the time the sale is recognised;

(c)   the buyer specifically acknowledges the deferred delivery instructions; and

(d)   the usual payment terms apply.

Revenue is not recognised when there is simply an intention to acquire or manufacture the goods in time for delivery. *[IAS 18.IE1].*

6.1.2 Goods shipped subject to conditions

The Appendix to IAS 18 identifies four scenarios where goods are shipped subject to various conditions: *[IAS 18.IE2]*

(a)   *installation and inspection*

Revenue is normally recognised when the buyer accepts delivery, and installation and inspection are complete. Revenue is recognised immediately upon the buyer's acceptance of delivery when:

(i)   the installation process is simple in nature, e.g. the installation of a factory-tested television receiver which only requires unpacking and connection of power and antennae; or

(ii)   the inspection is performed only for purposes of final determination of contract prices, for example, shipments of iron ore, sugar or soya beans.

(b)   *on approval when the buyer has negotiated a limited right of return*

If there is uncertainty about the possibility of return, revenue is recognised when the shipment has been formally accepted by the buyer or the goods have been delivered and the time period for rejection has elapsed. See the discussion at 2.1.3 above.

(c)   *consignment sales under which the recipient (buyer) undertakes to sell the goods on behalf of the shipper (seller)*

Revenue is recognised by the shipper when the goods are sold by the recipient to a third party.

(d)   *cash on delivery sales*

Revenue is recognised when delivery is made and cash is received by the seller or its agent.

The following extract from the financial statements of Sandvik illustrates a revenue recognition policy that reflects some of these requirements:

Extract 30.12: Sandvik AB (2008)

Accounting policies [extract]

Revenue [extract]

Revenue from sales and services [extract]

Revenue from the sale of goods is recognized in the income statement when the significant risks and rewards of ownership have been transferred to the buyer, that is, normally in connection with delivery. If the product requires installation at the buyer, and installation is a significant part of the contract, revenue is recognized when the installation is completed. Buy-back commitments may entail that sales revenue cannot be recognized if the agreement with the customer in reality implies that the customer has only rented the product for a certain period of time.

6.1.3   Layaway sales

The term 'layaway sales' applies to transactions where the goods are delivered only when the buyer makes the final payment in a series of instalments. This is fairly common in the retail sector, e.g. clothing and household goods. Revenue from such sales is recognised when the goods are delivered. However, when experience indicates that most such sales are consummated, revenue may be recognised when a significant deposit is received, provided the goods are on hand, identified and ready for delivery to the buyer. *[IAS 18.IE3]*.

6.1.4   Payments in advance

In certain sectors (e.g. furniture and kitchen retail) payment or partial payment is received from the customer when he places his order for the goods. This is often well in advance of delivery for goods which are not presently held in inventory, if, for example, the goods are still to be manufactured or will be delivered directly to the customer by a third party. In such cases, revenue is recognised when the goods are delivered to the buyer. *[IAS 18.IE4]*.

In other sectors – for example, utilities – companies receive advance payments from customers for services to be provided in the future. In some cases, these advance payments are long term in nature, and the issue that arises is whether or not interest should be accrued on these long term advances received for the delivery of such services and, if so, how revenue should be measured in these circumstances.

IAS 18 requires entities to measure revenue 'at the fair value of the consideration received or receivable'. *[IAS 18.9]*. The standard elaborates on this requirement by referring to the situation in which an entity either provides interest-free credit to the buyer or accepts a note receivable bearing a below-market interest rate from the buyer as consideration for the sale of goods. If the arrangement effectively constitutes a financing transaction, IAS 18 requires that the entity determine the fair value of the consideration by discounting all future receipts using an imputed rate of interest. *[IAS 18.11]*. Although IAS 18 does not address the reverse situation of the receipt of interest-free advances from customers, a similar rationale may be applied to justify the accruing of interest, i.e. there is a financing element to the transaction and this must be taken account of if revenue is to be measured at the fair value of the consideration at the time the good or service is provided.

However, in drafting IFRIC 18 the Interpretations Committee considered the concept of accruing interest on advance payments received from customers but the majority of respondents commenting on the draft disagreed that this was necessary. The Interpretations Committee subsequently agreed with this majority view and noted that 'paragraph 11 of IAS 18 requires taking the time value of money into account only when payments are deferred'. *[IFRIC 18.BC22]*.

Given this lack of clarity we believe it is a policy choice of whether or not to accrue interest on advance payments received from customers. If interest is accrued it will be calculated based upon the incremental borrowing rate of the entity and revenue will ultimately be recognised based upon the nominal value of the advance payments received from customers plus this accrued interest. In fact accruing interest would seem to be more consistent with the principles of IAS 18 and hence it would be difficult to justify a change in accounting policy from accruing interest to not doing so. Whichever accounting policy is adopted, it should be applied consistently.

6.1.5   *Sale and repurchase agreements*

Sale and repurchase agreements take many forms: the seller concurrently agrees to repurchase the same goods at a later date, or the seller has a call option to repurchase, or the buyer has a put option to require the repurchase, by the seller, of the goods.

In a sale and repurchase agreement for an asset other than a financial asset, the terms of the agreement need to be analysed to ascertain whether, in substance, the seller has transferred the risks and rewards of ownership to the buyer and hence revenue is recognised. When the seller has retained the risks and rewards of ownership, even though legal title has been transferred, the transaction is a financing arrangement and does not give rise to revenue. Sale and leaseback arrangements including repurchase agreements and options are discussed in Chapter 26 at 7. For a sale and repurchase agreement on a financial asset, IAS 39 applies (see Chapter 50). *[IAS 18.IE5]*.

Chapter 30

6.1.6   *Instalment sales*

The term 'instalment sales' refers to sales where the goods are delivered to the customer, but payment is made by a number of instalments that include financing charges In such cases, revenue attributable to the sale price, exclusive of interest, is recognised at the date of sale. The sale price is the present value of the consideration, determined by discounting the instalments receivable at the imputed rate of interest. The interest element is recognised as revenue as it is earned, using the effective interest method set out in IAS 39. *[IAS 18.IE8]*. The application of the effective interest rate method is discussed in Chapter 49 at 5.

6.2   Receipt of initial fees

The practice that has developed in certain industries of charging an initial fee at the inception of a service, followed by subsequent service fees, can present revenue allocation problems. This is because it is not always altogether clear what the initial fee represents; consequently, it is necessary to determine what proportion (if any) of the initial fee has been earned on receipt, and how much relates to the provision of future services. In some cases, large initial fees are paid for the provision of a service, whilst continuing fees are relatively small in relation to future services to be provided. If it is probable that the continuing fees will not cover the cost of the continuing services to be provided plus a reasonable profit, then a portion of the initial fee should be deferred over the period of the service contract such that a reasonable profit is earned throughout the service period. Accounting for initial fees has proved problematic and the Interpretations Committee has addressed the issue inconclusively – see 6.2.4 below.

6.2.1   *Franchise fees*

Franchise agreements between franchisors and franchisees can vary widely both in complexity and in the extent to which various rights, duties and obligations are explicitly addressed. There is no standard form of franchise agreement which would dictate standard accounting practice for the recognition of all franchise fee revenue. Only a full understanding of the franchise agreement will reveal the substance of a particular arrangement so that the most appropriate accounting treatment can be determined; nevertheless, the following are the more common areas which are likely to be addressed in any franchise agreement and which will be relevant to franchise fee revenue reporting:[48]

(a)   *rights transferred by the franchisor:* the agreement gives the franchisee the right to use the trade name, processes, know-how of the franchisor for a specified period of time or in perpetuity.

(b)   *the amount and terms of payment of initial fees:* payment of initial fees (where applicable) may be fully or partially due in cash, and may be payable immediately, over a specified period or on the fulfilment of certain obligations by the franchisor.

(c)   *amount and terms of payment of continuing franchise fees:* the franchisee will normally be required to pay a continuing fee to the franchisor – usually on the basis of a percentage of gross revenues.

(d) *services to be provided by the franchisor initially and on a continuing basis:* the franchisor will usually agree to provide a variety of services and advice to the franchisee, such as:

- site selection;
- the procurement of fixed assets and equipment – these may be either purchased by the franchisee, leased from the franchisor or leased from a third party (possibly with the franchisor guaranteeing the lease payments);
- advertising;
- training of franchisee's personnel;
- inspecting, testing and other quality control programmes; and
- bookkeeping services.

(e) *acquisition of equipment, stock and supplies:* the franchisee may be required to purchase these items either from the franchisor or from designated suppliers. Some franchisors manufacture products for sale to their franchisees, whilst others act as wholesalers.

The Appendix to IAS 18 includes a broad discussion of the receipt of franchise fees, stating that they are recognised as revenue on a basis that reflects the purpose for which the fees were charged. *[IAS 18.IE18]*. The standard states that the following methods of franchise fee recognition are appropriate: *[IAS 18.IE18]*

Supplies of equipment and other tangible assets: the amount, based on the fair value of the assets sold, is recognised as revenue when the items are delivered or title passes.

Supplies of initial and subsequent services: fees for the provision of continuing services, whether part of the initial fee or a separate fee, are recognised as revenue as the services are rendered. When the separate fee does not cover the cost of continuing services together with a reasonable profit, part of the initial fee, sufficient to cover the costs of continuing services and to provide a reasonable profit on those services, is deferred and recognised as revenue as the services are rendered.

The franchise agreement may provide for the franchisor to supply equipment, inventories, or other tangible assets, at a price lower than that charged to others or a price that does not provide a reasonable profit on those sales. In these circumstances, part of the initial fee, sufficient to cover estimated costs in excess of that price and to provide a reasonable profit on those sales, is deferred and recognised over the period the goods are likely to be sold to the franchisee. The balance of an initial fee is recognised as revenue when performance of all the initial services and other obligations required of the franchisor (such as assistance with site selection, staff training, financing and advertising) has been substantially accomplished.

The initial services and other obligations under an area franchise agreement may depend on the number of individual outlets established in the area. In this case, the fees attributable to the initial services are recognised as revenue in proportion to the number of outlets for which the initial services have been substantially completed.

Chapter 30

If the initial fee is collectible over an extended period and there is a significant uncertainty that it will be collected in full, the fee is recognised as cash instalments are received.

Continuing Franchise Fees: fees charged for the use of continuing rights granted by the agreement, or for other services provided during the period of the agreement, are recognised as revenue as the services are provided or the rights used.

Agency Transactions: transactions may take place between the franchisor and the franchisee which, in substance, involve the franchisor acting as agent for the franchisee. For example, the franchisor may order supplies and arrange for their delivery to the franchisee at no profit. Such transactions do not give rise to revenue.

In summary, it is necessary to break down the initial fee into its various components, e.g. the fee for franchise rights, fee for initial services to be performed by the franchisor, fair value of tangible assets sold etc. The individual components may be recognised at different stages. The portion that relates to the franchise rights may be recognised in full immediately unless part of it has to be deferred because the continuing fee does not cover the cost of continuing services to be provided by the franchisor plus a reasonable profit. In this case a portion of the initial fee should be deferred and recognised as services are provided. The fee for initial services should only be recognised when the services have been 'substantially performed' (it is unlikely that substantial performance will have been completed before the franchisee opens for business). The portion of the fee which relates to tangible assets may be recognised when title passes. If the collection period for the initial fees is extended and there is doubt as to the ultimate collectability, recognition of revenue should be deferred.

6.2.2   Advance royalty or licence receipts

The general guidance relating to licence fees and royalties states that 'fees and royalties paid for the use of an entity's assets (such as trademarks, patents, software, music copyright, record masters and motion picture films) are normally recognised in accordance with the substance of the agreement. As a practical matter, this may be on a straight line basis over the life of the agreement, for example, when a licensee has the right to use certain technology for a specified period of time.' *[IAS 18.IE20]*.

Therefore, under normal circumstances, the accounting treatment of advance royalty or licence receipts is straightforward; under the accruals concept the advance should be treated as deferred income when received, and released to the profit and loss account when earned under the terms of the royalty/licence agreement. Bayer provides an example of such an approach:

Extract 30.13: Bayer AG (2007)

Notes [extract]

4.   Basic principles, methods and critical accounting policies [extract]

Net sales and other operating income [extract]

Some of the Bayer Group's revenues are generated on the basis of licensing agreements under which third parties are granted rights to its products and technologies. Payments relating to the sale or outlicensing of technologies or technological expertise – once the respective agreements have become effective – are immediately recognized in income if all rights relating to the technologies and all obligations resulting from them have been relinquished under the contract terms and Bayer has no continuing obligation to perform under the agreement. However, if rights to the technologies continue to exist or obligations resulting from them have yet to be fulfilled, the payments received are recorded in line with the actual circumstances. Upfront payments and similar non-refundable payments received under these agreements are recorded as other liabilities and recognized in income over the estimated performance period stipulated in the agreement. Revenues such as license fees or rentals are recognized according to the same principles.

However, in some industries the forms of agreement are such that advance receipts comprise a number of components, each requiring different accounting treatments. In the record and music industry, a record company will normally enter into a contractual arrangement with either a recording artist or a production company to deliver finished recording masters over a specified period of time. The albums are then manufactured and shipped to retailers for ultimate sale to the customer. The recording artist will normally be compensated through participating in the record company's sales and licence fee income (i.e. a royalty), but may also receive a non-returnable fixed fee on delivery of the master to the record company.

Example 30.1:   Revenue recognition for licensors in the record and music industry

For each recording master delivered by a pop group, THRAG, the group (which operates through a service company) receives a payment of €1,000,000. This amount comprises:

- a non-returnable, non-recoupable payment of €100,000;
- a non-returnable but recoupable advance of €600,000; and
- a returnable, recoupable advance of €300,000.

The recoupable advances of €900,000 can be recouped against royalties on net sales earned both on the album concerned and on earlier and subsequent albums. This is achieved by computing the total royalties on net sales on all albums delivered under THRAG's service company's agreement with its recording company, and applying against this total the advances and royalties previously paid on those albums.

It is clear that the non-recoupable advance of €100,000 should be recognised in income when received, since it is not related to any future performance; at the other end of the spectrum, recognition of the returnable advance should be deferred and recognised only when recouped. However, the question arises as to whether the non-returnable but recoupable advance on royalties should be recognised immediately or deferred. If one accepts that revenue may be recognised when it is absolutely assured, there is an argument to justify the immediate recognition of the recoupable advance, since it is non-returnable. Conversely, some might argue that although the advance is non-returnable, it is not earned until it is recouped; furthermore, immediate recognition of royalty advances is likely to lead to a significant distortion of reported income, resulting in there being little correlation between reported income and album sales.

However, in our view, from the perspective of THRAG, the earnings process on the non-returnable but recoupable advance of €600,000 is complete. This is because THRAG has no other service obligation to fulfil, and the fact that the advance is recoupable is a risk of the record company. Consequently, it should be recognised in revenue immediately on delivery of the master.

Similar recognition principles should be applied in the case of advance fees paid on the sale of film/TV rights.

6.2.3   *Financial service fees*

The Appendix to IAS 18 includes a series of illustrative examples that relate to financial service fees, pointing out that the recognition of revenue for financial service fees depends on the purposes for which the fees are assessed and the basis of accounting for any associated financial instrument. *[IAS 18.IE14]*. The description of fees for financial services may not be indicative of the nature and substance of the services provided. Therefore, it is necessary to distinguish between fees that are an integral part of the effective interest rate of a financial instrument, fees that are earned as services are provided, and fees that are earned on the execution of a significant act. The Appendix to IAS 18 makes this distinction as follows: *[IAS 18.IE14]*

6.2.3.A   *Fees that are an integral part of the effective interest rate of a financial instrument*

Such fees are generally treated as an adjustment to the effective interest rate. However, when the financial instrument is measured at fair value with the change in fair value recognised in profit or loss the fees are recognised as revenue when the instrument is initially recognised.

- *Origination fees received by the entity relating to the creation or acquisition of a financial asset other than one that under IAS 39 is classified as a financial asset 'at fair value through profit or loss':* Such fees may include compensation for activities such as evaluating the borrower's financial condition, evaluating and recording guarantees, collateral and other security arrangements, negotiating the terms of the instrument, preparing and processing documents and closing the transaction. These fees are an integral part of generating an involvement with the resulting financial instrument and, together with the related transaction costs (as defined in IAS 39), are deferred and recognised as an adjustment to the effective interest rate.

Deutsche Bank discloses a policy that reflects this requirement:

Extract 30.14: Deutsche Bank AG (2010)

Notes to the Consolidated Financial Statements [extract]

01 – Significant Accounting Policies [extract]

Commission and Fee Income [extract]

The recognition of fee revenue (including commissions) is determined by the purpose of the fees and the basis of accounting for any associated financial instruments. If there is an associated financial instrument, fees that are an integral part of the effective interest rate of that financial instrument are included within the effective yield calculation. However, if the financial instrument is carried at fair value through profit or loss, any associated fees are recognized in profit or loss when the instrument is initially recognized, provided there are no significant unobservable inputs used in determining its fair value. Fees earned from services that are provided over a specified service period are recognized over that service period. Fees earned for the completion of a specific service or significant event are recognized when the service has been completed or the event has occurred.

Loan commitment fees related to commitments that are not accounted for at fair value through profit or loss are recognized in commissions and fee income over the life of the commitment if it is unlikely that the Group will enter into a specific lending arrangement. If it is probable that the Group will enter into a specific lending arrangement, the loan commitment fee is deferred until the origination of a loan and recognized as an adjustment to the loan's effective interest rate.

- *Commitment fees received by the entity to originate a loan when the loan commitment is outside the scope of IAS 39:* If it is probable that the entity will enter into a specific lending arrangement and the loan commitment is not within the scope of IAS 39, the commitment fee received is regarded as compensation for an ongoing involvement with the acquisition of a financial instrument and, together with the related transaction costs (as defined in IAS 39), is deferred and recognised as an adjustment to the effective interest rate. If the commitment expires without the entity making the loan, the fee is recognised as revenue on expiry. Loan commitments that are within the scope of IAS 39 are accounted for as derivatives and measured at fair value.

- *Origination fees received on issuing financial liabilities measured at amortised cost:* These fees are an integral part of generating an involvement with a financial liability. When a financial liability is not classified as 'at fair value through profit or loss', the origination fees received are included, with the related transaction costs (as defined in IAS 39) incurred, in the initial carrying amount of the financial liability and recognised as an adjustment to the effective yield. An entity distinguishes fees and costs that are an integral part of the effective interest rate for the financial liability from origination fees and transaction costs relating to the right to provide services, such as investment management services.

6.2.3.B   Fees earned as services are provided

The following are examples of situations where revenue is recognised over the period of the related service:

- *Fees charged for servicing a loan:* These fees are recognised as revenue as the services are provided.

- *Commitment fees to originate a loan when the loan commitment is outside the scope of IAS 39:* If it is unlikely that a specific lending arrangement will be entered into and the loan commitment is outside the scope of IAS 39, the commitment fee is recognised as revenue on a time proportion basis over the commitment period. Loan commitments that are within the scope of IAS 39 are accounted for as derivatives and measured at fair value.

- *Investment management fees:* Fees charged for managing investments are recognised as revenue as the services are provided. Incremental costs that are directly attributable to securing an investment management contract are recognised as an asset if they can be identified separately and measured reliably and if it is probable that they will be recovered. As in IAS 39, an incremental cost is one that would not have been incurred if the entity had not secured the investment management contract. The asset represents the entity's contractual right to benefit from providing investment management services, and is amortised as the entity recognises the related revenue. If the entity has a portfolio of investment management contracts, it may assess their recoverability on a portfolio basis. Some financial services contracts involve both the origination of one or more financial instruments and the provision of investment management services. An example is a long-term monthly saving contract linked to the management of a pool of equity securities. The provider of the contract distinguishes the

Chapter 30

transaction costs relating to the origination of the financial instrument from the costs of securing the right to provide investment management services.

6.2.3.C   *Fees that are earned on the execution of a significant act*

The fees are recognised as revenue when the significant act has been completed, as in the examples below.

- *Commission on the allotment of shares to a client:* The commission is recognised as revenue when the shares have been allotted.

- *Placement fees for arranging a loan between a borrower and an investor:* The fee is recognised as revenue when the loan has been arranged.

- *Loan syndication fees:* A syndication fee received by an entity that arranges a loan and retains no part of the loan package for itself (or retains a part at the same effective interest rate for comparable risk as other participants) is compensation for the service of syndication. Such a fee is recognised as revenue when the syndication has been completed.

The following extracts from the financial statements of Barclays and HSBC illustrate the approach followed in practice:

Extract 30.15: Barclays PLC (2007)

Consolidated accounts Barclays PLC

Significant Accounting Policies [extract]

6.   Interest, fees and commissions [extract]

Fees and commissions

Unless included in the effective interest calculation, fees and commissions are recognised on an accruals basis as the service is provided. Fees and commissions not integral to effective interest arising from negotiating, or participating in the negotiation of a transaction from a third party, such as the acquisition of loans, shares or other securities or the purchase or sale of businesses, are recognised on completion of the underlying transaction. Portfolio and other management advisory and service fees are recognised based on the applicable service contracts. Asset management fees related to investment funds are recognised over the period the service is provided. The same principle is applied to the recognition of income from wealth management, financial planning and custody services that are continuously provided over an extended period of time.

Commitment fees, together with related direct costs, for loan facilities where draw down is probable are deferred and recognised as an adjustment to the effective interest on the loan once drawn. Commitment fees in relation to facilities where draw down is not probable are recognised over the term of the commitment.

Extract 30.16: HSBC Holdings plc (2008)

Notes on the Financial Statements [extract]

2   Summary of significant accounting policies [extract]

(b)   Non-interest income [extract]

Fee income is earned from a diverse range of services provided by HSBC to its customers. Fee income is accounted for as follows:

- income earned on the execution of a significant act is recognised as revenue when the act is completed (for example, fees arising from negotiating, or participating in the negotiation of, a transaction for a third party, such as the arrangement for the acquisition of shares or other securities);

> – income earned from the provision of services is recognised as revenue as the services are provided (for example, asset management, portfolio and other management advisory and service fees); and
>
> – income which forms an integral part of the effective interest rate of a financial instrument is recognised as an adjustment to the effective interest rate (for example, certain loan commitment fees) and recorded in 'Interest income' (Note 2a).

6.2.4   Initial and ongoing fees received by a fund manager

Fund managers' activities generate a number of different fees and commissions, including the payment and receipt of initial fees followed by further payments and receipts (so-called 'trail' or 'trailing' commissions) and performance fees depending on the value of investments under management.

The Interpretations Committee has considered on a number of occasions the appropriate accounting for initial fees and trail commissions and failed to come to any conclusion, most recently in July 2008.[49] The Interpretations Committee has focused on the accounting treatment by the party that receives the fee, usually the financial adviser to the investor.

These fees are typically paid by an investor who makes an investment in a fund, and they are non-refundable regardless of how long the investor chooses to remain invested. An investor may pay a non-refundable fee (for example 5% of the initial investment) on investing in a fund and ongoing fees (say 1% of the fund assets per annum) for continuing fund management. Units in the fund may be sold by an adviser from an in-house sales department of the same group as the fund manager or by a separate financial adviser. If they are sold by a separate financial adviser, that adviser will retain the 5 per cent upfront fee. There are considerable difficulties in determining the appropriate accounting and they demonstrate a tension between different accounting standards that can lead to different accounting treatments.

The upfront fee is a fixed sum receivable at the commencement of the arrangement. Various parties have argued that the initial fee should be recognised as revenue when receivable, or alternatively that it should be spread over the estimated life of the investment. Some members of the Interpretations Committee viewed the fact that the upfront fee is the same, regardless of whether it is retained by a separate financial adviser (which is independent of the group that includes the fund manager and therefore has no further involvement with the transaction) or by an adviser from an in-house sales department of the same group as the fund manager, as evidence that upfront services were delivered and that the fair value of those services can be measured reliably. Other members noted that the receipt of a non refundable initial fee does not, in itself, give evidence that an upfront service has been provided or that the fair value of the consideration paid in respect of any upfront services is equal to the initial fee received.[50]

Trail commissions raise additional problems. They are paid periodically in arrears and the amounts payable vary with values (e.g. of funds under management). In July 2008 the Interpretations Committee was again unable to determine whether there were future services but revenue recognition remains an issue even if it is assumed that there are no services provided during the arrangement. Some argue

Chapter 30

that IAS 18 should be used; revenue ought to be taken when the conditions are met as two of the basic criteria for revenue recognition cannot be demonstrated at inception (that the amount of revenue can be measured reliably and that is probable that the economic benefits associated with the transaction will flow to the entity). *[IAS 18.14].* Paragraph 20 of the Appendix notes, in the context of licence fees or royalty whose receipt is contingent on the occurrence of a future event, that revenue is recognised only when it is probable that the fee will be received, which is normally when the event has occurred. Others argue that the initial fee and trail commissions together comprise the revenue earned by the financial advisor. The fair value can be estimated and ought to be recognised at inception, using IAS 39 as the relevant accounting standards.

Similar arrangements can be found in many industries, not all of which are financial services. For example, 'revenue share' arrangements in telecommunications share many features: an upfront commission is paid to the distributor, who receives further sums if the customer remains on the same network tariff. The corresponding treatment of the cost to the operator is also debated: is it an upfront liability as defined by IAS 32 – *Financial Instruments: Presentation*, expensed as incurred and measured using IAS 39 principles, or is it recognised when incurred under IAS 37 – *Provisions, Contingent Liabilities and Contingent Assets?* It is a widespread and complex problem and the arrangements create issues for the entity making the payment as well as the recipient. The Interpretations Committee decided not to add this issue to its agenda. While industry practice varies, some asset management groups take the view that some front-end fees are earned over the period in which it is expected that services will be provided and other fees earned as conditions are met:

Extract 30.17: Henderson Group plc (2008)

2   Accounting policies [extract]

2.1   Significant accounting policies

Income recognition

Fee income and commission receivable

Fee income includes annual management charges, transaction fees and performance fees. Annual management charges and transaction fees are recognised in the accounting period in which the associated investment management or transaction services are provided. Performance fees are recognised when the prescribed performance hurdles have been achieved and it is probable that the fee will crystallise as a result. The Group's policy is to accrue 95% of the expected fee calculation on satisfaction of the recognition criteria it has established for performance fees, with the balance of 5% credited on cash settlement.

Initial fees and commission receivable are deferred and amortised over the anticipated period in which services will be provided, determined by reference to the average term of investors in each product on which commissions are earned. Other income is recognised in the accounting period in which services are rendered.

In this extract, the company discloses its policy for performance fees. This is another area where practice varies, particularly in interim financial statements; some asset management groups accrue fees on a mark to market basis; most take nothing.

6.2.5   Insurance agency commissions

The critical event for the recognition of insurance agency commissions is the commencement of the policy. Hence, the Appendix to IAS 18 states that insurance agency commissions received or receivable which do not require the agent to render further service are recognised as revenue by the agent on the effective commencement or renewal dates of the related policies. However, when it is probable that the agent will be required to render further services during the life of the policy, the commission, or part thereof, is deferred and recognised as revenue over the period during which the policy is in force. *[IAS 18.IE13]*.

Some insurance agency commissions have similar features to the investment fund initial fee and 'trail commissions' noted above so there is a similar degree of uncertainty regarding the recognition and measurement of revenue.

6.2.6   Credit card fees

It is common practice in some countries for credit card companies to levy a charge, payable in advance, on its cardholders. Although such charges may be seen as commitment fees for the credit facilities offered by the card, they clearly cover the many other services available to cardholders as well. Accordingly, we would suggest that the fees that are periodically charged to cardholders should be deferred and recognised on a straight-line basis over the period the fee entitles the cardholder to use the card.[51]

6.2.7   Entrance and membership fees

The issue of entrance and membership fees is dealt with briefly in the Appendix to IAS 18, which states that revenue recognition depends on the nature of the services provided. If the fee permits only membership, and all other services or products are paid for separately, or if there is a separate annual subscription, the fee is recognised as revenue when no significant uncertainty as to its collectability exists. If the fee entitles the member to services or publications to be provided during the membership period, or to purchase goods or services at prices lower than those charged to non-members, it is recognised on a basis that reflects the timing, nature and value of the benefits provided. *[IAS 18.IE17]*.

6.3   Subscriptions to publications

Publication subscriptions are generally paid in advance and are non-refundable. As the publications will still have to be produced and delivered to the subscriber, the subscription revenue cannot be regarded as having been earned until production and delivery takes place. This is the approach adopted by IAS 18, which requires that revenue is recognised on a straight-line basis over the period in which the items are despatched when the items involved are of similar value in each time period. When the items vary in value from period to period, revenue is recognised on the basis of the sales value of the item despatched in relation to the total estimated sales value of all items covered by the subscription. *[IAS 18.IE7]*.

Chapter 30

Reed Elsevier discloses its policy for recognising revenue from subscriptions as follows:

Extract 30.18: Reed Elsevier (2007)

Combined financial statements [extract]

Accounting policies [extract]

Revenue

Revenue represents the invoiced value of sales less anticipated returns on transactions completed by performance, excluding customer sales taxes and sales between the combined businesses.

Revenues are recognised for the various categories of turnover as follows: subscriptions – on periodic despatch of subscribed product or rateably over the period of the subscription where performance is not measurable by despatch; circulation – on despatch; advertising – on publication or over the period of online display; exhibitions – on occurrence of the exhibition; educational testing contracts – over the term of the contract on percentage completed against contract milestones.

Where sales consist of two or more independent components whose value can be reliably measured, revenue is recognised on each component, as it is completed by performance, based on attribution of relative value.

6.4   Installation fees

Installation fees are recognised as revenue by reference to the stage of completion of the installation, unless they are incidental to the sale of a product in which case they are recognised when the goods are sold. *[IAS 18.IE10]*. However, in certain circumstances where the installation fees are linked to a contract for future services (for example, in the telecommunications industry: see 6.7 below) it may be more appropriate to defer such fees over either the contract period or the average expected life of the customer relationship, depending on the circumstances.

6.5   Advertising revenue

The Appendix to IAS 18 adopts the performance of the service as the critical event for the recognition of revenue derived from the rendering of advertising services. Consequently, media commissions are recognised when the related advertisement or commercial appears before the public. Production commissions are recognised by reference to the stage of completion of the project. *[IAS 18.IE12]*. The special case of barter transactions involving advertising services is addressed at 3.11 above.

German television corporation ProSiebenSat.1's revenues are derived mainly from the sale of advertising time on television as disclosed in its accounting policy:

Extract 30.19: ProSiebenSat.1 Media AG (2008)

Notes to the consolidated financial statements [extract]

[6]   ACCOUNTING POLICIES [extract]

Recognition of revenues [extract]

The ProSiebenSat.1 Group's revenues are mainly advertising revenues derived from the sale of advertising time on television. Advertising revenues are net of volume discounts, agency commissions, cash discounts and value-added tax. Other revenues besides advertising revenues derive from cooperative media agreements and call revenues from transaction television, revenues from pay TV activities, revenues from the sale of print products, revenues from the sale of radio advertising, revenues from the marketing of rights and other merchandising services, revenues from the sale of Club articles, revenues from new media services (such as teletext, Internet, mobile telephony and added-value telephone services), and revenues from the sale of programming rights and ancillary programming rights.

Revenues are recognized when the principal risks and opportunities associated with ownership have been transferred to the buyer, the amount of the revenue can be determined reliably, an economic benefit from the sale is sufficiently probable, the costs associated with the sale can be determined reliably, and the selling company neither has the authority to decide the disposition of the sold items such as would normally be associated with ownership, nor has any lasting power of disposition over the items. Specifically, advertising revenues from both television and radio are considered realized when advertising spots are broadcast. Revenues from pay TV activities and from the sale of print products are considered realized when the service is provided. Revenues from the sale of merchandising licenses are realized at the agreed guarantee amount as of the inception of the license for the customer. Revenues from the sale of programming assets and ancillary programming rights are considered realized when the license term for the purchaser of the programming has begun and broadcast-ready materials have been delivered to the purchaser.

6.6 Software revenue recognition

The accounting problems in the software services industry relate to such issues as: when to recognise revenue from contracts to develop software, software licensing fees, customer support services and data services. However, these issues have not been addressed in the IFRS literature. IAS 18 provides only one sentence of guidance: fees from the development of customised software are recognised as revenue by reference to the stage of completion of the development, including completion of services provided for post delivery service support. *[IAS 18.IE19].* Because of the nature of the products and services involved, applying the general revenue recognition principles to software transactions can sometimes be difficult. As a result, software companies have used a variety of methods to recognise revenue, often producing significantly different financial results from similar transactions.

The problem of software revenue recognition was recognised in the US by the FASB and SEC who encouraged the AICPA to provide guidance on software revenue recognition methods. As a result of practical experiences, in 1997 the AICPA issued SOP 97-2 – *Software Revenue Recognition*, now codified in ASC 985-605.

Whilst this US GAAP guidance is not mandatory for companies reporting under IFRS, many of them benefit by using the hierarchy in IAS 8 to adopt the US requirements in the absence of an IFRS pronouncement of comparable detail. Set out below is a broad overview of this guidance but the detailed requirements are beyond the scope of this publication.

6.6.1 The basic principles of SOP 97-2, now codified in ASC 985-605

Software arrangements range from those that simply provide a licence for a single software product, to those that require significant production, modification or customisation of the software. Arrangements may also include multiple products or services. The codified guidance in ASC 985-605 states that if the arrangement does not require significant production, modification or customisation of existing software (i.e. contract accounting does not apply – see below), revenue should be recognised when all of the following criteria are met:[52]

Chapter 30

- persuasive evidence of an arrangement exists;

- delivery has occurred (and no future elements to be delivered are essential to the functionality of the delivered element);

- the vendor's fee is fixed or determinable (the 'determinable' criterion relates to the issue as to whether the fee is subject to factors such as acceptance, refund, extended payment terms); and

- collectability is probable (i.e. whether the customer has the ability to pay and will pay).

With respect to 'persuasive evidence of an arrangement', ASC 985-605 requires that if a vendor has a customary practice of obtaining written contracts, revenues should not be recognised until the contract is signed by both parties.[53] Therefore, in the absence of a signed contract, revenue should not be recognised even if the software has been delivered and payment received.

ASC 985-605 states that the fee should be allocated to the various elements based on vendor-specific objective evidence ('VSOE') of fair value, regardless of any separate prices stated within the contract for each element.[54] It requires deferral of all revenue from multiple-element arrangements that are not accounted for using long-term contract accounting if there is insufficient VSOE to allocate revenue to the various elements of the arrangement.

The licence fee under an arrangement with multiple elements should be allocated to the elements according to VSOE. A portion of the licence fee should be allocated to elements that are deliverable on a when-and-if-available basis, whereby a vendor agrees to deliver software only when or if it becomes available while the agreement is in effect. However, absent such features and if all other criteria are met, this means that revenue may be recognised on entering into the arrangement in respect of a licence that allows the customer to use the software for a finite period.

If there is VSOE for the fair values of the undelivered elements in an arrangement, but not for one or more of the delivered elements in the arrangement, that fee can be recognised using the 'residual method'.[55] This means deducting the values for which there is VSOE from the total revenue and treating the remaining balance as the share of revenue for the element for which there is no VSOE. These requirements under US GAAP only apply to sales of computer software which are scoped into ASC 985. The US GAAP requirements in respect of other arrangements were always different to these and have recently been significantly amended by EITF 08-01 – *Revenue Arrangements with Multiple Deliverables*, described at 4.3 above.

6.6.2   Accounting for software arrangements with multiple elements

Software arrangements may provide licences for many products or services such as additional software products, upgrades/enhancements, rights to exchange or return software, post-contract customer support (PCS) or other services including elements deliverable only on a 'when-and-if-available' basis. These are referred to in US GAAP as 'multiple elements'.

We have noted at 3.6 above that in certain circumstances it is necessary to apply the recognition criteria to the separately identifiable components of a single transaction in order to reflect the substance of the transaction. *[IAS 18.13]*. However, IAS 18 does not establish more detailed criteria for segmenting and combining revenue transactions and in particular it contains little guidance on the allocation of revenue to those elements.

If there is a discount, a proportionate amount must be applied to each element included in the arrangement based on relative fair values without regard to the discount. No portion of the discount should be allocated to any upgrade rights and the residual method attributes the discount entirely to the delivered elements.[56]

If there is insufficient VSOE, ASC 985-605 provides that all revenue from the arrangement should be deferred until the earlier of the date on which such sufficient VSOE is obtained or all elements of the arrangement have been delivered.[57]

VSOE is a complex area and there are many detailed rules and requirements that expand the basic points made above and deal with areas such as upgrades, post-contract customer support, extended payment terms, rights of return and services. It is not necessary under IFRS to demonstrate VSOE in order to allocate revenue on the basis of the fair value of individual components.

6.6.3 Accounting for arrangements which require significant production, modification or customisation of software

Where companies are running well-established computer installations with systems and configurations that they do not wish to change, off-the-shelf software packages are generally not suitable for their purposes. For this reason, some software companies will enter into a customer contract whereby they agree to customise a generalised software product to meet the customer's specific requirements. A simple form of customisation is to modify the system's output reports so that they integrate with the customer's existing management reporting system. However, customisation will often entail more involved obligations; for example, having to translate the software so that it is able to run on the customer's specific hardware configuration, data conversion, system integration, installation and testing.

The question that arises, therefore, is the basis on which a software company recognises revenue when it enters into a contract that involves significant obligations. It is our view that the principles laid down in IAS 11 should be applied in this situation. This is supported by IAS 18, which states that the requirements of IAS 11 are generally applicable to the recognition of revenue and the associated expenses for a transaction involving the rendering of services. *[IAS 18.21]*. Accounting under IAS 11 is described in Chapter 25.

Consequently, where the software company is able to make reliable estimates as to the extent of progress towards completion of a contract, the related revenues and the related costs, and where the outcome of the contract can be assessed with reasonable certainty, the percentage-of-completion method of profit recognition should be applied.

Chapter 30

One company that follows this approach is SAP AG:

Extract 30.20: SAP AG (2007)

Notes to the Consolidated Financial Statements 2007 [extract]
3.   Summary of significant accounting policies [extract]
Revenue Recognition [extract]

Revenue for arrangements that involve significant production, modification, or customization of the software and those in which the services are not available from third-party vendors and are therefore deemed essential to the software, is recognized on a time-and-material basis or using the percentage of completion method of accounting, based on direct labor costs incurred to date as a percentage of total estimated project costs required to complete the project. If we do not have a sufficient basis to measure the progress of completion or to estimate the total contract revenues and costs, revenue is recognized only to the extent of contract cost incurred for which we believe recoverability to be probable.

Under ASC 985-605, if an arrangement to deliver software or a software system, either alone or together with other products or services, requires significant production, modification or customisation of software, the entire arrangement should be accounted for in accordance with ASC 605-35 – *Revenue – Construction-Type and Production-Type Contracts.*[58]

6.7   Revenue recognition issues in the telecommunications sector

There are significant revenue recognition complexities that affect the telecommunications sector, and about which IFRS is effectively silent. The complexities differ depending upon the type of telecommunications services being considered. For example fixed line (principally voice and data) services have recognition issues that may differ from wireless (principally mobile voice and data) services. It is the latter wireless services that currently provide many of the accounting challenges: wireless is a sector that is growing rapidly; there is a wide range of offerings; and there are considerable differences between the regulatory frameworks in different jurisdictions. The wireless revenue recognition problems fall into two broad groupings:

- recording of revenue in respect of multiple deliverable arrangements; and
- whether revenue should be recorded gross or net.

A number of general factors underlie the accounting issues. For example: local regulatory laws may dictate the way business is done by the operators; there may be restrictions on the discounting of handsets; handsets may be branded in some countries but not in others; both branded and unbranded handsets may co-exist in the same country; and there may be varying degrees of price protection.

The sector is continuing to develop rapidly and it is likely that new business models being adopted by operators – in particular the convergence of fixed line voice and broadband services with wireless services – will give rise to new revenue recognition challenges.

6.7.1   *Recording revenue for multiple service elements ('bundled offers')*

IAS 18 notes that in some instances revenue is recognised for the separately identifiable components of a single transaction and refers specifically to situations where the selling price of a product includes an identifiable amount for subsequent servicing, in which case that amount is deferred and recognised as revenue over the period during which the service is performed. *[IAS 18.13]*. This is directly relevant to some aspects of multiple deliverable arrangements offerings, where customers are offered a 'bundle' of assets and services.

When a consumer enters into a mobile phone contract with a provider, he is provided with a package that frequently includes a handset, a talktime allowance, text messages and other services such as data bundles (internet access),etc. Certain operators have started offering a bundle of fixed line broadband and mobile services.

Consumers may pay for their bundle of assets and services in a number of different ways: a payment for the handset (which may be discounted); connection charges related to activation of the handset, usually unrelated to connection costs and contracts that provide for monthly fixed or usage-based payments; non-binding contracts that provide for prepayments by credit card or by voucher, and which may or may not be discounted at the point of sale. None of these payments may relate directly to the cost of the services being provided by the operator, and operators also may be involved in loyalty programs that entail the provision of future free services.

As there is no specific guidance within IFRS on the subject of multiple deliverable arrangements beyond the brief references in paragraph 13 of IAS 18 referred to above, many companies use the hierarchy in IAS 8 to consider any relevant US guidance in the absence of a comparable IFRS pronouncement, particularly if they either have a US listing or have ambitions of a US listing. However, it needs to be made clear that – whilst US GAAP might provide useful guidance in this area – the IAS 8 hierarchy does not require companies to refer to it.

6.7.1.A   *Accounting for handsets and airtime*

Many of the mobile operators that provide telephone handsets to customers who subscribe to service contracts do so at heavily discounted prices or even free of charge. In March 2006, the Interpretations Committee was asked whether:

- the contracts should be treated as comprising two separately identifiable components, i.e. the sale of a telephone and the rendering of telecommunication services, as discussed in paragraph 13 of IAS 18 (under which revenue would be attributed to each component); or

- the telephones should be treated as a cost of acquiring the new customer, with no revenue being attributed to them.

The Interpretations Committee did not take this issue on to its agenda; instead, it published the following 'rejection notice' in the March 2006 issue of IFRIC Update:

'The IFRIC acknowledged that the question is of widespread relevance, both across the telecommunications industry and, more generally, in other sectors. IAS 18 does

Chapter 30

not give guidance on what it means by "separately identifiable components" and practices diverge.

'However, the IFRIC noted that the terms of subscriber contracts vary widely. Any guidance on accounting for discounted handsets would need to be principles-based to accommodate the diverse range of contract terms that arise in practice. The IASB is at present developing principles for identifying separable components within revenue contracts. In these circumstances, the IFRIC does not believe it could reach a consensus on a timely basis. The IFRIC, therefore, decided not to take the topic onto its agenda.'[59]

The Interpretations Committee did not publish its views on how (or whether) revenue ought to be attributed to each component if the transaction is treated as falling under paragraph 13. However, although IAS 18 requires revenue to be measured at its fair value, it is not definitive on the method of allocation. Usually, an allocation of revenue based on relative fair values would be considered an appropriate basis but this is not an explicit requirement and there are other bases allowed in IAS 18 and in IFRS more generally. When discussing servicing fees included in the price of the product, the standard requires them to be deferred, but states only that 'the amount deferred is that which will cover the expected costs of the services under the agreement, together with a reasonable profit on those services'. *[IAS 18.IE11]*. There is no further explanation of what constitutes a 'reasonable profit' but the requirement is quite clearly not to allocate revenue on a relative fair value basis. Another allocation example comes from IFRIC 13, which was not issued until June 2007, a year after the Committee's deliberations. As noted in 6.14 below, IFRIC 13 does not specify whether the amount allocated to the award credits should be a residual method or a relative fair value method, stating that the allocation to the award should be:

(a)   equal to their fair value (irrespective of the fair values of the other elements); or

(b)   a proportion of the total consideration based on the fair value of the award credits relative to the fair values of the other elements of the sale.

Most telecommunications operators have an accounting policy under which handsets and airtime are separately identifiable components but they apply a form of 'residual method' to the amount of revenue taken for the sale of the handset, recognising no more than the amount contractually receivable for it which may, *inter alia*, be equivalent to the so-called 'cash cap' under US GAAP, now in ASC 605-25-30-5. This states, 'The amount allocable to a delivered item or items is limited to the amount that is not contingent upon the delivery of additional items or meeting other specified performance conditions (the noncontingent amount)'. An example of this is France Télécom's policy with respect to bundled offers:

Extract 30.21: France Télécom (2010)

CONSOLIDATED FINANCIAL STATEMENTS [extract]

NOTE 2 Accounting policies [extract]

2.8 Revenues [extract]

Separable components of bundled offers

Numerous service offers on the Group's main markets include two components: an equipment component (e.g. a mobile handset) and a service component (e.g. a talk plan).

For the sale of multiple products or services, the Group evaluates all deliverables in the arrangement to determine whether they represent separate units of accounting. A delivered item is considered a separate unit of accounting if (i) it has value to the customer on a standalone basis and (ii) there is objective and reliable evidence of the fair value of the undelivered item(s).

The total fixed or determinable amount of the arrangement is allocated to the separate units of accounting based on its relative fair value. However, when an amount allocated to a delivered item is contingent upon the delivery of additional items or meeting specified performance conditions, the amount allocated to that delivered item is limited to the non contingent amount. The case arises in the mobile business for sales of bundled offers including a handset and a telecommunications service contract. The handset is considered to have value on a standalone basis to the customer, and there is objective and reliable evidence of fair value for the telecommunications service to be delivered. As the amount allocable to the handset generally exceeds the amount received from the customer at the date the handset is delivered, revenue recognized for the handset sale is generally limited to the amount of the arrangement that is not contingent upon the rendering of telecommunication services, i.e. the amount paid by the customer for the handset.

6.7.1.B   'Free' services

'Free' services are often included in the monthly service arrangement for contract subscribers as an additional incentive to encourage subscribers to sign up for a fixed contract period, typically twelve months.

'Free' services can either be provided up-front as inclusive services for a fixed monthly fee, or as an incentive after a specific threshold has been exceeded, intended to encourage subscribers to spend more than their specified amount.

These 'free' services may be provided to subscribers either in the form of 'free' talktime (e.g. 300 free minutes each month) or free credit (e.g. €50 to spend on any of the services offered each month). The matter is further complicated as increasing competition has led to the bundling of 'free' services, including talktime (voice and video), MMS, SMS and content downloads (e.g. wallpapers, ringtones, games).

As a result, one of the challenges that mobile operators will increasingly face is the allocation of the monthly fee between each element within the bundle. This information is a key requirement of investment analysts. A significant degree of estimation is involved, as the usage profile for an operator's subscribers has to be determined before the monthly revenue can be allocated.

The following example illustrates the accounting for free minutes granted at subscription date by a mobile operator to a subscriber:

Example 30.2:   Accounting for free minutes

An operator enters into a service contract with a customer for a period of 12 months. Under the contract specifications, the customer is offered for the first 2 months 60 free minutes talktime per month and for the remaining 10 months of the contract the customer will pay a fixed fee of €30 per month for 60 minutes of communication per month. The operator considers the recoverability of the amounts due under the contract from the customer to be probable.

In our view, since the free minutes offer is linked to the non-cancellable contract, the fee receivable for the non-cancellable contract is spread over the entire contract term.

Consequently, the fixed fee of €300 (€30 × 10 months) to be received from the subscriber would be recognised on a straight line basis over the 12 month contract period, being the stage of completion of the contract. The operator therefore would recognise €25 each month over the twelve month period (€30 × 10/12 = €25).

Chapter 30

6.7.1.C   Connection and up-front fees

Connection fees can be a feature of both the wireless (mobile) and the fixed line activities.

When the mobile telecoms industry was in its infancy, upfront costs such as connection fees, contract handling fees, registration fees, fees for changing plans etc., were commonly charged by operators. Such charges have been phased out over the years and are no longer a common feature in a number of markets.

Nevertheless, there are still occasions in which a telecommunications operator charges its subscribers a one-time non-refundable fee for connection to its network. The contract for telecommunications services between the operator and the subscriber has either a finite or an indefinite life and includes the provision of the network connection and ongoing telecommunications services. The direct/incremental costs incurred by the operator in providing the connection service are primarily the technician's salary and related benefits; this technician provides both connection and physical installation services at the same time.

In such cases, the connection service and the telecommunications services have to be analysed in accordance with their economic substance in order to determine whether they should be combined or segmented for revenue recognition purposes. When the connection transaction is bundled with the service arrangement in such a way that the commercial effect cannot be understood without reference to the two transactions as a whole, the connection fee revenue should be recognised over the expected term of the customer relationship under the arrangement which generated the connection. In our view, the expected term of the customer relationship may not necessarily be the contract period, but may be the estimated average life of the customer relationship, provided that this can be estimated reliably.

Vodafone is an example of a company that defers customer connection fees over the expected life of the customer relationship.

Extract 30.22: Vodafone Group Plc (2008)

Critical Accounting Estimates [extract]

Revenue recognition and presentation [extract]

Customer connection fees, when combined with related equipment revenue, in excess of the fair value of the equipment are deferred and recognised over the expected life of the customer relationship. The life is determined by reference to historical customer churn rates. An increase in churn rates would reduce the expected customer relationship life and accelerate revenue recognition. Historically, changes to the expected customer relationship lives have not had a significant impact on the Group's results and financial position.

Charging fees remains relatively common for connection to a fixed telephone line. Upfront recognition of the non-refundable fee may be possible if there is a clearly demonstrable separate service and it is provided at the inception of the contract.

The guidance provided within IFRIC 18 – *Transfers of Assets from Customers* – which is explained at 6.13 below may be of some help in identifying what services have been provided in return for the upfront fee, but the Interpretation is not normally directly relevant because the upfront fee is not used to construct PP&E

required for connection as envisaged under paragraph 6 of that Interpretation. Nevertheless, it is a common practice amongst fixed line operators to defer activation revenue, as illustrated by the two relevant policies of Telkom Group, which are similar to Vodafone's mobile policies included above:

Extract 30.23: Telkom Group (2011)

Notes to the consolidated annual financial statements [extract]

Summary of significant accounting policies [extract]

Fixed-line [extract]

Subscriptions, connections and other usage [extract]

The Group provides telephone and data communication services under post-paid and prepaid payment arrangements. Revenue includes fees for installation and activation, which are deferred and recognised over the expected customer relationship period.

Deferred revenue and expenses [extract]

Activation revenue and costs are deferred and recognised systematically over the expected duration of the customer relationship because it is considered to be part of the customers' ongoing rights to telecommunication services and the operator's continuing involvement. Any excess of the costs over revenues is expensed immediately.

6.7.2 'Gross versus net' issues

The difficulty of deciding whether to record revenue gross or net is pervasive in the telecommunications sector. The problem occurs because of the difficulty in deciding whether the parties involved in any particular agreement are acting as principal or agent. IAS 18 states that 'in an agency relationship, the gross inflows of economic benefits include amounts collected on behalf of the principal and which do not result in increases in equity for the entity. The amounts collected on behalf of the principal are not revenue. Instead, revenue is the amount of commission.' *[IAS 18.8].*

There is guidance to the Appendix of IAS 18 to help determine whether an entity is acting as a principal or as an agent. *[IAS 18.IE21].* This guidance is discussed at 3.3 above but does not necessarily help decide the matter in many telecoms scenarios. A frequent arrangement is where there is data content provided by third parties that is subject to a separate provider agreement.

Content, such as music, navigation and other downloads such as 'apps' can either be included in the monthly price plan, or purchased separately on an *ad hoc* basis. Operators can either develop the content in-house, or use third party providers to offer a range of services to their subscribers, with charges based either on duration (news, traffic updates etc.) or on quantity (number of ringtones, games etc.).

The issue is whether the operator should report the content revenue based on the gross amount billed to the subscriber because it has earned revenue from the sale of the services or the net amount retained (that is, the amount billed to the subscriber less the amount paid to a supplier) because it has only earned a commission or fee. Is the substance of the transaction with the supplier one of buying and on-selling goods or selling goods on consignment (i.e. an agency relationship)? The two most important considerations of those listed in IAS 18's Illustrative examples

Chapter 30

paragraph 21, for most of these arrangements, are whether the operator has the primary responsibility for providing the services to the customer or for fulfilling the order, for example by being responsible for the acceptability of the services ordered or purchased by the customer, and whether it has discretion in establishing prices, either directly or indirectly, for example by providing additional goods or services. Inventory risk is unlikely to be relevant for a service provision and credit risk may be only a weak indicator as the amounts are individually small and may be paid to access the download.

Therefore, if the content is an own-brand product or service then the revenue receivable from subscribers should be recorded as revenue by the operator, and the amounts payable to the third party content providers should be recorded as costs.

By contrast, if the content is a non-branded product/service that is merely using the mobile operator's network as a medium to access its subscriber base, then the amounts receivable from subscribers should not be recorded as revenue. The operator's revenue will comprise only the commissions receivable from the content providers for the use of the operator's network.

Vivendi discloses that it bases the decision on whether it is an agent or principal status on who has responsibility for content and setting the price to subscribers, as follows:

Extract 30.24: Vivendi SA (2010)

Notes to the Consolidated Financial Statements [extract]

Note 1. Accounting Policies and Valuation Methods [extract]

1.3. Principles governing the preparation of the Consolidated Financial Statements [extract]

1.3.4. Revenues from operations and associated costs [extract]

1.3.4.3. SFR, Maroc Telecom Group and GVT [extract]

Content sales

Sales of services provided to customers managed by SFR and Maroc Telecom Group on behalf of content providers (mainly premium rate numbers) are accounted for gross, or net of the content providers' fees when the provider is responsible for the content and for setting the price payable by subscribers.

6.7.3   Accounting for roll-over minutes

Where an operator offers a subscriber a finite number of call minutes for a fixed amount per period with the option of rolling over any unused minutes, the question arises as to how the operator should account for the unused minutes that the subscriber holds. The operator is not obliged to reimburse the subscriber for unused minutes, but is obliged (normally subject to a ceiling) to provide the accumulated unused call minutes to the subscriber until the end of the contract, after which they expire.

In such cases, revenue is recognised at the time the minutes are used. Any minutes unused at the end of each month should be recognised as deferred revenue.

However, in some instances, the operator has relevant and reliable evidence that shows that a portion of those unused minutes will not be used before the expiration of the validity period. In that case, the operator could consider an alternative revenue recognition policy that would take account of the probability of unused minutes at the end of the validity period in the computation of the revenue per minute used by the subscriber. This would result in allocating a higher amount of revenue per minute used.

When the validity period expires, any remaining balance of unused minutes would be recognised as revenue immediately, since the obligation of the operator to provide the contractual call minutes is extinguished.

6.7.4   *Accounting for the sale of pre-paid calling cards*

Prepaid cards are normally sold by an operator either through its own sales outlet or through distributors. The communication credit sold with the cards has an expiry date that varies from one operator to another, although, in certain limited jurisdictions, there is no expiry date. For example: prepaid cards may be sold with an initial credit of €10 covering 60 minutes of communication and the credit has a validity period of 90 days from the date of activation. If not used within this period, the credit is lost.

When the cards are sold through distributors, the distributor is usually obliged to sell the cards to the customers at the face value of the card. On sale of the card, the distributor pays the operator the face value less a commission. The distributor has a right to return unsold cards to the operator. Once the distributor has sold the cards, it has no further obligation to the operator.

In our view, when an operator sells calling cards directly, revenue is recognised at the time the minutes are used. Any minutes unused at the end of each month should be recognised as deferred revenue. However, in some instances, the operator has relevant and reliable evidence that shows that a portion of those unused minutes will not be used before the expiration of the validity period. In such cases, the operator could consider an alternative revenue recognition policy that would take account of the probability of unused minutes at the end of the validity period in the computation of the revenue per minute used by the subscriber. When the validity period expires, any remaining balance of unused minutes would be recognised as revenue immediately, since the obligation of the operator to provide the contractual call minutes is extinguished.

When an operator sells calling cards through a distributor, the revenue is required to be recognised based on the substance of the arrangement with the distributor.

It is usually the case that the distributor is in substance acting as an agent for the operator. The revenue associated with the sale of the calling card by the distributor to the subscriber is accounted for on a gross basis, recording revenue and commission, as. and when the subscriber uses the minutes. In our view, unless the distributor is also an operator or the calling card could be used on any operator's network (which is rare), it would be difficult to conclude that the distributor is the principal in the arrangement with the subscriber, because the distributor would not have the capacity to act as the principal under the terms of the service provided by the calling card to the subscriber (see 3.3 and 6.7.2 above).

Chapter 30

6.8　Excise taxes and goods and services taxes: recognition of gross versus net revenues

Many jurisdictions around the world raise taxes that are based on components of sales or production. These include excise taxes and goods and services or valued added taxes. In some cases these taxes are in effect collected by the entity from customers on behalf of the taxing authority. In other cases the taxpayer's role is more in the nature of principal than agent. The regulations (for example, excise taxes in the tobacco and drinks industries) differ significantly from one country to another. The practical accounting issue that arises concerns the interpretation of paragraph 8 of IAS 18: should excise taxes and goods and services taxes be deducted from revenue (net presentation) or included in the cost of sales and, therefore, revenue (gross presentation)?

Clearly, the appropriate accounting treatment will depend on the particular circumstances. In determining whether gross or net presentation is appropriate, the entity needs to consider whether it is acting in a manner similar to that of an agent or principal.

We believe that there are two main indicators that should be considered when determining whether the entity is acting as principal or agent. An additional two indicators relating to the nature of the tax itself should also be considered to determine whether a net or gross presentation is applicable. No one indicator is considered to be conclusive on its own. These indicators are:

Acting as Principal or Agent:

A whether the entity is exposed to financial risk in relation to the tax (e.g. non-recovery of the tax from the customers); and

B whether the entity has an obligation to change prices in line with changes in the rate or amount of the tax.

Nature of Taxes:

C basis of calculation – whether the tax is levied on sales proceeds or on units of production; and

D point of payment – whether the entity becomes liable to pay the tax at the point of sale or at the time of production.

Whether an entity is acting as principal or agent is a matter of judgement that depends on the relevant facts and circumstances of the particular tax in the country concerned. The factors that should be taken into account in determining gross or net treatment are summarised in the following table.

Indicator	Circumstances indicating:	
	<u>net</u> revenue recognition	<u>gross</u> revenue recognition
A Whether the entity is exposed to financial risk in relation to the tax (e.g. non-recovery of the tax from the customers) (i) who benefits from any short term fluctuations? (ii) who bears the inventory risk? (iii) who bears the credit risk?	• The tax is refundable in the event that stock becomes damaged or obsolete, or receivables are not collectible.	• The entity will not be refunded for the tax paid if the stock is not sold or the receivables are not collected.
B Whether the entity has an obligation to change prices in line with changes in the rate or amount of the tax.	• The tax is included in the selling price and the selling price can never fall below taxes paid. • The entity will change or is required (by law) to change the price of the product to reflect the tax increases but is unable to increase the price above tax increases. • The entity will reduce or is required (by law) to reduce the price of the product to reflect tax decreases.	• The entity has the discretion to determine the final selling price of the products. It bears the tax and makes the decision whether to pass the tax (entire/a portion of it) to the consumer.
C Basis of calculation – Whether the tax is levied on sales proceeds or on units of production.	• The tax is computed based on the sales price or units sold rather than producing activities.	• The tax is computed based on the number of units produced rather than sold. This suggests that it is a type of production tax.
D Point of payment – Whether the entity becomes liable to pay the tax at the point of sale or at the time of production. (This is likely to be a weak indicator that should not be considered without additional factors.)	• The tax is payable to the government only when the sale has occurred or the entity is required to make payment to the government at a date relatively close to the point of sale. The closer the payment is to the point of sale the more likely it is that the tax is similar to a sales tax.	• The tax is payable to the government when the unit is produced or the entity is required to make payment to the government at a date relatively close to the point of production. The closer the payment is to the point of production the more likely it is that the tax is a production tax.

Chapter 30

Clearly, it is important that companies disclose the policies that they have adopted in accounting for duty. BP is an example of a company that provides disclosure in this area:

Extract 30.25: BP p.l.c. (2008)

Notes on financial statements [extract]

1   Significant accounting policies [extract]

Customs duties and sales taxes

Revenues, expenses and assets are recognized net of the amount of customs duties or sales tax except:

– Where the customs duty or sales tax incurred on a purchase of goods and services is not recoverable from the taxation authority, in which case the customs duty or sales tax is recognized as part of the cost of acquisition of the asset or as part of the expense item as applicable.

– Receivables and payables are stated with the amount of customs duty or sales tax included.

   The net amount of sales tax recoverable from, or payable to, the taxation authority is included as part of receivables or payables in the balance sheet.

6.9   Sales incentives

Paragraph 10 of IAS 18 states that 'the amount of revenue arising on a transaction is usually determined by agreement between the entity and the buyer or user of the asset. It is measured at the fair value of the consideration received or receivable taking into account the amount of any trade discounts and volume rebates allowed by the entity.' *[IAS 18.10]*. Consequently, where an entity provides sales incentives to a customer when entering into a contract these are usually treated as rebates and will be included in the measurement of (i.e. deducted from) revenue when the goods are delivered or services provided.

Where the incentive is in the form of cash, revenue will be recognised at a reduced amount taking into account the rebate factor from the cash incentive.

Non-cash incentives take a variety of forms. Where the seller provides 'free postage' this would impose an additional cost on the entity but would not impact revenue. Where the seller provides free delivery and undertakes this service itself this would either be a separate component of a multiple element transaction to which some of the transaction price should be allocated, or more commonly, where risks and rewards of the good are not transferred to the customer until delivery, the total transaction price will not be recognised until that point.

Non-cash incentives may comprise products or services from third parties. Where these are provided as part of a sales transaction they will represent separate components of a multiple element transaction to which revenue must be attributed. The seller will need to determine whether they are acting as agent or principal for that element of the transaction. If the seller is acting as agent and has no further obligations in respect of that component then it will immediately recognise the margin on that element as its own revenue. If acting as principal it will recognise the full transaction price as revenue but it will need to defer any element that relates to the provision of the good or service by the third party if that party still needs to provide that good or service (for example where the incentive is in the form of a voucher that is redeemable by the third party at a later date).

Many of these non-cash incentives that are issued as part of a sales transaction will fall under the scope of IFRIC 13 (see 6.14 below). However even where it may be argued that they do not strictly fall under that Interpretation the main principle of IFRIC 13 (whereby fair value is attributed to the incentive and deferred from revenue until the related obligation is fulfilled) will still be applicable.

Where the sales incentive is in the form of a voucher that is issued independently of a sales transaction (e.g. one that entitles the customer to money off if they choose to make a purchase) there will be no impact on revenue. However the entity will need to assess whether this results in an onerous contract that would need to be provided for under IAS 37.

Prompt settlement discounts (for example, customers are offered a reduction of 5% of the selling price for paying an invoice within 7 days instead of the usual 60 days) should be estimated at the time of sale and deducted from revenues.

From the perspective of the buyer, cash incentives are accounted for as a liability when received until the buyer receives the goods, pays for the inventory (thereby reducing the cost of goods sold) and meets any additional obligations that might be attached to the incentives. Non-cash incentives, such as gifts, would only be considered part of inventories if they meet the definition of inventories.

Sanofi-aventis is an example of a company that provides various forms of sales incentives to its customers:

Extract 30.26: Sanofi-aventis SA (2007)

NOTES TO THE CONSOLIDATED FINANICIAL STATEMENTS

Year ended December 31, 2007 [extract]

B.   SUMMARY OF SIGNIFICANT ACCOUNTING POLICIES [extract]

B.14.   Revenue recognition

Revenue arising from the sale of goods is presented in the income statement under *net sales*. Net sales comprise revenue from sales of pharmaceutical products, vaccines, and active ingredients, net of sales returns, of customer incentives and discounts, and of certain sales-based payments paid or payable to the healthcare authorities.

Revenue is recognised when all of the following conditions have been met: the risks and rewards of ownership have been transferred to the customer; the Group no longer has effective control over the goods sold; the amount of revenue and costs associated with the transaction can be measured reliably; and it is probable that the economic benefits associated with the transaction will flow to the Group, in accordance with IAS 18 (Revenue).

Sanofi-aventis offers various types of price reductions on its products. In particular, products sold in the United States of America are covered by various programs (such as Medicare and Medicaid) under which products are sold at a discount. Rebates are granted to healthcare authorities, and under contractual arrangements with certain customers. Some wholesalers are entitled to chargeback incentives based on the selling price to the end customer, under specific contractual arrangements. Cash discounts may also be granted for prompt payment.

Returns, discounts, incentives and rebates as described above are recognized in the period in which the underlying sales are recognized, as a reduction of sales revenue.

These amounts are calculated as follows:

- Provisions for chargeback incentives are estimated on the basis of the relevant subsidiary's standard sales terms and conditions, and in certain cases on the basis of specific contractual arrangements with the customer. They represent management's best estimate of the ultimate amount of chargeback incentives that will eventually be claimed by the customer.

- Provisions for rebates based on attainment of sales targets are estimated and accrued as each of the underlying sales transactions is recognized.

- Provisions for price reductions under Government and State programs, largely in the United States, are estimated on the basis of the specific terms of the relevant regulations and/or agreements, and accrued as each of the underlying sales transactions is recognized.

- Provisions for sales returns are calculated on the basis of management's best estimate of the amount of product that will ultimately be returned by customers.

In each case, the provisions are subject to continuous review and adjustment as appropriate based on the most recent information available to management.

The Group believes that it has the ability to measure each of the above provisions reliably, using the following factors in developing its estimates:

- the nature and patient profile of the underlying product;

- the applicable regulations and/or the specific terms and conditions of contracts with governmental authorities, wholesalers and other customers;

- historical data relating to similar contracts, in the case of qualitative and quantitative rebates and chargeback incentives;

- past experience and sales growth trends for the same or similar products;

- actual inventory levels in distribution channels, monitored by the Group using internal sales data and externally provided data;

- the shelf life of the Group's products;

- market trends including competition, pricing and demand;

- the possibility of reusing returned goods.

Non-product revenues, mainly comprising royalty income from licence arrangements that constitute ongoing operations of the Group (see Note C), are presented in *Other revenues*.

6.10   Film exhibition and television broadcast rights

Revenue received from the licensing of films for exhibition at cinemas and on television should be recognised in accordance with the general recognition principles discussed in this chapter.

Contracts for the television broadcast rights of films normally allow for multiple showings within a specific period; these contracts usually expire either on the date of the last authorised telecast, or on a specified date, whichever occurs first. Rights for the exhibition of films at cinemas are generally sold either on the basis of a percentage of the box office receipts or for a flat fee.

The Appendix to IAS 18 states that an assignment of rights for a fixed fee or non refundable guarantee under a non cancellable contract which permits the licensee to exploit those rights freely and the licensor has no remaining obligations to perform is, in substance, a sale. When a licensor grants rights to exhibit a motion picture film in markets where it has no control over the distributor and expects to receive no further revenues from the box office receipts, revenue is recognised at the time of sale. *[IAS 18.IE20].*

Therefore, it is our view that the revenue from the sale of broadcast, film or exhibition rights may be recognised in full upon commencement of the licence period provided the following conditions are met:

(a)   a contract has been entered into;

(b)   the film is complete and available for delivery;

(c)   there are no outstanding performance obligations, other than having to make a copy of the film and deliver it to the licensee; and

(d)   collectability is reasonably assured.

This applies even if the rights allow for multiple showings within a specific period for a non-refundable flat fee and the contract expires either on the date of the last authorised telecast, or on a specified date, whichever occurs first. The sale can be recognised even though the rights have not yet been used by the purchaser. We do not believe it appropriate to recognise revenue prior to the date of commencement of the licence period since it is only from this date that the licensee is able to freely exploit the rights of the licence and hence has the rewards of ownership as required by paragraph 14(a) of IAS 18.

When the licensor is obliged to perform any significant acts or provide any significant services subsequent to delivery of the film to the licensee – for example to promote the film – it would be appropriate to recognise revenue as the acts or services are performed (or, as a practical matter, on a straight-line basis over the period of the licence).

Rights for the exhibition of a film at cinemas may be granted on the basis of a percentage of the box office receipts, in which case revenue should be recognised as the entitlement to revenue arises based on box office receipts.

If the fees only become payable when the box office receipts have exceeded a minimum level, IAS 18 suggests that revenue should not be recognised until the minimum level has been achieved. In the Appendix, it states that revenue that is contingent on the occurrence of a future event is recognised only when it is probable that the fee or royalty will be received, which is normally when the event has occurred. *[IAS 18.IE20]*.

In this instance the guidance in IAS 18 supports deferral until the contingency has occurred. This differs from the arguments based on IAS 32 described in 6.2.4 in the context of initial and ongoing fees, in which the full amount can be recognised at inception and the contingency affects measurement.

6.11   The disposal of property, plant and equipment

IAS 16 requires that the gain or loss arising from the derecognition of an item of PP&E be included in profit or loss when the item is derecognised unless IAS 17 requires otherwise on a sale and leaseback. IAS 16 prohibits recognition of any such gain as revenue *[IAS 16.68]* except in the case of entities that are in the business of renting and selling the same asset (see below).

An item is disposed of when the criteria in IAS 18 for recognising revenue from the sale of goods are met (see 3.7 above). IAS 17 applies to disposal by a sale and

Chapter 30

leaseback. *[IAS 16.69]*. IAS 18's criteria are essentially built around the transfer of significant risks and rewards of ownership. *[IAS 18.14-16]*. Although IAS 18 states that in most cases the transfer of the risks and rewards of ownership coincide with the transfer of legal title, it acknowledges that legal title sometimes passes at a different time. *[IAS 18.15]*.

There are two significant points in the earning process that could, depending on the circumstances of the sale, be considered to be the critical event for recognition. The first point is on exchange of contracts, at which time the vendor and purchaser are both bound by a legally enforceable contract of sale, whilst the second possible point of recognition is on completion of the contract, when legal title and beneficial ownership pass.

It is possible that the earnings process is sufficiently complete to permit recognition to take place on exchange of contracts. This is because the selling price would have been established, all material related expenses would have been ascertained and, usually, no significant uncertainties would remain. If, however, on exchange of contracts there are doubts that the sale will ultimately be completed, recognition should take place on the receipt of the sales proceeds at legal completion.

The issue arises most commonly with regard to the sale of real estate, but is not restricted to it. The two approaches had previously been supported by the Appendix to IAS 18, which stated that, in the case of real estate sales, revenue is normally recognised when legal title passes to the buyer; however, at the same time, it acknowledged that recognition might take place before legal title passes, provided that the seller has no further substantial acts to complete under the contract. *[IAS 18.IE9 (2008)]*. However, this paragraph was deleted with the introduction of IFRIC 15 (discussed at 6.11.2 below).

The evidence is that some companies delay profit recognition until legal completion, whilst others recognise profit before completion when the significant risks and returns have been transferred to the buyer. In our view, both approaches are acceptable and not affected by the amendment to IAS 18. However, care must be taken before recognising profits before completion and it may be that in many cases, legal completion is the more appropriate point at which to recognise revenue. However, whichever policy is adopted, it is important to ensure that all of the general conditions in IAS 18 have been met (see 3.7 above),

The two approaches are illustrated in the following extracts:

Extract 30.27: Hammerson plc (2008)

NOTES TO THE ACCOUNTS [extract]

1. SIGNIFICANT ACCOUNTING POLICIES [extract]

PROFITS ON SALE OF PROPERTIES

Profits on sale of properties are taken into account on the completion of contract, and are calculated by reference to the carrying value at the end of the previous year, adjusted for subsequent capital expenditure.

> **Extract 30.28: Liberty International PLC (2008)**
>
> **2 Accounting policies – group and company** [extract]
>
> **Revenue recognition** [extract]
>
> Where revenue is obtained by the sale of properties, it is recognised when the significant risks and returns have been transferred to the buyer. This will normally take place on exchange of contracts unless there are conditions attached. For conditional exchanges sales are recognised when these conditions are satisfied.

The gain or loss on derecognition of an item of PP&E is the difference between the net disposal proceeds, if any, and the carrying amount of the item. *[IAS 16.71]*. This means that any revaluation surplus relating to the asset disposed of is transferred within equity to retained earnings when the asset is derecognised and not reflected in profit or loss.

The consideration receivable on disposal of an item of PP&E is recognised initially at its fair value. If payment for the item is deferred, the consideration received is recognised initially at the cash price equivalent. The difference between the nominal amount of the consideration and the cash price equivalent is recognised as interest revenue in accordance with IAS 18 reflecting the effective yield on the receivable (see 3.5 above). *[IAS 16.72]*.

IFRS 5 – *Non-current Assets Held for Sale and Discontinued Operations* – lays down additional requirements for assets held for disposal; these requirements include measurement rules, which affect the measurement of the amount of the gain on disposal to be recognised. These are discussed in Chapter 4 at 2.2.

6.11.1 Sale of assets held for rental

Until 2008, IAS 16 prohibited classification as revenue any gains arising from the derecognition of items of property, plant and equipment. *[IAS 16.68]*. However, some entities are in the business of renting and subsequently selling the same asset. The IASB has agreed that the presentation of gross selling revenue, rather than a net gain or loss on the sale of the assets, would better reflect the ordinary activities of such entities. *[IAS 16.BC35C]*.

Therefore IAS 16 was amended to require that where an entity, in the course of its ordinary activities, routinely sells items of PP&E that it has held for rental to others to transfer the assets to inventories at their carrying amount when they cease to be rented and become held for sale. The proceeds from the sale of such assets are recognised as revenue in accordance with IAS 18. IFRS 5 does not apply when assets that are held for sale in the ordinary course of business are transferred to inventories. *[IAS 16.68A]*.

Paragraph 14 of IAS 7 – *Statement of Cash Flows* – has been amended to require presentation within operating activities of cash payments to manufacture or acquire such assets and cash receipts from rents and sales of such assets. *[IAS 7.14]*.

6.11.2 Pre-completion contracts and IFRIC 15

The recognition of revenue becomes more complex in the case of real estate developments where there are agreements for sale to the ultimate buyer prior to the completion of construction. Such 'forward sale' contracts are common in areas such as multiple-unit real estate developments (for example, residential apartment

Chapter 30

blocks) and commercial property developments that the developer has decided not to build speculatively and where agreements for sale are reached before construction is complete. In these situations, the developers start marketing the development before construction is complete (perhaps even before construction has started) and buyers enter into agreements to acquire either the entire building or a specific unit within the building development on completion of the construction. The contracts may require the buyer to pay a deposit and progress payments, which are refundable only if the developer fails to complete and deliver the unit. The balance of the purchase price may be payable only when the buyer gains possession, which often coincides with the point at which legal title is transferred to the buyer. However, legal title may transfer at different times, depending on national laws and practices.

The first issue that needs to be resolved is which standard is the relevant standard to apply: IAS 18 or IAS 11? IFRIC 15 was issued in July 2008 and applies to the accounting for revenue and associated expenses by entities that undertake the construction of real estate directly or through subcontractors. *[IFRIC 15.4]*. In substance the Interpretation argues that pre-completion sales contracts typically do not meet the IAS 11 definition of, and are distinguishable from, construction contracts. They are instead generally sales of goods for which IAS 18 is the applicable standard. This means that revenue is recognised only when the IAS 18 conditions are met. Such contracts may span more than one accounting period but this does not, by itself, justify the use of the percentage of completion method. Consequently there will be differences between IFRS and US GAAP, which requires a percentage of completion method for recognising profit from sales of units in condominium projects or time-sharing interests (provided specified criteria are met), but the Interpretations Committee considers that these differences should be resolved by harmonising standards.

The scope of the Interpretation includes agreements for the construction of real estate. Such agreements may include the delivery of other goods or services. *[IFRIC 15.5]*. As well as guidance as to the applicable standard, the Interpretation addresses when revenue from the construction of real estate should be recognised. *[IFRIC 15.6]*.

The Interpretations Committee has focused on IAS 11's definition of a construction contract as 'a contract specifically negotiated for the construction of an asset or a combination of assets...'. *[IAS 11.3]*. An agreement for the construction of real estate meets the definition of a construction contract when the buyer is able to specify the major structural elements of the design of the real estate before construction begins and/or specify major structural changes once construction is in progress (whether or not it exercises that ability). *[IFRIC 15.11]*. By contrast, the buyer may only have limited ability to influence the design of the real estate, for example to select a design from a range of options specified by the entity, or to specify only minor variations to the basic design. In practice many agreements only give the buyer the right of choice over a few options, such as types of flooring or kitchen fittings. In this case the agreement is for the sale of goods and is within the scope of IAS 18 rather than IAS 11. *[IFRIC 15.12]*.

The analysis assumes that there is revenue to be recognised, i.e. it assumes that the entity retains neither continuing managerial involvement to the degree usually associated with ownership nor effective control over the constructed real estate to an extent that would preclude recognition of some or all of the consideration as revenue. *[IFRIC 15.7]*. Examples are agreements in which the entity guarantees occupancy of the property for a specified period, or guarantees a return on the buyer's investment for a specified period. In such circumstances, recognition of revenue may be delayed or precluded altogether. *[IFRIC 15.IE9-10]*.

A feature of many of these agreements is that an entity may contract to deliver goods or services in addition to the construction of real estate, for example the sale of land or provision of property management services – and these may need to be split into their separate components. *[IAS 18.13]*. The fair value of the total consideration received or receivable for the agreement is allocated to each component. The entity will apply IFRIC 15 to the component for the construction of real estate in order to determine the appropriate accounting, *[IFRIC 15.8]*, as illustrated in the following flowchart:

Analysis of a single agreement for the construction of real estate

Analysis of the agreement, or components within it, will determine whether it is a construction contract, a contract for services or a contract for the sale of goods:

(a) if the agreement is a construction contract and its outcome can be estimated reliably, the entity should recognise revenue by reference to the stage of completion of the contract activity in accordance with IAS 11; *[IFRIC 15.13]*

(b) if the entity does not have to acquire and supply construction materials, the agreement may be for services and IAS 18 requires revenue to be recognised by reference to the stage of completion using IAS 11 principles; *[IFRIC 15.15]* (see 3.8 above) or

(c) if the entity has to provide services and construction materials as part of its contractual obligation to deliver the real estate to the buyer, the agreement is an agreement for the sale of goods – see 3.7 above. *[IFRIC 15.16]*. Under the agreement:

  (i) the entity may transfer to the buyer control and the significant risks and rewards of ownership of the work in progress in its current state as construction progresses, i.e. in a process of continuous transfer, and the percentage of completion method will apply; *[IFRIC 15.17]* or

  (ii) the entity may transfer to the buyer control and the significant risks and rewards of ownership of the real estate in its entirety at a single time (whether this be at completion, on or after delivery). In this case, the entity can recognise revenue only when all the criteria in paragraph 14 of IAS 18 are satisfied. *[IFRIC 15.18]*.

To meet the criteria in paragraph 14, as discussed at 3.7 above, means that, in addition to transferring significant risks and rewards of ownership, the entity retains neither continuing managerial involvement to the degree usually associated with ownership nor effective control over the goods sold. In addition, the amount of revenue can be measured reliably, it is probable that the economic benefits associated with the transaction will flow to the entity and the costs incurred or to be incurred in respect of the transaction can be measured reliably.

If the entity has to carry out any further work on the real estate itself that has already been delivered to the buyer, it should recognise a liability measured in accordance with IAS 37 and an expense for this work. Additional separately identifiable goods or services would already have been identified as a separate component and revenue allocated accordingly (see flowchart above). *[IFRIC 15.19]*.

When this Interpretation was in draft form the Interpretations Committee believed that the 'continuous transfer' of work in progress envisaged in (c)(i) above indicated that the contract was a construction contract and hence should be accounted for under IAS 11. However, in response to comments received, the Interpretations Committee accepted that these were not construction contracts but still argued that when the criteria for recognising revenue from the sale of goods are met continuously, it is appropriate to recognise revenue as the criteria are met. *[IFRIC 15.BC35(c)]*. The Interpretation states that the requirements of IAS 11 are generally applicable to the recognition of revenue and the associated expenses for such a transaction, *[IFRIC 15.17]*, i.e. they will give the best approximations in this type of arrangement.

Features of 'continuous transfer' include circumstances in which the buyer has a right to take over the work in progress during construction (albeit with a penalty) and to engage a different entity to complete it. During this process the builder will have access to the land and the work in progress in order to perform its contractual obligations. However, this access does not necessarily imply that the builder retains continuing managerial involvement to the degree usually associated with ownership to an extent that would preclude recognition of some or all of the consideration as revenue. The builder may have control over the activities related to the performance of its contractual obligation but not over the real estate itself. *[IFRIC 15.IE11]*.

The Interpretations Committee believe that arrangements involving this 'continuous transfer' of work in progress (in (c)(i) above) are uncommon. If a builder/developer 'pre-sells' a development to an institutional investor, this contractual arrangement is usually, in substance, a financing arrangement and the purchaser will not have the right to assume the work in progress. Revenue recognition will normally be deferred until a single point of time (as in (c)(ii) above), such as on completion.[60]

The following, based on the illustrative examples that accompany IFRIC 15, *[IFRIC 15.IE1-4]*, helps identify the different elements within these arrangements.

Example 30.3:   Applying IFRIC 15 to commercial real estate

An entity buys a plot of land for the construction of commercial real estate. It designs an office block and applies for building permission. The entity markets the office block to potential tenants and signs conditional lease agreements.

(a) It then markets the office block itself to potential buyers and signs with one of them a conditional agreement for the sale of land and the construction of the office block. The buyer cannot put the land or the incomplete office block back to the entity. When the entity receives the building permission and all agreements become unconditional, it constructs the office block.

The agreement should be separated into a component for the sale of land and a component for the construction of the office block. The component for the sale of land is a sale of goods within the scope of IAS 18.

Because all the major structural decisions were made by the entity and were included in the designs submitted to the planning authorities before the buyer signed the conditional agreement, it is assumed that there will be no major change in the designs after the construction has begun. Consequently, the construction of the office block is not a construction contract and is within the scope of IAS 18. Construction takes place on land the buyer owns before construction begins and the buyer cannot put the incomplete office block back to the entity. This indicates that the entity transfers to the buyer control and the significant risks and rewards of ownership of the work in progress in its current state as construction progresses. Therefore, the entity recognises revenue from the construction of the office block by reference to the stage of completion using the percentage of completion method.

(b) Alternatively, assume that the construction of the office block started before the entity signed the agreement with the buyer. In that event, the agreement should be separated into three components: a component for the sale of land, a component for the partially constructed office block and a component for the construction of the office block. The entity should apply the recognition criteria separately to each component. Assuming that the other facts remain unchanged, the entity recognises revenue from the component for the construction of the office block by reference to the stage of completion using the percentage of completion method.

Chapter 30

In this example, the sale of land is a separately identifiable component but this will not always be the case. IFRIC 15 notes that in some jurisdictions, a condominium is legally defined as the absolute ownership of a unit based on a legal description of the airspace the unit actually occupies, plus an undivided interest in the ownership of the common elements (that includes the land and actual building itself, all the driveways, parking, lifts, outside hallways, recreation and landscaped areas) that are owned jointly with the other condominium unit owners. The undivided interest in the ownership of the common elements does not give the buyer control over the significant risks and rewards of the land. The right to the unit and the interest in the common elements are not separable. *[IFRIC 15.IE5].* The following example is based on the Illustrative Examples paragraphs 6 to 8:

Example 30.4:   Applying IFRIC 15 to residential real estate

An entity is developing residential real estate and starts marketing individual units (apartments) while construction is still in progress. Buyers enter into a binding sale agreement that gives them the right to acquire a specified unit when it is ready for occupation. They pay a deposit that is refundable only if the entity fails to deliver the completed unit in accordance with the contracted terms. Buyers are also required to make progress payments between the time of the initial agreement and contractual completion. The balance of the purchase price is paid only on contractual completion, when buyers obtain possession of their unit. Buyers are able to specify only minor variations to the basic design but they cannot specify or alter major structural elements of the design of their unit.

(a) In Country A, no rights to the underlying real estate asset transfer to the buyer other than through the agreement. Consequently, the construction takes place regardless of whether sale agreements exist. The terms of the agreement and other facts and circumstances indicate that the agreement is not a construction contract. It is a forward contract that gives the buyer an asset in the form of a right to acquire, use and sell the completed real estate at a later date and an obligation to pay the purchase price in accordance with its terms. Although the buyer might be able to transfer its interest in the forward contract to another party, the entity retains control and the significant risks and rewards of ownership of the work in progress in its current state until the completed real estate is transferred. Therefore, revenue should be recognised at completion as it is only at this point that all of IAS 18's criteria are met.

(b) In Country B, the law requires the entity to transfer immediately to the buyer ownership of the real estate in its current state of completion and that any additional construction becomes the responsibility and property of the buyer as construction progresses. In this case it is possible that the entity transfers to the buyer control and the significant risks and rewards of ownership of the work in progress in its current state as construction progresses. For example, if the agreement is terminated before construction is complete, the buyer retains the work in progress and the entity has the right to be paid for the work performed. This might indicate that control is transferred along with ownership. If it does, the entity recognises revenue using the percentage of completion method taking into account the stage of completion of the whole building and the agreements signed with individual buyers.

Situation (b) involving the continuous transfer of work in progress is of a type that is generally uncommon. However in certain jurisdictions, such as France and Belgium, there are agreements defined by law (Vente en l'Etat Final d'Achèvement – otherwise known as 'VEFA' agreements) under which the seller of real estate does immediately transfer the rights of ownership of the floor area and existing work to the buyer, and additional construction work becomes the property of the buyer as it is performed.[61] These specific agreements were discussed by the Interpretations Committee in developing the Interpretation and may be an example of this continuous transfer. Although the Interpretations Committee considered that continuous transfer would not be common, there have been concerns about inconsistent treatments in different jurisdictions. The Committee was informed that diversity of views exists for similar types of fact patterns regarding the sale of residential apartments off plan where relevant public authorities are involved, usually to protect the buyer if the developer defaults. However, the Committee decided to defer further discussion on this matter until the criteria for the determination of the transfer of goods and services are finalised as part of the revenue recognition project.[62]

IAS 18 has fewer disclosure requirements than IAS 11 and therefore the Interpretations Committee have inserted a number of specific disclosures in IFRIC 15 that are required when these agreements are deemed to be 'continuous transfer' arrangements that are accounted for under IAS 18: *[IFRIC 15.20-21]*

(a) When an entity recognises revenue using the percentage of completion method for agreements that meet all the criteria in paragraph 14 of IAS 18 continuously as construction progresses it should disclose:

  (i) how it determines which agreements meet all the criteria in paragraph 14 of IAS 18 continuously as construction progresses;

  (ii) the amount of revenue arising from such agreements in the period; and

  (iii) the methods used to determine the stage of completion of agreements in progress.

(b) For the agreements described in the paragraph above that are in progress at the reporting date, the entity should also disclose:

  (i) the aggregate amount of costs incurred and recognised profits (less recognised losses) to date; and

  (ii) the amount of advances received.

The guidance in IFRIC 15 replaces the guidance on real estate sales that was previously included in the Appendix to IAS 18. The reference to revenue generally being recognised on the passing of legal title, *[IAS 18.IE9 (2008)]*, has been deleted but of course the general criteria of IAS 18 applicable to the sale of goods (see 3.7 above) will still be applicable.

6.12 Regulatory assets and liabilities

In many countries the provision of utilities (e.g. water, natural gas or electricity) to consumers is regulated by a government agency. Regulations differ between countries but often regulators operate a cost-plus system under which a utility is allowed to make a fixed return on investment. Consequently, the future price that a utility is allowed to charge its customers may be influenced by past cost levels and investment levels.

Under many national GAAPs (including US GAAP) accounting practices have been developed that allow an entity to account for the effects of regulation by recognising a 'regulatory liability' or 'regulatory asset' that reflects the decrease in future prices required by the regulator to compensate for an excessive return on investment, and vice versa where an increase would be permitted.

In July 2009 the IASB issued an exposure draft – *Rate-regulated Activities.*[63] This exposure draft favoured the US GAAP approach, requiring an entity to:[64]

(a)   recognise a regulatory asset or regulatory liability if the regulator permits the entity to recover specific previously incurred costs or requires it to refund previously collected amounts and to earn a specified return on its regulated activities by adjusting the prices it charges its customers; and

(b)   measure a regulatory asset or regulatory liability at the expected present value of the cash flows to be recovered or refunded as a result of regulation, both on initial recognition and at the end of each subsequent reporting period. This net present value will be an estimated probability-weighted average of the present value of the expected cash flows.

Since the issuance of this Exposure Draft the project has been discussed at a number of IASB meetings. The Board is clearly still divided on whether to require the recognition of regulatory assets and liabilities and, if so, how to measure these regulatory assets and liabilities. There are no further discussions planned for this project. The Board will consult on its agenda in 2011 and after that it will decide whether to include a project addressing rate regulated activities, and if so, what the scope of that project should be.[65] For further details, including our opinion of the proposals within the exposure draft, see Chapter 19 at 13.1 and Chapter 29 at 5.16.

6.13   Transfers of assets from customers and IFRIC 18

It is quite common for utilities, in particular, to receive contributions of assets from customers so that they can be connected to networks or receive services from them. IFRIC 18 – *Transfers of Assets from Customers* – was issued by the IASB in January 2009 to provide guidance in these situations.

This Interpretation applies to all agreements under which an entity receives from a customer, or another party, an item of PP&E (or cash to acquire or construct such an asset) that the entity must then use either to connect the customer to a network or to provide the customer ongoing access to a supply of goods or services or both. *[IFRIC 18.3-6]*. The Interpretation does not apply if this transfer is a government grant within the scope of IAS 20 – *Accounting for Government Grants and Disclosure of Government Assistance* – or the asset is used in a service concession within the scope of IFRIC 12 – *Service Concession Arrangements*; *[IFRIC 18.7]* see Chapter 28.

A typical arrangement is one in which a builder or individual householder must pay for power cables, pipes, or other connections for water, electricity or other supplies. However, the Interpretation will also apply to many outsourcing arrangements where the existing assets are contributed to the service provider or the customer must pay for assets or both. For example, in an arrangement under which an entity outsources its telephony, it is very common for it to transfer its existing assets to the service provider and for this to be reflected in the contract price.

The following flowchart illustrates the analysis and accounting to be applied under IFRIC 18:

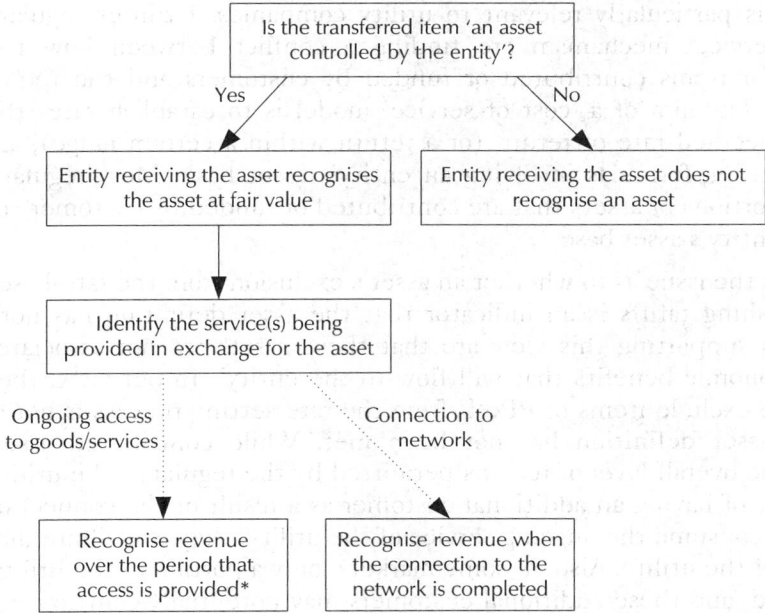

* If the agreement is silent, this is no longer than the life of the related asset.

The first step is to assess whether the item of PP&E received meets the definition of an asset. *[IFRIC 18.9]*. Paragraph 4.4(a) of the *Framework* defines an asset as 'a resource controlled by the entity as a result of past events and from which future economic benefits are expected to flow to the entity.'

In other words, whose asset is it? Something can only be an asset of the reporting entity if that entity controls it. The water pipes put in to connect the new house may be controlled by the householder from the house to the boundary of the property and the utility will control everything from the boundary. Note that a third party that has no direct connection to the ongoing service may have constructed and contributed the asset, e.g. the builder; this does not prevent the arrangement being within scope. In an outsourcing arrangement, the service provider may operate the equipment but may or may not have rights over its maintenance and replacement which will indicate who controls the asset.

Control is not determined solely by the transfer of legal ownership, and will require a careful assessment of the facts and circumstances. Factors that would indicate that the transferred asset is controlled by the receiving entity are that entity's ability to:

•   exchange the asset for other assets to deliver the same service;

•   employ the asset to produce other goods or services or settle a liability;

•   charge a price for others to use it; and

•   determine how the transferred asset is operated and maintained and when it is replaced.

Chapter 30

As well as establishing whether the entity controls the asset it also needs to determine whether the asset will be a source of future economic benefits.

IFRIC 18 is particularly relevant to utility companies. Utilities regulated under a 'cost of service' mechanism are finding a conflict between how the regulator accounts for items contributed or funded by customers and the requirements of IFRIC 18. The aim of a 'cost of service' model is to establish rates that earn the entity a specified rate of return (or a return within a certain range), and rates are often set using formulas involving an entity's asset base. Most regulators exclude assets or portions of assets that are contributed or funded by customer contributions from the entity's asset base.

This raises the issue as to whether an asset's exclusion from the rate-base calculation for establishing tariffs is an indicator that the asset definition has not been met. Arguments supporting this view are that these assets are not associated with any 'future economic benefits that will flow to the entity'. In our view, the regulator's decision to exclude items of PP&E from the rate setting process is not an indicator that the asset definition has not been met. While contributed assets may not increase the overall level of returns permitted by the regulator, the utility does have the benefit of having an additional customer as a result of the connection. As these customers consume the ongoing service of the utility, they contribute directly to the revenues of the utility. Also, in some markets, only a portion of the utility's business is regulated, and these additional customers may potentially contribute to revenues in unregulated portions of the utility's business. An entity's ability to sell the asset is also an indication that future economic benefits exists. Finally, contributed assets are usually only one of the many differences between the regulated asset and the asset in financial statements prepared under IFRS. For example, regulators may permit capitalisation of expenditure that would be considered repairs or maintenance under IAS 16 and treated as an expense.

Any asset transferred to the reporting entity will be measured initially at its fair value, which will become its cost for accounting purposes. *[IAS 18.12 and IFRIC 18.11].* It will be necessary to identify the separate services that are to be provided in exchange for the item of property, plant and equipment. *[IFRIC 18.14].* This is because revenue needs to be recognised as it is an exchange transaction involving dissimilar goods and services *[IFRIC 18.13]* (see 3.9 above). The nature of the services provided will determine the manner in which revenue is recognised.

The service may simply be connection of the customer to the network. This may be a separately identifiable service if connection represents stand-alone value to the customer. *[IFRIC 18.15].* Although IFRIC 18 does not provide a definition of stand-alone value, stand-alone selling price is defined in the Exposure Draft *Revenue from Contracts with Customers* as 'the price at which the entity would sell a good or service separately to the customer'[66] (see 5 above). US GAAP has a broader definition of stand-alone value – 'if they are sold separately by any vendor or the customer could resell the delivered item on a stand-alone basis'.[67]

Other factors that could be considered in determining if the connection has stand-alone value are:

- does the customer have a choice of service provider? If there is no choice in providers, this may indicate that connection does not have stand-alone value; and

- if the customer is able to choose the service provider, does the connection allow a future purchaser of the property to avoid connection charges with the new provider (i.e. a connection enhances the value of a property)? A connection that increases a property's value relative to a property that is not connected to the network indicates that the connection has stand-alone value.

Another feature that indicates the connection is a separately identifiable service is if the fair value of the connection service can be measured reliably. *[IFRIC 18.15]*. This may not always be straightforward, particularly when the connection is not sold separately.

It may be possible to identify the services that the entity is providing in exchange for the contributed asset by looking at how the ongoing goods and services are priced. Would the customer who made the contribution pay the same amount for the ongoing goods and services as others who have not done so? If so, this suggests that connection is the only service provided in exchange for the contributed asset. *[IFRIC 18.17]*. By contrast, a lower price than is available to other customers suggests that the future goods and services are, at least to some extent, provided in return for the contributed asset. *[IFRIC 18.16]*. The existence of any rate regulation, so common in the utilities industry, may make it harder to interpret this indicator. Prices established in a free market can be assumed to approximate a measure of the fair value of the ongoing service. Accordingly, it would be clear that if that price is the same for all customers irrespective of whether they contributed to the cost of the utility's assets, there is no ongoing benefit to those customers that made a contribution. However, where the price charged to customers is regulated, it does not follow that that price is a true measure of the fair value of the ongoing service obligation. In these circumstances this ongoing prices indicator can be inconclusive.

IFRIC 18 does not attribute a weighting or a priority to any of these features, and as a result, utility entities may find indicators that point to different conclusions. For example, many utilities have a legal obligation to provide ongoing services at set rates to all customers, indicating that the asset has been contributed in exchange for the connection, but the connection service may not have stand-alone value to the customer, which implies the opposite. In our opinion, no individual indicator is definitive and, as such, entities must consider all of them, along with other relevant facts and circumstances and exercise its own judgment in reaching its conclusion.

Once the services that have been provided in return for the asset have been indentified then the fair value of the total consideration received or receivable under the agreement, i.e. including the fair value of the contributed asset, is allocated to each service. *[IFRIC 18.19]*. This enables the entity to determine the period over which the revenue is recognised. If there are no ongoing goods and services provided in exchange, then revenue is recognised as soon as the connection is complete. The revenue for ongoing access will be recognised in accordance with the terms of the agreement if it has a specified term; otherwise the revenue will be recognised over a

Chapter 30

period not exceeding the useful life of the contributed item of PP&E. *[IFRIC 18.20]*. The following example based on Illustrative Example 3 in IFRIC 18 illustrates issues concerning revenue recognition (rather than asset recognition):

Example 30.5:   Recognising revenue when assets are transferred for services

An entity enters into an agreement with a customer involving the outsourcing of information technology (IT) functions. As part of the agreement, the customer transfers ownership of its existing IT equipment to the entity. Initially, the entity must use the equipment to provide the service required by the outsourcing agreement. The entity is responsible for maintaining the equipment and for replacing it when it decides to do so. The useful life of the equipment is estimated to be three years. The outsourcing agreement requires service to be provided for ten years for a fixed price that is lower than the price the entity would have charged if the IT equipment had not been transferred.

These facts indicate that the IT equipment is an asset of the entity, which will recognise the equipment and measure its cost on initial recognition at its fair value, together with a liability to provide the service. Because the price charged for the service is lower than the price the entity would charge without the transfer of the IT equipment, this service is a separately identifiable service included in the agreement. The facts also indicate that it is the only service to be provided in exchange for the transfer of the IT equipment. Therefore, the entity should recognise revenue arising from the exchange transaction when the service is performed, i.e. over the ten-year term of the outsourcing agreement.

Alternatively, assume that after the first three years, the price the entity charges under the outsourcing agreement increases to reflect the fact that it will then be replacing the equipment the customer transferred. In this case, the reduced price for the services provided under the outsourcing agreement reflects the useful life of the transferred equipment. For this reason, the entity should recognise revenue from the exchange transaction over the first three years of the agreement.

IFRIC 12 and IFRIC 13 may be used for guidance on allocating the fair value; in these Interpretations it is based on the fair values of the separate components. *[IFRIC 18.BC19]*. IFRIC 12 is discussed in Chapter 28 and IFRIC 13 at 6.14 below.

The analysis and accounting to be applied when the entity receives cash that it must use to construct or acquire the assets is similar to the above. The entity needs to assess whether the agreement is within scope of the Interpretation and, if so, it will need to assess whether an asset is required to be recognised. The PP&E acquired or constructed will be recognised in accordance with IAS 16 and revenue, at the amount of cash received, will be recognised according to each separately identifiable service provided, as explained above. *[IFRIC 18.21]*.

6.14   Customer loyalty programmes and IFRIC 13

Customer loyalty programmes are now an integral element of a wide range of businesses – from airlines to retail, and from consumer credit to mobile telecommunications. Customer loyalty programmes are used by companies to provide incentives to their customers to buy their products or use their services. Customer loyalty is recognised through the grant of award credits, such as 'points' or 'airmiles'; customers can then redeem the award credits for free or discounted goods or services.

The programmes operate in a variety of ways. Customers may be required to accumulate a specified minimum number or value of award credits before they are able to redeem them. Award credits may be linked to individual purchases or groups of purchases, or to continued custom over a specified period of time. A company may operate the customer loyalty programme itself or participate in a programme operated by a third party. The awards offered may include goods and services supplied by the company itself and/or rights to claim goods or services from another vendor. *[IFRIC 13.2].*

Until recently, IFRS lacked detailed guidance on how companies should account for customer loyalty programmes in general, and their liabilities under these schemes in particular. However, the matter was brought to the Interpretations Committee, and this ultimately led to the publication in 2007 of IFRIC 13 – *Customer Loyalty Programmes.*

In addressing the issue, the Interpretations Committee has rejected two approaches. It does not accept that an obligation for expenses is recognised as an expense at the time of the initial sale, measured by reference to the amount required to settle it, in accordance with IAS 37. Nor does it consider the accounting should depend on the nature of the customer loyalty programme, e.g. as a marketing expense or revenue, depending on significance. Instead it has concluded that some of the consideration received from the customer should be allocated to the award credits and deferred as a liability until the entity fulfils its obligations to deliver awards to customers. The liability is measured by reference to the value of the award credits to the customer (not their cost to the entity) and recognised as a deferral of revenue (not an expense). In support of this approach, it is argued that:

(a) award credits are an element of the market exchange of economic benefits between the entity and the customer. They represent rights granted to a customer, for which the customer is implicitly paying. They can be distinguished from marketing expenses because they are granted to the customer as part of a sales transaction; and

(b) award credits are separately identifiable from the other goods or services sold as part of the initial sale.

In the Interpretations Committee's view, paragraph 13 of IAS 18 applies if a single transaction requires two or more separate goods or services to be delivered at different times; it ensures that revenue for each item is recognised only when that item is delivered. In contrast, paragraph 19 of IAS 18 applies only if the entity has to incur further costs directly related to items already delivered – for example, to meet warranty claims. In the Interpretation Committee's view, loyalty awards are not costs that directly relate to the goods and services already delivered – rather, they are separate goods or services delivered at a later date. *[IFRIC 13.BC9(a)].*

Although the issue of customer loyalty programmes was discussed by the US Emerging Issues Task Force (EITF), no conclusion was reached. As a result, under US GAAP there is no specific authoritative accounting guidance on accounting for the issue of award credits, and in practice entities commonly recognise an expense on original sale or when the obligation is fulfilled. In the airline sector – where such arrangements are pervasive – the majority of airlines have historically used the first approach.

6.14.1 The scope of IFRIC 13

The Interpretation applies to customer loyalty award credits that an entity grants to its customers as part of a sales transaction (i.e. a sale of goods, rendering of services or use by a customer of entity assets) as a result of which, subject to meeting any further qualifying conditions, those customers can redeem the credits for free or discounted goods and services. *[IFRIC 13.3]*. In other words, it applies to schemes whereby the award credits offered to customers derive from a past transaction. This means that it does not apply to the distribution of 'money off' vouchers or other schemes that do not involve an initial sales transaction.

IFRIC 13 does not specifically address the situation where an operator of a loyalty programme (e.g. an airline) sells award credits to another entity (e.g. a credit card company) and that other entity grants the purchased award credits to its own customers who are also members of the loyalty programme. This type of transaction is a direct sale of the award credits to a third party and therefore is within the scope of IAS 18, as opposed to IFRIC 13. Consequently, since the cardholders/members can redeem the awards directly with the programme operator, it is our view that the programme operator still has an obligation that should be recognised through the deferral of some or all of the sales proceeds. Furthermore, the award credits granted to programme members directly by the programme operator versus those granted by third parties will, in both cases, have the same rights attaching to them and are indistinguishable from one another in the members' accounts.

However, where a programme operator sells its award credits to a third party, it is likely that the sale will involve a number of components. For example, an airline selling its airmiles to a credit card company is likely to be selling both a travel component (for redemption by the third party's customers) and a marketing component for allowing the third party access to its loyalty program and customer base. Consequently, in determining how much revenue should be recognised on the sale of the airmiles to the third party, the airline should determine how much of the consideration should be attributed to these components, since it is likely that the consideration related to marketing component may not require deferral. This is discussed in more detail in 6.14.3 below.

6.14.2 The requirements of IFRIC 13

Under IFRIC 13, an entity must account for award credits as a separately identifiable component of the sales transaction(s) in which they are granted (the 'initial sale'). The fair value of the consideration received or receivable in respect of the initial sale must be allocated between the award credits and the other components of the sale. *[IFRIC 13.5]*.

However, IAS 18 does not prescribe an allocation method for multiple-component sales. Its overall objective is to determine the amount the customer is paying for each component, which can be estimated by drawing on the entity's experience of transactions with similar customers. Hence, the Interpretation requires the consideration allocated to award credits to be measured by reference to their fair value.

The Interpretation does not specify whether the amount allocated to the award credits should be:

(a)   equal to their fair value (irrespective of the fair values of the other elements); or

(b)   a proportion of the total consideration based on the fair value of the award credits relative to the fair values of the other elements of the sale.

The Interpretations Committee noted that IAS 18 does not specify which of these methods should be applied, or in what circumstances and decided that the Interpretation should not be more prescriptive than IAS 18. The selection of one or other method is therefore left to management's judgement.

The measurement of fair value is discussed in more detail in 6.14.3 below.

However, since not all award credits will ultimately be redeemed, IFRIC 13 specifies the basis on which revenue should be recognised, depending on whether the awards are supplied by the entity itself or by a third party. If the entity supplies the awards itself, it should recognise the consideration allocated to award credits as revenue when award credits are redeemed and it fulfils its obligations to supply awards. The amount of revenue recognised should be based on the number of award credits that have been redeemed in exchange for awards, relative to the total number expected to be redeemed. *[IFRIC 13.7]*.

The practical application of this approach is illustrated in Example 1 of the illustrative examples appended to IFRIC 13, as follows:

Example 30.6: Awards supplied by the entity

A grocery retailer operates a customer loyalty programme. It grants programme members loyalty points when they spend a specified amount on groceries. Programme members can redeem the points for further groceries. The points have no expiry date. In one period, the entity grants 100 points. Management expects 80 of these points to be redeemed. Management estimates the fair value of each loyalty point to be $1, and defers revenue of $100.

Year 1

At the end of the first year, 40 of the points have been redeemed in exchange for groceries, i.e. half of those expected to be redeemed. The entity recognises revenue of (40 points ÷ 80 points) × $100 = $50.

Year 2

In the second year, management revises its expectations. It now expects 90 points to be redeemed altogether.

During the second year, 41 points are redeemed, bringing the total number redeemed to 40 + 41 = 81 points. The cumulative revenue that the entity recognises is (81 points ÷ 90 points) × $100 = $90. The entity has already recognised revenue of $50 in the first year, so it recognises $40 in the second year.

Year 3

In the third year, a further nine points are redeemed, taking the total number of points redeemed to 81 + 9 = 90. Management continues to expect that only 90 points will ever be redeemed, i.e. that no more points will be redeemed after the third year. So the cumulative revenue to date is (90 points ÷ 90 points) × $100 = $100. The entity has already recognised $90 of revenue ($50 in the first year and $40 in the second year), so it recognises the remaining $10 in the third year. All of the revenue initially deferred has now been recognised.

The IASB has clarified in *Improvements to IFRSs* issued in May 2010 that when the fair value of the award credit is calculated by reference to the value of the awards for which they could be redeemed, the value of the awards for which they could be redeemed must be adjusted to reflect expected forfeitures, as well as the discounts or incentives that would otherwise be offered to customers who have not earned award credits from an initial sale. *[IFRIC 13.AG2]*. Therefore each loyalty point issued could be redeemed for groceries valued at $1.25 but the fair value of the award credits is calculated at $100 being the 100 points issued multiplied by 80% (given the 20% forfeiture rate) of $1.25.

If a third party supplies the awards, the entity must assess whether it is collecting the consideration allocated to the award credits on its own account (i.e. as the principal in the transaction) or on behalf of the third party (i.e. as an agent for the third party).

(a)   If the entity is collecting the consideration on behalf of the third party, it must:

  (i)   measure its revenue as the net amount retained on its own account, i.e. the difference between the consideration allocated to the award credits and the amount payable to the third party for supplying the awards; and

  (ii)   recognise this net amount as revenue when the third party becomes obliged to supply the awards and entitled to receive consideration for doing so. These events may occur as soon as the award credits are granted. Alternatively, if the customer can choose to claim awards from either the entity or a third party, these events may occur only when the customer chooses to claim awards from the third party.

(b)   If the entity is collecting the consideration on its own account, it must measure its revenue as the gross consideration allocated to the award credits and recognise the revenue when it fulfils its obligations in respect of the awards. *[IFRIC 13.8].*

The practical application of this approach is illustrated in Example 2 of the illustrative examples appended to IFRIC 13, as follows:

Example 30.7:   Awards supplied by a third party

A retailer of electrical goods participates in a customer loyalty programme operated by an airline. It grants programme members one airmile with each $1 they spend on electrical goods. Programme members can redeem the airmiles for air travel with the airline, subject to availability. The retailer pays the airline $0.009 for each airmile.

In one period, the retailer sells electrical goods for consideration totalling $1 million and grants 1 million airmiles.

Allocation of consideration to airmiles

The retailer estimates that the fair value of an airmile is $0.01. It allocates to the airmiles 1 million × $0.01 = $10,000 of the consideration it has received from the sales of its electrical goods.

Revenue recognition

Having granted the airmiles, the retailer has fulfilled its obligations to the customer. The airline is obliged to supply the awards and entitled to receive consideration for doing so. Therefore the retailer recognises revenue from the airmiles when it sells the electrical goods.

Revenue measurement

If the retailer has collected the consideration allocated to the airmiles on its own account, it measures its revenue as the gross $10,000 allocated to them. It separately recognises the $9,000 paid or payable to the airline as an expense. If the retailer has collected the consideration on behalf of the airline, i.e. as an agent for the airline, it measures its revenue as the net amount it retains on its own account. This amount of revenue is the difference between the $10,000 consideration allocated to the airmiles and the $9,000 passed on to the airline.

Normally, the deferred consideration will exceed the unavoidable costs of meeting the obligation to supply the awards. However, if at any time the unavoidable costs of meeting the obligations to supply the awards are expected to exceed the consideration received and receivable for them (i.e. the consideration allocated to the award credits at the time of the initial sale that has not yet been recognised as revenue plus any further consideration receivable when the customer redeems the award credits), the entity has onerous contracts. A liability must be recognised for the excess in accordance with IAS 37. The need to recognise such a liability could arise if the expected costs of supplying awards increase, for example if the entity revises its expectations about the number of award credits that will be redeemed. *[IFRIC 13.9].*

6.14.3 *Measuring the fair value of award credits*

IAS 18 requires revenue to be measured at the fair value of the consideration received or receivable. *[IAS 18.9].* Hence the amount of revenue attributed to award credits should be the fair value of the consideration received for them.

IFRIC 13 requires also that the consideration allocated to the award credits must be measured by reference to their fair value but goes further and explains it as ', *i.e. the amount for which the award credits could be sold separately'. [IFRIC 13.6].* The brief Application Guidance set out in the Appendix to IFRIC 13 notes that this amount is often not directly observable and in such circumstances, it must be estimated. *[IFRIC 13.AG1].*

This can lead to some confusion as, for example, airlines also sell airmiles/award credits to third parties to use in their marketing programs. However, airlines would not consider the amount for which the credits are sold separately to be the same as the fair value of airmiles issued as part of sale of a ticket. The reason is that when airlines sell airmiles to third parties they are selling both a travel component (for redemption by the third party's customers) and a marketing component for allowing the third party access to their loyalty program and customer base. In such cases these sales would themselves be required to be accounted for under IAS 18 with an estimation required for the two components.

It is expected that in the majority of cases the fair value will need to be estimated. IFRIC 13 sets out in the application guidance that an entity may estimate the fair value of award credits by reference to the fair value of the awards for which they could be redeemed. It goes further and notes that if customers can choose from a range of different awards, the fair value of the award credits will reflect the fair values of the range of available awards, weighted in proportion to the frequency with which each award is expected to be selected. *[IFRIC 13.AG2].*

This means, for example, that airlines may be required to estimate the fair value of an airmile by reference to a weighted average ticket value using an equivalent restricted fare as a proxy for tickets representing the profile of actual redemptions. These would depend on which routes, classes of travel, and the time of flights for which the miles are redeemed. Therefore an airline would be expected to determine the fair value of the airmiles on a basis that is 'weighted in proportion to the frequency with which each award is expected to be selected'. In our view, companies

Chapter 30

will be required in a number of cases to maintain comprehensive redemption data covering all variables subject to estimation, and that this is likely to place an onerous burden on many companies that grant loyalty awards.

However, the Application Guidance goes on to state that, in some circumstances, other estimation techniques may be available. *[IFRIC 13.AG3]*. For example, if a third party will supply the awards and the entity pays the third party for each award credit it grants, it could estimate the fair value of the award credits by reference to the amount it pays the third party, adding a reasonable profit margin. The Application Guidance then ends merely by stating that 'Judgement is required to select and apply the estimation technique that satisfies the requirements of paragraph 6 of the consensus and is most appropriate in the circumstances.' *[IFRIC 13.AG3]*. Clearly, this provides preparers with substantial flexibility in choosing the estimation techniques that they apply in practice. At the same time, though, it needs to be recognised that in most cases the amount of revenue that is attributable to the award credits is not directly observable because the award credits are granted as part of a larger sale.

References

1 IAS 18 (Original), *Revenue Recognition*, IASC, December 1982, para. 4.
2 John H. Myers, '*The Critical Event and Recognition of Net Profit*', Accounting Review 34, October 1959, pp. 528-532.
3 SFAC No. 5, paras. 83-84.
4 FASB ASC 605-15-25-1.
5 FASB ASC 605-15-25-1.
6 FASB ASC 605-15-25-3.
7 IAS 18, Appendix, Sale of Goods.
8 FASB ASC 605-10-S99-1.
9 SFAC No. 5, para. 83.
10 SFAC No. 5, para. 83(b).
11 SFAC No. 5, para. 84(a).
12 SFAC No. 5, para. 84(d).
13 FASB ASC 605-10-S99.
14 FASB ASC 605-10-S99.
15 FASB ASC 605-25-25-5 amended by EITF 08-01.
16 FASB ASC 605-25-30-2 amended by EITF 08-01.
17 FASB ASC 605-25-25-5(b) prior to amendment by EITF 08-01.
18 FASB ASC 605-25-30-2 prior to amendment by EITF 08-01.
19 FASB ASC 605-25-65-1.
20 Exposure Draft (ED/2010/6), *Revenue from Contracts with Customers,* para. IN8, June 2010.
21 ED/2010/6, para. 86.
22 ED/2010/6, para. 6.
23 ED/2010/6, para. 85.
24 *IASB Update*, June 2011.
25 ED/2010/6, paras. 8-9.
26 ED/2010/6, para. 20.
27 *IASB Update*, February 2011.
28 *IASB Update*, February 2011.
29 *IASB Update*, April 2011.
30 *IASB Update*, April 2011.
31 *IASB Update*, April 2011.
32 ED/2010/6, para. 51.
33 ED/2010/6, para. 52.
34 *IASB Update*, April 2011.
35 ED/2010/6, para. 53.
36 *IASB Update*, April 2011.
37 ED/2010/6, paras. 25-26.
38 ED/2010/6, para. 30.
39 ED/2010/6, para. 31.
40 *IASB Update*, February 2011.
41 ED/2010/6, paras. B47-52.
42 *IASB Update*, April 2011.
43 ED/2010/6, paras. 54-56.
44 *IASB Update*, May 2011.
45 ED/2010/6, para. 57.
46 ED/2010/6, para. 69.
47 *IASB Update*, May 2011.
48 Based on the AICPA Industry Accounting Guide, *Accounting for Franchise Fee Revenue*, AICPA, 1973.
49 *IFRIC Update*, July 2008.
50 *IFRIC Update*, January 2007.

51 This is also the view taken under US GAAP; see FASB ASC 310-20-35-5.
52 FASB ASC 985-605-25-3.
53 FASB ASC 985-605-25-16.
54 FASB ASC 985-605-25-6.
55 FASB ASC 985-605-25-10.
56 FASB ASC 985-605-25-8.
57 FASB ASC 985-605-25-10.
58 FASB ASC 985-605-25-2.
59 *IFRIC Update*, March 2006, Page 7.
60 *IFRIC Update*, May 2008.
61 Agenda Paper 2B to the May 2008 IFRIC meeting, para. 12.
62 *IFRIC Update*, May 2011.
63 Exposure Draft, *Rate-regulated Activities,* July 2009.
64 Exposure Draft, *Rate-regulated Activities*, para. 2.
65 IASB Website, *www.iasb.org*, 17 February 2011.
66 ED/2010/6, Appendix.
67 FASB ASC 605-25-25-5.

Chapter 30

Chapter 31   Income taxes

List of examples

Chapter 31   Income taxes

1   INTRODUCTION

1.1   The nature of taxation

Accounting for taxation in financial statements must begin with some consideration of the nature of taxation. Although this might appear a simple question, taxation has certain characteristics which set it apart from other business expenses and which might justify a different treatment, in particular:

- tax payments are not typically made in exchange for goods or services specific to the business (as opposed to access to generally available national infrastructure assets and services); and

- the business has no say in whether or not the payments are to be made.

It is held by some that these characteristics mean that taxation is more in the nature of a distribution than an expense – in essence that the government is a stakeholder in the success of the business and participates in its results (generally in priority to other stakeholders).

Adoption of a 'distribution' view of taxation would render irrelevant most of the accounting questions which follow, since these are essentially concerned with the allocation of taxation expense between accounting periods (and to particular components of comprehensive income and equity within the same accounting period). If taxation were regarded as a distribution, however, these questions would not arise, since distributions are recognised when they are made rather than being allocated to accounting periods in the same way as items of expense.

In practice, however, a 'distribution' view of taxation is not adopted.[1] For all practical purposes, taxation is dealt with as an expense of the business, and the accounting standards which have been developed both by the IASB and by national standard setters are based on that premise.

1.2   Allocation between periods

The most significant accounting question which arises in relation to taxation is how to allocate tax expense between accounting periods. The recognition of transactions in the financial statements in a particular period is governed by the application of IFRS.

However, the timing of the recognition of transactions for the purposes of measuring the taxable profit is governed by the application of tax law, which sometimes prescribes an accounting treatment different from that used in the financial statements. The generally accepted view is that it is necessary for the financial statements to seek some reconciliation between these different treatments.

Accordingly IFRS requires an entity to recognise, at each reporting date, the tax consequences expected to arise in future periods in respect of the recovery of its assets and settlement of its liabilities recognised at that date. Broadly speaking, those tax consequences that are legal assets or liabilities at the reporting date are referred to as current tax. The other consequences, which are expected to become, or (more strictly) form part of, legal assets or liabilities in a future period, are referred to as deferred tax.

This is illustrated by Example 31.1, and the further discussion in 1.2.1 and 1.2.2, below.

Example 31.1:　PP&E attracting tax deductions in advance of accounting depreciation

An item of equipment is purchased on 1 January 2012 for €50,000 and is estimated to have a useful life of five years, at the end of which it will be scrapped. There is no change to the estimated residual amount of zero over the life of the equipment. The depreciation charge will therefore be €10,000 per year for five years.

The entity is tax-resident in a jurisdiction where the corporate tax rate is 30%. No tax deductions are given for depreciation charged in the financial statements. Instead, the cost may be deducted from taxes payable in the year that the asset is purchased. The entity's profit before tax, including the depreciation charge, for each of the five years ended 31 December 2012 to 31 December 2016 is €100,000. All components of pre-tax profit, other than the accounting depreciation, are taxable or tax-deductible.

The entity's tax computations for each year would show the following (all figures in €s)[2]:

	2012	2013	2014	2015	2016
Accounting profit	100,000	100,000	100,000	100,000	100,000
Accounting depreciation	10,000	10,000	10,000	10,000	10,000
Tax depreciation	(50,000)	–	–	–	–
Taxable profit	60,000	110,000	110,000	110,000	110,000
Tax payable @ 30%	18,000	33,000	33,000	33,000	33,000

1.2.1　No provision for deferred tax ('flow through')

If the entity in Example 31.1 above were to account only for the tax legally due in respect of each year ('current tax'), it would report the amounts in the table below in profit or loss. Accounting for current tax only is generally known as the 'flow through' method.

(€s)	2012	2013	2014	2015	2016	Total
Profit before tax	100,000	100,000	100,000	100,000	100,000	500,000
Current tax	18,000	33,000	33,000	33,000	33,000	150,000
Profit after tax	82,000	67,000	67,000	67,000	67,000	350,000
Effective tax rate (%)	18	33	33	33	33	30

The 'effective tax rate' in the last row of the table above is the ratio, expressed as a percentage, of the profit before tax to the charge for tax in the financial statements, and is regarded a key performance indicator by many preparers and users of financial statements. As can be seen from the table above, over the full five-year life of the asset, the entity pays tax at the statutory rate of 30% on its total profits of €500,000, but with considerable variation in the effective rate in individual accounting periods.

The generally held view is that simply to account for the tax legally payable as above is distortive, and that the tax should therefore be allocated between periods. Under IAS 12 – *Income Taxes* – this allocation is achieved by means of deferred taxation (see 1.2.2 below).

However, the flow-through method attracts the support of a number of respected commentators. They argue that the tax authorities impose a single annual tax assessment on the entity based on its profits as determined for tax purposes, not on accounting profits. That assessment is the entity's only liability to tax for that period, and any tax to be assessed in future years is not a present liability as defined in the IASB's *Conceptual Framework*. Supporters of flow-through acknowledge the distortive effect of transactions such as that in Example 31.1 above, but argue that this is better remedied by disclosure than by creating what they see as an 'imaginary' liability for deferred tax.

1.2.2   Provision for deferred tax (the temporary difference approach)

Over the last eighty years or so, numerous methods for accounting for deferred tax have evolved and been superseded. The approach currently required by IAS 12 is known as the temporary difference approach, which focuses on the difference between the carrying amount of an asset or liability in the financial statements and the amount attributed to it for tax purposes, known as its 'tax base'.

In Example 31.1 above, the carrying value of the PP&E in the financial statements at the end of each reporting period is:

(€s)	2012	2013	2014	2015	2016
PP&E	40,000	30,000	20,000	10,000	–

If the tax authority were to prepare financial statements based on tax law rather than IFRS, it would record PP&E of nil at the end of each period, since the full cost of €50,000 was written off in 2012 for tax purposes. There is therefore a difference, at the end of 2012, of €40,000 between the carrying amount of €40,000 of the asset in the financial statements and its tax base of nil. This difference is referred to as a 'temporary' difference because, by the end of 2016, the carrying value of the PP&E in the financial statements and its tax base are both nil, so that there is no longer a difference between them.

As discussed in more detail later in this chapter, IAS 12 requires an entity to recognise a liability for deferred tax on the temporary difference arising on the asset, as follows.

(€s)	2012	2013	2014	2015	2016
Net book value	40,000	30,000	20,000	10,000	–
Tax base	–	–	–	–	–
Temporary difference	40,000	30,000	20,000	10,000	–
Deferred tax[1]	12,000	9,000	6,000	3,000	–
Movement in deferred tax in period	12,000	(3,000)	(3,000)	(3,000)	(3,000)

[1]   Temporary difference multiplied by tax rate of 30%

IAS 12 argues that, taking the position as at 31 December 2012 as an example, the carrying amount of the PP&E of €40,000 implicitly assumes that the asset will ultimately be recovered or realised by a cash inflow of at least €40,000. Any tax that will be paid on that inflow represents a present liability. In this case, the entity pays tax at 30% and will be unable to make any deduction in respect of the asset for tax purposes in a future period. It will therefore pay tax of €12,000 (30% of €[40,000 – nil]) as the asset is realised. This tax is as much a liability as the PP&E is an asset, since it would be internally inconsistent for the financial statements simultaneously to represent that the asset will be recovered at €40,000 while ignoring the tax consequences of doing so. [IAS 12.16].

The deferred tax liability is recognised in the statement of financial position and any movement in the deferred tax liability during the period is recognised as deferred tax income or expense in profit or loss, with the following impact:

(€s)	2012	2013	2014	2015	2016	Total
Profit before tax	100,000	100,000	100,000	100,000	100,000	500,000
Current tax	18,000	33,000	33,000	33,000	33,000	150,000
Deferred tax	12,000	(3,000)	(3,000)	(3,000)	(3,000)	–
Total tax	30,000	30,000	30,000	30,000	30,000	150,000
Profit after tax	70,000	70,000	70,000	70,000	70,000	350,000
Effective tax rate (%)	30	30	30	30	30	30

It can be seen that the effect of accounting for deferred tax is to present an effective tax rate of 30% in profit or loss for each period. As will become apparent later in the Chapter, there is some tension in practice between the stated objective of IAS 12 (to recognise the appropriate amount of tax assets and liabilities in the statement of financial position) and what many users and preparers see as the real objective of IAS 12 (to align the pre- and post-tax effects of a transaction in the statement of comprehensive income).

This tension arises in part because earlier methods of accounting for income tax, which explicitly focused on tax income and expense rather than tax assets and liabilities, remain part of the professional 'DNA' of many preparers and users. Moreover, as will be seen later in the Chapter, there are a number of aspects of IAS 12 that are difficult to reconcile to the purported balance sheet approach of the standard, but which are in reality relics of the now superseded income statement approaches.

1.3   The development of IAS 12

The current version of IAS 12 was published in October 1996, and has been amended by a number of subsequent pronouncements. IAS 12 is based on the same principles as the US GAAP guidance (FASB ASC Topic 740 *Income Taxes*). However, there are important differences of methodology between the two standards which can lead to significant differences between the amounts recorded under IAS 12 and US GAAP. Some of the main differences between the standards are noted at relevant points in the discussion below.

In December 2010, the IASB issued an amendment to IAS 12 – *Deferred Tax: Recovery of Underlying Assets*. The amendment addresses the measurement of deferred tax associated with non-depreciable revalued property, plant and equipment (PP&E) and investment properties accounted for at fair value (see 8.3.6 and 8.3.7 below).

In addition, the SIC issued an interpretation of IAS 12, SIC-25 – *Income Taxes – Changes in the Tax Status of an Entity or its Shareholders.*[3]

In March 2009 the IASB issued an exposure draft (ED/2009/2 – *Income Tax*) of a standard to replace IAS 12. This was poorly received by commentators and there seems no prospect of a new standard in this form being issued in the foreseeable future. However, the ED gives some useful insights into the IASB's thinking on IAS 12, which are referred to where relevant in the text below.

The IASB continues to consider possible limited changes to IAS 12 with the aim of improving it or clarifying its existing provisions. This is discussed further at 15 below.

1.3.1   References to income taxes in standards other than IAS 12

There are numerous passing references in other standards and interpretations to income taxes, the more significant of which are noted at relevant points in the discussion below. The requirements of IFRS for accounting for income taxes in interim financial statements are discussed in Chapter 39 at 9.5.

2   OBJECTIVE AND SCOPE OF IAS 12

2.1   Objective

The stated objective of IAS 12 is 'to prescribe the accounting treatment for income taxes. The principal issue in accounting for income taxes is how to account for the current and future tax consequences of:

(a)   the future recovery (settlement) of the carrying amount of assets (liabilities) that are recognised in an entity's statement of financial position; and

(b)   transactions and other events of the current period that are recognised in an entity's financial statements.' *[IAS 12, Objective].*

IAS 12 requires this approach (the 'temporary difference approach') to be adopted, on the grounds that it is inherent in the recognition of an asset or liability that the reporting entity expects to recover or settle the carrying amount of that asset or liability. IAS 12 requires an entity to consider whether it is probable that recovery or settlement of that carrying amount will result in future tax payments larger (or smaller) than they would be if such recovery or settlement had no tax consequences. *[IAS 12.16, 25]*. If it is probable that such a larger or smaller tax payment will arise, in most cases IAS 12 requires an entity to recognise a deferred tax liability or deferred tax asset. This is discussed further at 3 to 9 and 11 below.

IAS 12 also requires an entity to account for the tax consequences of transactions and other events in a manner consistent with the accounting treatment of the transactions and other events themselves. *[IAS 12, Objective]*. In other words:

- tax effects of transactions and other events recognised in profit or loss are also recognised in profit or loss;

- tax effects of transactions and other events in other comprehensive income are also recognised in other comprehensive income;

- tax effects of transactions and other events recognised directly in equity are also recognised directly in equity; and

- deferred tax assets and liabilities recognised in a business combination affect:

  - the amount of goodwill arising in that business combination; or

  - the amount of the bargain purchase gain recognised.[4]

This is discussed in more detail at 10 and 12 below.

Finally the standard deals with:

- recognition of deferred tax assets arising for unused tax losses or unused tax credits (see 7.4 below);

- the presentation of income taxes in financial statements (see 13 below); and

- the disclosure of information relating to income taxes (see 14 below).

IAS 12 requires an entity to account for the tax consequences of recovering assets or settling liabilities at their carrying amount in the statement of financial position, not for the total tax expected to be paid (which will reflect the amount at which the asset or liability is actually settled, not its carrying amount at the reporting date). This is discussed further at 8.3 below.

IAS 12 may require an entity to recognise tax even on an accounting transaction that is not itself directly taxable, where the transaction gives rise to an asset (or liability) whose recovery (or settlement) will have tax consequences. For example, an entity might revalue a property. If (as is the case in many tax jurisdictions) no tax is payable on the revaluation, one might conclude that it has no tax effect. However, this is not the correct analysis under IAS 12, which focuses not on whether the revaluation itself is directly taxed, but rather on whether the profits out of which the increased carrying value of the property will be recovered will be subsequently taxed. This is discussed further at 8.3 below.

2.2 Overview

The overall requirements of IAS 12 can be summarised as follows:

- determine whether a tax is an 'income tax' (see 4 below);
- recognise income tax due or receivable in respect of the current period (current tax), measured using enacted or substantively enacted legislation (see 5 below), and having regard to any uncertain tax positions (see 9 below);
- determine whether there are temporary differences between the carrying amount of assets and liabilities and their tax bases (see 6 below), having regard to the expected manner of recovery of assets or settlement of liabilities (see 8 below);
- determine whether IAS 12 prohibits or restricts recognition of deferred tax on any temporary differences (see 7 below);
- recognise deferred tax on all temporary differences not subject to such a prohibition or restriction (see 7 below) measured using enacted or substantively enacted legislation (see 8 below), having regard to:
  - the expected manner of recovery of assets and settlement of liabilities (see 8 below); and
  - any uncertain tax positions (see 9 below);
- allocate any income tax charge or credit for the period to profit or loss, other comprehensive income and equity (see 10 below);
- present income tax in the financial statements as required by IAS 12 (see 13 below); and
- make the disclosures required by IAS 12 (see 14 below).

3 DEFINITIONS

IAS 12 uses the following terms with the meanings specified below. *[IAS 12.1-2,5].*

Income taxes include all domestic and foreign taxes which are based on taxable profits. Income taxes also include taxes, such as withholding taxes, which are payable by a subsidiary, associate or joint venture on distributions to the reporting entity.

Accounting profit is profit or loss for a period before deducting tax expense.

Taxable profit (tax loss) is the profit (loss) for a period, determined in accordance with the rules established by the taxation authorities, upon which income taxes are payable (recoverable).

Tax expense (tax income) is the aggregate amount included in the determination of profit or loss for the period in respect of current tax and deferred tax.

Current tax is the amount of income taxes payable (recoverable) in respect of the taxable profit (tax loss) or a period.

Deferred tax liabilities are the amounts of income taxes payable in future periods in respect of *taxable temporary differences* (see below).

Deferred tax assets are the amounts of income taxes recoverable in future periods in respect of *deductible temporary differences* (see below), together with the carryforward of unused tax losses and tax credits.

Temporary differences are differences between the carrying amount of an asset or liability in the balance sheet and its *tax base*. Temporary differences may be either:

- *taxable temporary differences*, which are temporary differences that will result in taxable amounts in determining taxable profit (tax loss) of future periods when the carrying amount of the asset or liability is recovered or settled; or

- *deductible temporary differences*, which are temporary differences that will result in amounts that are deductible in determining taxable profit (tax loss) of future periods when the carrying amount of the asset or liability is recovered or settled.

The *tax base* of an asset or liability is the amount attributed to that asset or liability for tax purposes.

4   SCOPE

IAS 12 should be applied in accounting for income taxes, defined as including:

- all domestic and foreign taxes which are based on taxable profits; and

- taxes, such as withholding taxes, which are payable by a subsidiary, associate or joint venture on distributions to the reporting entity. *[IAS 12.1-2]*.

IAS 12 does not apply to accounting for government grants, which fall within the scope of IAS 20 – *Accounting for Government Grants and Disclosure of Government Assistance*, or investment tax credits. However, it does deal with the accounting for any temporary differences that may arise from grants or investment tax credits. *[IAS 12.4]*.

A tax classified as an income tax is accounted for under IAS 12. Taxes other than income taxes are accounted for under IAS 37 – *Provisions, Contingent Liabilities and Contingent Assets*. The classification of a tax as an income tax affects its accounting treatment in several key respects:

- *Deferred tax*

    IAS 12 requires an entity to account for deferred tax in respect of income taxes. IAS 37 has no equivalent requirement for other taxes, recognising only legal or constructive obligations.

- *Recognition and measurement*

    IAS 12 requires tax to be recognised and measured according to a relatively tightly-defined accounting model. IAS 37 requires a provision to be recognised only where it is more likely than not that an outflow of resources will occur as a result of a past obligating event, and measured at the best estimate of the amount expected to be paid.

- *Presentation*

  IAS 1 – *Presentation of Financial Statements* – requires income tax assets, liabilities, income and expense to be presented in separate headings in profit or loss and the statement of financial position. There is no requirement for separate presentation of other taxes, but neither can they be included within the captions for 'income taxes'.

- *Disclosure*

  IAS 12 requires disclosures for income taxes significantly more detailed than those required by IAS 37 for other taxes.

4.1 What is an 'income tax'?

This is not as clear as might at first sight appear, since the definition is circular. Income tax is defined as a tax based on 'taxable profits', which are in turn defined as profits 'upon which income taxes are payable' (see 3 above).

It seems clear that those taxes that take as their starting profit the total net profit or loss before appropriations are income taxes. However, several jurisdictions raise 'taxes' on sub-components of net profit. These include:

- sales taxes;
- goods and services taxes;
- value added taxes;
- levies on the sale or extraction of minerals and other natural resources;
- taxes on certain goods as they reach a given state of production or are moved from one location to another; or
- taxes on gross production margins.

Taxes that are simply collected by the entity from one third party (generally a customer or employee) on behalf of another third party (generally local or national government) are generally not regarded as 'income taxes' for the purposes of IAS 12. This view is supported by the requirement of IAS 18 – *Revenue* – that taxes which are collected from customers by the entity on behalf of third parties do not form part of the entity's revenue *[IAS 18.8]* (and therefore, by implication, are not an expense of the entity either).

In cases where such taxes are a liability of the entity, they may often have some characteristics both of production or sales taxes (in that they are payable at a particular stage in the production or extraction process and may well be allowed as an expense in arriving at the tax on net profits) and of income taxes (in that they may be determined after deduction of certain allowable expenditure). This makes the classification of such taxes (as income taxes or not) difficult – see, for example, the discussion in Chapter 41 at 4.11.1.

In March 2006 the Interpretations Committee considered whether to give guidance on which taxes are within the scope of IAS 12. The Committee noted that the definition of 'income tax' in IAS 12 (i.e. taxes that are based on taxable profit) implies that:

- not all taxes are within the scope of IAS 12; but
- because taxable profit is not the same as accounting profit, taxes do not need to be based on a figure that is exactly accounting profit to be within the scope of IAS 12.

The latter point is also implied by the requirement in IAS 12 to disclose an explanation of the relationship between tax expense and accounting profit *[IAS 12.81(c)]* – see 14.2 below. The Interpretations Committee further noted that the term 'taxable profit' implies a notion of a net rather than gross amount, and that any taxes that are not in the scope of IAS 12 are in the scope of IAS 37 (see Chapter 29).

The Interpretations Committee drew attention to the variety of taxes that exist across the world and the need for judgement in determining whether some taxes are income taxes. The Committee therefore believed that guidance beyond the observations noted above could not be developed in a reasonable period of time and decided not to take a project on this issue onto its agenda.[5]

The Interpretations Committee's deliberations reinforce the difficulty of formulating a single view as to the treatment of taxes, such that the appropriate treatment will need to be addressed on a case-by-case basis depending on the particular terms of the tax concerned and the entity's own circumstances.

Where a tax is levied on multiple components of net income, it is more likely that the tax should be viewed as substantially a tax on income and therefore subject to IAS 12.

Even where such taxes are not income taxes, if they are deductible against current or future income taxes, they may nevertheless give rise to tax assets which do fall within the scope of IAS 12 (see 7.4 below).

4.2   Withholding and similar taxes

As noted at 4.1 above, IAS 12 also includes in its scope those taxes, such as withholding taxes, which are payable by a subsidiary, associate or joint venture on distributions to the reporting entity *[IAS 12.2]*. This gives rise to further questions of interpretation.

The most basic issue is what is meant by a 'withholding tax'. This is discussed at 10.3.2 below.

A second issue is whether the scope of IAS 12 covers only taxes on distributions from a subsidiary, associate or joint venture, or whether it extends to distributions from other entities in which the reporting entity has an investment. Such an investment will typically be accounted for at fair value under IAS 39 – *Financial Instruments: Recognition and Measurement* – or, where applied, IFRS 9 – *Financial Instruments*.

The rationale for the treatment as income taxes of taxes payable by a subsidiary, associate or joint venture on distributions to the investor is discussed further at 7.5 below. Essentially, however, the reason for considering withholding taxes within the scope of income tax accounting derives from the accounting treatment of the investments themselves. The accounting treatment for such investments – whether by full consolidation, proportionate consolidation or the equity method – results in the investor recognising profit that may be taxed twice: once as it is earned by the investee entity concerned, and again as that entity distributes the profit as dividend to the investor. IAS 12 ensures that the financial statements reflect both tax consequences.

Some argue that this indicates a general principle that an entity should account for all the tax consequences of realising the income of an investee as that income is recognised. On this analysis withholding taxes suffered on any investment income should be treated as income taxes. Others argue that the reference in IAS 12 to distributions from 'a subsidiary, associate or joint venture' should be read restrictively, and that no wider general principle is implied.

We believe that the first (wider) analysis is more appropriate. Accordingly, an entity should treat as income taxes the withholding taxes that could potentially be suffered on distributions from all investments, not just subsidiaries, associates and joint ventures. Whether or not any tax liability is recognised will depend on an analysis of the facts and circumstances in each particular case, in particular whether the investment concerned is expected to be recovered through receipt of dividend income or through sale (see 8.3 below).

4.3 Investment tax credits

Investment tax credits are not defined in IAS 12, but for the purposes of the following discussion they are taken to comprise government assistance and incentives for specific kinds of investment delivered through the tax system. Typically, a tax credit is given as a deduction from the tax liability, rather than as a deductible expense in computing the liability. As noted at 4 above, investment tax credits are not within the scope of IAS 12 (although any temporary differences that arise from them are in the scope of the standard). Moreover, government assistance provided by way of a reduction in taxable income is excluded from the scope of IAS 20 (see Chapter 27 at 2.2).

The fact that investment tax credits are excluded from the scope of both IAS 12 and IAS 20 does not prohibit an entity from applying either standard in accounting for them – particularly in the light of the 'GAAP hierarchy' in IAS 8 – *Accounting Policies, Changes in Accounting Estimates and Errors* (see Chapter 3). It simply reflects an acknowledgement by the IASB that such incentives occupy a wide spectrum, with some more in the nature of tax allowances and some more in the nature of government grants, so that it would not be appropriate to require application of a single standard in all circumstances.

In our view, factors that indicate that a particular credit may be more in the nature of a grant than an income tax include:

- where an entity does not have sufficient taxable profit for the credit to be offset in full, the balance is paid to the entity in any event;
- there are terms and conditions applicable to the credit other than being a taxpayer (e.g. a requirement to invest in a narrow geographical area or to employ a minimum number of people).

Where a tax credit is accounted for as income tax, it is generally treated as a discrete tax asset akin to a tax loss. However, where a credit is received in respect of a specific asset, an alternative analysis might be that the effect of a tax credit is to make the asset 'super-deductible' (i.e. eligible for tax deductions in excess of its cost). For example, if an entity pays tax at 30% and is allowed to deduct 100% of the cost of an item of PP&E costing €1,000 from its tax liability, it could be argued that the economic effect is the same as if the entity had been allowed to deduct €3,333 in respect of the asset in computing its taxable profit. The treatment of super-deductible assets is discussed further at 7.2.6 below.

In accordance with the general principles of IAS 8 (see Chapter 3), an entity should adopt a consistent accounting policy for each type of tax credit that it receives. The policy adopted should, in our view, take into account any generally accepted accounting practice by IFRS reporters in a specific tax jurisdiction for a particular tax allowance or incentive given in that jurisdiction. This may occasionally mean that an entity operating in a number of territories adopts different accounting treatments for apparently similar arrangements in different countries, but it at least ensures a measure of comparability between different entities operating in the same tax jurisdiction. Similar considerations apply in determining the meaning of 'substantively enacted' legislation in different jurisdictions (see 5.1 below).

4.4   Interest and penalties

Many tax regimes provide for interest and/or penalties to be paid on late payments of tax. This raises the question of whether or not such penalties fall within the scope of IAS 12. The issue is primarily one of presentation in the income statement. If such penalties and interest fall within the scope of IAS 12, they are presented as part of tax expense. If they do not fall within the scope of IAS 12, they should be included within profit before tax.

Some argue that penalties and interest have the characteristics of tax – they are paid to the tax authorities under tax legislation and in many jurisdictions are not a tax-deductible expense. Others contend that penalties and interest are distinct from the main tax liability and should not therefore form part of tax expense. Those who hold this view would point out, for example, that under IFRS the unwinding of the discount on discounted items is generally accounted for separately from the discounted expense.

The Interpretations Committee considered this issue in June 2004. It decided not to add the issue to its agenda, given that the disclosure requirements of IAS 12 and IAS 1 provide adequate transparency of these items.[6] The reference to IAS 12 indicates that the Interpretations Committee at the very least does not consider it inappropriate to account for interest and penalties as income taxes under IAS 12. Moreover, in the exposure draft of a possible replacement for IAS 12 issued in 2009, the IASB proposed that an entity should make an accounting policy decision whether to classify interest and penalties payable to tax authorities as tax expense.[7]

In our view:

- Where interest and penalties are not deductible in determining taxable income, there are reasonable grounds for treating them as either part of the tax charge or as an expense in arriving at profit before tax. Entities should determine their accounting policy for such items and apply it consistently.

- Where interest and penalties are tax-deductible, we believe that it is more generally appropriate to treat them as an expense in arriving at profit before tax.

4.5 Effectively tax-free entities

In a number of jurisdictions, certain classes of entity are exempt from income tax, and accordingly are not within the scope of IAS 12.

However, a more typical, and more complex, situation is that tax legislation has the effect that certain classes of entities, whilst not formally designated as 'tax-free' in law, are nevertheless exempt from tax provided that they meet certain conditions that, in practice, they are almost certain to meet. A common example is that, in many jurisdictions, some investment vehicles pay no tax, provided that they distribute all, or a minimum percentage, of their earnings to investors.

Accounting for the tax affairs of such entities raises a number of challenges, as discussed further at 8.4.1 below.

5 CURRENT TAX

Current tax is the amount of income taxes payable (recoverable) in respect of the taxable profit (tax loss) or a period. *[IAS 12.5]*.

Current tax for current and prior periods should, to the extent unpaid, be recognised as a liability. If the amount already paid in respect of current and prior periods exceeds the amount due for those periods, the excess should be recognised as an asset. *[IAS 12.12]*.

The benefit relating to a tax loss that can be carried back to recover current tax of a previous period should be recognised as an asset. When a tax loss is used to recover current tax of a previous period, an entity recognises the benefit as an asset in the period in which the tax loss occurs because it is probable that the benefit will flow to the entity and the benefit can be reliably measured. *[IAS 12.13-14]*.

Current tax should be measured at the amount expected to be paid to or recovered from the tax authorities by reference to tax rates and laws that have been enacted or substantively enacted by the end of the reporting period. *[IAS 12.46]*.

5.1 Enacted or substantively enacted tax legislation

IAS 12 requires current tax to be measured using tax rates or laws enacted 'or substantively enacted' at the balance sheet date. The standard comments that, in some jurisdictions, announcements of tax rates (and tax laws) by the government have the substantive effect of actual enactment, which may follow the announcement by a period of several months. In these circumstances, tax assets and liabilities are measured using the announced tax rate (and tax laws). *[IAS 12.48]*.

IAS 12 gives no guidance as to how this requirement is to be interpreted in different jurisdictions and both the IASB and the Interpretations Committee have resisted various requests for it. In most jurisdictions, however, a consensus has emerged as to the meaning of 'substantive enactment' for that jurisdiction (see 5.1.1 below). Nevertheless, apparently similar legislative processes in different jurisdictions may give rise to different treatments under IAS 12. For example, in most jurisdictions, tax legislation requires the formal approval of the head of state in order to become law. However, in some jurisdictions the head of state has real executive power (and could potentially not approve the legislation), whereas in others head of state has a more ceremonial role (and cannot practically fail to approve the legislation).

The view tends to be that in those jurisdictions where the head of state has executive power, legislation is not substantively enacted until actually enacted by the head of state. Where, however, the head of state's powers are more ceremonial, substantive enactment is generally regarded as occurring at the stage of the legislative process where no further amendment is possible.

5.1.1   *Meaning of substantive enactment in various jurisdictions*

The following table summarises the meaning of 'substantive enactment' in various jurisdictions as generally understood in those jurisdictions.[8]

Country	Point of substantive enactment
United Kingdom	A Finance Bill has been passed by the House of Commons and is awaiting only passage through the House of Lords and Royal Assent. Alternatively, a resolution having statutory effect has been passed under the Provisional Collection of Taxes Act 1968.
Canada	If there is a majority government, substantive enactment generally occurs with respect to proposed amendments to the Federal Income Tax Act when detailed draft legislation has been tabled for first reading in Parliament. If there is a minority government, proposed amendments to the Federal Income Tax Act would not normally be considered to be substantively enacted until the proposals have passed third reading in the House of Commons.
Australia	The Bill has been tabled in the Parliament and there is majority support for the passage of the Bill through both Houses of Parliament.
France	Signature of the legislation by the executive.
Germany	The Bundestag and Bundesrat pass the legislation.
Japan	The Diet passes the legislation.
United States	The legislation is signed by the President or there is a successful override vote by both houses of Congress.
South Africa	Changes in tax rates not inextricably linked to other changes in tax law are substantively enacted when announced in the Minister of Finance's Budget statement. Other changes in tax rates and tax laws are substantively enacted when approved by Parliament and signed by the President.

5.2 Uncertain tax positions

In recording the 'amount expected to be paid or recovered' as required by IAS 12, the entity will need to have regard to any uncertain tax positions. 'Uncertain tax position' is a term not defined in IAS 12, but is generally understood in practice to refer to an item, the tax treatment of which is unclear or is a matter of unresolved dispute between the reporting entity and the relevant tax authority. An uncertain tax position generally occurs where there is an uncertainty as to the meaning of the tax law, or to the applicability of the law to a particular transaction, or both.

Accounting for uncertain tax positions is a particularly challenging aspect of accounting for tax, discussed further at 9 below.

5.3 Intra-period allocation, presentation and disclosure

The allocation of current tax income and expense to components of total comprehensive income and equity is discussed at 10 below. The presentation and disclosure of current tax income expense and assets and liabilities are discussed at 13 and 14 below.

6 DEFERRED TAX – TAX BASES AND TEMPORARY DIFFERENCES

All deferred tax liabilities and many deferred tax assets represent the tax effects of temporary differences. Therefore, the first step in measuring deferred tax is to identify all temporary differences. The discussion in section 6 of this chapter addresses only whether a temporary difference exists. It does not necessarily follow that deferred tax is recognised in respect of that difference, since there are a number of situations, discussed at 7 below, in which IAS 12 prohibits the recognition of deferred tax on a temporary difference.

Temporary differences are differences between the carrying amount of an asset or liability in the balance sheet and its *tax base*. Temporary differences may be either:

- *taxable temporary differences*, which result in taxable amounts in determining taxable profit (tax loss) of future periods when the carrying amount of the asset or liability is recovered or settled; or

- *deductible temporary differences,* which result in amounts that are deductible in determining taxable profit (tax loss) of future periods when the carrying amount of the asset or liability is recovered or settled.

The *tax base* of an asset or liability is 'the amount attributed to that asset or liability for tax purposes'. *[IAS 12.5].*

In consolidated financial statements, temporary differences are determined by comparing the carrying amounts of an asset or liability in the consolidated financial statements with the appropriate tax base. The appropriate tax base is determined:

- in those jurisdictions in which a consolidated tax return is filed, by reference to that return; and

- in other jurisdictions, by reference to the tax returns of each entity in the group. *[IAS 12.11].*

As the definition of tax base is the one on which all the others relating to deferred tax ultimately depend, understanding it is key to a proper interpretation of IAS 12. A more detailed discussion follows at 6.1 and 6.2 below. However, the overall effect of IAS 12 can be summarised as follows:

A *taxable* temporary difference will arise when:

- *The carrying amount of an asset is higher than its tax base*

   For example, an item of PP&E is recorded in the financial statements at €8,000, but has a tax base of only €7,000. In future periods tax will be paid on €1,000 more profit than is recognised in the financial statements (since €1,000 of the remaining accounting depreciation is not tax-deductible).

- *The carrying amount of a liability is lower than its tax base*

   For example, a loan payable of €100,000 is recorded in the financial statements at €99,000, net of issue costs of €1,000 which have already been allowed for tax purposes (so that the loan is regarded as having a tax base of €100,000 – see 6.2.1.B below). In future periods tax will be paid on €1,000 more profit than is recognised in the financial statements (since the €1,000 issue costs will be charged to the income statement but not be eligible for further tax deductions).

Conversely, a *deductible* temporary difference will arise when:

- *The carrying amount of an asset is lower than its tax base*

   For example, an item of PP&E is recorded in the financial statements at €7,000, but has a tax base of €8,000. In future periods tax will be paid on €1,000 less profit than is recognised in the financial statements (since tax deductions will be claimed in respect of €1,000 more depreciation than is charged to the income statement in those future periods).

- *The carrying amount of a liability is higher than its tax base*

   For example, the financial statements record a liability for unfunded pension costs of €2 million. A tax deduction is available only as cash is paid to settle the liability (so that the liability is regarded as having a tax base of nil – see 6.2.2.A below). In future periods tax will be paid on €2 million less profit than is recognised in the financial statements (since tax deductions will be claimed in respect of €2 million more expense than is charged to the income statement in those future periods).

This may be summarised in the following table.

Asset/liability	Carrying amount higher or lower than tax base?	Nature of temporary difference	Resulting deferred tax (if recognised)
Asset	Higher	Taxable	Liability
Asset	Lower	Deductible	Asset
Liability	Higher	Deductible	Asset
Liability	Lower	Taxable	Liability

6.1 Tax base

6.1.1 Tax base of assets

The tax base of an asset is the amount that will be deductible for tax purposes against any taxable economic benefits that will flow to an entity when it recovers the carrying amount of the asset. If those economic benefits will not be taxable, the tax base of the asset is equal to its carrying amount. *[IAS 12.7]*.

In some cases the 'tax base' of an asset is relatively obvious. In the case of a tax-deductible item of PP&E, it is the tax-deductible amount of the asset at acquisition less tax depreciation already claimed (see Example 31.1 at 1.2 above). Other items, however, require more careful analysis.

For example, an entity may have accrued interest receivable of €1,000 that will be taxed only on receipt. When the asset is recovered, all the cash received is subject to tax. In other words, the amount deductible for tax on recovery of the asset, and therefore its tax base, is nil. Another way of arriving at the same conclusion might be to consider the amount at which the tax authority would recognise the receivable in notional financial statements for the entity prepared under tax law. At the balance sheet date the receivable would not be recognised in such notional financial statements, since the interest has not yet been recognised for tax purposes.

Conversely, an entity may have a receivable of €1,000 the recovery of which is not taxable. In this case, the tax base is €1,000 on the rule above that, where realisation of an asset will not be taxable, the tax base of the asset is equal to its carrying amount. This applies irrespective of whether the asset concerned arises from:

- a transaction already recognised in total comprehensive income and already subject to tax on initial recognition (e.g. in most jurisdictions, a sale);

- a transaction already recognised in total comprehensive income and exempt from tax (e.g. tax-free dividend income); or

- a transaction not affecting total comprehensive income at all (e.g. the principal of a loan receivable). *[IAS 12.7]*.

The effect of deeming the tax base of the €1,000 receivable to be equal to its carrying amount will be that the temporary difference associated with it is nil, and that no deferred tax is recognised in respect of it. This is appropriate given that, in the first case, the debtor represents a sale that has already been taxed and, in the second and third cases, the debtors represent items that are outside the scope of tax.

6.1.2   *Tax base of liabilities*

The tax base of a liability is its carrying amount, less any amount that will be deductible for tax purposes in respect of that liability in future periods. In the case of revenue which is received in advance, the tax base of the resulting liability is its carrying amount, less any amount of the revenue that will not be taxable in future periods. *[IAS 12.8]*.

As in the case of assets, the tax base of some items is relatively obvious. For example, an entity may have recognised a provision for environmental damage of CHF5 million, which will be deductible for tax purposes only on payment. The liability has a tax base of nil. Its carrying amount is CHF5 million, which is also the amount that will be deductible for tax purposes on settlement in future periods. The difference between these two (equal) amounts – the tax base – is nil. Another way of arriving at the same conclusion might be to consider the amount at which the tax authority would recognise the liability in notional financial statements for the entity prepared under tax law. At the balance sheet date the liability would not be recognised in such notional financial statements, since the expense has not yet been recognised for tax purposes.

Likewise, if the entity records revenue of £1,000 received in advance that was taxed on receipt, its tax base is nil. Under the definition above, the carrying amount is £1,000, none of which is taxable in future periods. The tax base is the difference between the £1,000 carrying amount and the amount *not* taxed in future periods (£1,000) – i.e. nil.

Again, if we were to consider a notional balance sheet of the entity drawn up by the tax authorities under tax law, this liability would not be included, since the relevant amount would, in the notional tax financial statements, have already been taken to income.

An entity may have a liability of (say) €1,000 that will attract no tax deduction when it is settled. In this case, the tax base is €1,000 (on the analogy with the rule in 6.1.1 above that where, realisation of an asset will not be taxable, the tax base of the asset is equal to its carrying amount). This applies irrespective of whether the liability concerned arises from:

- a transaction already recognised in total comprehensive income and already subject to a tax deduction on initial recognition (e.g. in most jurisdictions, the cost of goods sold or accrued expenses);

- a transaction already recognised in total comprehensive income and outside the scope of tax (e.g. non tax-deductible fines and penalties); or

- a transaction not affecting total comprehensive income at all (e.g. the principal of a loan payable). *[IAS 12.8]*.

This is appropriate given that, in the first case, the liability represents a cost that has already been deducted for tax purposes and, in the second and third cases, the liabilities represent items that are outside the scope of tax.

6.1.3   *Assets and liabilities whose tax base is not immediately apparent*

IAS 12 indicates that where the tax base of an asset or liability is not immediately apparent, it is helpful to consider the fundamental principle on which the standard is based: an entity should, with certain limited exceptions, recognise a deferred tax liability (asset) wherever recovery or settlement of the carrying amount of an asset or liability would make future tax payments larger (smaller) than they would be if such recovery or settlement were to have no tax consequences *[IAS 12.10]*. In other words: provide for the tax that would be payable or receivable if the assets and liabilities in the balance sheet were to be recovered or settled at book value.

In other words, in the basic 'equation' of IAS 12, i.e.

> carrying amount – tax base = temporary difference,

the true unknown is not in fact the temporary difference (as implied by the definitions of tax base and temporary difference) but the tax base (as implied by paragraph 10).

It will be apparent from the more detailed discussion at 6.2 below that this clarification is particularly relevant to determining the tax bases of certain financial liabilities, which often do not fit the general 'formula' of carrying amount less amount deductible on settlement.

6.1.4   Tax base of items not recognised as assets or liabilities in financial statements

Certain items are not recognised as assets or liabilities in financial statements, but may nevertheless have a tax base. Examples may include:

- research costs (which are required to be expensed immediately by IAS 38 – *Intangible Assets* – see Chapter 19);
- the cost of equity-settled share-based payment transactions (which under IFRS 2 – *Share-based Payment* – give rise to an increase in equity and not a liability – see Chapter 32); and
- goodwill written off to equity under previous IFRS or national GAAP.

Where such items are tax-deductible, their tax base is the difference between their carrying amount (i.e. nil) and the amount deductible in future periods. *[IAS 12.9]*. This may seem somewhat contrary to the definition of tax base, in which it is inherent that, in order for an item to have a tax base, that item must be an asset or liability, whereas none of the items above was ever recognised as an asset.[9] The implicit argument is that all these items were initially (and very briefly!) recognised as assets before being immediately written off in full.

Local tax legislation sometimes gives rise to liabilities that have a tax base but no carrying amount. For example, a subsidiary of the reporting entity may receive a tax deduction for a provision that has been recognised in the individual financial statements of that subsidiary prepared under local accounting principles. For the purposes of the entity's consolidated financial statements, however, the provision does not currently satisfy the recognition requirements of IAS 37, but is likely to do so in the future. In such situations we consider it as appropriate to regard the tax deduction received as giving rise to a deferred tax liability (by virtue of there being a provision with a tax base but no carrying amount) rather than current tax income.

Similar situations may arise where local tax legislation permits deductions for certain expenditure determined according to tax legislation without reference to any financial statements. Again, in those cases where an equivalent amount of expenditure is likely to be recognised in the financial statements at a later date, we would regard it as appropriate to regard the tax deduction received as giving rise to a deferred tax liability rather than current tax income.

6.1.5   Equity items with a tax base

The definition of 'tax base' refers to the tax base of an 'asset or liability'. This begs the question of whether IAS 12 regards equity items as having a tax base and therefore whether deferred tax can be recognised in respect of equity instruments (since deferred tax is the tax relating to temporary differences which, by definition, can only arise on items with a tax base – see above).

In February 2003 the Interpretations Committee considered this issue. It drew attention to the IASB's proposal at that time to amend the definition of 'tax base' so as to refer not only to assets and liabilities but also equity instruments as supporting the view that deferred tax should be recognised where appropriate on equity instruments. This was effectively the approach proposed in the exposure draft ED/2009/2 (see 1.3 above).[10]

An alternative analysis might be that equity items do not have a tax base, but that any tax effects of them are to be treated as items that are not recognised as assets or liabilities but nevertheless have a tax base (see 6.1.4 above).

Given the lack of explicit guidance in the current version of IAS 12 either analysis may be acceptable, provided that it is applied consistently. This is reflected in a number of the examples in the remainder of this chapter.

6.1.6   Items with more than one tax base

Some assets and liabilities have more than one tax base, depending on the manner in which they are realised or settled. These are discussed further at 8.3 below.

6.2   Examples of temporary differences

The following are examples of taxable temporary differences, deductible temporary differences and items where the tax base and carrying value are the same so that there is no temporary difference. They are mostly based on those given in IAS 12,[11] but include several others that are encountered in practice. It will be seen that a number of categories of assets and liabilities may give rise to either taxable or deductible temporary differences.

A temporary difference will not always result in a deferred tax asset or liability being recorded under IAS 12, since the difference may be subject to other provisions of the standard restricting the recognition of deferred tax assets and liabilities, which are discussed at 7 below. Moreover, even where deferred tax is recognised, it does not necessarily create tax income or expense, but may instead give rise to additional goodwill or bargain purchase gain in a business combination, or to a movement in equity.

6.2.1 Taxable temporary differences

6.2.1.A Transactions that affect profit or loss

- *Interest received in arrears*

  An entity with a financial year ending on 31 December 2012 holds a medium-term cash deposit on which interest of €10,000 is received annually on 31 March. The interest is taxed in the year of receipt. At 31 December 2012, the entity recognises a receivable of €7,000 in respect of interest accrued but not yet received. The receivable has a tax base of nil, since its recovery has tax consequences and no tax deductions are available in respect of it. The temporary difference associated with the receivable is €7,000 (€7,000 carrying amount less nil tax base).

- *Sale of goods taxed on a cash basis*

  An entity with a financial year end of 31 March 2012 has recorded revenue from the sale of goods of €40,000, together with a cost of the goods sold of €35,000, since the goods have been delivered. However, the transaction is taxed in the following financial year when the cash from the sale is collected.

  The entity will have recognised a receivable of €40,000 for the sale. The receivable has a tax base of nil, since its recovery has tax consequences and no tax deductions are available in respect of it. The temporary difference associated with the receivable is €40,000 (€40,000 carrying amount less nil tax base).

  There is also a deductible temporary difference of €35,000 associated with the (now derecognised) inventory, which has a carrying amount of zero but a tax base of €35,000 (since it will attract a tax deduction of €35,000 when the sale is taxed) – see 6.2.2.A below.

- *Depreciation of an asset accelerated for tax purposes*

  An entity with a financial year end of 30 June 2012 has an item of PP&E whose cost is fully tax deductible, but with deductions being given over a period shorter than the period over which the asset is being depreciated under IAS 16 – *Property, Plant and Equipment*. At 30 June 2012, the asset has been depreciated to £500,000 for financial reporting purposes but to £300,000 for tax purposes.

  Recovery of the PP&E has tax consequences since, although there is no deduction for accounting depreciation in the tax return, the PP&E is recovered through future taxable profits. There is a taxable temporary difference of £200,000 between the carrying value of the asset (£500,000) and its tax base (£300,000).

- *Capitalised development costs already deducted for tax*

  An entity incurred development costs of $1 million during year ended 31 December 2011. The costs were fully deductible for tax purposes in the tax return for that period, but were recognised as an intangible asset under IAS 38 in the financial statements. The amount carried forward at 31 December 2012 is $800,000.

Recovery of the intangible asset through use has tax consequences since, although there is no deduction for accounting amortisation in the tax return, the asset is recovered through future profits which will be taxed. There is a taxable temporary difference of $800,000 between the carrying value of the asset ($800,000) and its tax base (nil). Although the expenditure to create the asset is tax-deductible in the current period, its tax base is the amount deductible in *future* periods, which is nil, since all deductions were made in the tax return for 2012.

A similar analysis would apply to prepaid expenses that have already been deducted on a cash basis in determining the taxable profit of the current or previous periods.

6.2.1.B   *Transactions that affect the balance sheet*
- *Non-deductible and partially deductible assets*

    An entity acquires a building for €1 million. Any accounting depreciation of the building is not deductible for tax purposes, and no deduction will be available for tax purposes when the asset is sold or scrapped.

    Recovery of the building, whether in use or on sale, nevertheless has tax consequences since the building is recovered through future taxable profits of €1 million. There is a taxable temporary difference of €1 million between the carrying value of the asset (€1 million) and its tax base of zero.

    A similar analysis applies to an asset which, when acquired, is deductible for tax purposes, but for an amount lower than its cost. The difference between the cost and the amount deductible for tax purposes is a taxable temporary difference.

- *Deductible loan transaction costs*

    A borrowing entity records a loan at £9.5 million, being the proceeds received of £10 million (which equal the amount due at maturity), less transaction costs of £500,000, which are deducted for tax purposes in the period when the loan was first recognised. For financial reporting purposes, IAS 39 requires the costs, together with interest and similar payments, to be accrued over the period to maturity using the effective interest method.

    Inception of the loan gives rise to a taxable temporary difference of £500,000, being the difference between the carrying amount of the loan (£9.5 million) and its tax base (£10 million). This tax base does not conform to the general definition of the tax base of a liability – i.e. the carrying amount, less any amount that will be deductible for tax purposes in respect of that liability in future periods (see 6.1.2 above).

    The easiest way to derive the correct tax base is to construct a notional statement of financial position prepared by the tax authorities according to tax law. This would show a liability for the full £10 million (since the amortisation of the issue costs that has yet to occur in the financial statements has already occurred in the notional tax authority financial statements). This indicates that the tax base of the loan is £10 million.

A far simpler analysis of the purposes of IAS 12 might have been that the £9.5 million carrying amount comprises a loan of £10 million (with a tax base of £10 million, giving rise to temporary difference of zero) offset by prepaid transaction costs of £500,000 (with a tax base of zero, giving rise to a taxable temporary difference of £500,000). However, this is inconsistent with the analysis in IAS 39 that the issue costs are an integral part of the carrying value of the loan.

The consequence of recognising a deferred tax liability in this case is that the tax deduction for the transaction costs is recognised in profit or loss, not on inception of the loan, but as the costs are recognised through the effective interest method in future periods.

- *Non-deductible loan transaction costs*

  As in the immediately preceding example, a borrowing entity records a loan at £9.5 million, being the proceeds received of £10 million (which equal the amount due at maturity), less transaction costs of £500,000. In this case, however, the transaction costs are not deductible in determining the taxable profit of future, current or prior periods. For financial reporting purposes, IAS 39 requires the costs to be accrued over the period to maturity using the effective interest method.

  Just as in the preceding example (and perhaps rather counter-intuitively, given that the costs are non-deductible) inception of the loan gives rise to a taxable temporary difference of £500,000, being the difference between the carrying amount of the loan (£9.5 million) and its tax base (£10 million). This is because a notional statement of financial position prepared by the tax authorities according to tax law would show a liability for the full £10 million, since the transaction costs would never have been recorded (as they never occurred for tax purposes).

- *Liability component of compound financial instrument*

  An entity issues a convertible bond for €5 million which, in accordance with the requirements of IAS 32 – *Financial Instruments: Presentation*, is analysed as comprising a liability component of €4.6 million and a residual equity component of €400,000. The €400,000 discount is not deductible in determining taxable profit. There is a taxable temporary difference of €400,000 between the carrying amount of the liability component (€4.6 million) and its tax base (€5 million). This is discussed further at 7.2.8 below.

6.2.1.C Revaluations
- *Financial assets and property carried at valuation*

  An entity holds investments, accounted for at fair value through profit or loss, with a carrying amount of CHF2 million and an original cost (and tax base) of CHF1.3 million. There is a taxable temporary difference of CHF700,000 associated with the investments, being the amount on which the entity would pay tax if the investments were realised at their carrying value.

  A similar analysis would apply to investment property or PP&E carried at a value that exceeds cost, where no equivalent adjustment is made for tax purposes.

6.2.1.D   Tax re-basing
- *Withdrawal of tax depreciation for classes of PP&E*

An entity holds buildings with a carrying amount of £15 million and a tax base of £12 million, giving rise to a taxable temporary difference of £3 million. As part of a general fiscal reform package introduced by the government, future tax deductions for the buildings (their tax base) are reduced to £1 million. This increases the taxable temporary difference by £11 million to £14 million.

6.2.1.E   Business combinations and consolidation
- *Fair value adjustments*

Where the carrying amount of an asset is increased to fair value in a business combination, but no equivalent adjustment is made for tax purposes, a taxable temporary difference arises just as on the revaluation of an asset (see 6.2.1.C above).

- *Non-deductible or partially-deductible goodwill*

Where goodwill is not deductible, or only partially deductible, in determining taxable profit there will be a taxable temporary difference between the carrying amount of the goodwill and its tax base, similar to that arising on a non-deductible or partially-deductible asset (see 6.2.1.B above).

- *Intragroup transactions*

Although intragroup transactions are eliminated in consolidated financial statements, they may give rise to temporary differences. An entity in a group (A) might sell inventory with a cost and tax base of £1,000 to another group entity (B) for £900, which becomes the cost and tax base to B. If the carrying value in the consolidated financial statements remains £1,000 (i.e. the inventory is not actually impaired, notwithstanding the intragroup sale at a loss), a new taxable temporary difference of £100 emerges in the consolidated financial statements between the carrying value of £1,000 and the new tax base of £900.

- *Undistributed earnings of group investments*

A parent entity P holds in investment in subsidiary S. Retained earnings of $1 million relating to S are included in the consolidated financial statements of P. S must pay a non-refundable withholding tax on any distribution of earnings to P. There is therefore a taxable temporary difference in the consolidated financial statements of $1 million associated with the net assets representing the retained earnings, since their recovery (in the form of distribution to the parent) has tax consequences, with no offsetting tax deductions.

Similar temporary differences may arise on the retained earnings of branches, associates and joint ventures.

6.2.1.F   Foreign currency differences
- *Translation of foreign subsidiary to presentation currency*

A UK entity acquires the equity of a French entity, which therefore becomes its subsidiary, for €10 million. For UK tax purposes, the tax base of the investment is £8 million (the spot-rate equivalent of €10 million at the date of acquisition). The presentation currency of the UK entity's consolidated financial statements is sterling.

Between the date of acquisition and the first reporting date, the French entity makes no gains or losses, such that its net assets and goodwill as included in the consolidated financial statements, expressed in euros, remain €10 million. However, the exchange rate has moved, so that the sterling equivalent of €10 million at the reporting date, included in the consolidated balance sheet, is £9 million.

This gives rise to a £1 million taxable temporary difference between the £9 million carrying value of the investment and its £8 million tax base.

- *Functional currency different from currency used to compute tax*

  On 1 January 2012 an entity which, under IAS 21 – *The Effects of Changes in Foreign Exchange Rates*, has determined its functional currency as US dollars (see Chapter 17), purchases plant for $1 million, which will be depreciated to its estimated residual value of zero over 10 years. The entity is taxed in the local currency LC, and is entitled to receive tax deductions for the depreciation charged in the financial statements. The exchange rate is $1=LC2 at 1 January 2012 (so that the cost of the asset for local tax purposes is LC2 million). The exchange rate at 31 December 2012 is $1=LC2.5.

  At 31 December 2012 there is a taxable temporary difference of $180,000, being the difference between the net book value of the plant of $900,000 (cost $1,000,000 less depreciation $100,000) and its tax base of $720,000 (cost LC2,000,000 less depreciation LC200,000 = LC1,800,000 translated at year end rate of $1=LC2.5).

6.2.1.G   Hyperinflation

A taxable temporary difference (similar to those in 6.2.1.F above) arises when non-monetary assets are restated in terms of the measuring unit current at the end of the reporting period under IAS 29 – *Financial Reporting in Hyperinflationary Economies* – but no equivalent adjustment is made for tax purposes.

6.2.2   Deductible temporary differences

6.2.2.A   Transactions that affect profit of loss
- *Expenses deductible for tax on cash basis*

  An entity records a liability of €1 million for retirement benefit costs which are tax deductible only when paid. The tax base of the liability is zero, being its carrying amount (€1 million) less the amount deductible for tax purposes when the liability is settled (also €1 million). There is therefore a deductible temporary difference of €1 million (€1 million carrying amount less zero tax base) associated with the liability.

- *Depreciation of an asset delayed for tax purposes*

  An entity with a financial year end of 30 June 2012 has an item of PP&E that originally cost £1 million. The cost is fully tax deductible, with deductions being given over a period longer than the period over which the asset is being depreciated under IAS 16. At 30 June 2012, the asset has been depreciated to £300,000 for financial reporting purposes but to only £500,000 for tax purposes.

  Recovery of the PP&E has tax consequences since, although there is no deduction for accounting depreciation in the tax return, the PP&E is recovered through future taxable profits of £300,000. There is a deductible temporary difference of £200,000 between the carrying value of the asset (£300,000) and its tax base (£500,000).

- *Sale of goods taxed on a cash basis*

  An entity with a financial year end of 31 March 2012 has recorded revenue from the sale of goods of €40,000, together with a cost of the goods sold of €35,000, since the goods have been delivered. However, the transaction is taxed in the following financial year when the cash from the sale is collected.

  There is a deductible temporary difference of €35,000 associated with the (now derecognised) inventory, which has a carrying amount of zero but a tax base of €35,000 (since it will attract a tax deduction of €35,000 when the sale is taxed).

  There is also a taxable temporary difference of €40,000 associated with the receivable (see 6.2.1 A above).

- *Write-down of asset not deductible for tax purposes until realised*

  An entity purchases inventory for $1,000, which is also its tax base. The inventory is later written down to a net realisable value of $800. However, no loss is recognised for tax purposes until the inventory is sold. There is a deductible temporary difference of $200 between the $800 carrying amount of the inventory and its $1,000 tax base.

- *Deferred income taxed on receipt*

  In the year ended 31 December 2012, an entity received €2 million, being 5 years' rent of an investment property received in advance. In the statement of financial position as at 31 December, €1,800,000 is carried forward as deferred income. However, the whole €2 million is taxed in the tax return for the period.

  There is a deductible temporary difference of €1,800,000 associated with the deferred income, being its carrying amount (€1,800,000), less its tax base of zero, computed as the carrying amount (€1,800,000) less the amount not taxable in future periods (also €1,800,000 since the income has already been taxed).

- *Deferred non-taxable income*

  In the year ended 31 March 2012, an entity receives a government grant of £1 million, of which £700,000 is carried forward in the statement of financial position as at the period end.

There is a deductible temporary difference of £700,000 associated with the deferred income, being its carrying amount (£700,000), less its tax base of zero, computed as the carrying amount (£700,000) less the amount not taxable in future periods (also £700,000 since the income is tax free).

6.2.2.B   Transactions that affect the balance sheet
*   *Asset deductible for more than cost*

An entity invests NEK10 million in PP&E for which tax deductions of NEK13 million may be claimed. There is a deductible temporary difference of NEK 3 million between the NEK10 million carrying value of the PP&E and its tax base of NEK13 million.

6.2.2.C   Revaluations
*   *Financial assets and property carried at valuation*

An entity holds investments, accounted for at fair value through profit or loss, with a carrying amount of CHF2 million and an original cost (and tax base) of CHF2.5 million. There is a taxable temporary difference of CHF500,000 associated with the investments, being the amount for which the entity would receive a tax deduction if the investments were realised at their carrying value.

A similar analysis would apply to investment property or PP&E carried at a value below cost, where no equivalent adjustment is made for tax purposes.

6.2.2.D   Tax re-basing
*   *Indexation of assets for tax purposes*

An entity acquires land for $5 million, which is also its tax base at the date of purchase. A year later, as part of a general fiscal reform package introduced by the government, future tax deductions for the land (its tax base) are increased to $6 million. This creates a deductible temporary difference of $1 million in respect of the land.

6.2.2.E   Business combinations and consolidation
*   *Fair value adjustments*

Where a liability is recognised at fair value in a business combination, but the liability is deductible for tax purposes only on settlement, a deductible temporary difference arises similar to that arising on the initial recognition of a liability for an expense deductible for tax on a cash basis (see 6.2.2 A above).

*   *Intragroup transactions*

Although intragroup transactions are eliminated in consolidated financial statements, they may give rise to deductible temporary differences. An entity in a group (A) might sell inventory with a cost and tax base of £1,000 to another group entity (B) for £1,200, which becomes the cost and tax base to B. Since the carrying value in the consolidated financial statements remains £1,000, a new deductible temporary difference of £200 emerges in the consolidated financial statements between the carrying value of £1,000 and the new tax base of £1,200.

6.2.2.F   Foreign currency differences

• *Translation of foreign subsidiary to presentation currency*

A UK entity acquires the equity of a French entity, which therefore becomes its subsidiary, for €10 million. For UK tax purposes, the tax base of the investment is £8 million (the spot-rate equivalent of €10 million at the date of acquisition). The presentation currency of the UK entity's consolidated financial statements is sterling.

Between the date of acquisition and the first reporting date, the French entity makes no gains or losses, such that its net assets and goodwill as included in the consolidated financial statements, expressed in euros, remain €10 million. However, the exchange rate has moved, so that the sterling equivalent of €10 million at the reporting date, included in the consolidated balance sheet, is £7 million.

This gives rise to a £1 million deductible temporary difference between the £7 million carrying value of the investment and its £8 million tax base.

• *Functional currency different from currency used to compute tax*

On 1 January 2012 an entity which, under IAS 21 – *The Effects of Changes in Foreign Exchange Rates*, has determined its functional currency as US dollars (see Chapter 17), purchases plant for $1 million, which will be depreciated to its estimated residual value of zero over 10 years. The entity is taxed in the local currency LC, and is entitled to receive tax deductions for the depreciation charged in the financial statements. The exchange rate is $1=LC2 at 1 January 2012 (so that the cost of the asset for local tax purposes is LC2 million). The exchange rate at 31 December 2012 is $1=LC1.8.

At 31 December 2012 there is a deductible temporary difference of $100,000, being the difference between the net book value of the plant of $900,000 (cost $1,000,000 less depreciation $100,000) and its tax base of $1,000,000 (cost LC2,000,000 less depreciation LC200,000 = LC1,800,000 translated at year end rate of $1=LC1.8).

6.2.3   Assets and liabilities with no temporary difference (because tax base equals carrying amount)

• *Liability for expense already deducted for tax*

An entity accrues £200,000 for electricity costs in the year ended 31 March 2012. The expense is deductible for tax in that period. The temporary difference associated with the liability is zero, This is calculated as the carrying amount of £200,000 less the tax base of £200,000, being the carrying amount (£200,000) less amount deductible for tax in future periods (zero).

• *Liability for expense never deductible for tax*

An entity accrues €400,000 for a fine for environmental pollution, which is not deductible for tax. The temporary difference associated with the liability is zero. This is calculated as the carrying amount of €400,000 less the tax base of €400,000, being the carrying amount (€400,000) less amount deductible for tax in future periods (zero).

- *Loan repayable at carrying amount*

  An entity borrows $2 million. This is the carrying amount of the loan on initial recognition, which is the same as the amount repayable on final maturity of the loan. The temporary difference associated with the liability is zero, This is calculated as the carrying amount of $2 million less the tax base of $2 million, being the carrying amount ($2 million) less amount deductible for tax in future periods (zero).

- *Receivable for non-taxable income*

  In its separate financial statements an entity records a receivable for a £1 million dividend due from a subsidiary accounted for at cost. The dividend is not taxable. Accordingly it gives rise to a temporary difference of zero, since the tax base of any asset, the recovery of the carrying amount of which is not taxable, is taken to be the same as its carrying amount.

7 DEFERRED TAX – RECOGNITION

7.1 The basic principles

7.1.1 Taxable temporary differences (Deferred tax liabilities)

IAS 12 requires a deferred tax liability to be recognised in respect of all taxable temporary differences except those arising from:

- the initial recognition of goodwill; or
- the initial recognition of an asset or liability in a transaction that:
  - is not a business combination; and
  - at the time of the transaction, affects neither accounting profit nor taxable profit (tax loss).

These exceptions to the recognition principles do not apply to taxable temporary differences associated with investments in subsidiaries, branches and associates, and interests in joint ventures, which are subject to further detailed provisions of IAS 12 (see 7.5 below). *[IAS 12.15]*.

Examples of taxable temporary differences are given in 6.2.1 above.

7.1.2 Deductible temporary differences (Deferred tax assets)

IAS 12 requires a deferred tax asset to be recognised in respect of all deductible temporary differences to the extent that it is probable that taxable profit will be available against which the deductible temporary difference will be utilised except those arising from the initial recognition of an asset or liability in a transaction that:

- is not a business combination; and
- at the time of the transaction, affects neither accounting profit nor taxable profit (tax loss). *[IAS 12.24]*.

IAS 12 does not define 'probable' in this context. However, it is generally understood that, as in other IFRS, it should be taken to mean 'more likely than not'. The exposure draft ED/2009/2 (see 1.3 above) effectively clarified that this is the intended meaning.[12]

These exceptions to the recognition principles do not apply to deductible temporary differences associated with investments in subsidiaries, branches and associates, and interests in joint ventures, which are subject to further detailed provisions of IAS 12 (see 7.5 below).

Examples of deductible temporary differences are given in 6.2.2 above.

7.1.3　Interpretation issues

7.1.3.A　Accounting profit

The provisions of IAS 12 summarised above refer to a transaction that affects 'accounting profit'. In this context 'accounting profit' clearly means any item recognised in total comprehensive income, whether recognised in profit or loss or in other comprehensive income.

7.1.3.B　Taxable profit 'at the time of the transaction'

The provisions of IAS 12 summarised above also refer to a transaction which affects taxable profit 'at the time of the transaction'. Strictly speaking, no transaction affects taxable profit 'at the time of the transaction', since the taxable profit is affected only when the relevant item is included (some time later) in the tax return for the period. It is clear, however, that the intended meaning is that the transaction that gives rise to the initial recognition of the relevant asset or liability affects the current tax liability for the accounting period in which the initial recognition occurs.

Suppose that, in the year ended 31 December 2012, an entity received €2 million, being 5 years' prepaid rent of an investment property. In the statement of financial position as at 31 December, €1,800,000 is carried forward as deferred income. The whole €2 million is taxed on receipt and will therefore be included in the tax return for the period, which is not filed until 2013.

It could be argued that, in a literal legal sense, the transaction 'affects taxable profit' only in 2013. For the purposes of IAS 12, however, this argument is rejected. The transaction is regarded as affecting taxable profit during 2012 (since it affects the current tax for that period). This gives rise to the recognition, subject to the restrictions discussed at 7.4 below, of a deferred tax asset based on a deductible temporary difference of €1,800,000 (see 6.2.2.A above).

7.2　The initial recognition exception

The exceptions (summarised in 7.1 above) from recognising the deferred tax effects of certain temporary differences arising on the initial recognition of some assets and liabilities are generally referred to as the 'initial recognition exception' or 'initial recognition exemption', sometimes abbreviated to 'IRE'. 'Exception' is the more accurate description, since a reporting entity is required to apply it, rather than having the option to do so implicit in the term 'exemption'.

The initial recognition exception has its origins in the now superseded 'income statement' approaches to accounting for deferred tax. Under these approaches, deferred tax was not recognised on so-called 'permanent differences' – items of income or expense that appeared in either the financial statements or the tax return, but not in both. The majority of transactions to which the initial recognition exception applies would have been regarded as permanent differences under income statement approaches of accounting for deferred tax.

The purpose of the initial recognition exception is most easily understood by considering the accounting consequences that would follow if it did not exist, as illustrated in Example 31.2 below.

Example 31.2:   Rationale for initial recognition exception

An entity acquires an asset for €1,000 which it intends to use for five years and then scrap (i.e. the residual value is nil). The tax rate is 40%. Depreciation of the asset is not deductible for tax purposes. On disposal, any capital gain would not be taxable and any capital loss would not be deductible.

Although the asset is non-deductible, its recovery has tax consequences, since it will be recovered out of taxable income of €1,000 on which tax of €400 will be paid. The tax base of the asset it therefore zero, and a temporary difference of €1,000 arises on initial recognition of the asset.

Absent the initial recognition exception, the entity would recognise a deferred tax liability of €400 on initial recognition of the asset, being the taxable temporary difference of €1,000 multiplied by the tax rate of 40%. A debit entry would then be required to balance the credit for the liability.

One possibility might be to recognise tax expense in the statement of total comprehensive income. This would be meaningless, since the entity has clearly not suffered a loss simply by purchasing a non-deductible asset in an arm's length transaction for a price that (economically) must reflect the asset's non-deductibility.

A second possibility would be to gross up the asset by €400 to €1,400. However, IAS 12 states that to make such adjustments to the carrying value of the asset would make the financial statements 'less transparent'. *[IAS 12.22(c)]*.

A third possibility (broadly the guidance provided under US GAAP) would be to gross up the asset to the amount that would rationally have been paid for it, had it been fully tax-deductible, and recognise a corresponding amount of deferred tax. As the asset is non-deductible, the €1,000 cost must theoretically represent the anticipated minimum *post*-tax return from the asset. In order to achieve a post-tax return of €1,000, an entity paying tax at 40% needs to earn pre-tax profits of €1,667 (€1,000/[1 – 0.4]). Therefore, the cost of an equivalent fully-deductible asset would, all else being equal, be €1,667. On this analysis, the entity would gross up the asset to €1,667 and recognise deferred tax of €667 (€1,667 @ 40%).

The fourth possibility, which is what is actually required by IAS 12, is not to provide for deferred tax at all, where to do so would lead to one of the three outcomes above. However, in cases where provision for the deferred tax on a temporary difference arising on initial recognition of an asset or liability would not lead to one of the outcomes above, the initial recognition exception does not apply. This is the case in a business combination or a transaction affecting taxable profit or accounting profit (or both).

- *Business combination*

  In a business combination, the corresponding accounting entry for a deferred tax asset or liability forms part of the goodwill arising or the bargain purchase gain recognised. No deferred tax income or expense is recorded.

- *Transaction affecting taxable profit or accounting profit*

  In a transaction affecting taxable profit or accounting profit (or both), the corresponding accounting entry for a deferred tax asset or liability is recorded as deferred tax income or expense.

  This ensures that the entity recognises all future tax consequences of recovering the assets, or settling the liabilities, recognised in the transaction. The effect of this on the statement of total comprehensive income is broadly to recognise items the tax effects of the various components of income and expenditure in the same period(s) in which those items are recognised for financial reporting purposes (as illustrated in 1.2.2 above).

In short, the initial recognition exception may simply be seen as the least bad of the four theoretically possible options for dealing with 'day one' temporary differences.

7.2.1   Acquisition of tax losses

The initial recognition exception applies only to deferred tax relating to temporary differences. It does not apply to tax assets, such as purchased tax losses, that do not arise from deductible temporary differences. The definition of 'deferred tax assets' (see 3 above) explicitly distinguishes between deductible temporary differences and unused losses and tax credits. *[IAS 12.5].* There is therefore no restriction on the recognition of acquired tax losses other than the general criteria of IAS 12 for recognition of tax assets (see 7.4 below).

Under the general principles of IAS 12, acquired tax losses are initially recognised at the amount paid, subsequently re-assessed for recoverability (see 7.4.5 below) and re-measured accordingly (see 8 below). Changes in the recognised amount of acquired tax losses are generally recognised in profit or loss, on the basis that, as acquired losses, they do not relate to any pre-tax transaction previously accounted for by the entity (see 10 below). However, in some limited circumstances, changes to tax losses acquired as part of a business combination are required to be treated as an adjustment to goodwill (see 12.1.2 below).

7.2.2   Initial recognition of goodwill

7.2.2.A   Taxable temporary differences

In many jurisdictions goodwill is not tax-deductible either as it is impaired or on ultimate disposal, such that it gives rise to a temporary difference equal to its carrying amount (representing its carrying amount less its tax base of zero).

It may well be that the shares in the acquired entity have a tax base equal to their cost so that, economically, an amount equal to the goodwill is deductible on disposal of those shares. However, accounting for the tax effects of the shares in an acquired subsidiary (or other significant group investment) is subject to separate provisions of IAS 12, which are discussed at 7.5 below.

The initial recognition exception for taxable temporary differences on goodwill prevents the grossing-up of goodwill that would otherwise occur. Goodwill is a function of all the net assets of the acquired business, including deferred tax. If deferred tax is provided for on goodwill, the goodwill itself is increased, which means that the deferred tax on the goodwill is increased further, which means that the goodwill increases again, and so on. Equilibrium is reached when the amount of goodwill originally recorded is grossed up by the fraction $1/(1 - t)$, where t is the entity's tax rate, expressed as a decimal fraction. For example, an entity that pays tax at 30% and recognises CU1,400 of goodwill before recognising deferred tax would (absent the initial recognition exception) increase the goodwill to CU2,000 and recognise a deferred tax liability of CU600 (which is 30% of the restated goodwill of CU2,000).

IAS 12 takes the view that this would not be appropriate, since goodwill is intended to be a residual arising after fair values have been determined for the assets and liabilities acquired in a business combination, and recognition of deferred tax would increase that goodwill. *[IAS 12.21].*

7.2.2.B   Deductible temporary differences

Where the carrying amount of goodwill arising in a business combination is less than its tax base, a deductible temporary difference arises. IAS 12 requires a deferred tax asset to be recognised in respect of any deductible temporary difference, to the extent that it is probable that taxable profit will be available against which the temporary difference could be utilised. *[IAS 12.32A].* This contrasts the prohibition against recognising a deferred tax liability on any *taxable* temporary difference on initial recognition of goodwill (see 7.2.2.A above). A more general discussion of the criteria in IAS 12 for assessing the recoverability of deferred tax assets may be found at 7.4 below.

IAS 12 gives no guidance on the method to be used in calculating the resulting deferred tax asset, which is not entirely straightforward, as illustrated by the following example.

Example 31.3:   Deferred tax asset on initial recognition of goodwill

An entity that pays tax at 40% recognises, in the initial accounting for a business combination, goodwill of €1,000. Tax deductions of €1,250 are given for the goodwill over a 5 year period.

One approach would be to adopt an iterative method similar to that described in 7.2.2.A above, whereby recognition of a deferred tax asset on goodwill leads to a reduction of the goodwill, which in turn will lead to a further increase in the deferred tax asset, and so on. Equilibrium is reached when the goodwill is adjusted to an amount equal to $(g - bt)/(1 - t)$, where:

- g is the amount of goodwill originally recorded (before recognising a deferred tax asset),

- b is the tax base of the goodwill, and

- t is the tax rate, expressed as a decimal fraction.

Under this method, the entity would record goodwill of €833 (being [€1,000 − 0.4 × €1,250] ÷ 0.6) and a deferred tax asset of €167. This represents a deductible temporary difference of €417 (comprising the tax base of €1,250 less the adjusted carrying amount of €833), multiplied by the tax rate of 40%. On any subsequent impairment or disposal of the goodwill, the entity would report an effective tax rate of 40% (the statutory rate), comprised of pre-tax expense of €833 and tax income of €333 (the real tax deduction of €500 (€1,250 @ 40%), less the write-off of the deferred tax asset of €167).

An alternative approach might be to record a deferred tax asset based on the carrying amount of goodwill before calculating the deferred tax asset, and adjust the goodwill only once, rather than undertaking the iterative reduction in the goodwill described in the previous paragraph. In the example above this would lead to the entity recording a deferred tax asset of €100 (representing 40% of the deductible temporary difference of €250 between the tax base of the goodwill of €1,250 and its original carrying amount of €1,000) and goodwill of €900. On any subsequent impairment or disposal of the goodwill the entity would report an effective tax rate of 44% (higher than the statutory rate), comprised of pre-tax expense of €900 and tax income of €400 (the real tax deduction of €500 (€1,250 @ 40%), less the write-off of the deferred tax asset of €100).

We consider the first of these two approaches preferable, but in the absence of clear guidance for dealing with this issue, regard the second as acceptable.

7.2.2.C   Tax deductible goodwill

Where goodwill is tax-deductible, new temporary differences will arise after its initial recognition as a result of the interaction between tax deductions claimed and impairments (if any) of the goodwill in the financial statements. These temporary differences do not relate to the initial recognition of goodwill, and therefore deferred tax should be recognised on them, as illustrated by Example 31.14 at 7.2.4.C below. *[IAS 12.21B].*

7.2.3   Initial recognition of other assets and liabilities

Where a temporary difference arises on initial recognition of an asset or liability, its treatment depends on the circumstances which give rise to the recognition of the asset or liability.

If the temporary difference arises as the result of a business combination, deferred tax is recognised on the temporary difference with a corresponding adjustment to goodwill or any bargain purchase gain.

If the temporary difference arises in a transaction that gives rise to an accounting or taxable profit or loss, deferred tax is recognised on the temporary difference, giving rise to deferred tax expense or deferred tax income.

If the temporary difference arises in any other circumstances (i.e. neither in a business combination nor in a transaction that gives rise to an accounting or taxable profit or loss) no deferred tax is recognised. *[IAS 12.22].*

The application of the initial recognition exception to assets and liabilities is illustrated in Examples 31.4 to 31.7 below.

Example 31.4: Non-deductible PP&E

An entity paying tax at 35% acquires a building for €1 million. Any accounting depreciation of the building is not deductible for tax purposes, and no deduction will be available for tax purposes when the asset is sold or scrapped.

Recovery of the building, whether in use or on sale, has tax consequences since the building is recovered through future taxable profits of €1 million. There is a taxable temporary difference of €1 million between the €1 million carrying value of the asset and its tax base of zero.

Under the initial recognition exception, no deferred tax liability is provided for. The non-deductibility of the asset is reflected in an effective tax rate higher than the statutory rate (assuming that all other components of pre-tax profit are taxed at the statutory rate) as the asset is depreciated in future periods.

If the asset had been acquired as part of a larger business combination, the initial recognition would not have applied. Deferred tax of €350,000 (€1 million @ 35%) would have been provided for, with a corresponding increase in goodwill. As the asset is depreciated, the deferred tax liability is released to deferred tax income in the income statement, as illustrated in Example 31.1 above. This results in an effective tax rate equal to the statutory rate of 35% (assuming that all other components of pre-tax profit are taxed at the statutory rate).

Example 31.5: Inception of loan with tax-deductible issue costs

A borrowing entity paying tax at 30% records a loan at £9.5 million, being the proceeds received of £10 million (which equal the amount due at maturity), less transaction costs of £500,000, which are deducted for tax purposes in the period when the loan is first recognised. For financial reporting purposes, IAS 39 requires the costs, together with interest and similar payments, to be accrued over the period to maturity using the effective interest method.

Inception of the loan gives rise to a taxable temporary difference of £500,000, being the difference between the carrying amount of the loan (£9.5 million) and its tax base (£10 million). This analysis is explained in more detail at 6.2.1.B above.

Initial recognition of the transaction costs gives rise to no accounting loss (because they are included in the carrying amount of the loan). However, there is a tax loss (since the costs are included in the tax return for the period of inception). Accordingly, the initial recognition exception does not apply and a deferred tax liability of £150,000 (£500,000 @ 30%) is recognised.

Example 31.6: Inception of loan with non-deductible issue costs

A borrowing entity paying tax at 30% records a loan at £9.5 million, being the proceeds received of £10 million (which equal the amount due at maturity), less transaction costs of £500,000, which not deductible for tax purposes either in the period when the loan is first recognised or subsequently. For financial reporting purposes, IAS 39 requires the costs, together with interest and similar payments, to be accrued over the period to maturity using the effective interest method.

Inception of the loan gives rise to a taxable temporary difference of £500,000, being the difference between the carrying amount of the loan (£9.5 million) and its tax base (£10 million). This analysis is explained in more detail at 6.2.1.B above.

Initial recognition of the transaction costs gives rise to no accounting loss (because they are included in the carrying amount of the loan) or tax loss. Accordingly, the initial recognition exception applies and no deferred tax liability is recognised.

If the same loan (including the unamortised transaction costs) had been recognised as part of a larger business combination, the initial recognition would not have applied. Deferred tax of £150,000 (£500,000 @ 30%) would have been provided for, with a corresponding increase in goodwill (or decrease in any bargain purchase gain).

Example 31.7:   Purchase of PP&E subject to tax-free government grant

An entity acquires an item of PP&E for €1 million subject to a tax free government grant of €350,000. The asset is also fully-tax deductible (at €1 million). IAS 20 permits the grant to be accounted for either as deferred income or by deduction from the cost of the asset. Whichever treatment is followed, a deductible temporary difference arises:

- If the grant is accounted for as deferred income, there is a deductible temporary difference between the liability of €350,000 and its tax base of nil (carrying amount €350,000 less amount not taxed in future periods, also €350,000).

- If the grant is accounted for as a reduction in the cost of the PP&E, there is a deductible temporary difference between the carrying amount of the PP&E (€650,000) and its tax base (€1 million).

IAS 12 emphasises that the initial recognition exception applies, and no deferred tax asset should be recognised. *[IAS 12.33]*.

7.2.4   Changes to temporary differences after initial recognition

The initial recognition exception applies only to temporary differences arising on initial recognition of an asset or liability. It does not apply to new temporary differences that arise on the same asset or liability after initial recognition. When the exception has been applied to the temporary difference arising on initial recognition of an asset or liability, and there is a different temporary difference associated with that asset or liability at a subsequent date, it is necessary to analyse the temporary difference at that date between:

- any amount relating to the original temporary difference (on which no deferred tax is recognised); and

- the remainder, which has implicitly arisen after initial recognition of the asset or liability (on which deferred tax is recognised).

IAS 12 does not set out comprehensive guidance to be followed in making this analysis, but it does give a number of examples, from which the following general principles may be inferred:

- the new temporary difference is treated as part of the temporary difference arising on initial recognition to the extent that any change from the original temporary difference is due to:
  - the write-down (through depreciation, amortisation or impairment) of the original carrying amount of an asset with no corresponding change in the tax base (see 7.2.4.A below); or
  - the increase in the carrying amount of a liability arising from the amortisation of any discount recognised at the time of initial recognition of that liability, with no corresponding change in the tax base (see 7.2.4.A below);

- the new temporary difference is regarded as arising after initial recognition to the extent that any change from the original temporary difference is due to:
  - a change in the carrying value of the asset or liability, other than for the reasons set out above (see 7.2.4.B below); or
  - a change in the tax base due to items being recorded on the tax return (see 7.2.4.C below); and

- where the change in the temporary difference results from a change in the tax base due to legislative change, IAS 12 provides no specific guidance, and more than one treatment may be possible (see 7.2.4.D below).

7.2.4.A Depreciation, amortisation or impairment of initial carrying value

The following are examples of transactions where the initial temporary difference changes as the result of the amortisation of the original carrying amount, so that the adjusted temporary difference is regarded as part of the temporary difference arising on initial recognition, rather than a new difference.

Example 31.8: Impairment of non-deductible goodwill

Goodwill of £10 million (not tax-deductible) arose on a business combination in 2006. In accordance with IAS 12 no deferred tax liability was recognised on the taxable temporary difference of £10 million that arose on initial recognition of the goodwill. During the year ended 31 December 2012, following an impairment test, the carrying amount of the goodwill is reduced to £6 million.

No deferred tax is recognised on the new temporary difference of £6 million, because it is part of the temporary difference arising on the initial recognition of the goodwill. *[IAS 12.21A]*.

Example 31.9: Depreciation of non-deductible PP&E

During the year ended 31 March 2013 entity acquires an item of PP&E for €1 million which it intends to use for 20 years, with no anticipated residual value. No tax deductions are available for the asset. In accordance with IAS 12 no deferred tax liability was recognised on the taxable temporary difference of €1 million that arises on initial recognition of the PP&E.

The entity's accounting policy is to charge a full year's depreciation in the year of purchase, so that the carrying amount of the asset at 31 March 2013 is €950,000. No deferred tax is recognised on the current temporary difference of €950,000, because it is part of the temporary difference arising on the initial recognition of the PP&E. *[IAS 12.22(c)]*.

Example 31.10: Amortisation of non-deductible loan issue costs

A borrowing entity records a loan at £9.5 million, being the proceeds received of £10 million (which equal the amount due at maturity), less transaction costs of £500,000, which not deductible for tax purposes either in the period when the loan is first recognised or subsequently. For financial reporting purposes, IAS 39 requires the costs, together with interest and similar payments, to be accrued over the period to maturity using the effective interest method.

Inception of the loan gives rise to a taxable temporary difference of £500,000, being the difference between the carrying amount of the loan (£9.5 million) and its tax base (£10 million). This analysis is explained in more detail at 6.2.1.B above.

In accordance with IAS 12, no deferred tax liability was recognised on the taxable temporary difference of £10 million that arose on initial recognition of the loan.

One year later, the carrying amount of the loan is £9.7 million, comprising the proceeds received of £10 million (which equal the amount due at maturity), less unamortised transaction costs of £300,000. This gives rise to a new temporary difference of £300,000. No deferred tax is recognised on the current temporary difference, because it is part of the temporary difference arising on the initial recognition of the loan.

7.2.4.B   Change in carrying value due to revaluation

As illustrated in Example 31.4 at 7.2.3 above, a temporary difference arises when a non tax-deductible asset is acquired. Where the asset is acquired separately (i.e. not as part of a larger business combination) in circumstances giving rise to neither an accounting nor a taxable profit or loss, no deferred tax liability is recognised for that temporary difference.

If such an asset is subsequently revalued, however, deferred tax is recognised on the new temporary difference arising as a result of the revaluation, since this does not arise on initial recognition of the asset, as illustrated in Examples 31.11 and 31.12.

Example 31.11:   Revaluation of non-deductible asset (1)

On 1 January 2012 an entity paying tax at 30% acquires a non tax-deductible office building for €1,000,000 in circumstances in which IAS 12 prohibits recognition of the deferred tax liability associated with the temporary difference of €1,000,000.

Application of IAS 16 results in no depreciation being charged on the building.

On 1 January 2013 the entity revalues the building to €1,200,000. The temporary difference associated with the building is now €1,200,000, only €1,000,000 of which arose on initial recognition. Accordingly, the entity recognises a deferred tax liability based on the remaining temporary difference of €200,000 giving deferred tax expense at 30% of €60,000. This tax expense would be recognised other comprehensive income (see 10 below).

Example 31.12:   Revaluation of non-deductible asset (2)

On 1 January 2012 an entity paying tax at 30% acquires a non tax-deductible office building for €1,000,000 in circumstances in which IAS 12 prohibits recognition of the deferred tax liability associated with the temporary difference of €1,000,000. The building is depreciated over 20 years at €50,000 per year to a residual value of zero. The entity's financial year ends on 31 December.

At 1 January 2014, the carrying amount of the building is €900,000, and it is revalued upwards by €450,000 to its current market value of €1,350,000. As there is no change to the estimated residual value of zero, or to the life of the building, this will be depreciated over the next 18 years at €75,000 per year.

Following the revaluation, the temporary difference associated with the building is €1,350,000. Of this amount, only €900,000 arose on initial recognition, since €100,000 of the original temporary difference of €1,000,000 arising on initial recognition of the asset has been eliminated through depreciation of the asset (see 7.2.4.A above). The carrying amount (which equals the temporary difference, since the tax base is zero) and depreciation during the year ended 31 December 2014 may then be analysed as follows.

	Total carrying amount €	Arising on initial recognition €	Arising on revaluation €
1 January 2014	1,350,000	900,000	450,000
Depreciation[1]	75,000	50,000	25,000
31 December 2014	1,275,000	850,000	425,000

1   The depreciation is allocated pro-rata to the cost element and revalued element of the total carrying amount.

On 1 January 2014 the entity recognises a deferred tax liability based on the temporary difference of €450,000 arising on the revaluation (i.e. after initial recognition) giving a deferred tax expense of €135,000 (€450,000 @ 30%), recognised in other comprehensive income (see 10 below). This has the result that the effective tax rate shown in the financial statements for the revaluation is 30% (€450,000 gain with deferred tax expense of €135,000).

As can be seen from the table above, at the end of the period, €425,000 of the total temporary difference arose after initial recognition. The entity therefore provides for deferred tax of €127,500 (€425,000 @ 30%), and deferred tax income of €7,500 (the reduction in the liability from €135,000 to €127,500) recognised in profit or loss.

The deferred tax income can be explained as tax effect at 30% of the €25,000 depreciation relating to the revalued element of the building (see table above).

7.2.4.C   Change in tax base due to deductions in tax return

The following are examples of transactions where a new temporary difference emerges after initial recognition as the result of claiming tax deductions.

Example 31.13:   Tax deduction for land

An entity that pays tax at 35% acquires land with a fair value of €5 million. Tax deductions of €100,000 per year may be claimed for the land for the next 30 years (i.e. the tax base of the land is €3 million). In accordance with IAS 12, no deferred tax liability is recognised on the taxable temporary difference of €2 million that arises on initial recognition of the land.

In the period in which the land is acquired, the entity claims the first €100,000 annual tax deduction, and the original cost of the land is not depreciated or impaired. The taxable temporary difference at the end of the period is therefore €2.1 million (cost €5.0 million less tax base €2.9 million). Of this, €2 million arose on initial recognition and no deferred tax is recognised on this. However, the remaining €100,000 of the gross temporary difference arose after initial recognition. Accordingly the entity recognises a deferred tax liability of €35,000 (€100,000 @ 35%).

The analysis if the land had been impaired would be rather more complicated. The general issue of the treatment of assets that are tax-deductible, but for less than their cost, is discussed at 7.2.6 below.

Example 31.14:   Tax-deductible goodwill

On 1 January 2012 an entity with a tax rate of 35% acquires goodwill in a business combination with a cost of €1 million, which is deductible for tax purposes at a rate of 20% per year, starting in the year of acquisition.

During 2012 the entity claims the full 20% tax deduction and writes off €120,000 of the goodwill as the result of an impairment test. Thus at the end of 2012 the goodwill has a carrying amount of €880,000 and a tax base of €800,000. This gives rise to a taxable temporary difference of €80,000 that does not relate to the initial recognition of goodwill, and accordingly the entity recognises a deferred tax liability at 35% of €28,000.

If, during 2012, there had been no impairment of the goodwill, but the full tax deduction had nevertheless been claimed, at the end of the year the entity would have had goodwill with a carrying amount of €1 million and a tax base of €800,000. This would have given rise to a taxable temporary difference of €200,000 that does not relate to the initial recognition of goodwill, and accordingly the entity would have recognised a deferred tax liability at 35% of €70,000.

7.2.4.D   Temporary difference altered by legislative change

Any change to the basis on which an item is treated for tax purposes alters the tax base of the item concerned. For example, if the government decides that an item of PP&E that was previously tax-deductible is no longer eligible for tax deductions, the tax base of the PP&E is reduced to zero. Under IAS 12, any change in tax base normally results in an immediate adjustment of any associated deferred tax asset or liability, and the recognition of a corresponding amount of deferred tax income or expense.

However, where such an adjustment to the tax base occurs in respect of an asset or liability in respect of which no deferred tax has previously been recognised because of the initial recognition exception, the treatment required by IAS 12 is not entirely clear. The issue is illustrated by Example 31.15 below.

Example 31.15:   Asset non-deductible at date of acquisition later becomes deductible

During the year ended 31 March 2012 entity acquired an item of PP&E for €1 million which it intends to use for 20 years, with no anticipated residual value. No tax deductions were available for the asset. In accordance with IAS 12 no deferred tax liability was recognised on the taxable temporary difference of €1 million that arose on initial recognition of the PP&E.

During the year ended 31 March 2013, the government announces that it will allow the cost of such assets to be deducted in arriving at taxable profit. The deductions will be allowed in equal annual instalments over a 10-year period. As at 31 March 2013, the carrying amount of the asset and its tax base are both €900,000. The carrying amount is the original cost of €1 million less two years' depreciation at €50,000 per year. The tax base is the original cost of €1 million less one year's tax deduction at €100,000 per year.

Prima facie, therefore, there is no temporary difference associated with the asset. However, the treatment required by IAS 12 in Examples 27.13 and 14 above would lead to the conclusion that this temporary difference of nil should in fact be analysed into:

- a taxable temporary difference of €900,000 arising on initial recognition of the asset (being the €1 million difference arising on initial recognition less the €100,000 depreciation charged), and

- a deductible temporary difference of €900,000 arising after initial recognition (representing the fact that, since initial recognition, the government increased the tax base by €1 million which has been reduced to €900,000 by the €100,000 tax deduction claimed in the current period).

This analysis indicates that no deferred tax liability should be recognised on the taxable temporary difference (since this arose on initial recognition), but a deferred tax asset should be recognised on the deductible temporary difference of €900,000 identified above. A contrary view would be that this is inappropriate, since it is effectively recognising a gain on the elimination of a income tax liability that was never previously recognised.

As far as the tax income and expense in profit or loss is concerned, the difference between the two approaches is one of timing. Under the analysis that the overall temporary difference of zero should be 'bifurcated' into a an amount arising on initial recognition and an amount arising later, the change in legislation reduces income tax expense and the effective tax rate in the year of change. Under the analysis that the net temporary difference of zero is considered as a whole, the reduction in income tax expense and the effective tax rate is recognised prospectively over the remaining life of the asset.

In our view, the first approach ('bifurcation') is more consistent with the balance sheet approach of IAS 12 and therefore preferable, but, in the absence of specific guidance in the standard, the second approach may be acceptable.

7.2.5 *Intragroup transfers of assets with no change in tax base*

In many tax jurisdictions the tax deductions for an asset are generally related to the cost of that asset to the legal entity that owns it. However, in some jurisdictions, where an asset is transferred between members of the same group within that jurisdiction, the tax base remains unchanged, irrespective of the consideration paid.

Therefore, where the consideration paid for an asset in such a case differs from its tax base, a temporary difference arises in the acquiring entity's separate financial statements on transfer of the asset. The initial recognition exception applies to any such temporary difference. A further complication is that the acquiring entity acquires an asset that, rather than conforming to the fiscal norms of being either deductible for its full cost or not deductible at all, is deductible, but for an amount different from its cost. The treatment of such assets in the context of the initial recognition exception is discussed more generally at 7.2.6 below.

In the consolidated financial statements of any parent of the buying entity, however, there is no change to the amount of deferred tax recognised provided that the tax rate of the buying and selling entity is the same. Where the tax rate differs, the deferred tax will be remeasured using the buying entity's tax rate.

Where an asset is transferred between group entities and the tax base of the asset changes as a result of the transaction, there will be deferred tax income or expense in the consolidated financial statements. This is discussed further at 8.6 below.

7.2.6 *Partially deductible and super-deductible assets*

In many tax jurisdictions the tax deductions for an asset are generally related to the cost of that asset to the legal entity that owns it. However, in some jurisdictions, certain categories of asset are deductible for tax but for an amount either less than the cost of the asset ('partially deductible') or more than the cost of the asset ('super-deductible').

IAS 12 provides no specific guidance on the treatment of partially deductible and super-deductible assets acquired in a transaction to which the initial recognition exception applies. The issues raised by such assets are illustrated in Examples 31.16 and 31.17 below.

Example 31.16:   *Partially deductible asset*

An entity acquires an asset with a cost of €100,000 and a tax base of €60,000 in a transaction where IAS 12 prohibits recognition of deferred tax on the taxable temporary difference of €40,000 arising on initial recognition of the asset. The asset is depreciated to a residual value of zero over 10 years, and qualifies for tax deductions of 20% per year over 5 years. The temporary differences associated with the asset over its life will therefore be as follows.

Year	Carrying amount €	Tax base €	Temporary difference €
0	100,000	60,000	40,000
1	90,000	48,000	42,000
2	80,000	36,000	44,000
3	70,000	24,000	46,000
4	60,000	12,000	48,000
5	50,000	–	50,000
6	40,000	–	40,000
7	30,000	–	30,000
8	20,000	–	20,000
9	10,000	–	10,000
10	–	–	–

These differences are clearly a function both of:

- the €40,000 temporary difference arising on initial recognition relating to the non-deductible element of the asset, and
- the emergence of temporary differences arising from the claiming of tax deductions for the €60,000 deductible element in advance of its depreciation.

Whilst IAS 12 does not explicitly mandate the treatment to be followed here, the general requirement to distinguish between these elements of the gross temporary difference (see 7.2.4 above) suggests the following approach.

The total carrying amount of the asset is pro-rated into a 60% deductible element and a 40% non-deductible element, and deferred tax is recognised on the temporary difference between the 60% deductible element and its tax base. Under this approach, the temporary differences would be calculated as follows:

Year	Carrying amount a	40% non-deductible element b (40% of a)	60% deductible element c (60% of a)	Tax base d	Temporary difference c – d
0	100,000	40,000	60,000	60,000	–
1	90,000	36,000	54,000	48,000	6,000
2	80,000	32,000	48,000	36,000	12,000
3	70,000	28,000	42,000	24,000	18,000
4	60,000	24,000	36,000	12,000	24,000
5	50,000	20,000	30,000	–	30,000
6	40,000	16,000	24,000	–	24,000
7	30,000	12,000	18,000	–	18,000
8	20,000	8,000	12,000	–	12,000
9	10,000	4,000	6,000	–	6,000
10	–	–	–	–	–

If the entity pays tax at 30%, the amounts recorded for this transaction during year 1 (assuming that there are sufficient other taxable profits to absorb the tax loss created) would be as follows:

	€
Depreciation of asset	(10,000)
Current tax income[1]	3,600
Deferred tax charge[2]	(1,800)
Net tax credit	1,800
Post tax depreciation	(8,200)

1   €100,000 [cost of asset] × 60% [deductible element] × 20% [tax depreciation rate] × 30% [tax rate]
2   €6,000 [temporary difference] × 30% [tax rate] – brought forward balance [nil]

If this calculation is repeated for all 10 years, the following would be reported in the financial statements.

Year	Depreciation	Current tax credit	Deferred tax (charge)/ credit	Total tax credit	Effective tax rate
	a	b	c	d (=b+c)	e (=d/a)
1	(10,000)	3,600	(1,800)	1,800	18%
2	(10,000)	3,600	(1,800)	1,800	18%
3	(10,000)	3,600	(1,800)	1,800	18%
4	(10,000)	3,600	(1,800)	1,800	18%
5	(10,000)	3,600	(1,800)	1,800	18%
6	(10,000)	–	1,800	1,800	18%
7	(10,000)	–	1,800	1,800	18%
8	(10,000)	–	1,800	1,800	18%
9	(10,000)	–	1,800	1,800	18%
10	(10,000)	–	1,800	1,800	18%

This methodology has the result that, throughout the life of the asset, a consistent tax credit is reported in each period. The effective tax rate in each period corresponds to the effective tax rate for the transaction as a whole – i.e. cost of €100,000 attracting total tax deductions of €18,000 (€60,000 at 30%), an overall rate of 18%.

However, this approach cannot be said to be required by IAS 12 and other methodologies could well be appropriate, provided that they are applied consistently in similar circumstances.

Example 31.17:   Super-deductible asset

The converse situation to that in Example 31.16 exists in some jurisdictions which seek to encourage certain types of investment by giving tax allowances for an amount in excess of the expenditure actually incurred. Suppose that an entity invests $1,000,000 in PP&E with a tax base of $1,200,000 in circumstances where IAS 12 prohibits recognition of deferred tax on the deductible temporary difference of $200,000 arising on initial recognition of the asset. The asset is depreciated to a residual value of zero over 10 years, and qualifies for five annual tax deductions of 20% of its deemed tax cost of $1,200,000.

The methodology we propose in Example 31.16 could be applied 'in reverse' – i.e. with the tax base, rather than the carrying amount, of the asset being apportioned in the ratio 10:2 into a 'cost' element and a 'super deduction' element, and the temporary difference calculated by reference to the 'cost' element as follows.

Year	Book value a	Tax base b	'Super deduction' element c (=2/12 of b)	Cost element d (=10/12 of b)	Temporary difference a – d
0	1,000,000	1,200,000	200,000	1,000,000	–
1	900,000	960,000	160,000	800,000	100,000
2	800,000	720,000	120,000	600,000	200,000
3	700,000	480,000	80,000	400,000	300,000
4	600,000	240,000	40,000	200,000	400,000
5	500,000	–	–	–	500,000
6	400,000	–	–	–	400,000
7	300,000	–	–	–	300,000
8	200,000	–	–	–	200,000
9	100,000	–	–	–	100,000
10	–	–	–	–	–

If the entity pays tax at 30%, the amounts recorded for this transaction during year 1 (assuming that there are sufficient other taxable profits to absorb the tax loss created) would be as follows:

	$
Depreciation of asset	(100,000)
Current tax income[1]	72,000
Deferred tax charge[2]	(30,000)
Net tax credit	42,000
Profit after tax	(58,000)

1   $1,200,000 [deemed tax cost of asset] × 20% [tax depreciation rate] × 30% [tax rate]
2   $100,000 [temporary difference] × 30% [tax rate] – brought forward balance [nil]

If this calculation is repeated for all 10 years, the following would be reported in the financial statements.

Year	Depreciation a	Current tax credit b	Deferred tax (charge)/ credit c	Total tax credit d (=b+c)	Effective tax rate e (=d/a)
1	(100,000)	72,000	(30,000)	42,000	42%
2	(100,000)	72,000	(30,000)	42,000	42%
3	(100,000)	72,000	(30,000)	42,000	42%
4	(100,000)	72,000	(30,000)	42,000	42%
5	(100,000)	72,000	(30,000)	42,000	42%
6	(100,000)	–	30,000	30,000	30%
7	(100,000)	–	30,000	30,000	30%
8	(100,000)	–	30,000	30,000	30%
9	(100,000)	–	30,000	30,000	30%
10	(100,000)	–	30,000	30,000	30%

This results in an effective 42% tax rate for this transaction being reported in years 1 to 5, and a rate of 30% in years 6 to 10, in contrast to the true effective rate of 36% for the transaction as a whole – i.e. cost of $1,000,000 attracting total tax deductions of $360,000 ($1,200,000 at 30%). This is because, whilst in the case of a partially deductible asset as in Example 31.16 above there is an accounting mechanism (i.e. depreciation) for allocating the non-deductible cost on a straight-line basis, in the present case of a super deductible asset there is no ready mechanism for spreading the additional $60,000 tax deductions on a straight-line basis.

In individual cases it might be possible to argue that the additional tax deductions had sufficient of the characteristics of a government grant (e.g. if it were subject to conditions more onerous that those normally associated with tax deductions in the jurisdiction concerned) to allow application of the principles of IAS 20 so as to allocate the additional tax deductions over the life of the asset (see 4.3 above). However, it would be difficult to sustain such an approach as a matter of routine. IAS 12 is fundamentally a balance sheet approach, and a volatile tax rate must sometimes be accepted as an inevitable consequence of that approach.

Again, as in Example 31.16 above, no single approach can be said to be required by IAS 12 and other methodologies could well be appropriate, provided that they are applied consistently in similar circumstances.

7.2.7 Transactions involving the initial recognition of an asset and liability

As noted at 7.2 above, the initial recognition exception is essentially a pragmatic remedy to avoid accounting problems that would arise without it, particularly in transactions where one asset is exchanged for another (such as the acquisition of PP&E for cash).

However, experience has shown that the exception creates new difficulties of its own. In particular, it does not deal adequately with transactions involving the initial recognition of an equal and opposite asset and liability which subsequently unwind on different bases. Examples of such transactions include:

- recording a liability for decommissioning costs, for which the corresponding debit entry is an increase in PP&E (see 7.2.7.A below); and
- the inception of a finance lease by a lessee, which involves the recording of an asset and a corresponding financial liability see (7.2.7.B below).

7.2.7.A Decommissioning costs

The underlying issue is illustrated by the following example.

Example 31.18:   *Asset and liability giving rise to equal temporary differences on initial recognition*

On 1 January 2012 an entity paying tax at 40% recognises a provision for the clean-up costs of a mine that will require expenditure of €10 million at the end of 2016. A tax deduction for the expenditure will be given when it is incurred (i.e. as a reduction in the current tax liability for 2016).

In accordance with IAS 37, this provision is discounted (at a rate of 6%) to €7.5m, giving rise to the following accounting entry (see Chapter 29 at 5.5):

	€m	€m
PP&E	7.5	
Provision for clean-up costs		7.5

On initial recognition, the tax base of the PP&E is nil, since no deductions are available as it is recovered through future taxable profit of €7.5 million. The tax base of the provision is also nil (carrying amount of €7.5 million, less the amount deductible in future periods, also €7.5 million). Although deductions of €10 million are expected to be received, if the liability were settled at its carrying amount of €7.5 million, a deduction of only €7.5 million would be received – see 8.3.2.below.

There is therefore a taxable temporary difference of €7.5 million associated with the PP&E and a deductible temporary difference of the same amount associated with the provision. However, the initial recognition exception in IAS 12 prohibits recognition of deferred tax on either temporary difference.

Over the next five years an expense of €10 million (equivalent to the ultimate cash spend) will be recognised in profit or loss, comprising depreciation of the €7.5 million PP&E and accretion of €2.5 million finance costs on the provision. Given that this €10 million is fully tax-deductible, it would seem reasonable for the income statement to reflect €4 million of deferred tax credits over this period, giving rise to an effective tax rate of 40% in each period. However, the result is somewhat different.

Under the general approach of IAS 12 summarised in 7.2.4 above, the depreciation of the PP&E is regarded as reducing the temporary difference arising on initial recognition of the asset, and therefore gives rise to no tax effect. However, the accretion of €2.5 finance costs on the provision gives rise to an additional temporary difference arising after initial recognition, requiring recognition of a deferred tax asset (assuming that the general recognition criteria for assets are met – see 7.5 below). This gives rise to the following overall accounting entries for the year ended 31 December 2012.

	€m	€m
2012		
Depreciation (€7.5m ÷ 5)	1.50	
PP&E		1.50
Finance cost (€7.5m × 6%)	0.45	
Provision for clean-up costs		0.45
Deferred tax (balance sheet)	0.18	
Deferred tax (profit or loss) (40% × €0.45m)		0.18

If equivalent entries are made for the following periods, the following amounts will be included in subsequent income statements (all figures in € millions):

	2012	2013	2014	2015	2016	Total
Depreciation	1.50	1.50	1.50	1.50	1.50	7.50
Finance costs	0.45	0.47	0.50	0.53	0.55	2.50
Cost before tax	1.95	1.97	2.00	2.03	2.05	10.00
Current tax (income)					(4.00)	(4.00)
Deferred tax (income)/charge[1]	(0.18)	(0.19)	(0.20)	(0.21)	0.78	–
Cost after tax	1.77	1.78	1.80	1.82	(1.17)	6.00
Effective tax rate	9.2%	9.6%	10.0%	10.3%	157.1%	40.0%

1   In years 2012-2015 40% × finance cost for period. In 2016, reversal of cumulative deferred tax asset recognised in previous periods.

Absent the initial recognition exception, the entity would, on initial recognition of the provision and the addition to PP&E, establish a deferred tax asset of €3 million in respect of the provision (€7.5m @ 40%) and an equal liability in respect of the asset. This would result in the following amounts being included in subsequent income statements (all figures in € millions):

	2012	2013	2014	2015	2016	Total
Depreciation	1.50	1.50	1.50	1.50	1.50	7.50
Finance costs	0.45	0.47	0.50	0.53	0.55	2.50
Cost before tax	1.95	1.97	2.00	2.03	2.05	10.00
Current tax (income)					(4.00)	(4.00)
Deferred tax (income)/charge[1]	(0.78)	(0.79)	(0.80)	(0.81)	3.18	–
Cost after tax	1.17	1.18	1.20	1.22	1.23	6.00
Effective tax rate	40.0%	40.0%	40.0%	40.0%	40.0%	40.0%

1   In 2012 reduction in deferred tax liability in respect of PP&E €0.6m (€1.5m @ 40%) and increase in asset in respect of provision €0.18m (€0.45m @ 40%) – similarly for 2013-2015. The charge in 2016 represents the release of the remaining net deferred tax asset (equal to cumulative income statement credits in 2012-2015).

It is not clear that the accounting treatment strictly required by IAS 12, with its widely fluctuating effective tax rates – resulting in a post-tax profit in 2016 for what is in reality a post-tax loss-making transaction – appropriately reflects the economic reality that all expenditure is ultimately eligible for tax deductions at the standard rate of 40%. Indeed, it could be argued that the more realistic alternative treatment set out above is consistent with the underlying intention of the initial recognition exception (that the reporting entity should provide for deferred tax on initial recognition unless to do so would create an immediate net tax expense or credit in the statement of comprehensive income). That implied intention of the exception would not be breached by providing for deferred tax on initial recognition in such cases.

7.2.7.B   *Finance leases taxed as operating leases*

In a number of jurisdictions, tax deductions are given for finance leases as if they were operating leases (i.e. on the basis of lease payments made). The total cost for both accounting and tax purposes is obviously the same over the period of the lease, but for accounting purposes the cost comprises depreciation of the asset together with finance costs on the lease liability, rather than the cash paid, which is treated as a balance sheet movement. Strict application of the initial recognition exception will therefore lead to a result similar to that in set out the first table in Example 31.18 above.

That leads some to argue that, given that the asset and liability recognised at the inception of a finance lease (or on establishment of a decommissioning provision) are a single transaction, they should be regarded as effectively giving rise to a single (net) temporary difference of zero. This means that, as and when (net) temporary differences emerge after initial recognition, deferred tax may be recognised on those temporary differences, with the effect that the effective tax rate in the income statement reflects the statutory rate actually applicable to the transaction as a whole (as illustrated in the second table in Example 31.18 above).

Those who take this view might also argue that it is consistent with the implied, if not explicit, intention of the initial recognition exception that deferred tax should always be recognised unless it creates a 'day one' tax charge or credit in the statement of comprehensive income.

Others argue that this approach is not acceptable. The financial statements present a clearly separate asset and liability which do not meet any offset criteria. The initial recognition exception should therefore be applied to the asset and liability separately and not as if the two comprised some form of single net asset or liability.

The Interpretations Committee considered this issue on two occasions in 2005. *IFRIC Update* for April 2005 appeared to support the latter view:

> 'The [Interpretations Committee] noted that initial recognition exemption applies to each separate recognised element in the balance sheet, and no deferred tax asset or liability should be recognised on the temporary difference existing on the initial recognition of assets and liabilities arising from finance leases or subsequently.'[13]

However, only two months later, the Committee added:

> 'The [Interpretations Committee] considered the treatment of deferred tax relating to assets and liabilities arising from finance leases.
>
> While noting that there is diversity in practice in applying the requirements of IAS 12 to assets and liabilities arising from finance leases, the [Interpretations

Committee] agreed not to develop any guidance because the issue falls directly within the scope of the Board's short-term convergence project on income taxes with the FASB.'[14]

This appears to indicate that, whilst the Interpretations Committee regards the analysis that the asset and lease liability must be considered separately as consistent with the letter of IAS 12 as drafted, it accepts the alternative approach.

7.2.8 Initial recognition of compound financial instruments by the issuer

IAS 32 requires 'compound' financial instruments (those with both a liability feature and an equity feature, such as convertible bonds) to be accounted for by the issuer using so-called split accounting. This is discussed in more detail in Chapter 45 at 6, but in essence an entity is required to split the proceeds of issue of such an instrument (say €1 million) into a liability component, measured at its fair value based on real market rates for non-convertible debt rather than the nominal rate on the bond (say €750,000), with the balance being treated as an equity component (in this case €250,000).

Over the life of the instrument, the €750,000 carrying value of the liability element will be accreted back up to €1,000,000 (or such lower or higher sum as might be potentially repayable), so that the cumulative income statement interest charge will comprise:

(a) any actual cash interest payments made (which are tax-deductible in most jurisdictions); and

(b) the €250,000 accretion of the liability from €750,000 to €1,000,000 (which is not tax-deductible in most jurisdictions).

Where such an instrument is issued, IAS 12 requires the treatment in Example 31.19 to be adopted.[15]

Example 31.19: Compound financial instrument

An entity issues a zero-coupon convertible loan of €1,000,000 on 1 January 2012 repayable at par on 1 January 2015. In accordance with IAS 32, the entity classifies the instrument's liability component as a liability and the equity component as equity. The entity assigns an initial carrying amount of €750,000 to the liability component of the convertible loan and €250,000 to the equity component. Subsequently, the entity recognises the imputed discount of €250,000 as interest expense at the effective annual rate of 10% on the carrying amount of the liability component at the beginning of the year. The tax authorities do not allow the entity to claim any deduction for the imputed discount on the liability component of the convertible loan. The tax rate is 40%.

Temporary differences arise on the liability element as follows (all figures in € thousands).

	1.1.12	31.12.13	31.12.14	31.12.14
Carrying value of liability component[1]	750	825	908	1,000
Tax base	1,000	1,000	1,000	1,000
Taxable temporary difference	250	175	92	–
Deferred tax liability @ 40%	100	70	37	–

1 Figures for 2012-2014 = balance carried forward at end of previous period plus 10% accretion of notional interest.

The deferred tax arising at 1 January 2012 is deducted from equity. Subsequent reductions in the deferred tax balance are recognised in the income statement, resulting in an effective tax rate of

40%. For example, in 2013, the entity will accrete notional interest of €75,000 (closing loan liability €825,000 less opening balance €750,000) with deferred tax income of €30,000 (closing deferred tax liability €70,000 less opening liability €100,000).

Whilst this treatment is explicitly required by IAS 12, its conceptual basis is far from clear, and causes some confusion in practice. In the first instance, it apparently contravenes the prohibition on recognition of deferred tax on temporary differences arising on the initial recognition of assets and liabilities (other than in a business combination) that do not give rise to accounting or taxable profit or loss. IAS 12 argues that this temporary difference does not arise on initial recognition of a liability but as a result of the initial recognition of the equity component as a result of split accounting. *[IAS 12.23]*.

Even if this analysis is accepted, it remains unclear why the deferred tax should be deducted from equity. It may have been seen as an application of the general allocation principle of IAS 12 that the tax effects of transactions accounted for in equity should also be accounted for in equity – see 10 below. However, this would have been correct only if the accounting entry giving rise to the liability had been:

DR	Equity	€750,000	
	CR	Liability	€750,000

The actual entry was:

DR	Cash	€1,000,000	
	CR	Liability	€750,000
	CR	Equity	€250,000

Therefore, in fact the general allocation rule in IAS 12 would have required the deferred tax liability to be recognised as a charge to profit or loss. This would have resulted in a 'day one' tax expense, suggesting that that initial recognition exception ought, in principle, to have been applied here also.

The accounting treatment required by Example 31.19 above could be seen as no more than 'tax equalisation' accounting – i.e. the recognition of deferred tax of an amount that, when released to profit or loss, will yield an effective tax rate equivalent to the statutory rate. Some would question whether it is appropriate to represent as tax-deductible a charge to the income statement that in reality is not tax-deductible. Nevertheless, as noted above, this treatment is explicitly required by IAS 12.

7.2.9 Acquisition of subsidiary not accounted for as a business combination

Occasionally, an entity may acquire a subsidiary which is accounted for as the acquisition of an asset rather than as a business combination. This will be most often be the case where the subsidiary concerned is a 'single asset entity' holding a single item of property, plant and equipment which is not considered to comprise a business. Where an asset is acquired in such circumstances, the initial recognition exception applies, but there is room for debate as to the extent to which it applies, as illustrated by the following example.

Example 31.20:   Acquired subsidiary accounted for as asset purchase

An entity (P) acquires a subsidiary (S), whose only asset is a property, for $10 million. The transaction is accounted for as the acquisition of a property rather than as a business combination. The tax base of the property is $4 million and its carrying value in the financial statements of S (under IFRS) is $6 million. The taxable temporary difference of $2 million in the financial records of S arose after the initial recognition by S of the property, and accordingly a deferred tax liability of $800,000 has been recognised by S at its tax rate of 40%.

The question then arises as to whether any deferred tax should be recognised for the property in the financial statements of P.

One view would be that the initial recognition exception applies to the entire $6 million difference between the carrying value of the property of $10 million and its tax base of $4 million, in exactly the same way as if the property had been legally acquired as a separate asset rather than through acquisition of the shares of S. Under this approach, no deferred tax is recognised by P in respect of the property at the time of acquisition.

An alternative view might be that, although the acquisition of S is being treated as an asset acquisition rather than a business combination under IFRS 3, IAS 27 still requires P to consolidate S, and therefore to record the assets and liabilities (according to IFRS) of S in its consolidated financial statements. The deferred tax of $800,000 recognised by S should therefore be included in the financial statements of P. Under this approach, at the time of acquisition, the initial recognition exception applies only to the valuation uplift from $6 million to $10 million.

In our view, either analysis is acceptable, but should be applied consistently to similar transactions.

7.3   Assets carried at fair value or revalued amount

IAS 12 notes that certain IFRSs permit or require assets to be carried at fair value or to be revalued. These include:

* IAS 16 – *Property, Plant and Equipment*
* IAS 38 – *Intangible Assets*
* IAS 39 – *Financial Instruments: Recognition and Measurement*
* IAS 40 – *Investment Property*.

In most jurisdictions, the revaluation or restatement of an asset does not affect taxable profit in the period of the revaluation or restatement. Nevertheless, the future recovery of the carrying amount will result in a taxable flow of economic benefits to the entity and the amount that will be deductible for tax purposes (i.e. the original tax base) will differ from the amount of those economic benefits.

The difference between the carrying amount of a revalued asset and its tax base is a temporary difference and gives rise to a deferred tax liability or asset. IAS 12 clarifies that this is the case even if:

* the entity does not intend to dispose of the asset. In such cases, the revalued carrying amount of the asset will be recovered through use and this will generate taxable income which exceeds the depreciation that will be allowable for tax purposes in future periods; or
* tax on capital gains is deferred if the proceeds of the disposal of the asset are invested in similar assets. In such cases, the tax will ultimately become payable on sale or use of the similar assets. *[IAS 12.20]*. A discussion of the accounting for deferred taxable gains may be found at 7.7 below.

In some jurisdictions, the revaluation or other restatement of an asset to fair value affects taxable profit (tax loss) for the current period. In such cases, the tax base of the asset may be raised by amount equivalent to the revaluation gain, so that no temporary difference arises.

7.4 Restrictions on recognition of deferred tax assets

There is an essential difference between deferred tax liabilities and deferred tax assets. An entity's deferred tax liabilities will crystallise if the entity recovers its existing net assets at their carrying amount. However, in order to realise its net deferred tax assets in full, an entity must earn profits in excess of those represented by the carrying amount of its net assets in order to generate sufficient taxable profits against which the deductions represented by deferred tax assets can be offset. Accordingly IAS 12 restricts the recognition of deferred tax assets to the extent that it is probable that taxable profit will be available against which the underlying deductible temporary differences can be utilised. *[IAS 12.27]*.

7.4.1 Sources of 'probable' future taxable profit

It is 'probable' that there will be sufficient taxable profit if a deferred tax asset can be offset against a deferred tax liability relating to the same tax authority which will reverse in the same period as the asset, or in a period into which a loss arising from the asset may be carried back or forward. *[IAS 12.28]*. Any deferred tax liability used as the basis for recognising a deferred tax asset must represent a future tax liability against which the future tax deduction represented by the deferred tax asset can actually be offset. For example, in a tax jurisdiction where revenue and capital items are treated separately for tax purposes, a deferred tax asset representing a capital loss cannot be recognised by reference to a deferred tax liability relating to PP&E against which the capital loss could never be offset in a tax return.

Where there are insufficient deferred tax liabilities relating to the same tax authority to offset a deferred tax asset, the asset should be recognised to the extent that:

- it is probable that in future periods there will be sufficient taxable profits:
  - relating to the same tax authority;
  - relating to the same taxable entity; and
  - arising in the same period as the reversal of the deductible temporary difference or in a period into which a loss arising from the deferred tax asset may be carried back or forward – see also 7.4.2 below; or
- tax planning opportunities are available that will create taxable profit in appropriate periods – see 7.4.3 below. *[IAS 12.29]*.

Where an entity has a history of recent losses it should also consider the guidance in IAS 12 for recognition of such losses (see 7.4.4 below). *[IAS 12.31]*.

7.4.2   Future deductible temporary differences ignored

In assessing the availability of future taxable profits, an entity must ignore taxable profits arising from deductible temporary differences expected to originate in future periods. This is because those new deductible differences will themselves require future taxable profit in order to be utilised. *[IAS 12.29].*

For example, suppose that in 2012 an entity charges £100 to profit or loss for which a tax deduction is received in 2013. However, in 2013 a further £100 is charged to profit or loss, for which a deduction is made only in 2014, and so on for the foreseeable future. This will have the effect that, in 2012, the entity will pay tax on the £100 for which no deduction is made on the 2012 tax return. In the tax return for 2013, there will be a deduction for that £100, but this will be offset by the add-back in the same tax return for the equivalent £100 charged for accounting purposes in 2012. If this cycle of '£100 deduction less £100 add-back' is perpetuated in each tax return for the foreseeable future, there is never any real recovery of the tax paid on the £100 in 2012.

7.4.3   Tax planning opportunities

'Tax planning opportunities' are actions that the entity would take in order to create or increase taxable income in a particular period before the expiry of a tax loss or tax credit carryforward. IAS 12 notes that, in some jurisdictions, taxable profit may be created or increased by:

- electing to have interest income taxed on either a received or receivable basis;
- deferring the claim for certain deductions from taxable profit;
- selling, and perhaps leasing back, assets that have appreciated but for which the tax base has not been adjusted to reflect such appreciation; and
- selling an asset that generates non-taxable income (such as, in some jurisdictions, a government bond) in order to purchase another investment that generates taxable income.

Where tax planning opportunities advance taxable profit from a later period to an earlier period, the utilisation of a tax loss or tax credit carryforward still depends on the existence of future taxable profit from sources other than future originating temporary differences. *[IAS 12.30].*

The requirement to have regard to future tax planning opportunities applies only to the measurement of deferred tax assets. It does not apply to the measurement of deferred tax liabilities. Thus, for example, it would not be open to an entity subject to tax at 30% to argue that it should provide for deferred tax liabilities at some lower rate on the grounds that it intends to invest in assets attracting investment tax credits that will allow it to pay tax at that lower rate (see 8.3.1 below).

IAS 12 describes tax planning opportunities as actions that the entity 'would' take – not those it 'could' take. In other words, they are restricted to future courses of action that the entity would actually undertake to realise such a deferred tax asset, and do not include actions that are theoretically possible but practically implausible, such as the sale of an asset essential to the ongoing operations of the entity.

Chapter 31

Implementation of a tax planning opportunity may well entail significant direct costs or the loss of other tax benefits or both. Accordingly, any deferred tax asset recognised on the basis of a tax planning opportunity must be reduced by any cost of implementing that opportunity (measured, where applicable, on an after-tax basis).

Moreover, IAS 12 regards tax planning opportunities as a component of future net taxable profits. Thus, where a tax planning opportunity exists, but the entity is expected to remain loss-making (such that the opportunity effectively will simply reduce future tax losses), we believe that such an opportunity does not generally form the basis for recognising a deferred tax asset, except to the extent that it will create *net* future taxable profits (see also 7.4.4 below).

7.4.3.A   Available-for-sale debt securities

At its meeting in May 2010 the Interpretations Committee considered a request for guidance on the recognition of a deferred tax asset relating to an unrealised loss on available-for-sale ('AFS') debt securities. The request asked:

- whether an entity's ability and intent to hold the AFS debt securities until the unrealised losses reverse is a tax planning opportunity; and, if so
- whether recognition of a deferred tax asset relating to the unrealised loss can be assessed separately from other deferred tax assets.

Both views are accepted under US GAAP.

The Committee noted that the objective of IAS 12 focuses on the recovery of the carrying amount of an asset at the reporting date (see 2.1 above). The Committee also noted that an entity's intention to hold AFS debt securities to maturity does not represent a tax planning opportunity. In addition, the Committee noted that IAS 12 requires an entity to assess the probability of realising deferred tax assets on a combined basis.

Accordingly, the Committee tentatively concluded that IAS 12 provides sufficient guidance on the recognition of deferred tax assets and decided not to add this issue to its agenda.

Over the next few months, the Interpretations Committee considered responses received on this tentative agenda decision and discussions held by the Committee's staff with some of the respondents. The Committee has requested its staff to prepare further analysis, including consideration of clarifying IAS 12 to address the issue specifically.[16]

7.4.4   Unused tax losses and unused tax credits

A deferred tax asset should be recognised for the carryforward of unused tax losses and unused tax credits to the extent that it is probable that future taxable profit will be available against which the unused tax losses and unused tax credits can be utilised. *[IAS 12.34].*

The criteria for recognition are essentially the same as those for deductible temporary differences, as set out in 7.4.1 to 7.4.3 above. However, IAS 12 emphasises that the existence of unused tax losses is strong evidence that taxable profits (other than those represented by deferred tax liabilities) may not be available. Therefore, an entity with a history of recent losses recognises a deferred tax asset arising from unused tax losses or tax credits only to the extent that:

- it has sufficient taxable temporary differences; or
- there is other convincing evidence that sufficient taxable profit will be available against which the unused tax losses or unused tax credits can be utilised by the entity.

IAS 12 requires disclosure in respect of losses recognised in the circumstances in the last bullet above (see 14.3 below). *[IAS 12.35].*

Additionally, the entity should consider whether:

- the entity has sufficient taxable temporary differences relating to the same taxation authority and the same taxable entity, which will result in taxable amounts against which the unused tax losses or unused tax credits can be utilised before they expire;
- the entity will have taxable profits before the unused tax losses or unused tax credits expire;
- whether the unused tax losses result from identifiable causes which are unlikely to recur; and
- whether tax planning opportunities (see 7.4.3 above) are available to the entity that will create taxable profit in the period in which the unused tax losses or unused tax credits can be utilised.

To the extent that it is not probable that taxable profit will be available against which the unused tax losses or unused tax credits can be utilised, a deferred tax asset is not recognised. *[IAS 12.36].*

IAS 12 does not provide more specific guidance on the assessment of the availability of future taxable profits, and the Interpretations Committee has resisted calls for such guidance.[17] However, it would clearly be appropriate to give more weight to (say) revenues from existing orders and contracts than to those from merely anticipated future trading.

Some have suggested that the IASB should set time limits on the foresight period used, as has been done by some national standard setters. We consider that such generalised guidance would be inappropriate, particularly in the context of an international standard, which must address the great variety of tax systems that exist worldwide, and which impose a wide range of restrictions on the carryforward of tax assets. In any event, it may well be the case that a deferred tax asset recoverable in twenty years from profits from a currently existing long-term supply contract with a creditworthy customer may be more robust than one recoverable in one year from expected future trading by a start-up company.

A deferred tax asset can be recovered only out of future *taxable* profit. Evidence of future accounting profit is not necessarily evidence of future taxable profit (for example, if significant tax deductions or credits not reflected in the accounting profit are likely to be claimed by the entity in the relevant future periods).

7.4.5   *Re-assessment of deferred tax assets*

An entity must review its deferred tax assets, both recognised and unrecognised, at each reporting date.

7.4.5.A   *Previously recognised assets*

An entity should reduce the carrying amount of a deferred tax asset to the extent that it is no longer probable that sufficient taxable profit will be available to enable the asset to be recovered. Any such reduction should be reversed if it subsequently becomes probable that sufficient taxable profit will be available. *[IAS 12.56].*

7.4.5.B   *Previously unrecognised assets*

An entity recognises a previously unrecognised deferred tax asset to the extent that it has become probable that sufficient taxable profit will be available to enable the asset to be recovered. For example, an improvement in trading conditions may make it more probable that the entity will be able to generate sufficient taxable profit in the future for the deferred tax asset to meet the recognition criteria. Special considerations apply when an entity re-appraises deferred tax assets of an acquired business at the date of the business combination or subsequently (see 12.1.2 below). *[IAS 12.37].*

7.5   'Outside' temporary differences relating to subsidiaries, branches, associates and joint ventures

Investments in subsidiaries branches and associates or interests in joint ventures can give rise to two types of temporary difference:

* Differences between the tax base of the investment or interest – typically the original cost of the equity held in that investment or interest – and its carrying amount. 'Carrying amount' in this context means

    * in separate financial statements, the carrying amount of the relevant investment or interest, and

    * in financial statements other than separate financial statements, the carrying amount of the net assets (including goodwill) relating to the relevant investment or interest, whether accounted for by consolidation, proportionate consolidation or equity accounting.

    These differences are generally referred to in practice as 'outside' temporary differences, and normally arise in the tax jurisdiction of the entity that holds the equity in the investment or interest.

* In financial statements other than separate financial statements, differences between the tax bases of the individual assets and liabilities of the investment or interest and the carrying amounts of those assets and liabilities (as included in those financial statements through consolidation, proportionate consolidation, or equity accounting).

    These differences are generally referred to in practice as 'inside' temporary differences, and normally arise in the tax jurisdiction of the investment or interest.

This section is concerned with 'outside' temporary differences, the most common source of which is the undistributed profits of the investee entities, where distribution to the investor would trigger a tax liability. 'Outside' temporary differences may also arise from a change in the carrying value of an investment due to exchange movements, provisions, or revaluations.

The reversal of most 'inside' temporary differences is essentially inevitable as assets are recovered or liabilities settled at their carrying amount in the normal course of business. However, an entity may be able to postpone the reversal of some or all of its 'outside' differences more or less permanently. For example, if a distribution of the retained profits of a subsidiary would be subject to withholding tax, the parent may effectively be able to avoid such a tax by making the subsidiary reinvest all its profits into the business. IAS 12 recognises this essential difference in the nature of 'outside' and 'inside' temporary differences by setting different criteria for the recognition of 'outside' temporary differences.

7.5.1   Calculation of 'outside' temporary differences

As noted above, 'outside' temporary differences arise in both consolidated and separate financial statements and may well be different, due to the different bases used to account for subsidiaries, branches and associates or interests in joint ventures in consolidated and separate financial statements. *[IAS 12.38]*. This is illustrated by Example 31.21 below.

Example 31.21:   Temporary differences associated with subsidiaries, branches, associates and joint ventures

On 1 January 2012 entity H acquired 100% of the shares of entity S, whose functional currency is different from that of H, for €600m. The tax rate in H's tax jurisdiction is 30% and the tax rate in S's tax jurisdiction is 40%.

The fair value of the identifiable assets and liabilities (excluding deferred tax assets and liabilities) of S acquired by H is set out in the following table, together with their tax base in S's tax jurisdiction and the resulting temporary differences (all figures in € millions).

	Fair value	Tax base	(Taxable)/ deductible temporary difference
PP&E	270	155	(115)
Accounts receivable	210	210	–
Inventory	174	124	(50)
Retirement benefit obligations	(30)	–	30
Accounts payable	(120)	(120)	–
Fair value of net assets acquired excluding deferred tax	504	369	(135)
Deferred tax (135 @ 40%)	(54)		
Fair value of identifiable assets acquired and liabilities assumed	450		
Goodwill (balancing figure)	150		
Carrying amount	600		

No deferred tax is recognised on the goodwill, in accordance with the requirements of IAS 12 as discussed at 7.2.2 A above.

At the date of combination, the tax base, in H's tax jurisdiction, of H's investment in S is €600 million. Therefore, in H's jurisdiction, no temporary difference is associated with the investment, either in the consolidated financial statements of H (where the investment is represented by net assets and goodwill of €600 million), or in its separate financial statements, if prepared (where the investment is shown as an investment at cost of €600 million).

During 2012:

- S makes a profit after tax, as reported in H's consolidated financial statements, of €150 million, of which €80 million is paid as a dividend (after deduction of withholding tax) before 31 December 2011, leaving a net retained profit of €70 million.

- In accordance with IAS 21 – *The Effects of Changes in Foreign Exchange Rates*, H's consolidated financial statements record a loss of €15 million on retranslation to the closing exchange rate of S's opening net assets and profit for the period.

- In accordance with IAS 36 – *Impairment of Assets*, H's consolidated financial statements record an impairment loss of €10 million in respect of goodwill.

Thus in H's consolidated financial statements the carrying value of its investment in S is €645 million, comprising:

	€m
Carrying amount at 1.1.2012	600
Retained profit	70
Exchange loss	(15)
Impairment of goodwill	(10)
Carrying amount at 31.12.2012	645

7.5.1.A   Consolidated financial statements

Assuming that the tax base in H's jurisdiction remains €600 million, there is a taxable temporary difference of €45 million (carrying amount €645m less tax base €600m) associated with S in H's consolidated financial statements. Whether or not any deferred tax is required to be provided for on this difference is determined in accordance with the principles discussed in 7.5.2 below. Any tax provided for would be allocated to profit or loss, other comprehensive income or equity in accordance with the general provisions of IAS 12 (see 10 below). Irrespective of whether provision is made for deferred tax, H would be required to make disclosures in respect of this difference (see 14.2.2 below).

7.5.1.B   Separate financial statements

The amount of any temporary difference in H's separate financial statements would depend on the accounting policy adopted in those statements. IAS 27 – *Consolidated and Separate Financial Statements* – allows entities the choice of accounting for investments in group companies at either cost (less impairment) or at fair value – see Chapter 9 at 2. Suppose that, notwithstanding the impairment of goodwill required to be recognised in the consolidated financial statements, the investment in S taken as a whole is not impaired, and indeed its fair value at 31 December 2012 is €660 million.

If, in its separate financial statements, H accounts for its investment at cost of €600 million, there would be no temporary difference associated with S in H's separate financial statements, since the carrying amount and tax base of S would both be €600 million.

If, however, in its separate financial statements, H accounts for its investment at its fair value of €660 million, there would be a taxable temporary difference of €60 million (carrying amount €660m less tax base €600m) associated with S in H's separate financial statements. Whether or not any deferred tax is required to be provided for on this difference is determined in accordance with the principles discussed in 7.5.2 below. Any tax provided for would be allocated to profit or loss, other comprehensive income or equity in accordance with the general provisions of IAS 12 (see 10 below). Irrespective of whether provision is made for deferred tax, H would be required to make disclosures in respect of this difference (see 14.2 below).

7.5.2   *Taxable temporary differences*

IAS 12 requires a deferred tax liability to be recognised for all taxable temporary differences associated with investments (both domestic and foreign) in subsidiaries, branches and associates or interests in joint ventures, unless:

(a)   the parent, investor or venturer is able to control the timing of the reversal of the temporary difference; and

(b)   it is probable that the temporary difference will not reverse in the foreseeable future. *[IAS 12.39].*

IAS 12 does not currently define the meaning of 'probable' in this context. However, we consider that, as in other IFRS, it should be taken to mean 'more likely than not'. IAS 12 also does not elaborate on the meaning of 'foreseeable'. In our view, the period used will be a matter of judgment in individual circumstances.

What this means in practice is best illustrated by reference to its application to the retained earnings of subsidiaries, branches and joint ventures on the one hand, and those of associates on the other.

In the case of a subsidiary or a branch, the parent is able to control when and whether the retained earnings are distributed. Therefore, no provision need be made for the tax consequences of distribution of profits that the parent has determined will not be distributed in the foreseeable future. *[IAS 12.40].* In the case of a joint venture, provided that the investor can control the distribution policy, similar considerations apply. *[IAS 12.43].*

In the case of an associate, however, the investor cannot control distribution policy. Therefore provision should be made for the tax consequences of the distribution of the retained earnings of an associate, except to the extent that there is a shareholders' agreement that those earnings will not be distributed.

Some might consider this a counter-intuitive result. In reality, it is extremely unusual for any entity (other than one set up for a specific project) to pursue a policy of full distribution. To the extent that it occurs at all, it is much more likely in a wholly-owned subsidiary than in an associate; and yet IAS 12 effectively treats full distribution by associates as the norm and that by subsidiaries as the exception. Moreover, it seems to ignore the fact that equity accounting was developed as a regulatory response to the perceived ability of investors in associates to exert some degree of control over the amount and timing of dividends from them. This is discussed further in the introduction to Chapter 12.

In some jurisdictions, some or all of the temporary differences associated with such investments in subsidiaries, branches and associates or interests in joint ventures differences are crystallised on disposal of that investment or interest. Clearly, where the entity is contemplating such a disposal, it would no longer be able to assert that it is probable that the relevant temporary difference will not reverse in the foreseeable future.

The measurement of any deferred tax liability recognised is discussed at 8.3.8 below.

7.5.3   Deductible temporary differences

IAS 12 requires a deferred tax asset to be recognised for all deductible temporary differences associated with investments in subsidiaries, branches and associates or interests in joint ventures, only to the extent that it is probable that:

(a)   the temporary difference will reverse in the foreseeable future; and

(b)   taxable profit will be available against which the temporary difference can be utilised. *[IAS 12.44]*.

IAS 12 does not currently define the meaning of 'probable' in this context. However, we consider that, as in other IFRS, it should be taken to mean 'more likely than not'.

The guidance discussed in 7.4 above is used to determine whether or not a deferred tax asset can be recognised for such deductible temporary differences. *[IAS 12.45]*.

Any analysis of whether a deductible temporary difference gives rise to an asset must presumably make the same distinction between controlled and non-controlled entities as is required when assessing whether a taxable temporary difference gives rise to a liability (see 7.5.2 above). This may mean, in practical terms, that it is never possible to recognise a deferred tax asset in respect of a non-controlled investment (such as an associate), unless either the investee entity is committed to a course of action that would realise the asset or, where the asset can be realised by disposal, that it is probable that the reporting entity will undertake such a disposal.

The measurement of any deferred tax asset recognised is discussed at 8.3.9 below.

7.5.4   Anticipated intragroup dividends in future periods

Under IAS 10 – *Events after the Reporting Period* – and IAS 18, a dividend may be recognised as a liability of the paying entity and revenue of the receiving entity only when it has been declared by the paying entity. This raises the question of when a reporting entity should account for the tax consequences of a dividend expected to be paid by a subsidiary out of its retained profits as at the reporting date.

7.5.4.A   Consolidated financial statements of receiving entity

In our view, IAS 12 requires the group to make provision for the taxes payable on the retained profits of the group as at each reporting date based on the best evidence available to it at the reporting date. In other words, if in preparing its financial statements for 31 December 2012, an entity believes that, in order to meet the dividend expectations of its shareholders in 2013 and 2014, it will have to cause the retained earnings of certain overseas subsidiaries (as included in the group accounts at 31 December 2012) to be distributed, the group should provide for any tax consequences of such distributions in its consolidated financial statements for the period ended 31 December 2012.

It is not relevant that such dividends have not yet been recognised in the separate financial statements of the relevant members of the group. Indeed, such intragroup dividends will never be recognised in the group financial statements, as they will be eliminated on consolidation. What IAS 12 requires is a best estimate of the taxes ultimately payable on the net assets of the group as at 31 December 2012. However, for this reason it would not be appropriate to recognise any liability for the tax anticipated to be paid out of an intragroup dividend in a future period that is likely to be covered by profits made in *future* periods, since such profits do not form part of the net assets of the group as at 31 December 2012.

7.5.4.B   Separate financial statements of paying entity

Irrespective of whether a provision is made in the consolidated financial statements for the tax effects of an expected future intragroup dividend of the retained earnings of a subsidiary, the paying subsidiary would not recognise a liability for the tax effects of any distribution in its individual or separate financial statements until the liability to pay the dividend was recognised in those individual or separate financial statements.

7.5.5   Unpaid intragroup interest, royalties, management charges etc.

It is common for groups of companies to access the earnings of subsidiaries not only through distribution by way of dividend, but also by levying charges on subsidiaries such as interest, royalties or general management charges for central corporate services. In practice, such charges are often not settled but left outstanding on the intercompany account between the subsidiary and the parent. In some jurisdictions such income is taxed only on receipt.

This has led some to argue that, where settlement of such balances is within the control of the reporting entity, and it can be demonstrated that there is no foreseeable intention or need to settle such balances, such balances are economically equivalent to unremitted earnings, so that there is no need to provide for the tax consequences of settlement.

In February 2003 the Interpretations Committee considered the issue and indicated that it believes that the exemption from provision for deferred taxes on 'outside' temporary differences arising from subsidiaries, branches, associates and interests in joint ventures is intended to address the temporary differences arising from the undistributed earnings of such entities. The exception does not apply to the 'inside' temporary differences that exist between the carrying amount and the tax base of individual assets and liabilities within the subsidiary, branch, associate or interest in joint venture. Accordingly, the Interpretations Committee concluded that a deferred tax liability should be provided for the tax consequences of settling unpaid intragroup charges.[18]

7.5.6   Other overseas income taxed only on remittance

In May 2007 the Interpretations Committee considered the more general issue of whether deferred taxes should be recognised in respect of temporary differences arising because foreign income is not taxable unless it is remitted to the entity's home jurisdiction.

The Interpretations Committee resolved not to add this issue to its agenda, but to draw it to the attention of the IASB. This decision reflected the status of the IASB's project on income taxes (see 15 below) at that time – particularly the Board's decision to eliminate the notion of a 'branch'.[19]

7.6 'Tax-transparent' ('flow-through') entities

In many tax jurisdictions certain entities are not taxed in their own right. Instead the income of such entities is taxed in the hands of their owners as if it were income of the owners. An example might be a partnership which does not itself pay tax, but whose partners each pay tax on their share of the partnership's profits. Such entities are sometimes referred to as 'tax-transparent' or 'flow-through' entities.

The tax status of such an entity is of no particular relevance to the accounting treatment, in the investor's financial statements, of the tax paid on the income of the entity. An investor in such an entity will determine whether the entity is a subsidiary, associate, joint venture, branch or a financial asset investment and account for it accordingly. The investor then account for its own current tax payable as it arises in the normal way.

The investor will also determine whether the basis on which the investment has been accounted for (e.g. through consolidation, proportionate consolidation or equity accounting) has led to the recognition of assets or liabilities which give rise to temporary differences and recognise deferred tax on these in the normal way.

Finally, the investor will also determine whether there are 'outside' temporary differences associated with the investment as a whole and account for these as above.

Examples 31.22 and 31.23 illustrate the accounting treatment for, respectively, a consolidated and an equity-accounted tax-transparent entity.

Example 31.22: Tax-transparent entity (consolidated)

An entity (A) acquires 60% of a tax-transparent partnership (P) for $100 million in a transaction accounted for as a business combination. The aggregate fair value of the identifiable net assets of the partnership is $80 million and their tax base is $60m. A is directly liable to tax at 25% on 60% of the taxable profits of the partnership, in computing which it is entitled to offset 60% of the tax base of the assets. A elects to measure the non-controlling interest at its proportionate share of the net assets of the partnership.

The accounting entry to record the business combination is:

	$m	$m
Net assets	80	
Goodwill (balancing figure)	55	
Consideration paid		100
Deferred tax*		3
Non-controlling interest†		32

*   In recovering the carrying value of the net assets ($80m),
        A will pay tax on 60% of $20m ($80m – $60m) = $12m at 25% = $3m.

†   40% of $80m.

By contrast, if the partnership were a tax-paying entity, the accounting entry would be:

	$m	$m
Net assets	80	
Goodwill (balancing figure)	55	
Consideration paid		100
Deferred tax*		5
Non-controlling interest†		30

* In recovering the carrying value of the net assets ($80m), P will pay tax on $20m ($80m – $60m) at 25% = $5m.

† 40% of $75m (net assets excluding deferred tax $80m less deferred tax (as above) $5m).

Example 31.23:   Tax-transparent entity (equity-accounted)

The facts are the same as in Example 31.22 above, except that, due to an agreement between A and the other partners, P is a jointly-controlled entity, rather than a subsidiary, of A, which accounts for P using the equity method. In this case it is less clear how to account for the deferred tax liability, which, it must be remembered, is not a liability of P, but of A and therefore does not form part of the net assets and goodwill underlying A's investment in P.

One analysis might be that the deferred tax relates to a temporary difference arising on the initial recognition of the investment in P in a transaction that gives rise to no accounting or taxable profit, and therefore is not recognised under the initial recognition exception (see 7.2.3 above). On this view, the initial accounting entry is simply:

	$m	$m
Investment in P	100	
Consideration		100

Another analysis might be that the true cost of the investment in P comprises both the consideration paid to the vendor and the assumption by A of the deferred tax liability associated with its share of the underlying assets (other than goodwill) of the investment. On this view the initial accounting entry is:

	$m	$m
Investment in P	103	
Deferred tax (see Example 31.22 above)		3
Consideration		100

This second method has the merit that it results in the same implied underlying goodwill as arises on full consolidation in Example 31.22 above: $103m – $48m [60% of $80m] = $55m. However, it does raise the issue of an apparent 'day one' impairment, as discussed in more detail at 12.3 below.

In our view, either analysis is acceptable so long as it is applied consistently.

Any income tax relating to a tax-transparent entity accounted for using equity accounting forms part of the investor's tax charge. It is therefore included in the income tax line in profit or loss and not shown as part of the investor's share of the results of the tax-transparent entity.

7.7   Deferred taxable gains

Some tax regimes mitigate the tax impact of significant asset disposals by allowing some or all of the tax liability on such transactions to be deferred, typically subject to conditions, such as a requirement to reinvest the proceeds from the sale of the asset disposed of in a similar 'replacement' asset. The postponement of tax payments achieved in this way may either be for a fixed period (e.g. the liability must be paid in any event no later than ten years after the original disposal) or for an indefinite

Chapter 31

period (e.g. the liability crystallises when, and only when, the 'replacement' asset is subsequently disposed of).

As noted at 7.3 above, IAS 12 makes it clear that the ability to postpone payment of the tax liability arising on disposal of an asset – even for a considerable period – does not extinguish the liability. In many cases, the effect of such deferral provisions in tax legislation is to reduce the tax base of the 'replacement' asset. This will increase any taxable temporary difference, or reduce any deductible temporary difference, associated with the asset.

8   DEFERRED TAX – MEASUREMENT

8.1   Legislation at the end of the reporting period

Deferred tax should be measured by reference to the tax rates and laws, as enacted or substantively enacted by the end of the reporting period, that are expected to apply in the periods in which the assets and liabilities to which the deferred tax relates are realised or settled. *[IAS 12.47].*

When different tax rates apply to different levels of taxable income, deferred tax assets and liabilities are measured using the average rates that are expected to apply to the taxable profit (tax loss) of the periods in which the temporary differences are expected to reverse. *[IAS 12.49].*

IAS 12 comments that, in some jurisdictions, announcements of tax rates (and tax laws) by the government have the substantive effect of actual enactment, which may follow the announcement by a period of several months. In these circumstances, tax assets and liabilities are measured using the announced tax rate (and tax laws). *[IAS 12.48].*

IAS 12 gives no guidance as to how this requirement is to be interpreted in different jurisdictions and both the IASB and the Interpretations Committee have resisted various requests for it. In most jurisdictions, however, a consensus has emerged as to the meaning of 'substantive enactment' for that jurisdiction. Nevertheless, in practice apparently similar legislative processes in different jurisdictions may give rise to different treatments under IAS 12. For example, in most jurisdictions, tax legislation requires the formal approval of the head of state in order to become law. However, in some jurisdictions the head of state has real executive power (and could potentially not approve the legislation), whereas in others head of state has a more ceremonial role (and cannot practically fail to approve the legislation).

The view tends to be that, in those jurisdictions where the head of state has executive power, legislation is not substantively enacted until actually enacted by the head of state. Where, however, the head of state's powers are more ceremonial, substantive enactment is generally regarded as occurring at the stage of the legislative process where no further amendment is possible.

Some examples of the interpretation of 'substantive enactment' in particular jurisdictions are given at 5.1.1 above.

8.2   Uncertain tax positions

'Uncertain tax position' is a term not defined in IAS 12, but is generally understood in practice to refer to an item the tax treatment of which is unclear or is a matter of unresolved dispute between the reporting entity and the relevant tax authority. An uncertain tax position generally occurs where there is an uncertainty as to the meaning of the tax law, or to the applicability of the law to a particular transaction, or both.

Accounting for uncertain tax positions is a particularly challenging aspect of accounting for tax, discussed further at 9 below.

8.3   Expected manner of recovery of assets or settlement of liabilities

Deferred tax should be measured by reference to the tax consequences that would follow from the manner in which the entity expects, at the end of the reporting period, to recover or settle the carrying amount of the asset or liability to which it relates. *[IAS 12.51].*

8.3.1   *Tax planning strategies*

As discussed at 7.5.2 above, IAS 12 allows tax planning strategies to be taken into account in determining whether a deferred tax asset may be recognised. This raises the question of the extent to which tax planning strategies may be taken into account more generally in applying IAS 12.

For example, some jurisdictions may offer incentives in the form of a significantly reduced basis tax rate for entities that undertake particular activities, or invest in particular plant, property and equipment, or create a certain level of employment.

Some argue that, where an entity has the ability and intention to undertake transactions that will lead to its being taxed at a lower rate, it may take this into account in measuring deferred tax liabilities relating to temporary differences that will reverse in future periods when the lower rate is expected to apply.

In our view, this is not appropriate. IAS 12's references to tax planning opportunities are purely in the context of determining whether a deferred tax asset should be recognised. Such opportunities do not impact on the measurement of deferred tax until the entity has undertaken them, or is at least irrevocably committed to doing so.

8.3.2   *Carrying amount*

IAS 12 requires an entity to account for the tax consequences of recovering assets or settling liabilities at their *carrying amount*, and not, for example, the tax that might arise on a disposal at the current estimated fair value of the asset. This is illustrated by the example below.

Example 31.24:   Measurement of deferred tax based on carrying amount of asset

During 2007 an entity, which has an accounting date of 31 December and pays tax at 40%, purchased a business and assigned €3 million of the purchase consideration to goodwill. The goodwill originally had a tax base of €3 million, deductible only on disposal of the goodwill. Thus there was no temporary difference on initial recognition of the goodwill (and, even if there had been, no deferred tax would have been recognised under the initial recognition exception – see 7.2.2

above). During 2008 the entity disposed of another business giving rise to a taxable gain of €500,000. The tax law of the relevant jurisdiction allowed the gain to be deferred by deducting it from the tax base of the goodwill, which therefore became €2.5 million.

Since IFRS prohibits the amortisation of goodwill, but instead requires it to be measured at cost less impairment, in our view IAS 12 effectively requires any deferred tax to be measured at the amount that would arise if the goodwill were sold at its carrying amount. At the end of 2007, the goodwill was still carried at €3 million. The decrease in the tax base during the period through deferral of the taxable gain gave rise to a taxable temporary difference of €500,000 (€3 million carrying amount less €2.5 million tax base), which, since it arose *after* the initial recognition of the goodwill (see 7.2.4 above), gave rise to the recognition of a deferred tax liability of €200,000 (€500,000 @ 40%).

During 2009, the acquired business suffered a severe downturn in trading, such that the goodwill of €3 million was written off in its entirety. This gave rise to a deductible temporary difference of €2.5 million (carrying amount of zero less €2.5 million tax base). The deferred tax liability of €200,000 recognised at the end of 2007 was released. However, no deferred tax asset was recognised since it did not meet the criteria in IAS 12 for recognition of tax assets, since there was no expectation of suitable taxable profits sufficient to enable recovery of the asset (see 7.4 above).

During 2012, a new trading opportunity arises in the acquired business, with the result that, at the end of 2012, the value of the goodwill of that business is once more €3 million. However, in accordance with IAS 36, which prohibits the reinstatement of previously impaired goodwill (see Chapter 22 at 6.1), no accounting adjustment is made to the carrying value of goodwill.

If the goodwill were disposed of for its current fair value of €3 million, tax of €200,000 would arise. However, the entity recognises no deferred tax liability at the end of 2012, since IAS 12 requires the entity to recognise the tax (if any) that would arise on disposal of the goodwill for its *carrying amount* of zero. If the asset were sold for zero, a tax loss of €2.5 million would arise but, in accordance with the general provisions of IAS 12 discussed at 7.4 above, a deferred tax asset could be recognised in respect of this deductible temporary difference only if there were an expectation of suitable taxable profits sufficient to enable recovery of the asset.

This may mean that any deferred tax asset or liability recognised under IAS 12 will reflect the expected manner of recovery or settlement, but not the expected amount of recovery or settlement, where this differs from the current carrying amount.

8.3.3 Assets and liabilities with more than one tax base

IAS 12 notes that, in some jurisdictions, the manner in which an entity recovers (settles) the carrying amount of an asset (liability) may affect either or both of:

(a) the tax rate applicable when the entity recovers (settles) the carrying amount of the asset (or liability); and

(b) the tax base of the asset (or liability).

In such cases, an entity should measure deferred tax assets and liabilities using the tax rate and the tax base that are consistent with the expected manner of recovery or settlement. *[IAS 12.51A]*.

Assets which are treated differently for tax purposes depending on whether their value is recovered through use or sale are commonly referred to as 'dual-based assets'. This basic requirement of IAS 12 for dual-based assets can be illustrated with a simple example.

Example 31.25:   Calculation of deferred tax depending on method of realisation of asset

A building, which is fully tax-deductible, originally cost €1 million. At the balance sheet date it is carried at €1,750,000, but tax allowances of €400,000 have been claimed in respect of it. If the building were sold the tax base of the building would be €1.5 million due to inflation-linked increases in its tax base.

Any gain on sale (calculated as sale proceeds less tax base of €1.5 million) would be taxed at 40%. If the asset is consumed in the business, its depreciation will be charged to profits that are taxed at 30%. What deferred tax liability is required to be established under IAS 12?

If the intention is to retain the asset in the business, it will be recovered out of future income of €1.75 million, on which tax of €345,000 will be paid, calculated as:

	€000
Gross income	1,750
Future tax allowances for asset	
(£1m less £400,000 claimed to date)	(600)
	1,150
Tax at 30%	345

If, however, the intention is to sell the asset, the required deferred tax liability is only €100,000 calculated as:

	€000
Sales proceeds	1,750
Tax base	(1,500)
	250
Tax at 40%	100

IAS 12 provides further examples illustrating this requirement.[20]

8.3.4   Determining the expected manner of recovery of assets

Example 31.25 above, like the various similar examples in IAS 12, assumes that an asset will either be used in the business or sold. In practice, however, many assets are acquired, used for part of their life and then sold before the end of that life. This is particularly the case with long-lived assets such as property. We set out below that approach which we believe should be adopted in assessing the manner of recovery of:

- depreciable PP&E, investment properties and intangible assets (see 8.3.5 below);
- non-depreciable PP&E, investment properties and intangible assets (see 8.3.6 below); and
- other assets and liabilities (see 8.3.7 below).

8.3.5   Depreciable PP&E and intangible assets

Depreciable PP&E and investment properties are accounted for in accordance with IAS 16. Amortised intangibles are accounted for in accordance with IAS 38. IAS 16 and IAS 38, which are discussed in detail in Chapters 19 and 20, require the carrying amount of a depreciable asset to be separated into a 'residual value' and a 'depreciable amount'.

'Residual value' is defined as:

> '... the estimated amount that an entity would currently obtain from disposal of the asset, after deducting the estimated costs of disposal, if the asset were already of the age and condition expected at the end of its useful life'

and 'depreciable amount' as:

> '... the cost of an asset, or other amount substituted for cost, less its residual value'. *[IAS 16.6, IAS 38.8].*

It is inherent in the definitions of 'residual value' and 'depreciable amount' that, in determining residual value, an entity is effectively asserting that it expects to recover the depreciable amount of an asset through use and its residual value through sale. If the entity does not expect to sell an asset, but to use and scrap it, then the residual value (i.e. the amount that would be obtained from sale) must be nil.

Accordingly, we believe that, in determining the expected manner of recovery of an asset for the purposes of IAS 12, an entity should assume that, in the case of an asset accounted for under IAS 16 or IAS 38, it will recover the residual value of the asset through sale and the depreciable amount through use. This view is reinforced by the Basis for Conclusions on IAS 12 which notes that 'recognition of depreciation implies that the carrying amount of a depreciable asset is expected to be recovered through use to the extent of its depreciable amount, and through sale at its residual value'. *[IAS 12.BC6].*

Such an analysis is also consistent with the requirement of IAS 8 to account for similar transactions consistently (see Chapter 3 at 4.1.4). This suggests that consistent assumptions should be used in determining both the residual value of an asset for the purposes of IAS 16 and IAS 38 and the expected manner of its recovery for the purposes of IAS 12.

The effect of this treatment is as follows.

Example 31.26: Dual-based asset

As part of a business combination an entity purchases an opencast mine to which there is assigned a fair value of €10 million. The tax system of the jurisdiction where the mine is located provides that, if the site is sold (with or without the minerals *in situ*), €9 million will be allowed as a deduction in calculating the taxable profit on sale. The profit on sale of the land is taxed as a capital item. If the mine is exploited through excavation and sale of the minerals, no tax deduction is available.

The entity intends fully to exploit the mine and then to sell the site for retail development. Given the costs that any developer will need to incur in preparing the excavated site for development, the ultimate sales proceeds are likely to be nominal. Thus, for the purposes of IAS 16, the quarry is treated as having a depreciable amount of €10 million and a residual value of nil.

On the analysis above, there is a taxable temporary difference of €10 million associated with the depreciable amount of the asset (carrying amount of €10 million less tax base in use of nil), and a deductible temporary difference of €9 million associated with the residual value (carrying amount of nil less tax base on disposal of €9 million).

The entity will therefore provide for a deferred tax liability on the taxable temporary difference. Whether or not a deferred tax asset is recognised in respect of the deductible temporary difference will be determined in accordance with the criteria discussed in 7.4 above. In some tax regimes, capital profits and losses are treated more or less separately from revenue profits and losses to a greater or lesser degree, so that it may be difficult to recognise such an asset due to a lack of suitable taxable profits.

However, we acknowledge that this is not the only interpretation of IAS 12 adopted in practice. For example, in its 2005 financial statements BHP Billiton indicated that, where an asset has only a capital gains tax base deductible on sale, it computed deferred tax based on that tax base irrespective of the expected manner of recovery of the asset.

> *Extract 31.1: BHP Billiton Plc (2005)*
> **1   Accounting policies** [extract]
> The amount of deferred tax recognised is based on the expected manner and timing of realisation or settlement of the carrying amount of assets and liabilities, with the exception of items that have a tax base solely derived under capital gains tax legislation, using tax rates enacted or substantively enacted at period end. To the extent that an item's tax base is solely derived from the amount deductible under capital gains tax legislation, deferred tax is determined as if such amounts are deductible in determining future assessable income.

If applied to the fact pattern in Example 31.26 above, this treatment would result in the recognition of a deferred tax liability on a taxable temporary difference of €1 million (i.e. the extent to which the capital gains tax base does not exceed the carrying amount). An argument for this treatment would be that disposal of the asset will always attract a deduction of €9 million, and that the entity would be likely to dispose of the asset in such a way as to establish the tax loss. If the mine were immediately disposed of for that amount, the deduction would be fully recovered. As the mine is depleted, its carrying amount will fall below its tax base, giving rise to a gradually increasing deductible temporary difference. It may well not be possible to recognise a deferred tax asset on this difference for all the reasons set out in Example 31.26.

In our view, the difficulty with this treatment is that, as BHP Billiton acknowledged in explaining its accounting policy, it effectively provides for the tax consequences of recovery of the asset in a single sale transaction, although it appears more likely that it will in fact be recovered through ongoing extraction over an extended period, with no current tax deductions for the depletion cost. This is difficult to reconcile to:

- the requirement of IAS 12 to have regard to the expected manner of recovery of the mine in determining its tax base, and
- the overall objective of IAS 12 to 'account for the current and future tax consequences of ... the future recovery (settlement) of the carrying amount of assets (liabilities) that are recognised in an entity's balance sheet' (see 2.1 above).

8.3.6   Non-depreciable PP&E and intangible assets

During 2009 and 2010 the IASB received representations from various entities and bodies that it was often difficult and subjective to determine the manner of recovery of certain categories of asset for the purposes of IAS 12. This was particularly the case for investment properties accounted for at fair value under IAS 40, which are often traded opportunistically, without a particularly specific business plan, but yield rental income until disposed of. In many jurisdictions rental income is taxed at the standard rate, while gains on asset sales are tax-free or taxed at a significantly lower rate. The principal difficulty was that the then extant guidance (SIC-21) effectively required entities to determine what the residual amount of the asset would be if it were depreciated under IAS 16 rather than accounted for at fair value,[21] which many regarded as an exercise divorced from commercial reality.

To deal with these concerns, in December 2010 the IASB amended IAS 12 so as to give more specific guidance on determining the expected manner of recovery for non-depreciable assets measured using the revaluation model in IAS 16 (see 8.3.6.A below) and for investment properties measured using the fair value model in IAS 40 (see 8.3.7 below)

8.3.6.A PP&E accounted for using the revaluation model

IAS 16 allows plant, property and equipment (PP&E) to be accounted for using a revaluation model under which PP&E is regularly revalued to fair value (see Chapter 20 at 6). IAS 12 clarifies that where a non-depreciable asset is revalued, any deferred tax on the revaluation should be calculated by reference to the tax consequences that would arise if the asset were sold at book value irrespective of the basis on the carrying amount of the asset is measured. *[IAS 12.51B].* The rationale for this treatment is that, in accounting terms, the asset is never recovered through use, as it is not depreciated. *[IAS 12.BC6].*

IAS 12 clarifies that these requirements are subject to the general restrictions on the recognition of deferred tax assets (see 7.4 above). *[IAS 12.51E].*

An issue not explicitly addressed in IAS 12 is whether the term 'non-depreciable' asset refers to an asset that is not currently being depreciated or to one that does not have a limited useful life. This is explored further in the discussion of non-amortised intangible assets immediately below.

8.3.6.B Non-amortised intangible assets

Under IAS 38 an intangible asset with an indefinite life is not subject to amortisation.

The analysis in 8.3.5 and 8.3.6.A above would appear to lead to the conclusion that, where an intangible asset is not amortised, any deferred tax related to that asset should be measured on an 'on sale' basis. IAS 12 requires tax to be provided for based on the manner in which the entity expects to recover the 'carrying amount' of its assets. If the asset is not amortised under IAS 38, the financial statements are asserting that the carrying amount is never recovered through use.

However, an alternative analysis would be that the fact that an intangible asset is not being amortised does not of itself indicate that the expected manner of recovery is by sale. Rather an intangible asset is regarded as having an indefinite life when it is determined that there is no foreseeable limit to the period over which the asset is expected to generate net cash inflows for the entity. *[IAS 38.88].* This could still indicate an expectation of recovery through use.

An entity should consider which analysis is more appropriate in its particular circumstances. In many jurisdictions, however, either analysis may lead to an identical outcome, since many intangibles have no tax base either in use or on sale.

This will typically be the case where an intangible asset is recognised in consolidated financial statements, but not in the financial statements of any individual entity included in the consolidation (for example, because the asset was internally generated by an entity which is later acquired).

8.3.7 Investment properties

IAS 40 allows investment properties to be accounted for at fair value (see Chapter 21 at 6). IAS 12 requires any deferred tax asset or liability associated with such a property to be measured using a rebuttable presumption that the carrying amount of the investment property will be recovered through sale. *[IAS 12.51C]*. The same rebuttable presumption is also used when measuring any deferred tax asset or liability associated with an investment property acquired in a business combination if the entity intends to adopt the fair value model in accounting for the property subsequently. *[IAS 12.51D]*.

The presumption is rebutted if the investment property is depreciable and the entity's business model is to consume substantially all the economic benefits embodied in the investment property over time, rather than through sale. If the presumption is rebutted, the entity applies the normal requirements of IAS 12 for determining the manner of recovery of assets (see 8.3.1 to 8.3.5 above). *[IAS 12.51C]*.

IAS 12 clarifies that these requirements are subject to the general restrictions on the recognition of deferred tax assets (see 7.4 above). *[IAS 12.51E]*.

8.3.7.A Possible future developments

At its meeting in September 2011, the Interpretations Committee discussed a request for guidance as to whether the presumption of recovery through sale is rebutted only in the specific circumstances set out in the standard (see above), or in other situations as well.

The Committee tentatively decided not to add this item to its agenda, on the basis that IAS 12 clearly allows the presumption of recovery through use to be rebutted in other circumstances. However, the Committee also expressed the view that an entity should assume recovery of an investment property entirely through use or entirely through sale, on the grounds that the intention of the 2010 amendment was to eliminate subjectivity in making this determination.[22]

8.3.8 Other assets and liabilities

In a number of areas of accounting IFRS effectively requires a transaction to be accounted for in accordance with an assumption as to the ultimate settlement of that transaction that may not reflect the entity's expectation of the actual outcome.

For example, if the entity enters into a share-based payment transaction with an employee that gives the employee the right to require settlement in either shares or cash, IFRS 2 requires the transaction to be accounted for on the assumption that it will be settled in cash, however unlikely this may be. Similarly, if an entity issues a convertible bond that can also be settled in cash at the holder's option, IAS 32 requires the bond to be accounted for on the assumption that it will be repaid, however probable it is that the holders will actually elect for conversion. It may well be that such transactions have different tax consequences depending on the expected manner of settlement, as illustrated in Example 31.27 below.

Example 31.27:   Convertible bond deductible if settled

An entity issues a convertible bond for €1 million. After three years, the holders can elect to receive €1.2 million or 100,000 shares of the entity. If the bond were settled in cash, the entity would receive a tax deduction for the €200,000 difference between its original issue proceeds and the amount payable on redemption. If the bond is converted, no tax deduction is available.

Under IAS 32, the bond would be accreted from €1 million to €1.2 million over the three year issue period. The tax base remains at €1 million throughout, so that a deductible temporary difference of €200,000 emerges over the issue period. It is assumed that the deferred tax asset relating to this difference would meet the recognition criteria in IAS 12 (see 7.4 above).

For various reasons, it is extremely unlikely that the bond will be redeemed in cash.

Example 31.27 raises the issue of whether any deferred tax asset should be recognised in respect of the €200,000 temporary difference.

One view would be that no deferred tax asset should be recognised on the basis that there is no real expectation that the transaction will be settled in cash, thus allowing the entity to claim a tax deduction. The contrary view would be that the underlying rationale of IAS 12 is that, in order for the financial statements to be internally consistent, the tax effects of recognised assets and liabilities must also be recognised (see 2.1 above). Accordingly, a deferred tax asset should be recognised.

In our view, more weight should be given to the internal consistency of the financial statements.

8.3.9   'Outside' temporary differences relating to subsidiaries, branches, associates and joint ventures

In this section, an 'outside' temporary difference means a difference between the tax base of an investment in a subsidiary, associate or branch or an interest in a joint venture and carrying amount of that investment or interest (or the net assets and goodwill relating to it) included in the financial statements. Such differences, and the special recognition criteria applied to them by IAS 12, are discussed in more detail at 7.5 above.

Where deferred tax is recognised on such a temporary difference, the question arises as to how it should be measured. Broadly speaking, investors can realise an investment in one of two ways – either indirectly (by remittance of retained earnings or capital) or directly (through sale of the investment). In many jurisdictions, the two means of realisation have very different tax consequences.

IAS 12 indicates that the entity must apply the general rule (discussed in more detail above) that, where there is more than one method of recovering an investment, the entity should measure any associated deferred tax asset or liability by reference to the expected manner of recovery of the investment.[23] In other words, to the extent that the investment is expected to be realised through sale, the deferred tax is measured according to the tax rules applicable on sale, but to the extent that the temporary difference is expected to be realised through a distribution of earnings or capital, the deferred tax is measured according to the tax rules applicable on distribution.

Where the expected manner of recovery is through distribution, there may be tax consequences for more than one entity in the group. For example, the paying company may suffer a withholding tax on the dividend paid and the receiving company may suffer income tax on the dividend received. In such cases, provision should be made for the cumulative effect of all tax consequences. As discussed further at 10.3.3 below, a withholding tax on an intragroup dividend is not, from the perspective of the group financial statements, accounted for as a withholding tax, since the group is not making a distribution but transferring assets from a group entity to a parent of that entity.

8.3.10 'Single asset' entities

In many jurisdictions it is common for certain assets (particularly properties) to be bought and sold by transferring ownership of a separate legal entity formed to hold the asset (a 'single asset' entity) rather than the asset itself.

A 'single asset' entity may be formed for a number of reasons. For example, the insertion of a 'single asset' entity between that 'real' owner and the property may limit the 'real' owner's liability for obligations arising from ownership of the property. More pertinent to the current discussion, it may also provide shelter from tax liabilities arising on disposal of the property since, in many jurisdictions, the sale of shares is taxed at a lower rate than the sale of property.

This raises the question whether, in determining the expected manner of recovery of an asset for the purposes of IAS 12, an entity may have regard to the fact that an asset held by a 'single asset' entity can be disposed of by disposing of the shares of the entity rather than the asset itself.

A literal reading of IAS 12 might suggest that, where the reporting entity prepares consolidated financial statements (such that the asset held by the 'single asset' entity is included in those financial statements), it is not appropriate to have regard to the possible tax effects of disposing of the shares in the 'single asset' entity rather than the asset itself. This is because paragraph 51 of IAS 12 requires an entity to have regard to the expected manner of recovery or settlement of 'the carrying amount of its assets and liabilities'. Where consolidated financial statements are prepared, the asset recognised in the balance sheet is the property held by, not the shares in, the 'single asset' entity (which are eliminated on consolidation).

However, we consider that there could be specific limited circumstances where the manner in which the entity expects, at the end of the reporting period, to recover or settle the carrying amount of its assets and liabilities may also include the sale of a 'single asset' entity. These circumstances will typically be limited to situations where a property that is clearly not a business is already held by such an entity.

8.3.10.A Possible future developments

At its meeting in September 2011, the Interpretations Committee considered a request for guidance on the calculation of deferred tax relating to an asset held by a 'single asset' entity. The Committee tentatively decided not to add this item to its agenda but noted that, in its view, an entity must recognise deferred tax on the 'inside' temporary differences in a single asset entity, 'even if the entity does not expect to dispose of the asset separately from the entity which holds it'. In support of this tentative decision, the Committee cites various paragraphs of IAS 12, but curiously does not refer to paragraph 51.[24]

It would perhaps have been more helpful if the Interpretations Committee had explained how it reconciles its tentative preference for an accounting treatment which ignores the expected manner of recovery of the asset with the explicit requirement of paragraph 51 to have regard to it. It will be interesting to see how this issue is finally resolved.

8.3.11 *Change in expected manner of recovery of an asset or settlement of a liability*

A change in the expected manner recovery of an asset or settlement of a liability should be dealt with as an item of deferred tax income or expense for the period in which the change of expectation occurs, and recognised in profit or loss or in other comprehensive income or movements in equity for that period as appropriate (see 10 below).

8.4   Different tax rates applicable to retained and distributed profits

In some jurisdictions, the rate at which tax is paid depends on whether profits are distributed or retained. In other jurisdictions, distribution may lead to an additional liability to tax, or a refund of tax already paid. IAS 12 requires current and deferred taxes to be measured using the rate applicable to undistributed profits until a liability to pay a dividend is recognised, at which point the tax consequences of that dividend should also be recognised, as illustrated in Example 31.28 below. *[IAS 12.52A, 52B]*.

Example 31.28:   Different tax rates applicable to retained and distributed profits

An entity operates in a jurisdiction where income taxes are payable at a higher rate on undistributed profits (50%) with an amount being refundable when profits are distributed. The tax rate on distributed profits is 35%. At the balance sheet date, 31 December 2012, the entity does not recognise a liability for dividends proposed or declared after the balance sheet date. As a result, no dividends are recognised in the year 2012. Taxable income for 2012 is €100,000. Net taxable temporary differences have increased during the year ended 31 December 2012 by €40,000.

The entity recognises a current tax liability and a current income tax expense of €50,000 (€100,000 taxable profit @ 50%). No asset is recognised for the amount potentially recoverable as a result of future dividends. The entity also recognises a deferred tax liability and deferred tax expense of €20,000 (€40,000 @ 50%) representing the income taxes that the entity will pay when it recovers or settles the carrying amounts of its assets and liabilities based on the tax rate applicable to undistributed profits.

Subsequently, on 15 March 2013 the entity declares, and recognises as a liability, dividends of €10,000 from previous operating profits. At that point, the entity recognises the recovery of income taxes of €1,500 (€10,000 @ [50% – 35%]), representing the refund of tax due in respect of the dividends recognised as a liability, as a current tax asset and as a reduction of current income tax expense for the year ended 31 December 2013.

8.4.1   *Effectively tax-free entities*

In a number of jurisdictions certain types of entity, typically investment vehicles, are generally exempt from corporate income tax provided that they fulfil certain criteria, which generally include a requirement to distribute all, or a minimum percentage, of their annual income as a dividend to investors. This raises the question of how such entities should measure income taxes.

One view would be that, under the basic principle set out above, such an entity has a liability to tax at the normal rate until the dividend for a year becomes a liability. The liability for a dividend for an accounting period typically arises after the end of that period (as in Example 31.28 above). Under this analysis, therefore, such an entity would be required, at each period end, to record a liability for current tax at the standard corporate rate. That liability would be released in full when the dividend is recognised as a liability in the following period. This would mean that, on an ongoing basis, the income statement would show a current tax charge or credit comprising:

- a charge for a full liability for the current period, and
- a credit for the reversal of the corresponding liability for the prior period.

In addition, deferred tax would be recognised at the standard tax rate on all temporary differences.

A second view, which we prefer, would be that the provisions of IAS 12 regarding different tax rates for distributed and undistributed tax rates are intended to apply where the only significant factor determining the differential tax rate is the retention or distribution of profit. By contrast, the tax status of an investment fund typically depends on many more factors than whether or not profits are distributed, such as restrictions on its activities, the nature of its investments and so forth. On this view, the analysis would be that such an entity can choose to operate within one of two tax regimes (a 'full tax' regime or a 'no tax' regime), rather than that it operates in a single tax regime with a dual tax rate depending on whether profits are retained or distributed.

The IASB previously appeared to regard IAS 12 as favouring the first analysis, while accepting that the resulting accounting treatment – a cycle of raising full tax provisions and then reversing them – does not reflect economic reality. Accordingly, the exposure draft ED/2009/2 proposed that the measurement of tax assets and liabilities should include the effect of expected future distributions, based on the entity's past practices and expectations of future distributions.[25] Following the withdrawal of the exposure draft, the IASB intends to consider this issue further. However, no formal decision has been taken, or proposals issued for comment.

8.4.2 Withholding tax or distribution tax?

In practice, it is sometimes difficult to determine whether a particular transaction should be accounted for under the provisions of IAS 12 relating to different tax rates for distributed and undistributed profits, or in accordance with the provisions of the standard relating to withholding taxes.

The classification can significantly affect tax expense, because IAS 12 requires a withholding tax to be accounted for as a deduction from equity, whereas a higher tax rate for distributed profits is typically accounted for as a charge to profit or loss.

This issue is discussed further at 10.3 below.

Chapter 31

8.5   Discounting

IAS 12 prohibits discounting of deferred tax, on the basis that:

- it would be unreasonable to require discounting, given that it requires scheduling of the reversal of temporary differences, which can be impracticable or at least highly complex; and

- it would be inappropriate to permit discounting because of the lack of comparability between financial statements in which discounting was adopted and those in which it was not. *[IAS 12.53, 54]*.

Moreover, IAS 12 notes that when deferred tax is recognised in relation to an item that is itself discounted (such as a liability for post-employment benefits or a finance lease liability), the deferred tax, being based on the carrying amount of that item, is also effectively discounted. *[IAS 12.55]*.

8.6   Unrealised intragroup profits and losses in consolidated financial statements

As noted in 6.2.1 and 6.2.2 above, an unrealised intragroup profit or loss eliminated on consolidation will give rise to a temporary difference where the profit or loss arises on a transaction that alters the tax base of the item(s) subject to the transaction. Such an alteration in the tax base creates a temporary difference because there is no corresponding change in the carrying amount of the assets or liabilities in the consolidated financial statements, due to the intragroup eliminations.

IAS 12 does not specifically address the measurement of such items. However, IAS 12 generally requires an entity, in measuring deferred tax, to have regard to the expected manner of recovery or settlement of the tax. It would generally be consistent with this requirement to measure deferred tax on temporary differences arising from intragroup transfers at the tax rates and laws applicable to the 'transferee' company rather than those applicable to the 'transferor' company, since the 'transferee' company will be taxed when the asset or liability subject to the transfer is realised or sold.

This interpretation is reinforced by the fact that the measurement of deferred tax on intragroup transactions is an acknowledged difference between IAS 12 and US GAAP. Under US GAAP deferred tax on such intragroup temporary differences is measured using the 'transferor' company's tax rate and law as an explicit exception to the general application of the temporary difference approach. Under IAS 12 (which has no such exception), the 'transferee' company's tax rate and laws apply.

There are some jurisdictions where the tax history of an asset or liability subject to an intragroup transfer remains with the 'transferor' company. In such cases, the general principles of IAS 12 should be used to determine whether any deferred tax should be measured at the tax rate of the 'transferor' or the 'transferee' company.

The effect of the treatment required by IAS 12 is that tax income or expense may be recognised on transactions eliminated on consolidation, as illustrated by Examples 31.29 and 31.30.

Example 31.29:   Elimination of intragroup profit (1)

H, an entity taxed at 30%, has a subsidiary S, which is taxed at 34%. On 15 December 2012 S sells inventory with a cost of €100,000 to H for €120,000, giving rise to a taxable profit of €20,000 and tax at 34% of €6,800. If H were preparing consolidated financial statements for the year ended 31 December 2012, the profit made by S on the sale to H would be eliminated.

Under IAS 12, a deferred tax asset would be recognised on the unrealised profit of €20,000, based on H's 30% tax rate, i.e. €6,000. The additional €800 tax actually paid by S would be recognised in profit or loss for the period ended 31 December 2012, the accounting entry being:

	DR €	CR €
Current tax (profit or loss)	6,800	
Current tax (balance sheet)		6,800
Deferred tax (balance sheet)	6,000	
Deferred tax (profit or loss)		6,000

The net €800 tax charge to profit or loss (current tax charge €6,800 less deferred tax credit €6,000) reflects the fact that, by transferring the inventory from one tax jurisdiction to another with a lower tax rate, the group has effectively denied itself a tax deduction of €800 (i.e. €20,000 at the tax rate differential of 4%) for the inventory that would have been available had the inventory been sold by S, rather than H, to the ultimate third party customer.

Example 31.30:   Elimination of intragroup profit (2)

H, an entity taxed at 34%, has a subsidiary S, which is taxed at 30%. On 15 December 2012 S sells inventory with a cost of €100,000 to H for €120,000, giving rise to a taxable profit of €20,000 and tax at 30% of €6,000. If H were preparing consolidated financial statements for the year ended 31 December 2012, the profit made by S on the sale to H would be eliminated.

In this case, the consolidated financial statements would record current tax paid by S of €6,000 and a deferred tax asset measured at H's effective tax rate of 34% of €6,800, giving rise to the following entry:

	DR €	CR €
Current tax (profit or loss)	6,000	
Current tax (balance sheet)		6,000
Deferred tax (balance sheet)	6,800	
Deferred tax (profit or loss)		6,800

In this case there is a net €800 tax credit to profit or loss (current tax charge €6,000 less deferred tax credit €6,800). This reflects the fact that, by transferring the inventory from one tax jurisdiction to another with a higher tax rate, the group has put itself in the position of being able to claim a tax deduction for the inventory of €800 (i.e. €20,000 at the tax rate differential of 4%) in excess of that which would have been available had the inventory been sold by S, rather than H, to the ultimate third party customer.

8.6.1   Intragroup transfers of goodwill and intangible assets

It is common in some jurisdictions to sell goodwill and intangible assets from one entity in a group to another in the same group, very often in order either to increase tax deductions on an already recognised asset or to obtain deductions for a previously unrecognised asset. This raises the issue of how the tax effects of such transactions should be accounted for in the financial statements both of the individual entities concerned and in the consolidated financial statements, as illustrated by Example 31.31 below.

Example 31.31: Intragroup transfer of goodwill

A parent company P has two subsidiaries – A, which was acquired some years ago and B, which was acquired during the period ended 31 December 2009 at a cost of €10 million. For the purposes of this discussion, it is assumed that B had negligible identifiable assets and liabilities. Accordingly, P recorded goodwill of €10 million in its consolidated financial statements.

During 2012, B sells its business to A for its then current fair value of €12.5 million. As the goodwill inherent in B's business was internally generated, it was not recognised in the financial statements of B. Hence, the entire consideration of €12.5 million represents a profit to B, which is subject to current tax at 20% (i.e. €2.5 million). However, as a result of this transaction, A will be entitled to claim tax deductions (again at 20%) for this goodwill in ten equal annual instalments from 2013 to 2022. For the purposes of this discussion, it is assumed that A will have sufficient suitable taxable profits to be able to recover these deductions in full.

8.6.1.A   Individual financial statements of buyer

The buyer (A) accounts for the acquisition of B's business. As the business still has negligible identifiable assets and liabilities, this gives rise to goodwill of €12.5 million within A's own financial statements. A has acquired an asset for €12.5 million with a tax base of the same amount. There is therefore no temporary difference (and thus no deferred tax) to be accounted for in the financial statements of A.

8.6.1.B   Individual financial statements of seller

As described above, the individual financial statements of the seller (B) reflect a profit of €12.5 million and current tax of €2.5 million.

8.6.1.C   Consolidated financial statements

In the consolidated financial statements of P, the sale of the business from B to A will be eliminated on consolidation. However, the €2.5 million current tax suffered by B will be reflected in the consolidated financial statements, since this is a transaction with a third party (the tax authority), not an intragroup transaction. The question is what, if any, deferred tax arises as the result of this transaction.

One analysis would be that the tax base of consolidated goodwill has effectively been increased from nil to €12.5 million. This creates a deductible temporary difference of €2.5 million on which a deferred tax asset at 20% (€500,000) may be recognised. It could also be argued that there is an analogy here with the general treatment of deferred tax on intragroup profits and losses eliminated on consolidation (see Examples 31.29 and 31.30 above).

Under this analysis, the consolidated income statement would show a net tax charge of €2.0 million (€2.5 million current tax expense arising in B, less €0.5 million deferred tax income arising on consolidation). However, this is arguably inconsistent with the fact that the entity is not in an overall tax-paying position (since it has incurred a current tax loss of €2.5 million, but expects to receive tax deductions of the same amount over the next ten years). Clearly, there is an economic loss since the entity has effectively made an interest free loan equal to the current tax paid to the tax authority, but this is not relevant, since tax is not measured on a discounted basis under IAS 12 (see 8.5 above).

An alternative analysis might therefore be to argue that the goodwill reflected in the consolidated balance sheet still has no tax base. Rather, the tax base attaches to the goodwill recognised in the separate financial statements of A, which is eliminated on consolidation, and therefore has no carrying amount in the consolidated financial statements. Thus, applying the general principle illustrated in Examples 31.29 and 31.30 above, there is a deductible temporary difference of €12.5 million, being the difference between the carrying value of the goodwill (zero in the *consolidated* balance sheet) and its tax base (€12.5 million). Alternatively, as noted in 6.1.3 above, certain items may have a tax base, but no carrying amount, and thus give rise to deferred tax.

This analysis would allow recognition of a deferred tax asset of €2.5 million on a temporary difference of €12.5 million, subject to the recognition criteria for deferred tax assets. This would result in a net tax charge of nil (€2.5 million current tax expense arising in B less €2.5 million deferred tax income arising on consolidation).

In our view, there are arguments for either analysis and entities need to take a view on their accounting policy for such transactions and apply it consistently.

9   UNCERTAIN TAX POSITIONS

'Uncertain tax position' is a term widely used to refer to an item the tax treatment of which is unclear or is a matter of unresolved dispute between the reporting entity and the relevant tax authority. Uncertain tax positions generally occur where there is an uncertainty as to the meaning of the law, or to the applicability of the law to a particular transaction, or both. For example, the tax legislation may allow the deduction of research and development expenditure, but there may be disagreement as to whether a specific item of expenditure can be construed as relating to research and development.

Estimating the outcome of an uncertain tax position is often one of the most complex and subjective areas in accounting for tax. However, IAS 12 does not specifically address the measurement of uncertain tax positions, which are therefore implicitly subject to the general requirement of the standard to measure current tax at the amount expected to be paid or recovered *[IAS 12.46]* – see 5 above. This lack of specific guidance is seen by some as providing welcome flexibility and by others as a deficiency in the current standard.

Uncertain liabilities are generally accounted for under IAS 37. However, IAS 37 does not apply to income taxes (see Chapter 29 at 2.2.1.B). Therefore, whilst an entity might choose to apply IAS 37 to the measurement of uncertain tax positions by applying the 'GAAP hierarchy' in IAS 8 (see Chapter 3 at 4.4), it is not required to do so and, as a result, a number of methodologies for accounting for uncertain positions are seen in practice.

9.1   'One-step' and 'two-step' approaches to measurement

A key decision in developing any methodology is to decide whether to adopt what is often referred to as a 'one-step' approach or a 'two step' approach to the measurement of uncertain tax positions.

Under a 'one step' approach, each uncertain tax position is recognised, but the measurement of the position reflects the likelihood of the position crystallising. This was essentially the approach in the now superseded exposure draft ED/2009/2 published in March 2009 (see 1.3 above). Under a 'two-step' approach, a position is recognised only if there is a certain minimum probability – usually referred to as the 'recognition threshold' – that it will crystallise.

The use of a 'two-step' approach raises the linked issue of whether the uncertainty relating to a disputed deduction in a tax return should be considered in isolation as a potential asset, or as a component of the total liability to tax. This may affect the accounting outcome, since IFRS imposes a much higher recognition threshold for uncertain assets than for uncertain liabilities. In practice, most of the methods currently applied under IAS 12 implicitly regard the uncertainty as relating to the total liability for tax.

Where a 'two-step' approach is adopted, the recognition threshold selected for a liability is typically 'more likely than not' – i.e. more than 50%. This has doubtless been influenced by the 'more likely than not' recognition threshold for provisions in IAS 37 (see Chapter 29) and for uncertain tax positions under US GAAP (FASB ASC Topic 740 – *Income Taxes*).

The 'one-step' and 'two-step' methods both attract passionate support. Those who favour a 'two-step' approach argue that, until a minimum recognition threshold is reached, it is not possible to make an informed estimate of the likely outcome. Those who favour a 'one-step' approach argue that the determination of whether or not a recognition threshold has been reached is itself highly subjective. Also, a relatively small difference in view in the estimated probability of a liability crystallising (say from 51% to 49%) may result in a disproportionate impact on the amount of tax recognised.

It could be argued that, in practical terms, the real difference between the 'one-step' and 'two-step' approaches is less whether there is a recognition threshold than the level at which it is set. Even where a 'one-step' approach is adopted, it seems that in practice no liability is recognised where the probability of its crystallisation is very low.

9.2   Unit of account

Another key input to any methodology is to determine the unit of account for uncertain tax positions. In practice this might be an entire tax computation, individual uncertain positions, or a group of related uncertain positions (e.g. all positions in a particular tax jurisdiction, or all positions of a similar nature or relating to the same interpretation of tax legislation). This choice of unit of account is particularly important where a two-step approach is adopted, as illustrated by Example 31.32 below.

Example 31.32:   Uncertain tax positions – unit of account[26]

An entity has submitted a tax return indicating a current tax liability of £2.5 million. This £2.5 million is net of a deduction disputed by the tax authority, the tax effect of which is £500,000. In other words, if the tax authority's challenge is sustained the entity's tax liability will in fact be £3 million. The entity has received advice that the tax authority is extremely unlikely (say 10%) to sustain its challenge.

The entity's accounting policy for uncertain tax positions is that nothing is recognised for a position unless the position is considered more likely than not to occur. Where a position is considered more likely than not to occur, it is recognised and measured based on the probability of its occurrence.

If the entity regards the unit of account as the tax return as a whole, it is clearly more likely than not that the tax return will result in a payment of tax. Based on the advice the entity has received, there is a 90% probability that the liability will be £2.5 million and 10% probability that the liability will be £3 million. It would therefore record a current tax liability of 2.55 million (£2.5m × 0.9 + £3.0m × 0.1). This could equally have been calculated as £2.5m × 1 + £0.5m × 0.1 (i.e. the £2.5 million on the submitted return that is certain to be paid, with a 10% probability that an additional £500,000 will be paid).

If, however, the entity regards its unit of account as the disputed deduction, it would not recognise any liability for this at all, based on the advice received that the probability of the tax authority's challenge being sustained is only 10%. It would therefore recognise a current tax liability of only £2.5 million (i.e. the undisputed amount of the tax return).

9.3   Methodologies used in practice

A variety of acceptable methodologies for determining uncertain tax positions under IAS 12 are applied in practice. However, the chosen methodology should be applied consistently. The entity may also need to consider the relevance of the requirement of IAS 1 to disclose information about major sources of estimation uncertainty (see Chapter 3 at 5.2).

Methodologies seen in practice include both 'one-step' and 'two-step' approaches to recognition. Measurement bases may include a weighted average probability of outcomes, the most likely single outcome and an 'all or nothing approach' (i.e. no liability is recognised for an uncertain position with a probability of occurrence below the selected recognition threshold and a full liability for a position with a probability of occurrence above the threshold).

9.4   Tax authority practice

IAS 12 requires tax to be recognised and measured based on enacted or substantively enacted tax legislation *[IAS 12.46, 47]* – see 5 to 8 above. In some tax jurisdictions, however, the tax authority may – with the general consent of taxpayers – collect tax other than in accordance with the strict letter of the law. One example might be where the law as drafted would lead to a manifestly inequitable or unintended outcome for either the state or the taxpayer. Another example might be that the law allows a deduction in general terms (e.g. for 'refurbishment'), but the tax authority applies the law by reference to more detailed criteria (e.g. by allowing deductions for repainting, but not for replacement of windows).

Whether or not such an application of the tax law represents an uncertain tax position will be a matter for judgement in individual cases. Where the tax authority publishes its interpretations of the law, and these interpretations are generally accepted by taxpayers and upheld in legal proceedings, it may be appropriate to treat such interpretations as equivalent to tax law. Where, however, a particular interpretation appears to be followed only by individual officers of the tax authority, or accepted only in a relatively small number of tax returns, it would generally be more appropriate to treat such an interpretation as an uncertain tax position.

9.5 Detection risk

'Detection risk' is a term used in practice to refer to the risk that the tax authority examines the amounts reported to it by the entity and has full knowledge of all relevant information. US GAAP requires an entity to assess its uncertain tax positions on the assumption that the tax authority will examine them with full knowledge of relevant information, even if the entity believes that the possibility of such examination is remote, or if there is a long history of the tax authority not performing an examination or overlooking an issue. A similar requirement was proposed in the now superseded exposure draft ED/2009/2 published in March 2009 (see 1.3 above).

IAS 12 in its current form makes no explicit reference to detection risk. However, in our view, that does not mean that it can be ignored. In many jurisdictions, the tax law imposes a legal obligation on an entity operating in that jurisdiction to disclose its full liability to tax, or to assess its own liability to tax, and to make all relevant information available to the tax authorities. In such a tax jurisdiction it might be difficult, as a matter of corporate governance, for an entity to reconcile recording a tax provision calculated on the basis that the tax authority would not become aware of a particular position with the entity's legal obligation to disclose it.

9.6 Classification of uncertain tax positions

As noted above, uncertain tax positions generally relate to the provision for current tax. Any provision recognised for an uncertain current tax position should therefore normally be classified as current tax, and presented (or disclosed) as current or non-current in accordance with the general requirements of IAS 1 (see Chapter 3 at 3.1.1).

However, there are circumstances where an uncertain tax position affects the tax base of an asset or liability and therefore relates to deferred tax. For example, there might be doubt as to the amount of tax depreciation that can be deducted in respect of a particular asset, which in turn would lead to doubt as to the tax base of the asset. There may sometimes be an equal and opposite uncertainty relating to current and deferred tax. For example, there might be uncertainty as to whether a particular item of income is taxable, but – if it is – any tax payable will be reduced to zero by a loss carried forward from a prior period. As discussed at 13.1.1.C below, it is not appropriate to offset current and deferred tax items.

10   ALLOCATION OF TAX CHARGE OR CREDIT

Current and deferred tax is normally recognised as income or an expense in the profit or loss for the period, except to the extent that it arises from: *[IAS 12.58, 68A-68C]*

- an item that has been recognised directly outside profit or loss, whether in the same period or in a different period (see 10.1 to 10.6 below);

- a share-based payment transaction (see 10.7 below); or

- a business combination (see 12 below).

Where a deferred tax asset or liability is remeasured subsequent to its initial recognition, the change should be accounted for in profit or loss, unless it relates to an item originally recognised outside profit or loss, in which case the change should also be accounted for outside profit or loss. Such remeasurement might result from: *[IAS 12.60]*

- a change in tax law;

- a re-assessment of the recoverability of deferred tax assets (see 7.4 above); or

- a change in the expected manner of recovery of an asset or settlement of a liability (see 8.3.11 above).

Whilst IAS 12 as drafted refers only to remeasurement of 'deferred' tax, it seems clear that these principles should also be applied to any remeasurement of current tax.

Any current tax or deferred tax on items recognised outside profit or loss, whether in the same period or a different period, is also recognised directly outside profit or loss. Such items include: *[IAS 12.61A, 62, 62A]*

- revaluations of property, plant and equipment under IAS 16 (see 10.1 below);

- retrospective restatements or retrospective applications arising from corrections of errors and changes in accounting policy under IAS 8 – *Accounting Policies, Changes in Accounting Estimates and Errors* (see 10.2 below);

- exchange differences arising on translation of the financial statements of a foreign operation under IAS 21 – *The Effects of Changes in Foreign Exchange Rates* (see 7.5 above); and

- amounts taken to equity on initial recognition of a compound financial instrument by its issuer (so-called 'split accounting') under IAS 32 (see 7.2.8 above).

IAS 12 acknowledges that, in exceptional circumstances, it may be difficult to determine the amount of tax that relates to items recognised in other comprehensive income and/or equity. In these cases a reasonable pro-rata method, or another method that achieves a more appropriate allocation in the circumstances, may be used. IAS 12 gives the following examples of situations where such an approach may be appropriate:

- there are graduated rates of income tax and it is impossible to determine the rate at which a specific component of taxable profit (tax loss) has been taxed;

- a change in the tax rate or other tax rules affects a deferred tax asset or liability relating (in whole or in part) to an item that was previously recognised outside profit or loss; or

- an entity determines that a deferred tax asset should be recognised, or should no longer be recognised in full, and the deferred tax asset relates (in whole or in part) to an item that was previously recognised outside profit or loss. *[IAS 12.63]*.

IAS 12 requires tax not accounted for in profit or loss, whether in the same period or a different period, to be recognised:

- in other comprehensive income, if it relates to an item accounted for in other comprehensive income; and

- directly in equity, if it relates to an item accounted for directly in equity. *[IAS 12.61A]*.

This requirement to have regard to the previous history of a transaction in accounting for its tax effects is commonly referred to as 'backward tracing'.

10.1 Revalued and rebased assets

Where an entity depreciates a revalued item of PP&E, it may choose to transfer the depreciation in excess of the amount that would have arisen on a historical cost basis from revaluation surplus to retained earnings. In such cases, the relevant portion of any deferred tax liability recognised on the revaluation should also be transferred to retained earnings. A similar treatment should be adopted by an entity which has a policy of transferring revaluation gains to retained earnings on disposal of a previously revalued asset. *[IAS 12.64]*.

When an asset is revalued for tax purposes and that revaluation is related to an accounting revaluation of an earlier period, or to one that is expected to be carried out in a future period, the tax effects of both the asset revaluation and the adjustment of the tax base are credited or charged to equity in the periods in which they occur.

However, if the revaluation for tax purposes is not related to an accounting revaluation of an earlier period, or to one that is expected to be carried out in a future period, the tax effects of the adjustment of the tax base are recognised in the profit or loss. *[IAS 12.65]*.

In broad terms this means that, where an asset that is carried at cost is subject to a rebasing or revaluation for tax purposes, the effect will be recognised in profit or loss – subject, in the case of a deferred tax asset, to its qualifying for recognition at all under the criteria discussed in 7.4 above.

10.2 Retrospective restatements or applications

IAS 8 requires retrospective restatements or retrospective applications arising from corrections of errors and changes in accounting policy to be accounted for as an adjustment to equity in the period in which the retrospective restatement or application occurs.

Therefore, as noted above, IAS 12 requires the tax effect of a retrospective restatement or application to be dealt with as an adjustment to equity also. However, as drafted, IAS 12 can also be read as requiring any subsequent remeasurement of such tax effects to be accounted for in equity also. This would give rise to a rather surprising result, as illustrated by Example 31.33 below.

Example 31.33:   Remeasurement of deferred tax liability recognised as the result of retrospective application

An entity's date of transition to IFRS was 1 January 2004. As a result of the adoption of IAS 37 – *Provisions, Contingent Liabilities and Contingent Assets*, its first IFRS financial statements (prepared for the year ended 31 December 2005) showed an additional liability for environmental rectification costs of €5 million as an adjustment to opening reserves, together with an associated deferred tax asset at 40% of €2 million.

The environmental liability does not change substantially over the next few accounting periods, but during the year ended 31 December 2012 the tax rate falls to 30%. This requires the deferred tax asset to be remeasured to €1.5 million giving rise to tax expense of €500,000. Should this expense be recognised in profit or loss for the period or in equity?

If read literally, IAS 12 can be construed as requiring this expense to be accounted for in equity, as being a remeasurement of an amount originally recognised in equity. However, we question whether this was really the intention of IAS 12. We see a fundamental difference between an item that by its nature would always be recognised directly outside profit or loss (e.g. presentational foreign exchange differences or revaluations of plant, property and equipment) and an item which in the normal course of events would be accounted for in profit or loss, but when recognised for the first time as the result of a change in accounting policy (such as in Example 31.33 above) is dealt with as a 'catch up' adjustment to opening equity.

Such a 'catch up' adjustment is made in equity only because the entity is not presenting comparative information for all periods since it first commenced business. If it had done so, all the charge for environmental costs (and all the related deferred tax) would have been reflected in profit or loss in previous periods. In our view, once the tax effect of such an item has been recognised as a 'catch up' adjustment, any subsequent remeasurement of the tax should be allocated to profit or loss, other comprehensive income or equity based on the accounting treatment that would have been adopted in prior years if the new policy had always been in force.

10.3   Dividends and transaction costs of equity instruments

10.3.1 *Dividend subject to differential tax rate*

In some jurisdictions, the rate at which tax is paid depends on whether profits are distributed or retained. In other jurisdictions, distribution may lead to an additional liability to tax, or a refund of tax already paid. IAS 12 requires current and deferred taxes to be measured using the rate applicable to undistributed profits until a liability to pay a dividend is recognised, at which point the tax consequences of that dividend should also be recognised. This is discussed further at 8.4 above.

Where taxes are remeasured on recognition of a liability to pay a dividend, the difference should normally be recognised in profit or loss rather than directly in equity, even though the dividend itself is recognised directly in equity under IFRS. IAS 12 takes the view that any additional (or lower) tax liability relates to the original profit now being distributed rather than to the distribution itself. Where, however, the dividend is paid out of profit arising from a transaction that was originally recognised in other comprehensive income or equity, the adjustment to the tax liability should also be recognised in other comprehensive income or equity. *[IAS 12.52B].*

10.3.2 Dividend subject to withholding tax

Where dividends are paid by the reporting entity subject to withholding tax, the withholding tax should be included as part of the dividend charged to equity. *[IAS 12.65A].*

This provision of IAS 12 proves somewhat problematic in practice. There may be little economic difference, from the paying entity's perspective, between a requirement to pay a 5% 'withholding tax' on all dividends and a requirement to pay an additional 5% 'income tax' on distributed profit. Yet, the accounting treatment varies significantly depending on the analysis. If the tax is considered a withholding tax, it is treated as a deduction from equity in all circumstances. If, however, it is considered as an additional income tax, it will generally be treated as a charge to profit or loss (see 10.3.1 above). This distinction therefore relies on a clear definition of withholding tax, which IAS 12 unfortunately does not provide.

IAS 12 describes a withholding tax as a 'portion of the dividends [paid] to taxation authorities on behalf of shareholders'. *[IAS 12.65A].* However, this begs the question whether the determination of whether or not the tax is paid 'on behalf of shareholders' should be made by reference to the characterisation of the tax:

- in the paying entity's tax jurisdiction – in which case, there is the problem noted above that one jurisdiction's 'additional distribution tax' may be economically identical to another jurisdiction's 'withholding tax', or

- in the receiving entity's tax jurisdiction – in which case there would be the problem that the tax on a dividend paid to one shareholder be a 'withholding tax' (because credit is given for it on the shareholder's tax return) but the tax on a dividend paid to another shareholder the same time is not (because no credit is given for it on that shareholder's tax return).

This may be an area on which the IASB or the Interpretations Committee may be asked to provide guidance in due course.

10.3.3 Intragroup dividend subject to withholding tax

Where irrecoverable withholding tax is suffered on intragroup dividends, the withholding tax does not relate to an item recognised in equity in the consolidated financial statements (since the intragroup dividend to which it relates has been eliminated in those financial statements). The tax should therefore be accounted for in profit or loss for the period.

10.3.4 Incoming dividends

IAS 12 does not directly address the treatment of incoming dividends on which tax has been suffered (i.e. whether they should be shown at the amount received, or gross of withholding tax together with a corresponding tax charge).

However, in discussing the treatment prescribed for the paying company as summarised above, paragraph 65A of IAS 12 describes withholding tax as an amount 'paid to the tax authorities on behalf of shareholders'. It would therefore be most consistent with this treatment for the recipient to show dividends (and other income subject to withholding taxes) gross of withholding taxes, subject to the difficulties noted in 10.3.2 above to determining what exactly is a 'withholding tax'.

Some jurisdictions also give tax deductions for the 'underlying' tax suffered on dividends received. This is based on the concept that the dividend has been paid out of profits already subject to tax, so that to tax the full amount received again would amount to a punitive double taxation of the underlying profits. In our view, such underlying tax (which would form part of the tax charge, not the dividend, of the paying company) is not directly paid on behalf of the shareholder, and accordingly incoming dividends should not be grossed up for underlying tax.

10.3.5 Tax benefits of distributions and transaction costs of equity instruments

IAS 32 requires distributions to shareholders and transaction costs of equity instruments to be accounted for in equity net of any related income tax benefit (see Chapter 45 at 8.2). In the exposure draft *Improvements to IFRS* issued in June 2011, the IASB proposes deleting the reference to income tax benefit from IAS 32. This would mean that all tax effects of equity transactions would be allocated in accordance with the general principles of IAS 12. This proposal is unlikely to change the current accounting treatment of tax deductions for equity transactions required by IAS 32, other than to permit an entity to show such tax effects within equity gross rather than netted off the related pre-tax item. However, the proposals do not address the arguably far more pressing issue of the confusion caused by the lack of clear definition of withholding tax (see 10.3.2 above).

10.4   Gains and losses reclassified ('recycled') to profit or loss

Several IFRSs (notably IAS 21 and IAS 39) require certain gains and losses that have been accounted for outside profit or loss to be reclassified ('recycled') to profit or loss at a later date when the assets or liabilities to which they relate are realised or settled. Whilst IAS 12 requires any tax consequences of the original recognition of the gains or losses outside profit or loss also to be accounted for outside profit or loss, it is silent on the treatment to be adopted when the gains or losses are reclassified. In our view, any tax consequences of reclassified gains or losses originally recognised outside profit or loss should also be reclassified through profit or loss in the same period as the gains or losses to which they relate. Indeed, such reclassification is often an automatic consequence of the reversal of previously recognised deferred tax income or expense and its 're-recognition' as current tax income or expense, as illustrated in Example 31.34.

Example 31.34: Tax on reclassified ('recycled') items

On 1 January 2012 an entity purchases for €2,000 an equity security that it classifies as available-for-sale ('AFS'). At 31 December 2011 it restates the security to its fair value of €2,400. On 1 July 2012 it disposes of the investment for €2,100.

The entity's tax rate for 2012 is 40% and for 2012 35%. The change of rate was made in legislation enacted (without previous substantive enactment) on 1 May 2013. The entity is subject to tax on disposal of the investment (based on disposal proceeds less cost) in the period of disposal.

The accounting entries for this transaction would be as follows.

	€	€
1 January 2012		
AFS asset	2,000	
Cash		2,000
31 December 2012		
AFS asset [€2,400 – €2,000]	400	
Deferred tax (balance sheet) [€400 @ 40%]		160
Other comprehensive income ('OCI')		240
Recognition of increase in value of asset, and related deferred tax		
1 May 2013		
Deferred tax (balance sheet) [€400 @ (35% – 40%)]	20	
OCI		20
Remeasurement of deferred tax (assuming no change in the fair value of the AFS asset since 31 December 2011)		
1 July 2013		
Cash	2,100	
OCI (reclassification of €400 (before tax) credited 31.12.12)	400	
AFS asset		2,400
Profit on disposal of AFS asset [cash €2,100 less original cost €2,000]		100
Deferred tax (balance sheet)	140	
Deferred tax income (OCI)		140
Current tax (profit or loss)	35	
Current tax (balance sheet) [35% of €100 pre-tax profit]		35

10.5 Gain/loss in profit or loss and loss/gain outside profit or loss offset for tax purposes

It often happens that a gain or loss accounted for in profit or loss can be offset for tax purposes against a gain or loss accounted for in other comprehensive income (or an increase or decrease in equity). This raises the question of how the tax effects of such transactions should be accounted for, as illustrated by Example 31.35 below.

Example 31.35: Loss in other comprehensive income and gain in profit or loss offset for tax purposes

During the year ended 31 December 2012, an entity that pays tax at 35% makes a taxable profit of €50,000 comprising:

- €80,000 trading profit less finance costs accounted for in profit or loss; and
- €30,000 foreign exchange losses accounted for in other comprehensive income ('OCI').

Should the total tax liability of €17,500 (35% of €50,000) be presented as either:

(a) a charge of €17,500 in profit or loss; or

(b) a charge of €28,000 (35% of €80,000) in profit or loss and a credit of €10,500 (35% of €30,000) in OCI?

In our view, (b) is the appropriate treatment, since the amount accounted for in OCI represents the difference between the tax that would have been paid absent the exchange loss accounted for in OCI and the amount actually payable. This indicates that this is the amount that, in the words of paragraph 61A of IAS 12, 'relates to' items that are recognised outside profit or loss.

Similar issues may arise where a transaction accounted for outside profit or loss generates a suitable taxable profit that allows recognition of a previously unrecognised tax asset relating to a transaction previously accounted for in profit or loss, as illustrated by Example 31.36 below.

Example 31.36:   *Recognition of deferred tax asset in profit or loss on the basis of tax liability accounted for outside profit or loss*

An entity that pays tax at 30% has brought forward unrecognised deferred tax assets (with an indefinite life) totalling £1 million, relating to trading losses accounted for in profit or loss in prior periods. On 1 January 2012 it invests £100,000 in government bonds, which it holds until they are redeemed for the same amount on maturity on 31 December 2015. For tax purposes, any gain made by the entity on disposal of the bonds can be offset against the brought forward tax losses. The tax base of the bonds remains £100,000 at all times.

The entity elects to account for the bonds as available-for-sale and therefore carries them at fair value (see Chapter 49 at 2.4). Over the period to maturity the fair value of the bonds at each balance sheet date (31 December) is as follows:

	£000
2012	110
2013	115
2014	120
2015	100

Under IAS 39 the movements in value would all be accounted for in other comprehensive income ('OCI') – see Chapter 49 at 2.4. Taken in isolation, the valuation gains in 2012 to 2014 would give rise to a deferred tax liability (at 30%) of £3,000 (2012), £4,500 (2013) and £6,000 (2014). However, these liabilities arise from taxable temporary differences that can be offset against the losses brought forward (see 7.4 above), and accordingly the (equal and opposite) deferred tax liability and deferred tax asset are offset in the balance sheet (see 13.1.1 below). This raises the question as to whether there should be either:

(a) no tax charge or credit in either profit or loss or OCI in any of the periods affected; or

(b) in each period, a deferred tax charge in OCI (in respect of the taxable temporary difference arising from valuation gains on the bonds) and deferred tax income in profit or loss (representing the recognition of the previously unrecognised deferred tax asset).

In our view, the treatment in (b) should be followed. The fact that no deferred tax is presented in the balance sheet arises from the offset of a deferred tax asset and deferred tax liability – it does not imply that there is no deferred tax. Moreover, although the recognition of the deferred tax asset is possible only as the result of the recognition of a deferred tax liability arising from a transaction accounted for in OCI, the asset itself relates to a trading loss previously accounted for in profit or loss. Accordingly, the deferred tax credit arising from the recognition of the asset is properly accounted for in profit or loss.

10.6   Defined benefit pension plans

IAS 19 – *Employee Benefits* – currently permits, and as amended will require, an entity, in accounting for a defined benefit post-employment benefit plan, to recognise actuarial gains and losses relating to the plan in full in other comprehensive income ('OCI') (see Chapter 33 at 5.3.1.B and 8). At the same time, a calculated current service cost and finance income and expense relating to the plan assets and liabilities are recognised in profit or loss. The current and amended versions of IAS 19 require different amounts to be recognised in profit or loss – see Chapter 33 at 8 for further discussion.

In many jurisdictions, tax deductions for post-employment benefits are given on the basis of cash contributions paid to the plan fund (or benefits paid when a plan is unfunded).

This significant difference between the way in which defined plans are treated for tax and financial reporting purposes can make the allocation of tax deductions for them between profit or loss and OCI somewhat arbitrary, as illustrated by Example 31.37 below.

Example 31.37:   Tax deductions for defined benefit pension plans

At 1 January 2011 an entity that pays tax at 40% has a fully-funded defined benefit pension scheme. During the year ended 31 December 2012 it records a total cost of €1 million, of which €800,000 is allocated to profit or loss and €200,000 to other comprehensive income ('OCI'). In January 2013 it makes a funding payment of €400,000, a tax deduction for which is received through the current tax charge for the year ended 31 December 2013.

Assuming that the entity is able to recognise a deferred tax asset for the entire €1 million charged in 2012, it will record the following entry for income taxes in 2012.

	€	€
Deferred tax asset [€1,000,000 @ 40%]	400,000	
Deferred tax income (profit or loss) [€800,000 @ 40%]		320,000
Deferred tax income (OCI) [€200,000 @ 40%]		80,000

When the funding payment is made in January 2013, the accounting deficit on the fund is reduced by €400,000. This gives rise to deferred tax expense of €160,000 (€400,000 @ 40%), as some of the deferred tax asset as at 31 December 2012 is released, and current tax income of €160,000. The difficulty is how to allocate this movement between profit or loss and OCI, as it is ultimately a matter of arbitrary allocation as to whether the funding payment is regarded as making good (for example):

*   €400,000 of the €800,000 deficit previously accounted for in profit or loss;

*   the whole of the €200,000 of the deficit previously accounted for in OCI and €200,000 of the €800,000 deficit previously accounted for in profit or loss; or

*   a pro-rata share of those parts of the total deficit accounted for in profit or loss and OCI.

Indeed, for an entity that has adopted the transitional provision of IFRS 1 – *First-time Adoption of International Financial Reporting Standards* – that allows all cumulative actuarial gains and losses to be recognised on transition to IFRS, it will be quite impossible to determine how much of those cumulative gains and losses would have been accounted for in the profit or loss, and how much in OCI, if IFRS had always been applied.

In the example above, the split is of relatively minor significance, since the entity was able to recognise 100% of the potential deferred tax asset associated with the pension liability. This means that, as the scheme is funded, there will be an equal and opposite amount of current tax income and deferred tax expense. The only real issue is therefore one of presentation, namely whether the gross items comprising this net nil charge are disclosed within the tax charge in profit or loss or in OCI.

In other cases, however, there might be an amount of net tax income or expense that needs to be allocated. Suppose that, as above, the entity recorded a pension cost of €1 million in 2012 but determined that the related deferred tax asset did not meet the criteria for recognition under IAS 12. In 2013, the entity determines that an asset of €50,000 can be recognised in view of the funding payments and taxable profits anticipated in 2013 and later years. This results in a total tax credit of €210,000 (€160,000 current tax, €50,000 deferred tax) in 2013, raising the question of whether it should be allocated to profit or loss, to OCI, or allocated on a pro-rata basis. This question might also arise if, as the result of newly enacted tax rates, the existing deferred tax balance were required to be remeasured.

In our view, these are instances of the exceptional circumstances envisaged by IAS 12 when a strict allocation of tax between profit or loss and OCI is not possible (see 10 above). Accordingly, any reasonable method of allocation may be used, provided that it is applied on a consistent basis.

One approach might be to compare the funding payments made to the scheme in the previous few years with the charges made to profit or loss under IAS 19 in those periods. If, for example, it is found that the payments were equal to or greater than the charges to profit or loss, it might reasonably be concluded that the funding payments have 'covered' the charge recognised in profit or loss, so that any surplus or deficit on the balance sheet is broadly represented by items that have been accounted for in OCI.

However, a surplus may also arise from funding the scheme to an amount greater than the liability recognised under IAS 19 (for example under a minimum funding requirement imposed by local legislation or agreed with the pension fund trustees). In this case, the asset does not result from previously recognised income but from a reduction in another asset (i.e. cash). The entity should assess the expected manner of recovery of any asset implied by the accounting treatment of the surplus – i.e. whether it has been recognised on the basis that it will be 'consumed' (resulting in an accounting expense) or refunded to the entity in due course. The accounting treatment of refunds is discussed further in Chapter 33, and at 10.6.1 below.

The entity will account for the tax consequences of the expected manner of recovery implied by the accounting treatment. Where it is concluded that the asset will be 'consumed' (resulting in accounting expense), the entity will need to determine whether such an expense is likely to be recognised in profit or loss or in OCI in a future period.

10.6.1 Tax on refund of pension surplus

In some jurisdictions, a pension fund may be permitted or required to make a refund to the sponsoring employee of any surplus in the fund not required to settle the known or anticipated liabilities of the fund. It may be that such a refund is subject to tax. IFRIC 14 – IAS 19 – *The Limit on a Defined Benefit Asset, Minimum Funding Requirements and their Interaction* – requires any asset recorded in respect of such a refund to be shown net of any tax other than an income tax (see Chapter 33). In determining whether such a tax is an income tax of the entity, the general principles in 4.1 above should be applied. For example, a tax levied on the pension fund, and not the sponsoring entity, in respect of the gross amount of the refund, without regard to the sponsoring entity's other taxable income, or to whether the entity received tax deductions on contributions to the fund, is clearly not an income tax of the sponsoring entity.

10.7 Share-based payment transactions

The accounting treatment of share-based payment transactions, some knowledge of which is required to understand the discussion below, is dealt with in Chapter 32.

In many tax jurisdictions, an entity receives a tax deduction in respect of remuneration paid in shares, share options or other equity instruments of the entity. The amount of any tax deduction may differ from the related remuneration expense, and may arise in a later accounting period. For example, in some jurisdictions, an entity may recognise an expense for employee services in accordance with IFRS 2 (based on the fair value of the award at the date of grant), but not receive a tax deduction until the share options are exercised (based on the intrinsic value of the award at the date of exercise).

As noted in 6.1.4 above, IAS 12 effectively considers the cumulative expense associated with share-based payment transactions as an asset that has been fully expensed in the financial statements in advance of being recognised for tax purposes, thus giving rise to a deductible temporary difference. *[IAS 12.68A, 68B].*

If the tax deduction available in future periods is not known at the end of the period, it should be estimated based on information available at the end of the period. For example, if the tax deduction will be dependent upon the entity's share price at a future date, the measurement of the deductible temporary difference should be based on the entity's share price at the end of the period. *[IAS 12.68B].*

10.7.1 Allocation of tax deduction between profit or loss and equity

Where the amount of any tax deduction (or estimated future tax deduction) exceeds the amount of the related cumulative remuneration expense, the current or deferred tax associated with the excess should be recognised directly in equity. *[IAS 12.68C].* This treatment is illustrated by Example 31.38 below.

Example 31.38:   Tax deductions for share-based payment transactions – allocation to profit or loss and equity

At the start of year 1, an entity with a tax rate of 40% grants options, which vest at the end of year 3 and are exercised at the end of year 5. Tax deductions are received at the date of exercise of the options, based on their intrinsic value at the date of exercise. Details of the expense recognised for employee services received and consumed in each accounting period, the number of options expected to vest by the entity at each year-end during the vesting period and outstanding after the end of the vesting period, and the intrinsic value of the options at each year-end, are as follows:

Year	IFRS 2 expense for period £	Cumulative IFRS 2 expense £	Number of options	Intrinsic value per option £	Total intrinsic value £
1	188,000	188,000	50,000	5	250,000
2	185,000	373,000	45,000	8	360,000
3	190,000	563,000	40,000	13	520,000
4		563,000	40,000	17	680,000
5		563,000	40,000	20	800,000

The tax base of, and the temporary difference and deferred tax asset associated with, the employee services is calculated as follows. Since the book value of the employee services is in all cases zero, the temporary difference associated with the services is at all times equal to their tax base as set out below.

Year	Intrinsic value (see table above) £ a	Expired portion of vesting period [1] b	Tax base (and temporary difference) £ c = a × b	Tax asset [2] £ 40% of c	Tax income [3] £
1	250,000	1/3	83,333	33,333	33,333
2	360,000	2/3	240,000	96,000	62,667
3	520,000	3/3	520,000	208,000	112,000
4	680,000	3/3	680,000	272,000	64,000
5	800,000	3/3	800,000	320,000	48,000

1 The expired portion of the vesting period is consistent with that used to calculate the cumulative charge employee costs under IFRS 2 (see Chapter 32).

2 Deferred tax asset in years 1 to 4 and current tax asset in year 5.

3 Year-on-year increase in asset.

By comparing the 'Cumulative IFRS 2 expense' column in the first table with the 'Tax base (and temporary difference)' column in the second table it can be seen that in years 1 to 3 the expected tax deduction is lower than the cumulative expense charged, and is therefore dealt with entirely in profit or loss. However in years 4 and 5 the expected (and in year 5 the actual) tax deduction is higher than the cumulative expense charged. The tax relating to the cumulative expense charged is dealt with in profit or loss, and the tax relating to the excess of the tax-deductible amount over the amount charged in profit or loss is dealt with in equity as follows:

	DR	CR
Year 1		
Deferred tax (balance sheet)	33,333	
Deferred tax (profit or loss)		33,333
Year 2		
Deferred tax (balance sheet)	62,667	
Deferred tax (profit or loss)		62,667

Chapter 31

Year 3

Deferred tax (balance sheet)	112,000	
Deferred tax (profit or loss)		112,000

Year 4

Deferred tax (balance sheet)	64,000	
Deferred tax (profit or loss)[1]		17,200
Equity		46,800

Year 5

Deferred tax (profit or loss)	225,200	
Deferred tax (equity)	46,800	
Deferred tax (balance sheet)		272,000
Current tax (balance sheet)	320,000	
Current tax (profit or loss)[2]		225,200
Current tax (equity)		94,800

1   Cumulative tax credit to profit or loss restricted to 40% of cumulative expense of £563,000 = £225,200. Amount credited in years 1 to 3 is £(33,333 + 62,667 + 112,000) = £212,000. Therefore amount recognised in profit or loss is £(225,200 – 212,000) = £17,200.

2   Current tax credit in profit or loss is restricted to £225,000 as explained in note 1 above. The £48,000 net increase in total cumulative tax income since year 4 (£320,000 – £272,000) is dealt with entirely in equity (current tax income €94,800 less deferred tax charge €46,800).

Example 31.38 above is based on Example 5 in Appendix B to IAS 12 (as inserted by IFRS 2). However, the example included in IAS 12 states that the cumulative tax income is based on the number of options 'outstanding' at each period end. This is inconsistent with the methodology in IFRS 2 (see Chapter 32), which would require the share-based payment expense during the vesting period to be based on the number of options expected to vest (as that term is defined in IFRS 2), not the total number of options outstanding, at the period end. It would only be once the vesting period is complete that the number of options outstanding becomes relevant. We assume that this is simply a drafting slip by the IASB.

IAS 12 asserts that the allocation of the tax deduction between profit or loss and equity illustrated in Example 31.38 is appropriate on the basis that the fact that the tax deduction (or estimated future tax deduction) exceeds the amount of the related cumulative remuneration expense 'indicates that the tax deduction relates not only to remuneration expense but also to an equity item.' *[IAS 12.68C].*

However, some (including the IASB itself in the exposure draft that preceded IFRS 2) take the view that any tax deductions in excess of the amount charged to profit or loss relate to an increase in the fair value of the award from the date of grant to the date of exercise, which, under the 'grant date measurement' model in IFRS 2, is not recognised in equity, or indeed anywhere in the financial statements. The 'excess' tax deduction therefore does not meet the criteria for recognition in equity in IAS 12, and would (on application of the normal rules in IAS 12) be accounted for in profit or loss by default.

The treatment required by IFRS 2 seems to have been adopted for consistency with US GAAP. However, as the IASB acknowledges, while the final cumulative allocation of tax between profit or loss and equity is broadly consistent with that required by US GAAP, the basis on which it is measured and reported at reporting dates before exercise date is quite different. *[IFRS 2.BC311-BC329].*

10.7.2 Determining the tax base

IAS 12 does not specify exactly how the tax base of a share-based payment transaction is to be determined. However, the worked example in Appendix 5 of IAS 12 (the substance of which is reproduced at 10.7.1 above) calculates the tax base as:

- the amount that would be deductible for tax if the event triggering deduction occurred at the end of the reporting period; multiplied by

- the expired portion of the vesting period at the end of the reporting period.

IFRS 2 treats certain share-based payment awards as, in effect, a parcel of a number of discrete awards, each with a different vesting period. This may be the case where an award is subject to graded vesting, has been modified, or has separate equity and liability components (see Chapter 32). In order to determine the tax base for such an award, it is necessary to consider separately the part, or parts, of the award with the same vesting period, as illustrated in Example 31.39 below.

Example 31.39: Tax deductions for share-based payment transactions – 'multi-element' awards

An entity awards 550 free shares to an employee, with no conditions other than continuous service. 100 shares vest after one year, 150 shares after two years and 300 shares after three years. Any shares received at the end of years 1 and 2 have vested unconditionally.

At the date the award is granted, the fair value of a share delivered in one year's time is €3.00; in two years' time €2.80; and in three years' time €2.50.

Under IFRS 2, the analysis is that the employee has simultaneously received an award of 100 shares vesting over one year, an award of 150 shares vesting over two years and an award of 300 shares vesting over 3 years (see Chapter 32 at 6.2.2). This would be accounted for as follows (assuming that the award was expected to vest in full at each reporting date and did actually vest in full – see Chapter 32):

Year	Calculation of cumulative expense	Cumulative expense (€)	Expense for period (€)
1	[100 shares × €3.00] + [150 shares × €2.80 × 1/2] + [300 shares × €2.50 × 1/3]	760	760
2	[100 shares × €3.00] + [150 shares × €2.80 × 2/2] + [300 shares × €2.50 × 2/3]	1,220	460
3	[100 shares × €3.00] + [150 shares × €2.80 × 2/2] + [300 shares × €2.50 × 3/3]	1,470	250

The entity receives a tax deduction at 30% for the awards based on the fair value of the shares delivered. The fair value of a share at the end of years 1, 2 and 3 is, respectively, €3.60, €2.00 and €6.00.

At the end of year 1, a current tax deduction of €108 (100 shares × €3.60 @ 30%) is receivable in respect of the 100 shares that vest. The tax base of the shares expected to vest in years 2 and 3 is calculated by reference to the year-end share price of €3.60 as:

- in respect of the 150 shares expected to vest at the end of year 2, €270 (150 shares × €3.60 × 1/2). This will give rise to a deferred tax asset of €81 (€270 @ 30%); and

- in respect of the 300 shares expected to vest at the end of year 3, €360 (300 shares × €3.60 × 1/3). This will give rise to a deferred tax asset of €108 (€360 @ 30%).

The total deferred tax asset at the end of year is therefore €189 (€81 + €108).

At the end of year 2, a current tax deduction of €90 is receivable in respect of the 150 shares that vest (150 shares × €2.00 @ 30%). The tax base of the shares expected to vest in year 3 is calculated by reference to the year-end share price of €2.00 as €400 (300 shares × €2.00 × 2/3). This gives rise to a deferred tax asset of €120 (€400 @ 30%).

At the end of year 3, a current tax deduction of €540 (300 shares × €6.00 @ 30%) is receivable in respect of the 300 shares that vest.

When an award has multiple elements that vest at different times, the question arises as to whether the unit of account for applying the 'cap' on recognition of the tax benefit in profit or loss is the award as a whole or each element separately accounted for. In our view, the determination needs to be made for each element of the award separately. This is similar to our analysis in 10.7.3 below (multiple awards outstanding) and 10.7.4 below (awards for which a tax deduction is received on exercise which are exercised at different times).

Based on the information above, the total current and deferred tax income or expense (i.e. before allocation to profit or loss and equity) at the ends of years 1 to 3 would be as follows, assuming in each case that there is no restriction on the recognition of tax assets (see 7.4 above).

Year	Current tax asset and income €	Deferred tax asset €	Deferred tax income/(expense) €
1	108	189	189
2	90	120	(69)
3	540	–	(120)

The required accounting entries for income taxes are as follows:

Year 1

Current tax (balance sheet)	108	
Current tax (profit or loss)		90
Current tax (equity)[1]		18
Deferred tax (balance sheet)	189	
Deferred tax (profit or loss) (€63 + €75 – see below)		138
Deferred tax (equity)[2] (€18 + €33 – see below)		51

1   The current tax deduction relates to the 100 shares vesting in year 1, for which the charge to profit or loss is €300 (100 shares × €3.00). The tax deduction accounted for in profit or loss is therefore restricted to 30% of €300 = €90. The balance of €18 is credited to equity, and relates to the €0.60 difference between the grant date fair value of a 'Year 1' share at grant (€3.00) and at vesting (€3.60) – 100 shares × €0.60 = €60 @ 30% = €18.

2   The deferred tax income of €189 represents:

- €81 (see above) in respect of the 150 shares expected to vest in year 2, for which the charge to profit or loss is €210 (150 shares × €2.80 × 1/2). The tax deduction accounted for in profit or loss is restricted to 30% of €210 = €63, with the balance of €18 credited to equity; and

- €108 (see above) in respect of the 300 shares for which the expected charge to profit or loss is €250 (300 shares × €2.50 × 1/3). The tax deduction accounted for in profit or loss is therefore restricted to 30% of €250 = €75, with the balance of €33 credited to equity.

Year 2

Current tax (balance sheet)	90	
Current tax (profit or loss)[3]		90
Deferred tax (profit or loss)[4]	18	
Deferred tax (equity)[4]	51	
Deferred tax (balance sheet)[4]		69

3   The current tax deduction relates to the 150 shares vesting in year 2, for which the cumulative charge to profit or loss is €420 (150 shares × €2.80). The cumulative tax deduction accounted for in profit or loss would therefore be restricted to 30% of €420 = €126. The entire amount of current tax deduction received (€90) is therefore credited to profit or loss.

4   At the end of year 2, the deferred tax relates to the 300 shares expected to vest at the end of year 3, which has been measured based on the year end share price of €2.00. This is lower than the share price on which the IFRS 2 charge has been based. Therefore there is no requirement to allocate any deferred tax to equity, and the balance of deferred tax in equity is reduced to nil. The balance of the total €69 movement in the deferred tax balance is allocated to profit or loss.

The net tax credit in profit or loss in year 2 of €72 (current tax credit €90, less deferred tax charge €18) can be seen as representing:

Credit relating to IFRS 2 expense recognised in the period[5]	105
Charge relating to remeasurement of prior year deferred tax[6]	(33)
Total	72

5   In this case the tax credit recognised in profit or loss is not the 'expected' credit of €138 (IFRS 2 charge of €460 @ 30%). This is because the current tax deduction for the shares vesting in year 2 and the deferred tax deduction for the shares expected to vest in year 3 are based on the year-end share price of €2.00, which is lower than the share values used to calculate the IFRS 2 charge (€2.80 and €2.50). During the year, an IFRS 2 expense has been recognised for 75 'whole share equivalents' in respect of the shares vesting in year 2 (150 shares × 1/2) and 100 'whole share equivalents' in respect of the shares expected to vest in year 3 (300 shares × 1/3), a total of 175 'whole share equivalents'. Accordingly the credit for the year is €105 (175 × €2.00 × 30%).

6   In year 1 the deferred tax credit (based on the year 1 year end share price of €3.60) recognised in profit of loss in respect of the shares expected to vest in years 2 and 3 was €138. If this had been based on the year 2 year end share price of €2.00 this would have been only €105. [150 × 1/2 × €2.00] + [300 × 1/3 × €2.00] = €350 × 30% = €105. €138 − €105 = €33.

Year 3

Current tax (balance sheet)	540	
Current tax (profit or loss)		225
Current tax (equity)[7]		315
Deferred tax (profit or loss)	120	
Deferred tax (balance sheet)[8]		120

7   The current tax deduction relates to the 300 shares vesting in year 1, for which the cumulative charge to profit or loss is €750 (300 shares × €2.50). The tax deduction accounted for in profit or loss is therefore restricted to 30% of €750 = €225.

8   The deferred tax asset, all of which was – on a cumulative basis – recognised in profit or loss, is derecognised in profit or loss.

The net tax credit in profit or loss in year 3 of €105 (current tax credit €225, less deferred tax charge €120) can be seen as representing:

Credit relating to IFRS 2 expense recognised in the period[9]	75
Credit relating to remeasurement of prior year deferred tax[10]	30
Total	105

9 €250 @ 30%.

10 The opening balance deferred tax asset of €120 is based on the year 2 share price of €2.00. If this had been based on the year 3 share price of €6.00 it would have been €360. However, the amount recognised in profit or loss would have been restricted to €150 – 30% of the cumulative expense at the end of year 2 of €500 (300 shares × €2.50 × 2/3). €150 – €120 = €30.

10.7.3 Allocation when more than one award is outstanding

As noted above, IAS 12 requires that, 'where the amount of any tax deduction ... exceeds the amount of the related cumulative remuneration expense, the current or deferred tax associated with the excess should be recognised directly in equity'. Some have therefore argued that, as drafted, IAS 12 requires the cumulative expense for all outstanding share schemes to be compared in aggregate with the aggregate tax deduction for all share schemes. Others argue that the comparison should be made for each scheme separately. The effect of each treatment is illustrated in Example 31.40 below.

Example 31.40:   Tax deductions for share-based payment transactions – more than one award

An entity that pays tax at 30% has two outstanding share schemes, Scheme A and Scheme B. The entity receives tax deductions for share-based payment transactions based on their intrinsic value at the date of exercise.

At the balance sheet date, 31 March 2010, the cumulative expense charged for each scheme is £1 million. Scheme A has a negative intrinsic value at the balance sheet date, and is not expected to recover its value to the extent that employees will exercise their options. Accordingly no deferred tax asset is recognised for Scheme A. Scheme B has an intrinsic value of £1.5 million. The entity will therefore record a deferred tax asset of £450,000 (30% of £1.5 million), subject to the recognition criteria for deferred tax assets being satisfied.

Those who argue that comparison of share-based payment expense to tax deduction should be made on an aggregated basis would conclude that, because the cumulative potential tax deduction of £1.5 million (which relates only to Scheme B) is lower than the cumulative aggregate expense for both Scheme A and Scheme B (£2 million), the deferred tax income may be recognised entirely in profit or loss.

However, those who argue that comparison of share-based payment expense to tax deduction should be made on a discrete basis for each scheme would conclude that, because the cumulative tax deduction for Scheme B (£1.5 million) is higher than the cumulative aggregate expense for Scheme B (£1 million), only £300,000 of the deferred tax income (30% of £1 million) may be recognised in profit or loss, with the remaining £150,000 recognised in equity.

In our view, the comparison must be made on a discrete scheme-by-scheme basis. As noted in 10.7.2 above, it is clear from IAS 12 and the Basis for Conclusions to IFRS 2 that the IASB's intention was to exclude from profit or loss any tax deduction that is effectively given for the growth in fair value of an award that accrues after grant date.[27] This can be determined only on an award-by-award basis. Moreover, IAS 12 requires the amount of any tax deduction to be accounted for in equity when it 'exceeds the amount of the *related* cumulative remuneration expense'. In Example 31.40 above, the tax deduction on Scheme B cannot, in our view, be said to be 'related' to the remuneration expense for Scheme A. Accordingly, the expense relating to Scheme A is not relevant for determining the amount of tax income relating to Scheme B that is required to be accounted for in equity.

It may also be that what is regarded as a single scheme may need to be further sub-divided for the purposes of the comparison for reasons such as the following:

- where the same award is made to regular employees and also to top management, the fair value of the options granted to each population may nevertheless be different for the purposes of IFRS 2 given different exercise behaviours (see Chapter 32 at 8.5.2.A);

- an award is made to employees which attracts tax deductions in more than one tax jurisdiction;

- an award is made in the same tax jurisdiction to employees in different entities, not all of which are able to recognise a deferred tax asset.

10.7.4 Staggered exercise of awards

The example in IAS 12, the substance of which is included in Example 31.38 at 10.7.1 above, addresses a situation in which all vested awards are exercised simultaneously. In practice, however, vested awards are often exercised at different dates.

Once an award under a given scheme has vested, and different awards in that scheme are exercised at different times, the question arises as to whether the 'cap' on recognition of the tax benefit in profit or loss should be calculated by reference to the cumulative expense recognised in respect of the total number of awards vested, or in respect only of as yet unexercised vested awards. In our view, where a tax deduction is received on exercise, the calculation must be undertaken by reference to the cumulative expense recognised for outstanding unexercised options. This is illustrated by Example 31.41 below.

Example 31.41:   Tax deductions for share-based payment transactions – staggered exercise of award

At the start of year 1, an entity with a tax rate of 40% grants 20 options each to 5 employees. The options have a fair value of €5 and vest at the end of year 2. The options vest in full. 25 are exercised at the end of year 3 and 75 at the end of year 6. The entity is able to support the view that any deferred tax asset arising before exercise will be recoverable, and may therefore be recognised in full.

Tax deductions are given in the year of exercise, based on the intrinsic value of the options at the date of exercise. The intrinsic value of options at each balance sheet date is as follows:

Year	Intrinsic value per option
	€
1	3
2	8
3	8
4	1
5	7
6	6

On the basis of the information above:

- there would be an IFRS 2 charge of €250 in years 1 and 2 (20 options × 5 employees × €5 × 1/2 (portion of vesting period)
- current and deferred tax assets should be recognised at the end of each period as follows:

Current tax

Year	Number of options exercised	Intrinsic value per option €	Total intrinsic value €	Tax effect at 40% €
3	25	8	200	80
6	75	6	450	180

Deferred tax

Year	Number of options outstanding	Temporary difference per option €	Total temporary difference €	Tax effect at 40% €
1	100	1.5[1]	150	60
2	100	8	800	320
3	75	8	600	240
4	75	1	75	30
5	75	7	525	210
6	–	6	–	–

1 Intrinsic value €3 × 1/2 (expired portion of vesting period).

The required accounting entries for income taxes are as follows

	DR €	CR €
Year 1		
Deferred tax (balance sheet)	60	
Deferred tax (profit or loss)[1]		60
Year 2		
Deferred tax (balance sheet)[2]	260	
Deferred tax (profit or loss)[3]		140
Deferred tax (equity)		120
Year 3		
Deferred tax (profit or loss)[4]	50	
Deferred tax (equity)	30	
Deferred tax (balance sheet)[5]		80
Current tax (balance sheet)[6]	80	
Current tax (profit or loss)[4]		50
Current tax (equity)		30
Year 4		
Deferred tax (profit or loss)[7]	120	
Deferred tax (equity)	90	
Deferred tax (balance sheet)[8]		210
Year 5		
Deferred tax (balance sheet)[9]	180	
Deferred tax (profit or loss)[10]		120
Deferred tax (equity)		60

Year 6

Deferred tax (profit or loss)[11]	150	
Deferred tax (equity)	60	
Deferred tax (balance sheet)		210
Current tax (balance sheet)[12]	180	
Current tax (profit or loss)[13]		150
Current tax (equity)		30

1   The cumulative tax income is based on expected deductions of €150, which is less than the cumulative IFRS 2 charge of €250 (see above).

2   Year 2 year-end balance of €320 (see table above), less €60 recognised at end of year 1 = €140.

3   Cumulative deferred tax recognised in profit or loss must not exceed 40% × €500 (cumulative IFRS 2 charge) = €200. This limits the credit for year 2 to €200 less the €60 credited in year 1 = €140.

4   Reversal of deferred tax income previously recognised in profit or loss for the 25 options exercised: 25 × €5 [IFRS 2 charge per option] × 40% = €50. This also represents the limit on the amount of current tax deduction that can be recognised in profit or loss.

5   Year 3 year-end balance of €240 (see table above), less €320 recognised at end of year 2 = €80.

6   25 options × €8 intrinsic value × 40% = €80

In years 4 to 6, the amount of tax recognised in profit or loss is restricted by the cumulative IFRS 2 expense of €375 for the 75 options left outstanding (75 options × €5).

7   Cumulative (maximum) tax deduction already recognised in profit or loss is €375 @ 40% = €150. This needs to be reduced to €30 (year end deferred tax balance), giving rise to a charge of €150 − €30 = €120. This can be seen as representing the fact that, at the start of the period a cumulative potential tax deduction of €5 per award had been recognised in profit or loss. At the end of the period it is expected that deductions of only €1 per award will be available. Therefore there is a loss to be recognised in profit or loss of 75 awards × (€5 − €1) × 40% = €120.

8   Year 4 year-end balance of €30 (see table above), less €240 recognised at end of year 3 = €(210).

9   Year 5 year end balance of €210 (see table above), less €30 recognised at end of year 4 = €180.

10   Cumulative maximum tax deduction that can be recognised in profit or loss is €150 (see note 7). €30 cumulative deduction is brought forward, so that credit for period is limited to €150 − €30 = €120.

11   Reversal of deferred tax previously recognised. The amount previously taken to profit or loss was limited to €150 (see notes 7 and 9).

12   75 options × €6 × 40% = €180.

13   Deduction restricted to €375 [IFRS 2 charge] × 40% = €150.

It will be noted that the cumulative effect of the above entries in profit or loss is as follows (tax income in brackets):

Year	Deferred tax €	Current tax €	Total €
1	(60)		(60)
2	(140)		(140)
3	50	(50)	–
4	120		120
5	(120)		(120)
6	150	(150)	–
		Total	(200)

The cumulative effect of the above entries in equity is as follows (tax income in brackets):

Year	Deferred tax €	Current tax €	Total €
1			–
2	(120)		(120)
3	30	(30)	–
4	90		90
5	(60)		(60)
6	60	(30)	30
		Total	(60)

The overall effect is to take credit in profit or loss for the lower of total tax deductions actually received of €260 (€80 in year 3 and €180 in year 6) and the tax deductions on the IFRS 2 expense of €200 (40% of €500). The excess tax deductions of €60 are recognised in equity.

10.7.5 Replacement awards in a business combination

IFRS 3 – *Business Combinations* – contains some detailed provisions on the treatment of share-based payment awards issued by an acquirer to replace awards made by the acquired entity before the business combination occurred. These are discussed in Chapter 32 at 11.

IFRS 3 amends IAS 12 to include an illustrative example[28] for the treatment of tax deductions on such replacement awards, the substance of which is reproduced as Example 31.42 below.

Example 31.42: Deferred tax on replacement share-based awards in a business combination

On 1 January 2012 Entity A acquired Entity B. A paid cash consideration of €400 million to the former owners of B. At the acquisition date B had outstanding fully-vested employee share options with a fair value of €100 million. As part of the business combination B's outstanding share options are replaced by fully vested share options of A (replacement awards) with a market-based measure of €100 million and an intrinsic value of €80 million. In accordance with IFRS 3, the replacement awards are part of the consideration transferred for B (see Chapter 32 at 11).

A tax deduction will be given only when the options are exercised, based on the intrinsic value of the options at that date. A's tax rate is 40%.

A recognises a deferred tax asset of €32 million (intrinsic value of €80m × 40%) on the replacement awards at the acquisition date (see 10.7.1 above). IAS 12 does not indicate the calculation if only part of the fair value of the award were regarded as part of the consideration transferred. However, it would be consistent with the general approach indicated at 6.3.1 above to calculate the tax base of the award by adjusting the intrinsic value by the ratio of the expired vesting period at acquisition to the total vesting period of the award (as determined for the purposes of IFRS 3 – see Chapter 32 at 11).

A measures the identifiable net assets obtained in the business combination (excluding deferred tax assets and liabilities) at €450 million, with a combined tax base of €300 million, giving rise to a taxable temporary difference at the acquisition date of €150 million, on which deferred tax at 40% of €60 million is recognised. Goodwill is calculated as follows:

	€m
Cash consideration	400
Replacement options	100
Total consideration	500
Identifiable net assets (excluding deferred tax)	(450)
Deferred tax asset	(32)
Deferred tax liability	60
Goodwill	78

Reductions in the carrying amount of goodwill are not deductible for tax purposes. In accordance with the initial recognition exception in IAS 12 (see 7.2 above), A recognises no deferred tax liability for the taxable temporary difference associated with the goodwill recognised in the business combination. The accounting entry for the business combination is therefore as follows:

	DR	CR
	€m	€m
Goodwill	78	
Identifiable net assets	450	
Deferred tax asset	32	
Cash		400
Equity		100
Deferred tax liability		60

On 31 December 2012 the intrinsic value of the replacement awards is €120 million, in respect of which A recognises a deferred tax asset of €48 million (€120 m at 40%). This gives rise to deferred tax income of €16 million (€48 million recognised at 31 December 2012 less €32 million arising on acquisition). IAS 12 notes, somewhat redundantly, that this amount is credited to 'deferred tax income', but with no indication as to whether the amount should be recognised in profit or loss or in equity. In our view, the general principles of IAS 12 regarding tax deductions on share-based payment transactions suggest that the entire amount is recognised in equity. This is because the consolidated financial statements of A have never recognised any expense for the award in profit or loss (since it is attributed fully to the consideration transferred). Therefore none of the tax deductions can be recognised in profit or loss either.

10.7.6   *Share-based payment transactions subject to transitional provisions of IFRS 1 and IFRS 2*

IFRS 1 and IFRS 2 provide, respectively, first-time adopters and existing IFRS preparers with some transitional exemptions from accounting for share-based payment transactions. The accounting treatment of the tax effects of transactions to which these exemptions have been applied is discussed in Chapter 5 at 7.4.2. Whilst that discussion specifically addresses the tax effects of transactions subject to the exemption for first-time adopters of IFRS, it is equally applicable to the tax effects transactions subject to the exemptions in IFRS 2 for existing IFRS preparers.

10.8   Change in tax status of entity or shareholders

Sometimes there is a change in an entity's tax assets and liabilities as a result of a change in the tax status of the entity itself or that of its shareholders. SIC-25 clarifies that the effect of such a change should be recognised in profit or loss except to the extent that it involves a remeasurement of tax originally accounted for in other comprehensive income or in equity, in which case the change should also be dealt with in, respectively, other comprehensive income or equity. *[SIC-25.4].*

10.9   Previous revaluation of PP&E treated as deemed cost on transition to IFRS

In some cases IFRS 1 allows an entity, on transition to IFRS, to treat the carrying amount of property, plant, and equipment (PP&E) revalued under its pre-transition GAAP as a deemed cost for the purposes of IFRS (see Chapter 5 at 5.5).

Where an asset is carried at deemed cost on transition to IFRS, but the tax base of the asset remains at original cost (or an amount based on original cost), the pre-transition revaluation will give rise to a temporary difference (typically, a taxable temporary difference) associated with the asset. IAS 12 requires deferred tax to be recognised on any such temporary difference at transition.

If, after transition, the deferred tax is required to be remeasured (e.g. because of a change in tax rate, or a re-basing of the asset for tax purposes), and the asset concerned was revalued outside profit or loss under pre-transition GAAP, the question arises as to whether the resulting deferred tax income or expense should be recognised in, or outside, profit or loss. This is discussed in Chapter 5 at 7.4.1.

11   CONSOLIDATED TAX RETURNS AND OFFSET OF TAXABLE PROFITS AND LOSSES WITHIN GROUPS

In some jurisdictions one member of a group of companies may file a single tax return behalf of all, or some, members of the group. In other jurisdictions, it is possible for one member of a group to transfer tax losses to one or more other members of the group in order to reduce their tax liabilities. In some groups a company whose tax liability is reduced by such an arrangement may be required to make a payment to the member of the group that pays tax on its behalf, or transfers losses to it, as the case may be. In other groups no such charge is made.

Such transactions raise the question of the appropriate accounting treatment in the separate financial statements of the group entities involved – in particular, whether the company benefiting from such an arrangement should reflect income (or more likely a capital contribution) from another member of the group equal to the tax expense mitigated as a result of the arrangement.

Some argue that the effects of such transactions should be reflected in the separate financial statements of the entities involved, as is required by some national standards (e.g. those of the US and Australia). Others argue that, except to the extent that a management charge is actually made (see 11.1 below), there is no need to reflect such transactions in the separate financial statements of the entities involved. Those that take this view point out that it is inconsistent to require companies to show a capital contribution for tax losses ceded to them without charge, unless all other intragroup transactions are also restated on arm's-length terms – which would be somewhat radical. Moreover, IAS 24 – *Related Party Disclosures* – merely requires disclosure of the actual terms of such transactions, not that they be remeasured, either for financial reporting or disclosure purposes, on the same basis as a similar notional arm's length transaction (see Chapter 37).

At present, IAS 12 is silent on the issue and, in our view, neither approach can be said to either be prohibited or required. Accordingly, either approach may be adopted on a consistent basis.

The (now withdrawn) exposure draft of a standard to replace IAS 12 published in March 2009 (see 1.3 above) proposed that each entity within a group filing a consolidated tax return should recognise an appropriate share of the total tax liability shown in the return.

11.1   Payments for intragroup transfer of tax losses

Where one member of a group transfers tax losses to another member of the group, the entity whose tax liability is reduced may be required, as matter of group policy, to pay an amount of compensation the member of the group that transfers the losses to it. Such payments are known by different terms in different jurisdictions, but are referred to in the discussion below as 'tax loss payments'.

Tax loss payments are generally made in an amount equal to the tax saved by the paying company. In some cases, however, payment may be made in an amount equal to the nominal amount of the tax loss, which will be greater than the amount of tax saved. This raises the question of how such payments should be accounted for.

The first issue is whether such payments should be recognised:

* in total comprehensive income, or
* as a distribution (in the case of a payment from a subsidiary to a parent) or a capital contribution (in the case of a payment from a parent to a subsidiary).

The second issue is, to the extent that the payments are accounted for in total comprehensive income, whether they should be classified as:

* income tax, allocated between profit or loss, other comprehensive income or equity (see 10 above). The argument for this treatment is that the payments made or received are amounts that would otherwise be paid to or received from (or offset against an amount paid to) a tax authority.
* operating income or expense in profit or loss (on the grounds that, as a matter of fact, the payments are not made to or received from any tax authority).

IAS 12 is silent on these issues. However, there is a long-standing practice that such payments are treated as if they were income taxes. We believe that this practice is appropriate to the extent that the intragroup payment is for an amount up to the amount of tax that would otherwise have been paid by the paying company. Where a tax loss payment is made in excess of this amount, we consider that it is more appropriate to account for the excess not as an income tax but as either:

* a distribution or capital contribution (as applicable), or
* operating income or expense (as applicable).

The chosen treatment should be applied consistently.

12 BUSINESS COMBINATIONS

Additional deferred tax arises on business combinations as a result of items such as:

- the application of IAS 12 to the assets and liabilities of the acquired business in the consolidated financial statements, when it has not been applied in the separate financial statements of that business;

- where the acquired entity already applies IAS 12 in its own financial statements, the recognition in the fair value exercise of deferred tax in respect of assets and liabilities of the acquired entity where no deferred tax is provided in those financial statements. This may be the case where a temporary difference arose on initial recognition of an asset or liability in the acquired entity's own financial statements. Deferred tax would then be recognised in the acquirer's consolidated financial statements, because, in those statements, the difference arises on initial recognition in a business combination (see 7.2 above); and

- adjustments made to measure the assets and liabilities of the acquired business fair value, with consequential changes in the temporary differences associated with those assets and liabilities.

Any deferred tax assets or liabilities on temporary differences that arise on a business combination affect the amount of goodwill or bargain purchase gain. *[IAS 12.66].* Example 31.21 at 7.5.1 above illustrates the application of this principle.

12.1 Measurement and recognition of deferred tax in a business combination

IFRS 3 generally requires assets acquired and liabilities assumed in a business combination to be:

- recognised only to the extent that they were assets or liabilities of the acquired entity at the date of acquisition, *[IFRS 3.10]* and

- measured at fair value. *[IFRS 3.18].*

These provisions of IFRS 3 are discussed in more detail in Chapter 10 at 5. As exceptions to this general principles, IFRS 3 requires an acquirer to:

- recognise and measure a deferred tax asset or liability arising from the assets acquired and liabilities assumed in a business combination in 'accordance with IAS 12', *[IFRS 3.24],* and

- account for the potential tax effects of temporary differences and carryforwards of an acquiree that exist at the acquisition date or arise as a result of the acquisition 'in accordance with IAS 12'. *[IFRS 3.25].*

There are essentially two reasons underlying these exceptions. The first is that IAS 12 does not purport to measure future tax at fair value, but at an amount based on a prescribed model that takes no account of the time value of money. Secondly, and more subtly, IAS 12 requires a number of questions of both recognition and measurement to be resolved by reference to management's plans and expectations – in particular, the expected manner of recovery of assets (see 8.3 above) or the likelihood of recovering deferred tax assets (see 7.4 above). The expectations and plans of the acquirer may well differ from those of the acquired entity. For example, the acquired entity might have assessed, for the purposes of IAS 12, that an asset would be recovered through use, whereas the acquirer assesses it as recoverable through sale. The exceptions made by IFRS 3 allow the deferred tax recognised in a business combination to reflect the expectations of the acquirer rather than those of the acquiree.

Areas that give rise to particular difficulties of interpretation are:

- determining the manner of recovery of assets and settlement of liabilities at the date of the business combination (see 12.1.1 below); and
- deferred tax assets (see 12.1.2 below).

12.1.1 Determining the manner of recovery of assets and settlement of liabilities

As discussed at 8.3 above, IAS 12 requires deferred tax to be measured at an amount that reflects the tax consequences that would follow from the manner in which the entity expects to recover its assets or settle its liabilities. The expected manner of recovery or settlement may affect both the tax base of an asset or liability and the tax rate to be applied to any temporary difference arising.

As further noted above, the acquirer's assessment of the manner of recovery for the purposes of IAS 12 may well differ from that of the acquired entity. For example, the acquired entity might have intended to recover an asset through use, whereas the acquirer intends to sell it. In such a case, in our view, the requirement of IFRS 3 to recognise and measure deferred tax in accordance with IAS 12 has the effect that the expectations of the acquirer are used to determine the tax base of an item and the measurement of any deferred tax associated with the item.

12.1.1.A Changes in tax base consequent on the business combination

In some jurisdictions, a business combination may provide the opportunity to revise the tax base of an asset to an amount equal to the fair value assigned to it in accounting for the business combination. Most significantly, this may include the ability to create a tax base for an intangible asset or goodwill which may have had no tax base at all for the acquiree.

In some cases, the increase (as it generally is) in tax base may be more or less automatic. In others, the taxpayer may be required to make a formal claim or election for the increase to the tax authority. Sometimes further restructuring may be required – for example, it may be necessary for the business of the acquired entity to be transferred to another entity in the acquirer's group in the same tax jurisdiction.

An increase in a tax base that requires action by the relevant entity after the acquisition (such as making a claim or election or undertaking a restructuring) occurs after the business combination. However, some hold the view that the ability to increase a tax base following a business combination is a benefit that is taken into account by an informed buyer in negotiating the purchase price. Accordingly, it is argued, the increase is most appropriately reflected by adjusting the tax base of assets acquired as at the date of the business combination as if the increase had occurred at that date. This reduces any deferred tax liability and, therefore, any goodwill or 'bargain purchase' gain.

Those who support this view note that, if the increase in tax base is accounted for only when it legally occurs in the post-combination period, the net effect is to increase goodwill and reduce post-combination tax expense when in reality the entity may have done little more than fill in a form. It might also be difficult to sustain the higher carrying amount of goodwill arising from this treatment.

We believe that it is generally appropriate to anticipate an increase to a tax base that legally occurs following a business combination in accounting for the business combination where the increase:

- is automatic or requires only a notification to the tax authority;
- requires an application the tax authority that is not normally refused for transactions of a comparable nature; or
- is contingent on some post-acquisition restructuring, where this can be done without substantial difficulty.

Conversely, we believe that it would not generally be appropriate to account for an increase in a tax base until it occurs where the increase:

- relies on 'bespoke' tax planning that may be challenged by the tax authority;
- requires an application to the tax authority that in practice is frequently and successfully challenged for transactions of a comparable nature; or
- is contingent on some post-acquisition restructuring, where this will involve a substantial process, such as obtaining approval from regulators, unions, pension fund trustees etc.

12.1.2 Deferred tax assets arising on a business combination

12.1.2.A Assets of the acquirer

If, as a result of a business combination, the acquiring entity is able to recognise a previously unrecognised tax asset of its own (e.g. unused tax losses), the recognition of the asset is accounted for as income, and not as part of the accounting for the business combination. *[IAS 12.67]*.

12.1.2.B Assets of the acquiree

It may be the case that deferred tax assets of an acquired entity do not meet the recognition criteria of IAS 12 from the perspective of the acquired entity, but do meet the criteria from the perspective of the acquirer. In such cases, the general principles of IAS 12 require the acquirer's perspective to be applied as at the date of the business combination.

The potential benefit of the acquiree's income tax loss carryforwards or other deferred tax assets may not satisfy the criteria for separate recognition when a business combination is initially accounted for but may be realised subsequently.

Any changes in recognised deferred tax assets of an acquired entity are accounted for as follows: *[IFRS 3.67]*

- acquired deferred tax benefits recognised within the measurement period (see Chapter 10 at 5.6.2) that result from new information about facts and circumstances that existed at the acquisition date are applied to reduce the carrying amount of any goodwill related to that acquisition. If the carrying amount of that goodwill is zero, any remaining deferred tax benefits are recognised in profit or loss;

- all other acquired deferred tax benefits realised are recognised in profit or loss (or outside profit or loss if IAS 12 so requires – see 10 above). *[IAS 12.68]*.

12.1.3 Deferred tax liabilities of acquired entity

IAS 12 contains no specific provisions regarding the recognition of a deferred tax liability of an acquired entity after the date of the original combination. The recognition of such liabilities should therefore be accounted for in accordance with the normal rules of IAS 12 (i.e. in the period in which the liability arises), unless the failure to recognise the liability at the time of the combination was an error, in which case the provisions of IAS 8 should be applied – see Chapter 3 at 4.6.

12.2   Tax deductions for replacement share-based payment awards in a business combination

IFRS 3 contains some guidance on the treatment of tax deductions for share-based payment transactions made by an acquirer as a replacement for awards made by the acquired entity before the business combination. This is discussed in more detail at 10.7.5 above.

12.3   Apparent immediate impairment of goodwill created by deferred tax

The requirement of IAS 12 to recognise deferred tax on all temporary differences arising on net assets acquired in a business combination leads to the creation of goodwill which, on a literal reading of IAS 36 – *Impairment of Assets*, may then be required to be immediately impaired, as illustrated by Example 31.43 below.

Example 31.43:   Apparent 'day one' impairment arising from recognition of deferred tax in a business combination

Entity A, which is taxed at 40%, acquires Entity B for €100m in a transaction that is a business combination. The fair values and tax bases of the identifiable net assets of Entity B are as follows:

	Fair value (€m)	Tax base (€m)
Brand name	60	–
Other net assets	20	15

This will give rise to the following consolidation journal:

	€m	€m
Goodwill (balance)	46	
Brand name	60	
Other net assets	20	
Deferred tax[1]		26
Cost of investment		100

[1] 40% of (€[60m + 20m] – €15m)

The fair value of the consolidated assets of the subsidiary (excluding deferred tax) and goodwill is now €126m, but the cost of the subsidiary is only €100m. Clearly €26m of the goodwill arises solely from the recognition of deferred tax. However, IAS 36, paragraph 50, explicitly requires tax to be excluded from the estimate of future cash flows used to calculate any impairment. This raises the question of whether there should not be an immediate impairment write-down of the assets to €100m. In our view, this cannot have been the intention of IAS 36 (see the further discussion in Chapter 22 at 5.4).

12.4   Tax deductions for acquisition costs

12.4.1 *Business combinations accounted for under 'old' IFRS 3*

The discussion in this section is relevant to business combinations to which the current version of IFRS 3 (as revised in January 2008) is not applied. IFRS 3 generally requires transaction costs to be recognised as an expense, so that any tax deduction for those costs would be allocated to profit or loss, in accordance with the general principles discussed at 10 above. However, the previous version of IFRS 3 ('old IFRS 3') permitted certain acquisition costs to be treated as part of the consideration of the business.

In some jurisdictions, tax deductions are given for certain costs of an acquisition which, in the consolidated financial statements prepared under old IFRS 3, are effectively subsumed into the carrying amount of goodwill. This raises the question of how the effects of the tax deductions should be accounted for, as illustrated by Example 31.44 below.

Example 31.44:   Tax deduction for acquisition costs

Entity A, which pays tax at 40%, acquires 100% of Entity B for €1,000,000 on 1 January 2009. In addition A bears transaction costs, such as professional fees, of €50,000 so that the total purchase price recorded by A for B is €1,050,000. The transaction costs are deductible for tax purposes in the year ended 31 December 2009, so that A receives a current tax credit of €20,000 as a result of the transaction costs.

The tax base of the investment in B is €1,000,000, and, if it were sold, any gain arising would be taxable.

In the separate financial statements of A, the carrying amount of the investment in B is €1,050,000. In the consolidated financial statements of A, the net assets of and goodwill of B are carried at €1,050,000 (i.e. the transaction costs represent €50,000 of the goodwill recognised).

A has received a tax deduction of €20,000 in the period and so must record current tax income of this amount.

The issue then arises as to how to deal with the taxable temporary difference of €50,000 associated with the carrying amount of the net assets and goodwill of the investment (cost €1,050,000 less tax base €1,000,000).

One view might be that, in financial reporting terms, this temporary difference relates to the goodwill into which the transaction costs have been subsumed. This temporary difference did not arise on the initial recognition of goodwill since it results from the claiming of a tax deduction after the transaction costs had been incurred recognised in the financial statements. Therefore, a deferred tax liability is required to be recognised (see 7.2 above).

An alternative analysis would be that as no deduction is received for an item described as 'goodwill' in the tax return, the temporary difference should not be regarded as relating specifically to the goodwill. Rather it is an example of the more general category of differences associated with the carrying amount of an investment in a subsidiary (see 7.5 above). Therefore, a deferred tax liability should be recognised, but subject to the exemptions from recognising such liabilities discussed in 7.5 above.

12.4.2 Business combinations accounted for under 'new' IFRS 3

The discussion in this section is relevant to business combinations to which the current version of IFRS 3 (as revised in January 2008) is applied. Under the current version of IFRS 3 transaction costs are required to be expensed. However, in a number of jurisdictions, transaction costs are regarded as forming part of the cost of the investment, with the effect that a tax deduction for them is given only when the investment is subsequently sold or otherwise disposed of, rather than at the time that the costs are charged to profit or loss.

In such jurisdictions, there will be a deductible 'outside' temporary difference (see 7.5 above) between the carrying value of the net assets and goodwill of the acquired entity in the consolidated financial statements (which will exclude transaction costs) and tax base of the investment in the entity (which will include transaction costs). Whether or not a deferred tax asset is recognised in respect of such a deductible temporary difference will be determined in accordance with the general provisions of IAS 12 for such differences (see 7.5.3 above).

In the separate financial statements of the acquirer, there may be no temporary difference since the transaction costs may, under IAS 27, be included in the cost of the investment.

13   PRESENTATION

13.1   Balance sheet

Tax assets and liabilities should be shown separately from other assets and liabilities and current tax should be shown separately from deferred tax on the face of the balance sheet. Where an entity presents current and non-current assets and liabilities separately, deferred tax should not be shown as part of current assets or liabilities.[29]

13.1.1 Offset

13.1.1.A Current tax

Current tax assets and liabilities should be offset if, and only if, the entity:

- has a legally enforceable right to set off the recognised amounts; and
- intends either to settle them net or simultaneously. *[IAS 12.71].*

These restrictions are based on the offset criteria in IAS 32. Accordingly, while entities in many jurisdictions have a right to offset current tax assets and liabilities, and the tax authority permits the entity to make or receive a single net payment, IAS 12 permits offset in financial statements only where there is a positive intention for simultaneous net settlement. *[IAS 12.72].*

The offset restrictions also have the effect that, in consolidated financial statements, a current tax asset of one member of the group may be offset against a current tax liability of another only if the two group members have a legally enforceable right to make or receive a single net payment and a positive intention to recover the asset or settle the liability simultaneously. *[IAS 12.73].*

13.1.1.B Deferred tax

Deferred tax assets and liabilities should be offset if, and only if:

- the entity has a legally enforceable right to set off current tax assets and liabilities; and
- the deferred tax assets and liabilities concerned relate to income taxes raised by the same taxation authority on either:
  - the same taxable entity; or
  - different taxable entities which intend, in each future period in which significant amounts of deferred tax are expected to be settled or recovered, to settle their current tax assets and liabilities either on a net basis or simultaneously. *[IAS 12.74].*

The offset criteria for deferred tax are less clear than those for current tax. The position is broadly that, where in a particular jurisdiction current tax assets and liabilities relating to future periods will be offset, deferred tax assets and liabilities relating to that jurisdiction and those periods must be offset (even if the deferred tax balances actually recognised in the balance sheet would not satisfy the criteria for the offset of current tax).

IAS 12 suggests that this slightly more pragmatic approach was adopted in order to avoid the detailed scheduling of the reversal of temporary differences that would be necessary to apply the same criteria as for current tax. *[IAS 12.75].*

However, IAS 12 notes that, in rare circumstances, an entity may have a legally enforceable right of set-off, and an intention to settle net, for some periods but not for others. In such circumstances, detailed scheduling may be required to establish reliably whether the deferred tax liability of one taxable entity in the group will result in increased tax payments in the same period in which a deferred tax asset of a second taxable entity in the group will result in decreased payments by that second taxable entity. *[IAS 12.76].*

13.1.1.C Offset of current and deferred tax

IAS 12 contains no provisions allowing or requiring the offset of current tax and deferred tax. Accordingly, in our view, current and deferred tax may not be offset against each other and should always be presented gross.

13.2   Statement of comprehensive income

The tax expense (or income) related to profit or loss from ordinary activities should be presented as a component of profit or loss in the statement of comprehensive income. *[IAS 12.77]*.

The results of discontinued operations should be presented on a post-tax basis. *[IFRS 5.33]*.

The results of equity-accounted entities should be presented on a post-tax basis. *[IAS 1.IG6]*. Any income tax relating to a 'tax-transparent' equity-accounted entity (see 7.6 above) forms part of the investor's tax charge. It is therefore included in the income tax line in profit or loss and not shown as part of the investor's share of the results of the tax-transparent entity.

Components of other comprehensive income may be presented either:

*   net of related tax effects, or
*   before related tax effects with one amount shown for the total related income tax effects. *[IAS 1.91]*.

IAS 12 notes that, whilst IAS 21 requires certain exchange differences to be recognised within income or expense, it does not specify where exactly in the statement of comprehensive income they should be presented. Accordingly, exchange differences relating to deferred tax assets and liabilities may be classified as deferred tax expense (or income), if that presentation is considered to be the most useful to users of the financial statements. *[IAS 12.78]*. IAS 12 makes no reference to the treatment of exchange differences on current tax assets and liabilities but, presumably, the same considerations apply.

13.3   Statement of cash flows

Cash flows arising from taxes on income are separately disclosed and classified as cash flows from operating activities, unless they can be specifically identified with financing and investing activities. *[IAS 7.35]*.

IAS 7 – *Statement of Cash Flows* – notes that, whilst it is relatively easy to identify the expense relating to investing or financing activities, the related tax cash flows are often impracticable to identify. Therefore, taxes paid are usually classified as cash flows from operating activities. However, when it is practicable to identify the tax cash flow with an individual transaction that gives rise to cash flows that are classified as investing or financing activities, the tax cash flow is classified as an investing or financing activity as appropriate. When tax cash flows are allocated over more than one class of activity, the total amount of taxes paid is disclosed. *[IAS 7.36]*.

14   DISCLOSURE

IAS 1 notes that users would expect an entity subject to income taxes to disclose its accounting policies for income taxes, including those applicable to deferred tax liabilities and assets. *[IAS 1.120]*.

IAS 12 imposes extensive disclosure requirements as follows.

14.1 Components of tax expense

The major components of tax expense (or income) should be disclosed separately. These may include: *[IAS 12.79-80]*

(a)   current tax expense (or income);

(b)   any adjustments recognised in the period for current tax of prior periods;

(c)   the amount of deferred tax expense (or income) relating to the origination and reversal of temporary differences;

(d)   the amount of deferred tax expense (or income) relating to changes in tax rates or the imposition of new taxes;

(e)   the amount of the benefit arising from a previously unrecognised tax loss, tax credit or temporary difference of a prior period that is used to reduce current tax expense;

(f)   the amount of the benefit from a previously unrecognised tax loss, tax credit or temporary difference of a prior period that is used to reduce deferred tax expense;

(g)   deferred tax expense arising from the write-down, or reversal of a previous write-down, of a deferred tax asset; and

(h)   the amount of tax expense (or income) relating to those changes in accounting policies and errors which are included in the profit or loss in accordance with IAS 8 because they cannot be accounted for retrospectively (see Chapter 3 at 4.6).

14.2 Other disclosures

The following should also be disclosed separately: *[IAS 12.81]*

(a)   the aggregate current and deferred tax relating to items that are charged or credited to equity; and

(b)   the amount of income tax relating to each component of other comprehensive income;

(c)   an explanation of the relationship between tax expense (or income) and accounting profit in either or both of the following forms:

    (i)   a numerical reconciliation between tax expense (or income) and the product of accounting profit multiplied by the applicable tax rate(s), disclosing also the basis on which the applicable tax rate(s) is (are) computed; or

    (ii)   a numerical reconciliation between the average effective tax rate (i.e. tax expense (or income) divided by accounting profit) *[IAS 12.86]* and the applicable tax rate, disclosing also the basis on which the applicable tax rate is computed;

    This requirement is discussed further at 14.2.1 below.

(d)   an explanation of changes in the applicable tax rate(s) compared to the previous accounting period;

(e) the amount (and expiry date, if any) of deductible temporary differences, unused tax losses, and unused tax credits for which no deferred tax asset is recognised in the balance sheet;

(f) the aggregate amount of temporary differences associated with investments in subsidiaries, branches and associates and interests in joint ventures, for which deferred tax liabilities have not been recognised;

This is discussed further at 14.2.2 below.

(g) in respect of each type of temporary difference, and in respect of each type of unused tax losses and unused tax credits:

(i) the amount of the deferred tax assets and liabilities recognised in the balance sheet for each period presented;

(ii) the amount of the deferred tax income or expense recognised in the profit or loss, if this is not apparent from the changes in the amounts recognised in the balance sheet;

The analysis in (ii) will be required, for example, by any entity with acquisitions and disposals, or deferred tax accounted for in equity, since this will have the effect that the year-on-year balance sheet movement is not solely due to items recognised in profit or loss.

(h) in respect of discontinued operations, the tax expense relating to:

(i) the gain or loss on discontinuance; and

(ii) the profit or loss from the ordinary activities of the discontinued operation for the period, together with the corresponding amounts for each prior period presented;

(i) the amount of income tax consequences of dividends to shareholders of the entity that were proposed or declared before the financial statements were authorised for issue, but are not recognised as a liability in the financial statements.

Further disclosures are required in respect of the tax consequences of distributing retained earnings, which are discussed at 14.4 below;

(j) if a business combination in which the entity is the acquirer causes a change in the amount of a deferred tax asset of the entity (see 12.2.1 above), the amount of that change; and

(k) if the deferred tax benefits acquired in a business combination are not recognised at the acquisition date, but are recognised after the acquisition date (see 12.2.2 above), a description of the event or change in circumstances that caused the deferred tax benefits to be recognised.

Tax-related contingent liabilities and contingent assets (such as those arising from unresolved disputes with taxation authorities) are disclosed in accordance with IAS 37 (see Chapter 29 at 6). *[IAS 12.88]*.

Significant effects of changes in tax rates or tax laws enacted or announced after the reporting period on current and deferred tax assets and liabilities are disclosed in accordance with IAS 10 (see Chapter 36 at 2). *[IAS 12.88]*.

14.2.1 Tax (or tax rate) reconciliation

IAS 12 explains that the purpose of the tax reconciliation required by (c) above is to enable users of financial statements to understand whether the relationship between tax expense (or income) and accounting profit is unusual and to understand the significant factors that could affect that relationship in the future. The relationship may be affected by the effects of such factors as:

- revenue and expenses that are outside the scope of taxation;
- tax losses; and
- foreign tax rates. *[IAS 12.84].*

Accordingly, in explaining the relationship between tax expense (or income) and accounting profit, an entity should use an applicable tax rate that provides the most meaningful information to the users of its financial statements.

Often, the most meaningful rate is the domestic rate of tax in the country in which the entity is domiciled. In this case, the tax rate applied for national taxes should be aggregated with the rates applied for any local taxes which are computed on a substantially similar level of taxable profit (tax loss). However, for an entity operating in several jurisdictions, it may be more meaningful to aggregate separate reconciliations prepared using the domestic rate in each individual jurisdiction. *[IAS 12.85].* Where this latter approach is adopted, the entity may need to discuss the effect of significant changes in either tax rates, or the mix of profits earned in different jurisdictions, in order to meet requirement (d) at 14.2 above.

Example 31.45 illustrates how the selection of the applicable tax rate affects the presentation of the numerical reconciliation.

Example 31.45: Alternative presentations of tax reconciliation

In 2012 an entity has accounting profit of €3,000m (2009: €2,500m) comprising €1,500m (2009: €2,000m) in its own jurisdiction (country A) and €1,500m (2009: €500m) in country B. The tax rate is 30% in country A and 20% in country B. In country B, expenses of €200m (2009: €100m) are not deductible for tax purposes. There are no other differences between accounting profit and profit that is subject to current tax, or on which deferred tax has been provided for under IAS 12.

Thus the accounting tax charge in the financial statements for each period will be as follows

	2012 €m	2011 €m
Country A		
€1,500m/€2,000m @ 30%	450	600
Country B		
€[1,500 + 200]m/€[500 + 100]m @ 20%	340	120
Total tax charge	790	720

Reconciliation based on A's domestic tax rate

If the entity presents a tax reconciliation based on its own (i.e. country A's) domestic tax rate, the following presentation would be adopted.

	2012 €m	2011 €m
Accounting profit	3,000	2,500
Tax at domestic rate of 30%	900	750
Effect of:		
Expenses not deductible for tax purposes[1]	60	30
Overseas tax rates[2]	(170)	(60)
Tax expense	790	720

1   €200m/€100m @ 30%

2   B's taxable profit €1,700m/€600m @ (20% – 30%)

Reconciliation based on each jurisdiction's tax rate

If the entity presents a tax reconciliation based on each jurisdiction's domestic tax rate, the following presentation would be adopted.

	2012 €m	2011 €m
Accounting profit	3,000	2,500
Tax at domestic rates applicable to individual group entities[1]	750	700
Effect of:		
Expenses not deductible for tax purposes[2]	40	20
Tax expense	790	720

1   2012: A = €450m [€1,500m @ 30%], B = €300m [€1,500m @ 20%], total €750m

    2011: A = €600m [€2,000m @ 30%], B = €100m [€500m @ 20%], total €700m

2   €200m/€100m @ 20%

14.2.2 Temporary differences relating to subsidiaries, associates, branches and joint ventures

It will be noted that IAS 12 requires an entity to disclose the temporary differences associated with subsidiaries, associates, branches and joint ventures, as opposed to the unrecognised deferred tax on those temporary differences – see (f) under 14.2 above.

IAS 12 clarifies that this approach is adopted because it would often be impracticable to compute the amount of unrecognised deferred tax. Nevertheless, where practicable, entities are encouraged to disclose the amounts of the unrecognised deferred tax liabilities because financial statement users may find such information useful. *[IAS 12.87]*.

14.3   Reason for recognition of certain tax assets

Separate disclosure is required of the amount of any deferred tax asset that is recognised, and the nature of the evidence supporting its recognition, when:

(a)   utilisation of the deferred tax asset is dependent on future profits in excess of those arising from the reversal of deferred tax liabilities; and

(b)   the entity has suffered a loss in the current or preceding period in the tax jurisdiction to which the asset relates. *[IAS 12.82].*

In effect these disclosures are required when the entity has rebutted the presumption inherent in the recognition rules of IAS 12 that tax assets should not normally be recognised in these circumstances (see 7.4 above).

14.4   Dividends

As discussed at 8.4 above, where there are different tax consequences for an entity depending on whether profits are retained or distributed, tax should be measured on the rates applicable to retained profits except to the extent that there is a liability to pay dividends at the end of the reporting period, where the rate applicable to distributed profits should be used.

Where such differential tax rates apply, the entity should disclose the nature of the potential income tax consequences that would arise from a payment of dividends to shareholders. It should quantify the amount of potential income tax consequences that is practicably determinable and disclose whether there are any potential income tax consequences that are not practicably determinable. *[IAS 12.82A].* This will include disclosure of the important features of the income tax systems and the factors that will affect the amount of the potential income tax consequences of dividends. *[IAS 12.87A].*

The reason for this rather complicated requirement is that, as IAS 12 acknowledges, it can often be very difficult to quantify the tax consequences of a full distribution of profits (e.g. where there are a large number of overseas subsidiaries). Moreover, IAS 12 concedes that there is a tension between, on the one hand, the exemption from disclosing the deferred tax associated with temporary differences associated with subsidiaries and other investments (see 14.2.2 above) and, on the other hand, this requirement to disclose the tax effect of distributing undistributed profits – in some cases they could effectively be the same number.

However, to the extent that any liability can be quantified, it should be disclosed. This may mean that consolidated financial statements will disclose the potential tax effect of distributing the earnings of some, but not all, subsidiaries, associates, branches and joint ventures.

IAS 12 emphasises that, in an entity's separate financial statements, this requirement applies only to the undistributed earnings of the entity itself and not those of any of its subsidiaries, associates, branches and joint ventures. *[IAS 12.87A-87C].*

14.5   Example of disclosures

Examples of many of the disclosures required under IAS 12 are given by BP.

Extract 31.2: BP plc (2008)

Notes to the Consolidated Financial Statements [extract]
20   Taxation
Tax on profit

			$ million
	2008	2007	2006
Current tax			
Charge for the year	**13,468**	10,006	11,199
Adjustment in respect of prior years	**(85)**	(171)	442
	13,383	9,835	11,641
Innovene operations	**–**	–	159
Continuing operations	**13,383**	9,835	11,800
Deferred tax			
Origination and reversal of temporary differences in the current year	**(324)**	671	1,771
Adjustment in respect of prior years	**(442)**	(64)	(1,240)
	(766)	607	531
Tax on profit from continuing operations	**12,617**	10,442	12,331

Tax included in the statement of recognized income and expense

			$ million
	2008	2007	2006
Current tax	**(264)**	(178)	(51)
Deferred tax	**(2,492)**	241	985
	(2,756)	63	934
This comprises:			
Currency translation differences	**(100)**	(139)	201
Actuarial gain (loss) relating to pensions and other post-retirement benefits	**(2,602)**	427	820
Share-based payments	**190**	(213)	(26)
Cash flow hedges	**(194)**	(26)	47
Available-for-sale investments	**(50)**	14	(108)
	(2,756)	63	934

Reconciliation of the effective tax rate

The following table provides a reconciliation of the UK statutory corporation tax rate to the effective tax rate of the group on profit before taxation from continuing operations.

		$ million	
	2008	2007	2006
Profit before taxation from continuing operations	**34,283**	31,611	34,462
Tax on profit from continuing operations	**12,617**	10,442	12,331
Effective tax rate	**37%**	33%	36%
	% of profit before taxation from continuing operations		
UK statutory corporation tax rate	**28**	30	30
Increase (decrease) resulting from			
UK supplementary and overseas taxes at higher rates	**14**	7	11
Tax reported in equity-accounted entities	**(2)**	(2)	(3)
Adjustment in respect of prior years	**(2)**	(1)	(2)
Current year losses unrelieved (prior year losses utilized)	**(1)**	(1)	(1)
Other	**–**	–	1
Effective tax rate	**37**	33	36

Deferred tax

	Income statement			Balance sheet	
	2008	2007	2006	**2008**	2007
Deferred tax liability					
Depreciation	**1,248**	125	1,423	**23,342**	22,338
Pension plan surplus	**108**	127	173	**412**	2,136
Other taxable temporary differences	**(2,471)**	1,371	417	**3,626**	5,998
	(1,115)	1,623	2,013	**27,380**	30,472
Deferred tax asset					
Petroleum revenue tax	**121**	139	4	**(192)**	(325)
Pension plan and other post-retirement benefit plan deficits	**104**	(72)	71	**(2,414)**	(1,545)
Decommissioning, environmental and other provisions	**(333)**	(1,069)	(754)	**(4,860)**	(5,107)
Derivative financial instruments	**228**	450	(115)	**(331)**	(541)
Tax credit and loss carry forward	**118**	(466)	220	**(1,821)**	(1,822)
Other deductible temporary differences	**111**	2	(908)	**(1,564)**	(1,917)
	349	(1,016)	(1,482)	**(11,182)**	(11,257)
Net deferred tax (credit) charge and net deferred tax liability	**(766)**	607	531	**16,198**	19,215

$ million

Analysis of movements during the year	**2008**	2007
At 1 January	**19,215**	18,116
Exchange adjustments	**(67)**	42
Charge (credit) for the year on ordinary activities	**(766)**	607
Charge (credit) for the year in the statement of recognized income and expense	**(2,492)**	241
Acquisitions	**–**	199
Other movements	**308**	10
At 31 December	**16,198**	19,215

In 2008, there have been no changes in the statutory tax rates that have materially impacted the group's tax charge. The enactment, in 2007, of a 2% reduction in the rate of UK corporation tax on profits arising from activities outside the North Sea reduced the deferred tax charge by $189 million in that year.

Deferred tax assets are recognized to the extent that it is probable that taxable profit will be available against which the deductible temporary differences and the carry-forward of unused tax assets and unused tax losses can be utilized.

At 31 December 2008, the group had around $6.3 billion (2007 $5.0 billion) of carry-forward tax losses, predominantly in Europe, that would be available to offset against future taxable profit. A deferred tax asset has been recognized in respect of $4.2 billion of losses (2007 $3.2 billion). No deferred tax asset has been recognized in respect of $2.1 billion of losses (2007 $1.8 billion). Substantially all the tax losses have no fixed expiry date.

At 31 December 2008, the group had around $3.4 billion (2007 $4.1 billion) of unused tax credits in the UK and US. A deferred tax asset of $0.5 billion has been recognized in 2008 for these credits (2007 $0.8 billion), which is offset by a deferred tax liability associated with unremitted profits from overseas entities in jurisdictions with a lower tax rate than the UK. No deferred tax asset has been recognized in respect of $2.9 billion of tax credits (2007 $3.2 billion). The UK tax credits do not have a fixed expiry date. The US tax credits, amounting to $1.8 billion, expire ten years after generation, and substantially all expire in the period 2014-2018.

The major components of temporary differences at the end of 2008 are tax depreciation, US inventory holding gains (classified as other taxable temporary differences), provisions, and pension plan and other post-retirement benefit plan deficits.

The group profit and loss account reserve includes $18,347 million (2007 $16,335 million) of earnings retained by subsidiaries and equity-accounted entities.

14.6   Discontinued operations – interaction with IFRS 5

IFRS 5 – *Non-current Assets Held for Sale and Discontinued Operations* – requires the post-tax results of discontinued operations to be shown separately on the face of the statement of comprehensive income (and any separate income statement presenting the components of profit or loss). This may be done by giving the results of discontinued operations after those of continuing operations. This is discussed further in Chapter 4.

The definitions of income tax, tax expense and taxable profit in IAS 12 (see 3 above) do not distinguish between the results of continuing and discontinued operations, or the tax on those results. Thus, as drafted, IAS 12 applies not only to the tax income or expense on continuing operations (i.e. the amount shown in the 'tax line' in the income statement) but also to any tax income or expense relating to the results of discontinued operations separately disclosed after those of continuing operations.

However, IFRS 5 clarifies that items accounted for under that standard are not subject to the disclosure requirements of other standards, other than:

- specific disclosures in respect of non-current assets (or disposal groups) classified as held for sale or discontinued operations, or

- disclosures about the measurement of assets and liabilities within a disposal group that are not within the scope of the measurement requirements of IFRS 5, where such disclosures are not already provided in the other notes to the financial statements. *[IFRS 5.5B].*

15   POSSIBLE FUTURE DEVELOPMENTS

The IASB's income taxes project had originally been one of the areas under discussion by the IASB and the FASB as part of the short-term convergence project of the two standard-setters aimed at eliminating differences between US GAAP and IFRS. This joint project had been expected to lead to the publication of exposure drafts of standards to replace IAS 12 and FASB ASC Topic 740. However, as the project progressed, it proved more difficult to reach agreement on a common approach than might have been expected, given the similarity of the two standards.

Since August 2008, the FASB has suspended its deliberations on the Income Taxes project.[30]

Notwithstanding the FASB's withdrawal from the project, in March 2009 the IASB published an exposure draft (ED/2009/2) of a standard proposed to replace IAS 12 (see 1.3 above). This exposure draft was not generally well received and was not proceeded with. As a result, the IASB's income taxes project has been restricted to the resolution of problems arising under IAS 12 in practice without changing the fundamental approach of the standard and preferably without increasing divergence from US GAAP.[31]

In its *Agenda Consultation 2011* issued in July 2011, the IASB recognises that IAS 12 is sometimes difficult to apply. An issue to be addressed within the current project is the accounting for uncertain tax positions (see 9 above), although resolution of this issue may first require completion of the non-financial liabilities project (see Chapter 29 at 7.1). The *Agenda Consultation* also refers to a possible 'fundamental review' of accounting for income taxes. It is not clear what this might entail, but there is perhaps a hint in the IASB's Press Release issued on the publication of the exposure draft ED/2009/2, which referred to 'the efforts of several national standard setters, in particular the UK Accounting Standards Board (ASB) and the German Accounting Standards Board (GASB), to undertake a fundamental review of income tax accounting'.[32] As at the time of writing, no further details of the work being undertaken by those national standard setters had so far been made public.

In September 2011, the Interpretations Committee issued for comment tentative agenda decisions relating to assessing the manner of recovery, for the purposes of IAS 12, of certain investment properties (see 8.3.7.A above) and assets held within a 'single asset' entity (see 8.3.10.A above).

References

1 This analysis is less relevant under the IASB's *Framework*, which would classify the state's 'participation' in an entity through taxation as a liability and expense, not an equity interest and distribution.

2 Throughout this chapter, the tax treatment described in examples is purely illustrative, and does not necessarily relate to a specific provision of tax law in a jurisdiction using the currency in the example.

3 SIC-25, *Income Taxes – Changes in the Tax Status of an Entity or its Shareholders*, SIC, July 2000.
4 For transactions not accounted for under IFRS 3 – *Business Combinations* as revised in January 2008: 'the amount of any excess of the acquirer's interest in the net fair value of the acquiree's identifiable assets, liabilities and contingent liabilities over the cost of the combination'.
5 *IFRIC Update*, March 2006.
6 *IFRIC Update*, June 2004.
7 ED/2009/2 *Income Tax*, IASB, March 2009, para. 39.
8 Based on a summary in *IASB Update*, February 2005.
9 In some cases research and share-based payment costs may be included as part of the cost of other assets, such as inventories or PP&E.
10 ED/2009/2, Appendix A, definition of 'tax basis',
11 IAS 12, paras. 17-20 and 26, Appendix A.
12 ED/2009/2, paras. 20 and 23.
13 *IFRIC Update*, April 2005.
14 *IFRIC Update*, June 2005.
15 IAS 12, para. 23, Appendix B, Example 4.
16 *IFRIC Update*, May, July and September 2010.
17 *IFRIC Update*, June 2005.
18 *IFRIC Update*, February 2003.
19 *IFRIC Update*, May 2007.
20 IAS 12,   para. 52   and   Appendix A, Examples A-C.
21 SIC-21, Income Taxes – *Recovery of Non-Depreciable Assets*, SIC, July 2000, para. 4.
22 *IFRIC Update*, September 2011.
23 IAS 12, Appendix B, Example 3.
24 *IFRIC Update*, September 2011.
25 ED/2009/2, paras. 27(d), B31-B32.
26 This example is illustrative only and does not imply any preference for the unit of account chosen by the entity in the example.
27 IAS 12, para. 68C;
   IFRS 2, paras. BC311-BC329
28 IAS 12, Appendix B, Example 6.
29 IAS 1, paras. 54-56, IAS 1 (2007), paras. 68-70.
30 FASB website, September 2011.
31 IASB website, September 2011.
32 Press Release: 'IASB seeks comments on a proposed new standard on income tax accounting', IASB, 31 March 2009.

Chapter 32   Share-based payment

Chapter 32

Chapter 32

Chapter 32

List of examples

Chapter 32

Chapter 32   Share-based payment

1   INTRODUCTION

1.1   Background

Share-based payment is one of the most controversial projects so far tackled by the IASB, arousing as it does strong passions not only among the IASB's normal constituency but also at the highest political levels. The reason for this is that most share-based payment transactions undertaken by entities are awards of shares and options as remuneration to employees, in particular senior management and directors. In several countries, shares and options now comprise the greatest element of the total remuneration package of senior personnel, a trend encouraged by the current consensus that it is a matter of good corporate governance to promote significant long-term shareholdings by senior management, so as to align their economic interests with those of shareholders.

One advantage of shares and options as remuneration is that they need not entail any cash cost to the entity. If an executive is entitled under a bonus scheme to a free share, the entity can satisfy this award simply by printing another share certificate, which the executive can sell, so that the cash cost of the award is effectively borne by shareholders rather than by the entity itself. However, this very advantage was the source of the controversy surrounding share-based remuneration.

Investors became increasingly concerned that share-based remuneration was resulting in a significant cost to them, through dilution of their existing shareholdings. As a result, there emerged an increasing consensus among investors that awards of shares and share options should be recognised as a cost in the financial statements.

The opposing view, held by most entities, was that the financial statements were simply reflecting the economic reality that such awards are ultimately a cost to other shareholders and not to the entity. Moreover, it was said (not entirely accurately) that the information that shareholders were alleging had been withheld from them had been available all the time, in the disclosure of diluted earnings per share. Another powerful argument for those opposed to expensing options was to point out that some patently successful companies, particularly in the new technology sector, would never have shown a profit if they had been required to book an accounting expense for options. Some US critics argue that a key factor in US economic success has been the much greater 'social mobility' of wealth in the US than in Europe, and point to the important role played by stock options in achieving this.

The strength of feeling amongst opponents of expensing share-based remuneration was graphically illustrated in the early 1990s when the FASB in the US attempted to issue an accounting standard requiring options to be expensed, only to be forced into a partial climb-down by an unprecedented political campaign, at one stage involving a lobby of the FASB by US companies with bands and cheer-leaders. As a result, the US standard issued by the FASB at that stage, FAS 123 – *Accounting for stock based compensation* – was a compromise which required the fair value of shares or options issued to employees to be disclosed, but merely recommended, without requiring, those fair values to be expensed in the financial statements. Even so, this represented a significant achievement compared to that of most other national standard setters. However, in December 2004, following the issue of IFRS 2 – *Share-based Payment* – earlier that year (see 1.2 below), the FASB issued FASB ASC 718 – *Compensation – Stock Compensation* (formerly FAS 123(R) – *Share-Based Payment*) – which requires the fair value of share awards to be expensed.

1.2   Development of IFRS 2

In November 2002, the IASB issued an exposure draft ED 2 – *Share-based Payment* – proposing that share-based payments for goods and services should be expensed. Essentially, the proposal was that an expense should be recognised for all awards to employees for which service is rendered (whether ultimately vesting or not) measured at the fair value at grant date, rather than at vesting date.

Perhaps sensing that the tide was turning in favour of those advocating that share-based remuneration should be expensed, the IASB's chairman Sir David Tweedie felt sufficiently confident of the outcome as to stake the credibility of the then newly-structured Board on achieving a workable standard. However, the exposure draft proved highly controversial. Those who supported it in principle nevertheless had concerns on nearly every detail of the accounting treatment proposed, in particular the fact that it did not permit 'truing up', i.e. reversing any expense previously charged for an award that never actually crystallises. More fundamentally, many questioned whether there yet existed a methodology sufficiently robust for valuing shares and share options subject to the restrictions and performance conditions typically associated with employee share awards. There also remained a significant minority who still questioned the whole principle of expensing options and other share awards.

Despite these comments, the IASB finalised its proposals with the publication of IFRS 2 – *Share-based Payment* – on 19 February 2004, although some significant changes had been necessary. In particular, IFRS 2 requires an expense to be recognised only for awards that vest (or are considered by IFRS 2 to vest), but (in the case of awards settled in shares) based on their fair value at the date of grant. Nevertheless, IFRS 2 remains contentious: for example, there is still only limited provision for 'truing up', with the result that significant costs can potentially be recognised for awards that ultimately have no value to their recipients, and give rise to no dilution of the interests of other shareholders. Some commentators continue to question whether existing option valuation models can produce a reliable valuation of employee share awards.

The IASB has issued two amendments to the original version of IFRS 2:

- *Vesting Conditions and Cancellations,*[1] issued in January 2008 ('the January 2008 amendment'). Entities are required to apply IFRS 2 as modified by this amendment for periods beginning on or after 1 January 2009. Application to earlier periods is permitted provided that fact is disclosed *[IFRS 2.62]*; and

- *Group Cash-settled Share-based Payment Transactions,*[2] issued in June 2009 ('the June 2009 amendment'). Entities are required to apply IFRS 2 as modified by this amendment for periods beginning on or after 1 January 2010. Application to earlier periods is permitted provided that fact is disclosed. *[IFRS 2.63]*.

The requirements of IFRS 2 arising from the January 2008 amendment are discussed principally at 3.2 and 6.4 below, and those arising from the June 2009 amendment at 2.2.2 and 12 below. However, as noted below, and at 1.3, this Chapter does not generally deal with the requirements of IFRS 2 before these amendments.

Improvements to IFRSs issued in April 2009 made a minor amendment to the scope of IFRS 2 (the April 2009 amendment), discussed at 2.2.3.D below.

The Interpretations Committee has issued two interpretations of IFRS 2:

- IFRIC 8 – *Scope of IFRS 2;* and
- IFRIC 11 – *IFRS 2 – Group and Treasury Share Transactions.*

The June 2009 amendment withdrew these two interpretations, incorporating their provisions into IFRS 2. A more detailed discussion of IFRS 2 before the June 2009 amendment may be found in Ernst & Young's *International GAAP 2009.*

SIC-12 – *Consolidation – Special Purpose Entities* – is relevant to the accounting for employee benefit trusts and similar entities for accounting periods beginning before 1 January 2013 (see 12.3 below). For later periods IFRS 10 – *Consolidated Financial Statements* – will be the applicable standard.

IFRS 3 – *Business Combinations* (as revised in 2008 and amended in 2010) amends IFRS 2 and provides guidance on replacement share-based payment awards made by the acquirer in a business combination (see 11 below).

IFRS 2 is supplemented by implementation guidance. However, as noted above the first paragraph of the implementation guidance, this 'accompanies, but is not part of, IFRS 2'.

1.3 Scope of the chapter and referencing convention

This Chapter generally discusses the requirements of IFRS 2 for accounting periods beginning on or after 1 January 2012 and is based on the original version of IFRS 2 as amended in January 2008, April 2009 and June 2009 (see 1.2 above). This amended version of IFRS 2 is referred to as 'IFRS 2' throughout the Chapter.

This Chapter does not discuss IFRS 2 as originally issued (i.e. before the January 2008 amendment) or the version that applied before the June 2009 amendment. A summary of the main changes made by the January 2008 amendment and the requirements of the standard prior to the June 2009 amendment may be found in Ernst & Young's *International GAAP 2009*.

1.4   Overall approach of IFRS 2

IFRS 2 is a complex standard, in part because its overall accounting approach is something of a hybrid. Essentially the total cost (i.e. measurement) of an award is calculated by determining whether it is a liability or an equity instrument, using criteria somewhat different from those in IAS 32 – *Financial Instruments: Presentation* – (see 1.4.1 below), but then applying the measurement principles generally applicable to liabilities or equity instruments under IAS 32 and IAS 39 – *Financial Instruments: Recognition and Measurement*. However the periodic allocation (i.e. recognition) of the cost[3] is determined using something more akin to a straight-line accruals methodology, which would not generally be used for financial instruments.

This inevitably has the result that, depending on its legal form, a transaction of equal value to the recipient can result in several different potential charges in profit or loss, causing some to call into question the comparability of the information provided. Moreover, IFRS 2 is in many respects a rules-based 'anti-avoidance' standard, which often requires an expense to be recorded for transactions that either have no ultimate value to the counterparty or to which, in some cases, the counterparty actually has no entitlement at all. IFRS 2 has an unusually long Basis for Conclusions – longer in fact than the standard and implementation guidance combined, begging the question of whether a standard with clear conceptual foundations would have required such copious justification.

1.4.1   Classification differences between IFRS 2 and IAS 32/IAS 39

As noted above, not only are there differences between the accounting treatment of liabilities or equity under IFRS 2 as compared with that under IAS 32 and IAS 39, but the classification of a transaction as a liability or equity transaction under IFRS 2 may differ from that under IAS 32.

The most important difference between IAS 32 and IFRS 2 is that a transaction involving the delivery of equity instruments within the scope of IFRS 2 is always accounted for as an equity transaction, whereas a similar transaction within the scope of IAS 32 might well be classified as a liability if the number of shares to be delivered varies.

The IASB offers some (pragmatic rather than conceptual) explanation for these differences in the Basis for Conclusions to IFRS 2. First, it is argued that to apply IAS 32 to share option plans would mean that a variable share option plan (i.e. one where the number of shares varied according to performance) would give rise to a more volatile (and typically greater) cost than a fixed plan (i.e. one where the number of shares to be awarded is fixed from the start), even if the same number of shares was ultimately delivered under each plan, which would have 'undesirable consequences'. *[IFRS 2.BC109]*. Second, it is argued that this is just one of several inconsistencies between IAS 32 and IFRS 2 which will be addressed in the round as part of the IASB's review of accounting for debt and equity. *[IFRS 2.BC110].* It is noteworthy, however, that the IASB's current project on financial instruments with characteristics of equity excludes from its scope instruments currently accounted for under IFRS 2.[4]

2 THE OBJECTIVE AND SCOPE OF IFRS 2

2.1 Objective

The stated objective of IFRS 2 is 'to specify the financial reporting by an entity when it undertakes a share-based payment transaction. In particular, it requires an entity to reflect in its profit or loss and financial position the effects of share-based payment transactions, including expenses associated with transactions in which share options are granted to employees'. *[IFRS 2.1].*

2.2 Scope

2.2.1 Definitions

The following definitions from Appendix A to IFRS 2 are relevant to the scope of IFRS 2.

A *share-based payment arrangement* is 'an agreement between the entity (or another group entity or any shareholder of any group entity) and another party (including an employee) that entitles the other party to receive

(a)   cash or other assets of the entity for amounts that are based on the price (or value) of equity instruments (including shares or share options) of the entity or another group entity, or

(b)   equity instruments (including shares or share options) of the entity or another group entity,

provided the specified vesting conditions, if any, are met.'

A *share-based payment transaction* is 'a transaction in which the entity

(a)   receives goods or services from the supplier of those goods or services (including an employee) in a share-based payment arrangement, or

(b)   incurs an obligation to settle the transaction with the supplier in a share-based payment arrangement when another group entity receives those goods or services.'

An *equity-settled share-based payment transaction* is 'a share-based payment transaction in which the entity

(a)   receives goods or services as consideration for its own equity instruments (including shares or share options), or

(b)   receives goods or services but has no obligation to settle the transaction with the supplier.'

A *cash-settled share-based payment transaction* is 'a share-based payment transaction in which the entity acquires goods or services by incurring a liability to transfer cash or other assets to the supplier of those goods or services for amounts that are based on the price (or value) of equity instruments (including shares or share options) of the entity or another group entity'.

A *group entity* in the four definitions above means any parent, subsidiary, or subsidiary of any parent, of the entity.

An *equity instrument* is 'a contract that evidences a residual interest in the assets of an entity after deducting all of its liabilities'.

An *equity instrument granted* is 'the right (conditional or unconditional) to an equity instrument of the entity conferred by the entity on another party, under a share-based payment arrangement'.

A *share option* is 'a contract that gives the holder the right, but not the obligation, to subscribe to the entity's shares at a fixed or determinable price for a specified period of time'.

It will be seen from these definitions that IFRS 2 applies not only to awards of shares and share options but also to awards of cash (or other assets) of a value equivalent to the value, or a movement in the value, of a particular number of shares. Such cash awards may arise in a number of situations. For example:

- an entity may wish to extend its share scheme to the employees of overseas subsidiaries in jurisdictions where it may be difficult, or even illegal, to trade in the entity's shares, or where delivering shares would not give the same tax benefits to employees as would apply in the parent's own jurisdiction; or

- the entity may not wish to dilute existing shareholdings by significant share awards to employees.

In such cases, the employees may instead be offered cash equivalent to the value of the shares that they would otherwise have obtained.

2.2.2   Transactions within the scope of IFRS 2

Subject to the exceptions noted in 2.2.3 below, IFRS 2 must be applied to all share-based payment transactions, including:

(a)   equity-settled share-based payment transactions (discussed at 4 to 8 below);

(b)   cash-settled share-based payment transactions (discussed at 9 below); and

(c)   transactions where either the entity or the supplier of goods or services can choose whether the transaction is to be equity-settled or cash-settled (discussed at 10 below). *[IFRS 2.2].*

Whilst the boundaries between these types of transaction are reasonably self-explanatory, there may – as discussed in more detail at 9 and 10 below – be transactions that an entity may intuitively regard as equity-settled which are in fact required to be treated as cash-settled under IFRS 2.

Although IFRS 2 was primarily a response to concerns over share-based remuneration, its scope is not restricted to transactions with employees. For example, if an external supplier of goods or services, including another group entity, is paid in shares or share options, or cash of equivalent value, IFRS 2 must be applied. Goods include:

- inventories;
- consumables;
- property, plant and equipment;
- intangibles; and
- other non-financial assets. *[IFRS 2.5]*.

It will be seen that 'goods' do not include financial assets, which raises some further issues (see 2.2.3.F below). The scope of IFRS 2 extends to:

- certain transactions by shareholders and other group entities (see 2.2.2.A below);
- transactions with employee benefit trusts and similar vehicles (see 2.2.2.B below);
- transactions where the identifiable consideration received appears to be less than the consideration given (see 2.2.2.C below);
- 'all employee' share plans (see 2.2.2.D below); and
- vested transactions (see 2.2.2.E below).

2.2.2.A   Transactions by shareholders and other group entities

The definitions of 'share-based payment arrangement' and 'share-based payment transaction' at 2.2.1 above have the effect that the scope of IFRS 2 is not restricted to transactions where the reporting entity acquires goods or services in exchange for its own equity instruments (or cash or other assets based on the cost or value of those equity instruments). Within a group of companies it is common for one member of the group (typically the parent) to settle a share-based payment transaction in which services are provided to another member of the group (typically a subsidiary). This transaction is within the scope of IFRS 2 for the entity receiving the services, the entity settling the transaction and the group as a whole.

Accordingly, IFRS 2 requires an entity to account for a transaction in which it either:

- receives goods or services when another entity in the same group (or a shareholder of any group entity) has the obligation to settle the share-based payment transaction, or
- has an obligation to settle a share-based payment transaction when another entity in the same group receives the goods or services

unless the transaction is clearly for a purpose other than payment for goods or services supplied to the entity receiving them. *[IFRS 2.3A]*.

Moreover, the definitions of 'equity-settled share-based payment transaction' and 'cash-settled share-based payment transaction' have the effect that the analysis of the transaction as equity-settled or cash-settled (and its accounting treatment) may differ when viewed from the perspective of the entity receiving the goods or services, the entity settling the transaction and the group as a whole. *[IFRS 2.43A]*.

We consider seven scenarios below, based on the simple structure in Figure 32.1 below. These scenarios are by no means exhaustive, but cover most of the situations most commonly seen in practice.

Figure 32.1:   Scope of IFRS 2

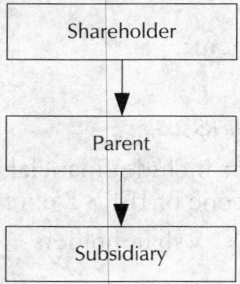

The shareholder is not a group entity.

Scenario 1

Parent awards equity shares in Parent to employees of Subsidiary in exchange for services to Subsidiary. Parent settles the award with the employees of Subsidiary. *[IFRS 2.43B-43C, B52(a), B53-B54].*

Consolidated financial statements of Parent

Under the definition of 'share-based payment transaction', 'the entity [i.e. the Parent group] ... receives goods or services ... in a share-based payment arrangement'. A share-based payment arrangement includes 'an agreement between the entity ... and another party (including an employee) that entitles the other party to receive ... equity instruments of the entity ... .'

The transaction is classified as an equity-settled transaction, because it is settled in an equity instrument of the group.

Separate financial statements of Parent

Under the definition of 'share-based payment transaction', the 'entity [i.e. the Parent as a single entity] ... incurs an obligation to settle the transaction with the supplier in a share-based payment arrangement when another group entity receives those goods or services'.

The transaction is classified as an equity-settled transaction, because it is settled in an equity instrument of Parent.

Subsidiary

Under the definition of 'share-based payment transaction', 'the entity [i.e. Subsidiary] ... receives goods or services ... in a share-based payment arrangement'. A 'share-based payment arrangement' includes 'an agreement between ... another group entity [i.e. Parent] ... and another party (including an employee) that entitles the other party to receive ... equity instruments of ... another group entity.'

The transaction is classified as an equity-settled transaction, because Subsidiary 'has no obligation to settle the transaction with the supplier'.

Even if Subsidiary is not a party to the agreement with its employees, it nevertheless records a cost for this transaction. In effect, the accounting treatment is representing that Subsidiary has received a capital contribution from Parent, which Subsidiary has then 'spent' on employee remuneration. This treatment is often referred to as 'push-down' accounting – the idea being that a transaction undertaken by one group entity (in this case, Parent) for the benefit of another group entity (in this case, Subsidiary) is 'pushed down' into the financial statements of the beneficiary entity.

Scenario 2

Shareholder awards equity shares in Parent to employees of Subsidiary in exchange for services to Subsidiary. Shareholder settles the award with the employees of Subsidiary. *[IFRS 2.B48(b)]*.

Consolidated financial statements of Parent

Under the definition of 'share-based payment transaction', 'the entity [i.e. the Parent group] ... receives goods or services ... in a share-based payment arrangement'. A 'share-based payment arrangement' includes 'an agreement between ... any shareholder ... and another party (including an employee) that entitles the other party to receive ... equity instruments (including shares or share options) of the entity...'.

The transaction is classified as an equity-settled transaction, because the Parent group 'has no obligation to settle the transaction with the supplier'.

Separate financial statements of Parent

Scenario 2 is not within the scope of IFRS 2 for the separate financial statements of Parent, because Parent (as a separate entity) receives no goods or services, nor does it settle the transaction.

Subsidiary

Under the definition of 'share-based payment transaction', 'the entity [i.e. Subsidiary] ... receives goods or services ... in a share-based payment arrangement'. A 'share-based payment arrangement' includes 'an agreement between ... any shareholder of any group entity [i.e. Shareholder] ... and another party (including an employee) that entitles the other party to receive equity instruments of ... another group entity [i.e. Parent].'

The transaction is classified as an equity-settled transaction, because Subsidiary 'has no obligation to settle the transaction with the supplier'.

IFRS 2 explicitly does not address the accounting treatment for such a transaction within the financial statements of a non-group shareholder. *[IFRS 2.BC22G]*. We discuss at 12.8 below the accounting treatment of such transactions in the financial statements of a shareholder that is an investor in a joint venture or associate.

Scenario 3

Subsidiary awards equity shares in Parent to employees of Subsidiary in exchange for services to Subsidiary. Subsidiary settles the award with the employees of Subsidiary. *[IFRS 2.43B, B52(b), B55]*.

Consolidated financial statements of Parent

Under the definition of 'share-based payment transaction', 'the entity [i.e. the Parent group] ... receives goods or services ... in a share-based payment arrangement'. A 'share-based payment arrangement' includes 'an agreement between the entity ... and another party (including an employee) that entitles the other party to receive ... equity instruments (including shares or share options) of the entity'.

The transaction is classified as an equity-settled transaction, because the Parent group 'receives goods or services as consideration for its own equity instruments (including shares or share options)...'.

Separate financial statements of Parent

Scenario 3 is not within the scope of IFRS 2 for the separate financial statements of Parent, because Parent (as a separate entity) receives no goods or services, nor does it settle the transaction.

Subsidiary

Under the definition of 'share-based payment transaction', 'the entity [i.e. Subsidiary] ... receives goods or services ... in a share-based payment arrangement'. A 'share-based payment arrangement' includes 'an agreement between ... [a] group entity [i.e. Subsidiary] ... and another party (including an employee) that entitles the other party to receive equity instruments of ... another group entity [i.e. Parent]'.

The transaction is classified as a cash-settled transaction because Subsidiary has the obligation to settle the award with equity instruments issued by Parent – i.e. a financial asset in Subsidiary's separate financial statements – rather than with Subsidiary's own equity instruments.

However, for the approach in this Scenario to apply, it must be the case that Subsidiary grants the award as a principal rather than as agent for Parent. If Subsidiary appears to be granting an award but is really doing so only on the instructions of Parent, as will generally be the case in certain jurisdictions, then the approach in Scenario 1 above is more likely to apply. This is discussed in more detail at 12.2.5.B below.

Scenario 4

Subsidiary awards equity shares in Subsidiary to employees of Subsidiary in exchange for services to Subsidiary. Subsidiary settles the award with the employees of Subsidiary. *[IFRS 2.43B, B49].*

Consolidated financial statements of Parent

Under the definition of 'share-based payment transaction', 'the entity [i.e. the Parent group] ... receives goods or services ... in a share-based payment arrangement'. A share-based payment arrangement includes 'an agreement between the entity ... and another party (including an employee) that entitles the other party to receive ... equity instruments ... of the entity ... .'

The transaction is classified as an equity-settled transaction, because it is settled in an equity instrument of the group. In the consolidated financial statements of Parent, shares of Subsidiary not held by Parent are a non-controlling (minority) interest, classified as equity (see Chapter 8 at 4).

Subsidiary

Under the definition of 'share-based payment transaction', 'the entity [i.e. Subsidiary] ... receives goods or services ... in a share-based payment arrangement'.

The transaction is classified as an equity-settled transaction, because it is settled in an equity instrument of Subsidiary.

Scenario 5

Parent awards equity shares in Subsidiary to employees of Subsidiary in exchange for services to Subsidiary. Parent settles the award with the employees of Subsidiary. *[IFRS 2.43B-43C, B50].*

Consolidated financial statements of Parent

Under the definition of 'share-based payment transaction', 'the entity [i.e. the Parent group] ... receives goods or services ... in a share-based payment arrangement'. A share-based payment arrangement includes 'an agreement between the entity ... and another party (including an employee) that entitles the other party to receive ... equity instruments of the entity ... .'

The transaction is classified as an equity-settled transaction, because it is settled in an equity instrument of the group. In the consolidated financial statements of Parent, shares of Subsidiary not held by Parent are a non-controlling (minority) interest, classified as equity (see Chapter 8 at 4).

Separate financial statements of Parent

Under the definition of 'share-based payment transaction', the 'entity [i.e. the Parent as a single entity] ... incurs an obligation to settle the transaction with the supplier in a share-based payment arrangement when another group entity [i.e. Subsidiary] receives those goods or services'. The transaction is a share-based payment arrangement for Subsidiary (see below) and the consolidated financial statements of Parent (see above).

The transaction is classified as a cash-settled transaction, because it is settled not in an equity instrument issued by Parent, but in an equity instrument issued by a subsidiary held by Parent – i.e. a financial asset in Parent's separate financial statements.

Subsidiary

Under the definition of 'share-based payment transaction', 'the entity [i.e. Subsidiary] ... receives goods or services ... in a share-based payment arrangement'. A 'share-based payment arrangement' includes 'an agreement between ... another group entity [i.e. Parent] ... and another party (including an employee) that entitles the other party to receive equity instruments of the entity... .'

The transaction is classified as an equity-settled transaction, because Subsidiary 'has no obligation to settle the transaction with the supplier'.

Scenario 6

Parent awards cash based on the value of shares in Parent to employees of Subsidiary in exchange for services to Subsidiary. Parent settles the award with the employees of Subsidiary. *[IFRS 2.43C, B56-B58]*.

Consolidated financial statements of Parent

Under the definition of 'share-based payment transaction', 'the entity [i.e. the Parent group] ... receives goods or services ... in a share-based payment arrangement'. A 'share-based payment arrangement' includes 'an agreement between the entity ... and another party (including an employee) that entitles the other party to receive ... cash ... of the entity ... based on the price (or value) of equity instruments ... of the entity ... .'

The transaction is classified as a cash-settled transaction, because it is settled in cash of the group.

Separate financial statements of Parent

Under the definition of 'share-based payment transaction', the 'entity [i.e. the Parent as a single entity] ... incurs an obligation to settle the transaction with the supplier in a share-based payment arrangement when another group entity [i.e. Subsidiary] receives those goods or services'.

The transaction is classified as a cash-settled transaction, because it is settled in cash of Parent.

Subsidiary

IFRS 2 contains detailed guidance for the accounting treatment of such transactions by the employing subsidiary (see 12 below), from which it may reasonably be inferred that the IASB intended them to be in the scope of IFRS 2 for the subsidiary.

However, this is strictly not the case when the drafting of IFRS 2 is examined closely. In order to be a share-based payment *transaction* (and therefore in the scope of IFRS 2) for the reporting entity, a transaction must also be a share-based payment *arrangement*. A share-based payment arrangement is defined as one in which the counterparty receives (our emphasis added):

- equity of the entity *or any other group entity*, or
- cash or other assets *of the entity*.

As drafted, the definition has the effect that a transaction settled in equity is in the scope of IFRS 2 for a reporting entity, whether the equity used to settle is the entity's own equity or that of another group entity. Where a transaction is settled in cash, however, the definition has the effect that a transaction is in the scope of IFRS 2 for a reporting entity only when that entity's own cash (or other assets) is used in settlement, and not when another group entity settles the transaction.

However, given the guidance referred to above in IFRS 2 for the accounting treatment for the reporting entity of transactions settled in cash by another group entity, we believe that the exclusion of such transactions from the definition of 'share-based payment arrangement' should be disregarded as an unfortunate drafting slip.

The transaction is classified as an equity-settled transaction by Subsidiary, because Subsidiary 'has no obligation to settle the transaction with the supplier'.

Scenario 7

Shareholder awards cash based on the value of shares in Parent to employees of Subsidiary in exchange for services to Subsidiary. Shareholder settles the award with the employees of Subsidiary.

For the reasons set out in Scenario 6 above, this transaction is not strictly in the scope of IFRS 2 as drafted either for the consolidated financial statements of Parent or for the separate financial statements of Parent or Subsidiary. As noted in Scenario 6 above, the definition of 'share-based payment arrangement' as drafted excludes any arrangement that is settled in cash by a party other than the reporting entity. Moreover, whilst IFRS 2 gives detailed guidance that effectively appears to 'over-ride' the definition in respect of a transaction settled by another group entity (see Scenario 6 above), there is no such over-riding guidance in respect of a transaction settled in cash by a non-group shareholder.

Nevertheless, we believe that the transaction should be treated as within the scope of IFRS 2 for the consolidated financial statements of Parent and the separate financial statements of Subsidiary. One of the original objectives of the project that led to the issue of the June 2009 amendment to IFRS 2 was to address a concern that, as originally issued, IFRS 2 did not require an entity to account for a cash-settled share-based payment transaction settled by an external shareholder.

Whether accounted for or not, any payments by a shareholder would potentially be disclosable under IAS 24 – *Related Party Disclosures*, as discussed in Chapter 37.

The accounting treatment of group share schemes is discussed in more detail at 12 below.

2.2.2.B   Transactions with employee benefit trusts and similar vehicles

In some jurisdictions, it is common for an entity to establish a trust to hold shares in the entity for the purpose of satisfying, or 'hedging' the cost of, share-based awards to employees. In such cases, it is often the trust, rather than any entity within the legal group, that actually makes share-based awards to employees. For accounting periods beginning before 1 January 2013 such trusts will normally be consolidated by the sponsoring employer in accordance with IAS 27 – *Consolidated and Separate Financial Statements* – as interpreted by SIC-12. For later accounting periods, consolidation of the trust will need to be assessed in accordance with the requirements of IFRS 10 (see 12.3 below).

Awards by such trusts are within the scope of IFRS 2, irrespective of whether or not the trust is consolidated, since:

- where the trust is consolidated, it is an award by a group entity; and
- where the trust is not consolidated, it is an award by a shareholder.

2.2.2.C   Transactions where the identifiable consideration received appears to be less than the consideration given

A share-based payment transaction as defined (see 2.2.1 above) involves the receipt of goods or services by the reporting entity. Nevertheless, IFRS 2 also applies to share-based payment transactions (other than those excluded from the scope of IFRS 2 – see 2.2.3 below) where no specifically identifiable goods or services have been (or will be) received. *[IFRS 2.2]*.

IFRS 2 asserts that, if the identifiable consideration received (if any) appears to be less than the fair value of consideration given, the implication is that, in addition to the identifiable goods and services acquired, the entity must also have received some unidentifiable consideration equal to the difference between the fair value of the share-based payment and the fair value of any identifiable consideration received. Accordingly, the cost of the unidentified consideration must be accounted for in accordance with IFRS 2. *[IFRS 2.13A]*.

For example, if an entity agrees to pay a supplier of services with a clearly identifiable market value of £1,000 by issuing shares with a value of £1,500, IFRS 2 requires the entity to recognise an expense of £1,500. This is notwithstanding the normal requirement of IFRS 2 that an equity-settled share-based payment transaction with a non-employee be recognised at the fair value of the goods or services received (see 5.1 and 5.4 below).

This requirement did not appear in IFRS 2 as originally published, but was introduced later by IFRIC 8, and more recently incorporated into IFRS 2 by the June 2009 amendment. The reason for the change is alluded to in an illustrative example. *[IFRS 2.IG5D, IG Example 1]*. As part of general economic reforms in South Africa, under arrangements generally referred to as black economic empowerment or 'BEE' (discussed further at 15.4 below), various entities issued or transferred significant numbers of shares to bodies representing historically disadvantaged communities. Some held that these transactions did not fall within the scope of IFRS 2 as originally drafted because the entities concerned were not purchasing goods or services. Rather, BEE arrangements were simply meant to replicate a transfer of shares from one group of shareholders to another. Accordingly, it was argued, such transactions did not fall within the scope of IFRS 2, since it is intrinsic to the definition of a 'share-based payment transaction' (see 2.2.1 above) that goods or services are received.

IFRS 2 rejects this argument. It effectively takes the view that, since the directors of an entity would not issue valuable consideration for nothing, something must have been received. *[IFRS 2.BC18C]*. IFRS 2 suggests that a transfer of equity under BEE and similar schemes is made 'as a means of enhancing [the entity's] image as a good corporate citizen'. *[IFRS 2, IG Example 1]*.

There seems little doubt that this aspect of IFRS 2 is in part an 'anti-avoidance' measure. As discussed in 4 to 8 below, the general measurement rule in IFRS 2 is that share-based payment transactions with employees are measured by reference to the fair value of the consideration given and those with non-employees by reference to the fair value of the consideration received. We argue at 5.2.2 below that the requirement to measure transactions with employees by reference to the consideration given is essentially an anti-avoidance provision. It essentially prevents entities from recognising a low cost for employee share options on the grounds that little incremental service is provided for them beyond that already provided for cash-based remuneration. The provisions of IFRS 2 under discussion here remove the potential for a similar abuse in accounting for transactions with non-employees.

Nevertheless, the IASB acknowledges that there may be rare circumstances in which a transaction may occur in which no goods or services are received by the entity. For example, a principal shareholder of an entity, for reasons of estate planning, may transfer shares to a relative. In the absence of indications that the relative has provided, or is expected to provide, goods or services to the entity in exchange for the shares, such a transfer would be outside the scope of IFRS 2. *[IFRS 2.BC18D]*.

2.2.2.D   'All employee' share plans

Many countries encourage wider share-ownership by allowing companies to award a limited number of free or discounted shares to employees without either the employee or the employer incurring tax liabilities which would apply if other benefits in kind to an equivalent value were given to employees.

Some existing national standards exempt some such plans from their scope, to some extent as the result of local political pressures. During the exposure period of ED 2, the IASB received some strong representations that IFRS should give a similar exemption, on the grounds that not to do so would discourage companies from continuing with such schemes.

The IASB concluded that such an exemption would be wrong in principle and difficult to draft in practice. By way of concession, the Basis for Conclusions hints that if the IFRS 2 charge for such schemes is (as asserted by some of the proponents of an exemption) *de minimis*, then there would be no charge under IFRS 2 anyway, since, like all IFRSs, it applies only to material items. *[IFRS 2.BC8-17]*. However, our experience is that, in many cases, the charge is material.

2.2.2.E   Vested transactions

Once a transaction accounted for under IFRS 2 has vested in the counterparty (see 3 below), it does not necessarily cease to be in the scope of IFRS 2. This is made clear by the numerous provisions of IFRS 2 referring to the accounting treatment of vested awards.

Once shares have been delivered or beneficially transferred to the counterparty (e.g. as the result of the vesting of an award of shares, or the exercise of a vested option over shares), those shares should generally be accounted for under IAS 32 and IAS 39 rather than IFRS 2. If, however, the holder of such a share enjoys rights not applicable to all holders of that class of share, such as a right to put the share to the entity for cash, the share might still remain in the scope of IFRS 2. The significance of this is that issued equity instruments and financial liabilities not within the scope of IFRS 2 would typically fall within the scope of IAS 32 and IAS 39, which might require a significantly different accounting treatment from that required by IFRS 2. See, for example:

- the discussion at 2.2.4.B below of the treatment in consolidated financial statements of an award with a right to put the share to the parent entity; and

- the discussion at 2.2.4.H below which highlights that a share option with a foreign currency strike price is accounted for as an equity instrument under IFRS 2, but as a liability under IAS 32 and IAS 39.

2.2.3   Transactions not within the scope of IFRS 2

The following transactions are outside the scope of IFRS 2:

- transactions with shareholders as a whole and with shareholders in their capacity as such (see 2.2.3.A below);

- transfers of assets in certain group restructuring arrangements (see 2.2.3.B below);

- business combinations (see 2.2.3.C below);
- combinations of businesses under common control and the contribution of a business to form a joint venture (see 2.2.3.D below); and
- transactions in the scope of IAS 32 – *Financial Instruments: Presentation* – and IAS 39 – *Financial Instruments: Recognition and Measurement* (see 2.2.3.E below). The scope exemptions in IFRS 2 combined with those in IAS 32 and IAS 39 appear to have the effect that there is no specific guidance in IFRS for accounting for certain types of investments when acquired for shares (see 2.2.3.F below).

However, there is no exemption from IFRS 2 for share schemes aimed mainly at lower- and middle-ranking employees, referred to in different jurisdictions by terms such as 'all-employee share schemes', 'employee share purchase plans' and 'broad-based plans' (see 2.2.2.D above).

2.2.3.A   Transactions with shareholders in their capacity as such

IFRS 2 does not apply to transactions with employees (and others) purely in their capacity as shareholders. For example, an employee may already hold shares in the entity as a result of previous share-based payment transactions. If the entity then raises funds through a rights issue, whereby all shareholders (including the employee) can acquire additional shares for less than the current fair value of the shares, such a transaction is not a 'share-based payment transaction' for the purposes of IFRS 2. *[IFRS 2.4]*.

2.2.3.B   Transfer of assets in group restructuring arrangements

In some group restructuring arrangements, one entity will transfer a group of net assets, which does not meet the definition of a business, to another entity in return for shares. Careful consideration of the precise facts and circumstances is needed in order to determine whether, for the separate or individual financial statements of any entity affected by the transfer, such a transfer falls within the scope of IFRS 2. If the transfer is considered primarily to be a transfer of goods by their owner in return for shares then, in our view, this should be accounted for under IFRS 2. However, if the transaction is for another purpose and is driven by the group shareholder in its capacity as such, the transaction may be outside the scope of IFRS 2 (see 2.2.3.A above). Accounting for intra-group asset transfers in return for shares is considered further in Chapter 9 at 4.4.1.

2.2.3.C   Business combinations

IFRS 2 does not apply to share-based payments to acquire goods (such as inventories or property, plant and equipment) in the context of a business combination to which IFRS 3 – *Business Combinations* – applies. However, equity instruments granted to the employees of the acquiree in their capacity as employees (e.g. in return for continued service) are within the scope of IFRS 2, as are the cancellation, replacement or modification of a share-based payment transaction as the result of a business combination or other equity restructuring (see 11 below). *[IFRS 2.5]*.

Thus, if a vendor of an acquired business remains as an employee of that business following the business combination and receives a share-based payment for transferring control of the entity and for remaining in continuing employment, it is necessary to determine how much of the share-based payment relates to the acquisition of control (which forms part of the cost of the combination, accounted for under IFRS 3) and how much relates to the provision of future services (which is a post-combination operating expense accounted for under IFRS 2). Guidance on this issue is given in IFRS 3 – see Chapter 10 at 7.

2.2.3.D   Common control transactions and formation of joint ventures

IFRS 2 also does not apply to a combination of entities or businesses under common control (see Chapter 11), or the contribution of a business on the formation of a joint venture (see Chapter 13).

These exemptions apply for annual periods beginning on or after 1 July 2009. Earlier application is permitted. If an entity applies IFRS 3 as revised in 2008 for an earlier period, the amendments are also applied for that earlier period. *[IFRS 2.5, 61].*

In practical terms, this is very much a 'technical' amendment to reflect what had always been understood to be the intention of IFRS 2. In practice, such transactions had not generally been accounted for under IFRS 2 before this amendment.

It should be noted that the contribution of assets (which do not constitute a business) to a joint venture in return for shares is within the scope of IFRS 2 (see 2.2.2 above).

IFRS 2 does not directly address other types of transactions involving joint ventures or transactions involving associates. These are discussed further at 12.8 below.

2.2.3.E   Transactions in the scope of IAS 32 and IAS 39

IFRS 2 does not apply to transactions within the scope of IAS 32 or IAS 39 (see Chapter 43 at 2). Therefore, if an entity enters into a share-based payment transaction to purchase a commodity surplus to its production requirements or with a view to short-term profit taking, the contract is treated as a financial instrument under IAS 32 and IAS 39 rather than a share-based payment transaction under IFRS 2. *[IFRS 2.6].*

Some practical examples of scope issues involving IFRS 2 and IAS 32 / IAS 39 are discussed at 2.2.4 below.

2.2.3.F   Transactions in financial assets not in the scope of IAS 32 and IAS 39

As noted in 2.2.2 above, IFRS 2 applies to share-based payment transactions involving goods or services, with 'goods' defined so as to exclude financial assets, presumably on the basis that these fall within IAS 32 and IAS 39. However, investments in subsidiaries, associates and corporate joint ventures in the separate financial statements of the investing entity are financial assets as defined in IAS 32 (and hence outside the scope of IFRS 2), but are outside the scope of IAS 39 where the entity chooses to account for them at cost (see Chapter 9 at 2.1 and Chapter 43 at 3.1).

Moreover, IFRS has no general requirements for accounting for the issue of equity instruments. Rather, consistent with the position taken by the *Framework* that equity is a residual rather than an item 'in its own right', the amount of an equity instrument is normally measured by reference to the item (expense or asset) in consideration for which the equity is issued, as determined in accordance with IFRS applicable to that other item.

This means that, when (as is commonly the case) an entity acquires an investment in a subsidiary, associate or joint venture for the issue of equity instruments, there is no explicit guidance in IFRS as to the required accounting in the separate financial statements of the investor, and in particular as to how the 'cost' of such an item is to be determined. This is discussed further in Chapter 9 at 2.1.1.A.

2.2.4 Some practical applications of the scope requirements

2.2.4.A Remuneration in non-equity shares and put rights over equity shares

A transaction is within the scope of IFRS 2 only where it involves the delivery of an equity instrument, or cash based on the price or value of an 'equity instrument' (see 2.2.1 above).

In some jurisdictions, there can be fiscal advantages in giving an employee, in lieu of a cash payment, a share that carries a right to a 'one-off' dividend, or is mandatorily redeemable, at an amount equivalent to the intended cash payment. Such a share would almost certainly be classified as a liability under IAS 32 (see Chapter 45). Accordingly, payment in such a share would not fall in the scope of IFRS 2, since the consideration paid by the entity for services received is a financial liability rather than an equity instrument (see the definitions in 2.2.1 above).

If, however, the amount of remuneration delivered in this way were equivalent to the value of a particular number of equity instruments issued by the entity, then the transaction would be in scope of IFRS 2 as a cash-settled share-based payment transaction, since the entity would have incurred a liability (i.e. by issuing the redeemable shares) for an amount based on the price of its equity instruments.

Similarly, if an entity grants an award of equity instruments to an employee together with a put right whereby the employee can require the entity to purchase those shares for fair value, both elements of that transaction are in the scope of IFRS 2 as a single cash-settled transaction (see 9 below). This is notwithstanding the fact that, under IAS 32, the share and the put right might well be analysed as a single synthetic instrument and classified as a liability with no equity component (see Chapter 45). Differences between the classification of instruments between IFRS 2 and IAS 32 are discussed further at 1.4.1 above.

2.2.4.B Equity-settled award of subsidiary with put option against the parent – treatment in consolidated accounts of parent

It is sometimes the case that a subsidiary entity grants an award over its own equity instruments and, either on the same date or later, the parent entity separately grants the same counterparty a put option to sell the equity instruments of the subsidiary to the parent for cash. Accounting for such an arrangement in the separate financial statements of the subsidiary and the parent will be determined in accordance with the general principles of IFRS 2 (see 2.2.2.A above). However, IFRS 2 does not explicitly address the accounting treatment of such arrangements in the parent's consolidated financial statements.

In our view, the analysis differs according to whether the put option is granted during or after the vesting period.

If the put option is granted during the vesting period (whether at the same time as the grant of the equity instruments or later), the two transactions should be treated as linked and accounted for in the consolidated financial statements as a single cash-settled transaction from the date the put option is granted. This reflects the fact that this situation is similar in group terms to a modification of an award to add a cash-settlement alternative – see 10.1.4 below.

If the put option is only granted once the equity instruments have vested, the accounting will depend on whether the equity instruments in the original share-based payment transaction are unexercised options or whether they are shares. If they are unexercised options, the vested award remains within the scope of IFRS 2 (see 2.2.2.E above) and so the put option should be treated as a linked transaction. Its effect in group terms is to modify the original award from an equity- to a cash-settled transaction until final settlement date. However, if the equity instruments are shares (free shares or exercised options), rather than unexercised options, they are no longer within the scope of IFRS 2. In such cases, the parent entity will need to evaluate whether or not the grant of the put option, as a separate transaction which modifies the terms of certain of the subsidiary's equity instruments, falls within the scope of IFRS 2.

2.2.4.C   Increase in ownership interest with no change in number of shares held

An increasingly common arrangement, typically found in entities with venture capital investors, is one where an employee (typically part of the key management) subscribes initially for, say, 1% of the entity's equity with the venture capitalist holding the other 99%. The employee's equity interest will subsequently increase by a variable amount depending on the extent to which certain targets are met. This is achieved not by issuing new shares but by cancelling some of the venture capitalist's shares. In our view, such an arrangement falls within the scope of IFRS 2 as the employee is rewarded with an increased equity stake in the entity if certain targets are achieved. The increased equity stake is consistent with the definition in Appendix A of IFRS 2 of an equity instrument as 'a contract that evidences a residual interest...' notwithstanding the fact that no additional shares are issued.

In such arrangements, it is often asserted that the employee has subscribed for a share of the equity at fair value. However, the subscription price paid must represent a fair value using an IFRS 2 valuation basis in order for there to be no additional IFRS 2 expense to recognise (see 2.2.4.D below).

Chapter 32

2.2.4.D Awards for which the counterparty has paid 'fair value'

In certain situations, such as where a special class of share is issued, the counterparty might be asked to subscribe a certain amount for the share which is agreed as being its 'fair value' for taxation or other purposes. This does not mean that such arrangements fall outside the scope of IFRS 2, either for measurement or disclosure purposes, if the arrangement meets the definition of a share-based payment transaction. In many cases, the agreed 'fair value' will be lower than a fair value measured in accordance with IFRS 2 because it will reflect the impact of non-market vesting conditions which are excluded from an IFRS 2 fair value. This is addressed in more detail at 15.3.5 below.

2.2.4.E Cash bonus dependent on share price performance

An entity might agree to pay its employees a €100 cash bonus if its share price remains at €10 or more over a given period. Intuitively, this does not appear to be in the scope of IFRS 2, since the employee is not being given cash of equivalent value to a particular number of shares. However, it could be argued that it does fall within the scope of IFRS 2 on the basis that the entity has incurred a liability, and the amount of that liability is 'based on' the share price – it is nil if the share price is below €10 and €100 if the share price is €10 or more. In our view, either interpretation is acceptable.

2.2.4.F Cash-settled awards based on 'enterprise value'

As noted at 2.2.1 above, IFRS 2 includes within its scope transactions in which the entity acquires goods or services by incurring a liability 'based on the price (or value) of equity instruments (including shares or share options) of the entity or another group entity'. Employees of an unquoted entity may receive a cash award based on the value of the equity of that entity. Such awards are typically, but not exclusively, made by venture capital investors to the management of entities in which they have invested and which they aim to sell in the medium term. Further discussion of the accounting implications of such awards may be found at 15.3 below.

Where employees of an unquoted entity receive a cash award based on the value of the equity, there is no quoted share price and an 'enterprise value' has therefore to be calculated as a surrogate for it. This begs the question of whether such awards are within the scope of IFRS 2 (because they are based on the value of the entity's equity) or that of IAS 19 – *Employee Benefits*.

There is unlikely to be any significant difference in the cost ultimately recorded under either standard. However, the disclosures required if IFRS 2 is the applicable standard are more onerous than those required by IAS 19.

In order for an award to be within the scope of IFRS 2, any calculated 'enterprise value' must represent the fair value of the entity's equity. Where the calculation uses techniques recognised by IFRS 2 as yielding a fair value for equity instruments (as discussed at 8 below), we believe that the award should be regarded as within the scope of IFRS 2.

Appendix B of IFRS 2 notes that an unquoted entity may have calculated the value of its equity based on net assets or earnings (see 8.5.3.B below). *[IFRS 2.B30]*. In our view, this is not intended to imply that it is always appropriate to do so, but simply to note that it may be appropriate in some cases.

Where, for example, the enterprise value is based on a constant formula, such as a fixed multiple of earnings before interest, tax, depreciation and amortisation ('EBITDA'), in our view it is unlikely that this will represent a good surrogate for the fair value of the equity on an ongoing basis, even if it did so at the inception of the transaction. It is not difficult to imagine scenarios in which the fair value of the equity of an entity could be affected with no significant change in EBITDA, for example as a result of changes in interest rates and effective tax rates, or a significant impairment of assets. Alternatively, there might be a significant shift in the multiple of EBITDA equivalent to fair value, for example if the entity were to create or acquire a significant item of intellectual property.

The treatment of equity-settled awards based on the market price of an unquoted entity raises similar issues, as discussed more fully at 6.3.8 below.

2.2.4.G   Employment taxes relating to share-based payment transactions

In many jurisdictions, share-based payment transactions are subject to employment taxes similar to those levied on cash-based remuneration. The accounting treatment of such taxes is discussed in more detail at 14 below.

2.2.4.H   Awards with a foreign currency strike price

Many entities award their employees options with a foreign currency strike price. This will arise most commonly in a multinational group where employees of overseas subsidiaries are granted options on terms that they can pay the option strike price in their local currency. They may also arise where an entity, which has a functional currency different from that of the country in which it operates (e.g. an oil company based in the United Kingdom with a functional currency of United States dollars), grants its UK-based employees options with a strike price in pounds sterling, which is a foreign currency from the perspective of the currency of the financial statements.

Under IAS 32, as currently interpreted, such an award could not be regarded as an equity instrument because the strike price to be tendered is not, in terms of the reporting entity's own currency, a fixed amount (see Chapter 45 at 5.2.2). However, under IFRS 2, as discussed at 2.2.1 above, equity instruments include options, which are defined as the right to acquire shares for a 'fixed *or determinable* price'. Moreover, it is quite clear from the Basis for Conclusions in IFRS 2 that an award which ultimately results in an employee receiving equity is equity-settled under IFRS 2 whatever its status under IAS 32 might be (see 1.4.1 above). Thus an option over equity with a foreign currency strike price is an equity instrument if accounted for under IFRS 2.

The fair value of such an award should be assessed at grant date and, where the award is treated as equity-settled, not subsequently revised for foreign exchange movements (on the general rule that an entity should not reflect changes in the value of an equity instrument in its financial statements). This applies to the separate financial statements of a parent or subsidiary entity as well as to consolidated financial statements. Where the award is treated as cash-settled, however, the periodic reassessment of fair value required by IFRS 2 will take account, *inter alia*, of any movement in exchange rates.

2.2.4.I Holding own shares to satisfy or 'hedge' awards

Entities often seek to hedge the cost of share-based payment transactions, most commonly by buying their own equity instruments in the market. For example, an entity could grant an employee options over 10,000 shares and buy 10,000 of its own shares into treasury at the date that the award is made. If the award is share-settled, the entity will deliver the shares to the counterparty. If it is cash-settled, it can sell the shares to raise the cash it is required to deliver to the counterparty. In either case, the cash cost of the award is capped at the market price of the shares at the date the award is made, less any amount paid by the employee on exercise. It could of course be argued that such an arrangement is not a true hedge at all. If the share price goes down so that the option is never exercised, the entity is left holding 10,000 of its own shares that cost more than they are now worth.

Whilst these strategies may provide a hedge of the cash cost of share-based payment transactions that are eventually exercised, they will not have any effect in hedging the charge to profit or loss required by IFRS 2 for such transactions. This is because purchases and sales of own shares are accounted for as movements in equity and are therefore never included in profit or loss (see 4.1 below). In any event, IAS 39 does not recognise a hedge of, or using, own equity as a valid hedging relationship (see Chapter 51).

2.2.4.J Convertible bonds and limited recourse loans

In certain circumstances, instruments such as limited recourse loans and convertible bonds will fall within the scope of IFRS 2 rather than IAS 32/IAS 39 because of the link both to the entity's equity instruments and to services received in exchange. Convertible bonds are discussed in more detail at 10.1.6 below and limited recourse loans at 15.1 below.

2.2.4.K Shares or warrants issued in connection with a financial liability

As noted at 2.2.3.F above, IFRS 2 does not apply to transactions within the scope of IAS 32 and IAS 39. However, if shares or warrants are granted to the lender by the counterparty as part of a financing arrangement, the measurement of those shares or warrants might fall within the scope of IFRS 2. The determination of the relevant standard is likely to require significant judgement based on the precise terms of individual transactions. If the shares or warrants are considered to be in lieu of a cash fee for the lender's services then IFRS 2 would be the appropriate standard, but if the shares or warrants are considered instead to be part of the overall return to the lender then IAS 32 and IAS 39 are more likely to apply.

3   GENERAL RECOGNITION PRINCIPLES

The recognition rules in IFRS 2 are based on a so-called 'service date model'. In other words, IFRS 2 requires the goods or services received or acquired in a share-based payment transaction to be recognised when the goods are acquired or the services rendered. *[IFRS 2.7].* For awards to employees (or others providing similar services), this contrasts with the measurement rules, which normally require a share-based payment transaction to be measured as at the date on which the transaction was entered into, which may be some time before or after the related services are received – see 4 to 7 below.

Where the goods or services received or acquired in exchange for a share-based payment transaction do not qualify for recognition as assets they should be expensed. *[IFRS 2.8].* The standard notes that typically services will not qualify as assets and should therefore be expensed immediately, whereas goods will generally be initially recognised as assets and expensed later as they are consumed. However, some payments for services may be capitalised (e.g. as part of the cost of PP&E or inventories) and some payments for goods may be expensed immediately (e.g. where they are for items included within development costs written off as incurred). *[IFRS 2.9].*

The corresponding credit entry is, in the case of an equity-settled transaction, an increase in equity and, in the case of a cash-settled transaction, a liability (or decrease in cash or other assets). *[IFRS 2.7].*

The primary focus of the discussion in the remainder of this Chapter is the application of these rules to transactions with employees. The accounting treatment of transactions with non-employees is addressed further at 5.1 and 5.4 below.

3.1   Vesting conditions

Under IFRS 2, the point at which a cost is recognised for goods or services depends on the concept of 'vesting'.

A share-based payment to a counterparty is said to *vest* when it becomes an entitlement of the counterparty. Under IFRS 2, a share-based payment arrangement vests when the counterparty's entitlement is no longer conditional on the satisfaction of any vesting conditions. *[IFRS 2 Appendix A].*

Vesting conditions are the conditions that determine whether the entity receives the services that entitle the counterparty to receive cash, other assets or equity instruments of the entity, under a share-based payment arrangement. Vesting conditions are either service conditions or performance conditions. *[IFRS 2 Appendix A].*

Service conditions require the counterparty to complete a specified period of service. *[IFRS 2 Appendix A].* For example, if an employee is granted a share option with a service condition of remaining in employment for three years, the award vests three years after the date of grant if the employee is still employed at that date.

Performance conditions require the counterparty to complete a specified period of service and specified performance targets to be met (such as a specified increase in the entity's profit over a specified period of time). A performance condition might include a market condition (see 6.3 below). *[IFRS 2 Appendix A]*. As discussed more fully at 3.2 below, performance conditions refer to performance by an employee (such as a personal sales target) or performance by the entity as a whole, rather than some external performance indicator, such as a general stock market index.

Thus a condition that an award vests if, in three years' time, earnings per share has increased by 10% and the employee is still in employment, is a performance condition. If, however, the award vests in three years' time if earnings per share has increased by 10%, irrespective of whether the employee is still in employment, that condition is not a performance condition, but a 'non-vesting' condition (see 3.2 below).

3.2 Conditions that are neither service conditions nor performance conditions ('non-vesting' conditions)

Some share-based payment transactions, particularly those with employees, are dependent on the satisfaction of conditions that are neither service conditions nor performance conditions. For example, an employee might be given the right to 100 shares in three years, subject only to the employee not working in competition with the reporting entity during that time. An undertaking not to work for another entity does not 'determine whether the entity receives ... services' – the employee could sit on a beach for three years and still be entitled to collect the award. Accordingly, such a condition is not regarded as a vesting condition for the purposes of IFRS 2, but is instead referred to as a 'non-vesting condition'. The accounting impact of non-vesting conditions is discussed in detail at 6.4 below.

IFRS 2 does not explicitly define a 'non-vesting condition', but uses the term to describe a condition that is neither a service condition nor a performance condition. However, the identification of such conditions is not always straightforward.

As noted at 3.1 above, IFRS 2 defines vesting conditions as conditions that determine whether the entity receives the services that entitle the counterparty to receive payment in equity or cash. Performance conditions are those that require the counterparty to complete a specified period of service and specified performance targets to be met (such as a specified increase in the entity's profit over a specified period of time).

The Basis for Conclusions to IFRS 2 adds that the feature that distinguishes a performance condition from a non-vesting condition is that the former has an explicit or implicit service requirement and the latter does not. *[IFRS 2.BC171A]*.

From this it appears to follow that:

- *A performance condition must be specific to the performance of the entity (or of the individual within the entity)*

  For example, a condition that requires the entity's profit before tax or its share price to reach a minimum level is a performance condition, provided that there is also a requirement for the employee to provide services (see below).

However, a condition that does not relate directly to the performance of the entity is a non-vesting condition. Examples given by IFRS 2 include:

- a requirement to make monthly savings during the vesting period;
- a requirement for a commodity index to reach a minimum level;
- restrictions on the transfer of vested equity instruments; or
- an agreement not to work for a competitor after the award has vested. *[IFRS 2.BC171B, IG24].*

The Interpretations Committee discussed some of the above conditions as part of its project on vesting and non-vesting conditions (see 3.2.1 below).

- *Any condition applicable to an award that does not also have a service condition (whether explicit or implied) is a non-vesting condition.*

  For a condition to be a performance condition, however, it is not sufficient that the condition is specific to the performance of the entity. There must also be an explicit or implied service condition. For example, a condition that requires the entity's profit before tax or its share price to reach a minimum level, but without any requirement for the employee to provide services, is not a performance condition, but a non-vesting condition.

  Thus, whilst conditions that are not related to the performance of the entity are always, by their nature, non-vesting conditions, conditions that relate to the performance of the entity may or may not be non-vesting conditions depending on whether there is also a requirement for the counterparty to render service.

  IFRS 2 defines a performance condition as one that requires the counterparty to complete a 'specified period of service' and 'specified performance targets' to be met. This raises the question of whether the 'specified period of service' must be the same as, or at least as long as, the period required to satisfy the performance target. An example might be an award granted on 1 January 2011 which vests if the employee remains in employment for the two years ended 31 December 2012 and the entity achieves a target cumulative profit for the three years ended 31 December 2013.

  In our view, in order for the performance target to be treated as a performance condition, the terms of the award must require the employee to remain in service for substantially all the period required to achieve the performance target. Thus, we believe that, in the example in the previous paragraph, the profit target is not a performance condition since it relates to a three-year period, while the terms of the award require the employee to provide service for only two of those years.

  The Interpretations Committee discussed this issue as part of its project on vesting and non-vesting conditions (see 3.2.1 below).

Within these broad parameters, however, there remains considerable room for judgement. In 6.3.1 below we discuss an entity, engaged in investment management and listed only in London, which grants options to an employee responsible for the Far East equities portfolio. The options have a condition linked to movements in a general index of shares of entities listed in Hong Kong, so as to compare the performance of the portfolio of investments for which the employee is responsible with that of the overall market in which they are traded.

We conclude (see 6.3.1 below) that this condition is not a market condition, and is probably a non-vesting condition. This conclusion is based on the analysis – which, we imagine, is what the IASB intended – that such a condition is directly analogous to a requirement for a commodity index to reach a particular level, which IFRS 2 gives as a specific example of a non-vesting condition (see above). On the other hand, it might be argued that it is a performance condition, if (as is likely to be the case) the entity's profits are based in whole or in part on a percentage of the performance of assets under management, so that increases in an index based on identical assets are in fact strongly and directly linked to the entity's performance.

The concept of a 'non-vesting condition', like much of IFRS 2 itself, had its origins as an anti-avoidance measure. It arose from a debate on how to account for employee share option schemes linked to a savings contract. In some jurisdictions, options are awarded to an employee on condition that the employee works for a fixed minimum period and, during that period, makes regular contributions to a savings account, which is then used to exercise the option. The employee is entitled to withdraw from the savings contract before vesting, in which case the right to the award lapses.

Entities applying IFRS 2 as originally issued almost invariably treated an employee's obligation to save as a vesting condition. Therefore, a cessation by the employee to save was treated as a failure to meet a vesting condition, and accordingly accounted for as a forfeiture, with the reversal of an expense so far recorded (see 6.1 and 6.2 below).

Some saw in this a scope for abuse of the general principle of IFRS 2 that, if a share-based payment transaction is cancelled, any amount not yet expensed for it is immediately recognised in full (see 7 below). The concern was that, if such a plan were 'out of the money', the employer, rather than cancel the plan (and thereby trigger an acceleration of expense) would 'encourage' the employee to stop saving (and thereby create a reversal of any expense already charged).

The broad effect of the January 2008 amendment to IFRS 2 was to remove this perceived anomaly from the standard.

However, it has become apparent that the concept of the 'non-vesting' condition is not clear. This has resulted in differing views on the appropriate classification of certain types of conditions. Examples of such ambiguous conditions include a vesting requirement that the entity opens a number of retail outlets or that the entity floats or is sold (see also 15.3.3 below). One view would be that these conditions are not direct measures of the entity's performance, and are therefore non-vesting conditions. A contrary view is that they are so strongly correlated to underlying business performance as to amount to performance conditions.

A secondary issue is the accounting treatment of awards with interactive vesting conditions and non-vesting conditions. For example, an award might vest if the entity floats or is sold and the holder of the award is in employment at that time. Should this be construed (or at least accounted for) as having:

Chapter 32

- a single non-market vesting condition, or
- two distinct conditions – a non-market vesting condition (being in employment) and a non-vesting condition (the entity floating or being sold)?

This is discussed further at 15.3.3 below.

The Interpretations Committee took a number of the above issues onto its agenda in January 2010 and this project is discussed further at 3.2.1 below.

3.2.1 *Vesting and non-vesting conditions: possible future developments*

At its January 2010 meeting the Interpretations Committee added to its agenda a request for clarification of the following:

- the basis on which vesting conditions, especially performance conditions, can be distinguished from non-vesting conditions, especially the distinction between a service condition, a performance condition and a non-vesting condition; and
- the interaction of multiple conditions.

As part of the request for clarification, the following two application issues were raised (see also the discussion at 3.2 above):

- whether there needs to be a direct link between a performance target and an individual employee's service in order for that target to be a performance condition; and
- when determining whether the target qualifies as a performance condition, does it matter whether the specified service period is shorter or longer than the period over which the performance target should be met?[5]

In July 2010 the Interpretations Committee made the following tentative decisions:

- a performance condition should be defined by reference to the operations or activities of the entity rather than by reference to any attributes of performance conditions in general;
- there should be no change to the accounting for save as you earn ('SAYE') plans; and
- IPO and change of control conditions should be deemed to constitute a performance condition.[6]

The Interpretations Committee completed its discussion of the project's technical issues in September 2010 and tentatively decided that:

- a non-compete provision should be presumed to be a 'contingent feature'[7]; and
- in order for a performance target to constitute a performance vesting condition, the performance target should fully coincide with an explicit or implicit service requirement for the entire period between the grant date and the performance target date.

The Interpretations Committee decided to ask the IASB for its recommendations on how to proceed with the above issues.[8]

The IASB discussed the Interpretations Committee's suggestions at its September 2010 meeting but did not support the amendments proposed by the Committee. The Interpretations Committee was asked to consider whether any of the issues being addressed could be dealt with as annual improvements. The IASB also asked the Interpretations Committee to review other requests that it had received in relation to IFRS 2 with a view to developing an agenda proposal that could be considered as part of the 2011 agenda-setting process.[9]

In November 2010 the Interpretations Committee proposed that the definitions of service and performance conditions be clarified through the next annual improvements cycle and prioritised the following issues:

- the correlation between an employee's responsibility [i.e. the individual's actions] and the performance target;

- whether a share market index target may be classified as a performance condition;

- whether a performance target that refers to a longer period than the required service period may be classified as a performance condition [rather than a non-vesting condition]; and

- whether termination of employment should be treated as a forfeiture or cancellation.

In addition to this, the Interpretations Committee concluded that the classification of a non-compete provision and the question of how to account for the interaction of multiple vesting conditions should be referred to the IASB for consideration as future agenda items.[10] This conclusion was re-iterated in March 2011 when the Committee reviewed the various IFRS 2 issues submitted to it over the previous six years.[11]

3.3 Vesting period

The *vesting period* is the period during which all the specified vesting conditions of a share-based payment arrangement are to be satisfied. *[IFRS 2 Appendix A].* This is not the same as the exercise period or the life of the option, as illustrated by Example 32.1 below.

Example 32.1:   Meaning of 'vesting period' – award with vesting conditions only

An employee is awarded options that can be exercised, if the employee remains in service for at least three years from the date of the award, at any time between three and ten years from the date of the award. For this award, the vesting period is three years; the exercise period is seven years; and the life of the option is ten years. However, as discussed further in 8 below, for the purposes of calculating the cost of the award under IFRS 2, the life of the award is taken as the period ending with the date on which the counterparty is most likely actually to exercise the option, which may be some time before the full ten year life expires.

It is also important to distinguish between vesting conditions and other restrictions on the exercise of options and/or trading in shares, as illustrated by Example 32.2 below.

Example 32.2:   Meaning of 'vesting period' – award with vesting conditions and other restrictions

An employee is awarded options that can be exercised, if the employee remains in service for at least three years from the date of the award, at any time between five and ten years from the date of the award. In this case, the vesting period remains three years as in Example 32.1 above, provided that the employee's entitlement to the award becomes absolute at the end of three years – in other words, the employee has to provide no services to the entity in years 4 and 5. The restriction on exercise of the award in the period after vesting is a non-vesting condition, which would be reflected in the original valuation of the award at the date of grant (see 4, 5 and 8 below).

The implications of vesting conditions, non-vesting conditions and vesting periods for equity-settled transactions are discussed in 4 to 7 below and for cash-settled transactions in 9 below.

4   EQUITY-SETTLED TRANSACTIONS – OVERVIEW

4.1   Summary of accounting treatment

The detailed provisions of IFRS 2 are complex, but their key points can be summarised as follows.

(a)   All equity-settled transactions are measured at fair value. However, transactions with employees are normally measured using a 'grant date model' (i.e. the transaction is recorded at the fair value of the equity instrument at the date when it is originally granted), whereas transactions with non-employees are normally measured using a 'service date model' (i.e. the transaction is recorded at the fair value of the goods or services received at the date they are received). As noted in 3 above, all transactions, however *measured*, are *recognised* using a 'service date model'.

(b)   Where an award is made subject to future fulfilment of conditions, a 'market condition' (i.e. one related to the market price of the entity's equity instruments) or a 'non-vesting condition' (i.e. one that is neither a service condition nor a performance condition) is taken into account in determining the fair value of the award. However, the effect of conditions other than market or non-vesting conditions is ignored in determining the fair value of the award.

(c)   Where an award is made subject to future fulfilment of vesting conditions, its cost is recognised over the period during which the conditions are fulfilled. The corresponding credit entry is recorded within equity (see 4.2 below).

(d)   Until an equity instrument has vested (i.e. the entitlement to it has become unconditional) any amounts recorded are in effect contingent and will be adjusted if more or fewer awards vest than were originally anticipated to do so. However, an equity instrument awarded subject to a market condition or a non-vesting condition is considered to vest irrespective of whether or not that market or non-vesting condition is fulfilled, provided that all other vesting conditions (if any) are satisfied.

(e)   No adjustments are made, either before or after vesting, to reflect the fact that an award has no value to the person entitled to it (e.g. in the case of a share option, because the option exercise price is above the current market price of the share).

(f)   If an equity instrument is cancelled, whether by the entity or the counterparty (see (g) below) before vesting, any amount remaining to be expensed is charged in full at that point. If an equity instrument is modified before vesting (e.g. in the case of a share option, by changing the performance conditions or the exercise price), the financial statements must continue to show a cost for at least the fair value of the original instrument, as measured at the original grant date, together with any excess of the fair value of the modified instrument over that of the original instrument, as measured at the date of modification.

(g) Where an award lapses during the vesting period due to a failure by the counterparty to satisfy a non-vesting condition within the counterparty's control, or a failure by the entity to satisfy a non-vesting condition within the entity's control, the lapse of the award is accounted for as if it were a cancellation (see (f) above).

(h) In determining the cost of an equity-settled transaction under IFRS 2, whether the entity satisfies its obligations under the transaction with a fresh issue of shares or by purchasing own shares in the financial markets is completely irrelevant to the charge in profit or loss, although there is clearly a difference in the cash flows. Where own shares are purchased, they are accounted for as treasury shares under IAS 32 (see Chapter 45 at 9). *[IFRS 2.BC330-333].*

The requirements summarised in (d) to (g) above can have the effect that IFRS 2 requires a cost to be recorded for an award that ultimately has no value to the counterparty, because the award either does not vest or vests but is not exercised. These rather counter-intuitive requirements of IFRS 2 are in part 'anti-abuse' provisions to prevent entities from applying a 'selective' grant date model, whereby awards that increase in value after grant date remain measured at grant date while awards that decrease in value are remeasured. This is discussed further in the detailed analysis at 5 to 7 below.

4.2 The credit entry

As noted at (c) in the summary in 4.1 above, the basic accounting entry for an equity-settled share-based payment transaction is:

DR   Profit or loss for the period (employee costs)

    CR   Equity.

IFRS 2 does not prescribe whether the credit should be to a separate component of equity, or, if the entity chooses to treat it as such, how it should be described.

The IASB presumably adopted this non-prescriptive approach so as to ensure there was no conflict between, on the one hand, the basic requirement of IFRS 2 that there should be a credit in equity and, on the other, the legal requirements of various jurisdictions as to exactly how that credit should be allocated within equity.

Occasionally there will be a credit to profit or loss (see for instance Example 32.11 at 6.2.4 below) and a corresponding reduction in equity.

A share-based payment transaction may be settled in equity instruments of a subsidiary of the reporting entity. This is most commonly the case where the subsidiary is partly-owned with traded shares held by external shareholders. In the consolidated financial statements, the credit entry for such transactions will need to be determined in accordance with the requirements of IAS 27 for changes in ownership interests (see Chapter 8 at 3).

5   EQUITY-SETTLED TRANSACTIONS – COST OF AWARDS

5.1   Cost of awards – overview

The general measurement rule in IFRS 2 is that an entity must measure the goods or services received, and the corresponding increase in equity, directly, at the fair value of the goods or services received, unless that fair value cannot be estimated reliably. If the fair value of the goods or services received cannot be estimated reliably, the entity must measure their value, and the corresponding increase in equity, indirectly, by reference to the fair value of the equity instruments granted. *[IFRS 2.10].* 'Fair value' is the amount for which an asset could be exchanged, a liability settled, or an equity instrument granted could be exchanged, between knowledgeable, willing parties in an arm's length transaction. *[IFRS 2 Appendix A].*

Thus, on their own, the general measurement principles of IFRS 2 would suggest that the reporting entity must determine in each case whether the fair value of the equity instruments granted or that of the goods or services received is more reliably determinable. However, IFRS 2 goes on to clarify that:

- in the case of transactions with employees, the fair value of the equity instruments must be used (see 5.2 below), except in those extremely rare cases where it is not possible to measure this fair value reliably, when the intrinsic value of the equity instruments may be used instead (see 5.5 below); but

- in the case of transactions with non-employees, there is a rebuttable presumption that the fair value of the goods or services provided is more reliably determinable (see 5.4 below).

Moreover, transactions with employees are measured at the date of grant (see 5.2 below), whereas those with non-employees are measured at the date when goods or services are received (see 5.4 below).

The overall position can be summarised by the following matrix.

Counterparty	Measurement basis	Measurement date	Recognition date
Employee	Fair value of equity instruments awarded	Grant date	Service date
Non-employee	Fair value of goods or services received	Service date	Service date

The Basis for Conclusions addresses the issue of why the accounting treatment for apparently identical transactions should, in effect, depend on the identity of the counterparty.

The main argument put forward to justify the approach adopted for transactions with employees is essentially that, once an award has been agreed, the value of the services provided pursuant to the transaction does not change significantly with the value of the award. *[IFRS 2.BC88-96].* However, some might question this proposition, on the grounds that employees are more likely to work harder when the value of their options is rising than when it has sunk irretrievably.

As regards transactions with non-employees, the IASB offers two main arguments for the use of measurement at service date.

The first is that, if the counterparty is not firmly committed to delivering the goods or services, the counterparty would consider whether the fair value of the equity instruments at the delivery date is sufficient payment for the goods or services when deciding whether to deliver the goods or services. This suggests that there is a high correlation between the fair value of the equity instruments at the date the goods or services are received and the fair value of those goods or services. *[IFRS 2.BC126].* This argument is clearly vulnerable to the challenge that it has no relevance where (as would more likely be the case) the counterparty is firmly committed to delivering the goods or services.

The second is that non-employees generally provide services over a short period commencing some time after grant date, whereas employees generally provide services over an extended period beginning on the grant date. This leads to a concern that transactions with non-employees could be entered into well in advance of the due date for delivery of goods or services. If an entity were able to measure the expense of such a transaction at the grant date fair value, the result, assuming that the entity's share price rises, would be to understate the cost of goods and services delivered. *[IFRS 2.BC126-127].*

The true reason for the IASB's approach may have been political as much as theoretical. One effect of a grant date measurement model is that, applied to a grant of share options that is eventually exercised, it 'freezes' the accounting cost at the (typically) lower fair value at the date of grant. This excludes from the post-grant financial statements the increased cost and volatility that would be associated with a model that constantly remeasured the award to fair value until exercise date. The IASB might well have perceived it as a marginally easier task to persuade the corporate sector of the merits of a 'lower cost, zero volatility' approach as opposed to a 'fair value at exercise date' model (such as is used for cash-settled awards – see 9 below).

The price to be paid in accounting terms for the grant date model is that, when an award falls in value after grant date, it continues to be recognised at its higher grant date value. It is therefore quite possible that, during a period of general economic downturn (as at the time of writing), financial statements will show significant costs for options granted in previous years, but which are currently worthless. This could well lead to (in fact, sometimes groundless) accusations of rewarding management for failure.

5.2 Transactions with employees

These will comprise the great majority of transactions accounted for under IFRS 2, and include all remuneration in the form of shares, share options and any other form of reward settled in equity instruments of the entity or a member of its group.

5.2.1   Who is an 'employee'?

Given the important difference between the accounting treatment of equity-settled transactions with employees and that of those with non-employees, it is obviously important for IFRS 2 to define what is meant by employees. In fact IFRS 2 strictly refers to 'employees and others providing similar services' *[IFRS 2.11]*, who are defined as individuals who render personal services to the entity and either:

(a)   the individuals are regarded as employees for legal or tax purposes;

(b)   the individuals work for the entity under its direction in the same way as individuals who are regarded as employees for legal or tax purposes; or

(c)   the services rendered are similar to those rendered by employees.

The term encompasses all management personnel, i.e. those persons having authority and responsibility for planning, directing and controlling the activities of the entity, including non-executive directors. *[IFRS 2 Appendix A]*.

The implication of (a) and (b) above is that it is not open to an entity to argue that an individual who is not an employee as a matter of law is therefore automatically a non-employee for the purposes of IFRS 2.

The implication of (b) and (c) above is that, where a third party provides services pursuant to a share-based payment transaction that could be provided by an employee (e.g. where an external IT consultant works alongside an in-house IT team), that third party is treated as an employee rather than a non-employee for the purposes of IFRS 2.

Conversely, however, where an entity engages a consultant to undertake work for which there is not an existing in-house function, the implication is that such an individual is not regarded as an employee. In other words, in our view, the reference in (c) to 'services ... similar to those rendered by employees' is to services rendered by employees that the entity actually has, rather than to employees that the entity might have if it were to recruit them. Otherwise, the distinction in IFRS 2 between employees and non-employees would have no effect, since it would always be open to an entity to argue that it could employ someone to undertake any task instead of engaging a contractor.

Exceptionally there might be cases where the same individual is engaged in both capacities. For example, a director of the entity might also be a partner in a firm of lawyers and be engaged in that latter capacity to advise the entity on a particular issue. It might be more appropriate to regard payment for the legal services as made to a non-employee rather than to an employee.

Related questions of interpretation arise where an award is made to an employee of an associate or joint venture (see 12.8 below).

The effect of a change of status from employee to non-employee (or vice versa) is addressed at 5.4.1 below.

5.2.2   Basis of measurement

As noted above, IFRS 2 requires equity-settled transactions with employees to be measured by reference to the fair value of the equity instruments granted at 'grant date' (see 5.3 below). *[IFRS 2.11]*. IFRS 2 asserts that this approach is necessary because shares, share options and other equity instruments are typically only part of a larger remuneration package, such that it would not be practicable to determine the value of the work performed in consideration for the cash element of the total package, the benefit-in-kind element, the share option element and so on. *[IFRS 2.12].*

In essence, this is really an anti-avoidance provision. The underlying concern is that, if an entity were able to value options by reference to the services provided for them, it might assert that the value of those services was zero, on the argument that its personnel are already so handsomely rewarded by the non-equity elements of their remuneration package (such as cash and health benefits), that no additional services are (or indeed could be) obtained by granting options.

5.3 Grant date

As noted above, IFRS 2 requires equity-settled transactions with employees to be accounted for at fair value at grant date, defined as 'the date at which the entity and another party (including an employee) agree to a share-based payment arrangement, being when the entity and the counterparty have a shared understanding of the terms and conditions of the arrangement'. *[IFRS 2 Appendix A].*

IFRS 2 and the accompanying implementation guidance emphasise that this occurs only when all the conditions are known and agreed. Thus, for example, if an entity makes an award 'in principle' to an employee of options whose terms are subject to review or approval by a remuneration committee or the shareholders, 'grant date' is the later date when the necessary formalities have been completed. *[IFRS 2 Appendix A, IG1-3].* The implementation guidance to IFRS 2 notes that employees may begin rendering services in consideration for an award before it has been formally ratified. For example, a new employee might join the entity on 1 January 2012 and be granted options relating to performance for a period beginning on that date, but subject to formal approval by the remuneration committee at its quarterly meeting on 15 March 2012. In that case, the entity would typically begin expensing the award from 1 January 2012 based on a best estimate of its fair value, but would subsequently adjust that estimate so that the ultimate cost of the award was its actual fair value at 15 March 2012. *[IFRS 2.IG4].* This reference to formal approval could be construed as indicating that, in fact, IFRS 2 requires not merely that there is a mutual understanding of the award (which might well have been in existence since 1 January 2012), but also that the entity has completed all processes necessary to make the award a legally binding agreement.

In practice, it is not always clear when a mutual understanding of the award (and, therefore, grant date) has occurred. This is discussed further at 5.3.1 below.

5.3.1 Determination of grant date

As noted in the discussion in 5.2 above, the determination of grant date is critical to the measurement of equity-settled share-based transactions with employees, since grant date is the date at which such transactions must be measured.

Grant date is defined as the date on which the reporting entity and the counterparty have a 'shared understanding of the terms of the arrangement' (see 5.3 above).

In practice, issues of interpretation can arise as to:

- how precise the shared understanding of the terms of the award must be; and
- exactly what level of communication between the reporting entity and the counterparty is sufficient to ensure the appropriate degree of 'shared understanding'.

We discuss some of these issues in more detail below.

5.3.2   Communication of awards to employees and services in advance of grant date

As discussed at 5.3 above, the implementation guidance to IFRS 2 indicates that, in order for a grant to have been made, there must not merely be a mutual understanding of the terms, but there must also be a legally enforceable arrangement. Thus, if an award requires board or shareholder approval for it to be legally binding on the reporting entity, for the purposes of IFRS 2 it has not been granted until such approval has been given, even if the terms of the award are fully understood at an earlier date. However, if services are effectively being rendered for the award from a date earlier than the grant date as defined in IFRS 2, the cost of the award should be recognised over a period starting with that earlier date.

The implications of this requirement are illustrated in Example 32.3 below. It is important, however, to retain a sense of proportion. In cases where the share price is not particularly volatile, whether the grant date is, say, 1 January or 1 April may not make a great difference to the valuation of the award, particularly when set beside the range of acceptable valuations resulting from the use of estimates in the valuation model.

Example 32.3:   Determination of grant date

Scenario 1

On 1 January 2012 an entity advises employees of the terms of a share award designed to reward performance over the three years ended 31 December 2014. The award is subject to board approval, which is given on 1 March 2012. Grant date is 1 March 2012. However, the cost of the award would be recognised over the three year period beginning 1 January 2012, since the employees would have effectively been rendering service for the award from that date.

Scenario 2

On 1 January 2012 an entity's board resolves to implement a share scheme designed to reward performance over the three years ended 31 December 2014. The award is notified to employees on 1 March 2012. Grant date is again 1 March 2012. *Prima facie*, in this case, the cost of the award would be recognised over the two years and ten months period beginning 1 March 2012, since the employees could not be regarded as rendering service in January and February for an award of which they were not aware at that time.

However, if a similar award is made each year, and according to a similar timescale, there might be an argument that, during January and February 2012, employees are rendering service for an award of which there is high expectation, and that the cost should therefore, as in Scenario 1, be recognised over the full three year period. The broader issue of the accounting treatment for awards of which there is a high expectation is addressed in the discussion of matching share awards at 10.5 below.

Scenario 3

On 1 January 2012 an entity advises employees of the terms of a share award designed to reward performance over the three years ended 31 December 2014. The award is subject to board approval, which is given on 1 March 2012. However, in giving such approval, the Board makes some changes to the performance conditions as originally communicated to employees on 1 January. The revised terms of the award are communicated to employees on 1 April 2012. Grant date is 1 April 2012. However, the cost of the award would be recognised over the three year period beginning 1 January 2012, since the employees would have effectively been rendering service for the award from that date.

5.3.3 Exercise price dependent on share price

Some share plans define the exercise price not in absolute terms, but as a factor of the share price. For example, the price might be expressed as:

- a percentage of the share price at exercise date; or
- a percentage of the lower of the share price at grant date and at exercise date.

The effect of this is that, although the actual exercise price is not known until the date of exercise, both the entity and the counterparty already have a shared understanding of how the price will be calculated. Accordingly, in our view, grant date is the date on which the terms and conditions (including the formula for calculating the exercise price) are determined and agreed by the entity and the counterparty, subject to the matters discussed at 5.3.2 above.

5.3.4 Exercise price paid in shares

Some share awards allow the exercise price to be paid in shares. In practical terms, this means that the number of shares delivered to the counterparty will be the total 'gross' number of shares awarded less as many shares as have, at the date of exercise, a fair value equal to the strike price.

In our view, this situation is analogous to that in 5.3.3 above in that, whilst the absolute 'net' number of shares awarded will not be known until the date of exercise, the basis on which that 'net' number will be determined is established in advance. Accordingly, in our view, grant date is the date on which the terms and conditions (including the ability to surrender shares to a fair value equal to the exercise price) are determined and agreed by the entity and the counterparty, subject to the matters discussed at 5.3.2 above.

Such a scheme could also be analysed as a share-settled share appreciation right (whereby the employee receives shares to the value of the excess of the value of the shares given over the exercise price), which is treated as an equity-settled award under IFRS 2.

5.3.5 Award of equity instruments to a fixed monetary value

Some entities may grant awards to employees of shares to a fixed value. For example, an entity might award as many shares as are worth €100,000, with the number of shares being calculated by reference to the share price as at the vesting date. The number of shares ultimately received will not be known until the vesting date. This begs the question of whether such an award can be regarded as having been granted until that date, on the argument that it is only then that the number of shares to be delivered – a key term of the award – is known, and therefore there cannot be a 'shared understanding' of the terms of the award until that later date.

In our view, this situation is analogous to those in 5.3.3 and 5.3.4 above in that, whilst the absolute number of shares awarded will not be known until the vesting date, the basis on which that number will be determined is established in advance. Accordingly, in our view, grant date is the date on which the terms and conditions are determined and agreed by the entity and the counterparty, subject to the matters discussed at 5.3.2 above.

However, the measurement of such awards raises further issues of the interpretation of IFRS 2, which we discuss at 8.10 below.

5.3.6   Awards over a fixed pool of shares (including 'last man standing' arrangements)

An award over a fixed pool of shares is sometimes granted to a small group of, typically senior, employees. Such awards might involve an initial allocation of shares to each individual but also provide for the redistribution of each employee's shares to the other participants should any individual leave employment before the end of the vesting period. This is often referred to as a 'last man standing' arrangement.

The accounting requirements of IFRS 2 for such an arrangement are unclear. In the absence of specific guidance, several interpretations are possible and we believe that an entity may make an accounting choice, provided that choice is applied consistently to all such arrangements.

The first approach is based on the view that the unit of account is all potential shares to be earned by the individual employee and that, from the outset, each employee has a full understanding of the terms and conditions of both the initial award and the reallocation arrangements. This means that there is a grant on day one with each individual's award being valued on the basis of:

- that employee's initial allocation of shares; plus
- an additional award with a non-vesting condition relating to the potential reallocation of other participants' shares.

Under this approach, the departure of an employee will be accounted for as a forfeiture (see 6 below) but the redistribution of that individual's shares to the other employees will have no accounting impact. This approach is likely to result in a total expense that is higher than the number of shares awarded multiplied by the grant date price per share.

The second approach, which we believe is consistent with US GAAP, also considers the individual employee's award to be the unit of account. Under this approach, there is an initial grant to all the employees and it is only these awards for which the fair value is measured at the date of the initial grant. Any subsequent reallocations of shares should be accounted for as a forfeiture of the original award and a completely new grant to the remaining employees. This approach accounts only for the specific number of shares that have been allocated to the individual employee as at the end of each reporting period. No account is taken in this approach of shares that might be allocated to the individual employee in the future due to another employee's forfeiture, even though the reallocation formula is known to the individual employees at the initial grant date.

A third view, which takes a pragmatic approach in the light of the issues arising from the two approaches outlined above, is to account for the award on the basis of the pool of shares granted rather than treating the individual employee as the unit of account. In our view this approach would be materially acceptable in many situations where there is a scheme with the same small number of participants from the outset. Under this approach, the grant date fair value of the total pool of shares is measured at the outset with the non-vesting condition effectively ignored for valuation purposes. Subsequent forfeitures and reallocations would have no effect on the accounting.

The 'last man standing' arrangement described above can be contrasted with a situation where an entity designates a fixed pool of shares to be used for awards to employees but where the allocation of leavers' shares is discretionary rather than pre-determined. In this situation, the valuation of the initial award would not take account of any potential future reallocations. If an employee left employment during the vesting period, that individual's award would be accounted for as a forfeiture and any reallocation of that individual's shares would be accounted for as a new grant with the fair value determined at the new grant date (i.e. a similar accounting treatment to that in approach two above).

A further type of award relating to a fixed pool of shares is one where an entity makes an award over a fixed number or percentage of its shares to a particular section of its workforce, the final allocation of the pool being made to those employed at the vesting date. In such an arrangement, some employees will typically join and leave the scheme during the original vesting period which will lead to changes in each employee's allocation of shares. Although employees are aware of the existence, and some of the terms, of the arrangement at the outset, the fact that there is no objective formula for determining the number of shares that each individual will ultimately receive means that there is no grant under IFRS 2 until the date of final allocation. However, because the employees render service under the arrangement in advance of the grant date – either from day one or from a later joining date – the entity should estimate the fair value of the award to each individual from the date services commence and expense this over the full service period of the award with a final truing up of the expense to the fair value of the award at the eventual grant date (see 5.3 above).

This has the effect that, where an entity decides to set aside a bonus pool of a fixed amount of cash (say £1 million), with the allocation to individual employees to be made at a later date, there is a known fixed cost of £1 million. However, where an entity decides to set aside a bonus pool of a fixed number of shares, with the allocation to individual employees to be made at a later date, the final cost is not determined until the eventual grant date.

5.3.7 Awards with multiple service periods

Entities frequently make awards that cover more than one reporting period, but with different performance conditions for each period, rather than a single cumulative target for the whole vesting period. In such cases, the grant date may depend on the precision with which the terms of the award are communicated to employees, as illustrated by Example 32.4 below.

Example 32.4:   Awards with multiple service periods

Scenario 1

On 1 January 2012, the entity enters into a share-based payment arrangement with an employee. The employee is informed that the maximum potential award is 40,000 shares, 10,000 of which will vest on 31 December 2012, and 10,000 more on each of 31 December 2013, 31 December 2014 and 31 December 2015. Vesting of each tranche of 10,000 shares is conditional on:

(a) the employee having been in continuous service until 31 December of the relevant year;

(b) revenue targets for each of those four years, as communicated to the employee on 1 January 2012, having been attained.

In this case, the terms of the award are clearly understood by both parties at 1 January 2012, and this is therefore the grant date under IFRS 2 (subject to issues such as any requirement for later formal approval – see 5.3 to 5.3.2 above). The cost of the award would be recognised using a 'graded' vesting period – see 6.2.2 below.

Scenario 2

On 1 January 2012, the entity enters into a share-based payment arrangement with an employee. The employee is informed that the maximum potential award is 40,000 shares, 10,000 of which will vest on 31 December 2012, and 10,000 more on each of 31 December 2013, 31 December 2014 and 31 December 2015. Vesting of each tranche of 10,000 shares is conditional on:

(a) the employee having been in continuous service until 31 December of the relevant year;

(b) revenue targets for each of those four years, to be communicated to the employee on 1 January of each year in respect of that year only, having been attained.

In this case, in our view, as at 1 January 2012, there is a clear shared understanding only of the terms of the first tranche of 10,000 shares that will potentially vest on 31 December 2012. There is no clear understanding of the terms of the tranches potentially vesting in 2013 to 2015 because their vesting depends on revenue targets for those years which have not yet been set.

Accordingly, each of the four tranches of 10,000 shares has a separate grant date – i.e. 1 January 2012, 1 January 2013, 1 January 2014 and 1 January 2015 – and a vesting period of one year from the relevant grant date.

5.3.8   Awards subject to modification by entity after original grant date

Some employee share awards are drafted in terms that give the entity discretion to modify the detailed terms of the scheme after grant date. Some have questioned whether this effectively means that the date originally determined as the 'grant date' is not in fact the grant date as defined in IFRS 2, on the grounds that the entity's right to modify means that the terms are not in fact understood by both parties in advance.

In our view, this is not an appropriate analysis. If it were, it could also mean that, in some jurisdictions, nearly all share-based awards to employees would be required to be measured at vesting date, which clearly was not the IASB's intention.

However, there may well be room for debate as to the extent to which an intervention by the entity after grant date constitutes modification or not.

5.3.8.A   Significant equity restructuring or transactions

Many schemes contain provisions designed to ensure that the value of awards is maintained following a major capital restructuring (such as a share split or share consolidation – see 7.8 below) or a major transaction with shareholders as a whole (such as the insertion of a new holding company over an existing group, a major share buyback or the payment of a special dividend). These provisions may allow the entity to make such adjustments as it sees fit to maintain the value of awards. In some cases the exercise of such powers may be relatively mechanistic (e.g. the adjustment of the number of shares subject to options following a share split). In some cases, more subjectivity will be involved (e.g. in determining whether a particular dividend is a 'special' dividend for the purposes of the scheme).

In our view, the presumption in such cases should be that the exercise of the entity's right to modify does not constitute a 'modification' as defined in IFRS 2. However, as the intention of such a provision is to preserve the value of the award before and after the restructuring, there would be no incremental value to account for even if the entity's exercise of such a discretion were regarded as a modification.

5.3.8.B   Interpretation of general terms

More problematic might be the exercise of any discretion by the entity to interpret the more general terms of a scheme. Suppose, for example, that an entity makes an award to its main executives with a performance condition based on total shareholder return (TSR) with a maximum payout if the entity is in the top quartile of a peer group of 100 entities (i.e. it is ranked between 1 and 25 in the peer group).

It might be that the entity is ranked 26 until shortly before the end of the performance period, at which point the entity ranked 25 suddenly announces that it is in financial difficulties and ceases trading shortly afterwards. This then means that the reporting entity moves up from 26 to 25 in the rankings. However, the entity might take the view that, in the circumstances, it could not be considered as having truly been ranked 25 in the peer group, so that a maximum payout is not justified.

In this case, there might be more of an argument that the entity's intervention constitutes a modification. However, as the effect would be to reduce the fair value of the award, it would have no impact on the accounting treatment (see 7.3.2 below).

If such an intervention were not regarded as a modification, then the results might be different depending on the nature of the award. Where an award is subject to a market condition, as here, or to a non-vesting condition, an expense might well have to be recognised in any event, if all the non-market vesting conditions (e.g. service) were satisfied – see 6.3 and 6.4 below.

However, suppose that the award had been based on a non-market vesting condition, such as an EPS target, which was met, but only due to a gain of an unusual, non-recurring nature, such as the revaluation of PP&E for tax purposes, giving rise to a deferred tax credit. The remuneration committee concludes that this should be ignored, with the effect that the award does not vest. If this is regarded as the exercise of a pre-existing right to ensure that the award vests only if 'normal' EPS reaches a given level, then there has been no modification. On this analysis, the award has not vested, and any expense previously recognised would be reversed. If, however, the committee's intervention is regarded as a modification, it would have no impact on the accounting treatment in this case, as the effect would be to reduce the fair value of the award and this would be ignored under the general requirements of IFRS 2 relating to modifications (see 7.3.2 below).

5.3.8.C   *'Good leaver' arrangements*

In some jurisdictions it is common for awards to contain a so-called 'good leaver' clause. A 'good leaver' clause is one which makes provision for an employee who leaves before the end of the full vesting period of an award nevertheless to receive some or all of the award on leaving.

In some cases the types of person who are 'good leavers' may be explicitly defined (common examples being persons who die or reach normal retirement age before the end of the full vesting period, or who work for a business unit that is sold or closed during the vesting period). In other cases, the entity may have the discretion to determine on a case-by-case basis whether a person should be treated as a 'good leaver'.

In addition, some schemes may specify the entitlement of a 'good leaver' on leaving (e.g. that the leaver receive a portion of the award pro-rata to the extent that the performance conditions have been met), whereas others leave the determination of the award to the entity at the time that the employee leaves.

Whichever situation applies, any expense relating to an award to a good leaver must be fully recognised by the leaving date because there is no service condition beyond the date of leaving.

In our view, an award which vests before the end of the original vesting period due to the operation of a 'good leaver' clause is measured at the original grant date only where – under the rules of the scheme as understood by both parties at the original grant date – the award is made:

- to a person clearly identified as a 'good leaver'; and
- in an amount clearly quantified or quantifiable.

Where a 'good leaver' clause has the effect that some part of the award vests in full before the end of the original vesting period, it will be necessary to recognise the cost of the award using a 'graded' vesting approach between grant date and the date of leaving (see 6.2.2 below). In practice, however, the precise application of this approach will depend on the exact terms of the arrangements in place, as well as being affected by precedents set by the company in respect of awards to previous leavers.

Where, as outlined above, the rules of the scheme make clear the categories of good leaver and their entitlement, the entity should assess how many good leavers there are likely to be and to what extent the service period is expected to be shorter than the full vesting period for these particular individuals. The grant date fair value of the estimated awards to good leavers should be separately determined, where significant, and the expense relating to good leavers recognised over the expected period between grant date and leaving employment. In this situation the entity would re-estimate the number of good leavers and adjust the cumulative expense at each reporting date. This would be a change of estimate rather than a modification of the award as it would all be in accordance with the original terms. We would not generally expect an entity to have significant numbers of good leavers under such an arrangement.

In some jurisdictions it is becoming increasingly common for entities to establish schemes where a significant number of the participants will potentially leave employment before the end of the full vesting period and be allowed to keep a pro rata share of the award. This gives rise to a much broader category of 'good leaver' and, in substance, indicates that the entire award to all participants vests on a graded basis over the vesting period as a whole. So, for example, an arrangement that gives employees 360 shares at the end of three years but, whether under the rules of the scheme or by precedent, allows the majority of leavers to take a pro rata share at their date of departure, should be treated as vesting at the rate of 10 shares per month for all employees (using the approach illustrated at 6.2.2 below).

In other cases, rather than a pro rata apportionment, any good leaver will be allowed to keep the entire award regardless of when they leave employment. If this is the case, and in substance there is no required minimum service period, then the award should be treated as immediately vested and fully expensed at the grant date.

The situations above deal with awards where the arrangements for leavers are clear as at the original grant date of the award. However, where – as is more usually the case – the entity determines only at the time that the employee leaves either that the employee is a 'good leaver', or the amount of the award, grant date should be taken as the later of the date on which such determination is made, or the date on which the award is notified to the employee. This is because the employee had no clear understanding, at the original grant date, of an entitlement to equity instruments other than through full vesting of the award.

In some cases, a good leaver will be allowed, on a discretionary basis, to keep existing awards that remain subject to the fulfilment of the conditions established at the original grant date. Whether this arrangement is accounted for as a cancellation of the old award plus a new grant or as a modification of the original award, any conditions that were previously treated as vesting conditions will become non-vesting conditions following the removal of the service requirement (see 3.1 and 3.2 above). The non-vesting conditions will need to be reflected in the measurement of the fair value of the award as at the date of modification or new grant (although the non-vesting conditions alone will not result in any incremental fair value). Any fair value that is unrecognised as at the date of the good leaver ceasing employment will need to be expensed immediately as there is no further service period over which to recognise the expense. There is further discussion of modifications at 7.3 below and of replacement awards granted on termination of employment at 7.5 below.

5.3.8.D Discretion to make further awards

Some schemes may give the entity the power to increase an award in circumstances where the recipient is considered to have delivered exceptional performance, or some such similar wording. In our view, unless the criteria for judging such exceptional performance are so clear as to be, in effect, performance conditions under IFRS 2, the presumption should be that any award made pursuant to such a clause is granted, and therefore measured, when it is made. We note at 10.5 below that there may be circumstances where an award described as 'discretionary' may not truly be so, since the entity has created an expectation amounting to a constructive obligation to make the award. However, we believe that it would be somewhat contradictory to argue that such expectations had been created in the case of an award stated to be for (undefined) exceptional performance only.

5.4   Transactions with non-employees

In accounting for equity-settled transactions with non-employees, the entity must adopt a rebuttable presumption that the value of the goods or services received provides the more reliable indication of the fair value of the transaction. The fair value to be used is that at the date on which the goods are obtained or the services rendered. *[IFRS 2.13]*. This implies that, where the goods or services are received on a number of dates over a period, the fair value at each date should be used, although in the case of a relatively short period there may be no great fluctuation in fair value.

If 'in rare cases' the presumption is rebutted, the entity may use as a surrogate measure the fair value of the equity instruments granted, but as at the date when the goods or services are received, not the original grant date. However, where the goods or services are received over a relatively short period where the share price does not change significantly, an average share price can be used in calculating the fair value of equity instruments granted. *[IFRS 2.13, IG5, IG6-7]*.

5.4.1   *Effect of change of status from employee to non-employee (or vice versa)*

IFRS 2 does not give specific guidance on how to account for an award when the status of the counterparty changes from employee to non-employee (or *vice versa*) but, in all other respects, the award remains unchanged. In our view, the accounting following the change of status will depend on the entity's assessment of whether or not the counterparty is performing the same or similar services before and after the change of status.

If it is concluded that the counterparty is providing the same or similar services before and after the change of status, the measurement approach remains unchanged.

However, if the services provided are substantially different, the accounting following the change of status will be determined by the counterparty's new status, as follows:

- for a change from non-employee to employee status, the expense for periods following the change should be measured as if the award had been granted at the date of change of status. This revised measurement only applies to the expense for the portion of the award that vests after the change of status and there is no effect on the expense recognised in prior periods;

- for a change from employee to non-employee status, the expense for periods following the change should be measured on the basis of the fair value of the counterparty's services as they are received – if this is reliably determinable. Otherwise, the fair value used is that of the equity instruments granted but measured at the date the services are received (see 5.4 above). There is no effect on the expense recognised in prior periods.

If the status of the counterparty changes and the terms of the award are modified in order to allow the award to continue to vest, the modification and change of status should be assessed in accordance with the general principles in IFRS 2 relating to the modification of awards (see 7.3 below).

5.5   Determining the fair value of equity instruments

As discussed in 5.2 to 5.4 above, IFRS 2 requires the following equity-settled transactions to be measured by reference to the fair value of the equity instruments issued rather than that of the goods or services received:

- all transactions with employees (except where it is impossible to determine fair value – see below); and

- transactions with non-employees where, exceptionally, the presumption that the fair value of goods or services provided is more reliably measurable is rebutted.

For all transactions measured by reference to the fair value of the equity instruments granted, IFRS 2 requires fair value to be measured at the 'measurement date' – i.e. grant date in the case of transactions with employees and service date in the case of transactions with non-employees. *[IFRS 2 Appendix A]*. Fair value should be based on market prices if available. *[IFRS 2.16]*. In the absence of market prices, a valuation technique should be used to estimate what the market price would have been on the measurement date in an arm's length transaction between informed and willing parties. The technique used should be a recognised technique and incorporate all factors that would be taken into account by knowledgeable and willing market participants. *[IFRS 2.17]*.

Appendix B to IFRS 2 contains more detailed guidance on valuation, which is discussed at 8 below. *[IFRS 2.18]*. IFRS 2 also deals with those 'rare' cases where it is not possible to value equity instruments reliably, where an intrinsic value approach may be used. This is more likely to apply in the case of awards of options rather than those of shares, and is discussed further at 8.8 below.

Paragraph 16 of IFRS 2 rather confusingly states that the fair value of equity instruments granted must take into account the terms and conditions on which they were granted, but this requirement is said to be 'subject to the requirements of paragraphs 19-22'. When those paragraphs are consulted, however, a somewhat different picture emerges, since they draw a distinction between:

- non-vesting conditions (i.e. those that are neither service conditions nor performance conditions);

- vesting conditions which are market conditions (i.e. those related to the entity's share price); and

- other vesting conditions (i.e. service and non-market performance conditions).

These are discussed in more detail at 6.2, 6.3, 6.4 and 8 below, but the essential difference is that, while non-vesting conditions and market conditions must be factored into any valuation, other vesting conditions must be ignored. *[IFRS 2.19-21A]*. As we explain in the more detailed discussion later, these essentially arbitrary distinctions originated in part as anti-avoidance measures.

The 'fair value' of equity instruments under IFRS 2 therefore takes account of some, but not all, conditions attached to an award rather than being a 'true' fair value. The approach to determining the fair value of share-based payments will continue to be that specified in IFRS 2 and share-based payments will be outside the scope of IFRS 13 – *Fair Value Measurement* – which applies more generally to the use of fair value under IFRSs with effect from 1 January 2013 (see Chapter 16).

5.5.1   *Reload features*

A 'reload feature' is a feature in a share option that provides for an automatic grant of additional share options (reload options) whenever the option holder exercises previously granted options using the entity's shares, rather than cash, to satisfy the exercise price. *[IFRS 2 Appendix A]*. IFRS 2 requires reload features to be ignored in the initial valuation of options that contain them. Instead any reload option should be treated as if it were a newly granted option at the time that it is granted. *[IFRS 2.22]*. This is discussed further at 8.9 below.

6   EQUITY-SETTLED TRANSACTIONS – ALLOCATION OF EXPENSE

6.1   Overview

Equity-settled transactions, particularly those with employees, raise particular accounting problems since they are often subject to vesting conditions (see 3.1 above) that can be satisfied only over an extended vesting period. This raises the issue of whether a share-based payment transaction should be recognised:

- when the relevant equity instrument is first granted;
- when it vests;
- during the vesting period; or
- during the life of the option.

An award of equity instruments that vests immediately is presumed, in the absence of evidence to the contrary, to relate to services that have already been rendered, and is therefore expensed in full at grant date. *[IFRS 2.14]*. This may lead to the immediate recognition of an expense for an award to which the employee may not be legally entitled for some time, as illustrated in Example 32.5.

Example 32.5:   Award with non-vesting condition only

An entity grants a director share options on condition that the director does not compete with the reporting entity for a period of at least three years. The 'non-compete' clause is considered to be a non-vesting condition (see 3.2 above and 6.4 below). As this is the only condition to which the award is subject, the award has no vesting conditions and therefore vests immediately. The fair value of the award at the date of grant, including the effect of the 'non-compete' clause, is determined to be €150,000. Accordingly, the entity immediately recognises a cost of €150,000.

This cost can never be reversed, even if the director goes to work for a competitor and loses the award. This is discussed more fully at 6.1.2 and 6.4 below.

Where equity instruments are granted subject to vesting conditions (as in many cases they will be, particularly where payments to employees are concerned), IFRS 2 creates a presumption that they are a payment for services to be received in the future, during the 'vesting period', with the transaction being recognised during that period, as illustrated in Example 32.6. *[IFRS 2.15]*.

Example 32.6:   Award with service condition only

An entity grants a director share options on condition that the director remain in employment for three years. The requirement to remain in employment is a service condition, and therefore a vesting condition, which will take three years to fulfil. The fair value of the award at the date of grant, ignoring the effect of the vesting condition, is determined to be €300,000. The entity will record a cost of €100,000 a year in profit or loss for three years, with a corresponding increase in equity.

In practice, the calculations required by IFRS 2 are unlikely to be as simple as that in Example 32.6. In particular:

- the final number of awards that vest cannot be known until the vesting date (because employees may leave before the vesting date, or because relevant performance conditions may not be met); and/or

- the length of the vesting period may not be known in advance (since vesting may depend on satisfaction of a performance condition with no, or a variable, time-limit on its attainment).

In order to deal with such issues, IFRS 2 requires a continuous re-estimation process as summarised in 6.1.1 below.

6.1.1   The continuous estimation process of IFRS 2

The overall objective of IFRS 2 is that, at the end of the vesting period, the cumulative cost recognised in profit or loss (or, where applicable, included in the carrying amount of an asset), should represent the product of:

- the number of equity instruments that have vested, or would have vested, but for the failure to satisfy a market condition (see 6.3 below) or a non-vesting condition (see 6.4 below); and

- the fair value (excluding the effect of any non-market vesting conditions, but including the effect of any market conditions or non-vesting conditions) of those equity instruments at the date of grant.

It is essential to appreciate that the 'grant date' measurement model in IFRS 2 seeks to capture the value of the contingent right to shares promised at grant date, to the extent that that promise becomes (or is deemed by IFRS 2 to become – see 6.1.2 below) an entitlement of the counterparty, rather than the value of any shares finally delivered. Therefore, if an option vests, but is not exercised because it would not be in the counterparty's economic interest to do so, IFRS 2 still recognises a cost for the award.

In order to achieve this outcome, IFRS 2 requires the following process to be applied:

(a)   at grant date, the fair value of the award (excluding the effect of any non-market vesting conditions, but including the effect of any market conditions or non-vesting conditions) is determined;

(b)   at each subsequent reporting date until vesting, the entity calculates a best estimate of the cumulative charge to profit or loss at that date, being the product of:

Chapter 32

(i)   the grant date fair value of the award determined in (a) above;

(ii)   the current best estimate of the number of awards that will vest (see 6.1.2 below); and

(iii) the expired portion of the vesting period;

(c)   the charge (or credit) to profit or loss for the period is the cumulative amount calculated in (b) above less the amounts already charged in previous periods. There is a corresponding credit (or debit) to equity *[IFRS 2.19-20]*;

(d)   once the awards have vested, no further accounting adjustments are made to the cost of the award, except in respect of certain modifications to the award – see 7 below; and

(e)   if a vested award is not exercised, an entity may (but need not) make a transfer between components of equity – see 6.1.3 below.

The overall effect of this process is that a cost is recognised for every award that is granted, except when it is forfeited, as that term is defined in IFRS 2 (see 6.1.2 below). *[IFRS 2.19]*.

6.1.2   *Vesting and forfeiture*

In normal English usage, and in many share scheme documents, an award is described as 'vested' when all the conditions needed to earn it have been met, and as 'forfeited' where it lapses before vesting because one or more of the conditions has not been met.

IFRS 2, however, uses the term 'forfeiture' in a much more restricted sense to mean an award that does not vest in IFRS 2 terms. This is a particularly complex aspect of IFRS 2, which is discussed in more detail at 6.2 to 6.4 below. Essentially:

- where an award is subject only to vesting conditions other than market conditions, failure to satisfy any one of the conditions is treated as a forfeiture by IFRS 2;

- where an award is subject only to market conditions and/or non-vesting conditions, it is always deemed to vest by IFRS 2; and

- where an award is subject to both

  - vesting conditions other than market conditions, and

  - market conditions and/or non-vesting conditions,

  failure to satisfy any one of the vesting conditions other than market conditions is treated as a forfeiture by IFRS 2. Otherwise (i.e. where all the vesting conditions other than market conditions are satisfied), the award is deemed to vest by IFRS 2 even if the market conditions and/or non-vesting conditions have not been satisfied.

The reference in the summary at 6.1.1 above to the 'best estimate of the number of awards that will vest' therefore really means the best estimate of the number of awards for which it is expected that all non-market vesting conditions will be met.

In practice, however, it is not always clear how that best estimate is to be determined, and in particular what future events may and may not be factored into the estimate. This is discussed further at 6.2 to 6.4 and 7.6 below.

6.1.3 Accounting after vesting

Once an equity-settled transaction has vested (or, in the case of a transaction subject to one or more market or non-vesting conditions, has been treated as vested under IFRS 2 – see 6.1.2 above), no further accounting entries are made to reverse the cost already charged, even if the instruments that are the subject of the transaction are subsequently forfeited or, in the case of options, are not exercised. However, the entity may make a transfer between different components of equity. *[IFRS 2.23]*. For example, an entity's accounting policy might be to credit all amounts recorded for share-based transactions to a separate reserve such as 'Shares to be issued'. Where an award lapses after vesting, it would then be appropriate to transfer an amount equivalent to the cumulative cost for the lapsed award from 'Shares to be issued' to another component of equity.

This prohibition against 'truing up' (i.e. reversing the cost of vested awards that lapse) is controversial, since it has the effect that a cost is still recognised for options that are never exercised, typically because they are 'underwater' (i.e. the current share price is lower than the option exercise price), so that it is not in the holder's interest to exercise the option. Some commentators have observed that an accounting standard that can result in an accounting cost for non-dilutive options does not meet the needs of those shareholders whose concerns about dilution were the catalyst for the share-based payment project in the first place (see 1.1 above).

The IASB counters such objections by pointing out that the treatment in IFRS 2 is perfectly consistent with that for other 'contingent' equity instruments, such as warrants, that ultimately result in no share ownership. Where an entity issues warrants for valuable consideration such as cash and those warrants lapse unexercised, the entity recognises no gain under IFRS. *[IFRS 2.BC218-221]*.

6.2 Vesting conditions other than market conditions

6.2.1 Awards with service conditions

Most share-based payment transactions with employees are subject to explicit or implied service conditions. The application of the general periodic allocation principles discussed in 6.1 above to awards subject only to service conditions is illustrated by Examples 32.7 and 32.8 below. *[IFRS 2.IG11]*.

Example 32.7:   Award with no re-estimation of number of awards vesting

An entity grants 100 share options to each of its 500 employees. Vesting is conditional upon the employees working for the entity over the next three years. The entity estimates that the fair value of each share option is €15. The entity estimates that 20% of the original 500 employees will leave during the three year period and therefore forfeit their rights to the share options.

If everything turns out exactly as expected, the entity will recognise the following amounts during the vesting period for services received as consideration for the share options.

Year	Calculation of cumulative expense	Cumulative expense (€)	Expense for period‡ (€)
1	50,000 options × 80%* × €15 × 1/3†	200,000	200,000
2	50,000 options × 80% × €15 × 2/3	400,000	200,000
3	50,000 options × 80% × €15 × 3/3	600,000	200,000

*   The entity expects 20% of employees to leave and therefore only 80% of the options to vest.

†   The vesting period is 3 years, and 1 year of it has expired.

‡   In each case the expense for the period is the difference between the calculated cumulative expense at the beginning and end of the period.

Example 32.8:   *Award with re-estimation of number of awards vesting due to staff turnover*

As in Example 32.7 above, an entity grants 100 share options to each of its 500 employees. Vesting is conditional upon the employee working for the entity over the next three years. The entity estimates that the fair value of each share option is €15.

In this case, however, 20 employees leave during the first year, and the entity's best estimate at the end of year 1 is that 15% of the original 500 employees will have left before the end of the vesting period. During the second year, a further 22 employees leave, and the entity revises its estimate of total employee departures over the vesting period from 15% to 12% of the original 500 employees. During the third year, a further 15 employees leave. Hence, a total of 57 employees (20 + 22 + 15) forfeit their rights to the share options during the three year period, and a total of 44,300 share options (443 employees × 100 options per employee) finally vest.

The entity will recognise the following amounts during the vesting period for services received as consideration for the share options.

Year	Calculation of cumulative expense	Cumulative expense (€)	Expense for period (€)
1	50,000 options × 85% × €15 × 1/3	212,500	212,500
2	50,000 options × 88% × €15 × 2/3	440,000	227,500
3	44,300 options × €15 × 3/3	664,500	224,500

Note that in Example 32.8 above, the number of employees that leave during year 1 and year 2 is not directly relevant to the calculation of cumulative expense in those years, but would naturally be a factor taken into account by the entity in estimating the likely number of awards finally vesting.

6.2.2   *Equity instruments vesting in instalments ('graded' vesting)*

An entity may make share-based payments that vest in instalments (sometimes referred to as 'graded' vesting). For example, an entity might grant an employee 600 options, 100 of which vest if the employee remains in service for one year, a further 200 after two years and the final 300 after three years. In today's more mobile labour markets, such awards are increasingly favoured over awards which vest only on an 'all or nothing' basis after an extended period.

IFRS 2 requires such an award to be treated as three separate awards, of 100, 200 and 300 options, on the grounds that the different vesting periods will mean that the three tranches of the award have different fair values. *[IFRS 2.IG11]*. This may well have the effect that, compared to the expense for an award with a single 'cliff' vesting, the expense for an award vesting in instalments will be for a different amount in total and require accelerated recognition of the expense in earlier periods, as illustrated in Example 32.9 below.

Example 32.9:   Award vesting in instalments ('graded' vesting)

An entity is considering the implementation of a scheme that awards 600 free shares to each of its employees, with no conditions other than continuous service. Two alternatives are being considered:

- All 600 shares vest in full only at the end of three years.
- 100 shares vest after one year, 200 shares after two years and 300 shares after three years. Any shares received at the end of years 1 and 2 would have vested unconditionally.

The fair value of a share delivered in one year's time is €3; in two years' time €2.80; and in three years' time €2.50.

For an employee that remains with the entity for the full three year period, the first alternative would be accounted for as follows:

Year	Calculation of cumulative expense	Cumulative expense (€)	Expense for period (€)
1	600 shares × €2.50 × 1/3	500	500
2	600 shares × €2.50 × 2/3	1,000	500
3	600 shares × €2.50 × 3/3	1,500	500

For the second alternative, the analysis is that the employee has simultaneously received an award of 100 shares vesting over one year, an award of 200 shares vesting over two years and an award of 300 shares vesting over 3 years. This would be accounted for as follows:

Year	Calculation of cumulative expense	Cumulative expense (€)	Expense for period (€)
1	[100 shares × €3.00] + [200 shares × €2.80 × 1/2] + [300 shares × €2.50 × 1/3]	830	830
2	[100 shares × €3.00] + [200 shares × €2.80 × 2/2] + [300 shares × €2.50 × 2/3]	1,360	530
3	[100 shares × €3.00] + [200 shares × €2.80 × 2/2] + [300 shares × €2.50 × 3/3]	1,610	250

At first sight, such an approach seems to be taking account of non-market vesting conditions in determining the fair value of an award, contrary to the basic principle of paragraph 19 of IFRS 2 (see 6.1.1 above). However, it is not the vesting conditions that are being taken into account *per se*, but the fact that the varying vesting periods will give rise to different lives for the award (which are required to be taken into account – see 7.2 and 8 below).

Provided all conditions are clearly understood at the outset, the accounting treatment illustrated in Example 32.9 would also apply even if the vesting of shares in each year also depended on a performance condition unique to that year (e.g. that profit in that year must reach a given minimum level), as opposed to a cumulative performance condition (e.g. that profit must have grown by a minimum amount by the end of year 1, 2 or 3). This is because there is an implied service condition covering a longer period. In other words, an award that vests at the end of year 3 conditional on profitability in year 3 is also implicitly conditional on the employee providing service for three years from the date of grant in order to be eligible to receive the award. This is discussed further at 5.3.7 above.

The accounting treatment illustrated in Example 32.9 is the only treatment for graded vesting permitted under IFRS 2. This contrasts with US GAAP[12] which permits, for awards with graded vesting where vesting depends solely on a service condition, a policy choice between the approach illustrated above and a straight-line recognition method.

6.2.3 Transactions with variable vesting periods due to non-market vesting conditions

An award may be made, the vesting period of which is subject to variation. For example, an award might be made contingent upon achievement of a particular target (such as achieving a given level of cumulative earnings) within a given period, but vesting immediately the target has been reached. Alternatively, an award might be contingent on levels of earnings growth over a period, but with vesting occurring more quickly if growth is achieved more quickly. Also some plans provide for 're-testing', whereby an original target is set for achievement within a given vesting period, but if that target is not met, a new target and/or a different vesting period are substituted.

In such cases, the entity needs to estimate the length of the vesting period at grant date, based on the most likely outcome of the performance condition. Subsequently, it is necessary continuously to re-estimate not only the number of awards that will finally vest, but also the date of vesting, as shown by Example 32.10. *[IFRS 2.15(b), IG12].* This contrasts with the treatment of awards with market conditions and variable vesting periods, where the initial estimate of the vesting period may not be revised (see 6.3.4 below).

Example 32.10: Award with non-market vesting condition and variable vesting period

At the beginning of year 1, the entity grants 100 shares each to 500 employees, conditional upon the employees remaining in the entity's employment during the vesting period. The shares will vest:

- at the end of year 1 if the entity's earnings increase by more than 18%
- at the end of year 2 if the entity's earnings increase by more than an average of 13% per year over the two year period
- at the end of year 3 if the entity's earnings increase by more than an average of 10% per year over the three year period.

The award is estimated to have a fair value of $30 per share at grant date. It is expected that no dividends will be paid during the whole three year period.

By the end of the first year, the entity's earnings have increased by 14%, and 30 employees have left. The entity expects that earnings will continue to increase at a similar rate in year 2, and therefore expects that the shares will vest at the end of year 2. The entity expects, on the basis of a weighted average probability, that a further 30 employees will leave during year 2, and therefore expects that an award of 100 shares each will vest for 440 (500 – 30 – 30) employees at the end of year 2.

By the end of the second year, the entity's earnings have increased by only 10% and therefore the shares do not vest at the end of that year. 28 employees have left during the year. The entity expects that a further 25 employees will leave during year 3, and that the entity's earnings will increase by at least 6%, thereby achieving the average growth of 10% per year necessary for an award after 3 years, so that an award of 100 shares each will vest for 417 (500 – 30 – 28 – 25) employees at the end of year 3.

By the end of the third year, 23 employees have left and the entity's earnings have increased by 8%, resulting in an average increase of 10.67% per year. Therefore, 419 (500 – 30 – 28 – 23) employees receive 100 shares at the end of year 3.

The entity will recognise the following amounts during the vesting period for services received as consideration for the shares.

Year	Calculation of cumulative expense	Cumulative expense ($)	Expense for period ($)
1	440 employees × 100 shares × $30 × 1/2*	660,000	660,000
2	417 employees × 100 shares × $30 × 2/3*	834,000	174,000
3	419 employees × 100 shares × $30	1,257,000	423,000

*   The entity's best estimate at the end of year 1 is that it is one year through a two year vesting period and at the end of year 2 that it is two years through a three year vesting period.

It will be noted that in Example 32.10, which is based on IG Example 2 in the implementation guidance to IFRS 2, it is assumed that the entity will pay no dividends (to any shareholders) throughout the maximum possible three year vesting period. This has the effect that the fair value of the shares to be awarded is (some might say, rather too conveniently) equivalent to their market value at the date of grant.

If dividends were expected to be paid during the vesting period, this would no longer be the case. Employees would be better off if they received shares after two years rather than three, since they would have a right to receive dividends from the end of year two. In practice, an entity is unlikely to suspend dividend payments in order to simplify the calculation of its share-based payment expense, and it is unfortunate that IG Example 2 is not more realistic.

One solution might be to use the approach in IG Example 4 in the implementation guidance to IFRS 2 (the substance of which is reproduced as Example 32.12 at 6.2.5 below). That Example deals with an award whose exercise price is either CHF12 or CHF16, dependent upon various performance conditions. Because vesting conditions other than market conditions must be ignored in determining the value of an award, the approach is in effect to treat the award as the simultaneous grant of two awards, whose value, in that case, varies by reference to the different exercise prices.

The same principle could be applied to an award of shares that vests at different times according to the performance conditions, by determining different fair values for the shares (in this case depending on whether they vest after one, two or three years). The charge during the vesting period would be based on a best estimate of which outcome will occur, and the final cumulative charge would be based on the actual outcome.

Such an approach appears to be taking account of non-market vesting conditions in determining the fair value of an award, contrary to the basic principle of paragraph 19 of IFRS 2 (see 6.1.1 above). However, it is not the vesting conditions that are being taken into account *per se*, but the fact that the varying vesting periods will give rise to different lives for the award (which are required to be taken into account – see 7.2 and 8 below).

Economically speaking, the entity in Example 32.10 has made a single award, the fair value of which must be a function of the weighted probabilities of the various outcomes occurring. However, under the accounting model for share-settled awards in IFRS 2, the probability of achieving non-market performance conditions is not taken into account in valuing an award. If this is required to be ignored, the only approach open is to proceed as above.

Some might object that this methodology is not relevant to the award in Example 32.10 above, since it is an award of shares rather than, in the case of Example 32.12 below, an award of options. However, an award of shares is no more than an award of options with an exercise price of zero. Moreover, the treatment in the previous paragraph is broadly consistent with the rationale given by IFRS 2 for the treatment of an award vesting in instalments (see 6.2.2 above).

In Example 32.10 above, the vesting period, although not known, is at least one of a finite number of known possibilities. The vesting period for some awards, however, may be more open-ended, such as an award that vests on a trade sale or flotation of the business. Such awards are discussed further at 15.3 below.

6.2.4 Transactions with variable number of equity instruments awarded depending on non-market vesting conditions

More common than awards with a variable vesting period are those where the number of equity instruments awarded varies, typically increasing to reflect the margin by which a particular minimum target is exceeded. In accounting for such awards, the entity must continuously revise its estimate of the number of shares to be awarded, as illustrated in Example 32.11 below (which is based on IG Example 3 in the implementation guidance to IFRS 2).

Example 32.11:   Award with non-market vesting condition and variable number of equity instruments

At the beginning of year 1, an entity grants an option over a variable number of shares (see below), estimated to have a fair value at grant date of £20 per share under option, to each of its 100 employees working in the sales department on the following terms. The share options will vest at the end of year 3, provided that the employees remain in the entity's employment, and provided that the volume of sales of a particular product increases by at least an average of 5% per year. If the volume of sales of the product increases by an average of between 5% and 10% per year, each employee will be entitled to exercise 100 share options. If the volume of sales increases by an average of between 10% and 15% each year, each employee will be entitled to exercise 200 share options. If the volume of sales increases by an average of 15% or more, each employee will be entitled to exercise 300 share options.

By the end of the first year, seven employees have left and the entity expects that a total of 20 employees will leave by the end of year 3. Product sales have increased by 12% and the entity expects this rate of increase to continue over the next two years, so that 80 employees will be entitled to exercise 200 options each.

By the end of the second year, a further five employees have left. The entity now expects only three more employees to leave during year 3, and therefore expects a total of 15 employees to have left during the three year period. Product sales have increased by 18%, resulting in an average of 15% over the two years to date. The entity now expects that sales will average 15% or more over the three year period, so that 85 employees will be entitled to exercise 300 options each.

By the end of year 3, a further seven employees have left. Hence, 19 employees have left during the three year period, and 81 employees remain. However, due to trading conditions significantly poorer than expected, sales have increased by a 3 year average of only 12%, so that the 81 remaining employees are entitled to exercise only 200 share options.

The entity will recognise the following amounts during the vesting period for services received as consideration for the options.

Year	Calculation of cumulative expense	Cumulative expense (£)	Expense for period (£)
1	80 employees × 200 options × £20 × 1/3	106,667	106,667
2	85 employees × 300 options × £20 × 2/3	340,000	233,333
3	81 employees × 200 options × £20	324,000	(16,000)

This Example reinforces the point that, under the methodology in IFRS 2, it is quite possible for an equity-settled transaction to give rise to a credit to profit or loss for a particular period during the period to vesting.

6.2.5 Transactions with variable exercise price due to non-market vesting conditions

Another mechanism for delivering higher value to the recipient of a share award so as to reflect the margin by which a particular target is exceeded might be to vary the exercise price depending on performance. IFRS 2 requires such an award to be dealt with, in effect, as two awards. The fair value of each award is determined, and the cost during the vesting period based on the best estimate of which award will actually vest, with the final cumulative charge being based on the actual outcome. *[IFRS 2.IG12, IG Example 4]*.

This is illustrated in Example 32.12 below.

Example 32.12: Award with non-market vesting condition and variable exercise price

An entity grants to a senior executive 10,000 share options, conditional upon the executive's remaining in the entity's employment for three years. The exercise price is CHF40. However, the exercise price drops to CHF30 if the entity's earnings increase by at least an average of 10% per year over the three year period.

On grant date, the entity estimates that the fair value of the share options, with an exercise price of CHF30, is CHF16 per option. If the exercise price is CHF40, the entity estimates that the share options have a fair value of CHF12 per option. During year 1, the entity's earnings increased by 12%, and the entity expects that earnings will continue to increase at this rate over the next two years. The entity therefore expects that the earnings target will be achieved, and hence the share options will have an exercise price of CHF30.

During year 2, the entity's earnings increased by 13%, and the entity continues to expect that the earnings target will be achieved. During year 3, the entity's earnings increased by only 3%, and therefore the earnings target was not achieved. The executive completes three years' service, and therefore satisfies the service condition. Because the earnings target was not achieved, the 10,000 vested share options have an exercise price of CHF40.

The entity will recognise the following amounts during the vesting period for services received as consideration for the options.

Year	Calculation of cumulative expense	Cumulative expense (CHF)	Expense for period (CHF)
1	10,000 options × CHF16 × 1/3	53,333	53,333
2	10,000 options × CHF16 × 2/3	106,667	53,334
3	10,000 options × CHF12	120,000	13,333

At first sight this may seem a rather surprising approach. In reality, has not the entity in Example 32.12 made a single award, the fair value of which must lie between CHF12 and CHF16, as a function of the weighted probabilities of either outcome occurring? Economically speaking, this is the case. However, under the accounting model for share-settled awards in IFRS 2, the probability of achieving non-market performance conditions is not taken into account in valuing an award. If this is required to be ignored, the only approach open is to proceed as above.

6.3   Market conditions

6.3.1   *What is a 'market condition'?*

IFRS 2 defines a market condition as 'a condition upon which the exercise price, vesting or exercisability of an equity instrument depends that is related to the market price of the entity's equity instruments, such as attaining a specified share price or a specified amount of intrinsic value of a share option, or achieving a specified target that is based on the market price of the entity's equity instruments relative to an index of market prices of equity instruments of other entities'. *[IFRS 2 Appendix A].*

The 'intrinsic value' of a share option means 'the difference between the fair value of the shares to which the counterparty has the (conditional or unconditional) right to subscribe or which it has the right to receive, and the price (if any) the counterparty is (or will be) required to pay for those shares'. *[IFRS 2 Appendix A].* In other words, an option to acquire for $8 a share with a fair value of $10 has an intrinsic value of $2. A performance condition based on the share price and one based on the intrinsic value of the option are effectively the same, since the values of each will obviously move in parallel.

An example of a market condition might be a condition based on total shareholder return (TSR). TSR is a measure of the increase or decrease in a given sum invested in an entity over a period on the assumption that all dividends received in the period had been used to purchase further shares in the entity. The market price of the entity's shares is an input to the calculation.

However, a condition linked to a purely internal financial performance measure such as profit or earnings per share is not a market condition. Such measures will affect the share price, but are not directly linked to it, and hence are not market conditions.

A condition linked to a general market index to which the reporting entity's share price is not an input is not a market condition, but a non-vesting condition (see 6.4 below). For example, suppose that an entity engaged in investment management and listed only in London grants options to an employee responsible for the Far East equities portfolio. The options have a condition linked to movements in a general index of shares of entities listed in Hong Kong, so as to compare the performance of the portfolio of investments for which the employee is responsible with that of the overall market in which they are traded. That condition would not be regarded as a market condition under IFRS 2, because even though it relates to the performance of a market, the reporting entity's own share price is not relevant to the satisfaction of the condition.

However, if the condition were that the entity's own share price had to outperform a general index of shares of entities listed in Hong Kong, that condition would be a market condition, because the reporting entity's own share price is then relevant to the satisfaction of the condition.

As discussed at 3.2.1 above, the Interpretations Committee has an ongoing project to clarify the distinction between vesting and non-vesting conditions.

6.3.2 Summary of accounting treatment

The key feature of the accounting treatment of an equity-settled transaction subject to a market condition is that the market condition is taken into account in valuing the award at the date of grant, but then subsequently ignored, so that an award is treated as vesting irrespective of whether the market condition is satisfied, provided that all other non-market vesting conditions are satisfied. *[IFRS 2.21, IG13]*. This can have rather controversial consequences, as illustrated by Example 32.13.

Example 32.13: Award with market condition

An entity grants an employee an option to buy a share on condition of remaining in employment for three years and the share price at the end of that period being at least €7. At the end of the vesting period, the share price is €6.80. The share price condition is factored into the initial valuation of the option, and the option is considered to vest provided that the employee remains for three years, irrespective of whether the share price does in fact reach €7. Thus, IFRS 2 sometimes treats as vesting (and recognises a cost for) awards that do not actually vest in the natural sense of the word. See also Example 32.15 at 6.3.4 below.

This treatment is clearly significantly different from that for transactions involving a non-market vesting condition, where no cost would be recognised where the conditions were not met. The Basis for Conclusions indicates that the IASB accepted this difference for two main reasons:

(a)   it was consistent with the approach in the US standard FAS 123; and

(b)   in principle, the same approach should have been adopted for all performance conditions. However, whereas market conditions can be readily incorporated into the valuation of options, other conditions cannot. *[IFRS 2.BC183-184]*.

In our view, the over-riding reason for the IASB's approach was almost certainly harmonisation with US GAAP, since the second reason given does not really stand up to scrutiny. As discussed in 6.2 above, the methodology prescribed by IFRS 2 for transactions with a vesting condition other than a market condition is to determine the fair value of the option ignoring the condition and then essentially to multiply that fair value by the estimated (and ultimately the actual) probability of that non-market vesting condition occurring, which in broad terms is no different from incorporating those probabilities in the valuation in the first place. Moreover, the January 2008 amendment to IFRS 2 (see 1.2 above) had the effect that certain conditions previously regarded as non-market vesting conditions (and therefore 'impossible' to incorporate in the determination of fair value) became non-vesting conditions (and therefore required to be incorporated in the determination of fair value)!

One of the reasons for adoption of this approach under US GAAP (not referred to in the Basis for Conclusions in IFRS 2) was as an 'anti-avoidance' measure. The concern was that the introduction of certain market conditions could effectively allow for the reversal of the expense for 'underwater' options (i.e. those whose exercise price is higher than the share price such that it is not in the holder's interest to exercise the option) for which all significant vesting conditions had been satisfied, contrary to the general principle in US GAAP (and IFRS 2) that no revisions should be made to the expense for an already vested option.

For example, an entity could grant an employee an option, when the share price is £10, exercisable at £10, provided that a certain sales target had been met within one year. If the target were achieved, IFRS 2 would require an expense to be recognised even if the share price at the end of the year were only £8, so that the employee would not rationally exercise the option. If, however, the performance conditions were that (a) the sales target was achieved and (b) the share price was at least £10.01, the effect would be (absent specific provision for market conditions) that the entity could reverse any expense for 'underwater' options. Whilst this concern is easily understood, some might question whether an accounting methodology designed to thwart the use of a hypothetical artificial market condition necessarily produces appropriate results when applied to the real market conditions actually found in most awards.

In any event, it appears that it may be possible to soften the impact of IFRS 2's rules for market-based conditions relatively easily by introducing a non-market vesting condition closely correlated to the market condition. For instance, the option in Example 32.13 above could be modified so that exercise was dependent not only upon the €7 target share price and continuous employment, but also on a target growth in earnings per share. Whilst there would not be a perfect correlation between earnings per share and the share price, it would be expected that they would move roughly in parallel, particularly if the entity has historically had a fairly consistent price/earnings ratio. Thus, if the share price target were not met, it would be highly likely that the earnings per share target would not be met either. This would allow the entity to show no cumulative cost for the option, since only one (i.e. not *all*) of the non-market related vesting conditions would have been met.

Similarly, entities in sectors where the share price is closely related to net asset value (e.g. property companies and investment trusts) could incorporate a net asset value target as a non-market performance condition that would be highly likely to be satisfied only if the market condition was satisfied.

The matrices below illustrate the interaction of market conditions and vesting conditions other than market conditions. Matrix 1 summarises the possible outcomes for an award with the following two vesting conditions:

- the employee remaining in service for three years ('service condition'); and
- the entity's total shareholder return ('TSR') relative to that of a peer group being in the top 10% of its peer group at the end of the period ('TSR target').

Matrix 1

	Service condition met?	TSR target met?	IFRS 2 expense?
1	Yes	Yes	Yes
2	Yes	No	Yes
3	No	Yes	No
4	No	No	No

It will be seen that, to all intents and purposes, the 'TSR target met?' column is redundant, as this is not relevant to whether or not the award is treated as vesting by IFRS 2. The effect of this is that the entity would recognise an expense for outcome 2, even though no awards truly vest.

Matrix 2 summarises the possible outcomes for an award with the same conditions as in Matrix 1, plus a requirement for earnings per share to grow by a general inflation index plus 10% over the period ('EPS target').

Matrix 2

	Service condition met?	TSR target met?	EPS target met?	IFRS 2 expense?
1	Yes	Yes	Yes	Yes
2	Yes	No	Yes	Yes
3	Yes	Yes	No	No
4	Yes	No	No	No
5	No	Yes	Yes	No
6	No	No	Yes	No
7	No	Yes	No	No
8	No	No	No	No

Again it will be seen that, to all intents and purposes, the 'TSR target met?' column is redundant, as this is not relevant to whether or not the award is treated as vesting by IFRS 2. The effect of this is that the entity would recognise an expense for outcome 2, even though no awards truly vest. However, no expense would be recognised for outcome 4, which is, except for the introduction of the EPS target, equivalent to outcome 2 in Matrix 1, for which an expense is recognised. This illustrates that the introduction of a non-market vesting condition closely related to a market condition may mitigate the impact of IFRS 2.

Examples of the application of the accounting treatment for transactions involving market conditions are given in 6.3.3 and 6.3.4 below.

6.3.3 Transactions with market conditions and known vesting periods

The accounting for these is essentially the same as that for transactions with no market conditions and a known vesting period, except that adjustments are made to reflect the changing probability of the achievement of the non-market vesting conditions only, as illustrated by Example 32.14 below. *[IFRS 2.19-21, IG13, IG Example 5].*

Example 32.14: Award with market condition and fixed vesting period

At the beginning of year 1, an entity grants to 100 employees 1,000 share options each, conditional upon the employees remaining in the entity's employment until the end of year 3. However, the share options cannot be exercised unless the share price has increased from €50 at the beginning of year 1 to more than €65 at the end of year 3.

If the share price is above €65 at the end of year 3, the share options can be exercised at any time during the next seven years, i.e. by the end of year 10. The entity applies a binomial option pricing model (see 8 below), which takes into account the possibility that the share price will exceed €65 at the end of year 3 (and hence the share options become exercisable) and the possibility that the share price will not exceed €65 at the end of year 3 (and hence the options will be forfeited). It estimates the fair value of the share options with this market condition to be €24 per option.

IFRS 2 requires the entity to recognise the services received from a counterparty who satisfies all other vesting conditions (e.g. services received from an employee who remains in service for the specified service period), irrespective of whether that market condition is satisfied. It makes no difference whether the share price target is achieved, since the possibility that the share price target might not be achieved has already been taken into account when estimating the fair value of the share options at grant date. However, the options are subject to another condition (i.e. continuous employment) and the cost recognised should be adjusted to reflect the ongoing best estimate of employee retention.

By the end of the first year, seven employees have left and the entity expects that a total of 20 employees will leave by the end of year 3, so that 80 employees will have satisfied all conditions other than the market condition (i.e. continuous employment).

By the end of the second year, a further five employees have left. The entity now expects only three more employees will leave during year 3, and therefore expects that a total of 15 employees will have left during the three year period, so that 85 employees will have satisfied all conditions other than the market condition.

By the end of year 3, a further seven employees have left. Hence, 19 employees have left during the three year period, and 81 employees remain. However, the share price is only €60, so that the options cannot be exercised. Nevertheless, as all conditions other than the market condition have been satisfied, a cumulative cost is recorded as if the options had fully vested in 81 employees.

The entity will recognise the following amounts during the vesting period for services received as consideration for the options (which in economic reality do not vest).

Year	Calculation of cumulative expense	Cumulative expense (€)	Expense for period (€)
1	80 employees × 1,000 options × €24 × 1/3	640,000	640,000
2	85 employees × 1,000 options × €24 × 2/3	1,360,000	720,000
3	81 employees × 1,000 options × €24	1,944,000	584,000

6.3.4   Transactions with variable vesting periods due to market conditions

Where a transaction has a variable vesting period due to a market condition, a best estimate of the most likely vesting period will have been used in determining the fair value of the transaction at the date of grant. IFRS 2 requires the expense for that transaction to be recognised over an estimated expected vesting period consistent with the assumptions used in the valuation, without any subsequent revision. *[IFRS 2.15(b), IG14].*

This may mean, for example, that, if the actual vesting period for an employee share option award turns out to be longer than that anticipated for the purposes of the initial valuation, a cost is nevertheless recorded in respect of all employees who reach the end of the *anticipated* vesting period, even if they do not reach the end of the *actual* vesting period, as shown by Example 32.15 below, which is based on Example 6 in the implementation guidance in IFRS 2.

Example 32.15:   Award with market condition and variable vesting period

At the beginning of year 1, an entity grants 10,000 share options with a ten year life to each of ten senior executives. The share options will vest and become exercisable immediately if and when the entity's share price increases from £50 to £70, provided that the executive remains in service until the share price target is achieved.

The entity applies a binomial option pricing model, which takes into account the possibility that the share price target will be achieved during the ten year life of the options, and the possibility that the target will not be achieved. The entity estimates that the fair value of the share options at grant date is £25 per option. From the option pricing model, the entity determines that the most likely vesting period is five years. The entity also estimates that two executives will have left by the end of year 5, and therefore expects that 80,000 share options (10,000 share options × 8 executives) will vest at the end of year 5.

Throughout years 1 to 4, the entity continues to estimate that a total of two executives will leave by the end of year 5. However, in total three executives leave, one in each of years 3, 4 and 5. The share price target is achieved at the end of year 6. Another executive leaves during year 6, before the share price target is achieved.

Paragraph 15 of IFRS 2 requires the entity to recognise the services received over the expected vesting period, as estimated at grant date, and also requires the entity not to revise that estimate. Therefore, the entity recognises the services received from the executives over years 1-5. Hence, the transaction amount is ultimately based on 70,000 share options (10,000 share options × 7 executives who remain in service at the end of year 5). Although another executive left during year 6, no adjustment is made, because the executive had already completed the expected vesting period of 5 years.

The entity will recognise the following amounts during the initial expected five year vesting period for services received as consideration for the options.

Year	Calculation of cumulative expense	Cumulative expense (£)	Expense for period (£)
1	8 employees × 10,000 options × £25 × 1/5	400,000	400,000
2	8 employees × 10,000 options × £25 × 2/5	800,000	400,000
3	8 employees × 10,000 options × £25 × 3/5	1,200,000	400,000
4	8 employees × 10,000 options × £25 × 4/5	1,600,000	400,000
5	7 employees × 10,000 options × £25	1,750,000	150,000

IFRS 2 does not specifically address the converse situation, namely where the award actually vests before the end of the anticipated vesting period. In our view, where this occurs, any expense not yet recognised at the point of vesting should be immediately accelerated. We consider that this treatment is most consistent with the overall requirement of IFRS 2 to recognise an expense for share-based payment transactions 'as the services are received'. *[IFRS 2.7]*. It is difficult to regard any services being received for an award after it has vested.

Moreover, the prohibition in IFRS 2 on adjusting the vesting period as originally determined refers to 'the estimate of the expected vesting period'. In our view, the acceleration of vesting that we propose is not the revision of an estimated period, but the substitution of a known vesting period for an estimate.

Suppose in Example 32.15 above, the award had in fact vested at the end of year 4. We believe that the expense for such an award should be allocated as follows:

Year	Calculation of cumulative expense	Cumulative expense (£)	Expense for period (£)
1	8 employees × 10,000 options × £25 × 1/5	400,000	400,000
2	8 employees × 10,000 options × £25 × 2/5	800,000	400,000
3	8 employees × 10,000 options × £25 × 3/5	1,200,000	400,000
4	8 employees × 10,000 options × £25 × 4/4	2,000,000	800,000

6.3.5 Transactions with multiple outcomes depending on market conditions

In practice, it is very common for an award subject to market conditions to give varying levels of reward that increase depending on the extent to which a 'base line' performance target has been met. Such an award is illustrated in Example 32.16 below.

Example 32.16:   Award with market conditions and graded outcomes

On 1 January 2012, the reporting entity grants an employee shares if the employee is still in employment on the third anniversary of grant, subject to the share price. The employee will receive:

- no shares if the share price is below €10.00
- 100 shares if the share price is in the range €10.00 – €14.99
- 150 shares if the share price is in the range €15.00 – €19.99
- 180 shares if the share price is €20.00 or above.

In effect the entity has made three awards, which need to be valued as follows:

(a)   100 shares if the employee remains in service for three years and the share price is in the range €10.00 – €14.99

(b)   50 (150 – 100) shares if the employee remains in service for three years and the share price is in the range €15.00 – €19.99; and

(c)   30 (180 – 150) shares if the employee remains in service for three years and the share price is €20.00 or more.

Each award would be valued, ignoring the impact of the three-year service requirement (a non-market vesting condition) but taking account of the share price target. This would result in each tranche of the award being subject to an increasing level of discount to reflect the relative probability of the share price target for each tranche of the award being met. All three awards would then be expensed over the three-year service period, and forfeited only if the awards lapsed as a result of the employee leaving during that period.

It can be seen that the (perhaps somewhat counterintuitive) impact of this is that an equity-settled award that increases in line with increases in the entity's share price may nevertheless have a fixed grant date value irrespective of the number of shares finally awarded.

6.3.6   Transactions with independent market conditions and non-market vesting conditions

The discussion at 6.3.2 above addressed the accounting treatment of awards with multiple conditions that must all be satisfied, i.e. a market condition *and* a non-market vesting condition. However, it is increasingly common for entities to make awards with multiple conditions, only one of which need be satisfied, i.e. the awards vest on satisfaction of either a market condition *or* a non-market vesting condition. IFRS 2 provides no explicit guidance on the treatment of such awards, which is far from clear, as illustrated by Example 32.17 below.

Example 32.17:   Award with independent market conditions and non-market vesting conditions

An entity grants an employee 100 share options that vest after three years if the employee is still in employment and the entity achieves either:

- cumulative total shareholder return (TSR) over three years of at least 15%, or
- cumulative profits over three years of at least £200 million.

The fair value of the award, ignoring vesting conditions, is £300,000. The fair value of the award, taking account of the TSR condition, but not the other conditions, is £210,000.

In our view, the entity has, in effect, simultaneously issued two awards – call them 'A' and 'B' – which vest as follows:

A   on achievement of three years' service plus minimum TSR,

B   on achievement of three years' service plus minimum earnings growth.

If the conditions for both awards are simultaneously satisfied, one or other effectively lapses.

It is clear that award A, if issued separately, would require the entity to recognise an expense of £210,000 if the employee were still in service at the end of the three year period. It therefore seems clear that, if the employee does remain in service, there should be a charge of £210,000 irrespective of whether the award actually vests. It would be anomalous for the entity to avoid recording a charge that would have been recognised if the entity had made award A in isolation simply by packaging it with award B.

If in fact the award vested because the earnings condition, but not the market condition, had been satisfied, it would then be appropriate to recognise a total expense of £300,000. This begs the question of whether the award should be accounted for:

(i)   On the assumption in years 1 and 2 that it will vest because of the earnings condition, with an adjustment in the final year if the award vests by virtue of the TSR condition (or the award does not vest, but the employee remains in service). This would give rise to annual expense as follows:

Year	Calculation of cumulative expense	Cumulative expense (£)	Expense for period (£)
1	300,000 × 1/3	100,000	100,000
2	300,000 × 2/3	200,000	100,000
3	210,000 × 3/3	210,000	10,000

(ii) On the assumption in years 1 and 2 that it will vest by virtue of the TSR condition being met (or the employee remaining in service), with a 'catch-up' adjustment in the final period, if the award vests by virtue of the earnings condition, but not the TSR condition, being satisfied. This would give rise to annual expense as follows:

Year	Calculation of cumulative expense	Cumulative expense (£)	Expense for period (£)
1	210,000 × 1/3	70,000	70,000
2	210,000 × 2/3	140,000	70,000
3	300,000 × 3/3	300,000	160,000

(iii) At each reporting date, on the basis of the probability, as assessed at that date, of the award vesting by virtue of the earnings condition, but not the TSR condition, being satisfied. Assume (for example) that the entity assesses at the end of year 1 that the award is likely to vest by virtue of the TSR condition, and at the end of year 2 that it is likely to vest by virtue of the earnings condition, and that the award actually does not vest, but the employee remains in service. This would give rise to annual expense as follows:

Year	Calculation of cumulative expense	Cumulative expense (£)	Expense for period (£)
1	210,000 × 1/3	70,000	70,000
2	300,000 × 2/3	200,000	130,000
3	210,000 × 3/3	210,000	10,000

We believe that treatment (iii) is most consistent with the general approach of IFRS 2 to awards with a number of possible outcomes.

Of course, as for other awards, the accounting treatment would also require an assessment of whether the employee was actually going to remain in service or not.

This begs the further question of how the award should be accounted for in a situation where both conditions are satisfied. It would clearly be inappropriate to recognise an expense of £510,000 (the sum of the separate fair values of the award) – this would be double-counting, because the employee receives only one package of 100 options. However, should the total expense be taken as £210,000 or £300,000? In our view, it is more appropriate to recognise a cost of £300,000 since the non-market vesting condition has been satisfied.

Ultimately, this is an issue which only the IASB can solve, since it arises from a problem of the IASB's own making – the fundamentally inconsistent treatment by IFRS 2 of awards with market conditions and those with non-market vesting conditions. In our experience, awards of this type are increasingly common, and, accordingly, there is an increasingly pressing need for a resolution of this issue.

6.3.7   Transactions with hybrid or interdependent market conditions and non-market vesting conditions

Awards may sometimes have a performance benchmark which depends simultaneously on a market condition and a non-market vesting condition, sometimes known as 'hybrid' conditions. For example, some entities have made share-based payment awards to employees with conditions that require achievement of:

- a particular price-earnings (PE) ratio (calculated by reference to share price, a market condition, and earnings, a non-market vesting condition); or

- a maximum level of discount of market capitalisation (a market condition) below net asset value (a non-market vesting condition).

Such awards are rather curious, in the sense that these ratios may remain fairly constant irrespective of the underlying performance of the entity, so that a performance condition based on them is arguably of limited motivational value.

In our view, in contrast to our suggested treatment of awards with independent market and non-market vesting conditions discussed in 6.3.6 above, awards with interdependent market conditions and non-market vesting conditions must be accounted for entirely as awards with market conditions. An indicator such as the PE ratio, or discount of market capitalisation below net asset value, is a market condition as defined since it is 'related to the market price of the entity's equity instruments' (see 6.3.1 above).

6.3.8   Awards based on the market value of a subsidiary or business unit

Typically, awards with a market condition are based on the market value of the (typically quoted) equity of the parent entity. However, there is an increasingly held view that the parent's share price is a somewhat blunt instrument for measuring the performance of the employees of a particular subsidiary or business unit. Indeed, it is not difficult to imagine situations in which a particular subsidiary might perform well but the parent's share price be dragged down by other factors, or conversely where the parent's share price might rise notwithstanding lacklustre results for that subsidiary.

Accordingly, entities are increasingly implementing share-based remuneration schemes which aim to reward employees by reference to the market value of the equity of the business unit for which they work. The detail of such schemes varies, but the general effect is typically as follows:

- at grant date, the employee is allocated a (real or notional) holding in the equity of the employing subsidiary, the market value of which is measured at grant date; and

- the employee is granted an award of as many shares of the listed parent as have a value, at a specified future date (generally at or shortly after the end of the vesting period), equal to the increase in the market value of the holding in the equity of the employing subsidiary over the vesting period.

Some argue that such a scheme contains a market condition, since it is based on the fair value of the subsidiary's shares, with the result that the grant date fair value is:

- discounted to reflect this market condition (see 6.3.2 above); and
- fixed, irrespective of how many parent company shares are finally issued, since the entity has effectively issued a market-based award with multiple outcomes based on the market value of the equity of a subsidiary (see 6.3.5 above).

In our view, however, the treatment of such schemes under IFRS 2 is not as straightforward as suggested by this analysis. A fundamental issue is whether any award dependent on the change in value of the equity of an unquoted entity contains a market condition at all. IFRS 2 defines a market condition (see 6.3.1 above) as one dependent on the 'market price' of the entity's equity. *Prima facie*, if there is no market, there is no market price.

Some would argue that there are generally accepted valuation techniques for unquoted equities which can yield a fair value as a surrogate for market value. The difficulty with that argument, in our view, is that the IASB refers in the definition of 'market condition' to 'market price' and not to 'fair value'. The latter term is, of course, used extensively elsewhere in IFRS 2, which suggests that the IASB does not see the two terms as equivalent. This concern is reinforced by that fact that, in the 'valuation hierarchy' in IAS 39 (see Chapter 49 at 4), a quoted market price is given as the preferred (but not the only) method of arriving at fair value, which is defined in the same way in Appendix A to IFRS 2 and in IAS 39. An entity implementing such an award must therefore consider whether the basis on which the subsidiary equity is valued truly yields a 'market price' or merely a fair value according to a hypothetical valuation model.

Awards based on the 'enterprise value' of an unquoted entity raise similar issues, as discussed more fully at 2.2.4.F above.

6.4 Non-vesting conditions

The accounting treatment for awards with non-vesting conditions has some similarities to that for awards with market conditions in that:

- the fair value of the award at grant date is reduced to reflect the impact of the condition; and
- an expense is recognised for the award irrespective of whether the non-vesting condition is met, provided that all vesting conditions (other than market conditions) are met. *[IFRS 2.21A].*

However, the accounting for non-vesting conditions differs from that for market conditions as regards the timing of the recognition of expense if the non-vesting condition is not satisfied (see 6.4.3 below).

As discussed at 3.2.1 above, the Interpretations Committee has an ongoing project to clarify the distinction between vesting and non-vesting conditions.

6.4.1   Awards with no conditions other than non-vesting conditions

The effect of the treatment required by IFRS 2 is that any award that has only non-vesting conditions (e.g. an option award to an employee that may be exercised on a trade sale or IPO of the entity, irrespective of whether the employee is still in employment at that time) must be expensed in full at grant date. This is discussed further at 3.2 above and 15.3 below, and illustrated in Example 32.5 at 6.1 above.

6.4.2   Awards with non-vesting conditions and variable vesting periods

IFRS 2 does not explicitly address the determination of the vesting period for an award with a non-vesting condition but a variable vesting period (e.g. an award which delivers 100 shares when the price of gold reaches a given level, but without limit as to when that level must be achieved, so long as the employee is still in employment when the target is reached). However, given the close similarity between the required treatment for awards with non-vesting conditions and that for awards with market conditions, we believe that entities should follow the guidance in the standard for awards with market conditions and variable vesting periods (see 6.3.4 above).

6.4.3   Failure to meet non-vesting conditions

As noted above, the accounting for non-vesting conditions differs from that for market conditions as regards the timing of the recognition of expense if the non-vesting condition is not satisfied. The treatment depends on the nature of the non-vesting condition, as follows:

- if a non-vesting condition within the control of the counterparty (e.g. making monthly savings) is not satisfied during the vesting period, the failure to satisfy the condition is treated as a cancellation (see 7.4 below), with immediate recognition of any expense for the award not previously recognised;

- if a non-vesting condition within the control of the entity (e.g. continuing to operate the scheme) is not satisfied during the vesting period, the failure to satisfy the condition is treated as a cancellation (see 7.4 below), with immediate recognition of any expense for the award not previously recognised *[IFRS 2.28A, IG24]*; but

- if a non-vesting condition within the control of neither the counterparty nor the entity (e.g. a financial market index reaching a minimum level) is not satisfied during the vesting period, any expense for the award not previously recognised is recognised over the remaining vesting period, unless the award is otherwise treated as forfeited by IFRS 2. *[IFRS 2.BC237A, IG24]*. In our view, the reference to the vesting period would include any deemed vesting period calculated as described in 6.4.2 above.

If an award is forfeited due to a failure to satisfy a non-vesting condition after the end of the vesting period (e.g. a requirement for an employee not to work for a competitor for a two year period after vesting), no adjustment is made to the expense previously recognised, consistent with the general provisions of IFRS 2 for accounting for awards in the post-vesting period (see 6.1.3 above). This would be the case even if shares previously issued to the employee were required to be returned to the entity on forfeiture.

7 EQUITY-SETTLED TRANSACTIONS – MODIFICATION, CANCELLATION AND SETTLEMENT

7.1 Background

It is quite common for equity instruments to be modified or cancelled before or after vesting. Typically this is done where the conditions for an award have become so onerous as to be virtually unachievable, or (in the case of an option) where the share price has fallen so far below the exercise price of an option that it is unlikely that the option will ever be 'in the money' to the holder during its life. In such cases, an entity may take the view that such equity awards are so unattainable as to have little or no motivational effect, and accordingly replace them with less onerous alternatives. Conversely, and more rarely, an entity may make the terms of a share award more onerous (possibly because of shareholder concern that targets are insufficiently demanding). In addition an entity may 'settle' an award, i.e. cancel it in return for cash or other consideration.

IFRS 2 contains detailed provisions for modification, cancellation and settlement. Whilst these provisions (like the summary of them below) are framed in terms of share-based payment transactions with employees, they apply to transactions with parties other than employees that are measured by reference to the fair value of the equity instruments granted (see 5.4 above). In that case, however, all references to 'grant date' should be taken as references to the date on which the third party supplied goods or rendered service. *[IFRS 2.26].*

In the discussion below, any reference to a 'cancellation' is to any cancellation, whether instigated by the entity or the counterparty. Cancellations include:

- a failure by the entity to satisfy a non-vesting condition (see 6.4 above) within the control of the entity; and

- a failure by the counterparty to satisfy a non-vesting condition (see 6.4 above) within the control of the counterparty. *[IFRS 2.28A, IG24].*

The discussion below is not relevant to cancellations and modifications of those equity-settled transactions that are (exceptionally) accounted for at intrinsic value (see 8.8 below).

The basic principles of the rules for modification, cancellation and settlement, which are discussed in more detail at 7.3 and 7.4 below, can be summarised as follows.

- As a minimum, the entity must recognise the amount that would have been recognised for the award if it remained in place on its original terms. This is discussed further at 7.4 below;

- If the value of an award to an employee is reduced (e.g. by reducing the number of equity instruments subject to the award or, in the case of an option, by increasing the exercise price), there is no reduction in the cost recognised in profit or loss *[IFRS 2.27, B42, B44];*

- However, where the effect of the modification, cancellation or settlement is to increase the value of the award to an employee (e.g. by increasing the number of equity instruments subject to the award or, in the case of an option, by reducing the exercise price), the incremental fair value must be recognised as a cost. The incremental fair value is the difference between the fair value of the original award and that of the modified award, both measured at the date of modification. *[IFRS 2.27, B43].*

Some argue that, when an award has been modified, and certainly when it has been cancelled altogether, it no longer exists, and that it is therefore not appropriate to recognise any cost for it. However, such a view is consistent with a vesting date measurement model rather than with the grant/service date measurement model of IFRS 2. The value of an award at grant date or service date cannot be changed by subsequent events.

Another reason given for the approach in IFRS 2 is that if entities were able not to recognise the cost of modified or cancelled options they would in effect be able to apply a selective form of 'truing up', whereby options that increased in value after grant would remain 'frozen' at their grant date valuation under the general principles of IFRS 2, whilst options that decreased in value could be modified or cancelled after grant date and credit taken for the fall in value. *[IFRS 2.BC222-237].*

7.2   Valuation requirements when an award is modified, cancelled or settled

These provisions have the important practical consequence that, when an award is modified, cancelled or settled, the entity must obtain a fair value not only for the modified award, but also for the original award, updated to the date of modification. If the award had not been modified, there would have been no need to obtain a valuation for the original award after the date of grant.

Whilst any modification of a performance condition clearly has an impact on the 'real' value of an award, it may have no direct effect on the value of the award for the purposes of IFRS 2. This is because, as discussed at 6.2 to 6.4 above, whilst a market condition or a non-vesting condition is taken into account in valuing an award, a non-market vesting condition is not. Accordingly, by implication, a change to a non market-related performance condition will not necessarily affect the expense recognised for the award under IFRS 2.

For example, if an award is contingent upon sales of a given number of units and the number of units required to be sold is decreased, the value of the award is clearly increased. However, as the performance condition is a non-market vesting condition, and therefore not relevant to the original determination of the value of the award, there is no incremental fair value required to be accounted for by IFRS 2. However, if the change makes the award more, rather than less, likely than not to vest, this change of estimate will give rise to an accounting charge (see 6.1 to 6.4 above).

If an award is modified by changing the service period, the situation is somewhat more complex. Whilst a service condition does not of itself change the fair value of the award for the purposes of IFRS 2, a change in service period may well indirectly change the life of the award, which is relevant to its value (see 8 below). For example, if an award was previously subject to a three year service period (and exercisable during a two week period immediately thereafter) and its terms are changed such that it now has a two year vesting period (and again exercisable during a two week period thereafter), the value of the award will change, because its life has been reduced by one year. Similar considerations apply where performance conditions are modified in such a way as to alter the anticipated vesting date.

The valuation requirements relating to cancelled and settled awards are considered further at 7.4 below.

7.3 Modification

When an award is modified, the entity must as a minimum recognise the cost of the original award as if it had not been modified (i.e. at the original grant date fair value, spread over the original vesting period, and subject to the original vesting conditions). *[IFRS 2.27, B42-43].*

In addition, a further cost must be recognised for any modifications that increase the fair value of the award. This additional cost is spread over the period from the date of modification until the vesting date of the modified award, which might not be the same as that of the original award. Where a modification is made after the original vesting period has expired, and is subject to no further vesting conditions, any incremental fair value should be recognised immediately. *[IFRS 2.27, B42-43].*

Whether a modification increases or decreases the fair value of an award is determined as at the date of modification, as illustrated by Example 32.18. *[IFRS 2.27, B42-44].*

Example 32.18: Does a modification increase or decrease the value of an award?

On 1 January 2011 an entity granted two executives, A and B, a number of options worth $100 each.

On 1 January 2012, A's options are modified such that they have a fair value of $85, their current fair value being $80. This is treated as an increase in fair value of $5 (even though the modified award is worth less than the original award when first granted). Therefore an additional $5 of expense would be recognised in respect of A's options.

On 1 January 2013, B's options are modified such that they have a fair value of $120, their current fair value being $125. This is treated as a reduction in fair value of $5 (even though the modified award is worth more than the original award when first granted). There is no change to the expense recognised for B's options.

This treatment ensures that movements in the fair value of the original award are not reflected in the entity's profit or loss, consistent with the treatment of other equity instruments under IFRS.

IFRS 2 provides further detailed guidance on this requirement as follows.

7.3.1 Modifications that increase the value of an award

7.3.1.A Increase in fair value of equity instruments granted

If the modification increases the fair value of the equity instruments granted, (e.g. by reducing the exercise price or changing the exercise period), the incremental fair value, measured at the date of modification, must be recognised over the period from the date of modification to the date of vesting for the modified instruments, as illustrated in Example 32.19 below. *[IFRS 2.B43(a), IG15, IG Example 7].*

Chapter 32

Example 32.19:   Award modified by repricing

At the beginning of year 1, an entity grants 100 share options to each of its 500 employees. Each grant is conditional upon the employee remaining in service over the next three years. The entity estimates that the fair value of each option is €15.

By the end of year 1, the entity's share price has dropped, and the entity reprices its share options. The repriced share options vest at the end of year 3. The entity estimates that, at the date of repricing, the fair value of each of the original share options granted (i.e. before taking into account the repricing) is €5 and that the fair value of each repriced share option is €8.

40 employees leave during year 1. The entity estimates that a further 70 employees will leave during years 2 and 3, so that there will be 390 employees at the end of year 3 (500 – 40 – 70).

During year 2, a further 35 employees leave, and the entity estimates that a further 30 employees will leave during year 3, so that there will be 395 employees at the end of year 3 (500 – 40 – 35 – 30).

During year 3, a total of 28 employees leave, and hence a total of 103 employees ceased employment during the original three year vesting period, so that, for the remaining 397 employees, the original share options vest at the end of year 3.

IFRS 2 requires the entity to recognise:

- the cost of the original award at grant date (€15 per option) over a three year vesting period beginning at the start of year 1, plus

- the incremental fair value of the repriced options at repricing date (€3 per option, being the €8 fair value of each repriced option less the €5 fair value of the original option) over a two year vesting period beginning at the date of repricing (end of year one).

This would be calculated as follows.

Year	Calculation of cumulative expense		Cumulative expense (€) (a+b)	Expense for period (€)
	Original award (a)	Modified award (b)		
1	390 employees × 100 options × €15 × 1/3		195,000	195,000
2	395 employees × 100 options × €15 × 2/3	395 employees × 100 options × €3 × 1/2	454,250	259,250
3	397 employees × 100 options × €15	397 employees × 100 options × €3	714,600	260,350

In effect, IFRS 2 treats the original award and the incremental value of the modified award as if they were two separate awards.

A similar treatment to that in Example 32.19 above is adopted where the fair value of an award subject to a market condition has its value increased by the removal or mitigation of the condition. *[IFRS 2.B43(c)].* Where a vesting condition other than a market condition is changed, the treatment set out in 7.3.1.C below is adopted. IFRS 2 does not specifically address the treatment of an award, the fair value of which is increased by the removal or mitigation of a non-vesting condition. It seems appropriate, however, to account for it in the same way as a modification caused by the removal or mitigation of a market condition – i.e. as in Example 32.19 above.

7.3.1.B   *Increase in number of equity instruments granted*

If the modification increases the number of equity instruments granted, the fair value of the additional instruments, measured at the date of modification, must be recognised over the period from the date of modification to the date of vesting for the modified instruments. If there is no further vesting period for the modified instruments, the incremental cost should be recognised immediately. *[IFRS 2.B43(b)]*.

7.3.1.C   *Removal or mitigation of non-market related vesting conditions*

Where a vesting condition, other than a market condition, is modified, the modified vesting condition should be taken into account when applying the general requirements of IFRS 2 as discussed in 6.1 to 6.4 above – in other words, the entity would continuously estimate the number of awards likely to vest and/or the vesting period. *[IFRS 2.B43(c)]*. This is consistent with the general principle of IFRS 2 that vesting conditions, other than market conditions, are not factored into the valuation of awards, but are reflected by recognising a cost for those instruments that ultimately vest pursuant to those conditions. See also the discussion at 7.2 above.

IFRS 2 does not provide an example that addresses this point specifically, but we assume that something along the lines of Example 32.20 below is intended.

Example 32.20:   Modification of non-market performance condition in employee's favour

At the beginning of year 1, the entity grants 1,000 share options to each member of its sales team, with exercise conditional upon the employee's remaining in the entity's employment for three years, and the team selling more than 50,000 units of a particular product over the three year period. The fair value of the share options is £15 per option at the date of grant.

At the end of year 1, the entity estimates that a total of 48,000 units will be sold, and accordingly records no cost for the award in year one.

During year 2, there is so severe a downturn in trading conditions that the entity believes that the sales target is too demanding to have any motivational effect, and reduces the target to 30,000 units, which it believes is achievable. It also expects 14 members of the sales team to remain in employment throughout the three year performance period. It therefore records an expense in year 2 of £140,000 (£15 × 14 employees × 1,000 options × 2/3). This cost is based on the originally assessed value of the award (i.e. £15) since the performance condition was never factored into the original valuation, such that any change in performance condition likewise has no effect on the valuation.

By the end of year 3, the entity has sold 35,000 units, and the share options vest. Twelve members of the sales team have remained in service for the three year period. The entity would therefore recognise a total cost of £180,000 (12 employees × 1,000 options × £15), giving an additional cost in year 3 of £40,000 (total charge £180,000, less £140,000 charged in year 2).

The difference between the accounting consequences for different methods of enhancing an award could cause confusion in some cases. For example, it may sometimes not be clear whether an award has been modified by increasing the number of equity instruments or by lowering the performance targets, as illustrated in Example 32.21.

Example 32.21:   Increase in number of equity instruments or modification of vesting conditions?

An entity grants a performance-related award which provides for different numbers of options to vest after 3 years, depending on different performance targets as follows.

Profit growth	Number of options
5% – 10%	100
over 10% – 15%	200
over 15%	300

During the vesting period, the entity concludes that the criteria are too demanding and modifies them as follows.

Profit growth	Number of options
5% – 10%	200
over 10%	300

This raises the issue of whether the entity has changed:

(a)   the performance conditions for the vesting of 200 or 300 options; or

(b)   the number of equity instruments awarded for achieving 5% - 10% or over 10% growth.

In our view, the reality is that the change is to the performance conditions for the vesting of 200 or 300 options, and should therefore be dealt with as in 7.3.1.C, rather than 7.3.1.B, above. Suppose, however, that the conditions had been modified as follows.

Profit growth	Number of options
5% – 10%	200
over 10% – 15%	300
over 15%	400

In that case, there has clearly been an increase in the number of equity instruments subject to an award for an increase of over 15% growth, which would have to be accounted for as such (i.e. under 7.3.1.B, rather than 7.3.1.C, above). In such a case, it might seem more appropriate to deal with the changes to the lower bands as changes to the number of shares awarded rather than changes to the performance conditions.

7.3.2   Modifications that decrease the value of an award

These do not occur very often, as their effect would be somewhat demotivating, although there have been occasional examples of an award being made more onerous – usually in response to criticism by shareholders that the original terms were insufficiently demanding. The general requirement of IFRS 2 is that, where an award is made more onerous (and therefore less valuable), the financial statements must still recognise the cost of the original award. This rule is in part an anti-avoidance measure since, without it, an entity could reverse the cost of an out-of-the-money award by, rather than cancelling the award and triggering an acceleration of expense as in 7.1 above, modifying it so that it was unlikely to vest (for example, by adding unattainable performance conditions).

Chapter 32

7.3.2.A   Decrease in fair value of equity instruments granted

If the modification decreases the fair value of the equity instruments (e.g. by increasing the exercise price or reducing the exercise period), the decrease in value is effectively ignored and the entity continues to recognise a cost for services as if the awards had not been modified. *[IFRS 2.B44(a)]*. Reductions in the fair value of an award by the addition of a market condition or by making an existing market condition more onerous are similarly ignored *[IFRS 2.B44(c)]*, as, presumably, are reductions in the fair value resulting from the addition of a non-vesting condition.

7.3.2.B   Decrease in number of equity instruments granted

If the modification reduces the number of equity instruments granted, IFRS 2 requires the reduction to be treated as a cancellation of that portion of the award (see 7.4 below). *[IFRS 2.B44(b)]*. Essentially this has the effect that any previously unrecognised cost of the cancelled instruments is immediately recognised in full, whereas the cost of an award whose value is reduced by other means continues to be spread in full over the remaining vesting period.

However, in situations where a decrease in the number of equity instruments is combined with other modifications so that the total fair value of the award remains the same or increases, it is unclear whether IFRS 2 requires an approach based on the value of the award as a whole or, as in the previous paragraph, one based on each equity instrument as the unit of account. This is considered further at 7.3.4 below.

7.3.2.C   Additional or more onerous non-market related vesting conditions

Where a non-market vesting condition is modified in a manner not beneficial to the employee, again it is ignored and a cost recognised as if the original award had not been modified, as shown by Example 32.22. *[IFRS 2.B44(c), IG15, IG Example 8]*.

Example 32.22: Award modified by changing non-market performance conditions

At the beginning of year 1, the entity grants 1,000 share options to each member of its sales team, conditional upon the employee remaining in the entity's employment for three years, and the team selling more than 50,000 units of a particular product over the three year period. The fair value of the share options is £15 per option at the date of grant. During year 2, the entity believes that the sales target is insufficiently demanding and increases it to 100,000 units. By the end of year 3, the entity has sold 55,000 units, and the share options are forfeited. Twelve members of the sales team have remained in service for the three year period.

On the basis that the original target would have been met, and twelve employees would have been eligible for awards, the entity would recognise a total cost of £180,000 (12 employees × 1,000 options × £15). The cumulative cost in years 1 and 2 would, as in the Examples above, reflect the entity's best estimate of the *original* 50,000 unit sales target being achieved at the end of year 3. If, conversely, sales of only 49,000 units had been achieved, any cost booked for the award in years 1 and 2 would have been reversed in year 3, since the original target of 50,000 units would not have been met.

7.3.3   Modifications with altered vesting period

As noted at 7.3.1 above, where an award is modified so that its value increases, IFRS 2 requires the entity to continue to recognise an expense for the grant date fair value of the unmodified award over its *original* vesting period, even where the vesting period of the modified award is longer. This appears to have the effect that an expense may be recognised for awards that do not actually vest, as illustrated by Example 32.23 (which is based on Example 32.19 above).

Example 32.23: *Award modified by reducing the exercise price and extending the vesting period*

At the beginning of year 1, an entity grants 100 share options to each of its 500 employees, with vesting conditional upon the employee remaining in service over the next three years. The entity estimates that the fair value of each option is €15.

By the end of year 1, the entity's share price has dropped, and the entity reprices its share options. The repriced share options vest at the end of year 4. The entity estimates that, at the date of repricing, the fair value of each of the original share options granted (i.e. before taking into account the repricing) is €5 and that the fair value of each repriced share option is €7.

40 employees leave during year 1. The entity estimates that a further 70 employees will leave during years 2 and 3, and a further 25 employees during year 4, such that there will be 390 employees at the end of year 3 (500 – 40 – 70) and 365 (500 – 40 – 70 – 25) at the end of year 4.

During year 2, a further 35 employees leave, and the entity estimates that a further 30 employees will leave during year 3 and 30 more in year 4, such that there will be 395 employees at the end of year 3 (500 – 40 – 35 – 30) and 365 (500 – 40 – 35 – 30 – 30) at the end of year 4.

During year 3, a total of 28 employees leave, and hence a total of 103 employees ceased employment during the original three year vesting period, so that, for the remaining 397 employees, the original share options would have vested at the end of year 3. The entity now estimates that only a further 20 employees will leave during year 4, leaving 377 at the end of year 4. In fact 25 employees leave, so that 372 satisfy the criteria for the modified options at the end of year 4.

In our view IFRS 2 requires the entity to recognise:

- the cost of the original award at grant date (€15 per option) over a three year vesting period beginning at the start of year 1, based on the ongoing best estimate of, and ultimately the actual, number of employees at the end of the *original three year* vesting period;

- the incremental fair value of the repriced options at repricing date (€2 per option, being the €7 fair value of each repriced option less the €5 fair value of the original option) over a three year vesting period beginning at the date of repricing (*end* of year one), but based on the ongoing best estimate of, and ultimately the actual, number of employees at the end of the *modified four year* vesting period.

This would be calculated as follows.

Year	Calculation of cumulative expense Original award	Modified award	Cumulative expense (£)	Expense for period (£)
1	390 employees × 100 options × €15 × 1/3		195,000	195,000
2	395 employees × 100 options × €15 × 2/3	365 employees × 100 options × €2 × 1/3	419,333	224,333
3	397 employees × 100 options × €15	377 employees × 100 options × €2 × 2/3	645,767	226,434
4	397 employees × 100 options × €15	372 employees × 100 options × €2	669,900	24,133

It may seem strange that a cost is being recognised for the original award in respect of the 25 employees who leave during year 4, who are never entitled to anything. However, in our view, this is consistent with:

- the overall requirement of IFRS 2 that the minimum cost of a modified award should be the cost that would have recognised if the award had not been modified; and

- IG Example 8 in IFRS 2 (the substance of which is reproduced in Example 32.22 above) where an expense is clearly required to be recognised to the extent that the original performance conditions would have been met if the award had not been modified.

Moreover, as Examples 32.22 and 32.23 illustrate, the rule in IFRS 2 requiring recognition of a minimum expense for a modified award (i.e. as if the original award had remained in place) applies irrespective of whether the effect of the modification is that an award becomes less valuable to the employee (as in Example 32.22) or more valuable to the employee (as in Example 32.23).

7.3.4 *Modifications that reduce the number of equity instruments granted but maintain or increase the value of an award*

As discussed at 7.3.2.A above, cancellation accounting has to be applied to a reduction in the number of equity instruments when a modification reduces both the number of equity instruments granted and the total fair value of the award. *[IFRS 2.B44(b)]*. This approach is consistent with the fact that part of the award has been removed without compensation to the employee. However, because of the demotivating effect and, in some jurisdictions, a requirement to pay compensation in such situations, a modification of this kind is rarely seen in practice. An entity is more likely to modify an award so that the overall fair value remains the same, or increases, even if the number of equity instruments is reduced. These types of modification are considered below.

Where an entity reduces the number of equity instruments but also makes other changes so that the total fair value of the modified award either remains the same as that of the original award as at the modification date or exceeds it, it is unclear whether the accounting should be based on an individual equity instrument or on the award as a whole. Examples 32.24 and 32.25 below illustrate the two situations and the two approaches.

Example 32.24: *Modification where number of equity instruments is reduced but total fair value is unchanged*

An entity granted an employee 200 share options on 1 January 2011. On 31 December 2012 the exercise price of the options is significantly higher than the market price and the options have a fair value of £5 per option. On this date, the entity modifies the award and exchanges the 200 underwater options for 100 'at the money' options with a fair value of £10 each. The fair value of the new awards of £1,000 (100 × £10) equals the fair value of the awards exchanged (200 × £5) so that, for the award as a whole, there is no incremental fair value.

One view is that the unit of account is an individual option. Taking this approach, the decrease in the number of options from 200 to 100 will be accounted for as a cancellation with an acceleration at the modification date of any unexpensed element of the grant date fair value of 100 options. The grant date fair value of the remaining 100 options continues to be recognised over the remainder of the vesting period.

The alternative view is that the total number of options exchanged is the more appropriate unit of account. In this case, the cancellation of the original options and the grant of replacement options are accounted for as a modification. There would therefore be no acceleration of expense in respect of the reduction in the number of options from 200 to 100 and the grant date fair value of the original award would continue to be recognised over the vesting period.

Example 32.25:   *Modification where number of equity instruments is reduced but total fair value is increased*

An entity has previously granted to its employees 1,000 share options with an exercise price equal to the market price of the shares at grant date. The grant date fair value is £10 per option. The entity's share price has declined significantly so that the share price is currently significantly less than the exercise price. The entity decides to reduce the exercise price of the options and, as part of the modification, it also reduces the number of options from 1,000 to 800. At the date of modification, the fair value of the original options is £7 per option and that of the modified options £11 per option.

One view is that the unit of account is an individual option. Taking this approach, the decrease in the number of options from 1,000 to 800 will be accounted for as a cancellation with an acceleration at the modification date of any remaining grant date fair value relating to those 200 options. The grant date fair value of the remaining 800 options continues to be recognised over the remainder of the vesting period together with the incremental fair value of those awards as measured at the modification date. In total the entity will recognise an expense of £13,200 (original grant date fair value of £10,000 (1,000 × £10) plus incremental fair value of £3,200 (800 × £(11 − 7)).

The alternative view is that the more appropriate unit of account is the total number of options as there are linked modifications forming one package. In this case, the incremental fair value is calculated as the difference between the total fair value before and after the modification. In total the entity will recognise an expense of £11,800 (original grant date fair value of £10,000 (1,000 × £10) plus incremental fair value on modification of £1,800 ((800 × £11) − (1,000 × £7)).

In both Examples above, the first view is based on paragraph B44(b) of IFRS 2 which states that 'if the modification reduces the number of equity instruments granted to an employee, that reduction shall be accounted for as a cancellation of that portion of the grant, in accordance with the requirements of paragraph 28'. This is perhaps further supported by paragraph B43(a) which, in providing guidance on accounting for a modification that increases the fair value of an equity instrument, appears only to refer to individual equity instruments when it states that 'the incremental fair value granted' in a modification is 'the difference between the fair value of the modified equity instrument and that of the original equity instrument, both estimated as at the date of modification'.

The alternative view is based on the overriding requirement in paragraph 27 of IFRS 2 for the grant date fair value of the equity instruments to be recognised unless the awards do not vest due to a failure to meet a vesting condition (other than a market condition). This requirement is applicable even if the award is modified after the grant date. The same paragraph also requires an entity to recognise the effect of modifications 'that increase the total fair value of the share-based payment arrangement or are otherwise beneficial to the employee'. This reference to 'total fair value' supports the view that the total award is the unit of account and is reiterated in paragraphs B42 and B44 which provide guidance, respectively, for situations where the total fair value decreases or increases as a consequence of the modification of an award. Supporters of the alternative view further consider that, in contrast to the cancellation accounting approach that is required in the very specific case where part of the award is, in effect, settled for no consideration (see 7.3.2.A above), a modification that reduces the number of equity instruments but maintains or increases the overall fair value of the award clearly provides the counterparty with a benefit. As a consequence, it is considered that no element of the grant date fair value should be accelerated as a cancellation expense.

Given the lack of clarity in IFRS 2, we believe that an entity may make an accounting policy choice as to whether it considers the unit of account to be an individual equity instrument or an award as a whole. However, once made, that accounting policy choice should be applied consistently to all modifications that reduce the number of equity instruments but maintain or increase the overall fair value of an award. Whatever the policy choice, the general requirements of IFRS 2 will still need to be applied in order to determine whether or not it is appropriate to treat an award modified in this way as a modification (in IFRS 2 terms) rather than as a new award (see 7.4.2 and 7.4.4 below).

7.3.5 *Modification of award from equity-settled to cash-settled (and vice versa)*

Occasionally an award that was equity-settled when originally granted is modified so as to become cash-settled, or an originally cash-settled award is modified so as to become equity-settled. Such modifications are discussed at 9.3.4 below.

7.4 Cancellation and settlement

Where an award is cancelled or settled (i.e. cancelled with some form of compensation), other than by forfeiture for failure to satisfy the vesting conditions:

(a) if the cancellation or settlement occurs during the vesting period, it is treated as an acceleration of vesting, and the entity recognises immediately the amount that would otherwise have been recognised for services over the vesting period;

(b) where the entity pays compensation for a cancelled award:

 (i) any compensation paid up to the fair value of the award at cancellation or settlement date (whether before or after vesting) is accounted for as a deduction from equity, as being equivalent to the redemption of an equity instrument;

 (ii) any compensation paid in excess of the fair value of the award at cancellation or settlement date (whether before or after vesting) is accounted for as an expense in profit or loss; and

 (iii) if the share-based payment arrangement includes liability components, the fair value of the liability is remeasured at the date of cancellation or settlement. Any payment made to settle the liability component is accounted for as an extinguishment of the liability; and

(c) if the entity grants new equity instruments during the vesting period and, on the date that they are granted, identifies them as replacing the cancelled or settled instruments, the entity is required to account for the new equity instruments as if they were a modification of the cancelled or settled award. Otherwise it accounts for the new instruments as an entirely new award. *[IFRS 2.28, 29].*

Chapter 32

The treatment of the cancelled or settled award in (a) above is similar, in its effect on profit or loss, to the result that would have occurred if:

- the fair value of the equity instruments issued had been recorded in full at grant date with a corresponding debit to a prepayment for 'services to be rendered';

- the prepayment were written off on a periodic basis until cancellation or settlement; and

- any remaining prepayment at the date of cancellation or settlement were written off in full.

It should be noted that the calculation of any additional expense in (b) above depends on the fair value of the award at the date of cancellation or settlement, not on the cumulative expense already charged. This has the important practical consequence that, when an entity pays compensation on cancellation or settlement of an award, it must obtain a fair value for the original award, updated to the date of cancellation or settlement. If the award had not been cancelled or settled, there would have been no need to obtain a valuation for the original award after the date of grant.

These requirements raise some further detailed issues of interpretation on a number of areas, as follows:

- the distinction between 'cancellation' and 'forfeiture' (see 7.4.1 below);

- the distinction between 'cancellation' and 'modification' (see 7.4.2 below);

- the calculation of the expense on cancellation (see 7.4.3 below); and

- replacement awards (see 7.4.4 and 7.5 below).

7.4.1   Distinction between cancellation and forfeiture

The above provisions of IFRS 2 apply when an award of equity instruments is cancelled or settled 'other than a grant cancelled by forfeiture when the vesting conditions are not satisfied'. *[IFRS 2.28]*. The significance of this is that the terms of many share-based awards provide that they are, or can be, 'cancelled' on forfeiture. IFRS 2 is clarifying that, where an award is forfeited (within the meaning of that term in IFRS 2), the entity should apply the accounting treatment for a forfeiture (i.e. reversal of expense previously recognised), even if the award is cancelled as a consequence of the forfeiture.

7.4.1.A   Termination of employment by entity

In some cases, however, it is not clear whether cancellation or forfeiture has occurred, particularly where options lapse as the result of a termination of employment by the entity. For example, an entity might grant options to an employee on 1 January 2012 on condition of his remaining in employment until at least 31 December 2014. During 2013, however, economic conditions require the entity to make a number of its personnel, including that employee, redundant, as a result of which his options lapse. Is this lapse a forfeiture or a cancellation for the purposes of IFRS 2?

Some argue that, as a result of the redundancy, the employee will be unable to render the service required in order for the options to vest. On this analysis, the lapse of the award should be treated as a forfeiture. This view is supported by column 1 of the table included in paragraph IG24 of the implementation guidance in IFRS 2 which gives, as an example of a forfeiture, an award where a requirement to remain in service 'is not met' – implying that it does not matter whether the failure to meet the condition is due to the actions of the employee or those of the employer.

Others, however, argue that, since the options lapse as a direct result of the employer's actions, the effect is equivalent to a cancellation of the award by the employer. This view is, somewhat ironically, also supported by the table included in paragraph IG24 of the implementation guidance referred to above, column 6 of which gives, as an example of a non-vesting condition, the continuation of the plan by the entity. On this analysis, if the entity chooses to terminate the plan, it breaches a non-vesting condition within its control, requiring cancellation accounting to be applied (see 7.1 above).

In our view, unlikely as it is that the IASB intended such an outcome, both analyses are supportable under IFRS 2, and an entity may adopt either treatment as a choice of accounting policy pending further clarification from the IASB or the Interpretations Committee. It should however be noted that the Interpretations Committee discussed this issue at its September 2010 meeting and tentatively concluded that termination of employment by the entity should be treated as a forfeiture (see 7.4.1.B below).

Another possible analysis might be that the lapse of an award on termination of employment for cause (such as gross misconduct) is a forfeiture, but a lapse on termination in other circumstances is a cancellation. The argument here would essentially be that refraining from gross misconduct is an implied term of any employment contract. An employee dismissed for such conduct has therefore not provided services of an appropriate nature, and the award is accordingly forfeited. We can see some theoretical merit in such an approach, but have the concern – from an auditor's perspective – that it is often difficult to determine the true reason for a termination of employment. There is the added complication that employees, particularly at senior levels of management, whose employment is in reality being terminated, will often agree to tender a letter of resignation for a number of reasons ranging from employment law to media relations.

At first sight, it might seem unlikely that an entity would not wish to treat the lapse of an award on a termination of employment as a forfeiture, given that this will give rise to a profit (as any cost previously recognised is reversed), whereas treatment as a cancellation will give rise to a loss (as any part of the grant date fair value not yet recognised as a cost is accelerated). However, where the employee is granted another award in compensation, the interaction between the rules in IFRS 2 for cancellation and those for replacement awards may make treatment as a cancellation less 'costly' in terms of the overall charge to profit or loss. This is discussed further at 7.5 below.

7.4.1.B Termination of employment by entity: possible future developments

The Interpretations Committee was asked for guidance on the accounting treatment of a share-based payment transaction when the employee's employment is terminated during the vesting period.

Chapter 32

At its September 2010 meeting, the Interpretations Committee considered this issue as part of its work in progress and tentatively decided that if an employee is unable to satisfy a service condition for any reason, including the termination of employment by the entity, the entity should account for this as a forfeiture rather than as a cancellation.[13]

In November 2010 the Interpretations Committee identified this issue as one of the priorities for clarification during its further discussion of the project on vesting and non-vesting conditions (see 3.2.1 above).[14]

7.4.2   *Distinction between cancellation and modification*

One general issue raised by IFRS 2 is where the boundary lies between 'modification' of an award in the entity's favour and outright cancellation of the award. As a matter of legal form, the difference is obvious. However, if an entity were to modify an award in such a way that there was no realistic chance of it ever vesting (for example, by introducing a requirement that the share price increase 1,000,000 times by vesting date), some might argue that this amounts to a *de facto* cancellation of the award. The significance of the distinction is that, whereas the cost of a 'modified' award continues to be recognised on a periodic basis (see 7.3 above), the remaining cost of a cancelled award is recognised immediately.

7.4.3   *Calculation of the expense on cancellation*

The basic accounting treatment for a cancellation and settlement is illustrated in Example 32.26 below.

Example 32.26:   Cancellation and settlement – basic accounting treatment

At the start of year 1 an entity grants an executive 30,000 options on condition that she remain in employment for three years. Each option is determined to have a fair value of $10.

At the end of year 1, the executive is still in employment and the entity charges an IFRS 2 expense of $100,000 (30,000 × $10 × 1/3). At the end of year 2, the executive is still in employment. However, the entity's share price has suffered a decline which the entity does not expect to have reversed by the end of year 3, such that the options, while still 'in the money' now have a fair value of only $6. Moreover, the entity is under pressure from major shareholders to end option schemes with no performance criteria other than continuing employment.

Accordingly, the entity cancels the options and in compensation pays the executive $6.50 per option cancelled, a total payment of $195,000 (30,000 options × $6.50).

IFRS 2 first requires the entity to record a cost as if the options had vested immediately. The total cumulative cost for the award must be $300,000 (300 options × $10). $100,000 was recognised in year 1, so that an additional cost of $200,000 is recognised.

As regards the compensation payment, the fair value of the awards cancelled is $180,000 (30,000 options × $6.00). Accordingly, $180,000 of the payment is accounted for as a deduction from equity, with the remaining payment in excess of fair value, $15,000, charged to profit or loss.

The net effect of this is that an award that ultimately results in a cash payment to the executive of only $195,000 (i.e. $6.50 per option) has resulted in a total charge to profit or loss of $315,000 (i.e. $10.50 per option, representing $10 grant date fair value + $6.50 compensation payment – $6.00 cancellation date fair value).

Example 32.26 illustrates the basic calculation of the cancellation 'charge' required by IFRS 2. In more complex situations, however, the amount of the 'charge' may not be so clear-cut, due to an ambiguity in the drafting of paragraph 28(a) of the standard, which reads as follows:

> 'the entity shall account for the cancellation or settlement as an acceleration of vesting, and shall therefore recognise immediately the amount that would otherwise have been recognised for services received over the remainder of the vesting period.'

There is something of a contradiction within this requirement as illustrated by Example 32.27.

Example 32.27: Cancellation and settlement – best estimate of cancellation expense

On 1 January 2011, an entity (A) granted 150 employees an award of free shares, with a grant date fair value of £5, conditional upon continuous service and performance targets over the 3-year period ending 31 December 2013. The number of shares awarded varies according to the extent to which targets (all non-market vesting conditions) have been met, and could result in each employee still in service at 31 December 2013 receiving a minimum of 600, and a maximum of 1,000 shares.

On 1 July 2012, A is acquired by B, following which all of A's share awards are cancelled. At the time of the cancellation, 130 of the original 150 employees were still in employment. At that time, it was A's best estimate that, had the award run to its full term, 120 employees would have received 900 shares each. Accordingly the cumulative expense recognised by A for the award as at the date of takeover would, under the normal estimation processes of IFRS 2 discussed at 6.1 to 6.4 above, be £270,000 (900 shares × 120 employees × £5 × 18/36).

How should A account for the cancellation of this award? The opening phrase of paragraph 28(a) – 'the entity shall account for the cancellation ...as an acceleration of vesting' – suggests that A should recognise a cost for all 130 employees in service at the date of cancellation. However, the following phrase – '[the entity] shall therefore recognise immediately the amount that would otherwise have been recognised for services received over the remainder of the vesting period' – suggests that the charge should be based on only 120 employees, the best estimate, as at the date of cancellation of the number of employees in whom shares will finally vest. In our view, either reading of paragraph 28(a) is possible.

There is then the issue of the number of shares per employee that should be taken into account in the cancellation charge. Should this be 1,000 shares per employee (the maximum amount that could vest) or 900 shares per employee (the amount expected by the entity at the date of cancellation actually to vest)?

In our view, the intention was probably that the cancellation charge should be based on the number of shares considered likely, at the date of cancellation, to vest for each employee (900 shares in this example).

In extreme cases, the entity might conclude, as at the date of cancellation, that no awards are likely to vest. In this situation, no cancellation expense would be recognised. However, there would need to be evidence that this was not just a rather convenient assessment made as at the date of cancellation. Typically, the previous accounting periods would also have reflected a cumulative IFRS 2 expense of zero on the assumption that the awards would not vest.

An effect of these requirements is that IFRS 2 creates an accounting arbitrage between an award that is 'out of the money' but not cancelled (which continues to be spread over the remaining period to vesting) and one which is formally cancelled (the cost of which is recognised immediately). Entities might well prefer to opt for cancellation so as to create a 'one off' charge to earnings rather than continue to show, particularly during difficult trading periods, significant periodic costs for options that no longer any real value. However, such early cancellation of an award precludes any chance of the cost of the award being reversed through forfeiture during, or at the end of, the vesting period.

7.4.4 Replacement awards

The required accounting treatment of replacement awards, whilst generally clear, nevertheless raises some issues of interpretation.

7.4.4.A Designation of award as replacement award

Whether or not an award is a 'replacement' award (and therefore recognised at only its incremental, not its full, fair value) is determined by whether or not the entity designates it as such on the date that it is granted. In other words, the accounting treatment effectively hinges on declared management intent, notwithstanding the IASB's systematic exclusion of management intent from many other areas of financial reporting. The Basis for Conclusions does not really explain the reason for this approach, which is also hard to reconcile with the fact that the value of an award is unaffected by whether, or when, the entity declares it to be a 'replacement' award for the purposes of IFRS 2. Presumably, the underlying reason is to prevent a retrospective, and possibly opportunistic, assertion that an award that has been in issue for some time is a replacement for an earlier award.

Entities need to ensure that designation occurs on grant date as defined by IFRS 2 (see 5.3 above). For example, if an entity writes to an employee on 15 March 2011 notifying the employee of its intention to procure that the remuneration committee will grant replacement options at its meeting on 15 May 2011, such notification (although formal and in writing) may not strictly meet IFRS 2's requirement for designation on grant date (i.e. 15 May 2011).

As drafted, IFRS 2 gives entities an apparently free choice to designate any newly granted awards as replacement awards. In our view, however, such designation cannot credibly be made unless there is evidence of some connection between the cancelled and replacement awards. This might be that the cancelled and replacement awards involve the same counterparties, or that the cancellation and replacement are part of the same arrangement.

7.4.4.B Incremental fair value of replacement award

Where an award is designated as a replacement award, it must be recognised, over its vesting period, at its incremental fair value. This is the difference between the fair value of the replacement award and the 'net fair value' of the cancelled or settled award, both measured at the date on which the replacement awards are granted. The net fair value of the cancelled or settled award is the fair value of the award, immediately before cancellation, less any compensation payment that is accounted for as a deduction from equity. *[IFRS 2.28(c)]*. Thus the 'net fair value' of the original award can never be less than zero (since any compensation payment in excess of the fair value of the cancelled award would be accounted for in profit or loss, not in equity – see Example 32.26 at 7.4.3 above).

There is some confusion within IFRS 2 as to whether a different accounting treatment is intended to result from, on the one hand, modifying an award and, on the other hand, cancelling it and replacing it with a new award on the same terms as the modified award. This is explored in Example 32.28 below, which is based on the same fact pattern as Example 32.19 at 7.3.1.A above.

Example 32.28:   Accounting arbitrage between modification and cancellation of award?

At the beginning of year 1, an entity grants 100 share options to each of its 500 employees. Each grant is conditional upon the employee remaining in service over the next three years. The entity estimates that the fair value of each option is €15.

By the end of year 1, the entity's share price has dropped. The entity cancels the existing options and issues options which it identifies as replacement options, which also vest at the end of year 3. The entity estimates that, at the date of cancellation, the fair value of each of the original share options granted is €5 and that the fair value of each replacement share option is €8.

40 employees leave during year 1. The entity estimates that a further 70 employees will leave during years 2 and 3, so that there will be 390 employees at the end of year 3 (500 – 40 – 70).

During year 2, a further 35 employees leave, and the entity estimates that a further 30 employees will leave during year 3, so that there will be 395 employees at the end of year 3 (500 – 40 – 35 – 30).

During year 3, a total of 28 employees leave, and hence a total of 103 employees ceased employment during the original three year vesting period, so that, for the remaining 397 employees, the replacement share options vest at the end of year 3.

The intention of the IASB appears to have been that the arrangement should be accounted for in exactly the same way as the modification in Example 32.19 above, since paragraph 233 of the Basis for Conclusions to IFRS 2 notes:

> '...the Board saw no difference between a repricing of share options and a cancellation of share options followed by the granting of replacement share options at a lower exercise price, and therefore concluded that the accounting treatment should be the same.'

However, it is not clear that this intention is actually reflected in the drafting of IFRS 2, paragraph 28 of which reads as follows:

> 'If a grant of equity instruments is cancelled or settled during the vesting period (other than a grant cancelled by forfeiture when the vesting conditions are not satisfied):
>
> (a)   the entity shall account for the cancellation or settlement as an acceleration of vesting, and shall therefore recognise immediately the amount that otherwise would have been recognised for services received over the remainder of the vesting period.
>
> (b)   any payment made to the employee on the cancellation or settlement of the grant shall be accounted for as the repurchase of an equity interest, i.e. as a deduction from equity, except to the extent that the payment exceeds the fair value of the equity instruments granted, measured at the repurchase date. Any such excess shall be recognised as an expense....
>
> (c)   if new equity instruments are granted to the employee and, on the date when those new equity instruments are granted, the entity identifies the new equity instruments granted as replacement equity instruments for the cancelled equity instruments, the entity shall account for the granting of replacement equity instruments in the same way as a modification of the original grant of equity instruments ...'

As a matter of natural construction, paragraph (a) requires the cancellation of the existing award to be treated as an acceleration of vesting – explicitly and without qualification. In particular there is no rider to the effect that the requirement of paragraph (a) is to be read as 'subject to paragraph (c) below'.

Paragraph (c) requires any 'new equity instruments' granted to be accounted for in the same way as a modification of the original grant of equity instruments. It does not require this treatment for the cancellation of the *original* instruments, because this has already been addressed in paragraph (a).

Moreover, in order to construe paragraphs (a) and (c) in a manner consistent with the Basis for Conclusions to the standard, it would be necessary to read paragraph (c) as effectively superseding paragraph (a). However, for this to be a valid reading, it would also be necessary to read paragraph (b) as also superseding paragraph (a), and this would produce a manifestly incorrect result, namely that, if an award is cancelled *and settled*, there is no need ever to expense any part of the cancelled award not yet expensed at the date of cancellation.

Therefore, the main text in IFRS 2 appears to require the entity to recognise:

- The entire cost of the original options at the end of year 1 (since cancellation has the effect that they are treated as vesting at that date), based on the 390 employees expected at the date to be in employment at the end of the vesting period. This is not the only possible interpretation of the requirement of paragraph 28(a) – see the broader discussion in Example 32.27 at 7.4.3 above.

- The incremental fair value of the replacement options at repricing date (€3 per option, being the €8 fair value of each replacement option less the €5 fair value of the cancelled option) over a two year vesting period beginning at the date of cancellation (end of year one), based on the (at first estimated and then actual) number of employees at the end of year 3.

This would be calculated as follows.

Year	Calculation of cumulative expense Original award	Replacement award	Cumulative expense (€)	Expense for period (€)
1	390 employees × 100 options × €15	–	585,000	585,000
2	390 employees × 100 options × €15	395 employees × 100 options × €3 × 1/2	644,250	59,250
3	390 employees × 100 options × €15	397 employees × 100 options × €3	704,100	59,850

By contrast, the accounting treatment implied by the Basis for Conclusions is as follows (see Example 32.19 above):

Year	Calculation of cumulative expense Original award (a)	Modified award (b)	Cumulative expense (€) (a+b)	Expense for period (€)
1	390 employees × 100 options × €15 × 1/3	–	195,000	195,000
2	395 employees × 100 options × €15 × 2/3	395 employees × 100 options × €3 × 1/2	454,250	259,250
3	397 employees × 100 options × €15	397 employees × 100 options × €3	714,600	260,350

It will be seen that both the periodic allocation of expense and the total expense differ under each interpretation. This is because, under the first interpretation, the cost of the original award is accelerated at the end of year 1 for all 390 employees expected at that date to be in employment at the end of the vesting period, whereas under the second interpretation a cost is recognised for the 397 employees whose awards finally vest. The difference between the two total charges of €10,500 (€714,600 – €704,100) represents 397 – 390 = 7 employees @ €1,500 [100 options × €15] each = €10,500.

We believe that either interpretation is valid, and an entity should adopt one or other consistently as a matter of accounting policy.

7.4.4.C   Replacement of vested awards

The rules for replacement awards summarised in paragraph (c) at 7.4 above apply 'if a grant of equity instruments is cancelled or settled during the vesting period ...'. *[IFRS 2.28].* This begs the question of the required treatment for a replacement award granted after the original award has vested. There is of course no question of accelerating the cost of the cancelled award in such cases, as it has already been recognised during the vesting period. The issue is rather the treatment of the new award itself. Whilst IFRS 2 does not explicitly address this point, it appears that such a replacement award should be treated as if it were a completely new award. In other words, its full fair value should be recognised immediately or, if there are any vesting conditions for the replacement award, over its vesting period.

By contrast, the rules for modification of awards discussed in 7.3 above apply whether the award has vested or not. Paragraphs 26 and 27 of IFRS 2 (modifications) are not restricted to events 'during the vesting period' in contrast to paragraph 28 (cancellation and settlement, including replacement awards), which is restricted to events 'during the vesting period'.

This has the effect that the accounting cost of modifying an already vested award (i.e. the incremental fair value of the modified award) may be lower than the cost of cancelling and replacing it, which requires the full fair value of the new award to be expensed. However, the fair value of the new award will be reduced by the fair value of the cancelled award that the employee has surrendered as part of the consideration for the new award. This analysis produces an accounting outcome similar to that of the modification of an unvested award.

7.5 Replacement award on termination of employment

When an employee's employment is terminated during the vesting period of an award of shares or options, the award will typically lapse in consequence. It is common in such situations, particularly where the employee was part of the senior management, for the entity to make an alternative award, or to allow the employee to retain existing awards, as part of the package of benefits agreed with the employee on termination of employment.

Generally, such an award is an *ex gratia* award – in other words, it is a voluntary award to which the outgoing employee had no legal entitlement. However, a number of plan rules set out, in a 'good leaver' clause (see 5.3.8.C above), the terms on which any *ex gratia* award may be made, usually by applying a formula to determine, or limit, how much of the original award can be considered to have vested. In many cases the award will be made on a fully vested basis, i.e. the employee has full entitlement without further conditions needing to be fulfilled. In some cases, however, an employee will be allowed to retain awards that remain subject to the fulfilment of the original conditions (other than future service). Whichever form the award takes, in IFRS 2 terms it will be treated as vesting at the date of termination of employment because any remaining conditions will be accounted for as non-vesting conditions in the absence of an explicit or implied service condition (see 3.2 above).

Because IFRS 2 is unclear about whether the termination of employment should be accounted for as a forfeiture or as a cancellation, there is more than one view as to how IFRS 2 requires such awards to be accounted for, as illustrated in Example 32.29 below.

It should be noted that the Interpretations Committee tentatively decided in September 2010 that if an employee is unable to satisfy a service condition for any reason, including termination of employment, this should be accounted for as a forfeiture rather than as a cancellation (see 7.4.1.B above). However, the Interpretations Committee did not specifically address the accounting for any replacement awards on termination of employment. The continued availability of an accounting policy choice, as illustrated in Example 32.29 below, should therefore be considered in the light of any further discussions by the Interpretations Committee.

Example 32.29:   Replacement award on termination of employment

On 1 January 2011, an executive is granted the right to 10,000 free shares on condition of remaining in service until 31 December 2013. The fair value of the award at grant date is £2.00 per share.

On 31 December 2012, the executive's employment is terminated and he therefore loses his right to any shares. However, as *ex gratia* (voluntary) compensation, the remuneration committee awards him 6,667 shares vesting immediately. At 31 December 2012, the share price was £4.00, and the fair value of the original award was £3.60 per share. (This is lower than the current share price because the holder of a share is entitled to receive any dividends paid during 2013, whereas the holder of an unvested right to a share is not – see 8.5.4 below).

This raises the question of how the *ex gratia* award of 6,667 shares should be accounted for. In our view, the starting point for any analysis is whether the entity, as a matter of accounting policy, accounts for the lapse of award on termination of employment by the entity as a forfeiture or as a cancellation (see 7.4.1.A and 7.4.1.B above).

The factors to be considered in determining the grant date in such cases are discussed further at 5.3.8.C above. For the purposes of this Example, it is assumed that the replacement award is treated as having been granted on 31 December 2012 rather than 1 January 2011.

If the lapse is treated as a forfeiture, the entity:

- reverses the cost already booked for the award of £13,333 (10,000 shares × £2 × 2/3); and
- recognises the cost of the *ex gratia* award (at the fair value at that award's grant date) of £26,668 (6,667 shares × £4)

This results in a net charge on termination of £13,335.

If the lapse is treated as a cancellation, the entity:

- accelerates the cost not yet booked for the original award of £6,667 (10,000 shares × £2 = £20,000, less £13,333 already recognised – see above); and
- treats the *ex gratia* award as a replacement award. The fair value of the replacement award of £26,668 (6,667 shares × £4 – see above) is compared to the fair value of the original award of £36,000 (10,000 shares × £3.60). Since the fair value of the replacement award is less than that of the original award, there is no incremental cost required to be recorded under IFRS 2.

This results in a net charge on termination of £6,667.

Some support a third analysis which argues that, of the original award of 10,000 shares:

- 3,333 are forfeited, giving rise to a reversal of expense previously charged of £4,444 (3,333 shares × £2 × 2/3);
- 6,667 have their terms modified, by changing the vesting period from one year (as at 31 December 2012) to immediate vesting. A service period is a non-market vesting condition which is not factored into the fair value of the award. Thus, although the modification clearly enhances the 'real' value of the award, it has no effect on its value for the purposes of IFRS 2 (see 7.3.1.C above). Therefore there is no incremental cost required to be recorded under IFRS 2, and the entity simply accelerates the cost (based on the original grant date fair value) not yet recognised for the awards of £4,444 (6,667 shares × £2 = £13,334, less the amount already recognised of £8,890 [6,667 shares × £2 × 2/3]).

This results in no profit or loss arising on the termination of employment. We do not believe that this approach is appropriate. In our view, the award must be considered as either forfeited and replaced as a whole, or as cancelled and replaced as a whole. An approach that treats some part of the award as forfeited and some as modified effectively treats the original award as 10,000 awards of one share rather than what we regard as its true economic substance of one award of 10,000 shares.

7.6 Possible future modification or replacement of award – impact on estimation process at reporting date

As discussed at 6.1.1 and 6.1.2 above, IFRS 2 requires an entity to determine a cumulative IFRS 2 charge at each reporting date by reference to the 'best available estimate' of the number of awards that will vest (within the special meaning of that term in IFRS 2).

In addition to the normal difficulties inherent in any estimation process, IFRS 2 brings the further complication that it is not entirely clear as to which anticipated future events should be taken into account in the estimation process and which should not, as illustrated by Example 32.30 below.

Example 32.30:   Estimation of number of awards expected to vest – treatment of anticipated future events

On 1 January 2012, an entity granted an award of 1,000 shares to each of its 600 employees at a particular manufacturing unit. The award vests on completion of three years' service at 31 December 2014. As at 31 December 2012, the entity firmly intends to close the unit, and terminate the employment of employees, as part of a rationalisation programme. This closure would occur on or around 1 July 2013. The entity has not, however, announced its intentions or taken any other steps so as to allow provision for the closure under IAS 37 – *Provisions, Contingent Liabilities and Contingent Assets* (see Chapter 29 at 5.2).

Under the original terms of the award, the award would lapse on termination of employment. However, the entity intends to compensate employees made redundant by changing the terms of their award so as to allow full vesting on termination of employment.

What is the 'best estimate', as at 31 December 2012, of the number of awards expected to vest? Specifically should the entity:

(a) ignore the intended closure altogether, on the grounds that there is no other recognition of it in the financial statements;

(b) take account of the impact of the intended closure on vesting of the current award, but ignore the intended modification to the terms of the award to allow vesting; or

(c) take account of both the intended closure and the intended modification of the award?

In our view, there is no basis in IFRS 2 for anticipating the modification of an award. The entity must account for awards in issue at the reporting date, not those that might be in issue in the future. Accordingly we do not consider approach (c) above to be appropriate.

Equally, we struggle to support approach (a) above. IFRS 2 requires the entity to use its 'best available estimate' and its best available estimate must be that the unit will be closed, and the employees' employment terminated, in 2013. This view is supported by the fact that, unlike IAS 36 – *Impairment of Assets* (see Chapter 22) and IAS 37 (see Chapter 29), IFRS 2 does not explicitly prohibit an entity from taking account of the consequences of reorganisations and similar transactions to which it is not yet committed.

Accordingly, we believe that approach (b) should be followed. The actual effect of doing so will depend on the view taken by the entity as to whether the loss of an award on termination of employment by the entity is a forfeiture or a cancellation (see 7.4.1.A and 7.4.1.B above).

If the entity takes the view that such a termination is a cancellation, we believe IFRS 2 requires a cancellation to be accounted for only when it happens (i.e. in 2013).

If, however, the entity takes the view that such a termination is a forfeiture, the entity's best estimate, at 31 December 2012, must be that the award currently in place will vest in no employees (because they will be made redundant before the end of the vesting period). It therefore reverses any cost previously recorded for the award. When the award is modified at the time of the redundancy in 2013 to allow full vesting, the entity will recognise the full cost of the modified award. This will have what many may see as the less than ideal result that the entity will recognise a credit in profit or loss in 2012 and a loss in 2013, even though there has been no change in management's best estimate of the overall outcome. This follows from the analysis, discussed above, that we do not believe that the entity can, in 2012, account for the award on the basis of what its terms may be in 2013.

7.7   Two awards running 'in parallel'

In some jurisdictions, it is not readily possible formally to cancel or modify an award. This may be because formal cancellation or modification may trigger either a legal requirement for the entity to pay compensation to the holder, or adverse tax consequences for the holder. In such cases, where an award has become unattractive (for example, because it is 'out-of-the-money'), the entity, rather than formally cancelling or modifying the award, may instead issue a second award. The second award cannot be designated as a replacement award, because the original award is still in place. Thus, the entity has two awards running 'in parallel'.

However, a mechanism is then put in place to ensure that the employee can effectively receive only one award. For instance, if the original award were 1,000 options, it might be replaced with a second award of 1,000 options, but with the proviso that, if options under one award are exercised, the number of options exercisable under the other award is correspondingly reduced, so that no more than 1,000 options can be exercised in total.

The accounting for such arrangements is discussed in Example 32.31 below.

Example 32.31:   Two option awards running in parallel

On 1 January 2011, the entity granted 1,000 options (the 'A options') to an employee, subject to non-market vesting conditions. The grant date fair value of an A option was €50.

As at 1 January 2012, the share price is significantly below the exercise price of an A option, which had a fair value at that date of €5. Without modifying or cancelling the A options, the entity awards the employee 1,000 new options (the 'B options'). The B options are subject to non-market vesting conditions different in nature from, and more onerous than, those applicable to the A options, but have a lower exercise price. The terms of the B options include a provision that for every A option that is exercised, the number of B options that can be exercised is reduced by one, and *vice-versa*. The fair value of a B option at 1 January 2012 is €15.

Clearly, the employee will exercise whichever series of options, A or B, has the higher intrinsic value. There are four possible outcomes:

1. Neither the A options nor the B options vest.
2. Only the A options vest.
3. Only the B options vest.
4. Both the A options and B options vest and the employee must choose which to exercise. Rationally, the employee would exercise the B options as they have the lower exercise price.

In our view, the B options are most appropriately accounted for as if they were a modification of the A options. As only one series of options can be exercised, we believe that the most appropriate treatment is to account for whichever award the entity believes, at each reporting date, is more likely to be exercised. This is analogous to the accounting treatment we suggest in Example 32.12 at 6.2.5 above and in Example 32.17 at 6.3.6 above.

If the entity believes that neither award will vest, any expense previously recorded would be reversed.

If the entity believes that only the A options will vest, it will recognise expense based on the grant date fair value of the A options (€50 each).

If the entity believes that only the B options will vest, or that both the A and B options will vest (so that, in either case, the B options will be exercised), it will recognise expense based on:

(a) the grant date fair value of the A options (€50 each) over the original vesting period of the A options, plus

(b) the incremental fair value of the B options, as at their grant date (€10 each, being their €15 fair value less the €5 fair value of an A option), over the vesting period of the B options.

A possible alternative analysis would have been that modification accounting is not applied, each award is accounted for separately, and the requirement that only one award can vest is treated as a non-vesting condition (i.e. it is a condition of exercising the A options that the B options are not exercised, and *vice-versa*) – see 6.4 above. This treatment would result in a charge representing the total fair value of both awards at their respective grant dates. This is because the entity would recognise an expense for whichever series of options was exercised plus a charge for the cancellation of the second series (by reason of the employee's failure to satisfy a non-vesting condition in the employee's control, namely refraining from exercising the first series of options).

7.8 Share splits and consolidations

It is common for an entity to divide its existing equity share capital into a larger number of shares (share splits) or to consolidate its existing share capital into a smaller number of shares (share consolidations). The impact of such splits and consolidations is not specifically addressed in IFRS 2, and a literal application of IFRS 2 could lead to some rather anomalous results.

Suppose that an employee has options over 100 shares in the reporting entity, with an exercise price of £1. The entity undertakes a '1 for 2' share consolidation – i.e. the number of shares in issue is halved such that, all other things being equal, the value of one share in the entity after the consolidation is twice that of one share before the consolidation.

IFRS 2 is required to be applied to modifications to an award arising from equity restructurings. *[IFRS 2.BC24]*. However, in most cases, a share scheme will provide that, following the consolidation, the employee holds options over only 50 shares with an exercise price of £2. All things being equal, it would be expected that the modified award would have the same fair value as the original award and, therefore, there would be no incremental expense to be accounted for.

It may be that the scheme has no such provision for automatic adjustment, such that the employee still holds options over 100 shares. The clear economic effect is that the award has been modified, since its value has been doubled. However, it could be argued that, on a literal reading of IFRS 2, no modification has occurred, since the employee holds options over 100 shares at the same exercise price before and after the consolidation. The Interpretations Committee discussed this issue at its July and November 2006 meetings but decided not to take it onto its agenda because it 'was not a normal commercial occurrence and ... unlikely to have widespread significance'.[15] This decision was re-confirmed by the Interpretations Committee in March 2011.[16] In our view, whilst it would seem appropriate to have regard to the substance of the transaction, and treat it as giving rise to a modification, it must be admitted that such a treatment can be argued not to be required by IFRS 2 as drafted, particularly given the decision of the Interpretations Committee not to discuss the issue further.

Sometimes, the terms of an award give the entity discretion to make modifications at a future date in response to more complex changes to the share structure, such as those arising from bonus issues, share buybacks and rights issues where the effect on existing options may not be so clear-cut. These are discussed further at 5.3.8 above.

8   EQUITY-SETTLED TRANSACTIONS – VALUATION

8.1   Introduction

This is a key issue for the implementation of IFRS 2. The IASB provides some guidance in Appendix B to the standard, which we summarise and elaborate upon below. Whilst the guidance is framed in terms of awards to employees which are valued at grant date, many of the general principles would apply equally to awards valued at service date. *[IFRS 2.B1].*

As discussed in more detail at 4 to 7 above, IFRS 2 requires a 'modified grant-date' approach, under which the fair value of an equity award is estimated on the grant date without regard to the possibility that any service conditions or non-market performance vesting conditions will not be met. Although the broad intention of IFRS 2 is to recognise the cost of the goods or services to be received, the IASB believes that, in the case of services from employees, the fair value of the share-based payment is more readily determinable than the fair value of the services received.

As noted at 5.1 above, IFRS 2 defines fair value as 'the amount for which an asset could be exchanged, a liability settled, or an equity instrument granted could be exchanged, between knowledgeable, willing parties in an arm's length transaction'.

IFRS 2 requires fair value to be determined based on the available information that ranks highest in the following hierarchy:

- Level 1 – observable market prices of identical instruments in active markets
- Level 2 – observable market prices of similar instruments in active markets
- Level 3 – valuation techniques.

While fair value may be readily determinable for awards of shares, market quotations are not available for long-term, non-transferable share options because these instruments are not generally traded.

As discussed further at 8.2.2 below, the fair value of an option at any point in time is made up of two basic components – intrinsic value and time value. Intrinsic value is the greater of (a) the market value of the underlying share less the exercise price of the option and (b) zero.

Time value reflects the potential of the option for future gain to the holder, given the length of time during which the option will be outstanding, and possible changes in the share price during that period. Because the information described in Levels 1 and 2 of the fair value hierarchy is not normally available for an employee share option, the IASB believes that the fair value of a share option awarded to an employee generally must be estimated using an option-pricing model. *[IFRS 2.BC130].* This is discussed further at 8.3 below.

The discussion below aims to provide guidance on the valuation of options and similar awards under IFRS 2. It is not intended to provide detailed instructions for constructing an option pricing model.[17]

The approach to determining the fair value of share-based payments will continue to be that specified in IFRS 2 and share-based payments will be outside the scope of IFRS 13 which applies more generally to the use of fair value under IFRSs with effect from 1 January 2013 (see Chapter 16).

8.2 Options

8.2.1 *Call options – overview*

Before considering the particular features of employee share options that make their valuation particularly difficult, a general overview of call options may be useful.

Call options give the holder the right, but not the obligation, to buy the underlying shares at a specified price (the 'exercise' or 'strike' price) on, or before, a specified date. Share-based payments take the form of call options over the underlying shares.

Options are often referred to as American or European. American options can be exercised at any time up to the expiry date, whereas European options can be exercised only on the expiry date itself.

The terms of employee options commonly have features of both American and European options, in that there is a period, generally two or three years, during which the option cannot be exercised (i.e. the vesting period). At the end of this period, if the options vest, they can be exercised at any time up until the expiry date. This type of option is known as a Window American option or Bermudan option.

A grant of shares is equivalent to an option with an exercise price of zero and will be exercised regardless of the share price on the vesting date. Throughout the discussion below, any reference to share options therefore includes reference to share grants or zero strike price options. Further discussion of grants of free shares may be found at 8.7.1 below.

8.2.2   Call options – valuation

As noted in 8.1 above, option value consists of intrinsic value and time value. Intrinsic value, for a call option, is the greater of:

•   the share price less the exercise price, and

•   zero.

Figure 32.2 below sets out the intrinsic value (or payoff) for a call option with an exercise price of $5.00.

Figure 32.2:   Intrinsic value of a call option

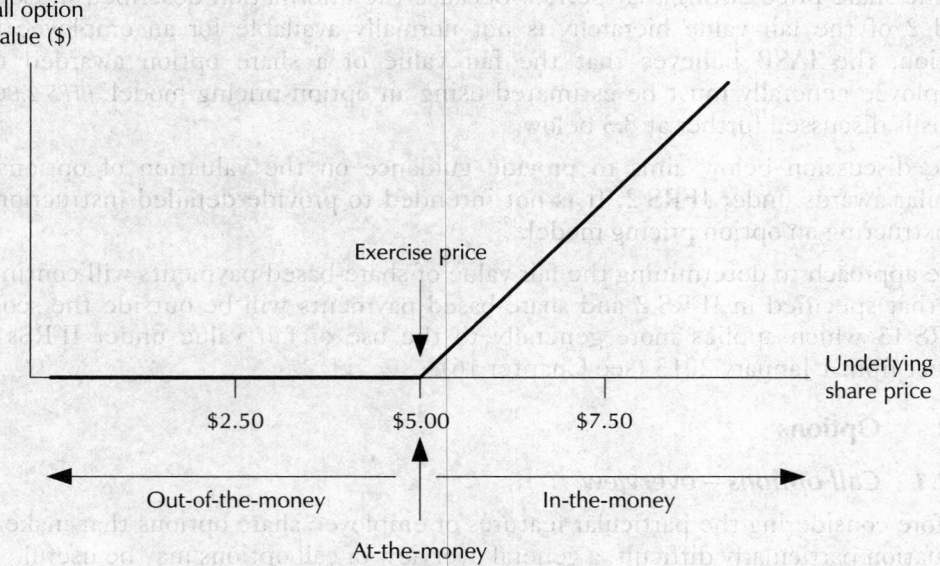

A call option is said to be 'in-the-money' when the share price is above the exercise price of the option and 'out-of-the-money' when the share price is less than the exercise price. An option is 'at-the-money' when the share price equals the exercise price of the option.

The time value of an option arises from the time remaining to expiry. As well as the share price and the exercise price, it is impacted by the volatility of the share price, time to expiry, dividend yield and the risk-free interest rate and the extent to which it is in- or out-of-the-money. For example, when the share price is significantly less than the exercise price, the option is said to be 'deeply' out-of-the-money. In this case, the fair value consists entirely of time value, which decreases the more the option is out-of-the-money.

The main inputs to the value of a simple option are:

- the exercise price of the option;
- the term of the option;
- the current market price of the underlying share;
- the expected future volatility of the price of the underlying share;
- the dividends expected to be paid on the shares during the life of the option (if any); and
- the risk-free interest rate(s) for the expected term of the option.

Their effect on each of the main components of the total value (intrinsic value and time value) is shown in Figure 32.3 below.

Figure 32.3:   Determinants of the fair value of a call option

The effect of these inputs on the value of a call option can be summarised as follows:

If this variable increases,	the option value ...
Share price	Increases
Exercise price	Decreases
Volatility	Increases
Time to expiry	Usually increases*
Interest rate	Increases
Dividend yield/payout	Decreases

*   When there is a dividend yield and the option is considerably in-the-money, an option may have a zero or negative time value. In this case, as the time to expiry increases, a European call option will reduce in value and an American call option will stay constant in value.

The factors to be considered in estimating the determinants of an option value in the context of IFRS 2 are considered in more detail at 8.5 below.

8.2.3   Factors specific to employee share options

In addition to the factors referred to in 8.2.2 above, employee share options are also affected by a number of specific factors that can affect their true economic value. These factors, not all of which are taken into account for IFRS 2 valuation purposes (see 8.4 and 8.5 below), include the following:

- non-transferability (see 8.2.3.A below);
- continued employment requirement (see 8.2.3.B below);
- vesting and non-vesting conditions (see 8.2.3.C below);
- periods during which holders cannot exercise their options – referred to in various jurisdictions as 'close', 'restricted' or 'blackout' periods (see 8.2.3.D below);
- limited ability to hedge option values (see 8.2.3.E below); and
- dilution effects (see 8.2.3.F below).

8.2.3.A   Non-transferability

Holders of 'ordinary' share options can choose to 'sell' their options (typically by writing a call option on the same terms) rather than exercise them. By contrast, employee share options are generally non-transferable, leading to early (and sub-optimal) exercise of the option. This will lower the value of the options.

8.2.3.B   Continued employment requirement

Holders of ordinary share options can maintain their positions until they wish to exercise, regardless of other circumstances. In contrast, employee share options cannot normally be held once employment is terminated. If the options have not vested, they will be lost. If the options have vested, the employee will be forced to exercise the options immediately or within a short timescale, or forfeit them altogether, losing all time value. This will lower the value of the options.

8.2.3.C   Vesting and non-vesting conditions

Holders of ordinary share options have an unconditional right to exercise their options. In contrast, employee share options may have vesting and non-vesting conditions attached to them, which may not be met, reducing their value. This is discussed in more detail in 8.4 below.

A non-market vesting condition, while reducing the 'true' fair value of an award, does not directly affect its valuation for the purposes of IFRS 2 (see 6.2 above). However, non-market vesting conditions may indirectly affect the value. For example, when an award vests on satisfaction of a particular target rather than at a specified time, its value may vary depending on the assessment of when that target will be met, since that may influence the expected life of the award, which is relevant to its fair value under IFRS 2 (see 8.2.2 above and 8.5.1 below).

8.2.3.D   Periods during which exercise is restricted

Holders of ordinary American or Bermudan share options can exercise at any time during the exercisable window. In contrast, employees may be subject to 'blackout' periods in which they cannot exercise their options, for example to prevent insider trading. While this could conceivably make a significant impact if the shares were significantly mis-priced in the market, in an efficient market blackout periods will only marginally decrease the value.

8.2.3.E   Limited ability to hedge option values

In the case of ordinary share options, it is reasonable to justify the theoretical valuation on the basis that, for any other value, arbitrage opportunities could arise through hedging. In contrast, employee share options are usually awarded only in relatively small amounts, and the employees are usually subject to restrictions on share trading (especially short selling the shares, as would be required to hedge an option). This, in combination with the non-transferability of the options (see 8.2.3.A above), means that exercising is the only way to remove exposure, which lowers the value of the options.

8.2.3.F   Dilution effects

When third parties write traded share options, upon exercise the writer delivers shares to the option holder, so that the exercise of the traded share options has no dilutive effect. By contrast, if an entity writes share options to employees and, when those share options are exercised, issues new shares (or uses shares previously repurchased and held in treasury) to settle the awards, there is a dilutive effect. As the shares will be issued at the exercise price rather than the current market price at the date of exercise, this actual or potential dilution may reduce the share price, so that the option holder does not make as large a gain as would arise on the exercise of similar traded options which do not dilute the share price.

8.3   Selection of an option-pricing model

Where, as will almost invariably be the case, there are no traded options over the entity's equity instruments that mirror the terms of share options granted to employees, IFRS 2 requires the fair value of options granted to be estimated using an option-pricing model. The entity must consider all factors that would be considered by knowledgeable, willing market participants in selecting a model. *[IFRS 2.B4-5].*

The IASB notes that it decided that it was not necessary or appropriate to prescribe the precise formula or model to be used for option valuation. There is no particular option pricing model that is regarded as theoretically superior to the others, and there is the risk that any model specified might be superseded by improved methodologies in the future. *[IFRS 2.BC131].*

The three most common option-pricing methodologies for valuing employee options are:

- the Black-Scholes-Merton formula (see 8.3.1 below);
- the binomial model (see 8.3.2 below); and
- the Monte Carlo Simulation (see 8.3.3 below).

It is important to understand all the terms and conditions of a share-based payment arrangement, as this will influence the choice of the most appropriate option pricing model.

IFRS 2 names the Black-Scholes-Merton formula and the binomial model as examples of acceptable models to use when estimating fair value *[IFRS 2.BC152]*, while noting that there are certain circumstances in which the Black-Scholes-Merton formula may not be the most appropriate model (see 8.3.1 below). Moreover, there may be instances where, due to the particular terms and conditions of the share-based payment arrangement, neither of these models is appropriate, and another methodology is more appropriate to achieving the intentions of IFRS 2. A model commonly used for valuing more complex awards is Monte Carlo Simulation (often combined with the Black-Scholes-Merton formula or the binomial model). This can deal with the complexities of a plan such as one based on relative total shareholder return (TSR), which compares the return on a fixed sum invested in the entity to the return on the same amount invested in a peer group of entities.

8.3.1   *The Black-Scholes-Merton formula*

The Black-Scholes-Merton methodology is commonly used for assessing the value of a freely-traded put or call option. In recent years the formula has been further developed to allow the incorporation of static dividends on shares. The assumptions underlying the Black-Scholes-Merton formula are as follows:

- the option can be exercised only on the expiry date (i.e. it is a European option);
- there are no taxes or transaction costs and no margin requirements;
- the volatility of the underlying asset is constant and is defined as the standard deviation of the continuously compounded rates of return on the share over a specified period;
- the risk-free interest rate is constant over time;
- short selling is permitted;
- there are no risk-free arbitrage opportunities;
- there are log normal returns (i.e. the continuously compounded rate of return is normally distributed); and
- security trading is continuous.

The main limitation of the Black-Scholes-Merton methodology is that it only calculates the option price at one point in time. It does not consider the steps along the way when there could be a possibility of early exercise of an American option (although as discussed at 8.4 below this can be partially mitigated by using an assumed expected term as an input to the calculation).

The Black-Scholes-Merton formula is an example of a closed-form model, which is a valuation model that uses an equation to produce an estimated fair value. The formula is as shown in Figure 32.4 below.

Figure 32.4:   *The Black-Scholes-Merton formula*

$$c = S_0 e^{-qT} N(d_1) - K e^{-rT} N(d_2)$$

Where :

$$d_1 = \frac{\ln(S_0 / K) + (r - q + \sigma^2 / 2)T}{\sigma\sqrt{T}}$$

$$d_2 = d_1 - \sigma\sqrt{T}$$

$c =$	price of a written call
$S_0 =$	price of the underlying share
$N =$	the cumulative probability distribution function for a standardised normal distribution
$q =$	dividend yield (continuously compounded)
$K =$	call option exercise price
$r =$	the continuously compounded risk-free rate
$\sigma =$	annualised volatility of the underlying share
$T =$	time to expiry (in years)

Note: 'e' represents the mathematical constant, the base of the natural logarithm (2.718282...), and 'ln' is the natural logarithm of the indicated value

Whilst the Black-Scholes-Merton formula is complex, its application in practice is relatively easy. It can be programmed into a spreadsheet, and numerous programs and calculators exist that use it to calculate the fair value of an option. As a result, the formula is used widely by finance professionals to value a large variety of options. However, a number of the assumptions underlying the formula may be better suited to valuing short-term, exchange-traded share options rather than employee share options.

The attributes of employee share options that render the Black-Scholes-Merton formula less effective as a valuation technique include:

- *Long term to expiry*

  The formula assumes that volatility, interest rates, dividends and share price are constant over the life of the option. While this may be appropriate when valuing short-term options, assuming constant values is less appropriate when valuing long-term options.

- *Non-transferability and early exercise*

  The formula assumes a fixed maturity/exercise date. While IFRS 2 provides for the use of an 'expected term' in place of the contractual life to reflect the possibility of early exercise resulting from the non-transferability of employee share options or other reasons (see 8.5 below), this may not adequately describe early exercise behaviour.

- *Vesting conditions and non-vesting conditions*

  The formula does not take into account any market-based vesting conditions or non-vesting conditions.

- *Blackout periods*

  As the formula assumes exercise on a fixed date, and does not allow earlier exercise, it does not take into consideration any blackout periods (see 8.2.3.D above).

In summary, application of the Black-Scholes-Merton formula is relatively simple, in part because many of the complicating factors associated with the valuation of employee share options cannot be incorporated into it directly and, therefore, must be derived outside of the formula (e.g. the input of an expected term).

IFRS 2 states that the Black-Scholes-Merton formula may not be appropriate for long-lived options which can be exercised before the end of their life and which are subject to variation in the various inputs to the model over the life of the option. However, IFRS 2 suggests that the Black-Scholes-Merton formula may give materially correct results for shorter lived options with a relatively short exercise period. [IFRS 2.B5].

The development of appropriate assumptions for use in the Black-Scholes-Merton formula is discussed at 8.5 below.

In certain circumstances it may be possible to use closed form solutions other than the Black-Scholes-Merton formula to value options where, for example, the share price has to reach a specified level for the options to vest. However, these other solutions are beyond the scope of the discussion in this Chapter.

8.3.2 The binomial model

The binomial model is one of a subset of valuation models known as lattice models, which adopt a flexible, iterative approach to valuation that can capture the unique aspects of employee share options. A binomial model produces an estimated fair value based on the assumed changes in prices of a financial instrument over successive periods of time. In each time period, the model assumes that at least two price movements are possible. The lattice represents the evolution of the value of either a financial instrument or a market variable for the purpose of valuing a financial instrument.

The concepts that underpin lattice models and the Black-Scholes-Merton formula are the same, but the key difference between a lattice model and a closed-form model is that a lattice model is more flexible. The valuations obtained using the Black-Scholes-Merton formula and a lattice model will be very similar if the lattice model uses identical assumptions to the Black-Scholes-Merton calculation (e.g. constant volatility, constant dividend yields, constant risk-free rate, the same expected life). However, a lattice model can explicitly use dynamic assumptions regarding the term structure of volatility, dividend yields, and interest rates.

Further, a lattice model can incorporate assumptions about how the likelihood of early exercise of an employee share option may increase as the intrinsic value of that option increases, or how employees may have a high propensity to exercise options with significant intrinsic value shortly after vesting.

In addition, a lattice model can incorporate market conditions that may be part of the design of an option, such as a requirement that an option is only exercisable if the underlying share price achieves a certain level (sometimes referred to as 'target share price' awards). The Black-Scholes-Merton formula is not generally appropriate for awards that have a market-based performance condition because it cannot handle that additional complexity.

Most valuation specialists believe that lattice models, through their versatility, generally provide a more accurate estimate of the fair value of an employee share option with market performance conditions or with the possibility of early exercise than a value based on a closed-form Black-Scholes-Merton formula. As a general rule, the longer the term of the option and the higher the dividend yield, the larger the amount by which the binomial lattice model value may differ from the Black-Scholes-Merton formula value.

To implement the binomial model, a 'tree' is constructed the branches (or time steps) of which represent alternative future share price movements over the life of the option. In each time step over the life of the option, the share price has a certain probability of moving up or down by a certain percentage amount. It is important to emphasise the assumption, in these models, that the valuation occurs in a risk-neutral world, where investors are assumed to require no extra return on average for bearing risks and the expected return on all securities is the risk free interest rate.

To illustrate how the binomial model is used, Example 32.32 below constructs a simple binomial lattice model with a few time steps. The valuation assumptions and principles will not differ in essence from those in a Black-Scholes-Merton valuation except that it will allow for early exercise of the option. The relevant difference between the two models is the specification of a very small number of time steps, for illustrative purposes, in the binomial lattice model (see also 8.3.2.A below). We discuss below how the model can be augmented for a more complex set of assumptions.

Example 32.32: Binomial model

A share option is issued with an exercise price of $10, being the share price on the grant date. This Example assumes a constant volatility (50%) and risk-free rate (5% continuously compounded) although, as discussed later, those static assumptions may not be appropriate when valuing a long-term share option. It is also assumed that: the grantor pays dividends with a yield of 2% (continuously compounded) on its shares; the term of the option is five years; and each branch of the tree represents a length of time of one year.

At t = 0 (the grant date), the model is started at the grant date share price ($10 in this Example). At each node (the base of any price time step), two possible price changes (one increase and one decrease) are computed based on the stock's volatility. The two new share prices are computed as follows:

The up-node price utilises the following formula:

$$u = e^{\sigma\sqrt{dt}} = e^{0.5*\sqrt{1}} = 1.6487$$

Where:

σ = annualised volatility of the underlying share

dt = period of time between nodes

The down-node is the inverse of the up-node:

$$d = \frac{1}{u} = \frac{1}{1.6487} = 0.6065$$

The probability of each upward and downward price movement occurring is calculated from:

- the probability of an upward movement in price:

$$p = \frac{e^{(r-q)dt} - d}{u - d} = \frac{e^{(.05-.02)*1} - 0.6065}{1.6487 - 0.6065} = 0.4068$$

Where:

r = continuously compounded risk free rate

q = dividend yield (continuously compounded)

dt = period of time between nodes

- the probability of a downward movement in price:

$$= 1 - p = 1 - 0.4068 = 0.5932$$

Using the above price multiples, the price tree can then be constructed as shown diagrammatically below – each rising node is built by multiplying the previous price by 'u' and each falling node is similarly calculated by multiplying the previous price by 'd'.

Assumptions:

Share price	$10
Exercise price	$10
Risk-free rate	5%
Dividend yield	2%
Volatility	50%
Life/Term	5 years

To calculate the option value:

- The option payoffs at the final time node (time 5 above) must be calculated. This is the share price less the exercise price, or zero if the payoff is negative.

- Then the option values must be calculated at the previous time point (time 4 above). This is done by calculating the expected value of the option for the branch paths available to the particular node being valued discounted at the risk-free rate. For example, for $S_{4,4}$ in the chart above the option value is the probability of going to node $S_{5,5}$ multiplied by the option value at that node plus the probability of going to node $S_{5,4}$ multiplied by the option value at that node, all discounted at the risk-free rate):

$$= e^{-r.dt}\{p.111.82 + (1-p)34.82\} = 0.95\{0.4068 * 111.82 + 0.5932 * 34.82\} = 62.92$$

This would be the value at node $S_{4,4}$ if the option were European and could not be exercised earlier. As the binomial model can allow for early exercise, the option value at node $S_{4,4}$ is the greater of the option value just calculated and the intrinsic value of the option which is calculated the same way as the end option payoff. In this case, as the intrinsic value is \$63.89 (\$73.89 – \$10.00), the node takes the value of \$63.89.

- The previous steps are then repeated throughout the entire lattice (i.e. for all nodes at time 4, then all nodes at time 3, etc.) until finally the option value is determined at time 0 – this being the binomial option value of \$4.42.

- Additionally, if there is a vesting period during which the options cannot be exercised, the model can be adjusted so as not to incorporate the early exercise condition stipulated in the previous point and allow for this only after the option has vested and has the ability to be exercised before expiry.

One of the advantages of a lattice model is its ability to depict a large number of possible future paths of share prices over the life of the option. In Example 32.32 above, the specification of an interval of 12 months between nodes provides an inappropriately narrow description of future price paths. The shorter the interval of time between each node, the more accurate will be the description of future share price movements.

Additions which can be made to a binomial model (or any type of lattice model) include the use of assumptions that are not fixed over the life of the option. Binomial trees may allow for conditions dependent on price and/or time, but in general do not support price-path dependent conditions and modifications to volatility. This may affect the structure of a tree making it difficult to recombine. In such cases, additional recombination techniques should be implemented, possibly with the use of a trinomial tree (i.e. one with three possible outcomes at each node).

For the first three assumptions above, the varying assumptions simply replace the value in the fixed assumption model. For instance in Example 32.32 above r = 0.05; in a time-dependent version this could be 0.045 at time 1, 0.048 at time 2 and so on, depending on the length of time from the valuation date to the individual nodes.

However, for a more complicated addition such as assumed withdrawal rates, the equation:

$$= e^{-r.dt}\{p.111.82 + (1-p)34.82\}$$

may be replaced with

$$= (1-g) * e^{-r.dt}\{p.111.82 + (1-p)34.82\} + g * \max(\text{intrinsic value},0)$$

where 'g' is the rate of employee departure, on the assumption that, on departure, the option is either forfeited or exercised. As with the other time and price dependent assumptions, the rate of departure could also be made time or price dependent (i.e. the rate of departure could be assumed to increase as the share price increases, or increase as time passes, and so forth).

8.3.2.A   Lattice models – number of time steps

When performing a lattice valuation, a decision must be taken as to how many time steps to use in the valuation (i.e. how much time passes between each node). Generally, the greater the number of time steps, the more accurate the final value. However, as more time steps are added, the incremental increase in accuracy declines. To illustrate the increases in accuracy, consider the diagram below, which values the option in Example 32.32 above as a European option. In this case, the binomial model has not been enhanced to allow for early exercise (i.e. the ability to exercise prior to expiry).

Whilst the binomial model is very flexible and can deal with much more complex assumptions than the Black-Scholes-Merton formula, there are certain complexities it cannot handle, which can best be accomplished by Monte Carlo Simulation – see 8.3.3 below.

The development of appropriate assumptions for use in a binomial model is discussed at 8.5 below.

In addition to the binomial model, other lattice models such as trinomial models or finite difference algorithms may be used. Discussion of these models is beyond the scope of this Chapter.

8.3.3   Monte Carlo Simulation

In order to value options with market-based performance targets where the market value of the entity's equity is an input to the determination of whether, or to what extent, an award has vested, the option methodology applied must be supplemented with techniques such as Monte Carlo Simulation.

TSR compares the return on a fixed sum invested in the entity to the return on the same amount invested in a peer group of entities. Typically, the entity is then ranked in the peer group and the number of share-based awards that vest depends on the ranking. For example, no award might vest for a low ranking, the full award might vest for a higher ranking, and a pro-rated level of award might vest for a median ranking.

The following table gives an example of a possible vesting pattern for such a scheme, with a peer group of 100 entities.

Ranking in peer group	Percentage vesting
Below 50	0%
50	50%
51 – 74	50% plus an additional 2% for each increase of 1 in the ranking
75 or higher	100%

Figure 32.5 below summarises the Monte Carlo approach.

Figure 32.5:   *Monte Carlo Simulation approach for share-based payment transactions*

The valuation could be performed using either:

- a binomial valuation or the Black-Scholes-Merton formula, dependent on the results of the Monte Carlo Simulation;
- the Monte Carlo Simulation on its own.

The framework for calculating future share prices uses essentially the same underlying assumptions as lie behind Black-Scholes-Merton and binomial models – namely a risk-neutral world and a log normal distribution of share prices.

For a given simulation, the risk-neutral returns of the entity and those of the peer group or index are projected until the performance target is achieved and the option vests. At this point, the option transforms into a 'vanilla' equity call option that may be valued using an option pricing model. This value is then discounted back to the grant date so as to give the value of the option for a single simulation.

When the performance target is not achieved and the option does not vest, a zero value is recorded. This process is repeated thousands or millions of times. The average option value obtained across all simulations provides an estimate of the value of the option, allowing for the impact of the performance target.

8.4   Adapting option-pricing models for share-based payment transactions

Since the option-pricing models discussed in 8.3 above were developed to value freely-traded options, a number of adjustments are required in order to account for the restrictions usually attached to share-based payment transactions, particularly those with employees. The restrictions not accounted for in these models include:

- non-transferability (see 8.4.1 below); and
- vesting conditions, including performance targets, and non-vesting conditions that affect the value for the purposes of IFRS 2 (see 8.4.2 below).

8.4.1   Non-transferability

As noted at 8.2.3.A above, employee options and other share-based awards are almost invariably non-transferable, except (in some cases) to the employee's estate in the event of death in service. Non-transferability often results in an option being exercised early (i.e. before the end of its contractual life), as this is the only way for the employee to realise its value in cash. Therefore, by imposing the restriction of non-transferability, the entity may cause the effective life of the option to be shorter than its contractual life, resulting in a loss of time value to the holder. *[IFRS 2.BC153-169].*

One aspect of time value is the value of the right to defer payment of the exercise price until the end of the option term. When the option is exercised early because of non-transferability, the entity receives the exercise price much earlier than it otherwise would. Therefore, as noted by IFRS 2, the effective time value granted by the entity to the option holder is less than that indicated by the option's contractual life.

IFRS 2 requires the effect of early exercise as a result of non-transferability and other factors to be reflected either by modelling early exercise in a binomial or similar model or by using expected life rather than contractual life as an input into the option-pricing model. This is discussed further at 8.5.1 below.

Reducing the time to expiry effectively reduces the value of the option. This is a simplified way of reducing the value of the employee stock option to reflect the fact that employees are unable to sell their vested options, rather than applying an arbitrary discount to take account of non-transferability.

8.4.2   Treatment of vesting and non-vesting conditions

Many share-based payment awards to employees have vesting and non-vesting conditions attached to them which must be satisfied before the award can be exercised. It must be remembered that a non-market vesting condition, while reducing the 'true' fair value of an award, does not directly affect its valuation for the purposes of IFRS 2 (see 6.2 above). However, non-market vesting conditions may indirectly affect the value. For example, when an award vests on satisfaction of a particular target rather than at a specified time, its value may vary depending on the assessment of when that target will be met, since that may influence the expected life of the award, which is relevant to its fair value under IFRS 2 (see 8.2.2 above and 8.5 below).

As discussed at 6.2 above, IFRS 2 requires a vesting condition, other than a market condition, to be taken into account by estimating the extent of forfeiture based on failure to vest (and making a corresponding adjustment to the number of equity instruments for which a cost is recognised), rather than by attempting to reflect the effect of the condition in the option-pricing model. If the actual numbers that vest differ from those originally estimated, adjustments are required so that the cumulative expense recognised over the vesting period reflects the number of instruments that actually vest (subject to the special provisions relating to awards subject to market conditions and/or non-vesting conditions – see 6.3 and 6.4 above).

8.4.2.A   Market-based performance measures and non-vesting conditions

As discussed at 6.3 and 6.4 above, IFRS 2 requires market-based vesting conditions and non-vesting conditions to be taken into account in estimating the fair value of the options granted. Moreover, the entity is required to recognise a cost for an award with a market condition or non-vesting condition if all the non-market vesting conditions attaching to the award are satisfied regardless of whether the market condition or non-vesting condition is satisfied. This means that a more sophisticated option pricing model may be required.

8.4.2.B   Non market-based vesting conditions

As discussed at 6.2 above, IFRS 2 requires non market-based vesting conditions to be ignored when estimating the fair value of share-based payment transactions. Instead, such vesting conditions are taken into account by adjusting the number of equity instruments included in the measurement of the transaction (by estimating the extent of forfeiture based on failure to vest) so that, ultimately, the amount recognised is based on the number of equity instruments that eventually vest.

8.5   Selecting appropriate assumptions for option-pricing models

IFRS 2 notes that, as discussed at 8.2.2 above, option pricing models take into account, as a minimum:

- the exercise price of the option;
- the life of the option (see 8.5.1 and 8.5.2 below);
- the current price of the underlying shares;
- the expected volatility of the share price (see 8.5.3 below);
- the dividends expected on the shares (if appropriate – see 8.5.4 below); and
- the risk-free interest rate for the life of the option (see 8.5.5 below). *[IFRS 2.B6]*.

Of these inputs, only the exercise price and the current share price are objectively determinable. The others are subjective, and their development will generally require significant analysis. The discussion below addresses the development of assumptions for use both in a Black-Scholes-Merton formula and in a lattice model.

IFRS 2 requires other factors that knowledgeable, willing market participants would consider in setting the price to be taken into account, except for those vesting conditions and reload features that are excluded from the measurement of fair value – see 5 and 6 above and 8.9 below. Such factors include:

- restrictions on exercise during the vesting period or during periods where trading by those with inside knowledge is prohibited by securities regulators; or

- the possibility of the early exercise of options (see 8.5.1 below). *[IFRS 2.B7-9].*

However, the entity should not consider factors that are relevant only to an individual employee and not to the market as a whole (such as the effect of an award of options on the personal motivation of an individual). *[IFRS 2.B10].*

The objective of estimating the expected volatility of, and dividends on, the underlying shares is to approximate the expectations that would be reflected in a current market or negotiated exchange price for the option. Similarly, when estimating the effects of early exercise of employee share options, the objective is to approximate the expectations about employees' exercise behaviour that would be developed by an outside party with access to detailed information at grant date. Where (as is likely) there is a range of reasonable expectations about future volatility, dividends and exercise behaviour, an expected value should be calculated, by weighting each amount within the range by its associated probability of occurrence. *[IFRS 2.B11-12].*

Such expectations are often based on past data. In some cases, however, such historical information may not be relevant (e.g. where the business of the entity has changed significantly) or even available (e.g. where the entity is unlisted or newly listed). An entity should not base estimates of future volatility, dividends or exercise behaviour on historical data without considering the extent to which they are likely to be reasonably predictive of future experience. *[IFRS 2.B13-15].*

8.5.1   Expected term of the option

IFRS 2 allows the estimation of the fair value of an employee share award to be based on its expected life, rather than its maximum term, as this is a reasonable means of reducing the value of the award to reflect its non-transferability.

Option value is not a linear function of option term. Rather, value increases at a decreasing rate as the term lengthens. For example, a two year option is worth less than twice as much as a one year option, if all other assumptions are equal. This means that to calculate a value for an award of options with widely different individual lives based on a single weighted average life is likely to overstate the value of the entire award. Accordingly, assumptions need to be made as to what exercise or termination behaviour an option holder will exhibit. Considerations include:

- vesting period – the expected term of the option must be at least as long as its vesting period. The length of time employees hold options after they vest may vary inversely with the length of the vesting period;

- past history of employee exercise and termination patterns for similar grants (adjusted for current expectations) – see 8.5.2 below;

- expected volatility of the underlying share – on average, employees tend to exercise options on shares with higher volatility earlier;

- periods during which exercise may be precluded and related arrangements (e.g. agreements that allow for exercise to occur automatically during such periods if certain conditions are satisfied);

- employee demographics (age, tenure, sex, position etc.); and

- time from vesting date – the likelihood of exercise typically increases as time passes.

As discussed at 8.4 above, IFRS 2 notes that the effect of early exercise can be reflected:

- in a pricing model such as the Black-Scholes-Merton formula, by treating the expected, rather than the contractual, life of the option as an input to the model (see 8.5.1.A below); or

- by using a binomial or similar model. *[IFRS 2.B16-17].*

8.5.1.A Expected term under the Black-Scholes-Merton formula

An estimate of expected term based on the types of inputs described above can be used in the Black-Scholes-Merton formula as well as a lattice model. However, the formula requires only a single expected term to be used. This is one of the reasons why the Black-Scholes-Merton formula may provide a higher valuation for the same options than a lattice model.

The difference in value that arises from using only a single expected term results, in part, from the convex shape of a typical option valuation curve, as illustrated below.

Chapter 32

It is assumed, for the purposes of this illustration, that an at-the-money option on a €10 share with a 10-year contractual term is equally likely to be exercised at the end of each year beginning with year two. An average expected term of six years [(2+3+4+...9)/9] would be used in a Black-Scholes-Merton calculation giving a fair value of €3.10 for the option. If, instead, nine separate valuations were performed, each with a different expected term corresponding to each of the possible terms (from two to ten years), the average of those valuations (also calculated using the Black-Scholes-Merton formula) would be €2.9854. The latter amount is lower than €3.10 because of the convex shape of the valuation curve, reflecting the fact that the value increases at a decreasing rate as the term lengthens. Therefore, the value of the share option with an average expected term of six years will exceed the value derived from averaging the separate valuations for each potential term.

In a lattice model, exercise can occur at any time based on the rules specified in the model regarding exercise behaviour. The lattice model can therefore be thought of as analogous to the calculation in the above example in which the fair value was calculated as the average of the valuations from periods two to ten. In contrast, the Black-Scholes-Merton valuation allows only a single expected term to be specified. Therefore, it is analogous to the valuation described in the above example based on a single average expected term of six years.

Therefore, even if the expected term derived from a lattice model were used as an input in the Black-Scholes-Merton formula (and all other inputs were identical), the two models would give different values.

To mitigate the impact of the convex shape of the valuation curve, an entity with a broad-based share option plan might consider stratifying annual awards into different employee groups for the purposes of estimating the expected option lives (see 8.5.2 below).

Determining a single expected term can be quite challenging, particularly for an entity seeking to base its estimate on the periods for which previously granted options were outstanding, which would have been highly dependent on the circumstances during those periods. For example, if the entity's share price had increased significantly during the option period (as would be the case for share options granted by certain entities at the beginning of a bull market), it is likely that employees would have exercised options very soon after vesting. Alternatively, if options were granted at the end of a bull market and the share price declined significantly after the grant date, it is likely that the options would be exercised much later (if at all). These relationships would exist because, as discussed previously, the extent to which an option is in-the-money has a significant impact on exercise behaviour. Accordingly, deriving a single expected term in these situations involves considerable judgment.

8.5.2   *Exercise and termination behaviour*

IFRS 2 notes that employees often exercise options early for a number of reasons, most typically:

- restrictions on transferability mean that this is the only way of realising the value of the option in cash;

- aversion to the risk of not exercising 'in the money' options in the hope that they increase in value; or

- in the case of leavers, a requirement to exercise, or forfeit, all vested options on or shortly after leaving (see 8.5.2.B below).

Factors to consider in estimating early exercise include:

(a)   the length of the vesting period, because the share option cannot be exercised until the end of the vesting period. Hence, determining the valuation implications of expected early exercise is based on the assumption that the options will vest;

(b)   the average length of time similar options have remained outstanding in the past;

(c)   the price of the underlying shares. Experience may indicate that employees tend to exercise options when the share price reaches a specified level above the exercise price;

(d)   the employee's level within the organisation. For example, experience might indicate that higher-level employees tend to exercise options later than lower-level employees (see also 8.5.2.A below); and

(e)   the expected volatility of the underlying shares. On average, employees might tend to exercise options on highly volatile shares earlier than on shares with low volatility. *[IFRS 2.B18].*

In addition, the pattern of terminations of employment after vesting may be relevant (see 8.5.2.B below).

In our view, past exercise behaviour should generally serve as the starting point for determining expected exercise behaviour. That behaviour should be analysed, correlated to the factors above, and extrapolated into the future. However, significant changes in the underlying share price or in other salient characteristics of the entity, changes in option plans, tax laws, share price volatility and termination patterns may indicate that past exercise behaviour is not indicative of expected exercise behaviour. The expected life may also be estimated indirectly, by using a modified option pricing model to compute an option value, an input to which is an assumption that the options will be expected to be exercised when a particular share price is reached.

Some entities, including recently listed entities, or entities for which all outstanding grants have been out-of-the-money for a long period, may simply not be able to observe any exercise behaviour or may not possess enough history to perform a reasonable analysis of past exercise behaviour. In these cases, in our view, entities may have to look to the exercise history of employees of similar entities to develop expectations of employee exercise behaviour. At present there is only limited publicly-available information about employee exercise patterns, but valuation professionals and human resource consultants may have access to relevant data, which we expect to become more broadly available in the future.

In the absence of extensive information regarding exercise behaviour, another solution could be to use a midpoint assumption – i.e. selecting as the expected date of exercise the midpoint between the first available exercise date (the end of the vesting period) and the last available exercise date (the contracted expiry date). However, this should be undertaken only when the entity is satisfied that this does not lead to a material misstatement. It is also plausible to assume exercise at the earliest possible time or to undertake a reasonable analysis of past behaviour and set up the amount of intrinsic value which, when exceeded, will trigger exercise of the option.

8.5.2.A   Grouping employees with homogeneous exercise behaviour

IFRS 2 emphasises that the estimated life of an option is critical to its valuation. Therefore, where options are granted to a group of employees, it will generally be necessary to ensure that either:

(a)   all the employees are expected to exercise their options within a relatively narrow time-frame; or

(b)   if not, that the group is divided into sub-groups of employees who are expected to exercise their options within a similar relatively narrow time-frame.

IFRS 2 suggests that it may become apparent that middle and senior management tend to exercise options later than lower-level employees, either because they choose to do so, or because they are encouraged or compelled to do so as a result of required minimum levels of ownership of equity instruments (including options) among more senior employees. *[IFRS 2.B19-21].*

8.5.2.B   Post-vesting termination behaviour

Most employee share options provide that, if employment is terminated, the former employee typically has only a short period (e.g. 90 days from the date of termination of employment) in which to exercise any vested options, the contractual expiry of which would otherwise be some years away. Accordingly, an entity should look at its prior termination patterns, adjust those patterns for future expectations and incorporate those expected terminations into a lattice model as expected early exercises.

Patterns of employee turnover are not necessarily linear and may be a non-linear function of a variety of factors, such as:

- employee demographics (age, sex, tenure, position, etc.);

- path of share price – for example, if options are deeply out-of-the-money, they may have little retention value and more employees may leave than if the options were at- or in-the-money; and

- economic conditions and other share prices.

8.5.3 *Expected volatility of share price*

Expected volatility is a measure of the amount by which a price is expected to fluctuate during a period. Share price volatility has a powerful influence on the estimation of the fair value of an option, much of the value of which is derived from its potential for appreciation. The more volatile the share price, the more valuable the option. It is therefore essential that the choice of volatility assumption can be properly supported.

IFRS 2 notes that the measure of volatility used in option pricing models is the annualised standard deviation of the continuously compounded rates of return on the share over a period of time. Volatility is typically expressed in annualised terms that are comparable regardless of the time period used in the calculation (for example, daily, weekly or monthly price observations).

The expected annualised volatility of a share is the range within which the continuously compounded annual rate of return is expected to fall approximately two-thirds of the time. For example, to say that a share with an expected continuously compounded rate of return of 12% has a volatility of 30% means that the probability that the rate of return on the share for one year will be between minus 18% (12% − 30%) and 42% (12% + 30%) is approximately two-thirds. If the share price is €100 at the beginning of the year, and no dividends are paid, the year-end share price would be expected to be between €83.53 (€100 × $e^{-0.18}$) and €152.20 (€100 × $e^{0.42}$) approximately two-thirds of the time.

The rate of return (which may be positive or negative) on a share for a period measures how much a shareholder has benefited from dividends and appreciation (or depreciation) of the share price. *[IFRS 2.B22-24].*

Paragraph B25 of IFRS 2 gives examples of factors to consider in estimating expected volatility including the following:

- *Implied volatility from traded share options*

  Implied volatility is the volatility derived by using an option pricing model with the traded option price (if available) as an input and solving for the volatility as the unknown on the entity's shares. It may also be derived from other traded instruments of the entity that include option features (such as convertible debt).

  Implied volatilities are often calculated by analysts and reflect market expectations for future volatility as well as imperfections in the assumptions in the valuation model. For this reason, the implied volatility of a share may be a better measure of prospective volatility than historical volatility (see below). However, traded options are usually short-term, ranging in general from one month to two years. If the expected lives are much longer than this, both the implied and historical volatilities will need to be considered;

- *Historical volatility*

  It may be relevant to consider the historical volatility of the share price over the most recent period that is generally commensurate with the expected term of the option (taking into account the remaining contractual life of the option and the effects of expected early exercise). However, this assumes that past share price behaviour is likely to be representative of future share price behaviour. Upon any restructuring of an entity, the question of whether or not past volatility will be likely to predict future volatility would need to be reassessed.

The historical volatilities of similar entities may be relevant for newly listed entities, unlisted entities or entities that have undergone substantial restructuring (see 8.5.3.A to 8.5.3.C below);

- *The length of time the entity's shares have been publicly traded*

A newly listed entity might have a high historical volatility, compared with similar entities that have been listed longer. Further guidance for newly listed entities is given in 8.5.3.A below;

- *'Mean-reverting tendency'*

This refers to the tendency of volatility to revert to its long-term average level, and other factors indicating that expected future volatility might differ from past volatility. For example, if an entity's share price was extraordinarily volatile for some identifiable period of time because of a failed takeover bid or a major restructuring, that period could be disregarded in computing historical average annual volatility. However, an entity should not exclude general economic factors such as the effect of an economic downturn on share price volatility;

- *Appropriate and regular intervals for price observations*

The price observations should be consistent from period to period. For example, an entity might use the closing price for each week or the opening price for the week, but it should not use the closing price for some weeks and the opening price for other weeks. Also, the price observations should be expressed in the same currency as the exercise price. In our view, at least thirty observations are generally required to calculate a statistically valid standard deviation. Our experience has been that, in general, it is more appropriate to make such observations daily or weekly rather than monthly.

8.5.3.A   Newly listed entities

As noted under 'Historical volatility' at 8.5.3 above, an entity should consider the historical volatility of the share price over the most recent period that is generally commensurate with the expected option term. If a newly listed entity does not have sufficient information on historical volatility, it should compute historical volatility for the longest period for which trading activity is available. It should also consider the historical volatility of similar entities. For example, an entity that has been listed for only one year and grants options with an average expected life of five years might consider the historical volatility of entities in the same industry, which are of a similar size and operate similar businesses, for the first six years in which the shares of those entities were publicly traded. *[IFRS 2.B26]*.

8.5.3.B   Unlisted entities

An unlisted entity will have neither historical nor current market information to consider when estimating expected volatility. IFRS 2 suggests that, in some cases, an unlisted entity that regularly issues options or shares might have set up an internal market for its shares. The volatility of those share prices could be considered when estimating expected volatility. Alternatively, if the entity has based the value of its shares on the share prices of similar listed entities, the entity could consider the historical or implied volatility of the shares of those similar listed entities. *[IFRS 2.B27-29].*

If the entity has not used a valuation methodology based on the share prices of similar listed entities, the entity could derive an estimate of expected volatility consistent with the valuation methodology used. For example, the entity might value its shares on a net asset or earnings basis, in which case it could consider the expected volatility of those net asset values or earnings. *[IFRS 2.B30].*

8.5.3.C   Listed entities that have undergone significant restructuring

An issue not specifically addressed by IFRS 2 is the approach required in the case of an entity that has been listed for some time but which has recently undergone significant restructuring or refocusing of the business (e.g. as a result of acquisitions, disposals or refinancing). In such cases, it may well be appropriate to adopt the approach advocated for newly listed entities in 8.5.3.A above.

8.5.3.D   Expected volatility under the Black-Scholes-Merton formula

In calculating the fair value of a share option using the Black-Scholes-Merton formula, a single expected volatility assumption must be used. That amount should be based on the volatility expected over the expected term of the option. Frequently, expected volatility is based on observed historical share price volatility during the period of time equal to the expected term of the option and ending on the grant date. Implied volatilities (i.e. volatilities implied by actual option prices on the entity's shares observed in the market) also may be considered in determining the expected volatility assumption (see 8.5.3 above).

When developing an expected volatility assumption, current and historical implied volatilities for publicly traded options and historical realised share volatilities should be considered for:

- shares of the grantor;
- shares of other entities in the grantor's industry and comparable entities; and
- stock market indices.

8.5.3.E   Expected volatility under lattice models

Expected volatility is more accurately taken into account by lattice models than by the Black-Scholes-Merton formula, because lattice models can accommodate dynamic assumptions regarding the term structure and path-dependence of volatility. For example, there is evidence that volatility during the life of an option depends on the term of the option and, in particular, that short-term options often exhibit higher volatility than similar options with longer terms. Additionally, volatility is path-dependent, in that it is often lower (higher) after an increase (decrease) in share price.

An entity that can observe sufficiently extensive trading of options over its shares may decide, when developing a term structure of expected volatility, to place greater weight on current implied volatilities than on historical observed and implied volatilities. It is likely that current implied volatilities are better indicators of the expectations of market participants about future volatility.

8.5.4   *Expected dividends*

The valuation of an award of options depends on whether or not the holder is entitled to dividends or dividend equivalents (whether in the form of cash payments or reductions in the exercise price) before the award is ultimately exercised. *[IFRS 2.B31-32, B34].* The accounting treatment of awards that entitle the holder to dividends before exercise is discussed further at 15.2 below.

Dividends paid on the underlying share will impact the share option value – the higher the expected dividend yield (i.e. dividend per share ÷ share price), the lower the option value. Option holders generally do not have dividend rights until they actually exercise the options and become shareholders. All other things being equal, a share option for a share yielding a high dividend is less valuable than one for a share yielding a low dividend.

Where employees are entitled to dividends or dividend equivalents, the options granted should be valued as if no dividends will be paid on the underlying shares, so that the input for expected dividends (which would otherwise reduce the valuation of an option) is zero. Conversely, where employees are not entitled to dividends or dividend equivalents, the expected dividends should be included in the application of the pricing model. *[IFRS 2.B31-32, B34].*

While option pricing models generally call for an expected dividend yield, they may be modified to use an expected dividend amount rather than a yield. Where an entity uses expected payments rather than expected yields, it should consider its historical pattern of increases in dividends. For example, if an entity's policy has generally been to increase dividends, its estimated option value should not assume a fixed dividend amount throughout the option's life unless there is evidence to support that assumption. *[IFRS 2.B35].*

Determination of the expected dividends over the expected term of the option requires judgment. Generally, the expected dividend assumption should be based on current expectations about an entity's anticipated dividend policy. For example, an entity that has demonstrated a stable dividend yield in past years, and has indicated no foreseeable plans to change its dividend policy, may simply use its historical dividend yield to estimate the fair value of its options. If an entity has never paid a dividend, but has publicly announced that it will begin paying a dividend yielding 2% of the current share price, it is likely that an expected dividend yield of 2% would be assumed in estimating the fair value of its options.

Generally assumptions about expected dividends should be based on publicly available information. Thus, an entity that does not pay dividends and has no plans to do so should assume an expected dividend yield of zero. However, an emerging entity with no history of paying dividends might expect to begin paying dividends during the expected lives of its employee share options. Such entities could use an average of their past dividend yield (zero) and the mean dividend yield of a comparable peer group of entities. *[IFRS 2.B36].*

8.5.4.A   Expected dividends under the Black-Scholes-Merton formula

Closed-form option-pricing models generally call for a single expected dividend yield as an input. That input should be determined based on the guidance at 8.5.4 above.

8.5.4.B   Expected dividends under the binomial model and other lattice models

Lattice models can be adapted to use an expected dividend amount rather than a dividend yield, and therefore can also take into account the impact of anticipated dividend changes. Such approaches might better reflect expected future dividends, since dividends do not always move in a fixed fashion with changes in the entity's share price. This may be a time- or price-dependent assumption, similar to those described in the discussion of the binomial model at 8.3.2 above. Expected dividend estimates in a lattice model should be determined based on the general guidance above. Additionally, when the present value of dividends becomes significant in relation to the share price, standard lattice models may need to be amended.

8.5.5   Risk-free interest rate

Typically, the risk-free interest rate is the implied yield currently available on zero-coupon government issues of the country in whose currency the exercise price is expressed, with a remaining term equal to the expected term of the option being valued (based on the remaining contractual life of the option and taking into account the effects of expected early exercise). It may be necessary to use an appropriate substitute, if no such government issues exist, or where the implied yield on zero-coupon government issues may not be representative of the risk-free interest rate (for example, in high inflation economies). An appropriate substitute should also be used if market participants would typically determine the risk-free interest rate by using that substitute. *[IFRS 2.B37].*

The risk free interest rate will not have an impact on most free share grants, since they have an exercise price of zero and therefore involve no cash outflow for the holder.

8.5.5.A   Risk-free interest rate under the Black-Scholes-Merton formula

The Black-Scholes-Merton formula expressed at 8.3.1 above uses a continuously compounded interest rate, which means that any interest rate calculated or obtained needs to be in this format. The continuously compounded interest rate is given by the formula:

continuously compounding rate = ln(1 + annual rate),

where ln represents a natural logarithm. For example, a 7.79% annual effective rate results in a continuously compounded rate of 7.50 per cent:

7.50% = ln(1 + 0.0779)

8.5.5.B   Risk-free interest rate under binomial and other lattice models

At each node in the lattice, the option values in the lattice should be discounted using an appropriate forward rate as determined by a yield curve constructed from the implied yield on zero coupon government bond issues. In stable economies this will have minimal impact and it is therefore likely that a flat risk-free rate that is consistent with the expected life assumption will be a reasonable estimate for this input.

8.6   Capital structure effects and dilution

Typically, traded share options are written by third parties, not the entity issuing the shares that are the subject of the option. When these share options are exercised, the writer delivers to the option holder shares acquired from existing shareholders. Hence the exercise of traded share options has no dilutive effect. By contrast, when share options written by the entity are exercised, new shares may be issued (either in form or in substance, if shares previously repurchased and held in treasury are used), giving rise to dilution. This actual or potential dilution may reduce the share price, so that the option holder does not make as large a gain on exercise as on exercising an otherwise similar traded option that does not dilute the share price. *[IFRS 2.B38-39].*

Whether or not this has a significant effect on the value of the share options granted depends on various factors, such as the number of new shares that will be issued on exercise of the options compared with the number of shares already issued. Also, if the market already expects that the option grant will take place, the market may have already factored the potential dilution into the share price at the date of grant. However, the entity should consider whether the possible dilutive effect of the future exercise of the share options granted might have an impact on their estimated fair value at grant date. Option pricing models can be adapted to take into account this potential dilutive effect. *[IFRS 2.B40-41].*

In practice, in our view, it is unlikely that a listed entity would be required to make such an adjustment unless it makes a very large, unanticipated grant of share options. Indeed, even in that case, if the potential dilution is material and is not already incorporated into the share price, it would be expected that the announcement of the grant would cause the share price to decline by a material amount. Unlisted entities should consider whether the dilutive impact of a very large option grant is already incorporated into the estimated share price used in their option-pricing model. If that is not the case, some adjustment to the fair value may be appropriate.

8.7   Other awards requiring the use of option valuation models

As noted at 8.1 above, the discussion in 8.3 to 8.5 above may well be relevant to share-based payments other than options. These include, but are not restricted to:

- awards of shares (see 8.7.1 below);
- non-recourse loans (see 8.7.2 below);
- share appreciation rights (SARs) (see 8.7.3 below); and
- performance rights (see 8.7.4 below).

8.7.1   Shares

IFRS 2 requires shares granted to employees to be valued at their market price (where one exists) or an estimated market value (where the shares are not publicly traded), in either case adjusted to take account of the terms and conditions on which the shares were granted, other than those vesting conditions that IFRS 2 requires to be excluded in determining the grant date fair value (see 6.2 above). *[IFRS 2.B2].*

For example, the valuation should take account of restrictions on the employee's right:

- to receive dividends in the vesting period (see below); or
- to transfer shares after vesting, but only to the extent that such restrictions would affect the price that a knowledgeable and willing market participant would pay for the shares. Where the shares are traded in a deep and liquid market, the effect may be negligible.

The valuation should not, however, take account of restrictions that arise directly from the existence of the vesting conditions (such as the right to transfer shares during the vesting period). *[IFRS 2.B3]*.

Whether dividends should be taken into account in measuring the fair value of shares depends on whether the counterparty is entitled to dividends or dividend equivalents (which might be paid in cash) during the vesting period. When the grant date fair value of shares granted to employees is estimated, no adjustment is required if the employees are entitled to receive dividends during the vesting period (as they are in no different a position in this respect than if they already held shares). However, where employees are not entitled to receive dividends during the vesting period, the valuation should be reduced by the present value of dividends expected to be paid during the vesting period. *[IFRS 2.B31, B33-34]*. The basis on which expected dividends during the vesting period might be determined is discussed in the context of the impact of expected dividends on the fair value of share options at 8.5.4 above.

The accounting treatment of awards which give the right to receive dividends during the vesting period is discussed further at 15.2 below.

8.7.2 Non-recourse loans

Non-recourse loans are loans granted by an entity to the employee to allow the employee to buy shares, and are discussed in more detail at 15.1 below. Generally, however, the loan is interest-free, with the dividends received being used to repay the loan. The loan acts like an option, in that, at the point in time when the holder decides to sell the shares to repay the loan, if the shares are worth less than the loan, the remaining part of the loan is forgiven, with the effect that, just as in the case of an option, the holder bears no risk of ownership.

8.7.3 Share appreciation rights (SARs)

A share appreciation right (SAR) is a grant whereby the employee will become entitled either to shares or, more commonly, to a future cash payment based on the increase in the entity's share price from a specified level over a period of time (see further discussion at 9 below on cash-settled awards). This essentially has the same payoff as a call option, except the award is generally cash- rather than equity-settled.

8.7.4 Performance rights

A performance right is the right to acquire further shares after vesting, upon certain criteria being met. These criteria may include certain performance conditions which can usually be modelled with either a binomial lattice model or a Monte Carlo Simulation. Such awards may be structured as matching share awards, as discussed in more detail at 10.5 below.

Chapter 32

8.8   Awards whose fair value cannot be measured reliably

IFRS 2 acknowledges that there may be rare cases where it is not possible to determine the fair value of equity instruments granted. In such cases, the entity is required to adopt a method of accounting based on the intrinsic value of the award (i.e. the price of the underlying share less the exercise price, if any, for the award). This is slightly puzzling in the sense that, for unlisted entities, a significant obstacle to determining a reliable fair value for equity instruments is the absence of a market share price, which is also a key input in determining intrinsic value. In fact, the intrinsic value model is arguably more onerous than the fair value model since, as discussed further in 8.8.1 and 8.8.2 below, it requires intrinsic value to be determined not just once, but at initial measurement date and each subsequent reporting date until exercise.

8.8.1   *Intrinsic value method – the basic accounting treatment*

Under the intrinsic value method:

(a)   the entity measures the intrinsic value of the award at each reporting date between grant date and settlement (whether through exercise, forfeiture or lapse);

(b)   at each reporting date during the vesting period the cumulative expense should be determined as the intrinsic value of the award at that date multiplied by the expired portion of the vesting period, with all changes in the cumulative expense recognised in profit or loss; and

(c)   once options have vested, all changes in their intrinsic value until settlement should be recognised in profit or loss. *[IFRS 2.24(a)].*

The cumulative expense during the vesting period, like that for awards measured at fair value, should always be based on the best estimate of the number of awards that will actually vest (see 6 above). However, the distinction between market vesting conditions, non-market vesting conditions and non-vesting conditions that would apply to equity-settled awards measured at fair value (see 6.1 to 6.4 above) does not apply in the case of awards measured at intrinsic value. *[IFRS 2.24(b)].* In other words, where an award measured at intrinsic value is subject to a market condition or non-vesting condition that is not met, there is ultimately no accounting expense for that award. This is consistent with a model requiring constant remeasurement.

The cost of awards measured at intrinsic value is ultimately revised to reflect the number of awards that are actually exercised. However, during the vesting period the cost should be based on the number of awards estimated to vest and thereafter on the number of awards that have vested. In other words, any post-vesting forfeiture or lapse should not be anticipated, but should be accounted for as it occurs. *[IFRS 2.24(b)].*

Example 32.33 illustrates the intrinsic value method.

Example 32.33: Intrinsic value method

At the beginning of year 1, an entity grants 1,000 share options to 50 employees.

The share options will vest at the end of year 3, provided the employees remain in service until then. The options can be exercised at the end of year 4, and then at the end of each subsequent year up to and including year 10. The exercise price, and the entity's grant date share price, is €60. At the date of grant, the entity concludes that it cannot estimate reliably the fair value of the share options granted.

At the end of year 1, the entity estimates that 80% of the share options will vest. At the end of year 2, the entity revises its estimate of the number of share options that it expects will vest to 86%.

During the vesting period, a total of seven employees leave, so that 43,000 share options vest.

The intrinsic value of the options, and the number of share options exercised during years 4-10, are as follows.

Year	Intrinsic value €	Number exercised
1	3	
2	5	
3	15	
4	28	6,000
5	40	8,000
6	30	5,000
7	36	9,000
8	45	8,000
9	48	5,000
10	55	2,000

The expense recognised under IFRS 2 will be as follows. In the period up to vesting the 'cumulative expense' methodology used in the examples in sections 6.1 to 6.4 above can be adopted to derive the expense for each period:

Year	Calculation of cumulative expense	Cumulative expense (€)	Expense for period (€)
1	50,000 options × €3 × 80% × 1/3	40,000	40,000
2	50,000 options × €5 × 86% × 2/3	143,333	103,333
3	43,000 options × €15	645,000	501,677

In years 4 to 10 it is more straightforward to calculate the expense directly. Since all options exercised during each year are exercised at the end of that year, the annual expense can be calculated as the change in intrinsic value during each year of the options outstanding at the *start* of the year.

Year		Expense for period (€)
4	43,000 options × €(28 − 15)	559,000
5	43,000 − 6,000 = 37,000 options × €(40 − 28)	444,000
6	37,000 − 8,000 = 29,000 options × €(30 − 40)	(290,000)
7	29,000 − 5,000 = 24,000 options × €(36 − 30)	144,000
8	24,000 − 9,000 = 15,000 options × €(45 − 36)	135,000
9	15,000 − 8,000 = 7,000 options × €(48 − 45)	21,000
10	7,000 − 5,000 = 2,000 options × €(55 − 48)	14,000

If, more realistically, the options had been exercisable, and were exercised, at other dates, it would have been necessary to record as an expense for those options the movement in intrinsic value from the start of the year until exercise date. For example, if the 6,000 options in year 4 had been exercised during the year when the intrinsic value was €20, the expense for that period would have been €511,000 comprising €481,000 change in value for the options outstanding at the end of year [37,000 options × €(28 − 15)] and €30,000 change in value of options exercised during the period [6,000 options × €(20 − 15)].

8.8.2   Modification, cancellation and settlement

The methodology of the intrinsic value method has the effect that modification or cancellation is dealt with automatically, and the rules for modification and cancellation of awards measured at fair value (see 7 above) therefore do not apply. *[IFRS 2.25].*

Where an award accounted for at intrinsic value is settled in cash, the following provisions apply, which are broadly similar to the rules for settlement of awards accounted for at fair value.

If settlement occurs before vesting, the entity must 'recognise immediately the amount that would otherwise have been recognised for services received over the remainder of the vesting period'. *[IFRS 2.25(a)].* The wording here is the same as that applicable to settlement of awards accounted for at fair value, which we discuss in more detail at 7.4.3 above.

Any payment made on settlement must be deducted from equity, except to the extent that it is greater than the intrinsic value of the award at settlement date. Any such excess is accounted for as an expense. *[IFRS 2.25(b)].*

8.9   Awards with reload features

Some share options contain a reload feature. Reloads commonly provide that, where an exercise price is satisfied in shares of the issuing entity rather than cash, there is a new grant of at-the-money options over as many shares as are equal to the exercise price of the exercised option. For example, if there were 100 options with an exercise price of $10, and the new share price were $15, 67 options (€1,000 ÷ €15) would be re-issued.

Even though the reload feature (i.e. the possibility that additional options would be issued in the future) is a feature of the original option, and can be readily incorporated into the valuation of the original option using a lattice model, the IASB concluded that the fair value of a reload feature should not be incorporated into the estimate of the fair value of the award at grant date. As a result, subsequent grants of reload awards under the reload feature would be accounted for as new awards and measured on their respective grant dates. *[IFRS 2.BC188-192].*

On the assumption that the exercise price of an award is at least the share price at grant date, the grant-date fair value of the reload award will generally be greater than the incremental value of the reload feature as at the date the original award was granted. This is because the reload award will only be granted if the original option is in-the-money and is exercised. As a result, the award would have increased in the period between the original grant date and the reload grant date, and the higher share price would be used to value the reload grant. However, from the perspective of the aggregate compensation cost, this result is mitigated by the fact that, as the value of the underlying share increases, fewer shares must be tendered to satisfy the exercise price requirement of the exercised option and, therefore, fewer reload options will be granted (as above when only 67 options are re-issued for the 100 originally issued).

If the reload feature were incorporated into the valuation of the original grant, then not only would a lower price be used, but the valuation would consider the possibility that the original option would never be exercised and, therefore, that the reload options would not be granted. Under the approach in IFRS 2, if the original award expires unexercised, no compensation cost results from the reload feature, so that the compensation cost is lower than would be the case if the value of the reload feature were incorporated into the measurement of the original award. Effectively, the approach in IFRS 2 incorporates subsequent share price changes into the valuation of a reload award.

8.10 Awards of equity instruments to a fixed monetary value

Entities may make an award of shares to a fixed monetary value (see 5.3.5 above). This is commonly found as part of a matching share award where an employee may be offered the choice of receiving cash or shares of an equivalent value, or a multiple of that value (see 10.5 below).

IFRS 2 does not address the valuation of such awards directly. Intuitively, it might seem obvious that an award which promises (subject to vesting conditions) shares to the value of €10,000 must have a grant date fair value of €10,000, adjusted for the time value of money, together with market conditions and non-vesting conditions. However, matters are not so clear-cut, as Example 32.34 illustrates:

Example 32.34: Award of shares to a fixed monetary value

On 1 January 2011, the reporting entity grants:

- to Employee A an award of 1,000 shares subject to remaining in employment until 31 December 2013; and

- to Employee B €10,000 subject to remaining in employment until 31 December 2013, to be paid in as many shares as are (on 31 December 2013) worth €10,000.

Both awards vest, and the share price on 31 December 2013 is €10, so that both employees receive 1,000 shares.

The IFRS 2 charge for A's award is clearly 1000 × the fair value as at 1 January 2011 of a share deliverable in three years' time. What is the charge for B's award – the same as for A's or €10,000, adjusted for the time value of money?

The Basis for Conclusions to IFRS 2 creates some confusion over this point. Paragraphs BC106 to BC118 discuss in general terms why IFRS 2 adopts a definition of equity instrument different from that in IAS 32. Paragraphs BC107 to BC109 particularly note that the IASB did not believe it appropriate that a fixed-cost award and a variable-cost award ultimately delivered in shares should be classified, and measured, (as would be the case under IAS 32) as, respectively, equity or a liability.

Whilst the primary focus of the discussion in the Basis for Conclusions is whether variable equity-settled awards should be liabilities (as they would be under IAS 32) or equity (as they are under IFRS 2), the reference to measurement as well as classification of awards can be read as meaning that the IASB believed that two awards that ultimately deliver 1,000 shares (as in Example 32.34 above) should have the same grant date fair value.

If the same grant date fair value per share were used for both employees' awards, Employee B's award would have to be valued as the number of shares that actually vest (which would need to be continually re-estimated until vesting) multiplied by the fair value of a share at grant date. This would have the somewhat counter-intuitive outcome that, if the value of the entity's equity falls, the IFRS 2 charge increases (since more shares are needed to deliver €10,000 of value), whereas if the value of the entity's equity rises, the IFRS 2 charge falls (since fewer shares are needed to deliver €10,000 of value).

For this reason, many take the view that this not an appropriate analysis, since an award of 1,000 shares (where the recipient bears share price risk) is fundamentally different in nature to an award of shares to a given value (where the entity bears share price risk) which happens to translate into 1,000 shares at vesting.

Some argue that an award of shares to a given monetary amount contains a market condition, since the number of shares ultimately delivered (and therefore vesting) depends on the market price of the shares on the date of delivery. This allows the award to be valued at a fixed amount at grant date. We acknowledge that a literal reading of the definition of 'market condition' in IFRS 2 supports this view, but question whether this can really have been intended. In our view, the essential feature of a share-based payment transaction subject to a market condition must be that the employee's ultimate entitlement to the award depends on the share price.

In our view, in the absence of clear guidance in IFRS 2, entities may take a number of views on how to value awards of shares to a given value, but should adopt a consistent approach for all such awards.

9   CASH-SETTLED TRANSACTIONS

Throughout the discussion in this section, 'cash' should be read as including 'other assets' in accordance with the definition of a cash-settled share-based payment transaction (see 2.2.1 above).

9.1   Scope of requirements

Cash-settled share-based payment transactions are usually easy to identify, and include such things as:

- share appreciation rights (SARs), where employees are entitled to a cash payment equivalent to the gain that would have arisen from a holding of a particular number of shares from the date of grant to the date of exercise; or

- phantom options, where employees are entitled to a cash payment equivalent to the gain that would have been made by exercising options at a notional price over a notional number of shares and then selling the shares at the date of exercise. *[IFRS 2.31]*.

However, IFRS 2 looks beyond the simple issue of whether an award entitles an employee to receive instruments that are in form shares or options to the terms of those instruments. For example, an award of shares or options over shares whose terms provide for their redemption either mandatorily according to their terms (e.g. on cessation of employment) or at the employee's option would be treated as a cash-settled, not an equity-settled, award under IFRS 2. *[IFRS 2.31].* This is consistent with the fact that IAS 32 would regard a share with these terms as a financial liability rather than an equity instrument of the issuer (see Chapter 45 at 4).

In some cases the boundary between equity-settled and cash-settled schemes may appear somewhat blurred, so that further analysis may be required to determine whether a particular arrangement is equity-settled or cash-settled. Some examples of such arrangements are discussed at 9.3 below.

9.2 Required accounting

9.2.1 Basic accounting treatment

It is clear that the ultimate cost of a cash-settled transaction must be the actual cash paid to the counterparty, which will be the fair value at settlement date. Moreover, the cumulative cost recognised until settlement is clearly a liability, not a component of equity.

The periodic determination of this liability is as follows:

- at each reporting date between grant and settlement the fair value of the award is determined;

- during the vesting period, the liability recognised at each reporting date is the fair value of the award at that date multiplied by the expired portion of the vesting period;

- from the end of the vesting period until settlement, the liability recognised is the full fair value of the liability at the reporting date.

All changes in the liability are recognised in profit or loss for the period. *[IFRS 2.30-33, IG Example 12].* Where the cost of services received in a cash-settled transaction is recognised in the carrying amount of an asset (e.g. inventory) in the entity's balance sheet, the carrying amount of the asset is not adjusted for changes in the fair value of the liability. *[IFRS 2.IG19].*

The fair value of the liability should be determined, initially and at each reporting date until it is settled, by applying an option pricing model, taking into account the terms and conditions on which the cash-settled transaction was granted, and the extent to which the employees have rendered service to date. It should be noted that IFRS 2 uses the term 'share appreciation rights' when referring to measurement of the liability but this should clearly be read as including any cash-settled share-based payment transaction. *[IFRS 2.33].*

This has the effect that, although the liability will ultimately be settled at its then intrinsic value, its measurement at reporting dates before settlement is based on its fair value. During the exposure period of ED 2, a number of respondents suggested that, for reasons of consistency and simplicity of calculation, cash-settled transactions should be measured at intrinsic value throughout their entire life. The IASB, while accepting these merits of the intrinsic value approach (together with the fact that it is also required under US GAAP), rejected it on the basis that, since it does not include a time value, it is not an adequate measure of either the liability or the cost of services consumed. *[IFRS 2.BC246-251].*

As noted at 5.5 above, the approach to determining the fair value of share-based payments will continue to be that specified in IFRS 2 and share-based payments will be outside the scope of IFRS 13 which applies more generally to the use of fair value under IFRSs with effect from 1 January 2013 (see Chapter 16).

9.2.2 *Application of the accounting treatment*

The treatment required by IFRS 2 for cash-settled transactions is illustrated by Example 32.35.

Example 32.35: *Cash-settled transaction*

An entity grants 100 cash share appreciation rights (SARs) to each of its 500 employees, on condition that the employees remain in its employment for the next three years. The SARs can be exercised on the third, fourth and fifth anniversary of the grant date.

During year 1, 35 employees leave. The entity estimates that a further 60 will leave during years 2 and 3 (i.e. the award will vest in 405 employees).

During year 2, 40 employees leave and the entity estimates that a further 25 will leave during year 3 (i.e. the award will vest in 400 employees).

During year 3, 22 employees leave, so that the award vests in 403 employees. At the end of year 3, 150 employees exercise their SARs (leaving 253 employees still to exercise).

Another 140 employees exercise their SARs at the end of year 4, leaving 113 employees still to exercise, who do so at the end of year 5.

The entity estimates the fair value of the SARs at the end of each year in which a liability exists as shown below. The intrinsic values of the SARs at the date of exercise (which equal the cash paid out) at the end of years 3, 4 and 5 are also shown below.

Year	Fair value £	Intrinsic value £
1	14.40	
2	15.50	
3	18.20	15.00
4	21.40	20.00
5		25.00

The entity will recognise the cost of this award as follows.

Year	Calculation of liability	Calculation of cash paid	Liability (£)	Cash paid (£)	Expense for period (£)*
1	405 employees × 100 SARs × £14.40 × 1/3		194,400	–	194,400
2	400 employees × 100 SARs × £15.50 × 2/3		413,333	–	218,933
3	253 employees × 100 SARs × £18.20	150 employees × 100 SARs × £15.00	460,460	225,000	272,127
4	113 employees × 100 SARs × £21.40	140 employees × 100 SARs × £20.00	241,820	280,000	61,360
5	–	113 employees × 100 SARs × £25.00	–	282,500	40,680

* Liability at end of period + cash paid in period – liability at start of period

The accounting treatment for cash-settled transactions is therefore (despite some similarities in the methodology) significantly different from that for equity-settled transactions. An important practical issue is that, for a cash-settled transaction, the entity must determine the fair value at each reporting date and not merely at grant date (and at the date of any subsequent modification or settlement) as would be the case for equity-settled transactions. However, as Example 32.35 shows, it is not actually necessary, although arguably required by IFRS 2, to determine the fair value of a cash-settled transaction at grant date, at least to determine the expense under IFRS 2. However, for entities subject to IAS 33 – *Earnings per Share* – the grant date fair value may be required in order to make the disclosures required by that standard – see Chapter 35 at 6.4.2.

IFRS 2 raises some issues of interpretation on detailed aspects of the methodology such as:

- determining the vesting period (see 9.2.2.A below);
- periodic allocation of cost (see 9.2.2.B below);
- treatment of non-market vesting conditions (see 9.2.2.C below);
- treatment of market conditions and non-vesting conditions (see 9.2.2.D below); and
- treatment of modification, cancellation and settlement (see 9.2.2.E below).

9.2.2.A Determining the vesting period

The rules for determining vesting periods are the same as those applicable to equity-settled transactions, as discussed in 6.1 to 6.4 above. Where an award vests immediately, IFRS 2 creates a presumption that, in the absence of evidence to the contrary, the award is in respect of services that have already been rendered, and should therefore be expensed in full at grant date. *[IFRS 2.32]*.

Where cash-settled awards are made subject to vesting conditions (as in many cases they will be, particularly where payments to employees are concerned), IFRS 2 creates a presumption that they are a payment for services to be received in the future, during the 'vesting period', with the transaction being recognised during that period, as illustrated in Example 32.35 above. *[IFRS 2.32]*.

9.2.2.B   Periodic allocation of cost

Paragraph 30 of IFRS 2 states that the required treatment for cash-settled transactions is simply to measure the fair value of the liability at each reporting date, which might suggest that the *full* fair value, and not just a time-apportioned part of it, should be recognised at each reporting date – as would be the case for any liability that is a financial instrument and measured at fair value under IAS 39.

However, paragraphs 32 and 33 clarify that the liability is to be measured at an amount that reflects 'the extent to which employees have rendered service to date', and the cost is to be recognised 'as the employees render service'. This, together with IG Example 12 in IFRS 2 (the substance of which is reproduced as Example 32.35 above), indicates that a spreading approach is to be adopted.

9.2.2.C   Non-market vesting conditions

As drafted, IFRS 2 does not specifically address the impact of vesting conditions in the context of cash-settled transactions – the provisions of IFRS 2 relating to vesting conditions are to be found in paragraphs 19-21 of IFRS 2, all of which fall under the main heading 'Equity-settled share-based payment transactions' immediately before paragraph 10.

Where a vesting condition is a minimum service period, IG Example 12 in IFRS 2 (broadly reproduced as Example 32.35 above) clearly indicates that, during the period to vesting, the liability should be estimated on the basis of the current best estimate of the number of awards that will vest, this estimate being made exactly as for an equity-settled transaction.

As regards other non-market performance conditions, based on the analogy of the treatment of service periods in IG Example 12, we believe that the liability until vesting date should be based on the current best estimate of the outcome of those conditions.

9.2.2.D   Market conditions and non-vesting conditions

There is no specific guidance in IFRS 2 as to whether, in the case of a cash-settled transaction, a distinction is to be drawn between non-vesting conditions or vesting conditions that are market conditions and other non-market vesting conditions, as would be the case for an equity-settled transaction (see 6.2 to 6.4 above). In our view, no such distinction need be drawn, since a cash-settled transaction must ultimately reflect the amount of cash paid. A cash-settled award is required to be valued at each reporting date, so that there will be no cost for an award subject to a market condition or non-vesting condition that is not satisfied. This is different from the accounting model for equity-settled transactions with market conditions or non-vesting conditions, which can result in a cost being recognised for awards subject to a market or non-vesting condition that is not satisfied (see 6.3 and 6.4 above).

9.2.2.E   Modification, cancellation and settlement

IFRS 2 provides no specific guidance on modification, cancellation and settlement of cash-settled awards. However, as cash-settled awards are accounted for using a full fair value model no such guidance is needed. It is clear that:

- where an award is modified, the liability recognised at and after the point of modification will be based on its new fair value, with the effect of any movement in the liability recognised immediately;

- where an award is cancelled the liability will be derecognised, with a credit immediately recognised in profit or loss; and

- where an award is settled, the liability will be derecognised, and any gain or loss on settlement immediately recognised in profit or loss.

9.3 What constitutes a cash-settled award?

There are a number of possible circumstances in which, on, or shortly after, settlement of an equity-settled award either:

- the entity incurs a cash outflow equivalent to that that would arise on cash-settlement (e.g. because it purchases shares in the market at fair value to deliver to counterparties); or

- the counterparty receives a cash inflow equivalent to that that would arise on cash-settlement (e.g. because the shares are sold in the market for cash on behalf of the counterparty).

Such situations raise the question of whether such schemes are in fact truly equity-settled or cash-settled.

Examples of relatively common mechanisms for delivering the cash-equivalent of an equity-settled award to employees are discussed below. It emerges from the analysis below that, in reality, IFRS 2 is driven by questions of form rather than substance. To put it rather crudely, what matters is often not so much whether the entity has written a cheque for the fair value of the award, but rather the name of the payee on the cheque.

The significance of this is that the analysis affects the profit or loss charge for the award, as illustrated by Example 32.36 below.

Example 32.36: Equity-settled award satisfied with market purchase of treasury shares

An entity awards an employee a free share with a fair value at grant date of £5 which has a fair value of £8 at vesting. At vesting the entity purchases a share in the market for £8 for delivery to the employee. If the scheme were treated as cash-settled, there would be a charge to profit or loss of £8 (the fair value at vesting date). If it were treated as equity-settled (as required in this case by IFRS 2), profit or loss would show a charge of only £5 (the fair value at grant date), with a further net charge of £3 in equity, comprising the £8 paid for the share accounted for as a treasury share (see Chapter 45 at 9) less the £5 credit to equity (being the credit entry corresponding to the £5 charge to profit or loss – see 4.2 above).

The analyses below all rely on a precise construction of the definition of cash-settled share-based payment transaction, i.e. one 'in which the entity acquires goods or services *by incurring a liability to transfer cash or other assets to the supplier of those goods or services* for amounts that are based on the price (or value) of the entity's shares or other equity instruments of the entity'. Thus, if the entity is not actually required – legally or constructively – to pay cash to the *counterparty*, there is no cash-settled transaction under IFRS 2, even though the arrangement may give rise to an external cash flow and, possibly, a liability under another standard.

9.3.1   *Market purchases of own equity used to satisfy awards*

It is common for an entity to choose to settle equity-settled transactions using shares previously purchased in the market rather than by issuing new shares. This does not mean that the transaction is cash-settled, since there is no obligation to deliver cash to the counterparty. *[IFRS 2.B48-49].*

The purchase of own shares is accounted for in accordance with the provisions of IAS 32 relating to treasury shares and other transactions over own equity (see Chapter 45 at 9).

Some have raised the question of whether the entity should recognise some form of liability to repurchase own equity in situations where the entity has a stated policy of settling equity-settled transactions using previously purchased treasury shares. In our view, the normal provisions of IAS 32 apply. For example, a public commitment to settle equity-settled transactions by purchasing treasury shares is no different in substance to a commitment to a share buyback programme. There would be no question under IAS 32 of recognising a liability to repurchase own equity on the basis merely of a declared intention. It is only when the entity enters into a forward contract or a call option with a third party that some accounting recognition of a future share purchase may be required.

9.3.2   *Market purchases of own equity following equity-settlement of award*

It sometimes happens that an entity, having issued shares in settlement of an equity-settled transaction, will shortly thereafter purchase a similar number of its own shares in the market. This raises the question of whether such a scheme would be considered as in substance cash-settled.

In our view, further enquiry into the detailed circumstances of the market purchase is required in order to determine the appropriate analysis under IFRS 2.

Broadly speaking, so long as there is no obligation (explicit or implicit) for the entity to settle in cash with the counterparty, such arrangements will not require a scheme to be treated as cash-settled under IFRS 2. This will be the case even where the entity, as a means of managing the dilutive impact on earnings per share of equity-settlement, routinely buys back shares broadly equivalent to the number issued in settlement.

However, in our view, there might be situations in which post-settlement market share purchases are indicative of an obligation to the counterparty, such that treatment as a cash-settled scheme would be appropriate.

For example, the shares might be quoted in a market which is not very deep, or in which the entity itself is a major participant. If the entity were to create an expectation by employees that any shares awarded can always be liquidated immediately, because the entity will ensure that there is sufficient depth in the market to do so, it could well be appropriate to account for such a scheme as cash-settled. The treatment of schemes in which the entity has a choice of settlement, but has created an expectation of cash-settlement, provides a relevant analogy (see 10.2.1 below).

A more extreme example of such a situation would be where the entity has arranged for the shares delivered to the counterparty to be sold on the counterparty's behalf by a broker (see 9.3.3 below), but has at the same time entered into a contract to purchase those shares from the broker. In that situation, in our view, the substance is that:

- the entity has created an expectation by the counterparty of a right to receive cash; and
- the broker is no more than an agent paying that cash to the counterparty on behalf of the entity.

Accordingly, it would be appropriate to account for such an arrangement as a cash-settled award.

In a situation where the entity had pre-arranged to purchase some, but not all, the shares from the broker, in our view it would generally be appropriate to treat the award as cash-settled only to the extent of the shares subject to the purchase agreement.

9.3.3 Broker settlement

Many recipients of share awards, particularly employees in lower and middle ranking positions within an entity, do not wish to become long-term investors in the entity and prefer instead to realise any equity-settled awards in cash soon after receipt. In order to facilitate this, the entity may either sell the shares in the market on the employees' behalf or, more likely, arrange for a third party broker to do so.

Such an arrangement (sometimes referred to as 'broker settlement') does not of itself create a cash-settled award, provided that the entity has not created any obligation to the employees. If, however, the entity has either created an expectation among employees that it will step in to make good any lack of depth in the market, or has indeed itself contracted to repurchase the shares in question, that may well mean that analysis as a cash-settled scheme is more appropriate (see also 9.3.2 above).

Broker settlement arrangements raise a general concern – at least for regulators and auditors – that an entity may be masking what are really issues of shares to raise cash to pay its employees as sales of shares on behalf of employees. If an entity were simply to issue shares (or reissue treasury shares) for cash, and then use that cash to pay an employee's salary, the normal accounting treatment for such a transaction would be to credit equity with the proceeds of issue or reissue of shares, and to charge the payment to the employee to profit or loss.

By contrast, a sale of shares on behalf of an employee is undertaken by the entity as agent and does not give rise an increase in equity and an expense, although an expense will be recognised for the award of shares under IFRS 2. However, the entity may enter into much the same transaction with a broker whether it is selling shares on its own behalf or on behalf of its employees. The challenge is therefore for the entity to be able to demonstrate the true economic nature of the transaction.

For this reason, some take the view that a sale of shares can be regarded as part of a broker settlement arrangement only if the shares are first legally registered in the name of the employee. Whilst we understand the concerns that lie behind this view, we nevertheless question whether legal registration is necessary to demonstrate a broker settlement arrangement. For example, suppose that 100 shares vest in each of

Chapter 32

10 employees who all express a wish that the entity sell the shares on their behalf, and the entity then sells 1,000 treasury shares on behalf of the employees, but without first re-registering title to the shares to the employees. We do not believe that the entity should automatically be precluded from regarding this as a broker settlement arrangement, particularly where the treasury shares are held not by the entity directly but through an employee benefit trust or similar entity (see 12.3 below) that is permitted to hold or sell shares only for the benefit of employees.

By contrast, the entity might regularly purchase and sell treasury shares, but identify some of the sales as being undertaken on behalf of employees only after they have occurred. Such an arrangement, in our view, is more difficult to construe as a true broker-settlement arrangement.

Where shares are sold on behalf of an employee, they will typically attract transaction costs, such as brokerage fees or taxes. If such costs are borne by the entity, they should, in our view, be included within profit or loss as an additional component of employment costs, rather than deducted from equity as a cost of a transaction in own shares.

This highlights a commercial disadvantage of broker settlement arrangements. The entity may have to:

- purchase shares in the market (incurring transaction costs) on behalf of an employee who does not want them and then sell them back into the market on the employee's behalf (incurring more transaction costs); or

- sell shares in the market (incurring transaction costs) on behalf of an employee who does not want them and then buy them back in the market on behalf of another employee who does want them (incurring more transaction costs).

In order to avoid this, entities may try to structure arrangements with their brokers involving back-to-back sale and purchase contracts, under which shares are never physically delivered, but the entity makes a cash payment to the broker in purported settlement of the purchase of shares on behalf of the entity and the broker passes it on to the employee in purported settlement of the sale of the shares on behalf of the employee.

In our view, such arrangements cannot be seen as equity-settled transactions with broker settlement, but must be regarded as cash-settled share-based payment transactions, using the broker as paying agent.

Related issues are raised by the 'drag along' and 'tag along' rights that are often a feature of awards designed to reward employees for a successful flotation or other exit event (see 15.3.6 below).

9.3.4   *Modification of award from equity-settled to cash-settled or from cash-settled to equity-settled*

During the life of an award, its terms will sometimes be modified so as to alter the manner of settlement. In other words, an award that at grant date was equity-settled is modified so as to become cash-settled, or *vice-versa*.

IFRS 2 provides no explicit guidance on such modifications. However, we believe that it is possible to arrive at a reasonable approach by analogy to the provisions of IFRS 2 in respect of:

- the modification of equity-settled awards during the vesting period (see 7.3 above);

- the addition of a cash-settlement alternative to an equity-settled award after grant date (see 10.1.4 below);

- the settlement of equity-settled awards in cash (see 7.4 above); and

- the settlement in equity of awards where the entity has a choice of settlement, but which have been accounted for as cash-settled during the vesting period (see 10.2 below).

9.3.4.A   Equity-settled award modified to cash-settled

Drawing on the principles within the guidance referred to at 9.3.4 above, in our view there are two alternative approaches to accounting for the modification of an award from equity-settled to cash-settled during the vesting period when all other conditions remain unchanged. The first approach is based more closely on the IFRS 2 treatment for the modification of an equity-settled award (see 7.3 above) and the second on that for the repurchase or settlement in cash of an equity instrument (see 7.4 above).

Both approaches take into account IG Example 9 in the implementation guidance to IFRS 2 (see 10.1.4 below) which shows the recognition of an expense for the post-modification remeasurement of the cash-settlement alternative in addition to an expense for the full grant date fair value of the equity-settled arrangement. Although this Example reflects a choice of settlement by the counterparty, rather than the elimination of a method of settlement (as is the case in a modification from equity-settlement to cash-settlement), we believe that an analogy may be drawn between the two situations because the addition of a cash alternative for the counterparty effectively results in the award being treated as cash-settled from the date of modification.

The two approaches are discussed in more detail below and illustrated in Example 32.37. In our view, either approach is acceptable in the absence of clear guidance in IFRS 2 but the choice of approach should be applied consistently to all such modifications.

Both approaches require the recognition, as a minimum, of an IFRS 2 expense which comprises the following elements:

- the grant date fair value of the original equity-settled award (see 7.3 above); plus

- any incremental fair value arising from the modification of that award (see 7.1 above); plus

- any remeasurement of the liability between its fair value at the modification date and the amount finally settled (see 10.1.4 below).

Over the vesting period as a whole, both approaches result in the same total IFRS 2 expense and liability/cash settlement amount with the net overall difference between the two being an adjustment to equity. However, the timing of recognition of any incremental fair value arising on modification will differ under the two approaches, as explained below.

Approach 1

- At the date of modification a liability is recognised based on the fair value of the cash-settled award as at that date and the extent to which the vesting period has expired.

- The entire corresponding debit is taken to equity. Any incremental fair value of the cash-settled award over that of the equity-settled award as at the modification date will be expensed over the period from the date of modification to the date of settlement of the cash-settled award (i.e. no expense is recognised at the date of modification).

- The total fair value of the cash-settled award is remeasured through profit or loss on an ongoing basis between the date of modification and the date of settlement.

As Approach 1 is based on the accounting treatment for a modification of an equity-settled award, no incremental fair value is recognised as an expense at the modification date. This means that, in cases where the fair value of the modified award is higher at the date of modification than that of the original award, the reduction in equity at the date of modification will be higher than the proportionate fair value at that date of the original equity-settled award. This situation reverses over the remainder of the vesting period when an expense (and corresponding credit to equity) will be recognised for the incremental fair value of the modified award.

Approach 2

- As for Approach 1, at the date of modification a liability is recognised based on the fair value of the cash-settled award as at that date and the extent to which the vesting period has expired.

- Unlike Approach 1, the corresponding debit is taken to equity only to the extent of the fair value of the original equity-settled award as at the date of modification. Any incremental fair value of the cash-settled award over the equity-settled award as at the modification date is expensed immediately on modification to the extent that the vesting period has expired. The remainder of any incremental value is expensed over the period from the date of modification to the date of settlement.

- As for Approach 1, the total fair value of the cash-settled award is remeasured through profit or loss on an ongoing basis between the date of modification and the date of settlement.

Approach 2 is based on the accounting treatment for a repurchase of an equity instrument where a reduction in equity up to the fair value of the equity instrument is recognised as at the date of repurchase with any incremental fair value of the repurchase arrangement being treated as an expense. Whilst Approach 2 avoids the potential problem of an immediate reduction in equity in excess of the fair value of the equity-settled award, its settlement approach could be seen as diverging from the basic IFRS 2 treatment for the modification of an equity-settled award where none of the incremental fair value arising on a modification is expensed at the date of modification.

Example 32.37: Modification of equity-settled award to cash-settled award

A   *Modified award with same fair value as original award*

On 1 January 2011 an entity granted an equity-settled award, with a fair value at that date of €500, and vesting if the employee is still in service on 31 December 2014. On 1 January 2013, the award is modified so as to become cash-settled, but its terms are otherwise unchanged. The fair value at that date of both alternatives is €150. The liability is actually settled for €180 on 31 December 2014.

	Approach 1			Approach 2		
	Expense	Equity	Liability	Expense	Equity	Liability
	€	€	€	€	€	€
Two years ended 31.12.2012	250	(250)	–	250	(250)	–
1.1.2013 – modification	–	75	(75)	–	75	(75)
Two years ended 31.12.2014	280	(175)	(105)	280	(175)	(105)
Totals	530	(350)	(180)	530	(350)	(180)

During 2011 and 2012 the entity recognises a cumulative expense of €250, being the proportion of the grant date fair value of the equity-settled award of €500 attributable to 2/4 of the vesting period.

At 1 January 2013, it is necessary to recognise a liability of €75 (€150 × 2/4 – see 9.2.2 above). The full amount of this liability is recognised as a reduction in equity under both Approaches as there is no difference between the fair value of the original and modified awards as at the modification date.

As the award is continuing, there is no acceleration at the modification date of the as yet unrecognised amount of the grant date fair value of the original award (€250, being €500 × 2/4), as would occur in an immediate settlement (see 7.4 above).

During 2013 and 2014 (the period from modification to settlement date), the entity recognises an increase of €105 in the fair value of the liability (€180 – €75). During this period it also recognises employee costs totalling €280, being the remaining grant date fair value of €250 (€500 total less €250 expensed prior to modification) plus the post-modification remeasurement of the liability of €30 (€180-€150). The balance of €175 is credited to equity.

In total the entity recognises an expense of €530, being the original grant date fair value of the equity-settled award of €500 plus the post-modification remeasurement of the liability of €30. This adjustment of €30 is consistent with the approach taken in IG Example 9 in the implementation guidance to IFRS 2 (see 10.1.4 and Example 32.40 below).

B   *Modified award with greater fair value than original award*

On 1 January 2011 an entity granted an equity-settled award, with a fair value at that date of €500, and vesting if the employee is still in service on 31 December 2014. On 1 January 2013, the award is modified so as to become cash-settled, with the new award having a higher fair value than the original award. At that date, the fair value of the original award is €150, but that of the cash-settled replacement award is €170. The liability is actually settled for €200 on 31 December 2014.

	Approach 1			Approach 2		
	Expense	Equity	Liability	Expense	Equity	Liability
	€	€	€	€	€	€
Two years ended 31.12.2012	250	(250)	–	250	(250)	–
1.1.2013 – modification	–	85	(85)	10	75	(85)
Two years ended 31.12.2014	300	(185)	(115)	290	(175)	(115)
Totals	550	(350)	(200)	550	(350)	(200)

During 2011 and 2012 the entity recognises a cumulative expense of €250, being the proportion of the grant date fair value of the equity-settled award of €500 attributable to 2/4 of the vesting period.

At 1 January 2013, it is necessary to recognise a liability of €85 (€170 × 2/4 – see 9.2.2 above). Under Approach 1 the difference between the fair value of the original equity-settled award and the modified award (€20 in total) is not recognised immediately as an expense but is spread over the remainder of the vesting period (i.e. starting from the date of modification). The liability of €85 is therefore recognised as a reduction in equity. Under Approach 2, the difference between the fair value of the original equity-settled award and the modified award is expensed immediately to the extent that the vesting period has already expired (€20 × 2/4) with the remainder being expensed in the post-modification period.

As the award is continuing, there is no acceleration at the modification date of the as yet unrecognised amount of the grant date fair value of the original award (€250, being €500 × 2/4) as would occur in an immediate settlement (see 7.4 above).

During 2013 and 2014 (the period from modification to settlement date), the entity recognises an increase of €115 in the fair value of the liability (€200 – €85). During this period, under Approach 1 it also recognises employee costs totalling €300, being the remaining grant date fair value of €250 (€500 total less €250 expensed prior to modification) plus the incremental modification fair value of €20 (€170-€150) plus the remeasurement of the liability of €30 (€200-€170) between modification date and settlement date. The balance of €185 is credited to equity. For Approach 2, the expense and the credit to equity during this period are €10 less than under Approach 1 because a proportionate amount of the incremental fair value was expensed immediately at the modification date.

In total the entity recognises an expense of €550, being the original grant date fair value of the equity-settled award of €500 plus the incremental fair value of €20 arising on modification of the award plus the post-modification remeasurement of the liability of €30. This remeasurement adjustment of €30 is consistent with the approach taken in IG Example 9 in the implementation guidance to IFRS 2 (see 10.1.4 and Example 32.40 below).

C   Modified award with lower fair value than original award

On 1 January 2011 an entity granted an equity-settled award, with a fair value at that date of €500, and vesting if the employee is still in service on 31 December 2014. On 1 January 2013, the award is modified so as to become cash-settled, but its terms are otherwise unchanged. At that date, the fair value of the original award is €150, but that of the cash-settled replacement award is €130. The liability is actually settled for €180 on 31 December 2014.

	Approach 1			Approach 2		
	Expense	Equity	Liability	Expense	Equity	Liability
	€	€	€	€	€	€
Two years ended 31.12.2012	250	(250)	–	250	(250)	–
1.1.2013 – modification	–	65	(65)	–	65	(65)
Two years ended 31.12.2014	300	(185)	(115)	300	(185)	(115)
Totals	550	(370)	(180)	550	(370)	(180)

During 2011 and 2012 the entity recognises a cumulative expense of €250, being the proportion of the grant date fair value of the equity-settled award of €500 attributable to 2/4 of the vesting period.

At 1 January 2013, it is necessary to recognise a liability of €65 (€130 × 2/4 – see 9.2.2 above). The full amount of this liability is recognised as a reduction in equity under both Approaches as the fair value of the modified award is lower than that of the original award. No gain is recognised for the reduction in fair value consistent with the general principle in IFRS 2 that the cost recognised for an equity-settled award must be at least the grant date fair value of the award.

As the award is continuing, there is no acceleration at the modification date of the as yet unrecognised amount of the grant date fair value of the original award (€250, being €500 × 2/4) as would occur in an immediate settlement (see 7.4 above).

During 2013 and 2014 (the period from modification to settlement date), the entity recognises an increase of €115 in the fair value of the liability (€180 – €65). During this period it also recognises employee costs totalling €300, being the remaining grant date fair value of €250 (€500 total less €250 expensed prior to modification) plus the remeasurement of the liability of €50 (€180-€130) between modification date and settlement date. The balance of €185 is credited to equity.

In total the entity recognises an expense of €550, being the original grant date fair value of the equity-settled award of €500 plus the post-modification remeasurement of the liability of €50. This adjustment of €50 is consistent with the approach taken in IG Example 9 in the implementation guidance to IFRS 2 (see 10.1.4 and Example 32.40 below).

Whilst the overall liability in Scenario C is the same as that in Scenario A above, the total expense and overall net credit to equity are higher even though the cash-settled award had a lower fair value at the modification date than that in Scenario A. This might appear illogical but is consistent with the approach in IG Example 9 and the requirement to recognise, as a minimum, the grant date fair value of the original equity-settled award together with any post-modification change in the fair value of the liability.

D   Modified award with greater fair value than original award but settled for less than modification date fair value

On 1 January 2011 an entity granted an equity-settled award, with a fair value at that date of €500, and vesting if the employee is still in service on 31 December 2014. On 1 January 2013, the award is modified so as to become cash-settled, with the new award having a higher fair value than the original award. At that date, the fair value of the original award is €150, but that of the cash-settled replacement award is €170. The liability is actually settled for €125 on 31 December 2014.

| | Approach 1 | | | Approach 2 | | |
	Expense	Equity	Liability	Expense	Equity	Liability
	€	€	€	€	€	€
Two years ended 31.12.2012	250	(250)	–	250	(250)	–
1.1.2013 – modification	–	85	(85)	10	75	(85)
Two years ended 31.12.2014	225	(185)	(40)	215	(175)	(40)
Totals	475	(350)	(125)	475	(350)	(125)

During 2011 and 2012 the entity recognises a cumulative expense of €250, being the proportion of the grant date fair value of the equity-settled award of €500 attributable to 2/4 of the vesting period.

At 1 January 2013, it is necessary to recognise a liability of €85 (€170 × 2/4 – see 9.2.2 above). Under Approach 1 the difference between the fair value of the original equity-settled award and the modified award (€20 in total) is not recognised immediately as an expense but is spread over the remainder of the vesting period (i.e. starting from the date of modification). The liability of €85 is therefore recognised as a reduction in equity. Under Approach 2, the difference between the fair value of the original equity-settled award and the modified award is expensed immediately to the extent that the vesting period has already expired (€20 × 2/4) with the remainder being expensed in the post-modification period.

As the award is continuing, there is no acceleration at the modification date of the as yet unrecognised amount of the grant date fair value of the original award (€250, being €500 × 2/4) as would occur in an immediate settlement (see 7.4 above).

During 2013 and 2014 (the period from modification to settlement date), the entity recognises an increase of €40 in the fair value of the liability (€125 – €85). During this period, under Approach 1 it also recognises employee costs totalling €225, being the remaining grant date fair value of €250 (€500 total less €250 expensed prior to modification) plus the incremental modification fair value of €20 less a reduction of €45 (€170-€125) in the fair value of the liability since modification date. The balance of €185 is credited to equity. For Approach 2, the expense and the credit to equity during this period are €10 less than under Approach 1 because a proportionate amount of the incremental fair value was expensed immediately at the modification date.

In total the entity recognises an expense of €475, being the original grant date fair value of the equity-settled award of €500 plus the incremental fair value of €20 arising on modification of the award less the post-modification remeasurement of the liability of €45. This remeasurement adjustment of €45 is consistent with the approach taken in IG Example 9 in the implementation guidance to IFRS 2 (see 10.1.4 and Example 32.40 below).

9.3.4.B   Cash-settled award modified to equity-settled

In the absence of specific guidance for modifications from cash-settlement to equity-settlement, we believe that it is appropriate to draw on the guidance in IFRS 2 for the settlement in equity of awards where there is a choice of settlement, but which have been accounted for as cash-settled during the vesting period (see 10.1.3.B and 10.2 below). Essentially, IFRS 2 requires the liability to be remeasured to fair value at the date of settlement and transferred to equity. Any excess of the fair value of the equity instruments used to settle the award over the fair value of the liability is recognised in profit or loss. This principle can be adapted to the modification of an award from cash- to equity-settlement so that, in effect, the original cash-settled award is treated as having been cancelled and replaced with an equity-settled award.

Within this overall approach, we believe that there are two alternative methodologies for the recognition of any incremental fair value of the equity-settled award as measured at the date of modification and an accounting policy choice may be made to recognise the excess either:

- immediately in profit or loss for the vested portion of the award (an approach that follows more closely the requirements of settlement accounting); or

- over the remaining vesting period (an approach that combines settlement accounting with the spreading approach applied when an equity-settled award is modified – see 7.3 above).

The two methodologies result in the same total expense and credit to equity by the end of the vesting period and differ only in the timing of recognition of part of the expense. Example 32.38 below illustrates the two approaches.

Example 32.38:   Modification of cash-settled award to equity-settled award

A   Modified award with same fair value as original award

In this situation there is no difference between accounting alternatives 1 and 2.

On 1 January 2011 an entity granted a cash-settled award, vesting over four years. On 1 January 2013, the award is modified so as to become equity-settled, but its terms are otherwise unchanged. The fair value of both alternatives at that date is €150.

As at 1 January 2013, the entity will have recognised a liability of €75 (€150 × 2/4 – see 9.2.2 above). This is transferred to equity. As there is no difference between the fair value of the original cash-settled award and the modified award, no further expense is recognised:

		€	€
1.1.2013	Liability	75	
	Equity		75

The remainder of the fair value of the equity-settled award, measured as at the date of modification, of €75 (€150 – €75) is recognised in profit or loss over the remaining vesting period, with a corresponding credit to equity:

		€	€
Two years ended 31.12.2014	Employee costs	75	
	Equity		75

B   Modified award with greater fair value than original award

On 1 January 2011 an entity granted a cash-settled award, vesting over four years. On 1 January 2013, the award is modified so as to become equity-settled, but its terms are otherwise unchanged. At that date, the fair value of the original award is €150, but that of the equity-settled replacement award is €190.

Accounting alternative 1: immediate recognition of increase in fair value as an expense

As at 1 January 2013, the entity will have recognised a liability of €75 (€150 × 2/4 – see 9.2.2 above). This is transferred to equity. The fair values of the original and modified awards, to the extent that they have vested, must be compared. These are respectively €75 (€150 × 2/4) and €95 (€190 × 2/4). The increase in value of €20 is recognised immediately as an expense at the date of modification, with a corresponding credit to equity:

		€	€
1.1.2013	Employee costs	20	
	Liability	75	
	Equity		95

The remainder of the fair value of the equity award, measured as at the date of modification, of €95 (€190 – €95) is recognised in profit or loss over the remaining two year vesting period from the date of modification (as in A above):

		€	€
Two years ended 31.12.2014	Employee costs	95	
	Equity		95

Accounting alternative 2: recognition of increase in fair value as an expense over the remainder of the vesting period

As at 1 January 2013, the entity will have recognised a liability of €75 (€150 × 2/4 – see 9.2.2 above). This is transferred to equity. The fair values of the original and modified awards, to the extent that they have vested, must be compared. These are respectively €75 (€150 × 2/4) and €95 (€190 × 2/4). The liability of €75 is transferred to equity at the date of modification and the increase in value of €20, is recognised as an expense over the two years to 31 December 2014, with a corresponding credit to equity (together with the remainder of the cost of the equity-settled award of €95 (€190 × 2/4):

		€	€
1.1.2013	Liability	75	
	Equity		75
Two years ended 31.12.2014	Employee costs	115	
	Equity		115

C   Modified award with lower fair value than original award

In this situation there is no difference between accounting alternatives 1 and 2.

On 1 January 2011 an entity granted a cash-settled award, vesting over four years. On 1 January 2013, the award is modified so as to become equity-settled. At that date, the fair value of the original award is €150, but that of the equity-settled replacement award is only €130.

As at 1 January 2013, the entity will have recognised a liability and employee costs of €75 (€150 × 2/4 – see 9.2.2 above). The fair values of the original and modified awards, to the extent that they have vested, are compared. These are respectively €75 (€150 × 2/4) and €65 (€130 × 2/4). Although the fair value of the modified award is lower than that of the original award, no gain is recognised. This is considered to be consistent with the requirements of IFRS 2 (see 10.1.3.B below) for an award that has been accounted for as cash-settled during the vesting period but which is settled with equity instruments (See also Chapter 45 at 7):

		€	€
1.1.2013	Liability	75	
	Equity		75

The remainder of the fair value of the equity award, measured as at the date of modification, of €65 (€130 × 2/4) is recognised in profit or loss over the remaining two year vesting period from the date of modification:

		€	€
Two years ended 31.12.2014	Employee costs	65	
	Equity		65

The Interpretations Committee discussed modification from cash- to equity-settlement in May 2011 but the discussions were solely in the context of an arrangement where a cash-settled award is cancelled and replaced with an equity-settled award with a higher fair value.

In addition to an approach based on settlement accounting (as discussed above and illustrated in Example 32.38), the Interpretations Committee considered whether the requirements in IFRS 2 for the modification of equity-settled awards could be fully applied by analogy to cash-settled awards that become equity-settled. The Interpretations Committee did not comment on the relative merits or shortcomings of the two approaches and simply observed that the amendments needed to IFRS 2 to provide specific guidance on this matter would be beyond the scope of the *Annual Improvements* process and better suited to a separate IASB project to improve IFRS 2.[18]

In our view, an approach that fully analogises to the modification of equity-settled awards (where the award remains equity-settled following modification) is less satisfactory than an approach based primarily on settlement because, for example:

- the grant date of the equity-settled award is unclear;

- a grant date fair value is needed for the cash-settled award and this will not necessarily have been determined at the time of granting the award (see 9.2.1 and 9.2.2 above). In our view, a retrospective calculation is unsatisfactory and runs counter to the requirements in IFRS 1 – *First-time Adoption of International Financial Reporting Standards*, for example, for an entity to use earlier fair values only if they have been publicly disclosed [IFRS 1.D2]; and

- the total expense recognised is potentially less than the fair value of the equity award at its only date of measurement.

10 TRANSACTIONS WITH CASH ALTERNATIVES

It is common for share-based payment transactions (particularly those with employees) to provide either the entity or the counterparty with the choice of settling the transaction either in shares (or other equity instruments) or in cash (or other assets). The general principle of IFRS 2 is that a transaction with a cash alternative, or the components of that transaction, should be accounted for:

(a)   as a cash-settled transaction if, and to the extent that, the entity has incurred a liability to settle in cash or other assets; or

(b)   as an equity-settled transaction if, and to the extent that, no such liability has been incurred. *[IFRS 2.34].*

More detailed guidance is provided as to how that general principle should be applied to transactions:

- where the counterparty has choice of settlement (see 10.1 below); and
- where the entity has choice of settlement (see 10.2 below).

10.1 Transactions where the counterparty has choice of settlement

Where the counterparty has the right to elect for settlement in either shares or cash, IFRS 2 regards the transaction as a compound transaction to which split accounting must be applied. The general principle is that the transaction must be analysed into a liability component (the counterparty's right to demand settlement in cash) and an equity component (the counterparty's right to demand settlement in shares). *[IFRS 2.35].* Once split, the two components are accounted for separately. Somewhat confusingly, the methodology of split accounting required by IFRS 2 is somewhat different from that required by IAS 32 for issuers of other compound instruments (see Chapter 45 at 6).

A practical issue is that, where a transaction gives the counterparty a choice of settlement, it will be necessary to establish a fair value for the liability component both at grant date and at each subsequent reporting date until settlement. By contrast, in the case of transactions that can be settled in cash only, no fair value is required at grant date, but is required at each subsequent reporting date until settlement (see 9 above). However, for entities subject to IAS 33, the grant date fair value is required in order to make the disclosures required by that standard – see Chapter 35 at 6.4.2.

10.1.1 Transactions in which the fair value is measured directly

Transactions with non-employees are normally measured by reference to the fair value of goods and services supplied at service date (i.e. the date at which the goods or services are supplied) – see 4 and 5 above.

Accordingly where an entity enters into such a transaction where the counterparty has choice of settlement, it determines the fair value of the liability component at service date. The equity component is the difference between the fair value (at service date) of the goods or services received and the fair value of the liability component. *[IFRS 2.35].*

10.1.2 Other transactions

All other transactions, including those with employees, are measured by reference to the fair value of the instruments issued at 'measurement date', being grant date in the case of transactions with employees and service date in the case of transactions with non-employees *[IFRS 2 Appendix A]* – see 4.1 and 5.1 above.

The fair value should take into account the terms and conditions on which the rights to cash or equity instruments were issued. *[IFRS 2.36]*. IFRS 2 does not elaborate further on this, but we assume that the IASB intends a reporting entity to apply:

• as regards the equity component of the transaction, the provisions of IFRS 2 relating to the impact of terms and conditions on the valuation of equity-settled transactions (see 4 to 6 above); and

• as regards the liability component of the transaction, the provisions of IFRS 2 relating to the impact of terms and conditions on the valuation of cash-settled transactions (see 9.2 above).

The entity should first measure the fair value of the liability component and then that of the equity component. The fair value of the equity component must be reduced to take into account the fact that the counterparty must forfeit the right to receive cash in order to receive shares. In practice, IG Example 13 in IFRS 2 (the substance of which is reproduced as Example 32.39 below) suggests that this will be done by establishing the fair value of the equity alternative and subtracting from it the fair value of the liability component. The sum of the two components is the fair value of the whole compound instrument. *[IFRS 2.37]*.

In many share-based payment transactions with a choice of settlement, the value of the share and cash alternatives is equal. The counterparty will have the choice between (say) 1,000 shares or the cash value of 1,000 shares. This will mean that the fair value of the liability component is equal to that of the transaction as a whole, so that the fair value of the equity component is zero. In other words, the transaction is accounted for as if it were a cash-settled transaction.

However, in some jurisdictions it is not uncommon, particularly in transactions with employees, for the equity-settlement alternative to have more value. For example, an employee might be able to choose at vesting between the cash value of 1,000 shares immediately or 2,000 shares (often subject to further conditions such as a minimum holding period, or a further service period). In such cases the equity component will have an independent value. *[IFRS 2.37]*. Such schemes are discussed in more detail at 10.5 below.

10.1.3 Accounting treatment

10.1.3.A During vesting period

Having established a fair value for the liability and equity components as set out in 10.1.1 and 10.1.2 above, the entity accounts for the liability component according to the rules for cash-settled transactions (see 9 above) and for the equity component according to the rules for equity-settled transactions (see 4 to 8 above). *[IFRS 2.38]*.

Example 32.39 below illustrates the accounting treatment for a transaction with an employee (as summarised in 10.1.2 above) where the equity component has a fair value independent of the liability component.

Example 32.39:   Award with employee choice of settlement with different fair values for cash-settlement and equity-settlement

An entity grants to an employee an award with the right to choose settlement in either:

- 1,000 phantom shares, i.e. a right to a cash payment equal to the value of 1,000 shares, or
- 1,200 shares.

Vesting is conditional upon the completion of three years' service. If the employee chooses the share alternative, the shares must be held for three years after vesting date.

At grant date, the entity estimates that the fair value of the share alternative, after taking into account the effects of the post-vesting transfer restrictions, is €48 per share. The fair value of the cash alternative is estimated as:

	€
Grant date	50
Year 1	52
Year 2	55
Year 3	60

The grant date fair value of the equity alternative is €57,600 (1,200 shares × €48). The grant date fair value of the cash alternative is €50,000 (1,000 phantom shares × €50). Therefore the fair value of the equity component excluding the right to receive cash is €7,600 (€57,600 – €50,000). The entity recognises a cost based on the following amounts.

	Equity component			Liability component		
Year	Calculation of cumulative expense	Cumulative expense (€)	Expense for year (€)	Calculation of cumulative expense	Cumulative expense (€)	Expense for year (€)
1	€7,600 × 1/3	2,533	2,533	1,000 phantoms × €52 × 1/3	17,333	17,333
2	€7,600 × 2/3	5,066	2,533	1,000 phantoms × €55 × 2/3	36,667	19,334
3	€7,600	7,600	2,534	1,000 phantoms × €60	60,000	23,333

This generates the following accounting entries.

	€	€
Year 1		
Profit or loss (employment costs)	19,866	
Liability		17,333
Equity		2,533
Year 2		
Profit or loss (employment costs)	21,867	
Liability		19,334
Equity		2,533
Year 3		
Profit or loss (employment costs)	25,867	
Liability		23,333
Equity		2,534

The above Example is based on IG Example 13 in IFRS 2, in which the fair value of the cash alternative is treated as being the share price at each reporting date. This is clearly an error of principle in the Example in IFRS 2 since, as discussed more fully at 9 above, the fair value of a cash award is not the same as the share price, a point reinforced by IG Example 12 in IFRS 2 (the basis for Example 32.35 at 9.2.2 above). Accordingly, in adapting IG Example 13 as Example 32.39 above, we have deliberately described the numbers used in respect of the liability component as 'fair value' and not as the 'share price'.

Example 32.39 also ignores the fact that transactions of this type often have different vesting periods for the two settlement alternatives. For instance, the employee might have been offered:

(a)   the cash equivalent of 1,000 shares in three years' time subject to performance conditions; or

(b)   subject to the performance criteria in (a) above being met over three years, 3,000 shares after a further two years' service.

IFRS 2 offers no guidance as to how such transactions are to be accounted for. Presumably, however, the equity component would be recognised over a five year period and the liability component over a three year period. This is discussed further in the discussion of 'matching' share awards at 10.5 below.

10.1.3.B   Settlement

At the date of settlement, the liability component is restated to fair value. If the counterparty elects for settlement in equity, the liability is transferred to equity as consideration for the equity instruments issued. If the liability is settled in cash, the cash is obviously applied to reduce the liability. *[IFRS 2.39-40].* In other words, if the transaction in Example 32.39 above had been settled in shares the accounting entry would have been:

	€	€
Liability*	60,000	
Equity†		60,000

*   There is no need to remeasure the liability in this case as it has already been stated at fair value at vesting date, which is the same as settlement date.

†   The precise allocation of this amount within equity, and its impact on distributable reserves, will depend on a number of factors, including jurisdictional legal requirements, which are not discussed here.

If the transaction had been settled in cash the entry would simply have been:

	€	€
Liability	60,000	
Cash		60,000

If the transaction is settled in cash, any amount taken to equity during the vesting period (€7,600 in Example 32.39 above) is not adjusted. However, the entity may transfer it from one component of equity to another (see 4.2 above). *[IFRS 2.40].*

10.1.4 Transactions with cash-settlement alternative for employee introduced after grant date

Such transactions are not specifically addressed in the main body of IFRS 2. However, IG Example 9 in the implementation guidance does address this issue, in the context of the rules for the modification of awards discussed in 7 above. The substance of this example is reproduced as Example 32.40 below.

Example 32.40:   Award with employee cash-settlement alternative introduced after grant

At the beginning of year 1, the entity grants 10,000 shares with a fair value of $33 per share to a senior executive, conditional upon the completion of three years' service. By the end of year 2, the fair value of the award has dropped to $25 per share. At that date, the entity adds a cash alternative to the grant, whereby the executive can choose whether to receive 10,000 shares or cash equal to the value of 10,000 shares on vesting date. The share price is $20 on vesting. The implementation guidance to IFRS 2 proposes the following approach.

For the first two years, the entity would recognise an expense of $110,000 per year, (representing 10,000 shares × $33 × 1/3), giving rise to the cumulative accounting entry by the end of year 2:

	$	$
Profit or loss (employee costs)	220,000	
Equity		220,000

The addition of a cash alternative at the end of year 2 constitutes a modification of the award, but does not increase the fair value of the award at the date of modification, which under either settlement alternative is $250,000 (10,000 shares × $25), excluding the effect of the non-market vesting condition as required by IFRS 2.

The fact that the employee now has the right to be paid in cash requires the 'split accounting' treatment set out in 10.1 above. Because of the requirement, under the rules for modification of awards (see 7.3 above), to recognise at least the fair value of the original award, the total fair value of the equity alternative of the award is deemed to remain $330,000. This is then reduced (in accordance with the rules in 10.1 above) to reflect the fact that the equity-settlement option would entail the sacrifice of the cash-settled option (modification date fair value $250,000), giving an implied value for the equity-settlement option of $80,000 ($330,000 – $250,000).

The award is now 2/3 through its vesting period, implying that the cumulative amount accounted for in equity should be only $53,333 ($80,000 × 2/3), as opposed to the $220,000 that has actually been accounted for in equity. Accordingly, the difference of $166,667 is transferred from equity to liabilities, the entry being:

	$	$
Equity	166,667	
Liability		166,667

The $166,667 carrying amount of the liability can be seen as representing 2/3 of the $250,000 fair value of the liability component at modification date.

From now on, the accounting for the equity component will be based on this implied value of $80,000. This results in the following accounting entry for the expense in year 3.

	$	$
Profit or loss	60,000*	
Liability		33,333†
Equity		26,667‡

*   Balancing figure.

†   Carried forward liability $200,000 (10,000 shares × year 3 fair value $20) less the brought forward liability $166,667.

‡ $80,000 equity component (as determined above) × 1/3.

This results in a total cumulative expense for the award of $280,000 ($220,000 for years 1 and 2 and $60,000 for year 3), which represents the actual cash liability at the end of year 3 of $200,000 plus the $80,000 deemed excess of the fair value of the equity component over the liability component at the end of year 2.

The $280,000 expense could also be analysed (as is done by the implementation guidance to IFRS 2 itself), as representing the grant date fair value of the award ($330,000) less the movement in the fair value of the liability alternative ($50,000, representing the fair value of $250,000 at the end of year 2 less the fair value of $200,000 at vesting). The implementation guidance may have adopted this approach to support an argument that, despite all appearances to the contrary, this methodology does not breach the fundamental principle of the modification rules for equity-settled transactions that the minimum expense recognised for a modified award should be the expense that would have been recognised had the award not been modified (see 7.3 above).

10.1.5 'Backstop' cash settlement rights

Some schemes may provide cash settlement rights to the holder so as to cover more or less remote contingencies. For example, an employee whose nationality and/or country of permanent residence is different from the jurisdiction of the reporting entity may be offered the option of cash settlement in case unforeseen future events make the transfer of equity from the entity's jurisdiction, or the holding or trading of it in the employee's country, inconvenient or impossible.

If the terms of the award provide the employee with a general right of cash-settlement, IFRS 2 requires the award to be treated as cash-settled. This is the case even if the right of cash settlement is unlikely to be exercised except in the most extreme circumstances (e.g. because it would give rise to adverse tax consequences for the employee as compared with equity settlement). If, however, the right to cash-settlement is exercisable only in specific circumstances, a more detailed analysis may be required (see 10.3 below).

10.1.6 Convertible bonds issued to acquire goods or services

In some jurisdictions entities issue convertible bonds to employees in exchange for services. When this occurs, such a bond is not accounted for under IAS 32, but under IFRS 2, since it falls within the scope of IFRS 2 as a transaction 'in which the entity receives or acquires goods or services and the terms of the arrangement provide either the entity or the supplier of those goods or services with a choice of whether the entity settles the transaction in cash (or other assets) or by issuing equity instruments' (see 2.2.1 and 2.2.2 above). *[IFRS 2.2(c)].*

As noted at 10.1 above, the methodology for splitting such an instrument into its liability and equity components under IFRS 2 differs from that under IAS 32. Moreover, under IAS 32 a convertible is (broadly) recognised at fair value on the date of issue, whereas under IFRS 2 the fair value is accrued over time as services are rendered.

It is therefore possible that, if an entity has issued to employees convertible bonds that have also been issued in the market, the accounting treatment for the bonds issued to employees will differ significantly from that of those issued in the market.

10.2 Transactions where the entity has choice of settlement

The accounting treatment for transactions where the entity has choice of settlement is quite different from transactions where the counterparty has choice of settlement, in that:

- where the counterparty has choice of settlement, a liability component and an equity component are identified (see 10.1 above); whereas

- where the entity has choice of settlement, the accounting treatment is binary – in other words the whole transaction is treated either as cash-settled or as equity-settled, depending on whether or not the entity has a present obligation to settle in cash, *[IFRS 2.41],* determined according to the criteria discussed in 10.2.1 below.

10.2.1 Transactions treated as cash-settled

IFRS 2 requires a transaction to be treated as a liability (and accounted for using the rules for cash-settled transactions discussed in 9 above) if:

(a) the choice of settlement has no commercial substance (for example, because the entity is legally prohibited from issuing shares);

(b) the entity has a past practice or stated policy of settling in cash; or

(c) the entity generally settles in cash whenever the counterparty asks for cash settlement. *[IFRS 2.41-42].*

These criteria are fundamentally different from those in IAS 32 for derivatives over own shares (which is what cash-settled share-based payment transactions are) not within the scope of IFRS 2. IAS 32 rejects an approach based on past practice or intention and broadly requires all derivatives over own equity that could result in the reporting entity being compelled to settle in cash as giving rise to a financial liability (see Chapter 45 at 4).

An important practical effect of these criteria is that some schemes that may appear at first sight to be equity-settled may in fact have to be treated as cash-settled. For example, if an entity has consistently adopted a policy of granting *ex gratia* cash compensation to all 'good' leavers (or all 'good' leavers of certain seniority) in respect of partially vested options, such a scheme may well be treated as cash-settled for the purposes of IFRS 2. 'Good leavers' are also discussed at 5.3.8.C above.

Another common example is that an entity may have a global share scheme with an entity option for cash settlement which it always exercises in respect of awards to employees in jurisdictions where it is difficult or illegal to hold shares in the parent. Such a scheme should be treated as a cash-settled scheme in respect of those jurisdictions. It would, however, in our view, be appropriate to account for the scheme in other jurisdictions as equity-settled (provided of course that none of the criteria in (a) to (c) above applied in those jurisdictions).

IFRS 2 gives no specific guidance as to the accounting treatment on settlement, but it is clear from other provisions of IFRS 2 that the liability should be remeasured to fair value at settlement date and:

- if cash settlement occurs, the cash paid is applied to reduce the liability; and

- if equity-settlement occurs, the liability is transferred into equity (see 10.1.3.B above).

10.2.1.A Economic compulsion for cash settlement

Some awards may nominally give the reporting entity the choice of settling in cash or equity, while in practice giving rise to an economic compulsion to settle only in cash. An example might be where an entity that is a subsidiary or owned by a small number of individuals, such as members of the same family, grants options to employees. In such cases there will normally be a very strong presumption that the entity will settle in cash in order to avoid diluting the existing owners' interests. Similarly, where the entity is not listed, there is little real benefit for an employee in receiving a share that cannot be realised except when another shareholder wishes to buy it or there is a change in ownership of the business as a whole.

In our view, such schemes are generally most appropriately accounted for as cash-settled schemes at inception. In any event, once the scheme has been operating for a while, it is likely that there will be a past practice of cash settlement such that the scheme is required to be treated as a liability under the general provisions of IFRS 2 summarised above.

10.2.2 Transactions treated as equity-settled

A transaction not meeting the criteria in 10.2.1 above should be accounted for as an equity-settled transaction using the rules for such transactions discussed in 4 to 8 above. *[IFRS 2.43]*.

However, when the transaction is settled the following approach is adopted:

(a) subject to (b) below:

    (i) if the transaction is cash-settled, the cash is accounted for as a deduction from equity; or

    (ii) if the transaction is equity-settled, there is a transfer from one component of equity to another (if necessary); and

(b) if the two methods of settlement are of different fair value at the date of settlement, and the entity chooses the method with the higher fair value, the entity recognises an additional expense for the excess fair value of the chosen method. *[IFRS 2.43]*.

This is illustrated in Examples 32.41 and 32.42 below.

Chapter 32

Example 32.41: Settlement of transaction treated as equity-settled where fair value of cash settlement exceeds fair value of equity settlement

An entity has accounted for a share-based payment transaction where it has the choice of settlement as an equity-settled transaction, and has recognised a cumulative expense of £1,000 based on the fair value at grant date.

At settlement date the fair value of the equity-settlement option is £1,700 and that of the cash-settlement option £2,000. If the entity settles in equity, no further accounting entry is required by IFRS 2. However, either at the entity's discretion or in compliance with local legal requirements, there may be a transfer within equity of the £1,000 credited to equity during the vesting period.

If the entity settles in cash, the entity must recognise an additional expense of £300, being the difference between the fair value of the equity-settlement option (£1,700) and that of the cash-settlement option (£2,000). The accounting entry is:

	£	£
Profit or loss (employee costs)	300	
Equity	1,700	
Cash		2,000

Example 32.42: Settlement of transaction treated as equity-settled where fair value of equity settlement exceeds fair value of cash settlement

As in Example 32.41, an entity has accounted for a share-based payment transaction where it has the choice of settlement as an equity-settled transaction, and has recognised a cumulative expense of £1,000 based on the fair value at grant date.

In this case, however, at settlement date the fair value of the equity-settlement option is £2,000 and that of the cash-settlement option £1,700. If the entity chooses to settle in equity, it must recognise an additional expense of £300, being the difference between fair value of the equity-settlement option (£2,000) and that of the cash-settlement option (£1,700). The accounting entry is:

	£	£
Profit or loss (employee costs)	300	
Equity		300

No further accounting entry is required by IFRS 2. However, either at the entity's discretion or in compliance with local legal requirements, there may be a transfer within equity of the £1,300 credited during the vesting period and on settlement.

If the entity settles in cash, no extra expense is recognised, and the accounting entry is:

	£	£
Equity	1,700	
Cash		1,700

It can be seen in this case that, if the transaction is settled in equity, an additional expense is recognised. If, however, the transaction had simply been an equity-settled transaction (i.e. with no cash alternative), there would have been no additional expense on settlement and the cumulative expense would have been only £1,000 based on the fair value at grant date.

10.2.3 Change in classification of award after grant date

IFRS 2 does not specify whether a transaction where the entity has a choice of settlement in equity or cash should be assessed as equity-settled or cash-settled only at the inception of the transaction or also at each reporting date until it is settled.

However, in describing the accounting treatment IFRS 2 states several times that the accounting depends on whether the entity '*has a present obligation* to settle in cash'. In our view, this suggests that IFRS 2 intends the position to be reviewed at each reporting date and not just considered at the inception of the transaction.

IFRS 2 does not specify the accounting treatment to be followed if such a change in classification is considered appropriate following a change in the entity's policy or intention. In our view, however, the most appropriate treatment is to account for such a change as if it were a modification of the manner of settlement of the award (see 9.3.4 above). In this situation, the entity is able to choose the manner of settlement which, in substance, is the same as choosing to modify the manner of settlement of an award which does not already give the entity a choice. These situations are distinct from those where the manner of settlement depends on the outcome of a contingency outside the entity's control (see 10.3 below).

10.3   Awards requiring cash settlement in specific circumstances (awards with contingent cash settlement)

Some awards, rather than giving a general right to cash settlement to either the entity or the counterparty, require cash settlement in certain specific and limited circumstances – what IAS 32 refers to as contingent settlement provisions (see Chapter 45 at 4.3). In the absence of specific guidance, questions then arise as to whether such an award should be accounted for as equity-settled or cash-settled and whether this should be re-assessed on an ongoing basis during the vesting period.

10.3.1 *Analysis 1 – Treat as cash-settled if contingency is outside entity's control*

One approach might be to observe that the underlying principle that determines whether an award is accounted for as an equity instrument or liability under IFRS 2 appears to be whether the reporting entity can unilaterally avoid cash-settlement (see 9.1 and 9.2 above). Thus, any award where the counterparty has a right to cash-settlement is treated as a liability in any event, irrespective of the probability of cash-settlement, since there is nothing that the entity could do to prevent cash-settlement. However, an award where the choice of settlement rests with the entity is accounted for as a liability only where the entity's own actions have effectively put it in a position where it has no real choice but to settle in cash.

This analysis would lead to the conclusion that it is first necessary to consider whether the event that requires cash-settlement is one over which the entity has control. If the event, however improbable, is outside the entity's control, the award should be treated as cash-settled. However, if the event is within the entity's control, the award should be treated as cash-settled only if the entity has a liability by reference to the criteria summarised in 9.1 and 9.2.1 above.

This analysis does not seem entirely satisfactory. For example, in a number of jurisdictions, it is common for an equity-settled share-based payment award to contain a provision to the effect that, if the employee dies in service, the entity will pay to the employee's estate the fair value of the award in cash. The analysis above would lead to the conclusion that the award must be classified as cash-settled, on the basis that it is beyond the entity's control whether or not an employee dies in service. This seems a somewhat far-fetched conclusion, and is moreover inconsistent with the accounting treatment that the entity would apply to any other death-in-service benefit under IAS 19. IAS 19 would generally require the entity to recognise a liability for such a benefit based on an actuarial estimate (see Chapter 33 at 3.6), rather than on a presumption that the entire workforce will die in service.

10.3.2 Analysis 2 – Treat as cash-settled if contingency is outside entity's control and probable

It was presumably considerations such as these that led the FASB staff to provide an interpretation[19] of the equivalent provisions of FASB ASC 718 – *Compensation – Stock Compensation* (formerly FAS 123(R) – *Share-Based Payment*) regarding awards that are cash-settled in certain circumstances. This interpretation states that a cash settlement feature that can be exercised only upon the occurrence of a contingent event that is outside the employee's control (such as an initial public offering) does not give rise to a liability until it becomes probable that that event will occur.[20]

In our view, this approach based on the probability of a contingent event that is outside the control of both the counterparty and the entity is also acceptable. The implied rationale (by reference to IFRS literature) is that:

- it is not necessary to have regard to the principles of IAS 32, given that IFRS 2 clearly notes a number of inconsistencies between IFRS 2 and IAS 32 (see 1.4.1 above); and

- it is therefore appropriate to have regard to the principles of IAS 37 in determining whether an uncertain future event gives rise to a liability. IAS 37 currently requires a liability to be recognised only when it is probable (i.e. more likely than not) to occur (see Chapter 29).

The impact of these two analyses can be illustrated by reference to an award that requires cash-settlement in the event of a change of control of the entity (see 10.3.3 below).

10.3.3 Awards requiring cash settlement on a change of control

It is not uncommon for an award to be compulsorily cash-settled if there is a change of control of the reporting entity. Such a provision ensures that there is no need for any separate negotiations to buy out all employee options, so as to avoid non-controlling (minority) interests arising in the acquired entity as equity-settled awards are settled after the change of control.

The question of whether or not a change of control is within the control of the entity is a matter that has become the subject of much recent discussion in the context of determining the classification of certain financial instruments by their issuer, and is considered more fully in Chapter 45 at 4.3.

If the view is taken, in a particular case, that a change of control is within the entity's control, the conclusion under either Analysis 1 or Analysis 2 above would be that the award should be treated as cash-settled only if the entity has a liability by reference to the criteria summarised in 10.2.1 above.

If, however, the view is taken, in a particular case, that a change of control is not within the control of the reporting entity, the conclusion will vary depending on whether Analysis 1 or Analysis 2 is followed. Under Analysis 1, an award requiring settlement in cash on a change of control outside the control of the entity would be treated as cash-settled, however unlikely the change of control may be. Under Analysis 2 however, an award requiring settlement in cash on a change of control outside the control of the entity would be treated as cash-settled only if a change of control were probable.

A difficulty with Analysis 2 is that it introduces rather bizarre inconsistencies in the accounting treatment for awards when the relative probability of their outcome is considered. As noted at 10.1.5 above, an award that gives the counterparty an absolute right to cash-settlement is accounted for as a liability, however unlikely it is that the counterparty will exercise that right. Thus, under this approach, the entity could find itself in the situation where it treats:

- as a liability: an award with a unrestricted right to cash-settlement for the counterparty, where the probability of the counterparty exercising that right is less than 1%; but

- as equity: an award that requires cash settlement in the event of a change of control which is assessed as having a 49% probability of occurring.

In our view, an entity may adopt either approach, but should do so consistently and state its policy for accounting for such transactions if material.

10.3.4 Accounting for change in manner of settlement where award is contingent on future events

When, under Analysis 2 above, the manner of settlement of an award changes as a consequence of a re-assessment of the probability of a contingent event, there is no settlement of the award or modification of its original terms. The award is such that there have been two potential outcomes, one equity-settled and one cash-settled, running in parallel since grant date. At each reporting date the entity should assess which outcome is more likely and account for the award on an equity- or cash-settled basis accordingly. In our view, any adjustments to switch between the cumulative cash-settled award and the cumulative equity-settled award should be taken to profit or loss in the current period. This is similar to the approach for an award with multiple independent vesting conditions (see 6.3.6 above).

Taking the approach that the two outcomes have both been part of the arrangement from grant date, the fair value of the equity-settled award would be measured only at the original grant date and would not be remeasured at the date of change in settlement method. As the cash-settled award would be remeasured on an ongoing basis, a switch in the manner of settlement during the vesting period could give rise to significant volatility in the cumulative expense. At the end of the vesting period, however, the cumulative expense will equate to either the grant date fair value of the equity-settled approach or the settlement value of the cash-settled approach depending on whether or not the contingent event has happened.

The above approach contrasts with that for an award where the manner of settlement is entirely within the entity's control. Where such a choice exists, a change in the manner of settlement would be treated as a modification with a potential catch-up through equity (see 10.2.3 above).

10.3.5 Manner of settlement contingent on future events: possible future developments

During 2009 the Interpretations Committee was asked to clarify how share-based payment transactions should be classified and measured if the manner of settlement is contingent on either:

- a future event that is outside the control of both the entity and the counterparty; or
- a future event that is within the control of the counterparty.

The Interpretations Committee noted that IFRS 2 does not provide guidance on share-based payment transactions for which the manner of settlement is contingent on a future event that is outside the control of both the entity and the counterparty. However, at its January 2010 meeting the Interpretations Committee decided not to add these issues to its agenda and recommended instead that they be dealt with by the IASB, in conjunction with a number of other IFRS 2 classification issues, in a post-implementation review of IFRS 2.[21] This view was reiterated by the Interpretations Committee in March 2011.[22]

10.4   Cash settlement alternative not based on share price

Some awards may provide a cash-settlement alternative not based on the share price. For example, an employee might be offered a choice between 500 shares or €1,000,000 on the vesting of an award. Whilst an award of €1,000,000, if considered in isolation, would obviously not be a share-based payment transaction, it nevertheless falls within the scope of IFRS 2, rather than – say – IAS 19, if it is offered as an alternative to a transaction that is within the scope of IFRS 2. The Basis for Conclusions to IFRS 2 states that the cash alternative may be fixed or variable and, if variable, may be determinable in a manner that is related, or unrelated, to the price of the entity's shares. *[IFRS 2.BC256].*

10.5   Matching share awards

As noted in the discussion at 10.1.2 above, in our view the rules in IFRS 2 for awards where there is a choice of equity- or cash-settlement do not deal adequately with awards where the equity and cash alternatives may have significantly different fair values and vesting periods. In some jurisdictions, an increasingly popular type of scheme giving rise to such issues is a matching share award.

Under a matching share award, the starting point is usually that an employee is awarded a bonus for a one year performance period. At the end of that period, the employee may then be either required or permitted to take all or part of that bonus in shares rather than cash. To the extent that the employee takes shares rather than cash, the employing entity may then be required or permitted to make a 'matching' award of an equal number of shares (or a multiple or fraction of that number). The matching award will typically vest over a longer period.

Whilst such schemes can appear superficially similar, the accounting analysis under IFRS 2 may vary significantly, according to whether:

- the employee has a choice, or is required, to take some of the 'base' bonus in shares; and/or
- the employer has a choice, or is required, to match any shares taken by the employee.

Examples 32.43 to 32.47 below set out an analysis of the five basic variants of such schemes, as summarised in the following matrix.

Employee's taking shares required or discretionary?	Employer's matching required or discretionary?	Example
Required	Required	32.43
Required	Discretionary	32.44
Discretionary	No provision for matching award	32.45
Discretionary	Required	32.46
Discretionary	Discretionary	32.47

Example 32.43: Mandatory investment by employee of cash bonus into shares with mandatory matching award by employer

On 1 January 2012 an employee is told that he is to participate in a bonus scheme which will pay £1,000 if certain performance criteria are met for the year ended 31 December 2012 and he remains in service. The bonus will be paid on 1 January 2013. 50% will be paid in cash and the employee will be required to invest the remaining 50% in as many shares as are worth £500 at 1 January 2013. Thus, if the share price were £2.50, the employee would receive £500 cash and 200 shares. These shares are fully vested.

If this first award is achieved, the entity is required to award an equal number of additional shares ('matching shares') – in this example 200 shares – conditional upon the employee remaining in service until 31 December 2014. The award of any matching shares will be made on 1 January 2013.

Annual bonus

The 50% of the bonus paid in cash is outside the scope of IFRS 2 and within that of IAS 19 (see Chapter 33). The 50% of the annual bonus settled in shares is an equity-settled share-based payment transaction within the scope of IFRS 2, since there is no discretion over the manner of settlement. The measurement date for this element of the bonus is 1 January 2012 and the vesting period is the year ended 31 December 2012, since all vesting conditions have been met as at that date. Notwithstanding that the two legs of the award strictly fall within the scope of two different standards, the practical effect will be to charge an expense over the year ended 31 December 2012.

Matching shares

The terms of the award of 200 matching shares have the effect that the entity has committed, as at 1 January 2012, to award shares with a value of £500 as at 1 January 2013, subject to satisfaction of:

- a performance condition relating to the year ended 31 December 2012; and
- a service condition relating to the three years ended 31 December 2014.

Those terms are understood by all parties at 1 January 2012, which is therefore the measurement date. The fact that the matching award is not formally made until 1 January 2013 is not relevant, since there has been a binding commitment to make the award, on terms understood both by the entity and the employee, since 1 January 2012 (see 5.3 above).

The vesting period is the three years ended 31 December 2014. As at 31 December 2012 only one of the vesting conditions (i.e. the performance condition) has been met. The further vesting condition (i.e. the service condition) is not met until 31 December 2014.

The discussion in 8.10 above is relevant to the valuation of the equity elements of the award.

Example 32.44: Mandatory investment by employee of cash bonus into shares with discretionary matching award by employer

On 1 January 2012 an employee is told that he is to participate in a bonus scheme which will pay £1,000 if certain performance criteria are met for the year ended 31 December 2012. The bonus will be paid on 1 January 2013. 50% will be paid in cash and the employee will be required to invest the remaining 50% in as many shares as are worth £500 at 1 January 2013. Thus, if the share price were £2.50, the employee would receive £500 cash and 200 shares. These shares are fully vested.

If this first award is achieved, the entity has the discretion, but not the obligation, to award an equal number of additional shares ('matching shares') – in this case 200 shares – conditional upon the employee remaining in service until 31 December 2014. The award of any matching shares will be made on 1 January 2013.

Annual bonus

The 50% of the bonus paid in cash is outside the scope of IFRS 2 and within that of IAS 19 (see Chapter 33). The 50% of the annual bonus settled in shares is an equity-settled share-based payment transaction within the scope of IFRS 2, since there is no discretion over the manner of settlement. The measurement date for this element of the bonus is 1 January 2012 and the vesting period is the year ended 31 December 2012, since all vesting conditions have been met as at that date. Notwithstanding that the two legs of the award strictly fall within the scope of two different standards, the practical effect will be to charge an expense over the year ended 31 December 2012.

Matching shares

In our view, it is necessary to consider whether the entity's discretion is real or not, this being a matter for judgement in the light of individual facts and circumstances.

In some cases the entity's discretion to make awards may be more apparent than real. For example, the awards may simply be documented as 'discretionary' for tax and other reasons. It may also be that the entity has consistently made matching awards to all eligible employees (or all members of a particular class of eligible employees), so that it has no realistic alternative but to make matching awards if it wants to maintain good staff relations. In such cases, it may be helpful to consider what the accounting for the 'matching' award would be if it were a pure cash award falling within paragraph 19 of IAS 19:

> 'An entity may have no legal obligation to pay a bonus. Nevertheless, in some cases, an entity has a practice of paying bonuses. In such cases, the entity has a constructive obligation because the entity has no realistic alternative but to pay the bonus. The measurement of the constructive obligation reflects the possibility that some employees may leave without receiving a bonus.'

This is discussed further in Chapter 33 at 6.1.3.

In making the determination of whether a constructive obligation would exist under IAS 19, it would be necessary to consider past data (e.g. the percentage of employees who have received matching awards having received the original award).

If it is concluded that the entity does not have a constructive obligation to make a matching award, the accounting treatment would follow the legal form of the transaction. On this view, the grant date (and therefore measurement date) would be 1 January 2013, and the vesting period two years from 1 January 2013 to 31 December 2014.

If it is concluded that the entity does have a constructive obligation to make a matching award, the effect is that the matching award of shares is equivalent to the mandatory matching award in Example 32.43 above, and should therefore be accounted for in the same way – i.e. the measurement date is 1 January 2012 and the vesting period is the three years ended 31 December 2014.

The discussion in 8.10 above is relevant to the valuation of the matching equity award.

Example 32.45:   Discretionary investment by employee of cash bonus into shares with no matching award

On 1 January 2012 an employee is told that he is to participate in a bonus scheme which will pay £1,000 if certain performance criteria are met for the year ended 31 December 2012. The bonus will be paid on 1 January 2013. 50% will be paid in cash and the employee will be permitted, but not required, to invest the remaining 50% in as many shares as are worth £500 at 1 January 2013. Thus, if the share price were £2.50, the employee could choose to receive either (a) £1,000 or (b) £500 cash and 200 shares. Any shares received are fully vested.

The 50% of the bonus automatically paid in cash is outside the scope of IFRS 2 and within that of IAS 19 (see Chapter 33).

The 50% of the bonus that may be invested in shares falls within the scope of IFRS 2 as a share-based payment transaction in which the terms of the arrangement provide the counterparty with the choice of settlement. This is the case even though the value of the alternative award is always £500 and does not depend on the share price (see 10.4 above).

The measurement date of the award is 1 January 2012 and the vesting period is the year ended 31 December 2012. The methodology set out in IFRS 2 for awards where the counterparty has a choice of settlement would lead to recognition over the vesting period of a liability component of £500 and an equity component of zero (see 10.1.2 above). If in fact the employee took shares at vesting, the £500 liability would be transferred to equity.

Example 32.46:   Discretionary investment by employee of cash bonus into shares with mandatory matching award by employer

On 1 January 2012 an employee is told that he is to participate in a bonus scheme which will pay £1,000 if certain performance criteria are met for the year ended 31 December 2012. The bonus will be paid on 1 January 2013. 50% will be paid in cash and the employee will be permitted, but not required, to invest the remaining 50% in as many shares as are worth £500 at 1 January 2013. Thus, if the share price were £2.50, the employee could choose to receive either (a) £1,000 or (b) £500 cash and 200 shares.

If the employee elects to reinvest the bonus in shares, the shares are not fully vested unless the employee remains in service until 31 December 2014. However, if the employee elects to receive 50% of the bonus in shares, the entity is required to award an equal number of additional shares ('matching shares'), in this case 200 shares, also conditional upon the employee remaining in service until 31 December 2014. The award of any matching shares will be made on 1 January 2013.

The 50% of the bonus automatically paid in cash is outside the scope of IFRS 2 and within that of IAS 19 (see Chapter 33).

The 50% of the bonus that may be invested in shares falls within the scope of IFRS 2 as a share-based payment transaction in which the terms of the arrangement provide the counterparty with the choice of settlement. This is the case even though the value of the alternative award is always £500 and does not depend on the share price (see 10.4 above).

The mandatory nature of the matching shares means that the award is a share-based payment transaction, entered into on (and therefore measured as at) 1 January 2012, in which the terms of the arrangement provide the counterparty with a choice of settlement between:

- at 1 January 2013: cash of £500, subject to performance in the year ended 31 December 2012; or
- at 31 December 2014: shares with a value of £1,000 as at 1 January 2013, subject to:
  (i)   performance in the year ended 31 December 2012; and
  (ii) service during the three years ended 31 December 2014.

The equity component as calculated in accordance with IFRS 2 will have a value in excess of zero (see 10.1.2 above). The measurement date of the equity component is 1 January 2012. However, as discussed at 10.1.3.A above, IFRS 2 does not specify how to deal with a transaction where the counterparty has the choice of equity- or cash-settlement but the liability and equity components have different vesting periods. In our view it is appropriate to recognise the liability and equity components independently over their different vesting periods, i.e. in this case:

- for the liability component (i.e. the fair value of the cash alternative), the year ended 31 December 2012;
- for the equity component (i.e. the excess of the total fair value of the award over the fair value of the cash alternative), the three years ended 31 December 2014.

Thus, at the end of the year ended 31 December 2012, the entity will have recorded:

- as a liability, the cost of the portion of the annual award that the employee may take in cash or equity;
- in equity, one-third of the cost of the matching award.

If the employee decides to take shares, the entity would simply transfer the amount recorded as a liability to equity and recognise the remaining cost of the matching shares over the following two years.

If, however, the employee elects to take cash, the position is more complicated. Clearly, the main accounting entry is to reduce the liability, with a corresponding reduction in cash, when the liability is settled. However, this raises the question of what is to be done with the one-third cost for the matching award already recognised in equity.

In our view, by electing to receive cash, the employee has effectively failed to exercise his option to receive additional equity at the end of 2014. This should therefore be accounted for as a failure to exercise (see 7 above), so that the amount already recognised in equity would not be reversed, but no further cost would be recognised. *[IFRS 2.40]*.

There is an argument that IFRS 2 could be read as requiring an election by the employee for cash at the end of 2012 to be treated as a cancellation of the matching award, due to the employee's failure to fulfil a non-vesting condition (i.e. not taking the cash alternative) for the matching award – see 3.2 and 6.4 above. This would require the remaining two-thirds of the matching award not yet recognised to be recognised immediately, resulting in an expense for an award that does not actually crystallise. Another view – which we prefer – would be that the requirement of paragraph 38 of IFRS 2 to 'account separately' for the liability and equity components of a transaction offering the employee alternative methods of settlement (see 10.1.3 above) suggests that not taking the cash alternative should not be considered as a non-vesting condition for the equity alternative.

Example 32.47: Discretionary investment by employee of cash bonus into shares with discretionary matching award by employer

On 1 January 2012 an employee is told that he is to participate in a bonus scheme which will pay £1,000 if certain performance criteria are met for the year ended 31 December 2012. The bonus will be paid on 1 January 2013. 50% will be paid in cash and the employee will be permitted, but not required, to invest the remaining 50% in as many shares as are worth £500. Thus, if the share price were £2.50, the employee could choose to receive either (a) £1,000 or (b) £500 cash and 200 shares. Any shares received under this part of the arrangement are fully vested.

If the employee elects to receive shares, the entity has the discretion, but not the obligation, to award additional shares ('matching shares') – in this case 200 shares – conditional upon the employee remaining in service until 31 December 2014. The award of any matching shares will be made on 1 January 2013.

The 50% of the bonus automatically paid in cash is outside the scope of IFRS 2 and within that of IAS 19 (see Chapter 33).

The 50% of the bonus that may be invested in shares falls within the scope of IFRS 2 as a share-based payment transaction in which the terms of the arrangement provide the counterparty with the choice of settlement. This is the case even though the value of the alternative award is always £500 and does not depend on the share price (see 10.4 above).

It is in our view necessary, as discussed in Example 32.44 above, to consider whether the entity's discretion to make an award of matching shares is real or not, this being a matter for judgement in the light of individual facts and circumstances.

If it is determined that the entity is effectively obliged to match any share award taken by the employee, then the award should be analysed as giving the employee the choice of settlement between:

- at 1 January 2013: cash of £500, subject to performance in the year ended 31 December 2012; or

- at 1 January 2013 shares with a value of £500 at 1 January 2013 subject to performance in the year ended 31 December 2012; and, at 31 December 2014: the same number of shares again subject to (i) performance in the year ended 31 December 2012 and (ii) service during the three years ended 31 December 2014.

In this case the grant date (and therefore measurement date) of all the equity awards would be taken as 1 January 2012. As regards the award due on 1 January 2013, this would be split into its equity and liability components, and in this case the equity component would have a value of zero (since the two components are essentially worth the same). Thus the entity would accrue a liability over the year to 31 December 2012. The matching share award would be expensed over the three years ending on 31 December 2014.

Thus, at the end of the year ended 31 December 2012, the entity will have recorded:

- as a liability, the cost of the portion of the annual award that the employee may take in cash or equity;

- in equity, one-third of the cost of the matching award.

If the employee decides to take shares, the entity would simply transfer the amount recorded as a liability to equity and recognise the remaining cost of the matching shares over the following two years.

If, however, the employee elects to take cash, the position is more complicated. Clearly, the main accounting entry is to reduce the liability, with a corresponding reduction in cash, when the liability is settled. However, what is to be done with the one-third cost for the matching award already recognised in equity?

In our view, by electing to receive cash, the employee has effectively failed to exercise his option to receive additional equity at the end of 2014. This should therefore be accounted for as a failure to exercise (see 7 above), so that the amount already recognised in equity would not be reversed, but no further cost would be recognised. [IFRS 2.40].

As in Example 32.46 above, there is an argument that IFRS 2 could be read as requiring an election by the employee for cash at the end of 2012 to be treated as a cancellation of the matching award, due to the employee's failure to fulfil a non-vesting condition (i.e. not taking the cash alternative) for the matching award – see 3.2 and 6.4 above This would require the remaining two-thirds of the matching award not yet recognised to be recognised immediately, resulting in an expense for an award that does not actually crystallise. Another view – which we prefer – would be that the requirement of paragraph 38 of IFRS 2 to 'account separately' for the liability and equity components of a transaction offering the employee alternative methods of settlement (see 10.1.3 above) suggests that not taking the cash alternative should not be considered as a non-vesting condition for the equity alternative.

If it is concluded that the entity has genuine discretion to make a matching award, the analysis is somewhat different.

The portion of the annual award that may be taken in shares should be analysed as giving the employee the choice, at 1 January 2013, between cash of £500 and shares worth £500 (the number of shares being determined by reference to the share price at that date). This would be split into its equity and liability components, and in this case the equity component would have a value of zero (since the two components are essentially worth the same). Thus the entity would accrue a liability over the year to 31 December 2012. If the employee elected to receive shares, this would be transferred to equity.

Any matching share award would be treated as being made on, and measured as at, 1 January 2013. The cost would be recognised over the two years ended 31 December 2014.

The discussion in 8.10 above is relevant to the valuation of the matching equity award.

If, in Examples 32.43 to 32.47 above, the employee had to retain his original holding of shares in addition to completing a further period of service in order for the matching award to vest, the requirement to retain the original shares would be treated as a non-vesting condition and taken into account in the grant date fair value of the matching award (see 6.4 above).

11 REPLACEMENT SHARE-BASED PAYMENT AWARDS ISSUED IN A BUSINESS COMBINATION

11.1 Background

It frequently occurs that an entity (A) acquires another (B) which, at the time of the business combination, has outstanding employee share options or other share-based awards. If no action were taken by A, employees of B would be entitled, once any vesting conditions had been satisfied, to shares in B. This is not a very satisfactory outcome for either party: A now has non-controlling (minority) shareholders in its hitherto wholly-owned subsidiary B, and the employees of B are the proud owners of unmarketable shares in an effectively wholly-owned subsidiary.

The obvious solution, adopted in the majority of cases, is for some mechanism to be put in place such that the employees of B end up holding shares in the new parent A. This can be achieved, for example, by:

- A granting the employees of B options over the shares of A in exchange for the surrender of their options over the shares of B; or

- changing the terms of the options so that they are over a special class of shares in B which are mandatorily convertible into shares of A.

This raises the question of how such a substitution transaction should be accounted for in the consolidated financial statements of A (the treatment in the single entity financial statements of B is discussed at 11.4 below).

The first guidance issued by the IASB on the accounting treatment to be adopted by A is contained in IFRS 3 as revised in January 2008. However, this version of IFRS 3 did not specifically address the accounting treatment where an acquirer replaces acquiree awards on a voluntary, rather than mandatory, basis or where acquiree awards are not replaced in a business combination.

The IASB considered the lack of guidance in these areas as part of its 2009 annual improvements project and, in its *Improvements to IFRSs* published in May 2010, amended IFRS 3.[23] The May 2010 amendment requires the provisions relating to awards that are required to be replaced also to be applied to share-based payment transactions of the acquiree that the acquirer chooses to replace, even if the acquiree awards would not expire as a consequence of the business combination (see 11.2 below). The IASB also included guidance on accounting for equity-settled share-based payment transactions of the acquiree that are not replaced as part of the business combination (see 11.3 below). The May 2010 amendment to IFRS 3 became effective for accounting periods beginning on or after 1 July 2010, with earlier application permitted provided this fact is disclosed. Application of the amendment should be on a prospective basis from the date when the entity first applied IFRS 3 (as revised in 2008). *[IFRS 3.64B]*.

The remainder of Section 11 of this Chapter discusses IFRS 3 as revised in 2008 and as amended in May 2010 (referred to as 'IFRS 3'). The requirements of IFRS 3 (as revised in 2008) prior to the May 2010 amendment are discussed in Chapter 28 of Ernst & Young's *International GAAP 2011*.

There is no specific guidance in IFRS for the replacement of awards in business combinations which are not accounted for under IFRS 3 (as revised in 2008). Further discussion on this may also be found in Chapter 28 of Ernst & Young's *International GAAP 2011*.

11.2   Replacement awards in business combinations accounted for under IFRS 3

A more comprehensive discussion of the requirements of IFRS 3 may be found in Chapter 10.

IFRS 3 requires an acquirer to measure a liability or an equity instrument related to the replacement of an acquiree's share-based payment awards in accordance with IFRS 2, rather than in accordance with the general principles of IFRS 3. References to the 'fair value' of an award in the following discussion therefore mean the fair value determined under IFRS 2, for which IFRS 3 uses the term 'market-based measure'. The May 2010 amendment clarifies that the fair value measurement is to be made as at the acquisition date. *[IFRS 3.30]*.

IFRS 3 notes that a transaction entered into by or on behalf of the acquirer or primarily for the benefit of the acquirer or the combined entity, rather than that of the acquiree (or its former owners) before the combination, is likely to be a transaction separate from the business combination itself. This includes a transaction that remunerates employees or former owners of the acquiree for future services. *[IFRS 3.52]*.

The Application Guidance in Appendix B to IFRS 3 and the illustrative examples accompanying the standard explain how this general principle is to be applied to replacement share-based payment transactions. Essentially, however, IFRS 3 appears to view an exchange of share options or other share-based payment awards in conjunction with a business combination as a form of modification (see 7.3 above). *[IFRS 3.B56]*.

11.2.1 Awards that the acquirer is 'obliged' to replace

Where the acquirer is 'obliged' to replace the acquiree awards (see below), either all or a portion of the fair value of the acquirer's replacement awards forms part of the consideration transferred in the business combination. *[IFRS 3.B56]*.

IFRS 3 regards the acquirer as 'obliged' to replace the acquiree awards if the acquiree or its employees have the ability to enforce replacement, for example if replacement is required by:

- the terms of the acquisition agreement;
- the terms of the acquiree's awards; or
- applicable laws or regulations.

The required treatment of replacement awards may be summarised as follows:

(a)   at the date of acquisition, the fair values of the replacement award and the original award are determined in accordance with IFRS 2;

(b)   the amount of the replacement award attributable to pre-combination service (and therefore included as part of the consideration transferred for the business) is determined by multiplying the fair value of the original award by the ratio of the vesting period completed, as at the date of the business combination, to the greater of:

- the total vesting period, as determined at the date of the business combination (being the period required to satisfy all vesting conditions, including conditions added to, or removed from, the original award by the replacement award); and

- the original vesting period;

(c)   any excess of the fair value of the replacement award over the amount determined in (b) above is recognised as a post-combination remuneration expense, in accordance with the normal principles of IFRS 2 (see 3 to 7 above). *[IFRS 3.B57-59].*

The requirements summarised in (a) to (c) above have the effect that any excess of the fair value of the replacement award over the original award is recognised as a post-combination remuneration expense. The requirement in (b) above has the effect that, if the replacement award requires service in the period after the business combination, an IFRS 2 cost is recognised in the post-combination period, even if the acquiree award being replaced had fully vested at the date of acquisition. It also has the effect that if a replacement award requires no service in the post-combination period, but the acquiree award being replaced would have done so, a cost must be recognised in the post-combination period. *[IFRS 3.B59].*

There is no specific guidance in IFRS 3 on how and when to recognise the post-combination remuneration expense in the consolidated financial statements of the acquirer. In our view, the expense should be recognised over the post-combination vesting period of the replacement award in accordance with the general principles of IFRS 2 (see 6.2 to 6.4 above).

The portions of the replacement award attributable to pre- and post-combination service calculated in (b) and (c) above are calculated, under the normal principles of IFRS 2, based on the best estimate of the number of awards expected to vest (or to be treated as vesting by IFRS 2). Rather than being treated as adjustments to the consideration for the business combination, any changes in estimates or forfeitures occurring after the acquisition date are reflected in remuneration cost for the period in which the changes occur in accordance with the normal principles of IFRS 2. Similarly, the effects of other post-acquisition events, such as modifications or the outcome of performance conditions, are accounted for in accordance with IFRS 2 as part of the determination of the remuneration expense for the period in which such events occur. *[IFRS 3.B60].* The application of these requirements is discussed in more detail at 11.2.3 below.

The requirements above to split an award into pre-combination and post-combination portions apply equally to equity-settled and cash-settled replacement awards. All changes after the acquisition date in the fair value of cash-settled replacements awards and their tax effects (recognised in accordance with IAS 12 – *Income Taxes*) are recognised in the post-combination financial statements when the changes occur. *[IFRS 3.B61-62]*. IFRS 3 does not specify where in the income statement any changes in the pre-combination element of a cash-settled award should be reflected and, in the absence of clear guidance, this will depend on an analysis of whether this is considered to be remuneration expense or whether it is actually closer to a change in a liability for contingent consideration.

The treatment of the income tax effects of replacement share-based payment transactions in a business combination is discussed further in Chapter 31 at 10.7.5.

11.2.1.A Illustrative examples of awards that the acquirer is 'obliged' to replace

IFRS 3 provides some examples in support of the written guidance summarised above, the substance of which is reproduced as Examples 32.48 to 32.51 below. *[IFRS 3.IE61-71]*. These deal with the following scenarios.

Is post-combination service required for the replacement award?	Has the acquiree award being replaced vested before the combination?	Example
Not required	Vested	32.48
Not required	Not vested	32.49
Required	Vested	32.50
Required	Not vested	32.51

In all the examples, it is assumed that the replacement award is equity-settled.

Example 32.48: Replacement award requiring no post-combination service replacing vested acquiree award

Entity A acquires Entity B and issues replacement awards with a fair value at the acquisition date of €1.1 million for awards of Entity B with a fair value at the acquisition date of €1.0 million. No post-combination services are required for the replacement awards and Entity B's employees had rendered all of the required service for the acquiree awards as of the acquisition date.

The amount attributable to pre-combination service, and therefore included in the consideration transferred in the business combination, is the fair value of Entity B's awards at the acquisition date (€1.0 million). The amount attributable to post-combination service is €0.1 million, the difference between the total value of the replacement awards (€1.1 million) and the portion attributable to pre-combination service (€1.0 million). Because no post-combination service is required for the replacement awards, Entity A immediately recognises €0.1 million as remuneration cost in its post-combination financial statements.

Example 32.49: Replacement award requiring no post-combination service replacing unvested acquiree award

Entity A acquires Entity B and issues replacement awards with a fair value at the acquisition date of €1.0 million for awards of Entity B also with a fair value at the acquisition date of €1.0 million. When originally granted, the awards of Entity B had a vesting period of four years and, as of the acquisition date, the employees of Entity B had rendered two years' service. The replacement award vests in full immediately.

The portion of the fair value of the replacement awards attributable to pre-combination services is the fair value of the award of Entity B being replaced (€1 million) multiplied by the ratio of the pre-combination vesting period (two years) to the greater of the total vesting period (now two years) and the original vesting period of Entity B's award (four years). Thus, €0.5 million (€1.0 million × 2/4 years) is attributable to pre-combination service and therefore included in the consideration transferred for the acquiree. The remaining €0.5 million is attributable to post-combination service, but, because no post-combination service is required for the replacement award to vest, Entity A recognises the entire €0.5 million immediately as remuneration cost in the post-combination financial statements.

Example 32.50:   Replacement award requiring post-combination service replacing vested award

Entity A acquires Entity B and issues replacement awards with a fair value at the acquisition date of €1.0 million for awards of Entity B also with a fair value at the acquisition date of €1.0 million. The replacement awards require one year of post-combination service. The awards of Entity B being replaced had a vesting period of four years. As of the acquisition date, employees of Entity B holding unexercised vested awards had rendered a total of seven years of service since the grant date.

Even though the Entity B employees have already rendered all of the service for their original awards, Entity A attributes a portion of the replacement award to post-combination remuneration cost, because the replacement awards require one year of post-combination service. The total vesting period is five years – the vesting period for the original Entity B award completed before the acquisition date (four years) plus the vesting period for the replacement award (one year). The fact that the employees have rendered seven years of service in total in the pre-combination period is not relevant to the calculation because only four years of that service were necessary in order to earn the original award.

The portion attributable to pre-combination services equals the fair value of the award of Entity B being replaced (€1 million) multiplied by the ratio of the pre-combination vesting period (four years) to the total vesting period (five years). Thus, €0.8 million (€1.0 million × 4/5 years) is attributed to the pre-combination vesting period and therefore included in the consideration transferred in the business combination. The remaining €0.2 million is attributed to the post-combination vesting period and is recognised as remuneration cost in Entity A's post-combination financial statements in accordance with IFRS 2, over the remaining one year vesting period.

Example 32.51:   Replacement award requiring post-combination service replacing unvested award

Entity A acquires Entity B and issues replacement awards with a fair value at the acquisition date of €1.0 million for awards of Entity B also with a fair value at the acquisition date of €1.0 million. The replacement awards require one year of post-combination service. When originally granted, the awards of Entity B being replaced had a vesting period of four years and, as of the acquisition date, the employees had rendered two years' service.

The replacement awards require one year of post-combination service. Because employees have already rendered two years of service, the total vesting period is three years. The portion attributable to pre-combination services equals the fair value of the award of Entity B being replaced (€1 million) multiplied by the ratio of the pre-combination vesting period (two years) to the greater of the total vesting period (three years) or the original vesting period of Entity B's award (four years). Thus, €0.5 million (€1.0 million × 2/4 years) is attributable to pre-combination service and therefore included in the consideration transferred for the acquiree. The remaining €0.5 million is attributable to post-combination service and therefore recognised as remuneration cost in Entity A's post-combination financial statements, over the remaining one year vesting period.

Chapter 32

11.2.2 *Awards that the acquirer is not 'obliged' to replace*

IFRS 3 notes that, in some situations, acquiree awards may expire as a consequence of a business combination. In such a situation, the acquirer might decide to replace those awards even though it is not obliged to do so. It might also be the case that the acquirer decides voluntarily to replace awards that would not expire and which it is not otherwise obliged to replace. Following the May 2010 amendment to IFRS 3 there is no difference in the basic approach to accounting for a replacement award that the acquirer is obliged to make and one that it makes on a voluntary basis (i.e. the approach is as set out at 11.2.1 above).

However, in situations where the acquiree awards would expire as a consequence of the business combination if they were not voluntarily replaced by the acquirer, none of the fair value of the replacement awards is treated as part of the consideration transferred for the business (and therefore included in the computation of goodwill), but the full amount is instead recognised as a remuneration cost in the post-combination financial statements. The IASB explains that this is because the new award by the acquirer can only be for future services to be provided by the employee as the acquirer has no obligation to the employee in respect of past services. *[IFRS 3.B56, BC311B].*

11.2.3 *Accounting for changes in vesting assumptions after the acquisition date*

Whilst the requirements outlined at 11.2.1 above to reflect changes in assumptions relating to the post-acquisition portion of an award through post-combination remuneration appear consistent with the general principles of IFRS 2 and IFRS 3, the application of the requirements to the pre-combination portion is less straightforward.

Paragraph B60 of IFRS 3 appears to require all changes to both the pre- and post-combination portions of the award to be reflected in post-combination remuneration expense. This could lead to significant volatility in post-combination profit or loss as a consequence of forfeitures, or other changes in estimates, relating to awards accounted for as part of the consideration for the business combination. It is also noteworthy that this approach appears to require the ongoing reassessment of an estimate of an equity-based transaction made as at the date of the business combination whereas, more generally, IFRS 3 does not permit the remeasurement of equity-settled contingent consideration.

An alternative approach relies on a combination of paragraphs B60 and B63(d). Whilst paragraph B60 is clear that no adjustment can be made to the purchase consideration, paragraph B63(d) refers to IFRS 2 providing 'guidance on subsequent measurement and accounting for *the portion of replacement share-based payment awards ... that is attributable to employees' future services*' (emphasis added). Supporters of this view therefore argue that the remeasurement requirements of paragraph B60 apply only to the portion of the replacement award that is attributed to future service and that the award should be split into two parts:

- a pre-combination element that is treated as if it were vested at the acquisition date and then accounted for in the same way as other contingent consideration settled in equity; and

- a post-combination portion that is treated as a new award and reflects only the employees' post-combination service.

A further alternative approach is based on the guidance in paragraph B59 of IFRS 3 which states that 'the acquirer attributes any excess of the market-based measure of the replacement award over the market-based measure of the acquiree award to post-combination service and recognises that excess as remuneration cost in the post-combination financial statements'. As for the second approach above, the pre-combination element is considered to be fixed and cannot be reversed. However, any subsequent changes in assumptions that give rise to an incremental expense over the amount recognised as pre-combination service should be recognised as part of the post-combination remuneration expense.

Whilst the second and third approaches above are more consistent with the general requirement under IFRS 2 that vested awards should not be adjusted, the first approach, based on paragraph B60, is arguably the most obvious reading of IFRS 3 as currently drafted. In the absence of clear guidance in the standard, we believe that an entity may make an accounting policy choice between the three approaches but, once chosen, the policy should be applied consistently.

The three approaches are illustrated in Example 32.52 below.

Example 32.52:   Accounting for post-acquisition changes in estimates relating to replacement awards

Entity A grants an award of 1,000 shares to each of two employees. The award will vest after three years provided the employees remain in service. At the end of year 2, Entity A is acquired by Entity B which replaces the award with one over its own shares but otherwise on the same terms. The fair value of each share at the date of acquisition is €1. At this date, Entity B estimates that one of the two employees will leave employment before the end of the remaining one year service period.

At the date of acquisition, Entity B recognises €667 (1 employee × 1,000 shares × €1 × 2/3) as part of the consideration for the business combination and expects to recognise a further €333 as an expense through post-acquisition profit or loss (1 × 1,000 × €1 × 1/3).

However, if the estimates made as at the date of the acquisition prove to be inaccurate and either both employees leave employment during year 3, or both remain in employment until the vesting date, there are three alternative approaches to the accounting as explained above:

- Approach 1 – all changes in estimates are reflected in post-acquisition profit or loss (drawing on paragraph B60 of IFRS 3);

- Approach 2 – changes to the estimates that affect the amount recognised as part of the purchase consideration are not adjusted for and changes affecting the post-acquisition assumptions are adjusted through post-acquisition profit or loss (drawing on paragraph B63(d) of IFRS 3); or

- Approach 3 – the amount attributable to pre-combination service, and treated as part of the business combination, is fixed and cannot be reversed. However, any changes in assumptions that give rise to an additional cumulative expense are reflected through post-acquisition profit or loss (drawing on paragraph B59 of IFRS 3).

Using the fact pattern above, and assuming that both employees leave employment in the post-acquisition period, the three alternative approaches would give rise to the following entries in accounting for the forfeitures:

- Approach 1 – a credit of €667 to post-acquisition profit or loss to reflect the reversal of the amount charged to the business combination. In addition to this, any additional expense that had been recognised in the post-acquisition period would be reversed.

- Approach 2 – the reversal through post-acquisition profit or loss of any additional expense that had been recognised in the post-acquisition period.

- Approach 3 – the reversal through post-acquisition profit or loss of any additional expense that had been recognised in the post-acquisition period.

If, instead, both employees remained in employment in the post-acquisition period and both awards vested, the three alternative approaches would give rise to the following entries:

- Approach 1 – an expense of €1,333 through post-acquisition profit or loss to reflect the remaining €333 fair value of the award to the employee who was expected to remain in service plus €1,000 for the award to the employee who was not expected to remain in service.

- Approach 2 – an expense of €666 (2 × €333) through post-acquisition profit or loss for the remaining 1/3 of the acquisition date fair value of the two awards. There is no adjustment to the business combination or to post-acquisition profit or loss for the €667 pre-acquisition element of the award that, as at the acquisition date, was not expected to vest.

- Approach 3 – an expense of €1,333 through post-acquisition profit or loss to reflect the remaining €333 fair value of the award to the employee who was expected to remain in service plus €1,000 for the award to the employee who was not expected to remain in service.

11.3   Acquiree award not replaced

It may occasionally happen that the acquirer does not replace unvested awards of the acquiree at the time of the acquisition. This might be the case where the acquired subsidiary is only partly-owned and is itself listed.

IFRS 3 distinguishes between vested and unvested share-based payment transactions of the acquiree that are outstanding at the date of the business combination but which the acquirer chooses not to replace.

If vested, the outstanding acquiree share-based payment transactions are treated by the acquirer as part of the non-controlling interest in the acquiree and measured at their IFRS 2 fair value at the date of acquisition.

If unvested, the outstanding share-based payment transactions are fair valued in accordance with IFRS 2 as if the acquisition date were the grant date. The fair value should be allocated to the non-controlling interest in the acquiree on the basis of the ratio of the portion of the vesting period completed to the greater of:

- the total vesting period; and

- the original vesting period of the share-based payment transactions.

The balance is treated as a post-combination remuneration expense in accordance with the general principles of IFRS 2. *[IFRS 3.B62A-B62B].*

11.4   Financial statements of the acquired entity

A replacement of an award based on the acquiree's equity with one based on the acquirer's equity is, from the perspective of the acquired entity, a cancellation and replacement, to be accounted for in accordance with the general principles of IFRS 2 for such transactions (see 7.4 above). However, in addition to considerations about whether this is accounted for as a separate cancellation and new grant or as a modification of the original terms, the acquiree needs to take into account its new status as a subsidiary of the acquirer.

If the acquirer is responsible for settling the award in its own equity with the acquiree's employees, the acquiree will continue to account for the award on an equity-settled basis. If, however, the acquiree is responsible for settling the award with shares of the acquirer, then the acquiree would have to switch from an equity-settled basis of accounting to a cash-settled basis of accounting (see 2.2.2.A and 9.3.4.A above).

Even if the acquiree continues to account for the award on an equity-settled basis, the share-based payment expense recorded in the consolidated financial statements (based on fair value at the date of the business combination) will generally not be the same as that in the financial statements of the acquired entity (based on fair value at the date of original grant plus any incremental value granted at the date of acquisition, if modification accounting is applied). The exact timing of the recognition of the expense in the financial statements of the acquired entity after the date of cancellation and replacement will depend on its interpretation of the requirements of IFRS 2 for the cancellation and replacement of options (see Example 32.28 at 7.4.4.B above).

12 GROUP SHARE SCHEMES

12.1 Typical features of a group share scheme

In this section we use the term 'share scheme' to encompass any transaction falling within the scope of IFRS 2, whether accounted for as equity-settled or cash-settled.

It is common practice for a group to operate a single share scheme covering several subsidiaries. Depending on the commercial needs of the entity, the scheme might cover all group entities, all group entities in a particular country or all employees of a particular grade throughout a number of subsidiaries.

The precise terms and structures of group share schemes are so varied that it is rare to find two completely identical arrangements. From an accounting perspective, however, group share schemes can generally be reduced to a basic prototype, as described below, which will serve as the basis of the discussion.

A group scheme typically involves transactions by several legal entities:

- the trust that administers the scheme. Such trusts are known by various names in different jurisdictions, but, for the sake of convenience, in this section we will use the term 'EBT' ('employee benefit trust') to cover all such vehicles by whatever name they are actually known. The accounting treatment of transactions with EBTs is discussed at 12.3 below;

- the subsidiary employing an employee who has been granted an award ('the employing subsidiary'); and

- the parent, over whose shares awards are granted.

In some cases the scheme may be directed by a group employee services entity. A share-based award is often granted to an employee by the parent, or a group employee services entity, which will in turn have an option exercisable against the EBT for the shares that it may be required to deliver to the employee. Less commonly, the trustees of the EBT make awards to the employees and enter into reciprocal arrangements with the parent.

If the parent takes the view that it will satisfy any awards using existing shares it will often seek to fix the cash cost of the award by arranging for the EBT to purchase in the market, on the day that the award is made, sufficient shares to satisfy all or part of the award. This purchase will be funded by external borrowings, a loan from the parent, a contribution from the employing subsidiary, or some combination. The cash received from the employee on exercise of the option can be used by the EBT to repay any borrowings.

If the parent takes the view that it will satisfy the options with a fresh issue of shares, these will be issued to the EBT, either:

(a)   at the date on which the employee exercises his option (in which case the EBT will subscribe for the new shares using the cash received from the employee together with any non-refundable contribution made by the employing subsidiary – see below). Such arrangements are generally referred to as 'simultaneous funding';

(b)   at some earlier date (in which case the EBT will subscribe for the new shares using external borrowings, a loan from the parent or a contribution from the employing subsidiary, or some combination. The cash received from the employee on exercise of the option may then be used by the EBT to repay any borrowings). Such arrangements are generally referred to as 'pre-funding'; or

(c)   some shares will be issued before the exercise date as in (b) above, and the balance on the exercise date as in (a) above.

As noted in (a) above, the employing subsidiary often makes a non-refundable contribution to the EBT in connection with the scheme, so as to ensure that employing subsidiaries bear an appropriate share of the overall cost of a group-wide share scheme.

12.2   Accounting treatment of group share schemes – summary

12.2.1 Background

From a financial reporting perspective, it is generally necessary to consider the accounting treatment in:

• the group's consolidated financial statements;
• the parent's separate financial statements; and
• the employing subsidiary's financial statements.

The accounting entries to be made will broadly vary according to:

- whether the award is satisfied using shares purchased in the market or a fresh issue of shares;
- whether any charge is made to the employing subsidiary for the cost of awards to its employees;
- whether an employee benefit trust (EBT) is involved. The accounting treatment of transactions undertaken with and by EBTs is discussed in more detail at 12.3 below; and
- the tax consequences of the award. However, for the purposes of the discussion and illustrative examples below, tax effects are ignored, since these will vary significantly by jurisdiction. A more general discussion of the tax effects of share-based payment transactions may be found at 14 below.

12.2.2 Scope of IFRS 2 for group share schemes

By virtue of the definition of 'share-based payment transaction' (see 2.2.1 and 2.2.2.A above), a group share-based payment transaction is in the scope of IFRS 2 for:

- the consolidated financial statements of the group (the accounting for which follows the general principles set out in 3 to 10 above),
- the separate or individual financial statements of the entity in the group that receives goods or services (see 12.2.3 below), and
- the separate or individual financial statements of the entity in the group (if different from that receiving the goods or services) that settles the transaction with the counterparty. This entity will typically, but not necessarily, be the parent (see 12.2.4 below).

IFRS 2 provides further guidance on the implication of its general principles to:

- transactions settled in the equity of the entity, or in the equity of its parent (see 12.2.5 below), and
- cash-settled transactions settled by a group entity other than the entity receiving the goods or services (see 12.2.6 below).

It is common practice in a group share scheme to require each participating entity in the group to pay a charge, either to the parent or to an EBT, in respect of the cost of awards made under the scheme to employees of that entity. This is generally done either as part of the group's cash-management strategy, or in order to obtain tax relief under applicable local legislation. The amount charged could in principle be at the discretion of the group, but is often based on either the fair value of the award at grant date or the fair value at vesting, in the case of an award of free shares, or exercise, in the case of an award of options.

IFRS 2 does not directly address the accounting treatment of such intragroup management charges and other recharge arrangements, which is discussed further at 12.2.7 below. *[IFRS 2.B46].*

Worked examples illustrating how these various principles translate into accounting entries are given at 12.4 to 12.6 below.

12.2.3 Entity receiving goods or services

The entity in a group receiving goods or services in a share-based payment transaction determines whether the transaction should be accounted for, in its separate or individual financial statements, as equity-settled or cash-settled. It does this by assessing the nature of the awards granted and its own rights and obligations. *[IFRS 2.43A]*.

The entity accounts for the transaction as equity-settled when either the awards granted are the entity's own equity instruments, or the entity has no obligation to settle the share-based payment transaction. Otherwise, the entity accounts for the transaction as cash-settled. Where the transaction is accounted for as equity-settled it is remeasured after grant date only to the extent permitted or required by IFRS 2 for equity transactions generally, as discussed at 3 to 6 above. *[IFRS 2.43B]*.

IFRS 2 notes that a possible consequence of these requirements is that the amount recognised by the entity may differ from the amount recognised by the consolidated group or by another group entity settling the share-based payment transaction. *[IFRS 2.43A]*. This is discussed further at 12.6 below.

The cost recognised by the entity receiving goods or services is always calculated according the principles set out above, regardless of any intragroup recharging arrangement. *[IFRS 2.43D]*. The accounting for such arrangements is discussed at 12.2.7 below.

12.2.4 Entity settling the transaction

A group entity which settles a share-based payment transaction in which another group entity receives goods or services accounts for the transaction as an equity-settled share-based payment transaction only if it is settled in the settling entity's own equity instruments. Otherwise, the transaction is accounted for as cash-settled. *[IFRS 2.43C]*.

IFRS 2 specifies only the credit entry – the classification of the transaction as equity- or cash-settled, and its measurement. IFRS 2 does not specify the debit entry, which is therefore subject to the general requirement of IFRS 2 that a share-based payment transaction should normally be treated as an expense, unless there is the basis for another treatment under other IFRS (see 3 above).

In our view, the settling entity should not normally treat the transaction as an expense. Instead:

- Where the settling entity is a parent (direct or indirect) of the entity receiving the goods or services, it accounts for the settlement under IAS 27 as an addition to the cost of its investment in the employing subsidiary (or of that holding company of the employing subsidiary which is the settling entity's directly-held subsidiary). It may then be necessary to review the carrying value of that investment to ensure that it is not impaired.

- In other cases (i.e. where the settling entity is a subsidiary (direct or indirect) or fellow subsidiary of the entity receiving the goods or services), it should treat the settlement as a distribution, and charge it directly to equity. Whether or not such a settlement is a legal distribution is a matter of law in the jurisdiction concerned.

We adopt this approach in the worked examples set out in 12.4 to 12.6 below.

12.2.5 Transactions settled in equity of the entity or its parent

12.2.5.A Awards settled in equity of subsidiary

Where a subsidiary grants an award to its employees and settles it in its own equity, the subsidiary accounts for the award as equity-settled.

The parent accounts for the award as equity-settled in its consolidated financial statements. In its separate financial statements, the parent does not account for the award under IFRS 2. In both cases, the transaction may have implications for other aspects of the financial statements, since its settlement results in the partial disposal of the subsidiary (see Chapter7).

Where the parent settles the award, it accounts for the transaction as equity-settled in its consolidated financial statements. In its separate financial statements, however, it accounts for the award as cash-settled, since it is settled not in its own equity, but in the equity of the subsidiary. From the perspective of the parent's separate financial statements, the equity of a subsidiary is a financial asset. *[IFRS 2.B50].*

12.2.5.B Awards settled in equity of the parent

Where the parent grants an award directly to the employees of a subsidiary and settles it in its own equity, the subsidiary accounts for the award as equity-settled, with a corresponding increase in equity as a contribution from the parent. *[IFRS 2.B53].*

The parent accounts for the award as equity-settled in both its consolidated and separate financial statements. *[IFRS 2.B54].*

Where a subsidiary grants an award of equity in its parent to its employees and settles the award itself, it accounts for the award as cash-settled, since it is settled not in its own equity, but in the equity of its parent. From the perspective of the subsidiary's separate or individual financial statements, the equity of the parent is a financial asset. *[IFRS 2.B55].*

This requirement potentially represents something of a compliance burden. For the purposes of the parent's consolidated financial statements the fair value of the award needs to be calculated once, at grant date. For the purposes of the subsidiary's financial statements, however, IFRS 2 requires the award to be accounted for as cash-settled, with the fair value recalculated at each reporting date.

It is, however, important to note that IFRS 2 requires this accounting treatment only for a subsidiary that 'grants' such an award. *[IFRS 2.B52, headings to B53 & B55].* In some jurisdictions it is normal for grants of share awards to be made by the parent, or an employee service company or EBT, rather than by the subsidiary, although the subsidiary may well make recommendations to the grantor of the award as to which of its employees should benefit.

In those cases, the fact that the subsidiary may communicate the award to the employee does not necessarily mean that the subsidiary itself has granted the award. It may simply be notifying the employee of an award granted by another group entity. In that case the subsidiary should apply the normal requirement of IFRS 2 to account for the award as equity-settled.

12.2.6 Cash-settled transactions not settled by the entity receiving goods or services

IFRS 2 considers arrangements in which the parent has an obligation to make the required cash payments to the employees of a subsidiary linked to the price of:

- the subsidiary's equity instruments, and
- the parent's equity instruments.

In both cases, the subsidiary has no obligation to settle the transaction and therefore accounts for the transaction as equity-settled, recognising a corresponding credit in equity as a contribution from its parent.

The subsidiary then subsequently remeasures the cost of the transaction only for any changes resulting from non-market vesting conditions not being met in accordance with the normal provisions of IFRS 2 discussed at 3 to 6 above. IFRS 2 points out that this will differ from the measurement of the transaction as cash-settled in the consolidated financial statements of the group. *[IFRS 2.B56-57]*.

In both cases, the parent has an obligation to settle the transaction in cash. Accordingly, the parent accounts for the transaction as cash-settled in both its consolidated and separate financial statements. *[IFRS 2.B58]*.

The requirement for the subsidiary to measure the transaction as equity-settled is somewhat controversial. The essential rationale for requiring the subsidiary to record the cost of a share-based payment transaction settled by its parent is to reflect that the subsidiary is effectively receiving a capital contribution from its parent. Many commentators, including ourselves, consider it more appropriate to measure that contribution by reference to the cash actually paid by the parent, rather than to use a notional accounting cost derived from a valuation model.

The IASB specifically considered this issue, but concluded that the approach adopted in IFRS 2 better reflects the perspective of the subsidiary as a separate reporting entity. An accounting treatment based on the cash paid by the parent would, in the IASB's view, reflect the perspective of the parent rather than that of the subsidiary. *[IFRS 2.BC268H-268K]*.

12.2.7 Intragroup recharges and management charges

As noted at 12.2.2 above, IFRS 2 does not deal with the accounting treatment of intragroup recharges and management charges that may be levied on the subsidiary that receives goods or services, the consideration for which is equity or cash of another group entity.

The accounting requirements of IFRS 2 for group share schemes derive from IFRIC 11 (now incorporated within IFRS 2 – see 1.2 above), which was based on an exposure draft (D17) published in 2005.

D17 proposed that any such payment made by a subsidiary should be charged directly to equity, on the basis that it represents a return of the capital contribution recorded as the credit to equity required by IFRS 2 (see 12.2.3 and 12.2.6 above) up to the amount of that contribution, and a distribution thereafter.[24]

In our view, whilst IFRS 2 clearly does not require this treatment, this is the preferable analysis. Indeed, the only alternative, 'mechanically' speaking, would be to charge the relevant amount to profit or loss. This would result in a double charge (once for the IFRS 2 charge, and again for the management charge or recharge) which we consider inappropriate when the recharge is directly related to the value of the share-based payment transaction. Accordingly, in the examples at 12.4 to 12.6 below, we apply the treatment originally proposed in D17 to any payments made by the subsidiary for participation in the group scheme.

Many intragroup recharge arrangements are based directly on the value of the underlying share-based payment – typically at grant date, vesting date or exercise date. In other cases, a more general management charge might be levied that reflects not just share-based payments but also a number of other arrangements or services provided to the subsidiary by the parent. Where there is a more general management charge of this kind, we believe that it is more appropriate for the subsidiary to recognise a double charge to profit or loss rather than debiting the management charge to equity as would be the case for a direct recharge.

Before the June 2009 amendment to IFRS 2, some took the view that, whilst any recharge up to the amount of the IFRS 2 charge should be charged to equity, any excess should be charged to profit or loss. The objective of this treatment is to ensure that profit or loss bears the full cash cost of the award where this is greater than the IFRS 2 charge. We can see some pragmatic attraction to this treatment, and acknowledge that it was not explicitly prohibited by IFRIC 11. However, it is difficult to reconcile this approach to the clear requirement of IFRS 2 (as amended) that the receiving entity should measure the goods or services received by reference to IFRS 2 'regardless' of any intragroup charging arrangements (see 12.2.3 above). Moreover, we struggle to see a satisfactory conceptual basis for this 'split' treatment, and in particular for why one part of a payment made under the same intragroup charging arrangement should be accounted for as a distribution and the remainder as an expense.

IFRS 2 also does not address the treatment by the parent of a recharge or management charge received by it. However, it would be consistent with the analysis above for the parent to account for it as a distribution from its subsidiary. This is illustrated in the examples at 12.4 to 12.6 below. The accounting treatment, in the separate financial statements of a parent, of a distribution from a subsidiary is more generally discussed in Chapter 9 at 2.3.

A further issue that arises in practice is the timing of recognition of the recharge by the parties to the arrangement. The treatment adopted might depend to some extent on the precise terms of the arrangement but, in our view, there are two possible approaches:

- to account for the recharge when it is actually levied or paid (which is consistent with accounting for a distribution); or

- to accrue the recharge over the life of the award or the recharge agreement even if, as is commonly the case, the actual recharge is only made at vesting or exercise date.

In our view, the first approach is preferable since this appears more consistent with the overall recognition of the arrangement through equity and with a situation where uncertainties are likely to exist during the vesting period about the existence of a present obligation and the estimated cash outflow. The alternative approach treats the recharge more like a provision or financial liability but, unlike the requirements of IAS 37 or IAS 39, reflects changes in the recognised amount through equity rather than profit or loss and builds up the recharge liability over the life of the award rather than recognising the liability in full when a present obligation has been identified.

The examples at 12.4 to 12.6 below illustrate our preferred treatment and recognise the recharge only when it becomes payable at the date of exercise.

Whichever accounting treatment is adopted, any adjustments to the amount to be recognised as a recharge, whether arising from a change in the IFRS 2 expense or other changes, should be recognised in the current period and previous periods should not be restated.

12.3   Employee benefit trusts ('EBTs') and similar entities

12.3.1 Background

For some time entities have established trusts and similar entities for the benefit of employees. These are known by various names in different jurisdictions, but, for the sake of convenience, in this section we will use the term 'EBT' ('employee benefit trust') to cover all such vehicles by whatever name they are actually known.

The commercial purposes of using such entities vary from employer to employer, and from jurisdiction to jurisdiction, but may include the following:

- An EBT, in order to achieve its purpose, needs to hold shares that have either been issued to it by the company or been bought by the EBT on the open market. In some jurisdictions, the direct holding of shares in an entity by the entity itself is unlawful.

- In the case of longer-term benefits the use of an EBT may 'ring fence' the assets set aside for the benefit of employees in case of the insolvency of the company.

- The use of an EBT may be necessary in order to achieve a favourable tax treatment for the company or the employees, or both.

The detailed features of an EBT will again vary from entity to entity, and from jurisdiction to jurisdiction, but typical features often include the following:

- The EBT provides a warehouse for the sponsoring entity's shares, for example by acquiring and holding shares that are to be sold or transferred to employees in the future. The trustees may purchase the shares with finance provided by the sponsoring entity (by way of cash contributions or loans), or by a third-party bank loan, or by a combination of the two. Loans from the entity are usually interest-free. In other cases, the EBT may subscribe directly for shares issued by the sponsoring company or acquire shares in the market.

- Where the EBT borrows from a third party, the sponsoring entity will usually guarantee the loan, i.e. it will be responsible for any shortfall if the EBT's assets are insufficient to meet its debt repayment obligations. The entity will also generally make regular contributions to the EBT to enable the EBT to meet its interest payments, i.e. to make good any shortfall between the dividend income of the EBT (if any) and the interest payable. As part of this arrangement the trustees may waive their right to dividends on the shares held by the EBT.

- Shares held by the EBT are distributed to employees through an employee share scheme. There are many different arrangements – these may include:

  - the purchase of shares by employees when exercising their share options under a share option scheme;

  - the purchase of shares by the trustees of an approved profit-sharing scheme for allocation to employees under the rules of the scheme; or

  - the transfer of shares to employees under some other incentive scheme.

- The trustees of an EBT may have a legal duty to act at all times in accordance with the interests of the beneficiaries under the EBT. However, most EBTs (particularly those established as a means of remunerating employees) are specifically designed so as to serve the purposes of the sponsoring entity, and to ensure that there will be minimal risk of any conflict arising between the duties of the trustees and the interest of the entity.

12.3.2 Accounting for EBTs

Historically, transactions involving EBTs were accounted for according to their legal form. In other words, any cash gifted or lent to the EBT was simply treated as, respectively, an expense or a loan in the financial statements of the employing entity.

However, this treatment gradually came to be challenged, not least by some tax authorities who began to question whether it was appropriate to allow a corporate tax deduction for the 'expense' of putting money into an EBT which in some cases might remain in the EBT for some considerable time (or even be lent back to the company) before being actually passed on to employees. Thus, the issue came onto the agenda of the national standard setters.

The accounting solution proposed by some national standard setters, such as in the United States and the United Kingdom, was to require a reporting entity to account for an EBT as an extension of the entity. The basis for this treatment was essentially that, as noted at 12.3.1 above, EBTs are specifically designed to serve the purposes of the sponsoring entity, and to ensure that there will be minimal risk of any conflict arising between the duties of the trustees and the interest of the entity, suggesting that they are under the de facto control of the entity.

For accounting periods beginning before 1 January 2013, an entity will generally be required to consolidate any EBT as a special purpose entity (SPE) in accordance with SIC 12 – *Consolidation – Special Purpose Entities*. The required treatment of EBTs in an employer's separate financial statements is somewhat less clear, and is discussed at 12.3.4 below. For accounting periods beginning on or after 1 January 2013, consolidation of the EBT will need to be determined in accordance with the general requirements of IFRS 10 (see Chapter 7).

SIC-12 is discussed in more detail in Chapter 6 at 2.2, but in most cases an EBT will exhibit all four of the characteristics of an SPE set out in paragraph 10 of SIC-12, namely:

(a)   its activities are conducted on behalf of the entity;

(b)   in substance the entity has the decision-making powers (by having the ability to appoint trustees who may be expected to have regard to the entity's wishes);

(c)   the entity obtains the majority of the benefits of the EBT (since the EBT incurs costs that would otherwise be borne directly by the entity); and

(d)   the entity retains the majority of the residual or ownership risks of the EBT (since it, and not the employees, bears the risk of any fall in the value of shares and other assets held by the EBT pending their transfer to employees).

Paragraphs BC70 to BC74 of the Basis for Conclusions to IFRS 2 are clearly written on the assumption that the trust referred to in paragraph BC70 is being included in the financial statements of the reporting entity. This further suggests that the IASB regards the consolidation of such entities as normal practice.

Consolidation of an EBT will have the following broad consequences for the consolidated financial statements of the reporting entity:

- Until such time as the entity's own shares held by the EBT vest unconditionally in employees:

  - any consideration paid for the shares should be deducted in arriving at shareholders' equity in accordance with IAS 32 (see Chapter 45 at 9); and

  - the shares should be treated as if they were cancelled when calculating earnings per share under IAS 33 (see Chapter 35 at 3.2).

- Other assets and liabilities (including borrowings) of the EBT should be recognised as assets and liabilities in the consolidated financial statements of the sponsoring entity.

- No gain or loss should be recognised in the profit or loss on the purchase, sale, issue or cancellation of the entity's own shares, as required by IAS 32. In our view, it is preferable, although not explicitly required by IFRS, for consideration paid or received for the purchase or sale of the entity's own shares in an EBT to be shown separately from other purchases and sales of the entity's own shares in the reconciliation of movements in shareholders' equity. This may be particularly relevant for entities in jurisdictions that distinguish between 'true' treasury shares (i.e. those legally held by the issuing entity) and those accounted for as such under IFRS (such as those held by an EBT).

- Any dividend income arising on own shares should be excluded in arriving at profit before tax and deducted from the aggregate of dividends paid and proposed. In our view, the deduction should be disclosed if material.

- Finance costs and any administration expenses should be charged as they accrue and not as funding payments are made to the EBT.

12.3.3 Illustrative Examples – awards satisfied by shares purchased by, or issued to, an EBT

The following Examples illustrate the accounting treatment required by SIC-12, and its interaction with that required by IFRS 2. Example 32.53 illustrates the treatment where an award is satisfied using shares previously purchased in the market. Example 32.54 illustrates the treatment where freshly issued shares are used.

Example 32.53: Interaction of SIC-12, IAS 32 and IFRS 2 (market purchase)

On 1 January 2012, the EBT of ABC plc made a market purchase of 100,000 shares of ABC plc at £2.50 per share. These were the only ABC shares held by the EBT at that date.

On 1 May 2012, ABC granted executives options over between 300,000 and 500,000 shares at £2.70 per share, which will vest on 31 December 2012, the number vesting depending on various performance criteria. It is determined that the cost to be recognised in respect of this award under IFRS 2 is 15p per share.

On 1 September 2012, the EBT made a further market purchase of 300,000 shares at £2.65 per share.

On 31 December 2012, options vested over 350,000 shares and were exercised immediately.

The accounting entries for the above transaction required by SIC-12, IAS 32 and IFRS 2 in the consolidated financial statements of ABC would be as follows. It should be noted that all these pronouncements require various entries to be recorded in 'equity'. Thus, some variation may be found in practice as to the precise characterisation of the reserves, in deference to local legal requirements and other 'traditions' in national GAAP which are retained to the extent that they do not conflict with IFRS.

	£	£
1 January 2012		
Own shares (equity)	250,000	
Cash		250,000
To record purchase of 100,000 £1 shares at £2.50/share		
1 May 2012 – 31 December 2012		
Profit or loss	52,500	
Equity†		52,500
To record cost of vested 350,000 options at 15p/option		
1 September 2012		
Own shares (equity)	795,000	
Cash		795,000
To record purchase of 300,000 £1 shares at £2.65/share		
31 December 2012		
Cash	945,000	
Equity†[1]		945,000
Receipt of proceeds on exercise of 350,000 options at £2.70/share		
Equity†	914,375	
Own shares (equity)[2]		914,375
Release of shares from EBT to employees		

1   This reflects the fact that the entity has had an increase in resources as a result of a transaction with an owner, which gives rise to no gain or loss and is therefore credited direct to equity.

2   It is necessary to transfer the cost of the shares 'reissued' by the EBT out of own shares, as the deduction for own shares would otherwise be overstated. The total cost of the pool of 400,000 shares immediately before vesting was £1,045,000 (£250,000 purchased on 1 January

2012 and £795,000 purchased on 1 September 2012), representing an average cost per share of £2.6125. £2.6125 × 350,000 shares = £914,375.

†   We recommend that, subject to any local legal restrictions, these amounts should all be accounted for in the same component of equity.

Example 32.53 illustrates the importance of keeping the accounting treatment required by IAS 32 for the cost of the shares completely separate from that for the cost of the award required by IFRS 2. In cash terms, ABC has made a 'profit' of £30,625, since it purchased 350,000 shares with a weighted average cost of £914,375 and sold them to the executives for £945,000. However, this 'profit' is accounted for entirely within equity, whereas a calculated IFRS 2 cost of £52,500 is recognised in profit or loss.

Example 32.54:   Interaction of SIC-12, IAS 32 and IFRS 2 (fresh issue of shares)

On 1 January 2012, the EBT of ABC plc subscribed for 100,000 £1 shares of ABC plc at £2.50 per share, paid for in cash provided by ABC by way of loan to the EBT. Under local law, these proceeds must be credited to the share capital account up to the par value of the shares issued, with any excess taken to a share premium account (additional paid-in capital). These were the only ABC shares held by the EBT at that date.

On 1 May 2012, ABC granted executives options over between 300,000 and 500,000 shares at £2.70 per share, which will vest on 31 December 2012, the number vesting depending on various performance criteria. It is determined that the cost to be recognised in respect of this award is 15p per share.

On 1 September 2012, the EBT subscribed for a further 300,000 shares at £2.65 per share, again paid for in cash provided by ABC by way of loan to the EBT.

On 31 December 2012, options vested over 350,000 shares and were exercised immediately.

The accounting entries for the above transaction required by SIC-12, IAS 32 and IFRS 2 in the consolidated financial statements of ABC would be as follows. It should be noted that all these pronouncements require various entries to be recorded in 'equity'. Thus, some variation may be found in practice as to the precise characterisation of the reserves, in deference to local legal requirements and other 'traditions' in national GAAP which are retained to the extent that they do not conflict with IFRS.

	£	£
1 January 2012		
Equity†1	250,000	
Share capital		100,000
Share premium		150,000
To record issue of 100,000 £1 shares to EBT at £2.50/share		
1 May 2012 – 31 December 2012		
Profit or loss	52,500	
Equity†		52,500
To record cost of vested 350,000 options at 15p/option		
1 September 2012		
Equity†1	795,000	
Share capital		300,000
Share premium		495,000
To record issue of 300,000 £1 shares at £2.65/share		
31 December 2012		
Cash	945,000	
Equity2†		945,000
Receipt of proceeds on exercise of 350,000 options at £2.70/share		

1   This entry is required to reconcile the requirement of local law to record an issue of shares with the fact that, in reality, there has been no increase in the resources of the reporting entity. All that has happened is that one member of the reporting group (the EBT) has transferred cash to another (the parent entity). In our view, this amount should not be accounted for within any 'Own shares reserve' in equity, which should be restricted to shares acquired from third parties.

2   This reflects the fact that the entity has had an increase in resources as a result of a transaction with an owner, which gives rise to no gain or loss and is therefore credited direct to equity.

†   We recommend that, subject to any local legal restrictions, these amounts should all be accounted for in the same component of equity.

12.3.4 Separate financial statements

In contrast to some national GAAPs, where an EBT is treated as a direct extension of the parent entity, such that the assets and liabilities of the EBT are included in both the separate and consolidated financial statements of the parent, under IFRS the accounting model is *prima facie* to treat the EBT as a subsidiary.

This means that the separate financial statements of the employing entity must show transactions and balances with, rather than the transactions, assets and liabilities of, the EBT. This raises some accounting problems, for some of which IFRS currently provides no real solution, as illustrated by Example 32.55 below. This has led the Interpretations Committee and others to discuss whether the 'separate entity' approach to accounting for EBTs is appropriate.

Example 32.55:   EBTs in separate financial statements

An entity lends its EBT €1 million which the EBT uses to make a market purchase of 200,000 shares in the entity. In the separate financial statements of the EBT the shares will be shown as an asset. In the consolidated financial statements, the shares will be accounted for as treasury shares, by deduction from equity.

In the separate financial statements of the entity, on the basis that the EBT is a separate entity, like any other subsidiary, the normal accounting entry would be:

	€	€
Loan to EBT	1,000,000	
Cash		1,000,000

The obvious issue with this approach is that it is, in economic substance, treating the shares held by the EBT (represented by the loan to the EBT) as an asset of the parent, whereas, if they were held directly by the parent, they would have to be accounted for as treasury shares, by deduction from equity. If the share price falls such that the EBT has no means of repaying the full €1,000,000, *prima facie* this gives rise to an impairment of the €1,000,000 loan. Again, however, this seems in effect to be recognising a loss on own equity.

Suppose now that employees are granted options over the shares with an exercise price of zero, which have a value under IFRS 2 of €1,200,000. The entity will therefore book an expense of €1,200,000 under IFRS 2. When the options are exercised, the shares are delivered to employees. At that point the €1,000,000 loan to the EBT clearly becomes irrecoverable (as it has no assets), and must be written off. Normally, the write-off of an investment or loan is an expense required to be recognised in profit or loss. However, to recognise the €1,000,000 investment write-off as an expense as well as the €1,200,000 IFRS 2 charge would clearly be a form of double counting.

Chapter 32

Some suggest that a solution to this problem is to say that the entity has effectively bought a gross-settled call option over its own shares from the EBT, whereby it can require the EBT to deliver 200,000 shares in return for a waiver of its €1,000,000 loan. Thus the accounting for the settlement of the call over the shares is as for any other gross-settled purchased call option over own equity under IAS 32 – see Chapter 45 at 10.2.1.

	€	€
Own shares (deduction from equity)	1,000,000	
Loan to EBT		1,000,000

When the shares are delivered to employees (some milliseconds later), the entry is:

	€	€
Other component of equity	1,000,000	
Own shares (deduction from equity)		1,000,000

If the entity is a parent company, and the shares are used to satisfy share awards to the employees not of the entity itself but of another member of the group, the parent could argue that a corresponding portion of the loan to the EBT should be transferred to the carrying amount of the investment in the relevant subsidiary. The argument for this treatment is that the transaction is, in its totality, equivalent to the parent making a cash capital contribution to the subsidiary, which then uses the cash to acquire shares in the parent for delivery to employees. Such a cash contribution would normally be accounted for in the first instance as an increase in the investment in the subsidiary rather than as an expense.

The precise timing of the transfer between the loan to the EBT and the investment in the relevant subsidiary (i.e. on initial purchase of the shares by the EBT, on final transfer to the employee or at some time in between) could depend on specific facts and circumstances, such as at what point the subsidiary, rather than the EBT, is exposed to any loss in value of the shares.

The Interpretations Committee discussed this issue at its meetings in May and July 2006, and considered whether the EBT should be treated as an extension of the sponsoring entity, such as a branch, or as a separate entity. The Interpretations Committee decided to explore how specific transactions between the sponsor and the EBT should be treated in the sponsor's separate or individual financial statements and whether transactions between the EBT and the sponsor's employees should be attributed to the sponsor.

Interestingly, the Interpretations Committee fell short of dismissing the 'extension of the parent company' approach and has not since revisited this topic other than to re-confirm in March 2011 that it had not become aware of additional concerns or of diversity in practice and hence it did not think it necessary for this to be considered for the IASB's agenda. Thus, in our view, whilst the requirement of SIC-12 to consolidate EBTs could be argued to give a clear steer towards treating the EBT as a separate entity in the separate financial statements of the employer, until there is any final clarification of this issue, it appears acceptable to treat an EBT as an extension of, or agent for, the employing entity. This treatment would result in outcomes essentially the same as those in Examples 32.53 and 32.54 above, while avoiding the problems highlighted in Example 32.55 above.

12.3.5 Financial statements of the EBT

The EBT may be required to prepare financial statements in accordance with requirements imposed by local law or by its own trust deed. The form and content of such financial statements are beyond the scope of this Chapter.

12.4 Illustrative example of group share scheme – equity-settled award satisfied by market purchase of shares

The discussion in 12.4.1 to 12.4.3 below is based on Example 32.56.

Example 32.56: Group share scheme (market purchase of shares)

On 1 July 2012 an employee of S Limited, a subsidiary of the H plc group, is awarded options under the H group share scheme over 3,000 shares in H plc at £1.50 each, exercisable between 1 July 2017 and 1 July 2018, subject to certain performance criteria being met in the three years ending 30 June 2015.

H plc is the grantor of the award, and has the obligation to settle it. On 1 January 2013, in connection with the award, the H plc group EBT purchases 3,000 shares at the then prevailing market price of £2.00 each, funded by a loan from H plc. On exercise of the option, S Limited is required to pay the differential between the purchase price of the shares and the exercise price of the option (50p per share) to the EBT.

For the purposes of IFRS 2, the options are considered to have a fair value at grant date of £1 per option. Throughout the vesting period of the option, H takes the view that the award will vest in full.

The option is exercised on 1 September 2017, at which point the EBT uses the option proceeds, together with the payment by S Limited, to repay the loan from H plc.

H plc and its subsidiaries have a 31 December year end.

12.4.1 Consolidated financial statements

So far as the consolidated financial statements are concerned, the transactions to be accounted for are:

- the purchase of the shares by the EBT and their eventual transfer to the employee; and
- the cost of the award.

Transactions between H plc or S Limited and the EBT are ignored since, under SIC-12, the EBT is consolidated (see 12.3 above). The accounting entries required are set out below. As in other examples in this Chapter, where an entry is shown as being made to equity the precise allocation to a particular component of equity will be a matter for local legislation and, possibly, local accounting 'tradition', to the extent that this is not incompatible with IFRS.

		£	£
y/e 31.12.2012	Profit or loss (employee costs)*	500	
	Equity		500
1.1.2013	Own shares (equity)	6,000	
	Cash		6,000
y/e 31.12.2013	Profit or loss (employee costs)*	1,000	
	Equity		1,000
y/e 31.12.2014	Profit or loss (employee costs)*	1,000	
	Equity		1,000
y/e 31.12.2015	Profit or loss (employee costs)*	500	
	Equity		500
1.9.2017	Cash (option proceeds)†	4,500	
	Equity‡	1,500	
	Own shares (equity)**		6,000

*   Total cost £3,000 (3000 options × £1) spread over 36 months. Charge for period to December 2012 is 6/36 × £3,000 = £500, and so on. In practice, where options are granted to a group of individuals, or with variable performance criteria, the annual charge will be based on a continually revised cumulative charge (see further discussion at 6.1 to 6.4 above).

†   3,000 options at £1.50 each.

‡   This reflects the fact that the overall effect of the transaction for the group *in cash terms* has been a 'loss' of £1,500 (£6,000 original cost of shares less £4,500 option proceeds received). However, under IFRS this is an equity transaction, not an expense.

**   £6,000 cost of own shares purchased on 1 January 2013 now transferred to the employee. In practice, it is more likely that the appropriate amount to be transferred would be based on the weighted average price of shares held by the EBT at the date of exercise, as in Example 32.53 at 12.3.3 above. In such a case there would be a corresponding adjustment to the debit to equity marked with ‡ above.

12.4.2 Parent

The parent has to consider the accounting treatment of the EBT (i.e. whether it is accounted for as a separate entity or an extension of the parent – see 12.3 above). This gives two possible accounting treatments:

- •   EBT treated as separate entity (see 12.4.2.A below); and
- •   EBT treated as extension of parent (see 12.4.2.B below).

We also discuss, at 12.4.2.C below, the accounting implications if the parent, rather than – as in Example 32.56 – a subsidiary, is the employing entity.

12.4.2.A   EBT treated as separate entity

The parent accounts for the share-based payment transaction under IFRS 2 as an equity-settled transaction, since the parent settles the award by delivering its own equity instruments to the employees of the subsidiary (see 12.2.4 above). However, as discussed at 12.2.4 above, instead of recording a cost, as in its consolidated financial statements, the parent records an increase in the carrying value of its subsidiary. It might then be necessary to consider whether the ever-increasing investment in subsidiary is supportable or is in fact impaired. As this is a matter to be determined in the light of specific facts and circumstances, it is not considered in this example. Any impairment charge would be recorded in profit or loss.

In addition to accounting for the share-based payment transaction, the parent records its transactions with the EBT and the purchase of shares.

This gives rise to the following entries:

		£	£
y/e 31.12.2012	Investment in subsidiary*	500	
	Equity		500
1.1.2013	Loan to EBT	6,000	
	Cash		6,000
y/e 31.12.2013	Investment in subsidiary*	1,000	
	Equity		1,000
y/e 31.12.2014	Investment in subsidiary*	1,000	
	Equity		1,000

y/e 31.12.2015	Investment in subsidiary*	500	
	Equity		500
1.9.2017	Cash	6,000	
	Loan to EBT		6,000

* Total adjustment to investment £3,000 (3000 shares × £1 fair value of each option) recognised over 36 months. Charge to period to December 2012 is 6/36 × £3,000 = £500, and so on. In practice, where options were granted to a group of individuals, or with variable performance criteria, the annual adjustment would be based on a continually revised cumulative adjustment (see further discussion at 6.1 to 6.4 above).

12.4.2.B EBT treated as extension of the parent

The parent accounts for the share-based payment transaction under IFRS 2 as an equity-settled transaction, since the parent settles the award by delivering its own equity instruments to the employees of the subsidiary (see 12.2.4 above). However, as discussed at 12.2.4 above, instead of recording a cost, as in its consolidated financial statements, the parent records an increase in the carrying value of its subsidiary. It might then be necessary to consider whether the ever-increasing investment in subsidiary is supportable or is in fact impaired. As this is a matter to be determined in the light of specific facts and circumstances, it is not considered in this example. Any impairment charge would be recorded in profit or loss.

In addition to accounting for the share-based payment transaction, the parent records the transactions of the EBT and the purchase of shares.

This gives rise to the following entries:

		£	£
y/e 31.12.2012	Investment in subsidiary*	500	
	Equity		500
1.1.2013	Own shares (equity)	6,000	
	Cash		6,000
y/e 31.12.2013	Investment in subsidiary*	1,000	
	Equity		1,000
y/e 31.12.2014	Investment in subsidiary*	1,000	
	Equity		1,000
y/e 31.12.2015	Investment in subsidiary*	500	
	Equity		500
1.9.2017	Cash†	6,000	
	Equity‡	1,500	
	Profit or loss§		1,500
	Own shares** (equity)		6,000

* Total adjustment to investment £3,000 (3000 shares × £1 fair value of each option) spread over 36 months. Charge to period to December 2012 is 6/36 × £3,000 = £500, and so on. In practice, where options were granted to a group of individuals, or with variable performance criteria, the annual adjustment would be based on a continually revised cumulative adjustment (see further discussion at 6.1 to 6.4 above).

† £4,500 option exercise proceeds from employee plus £1,500 contribution from S Limited.

‡   This is essentially a balancing figure representing the fact that the entity is distributing own shares with an original cost of £6,000, but has treated £1,500 of the £6,000 of the cash it has received as income (see § below) rather than as payment for the shares.

§   The £1,500 contribution by the subsidiary to the EBT has been treated as a distribution from the subsidiary (see 12.2.7 above) and recorded in profit or loss. It might then be necessary to consider whether, as a result of this payment, the investment in the subsidiary had become impaired (see Chapter 9 at 2.3). As this is a matter to be determined in the light of specific facts and circumstances, it is not considered in this example. Any impairment charge would be recorded in profit or loss.

** £6,000 cost of own shares purchased on 1 January 2013 now transferred to employee. In practice, it is more likely that the appropriate amount to be transferred would be based on the weighted average price of shares held by the EBT at the date of exercise, as in Example 32.53 at 12.3.3 above.

12.4.2.C Parent company as employing company

If, in Example 32.56, the employing entity were the parent, it would record an expense under IFRS 2. It would also normally waive £1,500 of its £6,000 loan to the EBT (i.e. the shortfall between the original loan and the £4,500 option proceeds received from the employee).

If the EBT is treated as an extension of the parent, the accounting entries for the parent would be the same as those for the group, as set out in 12.4.1 above.

If the EBT is treated as a separate entity, the accounting entries might be as follows:

		£	£
y/e 31.12.2012	Profit or loss*	500	
	Equity		500
1.1.2013	Loan to EBT	6,000	
	Cash		6,000
y/e 31.12.2013	Profit or loss*	1,000	
	Equity		1,000
y/e 31.12.2014	Profit or loss*	1,000	
	Equity		1,000
y/e 31.12.2015	Profit or loss*	500	
	Equity		500
1.9.2017	Own shares (Equity)†	1,500	
	Cash	4,500	
	Loan to EBT		6,000
	Equity	1,500	
	Own shares (Equity)		1,500

*   Total cost £3,000 (3000 options × £1) spread over 36 months. Charge for period to December 2012 is 6/36 × £3,000 = £500, and so on. In practice, where options were granted to a group of individuals, or with variable performance criteria, the annual charge would be based on a continually revised cumulative charge (see further discussion at 6.2 to 6.4 above).

†   This takes the approach of treating the parent as having a gross-settled purchased call option over its own equity (see Example 32.55 at 12.3.4 above), under which it can acquire 3,000 own shares from the EBT for the consideration of the waiver of £1,500 of the original £6,000 loan. The £4,500 cash inflow represents the £4,500 option exercise proceeds received by the EBT from the employee, which is then used to pay the balance of the original £6,000 loan.

12.4.3 *Employing subsidiary*

The employing subsidiary is required to account for the IFRS 2 expense and the contribution to the EBT on exercise of the award. This gives rise to the accounting entries set out below. The entries to reflect the IFRS 2 expense are required by IFRS 2 (see 12.2.3 above). The treatment of the contribution to the EBT as a distribution is based on the proposal in D17 (see 12.2.7 above).

		£	£
y/e 31.12.2012	Profit or loss*	500	
	Equity		500
y/e 31.12.2013	Profit or loss*	1,000	
	Equity		1,000
y/e 31.12.2014	Profit or loss*	1,000	
	Equity		1,000
y/e 31.12.2015	Profit or loss*	500	
	Equity		500
1.9.2017	Equity†	1,500	
	Cash		1,500

* Total cost £3,000 (3000 options × £1) spread over 36 months. Charge for period to December 2012 is 6/36 × £3,000 = £500, and so on. In practice, where options were granted to a group of individuals, or with variable performance criteria, the annual charge would be based on a continually revised cumulative charge (see further discussion at 6.1 to 6.4 above).

† This should be treated as a reduction of whatever component of equity was credited with the £3,000 quasi-contribution from the parent in the accounting entries above.

12.5 Illustrative example of group share scheme – equity-settled award satisfied by fresh issue of shares

Such schemes raise slightly different accounting issues. Again, these are most easily illustrated by way of an example. The discussion in 12.5.1 to 12.5.3 below is based on Example 32.57.

Example 32.57: Group share scheme (fresh issue of shares)

On 1 July 2012 an employee of S Limited, a subsidiary of the H plc group, is awarded options under the H group share scheme over 3,000 shares in H plc at £1.50 each, exercisable between 1 July 2017 and 1 July 2018, subject to certain performance criteria being met in the three years ending 30 June 2015. The fair value of the options on 1 July 2012 is £1 each.

H plc grants the award and has the obligation to settle it.

When preparing accounts during the vesting period H plc and its subsidiaries assume that the award will vest in full. The options are finally exercised on 1 September 2017, at which point H plc issues 3,000 new shares to the EBT at the then current market price of £3.50 for £10,500. The EBT funds the purchase using the £4,500 option proceeds received from the employee together with £6,000 contributed by S Limited, effectively representing the fair value of the options at exercise date (3,000 × [£3.50 – £1.50]). H plc and its subsidiaries have a 31 December year end.

12.5.1 Consolidated financial statements

The consolidated financial statements need to deal with:

- the charge required by IFRS 2 in respect of the award; and
- the issue of shares.

Transactions between H plc or S Limited and the EBT are ignored since, under SIC-12, the EBT is consolidated (see 12.3 above). The accounting entries required are set out below. As in other examples in this Chapter, where an entry is shown as being made to equity, the precise allocation to a particular component of equity will be a matter for local legislation and, possibly, local accounting 'tradition', to the extent that this is not incompatible with IFRS.

		£	£
y/e 31.12.2012	Profit or loss*	500	
	Equity		500
y/e 31.12.2013	Profit or loss*	1,000	
	Equity		1,000
y/e 31.12.2014	Profit or loss*	1,000	
	Equity		1,000
y/e 31.12.2015	Profit or loss*	500	
	Equity		500
1.9.2017	Cash	4,500	
	Equity†		4,500

*   Total cost £3,000 (3000 options × £1) spread over 36 months. Charge for period to December 2012 is 6/36 × £3,000 = £500, and so on. In practice, where options were granted to a group of individuals, or with variable performance criteria, the annual charge would be based on a continually revised cumulative charge (see further discussion at 6.1 to 6.4 above).

†   From the point of view of the consolidated group, the issue of shares results in an increase in net assets of only £4,500 (i.e. the exercise price received from the employee), since the £6,000 contribution from the employing subsidiary to the EBT is an intragroup transaction. However, it may be that, in certain jurisdictions, the entity is required to increase its share capital and share premium (additional paid in capital) accounts by the £10,500 legal consideration for the issue of shares. In that case, this entry would be expanded as below, which effectively treats the £6,000 consideration provided from within the group as a bonus issue.

		£	£
1.9.2017	Cash	4,500	
	Other equity	6,000	
	Share capital/premium		10,500

12.5.2 Parent

The parent has to consider the accounting treatment of the EBT (i.e. whether it is accounted for as a separate entity or an extension of the parent – see 12.3 above). This gives two possible accounting treatments:

- EBT treated as separate entity (see 12.5.2.A below); and
- EBT treated as extension of parent (see 12.5.2.B below).

We also discuss, at 12.5.2.C below, the accounting implications if the parent, rather than – as in Example 32.57 – a subsidiary, is the employing entity.

12.5.2.A EBT treated as separate entity

The parent accounts for the share-based payment transaction under IFRS 2 as an equity-settled transaction, since the parent settles the award by delivering its own equity instruments to the employees of the subsidiary (see 12.2.4 above). However, as discussed at 12.2.4 above, instead of recording a cost, as in its consolidated financial statements, the parent records an increase in the carrying value of its subsidiary. It might then be necessary to consider whether the ever-increasing investment in subsidiary is supportable or is in fact impaired. As this is a matter to be determined in the light of specific facts and circumstances, it is not considered in this example. Any impairment charge would be recorded in profit or loss.

In addition to accounting for the share-based payment transaction, the parent records its transactions with the EBT and the issue of shares.

This gives rise to the following entries:

		£	£
y/e 31.12.2012	Investment in subsidiary*	500	
	Equity		500
y/e 31.12.2013	Investment in subsidiary*	1,000	
	Equity		1,000
y/e 31.12.2014	Investment in subsidiary*	1,000	
	Equity		1,000
y/e 31.12.2015	Investment in subsidiary*	500	
	Equity		500
1.9.2017	Cash†	10,500	
	Share capital/premium		10,500

*   Total increase in investment £3,000 (3000 shares × £1 fair value of each option), recognised over 36 months. Increase in period to December 2012 is 6/36 × £3,000 = £500, and so on. In practice, where options were granted to a group of individuals, or with variable performance criteria, the annual adjustment would be based on a continually revised cumulative adjustment (see further discussion at 6.1 to 6.4 above).

†   £4,500 option exercise proceeds from employee plus £6,000 contribution from the subsidiary.

12.5.2.B EBT treated as extension of parent

The parent accounts for the share-based payment transaction under IFRS 2 as an equity-settled transaction, since the parent settles the award by delivering its own equity instruments to the employees of the subsidiary (see 12.2.4 above). However, as discussed at 12.2.4 above, instead of recording a cost, as in its consolidated financial statements, the parent records an increase in the carrying value of its subsidiary. It might then be necessary to consider whether the ever-increasing investment in subsidiary is supportable or is in fact impaired. As this is a matter to be determined in the light of specific facts and circumstances, it is not considered in this example. Any impairment charge would be recorded in profit or loss.

In addition to accounting for the share-based payment transaction, the parent records the transactions of the EBT and the issue of shares.

This gives rise to the following entries:

		£	£
y/e 31.12.2012	Investment in subsidiary*	500	
	Equity		500
y/e 31.12.2013	Investment in subsidiary*	1,000	
	Equity		1,000
y/e 31.12.2014	Investment in subsidiary*	1,000	
	Equity		1,000
y/e 31.12.2015	Investment in subsidiary*	500	
	Equity†		500
1.9.2017	Cash†	10,500	
	Equity‡	6,000	
	Profit or loss**		6,000
	Share capital/premium		10,500

* Total increase in investment £3,000 (3000 shares × £1 fair value of each option) spread over 36 months. Increase during period to December 2012 is 6/36 × £3,000 = £500, and so on. In practice, where options were granted to a group of individuals, or with variable performance criteria, the annual adjustment would be based on a continually revised cumulative adjustment (see further discussion at 6.1 to 6.4 above).

† £4,500 option exercise proceeds from employee plus £6,000 contribution from the subsidiary.

‡ This assumes that local law requires the entity to record share capital and share premium (additional paid-in capital) of £10,500, as in 12.5.2.A above. However, IFRS *prima facie* requires the £6,000 cash received by the EBT from the subsidiary to be treated as income (see ** below) rather than as part of the proceeds of the issue of shares. In order, in effect, to reconcile these conflicting analyses, £6,000 of the £10,500 required by law to be capitalised as share capital and share premium has been treated as an appropriation out of other equity.

** The £6,000 contribution by the subsidiary to the EBT has been treated as a distribution from the subsidiary (see 12.2.7 above) and recorded in profit or loss. It might then be necessary to consider whether, as a result of this payment, the investment in the subsidiary had become impaired (see Chapter 9 at 2.3). As this is a matter to be determined in the light of specific facts and circumstances, it is not considered in this Example. Any impairment charge would be recorded in profit or loss.

12.5.2.C Parent company as employing company

If, in Example 32.57, the employing entity were the parent rather than the subsidiary, it would clearly have to record an expense under IFRS 2. It would also have to fund the £6,000 shortfall between the option exercise proceeds of £4,500 and the £10,500 issue proceeds of the shares.

If the EBT is treated as an extension of the parent, the accounting entries for the parent would be the same as those for the group, as set out in 12.5.1 above.

In our view, the treatment in 12.5.1 above may also be appropriate for this specific transaction, even where the EBT is treated as a separate entity. The issue of shares requires the parent company to fund the EBT with £6,000 which immediately returns it to the parent, along with the £4,500 received from the employee, in exchange for an issue of shares. Whilst this 'circulation' of the £6,000 might have some significance for legal purposes it is, economically speaking, a non-transaction that could be ignored for accounting purposes under IFRS. It might, however, be relevant, under local law, to the amount of equity shown as share capital and share premium (additional paid-in capital), in which case the expanded entry in 12.5.1 above would be appropriate.

Where, however, the EBT is treated as a separate entity, and the cash used to subscribe for the shares arises from a prior transaction, such as an earlier loan to the EBT, matters are more complicated. Suppose that, during the life of the award under discussion, the company were to advance £50,000 to the EBT for general funding purposes. At that point it would clearly record the entry:

	£	£
Loan to EBT	50,000	
Cash		50,000

Suppose that, on exercise of the option, the EBT were to use some of that cash to fund the parent's 'top up' for the share issue. This effectively impairs the loan by £6,000 and leaves a 'missing debit' indicated by '?' in the journal below:

	£	£
Cash	10,500	
?	6,000	
Loan to EBT		6,000
Share capital/premium		10,500

This looks very much like an impairment loss on the loan required to be reported in profit or loss. On the other hand, it does not resemble a loss in any conventional sense. This suggests that another analysis may be possible.

Example 32.55 at 12.3.4 above addresses the situation where an EBT is pre-funded to enable it to buy the reporting entity's own shares in the market, and those shares are finally delivered to the entity for distribution to employees. Example 32.55 suggests that this could be construed as the execution of a gross-settled purchased call option by the entity.

If that analogy is extended, the present situation could be construed as comprising a back-to-back:

- gross-settled purchased call option (whereby the entity can require the EBT to provide 3,000 shares in return for waiver of £6,000 of its outstanding loan to the EBT), which triggers the exercise of

- a gross-settled written call option (whereby the EBT can require the entity to issue 3,000 fresh shares for £10,500 to the EBT, so that it can satisfy its obligations to the entity under the purchased call).

If these two call options are accounted for under IAS 32 (see Chapter 45 at 10.2), the write-off of the loan to the EBT can be effectively charged to equity, as follows:

	£	£
Cash	10,500	
Share capital/premium		10,500
Exercise by EBT of written call		
Own shares (Equity)	6,000	
Loan to EBT		6,000
Exercise by entity of purchased call		
Equity (other)	6,000	
Own shares (Equity)		6,000
Issue of shares to employee		

12.5.3 Employing subsidiary

The employing subsidiary is required to account for the IFRS 2 expense and the contribution to the EBT on exercise of the award. This gives rise to the accounting entries set out below. The entries to reflect the IFRS 2 expense are required by IFRS 2 (see 12.2.3 above). The treatment of the contribution to the EBT as a distribution is based on the proposal in D17 (see 12.2.7 above).

		£	£
y/e 31.12.2012	Profit or loss*	500	
	Equity		500
y/e 31.12.2013	Profit or loss*	1,000	
	Equity		1,000
y/e 31.12.2014	Profit or loss*	1,000	
	Equity		1,000
y/e 31.12.2015	Profit or loss*	500	
	Equity		500
1.9.2017	Equity†	6,000	
	Cash		6,000

*   Total cost £3,000 (3000 options × £1) spread over 36 months. Charge for period to December 2012 6/36 × £3,000 = £500, and so on. In practice, where options were granted to a group of individuals, or with variable performance criteria, the annual charge would be based on a continually revised cumulative charge (see further discussion at 6.1 to 6.4 above).

†   £3,000 of this payment should be treated as a reduction of whatever component of equity was credited with the £3,000 quasi-contribution from the parent in the accounting entries above. The remaining £3,000 would be treated as a distribution and charged to any appropriate component of equity.

Chapter 32

12.6 Illustrative example – cash-settled transaction not settled by the entity receiving goods or services

The discussion in 12.6.1 to 12.6.3 below is based on Example 32.58.

Example 32.58: Cash-settled scheme not settled by receiving entity

On 1 July 2012 an employee of S Limited, a subsidiary of the H plc group, is awarded a right, exercisable between 1 July 2017 and 1 July 2018, to receive cash equivalent to the value of 3,000 shares in H plc at the date on which the right is exercised. Exercise of the right is subject to certain performance criteria being met in the three years ending 30 June 2015. The cash will be paid to the employee not by S, but by H. Throughout the vesting period of the award, H and S take the view that it will vest in full.

The award does in fact vest, and the right is exercised on 1 September 2017.

The fair value of the award (per share-equivalent) at various relevant dates is as follows:

Date	Fair value
	£
1.7.2012	1.50
31.12.2012	1.80
31.12.2013	2.70
31.12.2014	2.40
31.12.2015	2.90
31.12.2016	3.30
1.9.2017	3.50

If the award had been equity-settled (i.e. the employee had instead been granted a right to 3,000 free shares), the grant date fair value of the award would have been £1.50 per share.

H plc and its subsidiaries have a 31 December year end.

12.6.1 Consolidated financial statements

The group has entered into a cash-settled transaction which is accounted for using the methodology discussed at 9.2 above. This gives rise to the following accounting entries:

		£	£
y/e 31.12.2012	Profit or loss*	900	
	Liability		900
y/e 31.12.2013	Profit or loss*	3,150	
	Liability		3,150
y/e 31.12.2014	Profit or loss*	1,950	
	Liability		1,950
y/e 31.12.2015	Profit or loss*	2,700	
	Liability		2,700
y/e 31.12.2016	Profit or loss*	1,200	
	Liability		1,200
y/e 31.12.2017	Profit or loss*	600	
	Liability		600
1.9.2017	Liability	10,500	
	Cash		10,500

*   Charge for period to 31 December 2012 is 6/36 × 3000 × £1.80 [reporting date fair value] = £900. Charge for year ended 31 December 2013 is 18/36 × 3000 × £2.70 = £4,050 less £900 charged in 2012 = £3,150 and so on (refer to Example 32.35 at 9.2.2 above). In practice, where options were granted to a group of individuals, or with variable performance criteria, the annual charge would be based on a continually revised cumulative charge (see further discussion at 9 above).

12.6.2 Parent company

The parent accounts for the share-based payment transaction under IFRS 2 as a cash-settled transaction, since the parent settles the award by delivering cash to the employees of the subsidiary (see 12.2.4 above). However, as discussed at 12.2.4 above, instead of recording a cost, as in its consolidated financial statements, the parent records an increase in the carrying value of its subsidiary. It might then be necessary to consider whether the ever-increasing investment in subsidiary is supportable or is in fact impaired. As this is a matter to be determined in the light of specific facts and circumstances, it is not considered in this example. Any impairment charge would be recorded in profit or loss.

This would result in the following accounting entries.

		£	£
y/e 31.12.2012	Investment in subsidiary*	900	
	Liability		900
y/e 31.12.2013	Investment in subsidiary*	3,150	
	Liability		3,150
y/e 31.12.2014	Investment in subsidiary*	1,950	
	Liability		1,950
y/e 31.12.2015	Investment in subsidiary*	2,700	
	Liability		2,700
y/e 31.12.2016	Investment in subsidiary*	1,200	
	Liability		1,200
y/e 31.12.2017	Investment in subsidiary*	600	
	Liability		600
1.9.2017	Liability	10,500	
	Cash		10,500

*   Increase in investment to 31 December 2012 is 6/36 × 3000 × £1.80 [reporting date fair value] = £900. Increase for year ended 31 December 2013 is 18/36 × 3000 × £2.70 = £4,050 less £900 charged in 2012 = £3,150 and so on (refer to Example 32.35 at 9.2.2 above). In practice, where options were granted to a group of individuals, or with variable performance criteria, the annual charge would be based on a continually revised cumulative charge (see further discussion at 9 above).

Where the parent entity was also the employing entity (and therefore receiving goods or services), it would apply the same accounting treatment in its separate financial statements as in its consolidated financial statements (see 12.6.1 above).

12.6.3 Employing subsidiary

The employing subsidiary accounts for the transaction as equity-settled, since it receives services, but incurs no obligation to its employees (see 12.2.3 and 12.2.6 above). This gives rise to the following accounting entries.

		£	£
y/e 31.12.2012	Profit or loss*	750	
	Equity		750
y/e 31.12.2013	Profit or loss*	1,500	
	Equity		1,500
y/e 31.12.2014	Profit or loss*	1,500	
	Equity		1,500
y/e 31.12.2015	Profit or loss*	750	
	Equity		750

* Charge for period to 31 December 2012 is $6/36 \times 3000 \times £1.50$ [grant date fair value] $= £750$, and so on. In practice, where options were granted to a group of individuals, or with variable performance criteria, the annual charge would be based on a continually revised cumulative charge (see further discussion at 6.1 to 6.4 above).

The effect of this treatment is that, while the group ultimately records a cost of £10,500, the subsidiary records a cost of only £4,500.

However, there may be cases where the subsidiary records a higher cost than the group. This would happen if, for example:

• the award vests, but the share price has fallen since grant date, so that the value of the award at vesting (as reflected in the consolidated financial statements) is lower than the value at grant (as reflected in the subsidiary's financial statements); or

• the award does not actually vest because of a failure to meet a market condition and/or a non-vesting condition (so that the cost is nil in the consolidated financial statements) but is treated by IFRS 2 as vesting in the subsidiary's financial statements, because it is accounted for as equity-settled (see 6.3 and 6.4 above).

12.7 Employee transferring between group entities

It is not uncommon for an employee to be granted an equity-settled share-based payment award while in the employment of one subsidiary in the group, but to transfer to another subsidiary in the group before the award is vested, but with the entitlement to the award being unchanged.

In such cases, each subsidiary measures the services received from the employee by reference to the fair value of the equity instruments at the date those rights to equity instruments were originally granted, and the proportion of the vesting period served by the employee with each subsidiary. *[IFRS 2.B59].* In other words, for an award with a three-year vesting period granted to an employee of subsidiary A, who transfers to subsidiary B at the end of year 2, subsidiary A will (cumulatively) record an expense of 2/3, and subsidiary B 1/3, of the fair value at grant date. However, any subsidiary required to account for the transaction as cash-settled in accordance with the general principles discussed at 12.2 above accounts not only for its portion of the grant date fair value, but also for any changes in the fair value of the award during the period of employment with that subsidiary. *[IFRS 2.B60].*

An employee, after transferring between group entities, may fail to satisfy a vesting condition other than a market condition, for example by leaving the employment of the group. In this situation each subsidiary adjusts the amount previously recognised in respect of the services received from the employee in accordance with the general principles of IFRS 2 (see 6.1 to 6.4 above). *[IFRS 2.B61].* This imposes upon the original employing entity the rather curious burden of tracking the service record of its former employee.

12.8 Share-based payments to employees of joint ventures or associates

The majority of share-based payment transactions with employees involve payments to employees of the reporting entity or of another entity in the same group. Occasionally, however, payments may be made to employees of significant investees of the reporting entity such as joint ventures or associates. For example, if one party to a joint venture is a quoted entity and the other not, it might be commercially appropriate for the quoted venturer to offer payments based on its quoted shares to employees of the joint venture, while the unquoted party contributes to the venture in other ways.

Such arrangements raise some questions of interpretation of IFRS 2, as illustrated by Example 32.59 below.

Example 32.59: Share-based payment to employees of associate

On 1 January 2012, an entity grants an award of free shares with a fair value at that date of €600,000 to employees of its 40% associate. The shares vest over the three-year period ended 31 December 2014. It is assumed throughout the vesting period of the award that it will vest in full, which is in fact the case. The associate and the investor both have a financial reporting date of 31 December.

12.8.1 Financial statements of the associate

For the financial statements of the associate, the transaction does not strictly fall within the scope of IFRS 2. In order for a transaction to be in the scope of IFRS 2 for a reporting entity, it must be settled in the equity of the entity itself, or that of another member of the same group. A group comprises a parent and its subsidiaries (see Chapter 6 at 2), and does not include associates.

Nevertheless, we believe that it would be appropriate, and preferable, for the associate to account for the transaction as if it did fall within the scope of IFRS 2 by applying the 'GAAP hierarchy' in IAS 8 – *Accounting Policies, Changes in Accounting Estimates and Errors* (see Chapter 3 at 4.3). The investor has effectively made a capital contribution to the associate (in the form of the investor's own equity), no less than if it made a capital contribution in cash which was then used to pay employees of the associate.

If the investor in the associate had instead granted an award settled in the equity of the associate, the transaction would have been in the scope of IFRS 2 for the associate, as being the grant of an award over the equity of the reporting entity by a shareholder of that entity (see 2.2.2.A above).

If the award is, or is treated as being, within the scope of IFRS 2 for the associate, the following entries are recorded:

		€000	€000
y/e 31.12.12	Employee costs†	200	
	Equity		200
y/e 31.12.13	Employee costs	200	
	Equity		200
y/e 31.12.14	Employee costs	200	
	Equity		200

† Grant date fair value of award €600,000 × 1/3. The credit to equity represents a capital contribution from the investor

12.8.2 Consolidated financial statements of the investor

The investor has entered into a share-based payment transaction since it has granted an award over its equity to third parties (the employees of the associates) in exchange for their services to a significant investee entity. However, employees of an associate are not employees of a group entity and are therefore not employees of the investor's group.

The issue for IFRS 2 purposes is, therefore, whether the award should be regarded as being made to persons providing similar services to employees (and therefore measured at grant date) or to persons other than employees or those providing similar services to employees (and therefore measured at service date) – see 5.2 to 5.4 above.

In our view, it is more appropriate to regard such awards as made to persons providing similar services to employees and therefore measured at grant date.

There are then, we believe, two possible approaches to the accounting. In any event, the investor's consolidated financial statements must show a credit to equity of €200,000 a year over the vesting period. The accounting issue is the analysis of the corresponding debit.

It seems clear that the investor must as a minimum recognise an annual cost of €80,000 (40% of €200,000), as part of its 'one-line' share of the result of the associate. The issue then is whether it should account for the remaining €120,000 as a further cost or as an increase in the cost of its investment in its associate.

The argument for treating the €120,000 as an expense is that the associate will either have recorded nothing or, under our preferred treatment set out in 12.8.1 above, an entry that results in no net increase in the equity of the associate. Therefore there has been no increase in the investor's share of the net assets of the associate, and there is therefore no basis for the investor to record an increase in its investment. This is broadly the approach required under US GAAP.

However, there may be cases where another shareholder has made, or undertaken to make, contributions to the associate that are not reflected in its recognised net assets (for example, an undertaking to provide knowhow or undertake mineral exploration). In such circumstances, it may be possible to conclude that the €120,000 is an increase in the cost of the associate. IAS 28 – *Investments in Associates* – defines the equity method of accounting as (emphasis added):

'a method of accounting whereby the investment is *initially recognised at cost and adjusted thereafter* for the post-acquisition change in the investor's share of net assets of the investee'. *[IAS 28.2]*.

Where an entity takes the view that the €120,000 is an increase in the cost of its investment, it is essential to ensure that the resulting carrying value of the investment is sustainable. This may be the case if, for example:

- the fair value of the investment in the associate exceeds its carrying amount;
- the investor has agreed to enter into the transaction while another major shareholder has agreed to bear equivalent costs.

In other circumstances, the carrying amount of the investment may not be sustainable, and the investor may need to recognise an impairment of its investment in accordance with IAS 36 (see Chapter 22).

12.8.3 Separate financial statements of the investor

The discussion below assumes that the investor accounts for its investment in the associate at cost in its separate financial statements (see Chapter 9).

The issues here are much the same as in 12.8.2 above. The investor has clearly entered into a share-based payment transaction since it has granted an award over its equity to third parties (the employees of the associates) in exchange for their services to a significant investee entity. As in 12.8.2 above, we believe that this is most appropriately characterised as a transaction with persons providing similar services to employees and therefore measured at its grant date fair value.

In any event, the investor's separate financial statements must show a credit to equity of €200,000 a year over the vesting period. However, as in 12.8.2 above, the analysis of the debit entry is more complex.

13   DISCLOSURES

IFRS 2 requires three main groups of disclosures, explaining:

- the nature and extent of share-based payment arrangements (see 13.1 below);
- the valuation of share-based payment arrangements (see 13.2 below); and
- the impact on the financial statements of share-based payment transactions (see 13.3 below).

13.1   Nature and extent of share-based payment arrangements

IFRS 2 requires an entity to 'disclose information that enables users of the financial statements to understand the nature and extent of share-based payment arrangements that existed during the period'. *[IFRS 2.44]*.

In order to satisfy this general principle, the entity must disclose at least:

(a)   a description of each type of share-based payment arrangement that existed at any time during the period, including the general terms and conditions of each arrangement, such as vesting requirements, the maximum term of options granted, and the method of settlement (e.g. whether in cash or equity). An entity with substantially similar types of share-based payment arrangements may aggregate this information, unless separate disclosure of each arrangement is necessary to satisfy the general principle above;

(b)   the number and weighted average exercise prices of share options for each of the following groups of options:

    (i)   outstanding at the beginning of the period;

    (ii)   granted during the period;

    (iii)   forfeited during the period;

    (iv)   exercised during the period;

    (v)   expired during the period;

    (vi)   outstanding at the end of the period; and

    (vii)   exercisable at the end of the period;

(c)   for share options exercised during the period, the weighted average share price at the date of exercise. If options were exercised on a regular basis throughout the period, the entity may instead disclose the weighted average share price during the period; and

(d)   for share options outstanding at the end of the period, the range of exercise prices and weighted average remaining contractual life. If the range of exercise prices is wide, the outstanding options must be divided into ranges that are meaningful for assessing the number and timing of additional shares that may be issued and the cash that may be received upon exercise of those options. *[IFRS 2.45].*

The reconciliation in (b) above should, in our view, reflect all changes in the number of equity instruments outstanding. In addition to awards with a grant date during the period, the reconciliation should include subsequent additions to earlier grants e.g. options or shares added to the award in recognition of dividends declared during the period (where this is part of the original terms of the award), and changes to the number of equity instruments as a result of demergers, share splits or consolidations and other similar changes.

As drafted, the requirements in (b) to (d) above appear to apply only to share options. However, since there is little distinction in IFRS 2 between the treatment of an option with a zero exercise price and the award of a free share, in our view the disclosures should not be restricted to awards of options.

13.2   Valuation of share-based payment arrangements

IFRS 2 requires an entity to 'disclose information that enables users of the financial statements to understand how the fair value of the goods or services received, or the fair value of the equity instruments granted, during the period was determined'. *[IFRS 2.46].*

As drafted, this requirement, and some of the detailed disclosures below, appear to apply only to equity-settled transactions. However, it would be clearly anomalous if detailed disclosures were required about the valuation of an award to be settled in shares, but not when it was to be settled in cash. In our view, therefore, the disclosures apply both to equity-settled and to cash-settled transactions.

If the entity has measured the fair value of goods or services received as consideration for equity instruments of the entity indirectly, by reference to the fair value of the equity instruments granted (i.e. transactions with employees and, in exceptional cases only, with non-employees), the entity must disclose at least the following:

(a)   for share options granted during the period, the weighted average fair value of those options at the measurement date and information on how that fair value was measured, including:

(i)   the option pricing model used and the inputs to that model, including the weighted average share price, exercise price, expected volatility, option life, expected dividends, the risk-free interest rate and any other inputs to the model, including the method used and the assumptions made to incorporate the effects of expected early exercise;

(ii)   how expected volatility was determined, including an explanation of the extent to which expected volatility was based on historical volatility; and

(iii)   whether and how any other features of the option grant were incorporated into the measurement of fair value, such as a market condition;

(b)   for other equity instruments granted during the period (i.e. other than share options), the number and weighted average fair value of those equity instruments at the measurement date, and information on how that fair value was measured, including:

(i)   if fair value was not measured on the basis of an observable market price, how it was determined;

(ii)   whether and how expected dividends were incorporated into the measurement of fair value; and

(iii)   whether and how any other features of the equity instruments granted were incorporated into the measurement of fair value;

(c)   for share-based payment arrangements that were modified during the period:

(i)   an explanation of those modifications;

(ii)   the incremental fair value granted (as a result of those modifications); and

(iii)   information on how the incremental fair value granted was measured, consistently with the requirements set out in (a) and (b) above, where applicable. *[IFRS 2.47].*

These requirements can be seen to some extent as an anti-avoidance measure. It would not be surprising if the IASB had concerns that entities might seek to minimise the impact of IFRS 2 by using unduly pessimistic assumptions that result in a low fair value for share-based payment transactions, and the disclosures above seem designed to deter entities from doing so. However, these disclosures give information about other commercially sensitive matters. For example, (a)(i) above effectively requires disclosure of future dividend policy for a longer period than is generally covered by such forecasts. Entities may need to consider the impact on investors and analysts of dividend yield assumptions disclosed under IFRS 2.

In our view, it is important for entities, in making these disclosures, to ensure that any assumptions disclosed, particularly those relating to future performance, are consistent with those used in other areas of financial reporting that rely on estimates of future events, such as the impairment of property, plant and equipment, intangible assets and goodwill, income taxes (recovery of deferred tax assets out of future profits) and pensions and other post-retirement benefits.

If the entity has measured a share-based payment transaction directly by reference to the fair value of goods or services received during the period, the entity must disclose how that fair value was determined (e.g. whether fair value was measured at a market price for those goods or services). *[IFRS 2.48]*.

As discussed in 5.4 above, IFRS 2 creates a rebuttable presumption that, for an equity-settled transaction with a counterparty other than an employee, the fair value of goods and services received provides the more reliable basis for assessing the fair value of the transaction. Where the entity has rebutted this presumption, and has valued the transaction by reference to the fair value of equity instruments issued, it must disclose this fact, and give an explanation of why the presumption was rebutted. *[IFRS 2.49]*.

13.3 Impact of share-based payment transactions on financial statements

IFRS 2 requires an entity to 'disclose information that enables users of the financial statements to understand the effect of share-based payment transactions on the entity's profit or loss for the period and on its financial position.' *[IFRS 2.50]*.

In order to do this, it must disclose at least:

(a) the total expense recognised for the period arising from share-based payment transactions in which the goods or services received did not qualify for recognition as assets and hence were recognised immediately as an expense, including separate disclosure of that portion of the total expense that arises from transactions accounted for as equity-settled share-based payment transactions;

(b) for liabilities arising from share-based payment transactions:

(i) the total carrying amount at the end of the period; and

(ii) the total intrinsic value at the end of the period of liabilities for which the counterparty's right to cash or other assets had vested by the end of the period (e.g. vested share appreciation rights). *[IFRS 2.51]*

The requirement in (b)(ii) above is slightly curious, in the sense that the IASB specifically rejected the suggestion of many respondents to ED 2 that cash-settled transactions should be accounted for using an intrinsic value methodology, rather than the fair value methodology required by IFRS 2, stating that the intrinsic value method 'is not an adequate measure of either the ... liability or the cost of services consumed'. *[IFRS 2.BC250]*. This rather begs the question of why the IASB requires disclosure of what is, in its eyes, a defective measure.

The disclosures section of IFRS 2 has a final paragraph requiring an entity to disclose additional information about its share-based payments should the information requirements set out above and in sections 13.1 and 13.2 be insufficient to meet the general disclosure principles of the standard. *[IFRS 2.52]*.

13.4   Example of IFRS 2 disclosures

An example of many of the disclosures required by IFRS 2 may be found in the financial statements of Aviva plc for the year ended 31 December 2010.

Extract 32.1: Aviva plc (2010)

Notes to the Consolidated Financial Statements [extract]

30 –   Equity compensation plans

(a) Description of the plans

The Group maintains a number of active share option and award plans and schemes (the Group's Share Plans). These are as follows:

(i) Savings-related options

These are options granted under the HM Revenue and Customs-approved Save As You Earn (SAYE) share option schemes in the UK and Irish Revenue-approved SAYE share option scheme in Ireland. Options are normally exercisable during the six-month period following either the third, fifth or seventh anniversary of the start of the relevant savings contract.

(ii) Executive share options

These are options granted on various dates until 2004, under the Aviva Executive Share Option Plan or predecessor plans, and in 2010, under the Aviva Executive Share Option Plan 2005. Options granted between 2001 and 2004 were subject to the satisfaction of conditions relating to both the Company's Return on Capital Employed (ROCE) and its relative Total Shareholder Return (TSR). The performance was measured over a three-year performance period and the options are normally exercisable between the third and tenth anniversary of their grant. The options granted in 2010 are described in the Directors' Remuneration Report.

(iii) Long-term incentive plan awards

These awards have been made under the Aviva Long Term Incentive Plan 2005 and are described in section (b) below and in the Directors' Remuneration Report.

(iv) Annual bonus plan awards

These awards have been made under the Aviva Annual Bonus Plan 2005, and are described in section (b) below and in the Directors' Remuneration Report.

(v) One Aviva, twice the value bonus plan awards

These are conditional awards first granted under the Aviva Annual Bonus Plan 2005 in 2008, and are described in section (b) below and in the Directors' Remuneration Report.

(vi) CFO recruitment share awards plan awards

The following awards were granted to Patrick Regan under the CFO Recruitment Share Awards Plan following his recruitment in 2010: the Replacement Restricted Share Award (RRSA), the Bonus Replacement Deferred Share Award (BRDSA) and the One Aviva Twice the Value Award (OATTV). The RRSA was awarded to compensate Mr Regan for the loss of share awards granted by his previous employer and the BRDSA was awarded to compensate Mr Regan for the loss of bonus from his previous employer. The awards are described in section (b) below and in the Directors' Remuneration Report. No further awards will be made under this plan.

(b) Outstanding options and awards

(i) Share options

At 31 December 2010, options to subscribe for ordinary shares of 25 pence each in the Company were outstanding as follows:

Aviva Savings Related Shave Option Scheme	Option Price p	Number of shares	Normally exercisable	Option Price p	Number of shares	Normally exercisable
	406	146,038	2010	563	1,113,993	2010, 2012 or 2014
	428	91,945	2011	410	2,599,581	2011, 2013 or 2015
	491	523,884	2010 or 2012	316	11,067,836	2012, 2014 or 2016
	593	290,792	2011 or 2013	310	6,050,688	2013, 2015 or 2017

Aviva Savings Related Shave Option Scheme (in euros)	Option Price c	Number of shares	Normally exercisable	Option Price c	Number of shares	Normally exercisable
	719	19,535	2010	509	256,558	2011 or 2013
	879	22,832	2011	360	1,122,071	2012 or 2014
	830	89,009	2010 or 2012	374	345,187	2013 or 2015

Aviva Executive Shave Option Plan	Option Price p	Number of shares	Normally exercisable
	1,035	291,730	2004 to 2011
	516	529,990	2005 to 2012
	512	694,984	2006 to 2013
	526	470,340	2007 to 2014
	386	1,529,647	2013

The following table summarises information about options outstanding at 31 December 2010:

Range of exercise prices	Outstanding options Number	Weighted average remaining contractual life Years	Weighted average exercise price p
£3.10 – £5.55	25,448,284	3	347.84
£5.56 – £8.00	1,516,626	1	569.20
£8.01 – £10.35	291,730	1	1,035.00

The comparative figures as at 31 December 2009 were:

Range of exercise prices	Outstanding options Number	Weighted average remaining contractual life Years	Weighted average exercise price p
£3.10 – £5.55	23,163,439	3	362.18
£5.56 – £8.00	2,725,129	1	576.28
£8.01 – £10.35	466,525	1	1,016.57

Chapter 32

(ii) Share awards

At 31 December 2010, awards issued under the Company's executive incentive plans over ordinary shares of 25 pence each in the Company were outstanding as follows:

Aviva Long Term Incentive Plan 2005	Number of shares	Vesting period	Number of shares	Vesting period
	3,669,927	2008 to 2010	7,599,920	2010 to 2012
	10,460,578	2009 to 2011		

One Aviva, twice the value Bonus Plan	Number of shares	Vesting period	Number of shares	Vesting period
	929,872	2008 to 2010	2,178,398	2010 to 2012
	2,420,778	2009 to 2011		

Aviva Annual Bonus Plan 2005	Number of shares	Vesting date	Number of shares	Vesting date
	1,775,320	2008 to 2010	5,051,579	2010 to 2012
	5,416,844	2009 to 2011		

CFO Recruitment Share Awards Plan	Award type	Number of shares	Vesting date
	RRSA	255,589	2010, 2011 and 2012
	BRDSA	43,231	2010 to 2012
	OATTV	55,051	2010 to 2012

The vesting of awards under the Aviva Long Term Incentive Plan 2005, the One Aviva, twice the value Bonus Plan and the OATTV award under the CFO Recruitment Share Awards Plan is subject to the attainment of performance conditions as described in the Directors' Remuneration Report. Shares which do not vest, lapse.

(iii) Shares to satisfy awards and options

Prior to March 2003, it was the practice to satisfy awards and options granted under the Group's Share Plans through shares purchased in the market and held by employee share trusts which were established for the purpose of satisfying awards under the Group's Share Plans and funded by the Company.

From March 2003 to July 2008, it was generally the Company's practice to satisfy the awards granted after March 2003 by the issue of new shares at the time of vesting. However, since July 2008, it has been the Company's practice to satisfy all awards and options using shares purchased in the market and held by employee trusts except where local regulations make it necessary to issue new shares.. Further details are given in note 31.

(c) Movements in the year

A summary of the status of the option plans as at 31 December 2009 and 2010, and changes during the years ended on those dates, is shown below.

	2010		2009	
	Number of options	Weighted average exercise price p	Number of options	Weighted average exercise price p
Outstanding at 1 January	26,355,093	395.90	26,278,223	477.82
Granted during the year	8,020,085	326.52	14,863,272	316.00
Exercised during the year	(73,755)	335.12	(146,330)	359.55
Forfeited during the year	(1,461,530)	380.82	(1,149,764)	459.77
Cancelled during the year	(2,788,423)	362.05	(8,604,422)	433.40
Expired during the year	(2,794,830)	516.95	(4,885,886)	513.42
Outstanding at 31 December	27,256,640	367.51	26,355,093	395.90
Exercisable at 31 December	3,319,816	564.95	6,709,247	550.41

(d) Expense charged to the income statement

The total expense recognised for the year arising from equity compensation plans was as follows:

	2010 £m	2009 £m
Equity-settled expense (note 10b)	50	56
Cash-settled expense	–	–
	50	56

(e) Fair value of options and awards granted after 7 November 2002

The weighted average fair value of options and awards granted during the year, estimated by using the Black-Scholes option-pricing model, were £1.32 and £2.39 (2009: £1.78 and £1.94) respectively.

(i) Share options

The fair value of the options was estimated on the date of grant, based on the following weighted average assumptions:

Weighted average assumption	2010	2009
Share price	402p	480p
Exercise price	310p	316p
Expected volatility	56%	55%
Expected life	5.00 years	5.00 years
Expected dividend yield	6.09%	5.06%
Risk-free interest rate	1.57%	2.47%

The expected volatility used was based on the historical volatility of the share price over a period equivalent to the expected life of the options prior to its date of grant. The risk-free interest rate was based on the yields available on UK government bonds as at the date of grant. The bonds chosen were those with a similar remaining term to the expected life of the options.

64,903 options granted after 7 November 2002 were exercised during the year *(2009: 144,590).*

(ii) Share awards

The fair value of the awards was estimated on the date of grant, based on the following weighted average assumptions:

Weighted average assumption	2010	2009
Share price	386.00p	216.25p
Expected volatility*	66%	60%
Expected volatility of comparator companies' share price*	65%	61%
Correlation between Aviva and competitors' share price*	57%	55%
Expected life	2.75 years	2.75 years
Expected dividend yield	7.70%	8.23%
Risk-free interest rate*	1.80%	1.76%

* For awards with market-based performance conditions.

The expected volatility used was based on the historical volatility of the share price over a period equivalent to the expected life of the options prior to its date of grant. The risk-free interest rate was based on the yields available on UK government bonds as at the date of grant. The bonds chosen were those with a similar remaining term to the expected life of the options.

Chapter 32

14 TAXES RELATED TO SHARE-BASED PAYMENT TRANSACTIONS

14.1 Income tax deductions for the entity

In many jurisdictions entities are entitled to receive tax deductions for share-based payment transactions. In many, if not most, cases the tax deduction is given for a cost different to that recorded under IFRS 2. For example, some jurisdictions give a tax deduction for the fair or intrinsic value of the award at the date of exercise; others may give a tax deduction for amounts charged to a subsidiary by its parent or a trust controlled by the parent in respect of the cost of group awards to the employees of that subsidiary. In either case, both the amount and timing of the expense for tax purposes will be different from the amount and timing of the expense required by IFRS 2.

The particular issues raised by share-based payment transactions are addressed in IAS 12, and discussed further in Chapter 31 at 10.7.

14.2 Employment taxes of the employer

In many jurisdictions, an employing entity is required to pay employment taxes or social security contributions on share options and other share-based payment transactions with employees, just as if the employees had received cash remuneration. This raises the question of how such taxes should be accounted for.

14.2.1 Applicable standard

The choice of accounting method does not affect the total expense ultimately recognised (which must always be the tax actually paid), but rather its allocation to different accounting periods. Some consider that such taxes are most appropriately accounted for under IAS 37 – *Provisions, Contingent Liabilities and Contingent Assets* (see 14.2.1.A below). However, others favour the alternatives set out in 14.2.1.B and 14.2.1.C below (IFRS 2 and IAS 19 – *Employee Benefits*). A reporting entity must therefore choose what it considers an appropriate policy in its particular circumstances.

Such taxes do not fall within the scope of IAS 39 since, like income taxes, they are not contractual liabilities (see Chapter 43 at 2.2.1).

14.2.1.A IAS 37

Some consider that, for the reasons set out in 14.2.1.B and 14.2.1.C below, employment taxes are in the scope neither of IFRS 2 nor of IAS 19. Accordingly, since the amount ultimately payable is uncertain, the most appropriate standard to apply is IAS 37 – *Provisions, Contingent Liabilities and Contingent Assets*.

Where IAS 37 is applied, the entity will recognise a provision for the employment tax when it has a present obligation to pay it as the result of a past event, it is probable (i.e. more likely than not) that it will be paid, and a reliable estimate can be made of the amount of the obligation (see Chapter 29 at 3.1).

Where IAS 37 is applied, however, there is some room for discussion as to what constitutes the critical past event that gives rise to the liability. Is it:

- the granting of the award;
- the event (typically exercise) that gives rise to a real tax liability; or
- the vesting of the award?

In our view, where IAS 37 is used to account for employment taxes, the critical event that gives rise to the liability for tax is the granting of the award and therefore, a liability for the tax should be recognised as soon as it becomes more likely than not that it will become payable. However, other analyses may be possible. It is of interest that:

- United States GAAP takes the view that the critical event is the event (typically exercise) that gives rise to a real tax liability. This is the case even for employment taxes relating to cash-settled awards, even though a liability is recognised for the awards themselves before exercise; while

- United Kingdom GAAP, where the national standard FRS 12 – *Provisions, Contingent Liabilities and Contingent Assets* – is essentially identical to IAS 37, regards the critical event as the granting of the award. However an interpretation of FRS 12[25] takes the view that the liability gradually accrues in line with the vesting of the award to which it relates. UK GAAP therefore recognises a liability for such taxes based on the intrinsic value of the award, and the expired portion of the vesting period, as at each reporting date. This is not unlike the methodology required by IAS 12 – *Income Taxes* – for measuring any deferred tax asset associated with a share-based payment transaction (see Chapter 31 at 10.7).

14.2.1.B IFRS 2

Some argue that, since the taxes are a payment of an amount of cash typically directly linked to the share price, they should be accounted for as a cash-settled share-based payment transaction under IFRS 2. This would require the taxes to be measured at each reporting date at fair value, multiplied by the expired vesting period of the award to which they relate (see 9.2.1 above).

A difficulty with this analysis is that IFRS 2 defines a cash-settled share-based payment transaction as one in which the entity incurs a liability to the 'supplier of ... goods or services'. The liability for such employment taxes is clearly due to the tax authorities, not to the supplier of goods and services (i.e. the employee). This leads some who support the application of IFRS 2 to accept that IFRS 2 is not directly applicable, but to argue that it is nevertheless the most appropriate standard to apply under the 'GAAP hierarchy' in IAS 8 (see Chapter 3 at 4.3). The objective of IFRS 2 (see 2.1 above) states that the standard is intended to apply to 'expenses associated with transactions in which share options are granted to employees'. However, the standard contains no explicit provisions relevant to this objective.

14.2.1.C IAS 19

Some argue that such payments are more appropriately accounted for under IAS 19 – *Employee Benefits* (see Chapter 33). Again the difficulty is that IAS 19 defines employee benefits as 'consideration ... given by an entity in exchange for employee services', which would appear to rule out payments to the tax authority, but for the fact that IAS 19 paragraph 8(a) refers to social security contributions as a component part of short-term employee benefits. However, many share-based payment transactions would, if they were within the scope of IAS 19, be classified as long-term benefits. That brings the added complication that IAS 19 would require the employment taxes due on long-term benefits to be accounted for, like the benefits themselves, using the projected unit credit method, which seems a somewhat unduly complex, and not altogether appropriate, approach in the circumstances.

In some situations the entity may require employees to discharge any liability to employment taxes. The accounting issues raised by such arrangements are discussed at 14.2.2 and 14.3 below.

14.2.2 Recovery of taxes from employees

In some jurisdictions, employers are required to pay employment taxes on share-based payment transactions. This detracts from one of the key attractions for an employer of a share-based payment transaction, namely that it entails no cash cost. This is particularly the case where the tax payable is based on the fair value of the award at vesting, where the employer's liability is potentially unlimited.

Accordingly, employers liable to such taxes are increasingly making it a condition of receiving a share-based award that the employee bear all or some of the cash cost of any related employment taxes. This may be done in a number of ways, including:

- direct payment to the entity;
- authorising the entity to deduct the relevant amount from the employee's salary; or
- surrendering as many shares to the entity as have a fair value equal to the tax liability.

The accounting treatment of schemes where the recovery of the cost from the employee is made through surrendering of a number of shares with an equivalent value is discussed at 14.3 below.

Where the scheme requires direct cash reimbursement of the cost, different considerations apply, as illustrated by Example 32.60 below.

Example 32.60: Recovery of employment tax on share-based payment from employee

On 1 January 2011, an entity granted an executive an award of free shares with a fair value of €100,000 on condition that the executive remain in employment for three years ending on 31 December 2013. In the jurisdiction concerned, an employment tax at the rate of 12% is payable when the shares vest, based on their fair value at the date of vesting. As a condition of obtaining the shares on vesting, the executive is required to pay cash equal to the tax liability to the employer.

When the shares vest on 31 December 2013, their fair value is €300,000, on which employment taxes of €36,000 are due. The executive pays this amount to the entity.

In our view, this arrangement can be construed in one of two ways, with somewhat different accounting outcomes:

- View 1: The executive's obligation to make whole the employer's tax liability means that this is, economically, not an award of free shares, but an option to acquire the shares for an exercise price equivalent to 12% of their market value at the date of exercise. The employer's tax liability is a separate transaction.

- View 2: The executive's obligation to make whole the employer's tax liability should be accounted for as such, separately from the share-based payment transaction.

In our view, either approach may be adopted, so long as it is applied consistently as a matter of accounting policy, The essential differences between View 1 and View 2, as illustrated below, are that:

- under View 1 the reimbursement received from the employee is credited to equity, whereas under View 2 it is credited to profit or loss; and

- under View 1, the IFRS 2 charge is lower than under View 2 reflecting the fact that under View 1 the award is construed as an option, not an award of free shares.

View 1   Reimbursement treated as exercise price

On this analysis, the award is construed as an option to acquire shares with an exercise price of 12% of the fair value, at vesting, of the shares. The grant date fair value of the award construed as an option is €88,000. The entity would process the following accounting entries (on a cumulative basis).

	€000	€000
Employee costs*	88	
Equity		88
Employee costs†	36	
Cash		36
Cash§	36	
Equity		36

* IFRS 2 charge.

† Employment taxes (12% of €300,000).

§ The receipt of cash from the employee to reimburse the tax is treated as the receipt of the exercise price for an option and credited to equity.

View 2   Reimbursement treated separately from the IFRS 2 charge

On this analysis, the award is construed as an award of free shares, with a grant date fair value of €100,000. The reimbursement is accounted for as such, giving rise to a credit to profit or loss. The entity would process the following accounting entries (on a cumulative basis).

	€000	€000
Employee costs*	100	
Equity		100
Employee costs†	36	
Cash		36
Cash§	36	
Employee costs		36

* IFRS 2 charge.

† Employment taxes (12% of €300,000).

§ The receipt of cash from the employee to reimburse the tax is treated as a reduction in employee costs.

It will be seen that View 1 results in a total employee expense of €124,000, while View 2 results in a total employee expense of €100,000.

14.2.3 Holding of own shares to 'hedge' tax liabilities

In many jurisdictions, an award of shares or options to an employee also gives rise to an employment tax liability for the employer, often related to the fair value of the award when it vests or, in the case of an option, is exercised. Employers may hold their own shares in order to hedge this liability (in an economic sense, if not under the criteria in IAS 39 – see 2.2.4.I above), and later sell as many shares as are needed to raise proceeds equal to the tax liability.

These are two separate transactions. The purchase and sale of own shares are treasury share transactions accounted for in accordance with IAS 32 (see Chapter 45 at 9). The accounting treatment of the employment tax liability is discussed at 14.2.1 above.

14.3   Sale of shares by employee to meet employee's tax liability

In some jurisdictions, an award of shares or options to an employee gives rise to a personal tax liability for the employee, often related to the fair value of the award when it vests or, in the case of an option, is exercised. In order to meet this tax liability, employees may wish to sell as many shares as are needed to raise proceeds equal to the tax liability (sometimes described as 'sell to cover').

This *in itself* does not, in our view, require the scheme to be considered as cash-settled, any more than if the employee wished to liquidate the shares in order to buy a car or undertake home improvements. However, if the manner in which the cash is passed to the employee gives rise to a legal or constructive obligation for the employer, then the scheme might well be cash-settled (see 9.3.1 to 9.3.3 above), to the extent of any such obligation.

In some jurisdictions where employees must pay income tax on share awards, the tax is initially collected from (and is a legal liability of) the employer, but with eventual recourse by the tax authorities to the employee for tax not collected from the employer. Such tax collection arrangements mean that even an equity-settled award results in a cash cost for the employer for the income tax.

In such a situation, the employer may require the employee, as a condition of taking delivery of any shares earned, to indemnify the entity against the tax liability, for example by:

- direct payment to the entity;
- authorising the entity to deduct the relevant amount from the employee's salary; or
- surrendering as many shares to the entity as have a fair value equal to the tax liability.

If the entity requires the employee to surrender the relevant number of shares, in our view the scheme must be treated as cash-settled to the extent of the indemnified amount, as explained in Example 32.61 below.

The issue of entities withholding a portion of shares in return for settling the counterparty's tax liability was discussed by the Interpretations Committee at its meetings between September 2010 and March 2011 (see below).

Example 32.61: Surrendering of vested shares by employee to indemnify liability of entity to pay employee's tax liability

An entity operates in a jurisdiction where the personal tax rate is 40%, and free shares are taxed at their fair value on vesting. The entity grants an award of 100 free shares with a grant date fair value of £3 each. The fair value at vesting date is £5, so that the employee's tax liability (required to be discharged in the first instance by the employer) is £200 (40% of £500). The award is to be satisfied using treasury shares with an original cost of £2.50 per share.

If the employee were required to surrender the 40 shares needed to settle the tax liability, in our view the substance of the transaction is that, at grant date, the entity is making an award of only 60 shares (with a grant date fair value of £3 each) and is bearing the cost of the employment tax itself. On this analysis, the entity will have recorded the following entries by the end of the vesting period:

	£	£
Employee costs	180	
Equity		180
Employee costs	200	
Employment tax liability		200

The award is then satisfied by delivery of 60 treasury shares (with a cost of £2.50 each) to the employee:

	£	£
Equity	150	
Treasury shares		150

The entity might well then sell the 40 shares 'surrendered' by the employee in order to raise the cash to pay the tax, but this would be accounted for as an increase in equity on the reissue of treasury shares, not as income (see 14.2.3 above).

If, however, the employee has a free choice as to how to indemnify the employer, the employer will have recorded the following entries by the end of the vesting period:

	£	£
Employee costs	300	
Equity		300
Receivable from employee	200	
Employment tax liability		200

The award is then satisfied by delivery of shares to the employee, and the employee indicates that he wishes to surrender 40 shares to discharge his obligation to the employer under the indemnity arrangement. The entity then receives 40 shares from the employee in settlement of the £200 receivable from him.

In practice, this would almost certainly be effected as a net delivery of 60 shares, but in principle there are two transactions, a release of 100 treasury shares, with a cost of £2.50 each, to the employee:

	£	£
Equity	250	
Treasury shares		250

and the re-acquisition of 40 of those shares at £5 each from the employee:

	£	£
Treasury shares	200	
Receivable from employee		200

The entity then settles the tax liability:

	£	£
Employment tax liability	200	
Cash		200

Even in this case, however, some might take the view that the substance of the arrangement is that the employee has the right to put 40 shares to the employer, and accordingly 40% of the award should be accounted for as cash-settled, resulting in essentially the same accounting as when the employee is required to surrender 40 shares, as set out above.

The Interpretations Committee was asked to consider the classification of a share-based payment transaction in which an entity withholds a specified portion of shares that would otherwise be issued to the counterparty at the date of exercise or vesting. The shares are withheld in return for the entity settling the counterparty's tax liability relating to the share-based payment. Should the portion of the share-based payment that is withheld be classified as cash-settled or equity-settled? In summarising the request following its September 2010 meeting, the Interpretations Committee notes, somewhat unusually in a request to interpret IFRSs, that liability classification would not be required for any portion of the award under US GAAP. It is noteworthy however that the summary by the Interpretations Committee does not make clear that, under US GAAP, withholding an amount for tax in excess of a prescribed minimum level would trigger the classification of the entire award as a liability.

At its September 2010 meeting, the Interpretations Committee also noted that 'the definitions in Appendix A [to IFRS 2] ... provide that an award is classified as cash-settled if the entity incurs a liability to transfer cash or other assets as a result of acquiring goods or services. In the circumstances considered by the Committee, cash is transferred to the tax authority, in settlement of the counterparty's tax obligation, in respect of the shares withheld'.[26]

The Interpretations Committee further noted that IFRS 2 provides sufficient guidance to address the issue and it does not expect diversity in practice. Therefore, a tentative decision was reached not to add the issue to the Committee's agenda. However, it was also recommended that the issue should be reconsidered by the IASB as part of a post-implementation review of IFRS 2 in order to determine whether it would be appropriate to amend IFRS 2 to permit the portion of the award withheld to be classified as equity-settled.[27]

As a result of comments received in relation to the tentative decision, the Interpretations Committee discussed the issue again in November 2010 and asked for some illustrative examples to be prepared before considering the matter further.[28]

The question was discussed again in March 2011 and the Interpretations Committee identified 'a number of issues arising from the submission for which the application of the requirements of IFRS 2 caused concern, such as separately classifying components of a single award'. To address these concerns would require an amendment to IFRS 2 and so the Committee decided to recommend that the IASB add this issue to a future agenda.[29]

It should be noted that the discussions by the Interpretations Committee apparently only addressed the narrow situation where the entity is required by law to withhold shares to meet the counterparty's tax liability. In such a situation we agree that IFRS 2 requires the shares withheld to be treated as a cash-settled award rather than as an equity-settled award. However, the submission did not address other types of arrangement that exist in practice, such as where either the entity or the counterparty is able to choose whether or not shares are withheld and/or directly sold in order to raise cash to settle the tax liability. In our view, this analysis is a necessary starting point in determining whether part of the arrangement should be treated as a separate cash-settled award.

15   OTHER PRACTICAL ISSUES

We discuss below the following aspects of the practical application of IFRS 2 that do not fit easily into any one of the sections above:

- limited recourse and full recourse loans (see 15.1 below);
- awards entitled to dividends during the vesting period (see 15.2 below);
- awards vesting or exercisable on a flotation (or change of control, trade sale etc.) (see 15.3 below); and
- arrangements under South African black economic empowerment ('BEE') legislation and similar arrangements (see 15.4 below).

15.1   Limited recourse and full recourse loans

In some jurisdictions, share awards to employees are made by means of so-called 'limited recourse loan' schemes. The detailed terms of such schemes vary, but typical features include the following:

- the entity makes an interest-free loan to the employee which is immediately used to acquire shares to the value of the loan on behalf of the employee;
- the shares may be held by the entity, or a trust controlled by it (see 12.3 above), until the loan is repaid;
- the employee is entitled to dividends, except that these are treated as paying off some of the outstanding loan;
- within a given period (say, five years) the employee must either have paid off the outstanding balance of the loan, at which point the shares are delivered to the employee, or surrendered the shares. Surrender of the shares by the employee is treated as discharging any outstanding amount on the loan, irrespective of the value of the shares.

The effect of such an arrangement is clearly equivalent to an option exercisable within five years with a strike price per share equal to the share price at grant date less total dividends since grant date – a view reinforced by the Interpretations Committee.[30] There is no real loan at the initial stage. The entity has no right to receive cash or anther financial asset, since the loan can be settled by the employee returning the (fixed) amount of equity 'purchased' at grant date.

Indeed, the only true cash flow in the entire transaction is any amount paid at the final stage if the employee chooses to acquire the shares at that point. The fact that the strike price is a factor of the share price at grant date and dividends paid between grant date and the date of repayment of the 'loan' is simply an issue for the valuation of the option.

Where, as is generally the case, such an award is subject to no future service or performance condition, IFRS 2 requires the cost to be recognised in full at grant date (see 6.1 above).

More recently, some more complex arrangements have begun to appear where the loan to the employee to acquire the shares is a full recourse loan (i.e. it cannot be discharged simply by surrendering the shares). However, the amount repayable on the loan is reduced not only by dividends paid on the shares, but also by the achievement of performance targets, such as the achievement of a given level of earnings.

The appropriate analysis of such awards is more difficult, as they could be viewed in two ways. One view would be that the employer has made a loan (which the employee has chosen to use to buy a share), accounted for under IAS 39, and has then entered into a performance-related cash bonus arrangement with the employee, accounted for under IAS 19. An alternative analysis would be that the transaction is a share option where the strike price varies according to the satisfaction of performance conditions and the amount of dividends on the shares, accounted for under IFRS 2. The different analyses give rise to potentially significantly different expenses. This will particularly be the case where one of the conditions for mitigation of the amount repayable on the loan is linked to the price of the employer's equity. As this is a market condition, the effect of accounting for the arrangement under IFRS 2 may be that an expense is recognised in circumstances where no expense would be recognised under IAS 19.

Such awards need to be carefully analysed, in the light of their particular facts and circumstances, in order to determine the appropriate treatment. Factors that could suggest that IFRS 2 is the more relevant standard would, in our view, include:

- the employee can use the loan only to acquire shares;
- the employee cannot trade the shares until the loan is discharged; or
- the entity has a practice of accepting (e.g. from leavers) surrender of the shares as full discharge for the amount outstanding on the loan and does not pursue any shortfall between the fair value of the shares and the amount owed by the employee. This would tend to indicate that, in substance, the loan is not truly full recourse.

15.2   Awards entitled to dividends during the vesting period

Some awards entitle the holder to receive dividends on unvested shares during the vesting period.

For example, in some jurisdictions, entities make awards of shares that are regarded as fully vested for the purposes of tax legislation (typically because the employee enjoys the full voting and dividend rights of the shares), but not for accounting purposes (typically because the shares are subject to forfeiture if a certain minimum service period is not achieved). In practice, the shares concerned are usually held by an EBT until the potential forfeiture period has expired.

Another variant of such an award that is sometimes seen is where an entity grants an employee an option to acquire shares in the entity which can be exercised immediately. However, if the employee exercises the option but leaves within a certain minimum period from the grant date, he is required to sell back the share to the entity (typically either at the original exercise price, or the lower of that price or the market value of the share at the time of the buy-back).

Such awards do not fully vest for the purposes of IFRS 2 until the potential forfeiture or buy-back period has expired. The cost of such awards should therefore be recognised over this period.

This raises the question of the accounting treatment of any dividends paid to employees during the vesting period. Conceptually, it could be argued that such dividends cannot be dividends for financial reporting purposes since the equity instruments to which they relate are not yet regarded as issued for financial reporting purposes (and would be excluded from the number of shares in issue for the purposes of IAS 33). This would lead to the conclusion that dividends paid in the vesting period should be charged to profit or loss as an employment cost.

However, the charge to be made for the award under IFRS 2 will already have been increased to take account of the fact that the recipient is entitled to receive dividends during the vesting period (see 8.5.4 above). Thus, it could be argued that also to charge profit or loss with the dividends paid is a form of double counting. Moreover, whilst the relevant shares may not have been fully issued for financial reporting purposes, the basic IFRS 2 accounting does build up an amount in equity over the vesting period. It could therefore be argued that – conceptually, if not legally – any dividend paid relates not to an issued share, but rather to the equity instrument represented by the cumulative amount that has been recorded for the award as a credit to equity, and can therefore appropriately be shown as a deduction from equity.

However, this argument is valid only to the extent that the credit to equity represents awards that are expected to vest. It cannot apply to dividends paid to employees whose awards are either known not to have vested or treated as expected not to vest when applying IFRS 2 (since there is no credit to equity for these awards). Accordingly, we believe that the most appropriate approach is to analyse the dividends paid so that, by the date of vesting, cumulative dividends paid on awards treated by IFRS 2 as vested are deducted from equity and those paid on awards treated by IFRS 2 as unvested are charged to profit or loss. The allocation for periods before that in which vesting occurs should be based on a best estimate of the final outcome, as illustrated by Example 32.62 below.

Example 32.62:   Award with rights to receive (and retain) dividends during vesting period

An entity grants 100 free shares to each of its 500 employees. The shares are treated as fully vested for legal and tax purposes, so that the employees are eligible to receive any dividends paid. However, the shares will be forfeited if the employee leaves within three years of the award being made. Accordingly, for the purposes of IFRS 2, vesting is conditional upon the employee working for the entity over the next three years. The entity estimates that the fair value of each share (including the right to receive dividends during the IFRS 2 vesting period) is €15. Employees are entitled to retain any dividend received even if the award does not vest.

20 employees leave during the first year, and the entity's best estimate at the end of year 1 is that 75 employees will have left before the end of the vesting period. During the second year, a further 22 employees leave, and the entity revises its estimate of total employee departures over the vesting period from 75 to 60. During the third year, a further 15 employees leave. Hence, a total of 57 employees (20 + 22 + 15) forfeit their rights to the shares during the three year period, and a total of 44,300 shares (443 employees × 100 shares per employee) finally vest.

The entity pays dividends of €1 per share in year 1, €1.20 per share in year 2, and €1.50 in year 3.

Under IFRS 2, the entity will recognise the following amounts during the vesting period for services received as consideration for the shares.

Year	Calculation of cumulative expense	Cumulative expense (€)	Expense for period (€)
1	100 shares × 425 employees × €15 × 1/3	212,500	212,500
2	100 shares × 440 employees × €15 × 2/3	440,000	227,500
3	100 shares × 443 × €15 × 3/3	664,500	224,500

On the assumption that all employees who leave during a period do so on the last day of that period (and thus receive dividends paid in that period), in our view the dividends paid on the shares should be accounted for as follows:

		€	€
Year 1	Profit or loss (employee costs)[1]	7,500	
	Equity[1]	42,500	
	Cash[2]		50,000
Year 2	Profit or loss (employee costs)[3]	3,300	
	Equity[3]	54,300	
	Cash[4]		57,600
Year 3	Profit or loss (employee costs)[5]	1,590	
	Equity[5]	67,110	
	Cash[6]		68,700

1   20 employees have left and a further 55 are anticipated to leave. Dividends paid to those employees (100 shares × 75 employees × €1 = €7,500) are therefore recognised as an expense. Dividends paid to other employees are recognised as a reduction in equity.

2   100 shares × 500 employees × €1.

3   22 further employees have left and a further 18 are anticipated to leave. The cumulative expense for dividends paid to leavers and anticipated leavers should therefore be €10,800 (100 shares × 20 employees × €1 = €2,000 for leavers in year 1 + 100 shares × 40 employees × [€1 + €1.20] for leavers and anticipated leavers in year 2 = €8,800). €7,500 was charged in year 1, so the charge for year 2 should be €10,800 − €7,500 = €3,300. This could also have been calculated as charge for leavers and expected leavers in current year €4,800 (100 shares × 40 [22 + 18] employees × €1.20) less reversal of expense in year 1 for reduction in anticipated final number of leavers €1,500 (100 shares × 15 [75 − 60] employees × €1.00). Dividends paid to other employees are recognised as a reduction in equity.

4   100 shares × 480 employees in employment at start of year × €1.20.

5   15 further employees have left. The cumulative expense for dividends paid to leavers should therefore be €12,390 (€2,000 for leavers in year 1 (see 3 above) + 100 shares × 22 employees × [€1 + €1.20] = €4,840 for leavers in year 2 + 100 shares × 15 employees × [€1 + €1.20 + €1.50] = €5,550 for leavers in year 3). A cumulative expense of €10,800 (see 3 above) was recognised by the end of year 2, so the charge for year 3 should be €12,390 − €10,800 = €1,590. This could

also have been calculated as charge for leavers in current year €2,250 (100 shares × 15 employees × €1.50) less reversal of expense in years 1 and 2 for reduction in final number of leavers as against estimate at end of year 2 €660 (100 shares × 3 [60 – 57] employees × [€1.00 + €1.20]). Dividends paid to other employees are recognised as a reduction in equity.

6   100 shares × 458 employees in employment at start of year × €1.50.

15.3   Awards vesting or exercisable on flotation (or change of control, trade sale etc.)

Entities frequently issue awards for which a significant event is a flotation, change of control or a trade sale of the business. It may be, as discussed at 10.3 above, that an award that would normally be only equity-settled becomes cash-settled on such an event.

However, it may also be that an award vests only on such an event, which raises various issues of interpretation, as discussed below.

15.3.1   Grant date

Sometimes such awards are structured so that they will vest on flotation, or that they will vest on flotation subject to further approval at that time. For awards in the first category, grant date as defined in IFRS 2 will be the date on which the award is first communicated to employees. For awards in the second category, grant date will be at or around the date of flotation, when the required further approval is given.

This means that the IFRS 2 cost of awards subject to final approval at flotation will generally be significantly higher than that of awards that do not require such approval. Moreover, as discussed further at 5.3 above, it may well be the case that employees begin rendering service for such awards before grant date (e.g. from the date on which the entity communicates its intention to make the award in principle). In that case, the entity would need to make an initial estimate of the value of the award for the purpose of recognising an expense from the date services have been provided, and continually re-assess that value up until the actual grant date. As with any award dependent on a non-market vesting condition (although it should be noted that the classification of a requirement to float as a non-market vesting condition is the matter of some discussion – see 15.3.3 below), an expense would be recognised only to the extent that the award is considered likely to vest.

15.3.2   Vesting period

Many awards that vest on flotation (or another similar event) have a time limit – in other words, the award lapses if flotation (or another similar event) has not occurred on or before a given future date. In principle, as discussed at 6.2.3 above, when an award has a variable vesting period, the reporting entity should make a best estimate of the likely vesting period at each reporting date and calculate the IFRS 2 charge on the basis of that best estimate.

However, the likely timing of a future flotation is notoriously difficult to assess months, let alone years, in advance. In such cases, it would generally be acceptable simply to recognise the cost over the full potential vesting period until there is real clarity that a shorter period may be more appropriate.

It is worth noting that, under IFRS, once an exit event becomes likely, the IFRS 2 expense will in some cases need to be recognised over a shorter vesting period than was originally envisaged as the probability of the exit event occurring will form the basis at the reporting date of the estimate of the number of awards expected to vest (see also the discussion at 7.6 above). This contrasts with the US GAAP approach where, in practice, an exit event that is a change in control or an initial public offering is only recognised when it occurs. It is therefore possible that, in a situation where a change in control or an initial public offering occurs shortly after the reporting date, the expense will need to be recognised in an earlier period under IFRS than under US GAAP.

15.3.3 Is flotation or sale a vesting condition?

As discussed at 3.2 above, it is unclear whether a requirement for a flotation or sale to occur in order for an award to vest is a vesting condition, as defined by IFRS 2, or a non-vesting condition. The argument as to why flotation or sale is not a vesting condition would be that flotation or sale may occur irrespective of the performance of the entity and is, in any event, outside the control of the entity. The counter-argument is essentially that the price achieved on flotation or sale, which typically affects the ultimate value of the award (see 15.3.4 below), does reflect performance. Moreover, flotation or sale, although not wholly within the control of the entity, is not wholly outside the control of the entity.

The view taken will clearly have a significant impact on the expense recorded. If the view is that flotation or sale is a non-vesting condition, an expense will always be recognised for such an award, provided that all non-market vesting conditions, such as a service condition, have been met, irrespective of whether the award truly vests or not.

Even if it is concluded that a requirement for a flotation or sale, together with a service condition, is a performance vesting condition, the conclusion could differ if the service period is shorter than the period during which flotation or a sale must be achieved. The issue of non-coterminous service and performance targets is considered further at 3.2 and 3.2.1 above.

The classification of flotation or sale as a vesting or non-vesting condition and the required treatment when a performance target is measured over a period exceeding the service period are part of the Interpretations Committee's wider project on vesting and non-vesting conditions. The Interpretations Committee reached a tentative decision in July 2010 that a requirement to float or be sold is a performance vesting condition rather than a non-vesting condition but, to date, no amendment has been made to IFRS 2 to clarify this point (see 3.2.1 above).

15.3.4 Awards requiring achievement of a minimum price

Some awards contingent on flotation (or another similar event) vest only if a minimum price per share is achieved. For example, an entity might grant all its employees options over its shares, the vesting of which is contingent upon a flotation or sale of the shares at a price of at least €5 per share within five years, and the employee being in employment at that time.

Even if it is concluded that the requirement for a flotation or sale to occur is a vesting condition (see 15.3.3 above), there remains the question of whether such an award comprises:

- *two* conditions:
  - a market condition (i.e. float or sell within five years at a share price of at least €5); and
  - a non-market vesting condition (i.e. being in employment at the time of flotation or sale);

or

- *three* conditions:
  - a market condition (share price at time of flotation or sale at least €5); and
  - two non-market vesting conditions:
    - flotation or sale achieved within five years; and
    - being in employment at the time of flotation or sale.

The significance of this is the issue discussed at 6.3 above, namely that an expense must always be recognised for all awards with a market condition, if *all* the non-market vesting conditions are satisfied, even if the market condition is not. In either case, however, there is a market condition which needs to be factored into the valuation of the award.

If the view is that 'flotation or sale at €5 within five years' is a single condition, the entity will recognise an expense for the award for all employees still in service at the end of the five year period, since the sole non-market vesting condition (i.e. service) will have been met.

If, on the other hand, the view is that 'flotation or sale within five years' and 'flotation or sale share price €5' are two separate conditions, and no flotation or sale occurs, no expense will be recognised since, of the two non-market vesting conditions (i.e. 'service' and 'flotation or sale within five years'), only one has been satisfied. However, even on this second analysis, if a sale or flotation is achieved at a price less than €5, an expense must be recognised, even though the award does not truly vest, since both non-market vesting conditions (i.e. 'service' and 'flotation or sale within five years') will have been met.

In our view, the appropriate analysis is to regard 'flotation or sale within five years' and 'flotation/sale share price €5' as two separate conditions.

There is, however a third possible analysis (see 15.3.3 above) which is that there are:

- *three* conditions:
  - a market condition (share price at time of flotation or sale at least €5);
  - a non-vesting condition (flotation or sale achieved within five years); and
  - a non-market vesting condition (being in employment at the time of flotation or sale).

Chapter 32

On this analysis, an expense would always be recognised for all employees still in service at the end of the five year period, since the sole non-market vesting condition (i.e. service) will have been met.

This provides a useful illustration of the practical difficulties created by the concept of the non-vesting condition (see 3.2 and 3.2.1 above).

15.3.5 Awards 'purchased for fair value'

Entities that are contemplating a flotation or trade sale may invite employees to subscribe for a special class of shares for a relatively nominal amount, which, in the event of a flotation or trade sale occurring, will be redeemable at a substantial premium. It may be argued that the initial subscription price paid represents the fair value of the share at the time, given the inherent high uncertainty as to whether a flotation or trade sale will in fact occur.

The premium paid on a flotation or trade sale will typically be calculated in part by reference to the price achieved. The question therefore arises as to whether such awards fall within the scope of IFRS 2. It might be argued for example that, as the employee paid full fair value for the award at issue, there has been no share-based payment and, accordingly, the instrument should be accounted for under IAS 32 and IAS 39.

In our view, it is necessary to consider whether the award has features that would not be expected in 'normal' equity – specifically a requirement for the holder of the shares to remain in employment until flotation. If this is the case, regardless of the amount subscribed, the terms suggest that the shares are being awarded in return for employee services and hence that the award is within the scope of IFRS 2. This may mean that, even if the award has no material fair value (and therefore gives rise to no expense), it may be necessary to make the disclosures required by IFRS 2.

Moreover, even if the amount paid by the employees can be demonstrated to be fair value, that amount would not necessarily constitute fair value under IFRS 2. Specifically, a 'true' fair value would take into account non-market vesting conditions (such as a requirement for the employee to remain in employment until flotation or a trade sale occurs). However, a valuation for IFRS 2 purposes would not take such conditions into account (see 5.5 and 6.2.1 above), and would therefore typically be higher than the 'true' fair value.

A non-equity share such as that described above might well be classified as a liability under IAS 32. However, if the redemption amount is linked to the flotation price of the 'real' equity, it is a cash-settled share-based payment transaction under IFRS 2 (see 2.2.4.A above).

It is common in such situations for the cost of satisfying any obligations to the special shareholders to be borne by shareholders rather than the entity itself. This raises a number of further issues, which are discussed at 2.2.2.A above.

15.3.6 'Drag along' and 'tag along' rights

An increasingly common form of award is for the management of an entity to be allowed to acquire a special class of equity at fair value (as in 15.3.5 above), but (in contrast to 15.3.5 above) with no redemption right on an exit event. However, rights are given:

- to any buyer of the 'normal' equity also to buy the special shares (sometimes called a 'drag along' right);
- to a holder of the special shares to require any buyer of the 'normal' equity also to buy the special shares (sometimes called a 'tag along' right).

Such schemes are particularly found in entities where the 'normal' equity is held by a provider of venture capital, which will generally be looking for an exit in the medium term.

It may well be that, under the scheme, the entity itself is required to facilitate the operation of the drag along or tag along rights, which may involve the entity collecting the proceeds from the buyer and passing them on to the holder of the special shares.

This raises the issue of whether such an arrangement is equity-settled or cash-settled. The fact that, in certain circumstances the entity is required to deliver cash to the holder of a share suggests that the arrangement is an award requiring cash settlement in specific circumstances, the treatment of which is discussed at 10.3 above.

However, if the terms of the award are such that the entity is obliged to pass on cash to the holder of the share only if, and to the extent that, proceeds are received from an external buyer, in our view, the arrangement may be economically no different to a broker settlement arrangement, as discussed at 9.3.3 above. This could allow the arrangement to be regarded as equity-settled, provided that consideration is given to all the factors (discussed at 9.3.3 above) that could suggest that the scheme is more appropriately regarded as cash-settled. In making such an assessment, care needs to be taken to ensure that the precise facts of the arrangement are considered. For example, a transaction where the entity has some discretion over the amount of proceeds attributable to each class of shareholder might indicate that it is inappropriate to treat the entity simply as an agent in the cash payment arrangement.

15.4   South African black economic empowerment ('BEE') and similar arrangements

As part of general economic reforms in South Africa, arrangements – commonly referred to as black economic empowerment or 'BEE' deals – have been put in place to encourage the transfer of equity, or economic interests in equity, to historically disadvantaged individuals.

An entity can enhance its BEE status in a number of ways (through employment equity, skills development or preferential procurement policies to name but a few). This section focuses on BEE deals involving transfers of equity instruments, or interests in equity instruments, to historically disadvantaged individuals.

Such transfers have generally been concluded at a discount to the fair value of the equity instruments concerned. As a result of having empowered shareholders, the reporting entity is able to claim its 'BEE credentials', thus allowing the reporting entity greater business opportunities in the South African economy. These arrangements raise a number of practical issues of interpretation, and indeed led to the scope of IFRS 2 being extended to include transactions where the consideration received appears less than the consideration given, as discussed further at 2.2.2.C above.

BEE deals are typically complex and their specific structures and terms may vary considerably. However, they do exhibit certain features with some regularity, as discussed below.

Typically BEE arrangements have involved the transfer of equity instruments to:

- empowerment companies controlled by prominent BEE qualifying individuals;
- BEE qualifying employees of the reporting entity; or
- beneficiaries in the BEE qualifying communities in which the entity operates.

Generally these individuals have not been able to raise sufficient finance in order to purchase the equity instruments. Accordingly, the reporting entity often facilitates the transaction and assists the BEE party in securing the necessary financing.

A BEE arrangement often involves the creation of a trust or corporate entity, with the BEE party holding beneficial rights in the trust which in turn holds equity instruments of the reporting entity (or a member of its group).

The awards made by the trust may be in the form of:

- the equity instruments originally transferred to the trust;
- units in the trust itself, usually with a value linked in some way to the value of the equity instruments of the reporting entity originally transferred to the trust; or
- payments made from the proceeds (dividends received, sale of equity instruments etc) that the trust generates.

The accounting issues arising from such schemes include:

- the nature of the trust (specifically, whether it is a special purpose entity (SPE) of the reporting entity);
- whether any charge arises under IFRS 2 and, if so, the grant date and therefore, under a grant date model, the amount of the charge; and
- whether awards are equity-settled or cash-settled.

15.4.1 Nature of the trust

The first issue to consider in any accounting analysis is whether any trust to which the equity instruments of the reporting entity have been transferred is an SPE of the entity under SIC-12 (see Chapter 6) or, with effect from 1 January 2013, whether the trust meets the requirements for consolidation under IFRS 10 (see Chapter 7). Factors that may indicate that the trust is an SPE include:

- the potential beneficiaries of the trust are restricted to persons in the employment of, or otherwise providing services to, the reporting entity;
- the reporting entity has the right to control (on 'autopilot' or otherwise), or does in practice control, the management of the trust; or
- the reporting entity assumes the residual risk associated with the trust.

The generic form of BEE deal normally requires the reporting entity either to finance the acquisition of the shares by the trust or to provide cross guarantees to the financiers of the trust. Alternative methodologies that have been employed include capital enhancements created in the trust by the sale of equity instruments at a severely discounted amount.

In summary, the BEE party generally injects only a notional amount of capital into the trust, which obtains financing to acquire the shares in the reporting entity and uses the dividend cash flows to service the debt it has raised. In such generic schemes, the BEE party faces a typical option return profile: the maximum amount of capital at risk is notional and the potential upside increase in value of the shares of the reporting entity accrues to the BEE party through the party's beneficial rights in the trust.

15.4.2 Measurement and timing of the accounting cost

If the analysis under 15.4.1 above is that the trust is an SPE of the reporting entity, the transfer of equity instruments to that entity is essentially the same as a transfer of own equity to an employee benefit trust, as discussed at 12.3 above. Such a transfer, considered alone, is an intra-entity transaction and therefore does not give rise to a charge under IFRS 2. The equity instruments held by the trust are therefore treated as treasury shares, and no non-controlling (minority) interests are recognised.

It is only when the trust itself makes an award to a third party that a charge arises, which will be measured at the time at which the transfer to the third party occurs. In a rising stock market this will lead to a higher charge than would have occurred had there been a grant, as defined in IFRS 2, on the date that the equity instruments were originally transferred to the trust. Generally, the value of the award is based on an option model and the BEE party is treated as the holder of an option.

Where the trust is not an SPE of the reporting entity, the presumption will be that the transfer of equity instruments to the trust crystallises an IFRS 2 charge at the date of transfer. However, it is important to consider the terms of the transaction in their totality. For example, if the entity has the right to buy back the equity instruments at some future date, the benefit transferred may in fact be an economic interest in the equity instruments for a limited period. This may, depending on the method used to determine the buy-back price, influence the measurement of any IFRS 2 charge (which would normally be based on the presumption that the benefits of a vested share had been passed in perpetuity).

Some have sought to argue that BEE credentials result in the recognition of an intangible asset rather than an expense. However, we concur with the conclusion of interpretive guidance issued in South Africa that BEE credentials do not qualify for recognition of intangible assets in terms of IAS 38 – *Intangible Assets* – and the difference between the fair value of the award and the consideration received should therefore be expensed.[31]

An issue to be considered in determining timing of the IFRS 2 expense is that many BEE transactions require the BEE party to be 'locked into' the transaction for a pre-determined period. During this period the BEE party or trust is generally prohibited from selling or transferring the equity instruments. As no specific performance is generally required during this period, it is not considered part of the vesting period (see 3.3 and 6 above). Rather, the restrictions would be considered to be post-vesting restrictions, and taken into account in calculating the fair value of the equity instruments (see 8.4.1 above).

15.4.3 Classification of awards as equity- or cash-settled

Certain schemes, particularly where the reporting entity is not listed, give the BEE party the right to put the shares back to the entity (or another group entity) after a certain date. This is often done to create liquidity for the BEE parties, should they decide to exit the scheme. Such a feature would require the scheme to be classified as cash-settled (see 9.1 above).

Similarly, where the BEE transaction is facilitated through a trust, the trust may have granted awards to beneficiaries in the form of units in the trust. The trustees may have the power to reacquire units from beneficiaries in certain circumstances (e.g. where the beneficiaries are employees, when they leave the employment of the entity). Where the trust does not have sufficient cash with which to make such payments, the reporting entity may be obliged, legally or constructively, to fund them.

Such arrangements may – in their totality – create a cash-settled scheme from the perspective of the reporting entity. In analysing a particular scheme, it should be remembered that, under IFRS 2, cash-settled schemes arise not only from legal liabilities, but also from constructive or commercial liabilities (e.g. to prevent a former employee having rights against what is essentially an employee trust) – see 10.2 above.

Finally, a transaction may be structured in such a way that the SPE trust holds equity instruments of the reporting entity for an indefinite period. Dividends received by the trust may be used to fund certain expenses in a particular community in which the reporting entity operates (e.g. tuition fees for children of the reporting entity's employees or the costs of certain community projects). The scheme may even make provision for the shares to be sold after a certain period with the eventual proceeds being distributed amongst members of the community.

In such a case it is necessary to consider the nature of the distribution requirement and whether or not the reporting entity (through the SPE trust) has a legal or constructive obligation under the scheme to make cash payments based on the price or value of the shares held by the trust. Where there is such an obligation, the arrangement would be classified as a cash-settled scheme. If however the trust merely acts as a conduit through which:

• dividend receipts by the trust are paid out to beneficiaries with the shares never leaving the trust; or

• proceeds from the sale of shares are distributed to beneficiaries,

the precise terms of the arrangement should be assessed to determine whether or not the arrangement meets the definition of a cash-settled share-based payment (see section 15.3.6 above for a discussion of similar considerations in the context of 'drag along' and 'tag along' rights).

Any dividend payments by the Group for the period that the SPE is consolidated should be treated as an equity distribution or as an expense, as appropriate, in accordance with the principles discussed at 15.2 above.

16 FIRST-TIME ADOPTION AND TRANSITIONAL PROVISIONS

16.1 First-time adoption provisions

These are discussed in Chapter 5 at 5.3. However, one provision may remain relevant for entities that have already adopted IFRS and would no longer generally be considered 'first-time adopters'.

IFRS 1 does not require an entity to account for equity-settled transactions:

- granted on or before 7 November 2002; or
- granted after 7 November 2002 but vested before the later of the date of transition to IFRS and 1 January 2005.

However, where such an award is modified, cancelled or settled, the rules regarding modification, cancellation and settlement (see 7 above) apply in full unless the modification occurred before the date of transition to IFRS. *[IFRS 1.D2]*. The intention of this provision is to prevent an entity from avoiding the recognition of a cost for a new award by structuring it as a modification to an earlier award not in the scope of IFRS 2.

There is slight ambiguity on this point in the wording of IFRS 1, paragraph D2 of which refers only to the *modification* of such awards. This could allow a literalistic argument that IFRS 1 does not prescribe any specific treatment when an entity cancels or settles (as opposed to modifying) an equity-settled award subject to the first-time adoption exception. However, paragraph D2 also requires an entity to apply 'paragraphs 26-29' of IFRS 2 to 'modified' awards. Paragraphs 26-29 deal not only with modification but also with cancellation and settlement, and indeed paragraphs 28 and 29 are not relevant to *modification* at all. This makes it clear, in our view, that the IASB intended IFRS 1 to be applied not only to the modification of such awards.

16.2 Transitional provisions

The original version of IFRS 2 published in February 2004 contained a number of transitional provisions that are now of limited application, and are therefore not discussed here. A fuller discussion appeared in *International GAAP 2008* and earlier editions.

The principal transitional provision likely to remain of relevance is that IFRS 2 as originally published in February 2004 did not require an entity to account for equity-settled transactions:

- granted on or before 7 November 2002; or
- granted after 7 November 2002 but vested before the effective date of IFRS 2 (the first date of the accounting period in which IFRS 2 first applied). *[IFRS 2.53, 60]*.

However, where such an award is modified, cancelled or settled after the effective date, the rules regarding modification, cancellation and settlement (see 7 above) apply in full. *[IFRS 2.57, 60]*. The intention of this provision is to prevent an entity from avoiding the recognition of a cost for a new award by structuring it as a modification to an earlier award not in the scope of IFRS 2.

As in paragraph D2 of IFRS 1 (see discussion at 16.1 above), there is slight ambiguity on this point in the wording of paragraph 57 of IFRS 2 as currently drafted.

Chapter 32

References

1 *Amendment to International Financial Reporting Standards: IFRS 2 Share-based Payment – Vesting Conditions and Cancellations*, IASB, January 2008 ('January 2008 amendment').

2 *Group Cash-settled Share-based Payment Transactions, Amendments to IFRS 2*, IASB, June 2009 ('June 2009 amendment').

3 For convenience, throughout this Chapter we refer to the recognition of a cost for share-based payments. In some cases, however, a share-based payment transaction may initially give rise to an asset (e.g. where employee costs are capitalised as part of the cost of PP&E or inventories).

4 *IASB Update*, February 2010.

5 *IFRIC Update*, January 2010.

6 *IFRIC Update*, July 2010.

7 'Contingent feature' is not currently a defined term in IFRS 2.

8 *IFRIC Update*, September 2010.

9 *IASB Update*, September 2010.

10 *IFRIC Update*, November 2010.

11 *IFRIC Update*, March 2011.

12 FASB ASC 718 – Compensation – Stock Compensation (formerly FAS123(R), *Share-Based Payment*), FASB, December 2004, [20-55-25].

13 *IFRIC Update*, September 2010.

14 *IFRIC Update*, November 2010.

15 *IFRIC Update*, July 2006.

16 *IFRIC Update*, March 2011.

17 More detailed guidance on this may be found in a publication such as Options, Futures, and Other Derivatives, John C. Hull.

18 *IFRIC Update*, May 2011.

19 FASB Staff Position 123(R)-4, *Classification of Options and Similar Instruments Issued as Employee Compensation That Allow for Cash Settlement upon the Occurrence of a Contingent Event*.

20 FASB ASC 718 – Compensation – Stock Compensation (formerly FAS123(R), *Share-Based Payment*), FASB, December 2004, para. 32, footnote 18a.

21 *IFRIC Update*, January 2010.

22 *IFRIC Update*, March 2011.

23 *Improvements to IFRSs*, IASB, May 2010 ('May 2010 amendment').

24 D17 – *IFRS 2 – Group and Treasury Share Transactions*, IASB, 2005, para. IE5.

25 UITF 25 – *National Insurance contributions on share option gains*, Urgent Issues Task Force of United Kingdom Accounting Standards Board, July 2000.

26 *IFRIC Update*, September 2010.

27 *IFRIC Update*, September 2010.

28 *IFRIC Update*, November 2010.

29 *IFRIC Update*, March 2011.

30 *IFRIC Update*, November 2005, p. 6.

31 AC 503, Accounting Practices Committee (South Africa), January 2010.

Chapter 33   Employee benefits

List of examples

Chapter 33

Chapter 33   Employee benefits

1   INTRODUCTION

This chapter principally deals with IAS 19 as published in 1998 and subject to numerous amendments up until 2010. In June 2011 the IASB issued a revised standard (IAS 19(2011)) which comes into mandatory force for periods beginning on or after 1 January 2013, with earlier adoption permitted. The new standard makes a number of significant changes to accounting for employee benefits and is discussed at 8 below.

Employee benefits typically form a very significant part of any entity's costs, and can take many and varied forms. Accordingly, IFRS devotes considerable attention to them in two separate standards. IFRS 2 – *Share-based Payment* – which was issued primarily in response to concerns over share-based remuneration and is discussed in Chapter 32. All other employee benefits are dealt with in IAS 19 – *Employee Benefits* – discussed in this Chapter.

Many issues raised in accounting for employee benefits can be straight forward, such as the allocation of wages paid to an accounting period, and are generally dealt with by IAS 19 accordingly. In contrast, accounting for the costs of retirement benefits in the financial statements of employers presents one of the most difficult challenges in the whole field of financial reporting. The amounts involved are large, the timescale is long, the estimation process is complex and involves many areas of uncertainty which have to be made the subject of assumptions. In addition the actuarial mechanisms used for allocating the costs to years of employment are complicated and their selection open to debate. Furthermore, the complexities for an International Standard are multiplied by the wide variety of arrangements found in different jurisdictions. In light of this it is perhaps not surprising that the requirements of IFRS in this area are complex and have changed frequently, sometimes radically, over the years.

In January 1983, the IASC issued IAS 19 – *Accounting for Retirement Benefits in the Financial Statements of Employers* – which was revised ten years later in November 1993 with the shortened title of *Retirement Benefit Costs*. Put simply, the original IAS 19 was an 'income statement standard' which sought to charge to income systematically the long-term cost of providing retirement benefits.

In October 1996, however, the IASC published an exposure draft proposing to make fundamental changes to IAS 19.[1] In particular, the whole focus of the standard was to be shifted from the income statement to the balance sheet. This led to the issue of a further revised version of IAS 19 in February 1998. The title of the standard was also changed to 'Employee Benefits' reflecting a broadening of its scope to cover pre-retirement and post-retirement benefits as well as disclosure requirements for employee equity compensation benefits (these latter requirements being superseded in 2004 by the publication of IFRS 2). In 1999, IAS 10 – *Events After the Balance Sheet Date* – made some minor consequential amendments to IAS 19. In October 2000 some further adjustments were made to IAS 19 relating to the treatment of assets in the form of insurance policies and reimbursement rights. The standard was revised again in 2002 to correct a perceived anomaly that in some circumstances the interaction of the standard's complex (indeed, conceptually conflicting) requirements could lead to the recognition of profits purely as a result of actuarial *losses* in a pension fund (and vice versa).

In April 2004, the IASB published an exposure draft of some further revisions to IAS 19.[2] This led to the publication, in December 2004, of a further amendment to the standard.[3] This amendment addressed four areas:

- the recognition of actuarial gains and losses. The revised standard now contains an option to recognise such gains and losses, in full as they occur, but outside of profit and loss;

- revised requirements for the treatment of plans that share risks and rewards between entities under common control;

- clarification of the treatment of multi-employer plans; and

- revised disclosure requirements.

In June 2005 the IASB published an exposure draft proposing some amendments to IAS 19 regarding termination benefits.[4]

In July 2007 the Interpretations Committee published Interpretation 14 which deals with the restriction of a defined benefit plan asset on recoverability grounds and the impact of minimum funding requirements.

The possible future development of the standard is discussed at 9 below.

2   OBJECTIVE AND SCOPE OF IAS 19

2.1   Objective

IAS 19 sets out its objective as follows:

'The objective of this Standard is to prescribe the accounting and disclosure for employee benefits. The Standard requires an entity to recognise:

(a)   a liability when an employee has provided service in exchange for employee benefits to be paid in the future; and

(b)   an expense when the entity consumes the economic benefit arising from service provided by an employee in exchange for employee benefits.'
[IAS 19, Objective].

It is fair to say the above is more of a summary than an objective (the objective of *all* accounting standards is to 'prescribe ... accounting and disclosure...' for some aspect of financial reporting) or at best an objective that is by definition self fulfilling. However, it provides the first glimpse of the direction taken by the standard. Driven by the balance sheet approach in the IASB's *Conceptual Framework* it approaches the issues from a balance sheet perspective although as we shall discuss later it currently stops short of a full fair value balance sheet treatment.

2.2   Scope

2.2.1 below deals with the general scope of the standard. The issue of employee benefits settled not by the employing entity but by a shareholder or other member of a group is discussed at 2.2.2.

2.2.1   *General scope requirements of IAS 19*

As mentioned above, the 1998 version of IAS 19 became entitled 'Employee Benefits', and as this name suggests it is not confined to pensions and other post-retirement benefits, but rather addresses all forms of consideration (aside of share based payments which are dealt with by IFRS 2 and discussed in Chapter 32) given by an employer in exchange for service rendered by employees. *[IAS 19.1, 7]*. In particular, in addition to post-retirement benefits employee benefits include: *[IAS 19.4]*

(a)   short-term benefits, including wages and salaries, paid annual leave, bonuses, benefits in kind, etc. The accounting treatment of these is discussed at 6.1;

(b)   long-term benefits, such as long-service leave, long-term disability benefits, long-term bonuses, etc. These are to be accounted for in a similar way to post-retirement benefits by using actuarial techniques and are discussed at 6.2 below;

(c)   termination benefits. These are to be provided for and expensed when the employer becomes committed to the redundancy plan, on a similar basis to that required by IAS 37 – *Provisions, Contingent Liabilities and Contingent Assets* – for provisions generally, and are discussed at 6.3 below.

The standard addresses only the accounting by employers, and excludes from its scope reporting by employee benefit plans themselves. These are dealt with in IAS 26 – *Accounting and Reporting by Retirement Benefit Plans*. *[IAS 19.1-2]*. The specialist nature of these requirements puts them beyond the scope of this book.

The standard makes clear it applies widely and in particular to benefits:

(a)   provided to all employees (whether full-time, part-time, permanent, temporary or casual staff and specifically including directors and other management personnel); *[IAS 19.6]*

(b)   however settled – including payments in cash or goods or services, whether paid directly to employees, their dependents (spouses, children or others) or any other party (such as insurance companies); *[IAS 19.5]* and

(c)   however provided, including:

(i)   under formal plans or other formal agreements between an entity and individual employees, groups of employees or their representatives;

(ii)   under legislative requirements, or through industry arrangements, whereby entities are required to contribute to national, state, industry or other multi-employer plans; or

(iii)   by those informal practices that give rise to a constructive obligation, that is where the entity has no realistic alternative but to pay employee benefits. An example of a constructive obligation is where a change in the entity's informal practices would cause unacceptable damage to its relationship with employees. *[IAS 19.3]*.

The standard does not define the term 'employee'. However, it is clear from the reference in (a) above to 'full-time, part-time, permanent, temporary or casual staff and specifically including directors' that the term is intended to apply widely. In particular, it is not necessary for there to be a contract of employment in order for an individual to be considered an employee for IAS 19 purposes. In our view the standard applies to anyone who is in substance an employee, and that will be a matter of judgement in light of all the facts and circumstances.

The following extract illustrates some of the variety of employee benefits addressed by the standard.

Extract 33.1: Telkom SA Limited (2006)

Notes to the consolidated annual financial statements [extract]

2.   Significant accounting policies [extract]

Employee benefits [extract]

Post-employment benefits

The Group provides defined benefit and defined contribution plans for the benefit of employees. These plans are funded by the employees and the Group, taking into account recommendations of the independent actuaries. The post retirement medical and telephone rebate liabilities are unfunded.

Defined contribution plans

The Group's funding of the defined contribution plans is charged to the income statement in the same year as the related service is provided.

Defined benefit plans

The Group provides defined benefit plans for pension, retirement, medical aid costs, and telephone rebates to qualifying employees. The Group's net obligation in respect of defined benefits is calculated separately for each plan by estimating the amount of future benefits earned in return for services rendered.

The amount recognised in the balance sheet represents the present value of the defined benefit obligations, calculated using the project unit credit method, as adjusted for unrecognised actuarial gains and losses, unrecognised past service costs and reduced by the fair value of plan assets. The amount of any surplus recognised is limited to unrecognised actuarial losses and past service costs plus the present value of available refunds and reductions in future contributions to the plan. To the extent that there is uncertainty as to the entitlement to the surplus, no asset is recognised.

Actuarial gains and losses are recognised as income or expense when the cumulative unrecognised gains and losses for each individual plan exceed 10% of the greater of the present value of the Group's obligation or the fair value of plan assets. These gains or losses are amortised on a straight-line basis over ten years for all the defined benefit plans.

Past service costs are recognised immediately to the extent that the benefits are vested, otherwise they are recognised on a straight-line basis over the average period the benefits become vested.

Leave benefits

Annual leave is provided for over the period that the leave accrues and is subject to a cap.

Workforce reduction

Workforce reduction expenses are payable when employment is terminated before the normal retirement age or when an employee accepts voluntary redundancy in exchange for benefits. Workforce reduction expenses are recognised when it is probable that the expenses will be incurred.

Deferred bonus incentives

Employees of the wholly owned subsidiaries of Vodacom, including the executive directors, are eligible for compensation benefits in the form of a Deferred Bonus Incentive Scheme. The benefit is recorded at the present value of the expected future cash flows
...

Short-term employee benefits

The cost of all short-term employee benefits is recognised during the period employees render services, unless the entity uses the services of employees in the construction of an asset, at which stage it is included as part of the related property, plant and equipment item.

2.2.2 *Employee benefits settled by a shareholder or another group entity.*

In some circumstances, employee benefits may be settled by a party other than the entity to which services were rendered by employees. Examples would include a shareholder or another entity in a group of entities under common control.

IAS 19 is silent on whether, and if so how, an entity receiving employee services in this way should account for them. IFRS 2, on the other hand, devotes quite some detail to this topic for employee services within its scope. Despite a certain infelicity in the drafting of IFRS 2, it generally requires the entity receiving employee services in this way to account for the cost of them.

An entity could make reference to the hierarchy in IAS 8 – *Accounting Policies, Changes in Accounting Estimates and Errors* (discussed in Chapter 3 at 4.3) when deciding on an accounting policy under IAS 19. Accordingly, these provisions of IFRS 2 could be applied by analogy to transactions within the scope of IAS 19.

The requirements of IFRS 2 are discussed in Chapter 32 at 2.2.2.A.

3 PENSIONS AND OTHER POST-EMPLOYMENT BENEFITS – DEFINED CONTRIBUTION AND DEFINED BENEFIT PLANS

3.1 The distinction between defined contribution plans and defined benefit plans

In common with most other accounting standards around the world, IAS 19 draws the natural, but important, distinction between defined contribution plans and defined benefit plans. The approach it takes is to define the former, with the latter being the default category. The relevant terms defined by the standard are as follows:

'*Post-employment benefits* are employee benefits (other than termination benefits) which are payable after the completion of employment'.

'*Post-employment benefit plans* are formal or informal arrangements under which an entity provides post-employment benefits for one or more employees'.

'*Defined contribution plans* are post-employment benefit plans under which an entity pays fixed contributions into a separate entity (a fund) and will have no legal or constructive obligation to pay further contributions if the fund does not hold sufficient assets to pay all employee benefits relating to employee service in the current and prior periods'.

'*Defined benefit plans* are post-employment benefit plans other than defined contribution plans'. *[IAS 19.7]*.

IAS 19 applies to all post-employment benefits (whether or not they involve the establishment of a separate entity to receive contributions and pay benefits) which include, for example, retirement benefits such as pensions; and post-employment life assurance or medical care. *[IAS 19.24]*. A less common benefit is the provision of services. Extract 33.1 at 2.2 above provides an example of a company providing telephone rebates to former employees.

Under defined benefit plans the employer's obligation is not limited to the amount that it agrees to contribute to the fund. Rather, the employer is obliged (legally or constructively) to provide the agreed benefits to current and former employees. Examples of defined benefit schemes given by IAS 19 are:

(a)   plans where the benefit formula is not linked solely to the amount of contributions;

(b)   guarantees, either directly or indirectly through a plan, of a specified return on contributions; and

(c)   those informal practices that give rise to a constructive obligation. For example, a history of increasing benefits for former employees to keep pace with inflation even where there is no legal obligation to do so. *[IAS 19.26-27]*.

The most significant difference between defined contribution and defined benefit plans is that, under defined benefit plans, both actuarial risk and investment risk fall on the employer. This means that if actuarial or investment experience is worse than expected, the employer's obligation may be increased. *[IAS 19.27]*. Consequently, because the employer is underwriting the actuarial and investment risks associated with the plan, the expense recognised for a defined benefit plan is not necessarily the amount of the contribution due for the period. *[IAS 19.49]*. Conversely, under defined contribution plans the benefits received by the employee are determined by the amount of contributions paid (either by the employer, or both the employer and the employee) together with investment returns, and hence actuarial and investment risk are borne by the employee. *[IAS 19.25]*.

3.2   Insured benefits

One factor that can complicate making the distinction between defined benefit and defined contribution plans is the use of external insurers. IAS 19 recognises that some employers may fund their post-employment benefit plans by paying insurance premiums and observes that the benefits insured need not have a direct or automatic relationship with the entity's obligation for employee benefits. However it makes clear that post-employment benefit plans involving insurance contracts are subject to the same distinction between accounting and funding as other funded plans. *[IAS 19.40]*.

Where insurance premiums are paid to fund post employment benefits, the employer should treat the plan as a defined contribution plan unless it has a legal or constructive obligation to:

(a)   pay the employee benefits directly when they fall due; or

(b)   pay further amounts if the insurer does not pay all future employee benefits relating to employee service in the current and prior periods.

If the employer has retained such a legal or constructive obligation it should treat the plan as a defined benefit plan. *[IAS 19.39]*. In that case, the employer recognises its rights under a 'qualifying insurance policy' as a plan asset and recognises other insurance policies as reimbursement rights. *[IAS 19.41]*. Plan assets are discussed at 5.2.1 below.

By way of final clarification, the standard notes that where an insurance policy is in the name of a specified plan participant or a group of plan participants and the employer does not have any legal or constructive obligation to cover any loss on the policy, the employer has no obligation to pay benefits to the employees and the insurer has sole responsibility for paying the benefits. In that case, the payment of fixed premiums under such contracts is, in substance, the settlement of the employee benefit obligation, rather than an investment to meet the obligation. Consequently, the employer no longer has an asset or a liability. Accordingly, it should treat the payments as contributions to a defined contribution plan. *[IAS 19.42]*. The important point here is that employee entitlements will be of a defined benefit nature unless the employer has no obligation whatsoever to pay them should the insurance fail or otherwise be insufficient.

The standard's analysis of insured plans described above, along with the definition of defined benefit and defined contribution plans seems comprehensive at first glance. However, there will be circumstances where careful consideration will be required and which reveal that the distinction may not be that cut and dried after all. For example, it is possible that an employer buys insurance on a regular basis (say annually), retaining no further obligation in respect of the benefits insured, but has an obligation (legal or constructive) to keep doing so in the future. In such a scenario the employer may be exposed to future actuarial variances reflected in a variable cost of purchasing the required insurance in future years (for example, due to changing mortality estimates by the insurer). An example would be where each year the employee earns an entitlement to a pension of (say) 2% of that year's (i.e. current as opposed to final) salary and that the employer purchases each year an annuity contract to commence on the date of retirement.

In our view the standard is not entirely clear as to the nature of such an arrangement. On the one hand, it could be argued that it is a defined contribution plan because the definition of defined contribution plans is met when:

• 'fixed' payments are paid to a separate fund; and

• the employer is not obliged to pay further amounts if the fund has insufficient assets to pay the benefits relating to employee service in the *current and prior periods*.

Further, as noted above the standard considers the payment of 'fixed' premiums to purchase insurance specific to an employee (or group thereof) with no retention of risk in respect of the insured benefits to be a defined contribution arrangement.

On the other hand, it could be argued that this is a defined benefit plan on the grounds that:

- the premiums of future years are not 'fixed' in any meaningful sense (certainly not in the same way as an intention simply to pay a one-off contribution of a given % of salary);

- the standard acknowledges that one factor that can mean insured arrangements are defined benefit in nature is when the employer retains an obligation indirectly through the mechanism for setting future premiums; and

- the standard observes that under defined benefit plans '...actuarial risk (that benefits will cost more than expected) and investment risk fall, in substance, on the entity. If actuarial or investment experience are worse than expected, the entity's obligation may be increased'. *[IAS 19.27]*.

Much would seem to depend on just what 'fixed' means in such circumstances. Although not expressly addressed by the standard, in our view such arrangements will very likely be defined benefit in nature, albeit with regular (and perhaps only partial) settlement and, if so, should be accounted for as such. This is because the employer has retained actuarial risks by committing to pay whatever it takes in future years to secure the requisite insurance. Naturally, for any schemes that are determined to be defined benefit plans, the next step would be to see whether the frequent settlement renders the output of the two accounting models materially the same. That would depend, inter alia, on the attribution of the benefit to years of service and the impact of an unwinding discount. The wide variety of possible arrangements in practice mean that careful consideration of individual circumstances will be required to determine the true substance of such arrangements.

3.3   Multi-employer plans

3.3.1   *Multi-employer plans other than those sharing risks between entities under common control*

3.3.1.A   *The treatment of multi-employer plans*

Multi-employer plans, other than state plans (see 3.4 below), under IAS 19 are defined contribution plans or defined benefit plans that:

(a)   pool assets contributed by various entities that are not under common control; and

(b)   use those assets to provide benefits to employees of more than one entity, on the basis that contribution and benefit levels are determined without regard to the identity of the entity that employs the employees concerned. *[IAS 19.7]*.

Accordingly, they exclude group administration plans, which simply pool the assets of more than one employer, for investment purposes and the reduction of administrative and investment costs, but keep the claims of different employers segregated for the sole benefit of their own employees. The standard observes that group administration plans pose no particular accounting problems because information is readily available to treat them in the same way as any other single employer plan and because they do not expose the participating employers to actuarial risks associated with the current and former employees of other entities. Accordingly, the standard requires group administration plans to be classified as defined contribution plans or defined benefit plans in accordance with the terms of the plan (including any constructive obligation that goes beyond the formal terms). *[IAS 19.33].*

The standard gives a description of one example of a multi-employer scheme as follows:

(a)   the plan is financed on a pay-as-you-go basis such that: contributions are set at a level that is expected to be sufficient to pay the benefits falling due in the same period; and future benefits earned during the current period will be paid out of future contributions; and

(b)   employees' benefits are determined by the length of their service and the participating entities have no realistic means of withdrawing from the plan without paying a contribution for the benefits earned by employees up to the date of withdrawal. Such a plan creates actuarial risk for the entity: if the ultimate cost of benefits already earned at the end of the reporting period is more than expected, it will be necessary for the entity either to increase its contributions or persuade employees to accept a reduction in benefits. Therefore, such a plan is a defined benefit plan. *[IAS 19.31].*

A multi-employer plan should be classified as either a defined contribution plan or a defined benefit plan in accordance with its terms in the normal way (see 3.1 above). If a multi-employer plan is classified as a defined benefit plan, IAS 19 requires that the employer should account for its proportionate share of the defined benefit obligation, plan assets and costs associated with the plan in the same way as for any other defined benefit plan (see 5 below). The employer should also disclose the same information as is required for any other defined benefit plan. *[IAS 19.29].*

The standard does, however, contain a practical exemption if insufficient information is available to use defined benefit accounting. This could be the case, for example, where:

(a)   the entity does not have access to information about the plan that satisfies the requirements of the standard; or

(b)   the plan exposes the participating entities to actuarial risks associated with the current and former employees of other entities, with the result that there is no consistent and reliable basis for allocating the obligation, plan assets and cost to individual entities participating in the plan. *[IAS 19.32].*

In such circumstances, an entity should: *[IAS 19.30, 32]*

(a)   account for the plan as if it were a defined contribution plan;

(b)   disclose that the plan is a defined benefit plan and the reason why insufficient information is available to account for the plan as a defined benefit plan; and

(c)   to the extent that a surplus or deficit in the plan may affect future contributions, disclose:

   (i)   any available information about that surplus or deficit;

   (ii)   the basis used to determine the surplus or deficit; and

   (iii)   any implications for the entity.

The standard notes that there may be a contractual agreement between the multi-employer plan and its participants that determines how the surplus in the plan will be distributed to the participants (or the deficit funded). In these circumstances, an entity participating in such a plan should account for it as a defined contribution plan as described above. In addition, the entity should recognise the asset or liability that arises from the contractual agreement and the resulting income or expense in profit or loss. *[IAS 19.32A].* The standard illustrates this with an example of an entity participating in a multi-employer defined benefit plan which it accounts for as a defined contribution plan because no IAS 19 valuations are prepared. A non-IAS 19 funding valuation shows a deficit of CU100 million in the plan. The plan has agreed under contract a schedule of contributions with the participating employers in the plan that will eliminate the deficit over the next five years. The entity's total contributions under the contract are CU8 million. IAS 19 requires the entity to recognise immediately a liability for the contributions adjusted for the time value of money and an equal expense in profit or loss. The important point here is that the standard makes clear that 'defined contribution accounting' is not the same as cash accounting. When extra payments to make good a deficit are contracted they should be provided for immediately.

IAS 19 also contains a reminder that IAS 37 requires an entity to disclose information about some contingent liabilities, and notes that such contingencies may arise (in the context of a multi-employer plan) from:

(a)   actuarial losses relating to the other participating entities because each entity that participates in a multi-employer plan shares in the actuarial risks of every other participating employer; or

(b)   any responsibility under the terms of a plan to finance any shortfall in the plan if other entities cease to participate. *[IAS 19.32B].* (See Chapter 29 at 4.6.)

3.3.1.B   What to do when 'sufficient information' becomes available

As discussed above, IAS 19 requires a multi-employer defined benefit plan to be treated for accounting purposes as a defined contribution plan when insufficient information is available to use defined benefit accounting. The standard does not address what to do when that situation changes because sufficient information becomes available in a period. Two possible approaches present themselves:

(a)   an immediate charge/credit to profit or loss equal to the deficit/surplus; or

(b)   an actuarial gain or loss.

Arguments in favour of (a) would be that *for accounting purposes* the scheme was a defined contribution scheme. Accordingly, starting defined benefit accounting is akin to introducing a new scheme. The defined benefit obligation recognised is essentially a past service cost. In addition, as discussed at 3.3.1.A above, the standard makes clear that while defined contribution accounting is being applied an asset or liability should be recognised where there is a contractual arrangement to share a surplus or fund a deficit. The receipt of full information could be considered to represent such an arrangement and hence require full recognition in the balance sheet with an equivalent item in profit or loss.

Arguments for (b) would be that the scheme has not changed and that defined contribution accounting was a proxy (and best available estimate) for what the defined benefit accounting should have been. Accordingly, any change to that estimate due to the emergence of new information is an actuarial variance.

Given the ambiguity of the standard either approach is acceptable if applied consistently.

3.3.2 Multi-employer plans sharing risks between entities under common control

IAS 19 provides that defined benefit plans that share risks between various entities under common control, for example a parent and its subsidiaries, are not multi-employer plans. *[IAS 19.34]*.

The test, described earlier, for allowing a defined benefit multi-employer plan to be accounted for as a defined contribution plan is that insufficient information is available. By completely excluding entities that are under common control from the definition of multi-employer plans the standard is essentially saying that for these employers sufficient information is deemed always to be available – at least for the plan as a whole. The standard requires that an entity participating in such a plan should obtain information about the plan as a whole measured in accordance with IAS 19 on the basis of assumptions that apply to the plan as a whole. *[IAS 19.34A]*. Whilst a subsidiary may not be in a position to demand such information (any more than participants in schemes described at 3.3.1 above) the standard is essentially saying that the parent must make the information available if it wants the subsidiary to be able to comply with IAS 19.

The standard then goes on to specify the accounting treatment to be applied in the individual financial statements of the participating entities. The requirements are somewhat opaque, and it is useful to set them out in full. What the standard says is this. 'If there is a contractual agreement or stated policy for charging the net defined benefit cost for the plan as a whole measured in accordance with IAS 19 to individual group entities, the entity shall, in its separate or individual financial statements, recognise the net defined benefit cost so charged. If there is no such agreement or policy, the net defined benefit cost shall be recognised in the separate or individual financial statements of the group entity that is legally the sponsoring employer for the plan. The other group entities shall, in their separate or individual financial statements, recognise a cost equal to their contribution payable for the period'. *[IAS 19.34A]*. This seems to raise more questions than it answers. For example it provides no clarity on:

(a) what the 'net defined benefit cost ... measured in accordance with IAS 19' actually means. In particular, how do actuarial gains and losses fit in? Are they part of this 'net cost'? Does it refer to items recognised in profit or loss only, all actuarial gains and losses or only recognised actuarial losses (including any recognised in other comprehensive income)? or

(b)   what is meant by an entity 'legally sponsoring the plan'. The pan-jurisdictional scope of IFRS make such a determination particularly difficult. Furthermore, it suggests that there is only one such legal sponsor – which may not be the case in practice.

A further difficulty with these provisions of the standard is whether it is ever likely in practice that entities would be charged that amount. Assuming 'charge' is intended to mean the cash contributions required from the various participating entities, it seems unlikely that those amounts will ever be amounts 'measured in accordance with IAS 19'. Naturally situations vary not just across but also within individual jurisdictions. However, it is typically the case that funding valuations will not be on an IAS 19 basis, so any amounts 'charged' will not be measured in accordance with IAS 19. Indeed, as discussed at 3.3.1 above, the standard gives non-IAS 19 funding valuations in a multi-employer plan as a reason why sufficient information to allow defined benefit accounting is not available.

Some further insight as to the IASB's intentions can be found in the basis for conclusions to the standard. Again, it is worth reproducing this in full. The standard says the following. 'The IASB noted that, if there were a contractual agreement or stated policy on charging the net defined benefit cost to group entities, that agreement or policy would determine the cost for each entity. If there is no such contractual agreement or stated policy, the entity that is the sponsoring employer by default bears the risk relating to the plan. The IASB therefore concluded that a group plan should be allocated to the individual entities within a group in accordance with any contractual agreement or stated policy. If there is no such agreement or policy, the net defined benefit cost is allocated to the sponsoring employer. The other group entities recognise a cost equal to any contribution collected by the sponsoring employer. This approach has the advantages of (a) all group entities recognising the cost they have to bear for the defined benefit promise and (b) being simple to apply'. *[IAS 19.BC10I-10J]*. Of particular note in the above is:

(a)   there is no mention of amounts charged being measured in accordance with IAS 19. Indeed, the third sentence refers to *any* such agreement or stated policy;

(b)   the focus is not on 'amounts charged' but rather an 'allocation' of the scheme across entities;

(c)   references are to a 'sponsoring employer' crucially not a *legally* sponsoring employer. The term is slightly clarified by the explanation that a sponsoring employer is one that by default bears the 'risks relating to the plan';

(d)   the discussion of employers other than the sponsoring employer is explicitly to 'amounts collected'.

Given the ambiguities in the standard we expect that, for entities applying IFRS at an individual company level, there may well be divergent treatments in practice.

The standard makes clear that, for each individual group entity, participation in such a plan is a related party transaction. Accordingly, the following disclosures are required:

(a)   the contractual agreement or stated policy for charging the net defined benefit cost or the fact that there is no such policy;

(b)   the policy for determining the contribution to be paid by the entity;

(c)   if the entity accounts for an *allocation* of the net defined benefit cost (as discussed above), all the information about the plan as a whole in accordance with the standard's normal rules (discussed at 7.2 below);

(d)   if the entity accounts for the *contribution payable* for the period (as discussed above), the information about the plan as a whole set out in (b)-(e), (j), (n), (o) and (q) at 7.2 below. The other disclosure requirements do not apply. *[IAS 19.34B].*

3.4   State plans

IAS 19 observes that state plans are established by legislation to cover all entities (or all entities in a particular category, for example a specific industry) and are operated by national or local government or by another body (for example an autonomous agency created specifically for this purpose) which is not subject to control or influence by the reporting entity. *[IAS 19.37].* The standard requires that state plans be accounted for in the same way as for a multi-employer plan (see 3.3.1 above). *[IAS 19.36].* It goes on to note that many state plans are:

*   funded on a pay-as-you-go basis;

*   with contributions set at a level that is expected to be sufficient to pay the required benefits falling due in the same period; and

*   future benefits earned during the current period will be paid out of future contributions.

Nevertheless, in most state plans, the entity has no legal or constructive obligation to pay those future benefits: its only obligation is to pay the contributions as they fall due and if the entity ceases to employ members of the state plan, it will have no obligation to pay the benefits earned by its own employees in previous years. For this reason, the standard considers that state plans are normally defined contribution plans. However, in the rare cases when a state plan is a defined benefit plan, IAS 19 requires it to be treated as such as a multi-employer plan. *[IAS 19.38].*

Some plans established by an entity provide both compulsory benefits which substitute for benefits that would otherwise be covered under a state plan and additional voluntary benefits. IAS 19 clarifies that such plans are not state plans. *[IAS 19.37].*

3.5   Plans that would be defined contribution plans but for the existence of a minimum return guarantee

It is common in some jurisdictions for the employer to make contributions to a defined contribution post-employment benefit plan and to guarantee a minimum level of return on the assets in which the contributions are invested. In other words the employee enjoys upside risk on the investments but has some level of protection from downside risk.

The existence of such a guarantee means the arrangement fails to meet the definition of a defined contribution plan (see 3.1 above) and accordingly is a defined benefit plan. Indeed, the standard is explicit as it uses plans which guarantee a specified return on contributions as an example of a defined benefit arrangement. *[IAS 19.26(b)]*. The somewhat thornier issue is how exactly to apply defined benefit accounting to such an arrangement, as this would require projecting forward future salary increases and investment returns, and discounting these amounts at corporate bond rates. Although this approach is clearly required by the standard, some would consider it inappropriate in such circumstances. This issue was debated by the Interpretations Committee, which published a draft interpretation on 8 July 2004 entitled D9 – *Employee Benefit Plans with a Promised Return on Contributions or Notional Contributions*. The approach taken in D9 was to distinguish two different types of benefits:

(a)   a benefit of contributions or notional contributions plus a guarantee of a fixed return (in other words, benefits which can be estimated without having to make an estimate of future asset returns); and

(b)   a benefit that depends on future asset returns.

For benefits under (a) above, it was proposed that IAS 19's defined benefit methodology be applied as normal. In summary, that means:

- calculating the benefit to be paid in the future by projecting forward the contributions or notional contributions at the guaranteed fixed rate of return;

- allocating the benefit to periods of service;

- discounting the benefits allocated to the current and prior periods at the rate specified in IAS 19 to arrive at the plan liability, current service cost and interest cost; and

- recognising any actuarial gains and losses in accordance with the entity's accounting policy.

For benefits covered by (b) above, it was proposed that the plan liability should be measured at the fair value at the balance sheet date of the assets upon which the benefit is specified (whether plan assets or notional assets). No projection forward of the benefits would be made, and discounting of the benefit would not therefore be required.

D9 suggested that plans with a combination of a guaranteed fixed return and a benefit that depends on future asset returns should be accounted for by analysing the benefits into a fixed component and a variable component. The defined benefit asset or liability that would arise from the fixed component alone would be measured and recognised as described above. The defined benefit asset (or liability) that would arise from the variable component alone would then be calculated as described above and compared to the fixed component. An additional plan liability would be recognised to the extent that the asset (or liability) calculated for the variable component is smaller (or greater) than the asset (or liability) recognised in respect of the fixed component.

The great complexity of these provisions was not wholeheartedly supported by respondents to the document. Also, many commentators pointed out that the proposals effectively re-wrote, rather than interpreted, the standard. In August 2005 the Interpretations Committee announced the withdrawal of D9, observing the following: 'The staff found the fixed/variable and modified fixed/variable approaches inadequate to give a faithful representation of the entity's obligation for more complex benefit structures. They believed that some aspects of the fixed/variable approach in D9 were not fully consistent with IAS 19. ... The staff ... recommended that the correct treatment for D9 plans should be determined as part of an IASB project.'

What this means is that the current text of IAS 19 applies. Accordingly the projected unit credit method will need to be applied to such benefits as it is to other defined benefit arrangements.

This issue was one of the topics the Board was seeking to address in its (relatively) short-term amendments to IAS 19. In March 2008 the Board published a discussion paper called Preliminary Views on Amendments to IAS 19 Employee Benefits. In this the Board observes that 'IAS 19 does not result in a faithful representation of the liability for some benefit promises that are based on contributions and a promised return on assets.' The discussion paper outlines an approach that the Board believed would overcome this measurement defect that is based on defining a new category of promises – 'contribution-based promises' – and measuring them at fair value. However, as discussed at 10 below, it now seems the board is no longer actively pursuing this project.

3.6 Death-in-service benefits

The provision of death-in-service benefits is a common part of employment packages (either as part of a defined benefit plan or on a stand alone basis). We think it is regrettable that IAS 19 provides no guidance on how to account for such benefits, particularly as E54 devoted considerable attention to the issue.[5] IAS 19 explains the removal of the guidance as follows: 'E54 gave guidance on cases where death-in-service benefits are not insured externally and are not provided through a post-employment benefit plan. The Board concluded that such cases will be rare. Accordingly, the Board agreed to delete the guidance on death-in-service benefits.' *[IAS 19.BC89]*.

In our view this misses the point – E54 also gave guidance on cases where the benefits *are* externally insured and where they are provided through a post-employment benefit plan. In our view the proposals in E54 were quite sensible, and it is worth reproducing them here.

'An enterprise should recognise the cost of death-in-service benefits ... as follows:

(a)   in the case of benefits insured or re-insured with third parties, in the period in respect of which the related insurance premiums are payable; and

(b)   in the case of benefits not insured or re-insured with third parties, to the extent that deaths have occurred before the end of the reporting period.

'However, in the case of death-in-service benefits provided through a post-employment benefit plan, an enterprise should recognise the cost of those benefits by including their present value in the post-employment benefit obligation.

'If an enterprise re-insures a commitment to provide death-in-service benefits, it acquires a right (to receive payments if an employee dies in service) in exchange for an obligation to pay the premiums.

'Where an enterprise provides death-in-service benefits directly, rather than through a post-employment benefit plan, the enterprise has a future commitment to provide death-in-service coverage in exchange for employee service in those same future periods (in the same way that the enterprise has a future commitment to pay salaries if the employee renders service in those periods). That future commitment is not a present obligation and does not justify recognition of a liability. Therefore, an obligation arises only to the extent that a death has already occurred by the end of the reporting period.

'If death-in-service benefits are provided through a pension plan (or other post-employment plan) which also provides post-employment benefits to the same employee(s), the measurement of the obligation reflects both the probability of a reduction in future pension payments through death in service and the present value of the death-in-service benefits (see [E 54's discussion of mutual compatibility of actuarial assumptions]).

'Death-in-service benefits differ from post-employment life insurance because post-employment life insurance creates an obligation as the employee renders services in exchange for that benefit; an enterprise accounts for that obligation in accordance with [the requirements for defined benefit plans]. Life insurance benefits that are payable regardless of whether the employee remains in service comprise two components: a death-in-service benefit and a post-employment benefit. An enterprise accounts for the two components separately.'

We suggest that the above may continue to represent valid guidance to the extent it does not conflict with extant IFRS. In particular, an appropriate approach could be that:

- death-in-service benefits provided as part of a defined benefit post-employment plan are factored into the actuarial valuation. In this case any insurance cover should be accounted for in accordance with the normal rules of IAS 19 (see 5.2.1 below). An important point here is that insurance policies typically cover only one year, and hence will have a low or negligible fair value. As a result, it will not be the case that the insurance asset is equal and opposite to the defined benefit obligation;

- other death-in-service benefits which are externally insured are accounted for by expensing the premiums as they become payable;

- other death-in-service benefits which are not externally insured are provided for as deaths in service occur.

The first bullet is particularly important. The measure of the post-employment benefit (like a pension) will be reduced to take account of expected deaths in service. Accordingly it would be inappropriate to ignore the death in service payments that would be made. The question that arises is how exactly to include those expected payments. This raises the same issue as disability benefits (discussed at 6.2.2.B below) – i.e. what to do with the debit entry. However, unlike disability benefits IAS 19 has no explicit special treatment for death-in-service benefits. Given the absence of specific guidance, the requirements are to apply the projected unit credit method to death in service benefits. As the benefit is fully vested, an argument could be made that the expected benefit should be accrued fully (on a discounted basis). Another approach would be to build up the credit entry in the balance sheet over the period to the expected date of death.

An alternative approach could be to view death-in-service benefits as being similar to disability benefits (perhaps the ultimate disability). Proponents of this view would argue that the recognition requirements for disability benefits (discussed at 6.2.2.B below) could also be applied to death-in-service.

In January 2008, the Interpretations Committee published its agenda decision explaining why it decided not to put death-in-service benefits onto its agenda.[6] In the view of the Interpretations Committee, 'divergence in this area was unlikely to be significant. In addition, any further guidance that it could issue would be application guidance on the use of the Projected Unit Credit Method'. In our view the second reason seems more credible that the first.

As part of its analysis, the 'rejection notice' sets out some of the Interpretation Committee's views on the subject. It observes the following:

(a)   in some situations, IAS 19 requires these benefits to be attributed to periods of service using the Projected Unit Credit Method;

(b)   IAS 19 requires attribution of the cost of the benefits until the date when further service by the employee will lead to no material amount of further benefits under the plan, other than from further salary increases;

(c)   the anticipated date of death would be the date at which no material amount of further benefit would arise from the plan;

(d)   using different mortality assumptions for a defined benefit pension plan and an associated death in service benefit would not comply with the requirement in paragraph 72 of IAS 19 to use actuarial assumptions that are mutually compatible.

Points (a) to (c) above support the analysis that a provision should be built up gradually from the commencement of employment to the expected date of death. They also suggest that making an analogy to the standard's specific rules on disability may not be appropriate. Point (c) is simply re-iterating a clear requirement of the standard. In our view, the above agenda decision of the Interpretations Committee is not as helpful as we would have liked. Aside of concerns over the status of rejection notices, the use of the phrase 'in some situations' in (a) above seems deliberate obfuscation. In September 2007, the Interpretations Committee published a tentative agenda decision which said 'If these benefits are provided as part of a defined benefit plan, IAS 19 requires them to be attributed to periods of service using the Projected Unit Credit Method.'[7] At the following meeting the Interpretations Committee discussed the comment letter received which noted that it could be argued that such attribution would be required only if the benefits were dependent on the period of service. No decision was reached on the final wording of the rejection notice because 'IFRIC ... was unable to agree on wording for its agenda decision'[8] This leaves us with the impression that the final 'authoritative' version is written deliberately to avoid addressing the point.

Given the standard's lack of explicit guidance on death-in-service benefits and given the Interpretations Committee's decision not to address the matter, it seems likely that practice will be mixed.

4   DEFINED CONTRIBUTION PLANS

4.1   Accounting requirements

4.1.1   *General*

Accounting for defined contribution plans is straightforward under IAS 19 because, as the standard observes, the reporting entity's obligation for each period is determined by the amounts to be contributed for that period. Consequently, no actuarial assumptions are required to measure the obligation or the expense and there is no possibility of any actuarial gain or loss to the reporting entity. Moreover, the obligations are measured on an undiscounted basis, except where they do not fall due wholly within twelve months after the end of the period in which the employees render the related service. *[IAS 19.43]*. Where discounting is required, the discount rate should be determined in the same way as for defined benefit plans, which is discussed at 5.2.2.E below. *[IAS 19.45]*. In general, though, it would seem unlikely for a defined contribution scheme to be structured with such a long delay between the employee service and the employer contribution.

IAS 19 requires that, when an employee has rendered services during a period, the employer should recognise the contribution payable to a defined contribution plan in exchange for that service:

(a)   as a liability, after deducting any contribution already paid. If the contribution already paid exceeds the contribution due for service before the end of the reporting period, the excess should be recognised as an asset when such prepayment will lead to a reduction in future payments or a cash refund; and

(b)   as an expense, unless another International Accounting Standard requires or permits capitalisation of such expense. *[IAS 19.44]*.

As discussed at 3.3.1A above, IAS 19 requires multi-employer defined benefit plans to be accounted for as defined contribution plans in certain circumstances. The standard makes clear that contractual arrangements to make contributions to fund a deficit should be fully provided for (on a discounted basis) even if they are to be paid over an extended period.

4.1.2   *Defined contribution plans with vesting conditions*

The Interpretations Committee received a request seeking clarification on the effect that vesting conditions have on the accounting for defined contribution plans. The Committee was asked whether contributions to such plans should be recognised as an expense in the period for which they are paid or over the vesting period. In the examples given in the submission, the employee's failure to meet a vesting condition could result in the refund of contributions to, or reductions in future contributions by, the employer.

The Committee decided not to add the issue to its agenda, noting that there is no significant diversity in practice in respect of the effect that vesting conditions have on the accounting for defined contribution post-employment benefit plans, nor does it expect significant diversity in practice to emerge in the future.

Explaining its decision, the Committee observed that each contribution to a defined contribution plan is to be recognised as an expense or recognised as a liability (accrued expense) over the period of service that obliges the employer to *pay* this contribution to the defined contribution plan. This period of service is distinguished from the period of service that entitles an employee to *receive* the benefit from the defined contribution plan (i.e. the vesting period). Refunds are recognised as an asset and as income when the entity/employer becomes entitled to the refunds, e.g. when the employee fails to meet the vesting condition.[9]

5 DEFINED BENEFIT PLANS

5.1 General

The standard notes that accounting for defined benefit plans is complex because actuarial assumptions are required to measure both the obligation and the expense, and there is a possibility of actuarial gains and losses. Moreover, the obligations are measured on a discounted basis because they may be settled many years after the employees render the related service. *[IAS 19.48]*. Also, IAS 19 makes clear that it applies not just to unfunded obligations of employers but also to funded plans. The details of pension scheme arrangements vary widely form jurisdiction to jurisdiction and, indeed, within them. Frequently though, they involve some entity or fund, separate from the employer, to which contributions are made by the employer (and sometimes employees) and from which benefits are paid. Typically, the employer (through either legal or constructive obligations) essentially underwrites the fund in the event that the assets in the fund are insufficient to pay the required benefits. This is the key feature which means such an arrangement is a defined benefit plan (see 3 above). *[IAS 19.49]*.

In addition to specifying accounting and disclosure requirements, IAS 19 provides what amounts to a work programme of the steps necessary to apply its rules, as follows:

(a) using actuarial techniques, make a reliable estimate of the amount of benefit that employees have earned in return for their service in the current and prior periods. This requires an entity to determine how much benefit is attributable to the current and prior periods and to make estimates (actuarial assumptions) about demographic variables (such as employee turnover and mortality) and financial variables (such as future increases in salaries and medical costs) that will influence the cost of the benefit;

(b) discount that benefit using the projected unit credit method in order to determine the present value of the defined benefit obligation and the current service cost;

(c) measure the fair value of any plan assets;

(d) determine the total amount of actuarial gains and losses and the amount of those actuarial gains and losses that should be recognised;

(e) where a plan has been introduced or changed, determine the resulting past service cost; and

(f) where a plan has been curtailed or settled, determine the resulting gain or loss. *[IAS 19.50].*

Retirement benefits will often be very significant in the context of an employer's financial statements. However, the standard acknowledges that in some circumstances estimates, averages and computational shortcuts may provide a reliable approximation. *[IAS 19.51].*

Where an employer has more than one defined benefit plan, it should apply the steps above for each material plan separately. *[IAS 19.50].*

The standard contains a detailed worked example illustrating how the various accounting entries are arrived at from the underlying data. *[IAS 19 Appendix A].*

5.2   Valuation of the plan surplus or deficit

5.2.1   Plan assets

5.2.1.A   Definition of plan assets

IAS 19 provides a definition of plan assets (which exclude unpaid contributions due from the employer to the fund, and any non-transferable financial instruments issued by the employer and are to be reduced by any liabilities of the fund not related to employee benefits – such as trade and other payables and derivative financial instruments *[IAS 19.103]*) as follows:

'*Plan assets* comprise:

(a) assets held by a long-term employee benefit fund; and

(b) qualifying insurance policies.

Assets held by a long-term employee benefit fund are assets (other than non-transferable financial instruments issued by the reporting entity) that:

(a) are held by an entity (a fund) that is legally separate from the reporting entity and exists solely to pay or fund employee benefits; and

(b) are available to be used only to pay or fund employee benefits, are not available to the reporting entity's own creditors (even in bankruptcy), and cannot be returned to the reporting entity, unless either:

(i) the remaining assets of the fund are sufficient to meet all the related employee benefit obligations of the plan or the reporting entity; or

(ii) the assets are returned to the reporting entity to reimburse it for employee benefits already paid.

A qualifying insurance policy is an insurance policy issued by an insurer that is not a related party (as defined in IAS 24 – *Related Party Disclosures*) of the reporting entity, if the proceeds of the policy:

(a)   can be used only to pay or fund employee benefits under a defined benefit plan;

(b)   are not available to the reporting entity's own creditors (even in bankruptcy) and cannot be paid to the reporting entity, unless either:

   (i)   the proceeds represent surplus assets that are not needed for the policy to meet all the related employee benefit obligations; or

   (ii) the proceeds are returned to the reporting entity to reimburse it for employee benefits already paid'. *[IAS 19.7].*

In 2004 IFRS 4 – *Insurance Contracts* – introduced a footnote to this definition to clarify that a qualifying insurance policy is not necessarily an insurance contract as defined in IFRS 4.

Whilst non-transferable financial instruments issued by the employer are excluded from the definition of plan assets, it is not uncommon for plans to own shares in the employer. Such shareholdings can sometimes be very substantial as illustrated in the following extract.

Extract 33.2: Novartis AG (2006)
Notes to the Novartis Group Consolidated Financial Statements [extract]
26.   Post-employment benefits of associates
26.1   Defined benefit plans [extract]

The number of Novartis AG shares held by pension and similar benefit funds at December 31, 2006 was 21.6 million shares with a market value of USD 1.2 billion (2005: 21.6 million shares with a market value of USD 1.1 billion). These funds sold no Novartis AG shares during the year ended December 31, 2006 (2005: 9.3 million). The amount of dividends received on Novartis AG share held as plan assets by these funds were USD 20 million for the year ended December 31, 2006 (2005: USD 26 million).

5.2.1.B   Measurement of plan assets

IAS 19 requires plan assets to be measured at their fair value, *[IAS 19.54],* which is defined as the amount for which an asset could be exchanged between knowledgeable, willing parties in an arm's length transaction. *[IAS 19.7].* For periods beginning before 1 January 2013, there is no further explanation in IAS 19 as to the meaning of fair value. However, it is defined in exactly the same way as in IAS 39 – *Financial Instruments: Recognition and Measurement.* That standard does contain further elaboration, and in particular makes clear that for quoted securities held, fair value usually means bid price with no deduction for transaction costs which may be incurred on disposal. *[IAS 39.46, AG72].* When no market price is available, IAS 19 notes that the fair value needs to be estimated, for example by discounting expected future cash flows at a discount rate reflecting both the risk and maturity date (or expected disposal date) of the asset. *[IAS 19.102].*

For periods beginning on or after 1 January 2013 the definition is changed to the following: Fair value is the price that would be received to sell an asset or paid to transfer a liability in an orderly transaction between market participants at the measurement date. (See IFRS 13 – *Fair Value Measurement.*) See Chapter 16. Where plan assets include qualifying insurance policies that exactly match the amount and timing of some or all of the benefits payable under the plan, the fair value of those insurance policies is deemed to be the present value of the related obligations, subject to any reductions required if the amounts receivable under the insurance policies are not recoverable in full. *[IAS 19.104]*.

Some employers may have in place arrangements to fund defined benefit obligations which do not meet the definition of qualifying insurance policies above but which do provide for another party to reimburse some or all of the expenditure required to settle a defined benefit obligation. In such a case, the expected receipts under the arrangement are not *classified* as plan assets under IAS 19 (and hence they are not presented as part of a net pension asset/liability – see 5.3 below). Instead, the employer should recognise its right to reimbursement as a separate asset, but only when it is virtually certain that another party will reimburse some or all of the expenditure required to settle a defined benefit obligation. The asset should be measured at fair value. In all other respects it should be treated in the same way as plan assets. In profit or loss, the expense relating to a defined benefit plan may be presented net of the amount recognised for a reimbursement. *[IAS 19.104A-104B]*.

The requirement that such rights are to be treated, aside of balance sheet presentation, in the same way as if they were plan assets extends to the use of the corridor mechanism discussed at 5.3.1 below. What this means is that whilst the reimbursement right is shown separately at its fair value, any cumulative unrecognised actuarial gains and losses in respect of it are included along with any other unrecognised gains and losses as part of the net pension asset or liability in the balance sheet. *[IAS 19.104C]*.

As is the case for qualifying insurance policies, for reimbursement rights that exactly match the amount and timing of some or all of the benefits payable fair value is determined as the present value of the related obligation. *[IAS 19.104D]*.

The standard illustrates the requirements regarding such rights as follows:

Example 33.1:   Reimbursement rights

	€
Present value of obligation	1,241
Unrecognised actuarial gains	17
Liability recognised in balance sheet	1,258
Rights under insurance policies that exactly match the amount and timing of some of the benefits payable under the plan. Those benefits have a present value of 1,092.	1,092

The unrecognised actuarial gains of 17 are the net cumulative actuarial gains on the obligation and on the reimbursement rights.

5.2.1.C   Contributions to defined benefit funds

Contributions to defined benefit plans under IAS 19 are a balance sheet movement – the reduction in cash for the employer being reflected by an increase in the plan assets. Perhaps because of this straightforward accounting, the standard provides no guidance on contributions, which it implicitly deals with as always being in the form of cash.

Although contributions are very commonly in cash, there is no reason why an employer could not contribute any other assets to a defined benefit plan and that raises the question of how to account for the disposal – particularly as from the point of transfer the assets will be measured at fair value under IAS 19. In our view, such transfers of non-cash assets should be treated as disposals, with proceeds equal to the assets' fair values. That would give rise to gains and losses in profit or loss (unless the asset in question was already carried at fair value) and, for certain assets (such as available for sale securities), the reclassification into profit or loss of amounts previously recognised in other comprehensive income.

5.2.2   Plan liabilities

5.2.2.A   Legal and constructive obligations

IAS 19 refers to the liabilities of defined benefit plans as the present value of defined benefit obligations, which it defines as '... the present value, without deducting any plan assets, of expected future payments required to settle the obligation resulting from employee service in the current and prior periods'. *[IAS 19.7, 55].*

The obligations should include not only the benefits set out in the plan, but also any constructive obligations that arise from the employer's informal practices which go beyond the formal plan terms, and should where relevant include an estimate of expected future salary increases (taking into account inflation, seniority, promotion and other relevant factors, such as supply and demand in the employment market). *[IAS 19.52, 83-84].*

A constructive obligation exists where a change in the employer's informal practices would cause unacceptable damage to its relationship with employees and which therefore leaves the employer with no realistic alternative but to pay those employee benefits. *[IAS 19.52].* The term constructive obligation is not defined by IAS 19; however as can be seen from the above it is very similar to the meaning of the term as used in IAS 37 where it is defined as follows:

'A constructive obligation is an obligation that derives from an entity's actions where:

(a)   by an established pattern of past practice, published policies or a sufficiently specific current statement, the entity has indicated to other parties that it will accept certain responsibilities; and

(b)   as a result, the entity has created a valid expectation on the part of those other parties that it will discharge those responsibilities'. *[IAS 37.10].*

However, IAS 19 goes on to add a subtly different nuance. The standard observes that it is usually difficult to cancel a retirement benefit plan whilst still retaining staff, and in light of this it requires that reporting entities assume (in the absence of evidence to the contrary) any currently promised benefits will continue for the remaining working lives of employees. *[IAS 19.53].* In our view this is a somewhat lower hurdle, and could bring into the scope of defined benefit accounting promises which are (strictly) legally unenforceable and which would not necessarily be considered constructive obligations under IAS 37.

Chapter 33

An employer's obligations (legal or constructive) may also extend to making changes to benefits in the future. The standard requires all such effects to be built into the computation of the obligation and gives the following examples of what they might comprise:

(a)   a past history of increasing benefits, for example, to mitigate the effects of inflation, and no indication that this practice will change in the future; or

(b)   actuarial gains have already been recognised in the financial statements and the employer is obliged (legally – under the terms of the plan or legislation – or constructively) to use any surplus in the plan for the benefit of plan participants. In this case, the increase in the obligation is an actuarial loss (and not a past service cost, discussed at 5.5.6 below. *[IAS 19.85, 98]*.

By contrast, any other future changes in the obligation (i.e. where no legal or constructive obligation previously existed) will be reflected in future current service costs, future past service costs or both (discussed at 5.5.1 and 5.5.6 respectively). *[IAS 19.86]*.

IAS 19 also deals with the situation where the level of defined benefits payable by a scheme varies with the level of state benefits. When this is the case any changes in state benefit may only be factored into the actuarial computations if they are enacted by the end of the reporting period or are predictable based on past history or other evidence. *[IAS 19.83, 97]*.

5.2.2.B   Actuarial methodology

Plan obligations are to be measured using the projected unit credit method, *[IAS 19.64]*, (sometimes known as the accrued benefit method pro-rated on service or as the benefit/years of service method). This method sees each period of service as giving rise to an additional unit of benefit entitlement and measures each unit separately to build up the final obligation. *[IAS 19.65]*. IAS 19 provides a simple example of what this entails as follows: *[IAS 19.65]*

Example 33.2:   The projected unit credit method

A lump sum benefit is payable on termination of service and equal to 1% of final salary for each year of service. The salary in year 1 is 10,000 and is assumed to increase at 7% (compound) each year. The discount rate used is 10% per annum. The following table shows how the obligation builds up for an employee who is expected to leave at the end of year 5, assuming that there are no changes in actuarial assumptions. For simplicity, this example ignores the additional adjustment needed to reflect the probability that the employee may leave the entity at an earlier or later date.

Year	1	2	3	4	5
Benefit attributed to:					
– prior years	0	131	262	393	524
– current year (1% of final salary)	131	131	131	131	131
– current and prior years	131	262	393	524	655
Opening Obligation	–	89	196	324	476
Interest at 10%	–	9	20	33	48
Current Service Cost	89	98	108	119	131
Closing Obligation	89	196	324	476	655

Note:
– The Opening Obligation is the present value of benefit attributed to prior years.
– The Current Service Cost is the present value of benefit attributed to the current year.
– The Closing Obligation is the present value of benefit attributed to current and prior years.

As can be seen in this simple example, the projected unit credit method also produces a figure for current service cost and interest cost (and, although not illustrated here, would where appropriate produce a figure for past service cost). These cost components are discussed at 5.5 below.

This example from the standard contains no underlying workings or proofs. The most useful would be as follows:

Final salary at year 5 (10,000 compounded at 7%)	$10,000 \times (1 + 0.07)^4 = 13,100$
1% of final salary attributed to each year	131
Expected final benefit	5 years $\times$ 1% $\times$ 131,000 = 655

Current service cost, being present value of 131 discounted at 10%: e.g.

Year 1	$131 \times (1 + 0.1)^{-4} = 89$
Year 2	$131 \times (1 + 0.1)^{-3} = 98$

Closing obligation, being years served multiplied by present value of 131: e.g.

Year 3	3 years $\times 131 \times (1 + 0.1)^{-2} = 324$

5.2.2.C *Attributing benefit to years of service*

The projected unit credit method requires benefits to be attributed to the current period (in order to determine current service cost) and the current and prior periods (in order to determine the present value of defined benefit obligations). IAS 19 requires benefits to be attributed to the periods in which the obligation to provide post-employment benefits arises. That is taken to be when employees render services in return for post-employment benefits which an entity expects to pay in future reporting periods. In the standard's view, actuarial techniques allow an entity to measure that obligation with sufficient reliability to justify recognition of a liability. *[IAS 19.68].*

In applying the projected unit credit method, IAS 19 normally requires benefits to be attributed to periods of service under the plan's benefit formula (as is the case in Example 33.2 above). If, however, an employee's service in later years will lead to a materially higher level of benefit, the benefit should be attributed on a straight-line basis from:

(a) the date when service by the employee first leads to benefits under the plan; until

(b) the date when further service by the employee will lead to no material amount of further benefits under the plan, other than from further salary increases. *[IAS 19.67].*

The standard considers that this requirement is necessary because the employee's service throughout the entire period will ultimately lead to benefit at that higher level. *[IAS 19.70]*.

The standard explains that employee service gives rise to an obligation under a defined benefit plan even if the benefits are conditional on future employment (in other words they are not vested). Employee service before the vesting date is considered to give rise to a constructive obligation because, at each successive balance sheet date, the amount of future service that an employee will have to render before becoming entitled to the benefit is reduced. In measuring its defined benefit obligation, an entity should consider the probability that some employees may not satisfy any vesting requirements. Similarly, although certain post-employment benefits, for example, post-employment medical benefits, become payable only if a specified event occurs when an employee is no longer employed, an obligation is considered to be created when the employee renders service that will provide entitlement to the benefit if the specified event occurs. The probability that the specified event will occur affects the measurement of the obligation, but does not determine whether for accounting purposes the obligation exists. *[IAS 19.69]*.

The obligation is considered to increase until the date when further service by the employee will lead to no material amount of further benefits, and accordingly all benefit should be attributed to periods ending on or before that date. *[IAS 19.70]*.

IAS 19 illustrates the attribution of benefits to service periods with a number of worked examples as follows: *[IAS 19.68-71]*

Example 33.3:   *Attributing benefits to years of service*

1. A defined benefit plan provides a lump-sum benefit of 100 payable on retirement for each year of service.

    A benefit of 100 is attributed to each year. The current service cost is the present value of 100. The present value of the defined benefit obligation is the present value of 100, multiplied by the number of years of service up to the end of the reporting period.

    If the benefit is payable immediately when the employee leaves the entity, the current service cost and the present value of the defined benefit obligation reflect the date at which the employee is expected to leave. Thus, because of the effect of discounting, they are less than the amounts that would be determined if the employee left at the end of the reporting period.

2. A plan provides a monthly pension of 0.2% of final salary for each year of service. The pension is payable from the age of 65.

    Benefit equal to the present value, at the expected retirement date, of a monthly pension of 0.2% of the estimated final salary payable from the expected retirement date until the expected date of death is attributed to each year of service. The current service cost is the present value of that benefit. The present value of the defined benefit obligation is the present value of monthly pension payments of 0.2% of final salary, multiplied by the number of years of service up to the end of the reporting period. The current service cost and the present value of the defined benefit obligation are discounted because pension payments begin at the age of 65.

3. A plan pays a benefit of 100 for each year of service. The benefits vest after ten years of service.

    A benefit of 100 is attributed to each year. In each of the first ten years, the current service cost and the present value of the obligation reflect the probability that the employee may not complete ten years of service.

4. A plan pays a benefit of 100 for each year of service, excluding service before the age of 25. The benefits vest immediately.

   No benefit is attributed to service before the age of 25 because service before that date does not lead to benefits (conditional or unconditional). A benefit of 100 is attributed to each subsequent year.

5. A plan pays a lump-sum benefit of 1,000 that vests after ten years of service. The plan provides no further benefit for subsequent service.

   A benefit of 100 (1,000 divided by ten) is attributed to each of the first ten years. The current service cost in each of the first ten years reflects the probability that the employee may not complete ten years of service. No benefit is attributed to subsequent years.

6. A plan pays a lump-sum retirement benefit of 2,000 to all employees who are still employed at the age of 55 after twenty years of service, or who are still employed at the age of 65, regardless of their length of service.

   For employees who join before the age of 35, service first leads to benefits under the plan at the age of 35 (an employee could leave at the age of 30 and return at the age of 33, with no effect on the amount or timing of benefits). Those benefits are conditional on further service. Also, service beyond the age of 55 will lead to no material amount of further benefits. For these employees, the entity attributes benefit of 100 (2,000 divided by 20) to each year from the age of 35 to the age of 55.

   For employees who join between the ages of 35 and 45, service beyond twenty years will lead to no material amount of further benefits. For these employees, the entity attributes benefit of 100 (2,000 divided by 20) to each of the first twenty years.

   For an employee who joins at the age of 55, service beyond ten years will lead to no material amount of further benefits. For this employee, the entity attributes benefit of 200 (2,000 divided by 10) to each of the first ten years.

   For all employees, the current service cost and the present value of the obligation reflect the probability that the employee may not complete the necessary period of service.

7. A post-employment medical plan reimburses 40% of an employee's post-employment medical costs if the employee leaves after more than ten and less than twenty years of service and 50% of those costs if the employee leaves after twenty or more years of service.

   Under the plan's benefit formula, the entity attributes 4% of the present value of the expected medical costs (40% divided by ten) to each of the first ten years and 1% (10% divided by ten) to each of the second ten years. The current service cost in each year reflects the probability that the employee may not complete the necessary period of service to earn part or all of the benefits. For employees expected to leave within ten years, no benefit is attributed.

8. A post-employment medical plan reimburses 10% of an employee's post-employment medical costs if the employee leaves after more than ten and less than twenty years of service and 50% of those costs if the employee leaves after twenty or more years of service.

   Service in later years will lead to a materially higher level of benefit than in earlier years. Therefore, for employees expected to leave after twenty or more years, the entity attributes benefit on a straight-line basis under paragraph 68 of the standard. Service beyond twenty years will lead to no material amount of further benefits. Therefore, the benefit attributed to each of the first twenty years is 2.5% of the present value of the expected medical costs (50% divided by twenty).

   For employees expected to leave between ten and twenty years, the benefit attributed to each of the first ten years is 1% of the present value of the expected medical costs. For these employees, no benefit is attributed to service between the end of the tenth year and the estimated date of leaving.

   For employees expected to leave within ten years, no benefit is attributed.

9.   Employees are entitled to a benefit of 3% of final salary for each year of service before the age of 55.

Benefit of 3% of estimated final salary is attributed to each year up to the age of 55. This is the date when further service by the employee will lead to no material amount of further benefits under the plan. No benefit is attributed to service after that age.

None of the illustrations above is controversial. The following points of note are brought out in the above:

- the scenarios in 3 and 5 are economically identical, and are attributed to years of service accordingly. In each case benefits only vest after ten years, however an obligation is to be built up over that period rather than at the end; and

- example 8 illustrates that accruing a 10% benefit over a period of 20 years of service which jumps to 50% once 20 years has been completed is an example of service in later years leading to a materially higher level of benefit. Accordingly the obligation is to be built-up on a straight-line basis over 20 years.

As regards example 9, the standard explains that where the amount of a benefit is a constant proportion of final salary for each year of service, future salary increases will affect the amount required to settle the obligation that exists for service before the end of the reporting period, but do not create an additional obligation. Therefore:

(a)   for the purpose of allocating benefits to years of service, salary increases are not considered to lead to further benefits, even though the amount of the benefits is dependent on final salary; and

(b)   the amount of benefit attributed to each period should be a constant proportion of the salary to which the benefit is linked. *[IAS 19.71].*

5.2.2.D   Actuarial assumptions

The long timescales and numerous uncertainties involved in estimating obligations for post-employment benefits require many assumptions to be made when applying the projected unit credit method. These are termed actuarial assumptions and comprise:

(a)   demographic assumptions about the future characteristics of current and former employees (and their dependants) who are eligible for benefits and deal with matters such as:

(i)   mortality, both during and after employment;

(ii)   rates of employee turnover, disability and early retirement;

(iii) the proportion of plan members with dependants who will be eligible for benefits; and

(iv)   claim rates under medical plans; and

(b)   financial assumptions, dealing with items such as:

(i)   the discount rate;

(ii)   future salary and benefit levels;

(iii) in the case of medical benefits, future medical costs, including, where material, the cost of administering claims and benefit payments; and

(iv)   the expected rate of return on plan assets. *[IAS 19.73].*

IAS 19's requirements in this regard are set out below, with the exception of the discount rate which is discussed at E below.

The standard requires that actuarial assumptions be unbiased (that is, neither imprudent nor excessively conservative *[IAS 19.74]*), mutually compatible and represent the employer's best estimates of the variables that will determine the ultimate cost of providing post-employment benefits.

The financial assumptions must be based on market expectations at the end of the reporting period, for the period over which the obligations are to be settled. *[IAS 19.72-73, 77]*. Actuarial assumptions are mutually compatible if they reflect the economic relationships between factors such as inflation, rates of salary increase, the return on plan assets and discount rates. For example, all assumptions which depend on a particular inflation level (such as assumptions about interest rates and salary and benefit increases) in any given future period should assume the same inflation level in that period. *[IAS 19.76]*.

Assumptions about medical costs should take account of inflation as well as specific changes in medical costs (including technological advances, changes in health care utilisation or delivery patterns, and changes in the health status of plan participants). *[IAS 19.88-89]*. The standard provides a quite detailed discussion of the factors that should be taken into account in making actuarial assumptions about medical costs, in particular it notes:

(a)   measuring post-employment medical benefits requires assumptions about the level and frequency of future claims, and the cost of meeting them. An employer should make such estimates based on its own experience, supplemented where necessary by historical data from other sources (such as other entities, insurance companies and medical providers); *[IAS 19.89]*

(b)   the level and frequency of claims is particularly sensitive to the age, health status and sex of the claimants, and may also be sensitive to their geographical location. This means that any historical data used for estimating future claims needs to be adjusted to the extent that the demographic mix of the plan participants differs from that of the population used as the basis for the historical data. Historical data should also be adjusted if there is reliable evidence that historical trends will not continue; *[IAS 19.90]* and

(c)   estimates of future medical costs should take account of any contributions that claimants are required to make based on the terms (whether formal or constructive) of the plan at the end of the reporting period. Changes in such terms will constitute past service costs or, where applicable, curtailments (discussed at 5.5.6 and 5.5.5 respectively). *[IAS 19.91]*.

The following extract shows a discussion of health care cost trend rates.

> *Extract 33.3: UBS AG (2006)*
>
> **Notes to the Financial Statements** [extract]
> **Note 31   Pension and Other Post-retirement Benefit Plans** [extract]
> **b)   Post-retirement medical and life plans** [extract]
>
> The assumed average health care cost trend rate used in determining post-retirement benefit expense is assumed to be 11% for 2006 and to decrease to an ultimate trend rate of 5% in 2013. On a country-by-country basis, the same discount rate is used for the calculation of the post-retirement benefit obligation from medical and life plans as for the defined benefit obligations arising from pension plans.
>
> Assumed health care cost trend rates have a significant effect on the amounts reported for health care plans. A one percentage point change in the assumed health care cost trend rates would change the US post-retirement benefit obligation and the service and interest cost components of the net periodic post-retirement benefit costs as follows:
>
> | CHF million | 1% increase | 1% decrease |
> |---|---|---|
> | Effect on total service and interest cost | 4 | (3) |
> | Effect on the post-retirement benefit obligation | 28 | (19) |

Clearly, the application of actuarial techniques to compute plan obligations is a complex task, and it seems likely that few entities would seek to prepare valuations without the advice of qualified actuaries. However, IAS 19 only encourages, but does not require that an entity takes actuarial advice. *[IAS 19.57]*.

However sophisticated actuarial projections may be, reality will (aside of the most simple scenarios) always diverge from assumptions. This means that when a surplus or deficit is estimated, it will almost certainly be different from the predicted value based on the last valuation. These differences are termed actuarial gains and losses. The standard observes that actuarial gains and losses may result from increases or decreases in either the present value of a defined benefit obligation or the fair value of any related plan assets. Causes of actuarial gains and losses could include, for example:

(a)   unexpectedly high or low rates of employee turnover, early retirement or mortality or of increases in salaries, benefits (if the formal or constructive terms of a plan provide for inflationary benefit increases) or medical costs;

(b)   the effect of changes in estimates of future employee turnover, early retirement or mortality or of increases in salaries, benefits (if the formal or constructive terms of a plan provide for inflationary benefit increases) or medical costs;

(c)   the effect of changes in the discount rate; and

(d)   differences between the actual return on plan assets and the expected return on plan assets.

Accounting for actuarial gains and losses is discussed at 5.3.1 below.

5.2.2.E   Discount rate

Due to the long timescales involved, post-employment benefit obligations are discounted. Also, the whole obligation should be discounted, even if some falls due within a year. *[IAS 19.66]*. The standard requires that the discount rate reflect the time value of money but not the actuarial or investment risk. Furthermore, the discount rate should not reflect the entity-specific credit risk borne by the entity's creditors, nor should it reflect the risk that future experience may differ from actuarial assumptions. *[IAS 19.79]*. The discount rate should reflect the estimated timing of benefit payments. For example, an appropriate rate may be quite different for a payment due in, say, ten years as opposed to one due in twenty. The standard observes that in practice, an acceptable answer can be obtained by applying a single weighted average discount rate that reflects the estimated timing and amount of benefit payments and the currency in which the benefits are to be paid. *[IAS 19.80]*.

The rate used should be determined 'by reference to' the yield (at the end of the reporting period) on high quality corporate bonds of currency and term consistent with the liabilities. In countries where there is no deep market in such bonds, the yields on government bonds should be used instead. *[IAS 19.78]*.

IAS 19 does not explain what is meant by the term 'high quality'. In practice it is considered, rightly in our view, to mean bonds rated AA.

The requirement that the rate be determined 'by reference to' high quality bond rates adds an important nuance.

The standard gives an example of this in the context of the availability of bonds with sufficiently long maturities. It observes that in some cases, there may be no deep market in bonds with a sufficiently long maturity to match the estimated maturity of all the benefit payments. In such cases, the standard requires the use of current market rates of the appropriate term to discount shorter-term payments, and estimation of the rate for longer maturities by extrapolating current market rates along the yield curve. It goes on to observe that the total present value of a defined benefit obligation is unlikely to be particularly sensitive to the discount rate applied to the portion of benefits that is payable beyond the final maturity of the available corporate or government bonds. *[IAS 19.81]*.

Of the three characteristics of corporate bonds stipulated by the standard (quality, currency and term) the above example is making an adjustment to observed yields with respect to term.

In June 2005 the Interpretations Committee discussed another form of extrapolation from observed inputs and published an explanation as to why it decided not to take the issue onto its agenda and hence not progress an interpretation. The question considered was, when there is no deep market in high quality corporate bonds in a country, whether the discount rate could be determined by reference to a synthetically constructed equivalent instead of using the yield on government bonds? The Interpretations Committee concluded that the standard 'is clear that a synthetically constructed equivalent to a high quality corporate bond by reference to the bond market in another country may not be used to determine the discount rate.' The Interpretations Committee further observed that the reference to 'in a country' could reasonably be read as including high quality corporate bonds that are available in a regional market to which the entity has access, provided that the currency of the regional market and the country were the same (e.g. the euro). This would not apply if the country currency differed from that of the regional market.[10]

It is more than a little difficult to know what to make of those observations. First, without a proper and detailed fact pattern one cannot know the details of the question being addressed and quite what a 'synthetically constructed equivalent' actually means. Second, as the observation is not a formal interpretation its status is questionable at best. Furthermore, the wording of the standard itself and of the Interpretations Committee's 'non-interpretation' implies that the defined benefit obligation is denominated in the same currency as government bonds in the country concerned. Whilst that may well be the case, there is no reason why employee benefits could not be denominated in another currency. In our view it would have been more helpful if the Interpretations Committee had progressed a formal interpretation to explore how and to what extent observed bond yields could form a starting point to extrapolate a discount rate. Whilst it would be wrong to understate the liabilities of the plan by using an inappropriately high rate (say, because the only relevant bonds in issue are not 'high quality') it would be equally wrong, in our view, to overstate them by using the default rate of government debt when a reliable rate could be estimated by reference to market yields. Indeed, the standard suggests this in its discussion of actuarial assumptions in general, requiring that they be unbiased, that is neither imprudent nor excessively conservative. *[IAS 19.72, 74]*.

IAS 19 also stipulates that the discount rate (and other financial assumptions) should be determined in nominal (stated) terms, unless estimates in real (inflation-adjusted) terms are more reliable, for example, in a hyper-inflationary economy (see Chapter 18 for a discussion of IAS 29 – *Financial Reporting in Hyperinflationary Economies*), or where the benefit is index-linked and there is a deep market in index-linked bonds of the same currency and term. *[IAS 19.76]*.

The basic part of this requirement – that a nominal rate be used – is consistent with the definition of the present value of a defined benefit obligation in that it should be '... the present value ... of expected future payments required to settle the obligation ...' (see 5.2.2.A above). In other words, as the future cash flows are stated at the actual amounts expected to be paid, the rate used to discount them should reflect that and not be adjusted to remove the effects of expected inflation. In contrast, the reference to the use of index-linked bonds seems to allow taking account of inflation through the discount rate (which would require expressing cash flows in current prices). This approach seems to be in conflict with the definition of the obligation, although in practice few index-linked corporate bonds exist (so it may be quite rare to have a deep market in them) so a more reliable approach may often be to take account of inflation via the projected cash flows.

5.2.2.F   Frequency of valuations

When it addresses the frequency of valuations, IAS 19 does not give particularly prescriptive guidance. Rather, its starting point is simply to require that the present value of defined benefit obligations, and the fair value of plan assets, should be determined frequently enough to ensure that the amounts recognised in the financial statements do not differ materially from the amounts that would be determined at the end of the reporting period. *[IAS 19.56]*. A reasonable argument could be launched that without a full valuation as at the end of the reporting period to compare with, it cannot be possible to know whether any less precise approach is materially different. However, it is reasonably clear that the intention of the standard is not necessarily to require full actuarial updates as at the year-end. This is because the standard goes on to observe that for practical reasons a valuation may be carried out before the end of the reporting period and that if such amounts determined before the end of the reporting period are used, they should be updated to take account of any material transactions or changes in circumstances up to the end of the reporting period. *[IAS 19.57]*. Much may turn on what is considered to be a 'material change', however it is expressly to include changes in market prices (hence requiring asset values to be those at the end of the reporting period) and interest rates, as well as financial actuarial assumptions. *[IAS 19.57, 77]*.

In this regard, it is also worth noting the observation in the standard that 'In some cases, estimates, averages and computational shortcuts may provide a reliable approximation of the detailed computations illustrated in this Standard.' *[IAS 19.51]*. It is worth remembering, though, that it is the amounts in the financial statements which must not differ materially from what they would be based on a balance sheet valuation. For funded schemes, the net balance sheet amount (before taking account of the corridor mechanism – see 5.3.1 below) is usually the difference between two very large figures – plan assets and plan liabilities. Such a net item is inevitably highly sensitive, in percentage terms, to a given percentage change in the gross amounts.

In summary, these rules will require a detailed valuation on an annual basis, but not necessarily as at the end of the reporting period. If not as at the end of the reporting period, the valuation will then need to be updated at the end of the reporting period to reflect *at least* changes in financial assumptions, asset values and discount rates. The need for updates in respect of other elements of the valuation will depend on individual circumstances.

5.3 Balance sheet treatment of the plan surplus or deficit

5.3.1 Actuarial gains and losses

The starting point under IAS 19 is that a plan surplus or deficit is reflected directly in the employer's balance sheet. However, not all of the movements in the amount of a surplus or deficit need be reflected in the balance sheet. Indeed, there is a range of options available regarding the treatment of actuarial gains and losses which reflect the history and evolution of the subject. At present, the options range from full recognition in profit or loss, through delayed recognition in profit or loss to full recognition in other comprehensive income.

The IASC encountered the same fundamental problem in developing its standard on pension accounting as some other standard setters around the world (notably the US and the UK which each have a conceptual framework similar to that in IFRS[11]). The zeal for balance sheet fair values which these respective conceptual frameworks demand leads inevitably to volatility considered by many to be unacceptable. For example, the investment portfolios of the pension funds of many companies exceed the market capitalisation of the company itself. Although asset allocations vary, many have a high equity weighting. Mark-to-market accounting for portfolios of that size and nature yields very large and volatile results, which will not be hedged by the liabilities determined under the projected unit method. As originally re-drafted in 1998, IAS 19 adopted an approach very similar to US GAAP which makes use of the so called corridor mechanism. The approach taken in 2000 by the UK's ASB to overcome earnings volatility was, in essence, to account for budgeted figures in profit or loss for the period with variances consigned (permanently) to other comprehensive income as actuarial gains and losses. In December 2004 the IASB amended IAS 19 to introduce a further option allowing this treatment for entities which recognise all actuarial gains and losses in full – a decision prompted largely as a result of the UK standard.

5.3.1.A   Recognition in profit and loss

In the 1998 revision to the standard the IASC decided to adopt a 'corridor' mechanism. In what at first glance appears to be a balance sheet approach, IAS 19 does not require immediate recognition of actuarial gains and losses. Instead an employer need only recognise in profit or loss a portion of the actuarial gains and losses to the extent that the net cumulative unrecognised actuarial gains and losses at the end of the previous reporting period exceeded the greater of:

(a)   10% of the present value of the defined benefit obligation; and

(b)   10% of the fair value of any plan assets.

The above 'corridor test' needs to be applied separately for each defined benefit plan.

As a minimum, an amount of cumulative gains/losses must be recognised each period equal to the excess outside the 'corridor' divided by the expected average remaining working lives of employees participating in the plan.

A plan which has been closed to future accrual (i.e. complete curtailment but without a settlement – curtailments and settlements are discussed at 5.5.5 below) no longer has any employees accruing benefits in it. Although the standard is not explicit, the phrase 'participating in the plan' could be read to mean the ongoing accrual of benefits. On that basis, for a plan closed to benefit accrual, cumulative amounts outside the corridor should be recognised in full.

An alternative view is that members 'participate' in a plan for every period until the benefits under the plan are settled in full.

A simple example of the mechanics of the corridor approach is included in Example 33.9 at 5.5.3 below. An entity may recognise actuarial gains and losses more quickly using any systematic method – as long as the same basis is applied to both gains and losses – even if they fall within the limits of the corridor. [IAS 19.92-93].

It is entirely possible that 10% of gross assets or liabilities will exceed the net balance sheet figure. This means that the balance sheet figure under IAS 19 could easily be 'wrong' by 100% or more, and even those actuarial movements that are recognised may be spread forward over a number of years. IAS 19 explains its corridor mechanism by observing that actuarial gains and losses may, in the long term, offset each other and that estimates of the obligation may be viewed as a range around a best estimate. Whilst permitting recognition of movements in the balance within this range, the standard stops short of requiring it. [IAS 19.95].

In June 2011 the IASB issued a revised IAS 19 which applies for periods beginning on or after 1 January 2013. This requires the full and immediate recognition of actuarial variances in other comprehensive income and prohibits all other methods. This is discussed at 8 below.

As a result of the above, IAS 19 requires the balance sheet figure relating to a defined benefit plan to be the net total of:

(a)   the present value of the defined benefit obligation at the end of the reporting period, before deducting the fair value of any plan assets (see 5.2.2 above);

(b)   plus actuarial gains and less actuarial losses not yet recognised (discussed below);

(c)   less past service cost not yet recognised (see 5.5.6 below); and

(d)   less the fair value of plan assets, at the end of the reporting period, out of which the obligations are to be settled directly (see 5.2.1 above). *[IAS 19.54-55].*

5.3.1.B   Recognition in other comprehensive income

In December 2004 IAS 19 was revised to allow a further treatment of actuarial gains and losses. If an entity adopts a policy of recognising actuarial gains and losses in the period in which they occur (i.e. full balance sheet recognition), it may recognise them in other comprehensive income rather than profit or loss. This treatment is allowed subject to the following conditions:

(a)   it must be applied to all of an entity's defined benefit plans and to all of its actuarial gains and losses;

(b)   any adjustments arising from the limit on recognition of an asset (see 5.3.2 below) must also be recognised in other comprehensive income; and

(c)   all amounts in relation to defined benefit plans which are recognised in other comprehensive income) must be recognised immediately in retained earnings. They should not be recognised in profit or loss in a subsequent period. *[IAS 19.93A-93D].*

5.3.2   Restriction of assets to their recoverable amounts

The balance sheet figure determined under IAS 19 may be an asset. An asset may arise where a defined benefit plan has been over-funded or in certain cases where actuarial gains are recognised. The standard justifies the recognition of an asset in such cases because:

(a)   the entity controls a resource, which is the ability to use the surplus to generate future benefits;

(b)   that control is a result of past events (contributions paid by the entity and service rendered by the employee); and

(c)   future economic benefits are available to the entity in the form of a reduction in future contributions or a cash refund, either directly to the entity or indirectly to another plan in deficit. *[IAS 19.59].*

When the mechanics above result in a balance sheet asset it is then subject to a ceiling test, and is restricted so as not to exceed the net total of:

(a) any unrecognised actuarial losses and past service cost (see 5.5.6 below); and

(b) the present value of any economic benefit available in the form of refunds from the plan or reductions in future contributions to the plan (determined by using the same discount rate as used for the plan liabilities). *[IAS 19.58]*.

The ceiling test is illustrated by the standard with the following example. *[IAS 19.60]*.

Example 33.4:   Restriction of assets to their recoverable amounts

A defined benefit plan has the following characteristics:

	€ million
Present value of the obligation	1,100
Fair value of plan assets	(1,190)
	(90)
Unrecognised actuarial losses	(110)
Unrecognised past service cost	(70)
Unrecognised increase in the liability on initial adoption of the Standard	(50)
Negative amount before any restriction	(320)
Present value of available future refunds and reductions in future contributions	90

The limit of the asset to be recognised is computed as follows:

Unrecognised actuarial losses	110
Unrecognised past service cost	70
Present value of available future refunds and reductions in future contributions	90
Limit	270

€270m is less than €320m. Therefore, the entity recognises an asset of €270m and discloses that the limit reduced the carrying amount of the asset by €50.

This ceiling test does not override the delayed recognition of certain actuarial losses under the corridor approach described above. IAS 19 provides a worked example illustrating the interaction between this ceiling test and the 'normal' delayed recognition allowed by the corridor approach. *[IAS 19.60]*.

Any adjustment required by the ceiling test is accounted for in profit or loss unless the entity has adopted a policy of recognising actuarial gains and losses directly in other comprehensive income. In this case, adjustments arising from the asset ceiling are also recognised in other comprehensive income – see 3.5.3.B above.

This limitation has proved quite problematic in practice and as a result was considered by the Interpretations Committee, initially in the context of statutory minimum funding requirements ('MFR'). This resulted in the publication, in July 2007, of IFRIC 14 entitled 'the limit on a defined benefit asset, minimum funding requirements and their interaction'. Whilst dealing with the interaction of the asset ceiling with MFR, IFRIC 14 also deals more generally with the restriction of a balance sheet asset on recoverability grounds. These issues are discussed in the following sections.

5.3.2.A   IFRIC Interpretation 14 – general requirements concerning the limit on a defined benefit asset

IFRIC 14 clarifies that economic benefits, in the form of refunds or reduced future contributions, are available if they can be realised at some point during the life of the plan or when the plan liabilities are settled. In particular, such economic benefits may be available even if they are not realisable immediately at the end of the reporting period. *[IFRIC 14.8]*. Furthermore, the benefit available does not depend on how the entity intends to use the surplus. There should be determined the maximum economic benefit that is available from refunds, reductions in future contributions or a combination of both. However, economic benefits should not be recognised from a combination of refunds and reductions in future contributions based on assumptions that are mutually exclusive. *[IFRIC 14.9]*. Perhaps unnecessarily, the interpretation requires the availability of a refund or a reduction in future contributions to be determined in accordance with the terms and conditions of the plan and any statutory requirements in the jurisdiction of the plan. *[IFRIC 14.7]*.

The interpretation observes that an unconditional right to a refund can exist whatever the funding level of a plan at the end of the reporting period. However, if the right to a refund of a surplus depends on the occurrence or non-occurrence of one or more uncertain future events not wholly within an entity's control, the entity does not have an unconditional right and should not recognise an asset. *[IFRIC 14.12]*. The interpretation further states that benefits are available as a refund only if the entity has an unconditional right to a refund: *[IFRIC 14.11]*

(a)   during the life of the plan, without assuming that the plan liabilities must be settled in order to obtain the refund; or

(b)   assuming the gradual settlement of the plan liabilities over time until all members have left the plan; or

(c)   assuming the full settlement of the plan liabilities in a single event (i.e. as a plan wind-up).

The economic benefit available as a refund should be measured as the amount of the surplus at the end of the reporting period (being the fair value of the plan assets less the present value of the defined benefit obligation) that the entity has a right to receive as a refund, less any associated costs. For example, if a refund would be subject to a tax other than income tax of the reporting entity, it should be measured net of the tax. *[IFRIC 14.13]*.

In measuring the amount of a refund available when the plan is wound up (point (c) above), the costs to the plan of settling the plan liabilities and making the refund should be included. For example, a deduction should be made for professional fees if these are paid by the plan rather than the entity, and the costs of any insurance premiums that may be required to secure the liability on wind-up. *[IFRIC 14.4]*.

Commonly, the trustees of a pension fund will be independent and have absolute discretion to set investment strategy, asset allocation and also the ability to buy annuities to settle liabilities.

These powers would allow the trustees to 'spend' any current or future surplus. Investing plan assets in ultra-cautious investments (yielding less that the unwinding discount on the obligation) could unwind any surplus over time. Settlements by way of buying annuities would absorb surpluses because of the cost of settlement typically exceeds the IAS 19 measure of the obligation.

These trustee powers raise the following questions:

- whether the exercise of such powers by the trustees are 'uncertain future events not wholly within [the entity's] control'; and

- if so, whether 'the entity's right to a refund of a surplus depends on the occurrence or non-occurrence of' them and accordingly no surplus could be recognised in any scenario where trustees have such powers.

Our view is that such a trustee powers should not, of themselves, preclude the recognition of a surplus (or, indeed, require the accrual of a liability for future MFR payments – discussed at 5.3.2.D below).

The reason for this is that the test in IFRIC 14 is whether the entity has an unconditional right to any surplus which may happen to exist at any future date. It is not concerned with whether such a surplus will exist, nor with the powers of others to influence that. Put another way, the question is whether any surplus existing in any of the three scenarios in (a) to (c) above would revert unconditionally to the employer. The fact that any surplus could be extinguished by uncertain future events not controlled by the employer is not relevant – it is the right to a surplus, not its existence, which is relevant. IFRIC 14 makes this clear for future actuarial losses and benefit improvements made by the employer *[IFRIC 14.BC10]*. Our view is that the same applies to asset allocation decisions (including settlements) whether decided by the employer or the trustees. Naturally, there will be different rules in different jurisdictions. The above arguments are predicated on clear reversion of any surplus should one exist following final settlement of obligations.

This view is further supported by the general requirements in IAS 19 surrounding settlements. Settlements are accounted for only when they happen, and this is so whether the decision to settle is taken by the employer or by trustees (see 5.5.5 below). Put simply, the test in (b) above is: if the scheme were to be run-off as reflected in the balance sheet, would the employer have an unconditional right to whatever is left? If the answer is 'Yes' (for example, because that is what the trust deed provides for), then measurement of a surplus follows the 'normal' IAS 19 methodology.

If the amount of a refund is determined as the full amount or a proportion of the surplus, rather than a fixed amount, an entity should make no adjustment for the time value of money, even if the refund is realisable only at a future date. *[IFRIC 14.15]*.

5.3.2.B   Economic benefits available as reduced future contributions when there are no minimum funding requirements for future service

IFRIC 14 addresses separately cases where there are minimum funding requirements relating to benefits to be awarded in future periods in exchange for services to be rendered in those periods, and cases where there are no such funding requirements.

This section deals with the situation where there are no such funding requirements. The implications of future service minimum funding requirements are discussed at 5.3.2.C below.

IFRIC 14 requires that the economic benefit available by way of reduced future contributions be determined as the future service cost to the entity for each period over the shorter of the expected life of the plan and the expected life of the entity. The future service cost to the entity excludes amounts that will be borne by employees. *[IFRIC 14.16]*.

Future service costs should be determined using assumptions consistent with those used to determine the defined benefit obligation and with the situation that exists at the end of the reporting period as determined by IAS 19. Accordingly, no future changes to the benefits to be provided by a plan should be assumed until the plan is amended, and a stable workforce in the future should be assumed unless the entity is demonstrably committed at the end of the reporting period to make a reduction in the number of employees covered by the plan. In the latter case, the assumption about the future workforce should include the reduction. The present value of the future service cost should be determined using the same discount rate as that used in the calculation of the defined benefit obligation (discount rates are discussed at 5.2.2.E above). *[IAS 19.58]*.

5.3.2.C IFRIC Interpretation 14 – The effect of a minimum funding requirement on the economic benefit available as a reduction in future contributions

IFRIC 14 defines minimum funding requirements as 'any requirements to fund a post-employment or other long-term defined benefit plan'. *[IFRIC 14.5]*. This is clearly quite a wide definition encompassing more than just statutory regimes.

The interpretation requires any minimum funding requirement at a given date to be analysed into contributions that are required to cover: *[IFRIC 14.18]*

(a)   any existing shortfall for past service on the minimum funding basis. These contributions do not affect future contributions for future service. However, they may give rise to a liability under IFRIC 14 (see 5.3.2.D below); *[IFRIC 14.19]* and

(b)   future service.

If there is a minimum funding requirement for contributions relating to future service, the economic benefit available as a reduction in future contributions is the sum of: *[IFRIC 14.20]*

(a)   any amount that reduces future minimum funding requirement contributions for future service because the entity made a pre-payment (that is, paid the amount before being required to do so); and

(b)   the estimated future service cost in each period in accordance (as discussed at 5.3.2.B above) the estimated minimum funding requirement contributions that would be required for future service in those periods if there were no pre-payment as described in (a).

The future minimum funding contributions required in respect of future service should be calculated taking into account the effect of any existing surplus on the minimum funding requirement basis but excluding the pre-payment discussed in (a) above. The assumptions used for this calculation should be consistent with the minimum funding requirement basis. For any factors not specified by the minimum funding requirement, the assumptions used should be consistent with those used to determine the defined benefit obligation and with the situation that exists at the end of the reporting period as determined by IAS 19. The estimate should include any changes expected as a result of the entity paying the minimum contributions when they are due. However, the estimate should not include the effect of expected changes in the terms and conditions of the minimum funding basis that are not substantively enacted or contractually agreed at the end of the reporting period. *[IFRIC 14.21].*

If the future minimum funding contribution required in respect of future service exceeds the future IAS 19 service cost in any given period, the present value of that excess reduces the amount of the asset available as a reduction in future contributions. However, the amount of the asset available as a reduction in future contributions can never be less than zero. *[IFRIC 14.22].*

The mechanics of the above requirements are illustrated in the following two examples based the illustrative examples accompanying IFRIC 14. Example 33.5 also illustrates the requirement in certain circumstances to recognise an additional liability for future MFR payments in respect of past service (discussed at 5.3.1.D below).

Example 33.5:   Deficit-clearing future minimum funding requirements when refunds are not available [IFRIC 14.IE3]

An entity has a funding level on the minimum funding requirement basis (which is measured on a different basis from that required under IAS 19) of 95% in Plan C. Under the minimum funding requirements, the entity is required to pay contributions to increase the funding level to 100% over the next three years. The contributions are required to make good the deficit on the minimum funding requirement basis (shortfall) and to cover the accrual of benefits in each year on the minimum funding basis.

Plan C also has an IAS 19 surplus at the end of the reporting period of €50m, which cannot be refunded to the entity under any circumstances. There are no unrecognised amounts.

The nominal amounts of the minimum funding contribution requirements in respect of the shortfall and the future IAS 19 service cost for the next three years are set out below.

Year	Total minimum contribution requirement	Minimum contributions required to make good the shortfall	Minimum contributions required to cover future accrual
	€m	€m	€m
1	135	120	15
2	125	112	13
3	115	104	11

The entity's present obligation in respect of services already received includes the contributions required to make good the shortfall but does not include the minimum contributions required to cover future accrual.

The present value of the entity's obligation, assuming a discount rate of 6% per year, is approximately 300, calculated as follows:

€120m/(1.06) + €112m /(1.06)^2 + €104m/(1.06)^3

When these contributions are paid into the plan, the present value of the IAS 19 surplus (i.e. the fair value of assets less the present value of the defined benefit obligation) would, other things being equal, increase from €50m to €350m. However, the surplus is not refundable although an asset may be available as a future contribution reduction.

As noted above, the economic benefit available as a reduction in future contributions is the present value of:

- the future service cost in each year to the entity; less
- any minimum funding contribution requirements in respect of the future accrual of benefits in that year

over the expected life of the plan.

The amounts available as a future contribution reduction are set out below.

Year	IAS 19 service cost €m	Minimum contributions required to cover future accrual €m	Amount available as contribution reduction €m
1	13	15	(2)
2	13	13	0
3	13	11	2
4+	13	9	4

Assuming a discount rate of 6%, the economic benefit available as a future contribution reduction is therefore equal to:

€(2)m/(1.06) + €0m/(1.06)^2 + €2m/(1.06)^3 + €4m/(1.06)^4 + €4m/(1.06)^5 + €4m/(1.06)^6 .... = €56m.

The asset available from future contribution reductions is accordingly limited to €56m.

As discussed at 5.3.2.D below, IFRIC 14 requires the entity to recognise a liability to the extent that the additional contributions payable will not be fully available. Therefore, the entity reduces the defined benefit asset by €294m (€50m + €300m – €56m).

As discussed at 5.3.2.D below, the €294m is recognised immediately in accordance with the policy adopted by the entity for recognising the effect of the asset ceiling and the entity recognises a net balance sheet liability of €244m. No other liability is recognised in respect of the obligation to make contributions to fund the minimum funding shortfall.

When the contributions of €300m are paid into the plan, the net balance sheet asset will become €56m (€300m – €244m).

Example 33.6: *Effect of a prepayment when a minimum funding requirement exceeds the expected future service charge [IFRIC 14.IE4]*

An entity is required to fund Plan D so that no deficit arises on the minimum funding basis. The entity is required to pay minimum funding requirement contributions to cover the service cost in each period determined on the minimum funding basis.

Plan D has an IAS 19 surplus of 35 at the beginning of 2012. There are no cumulative unrecognised net actuarial losses or past service costs. This example assumes that the discount rate and expected return on assets are both 0%, and that the plan cannot refund the surplus to the entity under any circumstances but can use the surplus for reductions of future contributions.

The minimum contributions required to cover future service are 15 for each of the next five years. The expected IAS 19 service cost is 10 in each year.

The entity makes a pre-payment of 30 at the beginning of 2012 in respect of years 2012 and 2013, increasing its surplus at the beginning of 2012 to 65. That prepayment reduces the future contributions it expects to make in the following two years, as follows:

Year	IAS 19 service cost	Minimum funding requirement: Before pre-payment	After pre-payment
2012	10	15	0
2013	10	15	0
2014	10	15	15
2015	10	15	15
2016	10	15	15
Total	50	75	45

At the beginning of 2012, the economic benefit available as a reduction in future contributions is the sum of:

- 30, being the prepayment of the minimum funding requirement contributions; and

- nil. The estimated minimum funding requirement contributions required for future service would be 75 if there was no prepayment. Those contributions exceed the estimated future service cost (50); therefore the entity cannot use any part of the surplus of 35.

Assuming a discount rate of 0%, the present value of the economic benefit available as a reduction in future contributions is equal to 30. Accordingly, the entity recognises an asset of 30 (because this is lower than the IAS 19 surplus of 65).

Two points worth noting in the above are as follows. The first is that, if IFRIC 14 did not allow the recognition of such prepayments the full surplus of 60 would have been written-off. The second, is that in the fact pattern of the question, it is unnecessary to know that the surplus before the prepayment was 35. This is because any surplus (other than the prepayment of MFR) would not be recognised because refunds are not available and future MFR exceed future service costs.

5.3.2.D   IFRIC Interpretation 14 – When a minimum funding requirement may give rise to a liability

If there is an obligation under a minimum funding requirement to pay contributions to cover an existing shortfall on the minimum funding basis in respect of services already received, the entity should determine whether the contributions payable will be available as a refund or reduction in future contributions after they are paid into the plan. *[IFRIC 14.23]*. Recovery through reduced future contributions is discussed at 5.3.2.B and C above.

If a surplus is recoverable by way of a refund (see 5.3.2.A above), a minimum funding requirement to cover a shortfall in respect of past services will neither restrict an IAS 19 asset nor trigger the recognition of a liability. IFRIC 14 illustrates this by way of an example upon which the following is based.

Example 33.7:   *Effect of the minimum funding requirement when there is an IAS 19 surplus and the minimum funding contributions payable are fully refundable to the entity* *[IFRIC 14.IE1]*

An entity has a funding level on the minimum funding requirement basis (which is measured on a different basis from that required under IAS 19) of 82% in Plan A. Under the minimum funding requirements, the entity is required to increase the funding level to 95% immediately. As a result, the entity has a statutory obligation at the end of the reporting period to contribute €200m to Plan A immediately. The plan rules permit a full refund of any surplus to the entity at the end of the life of the plan. The year-end valuations for Plan A are set out below.

	€million
Market value of assets	1,200
Present value of defined benefit obligation under IAS 19	(1,100)
Surplus	100
Defined benefit asset (before consideration of the minimum funding requirement)*	100

*For simplicity, it is assumed that there are no unrecognised amounts

Payment of the contributions of €200m will increase the IAS 19 surplus from €100m to €300m. Under the rules of the plan this amount will be fully refundable to the entity with no associated costs. Therefore, no liability is recognised for the obligation to pay the contributions. To the extent that the contributions payable would not be fully available IFRIC 14 requires the entity to recognise a liability. This is discussed below.

To the extent that the contributions payable will not be available after they are paid into the plan, a liability should be recognised when the obligation arises. The liability should reduce the defined benefit asset or increase the defined benefit liability so that no gain or loss is expected to result from the effect of the asset ceiling when the contributions are paid. *[IFRIC 14.24]*. It should be noted that before this is done, any adjustment required by IAS 19's rules regarding the restriction of the recognition of profits (losses) solely as a result of actuarial losses (gains) should first be accounted for (see 5.3.3 below). *[IFRIC 14.25]*.

The liability in respect of the minimum funding requirement and any subsequent re-measurement of it should be recognised immediately in accordance with the entity's policy for recognising the effect of the asset ceiling (see 5.3.2 above). In particular, any required adjustment should: *[IFRIC 14.26]*

(a) be recognised immediately in profit or loss if the effect of the asset ceiling is recognised in profit or loss; and

(b) be recognised immediately in other comprehensive income if the effect of the asset ceiling is recognised in other comprehensive income.

IFRIC 14 illustrates this by way of an example upon which the following is based.

Example 33.8:   *Effect of a minimum funding requirement when there is an IAS 19 deficit and the minimum funding contributions payable would not be fully available [IFRIC 14.IE2]*

An entity has a funding level on the minimum funding requirement basis (which is measured on a different basis from that required under IAS 19) of 77% in Plan B. Under the minimum funding requirements, the entity is required to increase the funding level to 100% immediately. As a result, the entity has a statutory obligation at the end of the reporting period to pay additional contributions of €300m to Plan B. The plan rules permit a maximum refund of 60% of the IAS 19 surplus to the entity and the entity is not permitted to reduce its contributions below a specified level which happens to equal the IAS 19 service cost. The year-end valuations for Plan B are set out below.

	€million
Market value of assets	1,000
Present value of defined benefit obligation under IAS 19	(1,100)
Deficit	(100)
Defined benefit (liability) (before consideration of the minimum funding requirement)*	100

* For simplicity, it is assumed that there are no unrecognised amounts

The payment of €300m would change the IAS 19 deficit of €100m to a surplus of €200m. Of this €200m, 60% (€120m) is refundable. Therefore, of the contributions of €300m, €100m eliminates the IAS 19 deficit and €120m (60% of €200m) is available as an economic benefit. The remaining €80m (40% of €200m) of the contributions paid is not available to the entity. As discussed above, IFRIC 14 requires the entity to recognise a liability to the extent that the additional contributions payable are not available to it. Accordingly, the entity increases the defined benefit liability by €80m and this is recognised immediately in accordance with the entity's adopted policy for recognising the effect of the asset ceiling. This results in a net balance sheet liability of €180m. No other liability is recognised in respect of the statutory obligation to pay contributions of €300m. When the contributions of €300m are paid, the net balance sheet asset will be €120m.

5.3.2.E   IFRIC Interpretation 14 – disclosure requirements

IFRIC 14 does not introduce any new disclosure requirements. However, it suggests that any restrictions on the current realisability of the surplus or a description of the basis used to determine the amount of the economic benefit available, may require disclosure under the provisions in IAS 1 – *Presentation of Financial Statements* – about key sources of estimation uncertainty. *[IFRIC 14.10]*. These requirements are discussed in Chapter 3 at 5.2.1.

5.3.3   Restriction of the recognition of profits (losses) solely as a result of actuarial losses (gains)

Only a few years after its publication an anomaly in the standard came to light. It was that in some circumstances the interaction of the standard's complex (indeed, conceptually conflicting) requirements could lead to the recognition of profits purely as a result of actuarial *losses* in a pension fund (and vice versa). Accordingly the standard was revised. The anomaly is best explained with a numerical example (based on Appendix C to IAS 19) as follows.

Example 33.9: *Restriction of the recognition of a profit solely as a result of an actuarial loss*

	A	B		C	D = A + C	E = B + C	F = lower of D and E	G
Year	Surplus in plan	Economic benefits available	Losses unrecognised due to the corridor		Unrestricted asset	Present value of future economic benefits	Asset ceiling, i.e. recognised asset	Gain recognised in year 2
1	100	0	0		100	0	0	
2	70	0	30		100	30	30	30

At the end of year 1, there is a surplus of 100 in the plan (column A in the table above), but no economic benefits are available to the entity either from refunds or reductions in future contributions (column B). There are no unrecognised gains and losses (column C). So, if there were no asset ceiling, an asset of 100 would be recognised, being the amount determined by the 'normal' output of the surplus in the scheme and the corridor mechanism (column D). The asset ceiling (see B above) restricts the asset to nil (column F).

In year 2 there is an actuarial loss in the plan of 30 that reduces the surplus from 100 to 70 (column A) the recognition of which is deferred under the corridor mechanism (column C). So, if there were no asset ceiling, an asset of 100 (column D) would be recognised. The asset ceiling before the standard was amended in this regard would be 30 (column E). An asset of 30 would be recognised (column F), giving rise to a gain in income (column G) even though all that has happened is that a surplus from which the entity cannot benefit has decreased.

A similarly counter-intuitive effect could arise with actuarial gains (to the extent that they reduce cumulative unrecognised actuarial losses).

The reason for this 'anomaly' is a direct consequence of the allowed deferral of actuarial gains and losses. Any resulting asset in the balance sheet is best characterised as a prepayment and to apply a recoverability test based on asset valuation principles to such an item is meaningless. Indeed, one member of the IASB observed the following when dissenting from the 2002 amendment 'Ms O'Malley dissents from this amendment of IAS 19. In her view, the perceived problem being addressed is an inevitable result of the interaction of two fundamentally inconsistent notions in IAS 19. The corridor approach allowed by IAS 19 permits the recognition of amounts on the balance sheet that do not meet the Framework's definition of assets. The asset ceiling then imposes a limitation on the recognition of some of those assets based on a recoverability notion. A far preferable limited amendment would be to delete the asset ceiling in paragraph 58. This would resolve the identified problem and at least remove the internal inconsistency in IAS 19. It is asserted that the amendment to the standard will result in a more representationally faithful portrayal of economic events. Ms O'Malley believes that it is impossible to improve the representational faithfulness of a standard that permits recording an asset relating to a pension plan that actually has a deficiency, or a liability in respect of a plan that actually has a surplus.' *[IAS 19 Appendix E].*

When the plan has a surplus, and the balance sheet asset is restricted (because the surplus cannot be fully recovered by refunds or reduced contributions) any actuarial loss or past service which arises but is deferred by the corridor mechanism *increases* the amount to which the asset is restricted. The credit entry is to income. *[IAS 19.58B]*.

To fix this problem, further overlaying requirements were added to the standard requiring that the application of the asset ceiling should not result in:

- a gain being recognised solely as a result of an actuarial loss or past service cost in the current period; or

- in a loss being recognised solely as a result of an actuarial gain in the current period.

Accordingly, whenever the asset is restricted (see 5.3.2 above) the following should be recognised immediately:

(a)   net actuarial losses of the current period and past service cost of the current period to the extent that they exceed any reduction in the present value of the economic benefits determined under the ceiling test. If there is no change or an increase in the present value of the economic benefits, the entire net actuarial losses of the current period and past service cost of the current period should be recognised immediately;

(b)   net actuarial gains of the current period after the deduction of past service cost of the current period to the extent that they exceed any increase in the present value of the economic benefits available. If there is no change or a decrease in the present value of the economic benefits, the entire net actuarial gains of the current period after the deduction of past service cost of the current period should be recognised immediately. *[IAS 19.58A]*.

What that means for the scenario in the above example is that, because there is no change in the economic benefits available, the entire actuarial loss of 30 is recognised immediately in year 2. Hence, the asset ceiling remains at nil and no net gain is recognised.

5.3.4   Business combinations

In a business combination, an entity recognises assets and liabilities arising from post-employment benefits at the present value of the obligation less the fair value of any plan assets (see Chapter 10 at 5.6.3). The present value of the obligation includes all of the following, even if the acquiree had not yet recognised them at the date of the acquisition:

(a)   actuarial gains and losses that arose before the date of the acquisition (whether or not they fell inside the 10% corridor); and

(b)   past service cost that arose from benefit changes, or the introduction of a plan, before the date of the acquisition. *[IAS 19.108]*.

5.4   Presentation of balance sheet amounts

Neither IAS 19 nor IAS 1 specifies where in the balance sheet an asset or liability in respect of a defined benefit plan should be presented, nor whether such balances should be shown separately on the face of the balance sheet or only in the notes –

this is left to the discretion of the reporting entity subject to the general requirements of IAS 1 discussed in Chapter 3 at 3.1. If the format of the balance sheet distinguishes current assets and liabilities from non-current ones, the question arises as to whether this split needs also to be made for pension balances. IAS 19 does not specify whether such a split should be made, on the grounds that it may sometimes be arbitrary. *[IAS 19.118, BC81].*

Employers with more than one plan may find that some are in surplus while others are in deficit. IAS 19 contains offset criteria closely modelled on those in IAS 32 – *Financial Instruments: Disclosure and Presentation. [IAS 19.117].* An asset relating to one plan may only be offset against a liability relating to another plan when there is a legally enforceable right to use a surplus in one plan to settle obligations under the other plan, and the employer intends to settle the obligations on a net basis or realise the surplus and settle the obligation simultaneously. *[IAS 19.116].* In our view these offset criteria are unlikely to be met in practice.

The following extract shows a company presenting a non-current asset and a non-current liability relating to pensions on the face of the balance sheet.

Extract 33.4: Jardine Matheson Holdings Limited (2006)

Consolidated Balance Sheet
At 31 December 2006

	Note	2006 US$m	Restated 2005 US$m
Assets			
Intangible assets	*8*	**1,825**	1,689
Tangible assets	*9*	**2,931**	2,404
Investment properties	*10*	**271**	179
Plantations	*11*	**460**	383
Associates and joint ventures	*12*	**6,476**	5,062
Other investments	*13*	**597**	686
Financing and other debtors	*14*	**1,052**	1,349
Deferred tax assets	*16*	**119**	103
Pension assets	*17*	**174**	152
Non-current assets		**13,905**	12,077
Stocks and work in progress	*18*	**1,478**	1,491
Trade, financing and other debtors	*19*	**2,262**	2,382
Current investments	*13*	**3**	–
Current tax assets		**142**	56
Bank balances and other liquid funds	*20*		
– non-finance companies		**2,355**	1,503
– finance companies		**173**	187
		2,528	1,690
		6,413	5,619
Non-current assets classified as held for sale	*21*	**60**	690
Current assets		**6,473**	6,309
Total assets		**20,378**	18,316

Equity			
Share capital	22	**154**	151
Share premium and capital reserves	24	**29**	21
Revenue and other reserves	25	**7,303**	5,607
Own shares held	27	**(892)**	(781)
Shareholders' funds		**6,594**	4,998
Minority interests	28	**4,509**	3,876
Total equity		**11,103**	8,874
Liabilities			
Long-term borrowings	29		
– non-finance companies		**2,074**	2,631
– finance companies		**723**	1,005
		2,797	3,636
Deferred tax liabilities	16	**557**	459
Pension liabilities	17	**151**	176
Non-current provisions	30	**20**	16
Other non-current liabilities	31	**190**	151
Non-current liabilities		**3,715**	4,438
Creditors and accruals	32	**2,920**	2,838
Current borrowings	29		
– non-finance companies		**1,522**	619
– finance companies		**954**	1,169
		2,476	1,788
Current tax liabilities		**101**	128
Current provisions	30	**63**	54
		5,560	4,808
Liabilities directly associated with non-current			
Assets classified as held for sale	21	**–**	196
Current liabilities		**5,560**	5,004
Total liabilities		**9,275**	9,442
Total equity and liabilities		**20,378**	18,316

An alternative approach is to include assets and liabilities relating to post-employments benefits within a suitable balance sheet caption and provide an analysis in the note, as illustrated by the following extract.

Extract 33.5: Novartis AG (2006)

Notes to the Novartis Group Consolidated Financial Statements [extract]
26.   Post-employment benefits of associates [extract]
26.1   Defined benefit plans [extract]

	Pension plans		Other post-employment benefit plans	
	2006	2005	**2006**	2005
	USD millions	USD millions	**USD millions**	USD millions
Amounts recognized in the balance sheet				
Prepaid benefit cost	**2 102**	1 919		
Accrued benefit liability	**–1 343**	–1 480	**–993**	–1 033
Net asset or (liability) in the balance sheet at the end of the year	**759**	439	**–993**	–1 033

Novartis includes the pension asset in the balance sheet caption 'Financial and other non-current assets'. The liability is included in the balance sheet caption 'Provisions and other non-current liabilities'. A separate note sub-analyses each caption into its various components.

5.5   Treatment of defined benefit plans in profit or loss

IAS 19 identifies six components of annual pension cost as follows:

(a)   current service cost;

(b)   interest cost;

(c)   the expected return on any plan assets (and any reimbursement rights);

(d)   actuarial gains and losses (if, and to the extent that, they are recognised in profit and loss);

(e)   past service cost (to the extent they are recognised);

(f)   the effect of any curtailments or settlements; and

(g)   the effect of the requirement to limit any balance sheet asset (unless it is recognised outside profit and loss). [IAS 19.61].

The standard requires the net total of the above to be recognised in profit or loss, unless another standard requires or permits its inclusion in the cost of an asset – for example IAS 2 – *Inventories* – and IAS 16 – *Property, Plant and Equipment*. Where the post-employment benefit costs are included in the cost of an asset the appropriate proportion of *all* the above items must be included. [IAS 19.62]. There is no guidance in the standard as to what an 'appropriate' proportion of these items might be, although both IAS 2 and IAS 16 are clear that only those costs which are directly attributable to the asset qualify for capitalisation. In our view, it is not necessarily the case that the appropriate proportion will be the same for all of the components and judgement will be required in deciding how much of each item can meaningfully be said to relate to the production of an asset.

In terms of income statement 'geography' the standard is far from clear. What is says is this. 'This Standard does not specify whether an entity should present current service cost, interest cost and the expected return on plan assets as components of a single item of income or expense in the statement of comprehensive income.' *[IAS 19.119]*. This sentence does not make clear whether it is the prominence of disclosure on the face of the statement (as opposed to just in the notes) or the inclusion of all the elements in one caption of the statement that the standard is not specifying. The standard does, however, seem to contemplate the inclusion of pension items in more than one income statement caption because it specifically requires disclosure of which captions the items are in (disclosure is discussed at 7.2 below). Also, the requirement in the final standard is a change from E54 which explicitly required all components of the charge/credit to be included in the same line item.[12] We believe that a number of approaches (within the general confines of IAS 1) would be acceptable. In particular, some entities may wish to locate the expected return on assets and the interest cost with other financial items.

Each of the components listed above is discussed below.

5.5.1   Current service cost

The current service cost, which should be determined using the projected unit credit method, is the increase in the present value of the defined benefit obligation resulting from employee service in the current period. *[IAS 19.7, 64]*. The basic computation is illustrated in Example 33.2 at 5.2.2.B above.

5.5.2   Interest cost

Interest cost is the increase during a period in the present value of a defined benefit obligation which arises because the benefits are one period closer to settlement. *[IAS 19.7]*. Interest cost is calculated by multiplying the discount rate at the beginning of the period by the present value of the defined benefit obligation (i.e. the gross obligation, not the net balance sheet amount) throughout that period, taking account of any material changes in the obligation. *[IAS 19.82]*. The standard gives no further explanation of what is meant by the requirement to multiply the discount rate not by the opening obligation but by the obligation 'throughout that period taking into account any material changes in the obligation.' The comprehensive worked example contained in Appendix A to the standard sheds no further light on this because it notes that 'To keep interest computations simple, all transactions are assumed to occur at the year end.'

At the extreme, it could be read as requiring a re-computation on, say, a monthly or weekly basis and to take account of all changes in scheme obligations (such as payments of benefits by the fund, accrual of further benefits by members, adjustments for leavers and joiners, changes in demographic assumptions etc). However, it seems unlikely that such an onerous requirement was intended by the IASC – particularly in light of the reference to 'material' changes and the fairly vague requirements in respect of the frequency of valuations (see 5.2.2.F above). It seems fairly likely this may be one of the areas where the '... estimates, averages and computational shortcuts [which] may provide a reliable approximation of the detailed computations ...' envisaged by the standard come into play. *[IAS 19.51]*. For example, entities might take the view that adjustments need to be made only for significant one-off changes in the scheme, such as settlements and curtailments, benefit improvements and updated actuarial valuations. Similar issues arise in relation to expected asset returns, discussed at 5.5.3 below.

5.5.3 *Expected return on plan assets (and any reimbursement rights)*

IAS 19 gives a definition of return on plan assets as follows: *[IAS 19.7]*

'The return on plan assets is interest, dividends and other revenue derived from the plan assets, together with realised and unrealised gains or losses on the plan assets, less any costs of administering the plan (other than those included in the actuarial assumptions used to measure the defined benefit obligation) and less any tax payable by the plan itself.'

The *expected* return on plan assets is just that – a forward-looking expectation or estimate. It is based on market expectations at the beginning of the period for returns over the entire life of the related obligation, and should reflect changes in the fair value of plan assets during the period arising from contributions to and benefits paid out of the fund. *[IAS 19.106]*. Clearly this is a very subjective assumption – an increase in which directly creates income at the expense of (possibly unrecognised) actuarial losses. This potential for accounting arbitrage received some debate and criticism. The IASB responded to the issue by requiring the disclosure of the basis used to determine the rate. *[IAS 19.120A(l)]*.

Expected and actual returns on plan assets are determined after deducting administration costs other than those included in the actuarial assumptions to measure the plan obligations. *[IAS 19.107]*. This clearly recognises that administration costs may, at least in some circumstances, be factored into the measurement of the defined benefit obligation.

Regrettably, however, the standard does not set out when each of the two approaches should be used, meaning that an accounting policy choice is required (for example, the administration costs of unfunded schemes, where there will be no expected return on assets to deduct them from, may lend themselves to be incorporated in the obligation instead).

For an ongoing plan it may make little practical difference. However, for a plan closed to the accrual of benefit including such costs in the obligation would result in all administration costs being accrued for (because the benefits are fully vested). A case could be made that this approach is more appropriate in those circumstances as the entity is obtaining no further benefits from the employees yet remains liable to administer the plan and pay the eventual benefits. The difference between the expected return and actual return on plan assets is an actuarial gain or loss. *[IAS 19.105]*. IAS 19 illustrates the computation of the expected and actual return on plan assets with a simple worked example upon which the following is based: *[IAS 19.106]*.

Chapter 33

Example 33.10:   Expected return on plan assets

At 1 January 2012, the fair value of plan assets was €10,000 and net cumulative unrecognised actuarial gains were €760. On 30 June 2012, the plan paid benefits of €1,900 and received contributions of €4,900. At 31 December 2012, the fair value of plan assets was €15,000 and the present value of the defined benefit obligation was €14,792. Actuarial losses on the obligation for 2012 were 60.

At 1 January 2012, the reporting entity made the following estimates, based on market prices at that date:

	%
Interest and dividend income, after tax payable by the fund	9.25
Realised and unrealised gains on plan assets (after tax)	2.00
Administration costs	(1.00)
Expected rate of return	10.25

For 2012, the expected and actual return on plan assets are as follows:

	€
Return on €10,000 held for 12 months at 10.25%	1,025
Return on €3,000 held for six months at 5% (equivalent to 10.25% annually, compounded every six months)	150
Expected return on plan assets for 2012	1,175
Fair value of plan assets at 31 December 2012	15,000
Less fair value of plan assets at 1 January 2012	(10,000)
Less contributions received	(4,900)
Add benefits paid	1,900
Actual return on plan assets	2,000

The difference between the expected return on plan assets (€1,175) and the actual return on plan assets (€2,000) is an actuarial gain of €825. Therefore, the cumulative net unrecognised actuarial gains are €1,525 (€760 plus €825 less €60). The limits of the corridor (see 5.3.1 above) are set at €1,500 (greater of: (i) 10% of €15,000 and (ii) 10% of €14,792). In the following year (2013), the entity recognises in profit and loss an actuarial gain of €25 (€1,525 less €1,500) divided by the expected average remaining working life of the employees concerned.

The expected return on plan assets for 2013 will be based on market expectations at 1 January 2013 for returns over the entire life of the obligation.

The requirement to compute the expected return not just by reference to the assets at the beginning of the year but to adjust for changes in them throughout the year, raises similar questions as to the required precision as noted in relation to interest costs (see 5.5.2 above). The example above conveniently assumes only one benefit payment and one contribution in the year, both on the same day, which is clearly for the purpose of providing a simple example rather than a reflection of likely reality. In our view, the 'estimates, averages and computational shortcuts' anticipated by the standard (see 5.5.2 above) may well be relevant here, with some employers experiencing fairly stable inflows and outflows of funds only considering it necessary to adjust for significant events (such as special contributions or major portfolio reallocations).

5.5.4   *Actuarial gains and losses*

Actuarial gains and losses comprise experience adjustments (the effects of differences between the previous actuarial assumptions and what has actually occurred) and the effects of changes in actuarial assumptions. These can result, for example, from:

(a)   unexpectedly high or low rates of: employee turnover, early retirement, mortality, increases in salaries or benefits, or medical costs;

(b)   the effect of changes in estimates of: future employee turnover, early retirement, mortality, increases in salaries or benefits, or medical costs;

(c)   the effect of changes in the discount rate; and

(d)   differences between the actual return on plan assets and the expected return on plan assets. *[IAS 19.7, 94].*

Under IAS 19 actuarial gains and losses need not be recognised in full as they occur. This is discussed at 5.3.1 above.

5.5.5   *Settlements and curtailments*

5.5.5.A   *Meaning of settlement*

A settlement occurs when an employer enters into a transaction that eliminates all further legal or constructive obligations for part or all of the benefits provided under a defined benefit plan, for example, when a lump-sum cash payment is made to, or on behalf of, plan participants in exchange for their rights to receive specified post-employment benefits. *[IAS 19.112].* IAS 19 observes that an employer may acquire an insurance policy to fund some or all of the employee benefits relating to employee service in the current and prior periods. The acquisition of such a policy is not a settlement if the employer retains a legal or constructive obligation to pay further amounts if the insurer does not pay the employee benefits specified in the insurance policy. *[IAS 19.113].* However, the acquisition of an insurance policy will mean an entity has an asset which needs to be measured at fair value. As discussed at 5.2.1B above, certain insurance policies are valued at an amount equal to the present value of the defined benefit obligation which they match. The cost of buying such a policy will typically greatly exceed its subsequent carrying amount. That raises the question of how to treat the resultant debit entry. One view might be that the loss is, in substance, very similar to a settlement loss and should be recognised in profit and loss. Another view is that because the loss results from exchanging one plan asset for another it is an actuarial loss. The typical bid-offer spread in quoted investments results in the same type, albeit typically less significant, of actuarial loss. In our view, either approach is acceptable if applied consistently and, where material, disclosed.

Chapter 33

5.5.5.B   *Meaning of curtailment*

IAS 19 describes a curtailment as occurring when an employer:

- is demonstrably committed to make a significant reduction in the number of employees covered by a plan, or

- amends the terms of a defined benefit plan such that a significant element of future service by current employees will no longer qualify for benefits or will qualify only for reduced benefits. *[IAS 19.111].*

A reduction in the extent to which future salary increases are linked to the benefits payable for past service constitutes a curtailment (and hence does not comprise a negative past service cost) *[IAS 19.111A].*

A curtailment may arise from an isolated event, such as the closing of a plant, discontinuance of an operation or termination or suspension of a plan. IAS 19 notes that curtailments are often linked to a restructuring, in which case the curtailment gain or loss should be accounted for at the same time as the related restructuring. *[IAS 19.111].*

5.5.5.C   *Recognition of gains and losses from settlements and curtailments*

Gains or losses on the settlement or curtailment of a defined benefit plan should be recognised when the settlement or curtailment occurs. The gain or loss should comprise:

(a)   any resulting change in the present value of the defined benefit obligation;

(b)   any resulting change in the fair value of the plan assets; and

(c)   any related actuarial gains and losses and past service cost that had not previously been recognised. *[IAS 19.109].*

Before determining the effect of a settlement or curtailment, the standard requires that the obligation and any related plan assets be remeasured using current actuarial assumptions including current market interest rates and other current market prices. *[IAS 19.110].* These should be taken account of in the normal way for the period preceding the settlement or curtailment (which, as shown in example 33.10 below, includes the corridor mechanism).

Where a curtailment relates to only some employees covered by a plan or only part of an obligation is settled, the gain or loss should include a proportionate share of the previously unrecognised past service costs and actuarial gains and losses.

The proportionate share is determined on the basis of the present value of the obligations before and after the curtailment or settlement, unless another basis is more rational in the circumstances. For example, it may be appropriate to apply any gain arising on a curtailment or settlement of the same plan to first eliminate any unrecognised past service cost relating to the same plan. *[IAS 19.115].*

The standard illustrates this as follows: *[IAS 19.115]*

Example 33.11: Curtailment gains

An entity discontinues a business segment and employees of the discontinued segment will earn no further benefits. This is a curtailment without a settlement. Using current actuarial assumptions (including current market interest rates and other current market prices) immediately before the curtailment, the entity has a defined benefit obligation with a net present value of 1,000, plan assets with a fair value of 820 and net cumulative unrecognised actuarial gains of 50. The entity had first adopted the Standard one year before. This increased the net liability by 100, which the entity chose to recognise over five years. The curtailment reduces the net present value of the obligation by 100 to 900.

Of the previously unrecognised actuarial gains and transitional amounts, 10% (= 100 ÷ 1,000) relates to the part of the obligation that was eliminated through the curtailment. Therefore, the effect of the curtailment is as follows:

	Before curtailment	Curtailment gain	After curtailment
Net present value of obligation	1,000	(100)	900
Fair value of plan assets	(820)	–	(820)
	180	(100)	80
Unrecognised actuarial gains	50	(5)	45
Unrecognised transitional amount (100 × 4/5)	(80)	8	(72)
Net liability recognised in balance sheet	150	(97)	53

This example illustrates determining the proportionate share of previously unrecognised amounts on the basis of the percentage change in the obligation resulting from the curtailment. As noted above, this is the default method but others should be used if more rational in the circumstances.

IAS 19 notes that a settlement occurs together with a curtailment when a plan is terminated such that the obligation is settled and the plan ceases to exist. However, if the plan is replaced by a new plan offering benefits that are, in substance, identical to the old one, the event is not a settlement or a curtailment. *[IAS 19.114]*.

This is the only mention in the standard of the closure of a defined benefit plan. Over recent years, the closure of plans to future accrual has become increasingly common in some jurisdictions. However, such closure is not always accompanied by full settlement – very often the plan will be left in place to 'run-off' the liability over time. Closure to future accrual is a curtailment, we would suggest that all previously unrecognised actuarial gains and losses should be recognised (assuming the closure is for all employees). An alternative would be to apply the approach in Example 33.11. In our view, in these circumstances the first approach is superior, but the second would be acceptable.

Closure to future accrual raises two particular accounting questions:

(a) having recognised some or all previously unrecognised actuarial gains and losses, is it still acceptable to defer the recognition of those arising subsequently using the corridor mechanism?

(b) is it still acceptable to spread forward these gains and losses over the remaining service lives of employees?

These deferral mechanisms are discussed at 5.3.1 above.

In our view, the most convincing justification for the corridor mechanism presented by the IASC was one of precision. In particular, the IASC considered that ' ... the purpose of the "corridor" is to deal with the inevitable imprecision in the measurement of defined benefit obligations.' *[IAS 19.BC54]*. Also, the standard observes that 'In the long term, actuarial gains and losses may offset one another. Therefore, estimates of post-employment benefit obligations may be viewed as a range (or "corridor") around the best estimate.' *[IAS 19.95]*. On that basis, it could be argued that the corridor remains appropriate for closed schemes. One quite powerful counterview is that the 'imprecision argument' is much less convincing for a closed scheme because for many schemes two significant uncertainties may have been resolved (future salary progression, if that is the case, and the impact of future staff retention rates on the computation of the liability in any event).

As for the smoothing of actuarial variances over service lives, the standard offers no explanation as to why this is appropriate in the first place. The option is to smooth variances over the working lives of employees 'participating' in the plan. The phrase 'participating in the plan' is not explained in the standard and several interpretations present themselves. This is discussed further at 5.3.1A above.

5.5.6   *Past service costs*

Past service cost is the change in the present value of the defined benefit obligation for employee service in prior periods, which occurs in the current period from the introduction of, or changes to, post-employment benefits or other long-term employee benefits. *[IAS 19.7]*. It excludes:

(a)   the effect of differences between actual and previously assumed salary increases on the obligation to pay benefits for service in prior years (there is no past service cost because actuarial assumptions allow for projected salaries, accordingly the effect of any such difference is an actuarial gain or loss, see 5.2.2 above);

(b)   under- and over-estimates of discretionary pension increases when an entity has a constructive obligation to grant such increases (there is no past service cost because actuarial assumptions allow for such increases, accordingly the effect of any such under or overestimate is an actuarial gain or loss, see 5.2.2 above);

(c)   estimates of benefit improvements that result from actuarial gains that have been recognised in the financial statements if the entity is obliged, by either the formal terms of a plan (or a constructive obligation that goes beyond those terms) or legislation, to use any surplus in the plan for the benefit of plan participants, even if the benefit increase has not yet been formally awarded (the resulting increase in the obligation is an actuarial loss and not past service cost, see 5.2.2 above);

(d)   the increase in vested benefits when, in the absence of new or improved benefits, employees complete vesting requirements (there is no past service cost because the estimated cost of benefits was recognised as current service cost as the service was rendered, accordingly the effect of any such increase is an actuarial gain or loss, see 5.2.2 above); and

(e)   the effect of plan amendments that reduce benefits for future service (a curtailment, see 5.5.5 above). *[IAS 19.98]*.

Where an entity reduces certain benefits payable under an existing defined benefit plan and, at the same time, increases other benefits payable under the plan for the same employees, the entity treats the change as a single net change. *[IAS 19.101]*.

Past service cost may be either positive (when benefits are introduced or changed so that the present value of the obligation rises) or negative (when existing benefits are changed so that the present value of the obligation falls). *[IAS 19.7]*. IAS 19 requires that in measuring its defined benefit liability, an employer should recognise past service cost as an expense (income) on a straight-line basis over the average period until the benefits become vested (although this is subject to the particular provisions relating to the restriction of assets discussed at 5.3.2 above). *[IAS 19.96, 100]*. This is on the grounds that past service awards are granted in return for employee service over the vesting period, and is regardless of the fact that the cost refers to employee service in previous periods. *[IAS 19.97]*. If benefits are vested immediately following the changes to a defined benefit plan, the past service cost should be recognised immediately. *[IAS 19.96]*. The standard illustrates these requirements with a worked example as follows: *[IAS 19.97]*

Example 33.12: Past service costs

An entity operates a pension plan that provides a pension of 2% of final salary for each year of service. The benefits become vested after five years of service. On 1 January 2012 the entity improves the pension to 2.5% of final salary for each year of service starting from 1 January 2008. At the date of the improvement, the present value of the additional benefits for service from 1 January 2008 to 1 January 2012 is as follows:

Employees with more than five years' service at 1/1/2012	150
Employees with less than five years' service at 1/1/2012 (average period until vesting: three years)	120
	270

The entity recognises 150 immediately because those benefits are already vested. The entity recognises 120 on a straight-line basis over three years from 1 January 2012.

Not requiring the full recognition of the rise in the defined benefit obligation represents a third departure from the 'balance sheet purity' of a full fair value balance sheet model (the other two being the corridor and spreading mechanisms discussed at 5.3.1 above).

If done rigorously, the mechanics of this approach could impose a burdensome extra layer of record keeping on employers. This is because the obligation computed under the projected unit method at and after the past service award would include an increase due to the benefit improvement (making assumptions about how many staff will remain until vesting). The deferral of a reducing portion of the unvested benefit is, in accounting terms, an asset which adjusts the amount recorded in the balance sheet. To achieve accounting accuracy any subsequent adjustment to the obligation due to experience adjustments or changes in assumptions relating to the level of benefit to vest would require an equivalent adjustment to the deferred past service cost. For example, if the number of staff for whom the benefit is expected to vest:

- falls, the resulting actuarial gain should be compensated for by an accelerated release of an appropriate portion of the deferred past service cost. Otherwise the accrual of the cost would be recorded as an asset and its reversal taken to income;

- rises, the actuarial loss is taken account of in full in the obligation (subject to the corridor etc) whereas if that level of vesting had been correctly predicted at the date of the past service award the cost would have qualified for deferral.

The IASC took the view that it would be impractical to track the impact of these complexities. Accordingly it provides that an amortisation schedule for past service cost should be established when the benefits are introduced or changed. Noting that it would be impracticable to maintain the detailed records needed to identify and implement subsequent changes in that amortisation schedule. Moreover, the standard argues that the effect is likely to be material only where there is a curtailment or settlement. For this reason an amendment to the amortisation schedule for past service cost is required only if there is a curtailment or settlement. [IAS 19.99].

6　OTHER EMPLOYEE BENEFITS

6.1　Short-term employee benefits

Short-term employee benefits are employee benefits (other than termination benefits) that are due to be settled within twelve months after the end of the period in which the employees render the related service. [IAS 19.7]. They include:

- wages, salaries and social security contributions;

- short-term compensated absences (such as paid annual leave and paid sick leave) where the compensation for the absences is due to be settled within twelve months after the end of the period in which the employees render the related service;

- profit sharing and bonuses payable within twelve months after the end of the period in which the employees render the related service; and

- non-monetary benefits (such as medical care, housing, cars and free or subsidised goods or services) for current employees. [IAS 19.8].

IAS 19 observes that accounting for short-term employee benefits is generally straightforward because no actuarial assumptions are required to measure the obligation or the cost and there is no possibility of any actuarial gain or loss. Moreover, short-term employee benefit obligations are measured on an undiscounted basis. [IAS 19.9].

6.1.1　General recognition criteria for short-term employee benefits

An entity should recognise the undiscounted amount of short-term benefits attributable to services that have been rendered in the period as an expense, unless another IFRS requires or permits the benefits to be included in the cost of an asset. This may particularly be the case under IAS 2 (see Chapter 24 at 3) and IAS 16 (see Chapter 20 at 4). Any difference between the amount of cost recognised and cash payments made should be treated as a liability or prepayment as appropriate. [IAS 19.10]. There are further requirements in respect of short-term compensated absences and profit sharing and bonus plans.

6.1.2 Short-term compensated absences

These include absences for vacation (holiday), sickness and short-term disability, maternity or paternity leave, jury service and military service. These can either be accumulating and non-accumulating absences. Accumulating absences are those that can be carried forward and used in future periods if the entitlement in the current period is not used in full. They can be either vesting entitlements (which entitle employees to a cash payment in lieu of absences not taken on leaving the entity) or non-vesting entitlement (where no cash compensation is payable). Non-accumulating absences are those where there is no entitlement to carry forward unused days. [IAS 19.12-13].

6.1.2.A Accumulating absences

The cost of accumulating absences should be recognised when employees render the service that increases their entitlement to future compensated absences. No distinction should be made between vesting and non-vesting entitlements (see above), on the basis that the liability arises as services are rendered in both cases. However, in measuring non-vesting entitlements, the possibility of employees leaving before receiving them should be taken into account. [IAS 19.11(a), 13].

The cost of accumulating absences should be measured as the additional amount that the entity expects to pay as a result of the unused entitlement that has accumulated at the end of the reporting period. In the case of unused paid sick leave, provision should be made only to the extent that it is expected that employees will use the sick leave in subsequent periods. The standard observes that in many cases, it may not be necessary to make detailed computations to estimate that there is no material obligation for unused compensated absences. For example, IAS 19 considers it unlikely that a sick leave obligation will be material unless if there is a formal or informal understanding that unused paid sick leave may be taken as paid vacation. [IAS 19.14-15].

The standard provides an example to illustrate the requirements for accumulating absences upon which the following is based: [IAS 19.15]

Example 33.13: Accumulating absences

An entity has 100 employees, who are each entitled to five working days of paid sick leave for each year. Unused sick leave may be carried forward for one calendar year. Sick leave is taken first out of the current year's entitlement and then out of any balance brought forward from the previous year (a LIFO basis). At 31 December 2012, the average unused entitlement is two days per employee. The entity expects, based on past experience which is expected to continue, that 92 employees will take no more than five days of paid sick leave in 2013 and that the remaining eight employees will take an average of six and a half days each.

The entity expects that it will pay an additional 12 days of sick pay as a result of the unused entitlement that has accumulated at 31 December 2012 (one and a half days each, for eight employees). Therefore, the entity recognises a liability equal to 12 days of sick pay.

6.1.2.B Non-accumulating absences

The cost of non-accumulating absences should be recognised as and when they arise, on the basis that the entitlement is not directly linked to the service rendered by employees in the period. This is commonly the case for sick pay (to the extent that unused past entitlement cannot be carried forward), maternity or paternity leave and compensated absences for jury service or military service. [IAS 19.11(b), 16].

6.1.3   *Profit sharing and bonus plans*

An entity should recognise the expected cost of profit sharing and bonus payments when, and only when:

- the entity has a present legal or constructive obligation to make such payments as a result of past events; and

- a reliable estimate of the obligation can be made. *[IAS 19.17]*.

The above are discussed in turn at 6.1.3.A and 6.1.3.B below. Statutory profit sharing arrangements based on taxable profit are discussed at 6.1.3.C.

6.1.3.A   *Present legal or constructive obligation*

A present obligation exists when, and only when, the entity has no realistic alternative but to make the payments. *[IAS 19.17]*. IAS 19 clarifies that where a profit-sharing plan is subject to a loyalty period (i.e. a period during which employees must remain with the entity in order to receive their share), a constructive obligation is created during the period in which the relevant profit is earned. However, the possibility of employees leaving during the loyalty period should be taken into account in measuring the cost of the plan. *[IAS 19.18]*. The standard attempts to illustrate the approach as follows:

Example 33.14:   *Profit sharing and bonus plans*

A profit-sharing plan requires an entity to pay a specified proportion of its net profit for the year to employees who serve throughout the year. If no employees leave during the year, the total profit-sharing payments for the year will be 3% of net profit. The entity estimates that staff turnover will reduce the payments to 2.5% of net profit.

The entity recognises a liability and an expense of 2.5% of net profit.

It is a little hard to know what to make of this example. Whilst claiming to illustrate accruing a bonus over a period *excluding* the loyalty period, it selects a fact pattern where the 'earning period' and the loyalty period both end at the end of the reporting period! Moreover, when preparing accounts for the year it will no longer be uncertain whether all eligible employees become entitled to the bonus, as that is determined at the year-end. That means the reduction in the accrual from 3% to 2.5% should be an observable fact not an estimate. The requirement to account for short-term bonuses over the period during which employees render service that increases the amount to be paid if they remain in service for a further period (in other words, excluding the loyalty period) is in marked contrast to the requirements for long-term bonuses. If the loyalty period exceeds one year from the end of the reporting period the bonus becomes an 'other long-term employee benefit' to which the projected unit method is applied. This is discussed at 6.2 below.

The standard also states that where an entity has a practice of paying bonuses, it has a constructive obligation to pay a bonus, even though there may be no legal obligation for it to do so. Again, however, in measuring the cost, the possibility of employees leaving before receiving a bonus should be taken into account. *[IAS 19.19]*.

6.1.3.B   *Reliable estimate of provision*

A reliable estimate of a legal or constructive obligation under a profit sharing or bonus plan can be made when, and only when:

- the formal terms of the plan contain a formula for determining the amount of the benefit;
- the entity determines the amounts to be paid before the financial statements are approved for issue; or
- past practice gives clear evidence of the amount of the entity's constructive obligation. *[IAS 19.20].*

IAS 19 states that an obligation under a profit sharing or bonus plan must be accounted for as expense and not a distribution of profit, since it results from employee service and not from a transaction with owners. *[IAS 19.21].* Where profit sharing and bonus payments are not due wholly within twelve months of the end of the period in which the employees render the relevant service, they should be accounted for as other long-term employee benefits (see 6.2 below). *[IAS 19.22].*

6.1.3.C   *Statutory profit sharing based on taxable profit.*

The Interpretations Committee was asked to clarify how to account for a statutory employee benefit whereby 10% of taxable profit is shared with employees. In particular, the request sought clarification as to whether analogy could be made to IAS 12 – *Income Taxes* – to account for temporary differences between accounting and taxable profit which would reverse in the future.

The Committee thought that such an approach was not acceptable. It decided not to add the item to its agenda saying 'The Committee noted that the statutory employee profit-sharing arrangement described in the request should be accounted for in accordance with IAS 19, and that IAS 19 provides sufficient guidance on amounts that should be recognised and measured, with the result that significantly divergent interpretations are not expected in practice. Consequently, the Committee decided not to add this issue to its agenda.'

6.2   Long-term employee benefits other than post-employment benefits

6.2.1   *Meaning of other long-term employee benefits*

These are employee benefits (other than post-employment benefits and termination benefits) that are not due to be settled within twelve months after the end of the period in which the employees render the related service. *[IAS 19.7].* They include:

- long-term compensated absences such as long-service or sabbatical leave;
- jubilee or other long-service benefits;
- long-term disability benefits;
- profit sharing and bonuses payable twelve months or more after the end of the period in which the employees render the related service; and
- deferred compensation paid twelve months or more after the end of the period in which it is earned. *[IAS 19.126].*

6.2.2   *Recognition and measurement*

For such benefits IAS 19 requires a simplified version of the accounting treatment required in respect of defined benefit plans (which is discussed in detail at 5 above).

The amount recognised as a liability for other long-term employee benefits should be the net total, at the end of the reporting period, of the present value of the defined benefit obligation and the fair value of plan assets (if any) out of which the obligations are to be settled directly. The net total of the following amounts should be recognised as expense or income, except to the extent that another IFRS requires or permits their inclusion in the cost of an asset:

(a)   current service cost;

(b)   interest cost;

(c)   the expected return on any plan assets and on any reimbursement right recognised as an asset;

(d)   actuarial gains and losses, which should all be recognised immediately;

(e)   past service cost, which should all be recognised immediately; and

(f)   the effect of any curtailments or settlements.

All assets, liabilities, income and expenditure relating to such benefits should be accounted for in the same way, and subject to the same restrictions on the recognition of assets and income, as those relating to a defined benefit pension plan (see 5.3.1 and 5.3.2 above), except that:

- actuarial gains and losses are recognised immediately (i.e. they are not limited to a 'corridor' – see 5.3.1 above);

- actuarial gains and losses are recognised in income, even if the entity adopts a policy of recognising actuarial gains and losses relating to post-employment benefits in equity; and

- all past service costs are recognised immediately (i.e. they are not spread over the period to vesting – see 5.5.6 above). *[IAS 19.127-129].*

6.2.2.A   Annually determined bonuses with a loyalty period greater than one year

It is quite common practice for certain employees (particularly more senior ones) to receive bonuses whereby the amount to be received is determined some time in advance of payment (the 'earning' period) with entitlement to it then only subject to the requirement for continued employment for a further period (the 'loyalty' period). Often the amount payable will be determined by reference to performance in the earning period – such as corporate financial performance – but that need not be the case. As discussed at 6.1.3.A above, when the arrangement meets the definition of a short-term benefit (i.e. all amounts due to be settled within a year after the end of the earning period), the standard considers that an obligation is created as 'employees render service that increases the amount to be paid *if they remain in service until the end of the specified period.*' [emphasis added]. In other words, for a typical 'annual' scheme (with payments based on, say, profits for the year) if the loyalty period ends within a year of the end of the reporting period then all the payments are accrued in the year (the earnings period) and not spread forward over the loyalty period.

Should the loyalty period be any longer than this (say, a year and a day), however, a very different model is used by IAS 19. In these circumstances, the arrangement is an 'other long-term employee benefit' to which the projected unit credit method should be applied. As discussed at 5.2.2 above this involves attributing benefits to years of service from:

- the date when service by the employee first leads to benefits under the plan (whether or not the benefits are conditional on further service); until

- the date when further service by the employee will lead to no material amount of further benefits under the plan, other than from further salary increases.

Accordingly, attributing benefits to periods of service under the plan's formula would lead to all benefits being attributed to the very last period. This is because the benefit does not vest until the end of the loyalty period. In these circumstances, IAS 19 requires the benefits to be attributed on a straight-line basis over the vesting period. This requirement is illustrated in items 5 to 8 in Example 33.3 at 5.2.2.C above. Crucially, there is no allowance to recognise the liability any earlier than this – in particular there is no reference to a shorter period during which 'the amount to be paid [increases] if they remain in service until the end of the specified period.'

That this is genuinely the intention of the standard seems to be confirmed by the fact that IFRS 2 makes the same requirement to allocate the cost of share-based payments over the full vesting period, including any loyalty period. *[IFRS 2.15].*

In light of this, choosing to allow 'special' simplified accruals accounting for such amounts when they are payable soon after the year-end seems to be just a pragmatic simplification in the standard. Inevitably that will produce slightly curious results when the vesting period ends just before as opposed to just after the period chosen (a year in IAS 19). In particular, the flip between short term accruals accounting and the long-term projected unit method will mean that a bonus determined within a year and payable one year later will all be charged in the first year, whereas if the recipient must remain employed one day longer for the benefit to vest it will be spread over two years and the cost will comprise part current service cost and part interest cost.

6.2.2.B   Long-term disability benefit

Where long-term disability benefit depends on the length of service of the employee, an obligation arises as the employee renders service, which is to be measured according to the probability that payment will be required and the length of time for which payment is expected to be made. If, however, the level of benefit is the same for all employees regardless of years of service, the cost is recognised only when an event causing disability occurs. *[IAS 19.130].*

It is not clear why the IASC made this distinction, since in principle both types of benefit are equally susceptible to actuarial measurement. If anything the cost of benefits applicable to all employees regardless of service is probably easier to quantify actuarially. It may be that the reason is another departure from the balance sheet purity of the standard because of unpalatable income statement results. Given

Chapter 33

that an exposure to disability benefits which grows with years of service is fully provided for (actuarially) as it grows over time, it would seem logical for full provision to be made immediately for an exposure which comes into being (in full) on the day the employee commences employment. The problem with such an approach would be what to do with the debit entry. It would not represent an asset as envisaged in the Conceptual Framework, which would tend to imply an instant charge to profit or loss. These issues are similar to those surrounding death-in-service benefits discussed at 3.6 above.

6.3   Termination benefits

Termination benefits are employee benefits payable as a result of either:

- an entity's decision to terminate an employee's employment before the normal retirement date; or
- an employee's decision to accept voluntary redundancy in exchange for those benefits. *[IAS 19.7]*.

They are accounted for differently from other employee benefits because the event that gives rise an obligation for them is the termination rather than the rendering of service by the employee. *[IAS 19.132]*.

6.3.1   Recognition

An entity should recognise termination benefits as a liability and an expense when, and only when, the entity is demonstrably committed (see below) to either:

- terminate the employment of an employee or group of employees before the normal retirement date; or
- provide termination benefits as a result of an offer made in order to encourage voluntary redundancy. *[IAS 19.133]*.

An entity is demonstrably committed to a termination when, and only when, the entity has a detailed formal plan for the termination and is without realistic possibility of withdrawal. The detailed plan should include, as a minimum:

- the location, function, and approximate number of employees whose services are to be terminated;
- the termination benefits for each job classification or function; and
- the time at which the plan will be implemented. Implementation should begin as soon as possible and the period of time to complete implementation should be such that material changes to the plan are not likely. *[IAS 19.134]*.

IAS 19 distinguishes between those benefits that are payable as a result of the termination of employment by the entity and those payable to employees on leaving, regardless of the reason for their departure.

Benefits resulting from a termination by the entity are 'termination benefits' as defined by the standard, whether the obligation is imposed by law, contractual agreement with employees or their representatives, custom, or a desire to act equitably. They are generally given as lump-sum payments, but may include enhancement of retirement benefits or of other post-employment benefits (either indirectly through an employee benefit plan or directly) and salary until the end of a specified notice period if the employee renders no further service that provides economic benefits to the entity. *[IAS 19.135]*. The restriction that salary over a notice period may only be considered a termination benefit if the employee renders no further service that provides economic benefits to the entity is an important one. In a corporate restructuring it may frequently be the case that some employees are paid (perhaps at enhanced rates) to stay on and achieve an orderly wind-down of the operations rather than leave once the termination is announced. Such payments would not fall to be treated as termination benefits.

By contrast benefits payable to employees on leaving (subject possibly to minimum service or vesting requirements) in all circumstances are not 'termination benefits' as defined in IAS 19, notwithstanding that they may be referred to as such in some jurisdictions. Benefits of this nature should be accounted for as post-employment benefits (see 5 above). It may also be that a type of hybrid arrangement operates, whereby employees receive a lower benefit for a voluntary termination at their request than for an involuntary one, and a higher benefit for an involuntary termination at the request of the entity. In such cases, only the difference between the lower and higher levels of benefit should be treated as a termination benefit. *[IAS 19.136]*.

The cost of termination benefits should be recognised immediately on the grounds that they do not provide an entity with future economic benefits. *[IAS 19.137]*. IAS 19 also points out that the recognition of termination benefits will often give rise to the need to account for a curtailment of retirement benefits or other employee benefits (see 5.5.5 above). *[IAS 19.138]*.

The treatment of termination benefits is a topic currently under review by the IASB as part of their 'convergence' project. This is discussed at 9.2.1 below.

6.3.2   *Measurement*

Where termination benefits fall due more than twelve months after the end of the reporting period, they should be discounted. The rate used should be determined in the same way as for defined benefit post-employment benefits discussed at 5.2.2.E above. *[IAS 19.78, 139]*.

Where an offer has been made to encourage voluntary redundancy, the termination benefits should be measured by reference to the number of employee expected to accept the offer. *[IAS 19.140]*.

7   DISCLOSURE REQUIREMENTS

7.1   Defined contribution plans

IAS 19 requires the disclosure of the expense recognised for defined contribution plans. *[IAS 19.46]*.

Where a multi-employer defined benefit plan is treated as a defined contribution plan (see 3.3 above) the following additional disclosures are required:

(a)   the fact that the plan is a defined benefit plan; and

(b)   the reason why sufficient information is not available to enable the entity to account for the plan as a defined benefit plan; and

(c)   to the extent that a surplus or deficit in the plan may affect the amount of future contributions:

(i)   any available information about that surplus or deficit;

(ii)   the basis used to determine that surplus or deficit; and

(iii) the implications, if any, for the entity. *[IAS 19.30, 123]*.

The standard provides an illustration of what the above disclosures might look like in Appendix B.

Where required by IAS 24, information should also be disclosed about contributions to defined contribution plans for key management personnel. *[IAS 19.47]*. (See Chapter 37 at 2.5.1).

7.2   Defined benefit plans

IAS 19 requires extensive disclosure in relation to defined benefit plans, which have evolved and grown over time.

IAS 19 explains that an entity should disclose information that enables users of financial statements to evaluate the nature of its defined benefit plans and the financial effects of changes in those plans during the period. *[IAS 19.120]*. It goes on specifically to require disclosure of the following:

(a)   the accounting policy for recognising actuarial gains and losses;

(b)   a general description of the type of plan. This description should distinguish, for example, flat salary pension plans from final salary pension plans and from post-employment medical plans. The description should include informal practices that give rise to constructive obligations included in the measurement of the defined benefit obligation. Further detail is not required;

(c)   a reconciliation of opening and closing balances of the present value of the defined benefit obligation showing separately, if applicable, the effects during the period attributable to each of the following:

(i)   current service cost;

(ii)   interest cost;

(iii) contributions by plan participants;

(iv)   actuarial gains and losses;

(v)   foreign currency exchange rate changes on plans measured in a currency different from the entity's presentation currency;

(vi)   benefits paid;

(vii) past service cost;

(viii) business combinations;

(ix)   curtailments; and

(x)   settlements.

(d) an analysis of the defined benefit obligation into amounts arising from plans that are wholly unfunded and amounts arising from plans that are wholly or partly funded;

(e) a reconciliation of the opening and closing balances of the fair value of plan assets and of the opening and closing balances of any reimbursement right recognised as an asset showing separately, if applicable, the effects during the period attributable to each of the following:

    (i) expected return on plan assets;

    (ii) actuarial gains and losses;

    (iii) foreign currency exchange rate changes on plans measured in a currency different from the entity's presentation currency;

    (iv) contributions by the employer;

    (v) contributions by plan participants;

    (vi) benefits paid;

    (vii) business combinations; and

    (viii) settlements.

(f) a reconciliation of the present value of the defined benefit obligation in (c) and the fair value of the plan assets in (e) to the assets and liabilities recognised in the balance sheet, showing at least:

    (i) the net actuarial gains or losses not recognised in the balance sheet (see 5.3.1 above);

    (ii) the past service cost not recognised in the balance sheet (see 5.5.6 above);

    (iii) any amount not recognised as an asset, because of the limit (to recoverable amount) set by IAS 19 (see 5.3.3 above);

    (iv) the fair value at the end of the reporting period of any reimbursement right recognised as an asset (with a brief description of the link between the reimbursement right and the related obligation) (see 5.2.1.B above); and

    (v) the other amounts recognised in the balance sheet;

(g) the total expense recognised in profit or loss for each of the following, and the line item(s) in which they are included:

    (i) current service cost;

    (ii) interest cost;

    (iii) expected return on plan assets;

    (iv) expected return on any reimbursement right recognised as an asset;

    (v) actuarial gains and losses;

    (vi) past service cost;

    (vii) the effect of any curtailment or settlement; and

    (viii) the effect of the limit (to recoverable amount) of an asset set by IAS 19;

Chapter 33

(h)   the total amount recognised in the statement of recognised income and expense for each of the following:

   (i)   actuarial gains and losses; and

   (ii)   the effect of the limit (to recoverable amount) of an asset set by IAS 19;

(i)   for entities that recognise actuarial gains and losses in the statement of recognised income and expense, the cumulative amount of actuarial gains and losses recognised in the statement of recognised income and expense;

(j)   for each major category of plan assets, which shall include, but is not limited to, equity instruments, debt instruments, property, and all other assets, the percentage or amount that each major category constitutes of the fair value of the total plan assets;

(k)   the amounts included in the fair value of plan assets for:

   (i)   each category of the entity's own financial instruments; and

   (ii)   any property occupied by, or other assets used by, the entity;

(l)   a narrative description of the basis used to determine the overall expected rate of return on assets, including the effect of the major categories of plan assets;

(m)   the actual return on plan assets, as well as the actual return on any reimbursement right recognised as an asset;

(n)   the principal actuarial assumptions used as at the end of the reporting period, including, when applicable:

   (i)   the discount rates;

   (ii)   the expected rates of return on any plan assets for the periods presented in the financial statements;

   (iii) the expected rates of return for the periods presented in the financial statements on any reimbursement right recognised as an asset;

   (iv)   the expected rates of salary increases (and of changes in an index or other variable specified in the formal or constructive terms of a plan as the basis for future benefit increases);

   (v)   medical cost trend rates; and

   (vi)   any other material actuarial assumptions used;

Each actuarial assumption should be disclosed in absolute terms (for example, as an absolute percentage) and not just as a margin between different percentages or other variables;

(o)   the effect of an increase of one percentage point and the effect of a decrease of one percentage point in the assumed medical cost trend rates on:

   (i)   the aggregate of the current service cost and interest cost components of net periodic post-employment medical costs; and

   (ii)   the accumulated post-employment benefit obligation for medical cost;

For the purposes of this disclosure, all other assumptions should be held constant. For plans operating in a high inflation environment, the disclosure should be the effect of a percentage increase or decrease in the assumed medical cost trend rate of a significance similar to one percentage point in a low inflation environment;

(p)   the amounts for the current annual period and previous four annual periods of:

   (i)   the present value of the defined benefit obligation, the fair value of the plan assets and the surplus or deficit in the plan; and

   (ii)   the experience adjustments arising on:

      (A)   the plan liabilities expressed either as (1) an amount or (2) a percentage of the plan liabilities at the end of the reporting period; and

      (B)   the plan assets expressed either as (1) an amount or (2) a percentage of the plan assets at the end of the reporting period; and

(q)   the employer's best estimate, as soon as it can reasonably be determined, of contributions expected to be paid to the plan during the annual period beginning after the end of the reporting period.

There is some flexibility allowed in aggregating disclosure where an employer has more than one plan. In these circumstances, the required disclosures may be made separately for each plan, in total or in such groupings as are considered most useful. Examples of possible groupings which may be considered useful include: geographical location (e.g. distinguishing between domestic and foreign plans) and plans which are subject to materially different risks (e.g. distinguishing flat salary pension plans from final salary pension plans and from post-retirement medical plans). When disclosures are given in total for a grouping of plans, they should be provided in the form of weighted averages or of relatively narrow ranges. *[IAS 19.122]*. The standard provides a detailed illustration of what its required disclosures might look like in Appendix B.

The standard also contains a reminder that:

- Where required by IAS 24 information about:

   (i)   related party transactions with post-employment benefit plans (see Chapter 37 at 2.2.6); and

   (ii)   post-employment benefits for key management personnel (see Chapter 44 at 2.6.1.); *[IAS 19.124]* and

- Where required by IAS 37 (see Chapter 29 at 6.2), information about contingent liabilities arising from post-employment benefit obligations. *[IAS 19.125]*.

One company subject to the above requirements is GlaxoSmithKline plc:

Extract 33.6: GlaxoSmithKline plc (2007)

Notes to the Financial Statements [extract]

28   Pensions and other post-employment benefits [extract]

Pension and other post-employment costs	2007 £m	2006 £m	2005 £m
UK pension schemes	108	159	124
US pension schemes	24	35	41
Other overseas pensions schemes	89	91	83
Unfunded post-retirement healthcare schemes	90	91	100
Other post-employment costs	2	1	2
	313	377	350
Analysed as:			
Funded defined benefit/hybrid pension schemes	171	237	198
Unfunded defined benefit pension schemes	17	19	25
Unfunded post-retirement healthcare schemes	90	91	100
Defined benefit schemes	278	347	323
Defined contribution pension schemes	33	29	25
Other post-employment costs	2	1	2
	313	377	350

The costs of the defined benefit pension and post-retirement healthcare schemes are charged in the income statement as follows:

Cost of sales	72	74	71
Selling, general and administration	129	175	177
Research and development	77	98	75
	278	347	323

GSK entities operate pension arrangements which cover the Group's material obligations to provide pensions to retired employees. These arrangements have been developed in accordance with local practices in the countries concerned. Pension benefits can be provided by state schemes; by defined contribution schemes, whereby retirement benefits are determined by the value of funds arising from contributions paid in respect of each employee, or by defined benefit schemes, whereby retirement benefits are based on employee pensionable remuneration and length of service. Some 'hybrid' defined benefit schemes also include defined contribution sections.

Contributions to defined benefit schemes are determined in accordance with the advice of independent, professionally qualified actuaries. Pension costs of defined benefit schemes for accounting purposes have been assessed in accordance with independent actuarial advice, using the projected unit method. In certain countries pension benefits are provided on an unfunded basis, some administered by trustee companies. Liabilities are generally assessed annually in accordance with the advice of independent actuaries. Formal, independent, actuarial valuations of the Group's main plans are undertaken regularly, normally at least every three years.

Actuarial movements in the year are recognised in full through the statement of recognised income and expense.

The UK discount rate is based on the iBoxx over 15 year AA index and the US discount rate is based on corporate bond yields which reflect the term of the expected benefit payments. The expected rate of return on bonds reflects the portfolio mix of index-linked, government and corporate bonds. An equity risk premium of between 3% and 4% is added to longer term government bond yields to give the expected rate of return on equities. Projected inflation rate and pension increases are long term predictions based on the yield gap between long term index-linked and fixed interest Gilts. In the UK, mortality rates are determined by adjusting the PA92 standard mortality tables to reflect recent scheme experience. These rates are then projected to reflect improvements in life expectancy in line with the medium cohort (i.e. improvements at recently observed higher levels which are assumed to continue to 2020) with minimum improvements thereafter of 1% per year for males and 0.5% for females. In the USA, mortality rates are calculated using he RP2000 fully generational table, projected using scale AA, with the white collar adjustment.

The mortality assumptions for the UK and US schemes were set following a review in December 2007. GSK expects to review these again in December 2008.

The average life expectancy assumed now for an individual at the age of 60 and projected to apply in 2027 for an individual then at the age of 60 is as follows:

	UK Male Years	UK Female Years	USA Male Years	USA Female Years
Current	26.8	28.0	24.4	26.1
Projected for 2027	29.2	29.8	25.9	27.0

The assets of funded schemes are generally held in separately administered trusts or are insured. Assets are invested in different classes in order to maintain a balance between risk and return. Investments are diversified to limit the financial effect of the failure of any individual investment. Following an asset liability study in 2007, the Group decided to adopt a strategy to reduce gradually the allocation of investment in equities. In the UK it is proposed that the strategy will be linked to the funding levels in the schemes and this will be considered further with the trustees of the UK schemes in 2008. The allocation of equities and property in the US scheme will be reduced from 80% of the total to 60% in 2008.

In the UK the defined benefit pension schemes operated for the benefit of former Glaxo Wellcome employees and former SmithKline Beecham employees remain separate. These schemes were closed to new entrants in 2001 and subsequent UK employees are entitled to join a defined contribution scheme. In the USA the former Glaxo Wellcome and SmithKline Beecham defined benefit schemes were merged during 2001. In addition, the Group operates a number of post-retirement healthcare schemes, the principal one of which is in the USA.

The Group has applied the following financial assumptions in assessing the defined benefit liabilities:

	UK 2007 % pa	UK 2006 % pa	UK 2005 % pa	USA 2007 % pa	USA 2006 % pa	USA 2005 % pa	Rest of World 2007 % pa	Rest of World 2006 % pa	Rest of World 2005 % pa
Rate of increase of future earnings	4.25	4.25	4.00	5.00	5.00	5.00	3.25	3.25	3.25
Discount rate	5.75	5.00	4.75	6.00	5.75	5.50	4.75	4.25	3.75
Expected pension increases	3.25	3.00	2.75	n/a	n/a	n/a	2.00	2.00	2.00
Cash balance credit/conversion rate	n/a	n/a	n/a	4.75	4.75	4.50	1.60	1.75	1.75
Inflation rate	3.25	3.00	2.75	2.50	2.50	2.50	1.75	1.75	1.75

The amounts recorded in the income statement and statement of recognised income and expense for the three years ended 31st December 2007 in relation to the defined benefit pension and post-retirement healthcare schemes were as follows:

2007				Pensions	Post-retirement benefits
	UK £m	USA £m	Rest of World £m	**Group £m**	**Group £m**
Amounts charged to operating profit					
Current service cost	138	60	57	**255**	30
Past service cost	–	(7)	1	**(6)**	–
Expected return on pension scheme assets	(389)	(141)	(37)	**(567)**	–
Interest on scheme liabilities	335	107	41	**483**	54
Settlements and curtailments	24	5	(6)	**23**	6
	180	24	56	**188**	90
Actuarial gains recorded in the statement of recognised income and expense	523	66	43	**632**	39

2006				Pensions	Post-retirement benefits
	UK £m	USA £m	Rest of World £m	**Group £m**	**Group £m**
Amounts charged to operating profit					
Current service cost	135	66	56	**257**	48
Past service cost	33	–	(2)	**31**	–
Expected return on pension scheme assets	(333)	(142)	(30)	**(505)**	–
Interest on scheme liabilities	307	113	42	**462**	57
Settlements and curtailments	17	(2)	(4)	**11**	(14)
	159	35	62	**256**	91
Actuarial losses recorded in the statement of recognised income and expense	111	169	10	**290**	139

2005				Pensions	Post-retirement benefits
	UK £m	USA £m	Rest of World £m	**Group £m**	**Group £m**
Amounts charged to operating profit					
Current service cost	117	63	52	**232**	46
Past service cost	–	–	–	**–**	1
Expected return on pension scheme assets	(285)	(126)	(28)	**(439)**	–
Interest on scheme liabilities	276	104	34	**414**	53
Settlements and curtailments	16	–	–	**16**	–
	124	41	58	**223**	100
Actuarial losses recorded in the statement of recognised income and expense	(490)	(109)	(93)	**(692)**	(102)

The total actuarial losses recorded in the statement of recognised income and expense since 1st January 2003 amount to £18 million.

The fair values of the assets and liabilities of the UK and US defined benefit pension schemes, together with aggregated data for other defined benefit pension schemes in the Group are as follows:

At 31st December 2007	UK Expected rate of return %	UK Fair value £m	USA Expected rate of return %	USA Fair value £m	Rest of World Average expected rate of return %	Rest of World Fair value £m	Group Fair Value £m
Equities	8.00	4,578	8.50	1,446	7.50	223	**6,247**
Property	7.00	338	7.50	213	7.00	20	**571**
Bonds	5.00	2,322	5.00	335	4.00	430	**3,087**
Other assets	6.00	55	4.75	10	4.25	212	**277**
Fair value of assets		7,293		2,004		885	**10,182**
Present value of scheme obligations		(7,371)		(1,945)		(1,022)	**(10,338)**
		(78)		59		(137)	**(156)**
Included in other non-current assets		10		215		30	**255**
Included in pensions and other post-employment benefits		(88)		(156)		(167)	**(411)**
		(78)		59		(137)	**(156)**
Actual return on plan assets		557		187		19	**763**

At 31st December 2006	UK Expected rate of return %	UK Fair value £m	USA Expected rate of return %	USA Fair value £m	Rest of World Average expected rate of return %	Rest of World Fair value £m	Group Fair Value £m
Equities	8.00	4,218	8.50	1,412	7.25	205	5,835
Property	7.00	210	7.50	169	6.75	11	390
Bonds	4.50	2,026	5.50	324	3.50	351	2,701
Other assets	5.00	100	5.00	48	3.75	174	322
Fair value of assets		6,554		1,953		741	9,248
Present value of scheme obligations		(7,444)		(1,949)		(952)	(10,345)
		(890)		4		(211)	(1,097)
Included in other non-current assets		–		160		19	179
Included in pensions and other post-employment benefits		(890)		(156)		(230)	(1,276)
		(890)		4		(211)	(1,097)
Actual return on plan assets		560		310		56	926

Chapter 33

At 31st December 2005	UK Expected rate of return %	UK Fair value £m	USA Expected rate of return %	USA Fair value £m	Rest of World Average expected rate of return %	Rest of World Fair value £m	Group Fair Value £m
Equities	7.75	3,895	8.50	1,440	7.00	192	5,527
Property	–	–	7.50	106	6.25	11	117
Bonds	4.25	1,764	5.50	352	3.50	302	2,418
Other assets	4.00	85	4.00	78	3.25	152	315
Fair value of assets		5,744		1,976		657	8,377
Present value of scheme obligations		(7,054)		(2,150)		(922)	(10,126)
		(1,310)		(174)		(265)	(1,749)
Included in other non-current assets		–		–		12	12
Included in pensions and other post-employment benefits		(1,310)		(174)		(277)	(1,761)
		(1,310)		(174)		(265)	(1,749)
Actual return on plan assets		932		129		63	1,124

Movements in defined benefit obligations	UK £m	USA £m	Rest of World £m	Pensions Group £m	Post-retirement benefits Group £m
Obligations at 1ˢᵗ January 2005	(5,735)	(1,750)	(761)	**(8,246)**	**(1,005)**
Exchange adjustments	–	(217)	14	**(203)**	**(138)**
Service cost	(117)	(63)	(52)	**(232)**	**(47)**
Interest cost	(276)	(104)	(34)	**(414)**	**(53)**
Settlements and curtailments	(16)	–	–	**(16)**	**–**
Actuarial losses	(1,137)	(112)	(128)	**(1,377)**	**(102)**
Scheme participants' contributions	(12)	–	(3)	**(15)**	**(9)**
Benefits paid	239	96	42	**377**	**46**
Obligations at 31ˢᵗ December 2005	(7,054)	(2,150)	(922)	**(10,126)**	**(1,308)**
Exchange adjustments	–	267	30	**297**	**151**
Service cost	(168)	(66)	(54)	**(288)**	**(48)**
Interest cost	(307)	(113)	(42)	**(462)**	**(57)**
Settlement and curtailments	(17)	2	12	**(3)**	**14**
Actuarial (losses)/gains	(116)	1	(16)	**(131)**	**139**
Scheme participants' contributions	(11)	–	(3)	**(14)**	**(8)**
Benefits paid	229	110	43	**382**	**54**
Obligations as 31ˢᵗ December 2006	(7,444)	(1,949)	(952)	**(10,345)**	**(1,063)**
Exchange adjustments	–	34	(80)	**(46)**	**9**
Service cost	(138)	(53)	(58)	**(249)**	**(30)**
Interest cost	(335)	(107)	(41)	**(483)**	**(54)**
Settlement and curtailments	(24)	(5)	4	**(25)**	**(6)**
Actuarial gains	355	20	61	**436**	**39**
Scheme participants' contributions	(38)	–	(5)	**(43)**	**–**
Benefits paid	253	115	49	**417**	**44**
Transfers	–	–	–	**–**	**89**
Recognised in the balance sheet at 31ˢᵗ December 2007	(7,371)	(1,945)	(1,002)	**(10,338)**	**(972)**
Unrecognised past service costs	–	–	–	**–**	**(47)**
Obligations at 31ˢᵗ December 2007	(7,371)	(1,945)	(1,002)	**(10,338)**	**(1,019)**

The UK defined benefit schemes include defined contribution sections with obligations totalling £693 million at 31ˢᵗ December 2007 (2006 – £609 million, 2005 – £515 million).

The liability for the US post-retirement healthcare scheme has been assessed using the same assumptions as for the US pension scheme, together with the assumption for future medical inflation of 8.5% (2006 – 9.25%), reducing by 0.75% per year to 5% in 2013 and thereafter. During 2007, the US post-retirement healthcare scheme was amended. The main change was an increase in the cap on company costs. At the year-end the plan obligation was £879 million. However, in accordance with IAS 19 the unvested part of a benefit improvement is not recognised immediately on the balance sheet but is recognised gradually through the income statement. At the year-end the unrecognised amount was £47 million and the amount recognised on the balance sheet was therefore £832 million (2006 – £927 million), 2005 – £1,133 million).

The Group provides certain medical benefits to disabled employees and their spouses in the USA. The obligations for these benefits which were transferred at a value of £89 million are now shown within other provisions.

Chapter 33

The defined benefit pension obligation is analysed as follows:

	2007 £m	2006 £m	2005 £m
Funded	(10,079)	(10,099)	(9,858)
Unfunded	(259)	(246)	(268)
	(10,338)	(10,345)	(10,126)

Post-retirement benefits are unfunded.

Movements in fair value of assets	Pensions				Post-retirement benefits
	UK £m	USA £m	Rest of World £m	Group £m	Group £m
Assets at 1st January 2005	4,561	1,638	547	6,746	–
Exchange adjustments	–	200	(4)	196	–
Expected return on assets	285	126	28	439	–
Actuarial gains	647	3	35	685	–
Employer contributions	478	105	90	673	37
Scheme participants' contributions	12	–	3	15	9
Benefits paid	(239)	(96)	(42)	(377)	(46)
Assets at 31st December 2005	5,744	1,976	657	8,377	
Exchange adjustments	–	(255)	(30)	(285)	–
Expected return on assets	333	142	30	505	–
Settlements and curtailments	–	–	(8)	(8)	–
Actuarial gains	227	168	26	421	–
Employer contributions	468	32	106	606	46
Scheme participants' contributions	11	–	3	14	8
Benefits paid	(229)	(110)	(43)	(382)	(54)
Assets at 31st December 2006	6,554	1,953	741	9,248	–
Exchange adjustments	–	(29)	68	39	–
Expected return on assets	389	141	37	567	–
Settlements and curtailments	–	–	2	2	–
Actuarial gains	168	46	(18)	196	–
Employer contributions	397	8	99	504	41
Scheme participants' contributions	38	–	5	43	3
Benefits paid	(253)	(115)	(49)	(417)	(44)
Assets at 31st December 2007	7,293	2,004	885	10,182	–

The UK defined benefit schemes include defined contribution sections with account balances totalling £693 million at 31st December 2007 (2006 – £609 million, 2005 – £515 million).

During 2007, the Group made special funding contributions to the UK pension schemes totalling £285 million (2006 – £346 million to the UK and US pension schemes). In 2006, GSK formalised an agreement with the trustees of the UK defined benefit pension schemes to make additional contributions of up to £325 million per year in addition to the normal contributions, over a four-year period ending 31st December 2009 in order to eliminate the then pension deficits on an IAS 19 basis.

Employer contributions for 2008, including special funding contributions, are estimated to be approximately £200 million in respect of defined benefit pension schemes and £40 million in respect of post-retirement benefits.

History of experience gains and losses	UK £m	USA £m	Rest of World £m	Pensions Group £m	Post-retirement benefits Group £m
2007					
Experience gains/(losses) of scheme assets (£m)	168	46	(18)	**196**	
Percentage of scheme assets at 31st December 2007	2%	2%	2%	**2%**	
Experience (losses)/gains of scheme liabilities (£m)	33	(30)	6	**9**	–
Percentage of scheme obligations at 31st December 2007	–	2%	1%	**–**	–
Fair value of assets	7,293	2,004	885	**10,182**	–
Present value of scheme obligations	(7,371)	(1,945)	(1,022)	**(10,338)**	**(1,019)**
(Deficits)/surpluses in the schemes	(78)	59	(137)	**(156)**	**(1,019)**

History of experience gains and losses	UK £m	USA £m	Rest of World £m	Pensions Group £m	Post-retirement benefits Group £m
2006					
Experience gains of scheme assets (£m)	227	168	26	**421**	
Percentage of scheme assets at 31st December 2006	3%	9%	4%	**5%**	
Experience (losses)/gains of scheme liabilities (£m)	(37)	(16)	(42)	**(95)**	17
Percentage of scheme obligations at 31st December 2006	–	1%	4%	**1%**	2%
Fair value of assets	6,554	1,953	741	**9,248**	–
Present value of scheme obligations	(7,444)	(1,949)	(952)	**(10,345)**	**(1,063)**
(Deficits)/surpluses in the schemes	(890)	4	(211)	**(1,097)**	**(1,063)**
2005					
Experience gains of scheme assets (£m)	647	3	35	**685**	
Percentage of scheme assets at 31st December 2005	11%	–	5%	**8%**	
Experience losses of scheme liabilities (£m)	(94)	(10)	(35)	**(139)**	(4)
Percentage of scheme obligations at 31st December 2005	1%	–	4%	**1%**	–
Fair value of assets	5,744	1,976	657	**8,377**	–
Present value of scheme obligations	(7,054)	(2,150)	(922)	**(10,126)**	**(1,308)**
Deficits in the schemes	(1,310)	(174)	(265)	**(1,749)**	**(1,308)**

Chapter 33

2004

Experience gains of scheme assets (£m)	196	86	23	**305**	
Percentage of scheme assets at 31st December 2004	4%	5%	4%	**5%**	
Experience (losses)/gains of scheme liabilities (£m)	(25)	(5)	(18)	**(48)**	47
Percentage of scheme obligations at 31st December 2004	–	–	2%	**1%**	5%
Fair value of assets	4,561	1,638	547	**6,746**	–
Present value of scheme obligations	(5,735)	(1,750)	(761)	**(8,246)**	(1,005)
Deficits in the schemes	(1,174)	(112)	(214)	**(1,500)**	(1,005)

2003

Experience gains of scheme assets (£m)	336	231	33	**600**	
Percentage of scheme assets at 31st December 2003	8%	15%	7%	**10%**	
Experience (losses)/gains of scheme liabilities (£m)	(183)	5	(19)	**(197)**	(123)
Percentage of scheme obligations at 31st December 2003	3%	–	3%	**2%**	13%
Fair value of assets	3,955	1,583	444	**5,982**	–
Present value of scheme obligations	(5,508)	(1,751)	(707)	**(7,966)**	(951)
Deficits in the schemes	(1,553)	(168)	(263)	**(1,984)**	(951)

Sensitivity analysis

Effect of changes in assumptions used on the annual defined benefit pension and post-retirement costs or the benefit obligations:

	£m
A 0.25% decrease in discount rate would have the following approximate effect:	
Increase in annual pension cost	8
Increase in annual post-retirement benefits cost	–
Increase in pension obligation	374
Increase in post-retirement benefits obligation	29
A one year increase in life expectancy would have the following approximate effect:	
Increase in annual pension cost	17
Increase in annual post-retirement benefits cost	3
Increase in pension obligation	231
Increase in post-retirement benefits obligation	38
A 0.25% decrease in expected rates of returns on assets would have the following approximate effect:	
Increase in annual pension cost	24
A 1% increase in the rate of future healthcare inflation would have the following approximate effect:	
Increase in annual post-retirement benefits cost	3
Increase in post-retirement benefits obligation	47
A 0.25% increase in inflation would have the following approximate effect:	
Increase in annual pension cost	26
Increase in pension obligation	317

7.3 Short-term employee benefits

IAS 19 has no specific disclosure requirements in respect of short-term employee benefits, but contains reminders that:

- IAS 24 requires disclosure of employee benefits for key management personnel (see Chapter 37); and
- IAS 1 requires disclosure of employee benefits expense. *[IAS 19.23].*

7.4 Long-term employee benefits

IAS 19 requires no specific disclosures in respect of other long-term benefits but notes that other IAS may require disclosure, for example where:

- the expense resulting from such benefits is material (as required by IAS 1 – see Chapter 3 at 3.2.6); or
- the expense relates to key management personnel (as required by IAS 24 – see Chapter 37 at 2.6.1). *[IAS 19.131].*

7.5 Termination benefits

IAS 19 contains no specific disclosure requirements for termination benefits, but notes that the following requirements of other IAS will be relevant:

- where an offer of termination benefits is made to employees and the number of employees who will accept it is uncertain, a contingent liability exists, details of which must be disclosed under IAS 37 (see Chapter 29 at 6.2), unless the possibility of an outflow in settlement is remote;
- termination benefits may be material, therefore the nature and amount of the expense will be disclosed as required by IAS 1 (see Chapter 3 at 3.2.6); and
- termination benefits payable to key management personnel will be disclosed under IAS 24 (see Chapter 37 at 2.6.1). *[IAS 19.142-143].*

8 IAS 19(2011) FOR PERIODS BEGINNING ON OR AFTER 1 JANUARY 2013

On 16 June 2011 the IASB issued a revised version of IAS 19 *Employee Benefits*, which is effective from 1 January 2013. Of the numerous changes, many are simple re-wording or clarifications. There are some fundamental changes and these are discussed in the rest of this section.

8.1 Full balance sheet recognition of defined benefit plans

The two methods of deferring the recognition of actuarial gains and losses on post-employment defined benefit plans (described at 5.3.1 above) have been removed. This means balance sheets will contain the net surplus or deficit in a plan, being the fair value of plan assets less the present value of the defined benefit obligation. *[IAS 19(2011).63].* Any surplus will continue to be restricted to the present value of any economic benefits available in the form of refunds from the plan or reductions in future contributions to the plan. *[IAS 19(2011).8, 64].* This will be a significant change for entities currently deferring the recognition of actuarial variances, introducing more balance sheet volatility.

Actuarial gains and losses will be recognised in other comprehensive income. *[IAS 19(2011).120]*. The option to recognise actuarial variance in full in profit or loss is withdrawn.

8.2   Amounts recognised in profit and loss

The following amounts will be recognised in profit or loss:

- current service cost;
- past service cost;
- gains and losses on curtailments;
- gains and losses on settlements; and
- net interest on the defined benefit asset or liability. *[IAS 19(2011).120]*

Under IAS 19(2011) past service costs will be recognised immediately rather than over the period during which they vest. Past service cost and curtailments will be recognised as an expense at the earlier of:

(a)   when they occur, being:

   (i)   for past service costs, when the change to the plan is made;

   (ii)   for a curtailment, when an entity significantly reduces the number of employees covered by a plan; and

(b)   when the entity recognises related restructuring costs in accordance with IAS 37 or termination benefits. *[IAS 19(2011).103-105]*.

Net interest on the net defined benefit liability or asset is computed by multiplying the net defined benefit liability (asset) by the discount rate used to measure the defined benefit liability, both as determined at the start of the annual reporting period, taking account of any changes in the net defined benefit liability (asset) during the period as a result of contributions and benefit payments. *[IAS 19(2011).123]*. The discount rate remains the yield on a high quality corporate bond (see 5.2.2.E above).

This means that asset returns are treated in a markedly different fashion. The treatment in IAS 19(1998) is to credit income with an expected rate of return based on the asset fair values at the start of the period (see 5.5.3 above). IAS 19(2011) replaces that return with the yield on high quality corporate bonds, irrespective of the composition of the assets concerned.

8.3   Short-term vs other long-term employee benefits

Under IAS 19(2011) a benefit is classified as short-term if it is expected to be settled within a year of the period end. *[IAS 19(2011).8]*. Those which are not are classified as other long-term employee benefits. In other words, the entitlement of the employee to require settlement is no longer the determining factor. In circumstances when employees can choose when the obligation is settled, an estimate of when they will do so is needed to determine the classification.

8.4 Termination benefits

IAS 19(2011) requires termination benefits to be recognised at the earlier of the following dates:

(a) when the entity can no longer withdraw the offer of those benefits; and

(b) when the entity recognises costs for a restructuring that is within the scope of IAS 37 and involves the payment of termination benefits. *[IAS 19(2011).165]*

The date in (a) above has a defined meaning in the standard which is different in different circumstances.

Where an employee's accepts an offer of benefits in exchange for the termination of employment, the time when an entity can no longer withdraw the offer is the earlier of:

(a) when the employee accepts the offer; and

(b) when a restriction (e.g. a legal, regulatory or contractual requirement or other restriction) on the entity's ability to withdraw the offer takes effect. *[IAS 19(2011).166].*

For benefits payable as a result of an entity's unilateral decision to terminate an employee's employment, the entity can no longer withdraw the offer when the entity has communicated to the affected employees a plan of termination meeting all of the following criteria:

(a) actions required to complete the plan indicate that it is unlikely that significant changes to the plan will be made;

(b) the plan identifies the number of employees whose employment is to be terminated, their job classifications or functions and their locations (but the plan need not identify each individual employee) and the expected completion date; and

(c) the plan establishes the termination benefits that employees will receive in sufficient detail that employees can determine the type and amount of benefits they will receive when their employment is terminated. *[IAS 19(2011).167]*

8.5 Disclosure requirements

IAS 19(2011), like its predecessor, has extensive disclosure requirements. The standard requires disclosure of information that:

(a) explains the characteristics of its defined benefit plans and risks associated with them;

(b) identifies and explains the amounts in its financial statements arising from its defined benefit plans; and

(c) describes how its defined benefit plans may affect the amount, timing and uncertainty of the entity's future cash flows. *[IAS 19(2011).135].*

To achieve the above, the standard sets out a long and detailed list of narrative and numerical disclosure.

The Board also noted that entities must comply with the general materiality requirements of IAS 1 (discussed in Chapter 3 at 4.1.5), including the requirement to disclose additional information if necessary, and that the financial statements need not contain disclosures that are not material. *[IAS 19(2011).BC209].*

One of the Board's objectives in regard to disclosure was to ensure that financial statements provide relevant information that is not obscured by excessive detail. *[IAS 19(2011).BC207].*

These references to excessive detail and non-disclosure of immaterial items suggest the Board is expecting entities to apply judgement regarding the level of detail to be provided rather than giving everything set out in the standard.

In our view this is a worthy aim and would, perhaps, have been better set out in the standard itself. It remains to be seen what entities will do in practice.

9   POSSIBLE FUTURE DEVELOPMENTS

As discussed at 8 above, the IASB published a revised standard in June 2011. This represents the first phase in what was originally to be a two phase project. The second phase was to be a comprehensive review of all aspects of the standard. The IASB's website is now entirely silent on the matter of a second phase and the revised standard contains the following. 'The discussion paper included proposals on contribution-based promises. The Board will consider whether to develop those proposals further if it undertakes a comprehensive review of employee benefit accounting.' *[IAS 19(2011).BC13].* The use of 'if' and the removal of the discussion of the project from the website, seem to suggest the Board has lost appetite for a second phase.

References

1 E54, *Exposure Draft E54 Proposed International Accounting Standard: Employee Benefits*, IASC, October 1996.
2 Exposure Draft, *Amendments to IAS 19 Employee Benefits – Actuarial Gains and Losses, Group Plans and Disclosures*, IASB, April 2004.
3 *Amendment to International Accounting Standard 19 Employee Benefits Actuarial Gains and Losses, Group Plans and Disclosures*, IASB, December 2004.
4 *Exposure Draft Of Proposed Amendments to IAS 37 Provisions, Contingent Liabilities and Contingent Assets and IAS 19 Employee Benefits*, IASB, June 2005.
5 E54.17-21.
6 *IFRIC Update*, January 2008, Page 3.
7 *IASB Update*, September 2007, Page 5.
8 *IASB Update*, November 2007, Page 2.
9 *IFRIC Update,* July 2011
10 *IFRIC Update*, June 2005, pages 4 and 5.
11 In the UK, *Statement of Principles for Financial Reporting*, ASB, December 1999. In the US, seven *Statements of Financial Accounting Concepts*, FASB, 1978-2000.
12 E54.109-110.

Chapter 34   Operating segments

List of examples

Chapter 34　　　　Operating segments

1　INTRODUCTION

1.1　Background

In January 2005 the IASB elected to replace its existing standard, IAS 14 – *Segment Reporting* – and converge with the requirements of FASB ASC Topic 280 – *Segment Reporting*.[1] It published IFRS 8 – *Operating Segments*, in November 2006.

IFRS 8 became mandatory for accounting periods beginning on or after 1 January 2009, with earlier application permitted. *[IFRS 8.35]*. The standard also amended IAS 34 – *Interim Financial Reporting* – and IAS 36 – *Impairment of Assets* – from that date (see Chapter 39 at 4.4 and Chapter 18 at 5.1.1 respectively).

While IFRS 8 was issued as a converged standard, it should be noted that it is different from its US counterpart, FASB ASC Topic 280, in three key respects. *[IFRS 8.BC60]*.

- IFRS 8 requires disclosures about 'non-current assets' including intangibles, when FASB ASC Topic 280 refers only to 'long-lived assets', which excludes intangible assets;

- IFRS 8 requires information to be given about segment liabilities (if this forms part of the data presented to the chief operating decision maker). There is no equivalent requirement in FASB ASC Topic 280; and

- whereas under the US standard entities managed under a matrix structure must determine operating segments based on products and services, this is not mandated in IFRS 8.

In its April 2009 *Improvements to IFRSs* the IASB amended its requirements concerning the disclosure of information about segment assets to apply only if such amounts are regularly provided to the chief operating decision maker. *[IFRS 8.23]*. The amendment, which applied for annual periods beginning on or after 1 January 2010, made the requirements of the standard the same for segment assets and segment liabilities and reflected the Board's understanding of the way that the segment asset disclosure requirements in FASB ASC Topic 280 had been interpreted for some time. *[IFRS 8.BC35A]*.

In Europe, the proposal to replace IAS 14 with IFRS 8 was controversial. Opponents to its introduction shared concerns expressed in the dissenting opinions of two IASB members that the lack of a defined measure of segment profit or loss and the absence of any requirement for that measure to be consistent with the attribution of assets to reportable segments would encourage the proliferation of non-GAAP measures that could mislead users.[2] These concerns were raised in the European Parliament together with questions about the governance of the IASB, as a result of which the process to endorse IFRS 8 in the European Union was not completed until November 2007, a year after the standard had been published.

During this period, the IFRS Foundation announced enhancements to oversight and due process to include a requirement for the IASB to conduct 'a review of issues identified as contentious as part of the consultation process related to all new IFRSs (including IFRS 8), major amendments to IFRSs and major IFRIC interpretations'. Such a review would be performed after at least two full years of implementation and be completed within three years of the pronouncement's effective date.[3] In its endorsement resolution, the European Parliament stated that the IASB should carry out a review of the new standard within 2 years of its implementation. Furthermore, it requires the European Commission to 'follow closely the application of IFRS 8 and report back to the Parliament not later than 2011, inter alia regarding the reporting of geographical segments, segment profit or loss, and use of non-IFRS measures' and underlines that if the Commission identifies deficiencies in application it has a duty to rectify them.[4]

IFRS 8 is the first standard for which the IASB committed to perform such a post-implementation review. This commitment has since been extended to the 2008 revisions of IFRS 3 – *Business Combinations* – and IAS 27 – *Consolidated and Separate Financial Statements* – and to those new IFRSs with an effective date of 2013. In its July 2011 Agenda Consultation, the IASB indicated that the post-implementation review of IFRS 8 will commence in the second half of 2011.[5]

1.2   The main features of IFRS 8

IFRS 8 is a disclosure standard. IFRS 8 specifies the way an entity should report information about its operating segments in annual financial statements and, as a consequential amendment to IAS 34 – *Interim Financial Reporting*, requires an entity to report selected information about its operating segments in interim financial reports (see Chapter 39). It also sets out requirements for related disclosures about an entity's products and services, geographical areas and major customers. *[IFRS 8.IN4]*. The disclosures required include:

- descriptive information about the entity's reportable segments, which are operating segments or aggregations of operating segments that meet the criteria in the standard for separate disclosure; *[IFRS 8.IN5]*
- segment revenues and a measure of profit or loss for each reportable segment, reconciled to the amounts disclosed in the entity's financial statements; *[IFRS 8.IN6]*
- a measure of segment assets, segment liabilities and particular income and expense items to the extent that such information is regularly provided to the chief operating decision maker of the entity, reconciled to the amounts disclosed in the entity's financial statements; *[IFRS 8.IN6]*

- unless the information is not available and the cost of its development would be excessive, information about the revenues derived from the entity's products and services (or groups of similar products and services), about the countries in which it earns revenues and holds assets, and about major customers, regardless of whether this information is used by management in making operating decisions; and *[IFRS 8.IN7]*

- descriptive information about the way that operating segments were determined, the products and services provided by the segments, differences between the measurements used in reporting segment information and those used in the entity's financial statements, and changes in the measurement of segment amounts from period to period. *[IFRS 8.IN8]*.

The process of identifying operating segments for external reporting purposes begins with the information used by the entity's chief operating decision maker to assess performance and to make decisions about future allocations of resources. *[IFRS 8.5]*. Entities applying IFRS 8 report on a single set of components according to the way that the business is sub-divided for management reporting purposes. *[IFRS 8.IN11]*.

If a component of an entity is managed as a separate segment, IFRS 8 requires it to be treated as such even if it sells exclusively or primarily to internal customers. *[IFRS 8.IN12]*.

IFRS 8 does not go so far as to require an entity to report all the information that is reviewed by the chief operating decision maker, recognising that such detail may not be useful to users of financial statements and could be cumbersome in its presentation. Instead it allows entities to aggregate components and to disclose information only for those segments that exceed certain quantitative criteria.[6]

Under IFRS 8, the amounts reported about identified segments are prepared according to the manner in which information is presented to the entity's chief operating decision maker. *[IFRS 8.IN13]*.

IFRS 8 requires an entity to describe the factors used to identify the entity's operating segments, including a description of the basis of organisation. This description would explain whether the organisation is structured according to products and services, geographical areas, regulatory environments or other factors and state whether operating segments have been aggregated for reporting purposes. In addition, the entity must describe the types of products and services from which each reportable segment derives its revenues. *[IFRS 8.IN15]*.

IFRS 8 specifies amounts which should be disclosed about each reportable segment, but only if those measures are included in the measure of profit or loss used by, or otherwise regularly provided to, the chief operating decision maker (see 5.2 below). *[IFRS 8.IN16]*. These specified amounts include a requirement to report separately interest revenue and interest expense by segment (but only if those measures are included in the measure of profit or loss used, or otherwise regularly provided to the by the chief operating decision maker) unless a majority of the segment's revenues is derived from interest and performance is assessed primarily on the basis of net interest revenue. *[IFRS 8.IN17]*.

Certain 'entity-wide disclosures' are also required to be provided under IFRS 8, even if the entity has only one reportable segment (see 5.8 below). Entity-wide information is disclosed for the entity as a whole about its products and services, geographical areas and major customers, regardless of the way the entity is organised and the information presented to the chief operating decision maker. *[IFRS 8.IN18]*. The amounts reported for this entity-wide information is based on the financial information used to produce the entity's financial statements. *[IFRS 8.32-33]*.

There is no 'competitive harm' exemption in IFRS 8 from the requirement to disclose segment information, or components of such information, for example on the grounds of commercial sensitivity, confidentiality or being otherwise detrimental to the entity's competitive position. *[IFRS 8.BC43-45]*.

1.3   Terms used in IFRS 8

The following terms are used in IFRS 8 with the meanings specified:

Term	Meaning
Operating segment	A component of an entity: *[IFRS 8.5 Appendix A]*. (a) that engages in business activities from which it may earn revenues and incur expenses (including revenues and expenses relating to transactions with other components or the same entity); (b) whose operating results are regularly reviewed by the entity's chief operating decision maker to make decisions about resources to be allocated to the segment and assess its performance; and (c) for which discrete financial information is available.
Chief operating decision maker	The function of allocating resources to and assessing the performance of the operating segments of an entity. This is not necessarily a manager with a specific title, but can be an entity's chief executive officer, chief operating officer, a group of executive directors or others. *[IFRS 8.7]*.
Segment manager	The function of being directly accountable to and maintaining regular contact with the chief operating decision maker to discuss operating activities, financial results, forecasts, or plans for the segment. *[IFRS 8.9]*.
Reportable segment	An operating segment or a group of two or more operating segments determined to be eligible for aggregation in accordance with IFRS 8.12; and which exceeds the quantitative thresholds in IFRS 8.13. *[IFRS 8.11]*.
Aggregation criteria	Two or more operating segments may be aggregated into a single operating segment if aggregation is consistent with the core principle of IFRS 8, they have similar economic characteristics, such as long-term average gross margins, and are similar in each of the following respects: *[IFRS 8.12]* (a) the nature of the products and services; (b) the nature of the production processes; (c) the type or class of customer for their products and services;

(d) the methods used to distribute their products or provide their services;

(e) if applicable, the nature of the regulatory environment, for example, banking, insurance or public utilities.

Quantitative thresholds	Information about an operating segment that meets any of the following criteria: *[IFRS 8.13]*
	(a) its reported revenue, including both sales to external customers and intersegment sales or transfers, is 10% or more of combined revenue, internal and external, of all operating segments; or
	(b) its reported profit or loss is, in absolute terms, 10% or more of the greater of, in absolute amount:
	(i) the combined profit of all operating segments that did not report a loss; and
	(ii) the combined reported loss of all operating segments that reported a loss; or
	(c) its assets are 10% or more of the combined assets of all operating segments.

2 OBJECTIVE AND SCOPE OF IFRS 8

2.1 Objective

The objective of IFRS 8 is expressed as a 'core principle', being that an entity shall disclose information to enable users of its financial statements evaluate the nature and financial effects of the business activities in which it engages and the economic environments in which it operates. *[IFRS 8.1]*.

2.2 Scope of IFRS 8

IFRS 8 applies to both the separate or individual financial statements of an entity and the consolidated financial statements of a group with a parent: *[IFRS 8.2]*

(a) whose debt or equity instruments are traded in a public market (a domestic or foreign stock exchange or an over-the-counter market, including local and regional markets), or

(b) that files, or is in the process of filing, its financial statements with a securities commission or other regulatory organisation for the purpose of issuing any class of instruments in a public market.

The Board has confirmed that for consolidated financial statements, the above test is applied to the parent entity alone. *[IFRS 8.BC23]*, Therefore, IFRS 8 does not apply to a group headed by a parent that has no listed financial instruments, even if the group includes a subsidiary that has any of its equity or debt instruments traded in a public market. The scope of IAS 33 – *Earnings per Share* – has been similarly redefined. *[IFRS 8.BC23]*. Of course, a subsidiary with publicly traded debt or equity instruments would be required to provide segment information under IFRS 8 in its own financial statements.

Chapter 34

2.2.1   The meaning of 'traded in a public market'

The standard describes a 'public market' to include a domestic or foreign stock exchange or an over-the-counter market, including local and regional markets, *[IFRS 8.2]*, but does not define what would make some markets 'public' and others not.

In our view, a market is 'public' where buyers and sellers (market participants) can transact with one another (directly; through agents; and including in a secondary market) at a price determined in that market. A public market does not exist where the buyers and sellers can transact only with the entity itself (or an agent acting on its behalf). The requirement for an entity to list its securities on a stock exchange is not the sole factor determining whether the entity is in the scope of IFRS 8. Its securities must be *traded* in a public market meeting the criteria noted above.

Example 34.1:   The meaning of 'public market' in the context of a fund

Many investment funds are listed on a public stock exchange for informational purposes, in particular to facilitate the valuation of portfolios by investors or because it is a requirement for the fund to be listed on a public stock exchange to make it eligible for investment by entities that are required to invest only in listed securities. However, in spite of such a listing, subscriptions and redemptions are handled by a fund administrator or a transfer agent (acting on behalf of the fund) and no transactions are undertaken on the public stock exchange. In addition, the prices for those transactions are determined by the fund agreement, such as on the basis of the fund's Net Asset Value, rather than the price quoted on the public stock exchange.

In our view the debt or equity instruments of such entities are not traded on a public market and so the entity would not fall within the scope of IFRS 8.

2.2.2   Consolidated financial statements presented with those of the parent

Where both the consolidated financial statements and the parent's separate or individual financial statements are contained in the same financial report, segment information is only required in the consolidated financial statements. *[IFRS 8.4]*.

2.2.3   Extending the scope of IFRS 8 to 'publicly accountable entities'

It had been proposed in the exposure draft that preceded IFRS 8 (ED 8 – *Operating Segments*) that the scope of the standard be extended to require entities which hold assets in a fiduciary capacity for a broad group of outsiders to provide segment information, even if those entities do not issue securities that are publicly traded. Examples included a non-listed bank, insurance company, securities broker/dealer, mutual fund or investment banking entity.[7] The IASB removed this requirement following concerns raised by respondents to the exposure draft that terms like 'fiduciary capacity' or wider concepts of public accountability would not be adequately defined until the Board had completed its project on small and medium-sized entities. When it issued IFRS 8, the IASB indicated that an amendment to the standard would be issued together with the IFRS for Small and Medium-sized Entities, to bring publicly accountable entities within the scope of IFRS 8. *[IFRS 8.BC18-20]*. Whilst an amendment to IFRS 8 was not a feature of the IFRS for Small and Medium-sized Entities issued in July 2009, the definition of a publicly accountable entity in the latter uses similar wording to the intended scope of ED 8.[8]

2.2.4 Entities providing segment information on a voluntary basis

In entities for which the standard is not mandatory, IAS 14 required and ED 8 proposed that any voluntary disclosures in financial statements that comply with IFRS should meet in full the requirements of the standard. This constraint was relaxed in light of responses to the exposure draft. The Board accepted that an entity outside the scope of IFRS 8 should be allowed to disclose information, for example about sales by segment, without triggering the need to comply fully with the standard, provided that such disclosure is not referred to as 'segment information'. *[IFRS 8.BC22].* Consequently, entities giving information about segments on a voluntary basis cannot describe that information as 'segment information' unless it has been prepared in compliance with IFRS 8. *[IFRS 8.3].*

3 IDENTIFYING A SINGLE SET OF OPERATING SEGMENTS

IFRS 8 adopts a 'bottom up' approach to determining the level of detail required for segment reporting in the notes to the financial statements. It requires the entity's revenue earning activities to be divided into operating segments (based on the same components used by management to run the business) and only allows that information to be aggregated for reporting purposes if specific criteria are met. This process can involve considerable judgement, as it may not always be immediately clear what activities are operating segments for the purposes of the standard or which layer of the entity's organisational structure represents the level at which those activities are managed. This is particularly the case when management information is presented in a number of different ways (for example by product, by geographical market and by legal entity) or where management structures distinguish operational, strategic and oversight responsibilities.

Notwithstanding such difficulties, the requirement is to identify a single set of components as constituting the entity's operating segments. *[IFRS 8.8].*

The process for determining operating segments is important not only to entities applying IFRS 8, but also to entities implementing the requirements of IAS 36 – *Impairment of Assets* – for testing indefinite-lived intangibles and goodwill for impairment. As such, IFRS 8 can affect the financial statements of entities to which the disclosure requirements in IFRS 8 do not apply, such as those without traded equity or debt. This is because a group of cash-generating units (CGUs) for impairment testing purposes cannot be larger than an operating segment (as determined below). *[IAS 36.80b].* See Chapter 22 at 5.1.

3.1 Definition of an operating segment

An operating segment is defined as a component of an entity: *[IFRS 8.5]*

(a) that engages in business activities from which it may earn revenues and incur expenses (including revenues and expenses relating to transactions with other components of the same entity);

(b) whose operating results are regularly reviewed by the entity's chief operating decision maker to make decisions about resources to be allocated to the segment and assess its performance; and

(c) for which discrete financial information is available.

This means that the search for an entity's operating segments starts with the smallest components of the business for which information about profit is presented for use by the entity's chief operating decision maker (sometimes referred to as 'CODM').

3.1.1   *Revenue earning business activities*

A significant feature of an operating segment is the potential for revenue generation rather than actually earning revenues in the reporting period. Accordingly, a start-up operation can be treated as an operating segment while it has yet to earn revenues. *[IFRS 8.5]*.

However, not every part of an entity is necessarily an operating segment. For example, a corporate headquarters or a functional department (such as a centralised data processing centre) that either does not earn revenues or for which revenues are only incidental to the activities of the entity would not be an operating segment for the purposes of the standard. Similarly, an entity's post-employment benefit plans would not be regarded as operating segments. *[IFRS 8.6]*.

3.1.2   *'Chief operating decision maker' and 'segment manager'*

Arguably the most important judgements made in implementing IFRS 8 relate to the identification of the entity's chief operating decision maker. The nature of what is ultimately disclosed in the financial statements about operating segments and the level of detail (or segmentation) required is directly related to the information regularly provided to the chief operating decision maker.

References in the standard to 'chief operating decision maker' are to the function of allocating resources and assessing performance of the operating segments and not to a manager with a specific title. Often the chief operating decision maker of an entity is its chief executive officer or chief operating officer, but the term could refer equally to a group of executive directors or others charged with that role. *[IFRS 8.7]*.

The determination of chief operating decision maker will not be the same for all entities applying IFRS 8 and will depend upon the particular facts and circumstances applying to each entity. However, in stating that the term could apply to a group of executive directors or others, *[IFRS 8.7]*, the standard is clear that the function of CODM is an executive role. The Interpretations Committee confirmed this view in 2011. While it is observed that in practice the functions of CODM are sometimes carried out by multiple persons and that all such persons involved in those activities would be part of the CODM group, the Committee noted that the CODM would not normally include non-executive directors.[9] For example, an entity may have a single board of executive and non-executive directors which reviews the performance of individual business units, makes decisions about the operating budgets for those businesses and reviews significant applications for investment. In that case, the full board could be identified as the chief operating decision maker. However, if the entity also has a sub-committee of executive directors or another grouping of key management personnel (sometimes referred to as an 'operational board'), this smaller group of executives would be identified as the chief operating decision maker. Essentially, the chief operating decision maker is found at the most senior executive decision-making level of an organisation and as such should be distinguished from higher levels of management fulfilling primarily an oversight or approval role and who, to reflect their non-executive function, are provided information at a more aggregated level as a matter of course.

Another important distinction to be made is between the function of 'segment manager' and chief operating decision maker. The segment manager is accountable to and maintains regular contact with the chief operating decision maker to discuss operating activities, financial results, forecasts or plans for the segment. The chief operating decision maker may also fulfil the role of segment manager for some operating segments and a single segment manager may be responsible for more than one operating segment. *[IFRS 8.9].* These considerations are relevant to the identification of an entity's operating segments and not to how they might be reported in the financial statements. Accordingly, separate operating segments which otherwise meet the definition at 3.1 above are not combined simply because they have a common segment manager. The standard is clear that such segments are only combined if they exhibit similar long-term economic characteristics and are similar in respect of the qualitative criteria set out at 3.2.1 below. *[IFRS 8.12].* In addition, because the oversight role of the CODM is separate from the operational role of the segment manager, it is possible that an entity could regard an investee accounted for by the equity method as an operating segment.

A common situation in practice is that detailed financial information is provided or available to the chief operating decision maker on a regular basis about various levels of management and operational activity within an entity. In these circumstances, the interplay between the three criteria at 3.1 above becomes very important, as the existence of more detailed internal reporting could otherwise lead to a determination that there are more operating segments. If the three criteria apply to more than one set of components of an entity, but there is only one set that has segment managers, generally the set of components with segment managers constitutes the operating segments. *[IFRS 8.8].*

Example 34.2:   Identifying operating segments – CODM and segment manager

The diagram above sets out the internal reporting structure of Entity A. The CODM receives financial information about the entity's operations, the most detailed of which (including revenue and operating profit) relates to the six business units (Shoes, Trousers, Shirts, Watches, Equipment and Souvenirs). However, these units do not have their own segment manager. Instead, the six business units are grouped into three divisions (Clothing, Accessories and Sporting Goods), each of which has a segment manager who reports directly to the CODM. The three divisions report financial information to the CODM who uses it to assess performance and allocate resources.

In this case, the entity decides that the operating segments as defined in IFRS 8 comprise the three divisions as opposed to the six business units, because only the divisions have segment managers.

Proper application of the requirements of IFRS 8 requires a clear understanding of what information is given to the chief operating decision maker and how the CODM uses that information, in conjunction with the segment managers. In the above example, the fact that the CODM receives detailed financial information about activities below the divisional level could raise doubts about the determination that the divisions represent the entity's operating segments, rather than the business units. In these circumstances, entities would be required to demonstrate that:

- The more detailed information is not used by the CODM to assess performance and allocate resources.

- Segment managers operate only at the divisional level and are not, in effect, managers for each of the business units in their division. As noted above, components otherwise meeting the characteristics of an operating segment under IFRS 8 are not combined simply because they share a segment manager.

It might be evident from the records of the discussions between segment managers and the CODM that results are monitored at divisional rather than at business unit level. It might equally be clear from the records of board meetings that more detailed information is not referred to by the CODM in its deliberations. However, there is evidence that when regulators and other enforcement agencies assess the quality of an entity's compliance with IFRS 8, they adopt the presumption that the CODM uses whatever detailed information is provided to him/her on a regular basis for its decision-making and assessment purposes. Such a presumption is not unreasonable, since at best the provision of information that management does not use is an inefficient use of resources.

3.1.3   *Availability of discrete financial information*

As noted above, a component of an entity can only be regarded as an operating segment if discrete financial information is available about that component. *[IFRS 8.5(c)]*. This requirement relates solely to the existence of discrete information that allows the chief operating decision maker to make decisions about the allocation of resources and to assess the performance of that component.

Accordingly, a component of an entity is still regarded as an operating segment if the only information available relates to the profitability of that component. Such information would be sufficient for the chief operating decision maker to review its operating results, assess performance and make decisions about resource allocation. *[IFRS 8.5(b)]*. The financial information is not rendered useless by the lack of, for example, a separate balance sheet or a separate statement of cash flows for that component.

However, it would be unlikely that a component of an entity could be regarded as an operating segment solely because the chief operating decision maker receives information about revenue from that component. Without a measure of the component's operating results it would be difficult to make meaningful assessments of the effect of allocating more or less resource to that activity. As such, information on revenue alone would have limited value in decision making. Therefore, the search for an entity's operating segments starts with the smallest components of the business for which information about profit is provided to the entity's chief operating decision maker.

3.1.4 When a single set of components is not immediately apparent

For many entities, the search for operating segments is concluded after applying the three criteria listed at 3.1 above.

However, in cases where a single set of operating segments cannot be identified clearly by applying the above criteria, for example in an entity where its business activities are reported internally and assessed in a variety of ways, IFRS 8 states that other factors should be considered, including the nature of the business activities of each component, the existence of a manager responsible for it, and the information presented to the board of directors. *[IFRS 8.8]*. Therefore, if an entity's activities are reported internally in a number of different ways, each with their own set of business components as defined above, but there is only one set to which segment managers are assigned, then that will comprise the operating segments to report in the financial statements for IFRS 8 purposes. *[IFRS 8.9]*. For example, if an entity's board of directors manages its business using information on revenues and costs analysed both by product grouping as well as by geographical market, but the management structure operates only on geographical lines, then the financial statements would include segmental information on a geographical basis.

A single set of operating segments must be identified, even where two or more sets of components of an entity are managed in a matrix structure, for example where financial information is available and performance is assessed and segment managers assigned not only on the basis of product and service lines worldwide but also by geographical area irrespective of products and service lines. In that situation the choice of a single set of components is a matter of judgement, made by reference to the core principle of the standard as set out in 2.1 above. *[IFRS 8.10]*. This requirement is different to FASB ASC Topic 280 and ED 8, which proposed that in such circumstances operating segments be drawn up on product and service lines.[10] The IASB agreed with respondents to the exposure draft that a default position mandating the use of components based on products and services was inconsistent with a management approach founded on what is important to the chief operating decision maker. *[IFRS 8.BC27]*.

3.2 Identifying externally reportable segments

Having identified a single set of internal operating segments, the standard describes how reportable segments are determined. As a minimum an entity must separately disclose information on reportable segments above a certain size (see 3.2.2 below). In addition, a previously identified reportable segment continues to be disclosed separately in the current period if management judges it to be of continuing significance, even if it no longer satisfies the quantitative thresholds. *[IFRS 8.17]*.

Thereafter, an entity is only compelled to give information on other segments (either individually or in certain circumstances on a combined basis) if the unallocated element is too large (see 3.2.4 below).

Chapter 34

The implementation guidance to IFRS 8 includes a diagram illustrating how to apply the main provisions of the standard for identifying reportable segments, which is reproduced below:

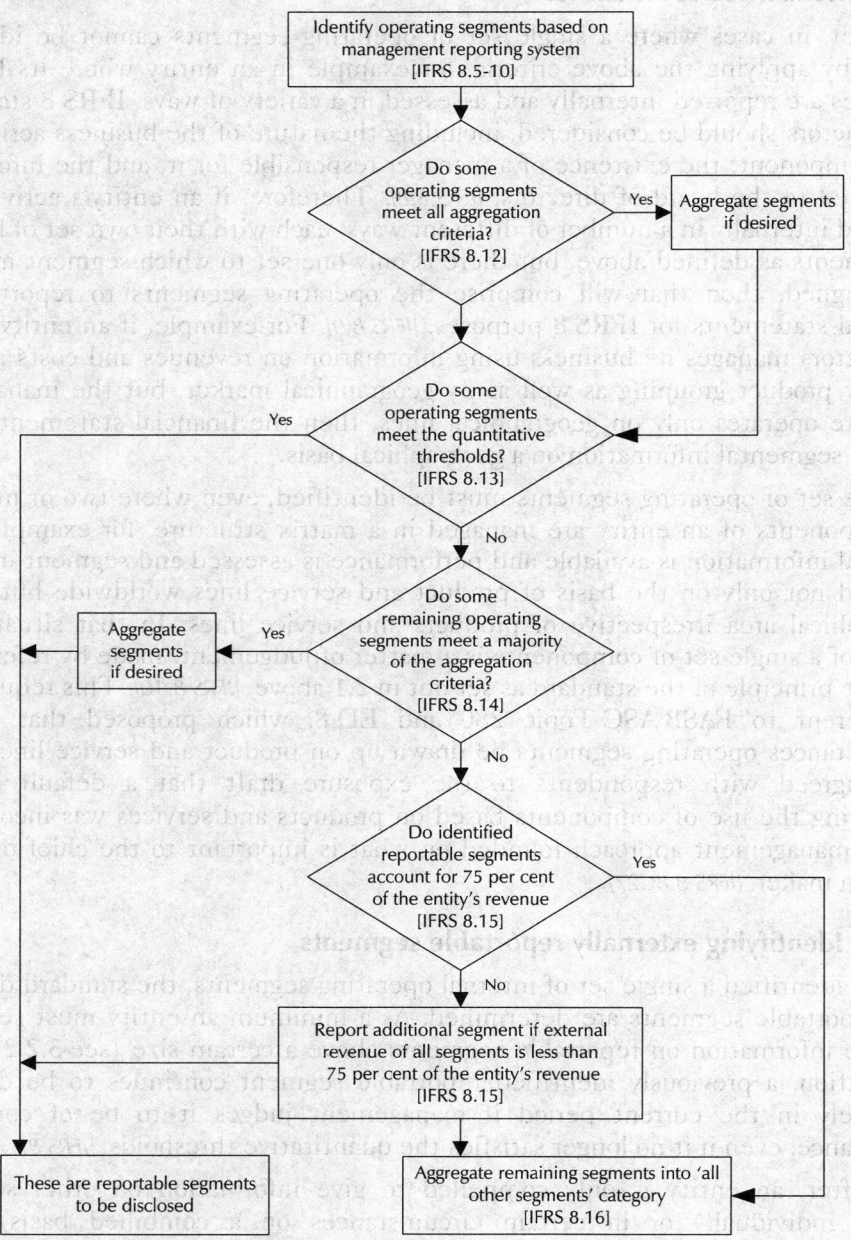

As indicated in the implementation guidance, the diagram is a visual supplement to the IFRS. It should not be interpreted as altering or adding to any requirements of the IFRS nor should it be regarded as a substitute for its requirements. *[IFRS 8.IG7].*

IFRS 8 does not permit the omission of segment information when management believe that its disclosure is commercially sensitive or potentially detrimental to the entity's competitive position. If the criteria for separate disclosure described at 3.2.2 and 3.2.4 below are met, an entity is compelled to give information on that operating segment in the financial statements. The IASB considered both a general 'competitive harm' exemption and a 'comply or explain' basis for disclosure and rejected both. *[IFRS 8.BC43-45]*.

3.2.1 Aggregation criteria – combining internally reported operating segments

Regardless of their size, two or more operating segments can be combined if they have similar economic characteristics (demonstrated, for example, by similar long-term average gross margins) and are similar in each of the following respects: *[IFRS 8.12]*

(a) the nature of the products and services;

(b) the nature of the production processes;

(c) the type or class of customer for the products and services;

(d) the methods used to distribute the products or provide the services; and

(e) if applicable, the nature of the regulatory environment.

At this stage in the process only segments which are similar in *all* the above respects can be combined. Further aggregation can only be achieved for segments which do not merit separate disclosure by virtue of their size (see 3.2.2 below).

Example 34.3: *Combining internally reported operating segments with similar characteristics*

In the information presented to the board of directors, a single-product company has six internally reported operating segments, Australia, France, Germany, Italy, UK and USA. The company dominates its markets in Australia and Germany and consequently enjoys superior operating profits. Its other markets are fragmented, competition is greater and therefore margins are lower. Can any segments be combined for external reporting purposes?

It would not be possible to combine operating segments with different underlying currency risks, as this is indicative of different economic characteristics. That would leave only France, Germany and Italy as candidates for combination, since they all operate within the Euro zone. However, Germany could not be included in a larger reportable segment because, whilst similar in all other ways, its long-term financial performance is not comparable to France and Italy, as evidenced by its superior operating profits. On this basis the company could only combine at this stage its operations in France and Italy for external segment reporting purposes.

It is important that entities do not overlook the requirement for operating segments to exhibit similar economic characteristics before considering the other factors allowing aggregation. The fact that certain operating segments have been selected by management as a separately reportable component of activities in the business would suggest that there are good commercial reasons why their performance is monitored separately by the chief operating decision maker and, therefore, might usefully be reported separately to users of the financial statements. Only if those components exhibit similar economic characteristics does their aggregation not compromise the entity's ability to achieve the core principle of IFRS 8, to disclose information that is useful to users of its financial statements. *[IFRS 8.BC32]*.

As can be seen in the above example, operating segments trading in clearly different economic environments (for example with unrelated functional currencies) should not be combined for segment reporting purposes (unless they are so small as to fall within the 'all other segments' category discussed at 3.2.4 below). As it states in the standard, the existence of similar long-term average gross margins would be a positive indicator. *[IFRS 8.12]*. So operating segments should not be combined if their long-term average gross margins are significantly different, even if they are similar in all the other respects noted above.

It follows that operating segments that have been profitable over the longer term should not be combined with segments that over the longer term have been consistently loss-making.

Nevertheless, the Interpretations Committee has acknowledged that IFRS 8 could usefully include further guidance on the meaning of 'similar economic characteristics' and the criteria for identifying similar segments listed in (a) to (e) above.[11]

3.2.2   Quantitative thresholds – operating segments which are reportable because of their size

IFRS 8 includes a number of quantitative measures for determining whether information on the identified operating segments should be reported separately. Accordingly, an operating segment (or combination of segments meeting the qualitative criteria for aggregation described at 3.2.1 above) merits separate disclosure if it meets any of the following thresholds: *[IFRS 8.13]*

(a)   its reported revenue (including both sales to external customers and intersegment sales or transfers) is 10% or more of the combined revenue (internal and external) of all operating segments; or

(b)   its reported profit or loss is, in absolute terms, 10% or more of the greater of:

(i) the combined profit of all operating segments that did not report a loss; or

(ii) the combined loss of all operating segments that reported a loss; or

(c)   its assets are 10% or more of the combined assets of all operating segments.

The definition in the standard of an operating segment includes a component of an entity earning revenues and incurring expenses relating to transactions with other components of the same entity. *[IFRS 8.5]*. Therefore an entity would have to report separately information on an operating segment that exceeds the above criteria, even if that segment earns a majority of its revenues from transactions with other components of the same entity.

Example 34.4: *Identifying reportable segments using the quantitative thresholds*

An entity divides its business into 9 operating units for internal reporting purposes and presents information to the Chief Operating Decision Maker as follows:

	Unit 1 £000	Unit 2 £000	Unit 3 £000	Unit 4 £000	Unit 5 £000	Unit 6 £000	Unit 7 £000	Unit 8 £000	Unit 9 £000	Total £000
Revenue:										
External	34,000	3,000	15,000	30,000	35,000	35,000	77,500	55,500	25,000	310,000
Internal	35,000	34,000	12,500	2,200	0	1,500	7,800	2,300	0	95,300
Total	69,000	37,000	27,500	32,200	35,000	36,500	85,300	57,800	25,000	405,300
Profit/(loss)	21,500	24,500	(4,500)	2,300	10,000	7,500	3,500	35,000	(21,250)	78,550
Assets	12,250	77,800	25,000	24,000	40,000	7,730	145,000	55,000	4,300	391,080

Assuming that none are eligible for aggregation under the qualitative aggregation criteria set out at 3.2.1 above, which units are required to be reported as operating segments in the entity's financial statements?

Applying the above quantitative thresholds, Units 1, 2, 5, 7, 8 and 9 should be identified as reportable segments, as follows:

- A Unit whose internal and external revenue is 10% or more of the total revenue of all segments is a reportable segment. On this criterion Unit 1 (17%), Unit 7 (21%) and Unit 8 (14%) are reportable segments.

- A Unit is a reportable segment if its profit or loss, in absolute terms, is 10% or more of the greater of the combined profits of all profitable segments or the combined losses of all segments in loss. The combined profit of all profitable segments is £104.3m, which is greater than the total of £25.75m for segments in loss. On this basis, Unit 1 (21%), Unit 2 (23%), Unit 8 (34%) and the loss-making Unit 9 (20%) are reportable segments.

- A Unit is also a reportable segment if the measure reported to the chief operating decision maker of its assets is 10% or more of the total reported measure of assets of all segments. On this test, Unit 5 (10%) joins the list of reportable segments, with Unit 2 (20%), Unit 7 (37%) and Unit 8 (14%) having been already identified under other criteria.

Only those segments that have similar economic characteristics (demonstrated, for example, by similar long-term average gross margins) and are similar in all of the qualitative criteria set out at 3.2.1 above could be combined into a larger segment for reporting purposes.

Even if an internally reported operating segment falls below all of the quantitative thresholds, it may still be considered as reportable, and separately disclosed, if management believes information about the segment would be useful to users of the financial statements. *[IFRS 8.13]*.

3.2.3 Combining small operating segments into a larger reportable segment

Operating segments which individually fall below the size criteria may be combined with other small operating segments into a single larger reporting segment provided that: *[IFRS 8.14]*

(a)   the operating segments being combined have similar economic characteristics; and

(b)   they share a majority of the criteria listed at 3.2.1 above.

For the avoidance of doubt, if an entity proposes to combine a small operating segment with one that exceeds any of the quantitative thresholds, they must share all of the criteria described in 3.2.1 above. The requirement that combining segments must demonstrate similar economic characteristics applies to combinations of both larger and smaller operating segments into reportable segments, without exception. Therefore, irrespective of their size, operating segments cannot be combined if they do not meet the criteria in 3.2.1.

3.2.4   'All other segments'

At this stage the entity has been divided into a single set of components, based on the elements reported to the chief operating decision maker. Components (operating segments) have been combined where permitted by the standard and the entity has identified a number of individual operating segments or groups of operating segments that are required to be disclosed separately in the financial statements because each exceeds the quantitative thresholds for a reportable segment. The entity may then be left with a number of operating segments which have not been identified as being reportable, as well as other business activities that are not an operating segment or part of an operating segment.

Information about other business activities and operating segments that are not reportable should be combined and disclosed in a separate category for 'all other segments'. *[IFRS 8.16]*. However, this residual category cannot be too large. If total external revenue for the operating segments already reported separately is less than 75% of the entity's revenue, the entity should identify additional operating segments for external reporting until the 75% target is reached. In this situation segments would have to be reported separately even if they fall below the quantitative thresholds described at 3.2.2 above and are not otherwise regarded as being significant. *[IFRS 8.15]*.

There is no requirement to identify as a reportable segment the next largest internally reported operating segment. The choice of additional reporting segments is aimed simply to reach the 75% threshold, as illustrated below.

Example 34.5:   Reaching the threshold of 75% of external revenue

In Example 34.4 above, Units 1, 2, 5, 7, 8 and 9 were identified as reportable segments. The total external revenue attributable to these reportable segments is £230m. This is only 74.2% of total external revenues and therefore less than the required 75% of total external revenue of £310m.

The entity is therefore required to identify additional segments as reportable segments, even if they do not meet the quantitative thresholds in 3.2.2 above. Unit 3, with external revenue of £15m (4.8%), Unit 4's external revenue of £30m (9.7%) and Unit 6's external revenue of £35m (11.3%) would each take the total above the required 75%. The entity can choose to present any of these as a reportable segment, leaving the others to be combined to form the item for 'all other segments'.

3.2.5   A 'practical limit' for the number of reported operating segments

IFRS 8 states that there may be a practical limit to the number of separately reportable segments beyond which segment information may become too detailed. Without prescribing such a limit, it suggests that an entity expecting to disclose more than 10 separate reportable segments should consider whether the practical limit has been reached. *[IFRS 8.19]*.

3.2.6 *Restatement of segments reported in comparative periods*

When an operating segment is identified as a reportable segment in accordance with the thresholds in 3.2.2 above for the first time, the prior period segment data that is presented for comparative purposes should be restated to reflect the newly reportable segment regardless of whether it would have satisfied the quantitative thresholds in the prior period. Only if the necessary information is not available and the cost to develop it would be excessive would prior periods not be restated. *[IFRS 8.18].*

4 MEASUREMENT

For an entity that does not present IFRS-compliant financial information to its chief operating decision maker, the measurement regime in IFRS 8 means that the values disclosed for segment revenue, profit or loss, and (when reported) assets or liabilities could be very different to those reported elsewhere in the financial statements. For example, management might include gains on sale of property, plant and equipment in its measure of segment revenue but not be permitted to do so in its financial statements. *[IAS 16.68].*

There is no requirement in IFRS 8 for segment information to be prepared in conformity with the accounting policies used to present the financial statements of the consolidated group or entity. IFRS 8 requires amounts reported to be the same as those measures used by the chief operating decision maker for determining resource allocation and for assessing performance. This requirement is interpreted strictly. For example, unless adjustments and eliminations made in preparing the financial statements are reflected in the information used by the chief operating decision maker, an entity is prohibited from restating reported segment profit or loss for those adjustments and eliminations. In addition, the standard prohibits any further allocation of revenues, expenses and gains and losses in determining segment profit or loss unless that measure is used by the chief operating decision maker. *[IFRS 8.25].* IFRS 8 does not require symmetry between the revenues and expenses included in segment result and the assets and liabilities allocated to segments; it simply requires disclosure of the nature and effect of any asymmetrical allocations to reportable segments, for example when depreciation expense is reflected in segment profit or loss, but the related depreciable assets are not allocated to that segment. *[IFRS 8.27(f)].* Only those assets and liabilities taken into account by the chief operating decision maker will be included in assets and liabilities reported for that segment. *[IFRS 8.25].*

The amounts presented for segment revenue, profit or loss, assets and liabilities need bear no relationship to the values reported elsewhere in the financial statements, if the *only* measure of each that is used by the chief operating decision maker is not prepared in accordance with the entity's accounting policies or even under IFRS. *[IFRS 8.26].* However, there is a constraint on this otherwise 'free-for-all', since in those cases where a number of measures of segment profit or loss, assets or liabilities are used by the chief operating decision maker, an entity is required to select for its segment disclosures the measurements that are most consistent with

Chapter 34

those used in preparing the financial statements. *[IFRS 8.26]*. A key judgement that can significantly affect the segment disclosures reported in the financial statements arises when an entity seeks to distinguish information used by the chief operating decision maker for determining resource allocation and for assessing performance from other information and supporting detail which is regularly provided. Whether, for example, it is appropriate to ignore IFRS-compliant measures provided to the chief operating decision maker on the basis that they are not used for determining resource allocation and for assessing performance depends on the facts and circumstances supporting that assertion. Nevertheless, it might be appropriate to apply a rebuttable presumption that management effort is not normally wasted in providing the chief operating decision maker with information that is not used.

Instead of defining the elements of segment information to be disclosed and requiring that they be prepared under the same policies and principles applied in producing the financial statements, IFRS 8 requires an entity to explain how it has measured segment profit or loss and segment assets and liabilities for each reportable segment and to reconcile this to the information reported under IFRS. *[IFRS 8.27]*. These requirements are discussed at 5.5 below.

5   INFORMATION TO BE DISCLOSED ABOUT REPORTABLE SEGMENTS

IFRS 8 establishes a general principle for an entity to disclose information to enable users of its financial statements to evaluate the nature and financial effects of the types of business activities in which the entity engages and the economic environments in which it operates. *[IFRS 8.20]*. This principle is met by disclosing the following information for each period for which a statement of comprehensive income or separate income statement is presented: *[IFRS 8.21]*

(a)   general information on segments identified for reporting;

(b)   reported segment profit or loss, including information about specified revenues and expenses included in reported segment profit or loss, segment assets and segment liabilities (if reported to the CODM) and the basis of measurement; and

(c)   reconciliations of the totals of segment revenues, reported segment profit or loss, segment assets, segment liabilities and other material segment items to the corresponding entity amounts in the financial statements.

Reconciliations of balance sheet amounts for reportable segments are required as at each date for which a balance sheet is presented. *[IFRS 8.21]*.

These requirements are addressed in more detail below and the information described therein should be given separately for each segment determined to be reportable using the process set out at 3.2 above. *[IFRS 8.11]*.

5.1   General information about reportable segments

The factors used to identify reportable segments should be described. This would include an explanation of the entity's basis of organisation, for example whether management has chosen to organise the entity by different products and services, by geographical area, by regulatory environment or by applying a combination of factors. The description would also indicate whether operating segments have been aggregated. The general information on reportable segments would include a description of the types of products and services from which each reportable segment derives its revenues. *[IFRS 8.22]*. The disclosures should also include a description of the sources of the revenue classified in the 'all other segments' category. *[IFRS 8.16]*.

In Extract 34.1 below, Daimler describes how its activities have been segmented into its principal business activities and specific product lines.

Extract 34.1: Daimler AG (2010)

Notes to Consolidated Financial Statements [extract]

32.   Segment reporting [extract]

Reportable segments. The reportable segments of the Group are Mercedes-Benz Cars, Daimler Trucks, Mercedes-Benz Vans, Daimler Buses and Daimler Financial Services. The segments are largely organized and managed separately according to nature of products and services provided, brands, distribution channels and profile of customers.

The vehicle segments develop and manufacture passenger cars and off-road vehicles, trucks, vans and buses. Mercedes-Benz Cars sells its passenger cars and off-road vehicles under the brand names Mercedes-Benz, smart and Maybach. Daimler Trucks distributes its trucks under the brand names Mercedes-Benz, Freightliner, Western Star and Fuso. The vans of the Mercedes-Benz Vans segment are primarily sold under the brand name Mercedes-Benz. Daimler Buses sells completely built-up buses under the brand names Mercedes-Benz, Setra and Orion. In addition, Daimler Buses produces and sells bus chassis. The vehicle segments also sell related spare parts and accessories.

The Daimler Financial Services segment supports the sales of the Group's vehicle segments worldwide. Its product portfolio mainly comprises tailored financing and leasing packages for customers and dealers. The segment also provides services such as insurance, fleet management, investment products and credit cards.

5.2   A measure of segment profit or loss, total assets and total liabilities

For each reportable segment, an entity is required to disclose a measure of profit or loss for each segment. An entity is also required to disclose a measure of total assets and total liabilities for each reportable segment, but only if such amounts are regularly provided to the chief operating decision maker. *[IFRS 8.23]*. This 'measure' means segment profit or loss and segment assets and liabilities as defined in the information used by the chief operating decision maker.

ED 8 had not proposed the disclosure of segment liabilities because it was not required in FASB ASC Topic 280. However respondents to the exposure draft pointed out the usefulness of this information and the Board accepted that the principle described as the management approach would require disclosure in the financial statements if indeed it were the case that this information was considered by the chief operating decision maker. *[IFRS 8.BC36-38]*.

Respondents to ED 8 had also suggested that a similar exemption apply to the disclosure of segment assets, particularly in service industries or other industries with low utilisation of physical assets and for which a measure of segment assets might not be used by the chief operating decision maker. *[IFRS 8.BC34]*. The IASB originally maintained the requirement in FASB ASC Topic 280 that a measure of total assets be disclosed for each reportable segment, regardless of whether it is used by the chief operating decision maker, but later reconsidered its position and determined that there would be no divergence from practice in the US under FASB ASC Topic 280. *[IFRS 8.BC35A]*. Accordingly, the IASB included in its *Improvements to IFRSs*, issued in April 2009, an amendment to require information to be disclosed for segment assets on the same basis as for segment liabilities. The amendment applied for annual periods beginning on or after 1 January 2010, with earlier application permitted, if disclosed. *[IFRS 8.35A]*.

5.3　Disclosure of other elements of revenue, income and expense

The following items should also be disclosed about each reportable segment if the specified amounts are included in the measure of segment profit or loss reviewed by the chief operating decision maker or are otherwise regularly provided in respect of those segments to the chief operating decision maker (even if not included in that measure of segment profit or loss): *[IFRS 8.23]*

(a)　revenues from external customers;

(b)　revenues from transactions with other operating segments of the same entity;

(c)　interest revenue;

(d)　interest expense;

(e)　depreciation and amortisation;

(f)　material items of income and expense disclosed in accordance with paragraph 97 of IAS 1 – *Presentation of Financial Statements*;

(g)　the entity's interest in the profit or loss of associates and joint ventures accounted for by the equity method;

(h)　income tax expense or income; and

(i)　material non-cash items other than depreciation and amortisation.

Interest revenue should be reported separately from interest expense for each reportable segment unless a majority of the segment's revenues are from interest and the chief operating decision maker relies primarily on net interest revenue to assess the performance of the segment and make decisions on the allocation of resources to it. In that case, the entity can report net interest revenue or expense for the segment provided that it discloses it has done so. *[IFRS 8.23]*.

It can be seen that whilst IFRS 8 indicates the line items of income or expense or other information that might merit disclosure by segment, what an entity actually reports in its financial statements is determined by the line items used by the chief operating decision maker to define segment profit or loss and segment assets, together with the other information otherwise regularly provided to the chief operating decision maker. *[IFRS 8.23-24]*. This means that different entities (even those with very similar activities) will make different disclosures, depending on what information is provided to the chief operating decision maker. Indeed, what is disclosed by one entity for each of its reportable segments might vary because, for example, the result of one segment is determined after deducting interest whilst that of other segments is drawn before interest; or because the information provided to the chief operating decision maker about one segment includes equity-accounted associates but for other segments does not. As such the disclosures made by an entity are tailored according to exactly what appears in the information presented to the chief operating decision maker.

Statoil provides segment disclosures based on its internal management reporting, with reportable segments determined based on differences in the nature of their operations, products and services, as follows:

Extract 34.2: Statoil ASA (2010)

Notes to the Consolidated Financial Statements [extract]

8.1.3   Segments [extract]

Segment data for the years 31 December 2010, 2009 and 2008 is presented below: [extract]

(in NOK million)	Exploration and Production Norway	International Exploration and Production	Natural Gas	Manufact- uring and Marketing	Fuel and retail	Other	Elimina- tions	Total
Year ended 31 December 2010								
Revenues and Other income, third party	4,101	8,358	84,480	367,782	62,283	1,511	0	528,515
Revenues and Other income, inter-segment	166,571	41,930	2,765	39,244	3,571	2,207	(256,268)	0
Net income from equity accounted investments	56	707	276	226	4	(136)	0	1,133
Total revenues and other income	170,728	50,995	87,521	407,232	65,858	3,582	(256,268)	529,648
Net operating income	115,615	12,623	8,511	(1,973)	2,354	170	(72)	137,228
Significant non-cash items recognised in segment profit or loss								
– Depreciation and amortisation	26,109	15,183	1,916	1,055	1,215	693	0	46,081
– Impairment losses	0	1,469	0	2,913	97	48	0	4,527
– Commodity derivatives	(1,866)	0	4,542	(226)	0	0	0	2,450
– Exploration expenditure written off	1,441	1,470	0	0	0	0	0	2,911
Equity accounted investments	133	8,842	2,629	712	43	1,525	0	13,884
Other segment non-current assets*	188,194	133,482	36,078	15,895	11,115	3,135	0	387,899
Assets classified as held for sale	0	44,890	0	0	0	0	0	44,890
Non-current assets, not allocated to segments*								47,573
Total non-current assets and assets classified as held for sale								494,246
Additions to PP&E and intangible assets**	31,902	40,385	2,995	3,348	829	969	0	80,428

*   Deferred tax assets, post employment benefit assets and financial instruments are not allocated to segments.
**   Excluding movements due to changes in asset retirement obligations.

5.4   Additional disclosures relating to segment assets

If any of the following items are either included in the measure of segment assets reviewed by the chief operating decision maker or otherwise regularly provided in respect of those segments (whether included in segment assets or not), an entity should also disclose for each segment: *[IFRS 8.24]*

(a)   the investment in equity-accounted associates and joint ventures; and

(b)   total expenditures for additions to non-current assets other than financial instruments, deferred tax assets, post-employment benefit assets and rights arising under insurance contracts.

The requirement in (b) above is subtly different to FASB ASC Topic 280, which uses the term 'long-lived assets' excluding intangible assets. The Board noted in ED 8 that it saw no reason to exclude intangible assets and has not departed from that position. Having reconsidered whether, in the interest of convergence, the standard should require a subtotal of tangible non-current assets to be presented, the Board concluded that the incremental benefits of disclosure were not significant, although entities are free to do so if they wish. *[IFRS 8.BC56-57]*.

5.5   Explanation of the measurements used in segment reporting

As noted at 4 above, instead of prescribing how an entity should calculate the values reported in its segmental disclosures, IFRS 8 requires an entity to explain how its measures of segment profit or loss, segment assets and segment liabilities have been determined. As a minimum, the following information is required: *[IFRS 8.27]*

(a)   the basis of accounting for any transactions between reportable segments;

(b)   if not apparent from the required reconciliations (see 5.6 below), the nature of any differences between the measurement of total reported segment profit or loss and the entity's profit or loss before income taxes and discontinued operations;

(c) .   the nature of any differences between the measurements of total reported segment assets and the entity's assets, if not apparent from the required reconciliations;

(d)   the nature of any differences between the measurements of total reported segment liabilities and the entity's liabilities, if not apparent from the required reconciliations;

(e)   the nature of any changes from prior periods in the measurement methods used to determine segment profit or loss, including the financial effect, if any, of those changes; and

(f)   the nature and effect of any asymmetrical allocations to reportable segments, such as where depreciation is included in segment profit but the related property, plant and equipment is not included in segment assets.

The kind of disclosures in (b), (c) and (d) above that are necessary for an understanding of the reported segment information could relate to the accounting policies used, including policies for the allocation of centrally incurred costs in arriving at segment profit or loss and for the allocation of jointly used assets and liabilities in determining segment assets and segment liabilities. *[IFRS 8.27]*.

In Extract 34.3 below, Daimler confirms that segment information is prepared using the same accounting policies as the IFRS financial statements; describes how 'EBIT' is the measure of segment profit or loss and explains how segment assets and liabilities are determined.

Extract 34.3: Daimler AG (2010)

Notes to Consolidated Financial Statements [extract]

32.   Segment reporting [extract]

Management Reporting and Controlling Systems. The Group's management reporting and controlling systems principally use accounting policies that are the same as those described in Note 1 in the summary of significant accounting policies under IFRS.

The Group measures the performance of its operating segments through a measure of segment profit or loss which is referred to as "EBIT" in our management and reporting system.

EBIT is the measure of segment profit/loss used in segment reporting and comprises gross profit, selling and general administrative expenses, research and non-capitalized development costs, other operating income and expense, and our share of profit/loss from companies accounted for using the equity method, net, as well as other financial income/expense, net.

Intersegment revenue is generally recorded at values that approximate third-party selling prices.

Segment assets principally comprise all assets. The industrial business segments' assets exclude income tax assets, assets from defined pension benefit plans and other post-employment benefit plans and certain financial assets (including liquidity).

Segment liabilities principally comprise all liabilities. The industrial business segments' liabilities exclude income tax liabilities, liabilities from defined pension benefit plans and other post-employment benefit plans and certain financial liabilities (including financing liabilities).

Pursuant to risk sharing agreements between Daimler Financial Services and the respective vehicle segments the residual value risk associated with the Group's operating leases and its finance lease receivables is primarily borne by the vehicle segments that manufactured the leased equipment. The terms of the risk sharing arrangement vary by segment and geographic region.

Non-current assets comprise of intangible assets, property plant and equipment and equipment on operating leases.

Capital expenditures for property, plant and equipment and intangible assets reflect the cash effective additions to these property, plant and equipment and intangible assets as far as they do not relate to capitalized borrowing costs or goodwill and finance leases.

The effects of certain legal proceedings are excluded from the operative results and liabilities of the segments, if such items are not indicative of the segments' performance, since their related results of operations may be distorted by the amount and the irregular nature of such events. This may also be the case for items that refer to more than one reportable segment.

With respect to information about geographical regions, revenue is allocated to countries based on the location of the customer; non-current assets are disclosed according to the physical location of these assets.

In its 2008 financial statements, Roche explained the basis of accounting for transactions between reportable segments.

Extract 34.4: Roche Holding Limited (2008)

Notes to the Roche Group Consolidated Financial Statements [extract]

1.   Summary of significant accounting policies [extract]

Segment reporting

Within the Group's consolidated financial statements, transactions and balances between consolidated subsidiaries, such as between Genentech, Chugai and other Roche Group subsidiaries, are eliminated on consolidation.

Genentech and Chugai are considered separately reportable operating segments for the purposes of the Group's operating segment disclosures in Note 2. Additional information relating to Genentech and Chugai results is given in Notes 3 and 4, respectively.

Profits on product sales between the Roche Pharmaceuticals, Genentech and Chugai operating segments are recorded as part of the segment results of the operating segment making the sale. Unrealised internal profits on inventories that have been sold by one operating segment to another but which have not yet been sold on to external customers as at the balance sheet date are eliminated as a consolidation entry at a Pharmaceuticals Division level.

Additionally the results of each operating segment may include income received from another operating segment in respect of:

● Royalties
● Licensing, milestone and other upfront payments
● Transfers in respect of research collaborations

These are recognised as income in the segment results of the operating segment receiving the income consistently with the accounting policies applied to third-party transactions and set out in these financial statements. Corresponding expenses are recorded in the other operating segment so that these eliminate at a Pharmaceuticals Division level.

5.6   Reconciliations

Reconciliations are required of all the following: *[IFRS 8.28]*

(a)   the total of revenue from reportable segments to the entity's revenue;

(b)   the total profit or loss for reportable segments to the entity's profit or loss before income taxes and discontinued operations. Where items such as income taxes have been allocated to arrive at segment profit or loss, the reconciliation can be made to the entity's profit or loss after those items;

(c)   if segment assets are reported (see 5.2 above), the total of the reportable segments' assets to the entity's assets;

(d)   if segment liabilities are reported (see 5.2 above), the total of reportable segments' liabilities to the entity's liabilities; and

(e)   for every other material item of information the entity chooses to give in its segment information, the total of each item from all reportable segments to the corresponding amount for the entity.

In each of the above reconciliations an entity must separately identify and describe all material reconciling items. For example, when reconciling segment profit or loss to the entity's profit or loss before income taxes and discontinued operations, each material adjustment arising from differences in accounting policies would have to be separately identified and described. *[IFRS 8.28].* In addition, the standard requires that information about the 'all other segments' category is shown separately from other reconciling items. *[IFRS 8.16].*

National Australia Bank evaluates operating segments' performance on the basis of cash earnings. This post-tax measure of reportable segments' profit or loss is reconciled to the consolidated financial statements as follows:

Extract 34.5: National Australia Bank Limited (2010)

Notes to the financial statements [extract]

2   Segment information [extract]

Reconciliations between reportable segments and statutory results [extract]

The tables below reconcile the information in the reportable segment tables presented above, which have been prepared on an ongoing cash earnings basis, to the relevant statutory information presented in the financial report. In addition to the sum of the eight reportable segments, the ongoing cash earnings basis includes the Group's Corporate Functions & Other segment and intra group eliminations. The MLC & NAB Wealth net adjustment represents income included from management results for the MLC & NAB Wealth business.

	Group	
	2010 $m	2009 $m
Cash earnings		
Group cash earnings – ongoing[1]	**4,581**	3,841
Non-cash earnings items (after tax)		
Distributions	**215**	245
Treasury shares	**106**	(256)
Fair value and hedge ineffectiveness	**(353)**	(79)
Investment earnings on shareholders' retained profits discount rate variation	**34**	(4)
Efficiency, quality and service initiatives	**(237)**	(179)
Litigation expense	**(12)**	(110)
Property revaluation	**(4)**	–
Provision for tax on NZ structured finance transactions	**128**	(542)
MLC reinsurance dispute	**(36)**	–
Amortisation of acquired intangibles	**(73)**	(6)
ExCaps taxation assessment	**–**	(309)
Due diligence, acquisition and integration costs	**(125)**	(12)
Net profit attributable to members of the Company	**4,224**	2,589

[1] Includes distributions

5.7   Restatement of previously reported information

When an entity changes its organisational structure in a manner that causes a change in the composition of its reportable segments, corresponding amounts for earlier periods should be restated unless the information is not available and the cost to develop it would be excessive. This requirement also applies to the presentation of segment information in respect of interim periods. *[IFRS 8.29].* Similarly, entities are expected to restate comparative segment information when first adopting IFRS 8, unless the necessary information is not available and the cost to develop it would be excessive. *[IFRS 8.36]*. As discussed at 5.8 below, this exemption is not the same as the test of impracticability in IAS 1, which makes no allowance for the cost of compliance. *[IAS 1.7, 41-43]*.

The exemption from restatement on grounds of excessive cost is applied to each individual item of disclosure. *[IFRS 8.29]*. This means that an entity should restate its comparative information for all the items it can, even if this results in some comparative information not being presented or restated, such as inter-segment revenues. When the composition of reportable segments has changed, an entity should disclose whether the corresponding items of segment information have been restated. *[IFRS 8.29]*.

Where corresponding information is not restated to reflect the new composition of reportable segments, the segment information for the current period should be presented on both the old and the new bases of segmentation. Only if the necessary information were unavailable and the cost of developing it excessive would an entity not have to show current information on the old basis of segmentation. *[IFRS 8.30]*.

5.8   Entity-wide disclosures

In addition to disclosing segment information derived from the formats and measurements presented to the chief operating decision maker, IFRS 8 requires certain entity-wide disclosures about products and services, geographical areas and major customers. The information described below is required even if the entity has only a single reportable segment, but need not be repeated if already provided as part of the disclosures on reportable segments set out above. *[IFRS 8.31]*. The amounts reported about products and services and about geographical areas in these entity-wide disclosures are measured using the same accounting policies and estimates as the entity's financial statements. *[IFRS 8.32-33]*. As such, the amounts disclosed in this part of the segment disclosures might well be different to the information already provided in other segment information (see 4 above).

Exemption from the requirements set out at 5.8.1 and 5.8.2 below is offered if the necessary information is unavailable and the cost to develop it would be excessive. If disclosure is not made on these grounds, that fact should be stated. *[IFRS 8.32-33]*. Some respondents to ED 8 expressed concern that the basis of this exemption was inconsistent with the test of impracticability in IAS 1, which makes no allowance for the cost of compliance. *[IAS 1.7]*. However, the IASB did not see any merit in divergence from FASB ASC Topic 280 in this respect and therefore retained the exemption from disclosure if the necessary information were unavailable and the cost of developing it excessive. *[IFRS 8.BC46-47]*.

This exemption is not available in respect of the disclosures about major customers set out at 5.9 below.

5.8.1   Information about products and services

An entity should report revenues from external customers for each product and service or for each group of similar products and services, measuring revenues on the same basis as the entity's financial statements. *[IFRS 8.32]*.

In Extract 34.2 at 5.3 above, Statoil provides segment disclosures based on its internal management reporting, with reportable segments relating to domestic and international exploration and production, natural gas and manufacturing activities. Accordingly, it also discloses external revenues by product group (and combines it with a geographical analysis of revenue), as follows:

Extract 34.6: Statoil ASA (2010)

Notes to the Consolidated Financial Statements [extract]

8.1.3   Segments [extract]

Geographical data for the years 31 December 2010, 2009 and 2008 is presented below: [extract]

(in NOK million)	Crude oil	Gas	NGL	Refined products	Other	Total sale
Year ended 31 December 2010						
Norway	227,122	72,643	47,551	47,332	16,725	411,373
USA	22,397	7,817	1,815	14,918	5,771	52,718
Sweden	0	0	0	18,810	4,612	23,422
Denmark	0	0	0	14,275	3,027	17,302
Other	4,508	4,380	205	12,150	2,457	23,700
Total revenues (excluding net income from equity accounted investments)	254,027	84,840	49,571	107,485	32,592	528,515

5.8.2   Information about geographical areas

IFRS 8 requires disclosure of the following geographical information: *[IFRS 8.33]*

(a)   revenues from external customers, analysed between amounts attributed to the entity's country of domicile and the total of those attributed to all foreign countries; and

(b)   non-current assets other than financial instruments, deferred tax assets, post-employment benefit assets and rights arising under insurance contracts, analysed between assets located in the entity's country of domicile and the total of those located in all foreign countries.

In addition, if revenues from external customers or assets attributed to an individual foreign country are material, separate disclosure of that country's revenues or assets is required. *[IFRS 8.33]*. The standard does not indicate what might be regarded as 'material', but given the criteria for a reportable segment and a major customer for reporting purposes (see 3.2.2 above and 5.9 below respectively) it would seem appropriate to consider the need for separate disclosure in respect of a foreign country accounting for more than 10% of total external revenues or more than 10% of total non-current assets.

The basis on which revenues from external customers are attributed to individual countries should be disclosed. An entity can elect to provide, in addition to the information required above, subtotals of geographical information about groups of countries. *[IFRS 8.33].* In Extract 34.7 below, BAE Systems provides this more detailed level of disclosure.

Extract 34.7: BAE Systems plc (2010)

Notes to the Group accounts [extract]

3. Segmental analysis [extract]

Analysis of non-current assets by geographical location

	Carrying value of non-current assets	
		Restated[6]
	2010	2009
Asset location	£m	£m
United Kingdom	2,582	2,587
Rest of Europe	1,105	1,190
Saudi Arabia	734	729
United States	10,022	9,838
Asia and Pacific	621	589
Africa, Central and South America	31	47
Non-current operating group assets	**15,095**	**14,980**
Financial instruments	354	310
Inventories	644	887
Trade and other receivables	3,559	3,764
Total operating group assets	**19,652**	**19,941**
Tax	1,211	1,563
Retirement benefit obligations (note 21)	49	42
Cash (as defined by the Group) (note 27)	3,118	3,943
Consolidated total assets	**24,030**	**25,489**

6 Restated following finalisation of the fair values recognised on acquisition of the 45% shareholding in BVT Surface Fleet Limited (see note 29).

Analysis of sales and revenue by geographical location – continuing operations [extract]

	Revenue	
	2010	2009
Customer location	£m	£m
United Kingdom	4,161	3,562
Rest of Europe	2,036	1,811
Saudi Arabia	2,994	2,607
Rest of Middle East	162	64
United States	10,126	10,902
Canada	77	119
Australia	1,027	672
Rest of Asia and Pacific	257	226
Africa, Central and South America	257	411
	21,097	**20,374**

5.9   Information about major customers

IFRS 8 also requires an entity to give disclosures indicating the extent of its reliance on its major customers. If revenues from a single external customer account for 10% or more of the entity's total revenues, the entity should disclose: *[IFRS 8.34]*

(a)   that fact;

(b)   the total amount of revenues from each such customer; and

(c)   the identity of the reportable segment or segments reporting the revenues.

Disclosure is not required of the name of each major customer, nor the amounts of revenue reported in each segment for that customer. Nevertheless, Roche elects to provide the customers' names in the following extract.

Extract 34.8: Roche Holding Limited (2010)

Notes to the Roche Group Consolidated Financial Statements [extract]

2.   Operating segment information [extract]

Major customers

The US national wholesale distributor, AmerisourceBergen Corp., represented approximately 6 billion Swiss francs (2009: 6 billion Swiss francs) of the Group's revenues. Approximately 99% of these revenues were in the Pharmaceuticals operating segment, with the residual in the Diagnostics segment. The Group also reported substantial revenues from the US national wholesale distributors, Cardinal Health Inc. and McKesson Corp., and in total these three customers represented approximately a quarter of the Group's revenues.

5.9.1   *Customers known to be under common control*

For the purposes of the above disclosures, a group of entities known to a reporting entity to be under common control are to be considered a single customer. *[IFRS 8.34]*.

However, judgement is required to assess whether a government (including government agencies and similar bodies whether local, national or international), and entities known to the reporting entity to be under the control of that government are considered a single customer. The assessment of whether entities should be regarded as a single customer for these purposes should take into account the extent of economic integration between those entities. *[IFRS 8.34]*.

The requirement to exercise judgement to assess whether a government and entities controlled by that government should be regarded as a single customer was introduced as part of the revision of IAS 24 – *Related Party Disclosures* – and is effective for annual periods beginning on or after 1 January 2011. *[IFRS 8.36B]*. Previously the standard made no distinction between government-controlled and privately controlled entities, despite the fact that respondents to ED 8 had noted the difficulty presented by this requirement for an entity with a number of customers under common state control. *[IFRS 8.BC58]*. The IASB's Project Summary on the revision of IAS 24 had stated that IASB staff had been asked to develop guidance on the factors relevant to determining the extent of economic integration,[12] but the final amendment was issued without it.

BAE Systems identifies revenues from three principal governments.

Extract 34.9: BAE Systems plc (2010)

Notes to the Group accounts [extract]

3.   Segmental analysis [extract]

Analysis of revenue by major customer – continuing operations
Revenue from the Group's three principal customers, which individually represent
over 10% of total revenue, is as follows:

	2010 £m	2009 £m
UK Ministry of Defence[1]	5,060	4,101
US Department of Defense	7,696	8,381
Kingdom of Saudi Arabia Ministry of Defence and Aviation	2,870	2,602

[1]Revenue from the UK Ministry of Defence includes £1.3 bn (2009 £1.1bn) generated under the Typhoon workshare agreement with Eurofighter GmbH. This revenue is included within Rest of Europe in the analysis by geographical location above.

Revenue from the UK Ministry of Defence and the US Department of Defense was generated by all four principal operating groups. Revenue from the Kingdom of Saudi Arabia Ministry of Defence and Aviation was generated by the International operating group.

In its segment disclosures made under FASB ASC Topic 280, Lockheed Martin provides more detailed information about customer revenues by segment as well as total revenues for foreign governments and commercial customers.

Extract 34.10: Lockheed Martin Corporation (2010)

Notes to the consolidated financial statements [extract]

Note 5   Information on business segments [extract]

Net Sales by Customer Category

(In millions)	2010	2009	2008
U.S. Government			
Aeronautics	$10,720	$10,151	$9,268
Electronic Systems	10,242	9,699	9,405
Information Systems & Global Services	9,437	9,128	8,588
Space Systems	7,995	8,405	7,685
Total	$38,394	$37,383	$34,946
Foreign governments (a) (b)			
Aeronautics	$2,478	$1,990	$2,043
Electronic Systems	3,749	3,432	3,049
Information Systems & Global Services	417	256	160
Space Systems	20	27	15
Total	$6,664	$5,705	$5,267
Commercial and Other (b)			
Aeronautics	$ 37	$ 60	$162
Electronic Systems	372	401	349
Information Systems & Global Services	105	224	321
Space Systems	231	222	327
Total	$745	$907	$1,159
	$45,803	$43,995	$41,372

(a) Sales made to foreign governments through the U.S. Government, or "foreign military sales," are included in the foreign governments category.

(b) International sales, including export sales reflected in the foreign governments and commercial categories, were approximately $7.1 billion, $6.3 billion and $5.7 billion in 2010, 2009 and 2008.

5.10 Disclosure of commercially sensitive information

The criteria for determining the externally reportable segments, as discussed at 3.2 above, attempt to define which internally reported operating units can be combined; those which must be reported separately; and those which are included in an unallocated reconciling item. The interaction between these criteria, in particular with the requirement that segments cannot be combined if they exhibit different long-term financial performance, leaves entities open to the risk of having to disclose information that management would be concerned about sharing with competitors, customers, suppliers or employees.

However, IFRS 8 does not permit the omission of segment information when management believes that its disclosure is commercially sensitive or potentially detrimental to the entity's competitive position. Indeed, IAS 1 requires an entity not only to present information in a manner that provides relevant, reliable, comparable and understandable information, but also to provide *additional* disclosures if compliance with an individual standard is insufficient to enable users to understand the entity's financial position and financial performance. *[IAS 1.17]*. The only justification for failing to meet these requirements is if disclosure would be so misleading that it would conflict with the objective of financial statements set out in the IASB *Framework*. *[IAS 1.19]*.

Given that the objective of IFRS 8 is to disclose information to help users of financial statements evaluate the nature and financial effects of the entity's business activities and the economic environments in which it operates, *[IFRS 8.1]*, this possibility would seem to be remote. The IASB rejected similar concerns raised by respondents to ED 8, noting that entities would be unlikely to suffer competitive harm from the required disclosures since most competitors have sources of detailed information about an entity other than its financial statements. *[IFRS 8.BC44]*.

6 TRANSITIONAL PROVISIONS

There are no special arrangements for entities applying IFRS 8 for the first time, with the standard requiring comparative information to be restated. Only where the necessary information is both unavailable and incapable of being developed without excessive cost is an entity exempt from full restatement. *[IFRS 8.36]*. Accordingly, an entity should ensure that internal reporting systems can provide the information needed to meet the disclosure requirements of IFRS 8 for all periods presented in its financial statements.

Chapter 34

References

1 *IASB Update*, January 2005, p.4.
2 IFRS 8 D01-D04.
3 Press Release, *Summary of the IASC Foundation Trustees meeting 2 and 3 July 2007, Madrid,* IFRS Foundation, 18 July 2007.
4 European Parliament, *Resolution on the draft Commission regulation amending Regulation (EC) No. 1725/2003 adopting certain international accounting standards in accordance with Regulation (EC) No. 1606/2002 of the European Parliament and of the Council as regards: International Financial Reporting Standard (IFRS) 8 concerning disclosure of operating segments (C6-0000/0000),* 7 November 2007, D and 6.
5 Request for Views *Agenda Consultation 2011,* IASB, July 2011, p. 11.
6 IFRS 8, Basis for Conclusions, Appendix A, 72.
7 ED 8, *Operating Segments*, IASB, January 2006, 2.
8 *IFRS for Small and Medium-sized Entities,* IASB, July 2009, 1.3.
9 *IFRIC Update,* July 2011, p. 5.
10 ED 8.9.
11 *IFRIC Update,* September 2011, p. 5.
12 Project Summary, *Related Party Disclosures, Update on the Other Amendments Proposed in the 2007 Exposure Draft,* IASB, July 2009.

Chapter 35   Earnings per share

Chapter 35

List of examples

Chapter 35

Chapter 35   Earnings per share

1   INTRODUCTION

Earnings per share (EPS) is one of the most widely quoted statistics in financial analysis. It came into great prominence in the US during the late 1950s and early 1960s due to the widespread use of the price earnings ratio (PE) as a yardstick for investment decisions. As a result, standard setters in some jurisdictions (notably the USA and the UK) have had rules on EPS for many years. However, it was not until 1997 that an international accounting standard on the subject was published.

IAS 33 – *Earnings per Share* – was introduced for accounting periods beginning on or after 1 January 1998. In December 2003, as part of the improvements project, the IASB updated IAS 33 to provide more detailed guidance in some complex areas. The requirements of IAS 33 are discussed at 2 to 7 below, and the standard's illustrative examples of particular issues are included in the text of the chapter, whilst its comprehensive worked example is included as an Appendix.

2   OBJECTIVE AND SCOPE OF IAS 33

2.1   Objective

IAS 33 sets out its objective as follows: 'to prescribe principles for the determination and presentation of earnings per share, so as to improve performance comparisons between different entities in the same reporting period and between different reporting periods for the same entity. Even though earnings per share data have limitations because of the different accounting policies that may be used for determining "earnings", a consistently determined denominator enhances financial reporting. The focus of this Standard is on the denominator of the earnings per share calculation.' *[IAS 33.1].*

The standard requires the computation of both basic and diluted EPS, explaining the objective of each as follows:

• the objective of basic earnings per share information is to provide a measure of the interests of each ordinary share of a parent entity in the performance of the entity over the reporting period; *[IAS 33.11]* and

• the objective of diluted earnings per share is consistent with that of basic earnings per share – to provide a measure of the interest of each ordinary share in the performance of an entity – while giving effect to all dilutive potential ordinary shares outstanding during the period. *[IAS 33.32]*.

The underlying logic here is that EPS, including diluted EPS, should be an historical performance measure. This impacts particularly on the reporting of diluted EPS, in steering it away from an alternative purpose: to warn of potential future dilution. Indeed the tension between these differing objectives is evident in the standard. As discussed more fully at 6.4.6 below, IAS 33 sets out a very restrictive regime for including certain potentially dilutive shares in the diluted EPS calculation. Yet diluted EPS is only to take account of those potential shares that would dilute earnings from *continuing* operations which seems to have more of a forward looking 'warning signal' flavour.

2.2 Scope

IAS 33 applies to:

(a) the separate or individual financial statements of an entity:

(i) whose ordinary shares or potential ordinary shares are traded in a public market (a domestic or foreign stock exchange or an over-the-counter market, including local and regional markets); or

(ii) that files, or is in the process of filing, its financial statements with a securities commission or other regulatory information for the purpose of issuing ordinary shares in a public market; and

(b) the consolidated financial statements of a group with a parent:

(i) whose ordinary shares or potential ordinary shares are traded in a public market (a domestic or foreign stock exchange or an over-the-counter market, including local and regional markets); or

(ii) that files, or is in the process of filing, its financial statements with a securities commission or other regulatory information for the purpose of issuing ordinary shares in a public market.

IAS 33 also applies to any other entity that discloses earnings per share. *[IAS 33.3]*. Where both the parent's and consolidated financial statements are presented, the standard only requires consolidated earnings per share to be given. If the parent chooses to present EPS data based on its separate financial statements the standard requires that the disclosures be restricted to the face of the parent-only statement of comprehensive income (or separate income statement) and not be included in the consolidated financial statements. *[IAS 33.4]*.

3 THE BASIC EPS

IAS 33 requires the computation of basic EPS for the profit or loss (and, if presented, the profit or loss from continuing operations) attributable to ordinary equity holders. *[IAS 33.9]*. It defines, or rather describes, basic earnings per share in the following manner: 'Basic earnings per share shall be calculated by dividing profit or loss attributable to ordinary equity holders of the parent entity (the numerator) by the weighted average number of ordinary shares outstanding (the denominator) during the period.' *[IAS 33.10]*.

The components of the calculation are illustrated in the following extract.

Extract 35.1: Deutsche Post AG (2007)

Notes [extract]
20   Earnings per share [extract]

Basic earnings per share are computed in accordance with IAS 33 (Earnings per Share) by dividing consolidated net profit by the average number of shares. Basic earnings per share for financial year 2007 were €1.15 (previous year: €1.60).

	2006	2007
Consolidated net profit attributable to Deutsche Post AG shareholders (€m)	1,916	1,389
Weighted average number of shares outstanding	1,196,244,814	1,205,101,455
Basic earnings per share (€)	1.60	1.15

To compute diluted earnings per share, the average number of shares outstanding is adjusted for the number of all potentially dilutive shares. There were 13,184,482 stock options for executives as of the reporting date (previous year: 21,854,658), of which 2,489,720 were dilutive (previous year: 3,395,362).

	2006	2007
Consolidated net profit attributable to Deutsche Post AG shareholders (€m)	1,916	1,389
Weighted-average number of shares outstanding	1,196,244,814	1,205,101,455
Potentially dilutive shares	3,395,362	2,489,720
Weighted-average number of shares for diluted net income	1,199,640,176	1,207,591,175
Diluted earnings per share (€)	1.60	1.15

3.1   Earnings

The starting point for determining the earnings figure to be used in the basic EPS calculation (both for total earnings and, if appropriate, earnings from continuing operations) is the net profit or loss for the period attributable to ordinary equity holders. *[IAS 33.12]*. This will, in accordance with IAS 1 – *Presentation of Financial Statements* – include all items of income and expense, including, dividends on preference shares classified as liabilities and tax and is stated after the deduction of non-controlling interests *[IAS 33.13, A1, IAS 1.83, 88]*. This is then adjusted for the after-tax amounts of preference dividends, differences arising on the settlement of preference shares, and other similar effects of preference shares classified as equity. *[IAS 33.12]*. These adjustments are discussed at 5.2 below.

3.2   Number of shares

An ordinary share is defined as 'an equity instrument that is subordinate to all other classes of equity instruments'. *[IAS 33.5]*. 'Equity instrument' has the same meaning as in IAS 32 – *Financial Instruments: Presentation* – that is 'any contract that evidences a residual interest in the assets of an entity after deducting all of its liabilities' *[IAS 33.8, IAS 32.11]*. IAS 33 goes on to observe that ordinary shares participate in profit for the period only after other types of share such as preference shares have participated. *[IAS 33.6]*. The standard also clarifies that there may be more than one class of ordinary share and requires the computation and presentation of EPS for each class that has a different right to share in profit for the period. *[IAS 33.6, 66]*. In practice, it is usually straightforward to determine which instruments are ordinary shares for EPS purposes. The treatment of different classes of shares is discussed at 5.4 below.

The basic rule in IAS 33 is that all outstanding ordinary shares are brought into the basic EPS computation – time-weighted for changes in the period (changes in ordinary shares is discussed at 4 below). *[IAS 33.19]*. There are three exceptions to this:

- ordinary shares that are issued as partly paid are included in the weighted average as a fraction of a share based on their dividend participation relative to fully paid shares (so, if although only partly paid they ranked equally for dividends they would be included in full); *[IAS 33.A15]*

- treasury shares, which are presented in the financial statements as a deduction from equity are not considered outstanding for EPS purposes for the period they are held in treasury. Although not stated explicitly in the standard itself, this requirement is clearly logical (as although the shares are still in issue, they are accounted for as if redeemed) and is illustrated in one of the examples appended to the standard (see Example 35.1 at 4.1 below). *[IAS 33.IE2]*. Extract 35.6 at 6.4.2 A below shows a company presenting the deduction of treasury shares in the EPS calculation; and

- shares that are contingently returnable (that is, subject to recall) are not treated as outstanding until they cease to be subject to recall, and hence are excluded from basic EPS until that time. *[IAS 33.25]*.

The standard contains some specific guidance on when newly issued ordinary shares should be considered outstanding. In general shares are to be included from the date consideration is receivable (considered by the standard generally to be the date of their issue), for example: *[IAS 33.21]*

- shares issued in exchange for cash are included when cash is receivable;

- shares issued on the voluntary reinvestment of dividends on ordinary or preference shares are included when the dividends are reinvested;

- shares issued as a result of the conversion of a debt instrument to ordinary shares are included as of the date interest ceases accruing;

- shares issued in place of interest or principal on other financial instruments are included as of the date interest ceases accruing;

- shares issued in exchange for the settlement of a liability of the entity are included as of the settlement date;

- shares issued as consideration for the acquisition of an asset other than cash are included as of the date on which the acquisition is recognised;

- shares issued in exchange for the rendering of services to the entity are included as the services are rendered; and

- shares that will be issued upon the conversion of a mandatorily convertible instrument are included in the calculation of basic earnings per share from the date the contract is entered into. *[IAS 33.23]*.

Most of these provisions are straightforward, however some are worthy of note.

Shares issued in exchange for services will be accounted for in accordance with IFRS 2 – *Share-based Payment*, with a charge to income matched by a credit to equity. IAS 33 has some guidance on the inclusion of such potential shares in *diluted* EPS (see 6.4.5 below), however there is no further elaboration of the meaning of 'included as the services are rendered'. What seems to be implicit in the phrase is that the shares concerned vest unconditionally as services are rendered. On that basis, clearly it would be appropriate to include shares in basic EPS as entitlement to them vests, notwithstanding that the actual issue of shares may be at a different time. However, a very common form of share-based remuneration involves entitlement to shares vesting at the end of an extended period conditional on future events (typically continued employment and sometimes specific future performance). In our view, such arrangements are clearly conditionally issuable shares and should be excluded from basic EPS until vesting. Indeed, when discussing employee share schemes in the context of diluted EPS the standard is explicit, as follows. 'Employee share options with fixed or determinable terms and non-vested ordinary shares are treated as options in the calculation of diluted earnings per share, even though they may be contingent on vesting. They are treated as outstanding on the grant date. Performance-based employee share options are treated as contingently issuable shares because their issue is contingent upon satisfying specified conditions in addition to the passage of time.' *[IAS 33.48]*. Contingently issuable shares are discussed at 6.4.6 below.

In respect of the final bullet point, the standard does not define what a mandatorily convertible instrument is. One view would be that the requirement to account for the shares in EPS from inception must mean it refers to instruments where the proceeds also are received at inception. On that basis, it would exclude a forward contract for the issue of shares which (as required by the first bullet above) would increase the denominator of basic EPS only from the time the cash is receivable. Similarly, in the reverse situation of a forward contract to redeem ordinary shares the shares would only be removed from basic EPS when the consideration becomes payable. Another view would be that all binding agreements to issue or redeem ordinary shares should be reflected in basic EPS when the entity becomes party to the arrangement. A further possible complexity is the question of whether or not a symmetrical treatment for the issue and redemption of shares should be applied for EPS purposes. Whilst that certainly seems logical, it is not beyond question in all circumstances particularly given the asymmetrical accounting treatment for certain derivatives over own shares required by IAS 32 (discussed in Chapter 45 at 10).

Chapter 35

More generally, the standard goes on to say the timing of inclusion is determined by the attaching terms and conditions, and also that due consideration should be given to the substance of any contract associated with the issue. *[IAS 33.21]*. Ordinary shares that are issuable on the satisfaction of certain conditions (contingently issuable shares) are to be included in the calculation of basic EPS only from the date when all necessary conditions have been satisfied; in effect when they are no longer contingent. *[IAS 33.24]*. This provision is interpreted strictly, as illustrated in Example 7 appended to the standard (see Example 35.14 at 6.4.6 A below). In that example earnings in a year, by meeting certain thresholds, would trigger the issue of shares. Because it is not certain that the condition is met until the last day of the year (when earnings become known with certainty) the new shares are excluded from basic EPS until the following year. Where shares will be issued at some future date (that is, solely after the passage of time) they are not considered contingently issuable by IAS 33, as the passage of time is a certainty. *[IAS 33.24]*. In principle, this would seem to mean that they should be included in basic EPS from the agreement date. However, careful consideration of the individual facts and circumstances would be necessary.

The calculation of the basic EPS is often simple but a number of complications can arise; these may be considered under the following two headings:

(a)   changes in ordinary shares outstanding; and

(b)   matters affecting the numerator.

These are discussed in the next two sections.

4   CHANGES IN OUTSTANDING ORDINARY SHARES

Changes in ordinary share outstanding can occur under a variety of circumstances, the most common of which are dealt with below. Whenever such a change occurs during the accounting period, an adjustment is required to the number of shares in the EPS calculation for that period; furthermore, in certain situations the EPS for previous periods will also have to be recalculated.

4.1   Weighted average number of shares

Implicit in the methodology of IAS 33 is a correlation between the capital of an entity (or rather the income generating assets it reflects) and earnings. Accordingly, to compute EPS as a performance measure requires adjusting the number of shares in the denominator to reflect any variations in the period to the capital available to generate that period's earnings. The standard observes that using the weighted average number of ordinary shares outstanding during the period reflects the possibility that the amount of shareholders' capital varied during the period as a result of a larger or smaller number of shares being outstanding at any time. The weighted average number of ordinary shares outstanding during the period is the number of ordinary shares outstanding at the beginning of the period, adjusted by the number of ordinary shares bought back or issued during the period multiplied by a time-weighting factor. The time-weighting factor is the number of days that the shares are outstanding as a proportion of the total number of days in the period;

IAS 33 notes that a reasonable approximation of the weighted average is adequate in many circumstances. *[IAS 33.20]*. Computation of a weighted average number of shares is illustrated in the following example:

Example 35.1:   Calculation of weighted average number of shares [IAS 33.IE2]

		Shares issued	Treasury shares*	Shares outstanding
1 January 2012	Balance at beginning of year	2,000	300	1,700
31 May 2012	Issue of new shares for cash	800	–	2,500
1 December 2012	Purchase of treasury shares for cash	–	250	2,250
31 December 2012	Balance at year end	2,800	550	2,250

Calculation of weighted average:
$(1,700 \times 5/12) + (2,500 \times 6/12) + (2,250 \times 1/12)$ = 2,146 shares *or*
$(1,700 \times 12/12) + (800 \times 7/12) - (250 \times 1/12)$ = 2,146 shares

*   Treasury shares are equity instruments reacquired and held by the issuing entity itself or by its subsidiaries.

The use of a weighted average number of shares is necessary because the increase in the share capital would have affected earnings only for that portion of the year during which the issue proceeds were available to management for use in the business.

The following extract illustrates the approach taken by Nordea Bank AB to quantify the impact on the weighted average number of shares of shares repurchased and traded during the period.

Extract 35.2: Nordea Bank AB (publ) (2007)

Notes to the financial statements [extract]
Note 14:   Earnings per share (EPS) [extract]

Group	31 Dec 2007	31 Dec 2006
Profit attributable to shareholders of Nordea Bank AB (publ) (EURm)	3,121	3,145
Weighted average number of shares outstanding (in millions)	2,591	2,592
Weighted average number of shares outstanding after full dilution (in millions):	2,592	2,592
Earnings per share, EUR	1.20	1.21
Earnings per share, after full dilution, EUR	1.20	1.21
Weighted average number of shares outstanding (in millions):		
Number of shares outstanding at beginning of year	2,594	2,594
Adjustment for average own shares referring to Nordea Bank AB (publ)'s repurchase of own shares	2	–
Adjustment for average own shares in trading portfolio	–5	–2
Weighted average number of shares outstanding at end of year	2,591	2,592
Adjustment for weighted average number of additional ordinary shares outstanding after full dilution	1	–
Weighted average number of shares outstanding after full dilution, at end of year	2,592	2,592

Chapter 35

4.2   Purchase and redemption of own shares

An entity may, if it is authorised to do so by its constitution and it complies with any relevant legislation, purchase or otherwise redeem its own shares. Assuming this is done at fair value, then the earnings should be apportioned over the weighted average share capital in issue for the year. This was illustrated in Example 35.1 above in relation to the purchase of treasury shares. If, on the other hand, the repurchase is at significantly more than market value then IAS 33 requires adjustments to be made to EPS for periods before buy-back. This is discussed at 4.3.5 below.

4.3   Changes in ordinary shares without corresponding changes in resources

IAS 33 requires the number of shares used in the calculation to be adjusted (for all periods presented) for any transaction (other than the conversion of potential ordinary shares) that changes the number of shares outstanding without a corresponding change in resources. *[IAS 33.26].* This is also to apply where some, but curiously not all, such changes have happened after the year-end but before the approval of the financial statements.

The standard gives the following as examples of changes in the number of ordinary shares without a corresponding change in resources:

(a)   a capitalisation or bonus issue (sometimes referred to as a stock dividend);

(b)   a bonus element in any other issue, for example a bonus element in a rights issue to existing shareholders;

(c)   a share split; and

(d)   a reverse share split (share consolidation). *[IAS 33.27].*

Another example not mentioned by the standard would be any bonus element in a buy-back, such as a put warrant involving the repurchase of shares at significantly more than their fair value.[1] The adjustments required to EPS for each of these is discussed below.

As noted above, IAS 33 requires retrospective adjustment for all such events that happen in the reporting period. However, it only requires restatement for those in (a), (c) and (d) if they happen after the year-end but before the financial statements are authorised for issue. *[IAS 33.64].* We are not convinced that this was the intention of the board, and suspect that it may be the result of less than precise drafting (particularly as the paragraph requiring restatement for these post-balance sheet changes also applies to events that have happened during the reporting period, but refers only to the same items) – however it is what the standard literally requires.

4.3.1   *Capitalisation, bonus issue, share split and share consolidation*

4.3.1.A   *Capitalisation, bonus issues and share splits*

A capitalisation or bonus issue or share split has the effect of increasing the number of shares in issue without any inflow of resources, as further ordinary shares are issued to existing shareholders for no consideration. Consequently, no additional earnings will be expected to accrue as a result of the issue. The additional shares should be treated as having been in issue for the whole period and also included in the EPS calculation of all earlier periods presented so as to give a comparable result. For example, on a two-for-one bonus issue, the number of ordinary shares outstanding before the issue is multiplied by three to obtain the new total number of ordinary shares, or by two to obtain the number of additional ordinary shares. *[IAS 33.28].*

The EPS calculation involving a bonus issue is illustrated in the following example.

Example 35.2:   A bonus issue [IAS 33.IE3]

Profit attributable to ordinary equity holders of the parent entity 2011	€180
Profit attributable to ordinary equity holders of the parent entity 2012	€600
Ordinary shares outstanding until 30 September 2012	200

Bonus issue 1 October 2012	2 ordinary shares for each ordinary share outstanding at 30 September 2012 $200 \times 2 = 400$
Basic earnings per share 2012	$\dfrac{€600}{(200 + 400)} = €1.00$
Basic earnings per share 2011	$\dfrac{€180}{(200 + 400)} = €0.30$

Because the bonus issue was without consideration, it is treated as if it had occurred before the beginning of 2011, the earliest period presented.

Again, although the standard is silent on the matter, we believe that any financial ratios disclosed for earlier periods, which are based on the number of equity shares at a year-end (e.g. dividend per share) should also be adjusted by in a similar manner.

4.3.1.B   Stock dividends

Stock or scrip dividends refer to the case where an entity offers its shareholders the choice of receiving further fully paid up shares in the company as an alternative to receiving a cash dividend. It could be argued that the dividend foregone represents payment for the shares, usually at fair value, and hence no restatement is appropriate. Alternatively, the shares could be viewed as being, in substance, bonus issues which require the EPS for the earlier period to be adjusted. IAS 33 seems to suggest the latter view, as it notes that capitalisation or bonus issues are sometimes referred to as stock dividends. However, entities often refer to these arrangements as dividend reinvestment plans which suggests the acquisition of new shares for valuable consideration.

In our view, this distinction should be a factual one. If an entity (say, through proposal and subsequent approval by shareholders) has a legal obligation to pay a dividend in cash or, at the shareholder's option, shares then the cash payment avoided if the scrip dividend is taken up is consideration for the shares. This may be equivalent to an issue at fair value or it may contain some bonus element requiring retrospective adjustment of EPS. In practice the fair value of shares received as a scrip alternative may exceed the cash alternative; this is often referred to as an enhanced scrip dividend. In these cases IAS 33 will require a bonus element to be identified, and prior EPS figures

Chapter 35

restated accordingly. This is essentially the same as adjustments for the bonus element in a rights issue, discussed at 4.3.3 below. Furthermore, in this scenario, during the period between the obligation coming into existence and its settlement (in cash or shares) it could be argued to represent a written call option and hence potentially affect diluted EPS (see 6.4.2 B below). Given that the standard is silent on this aspect of some stock dividends we doubt that such an approach was intended. In any event it strikes us as unlikely in most cases that the effect would be significant. Conversely, if the entity issues fresh shares *instead of* a dividend it is a bonus issue requiring full retrospective adjustment to EPS.

4.3.1.C   Share consolidations

Occasionally, entities will consolidate their equity share capital into a smaller number of shares. Such a consolidation generally reduces the number of shares outstanding without a corresponding outflow of resources, and this would require an adjustment to the denominator for periods before the consolidation. *[IAS 33.29]*.

4.3.2   Share consolidation with a special dividend

Share consolidations as discussed above normally do not involve any outflow of funds from the entity. However, entities may return surplus cash to their shareholders by paying special dividends accompanied by a share consolidation, the purpose of which is to maintain the value of each share following the payment of the dividend. This issue is specifically addressed by IAS 33 as revised in 2003 (the original standard being silent on the issue), perhaps because such schemes had been quite common when it was being revised. The normal rule of restating the outstanding number of shares for all periods for a share consolidation is not applied when the overall effect is a share repurchase at fair value because in such cases the reduction of shares *is* the result of a corresponding reduction in resources. In such cases the weighted average number of shares is adjusted for the consolidation from the date the special dividend is recognised. *[IAS 33.29]*.

One IAS reporter in this situation was Intercontinental Hotels Group PLC as shown in Extract 35.3 below.

Extract 35.3: Intercontinental Hotels Group PLC (2007)

Notes to the financial statements [extract]
Note 9:   Earnings per ordinary share [extract]

Basic earnings per ordinary share is calculated by dividing the profit for the year available for IHG equity holders by the weighted average number of ordinary shares, excluding investment in own shares, in issue during the year.

Diluted earnings per ordinary share is calculated by adjusting basic earnings per ordinary share to reflect the notional exercise of the weighted average number of dilutive ordinary share options outstanding during the year.

On June 1, 2007, shareholders approved a share capital consolidation on the basis of 47 new ordinary shares for every 56 existing ordinary shares, together with a special dividend of 200 pence per existing ordinary share. The overall effect of the transaction was that of a share repurchase at fair value, therefore no adjustment has been made to comparative data.

Adjusted earnings per ordinary share is disclosed in order to show performance undistorted by exceptional items, to give a more meaningful comparison of the Company's performance.

There is undoubtedly a conceptual attraction in trying to standardise adjustments made to prior years' EPS figures. However, in our view the approach taken by the standard is rather piecemeal, in that restatement is only ever triggered by a change in the number of shares, and it will not necessarily achieve the objective of standardising the restatement of EPS. Capital may be returned to shareholders in various different ways, including demergers and group reconstructions, as well as share buybacks and special dividends. In many such cases the number of shares in issue is only reduced if the entity opts to consolidate its shares. The natural consequence of returning capital is that earnings will fall, so it is debatable whether a fall in EPS in these circumstances should be regarded as a distortion that needs to be corrected at all. Of course, if an entity buys back its shares, the number of shares will automatically be reduced and therefore affect the EPS calculation in a way that other returns of capital do not, but this does not necessarily mean that a special dividend should be treated as if it were a share buyback. However, the standard is now clear, so entities must apply these provisions so that this specific type of return of capital will fall to be treated as a share repurchase, but only when the entity also chooses to consolidate its shares.

4.3.3   *Rights issue*

A rights issue is a popular method through which entities are able to access the capital markets for further capital. Under the terms of such an issue, existing shareholders are given the opportunity to acquire further shares in the entity on a pro-rata basis to their existing shareholdings.

The 'rights' shares will usually be offered either at the current market price or at a price below that. In the former case, the treatment of the issue for EPS purposes is as discussed in 4.1 above. However, where the rights price is at a discount to market it is not quite as straightforward, since the issue is equivalent to a bonus issue (see 4.3.1 above) combined with an issue at full market price. In such cases, IAS 33 requires an adjustment to the number of shares outstanding before the rights issue to reflect the bonus element inherent in it. *[IAS 33.26-27]*.

The bonus element of the rights issue available to all existing shareholders is given by the following adjustment factor, sometimes referred to as the bonus fraction: *[IAS 33.A2]*

$$\frac{\text{Fair value per share immediately before the exercise of rights}}{\text{Theoretical ex-rights fair value per share}}$$

The fair value per share immediately before the exercise of rights is the *actual* price at which the shares are quoted inclusive of the right to take up the future shares under the rights issue. Where the rights are to be traded separately from the shares the fair value used is the closing price on the last day on which the shares are traded inclusive of the right. *[IAS 33.A2]*.

The 'ex-rights fair value' is the *theoretical* price at which the shares would be expected to be quoted, other stock market factors apart, after the rights issue shares have been issued. It is calculated by adding the aggregate fair value of the shares immediately before the exercise of the rights to the proceeds from the exercise, and dividing by the number of shares outstanding after the exercise. *[IAS 33.A2]*. The EPS calculation involving a rights issue is illustrated in the following example.

Example 35.3:   Rights issue at less than full market price [IAS 33.IE4]

	2010	2011	2012
Profit attributable to ordinary equity holders of the parent entity	€1,100	€1,500	€1,800

Shares outstanding before rights issue	500 shares
Rights issue	One new share for each five outstanding shares (100 new shares total) Exercise price: €5.00 Date of rights issue: 1 January 2011 Last date to exercise rights: 1 March 2011
Market price of one ordinary share immediately before exercise on 1 March 2011	€11.00
Reporting date	31 December

Calculation of theoretical ex-rights value per share

$$\frac{\text{Fair value of all outstanding shares before the exercise of rights} + \text{Total amount received from exercise of rights}}{\text{Number of shares outstanding before exercise} + \text{Number of shares issued in the exercise}} =$$

$$\frac{(€11.00 \times 500 \text{ shares}) + (€5.00 \times 100 \text{ shares})}{500 \text{ shares} + 100 \text{ shares}}$$

Theoretical ex-rights value per share = €10.00

Calculation of adjustment factor

$$\frac{\text{Fair value per share before exercise of rights}}{\text{Theoretical ex - rights value per share}} = \frac{€11.00}{€10.00} = 1.10$$

Calculation of basic earnings per share

	2010	2011	2012
2010 basic EPS as originally reported: €1,100 ÷ 500 shares =	€2.20		
2010 basic EPS restated for rights issue: €1,100 ÷ (500 shares × 1.1) =	€2.00		
2011 basic EPS including effects of rights issue: $\dfrac{€1,500}{(500 \times 1.1 \times 2/12) + (600 \times 10/12)} =$		€2.54	
2012 basic EPS: €1,800 ÷ 600 shares =			€3.00

Rather than multiplying the denominator by 11/10ths, the previous year's EPS (and any EPS disclosures in a historical summary) could alternatively be arrived at by multiplying the original EPS by 10/11ths.

Whilst the rights are outstanding they represent, strictly speaking, a written call option over the entity's shares which could have implications for diluted EPS (see 6.4.2 below).

It is possible that shares could be issued as a result of open offers, placings and other offerings of equity shares not made to existing shareholders, at a discount to the market price. In such cases it would be necessary to consider whether the issue contained a bonus element, or rather simply reflected differing views on the fair value of the shares. In our opinion the latter seems a far more realistic alternative. Accordingly the shares should be dealt with on a weighted average basis without calculating any bonus element when computing the EPS.

4.3.4 B share schemes

One method by which some entities have returned capital to shareholders is the so-called 'B share scheme'. These schemes involve issuing 'B shares' (usually undated preference shares with low or zero coupons) to existing shareholders, either as a bonus issue or via a share split. These are then repurchased for cash and cancelled, following which the ordinary shares are consolidated. The overall effect is intended to be the same as a repurchase of ordinary shares at fair value, and accordingly no retrospective adjustment to EPS is necessary. *[IAS 33.29]*. A typical example is Cairn Energy PLC as shown in the following extract.

Extract 35.4: Cairn Energy PLC (2007)

Notes to the accounts [extract]

27.   Share Capital [extract]

Group and Company	Number 5p B Shares '000	Number 10p Ordinary '000	Number 6₂/₁₃p Ordinary '000
Authorised ordinary shares			
At 1 January 2006 and 1 January 2007	–	225,000	–
Consolidation of Shares	160,468	(225,000)	365,625
B Shares repurchased and cancelled	(160,468)	–	–
At 31 December 2007	–	–	365,625

	Number 5p B Shares '000	Number 10p Ordinary '000	Number 6₂/₁₃p Ordinary '000	Number 10p Ordinary $'000	6₂/₁₃p Ordinary $'000
Allotted, issued and fully paid ordinary shares					
At 1 January 2006	–	159,767	–	25,775	–
Issued and allotted for employee share options	–	520	–	95	–
At 1 January 2007	–	160,287	–	25,870	–
Issued and allotted for employee share options pre-consolidation	–	181	–	36	–
Consolidation of shares	160,468	(160,468)	130,380	(25,906)	15,795
B Shares repurchased and cancelled	(160,468)	–	–	–	–
Issued and allotted for employee share options post-consolidation	–	–	183	–	50
At 31 December 2007	–	–	130,563	–	15,845

Chapter 35

At an extraordinary general meeting held on 22 March 2007, it was resolved that the 160,467,920 existing ordinary shares of 10 pence each be replaced by 130,380,285 new ordinary shares of 6 2/13 pence each and 160,467,920 B shares of 5 pence each. The effective date of this transaction was 23 March 2007.

The B share scheme allowed Cairn to return to shareholders $936m (including expenses) of the proceeds from the flotation of its Indian business, Cairn India. The B shares were not listed on the Official List nor admitted to trading on the London Stock Exchange. As at the Balance Sheet date, all B shares had been fully converted to cash.

In order to make the market price of a Cairn share comparable before and after the return of cash to shareholders, a share consolidation was carried out to convert 16 existing ordinary shares of 10 pence each to 13 new ordinary shares of 6 2/13 pence each.

Following the share capital consolidation, Cairn's authorised equity share capital was 365,625,000 shares of 6 2/13 pence each.

12.   Earnings per ordinary share [extract]

The earnings per ordinary share are calculated on a profit of $1,519,653,000 (2006 (restated): loss $97,122,000) and on a weighted average of 135,637,411 ordinary shares (2006: 157,654,751). The weighted average of ordinary shares excludes share held by the Cairn Energy PLC Employees' Share Trust. No retrospective adjustment was made to the weighted average number of shares, relating to the share consolidation of 23 March 2007, as there was a corresponding change in resources in the form of the return of cash to shareholders (see Notes 27 and 29).

The diluted earnings per ordinary share are calculated on a profit of $1,519,511,000 and on 135,844,139 ordinary shares. The profit of $1,519,511,000 reflects the reduced profit attributable to equity holders of the parent after potential Cairn India share option issues. The figure of 135,844,139 ordinary shares is the basic weighted average of 135,637,411 ordinary shares and the 206,728 dilutive potential ordinary shares relating to share options.

In respect of 2006, 587,128 potential ordinary shares were anti-dilutive.

4.3.5   Put warrants priced above market value

As noted at 4.3 above, an example of a change in the number of shares outstanding without a corresponding change in resources not mentioned by the standard would be any bonus element in a buy-back, such as a put warrant involving the repurchase of shares at significantly more than their fair value. The accounting requirements for such instruments are discussed in Chapter 45 at 10.

Unfortunately IAS 33 does not give an illustrative calculation for a put warrant at significantly more than fair value, but it does for the familiar rights issue (rights issues are discussed at 4.3.3 above). In a rights issue new shares are issued at a discount to market value, whereas with put warrants shares are bought back at a premium to market value. In both cases the remaining shares are viewed as being devalued for the purposes of comparing EPS over time. Applying the logic of adjusting EPS when there is a change in the number of shares without a corresponding change in resources seems to require that put warrants are treated as a reverse rights issue. This would mean calculating a similar 'adjustment factor', and applying it to the number of shares outstanding before the transaction. The difference in the calculation would be that the number of shares issued and the consideration received for them would be replaced by negative amounts representing the number of shares put back to the entity and the amount paid for them.

An illustration of what this might entail is as follows:

Example 35.4: Put warrants priced above market value

The following example takes the same scenario as Example 35.3 above (a rights issue), altered to illustrate a put warrant scheme. In that example the shares are issued at a discount of €6.00 to the €11.00 market price on a one for five basis two months into the year. Reversing this would give a put warrant to sell shares back to the company at a €6 premium, again on a one for five basis. All other details have been left the same for comparability, although in reality the rising earnings following a rights issue may well become falling earnings after a buy-back. The calculation would then become:

Calculation of theoretical ex-warrant value per share

$$\frac{\text{fair value of all outstanding shares before the exercise of warrants} - \text{total amount paid on exercise of warrants}}{\text{shares outstanding before exercise} - \text{shares cancelled in the exercise}} =$$

$$\frac{(€11 \times 500) - (€17 \times 100)}{500 - 100} = €9.50$$

Calculation of adjustment factor

$$\frac{\text{Fair value per share before exercise of warrants}}{\text{Theoretical ex - warrant value per share}} = \frac{€11}{€9.5} = 1.16$$

Calculation of basic earnings per share

	2010 €	2011 €	2012 €
2010 EPS as originally reported: €1,100 ÷ 500 shares =	2.20		
2010 EPS restated for warrants: €1,100 ÷ (500 shares × 1.16) =	1.90		

	2010 €	2011 €	2012 €
2011 EPS including effects of warrants:			
$$\frac{€1,500}{(500 \times 1.16 \times 2/12) + (400 \times 10/12)} =$$		3.49	
2012 basic EPS: €1,800 ÷ 400 shares =			3.49

Whilst the above seems a sensible interpretation of the requirements, as the procedure is not specified there may be scope for other interpretations.

4.4   Options exercised during the year

Shares issued as a result of options being exercised should be dealt with on a weighted average basis in the basic EPS. *[IAS 33.38]*. Furthermore, options that have been exercised during the year will also affect diluted EPS calculations. If the options in question would have had a diluting effect on the basic EPS had they been exercised at the beginning of the year, then they should be considered in the diluted EPS calculation as explained in 6.4.2 below, but on a weighted average basis for the period up to the date of exercise. The exercise of options is a 'conversion of potential ordinary shares'. The standard excludes such conversions from the general requirement (see 4.3 above) to adjust prior periods' EPS when a change in the number of shares happens without a corresponding change in resources. *[IAS 33.26].*

4.5   Post balance sheet changes in capital

The EPS figure should not reflect any changes in the capital structure occurring after the reporting period, but before the financial statements are approved, which was effected for fair value. This is because any proceeds received from the issue were not available for use during the period. However, EPS for all periods presented should be adjusted for any bonus element in certain post year-end changes in the number of shares, as discussed at 4.3 above. When this is done that fact should be stated. *[IAS 33.64].*

4.6   Issue to acquire another business

4.6.1   Acquisitions

As a result of a share issue to acquire another business, funds or other assets will flow into the business and extra profits will be expected to be generated. When calculating EPS, it should be assumed that the shares were issued on the acquisition date (even if the actual date of issue is later), since this will be the date from which the results of the newly acquired business are recognised. *[IAS 33.21(f), 22].*

4.6.2   Reverse acquisitions

Reverse acquisition is the term used to describe a business combination whereby the legal parent entity after the combination is in substance the acquired and not the acquiring entity (discussed in Chapter 10 at 14). IAS 33 is silent on the subject, however, an appendix to IFRS 3 – *Business Combinations* – contains a discussion of the implications for EPS of such transactions. Following a reverse acquisition the equity structure appearing in the consolidated financial statements will reflect the equity of the legal parent, including the equity instruments issued by it to effect the business combination. *[IFRS 3.B25].*

For the purposes of calculating the weighted average number of ordinary shares outstanding during the period in which the reverse acquisition occurs:

(a)   the number of ordinary shares outstanding from the beginning of that period to the acquisition date shall be computed on the basis of the weighted average number of ordinary shares of the legal acquiree (accounting acquirer) outstanding during the period multiplied by the exchange ratio established in the merger agreement; and

(b)   the number of ordinary shares outstanding from the acquisition date to the end of that period shall be the actual number of ordinary shares of the legal acquirer (the accounting acquiree) outstanding during that period. *[IFRS 3.B26].*

The basic EPS disclosed for each comparative period before the acquisition date is calculated by dividing the profit or loss of the legal subsidiary attributable to ordinary shareholders in each of those periods by the legal acquiree's historical weighted average number of ordinary shares outstanding multiplied by the exchange ratio established in the acquisition agreement *[IFRS 3.B27]*.

IFRS 3 presents an illustrative example of a reverse acquisition, including the EPS calculation, see Chapter 10 at 14.5.

4.6.3 Establishment of a new parent undertaking

Where a new parent entity is established by means of a share for share exchange and the pooling of interest method has been adopted (discussed in Chapter 11 at 3.1, the number of shares taken as being in issue for both the current and preceding periods would be the number of shares issued by the new parent entity. However, EPS calculations for previous periods in the new parent entity's financial statements would have to reflect any changes in the number of outstanding ordinary shares of the former parent entity that may have occurred in those periods, as illustrated in the example below:

Example 35.5:   Calculation of EPS where a new holding company is established

Entity A has been established as the newly formed parent entity of Entity B in a one for one share exchange on 30 June 2012. At that date, Entity B has 1,000,000 €1 ordinary shares in issue. Previously, on 30 June 2011 Entity B had issued 200,000 €1 ordinary shares for cash at full market price. Both entities have a 31 December year-end and the trading results of Entity B are as follows:

	2012 €	2011 €
Profit for equity shareholders after taxation	500,000	300,000

The earnings per share calculation of Entity A is shown below:

	2012	2011
Number of equity shares	$800,000 \times \dfrac{6}{12} =$	400,000
	$1,000,000 \times \dfrac{6}{12} =$	500,000
	1,000,000	900,000
EPS	$\dfrac{500,000}{1,000,000} = €0.50$	$\dfrac{300,000}{900,000} = €0.33$

If, in the above example, the share exchange did not take place on a one for one basis, but Entity A issued three shares for every one share held in Entity B, then the number of shares issued by Entity B in 2011 would have to be apportioned accordingly before carrying out the weighted average calculation. The earnings per share calculation would, therefore, have been as follows:

	2012		*2011*
Number of equity shares	$2,400,000 \times \dfrac{6}{12} =$		1,200,000
	$3,000,000 \times \dfrac{6}{12} =$		1,500,000
	3,000,000		2,700,000
EPS	$\dfrac{500,000}{3,000,000} = €0.17$		$\dfrac{300,000}{2,700,000} = €0.11$

4.7   Adjustments to EPS in historical summaries

In order to ensure comparability of EPS figures, the previously published EPS figures for all periods presented in IFRS financial statements should be adjusted for subsequent changes in capital not involving full consideration at fair value (apart from the conversion of potential ordinary shares) in the manner described in 4.3 above; they should also be adjusted, in our view, for certain group reconstructions. Often entities will include EPS figures in historical summaries (typically five years) in the analyses and discussions accompanying (but not part of) the financial statements. We suggest that all such analyses need similar adjustments in order to be meaningful. We would also suggest that the resultant figures should be described as restated.

5   MATTERS AFFECTING THE NUMERATOR

5.1   Earnings

The earnings figure on which the basic EPS calculation is based should be the consolidated net profit or loss for the year after tax, non-controlling interests and after adjusting for returns to preference shareholders that are not already included in net profit (as will be the case for preference shares classified as liabilities under IAS 32).

5.2   Preference dividends

The adjustments to net profit attributable to ordinary shareholders in relation to returns to preference shareholders should include:

- the after-tax amount of any preference dividends on non-cumulative preference shares declared in respect of the period; *[IAS 33.14(a)]*

- the after-tax amount of the preference dividends for cumulative preference shares required for the period, whether or not the dividends have been declared. This does not include the amount of any preference dividends for cumulative preference shares paid or declared during the current period in respect of previous periods; *[IAS 33.14(b)]*

- any original issue discount or premium on increasing rate preference shares which is amortised to retained earnings using the effective interest method. Increasing rate preference shares are those that provide: a low initial dividend to compensate an entity for selling them at a discount; or an above-market dividend in later periods to compensate investors for purchasing them at a premium (see Example 35.6 below); *[IAS 33.15]*

- the excess of the fair value of the consideration paid to shareholders over the carrying amount of the preference shares when the shares are repurchased under an entity's tender offer to the holders. As this represents a return to the holders of the shares (and a charge to retained earnings for the entity) it is deducted in calculating profit or loss attributable to ordinary equity holders of the parent entity; *[IAS 33.16]*

- the excess of the fair value of the ordinary shares or other consideration paid over the fair value of the ordinary shares issuable under the original conversion terms when early conversion of convertible preference shares is induced through favourable changes to the original conversion terms or the payment of additional consideration. This is a return to the preference shareholders, and accordingly is deducted in calculating profit or loss attributable to ordinary equity holders of the parent entity; *[IAS 33.17]* and

- any excess of the carrying amount of preference shares over the fair value of the consideration paid to settle them. This reflects a gain to the entity and is added in calculating profit or loss attributable to ordinary equity holders. *[IAS 33.18]*.

The computation of EPS involving increasing rate preference shares is illustrated in the following example.

Example 35.6:   Increasing rate preference shares [IAS 33.IE1]

Entity D issued non-convertible, non-redeemable class A cumulative preference shares of €100 par value on 1 January 2012. The class A preference shares are entitled to a cumulative annual dividend of €7 per share starting in 2014. At the time of issue, the market rate dividend yield on the class A preference shares was 7 per cent a year. Thus, Entity D could have expected to receive proceeds of approximately €100 per class A preference share if the dividend rate of €7 per share had been in effect at the date of issue.

In consideration of the dividend payment terms, however, the class A preference shares were issued at €81.63 per share, i.e. at a discount of €18.37 per share. The issue price can be calculated by taking the present value of €100, discounted at 7 per cent over a three-year period. Because the shares are classified as equity, the original issue discount is amortised to retained earnings using the effective interest method and treated as a preference dividend for earnings per share purposes. To calculate basic earnings per share, the following imputed dividend per class A preference share is deducted to determine the profit or loss attributable to ordinary equity holders of the parent entity:

Year paid	Carrying amount of class A preference shares 1 January	Imputed dividend [1]	Carrying amount of class A preference shares 31 December [2]	Dividend
	€	€	€	€
2012	81.63	5.71	87.34	–
2013	87.34	6.12	93.46	–
2014	93.46	6.54	100.00	–
Thereafter:	100.00	7.00	107.00	(7.00)

[1] at 7%

[2] This is before dividend payment.

5.3   Retrospective adjustments

Where comparative figures have been restated (for example, to correct a material error or as a result of a change in accounting policy), earnings per share for all periods presented should also be restated. *[IAS 33.64]*.

5.4   Participating equity instruments and two class shares

As noted at 3.2 above, IAS 33 envisages entities having more than one class of ordinary shares and requires the calculation and presentation of EPS for each such class. *[IAS 33.66]*. Although perhaps not exactly obvious from the definition, some instruments that have a right to participate in profits are viewed by the standard as ordinary shares. The standard observes that the equity of some entities includes:

(a)   instruments that participate in dividends with ordinary shares according to a predetermined formula (for example, two for one) with, at times, an upper limit on the extent of participation (for example, up to, but not beyond, a specified amount per share); and

(b)   a class of ordinary shares with a different dividend rate from that of another class of ordinary shares but without prior or senior rights. *[IAS 33.A13]*.

In our view whilst category (a) could encompass some participating preference shares (as illustrated in Example 35.7 below), not all participating preference shares would necessarily fall to be treated as ordinary shares for EPS purposes. This is because the participation features of some instruments could mean that they are not subordinate to all other classes of equity instrument. The meaning of ordinary shares for EPS purposes is discussed at 3.2 above.

To calculate basic (and diluted) earnings per share:

(a)   profit or loss attributable to ordinary equity holders of the parent entity is adjusted (a profit reduced and a loss increased) by the amount of dividends declared in the period for each class of shares and by the contractual amount of dividends (or interest on participating bonds) that must be paid for the period (for example, unpaid cumulative dividends);

(b)   the remaining profit or loss is allocated to ordinary shares and participating equity instruments to the extent that each instrument shares in earnings as if all of the profit or loss for the period had been distributed. The total profit or loss allocated to each class of equity instrument is determined by adding together the amount allocated for dividends and the amount allocated for a participation feature; and

(c)   the total amount of profit or loss allocated to each class of equity instrument is divided by the number of outstanding instruments to which the earnings are allocated to determine the earnings per share for the instrument.

For the calculation of diluted earnings per share, all potential ordinary shares assumed to have been issued are included in outstanding ordinary shares. *[IAS 33.A14]*. This is discussed at 6.4 below.

Participating equity instruments and two-class ordinary shares are illustrated with the following example.

Example 35.7:   *Participating equity instruments and two-class ordinary shares*
[IAS 33.IE11]

Profit attributable to equity holders of the parent entity	€100,000
Ordinary shares outstanding	10,000
Non-convertible preference shares	6,000
Non-cumulative annual dividend on preference shares	€5.50 per share
(before any dividend is paid on ordinary shares)	

After ordinary shares have been paid a dividend of €2.10 per share, the preference shares participate in any additional dividends on a 20:80 ratio with ordinary shares (i.e. after preference and ordinary shares have been paid dividends of €5.50 and €2.10 per share, respectively, preference shares participate in any additional dividends at a rate of one-fourth of the amount paid to ordinary shares on a per-share basis).

Dividends on preference shares paid	€33,000	(€5.50 per share)
Dividends on ordinary shares paid	€21,000	(€2.10 per share)

Basic earnings per share is calculated as follows:

	€	€
Profit attributable to equity holders of the parent entity		100,000
Less dividends paid:		
Preference	33,000	
Ordinary	21,000	
		(54,000)
Undistributed earnings		46,000

Allocation of undistributed earnings:
Allocation per ordinary share = A
Allocation per preference share = B; B = 1/4 A

$$\text{(A } 10{,}000) + (1/4 \text{ A } 6{,}000) = €46{,}000$$
$$A = €46{,}000 \div (10{,}000 + 1{,}500)$$
$$A = €4.00$$
$$B = 1/4 \text{ A}$$
$$B = €1.00$$

Basic per share amounts:

	Preference shares	Ordinary shares
Distributed earnings	€5.50	€2.10
Undistributed earnings	€1.00	€4.00
Totals	€6.50	€6.10

NB. This example does not illustrate the classification of the components of convertible financial instruments as liabilities and equity or the classification of related interest and dividends as expenses and equity as required by IAS 32.

It is worth noting that this calculation provided by the standard does not actually follow the procedure specified by IAS 33. As noted above, the method outlined by the standard is to allocate dividends and then all remaining profits to the different classes of share then divide this by the number of shares in each class. The above example computes dividends and then remaining profit on a per-share basis and then combines them.

Chapter 35

5.5   Other bases

It is not uncommon for entities to supplement the EPS figures required by IAS 33 by voluntarily presenting additional amounts per share. For additional *earnings* per share amounts, the standard requires that:

(a)   the denominator used should be that required by IAS 33;

(b)   basic and diluted amounts be disclosed with equal prominence and presented in the notes;

(c)   an indication of the basis on which the numerator is determined, including whether amounts per share are before or after tax; and

(d)   if the numerator is not reported as a component of the statement of comprehensive income or separate statement of profit or loss, a reconciliation between it and a line item that is reported in the statement of comprehensive income. *[IAS 33.73, 73A].*

The requirement in (b) is a curious one – or at least curiously phrased. The wording of the standard requires that additional EPS figures be 'presented in the notes'. Some commentators have asserted that this amounts to banning the presentation of such figures on the face of the statement of comprehensive income (or separate income statement if one is presented). In our view, however, it is clear that a requirement to put a disclosure in the notes simply does not amount to a prohibition on also presenting it elsewhere as well. This view is reflected in the fact that alternative EPS figures quite commonly appear on the face of income statements prepared under IFRS.[2]

In September 2007 the IASB indicated that it intended to modify IAS 33 to prohibit the presentation of alternative EPS figures on the face of the income statement as part of the annual improvements project. *[IAS 1.BC103].* However, that project was ultimately finalised without addressing this issue.

In August 2008 the IASB published an exposure draft proposing changes to IAS 33 (see 8 below). One of the proposals in the exposure draft was to amend the standard so as to prohibit the presentation of alternative EPS in the statement of comprehensive income (or separate income statement) and allow it only in the notes.[3]

The requirements discussed above apply to voluntarily presented *earnings* per share figures. The standard does not mention the presentation of other 'per share' figures. We believe that if the per share disclosure is of some measure of performance over time (say, cash flow per share) then it would be necessary to use the same denominator as required by the standard for EPS. Other measures may relate to a point in time (say, net assets per share). In such cases the quantity of shares as at the measurement date would be a more appropriate denominator.

6   DILUTED EARNINGS PER SHARE

6.1   The need for diluted EPS

The presentation of basic EPS seeks to show a performance measure, by computing how much profit an entity has earned for each of the shares in issue for the period.

Entities often enter into commitments to issue shares in the future which would result in a change in basic EPS. IAS 33 refers to such commitments as potential ordinary shares, which it defines as 'a financial instrument or other contract that may entitle its holder to ordinary shares'. *[IAS 33.5]*.

Examples of potential ordinary shares given by IAS 33 are:

(a)   financial liabilities or equity instruments, including preference shares, that are convertible into ordinary shares;

(b)   options and warrants (whether accounted for under IAS 32 or IFRS 2);

(c)   shares that would be issued upon the satisfaction of conditions resulting from contractual arrangements, such as the purchase of a business or other assets. *[IAS 33.7]*.

When potential shares are actually issued, the impact on basic EPS will be two-fold. First, the number of shares in issue will change; second, profits could be affected, for example by lower interest charges or the return made on cash inflows. Scenarios whereby such an adjustment to basic EPS is unfavourable are described by the standard as dilution, defined as 'a reduction in earnings per share or an increase in loss per share resulting from the assumption that convertible instruments are converted, that options or warrants are exercised, or that ordinary shares are issued upon the satisfaction of specified conditions'. *[IAS 33.5]*. This potential fall in EPS is quantified by computing diluted EPS, and as a result:

(a)   profit or loss attributable to equity holders is increased by the after-tax amount of dividends and interest recognised in the period in respect of the dilutive potential ordinary shares and is adjusted for any other changes in income or expense that would result from the conversion of the dilutive potential ordinary shares; and

(b)   the weighted average number of ordinary shares outstanding is increased by the weighted average number of additional ordinary shares that would have been outstanding assuming the conversion of all dilutive potential ordinary shares. *[IAS 33.32]*.

6.2   Calculation of diluted EPS

IAS 33 requires a diluted EPS figure to be calculated for the profit or loss attributable to ordinary equity holders of the parent and, if presented, profit or loss from continuing operations attributable to them. *[IAS 33.30]*. For these purposes, the profit or loss attributable to ordinary equity holders and the weighted average number of shares outstanding should be adjusted for the effects of all potential ordinary shares. *[IAS 33.31]*. In calculating diluted EPS, the number of shares should be that used in calculating basic EPS, plus the weighted average number of shares that would be issued on the conversion of all the dilutive potential ordinary shares into ordinary shares. As is the case for outstanding shares in the basic EPS calculation, potential ordinary shares should be weighted for the period they are outstanding. *[IAS 33.36, 38]*. Accordingly, potential ordinary shares:

- should be deemed to have been converted into ordinary shares at the beginning of the period or, if not in existence at the beginning of the period, the date of their issue; *[IAS 33.36]*

- which are cancelled or allowed to lapse should be included only for the period they are outstanding; and

- which convert into ordinary shares during the period are included up until the date of conversion (from which point they will be included in the basic EPS). *[IAS 33.38]*.

The number of dilutive potential ordinary shares should be determined independently for each period presented, and not subsequently revisited. In particular, prior periods' EPS are not restated for changes in assumptions about the conversion of potential shares into shares. IAS 33 also stresses, unnecessarily in our view, that the number of dilutive potential ordinary shares included in the year-to-date period is not a weighted average of the dilutive potential ordinary shares included in each interim computation. *[IAS 33.37, 65]* The reason the standard stresses this point is probably that it represents a change from the proposal in the draft 'improved' standard.[4]

6.2.1   Diluted earnings

The earnings figure should be that used for basic EPS adjusted to reflect any changes that would arise if the potential shares outstanding in the period were actually issued. Adjustment is to be made for the post-tax effects of:

(a)   any dividends or other items related to dilutive potential ordinary shares deducted in arriving at the earnings figure used for basic EPS;

(b)   any interest recognised in the period related to dilutive potential ordinary shares; and

(c)   any other changes in income or expense that would result from the conversion of the dilutive potential ordinary shares. *[IAS 33.33]*.

These adjustments will also include any amounts charged in accordance with the effective interest method prescribed by IAS 39 – *Financial Instruments: Recognition and Measurement* – as a result of allocating transaction costs, premiums or discounts over the term of the instrument. *[IAS 33.34]*. Instruments with a choice of settlement method may also require adjustments to the numerator as discussed at 6.2.2 below.

An example of an adjustment covered by (b) above is shown in the extract below.

Extract 35.5: Roche Holdings Ltd (2007)

Notes to the Roche Group Consolidated Financial Statements [extract]
29.   Earnings per share and non-voting equity security [extract]

Basic earnings per share and non-voting equity security

For the calculation of basic earnings per share and non-voting equity security, the number of shares and non-voting equity securities is reduced by the weighted average number of its own non-voting equity securities held by the Group during the period.

Basic earnings per share and non-voting equity security

	Continuing businesses		Group	
	2007	2006	**2007**	2006
Net income attributable to Roche shareholders (millions of CHF)	**9,761**	7,860	**9,761**	7,880
Number of shares (millions)	**160**	160	**160**	160
Number of non-voting equity securities (millions)	**703**	703	**703**	703
Weighted average number of own non-voting equity securities held (millions)	**(4)**	(11)	**(4)**	(11)
Weighted average number of shares and non-voting equity securities in issue (millions)	**859**	852	**859**	852
Basic earnings per shares and non-voting equity security (CHF)	**11.36**	9.22	**11.36**	9.24

Diluted earnings per share and non-voting equity security

For the calculation of diluted earnings per share and non-voting equity security, the net income and weighted average number of shares and non-voting equity securities outstanding are adjusted for the effects of all dilutive potential shares and non-voting equity securities.

Potential dilutive effects arise from the convertible debt instruments and the employee stock option plans. If the outstanding convertible debt instruments were to be converted then this would lead to a reduction in interest expense and an increase in the number of shares which may have a net dilutive effect on the earnings per share. The exercise of outstanding vested employee stock options would have a dilutive effect. The exercise of the outstanding vested Genentech employee stock options would have a dilutive effect if the net income of Genentech is positive. The diluted earnings per share and non-voting equity security reflects the potential impacts of these dilutive effects on the earnings per share figures.

Diluted earnings per share and non-voting equity security

	Continuing businesses		Group	
	2007	2006	**2007**	2006
Net income attributable to Roche shareholders (millions of CHF)	**9,761**	7,860	**9,761**	7,880
Elimination of interest expense, net of tax, of convertible debt instruments, where dilutive (millions of CHF)	**4**	25	**4**	25
Increase in minority share of Group net income, net of tax, assuming all outstanding Genentech stock options exercised (millions of CHF)	**(141)**	(100)	**(141)**	(100)
Net income used to calculate diluted earnings per share (million of CHF)	**9,624**	7,785	**9,624**	7,805
Weighted average number of shares and non-voting equity securities in issue (millions)	**859**	852	**859**	852
Adjustment for assumed conversion of convertible debt instruments, where dilutive	**1**	7	**1**	7
Adjustment for assumed exercise of equity compensation plans, where dilutive (millions)	**2**	3	**2**	3
Weighted average number of shares and non-voting equity securities in issue used to calculate diluted earnings per share (millions)	**862**	862	**862**	862
Diluted earnings per share and non-voting equity security (CHF)	**11.16**	9.03	**11.16**	9.05

The standard notes that certain earnings adjustments directly attributable to the instrument could have a knock-on impact on other items of income or expense which will need to be accounted for. For example, the lower interest charge following

Chapter 35

conversion of convertible debt could lead to higher charges under profit sharing schemes. *[IAS 33.35]*.

No imputed earnings are taken into account in respect of the proceeds to be received on exercise of share options or warrants. The effect of such potential ordinary shares on the diluted EPS is reflected in the computation of the denominator. This is discussed at 6.4.2 below.

6.2.2   *Diluted number of shares*

IAS 33 discusses a number of specific types of potential ordinary shares and how they should be brought into the calculation, which are discussed at 6.4 below.

More generally, the standard also discusses scenarios where the method of conversion or settlement of potential ordinary shares is at the discretion of one of the parties, as follows:

(a)   The number of shares that would be issued on conversion should be determined from the terms of the potential ordinary shares. When more than one basis of conversion exists, the calculation should assume the most advantageous conversion rate or exercise price from the standpoint of the holder of the potential ordinary shares; *[IAS 33.39]*

(b)   When an entity has issued a contract that may be settled in shares or cash at its option, it should presume that the contract will be settled in shares. The resulting potential ordinary shares would be included in diluted earnings per share if the effect is dilutive. *[IAS 33.58]*. When such a contract is presented for accounting purposes as an asset or a liability, or has an equity component and a liability component, the numerator should be adjusted for any changes in profit or loss that would have resulted during the period if the contract had been classified wholly as an equity instrument. That adjustment is similar to the adjustments discussed at 6.2.1 above; *[IAS 33.59]* and

(c)   For contracts that may be settled in ordinary shares or cash at the holder's option, the more dilutive of cash settlement and share settlement should be used in calculating diluted earnings per share. *[IAS 33.60]*.

An example of an instrument covered by (b) above is a debt instrument that, on maturity, gives the issuer the unrestricted right to settle the principal amount in cash or in its own ordinary shares (see Example 35.10 at 6.4.1 A below). An example of an instrument covered by (c) is a written put option that gives the holder a choice of settling in ordinary shares or cash. *[IAS 33.61]*.

In our view, the standard's requirements in (b) and (c) above relating to settlement options are somewhat confused. In particular they seem to envisage a binary accounting model based on the strict legal form of settlement (cash or shares). However, IAS 32 sets out rules for *three* different settlement methods – net cash, net shares and gross physical settlement (discussed in Chapter 45 at 10). One consequence of the above is that, if taken literally, the numerator is only required to be adjusted to remove items of income or expense arising from a liability when there is a choice of settlement method. However, mandatory net share settlement also gives rise to a liability and income/expense under IAS 32. In our view any such income statement items should be removed for diluted EPS purposes.

6.3 Dilutive potential ordinary shares

Only those potential shares whose issue would have a dilutive effect on EPS are brought into the calculation. Potential ordinary shares are 'antidilutive' when their conversion to ordinary shares would increase earnings per share or decrease loss per share. *[IAS 33.5, 43]*. The calculation of diluted earnings per share should not assume conversion, exercise, or other issue of potential ordinary shares that would have an antidilutive effect on earnings per share. *[IAS 33.43]*. The standard gives detailed guidance for determining which potential shares are deemed to be dilutive, and hence brought into the diluted EPS calculation. This guidance covers the element of profit which needs to be diluted to trigger inclusion, and the sequence in which potential shares are tested to establish cumulative dilution. Each is discussed below.

6.3.1 *Dilution judged by effect on profits from continuing operations*

Potential ordinary shares are only to be treated as dilutive if their conversion to ordinary shares would decrease earnings per share or increase loss per share from *continuing* operations. The 'control number' that this focuses on is therefore the net result from continuing operations, which is the net profit or loss attributable to the parent entity, after deducting items relating to preference shares (see 5.2 above) and after excluding items relating to discontinuing operations. *[IAS 33.42]*. The same denominator is required to be used to compute diluted EPS from continuing operations and total diluted EPS. By determining which potential shares are to be included by reference to their impact on continuing EPS can produce some slightly curious results for total EPS. For example, it is possible to exclude instruments which would dilute basic EPS (but not continuing EPS), and include items which are anti-dilutive as regards total profit. This latter point is acknowledged by the standard as follows.

'To illustrate the application of the control number notion ... assume that an entity has profit from continuing operations attributable to the parent entity of CU 4,800, a loss from discontinuing operations attributable to the parent entity of (CU 7,200), a loss attributable to the parent entity of (CU 2,400), and 2,000 ordinary shares and 400 potential ordinary shares outstanding. The entity's basic earnings per share is CU 2.40 for continuing operations, (CU 3.60) for discontinuing operations and (CU 1.20) for the loss. The 400 potential ordinary shares are included in the diluted earnings per share calculation because the resulting CU 2.00 earnings per share for continuing operations is dilutive, assuming no profit or loss impact of those 400 potential ordinary shares. Because profit from continuing operations attributable to the parent entity is the control number, the entity also includes those 400 potential ordinary shares in the calculation of the other earnings per share amounts, even though the resulting earnings per share amounts are antidilutive to their comparable basic earnings per share amounts, i.e. the loss per share is less [(CU 3.00) per share for the loss from discontinuing operations and (CU 1.00) per share for the loss].' *[IAS 33.A3]*.

6.3.2 Dilution judged by the cumulative impact of potential shares

Where a entity has a number of different potential ordinary shares, in deciding whether they are dilutive (and hence reflected in the calculation), each issue or series of potential ordinary shares is to be considered in sequence from the most to the least dilutive. Only those potential shares which produce a cumulative dilution are to be included. This means that some potential shares which would dilute basic EPS if viewed on their own may need to be excluded. This results in a diluted EPS showing the maximum overall dilution of basic EPS. The standard observes that options and warrants should generally be included first as they do not affect the numerator in the diluted EPS calculation (but see the discussion at 6.4.2 below). *[IAS 33.44].* The way this is to be done is illustrated in the following example.

Example 35.8: *Calculation of weighted average number of shares: determining the order in which to include dilutive instruments* *[IAS 33.IE9]*

Earnings	€
Profit from continuing operations attributable to the parent entity	16,400,000
Less dividends on preference shares	(6,400,000)
Profit from continuing operations attributable to ordinary equity holders of the parent entity	10,000,000
Loss from discontinuing operations attributable to the parent entity	(4,000,000)
Profit attributable to ordinary equity holders of the parent entity	6,000,000
Ordinary shares outstanding	2,000,000
Average market price of one ordinary share during year	€75.00

Potential Ordinary Shares

Options	100,000 with exercise price of €60
Convertible preference shares	800,000 shares with a par value of €100 entitled to a cumulative dividend of €8 per share. Each preference share is convertible to two ordinary shares.
5% convertible bonds	Nominal amount €100,000,000. Each €1,000 bond is convertible to 20 ordinary shares. There is no amortisation of premium or discount affecting the determination of interest expense.
Tax rate	40%

Increase in Earnings Attributable to Ordinary Equity Holders on Conversion of Potential Ordinary Shares

	Increase in earnings €	Increase in number of ordinary shares	Earnings per incremental share €
Options			
Increase in earnings	Nil		
Incremental shares issued for no consideration			
$100,000 \times (€75 - €60) \div €75 =$		20,000	Nil
Convertible preference shares			
Increase in earnings			
$€800,000 \times 100 \times 0.08 =$	6,400,000		
Incremental shares			
$2 \times 800,000 =$		1,600,000	4.00

5% convertible bonds

Increase in earnings			
€100,000,000 × 0.05 × (1 − 0.40) =	3,000,000		
Incremental shares			
100,000 × 20 =		2,000,000	1.50

The order in which to include the dilutive instruments is therefore:

(1) Options
(2) 5% convertible bonds
(3) Convertible preference shares

Calculation of Diluted Earnings per Share

	Profit from continuing operations attributable to ordinary equity holders of the parent entity (control number)	Ordinary shares	Per share	
	€		€	
As reported	10,000,000	2,000,000	5.00	
Options	—	20,000		
	10,000,000	2,020,000	4.95	Dilutive
5% convertible bonds	3,000,000	2,000,000		
	13,000,000	4,020,000	3.23	Dilutive
Convertible preference shares	6,400,000	1,600,000		
	19,400,000	5,620,000	3.45	Antidilutive

Because diluted earnings per share is increased when taking the convertible preference shares into account (from €3.23 to €3.45), the convertible preference shares are antidilutive and are ignored in the calculation of diluted earnings per share. Therefore, diluted earnings per share for profit from continuing operations is €3.23:

	Basic EPS		Diluted EPS	
	€		€	
Profit from continuing operations attributable to ordinary equity holders of the parent entity	5.00		3.23	
Loss from discontinuing operations attributable to ordinary equity holders of the parent entity	(2.00)	(a)	(0.99)	(b)
Profit attributable to ordinary equity holders of the parent entity	3.00	(c)	2.24	(d)

(a) (€4,000,000) ÷ 2,000,000 = (€2.00)
(b) (€4,000,000) ÷ 4,020,000 = (€0.99)
(c) €6,000,000 ÷ 2,000,000 = €3.00
(d) (€6,000,000 + €3,000,000) ÷ 4,020,000 = €2.24

This example does not illustrate the classification of the components of convertible financial instruments as liabilities and equity or the classification of related interest and dividends as expenses and equity as required by IAS 32.

6.4 Particular types of dilutive instruments

6.4.1 *Convertible instruments*

In order to secure a lower rate of interest, entities sometimes attach benefits to loan stock, debentures or preference shares in the form of conversion rights. These permit the holder to convert his holding in whole or part into equity capital. The right is normally exercisable between specified dates. The ultimate conversion of the instrument will have the following effects:

Chapter 35

(a)   there will be an increase in earnings by the amount of the interest (or items relating to preference shares) no longer payable. As interest is normally allowable for tax purposes, the effect on earnings may be net of a tax deduction relating to some or all of the items; and

(b)   the number of ordinary shares in issue will increase. The diluted EPS should be calculated assuming that the instrument is converted into the maximum possible number of shares. *[IAS 33.49].*

Convertible preference shares will be antidilutive whenever the amount of the dividend on such shares declared in or accumulated for the current period per ordinary share obtainable on conversion exceeds basic earnings per share. Similarly, convertible debt will be antidilutive whenever its interest (net of tax and other changes in income or expense) per ordinary share obtainable on conversion exceeds basic earnings per share. *[IAS 33.50].*

A curious feature of the standard is the different treatment applied to the conversion feature in a convertible instrument to that applied to a stand alone option or warrant (see 6.4.2 below). IAS 32 requires split accounting for embedded conversion rights in a host convertible instrument (see Chapter 45 at 6). The effect of that is that for accounting purposes convertible instruments are treated in the same way as an equivalent non-convertible instrument accompanied by a stand alone warrant. It is somewhat illogical, therefore, that IAS 33 requires a different treatment to assess the dilution arising from separate and embedded warrants and options. In January 2006 the IASB indicated that it intended to address this, and proposed extending the so called treasury stock method to convertible instruments.[5] In March 2007, the IASB indicated that its earlier deliberations on the subject had been superseded by revised proposals. The revised proposals are discussed at 8 below.

6.4.1.A   Convertible debt

The EPS calculation for convertible bonds is illustrated in the following example:

Example 35.9:   Treatment of convertible bonds in diluted EPS calculations [IAS 33.IE6]

Profit attributable to ordinary equity holders of the parent entity	€1,004
Ordinary shares outstanding	1,000
Basic earnings per share	€1.00
Convertible bonds	100
Each block of 10 bonds is convertible into three ordinary shares	
Interest expense for the current year relating to the liability component of the convertible bonds	€10
Current and deferred tax relating to that interest expense	€4

Note: the interest expense includes amortisation of the discount arising on initial recognition of the liability component (see IAS 32 – *Financial Instruments: Disclosure and Presentation*).

Adjusted profit attributable to ordinary equity holders of the parent entity	€1,004 + €10 – €4 = €1,010
Number of ordinary shares resulting from conversion of bonds	30
Number of ordinary shares used to calculate diluted earnings per share	1,000 + 30 = 1,030
Diluted earnings per share	€1,010 ÷ 1,030 = €0.98

This example does not illustrate the classification of the components of convertible financial instruments as liabilities and equity or the classification of related interest and dividends as expenses and equity as required by IAS 32.

As discussed at 6.2.2 above, the standard also discusses the impact on diluted EPS of different settlement options. As discussed earlier, we believe this should be taken to mean that for diluted EPS purposes earnings should be adjusted to remove any items that arose from an instrument being classified as an asset or liability rather than equity. The standard claims to illustrate settlement options with the following example.

Example 35.10: *Convertible bonds settled in shares or cash at the issuer's option.*
          [IAS 33.IE8]

An entity issues 2,000 convertible bonds at the beginning of Year 1. The bonds have a three-year term, and are issued at par with a face value of €1,000 per bond, giving total proceeds of €2,000,000. Interest is payable annually in arrears at a nominal annual interest rate of 6 per cent. Each bond is convertible at any time up to maturity into 250 common shares. The entity has an option to settle the principal amount of the convertible bonds in ordinary shares or in cash.

When the bonds are issued, the prevailing market interest rate for similar debt without a conversion option is 9 per cent. At the issue date, the market price of one common share is €3. Income tax is ignored.

Profit attributable to ordinary equity holders of the parent entity Year 1	€1,000,000
Ordinary shares outstanding	1,200,000
Convertible bonds outstanding	2,000
Allocation of proceeds of the bond issue:	
Liability component	* €1,848,122
Equity component	€151,878
	€2,000,000

The liability and equity components would be determined in accordance with IAS 32. These amounts are recognised as the initial carrying amounts of the liability and equity components. The amount assigned to the issuer conversion option equity element is an addition to equity and is not adjusted.

*   This represents the present value of the principal and interest discounted at 9% – €2,000,000 payable at the end of three years; €120,000 payable annually in arrears for three years.

Basic earnings per share Year 1:

$$\frac{€\,1,000,000}{1,200,000} = €0.83 \text{ per ordinary share}$$

Diluted earnings per share Year 1:

It is presumed that the issuer will settle the contract by the issue of ordinary shares. The dilutive effect is therefore calculated in accordance with paragraph 59 of the Standard.

$$\frac{€\,1,000,000 + €\,166,331^{(a)}}{1,200,000 + 500,000^{(b)}} = €\,0.69 \text{ per ordinary share}$$

(a)   Profit is adjusted for the accretion of €166,331 (€1,848,122 × 9%) of the liability because of the passage of time.

(b)   500,000 ordinary shares = 250 ordinary shares × 2,000 convertible bonds

It is a little hard to know what to make of this example, which seems to raise more questions than it answers without actually illustrating any impact on the calculation. As regards settlement options, it really adds nothing to the text of the standard and the basic approach to convertibles shown in Example 35.9 above – aside of saying that, because the issuer can choose to settle in shares or cash, share settlement is assumed

Chapter 35

and a diluted EPS calculated at all. Furthermore, the description of the terms that the entity 'has an option to settle the principal in shares or cash' is far from precise, and its meaning far from clear. Given that a component of the instrument is classified as a liability, we presume that the settlement option means that if the holder does not convert, the issuer could choose to deliver a *variable* quantity of shares having a value equal to the principal (€2,000,000). This is because all of the instrument would be equity if the quantity of shares was fixed (discussed in Chapter 45 at 5). That would then mean that the number of shares to be issued would either be:

- 500,000 assuming the holder converts; or
- such a quantity that has a value at the repayment date of €2,000,000.

Regrettably, neither the text of the standard nor the example appended to it gives any indication of which of these should be used, or how the latter should be calculated. One possible approach would be to compare the principal of the convertible debt at the end of the reporting period with the market value of the entity's shares at that date. This would then enable the more dilutive of the two options to be used.

6.4.1.B   Convertible preference shares

The rules for convertible preference shares are very similar to those detailed above in the case of convertible debt, i.e. dividends and other returns to preference shareholders are added back to earnings used for basic EPS and the maximum number of ordinary shares that could be issued on conversion should be used in the calculation.

As discussed at 5.2 above, one possible return to preference shareholders is a premium payable on redemption or induced early conversion in excess of the original terms. IAS 33 notes that the redemption or induced conversion of convertible preference shares may affect only a portion of the previously outstanding convertible preference shares. In such cases, the standard makes clear that any excess consideration is attributed to those shares that are redeemed or converted for the purpose of determining whether the remaining outstanding preference shares are dilutive. In other words, the shares redeemed or converted are considered separately from those shares that are not redeemed or converted. *[IAS 33.51].*

6.4.1.C   Participating equity instruments and two class shares with conversion rights

The treatment for basic EPS of participating equity instruments and two class shares is discussed at 5.4 above. When discussing these instruments the standard observes that when calculating diluted EPS;

- conversion is assumed for those instruments that are convertible into ordinary shares if the effect is dilutive;
- for those that are not convertible into a class of ordinary shares, profit or loss for the period is allocated to the different classes of shares and participating equity instruments in accordance with their dividend rights or other rights to participate in undistributed earnings. *[IAS 33.A14].*

What the standard seems to be hinting at here, without directly addressing, is how to present EPS for two or more classes of ordinary shares (say, class A and class B) when one class can convert into another (say, class B can convert into class A). It this scenario, in our view the basic EPS for each class should be calculated based on profit entitlement (see 5.4 above). For diluted EPS it would be necessary to attribute to class A the profits attributed to class B in the basic EPS – if the overall effect were dilutive to class A, conversion should be assumed.

6.4.2 Options, warrants and their equivalents

6.4.2.A The numerator

IAS 33 contains a fair quantity of detailed guidance on the treatment for diluted EPS purposes of options, warrants and their equivalents which it defines as 'financial instruments that give the holder the right to purchase ordinary shares'. *[IAS 33.5]*. However, it was largely written before the significant developments in accounting for such instruments (IFRS 2 and IAS 32). Although the standard was updated as part of the 'improvements' project in 2003 and further amended as a consequence of IFRS 2, in our view the result is a somewhat unclear patchwork.

IAS 33 clearly states that 'Options and warrants ... do not affect the numerator of the calculation' *[IAS 33.44]* and this text was added in 2003 as part of the improvements project, so clearly drafted against the back drop of the impending move to expensing share-based payments and also the (then) recent changes to IAS 32 regarding accounting for derivatives over an entity's own shares. As regards employee share options in particular, neither IAS 33 (as updated by IFRS 2) nor the worked example appended to it (see Example 35.13 at 6.4.5 below) make reference to removing either some or all the charge when computing diluted EPS. However, this seems to sit somewhat awkwardly (particularly for options outside the scope of IFRS 2) with the general requirement for calculating diluted EPS that earnings be adjusted for the effects of 'any other changes in income or expense that would result from the conversion of the dilutive potential ordinary shares.' *[IAS 33.33]*. Furthermore, IAS 33 explicitly requires an adjustment to the numerator in some circumstances:

(a)   as discussed at 6.2.2 above, adjustment to the numerator may be required for a contract (which could include options and warrants) that may be settled in ordinary shares or cash at the entity's option when such a contract is presented for accounting purposes as an asset or a liability, or has an equity component and a liability component. In such a case, the standard requires that 'the entity shall adjust the numerator for any changes in profit or loss that would have resulted during the period if the contract had been classified wholly as an equity instrument'. For contracts that may be settled in ordinary shares or cash at the holder's option, 'the more dilutive of cash settlement and share settlement shall be used in calculating diluted earnings per share'; *[IAS 33.59-60]*

(b)   where an option agreement requires or permits the tendering of debt in payment of the exercise price (and, if the holder could choose to pay cash, that tendering debt is more advantageous to him) the numerator should be adjusted for the after tax amount of any such debt assumed to be tendered (see E below); and *[IAS 33.A7]*

(c)   where option proceeds are required to be applied to redeem debt or other instruments of the entity (see F below). *[IAS 33.A9]*.

For situations covered by (b) and (c) above the standard's specific requirements for adjusting the numerator should be followed. In other circumstances, the interaction of these complex and conflicting requirements with each other and with IFRS 2 and IAS 32 seem to lead to the following requirements when computing the numerator for diluted EPS:

(a)   for instruments accounted for under IAS 32:

    (i)   for a contract classified wholly as an equity instrument, no adjustment to the numerator will be necessary; and

    (ii)   for a contract not classified wholly as an equity instrument, the numerator should be adjusted for any changes in profit or loss that would have resulted if it had been classified wholly as an equity instrument; and

(b)   for instruments accounted for under IFRS 2:

    (i)   for those treated as equity settled, the IFRS 2 charge should *not* be adjusted for; and

    (ii)   for those treated as cash settled, the numerator should be adjusted for any changes in profit or loss that would have resulted if the instrument had been classified wholly as an equity instrument.

In respect of (b), part (i) is supported by the IASB's view regarding share-based payments as follows. 'Some argue that any cost arising from share-based payment transactions is already recognised in the dilution of earnings per share (EPS). If an expense were recognised in the income statement, EPS would be "hit twice". However, the Board noted that this result is appropriate. For example, if the entity paid the employees in cash for their services and the cash was then returned to the entity, as consideration for the issue of share options, the effect on EPS would be the same as issuing those options direct to the employees. The dual effect on EPS simply reflects the two economic events that have occurred: the entity has issued shares or share options, thereby increasing the number of shares included in the EPS calculation – although, in the case of options, only to the extent that the options are regarded as dilutive – and it has also consumed the resources it received for those options, thereby decreasing earnings. ... In summary, the Board concluded that the dual effect on diluted EPS is not double-counting the effects of a share or share option grant – the same effect is not counted twice. Rather, two different effects are each counted once.'[6]

As for part (ii) of (b) above, this is the explicit requirement of IAS 33 when the entity can choose cash or share settlement. It is, in our view, also implicit in the requirement of the standard that for contracts that may be settled in ordinary shares or cash at the holder's option, the more dilutive of cash settlement and share settlement should be used in calculating diluted earnings per share. This would also explain why IFRS 2 requires the computation of grant date fair values for cash settled share based payments when that information is not actually required for accounting purposes (see Chapter 32 at 9).

One company which adjusts the numerator of the calculation for the effects of own equity derivatives is UBS as shown in the following extract.

Extract 35.6: UBS AG (2007)

Notes to the Financial Statement [extract]
Note 8   Earnings per Share (EPS) and Shares Outstanding [extract]

	For the year ended			% change from
	31.12.07	31.12.06	31.12.05	31.12.06
Basic earnings (CHF million)				
Net profit attributable to UBS				
shareholders	(4,384)	12,257	14,029	
from continuing operations	(4,785)	11,469	9,748	
from discontinued operations	401	788	4,281	(49)
Diluted earnings (CHF million)				
Net profit attributable to UBS				
shareholders	(4,384)	12,257	14,029	
Less: (Profit)/loss on equity				
derivative contracts	(16)	(8)	(22)	(100)
Net profit attributable to UBS				
shareholders for diluted EPS	(4,400)	12,249	14,007	
from continuing operations	(4,801)	11,461	9,749	
from discontinued operations	401	788	4,258	(49)
Weighted average shares outstanding				
Weighted average share outstanding[1]	1,926,328,078	1,976,405,800	2,013,987,754	(3)
Potentially dilutive ordinary shares				
resulting from unvested				
exchangeable shares, options and				
warrants outstanding[2]	1,370,654	82,429,012	83,203,786	(98)
Weighted average shares				
outstanding for diluted EPS	1,927,698,732	2,058,834,812	2,097,191,540	(6)
Earnings per share (CHF)				
Basic	(2.28)	6.20	6.97	
from continuing operations	(2.49)	5.80	4.84	
from discontinued operations	0.21	0.40	2.13	(48)
Diluted	(2.28)	5.95	6.68	
from continuing operations	(2.49)	5.57	4.65	
from discontinued operations	0.21	0.38	2.03	(45)

1   Includes an average of 490,118 and 143,809 exchangeable shares for the year ended 31 December 2007 and
    31 December 2006, respectively, that can be exchange into the same number of UBS shares
2   Due to the net loss in 2007, 50,132,221 potential ordinary shares from unexercised employee shares and in-the-
    money options are not considered as they have an anti-dilutive effect for the year ended 31 December 2007. Total
    equivalent shares outstanding on out-of-the-money options that were not dilutive for the respective periods but
    could potentially dilute earnings per share in the future were 119,309,645; 37,229,136 and 29,117,750; for the years
    ended 31 December 2007, 31 December 2006 and 31 December 2005, respectively.

Shares outstanding

	As of			% change from
	31.12.07	31.12.06	31.12.05	31.12.06
Total ordinary shares issued	2,073,547,344	2,105,273,286	2,117,265,044	(2)
Second trading line treasury shares				
2005 program			67,770,000	
2006 program		22,600,000		
Other treasury shares	158,105,524	141,875,699	140,749,748	11
Total treasury shares	158,105,524	164,475,699	208,519,748	(4)
Shares outstanding	1,915,441,820	1,940,797,587	1,968,745,296	(1)

Chapter 35

6.4.2.B   *Written call options*

Entities may issue options or warrants which give holders the right to subscribe for shares at fixed prices on specified future dates. If the options or warrants are exercised then:

(a)   the number of shares in issue will be increased; and

(b)   funds will flow into the company and these will produce income.

For calculating diluted EPS, IAS 33 requires the exercise of all dilutive options and warrants to be assumed. *[IAS 33.45]*. Options and warrants are considered dilutive when they would result in the issue of ordinary shares for less than the average market price of ordinary shares during the period. The amount of the dilution is taken to be the average market price of ordinary shares during the period minus the issue price. *[IAS 33.46]*.

Under IAS 33 the effects of such potential ordinary shares on the diluted EPS are reflected in the computation of the denominator using a method sometimes called the 'treasury stock method'.

For this purpose, the weighted average number of shares used in calculating the basic EPS is increased, but not by the full number of shares that would be issued on exercise of the instruments. To work out how many additional shares to include in the denominator, the assumed proceeds from these issues are to be treated as having been received in exchange for:

- a certain number of shares at their average market price for the period (i.e. no EPS impact); and

- the remainder for no consideration (i.e. full dilution with no earnings enhancement). *[IAS 33.45-46]*.

This means that the excess of the total number of potential shares over the number that could be issued at their average market price for the period out of the issue proceeds is included within the denominator; the calculation is illustrated as follows:

Example 35.11:   Effects of share options on diluted earnings per share [IAS 33.IE5]

Profit attributable to ordinary equity holders of the parent entity for year	€1,200,000
Weighted average number of ordinary shares outstanding during year	500,000 shares
Average market price of one ordinary share during year	€20.00
Weighted average number of shares under option during year	100,000 shares
Exercise price for shares under option during year	€15.00

Calculation of earnings per share

	Earnings	*Shares*	*Per share*
Profit attributable to ordinary equity holders of the parent entity for year	€1,200,000		
Weighted average shares outstanding during year		500,000	
Basic earnings per share			€2.40
Weighted average number of shares under option		100,000	
Weighted average number of shares that would have been issued at average market price:			
(100,000 × €15.00) ÷ €20.00		(75,000)	
Diluted earnings per share	€1,200,000	525,000	€2.29

*   Earnings have not increased because the total number of shares has increased only by the number of shares (25,000) deemed to have been issued for no consideration.

The number of shares viewed as fairly priced (and hence neither dilutive nor antidilutive) for this purpose is calculated on the basis of the average price of the ordinary shares during the reporting period. *[IAS 33.46]*. The standard observes that, in theory, calculating an average share price for the period could include every market transaction in the shares. However, it notes that as a practical matter an average (weekly or monthly) will usually be adequate. *[IAS 33.A4]*. The individual prices used should generally be the closing market price unless prices fluctuate widely, in which case the average of high and low prices may be more representative. Whatever method is adopted, it should be used consistently unless it ceases to yield a representative price. For example, closing prices may have been used consistently in a series of relatively stable periods then a change to high/low average could be appropriate when prices begin to fluctuate more widely. *[IAS 33.A5]*.

The shares would be deemed to have been issued at the beginning of the period or, if later, the date of issue of the warrants or options. Options which are exercised or lapse in the period are included for the portion of the period during which they were outstanding. *[IAS 33.36, 38]*

The following extract provides an example of an entity's description of the diluted EPS effects of options.

Chapter 35

Extract 35.7: Del Monte Pacific Limited (2006)

NOTES TO THE FINANCIAL STATEMENT
YEAR ENDED 31 DECEMBER 2006 [extract]
23   EARNINGS PER SHARE [extract]

Basic earnings per share is calculated by dividing the net profit attributable to shareholders by the weighted average number of ordinary shares in issue during the year.

	Group	
	2006	2005
Net profit attributable to shareholders (US$'000)	21,037	18,734
Issued ordinary shares at beginning of the year ('000)	1,081,781	1,074,483
Effect of share options exercised ('000)	–	4,649
Weighted average number of ordinary shares in issue ('000)	1,081,781	1,079,132
Basic earnings per share (in US cents)	1.94	1.74

For the diluted earnings per share, the weighted average number of ordinary shares in issue is adjusted to assume conversation of all dilutive potential ordinary shares which are the share options granted to employees.

For the diluted earnings per share in relation to the share options, a calculation is done to determine the number of shares that could have been acquired at market price (determined as the average share price of the Company's shares for the financial year) based on the monetary value of the subscription rights attached to outstanding share options. This calculation serves to determine the 'unpurchased' shares to be added to the ordinary shares outstanding for the purpose of computing the dilution. For the share options calculation, no adjustment is made to net profit attributable to shareholders.

	Group	
	2006	2005
Net profit attributable to shareholders (US$'000)	21,037	18,734
Weighted average number of ordinary shares in issue ('000)	1,081,781	1,079,132
Adjustments for share options ('000)	–	798
Weighted average number of ordinary shares for diluted earnings per share ('000)	1,081,781	1,079,930
Diluted earnings per share (in US cents)	1.94	1.74

Although the standard seems to require that the fair value used should be the average for the reporting period for all outstanding options or warrants, in our view, for instruments issued, lapsed or exercised during the period a credible case could be made for using an average price for that part of the reporting period that the instrument was outstanding. Indeed, this view is supported by the comprehensive example included in the standard (see the appendix to this chapter), where in computing the number of warrants to be included in calculating the diluted EPS for the full year, the average price used was not that for the full year, but only for the period that the warrants were outstanding.

One practical problem with this requirement is that the average market price of ordinary shares for the reporting period may not be available. Examples would include an entity only listed for part of the period, or an unlisted entity giving voluntary disclosures. In such cases estimates of the market price would need to be made.

6.4.2.C   Written put options and forward purchase agreements

Contracts that require the entity to repurchase its own shares, such as written put options and forward purchase contracts, should be reflected in the calculation of diluted earnings per share if the effect is dilutive. If these contracts are 'in the money' during the period (i.e. the exercise or settlement price is above the average market price for that period), IAS 33 requires the potential dilutive effect on EPS to be calculated as follows:

- it should be assumed that at the beginning of the period sufficient ordinary shares are issued (at the average market price during the period) to raise proceeds to satisfy the contract;

- the proceeds from the issue are then assumed to be used to satisfy the contract (i.e. to buy back ordinary shares); and

- the incremental ordinary shares (the difference between the number of ordinary shares assumed issued and the number of ordinary shares received from satisfying the contract) should be included in the calculation of diluted earnings per share. [IAS 33.63].

The standard illustrates this methodology as follows: '... assume that an entity has outstanding 120 written put options on its ordinary shares with an exercise price of CU 35. The average market price of its ordinary shares for the period is CU 28. In calculating diluted earnings per share, the entity assumes that it issued 150 shares at CU 28 per share at the beginning of the period to satisfy its put obligation of CU 4,200. The difference between the 150 ordinary shares issued and the 120 ordinary shares received from satisfying the put option (30 incremental ordinary shares) is added to the denominator in calculating diluted earnings per share.' *[IAS 33.A10]*.

6.4.2.D   Options over convertible instruments

Although not common, it is possible that an entity grants options or warrants to acquire not ordinary shares directly but other instruments convertible into them (such as convertible preference shares or debt). In this scenario, IAS 33 sets a dual test:

- exercise is assumed whenever the average prices of both the convertible instrument and the ordinary shares obtainable upon conversion are above the exercise price of the options or warrants; but

- exercise is not assumed unless conversion of similar outstanding convertible instruments, if any, is also assumed. *[IAS 33.A6]*.

6.4.2.E   Settlement of option exercise price with debt or other instruments of the entity

The standard notes that options or warrants may permit or require the tendering of debt or other instruments of the entity (or its parent or a subsidiary) in payment of all or a portion of the exercise price. In the calculation of diluted earnings per share, those options or warrants have a dilutive effect if (a) the average market price of the related ordinary shares for the period exceeds the exercise price or (b) the selling price of the instrument to be tendered is below that at which the instrument may be tendered under the option or warrant agreement and the resulting discount establishes an effective exercise price below the market price of the ordinary shares obtainable upon exercise. In the calculation of diluted EPS, those options or warrants should be assumed to be exercised and the debt or other instruments assumed to be tendered. If tendering cash is more advantageous to the option or warrant holder and the contract permits it, tendering of cash should be assumed. Interest (net of tax) on any debt assumed to be tendered is added back as an adjustment to the numerator. *[IAS 33.A7]*.

Similar treatment is given to preference shares that have similar provisions or to other instruments that have conversion options that permit the investor to pay cash for a more favourable conversion rate. *[IAS 33.A8]*.

6.4.2.F   Specified application of option proceeds

IAS 33 observes that the underlying terms of certain options or warrants may require the proceeds received from the exercise of those instruments to be applied to redeem debt or other instruments of the entity (or its parent or a subsidiary). In which case it requires that in 'the calculation of diluted earnings per share, those options or warrants are assumed to be exercised and the proceeds applied to purchase the debt at its average market price rather than to purchase ordinary shares. However, the excess proceeds received from the assumed exercise over the amount

Chapter 35

used for the assumed purchase of debt are considered (i.e. assumed to be used to buy back ordinary shares) in the diluted earnings per share calculation. Interest (net of tax) on any debt assumed to be purchased is added back as an adjustment to the numerator.' *[IAS 33.A9]*.

In our view this drafting is far from clear, and with it the intentions of the IASB. However, it seems to have in mind what one might call an 'in substance convertible bond' made up of a straight option and a requirement that the proceeds be used to redeem debt. On that basis, the phrase 'rather than purchase ordinary shares' presumably means that the 'normal' treasury stock rules for options are not applied, but rather more shares are brought into the denominator and interest is added back to the numerator. Put another way, we believe this provision is trying to achieve consistency with the requirements for convertible debt.

6.4.3   *Purchased options and warrants*

IAS 33 states that a holding by an entity of options over its own shares will always be antidilutive because:

- put options would only be exercised if the exercise price were higher than the market price; and

- call options would only be exercised if the exercise price were lower than the market price.

Accordingly, the standard requires that such instruments are not included in the calculation of diluted EPS. *[IAS 33.62]*.

This ostensibly rather neat dismissal of the issue strikes us as another example of IAS 33 failing to recognise the accounting requirements of IAS 32. It is true that the application of the treasury stock method to an option which is in-the-money from the entity's perspective (by reference to the average share price for the period) would *reduce* the number of shares in the denominator, and hence be anti-dilutive. However, dependent upon the settlement mechanism and the share price at the beginning and end of the period, the option could have resulted in a gain being reported (see Chapter 45 at 10). It is possible that the removal of the gain from the numerator could have a greater dilutive effect than the reduction in the denominator and hence render the option dilutive. If that is the case, we believe the option should be included in the diluted EPS calculation.

6.4.4   *Partly paid shares*

As noted at 3 above, shares issued in partly paid form are to be included in the basic EPS as a fraction of a share, based on dividend participation. As regards diluted EPS they are to be treated, to the extent that they are not entitled to participate in dividends, as the equivalent of options or warrants. The unpaid balance is assumed to represent proceeds used to purchase ordinary shares. The number of shares included in diluted earnings per share is the difference between the number of shares subscribed and the number of shares assumed to be purchased. *[IAS 33.A16]*. The mechanics of this treatment are not further spelt out in the standard, but curiously the phrase 'treated as a fraction of an ordinary share' is not repeated. Instead, it is 'the number of shares subscribed' which the standard says should be compared to the number assumed purchased to measure dilution. Unfortunately 'the number of shares subscribed' is not defined. Whilst this could be read to mean that the remaining unpaid consideration is to be treated as the exercise price for options over *all* of the shares issued in partly paid form, the results would make little sense. In our view, the more sensible interpretation is that the unpaid capital should be viewed as the exercise price for options over the proportion of the shares not reflected in the basic EPS. This would mean that if the average share price for the period were the same as the total issue price, then no dilution would be reported. Furthermore, an issue of partly paid shares, say 50% paid with 50% dividend entitlement is, economically identical to an issue of half the quantity as fully paid (with full dividend entitlement) and a forward contract for the remaining half. In that scenario, the issued shares would be incorporated into the basic and diluted EPS in full from the date of issue. The forward contract would be included in diluted EPS calculation by comparing the contracted number of shares with the number of shares that could be bought out of proceeds based on the average share price for the period. In our view, these economically identical transactions should produce the same diluted EPS – that would be achieved by interpreting 'the number of shares subscribed' as the number *economically* subscribed, i.e. the proportion of part-paid shares not already included in basic EPS.

An illustration of what the calculation would look like is as follows:

Example 35.12: Partly paid shares

Capital structure

Issued share capital as at 31 December 2011:
2,000,000 ordinary shares of 10c each

Issued on 1 January 2012:
500,000 part paid ordinary shares of 10c each. Full consideration of 50c per share (being fair value at 1 January 2012) paid up 50% on issue. Dividend participation 50% until fully paid. New shares remain part paid at 31 December 2012.

Average fair value of one ordinary share for the period 60c.

Trading results

Net profit attributable to ordinary shareholders for the year ended 31 December 2012: €100,000.

Computation of basic and diluted EPS

	Net profit attributable to ordinary shareholders €	Ordinary shares No.	Per share
Fully paid shares	100,000	2,000,000	
Partly paid shares (1)		250,000	
Basic EPS	100,000	2,250,000	4.44c
Dilutive effect of partly paid shares (2)		41,667	
Diluted EPS	100,000	2,291,667	4.36c

(1) 50% dividend rights for 500,000 shares.

(2) Outstanding consideration of €125,000 (500,000 × 25c), using fair value of 60c this equates to 208,333 shares, hence the number of dilutive shares deemed issued for free is 41,667 (250,000 – 208,333).

The example assumes the fair value of the shares over the year is higher than the issue price, which explains why some extra shares fall to be included in the diluted EPS. If the average fair value remained at the issue price of 50c then no additional shares would be included for diluted EPS.

6.4.5 Share based payments

Share options and other incentive schemes are an increasingly common feature of employee remuneration, and can come in many forms. For diluted EPS purposes, IAS 33 identifies two categories and specifies the diluted EPS treatment for each. The categories are:

(a)   performance-based employee share options; and

(b)   employee share options with fixed or determinable terms and non-vested ordinary shares. *[IAS 33.48]*.

Before moving on to the diluted EPS treatment, it is worth noting an issue that arises from the way IAS 33 phrases this categorisation and subsequent guidance. The drafting does not make clear whether the two categories cover all possible schemes. In our view all schemes should fall to be treated as either category (a) or category (b). Any arrangements where entitlement is subject to future performance would fall into category (a) with category (b) being the default for all other arrangements.

Schemes in the first category are to be treated as contingently issuable shares (see 6.4.6 below) because their issue is contingent upon satisfying specified conditions in addition to the passage of time. *[IAS 33.48]*. This gives rise to an apparent paradox relating to shares held in treasury (and shown as a deduction from equity). Frequently employee share schemes will be arranged in this way, with shares released from treasury to satisfy the exercise of options. The rules for, and indeed the title, 'contingently issuable shares' seems to refer to shares which do not exist at the end of the reporting period, but may be issued subsequently. Shares held in treasury to satisfy employee options are obviously already 'in issue', so a literal reading of the standard would seem to imply that these have no dilutive impact. In our view this makes little sense, and does not seem to be what the standard setters intended. A sensible interpretation would be to consider the vesting of treasury shares, and hence ceasing to be treated as cancelled for EPS purposes (see 3.2 above), as an issue for calculating diluted EPS.

Those in the second category are to be treated as options (see 6.4.2 above). They should be regarded as outstanding from the grant date, even if they vest, and hence can be realised by the employees, at some later date. *[IAS 33.48]*. An example would be an unexpired loyalty period. This means that some shares may be included in diluted EPS which never, in fact, get issued to employees because they fail to remain with the company for this period. Whilst this requirement is clear, it sits rather awkwardly with the rules for contingently issuable shares which, as discussed at 6.4.6 below, tend to restrict the number of potential shares accounted for. Furthermore, for share options and other share-based payment arrangements to which IFRS 2 applies, the proceeds figure to be used in calculating the dilution under such schemes should include the fair value (as determined in accordance with IFRS 2) of any goods or services to be supplied to the entity in the future under the arrangement. *[IAS 33.47A]*. An example illustrating the this latter point is as follows:

Example 35.13:   Determining the exercise price of employee share options [IAS 33.IE5A]

Weighted average number of unvested share options per employee	1,000
Weighted average amount per employee to be recognised over the remainder of the vesting period for employee services to be rendered as consideration for the share options, determined in accordance with IFRS 2	€1,200.00
Cash exercise price of unvested share options	€15.00
Calculation of adjusted exercise price	
Fair value of services yet to be rendered per employee:	€1,200.00
Fair value of services yet to be rendered per option: (€1,200 ÷ 1,000)	€1.20
Total exercise price of share options: (€15.00 + €1.20)	€16.20

Whilst the standard requires that the additional deemed proceeds is the *fair value* of goods or services yet to be received (which could, in theory, vary over time), the example seems to clarify that it is the IFRS 2 expense yet to be charged to income.

What this requirement seeks to reflect is that for such options the issuer will receive not just the cash proceeds (if any) under the option when it is exercised but also valuable goods and services over its life. This will result in the dilutive effect of the options increasing over time as the deemed proceeds on exercise of the options reduces.

6.4.6   Contingently issuable shares

As part of the improvements project, IAS 33 was updated to contain considerable detailed guidance, including a numerical worked example, on contingently issuable shares. Contingently issuable ordinary shares are defined as 'ordinary shares issuable for little or no cash or other consideration upon satisfaction of specified conditions in a contingent share agreement.' A contingent share agreement is, perhaps unnecessarily, also defined by the standard as 'an agreement to issue shares that is dependent on the satisfaction of specified conditions.' *[IAS 33.5].* The basic rule is that the number of contingently issuable shares to be included in the diluted EPS calculation is 'based on the number of shares that would be issuable if the end of the period were the end of the contingency period'. *[IAS 33.52].* This requirement to look at the status of the contingency at the end of the reporting period, rather than to consider the most likely outcome, seems to have the overall result of *reducing* the amount of dilution disclosed. Furthermore, these detailed rules on contingently issuable shares are arguably at odds with the more general requirement of 'giving effect to *all* dilutive potential ordinary shares outstanding during the period'. *[IAS 33.32].* (Emphasis added).

The standard's discussions cover three broad categories: earnings-based contingencies, share-price-based contingencies, and other contingencies. These are discussed in turn below.

The number of shares contingently issuable may depend on future earnings and future prices of the ordinary shares. In such cases, the standard makes clear that the number of shares included in the diluted EPS calculation is based on both conditions (i.e. earnings to date and the current market price at the end of the reporting period). In other words, contingently issuable shares are not included in the diluted EPS calculation unless both conditions are met. *[IAS 33.55].*

6.4.6.A   *Earnings-based contingencies*

The standard discusses the scenario where shares would be issued contingent upon the attainment or maintenance of a specified amount of earnings for a period. In such a case the standard requires that 'if that amount has been attained at the end of the reporting period but must be maintained beyond the end of the reporting period for an additional period, then the additional ordinary shares are treated as outstanding, if the effect is dilutive, when calculating diluted earnings per share. In that case, the calculation of diluted earnings per share is based on the number of ordinary shares that would be issued if the amount of earnings at the end of the reporting period were the amount of earnings at the end of the contingency period'. *[IAS 33.53]*. Although perhaps not the clearest of drafting, this seems to be saying that earnings-based contingencies need to be viewed as an absolute cumulative hurdle which either is met or not met at the reporting date. Often, such contingencies may be contractually expressed in terms of *annual* performance over a number of years, say an average of €1million profit per year for three years. In our view, 'the attainment or maintenance of a specified amount of earnings for a period' in this scenario would mean generating a total of €3million of profits. If that is achieved by the end of a reporting period, the shares are outstanding for diluted EPS purposes and included in the computation if the effect is dilutive. It could, perhaps, be argued that the potential shares should be considered outstanding if profits of €1million were generated at the end of the first year. However, the requirement that the calculation be 'based on the number of ordinary shares that would be issued if the amount of earnings at the end of the reporting period were the amount of earnings at the end of the contingency period' means that the test must be: would shares be issued if the current earnings of €1million were all the profits earned by the end of the three year contingency period? In this example the answer is no, as that amount of earnings would fall short of averaging €1million per year. The standard then notes that, because earnings may change in a future period, the calculation of basic EPS does not include such contingently issuable shares until the end of the contingency period because not all necessary conditions have been satisfied. *[IAS 33.53]*.

An earnings-based contingency is illustrated in the following example:

Example 35.14:   Contingently issuable shares *[IAS 33.IE7]*

Ordinary shares outstanding during 2012	1,000,000 (there were no options, warrants or convertible instruments outstanding during the period)

An agreement related to a recent business combination provides for the issue of additional ordinary shares based on the following conditions:

5,000 additional ordinary shares for each new retail site opened during 2012
1,000 additional ordinary shares for each €1,000 of consolidated profit in excess of €2,000,000 for the year ended 31 December 2012

Retail sites opened during the year:

one on 1 May 2012
one on 1 September 2012

Consolidated year-to-date profit attributable
to ordinary equity holders of the parent
entity:

€1,100,000 as of 31 March 2012
€2,300,000 as of 30 June 2012
€1,900,000 as of 30 September 2011 (including a
€450,000 loss from a discontinuing operation)
€2,900,000 as of 31 December 2012

Basic earnings per share

	First quarter	Second quarter	Third quarter	Fourth quarter	Full year
Numerator (€)	1,100,000	1,200,000	(400,000)	1,000,000	2,900,000
Denominator:					
Ordinary shares outstanding	1,000,000	1,000,000	1,000,000	1,000,000	1,000,000
Retail site contingency	–	3,333 (a)	6,667 (b)	10,000	5,000 (c)
Earnings contingency (d)	–	–	–	–	–
Total shares	1,000,000	1,003,333	1,006,667	1,010,000	1,005,000
Basic earnings per share (€)	1.10	1.20	(0.40)	0.99	2.89

(a)   5,000 shares × 2/3
(b)   5,000 shares + (5,000 shares × 1/3)
(c)   (5,000 shares × 8/12) + (5,000 shares × 4/12)
(d)   The earnings contingency has no effect on basic earnings per share because it is not certain
      that the condition is satisfied until the end of the contingency period. The effect is negligible
      for the fourth-quarter and full-year calculations because it is not certain that the condition is
      met until the last day of the period.

Diluted earnings per share

	First quarter	Second quarter	Third quarter	Fourth quarter	Full year
Numerator (€)	1,100,000	1,200,000	(400,000)	1,000,000	2,900,000
Denominator:					
Ordinary shares outstanding	1,000,000	1,000,000	1,000,000	1,000,000	1,000,000
Retail site contingency	–	5,000	10,000	10,000	10,000
Earnings contingency	– (e)	300,000 (f)	(g)	900,000 (h)	900,000 (h)
Total shares	1,000,000	1,305,000	1,010,000	1,910,000	1,910,000
Diluted earnings per share (€)	1.10	0.92	(0.40) (i)	0.52	1.52

(e)   Year-to-date profits do not exceed €2,000,000 at 31 March 2012. The Standard does not
      permit projecting future earnings levels and including the related contingent shares.
(f)   [(€2,300,000 – €2,000,000) ÷ 1,000] × 1,000 shares = 300,000 shares.
(g)   Year-to-date profit is less than €2,000,000.
(h)   [(€2,900,000 – €2,000,000) ÷ 1,000] × 1,000 shares = 900,000 shares.
(i)   Because the loss during the third quarter is attributable to a loss from a discontinuing
      operation, the antidilution rules do not apply. The control number (i.e. profit or loss from
      continuing operations attributable to the equity holders of the parent entity) is positive.
      Accordingly, the effect of potential ordinary shares is included in the calculation of diluted
      earnings per share.

Chapter 35

Curiously, this example from IAS 33 illustrates *quarterly* financial reporting. However, the principles are the same whether the reporting period is illustrated as three months or one year. The example does illustrate that the earnings target is a cumulative hurdle over the entire contingency period (four reporting periods in the example) rather than including potential shares based on the assumption that the level of quarterly profit would be maintained for the four quarters.

The standard only discusses earnings criteria based on *absolute* measures; in the example above a cumulative profit of in excess of €2,000,000. In our experience such criteria are rare. In practice criteria are often phrased in terms of *relative* performance against an external benchmark. Examples would be earnings growth targets of inflation plus 2% or EPS growth being in the top quartile of a group of competitors. For contingencies such as these it is impossible to establish an absolute target in order to ask whether it is met at the period end. For example, consider the earnings contingency in IAS 33, discussed above, to achieve profits in excess of €2,000,000 over four quarters. If this instead required the profits to be €2,000,000 adjusted in line with inflation, it would be impossible to know how many shares would be issued if the cumulative profit at the end of the second quarter of €2,300,000 were the amount of earnings at the end of the contingency period. Until the end of the year the absolute level of profit required would be unknown; it would be more or less than €2,000,000 depending on the level of inflation or deflation over the period.

There would seem to be (at least) two different ways of interpreting the requirements of IAS 33 in such a scenario, each resulting in a different diluted EPS figure. One approach would be to consider such criteria as being based on 'a condition other than earnings or market price'. That would mean (as discussed under C below) that the number of shares brought into diluted EPS would be based on the status of the condition at the end of the reporting period. *[IAS 33.56]*. So, if the target was earnings for the year in excess of €2,000,000 adjusted in line with inflation and at the end of the second quarter inflation had been 4%, then the target would become €2,080,000 and hence 220,000 shares would be included for diluted EPS for the second quarter. An alternative approach would be to regard it as an earnings-based contingency and make an assumption as to future inflation over the contingency period. This would allow a cumulative hurdle to be calculated and compared with actual earnings to date. So if at the end of the second quarter it was estimated that the annual inflation for the year was 5%, then the target would become €2,100,000 and hence 200,000 shares would be included for diluted EPS for the second quarter. Given the lack of clarity in the standard, it seems likely that either of the above approaches may be selected in practice.

6.4.6.B   Share-price-based contingencies

The provisions here are more straightforward. In these cases, if the effect is dilutive, the calculation of diluted EPS is based on the number of shares that would be issued if the market price at the end of the reporting period were the market price at the end of the contingency period. If the condition is based on an average of market prices over a period of time that extends beyond the end of the reporting period, the average for the period of time that has lapsed should be used. Again the standard explains that, because the market price may change in a future period, the calculation of basic earnings per share does not include such contingently issuable ordinary shares until the end of the contingency period because not all necessary conditions have been satisfied. *[IAS 33.54]*.

6.4.6.C   Other contingencies

The requirement regarding contingencies not driven by earnings or share price is as follows: 'assuming that the present status of the condition remains unchanged until the end of the contingency period, the contingently issuable ordinary shares are included in the calculation of diluted earnings per share according to the status at the end of the reporting period.' *[IAS 33.56]*.

The standard illustrates the 'other contingency' rules by the example of shares being issued depending upon the opening of a specified number of retail sites, and such a contingency is included in the standard's numerical example (see Example 35.14 above). As is the case for earnings-based contingencies discussed above, it would seem that such conditions are always deemed to be expressed as a cumulative hurdle which may or may not be met by the end of the reporting period. Accordingly, the required treatment would be the same if the condition had been expressed in terms of achieving a certain average annual level of shop openings.

6.4.7   Potential ordinary shares of investees

A subsidiary, joint venture or associate may issue to parties other than the parent, venturer or investor potential ordinary shares that are convertible into either ordinary shares of the subsidiary, joint venture or associate, or ordinary shares of the parent, venturer or investor (the reporting entity). If these potential ordinary shares of the subsidiary, joint venture or associate have a dilutive effect on the basic EPS of the reporting entity, they should be included in the calculation of diluted earnings per share. *[IAS 33.40]*.

The standard requires that such potential ordinary shares should be included in the calculation of diluted EPS as follows:

(a)   instruments issued by a subsidiary, joint venture or associate that enable their holders to obtain ordinary shares of the subsidiary, joint venture or associate should be included in calculating the diluted EPS data of the subsidiary, joint venture or associate. Those EPS are then included in the reporting entity's EPS calculations based on the reporting entity's holding of the instruments of the subsidiary, joint venture or associate; and

(b)   instruments of a subsidiary, joint venture or associate that are convertible into the reporting entity's ordinary shares should be considered among the potential ordinary shares of the reporting entity for the purpose of calculating diluted EPS. Similarly, options or warrants issued by a subsidiary, joint venture or associate to purchase ordinary shares of the reporting entity should be considered among the potential ordinary shares of the reporting entity in the calculation of consolidated diluted EPS. *[IAS 33.A11]*.

For the purpose of determining the EPS effect of instruments issued by a reporting entity that are convertible into ordinary shares of a subsidiary, joint venture or associate, the standard requires that the instruments are assumed to be converted and the numerator (profit or loss attributable to ordinary equity holders of the parent entity) adjusted as necessary in accordance with the normal rules (see 6.2.1 above). In addition to those adjustments, the numerator is adjusted for any change in the profit or loss recorded by the reporting entity (such as dividend income or equity method income) that is attributable to the increase in the number of ordinary shares of the subsidiary, joint venture or associate outstanding as a result of the assumed conversion. The denominator of the diluted EPS calculation is not affected because the number of ordinary shares of the reporting entity outstanding would not change upon assumed conversion. *[IAS 33.A12].*

The computation under (a) above is illustrated in the following example.

Example 35.15:   Warrants issued by a subsidiary [IAS 33.IE10]

Parent:

Profit attributable to ordinary equity holders of the parent entity	€12,000 (excluding any earnings of, or dividends paid by, the subsidiary)
Ordinary shares outstanding	10,000
Instruments of subsidiary owned by the parent	800 ordinary shares
	30 warrants exercisable to purchase ordinary shares of subsidiary
	300 convertible preference shares

Subsidiary:

Profit	€5,400
Ordinary shares outstanding	1,000
Warrants	150, exercisable to purchase ordinary shares of the subsidiary
Exercise price	€10
Average market price of one ordinary share	€20
Convertible preference shares	400, each convertible into one ordinary share
Dividends on preference shares	€1 per share

No inter-company eliminations or adjustments were necessary except for dividends. For the purposes of this illustration, income taxes have been ignored.

Subsidiary's earnings per share

Basic EPS   €5.00   calculated: $\dfrac{€5,400^{(a)} - €400^{(b)}}{1,000^{(c)}}$

Diluted EPS   €3.66   calculated: $\dfrac{€5,400^{(d)}}{1,000 + 75^{(e)} + 400^{(f)}}$

(a)   Subsidiary's profit.
(b)   Dividends paid by subsidiary on convertible preference shares.
(c)   Subsidiary's ordinary shares outstanding.
(d)   Subsidiary's profit attributable to ordinary equity holders (€5,000) increased by €400 preference dividends for the purpose of calculating diluted earnings per share.
(e)   Incremental shares from warrants, calculated: $[(€20 - €10) \div €20] \times 150$.
(f)   Subsidiary's ordinary shares assumed outstanding from conversion of convertible preference shares, calculated: 400 convertible preference shares × conversion factor of 1.

Consolidated earnings per share

Basic EPS   €1.63   calculated: $$\frac{€12,000^{(g)} + €4,300^{(h)}}{10,000^{(i)}}$$

Diluted EPS   €1.61   calculated: $$\frac{€12,000 + €2,928^{(j)} + €55^{(k)} + €1,098^{(l)}}{10,000}$$

(g)   Parent's profit attributable to ordinary equity holders of the parent entity.
(h)   Portion of subsidiary's profit to be included in consolidated basic earnings per share, calculated: (800 × CU 5.00) + (300 × €1.00).
(i)   Parent's ordinary shares outstanding.
(j)   Parent's proportionate interest in subsidiary's earnings attributable to ordinary shares, calculated: (800 ÷ 1,000) × (1,000 shares × €3.66 per share)
(k)   Parent's proportionate interest in subsidiary's earnings attributable to warrants, calculated: (30 ÷ 150) × (75 incremental shares × €3.66 per share)
(l)   Parent's proportionate interest in subsidiary's earnings attributable to convertible preference shares, calculated: (300 ÷ 400) × (400 shares from conversion × €3.66 per share)

This example does not illustrate the classification of the components of convertible financial instruments as liabilities and equity or the classification of related interest and dividends as expenses and equity as required by IAS 32.

Extract 35.5 above illustrates these requirements.

6.4.8   Contingently issuable potential ordinary shares

The standard requires that contingently issuable potential ordinary shares (other than those covered by a contingent share agreement, such as contingently issuable convertible instruments) to be included in the diluted EPS calculation as follows:

(a)   determine whether the potential ordinary shares may be assumed to be issuable on the basis of the conditions specified for their issue in accordance with the standard's contingent ordinary share provisions (see 6.4.6) above; and

(b)   if those potential ordinary shares should be reflected in diluted EPS, determine their impact on the calculation of diluted earnings per share by following the provisions of the standard for that type of potential ordinary share.

However, exercise or conversion is not to be assumed for the purpose of calculating diluted earnings per share unless exercise or conversion of similar outstanding potential ordinary shares that are not contingently issuable is assumed. *[IAS 33.57]*.

This two-stage test (essentially, are the contingencies met and are the resulting potential shares dilutive?) is a perfectly logical stance for the standard to take. However, we are mystified by the somewhat cryptic scope of these provisions in that they apply to 'contingently issuable potential ordinary shares (other than those covered by a contingent share agreement, such as contingently issuable convertible instruments)'. A contingent share agreement is defined as 'an agreement to issue shares that is dependent on the satisfaction of specified conditions'. *[IAS 33.5]*. We fail to see how a contingent agreement to issue *potential* ordinary shares could be 'covered' by an agreement 'to issue shares'. In our view the methodology described above seems appropriate for a contingently issuable convertible bond.

Chapter 35

7   PRESENTATION, RESTATEMENT AND DISCLOSURE

7.1   Presentation

As discussed in Chapter 3 at 3.2.1, IAS 1 requires that all items of income and expense be presented either:

(a)   in a single statement of profit or loss and comprehensive income; or

(b)   in two separate statements:

  (i)   a statement of profit or loss; and

  (ii)   a statement, beginning with profit or loss, presenting items of other comprehensive income. *[IAS 1.10A].*

If the approach in (b) is followed, the separate statement of profit or loss must be displayed immediately before the statement of comprehensive income. *[IAS 1.10A].*

If (a) is adopted, the EPS presentational requirements below apply to that single statement. If (b) is chosen, the requirements apply to the separate statement of profit or loss only and not the separate statement of comprehensive income. *[IAS 33.4A, 67A, 68A].*

IAS 33 requires the presentation of basic and diluted EPS (with equal prominence and even if the amounts are negative – i.e. a loss per share) for each period for which a statement of comprehensive income (or separate income statement) is presented. *[IAS 33.66, 69].* This is required for the profit or loss attributable to ordinary equity holders for:

(a)   overall profit;

(b)   profit or loss from continuing operations; and

(c)   profit or loss from discontinued operations, if any. *[IAS 33.66, 68].*

In the case of (a) and (b), separate figures are required for each class of ordinary shares with a different right to share in profits for the period. The figures for (a) and (b) must be displayed on the face of the statement. *[IAS 33.66].* Those for (c) may be either on the face or in the notes. *[IAS 33.68].* The standard (somewhat unnecessarily given the requirement to show basic and diluted EPS for all periods) states that if diluted EPS is given for at least one period it must be given for all periods presented. In what some might view as a further statement of the obvious, IAS 33 notes that if basic and diluted EPS are equal, dual presentation can be accomplished in one line in the statement. *[IAS 33.67].* It stops short, however, of explaining that this is only true if the caption is amended to address both.

Regarding (c), the wording of the standard is not very clear. In particular, if an entity has more than one discontinued operation it does not clarify whether separate EPS disclosures are required for each or whether one aggregate figure is needed. The wording leans to the former, as it uses the singular – 'An entity that reports a discontinued operation shall disclose the basic and diluted amounts per share for the discontinued operation ...'. However, IFRS 5 – *Non-current Assets Held for Sale and Discontinued Operations* – only requires the statement of comprehensive income (or separate income statement) to identify the total result from all discontinued operations. *[IFRS 5.33].* In light of this, we believe aggregate figures are acceptable.

7.2 Restatement

IAS 33 contains requirements to restate prior periods' EPS for events that change the number of shares outstanding without a corresponding change in resources. Additionally it specifies circumstances when EPS should not be restated.

Basic and diluted EPS for all periods presented should be adjusted for:

- events (other than the conversion of potential ordinary shares) which change the number of ordinary shares without a corresponding change in resources (discussed at 4.3 above); *[IAS 33.26, 64]*.

- the effects of errors and adjustments resulting from changes in accounting policies accounted for retrospectively (see 5.3 above); *[IAS 33.64]* and

- in our opinion, the effects of business combinations that are accounted for as a uniting of interests (discussed at 4.6 above).

No adjustment should be made:

- to basic or diluted EPS when a share consolidation is combined with a special dividend where the overall commercial effect is that of a share repurchase at fair value (discussed at 4.3.2 above); *[IAS 33.29]*

- to previously reported diluted EPS due to changes in the prices of ordinary shares which would have given a different dilutive effect for options and warrants; *[IAS 33.47]*

- to prior period diluted EPS as a result of a contingency period coming to an end without the conditions attaching to contingently issuable shares being met; *[IAS 33.52]* or

- to prior period diluted EPS for changes in the assumptions used in the calculations or for the conversion of potential ordinary shares into ordinary shares. *[IAS 33.65]*.

7.3 Disclosure

IAS 33 requires disclosure of the following:

(a) the amounts used as the numerators in calculating basic and diluted EPS, and a reconciliation of those amounts to profit or loss attributable to the parent entity for the period. The reconciliation should include the individual effect of each class of instruments that affects EPS;

(b) the weighted average number of ordinary shares used as the denominator in calculating basic and diluted earnings per share, and a reconciliation of these denominators to each other. The reconciliation should include the individual effect of each class of instruments that affects EPS;

(c) instruments (including contingently issuable shares) that could potentially dilute basic EPS in the future, but were not included in the calculation because they were antidilutive for the period(s) presented; and

(d) a description of ordinary share transactions or potential ordinary share transactions (other than those accounted for in EPS for the year – see 4.3 above – in which case that fact should be stated), that occur after the end of the reporting period and that would have changed significantly the number of ordinary shares or potential ordinary shares outstanding at the end of the period if those transactions had occurred before the end of the reporting period. *[IAS 33.70]*.

Examples of transactions in (d) include:

(a)   an issue of shares for cash;

(b)   an issue of shares when the proceeds are used to repay debt or preference shares outstanding at the end of the reporting period;

(c)   the redemption of ordinary shares outstanding;

(d)   the conversion or exercise of potential ordinary shares outstanding at the end of the reporting period into ordinary shares;

(e)   an issue of options, warrants, or convertible instruments; and

(f)   the achievement of conditions that would result in the issue of contingently issuable shares.

The standard observes that EPS amounts are not adjusted for such transactions occurring after the reporting period because such transactions do not affect the amount of capital used to produce profit or loss for the period. *[IAS 33.71]*. Changes in ordinary shares are discussed at 4 above.

The standard observes that financial instruments and other contracts generating potential ordinary shares may incorporate terms and conditions that affect the measurement of basic and diluted earnings per share. These terms and conditions may determine whether any potential ordinary shares are dilutive and, if so, the effect on the weighted average number of shares outstanding and any consequent adjustments to profit or loss attributable to ordinary equity holders. The disclosure of the terms and conditions of such financial instruments and other contracts is encouraged by IAS 33, if not otherwise required by IFRS 7 – *Financial Instruments: Disclosures* (discussed in Chapter 52). *[IAS 33.72]*.

8   FUTURE DEVELOPMENTS

In August 2008 the IASB published an exposure draft of proposed amendments to IAS 33 as part of its convergence project with the FASB.[7] The proposals aimed to achieve convergence of the denominator of the EPS calculation and to clarify and simplify the calculation of EPS.

The proposals aimed to achieve convergence by:[8]

• establishing a principle to determine which instruments are included in the calculation of basic EPS. According to this principle, the weighted average number of ordinary shares includes only those instruments that give (or are deemed to give) their holder the right to share currently in profit or loss of the period. As a consequence, if ordinary shares issuable for little or no cash or other consideration or mandatorily convertible instruments do not meet this condition, they will not be included in basic EPS.

• clarifying the treatment of contracts for the purchase of own ordinary shares for cash or other financial assets. Such contracts include gross physically settled written put options, forward purchase contracts and mandatorily redeemable ordinary shares. The exposure draft treats those contracts as if the entity had already repurchased the shares.

- amending the calculation of diluted EPS for participating instruments and two-class ordinary shares. The proposed amendment introduces a test to determine whether a convertible financial instrument would have a more dilutive effect if conversion is assumed. The diluted EPS calculation should assume the more dilutive treatment.

The proposals aimed to clarify and simplify the calculation of EPS as follows.[9]

- Instruments measured at fair value through profit or loss to be ignored for diluted EPS purposes. This is because the Boards believe changes in fair value reflect the economic effect of such instruments on current equity holders for the period. In other words, the changes in fair value reflect the benefits received, or detriments incurred, by the current equity holders during the period.

- Using the year-end share price, rather than the average for the period, to calculate the dilutive effect of options, warrants and their equivalents.

- Providing explicit requirements for the diluted EPS calculation of forward contracts to sell an entity's own shares. The proposal is to clarify that for the calculation of diluted EPS an entity assumes that ordinary shares relating to such a contract are sold and the effect is dilutive.

- Contracts to repurchase an entity's own shares and contracts that may be settled in ordinary shares or cash would either be measured at fair value through profit or loss or the liability for the present value of the redemption amount would meet the definition of a participating instrument. Accordingly, either no adjustments would be required in calculating diluted EPS or the application guidance on participating instruments and two-class ordinary shares would apply. Therefore, the Board proposes to delete the current requirements for contracts that may be settled in ordinary shares or cash in and for contracts to repurchase an entity's own shares.

The Board reviewed a summary of responses to the ED in its meeting in April 2009. In the light of other priorities, the Board directed the staff to consider towards the end of 2009 when would be the best time for the Board to start reviewing the responses in more detail.[10] At the time of writing, the project is described as deferred and its future will be decided as part of the IASB's wider consultation on its agenda (see Chapter 1).

9   APPENDIX

CALCULATION AND PRESENTATION OF BASIC AND DILUTED EARNINGS PER SHARE (COMPREHENSIVE EXAMPLE)

Reproduced below is IAS 33's comprehensive worked example of the computation and presentation of EPS. *[IAS 33.IE12].* It illustrates four quarters and then the full year, but the principles and calculations would be the same whatever the length of the periods considered.

Chapter 35

This example illustrates the quarterly and annual calculations of basic and diluted earnings per share in the year 20X1 for Company A, which has a complex capital structure. The control number is profit or loss from continuing operations attributable to the parent entity. Other facts assumed are as follows:

Average market price of ordinary shares: The average market prices of ordinary shares for the calendar year 20X1 were as follows:

First quarter	CU 49
Second quarter	CU 60
Third quarter	CU 67
Fourth quarter	CU 67

The average market price of ordinary shares from 1 July to 1 September 20X1 was CU 65.

Ordinary shares: The number of ordinary shares outstanding at the beginning of 20X1 was 5,000,000. On 1 March 20X1, 200,000 ordinary shares were issued for cash.

Convertible bonds: In the last quarter of 20X0, 5 per cent convertible bonds with a principal amount of CU 12,000,000 due in 20 years were sold for cash at CU 1,000 (par). Interest is payable twice a year, on 1 November and 1 May. Each CU 1,000 bond is convertible into 40 ordinary shares. No bonds were converted in 20X0. The entire issue was converted on 1 April 20X1 because the issue was called by Company A.

Convertible preference shares: In the second quarter of 20X0, 800,000 convertible preference shares were issued for assets in a purchase transaction. The quarterly dividend on each convertible preference share is CU 0.05, payable at the end of the quarter for shares outstanding at that date. Each share is convertible into one ordinary share. Holders of 600,000 convertible preference shares converted their preference shares into ordinary shares on 1 June 20X1.

Warrants: Warrants to buy 600,000 ordinary shares at CU 55 per share for a period of five years were issued on 1 January 20X1. All outstanding warrants were exercised on 1 September 20X1.

Options: Options to buy 1,500,000 ordinary shares at CU 75 per share for a period of 10 years were issued on 1 July 20X1. No options were exercised during 20X1 because the exercise price of the options exceeded the market price of the ordinary shares.

Tax rate: The tax rate was 40 per cent for 20X1.

20X1	Profit (loss) from continuing operations attributable to the parent entity (a) CU	Profit (loss) attributable to the parent entity CU	
First quarter	5,000,000	5,000,000	
Second quarter	6,500,000	6,500,000	
Third quarter	1,000,000	(1,000,000)	(b)
Fourth quarter	(700,000)	(700,000)	
Full year	11,800,000	9,800,000	

(a) This is the control number (before adjusting for preference dividends).

(b) Company A had a CU 2,000,000 loss (net of tax) from discontinuing operations in the third quarter.

First Quarter 20X1

Basic EPS calculation	CU
Profit from continuing operations attributable to the parent entity	5,000,000
Less: preference shares dividends	(40,000) (c)
Profit attributable to ordinary equity holders of the parent entity	4,960,000

Dates	Shares Outstanding	Fraction of period	Weighted-average shares
1 January 28 February	5,000,000	2/3	3,333,333
Issue of ordinary shares on 1 March	200,000		
1 March 31 March	5,200,000	1/3	1,733,333
Weighted-average shares			5,066,666

Basic EPS   **CU 0.98**

(c)   800,000 shares × CU 0.05

Diluted EPS calculation

Profit attributable to ordinary equity holders of the parent entity		CU 4,960,000
Plus: profit impact of assumed conversions		
Preference share dividends	CU 40,000 (d)	
Interest on 5% convertible bonds	CU 90,000 (e)	
Effect of assumed conversions		CU 130,000
Profit attributable to ordinary equity holders of the parent entity including assumed conversions		CU 5,090,000

Weighted-average shares		5,066,666
Plus: incremental shares from assumed conversions		
Warrants	0 (f)	
Convertible preference shares	800,000	
5% convertible bonds	480,000	
Dilutive potential ordinary shares		1,280,000
Adjusted weighted-average shares		6,346,666

Diluted EPS   **CU 0.80**

(d)   800,000 shares × CU 0.05

(e)   (CU 12,000,000 × 5%) ÷ 4; less taxes at 40%

(f)   The warrants were not assumed to be exercised because they were antidilutive in the period (CU 55 [exercise price] > CU 49 [average price]).

Second Quarter 20X1

Basic EPS calculation			*CU*
Profit from continuing operations attributable to the parent entity			6,500,000
Less: preference shares dividends			(10,000) (g)
Profit attributable to ordinary equity holders of the parent entity			6,490,000

Dates	*Shares outstanding*	*Fraction of period*	*Weighted-average shares*
1 April	5,200,000		
Conversion of 5% bonds on 1April	480,000		
1 April – 31 May	5,680,000	2/3	3,786,666
Conversion of preference shares on 1June	600,000		
1 June – 30 June	6,280,000	1/3	2,093,333
Weighted-average shares			5,880,000
Basic EPS			**CU 1.10**

(g)   200,000 shares × CU 0.05

Diluted EPS calculation		
Profit attributable to ordinary equity holders of the parent entity		CU 6,490,000
Plus: profit impact of assumed conversions		
Preference share dividends	CU 10,000 (h)	
Effect of assumed conversions		CU 10,000
Profit attributable to ordinary equity holders of the parent entity including assumed conversions		CU 6,500,000
Weighted-average shares		5,880,000
Plus: incremental shares from assumed conversions		
Warrants	50,000 (i)	
Convertible preference shares	600,000 (j)	
Dilutive potential ordinary shares		650,000
Adjusted weighted-average shares		6,530,000
Diluted EPS		**CU 1.00**

(h)   200,000 shares × CU 0.05

(i)   CU 55 × 600,000 = CU 33,000,000; CU 33,000,000 ÷ CU 60 = 550,000;
       600,000 – 550,000 = 50,000 shares *or*
       [(CU 60 – CU 55) ÷ CU 60] × 600,000 shares = 50,000 shares

(j)   (800,000 shares × 2/3) + (200,000 shares × 1/3)

Third Quarter 20X1

Basic EPS calculation			CU
Profit from continuing operations attributable to the parent entity			1,000,000
Less: preference shares dividends			(10,000)
Profit from continuing operations attributable to ordinary equity holders of the parent entity			990,000
Loss from discontinuing operations attributable to the parent entity			(2,000,000)
Loss attributable to ordinary equity holders of the parent entity			(1,010,000)

Dates	Shares outstanding	Fraction of period	Weighted-average shares
1 July – 31 August	6,280,000	2/3	4,186,666
Exercise of warrants on 1 September	600,000		
1 September – 30 September	6,880,000	1/3	2,293,333
Weighted-average shares			6,480,000

Basic EPS	
Profit from continuing operations	**CU 0.15**
Loss from discontinuing operations	**(CU 0.31)**
Loss	**(CU 0.16)**

Diluted EPS calculation		
Profit from continuing operations attributable to ordinary equity holders of the parent entity		CU 990,000
Plus: profit impact of assumed conversions		
Preference shares dividends	CU 10,000	
Effect of assumed conversions		CU 10,000
Profit from continuing operations attributable to ordinary equity holders of the parent entity including assumed conversions		CU 1,000,000
Loss from discontinuing operations attributable to the parent entity		(CU 2,000,000)
Loss attributable to ordinary equity holders of the parent entity including assumed conversions		(CU 1,000,000)

Weighted-average shares		6,480,000
Plus: incremental shares from assumed conversions		
Warrants	61,538 (k)	
Convertible preference shares	200,000	
Dilutive potential ordinary shares		261,538
Adjusted weighted-average shares		6,741,538

Diluted EPS	
Profit from continuing operations	**CU 0.15**
Loss from discontinuing operations	**(CU 0.30)**
Loss	**(CU 0.15)**

(k) [(CU 65 – CU 55) ÷ CU 65] × 600,000 = 92,308 shares; 92,308 × 2/3 = 61,538 shares

Note: The incremental shares from assumed conversions are included in calculating the diluted per-share amounts for the loss from discontinuing operations and loss even though they are antidilutive. This is because the control number (profit from continuing operations attributable to ordinary equity holders of the parent entity, adjusted for preference dividends) was positive (i.e. profit, rather than loss).

Chapter 35

Fourth Quarter 20X1

Basic and diluted EPS calculation			CU
Loss from continuing operations attributable to the parent entity			(700,000)
Add: preference shares dividends			(10,000)
Loss attributable to ordinary equity holders of the parent entity			(710,000)

Dates	Shares outstanding	Fraction of period	Weighted-average shares
1 October – 31 December	6,880,000	3/3	6,880,000
Weighted-average shares			6,880,000

Basic and diluted EPS

Loss attributable to ordinary equity holders of the parent entity	**(CU 0.10)**

Note: The incremental shares from assumed conversions are not included in calculating the diluted per-share amounts because the control number (loss from continuing operations attributable to ordinary equity holders of the parent entity adjusted for preference dividends) was negative (i.e. a loss, rather than profit).

Full Year 20X1

Basic EPS calculation	CU
Profit from continuing operations attributable to the parent entity	11,800,000
Less: preference shares dividends	(70,000)
Profit from continuing operations attributable to ordinary equity holders of the parent entity	11,730,000
Loss from discontinuing operations attributable to the parent entity	(2,000,000)
Profit attributable to ordinary equity holders of the parent entity	9,730,000

Dates	Shares Outstanding	Fraction of period	Weighted-average shares
1 January – 28 February	5,000,000	2/12	833,333
Issue of ordinary shares on 1 March	200,000		
1 March – 31 March	5,200,000	1/12	433,333
Conversion of 5% bonds on 1 April	480,000		
1 April – 31 May	5,680,000	2/12	946,667
Conversion of preference shares on 1 June	600,000		
1 June – 31 August	6,280,000	3/12	1,570,000
Exercise of warrants on 1 September	600,000		
1 September – 31 December	6,880,000	4/12	2,293,333
Weighted-average shares			6,076,667

Basic EPS

Profit from continuing operations	**CU 1.93**
Loss from discontinuing operations	**(CU 0.33)**
Profit	**CU 1.60**

Diluted EPS calculation

Profit from continuing operations attributable to ordinary equity holders of the parent entity		CU 11,730,000
Plus: profit impact of assumed conversions		
Preference share dividends	CU 70,000	
Interest on 5% convertible bonds	CU 90,000 (l)	
Effect of assumed conversions		CU 160,000
Profit from continuing operations attributable to ordinary equity holders of the parent entity including assumed conversions		CU 11,890,000
Loss from discontinuing operations attributable to the parent entity		(CU 2,000,000)
Profit attributable to ordinary equity holders of the parent entity including assumed conversions		CU 9,890,000
Weighted-average shares		6,076,667
Plus: incremental shares from assumed conversions		
Warrants	14,880 (m)	
Convertible preference shares	450,000 (n)	
5% convertible bonds	120,000 (o)	
Dilutive potential ordinary shares		584,880
Adjusted weighted-average shares		6,661,547
Diluted EPS		
Profit from continuing operations		**CU 1.78**
Loss from discontinuing operations		**(CU 0.30)**
Profit		**CU 1.48**

(l) (CU 12,000,000 × 5%) ÷ 4; less taxes at 40%

(m) [(CU 57.125* – CU 55) ÷ CU 57.125] × 600,000 = 22,320 shares; 22,320 × 8/12 = 14,880 shares
    * The average market price from 1 January 20X1 to 1 September 20X1

(n) (800,000 shares × 5/12) + (200,000 shares × 7/12)

(o) 480,000 shares × 3/12

The following illustrates how Company A might present its earnings per share data in its statement of comprehensive income. Note that the amounts per share for the loss from discontinuing operations are not required to be presented on the face of the statement of comprehensive income.

	For the year ended 20X1 CU
Earnings per ordinary share	
Profit from continuing operations	1.93
Loss from discontinuing operations	(0.33)
Profit	1.60
Diluted earnings per ordinary share	
Profit from continuing operations	1.78
Loss from discontinuing operations	(0.30)
Profit	1.48

Chapter 35

The following table includes the quarterly and annual earnings per share data for Company A. The purpose of this table is to illustrate that the sum of the four quarters' earnings per share data will not necessarily equal the annual earnings per share data. The Standard does not require disclosure of this information.

	First quarter CU	Second quarter CU	Third quarter CU	Fourth quarter CU	Full year CU
Basic EPS					
Profit (loss) from continuing operations	0.98	1.10	0.15	(0.10)	1.93
Loss from discontinuing operations	–	–	(0.31)	–	(0.33)
Profit (loss)	0.98	1.10	(0.16)	(0.10)	1.60
Diluted EPS					
Profit (loss) from continuing operations	0.80	1.00	0.15	(0.10)	1.78
Loss from discontinuing operations	–	–	(0.30)	–	(0.30)
Profit (loss)	0.80	1.00	(0.15)	(0.10)	1.48

This example does not illustrate the classification of the components of convertible financial instruments as liabilities and equity or the classification of related interest and dividends as expenses and equity as required by IAS 32.

References

1 A put warrant, involving the repurchase of shares at significantly more than their fair value is included as an example in the equivalent standard in the UK which was developed at the same time as, and is very similar to, IAS 33.

2 See, for example, the financial statements of: SPORTECH PLC (2010) and L'Oréal (2010).

3 *Exposure Draft, Simplifying Earnings per Share: Proposed amendments to IAS 33*, IASB, August 2008, para. 67.

4 Proposed Improvements to International Accounting Standard IAS 33, IASB, December 2003, Invitation to Comment Question 2 and Appendix B, examples 7 and 12.

5 *IASB Update*, January 2006, page 2.

6 IFRS 2, paras. BC54-BC57.

7 *Exposure Draft, Simplifying Earnings per Share: Proposed amendments to IAS 33*, IASB, August 2008.

8 *Exposure Draft, Simplifying Earnings per Share: Proposed amendments to IAS 33*, para. IN2.

9 *Exposure Draft, Simplifying Earnings per Share: Proposed amendments to IAS 33*, paras. IN5-IN8.

10 *IASB Update*, April 2009.

Chapter 36   Events after the reporting period

List of examples

Chapter 36

Events after the reporting period

1 INTRODUCTION

IAS 10 – *Events after the Reporting Period* – deals with accounting for, and disclosure of, events after the reporting period, which are defined as 'those events, favourable and unfavourable, that occur between the end of the reporting period and the date when the financial statements are authorised for issue'. *[IAS 10.3]*. Therefore, the definition includes all events occurring between those dates – irrespective of whether they relate to conditions that existed at the end of the reporting period. The principal issue is determining which events after the reporting period to reflect in the financial statements.

The financial statements of an entity present, among other things, an entity's financial position at the end of the reporting period. Therefore, it is appropriate to adjust the financial statements for all events that offer greater clarity concerning the conditions that existed at the end of the reporting period, that occur prior to the date the financial statements are authorised for issuance. Therefore, the standard requires that entities adjust the amounts recognised in the financial statements for 'adjusting events' that provide evidence of conditions that existed at the end of the reporting period. An entity does not recognise events after the reporting period that relate to conditions that only arose after that date ('non-adjusting events') in the financial statements. However, if non-adjusting events are significant, the standard requires certain disclosures about them.

One exception to the standard's general rule for non-adjusting events is when the going concern basis becomes no longer appropriate. This is treated as an adjusting event.

The requirements of IAS 10 and practical issues resulting there from are dealt with at 2 and 3 below.

2   REQUIREMENTS OF IAS 10

2.1   Objective, scope and definitions

The objective of IAS 10 is to prescribe:

- when an entity adjusts its financial statements for events after the reporting period; and

- the required disclosures about the date when the financial statements were authorised for issue and about events after the reporting period.

The standard does not permit an entity to prepare its financial statements on a going concern basis if events after the reporting period indicate that the going concern assumption is not appropriate. *[IAS 10.1]*. This requirement is discussed further at 2.2.2 below. The going concern basis is discussed in Chapter 3 at 4.1.2.

IAS 10 defines events after the reporting period as 'those events, favourable and unfavourable, that occur between the end of the reporting period and the date when the financial statements are authorised for issue'. *[IAS 10.3]*. This definition therefore includes events that provide additional evidence about conditions that existed at the end of the reporting period, as well as those that do not. The former are adjusting events, the latter are non-adjusting events. *[IAS 10.3]*. Adjusting and non-adjusting events are discussed further at 2.1.2 and 2.1.3 below, respectively.

2.1.1   *Date when financial statements are authorised for issue*

Given the definition above, the meaning of 'the date when the financial statements are authorised for issue' is clearly important. The standard observes that the process for authorising financial statements for issue varies depending upon the management structure, statutory requirements, and procedures followed in preparing and finalising the financial statements. *[IAS 10.4]*.

The standard identifies two particular instances of the different meaning of 'authorised for issue', as follows:

(a)   an entity may be required to submit its financial statements to its shareholders for approval (as in France, for example) after the financial statements have been issued. In such cases, the financial statements are considered authorised for issue on the date of issue, not the date when shareholders approve them; *[IAS 10.5]* and

(b)   the management of an entity may be required to issue its financial statements to a supervisory board (made up solely of non-executives) for approval. Such financial statements are considered 'authorised for issue' when management authorises them for issue to the supervisory board. *[IAS 10.6]*.

These two meanings are illustrated with two examples, as follows.

Example 36.1:   Financial statements required to be approved by shareholders

The management of an entity completes draft financial statements for the year to 31 December 2011 on 28 February 2012. On 17 March 2012, the board of directors reviews the financial statements and authorises them for issue. The entity announces its profit and certain other financial information on 18 March 2012. The financial statements are made available to shareholders and others on 1 April 2012. The shareholders approve the financial statements at their annual meeting on 11 May 2012 and the approved financial statements are filed with a regulatory body on 13 May 2012.

The financial statements are authorised for issue on 17 March 2012 (date of board authorisation for issue).

Example 36.2:   *Financial statements required to be approved by supervisory board*

On 17 March 2012, the management of an entity authorises for issue to its supervisory board financial statements for the year to 31 December 2011. The supervisory board consists solely of non-executives and may include representatives of employees and other outside interests. The supervisory board approves the financial statements on 25 March 2012. The financial statements are available to shareholders and others on 1 April 2012. The shareholders approve the financial statements at their annual meeting on 11 May 2012 and the financial statements are filed with a regulatory body on 13 May 2012.

The financial statements are authorised for issue on 17 March 2012 (date of management authorisation for issue to the supervisory board).

An uncommon, but possible situation may occur, wherein the financial statements are changed after they are authorised for issue to the supervisory board. The following example illustrates such a situation.

Example 36.3:   *Financial statements required to be approved by supervisory board – changes are made by supervisory board*

Same facts as in Example 36.2 above, except that the supervisory board reviews the financial statements on 25 March 2012 and proposes changes to certain note disclosures. The management of the entity incorporates the suggested changes and re-authorises those financial statements for issue to the supervisory board on 27 March 2012. The supervisory board then approves the financial statements on 30 March 2012.

The financial statements are authorised for issue on 27 March 2012 (date of management re-authorisation for issue to the supervisory board).

A fourth example illustrates when the entity releases preliminary information, but not complete financial statements, before the date of the authorisation for issue.

Example 36.4:   *Release of financial information before date of authorisation for issue*

The management of an entity completes the primary financial statements (e.g. balance sheet, statement of comprehensive income, cash flow statement) for the year to 31 December 2011 on 21 January 2012, but has not yet completed the explanatory notes. On 26 January 2012, the board of directors (which includes management and non-executives) reviews the primary financial statements and authorises them for public media release. The entity announces its profit and certain other financial information on 28 January 2012. On 11 February 2012, management issues the financial statements (with full explanatory notes) to the board of directors, which approves the financial statements for filing on 18 February 2012. The entity files the financial statements with a regulatory body on 21 February 2012.

The financial statements are authorised for issue on 18 February 2012 (date the board of directors, approves the financial statements for filing).

Example 36.4 illustrates that events after the reporting period include those events that arise between the date of the preliminary announcement and the date on which the financial statements are authorised for issue. Accordingly, the information in the financial statements might differ from the equivalent information in the preliminary announcement. As governance structures vary by jurisdiction, entities may be allowed to organise their procedures differently, and adjust the financial reporting process accordingly.

Chapter 36

An example of a company covered by (a) above is Holcim as illustrated in the following extract:

> *Extract 36.1: Holcim Ltd (2007)*
>
> **41   Authorization of the financial statements for issuance** [extract]
>
> The consolidated financial statements were authorized for issuance by the Board of Directors of Holcim Ltd on February 22, 2008 and are subject to shareholder approval at the annual general meeting of shareholders scheduled for May 7, 2008.

For (b) above, the phrase 'made up solely of non-executives' is not defined by the standard, although the standard contemplates a supervisory board including representatives of employees and other outside interests. However, it seems to draw a distinction between those responsible for the executive management of an entity (and the preparation of its financial statements) and those in a position of high-level oversight (including reviewing and approving the financial statements). This situation seems to describe the typical two-tier board system seen in some jurisdictions (for example, Germany). An example of a company with this structure is Bayer, as illustrated in the following Extract.

> *Extract 36.2: Bayer AG (2007)*
>
> **Corporate Governance** [extract]
>
> **Supervisory Board: oversight and control functions** [extract]
>
> The role of the 20-member Supervisory Board is to oversee and advise the Board of Management. Under the German Codetermination Act, half the members of the Supervisory Board are elected by the stockholders, and half by the company's employees. The Supervisory Board is directly involved in decisions on matters of fundamental importance to the company, regularly conferring with the Board of Management on the company's strategic alignment and the implementation status of the business strategy.
>
> The Chairman of the Supervisory Board coordinates its work and presides over the meetings. Through regular discussions with the Board of Management, the Supervisory Board is kept constantly informed of business policy, corporate planning and strategy. The annual budget, the financial statements of Bayer AG and the consolidated financial statements of the Bayer Group must be submitted to the Supervisory Board to obtain its approval, which must also take the auditor's report into account.

If an entity re-issues financial statements (whether to correct for an error or to include events that occurred after the financial statements were originally authorised for issue), there is a new date of authorisation for issue. The financial statements should then appropriately reflect all adjusting and non-adjusting events (including those that occurred in the interim period between the original and new date of authorisation for issue). This means an entity cannot 'dual date' its financial statements. That is, an entity cannot retain the original date of authorisation of the financial statements with a second authorisation date for specific events occurring between the two dates. The re-issued financial statements must reflect all adjusting and non-adjusting events occurring up to the new date of authorisation.

2.1.2 Adjusting events

Adjusting events are 'those that provide evidence of conditions that existed at the end of the reporting period.' *[IAS 10.3(a)]*.

Examples of adjusting events are as follows: *[IAS 10.9]*

(a) a settlement after the reporting period of a court case that confirms that the entity had a present obligation at the end of the reporting period. In this situation, an entity adjusts any previously recognised provision related to this court case under IAS 37 – *Provisions, Contingent Liabilities and Contingent Assets*, or recognises a new provision. The standard explains that mere disclosure of a contingent liability is not sufficient because the settlement provides additional evidence of conditions that existed at the end of the reporting period that would be considered in accordance with IAS 37 (see Chapter 29 at 3.1.1 and 3.2.1);

(b) the receipt of information after the reporting period indicating that an asset was impaired at the end of the reporting period, or that the amount of a previously recognised impairment loss for that asset needs to be adjusted. For example:

(i) the bankruptcy of a customer that occurs after the reporting period usually confirms that a loss existed at the end of the reporting period on a trade receivable and that the entity needs to adjust the carrying amount of the trade receivable; and

(ii) the sale of inventories after the reporting period may give evidence about their net realisable value at the end of the reporting period;

(c) the determination after the reporting period of the cost of assets purchased, or the proceeds from assets sold, before the end of the reporting period;

(d) the determination after the reporting period of the amount of profit-sharing or bonus payments, if the entity had a present legal or constructive obligation at the end of the reporting period to make such payments as a result of events before that date;

(e) the discovery of fraud or errors that show that the financial statements are incorrect (see 3.5 below).

In addition, IAS 33 – *Earnings per Share* – requires an adjustment to earnings per share for certain share transactions after the reporting period (such as bonus issues, share splits or share consolidations discussed in Chapter 35 at 4.5), even though the transactions themselves are non-adjusting events (see 2.1.3 below). *[IAS 10.22]*.

2.1.3 Non-adjusting events

The standard states that non-adjusting events are 'those that are indicative of conditions that arose after the reporting period'. *[IAS 10.3(b)]*.

As examples of non-adjusting events, the standard gives the following events after the reporting period: *[IAS 10.11-12, 22]*

(a)   major business combinations (IFRS 3 – *Business Combinations* – requires specific disclosures in such cases, see Chapter 10 at 16.1.2) or dispositions of major subsidiaries;

(b)   announcing a plan to discontinue an operation;

(c)   a major purchase of assets, classification of assets as held for sale in accordance with IFRS 5 – *Non-current Assets Held for Sale and Discontinued Operations*, other disposal of assets, or expropriation of major assets by government (see Chapter 4 at 5);

(d)   the destruction of a major production plant by a fire;

(e)   announcing, or commencing the implementation of a major restructuring (discussed in Chapter 29 at 5.2);

(f)   a major ordinary share transaction or potential ordinary share transactions (although as noted at 2.1.2 above, some transactions in ordinary shares are adjusting events for the purposes of computing earnings per share);

(g)   an abnormally large change in asset prices or foreign exchange rates;

(h)   a change in tax rates or the enactment or announcement of tax laws that significantly affect current and deferred tax assets and liabilities (discussed in Chapter 31 at 8.1);

(i)   entry into significant commitments or contingent liabilities, for example, by issuing significant guarantees;

(j)   start of major litigation arising solely out of events that occurred after the reporting period;

(k)   a decline in market value of investments; and

(l)   a declaration of dividends to holders of equity instruments (as defined in IAS 32 – *Financial Instruments: Presentation* – discussed in Chapter 45 at 8).

The reference in (a) and (c) above to asset disposals as examples of non-adjusting events is not quite the whole story, as they may indicate an impairment of assets, which may be an adjusting event. In addition, (b) and (e) above, regarding announcements of plans to discontinue an operation or to restructure a business, respectively, may also lead to an impairment charge (see Chapter 22 at 2).

For market value declines in investments, as in (k) above, the standard notes that the decline in market value does not *normally* relate to the condition of the investments at the end of the reporting period, but reflects circumstances that arose subsequently. Therefore, in those circumstances the amounts recognised in financial statements for the investments are not adjusted. Similarly, the standard states that an entity does not update the amounts disclosed for the investments as at the end of the reporting period, although it may need to give additional disclosure if material, as discussed at 2.3 below. [IAS 10.11].

However, the assertion that a decline in market value of investments does not *normally* relate to conditions at the end of the reporting period is similar wording to that used for bankruptcy and the sale of inventories (see 2.1.2(b) above). Therefore, the standard requires an assessment of the circumstances in order to determine which conditions actually existed at the end of the reporting period – although this can be difficult in practice, particularly when fraud is involved (see 3.5 below).

In respect of dividend declarations, as in (1) above, IAS 10 takes a strict balance sheet approach. Dividends are only recognised as a liability if 'declared' on or by the end of the reporting period. If an entity declares dividends to holders of equity instruments (as defined in IAS 32) after the reporting period, the entity shall not recognise those dividends as a liability at the end of the reporting period. *[IAS 10.13]*. While an entity may have a past practice of paying dividends, such dividends are not 'declared', and therefore not recognised as an obligation.

IFRIC 17 – *Distributions of Non-cash Assets to Owners* – states that an entity recognises a liability to pay a dividend when the dividend is appropriately authorised and is no longer at the discretion of the entity, which is the date: *[IFRIC 17.10]*

- when declaration of the dividend, e.g. by management or the board of directors, is approved by the relevant authority, e.g. the shareholders, if the jurisdiction requires such approval; or
- when the dividend is declared, e.g. by management or the board of directors, if the jurisdiction does not require further approval.

IAS 10 contains a reminder that an entity discloses dividends, both proposed and declared, in the notes to the financial statements in accordance with IAS 1 – *Presentation of Financial Statements* (see Chapter 3 at 5.5). *[IAS 10.13]*.

Similar issues arise regarding the declaration of dividends by subsidiaries and associates. Although IAS 10 does not specifically address such items, IAS 18 – *Revenue* – requires that a shareholder recognise dividends when its right to receive payment is established. *[IAS 18.30(c)]*. Accordingly, a shareholder does not recognise such dividend income until the period in which the dividend is declared.

2.2 The treatment of adjusting events

2.2.1 Events requiring adjustment to the amounts recognised, or disclosures, in the financial statements

IAS 10 requires that the amounts recognised in the financial statements be adjusted to take account of an adjusting event. *[IAS 10.8]*. The standard also notes that an entity may receive information after the balance sheet date about conditions existing at that date relating to disclosures made in the financial statements but not affecting the amounts recognised in them. *[IAS 10.20]*. In such cases, the standard requires the entity to update the disclosures that relate to those conditions for the new information. *[IAS 10.19]*.

For example, evidence may become available after the reporting period about a contingent liability that existed at the end of the reporting period. In addition to considering whether to recognise or change a provision under IAS 37, IAS 10 requires an entity to update its disclosures about the contingent liability for that evidence. *[IAS 10.20]*.

2.2.2 *Events indicating that the going concern basis is not appropriate*

IAS 10 states that if management determines after the reporting period either that it intends to liquidate the entity or to cease trading, or that it has no realistic alternative but to do so, the financial statements are not prepared on the going concern basis. *[IAS 10.14]*.

The standard states that deterioration in operating results and financial position after the reporting period may indicate a need to consider whether the going concern assumption is still appropriate. If the going concern assumption is no longer appropriate, the standard states that the effect is so pervasive that it results in a fundamental change in the basis of accounting, rather than an adjustment to the amounts recognised in the original basis of accounting. *[IAS 10.15]*. As noted in Chapter 3 at 4.1.2, IFRS contains no guidance on this 'fundamental change in the basis of accounting.' Accordingly, entities will need to consider carefully their individual circumstances to arrive at an appropriate basis.

The standard also contains a reminder of the requirements under IAS 1 related to the going concern basis: *[IAS 10.16, IAS 1.25]*

(a)   When the financial statements are not prepared on a going concern basis, that fact should be disclosed, together with the basis on which the financial statements have been prepared and the reason why the entity is not regarded as a going concern; or

(b)   When management is aware of material uncertainties related to events or conditions that may cast significant doubt upon the entity's ability to continue as a going concern, a disclosure of those uncertainties should be made.

While IFRSs are generally written from the perspective that an entity is a going concern, they are also applicable when another basis of accounting is used to prepare financial statements. Various IFRSs acknowledge that financial statements may be prepared on either a going concern basis or an alternative basis of accounting. *[IAS 1.25, IAS 10.14, Framework 4.1]*. Such IFRSs do not specifically exclude the application of IFRS when an alternative basis of accounting, such as liquidation basis of accounting, is used. Therefore, in our view, financial statements prepared on a basis of accounting other than a going concern basis following the above-mentioned guidance under IFRSs, are capable of compliance with IFRS.

When an entity prepares financial statements on a basis other than a going concern basis, certain deviations from specific sections or paragraphs of IFRSs may be appropriate. Significant judgment may be involved in determining the degree of acceptable deviation from IFRSs which are not more than is required to 'present fairly' the financial statements prepared on the stated basis of accounting. Adequate disclosure as required under (a) above is important in such circumstances to allow users of financial statements to understand how the financial statements have been prepared.

Regarding (b), the events or conditions requiring disclosure may arise after the reporting period. *[IAS 10.16(b)]*.

2.3 The treatment of non-adjusting events

IAS 10 prohibits the adjustment of amounts recognised in financial statements to reflect non-adjusting events. *[IAS 10.10]*. The standard indicates that if non-adjusting events are material, non-disclosure could influence the economic decisions of users of the financial statements. Accordingly, an entity should disclose the following for each material category of non-adjusting event: *[IAS 10.21]*

(a)   the nature of the event; and

(b)   an estimate of its financial effect, or a statement that such an estimate cannot be made.

To illustrate how these requirements have been applied in practice, example disclosures for certain types of non-adjusting events are given below.

Possibly the non-adjusting events that appear most regularly in financial statements are the acquisition/disposal of a non-current asset, such as an investment in a subsidiary or a business, subsequent to end of the reporting period. Extract 36.3 contains examples of the disclosures required for 2.1.3(a) and (l) above related to business combinations and disposals, and declaration of dividends, respectively:

Extract 36.3: Reed Elsevier (2007)

Notes to the combined financial statements [extract]

36.   Post balance sheet events [extract]

On 18 January 2008, Reed Elsevier PLC paid a special distribution of 82.0p per ordinary share and Reed Elsevier NV paid a special distribution of €1.767 per ordinary share, from the net proceeds of the disposal of Harcourt Education. The aggregate special distribution, announced on 12 December 2007, of £2,013m was recognised when paid in January 2008.

The special distributions were accompanied by a consolidation of the ordinary share capital of Reed Elsevier PLC and Reed Elsevier NV on the basis of 58 new ordinary shares for every 67 existing ordinary shares, being the ratio of the aggregate special distribution to the combined market capitalisation of Reed Elsevier PLC and Reed Elsevier NV (excluding the 5.8% indirect equity interest in Reed Elsevier NV held by Reed Elsevier PLC) as at the date of the announcement of the special distributions.

On 30 January 2008 the sale of Harcourt Assessment and the remaining Harcourt International businesses, first announced in May 2007, completed following receipt of regulatory clearance in the United States. Proceeds received on disposal were £330m.

On 20 February 2008, Reed Elsevier approved a plan to divest Reed Business Information. In the year to 31 December 2007, Reed Business Information reported revenues of £906m, operating profits of £89m and adjusted operating profits of £119m. On 20 February 2008, Reed Elsevier entered into a definitive merger agreement with ChoicePoint, Inc to acquire the company for cash. Taking into account ChoicePoint's estimated net debt of $0.6bn, the total value of the transaction is $4.1bn. The ChoicePoint board will convene a meeting of ChoicePoint shareholders to approve the merger and is unanimous in its recommendation of the merger. The merger is subject to customary regulatory approvals and is expected to be completed later in the year. The transaction will be financed initially through committed new bank facilities, to be later refinanced through the issuance of term debt.

ChoicePoint provides unique information and analytics to support underwriting decisions within the property and casualty insurance sector; screening and authentication services for employment, real estate leasing and customer enrolment; and public information solutions primarily to banking, professional services and government customers. In 2007 ChoicePoint reported revenues of £491m, operating income (before goodwill and asset write downs) of £112m and earnings before interest, tax, depreciation and amortisation of £144m.

Extract 36.4 contains examples of the disclosures required for ordinary share transactions, as described at 2.1.3(f) above:

Extract 36.4: Northern Rock (2007)

Notes to the accounts [extract]

45.   Events after the balance sheet date [extract]

On 10 January 2008, the Company sold its Lifetime mortgage portfolio to JP Morgan at a premium of 2.25% to the balance sheet value. Proceeds of the sale amounted to approximately £2.2bn and were used to reduce the level of the Bank of England facility.

On 22 February 2008 the entire share capital of the Company was transferred to the Treasury Solicitor in accordance with The Northern Rock plc Transfer Order 2008 taking Northern Rock into a period of temporary public ownership. Details of the impact of temporary public ownership are given throughout the Annual Report and Accounts as it affects the Company's operations and financial disclosures.

On 29 March 2008 the Bank of England and HM Treasury agreed to extend the existing on demand loan facilities as set out in note 28 above to 30 April 2008. On 29 March 2008 the Bank of England and HM Treasury confirmed that they intend to make arrangements to provide an additional committed secured revolving loan reserve facility to the Company in addition to the existing facilities as set out in note 28 above.

Extract 36.5 contains examples of the disclosures required for changes in tax laws, as described at 2.1.3(h) above:

Extract 36.5: British Energy (2008)

Notes to the Financial Statements [extract]

38.   Non-adjusting Post Balance Sheet Events [extract]

On 21 March 2007, the Government announced its intention to phase out industrial buildings allowances with effect from 1 April 2008. The phasing out of industrial buildings allowances was not included in the 2007 Finance Act and so is not considered to be substantively enacted at the balance sheet date. An estimate of the financial effect of this change, calculated at 28%, is that it would increase the net deferred tax liability by £37m to £82m.

Extract 36.6 contains examples of the disclosures required for a decline in market value of investments, as in 2.1.3(k) above:

Extract 36.6: Imperial Innovations (2008)

Notes to the Financial Statements [extract]

31.   Post Balance Sheet Events [extract]

Since the year end and as at 7 October 2008, the latest practical date prior to the approval of the accounts, the value of the Group's most significant asset Ceres Power Holdings plc (CWR.L) has reduced by £2.9 million (32%). This has had the effects of reducing investments by £2.9 million and of reducing the provision for liabilities and charges by £1.4m million since the year end. This is a non-adjusted post balance sheet event since it does not relate to conditions existing at the balance sheet date.

The list of examples of non-adjusting events in IAS 10, and summarised at 2.1.3 above, is not all-inclusive. IAS 10 requires disclosure of any material non-adjusting event. Extract 36.7 contains examples of the disclosures required for other non-adjusting events, which are not specifically listed by IAS 10:

> *Extract 36.7: GlaxoSmithKline (2007)*
>
> **Notes to the financial statements** [extract]
>
> **40.   Post balance sheet events** [extract]
>
> On 25th January 2008, the FDA issued a not approvable letter in respect of Merck's NDA seeking approval for over-the-counter Mevacor. This triggered repayment to GSK of the upfront fee GSK had paid to Merck in 2007 for the US OTC rights.
>
> On 18th February 2008, GSK's long-term Standard and Poor's debt rating was revised from AA with negative outlook to A+ stable. Standard and Poor's also revised GSK's short-term rating for paper issued under the Group's commercial paper programme from A-1+ to A-1.

2.4   Other disclosure requirements

The disclosures required in respect of non-adjusting events are discussed at 2.3 above. As IAS 10 only requires consideration to be given to events that occur up to the date when the financial statements are authorised for issue, it is important for users to know that date, since the financial statements do not reflect events after that date. *[IAS 10.18]*. Accordingly, the standard requires disclosure of the date the financial statements were authorised for issue. *[IAS 10.17]*. Furthermore, IAS 10 requires disclosure of who authorised the financial statements for issue and, if the owners of the entity or others have the power to amend them after issue, disclosure of that fact. *[IAS 10.17]*. In practice, this information can be presented in a number of ways:

(a)   on the face of a primary statement. For example, entities that are required to have the balance sheet signed could include the information at that point;

(b)   in the note dealing with other IAS 10 disclosures, or another note, such as the summary of significant accounting policies; or

(c)   in a separate statement, such as a statement of directors' responsibilities for the financial statements, (that is, outside of the financial statements, as permitted in certain jurisdictions).

Strictly speaking, this information is required to be presented within the financial statements. So, if (c) were chosen, either the whole report would need to be part of the financial statements or the information could be incorporated into them by way of a cross-reference.

The financial statements should also disclose new standards that are issued but are not yet effective for the entity (see Chapter 3 at 5.1.2.C).

3   PRACTICAL ISSUES

The standard alludes to practical issues, such as those discussed below. It states that a decline in market value of investments after the reporting period *does not normally* relate to conditions at the end of the reporting period (see 2.1.3 above). At the same time, the standard asserts that the bankruptcy of a customer that occurs after the reporting period *usually* confirms that a loss on a trade receivable existed at the end of the reporting period (see 2.1.2(b)(i) above). Judgment of the facts and

Chapter 36

circumstances is required to determine whether an event that occurs after the reporting period provides evidence about a condition that existed at the end of the reporting period, or whether the condition arose subsequent to the reporting period.

3.1   Valuation of inventory

The sale of inventories after the reporting period is normally a good indicator of the net realisable value (NRV) at that date. IAS 10 states that such sales 'may give evidence about... net realisable value at the end of the reporting period'. *[IAS 10.9(b)(ii)]*. However, in some cases, NRV decreases because of conditions that did not exist at the end of the reporting period.

Therefore, the problem is determining why NRV decreased. Did it decrease because of circumstances that existed at the end of the reporting period, which subsequently became known; or did it decrease because of circumstances that arose subsequently? A decrease in price is merely a response to changing conditions; so it is important to assess the reasons for these changes.

Some examples of changing conditions are as follows:

(a)   Price reductions caused by a sudden increase in cheap imports

Whilst it is arguable that the 'dumping' of cheap imports after the reporting period is a condition that arises subsequent to that date, it is more likely that this is a reaction to a condition that already existed, such as overproduction in other parts of the world. Thus, it might be more appropriate in such a situation to adjust the value of inventories based on its subsequent NRV.

(b)   Price reductions caused by increased competition

The reasons for price reductions and increased competition do not generally arise overnight, but normally occur over a period. For example, a competitor may have built up a competitive advantage by investing in machinery that is more efficient. In these circumstances, it is appropriate for an entity to adjust the valuation of its inventories, as its own investment in production machinery is inferior to its competitor's, and this situation existed at the end of the reporting period.

(c)   Price reductions caused by the introduction of an improved competitive product

It is unlikely that a competitor developed and introduced an improved product overnight. Therefore, it is correct to adjust the valuation of inventories to their NRV after that introduction, because the entity's failure to maintain its competitive position in relation to product improvements existed at the end of the reporting period.

Competitive pressures that caused a decrease in NRV after the reporting period are generally additional evidence of conditions that developed over a period and existed at the end of the reporting period. Consequently, their effects normally require adjustment in the financial statements.

However, for certain types of inventory, there is clear evidence of a price at the end of the reporting period, and it is inappropriate to adjust the price of that inventory to reflect a subsequent decline. An example is inventories for which there is a price on an appropriate commodities market. In addition, inventory may be physically damaged or destroyed after the reporting period (say, by fire, flood, or other disaster). In these cases, the entity does not adjust the financial statements.

3.2 Percentage of completion estimates

Events after the reporting period frequently give evidence about the profitability of construction contracts (or other contracts for which revenue is recognised using percentage of completion) that are in progress at the end of the reporting period.

IAS 11 – *Construction Contracts* – requires an assessment to be made of the *outcome* of a contract, as of the end of the reporting period, to recognise revenue under the percentage of completion method (see Chapter 25 at 3). *[IAS 11.22]*. In such assessment, consideration should be given to events that occur after the reporting period, and a determination made as to whether they are adjusting or non-adjusting events for which the financial statement effect is included in the percentage of completion calculation.

3.3 Insolvency of a debtor

The insolvency of a debtor or inability to pay debts usually builds up over a period. Consequently, if a debtor has an amount outstanding at the end of the reporting period, and this amount is written off because of information received after the reporting period, the event is normally adjusting. IAS 10 states that 'the bankruptcy of a customer that occurs after the reporting period usually confirms that a loss existed at the end of the reporting period'. *[IAS 10.9(b)(i)]*. If, however, there is evidence to show that the insolvency of the debtor resulted solely from an event occurring after the reporting period, then the event is a non-adjusting event.

3.4 Valuation of investment property at fair value and tenant insolvency

The fair value of investment property reflects, among other things, the quality of tenants' covenants and the future rental income from the property. If a tenant ceases to be able to meet its lease obligations due to insolvency after the reporting period, an entity considers how this event is reflected in the valuation at the end of the reporting period.

IAS 40 – *Investment Property* – requires that the fair value of investment property shall reflect market conditions at the end of the reporting period. *[IAS 40.38]*. In addition, professional valuations generally reference the state of the market at the date of valuation without the use of hindsight. Consequently, the insolvency of a tenant is not *normally* an adjusting event to the fair value of the investment property (it is, however, an adjusting event for any amounts due from the tenant at the end of the reporting period), because the investment property still holds value in the market. This conclusion is consistent with the treatment of investment property measured using the alternative cost model. IAS 10 states that a decline in market value of investments after the reporting period and before the date the financial statements are authorised for issue is a non-adjusting event, as the decline does not *normally* relate to a condition at the end of the reporting period (see 2.1.3 above).

3.5   Valuation of investments and fraud

The fair value of an investment may be based on its trading price in an active market. If no active market exists, the fair value may be derived from a model, such as in a cash flow forecast, and is based on the conditions that existed at the end of the reporting period.

In practice, such forecasts are prepared after the reporting period when some of the actual results of the subsequent period are available. However, it is often difficult to determine whether a difference between an actual and forecast cash flow after the reporting period resulted from conditions that existed at the end of the reporting period or relate to an event after the reporting period.

The valuation for investments carried at fair value that are traded in an active market is easier, because that market price records the conditions at the end of the reporting period. The standard states that a decline in market value of investments after the reporting period *does not normally* relate to conditions that existed at the end of the reporting period (see 2.1.3 above).

However, when fraud is discovered after the reporting period, the determination of whether a condition existed at the end of the reporting period becomes even more difficult. In some cases, an investment has a significantly lower value than previously believed. Is this an adjusting or non-adjusting event?

Consideration should be given to all facts and circumstances related to the investment. Generally, if a fraud is discovered after the reporting period but before the financial statements are authorised for issue, and the security is found never to have existed, this is an adjusting event because the discovery of fraud provides new information about the conditions that existed as of the end of the reporting period.

However, if fraud is discovered after the reporting period but before the financial statements are authorised for issue, and the fair value of the security (subsequent to the reporting period) is much lower than the original (fraudulent) amount, this is generally a non-adjusting event. This is because a decline in the value of an investment, whether based on a market price, or a valuation model, after the reporting period is a change in estimate that resulted from new information or developments. *[IAS 8.5]*. For traded securities, the fact that the entity could have sold the security at the end of the reporting period and received the original (fraudulent) amount is further support that the decline in fair value after the reporting period does not provide evidence about a condition that existed as of the end of the reporting period.

Determining whether the discovery of fraud is an adjusting event is a complex task, and requires careful consideration of the facts and circumstances.

Chapter 37   Related party disclosures

List of examples

Chapter 37

Chapter 37   Related party disclosures

1   INTRODUCTION

Related party relationships and transactions between related parties are a normal feature of business. Many entities carry on their business activities through subsidiaries, joint ventures, and associates and there are inevitably transactions between these parties. It is also common for entities under common control, which are not a group for financial reporting purposes, to transact with each other. These are matters addressed by IAS 24 – *Related Party Disclosures.*

A revised version of IAS 24 was issued in November 2009. It is mandatory for accounting periods beginning on or after 1 January 2011. The adoption of this revised standard is discussed at 2.1.1 below. The previous version of IAS 24 was issued in December 2003 and applied to accounting periods beginning before 1 January 2011.

1.1   The related party issue

The problems posed by related party relationships and transactions are described in IAS 24 as follows:

> 'A related party relationship could have an effect on the profit or loss and financial position of an entity. Related parties may enter into transactions that unrelated parties would not. For example, an entity that sells goods to its parent at cost might not sell on those terms to another customer. Also, transactions between related parties may not be made at the same amounts as between unrelated parties.
>
> 'The profit or loss and financial position of an entity may be affected by a related party relationship even if related party transactions do not occur. The mere existence of the relationship may be sufficient to affect the transactions of the entity with other parties. For example, a subsidiary may terminate relations with a trading partner on acquisition by the parent of a fellow subsidiary engaged in the same activity as the former trading partner. Alternatively, one party may refrain from acting because of the significant influence of another – for example, a subsidiary may be instructed by its parent not to engage in research and development.' *[IAS 24.6-7].*

Chapter 37

Chapter 37

1.2 Possible solutions

1.2.1 Remeasurement of related party transactions at fair values

One solution to the problems posed by related party relationships and transactions is to adjust the financial statements to value related party transactions as if they occurred with an independent third party and recognise any such transactions at an arm's length price. However, the consensus for over thirty years is that it often is impossible to establish what would have been the terms of any non-arm's length transaction had it been bargained on an arm's length basis. This is because no comparable transactions may have taken place and, in any event, the transaction might never have taken place at all if it had been bargained using different values.

1.2.2 Disclosure of transactions

Because of this problem, accounting standards internationally require disclosure of related party transactions and relationships, rather than adjustment of the financial statements. This approach is adopted by the IASB in IAS 24. The purpose of the disclosures is to give users of the financial statements information about transactions, outstanding balances, including commitments, and relationships with related parties that may affect their assessment of an entity's operations, including assessments of the risks and opportunities facing an entity. [IAS 24.8].

The main issues in determining the disclosures are as follows:

* identification of related parties;
* types of related party transactions and arrangements; and
* the type, extent, and measurement of the information disclosed.

1.3 Reasons for revising IAS 24

IAS 24 was revised in order to correct two perceived problems with the old standard:

(a) a practical problem regarding the lack of a disclosure exemption for government-controlled entities with other such entities; and

(b) a technical problem that some definitions of a related party were difficult to understand or apparently flawed (e.g. because Entity A could be defined as a related party of Entity B without Entity B necessarily being a related party of Entity A).

The main changes introduced by the revised version are summarised at 2.1.4 below.

2 REQUIREMENTS OF IAS 24

2.1 Effective date and transition, objective, scope and main changes introduced by the revised IAS 24

2.1.1 Effective date and transition

The revised version of IAS 24 applies for accounting periods beginning on or after 1 January 2011. Early application was permitted, either of the whole standard or of the partial exemption given in respect of the disclosures for government-related entities (see 2.6.3 below). Disclosure of any early application was required whether that early application was of the whole standard or in respect of the partial exemption. *[IAS 24.28]*.

The revised standard must be applied retrospectively when first adopted. *[IAS 24.28]*. This means that comparatives must be given for all disclosures required by the revised version of IAS 24 even if disclosure was not previously required by the older version (for example, because the definition of a related party has changed). On adoption of the revised standard, an entity should also consider the requirements to present a minimum of three statements of financial position and related notes whenever an entity applies an accounting policy retrospectively or makes a retrospective restatement of items in its financial statements. *[IAS 1.39]*. This may require the disclosure of balances with related parties as at the date of the beginning of the earliest comparative period presented. In determining whether to make the additional disclosures, entities will need to consider the provisions of IAS 1 – *Presentation of Financial Statements* – relating to materiality.

2.1.2 Objective

IAS 24 states that its objective 'is to ensure that an entity's financial statements contain the disclosures necessary to draw attention to the possibility that its financial position and profit or loss may have been affected by the existence of related parties and by transactions and outstanding balances, including commitments, with such parties'. *[IAS 24.1]*.

Accordingly, IAS 24 requires disclosure of related party transactions and outstanding balances, including commitments, together with the names of any parties who control the reporting entity.

2.1.3 Scope

IAS 24 applies in: *[IAS 24.2]*

(a) identifying related party relationships and transactions;

(b) identifying outstanding balances, including commitments, between an entity and its related parties;

(c) identifying the circumstances in which disclosure of the items in (a) and (b) is required; and

(d) determining the disclosures to be made about those items.

The standard explicitly requires disclosure of related party relationships. transactions and outstanding balances, including commitments, in the consolidated and separate financial statements of a parent, venturer, or investor presented in accordance with IAS 27 – *Consolidated and Separate Financial Statements* – (when IFRS 10 – *Consolidated Financial Statements* – is adopted, the words 'venturer or investor' are replaced by 'or investors with joint control of, or significant influence over an investee'). The standard also applies to individual financial statements. *[IAS 24.3, IFRS 10.D19]*.

All entities within a group that prepare their financial statements under IFRS must disclose related party transactions and outstanding balances with other entities in the group in their financial statements. *[IAS 24.4]*. There are no disclosure exemptions for subsidiaries or for parent companies that produce separate financial statements even where those separate financial statements are issued with the consolidated financial statements.

The IASB consider that the financial statements of an entity that is part of a consolidated group may include the effects of extensive intragroup transactions and concluded that the disclosures required by IAS 24 are essential to understanding the financial position and financial performance of such an entity and therefore should be required for separate financial statements presented in accordance with IAS 27. The IASB also believe that disclosure of such transactions is essential because the external users need to be aware of the interrelationships between related parties, including the level of support provided by related parties, to assist in their economic decisions. *[IAS 24.BC16-17].*

The standard notes that 'intragroup related party transactions and outstanding balances are eliminated in the preparation of consolidated financial statements of the group'. *[IAS 24.4].* This implies that disclosure of such transactions and balances is not required in the group's consolidated financial statements since, so far as those financial statements are concerned, such items do not exist.

2.1.4   Main changes introduced by the revised IAS 24

2.1.4.A   Disclosure exemption for government-controlled entities

IAS 24 now provides an exemption from the disclosure requirements relating to related party transactions and outstanding balances, including commitments, for reporting entities that are controlled, jointly controlled or significantly influenced by a government and with another entity that is a related party because that same government has control, joint control or significant influence over both the reporting entity and that other entity. *[IAS 24.25].*

This exemption is conditional on certain disclosures being made including the name of the government and an indication of the nature and amount of individually and collectively significant transactions with that government or any other government-related entity. *[IAS 24.26].*

2.1.4.B   Changes to the definition of a related party

The definition of a related party has been changed in the revised standard in the following ways:

- where an investor has significant influence over an associate, any subsidiary of the investor is also a related party to the associate; *[IAS 24.BC21]*
- in the individual financial statements of a subsidiary, an associate of the subsidiary's controlling investor is also a related party; *[IAS 24.BC22]*
- the related parties definition now excludes associates that were previously related because a person significantly influences one entity and a close member of that person's family significantly influences another entity; *[IAS 24.BC25]*
- where investees controlled or jointly controlled by key management personnel of a reporting entity are related to that entity, the reciprocal of this is also treated as a related party (i.e. from the standpoint of the investee, the entity is a related party); *[IAS 24.BC26]*

- when a person has joint control over the reporting entity and a close member of that person's family has joint control or significant influence over another entity, the reciprocal of this is also treated as a related party (i.e. from the standpoint of the other entity, the reporting entity is a related party); *[IAS 24.BC27-29]* and

- there is no longer a reference to 'significant voting power' in the definition of a related party. The IASB considered that the phrase was undefined, used inconsistently and created unnecessary complexity. *[IAS 24.BC31]*.

The reporting entities most likely to be affected by these changes are those that have transactions and outstanding balances, including commitments, with associates of their parent or transactions and outstanding balances, including commitments, with subsidiaries of those that exercise significant influence over them.

2.1.4.C *Disclosures of commitments*

The previous version of IAS 24 did not have an explicit requirement to disclose commitments to related parties. The revised standard adds explicit disclosure requirements for commitments (including executory contracts) with related parties.

The Board concluded that commitments were one type of related party transaction but to avoid doubt decided to make explicit reference to them. *[IAS 24.BC49]*.

2.2   Identification of a related party and related party transactions

A related party is defined as 'a person or entity that is related to the entity that is preparing its financial statements (the "reporting entity")'. *[IAS 24.9]*.

The standard contains a, multi-part definition of 'related party,' which is discussed in the following sections. The standard emphasises attention to the substance of the relationship and not merely the legal form. *[IAS 24.10]*.

This definition is also included in the IASB's glossary which implies that preparers should use this definition of 'related party' when applying concepts elsewhere in IFRS where this term or similar terms are used and not otherwise defined.

A related party transaction is a transfer of resources, services or obligations between a reporting entity and a related party, regardless of whether a price is charged. *[IAS 24.9]*.

The following are considered to be related parties of the reporting entity:

- certain persons or close family members (see 2.2.1 below);
- entities that are members of the same group (see 2.2.2 below);
- entities that are associates or joint ventures (see 2.2.3 below);
- entities that are joint ventures of the same third party (see 2.2.4 below);
- entities that are joint ventures and associates of the same third entity (see 2.2.5 below);
- post-employment benefit plans (see 2.2.6 below);
- entities under common control or joint control of certain persons or close family members (see 2.2.7 below);

Chapter 37

- entities under significant influence of certain persons or close family members (see 2.2.8 below); and
- government-related entities (see 2.2.9 below).

2.2.1   *Persons or close family members that are related parties*

A person or close family member of that person's family is related to a reporting entity if that person: *[IAS 24.9]*

(i)   has control or joint control over the reporting entity;

(ii)   has significant influence over the reporting entity; or

(iii)   is a member of the key management personnel of the reporting entity or of a parent of the reporting entity.

Close members of a family of a person are defined as 'those family members who may be expected to influence, or be influenced by, that person in their dealings with the entity' and include: *[IAS 24.9]*

(a)   that person's children and spouse or domestic partner;

(b)   children of that person's spouse or domestic partner; and

(c)   dependants of that person or that person's spouse or domestic partner.

As well as the specific family members mentioned above, the definition also applies to any other family members who may be expected to influence or be influenced by that person in their dealings with the reporting entity. For example, this may include parents, siblings or relatives that are even more distant.

Relationships involving a person or close family members as investors are illustrated in the following examples, which are based on illustrative examples published by the IASB which accompany, but are not part of IAS 24.

Example 37.1:   Person as investor

Mrs X has an investment in Entity A and Entity B.

For Entity A's financial statements, if Mrs X controls or jointly controls Entity A, Entity B is related to Entity A when Mrs X has control, joint control or significant influence over Entity B.

For Entity B's financial statements, if Mrs X controls or jointly controls Entity A, Entity A is related to Entity B when Mrs X has control, joint control or significant influence over Entity B.

If Mrs X has significant influence over both Entity A and Entity B, Entities A and B are not related to each other.

If Mrs X is a member of the key management personnel of both Entity A and Entity B, Entities A and B are not, in the absence of any other indicator of a related party relationship, related to each other.

Example 37.2:   *Close members of the family holding investments*

Mr X is the spouse of Mrs X. Mr X has an investment in Entity A and Mrs X has an investment in Entity B.

For Entity A's financial statements, if Mr X controls or jointly controls Entity A, Entity B is related to Entity A when Mrs X has control, joint control or significant influence over Entity B.

For Entity B's financial statements, if Mr X controls or jointly controls Entity A, Entity A is related to Entity B when Mrs X has control, joint control or significant influence over Entity B.

If Mr X has significant influence (but not control or joint control) over Entity A and Mrs X has significant influence (but not control or joint control) over Entity B, Entities A and B are not related to each other.

If Mr X is a member of the key management personnel of Entity A and Mrs X is a member of the key management personnel of Entity B, Entities A and B are not related to each other.

2.2.1.A   Control

'Control' is the power to govern the financial and operating policies of an entity so as to obtain benefits from its activities. *[IAS 24.9]*. This is the same definition as used in IAS 27 and implies that the same criteria used in IAS 27 should be applied to determine control under IAS 24. When IFRS 10 is adopted, the definition of 'control' in IAS 24 is amended to be simply a cross-reference to the definition in IFRS 10. IFRS 10 states that 'an investor controls an investee when the investor is exposed, or has rights, to variable returns from its involvement with the investee and has the ability to affect those returns through its power over the investee'. *[IFRS 10 Appendix A]*. IFRS 10 applies for annual periods beginning on or after 1 January 2013 but can be adopted in earlier periods.

2.2.1.B   Joint control

'Joint control' is the contractually agreed sharing of control over an economic activity. *[IAS 24.9]*. This is similar but not identical to the definition of joint control used in IAS 31 – *Interests in Joint Ventures* – which additionally requires that joint control 'exists only when the strategic financial and operating decisions relating to the entity require the unanimous consent of the parties sharing control (the venturers)'. *[IAS 31.3]*. IAS 24 does not explain why its description of 'joint control' is slightly different to that in IAS 31. Under IAS 24, joint control would appear to exist regardless of whether the strategic and financial operating decisions of an entity require the unanimous consent of the venturers. This inconsistency in the definition of 'joint control' is eliminated when IFRS 11 – *Joint Arrangements* – is adopted. When IFRS 11 is adopted, the definition of 'joint control' in IAS 24 is then amended to be simply a cross-reference to the definition in IFRS 11. IFRS 11 defines joint

Chapter 37

control as 'the contractually sharing of control of an arrangement, which exists only when decisions about the relevant activities require the unanimous consent of the parties sharing control'. *[IFRS 11 Appendix A]*. IFRS 11 applies for annual periods beginning on or after 1 January 2013 but can be adopted in earlier periods.

2.2.1.C   Significant influence

'Significant influence' is the power to participate in the financial and operating policy decisions of an entity, but is not control over those policies. Significant influence may be gained by share ownership, statute or agreement. *[IAS 24.9]*. In contrast, IAS 28 – *Investments in Associates* – defines significant influence as 'the power to participate in the financial and operating policy decisions of the investee but is not control or joint control over those policies'. *[IAS 28.2]*. IAS 24 does not explain why its description of 'significant influence' is slightly different to that in IAS 28 and in what circumstances significant influence may be exercised in IAS 24 and not IAS 28. In practice, we would expect consistency between the two standards. This inconsistency between the two standards in the definition of 'significant influence' is eliminated when IAS 28, as revised in 2011, is adopted. When IAS 28, as revised in 2011, is adopted the definition of 'significant influence' in IAS 24 is amended to be simply a cross-reference to the definition in IAS 28. IAS 28, as revised in 2011, defines significant influence as 'the power to participate in the financial and operating policy decisions of the investee but is not control or joint control of those policies'. *[IAS 28 (2011).3]*. IAS 28, as revised in 2011, applies for annual periods beginning on or after 1 January 2013 but can be adopted in earlier periods.

2.2.1.D   Key management personnel

'Key management personnel' are those persons with authority and responsibility for planning, directing and controlling the activities of an entity, directly or indirectly, including any director (whether executive or otherwise) of that entity. *[IAS 24.9]*.

A related party includes all key management personnel of a reporting entity and of a parent of the reporting entity. This means that all key management personnel of all parents (i.e. the immediate parent, any intermediate parent and the ultimate parent) of a reporting entity are related parties. The wording in the previous version of IAS 24 was more ambiguous.

The definition of key management personnel is not restricted to directors. It also includes other individuals with authority and responsibility for planning, directing and controlling the activities of an entity. The main intention of the definition is presumably to ensure that transactions with persons with responsibilities similar to those of directors, and the compensation paid to such persons, do not escape disclosure simply because they are not directors. Otherwise, there would be an obvious loophole in the standard.

However, it is not clear whether many individuals who are not directors fall within this heading. The type of person most likely to be a member of 'key management' (apart from directors of the entity) is probably a divisional chief executive or a director of a subsidiary of the entity, but not of the entity itself, who nevertheless participates in the management of the reporting entity. One might argue that, if the individual is truly part of the 'key management' of the group, he or she would be on the parent entity's board. However, this view is inconsistent with the view of the IASB that 'key management' may be found outside the boardroom.

'Key management personnel' are normally employees of the reporting entity (or of another entity in the same group). However, the definition does not restrict itself to employees. Therefore, seconded staff and persons engaged under management or outsourcing contracts may also have a level of authority or responsibility such that they are 'key management personnel.'

The definition of key management personnel refers to 'persons'. In some jurisdictions, the term 'person' includes both a 'corporate person' and a 'natural person'. Additionally, in some jurisdictions, the responsible entity of funds or trusts (i.e. the body acting as key management personnel) must be a corporate entity and, by law, has the authority and responsibility for planning, directing and controlling the activities of the fund for the benefit of the fund's investors in accordance with the fund's constitution and relevant statutes. We therefore believe that, although the definition of 'key management personnel' appears to restrict its application to natural persons, the definition could also include a corporate entity. A further issue is whether staff acting for the corporate 'director' could be considered to be key management personnel of the reporting entity. This determination is important for complying with the disclosure requirements for key management personnel (see 2.5.1 below).

The issue of whether key management personnel can include an entity as opposed to individuals was discussed by the IFRS Interpretations Committee (the 'Interpretations Committee') in September 2010. The tentative view of the Interpretations Committee was that an entity could not be a member of key management personnel (KMP) but any management entity which provides KMP services to a reporting entity should be a related party of that reporting entity in respect of those KMP services and therefore any service fee should be disclosed. Any individuals who are employees or directors of the management entity and are acting as KMP of the reporting entity should not be identified as a related party unless they qualify as related parties for other reasons. The Interpretations Committee recommended that the IASB amend IAS 24 to this effect as part of its Annual Improvements project.[1] However, at its October 2010 meeting, the IASB expressed concerns about unintended consequences of these proposed amendments and asked the staff to perform further work to ensure consistency of the proposal with the objective of IAS 24 and to bring some examples back to the IASB.[2] There has been no further discussion of this issue by the IASB since October 2010 and it is not included in the *Improvements to IFRSs* Exposure Draft *(ED/2011/2)* published in June 2011.

2.2.2 *Entities that are members of the same group*

'An entity is related to a reporting entity if:

(i) The entity and the reporting entity are members of the same group (which means that each parent, subsidiary and fellow subsidiary is related to the others).' *[IAS 24.9(b)].*

IAS 27 defines a group as 'a parent and all its subsidiaries'. *[IAS 27.4]*. IFRS 10 defines a group as 'a parent and its subsidiaries'. *[IFRS 10 Appendix A]*.

IAS 27 defines a subsidiary as 'an entity, including an unincorporated entity such as a partnership, that is controlled by another entity (known as the parent)'. *[IAS 27.4]*. IFRS 10 defines a subsidiary as 'an entity that is controlled by another entity'. *[IFRS 10 Appendix A]*.

Therefore, all entities that are controlled by the same ultimate parent are related parties. This would include entities less than 50% owned that are considered to be subsidiaries under the control definitions of IAS 27 or IFRS 10. There are no exceptions to this rule.

Example 37.3:   Entities that are members of the same group

Entities H, S and A are all related parties to each other as they are members of the same group. Both Entity S and Entity A are subsidiaries of Entity H. Related party disclosures will be required in the financial statements of both Entity S and Entity A and in the separate financial statements of Entity H.

2.2.3   *Entities that are associates or joint ventures*

'An entity is related to a reporting entity if:

...

> (ii)   One entity is an associate or joint venture of the other entity (or an associate or joint venture of a member of a group of which the other entity is a member)'. *[IAS 24.9(b)]*.

Any entity that a reporting entity determines is an associate under IAS 28 or a joint venture under IAS 31 is a related party. This requirement applies also to investments held by a venture capital organisation, mutual fund, unit trust or similar entity, even where the investment is accounted for at fair value through profit or loss or held for trading under IAS 39 – *Financial Instruments: Recognition and Measurement* – rather than under the equity method or using the proportionate consolidation method. Likewise, any reporting entity which is an associate or joint venture of another entity must treat that investor as a related party.

In the definition of a related party, an associate includes subsidiaries of the associate. Therefore, for example, an associate's subsidiary and the investor that has significant influence over the associate are related to one another. *[IAS 24.12]*.

The definition means that an associate of a reporting entity's parent is also a related party of the reporting entity. This is a change from the wording of the previous version of IAS 24 where these entities were not related.

However, the definition does not cause investors in a joint venture or an associate to be related to each other (see 2.3 below). Investors in joint operations are also not related to each other.

The application of these requirements is illustrated in the example below, which is based on an illustrative example accompanying IAS 24:

Example 37.4:   Associates of the reporting entity's group that are related parties

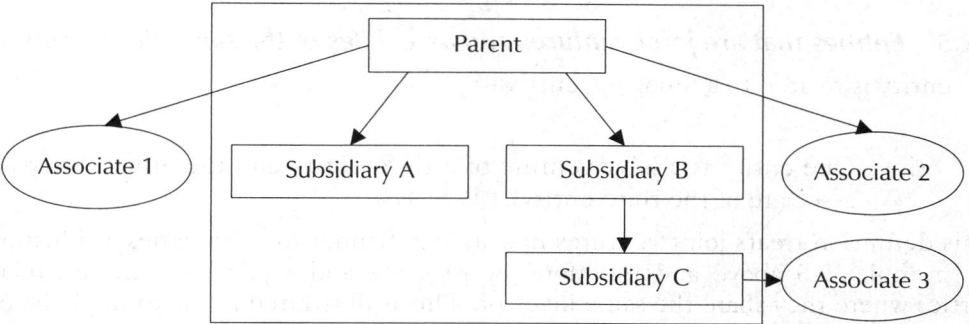

In Parent's separate financial statements, Associates 1, 2 and 3 are related parties. For Parent's consolidated financial statements, Associates 1, 2 and 3 are related to the group.

For Subsidiary A's financial statements, Associates 1, 2 and 3 are related parties. For Subsidiary B's separate financial statements, Associates 1, 2 and 3 are related parties. For Subsidiary C's financial statements, Associates 1, 2 and 3 are related parties.

For the financial statements of Associates 1, 2 and 3, Parent and Subsidiaries A, B and C are related parties. Associates 1, 2 and 3 are not related to each other.

2.2.4   Entities that are joint ventures of the same third party

'An entity is related to a reporting entity if:

...

      (iii)   Both entities are joint ventures of the same third party'. *[IAS 24.9(b)]*.

This is illustrated by the following example:

Example 37.5:   Entities that are joint ventures of the same third party

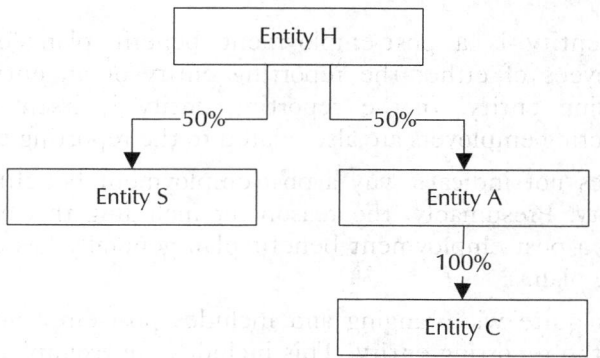

In this example, Entities S and A are joint ventures of Entity H and are therefore related parties. Entity C, as a subsidiary of Entity A, is also a related party of Entity H and Entity S.

If, however, Entities S and A were only associates (rather than joint ventures) of the same third party then they would not be related parties. In making this distinction between joint ventures and associates the IASB considered that 'significant influence' was not as close a relationship as control or joint control. *[IAS 24.BC19(a)]*.

In the definition of a related party, a joint venture includes subsidiaries of the joint venture. Therefore, for example, a joint venture's subsidiary and the investor that has significant influence over the joint venture are related to each other. *[IAS 24.12]*.

2.2.5   *Entities that are joint ventures and associates of the same third entity*

'An entity is related to a reporting entity if:

...

(iv)   One entity is a joint venture of a third entity and the other entity is an associate of the third entity'. *[IAS 24.9(b)]*.

This definition treats joint ventures in a similar manner to subsidiaries as illustrated in Example 37.3 above and therefore an associate and a joint venture are related parties where they share the same investor. This is illustrated in the example below:

Example 37.6:   Entities that are joint ventures and associates of the same third entity

Entity S is a joint venture of Entity H and Entity A is an associate of Entity H. Therefore, Entities S and A are related parties.

However, Entities Z and H are not related parties (see 2.3 below).

2.2.6   *Post-employment benefit plans*

'An entity is related to a reporting entity if:

...

(v)   The entity is a post-employment benefit plan for the benefit of employees of either the reporting entity or an entity related to the reporting entity. If the reporting entity is itself such a plan, the sponsoring employers are also related to the reporting entity'. *[IAS 24.9(b)]*.

The standard does not indicate why a post-employment benefit plan is a related party of the entity. Presumably, the reason for including this category is that an entity sponsoring a post-employment benefit plan generally has at least significant influence over the plan.

The definition is quite wide-ranging and includes post-employment plans of any entity related to the reporting entity. This includes, for example, post-employment benefit plans of an associate or joint venture of the reporting entity or a post-employment benefit plan of an associate of the reporting entity's parent.

IAS 24 also amended the definition of a related party such that the sponsoring employers are related parties of a post-employment benefit plan. Under the previous a sponsoring employer was not a related party of the plan itself.

2.2.7 Entities under common control or joint control

'An entity is related to a reporting entity if:

...

(vi) The entity is controlled or jointly controlled by a person identified in (a) above (i.e. a person or a close member of that person's family who has control or joint control over the reporting entity)'. *[IAS 24.9].*

This is intended to cover situations whereby different entities are controlled or jointly controlled by the same person(s). This situation is illustrated by Examples 37.1 and 37.2 above. The situation whereby one company owns another is covered by Example 37.3 above.

2.2.8 Entities under significant influence

'An entity is related to a reporting entity if:

...

(vii) A person identified in (a) (i) (i.e. a person who controls or who has joint control over the reporting entity) has significant influence over the entity or is a member of the key management personnel of the entity (or of a parent of the entity)'. *[IAS 24.9(b)].*

The persons referred to above are those who control or jointly control the reporting entity and have significant influence over (see 2.2.1.C), or are members of the key management personnel (see 2.2.1.D) of another entity. Entities that simply share the same key management personnel in the absence of any control or joint control by those persons are not related parties (see 2.3 below).

This is illustrated below:

Example 37.7:   *Persons who control an entity and are a member of the key management personnel of another entity*

Mrs X has a 100% investment in Entity A and is a member of the key management personnel of Entity S. Entity M has a 100% investment in Entity S.

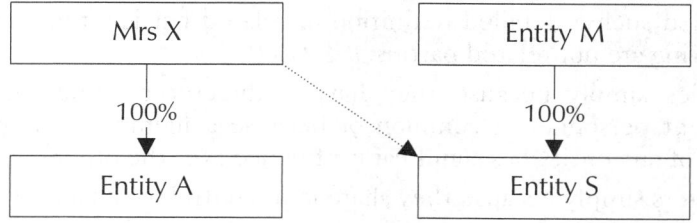

For Entity S's financial statements, Entity A is related to Entity S because Mrs X controls Entity A and is a member of the key management personnel of Entity S.

For Entity S's financial statements, Entity A is also related to Entity S if Mrs X is a member of the key management personnel of Entity M and not of Entity S.

This outcome would be the same if Mrs X has joint control over Entity A (if Mrs X only had significant influence over Entity A and not control or joint control then Entities A and S would not be related parties).

For Entity A's financial statements, Entity S is related to Entity A because Mrs X controls A and is a member of Entity S's key management personnel. This outcome would be the same if Mrs X has joint control over Entity A and will also be the same if Mrs X is a member of the key management personnel of Entity M and not Entity S.

For Entity M's consolidated financial statements, Entity A is a related party of the Group if Mrs X is a member of the key management personnel of the Group. If Mrs X is only a member of the key management personnel of Entity S and not the Group then Entity A is not a related party of the Entity M Group.

2.2.9   *Government-related entities*

A 'government-related entity' is an entity that is controlled, jointly controlled or significantly influenced by a government. *[IAS 24.9]*.

'Government' in this context refers to government, government agencies and similar bodies whether local, national or international. *[IAS 24.9]*. This is the same definition used in IAS 20 – *Accounting for Government Grants and Disclosure of Government Assistance*. The Board decided that it would not provide a more comprehensive definition or additional guidance on how to determine what is meant by 'government'. In the Board's view, a more detailed definition could not capture every conceivable government structure across every jurisdiction. In addition, judgement is required by a reporting entity when applying the definition because every jurisdiction has its own way of organising government-related activities. *[IAS 24.BC41]*. This implies that there may well be diversity in practice across different jurisdictions in defining what is meant by 'government'.

Where an entity is controlled, jointly controlled or significantly influenced by a government then relationships, transactions and outstanding balances, including commitments, with that government are covered by IAS 24. Similarly, transactions and outstanding balances, including commitments, with other entities controlled, jointly controlled or significantly influenced by that government are covered by IAS 24.

Related party transactions with government-related entities are subject to certain disclosure exemptions. These are discussed at 2.6 below.

2.3   Parties that are not related parties

Having included such a detailed definition of related parties, the standard clarifies that the following are not related parties: *[IAS 24.11]*

- two entities simply because they have a director or other member of key management personnel in common or because a member of key management personnel of one entity has significant influence over the other entity;

- two venturers simply because they share joint control over a joint venture;

- providers of finance, trade unions, public utilities and departments and agencies of a government that does not control, jointly control or significantly influence the reporting entity, simply by virtue of their normal dealings with the entity (even though they may affect the freedom of action of an entity or participate in its decision-making process); and

- a customer, supplier, franchisor, distributor or general agent with whom an entity transacts a significant volume of business, simply by virtue of the resulting economic dependence.

The reason for these exclusions is that, without them, many entities that are not normally regarded as related parties could fall within the definition of related party. For example, a small clothing manufacturer selling 90% of its output to a high street chain could be under the effective economic control of that customer.

These exclusions are effective only where these parties are 'related' to the reporting entity simply because of the relationship noted above. If there are other reasons why a party is a related party, the exclusions do not apply. Consider the following examples:

- A water company that supplies the reporting entity is not a related party if the only link between the two is the supply of water. If, however, the water company is also an associate of the reporting entity, the exclusion does not apply; the two are related parties, and the transactions relating to the supply of water are disclosed if material.

- Two shareholders are not related parties simply because one holds a controlling interest and the other shareholder (not in the group) holds a non-controlling interest. Even if the investor holding the non-controlling interest in the subsidiary exercises significant influence over the subsidiary but is otherwise not related to the parent, only the subsidiary and the parent are related parties in the consolidated and separate financial statements of the parent. However, if the two shareholders are close members of the same family and the shareholder with the non-controlling interest has significant influence over or significant voting power in that that subsidiary, the exclusion does not apply. In this situation, the two shareholders are related parties, and the transactions and outstanding balances, including commitments, between them should be disclosed if material.

- Two entities are not related parties simply because they share common key management personnel. However, if the common member of key management personnel exerts control over one or more of the entities then they are related parties.

- An administrator, custodian, broker and fund manager of the same fund are not related parties, to each other or to the fund to which they provide services simply because they each provide services to the fund, even if any of the parties are economically dependent upon the income from such services. However, any such party could meet the definition of 'key management personnel' of the fund if it provides key management personnel services. In addition, any shared ownership (e.g. control, joint control, or significant influence) between such parties should be evaluated to determine if the parties are related. As discussed at 2.2.1.D above, the IASB is considering a recommendation of the Interpretations Committee to amend IAS 24 so that an entity cannot meet the definition of key management personnel but that any management entity which provides key management personnel services to a reporting entity should be a related party in respect of such services and therefore any service fee should be disclosed. The IASB has asked the staff to perform further work to ensure consistency of the proposal with the objective of IAS 24 and to bring some examples to the IASB before further discussing the staff proposal.

In addition, an unconsolidated structured entity as defined by IFRS 12 – *Disclosure of Interests in Other Entities* – is not a related party to a reporting entity unless it would otherwise meet the definition of a related party (e.g. because the structured entity is an associate of the reporting entity).

2.4   Disclosure of controlling relationships

IAS 24 asserts that, in order to enable users of financial statements to form a view about the effects of related party relationships on an entity, it is appropriate to disclose the related party relationship when control exists, irrespective of whether there have been transactions between the related parties. *[IAS 24.14]*.

Accordingly, the standard requires an entity to disclose the name of its parent and, if different, the ultimate controlling party. The use of the word 'party' means that the disclosure applies to both individuals and to entities. Disclosure must be made even if the parent or ultimate controlling party does not prepare financial statements. If neither the entity's parent nor the ultimate controlling party produces consolidated financial statements available for public use, the name of the next most senior parent that does so must also be disclosed. *[IAS 24.13]*. The 'next most senior parent' is the first parent in the group above the immediate parent that produces consolidated financial statements available for public use. *[IAS 24.16]*. Consequently, in some circumstances, an entity may need to disclose the names of three parents.

In the situation when the ultimate controlling party is an individual, rather than an entity, the reporting entity is likely to have to disclose the name of the next most senior parent in addition since the individual undoubtedly does not produce financial statements for public use. IAS 1 also requires disclosure of the 'ultimate parent' of the group, which is not necessarily synonymous with the 'ultimate controlling party,' where that party is an individual. *[IAS 1.126(c)]*.

Where the controlling party is a trust, it will be necessary to determine whether the trust itself is controlled by a person or persons who will need to be disclosed as the ultimate controlling party.

The ultimate controlling party could be a group of individuals or entities acting together. IAS 24 is silent on the issue of individuals or entities acting together to exercise joint control. However, IFRS 3 – *Business Combinations* – states that a group of individuals can be regarded as a controlling party when, as a result of contractual arrangements, they collectively have the power to govern that entity's financial and operating policies so as to obtain benefits from its activities. *[IFRS 3.B2]*. In such circumstances, these entities or individuals should be identified as the controlling party. Where there is no such contractual arrangement, IFRS is silent on whether a group of individuals acting in an informal way could be considered to be the ultimate controlling party of an entity. However, as discussed at 2.2 above, IAS 24 emphasises attention to the substance of any related party relationship and not merely the legal form. It is likely that such an informal arrangement would at least give such individuals collectively significant influence over the reporting entity and such individuals would therefore be related parties under IAS 24.

The standard also requires that an entity disclose relationships between a parent and its subsidiaries, irrespective of whether there are transactions between them. *[IAS 24.13]*. This requirement suggests that a parent entity must disclose its relationships with its subsidiaries in addition to the explicit requirement to disclose the name of the parent and, if different, the ultimate controlling party. However, the standard does not indicate what information is required. All that is stated is that the requirement to disclose related party relationships between a parent and its subsidiaries is 'in addition to the disclosure requirements in IAS 27, IAS 28 and IAS 31'. *[IAS 24.15]*. The references to IAS 28 and IAS 31 are puzzling since associates and joint ventures are not subsidiaries and IAS 24 contains no explicit requirement to disclose the name of entities exercising significant influence over an entity. IAS 27 requires a listing of significant investments in subsidiaries, jointly controlled entities and associates for a parent which elects not to prepare consolidated accounts *[IAS 27.42(b)]* but not for the consolidated financial statements themselves. IAS 31 requires a listing of significant joint ventures. *[IAS 31.56]*. IAS 28 contains no requirement to disclose a list of significant associates. However, when IFRS 12 is adopted, IAS 24 is amended to state that the requirement to disclosure related party relationships between a parent and its subsidiaries is in addition to the disclosure requirements of IAS 27 and IFRS 12. *[IFRS 12.D2]*. This removes the ambiguous references to associates and joint ventures. IFRS 12 requires an entity to disclose information to enable users to understand the composition of a group *[IFRS 12.10(a)(i)]*. IFRS 12 applies for annual periods beginning on or after 1 January 2013 but can be adopted in earlier periods. However, it remains unclear exactly what 'related party relationships between a parent and its subsidiaries' are required to be disclosed by paragraph 15 of IAS 24 other than the name of the parent and, if different, the name of the ultimate controlling party since the disclosure of the nature of related party relationships and information about transactions and outstanding balances is a separate requirement of paragraph 18 (see 2.6.2 below). IAS 24 does not require a reporting entity to disclose the name of a related party exercising significant influence unless it invokes the exemption in respect of disclosures with government-related entities (see 2.6.3 below).

RBS Group identified and disclosed an ultimate controlling party in its financial statements for the year ended 31 December 2010 as follows:

Extract 37.1: The Royal Bank of Scotland Group plc (2010)
NOTES TO THE CONSOLIDATED FINANCIAL STATEMENTS [extract]
43.   RELATED PARTIES [extract]

UK Government

On 1 December 2008, the UK Government through HM Treasury became the ultimate controlling party of The Royal Bank of Scotland Group plc. The UK government's shareholding is managed by UK Financial Investments Limited, a company wholly owned by the UK Government. As a result, the UK Government and UK Government controlled bodies became related parties of the Group.

2.5   Disclosable transactions

A related party transaction is defined as 'a transfer of resources, services or obligations between related parties, regardless of whether a price is charged.' *[IAS 24.9]*. Read literally, this definition requires many transactions to be disclosed more than once. For example, if an entity buys goods on credit from a related party and pays for them 30 days later, both the original purchase and the final payment represent a 'transfer of resources ... between related parties' and, therefore on a literal reading, are required to be separately disclosed. However, we doubt that this reading is the IASB's intention, and the nature of the disclosures required by IAS 24 seems to support this view. This definition also appears to exclude those commitments which do not transfer resources.

The definition of a related party transaction implies that transactions are disclosable only for the period in which parties are related. For example, where a reporting entity has disposed of a subsidiary during the reporting period, only transactions with the subsidiary up to the date of disposal are related party transactions in the financial statements of the reporting entity. Similarly, if a person became a member of key management personnel of a reporting entity during a reporting period, no disclosure is required of any remuneration paid to that person before that person's appointment as key management personnel.

2.5.1   *Key management personnel compensation*

IAS 24 requires disclosure of key management personnel compensation.

'Compensation' includes all employee benefits (as defined in IAS 19 – *Employee Benefits*) including employee benefits to which IFRS 2 – *Share-based Payment* – applies. Employee benefits are all forms of consideration given by an entity, or on behalf of the entity, in exchange for services rendered to the entity. *[IAS 19.7]*. Employee benefits also include such consideration paid on behalf of a parent of the entity in respect of the entity. *[IAS 24.9]*. Therefore, the compensation disclosed by an entity in its financial statements is that which is for services to that entity, irrespective of whether it is paid by the reporting entity or by another entity or individual on behalf of the entity.

Under IAS 24, compensation includes: *[IAS 24.9]*

(a)   short-term employee benefits, such as wages, salaries and social security contributions, paid annual leave and paid sick leave, profit-sharing and bonuses (if payable within twelve months of the end of the reporting period) and non-monetary benefits (such as medical care, housing, cars and free or subsidised goods or services) for current employees;

(b)   post-employment benefits such as pensions, other retirement benefits, post-employment life insurance and post-employment medical care;

(c)   other long-term employee benefits, including long-service leave or sabbatical leave, jubilee or other long-service benefits, long-term disability benefits and, if they are not payable wholly within twelve months after the end of the reporting period, profit-sharing, bonuses and deferred compensation;

(d)   termination benefits; and

(e)   share-based payment.

These requirements raise some issues of interpretation which are discussed further at 2.6.1 below.

For an illustrative example of a disclosure of key management personnel compensation see Extract 37.2 at 2.6.1 below.

2.5.2 Other transactions, including commitments

IAS 24 gives the following as examples of transactions to be disclosed, if they are with a related party, which are not intended to be exhaustive: *[IAS 24.21]*

- purchases or sales of goods (finished or unfinished);
- purchases or sales of property and other assets;
- rendering or receiving of services;
- leases;
- transfers of research and development;
- transfers under licence agreements;
- transfers under finance arrangements (including loans and equity contributions in cash or in kind);
- provisions of guarantees or collateral;
- commitments to do something if a particular event occurs or does not occur in the future, including executory contracts (recognised and unrecognised); and
- settlement of liabilities on behalf of the entity or by the entity on behalf of that related party.

The standard does not contain any exemptions based on the nature of the transaction. Consequently, related party transactions include transactions such as dividend payments and the issue of shares under rights issues to major shareholders or key management personnel (i.e. those that fall within the definition of related parties), even where they participate on the same basis as other shareholders. However, for dividend payments, a preparer might conclude that no additional disclosures are necessary beyond those required by IAS 1 to explain the potential effect of the relationship on the financial statements. *[IAS 1.137].*

The standard also includes transactions with those individuals identified as related parties where their dealings with the entity are in a private capacity, rather than in a business capacity.

As indicated at 2.5 above, disclosure is required irrespective of whether or not consideration is received, which means that the standard applies to gifts of assets or services and to asset swaps. Common examples of such transactions include:

- administration by an entity of another entity within a group (or of its post-employment benefit plan) free of charge;
- transfer of tax assets from one member of a group to another without payment;
- rent-free accommodation or the loan of assets at no charge; or
- guarantees by directors of bank loans to the entity.

Chapter 37

2.5.2.A   Commitments

The disclosure of commitments in respect of related party transactions is a new requirement introduced by the revised version of IAS 24. The IASB considered that commitments were a type of transaction and, to avoid doubt about this, made an explicit reference to them. *[IAS 24.BC49(a)]*.

'Commitments' is not defined in IFRS and therefore preparers will have to exercise judgement in determining the transactions covered by the disclosure requirement. However, IFRS 12 states that the commitments relating to joint ventures requiring disclosure under IAS 24 are those that may give rise to a future outflow of cash or other resources. *[IFRS 12.B18]*.

The IASB's definition of a commitment specifically includes executory contracts which are excluded from the scope of IAS 37 – *Provisions, Contingent Liabilities and Contingent Assets* – unless they are onerous to the reporting entity. *[IAS 37.3]*. An executory contract is a contract under which neither party has performed any of its obligations or both parties have partially performed their obligations to an equal extent. *[IAS 37.3]*. An example would be a contract to buy an asset at a future date where neither the asset has changed hands nor any consideration been paid. In the first year of application of the revised version of IAS 24, entities will be required to disclose comparative commitments (if not previously disclosed) at the end of the previous reporting period(s).

The words 'commitments to do something if a particular event occurs or does not occur in the future' can potentially have a wide application. One obvious type of arrangement to which this applies would be some form of commitment by a subsidiary to its parent to undertake certain trading or research and development activities.

With respect to the type of transaction that the IASB is expecting to be disclosed, IFRS 12 provides a list of illustrative but not exhaustive examples of the type of unrecognised commitments that could relate to joint ventures. Some of these could equally apply to other related party arrangements. IFRS 12 clarifies that the commitments required to be disclosed under IAS 24 in respect of joint ventures include an entity's share of commitments made jointly with other investors with joint control of a joint venture. *[IFRS 12.B18]*.

IFRS 12 gives the following commitments relating to joint ventures:

- unrecognised commitments to contribute funding or resources as a result of, for example:
    - the constitution or acquisition agreements of a joint venture (that, for example, require an entity to contribute funds over a specific period);
    - capital intensive projects undertaken by a joint venture;
    - unconditional purchase obligations, comprising procurement of equipment, inventory or services that an entity is committed to purchasing from, or on behalf of, a joint venture;
    - unrecognised commitments to provide loans or other financial support to a joint venture;

- unrecognised commitments to contribute resources to a joint venture, such as assets or services; and

- other non-cancellable unrecognised commitments relating to a joint venture.

- unrecognised commitments to acquire another party's ownership interest (or a portion of that ownership interest) in a joint venture if a particular event occurs or does not occur in the future. *[IFRS 12.B19]*.

Provisions of guarantees, which are a form of commitment, require separate disclosure. Disclosure of commitments to purchase property, plant and equipment and intangible assets in aggregate are separately required by IAS 16 – *Property, Plant and Equipment* – and IAS 38 – *Intangible Assets* – respectively. *[IAS 16.74(c), IAS 38.122(e)]*.

2.5.3 Materiality

In determining whether an entity discloses related party transactions in financial statements, the general concept of materiality is applied. IAS 24 does not refer specifically to materiality since this requirement is in IAS 1, which states that 'an entity need not provide a specific disclosure required by an IFRS if the information is not material.' *[IAS 1.31]*. Omissions or misstatements of items material within IAS 1 'if they could, individually or collectively, influence the economic decisions of users taken on the basis of the financial statements. Materiality depends on the size and nature of the omission or misstatement judged in the surrounding circumstances. The size or nature of the item, or a combination of both, could be the determining factor.' *[IAS 1.7]*.

This may have the effect that any related party transaction whose disclosure is considered sensitive (for tax reasons perhaps) is by definition material, because it is expected by the reporting entity to influence a user of the financial statements. Therefore, it may not be possible to avoid disclosing such items on the grounds that they are financially immaterial. In addition, a transaction conducted at advantageous terms to either the related party or the reporting entity is more likely to be material than one conducted at arm's length. Since IAS 24 requires disclosure of related party transactions irrespective of whether or consideration is received, then, even if the materiality judgement is based on the amount of the transaction, disclosure cannot be avoided on the argument that, since there is no consideration, the transaction must be immaterial.

2.5.4 Aggregation of items of a similar nature

Presumably in order to minimise the volume of disclosures, IAS 24 permits aggregation of items of a similar nature, except when separate disclosure is necessary for an understanding of the effects of the related party transactions on the financial statements of the entity. *[IAS 24.24]*. The standard does not expand on this requirement, but it seems appropriate that, for example, purchases or sales of goods with other subsidiaries within a group can be aggregated, but any purchases or sales of property, plant, and equipment or of intangible assets with such entities are shown as a separate category. However, the level of aggregation is limited by the separate disclosure of transactions with particular categories of related parties (see 2.6.2 below).

Chapter 37

2.6   Disclosures required for related party transactions

There is no requirement in IAS 24 to disclose information about related party transactions in one comprehensive note. However, it may be more useful to users of the financial statements to present information this way.

IAS 1 requires that, except where a standard permits otherwise (which IAS 24 does not), comparative information in respect of the previous period must be disclosed for all amounts reported in the current period's financial statements. *[IAS 1.38].*

2.6.1   *Disclosures required for key management personnel compensation*

As discussed at 2.5.1 above, IAS 24 requires disclosure of key management personnel compensation. Where this disclosure is included in a remuneration report presented outside the financial statements (as permitted in certain jurisdictions), the financial statements must give a clear and unambiguous cross-reference to the remuneration report, indicating which portions of such report are included by the cross-reference in the financial statements.

There is no requirement in IAS 24 to disclose individual key management personnel remuneration. Instead, the standard requires an entity to disclose key management personnel compensation in total and for each of the following categories: *[IAS 24.17]*

- short-term employee benefits;
- post-employment benefits;
- other long-term benefits;
- termination benefits; and
- share-based payment.

It is unclear from the standard the basis on which the amount for each of the categories above is determined. There are alternative views that the disclosure is the amount:

- paid or payable by the entity (or on its behalf);
- recognised as expense under the relevant standard by the entity (or on its behalf);
- attributed to the benefit for tax purposes;
- due under contract by the entity (or due on its behalf); or
- determined on some other basis.

In the Basis for Conclusions accompanying the standard, the IASB noted that the guidance on compensation in IAS 19 is sufficient to enable an entity to disclose the relevant information, *[IAS 24.BC10],* which suggests that the IASB is expecting the amounts to be based on the expense recognised under the relevant standards. It is helpful to remember that the definition of compensation states that 'employee benefits are all forms of consideration paid, payable or provided by the entity, or on behalf of the entity in exchange for services rendered...' *[IAS 24.9].*

Issues relating to each of the categories are discussed below.

2.6.1.A   Short-term employee benefits

As indicated at 2.5.1 above, these include wages, salaries and social security contributions, paid annual leave and paid sick leave, profit-sharing and bonuses (if payable within twelve months of the end of the reporting period). Most of these should not cause difficulty, since the expense for such items under IAS 19 is generally equivalent to the amount payable for the period. However, there are instances when adjustments are necessary. For example, if the total expense under IAS 19 for a profit-sharing plan includes a deduction for anticipated staff turnover, this deduction may need to be adjusted in determining the amount disclosed for key management personnel. That is, the turnover rate for staff as a whole is likely different from the turnover rate for key management personnel, and the deduction should be adjusted accordingly for disclosure purposes.

Non-monetary benefits (such as medical care, housing, cars and free or subsidised goods or services) must also be included within the amount disclosed for short-term employee benefits. *[IAS 24.9]*. In some cases these might have been provided at no direct cost to the entity. In such circumstances it would appear reasonable to either attribute a value for non-monetary benefits, so as to describe them quantitatively, or to describe such benefits qualitatively.

2.6.1.B   Post-employment benefits

As indicated at 2.5.1 above, these include pensions, other retirement benefits, post-employment life insurance and post-employment medical care. The inclusion of this category suggests that amounts are disclosed while members of key management are providing services. If amounts were only disclosed when the benefits are payable, then in many cases there would be no disclosure since the individuals would no longer be members of key management. For defined contribution plans, it seems appropriate that the amount included is based on the total expense recognised under IAS 19, which is the equivalent of the contributions payable to the plan for service rendered in the period.

The main issue related to defined benefit plans is to determine an appropriate calculation for the disclosable cost for the period. Normally, for defined benefit plans, the expense recognised under IAS 19 differs from the contributions payable to the plan. Disclosing the contributions payable is generally not appropriate, particularly where the entity is benefiting from a contribution holiday, since the amount payable does not reflect the benefits provided by the entity in exchange for the services rendered. One approach is to include an amount based on the expense recognised. However, this approach requires an apportionment of the total expense, for example, based on the proportion of the pensionable salaries of key management to that of all employees within the plan. The total expense recognised under IAS 19 for defined benefit plans includes items such as interest, recognised actuarial gains and losses and the effects of curtailments and settlements. One view is that these are included to the extent that they relate to the individuals concerned. An alternative view is that, since these items relate more to the overall plan, they are not included, and the amount included is the current service cost and, where applicable, past service cost related to those individuals. An entity might obtain an actuarial valuation of such amounts, or by apportion these elements appropriately.

2.6.1.C   Other long-term benefits

As indicated at 2.5.1 above, these include long-service leave or sabbatical leave, jubilee or other long-service benefits, long-term disability benefits and, if they are not payable wholly within twelve months after the end of the reporting period, profit-sharing, bonuses and deferred compensation. Since the accounting for such items under IAS 19 is on a similar basis to that for post-employment benefits similar issues to those discussed at 2.6.1.B above are applicable.

2.6.1.D   Termination benefits

These should not cause difficulty, since an entity generally recognises such items, particularly for key management personnel, under IAS 19 (only when the entity is obliged to make the termination payment to the individual concerned).

2.6.1.E   Share-based payment transactions

This category includes share options, share awards or cash-settled awards granted in return for service by the members of key management. Such compensation is accounted for under IFRS 2. For equity-settled share based payment transactions, such as share options or share awards, IFRS 2 broadly requires measurement of their fair value at grant date, and that expense is recognised over the period that employees render services. For cash-settled share-based payment transactions, IFRS 2 requires measurement and recognition based on the cash ultimately paid.

One approach is to disclose an amount based on the expense under IFRS 2. An alternative approach is to disclose amounts based on the fair value that the individual received (based on the value of the shares at date of vesting, or at date of exercise of share options or the cash that is ultimately payable) at those later dates, rather than over the period of the service. An entity should adopt a consistent accounting policy for determining the amounts disclosed. An entity should also disclose other share transactions with key management personnel.

2.6.1.F   Reporting entity part of a group

One additional practical difficulty for an entity in a group is that the disclosure of its key management personnel compensation is for the services rendered to the reporting entity. Accordingly, where key management personnel of the reporting entity also provide services to other entities within the group, an apportionment of the compensation is necessary. Likewise, where the reporting entity receives services from key management personnel that are also key management personnel of other entities within the group, the reporting entity may have to impute the compensation received. Such apportionments and allocations required judgment and an assessment of the time commitment involved.

In respect of the accounting for share-based payment transactions by individual members of a group, IFRS 2 does not clarify which amount is disclosed by a subsidiary for related party transactions Various alternatives would appear

Related party disclosures

appropriate (e.g. the IFRS 2 charge in the group, the IFRS 2 charge in the subsidiary or the vesting/exercise date value), so long as the method is applied consistently.

2.6.1.G   Key management personnel compensated by other entities

A reporting entity also applies the principles set out in 2.6.1.F above to situations in which the other entity is a third party, outside of the group, but is a related party.

An example of the disclosure of key management personnel compensation can be found in the financial statements of BP plc.

Extract 37.2: BP plc (2010)

Notes on Financial Statements [extract]
43   Remuneration of directors and senior management [extract]
Remuneration of directors and senior management

	2010	2009	$'million 2008
Total for all senior management			
Short-term employee benefits	25	36	34
Post-retirement benefits	3	3	4
Share-based payments	29	20	20

Senior management, in addition to executive and non-executive directors, includes other senior managers who are members of the executive management team.

Short-term employee benefits

In addition to fees paid to the non-executive chairman and non-executive directors, these amounts comprise, for executive directors and senior managers, salary and benefits earned during the year, plus cash bonuses awarded for the year. Deferred annual bonus awards, to be settled in shares, are included in share-based payments. Short-term employee benefits includes compensation for loss of office of $3 million (2009 $6 million and 2008 $3 million).

Post-retirement benefits

The amounts represent the estimated cost to the group of providing defined benefit pensions and other post-retirement benefits to senior management in respect of the current year of service measured in accordance with IAS 19 'Employee benefits'.

Share-based payments

This is the cost to the group of senior management's participation in share-based payment plans, as measured by the fair value of options and shares granted in accordance with IFRS 2 'Share-based payments'. The main plans in which senior management have participated are the EDIP, DAB and RSP. For details of these plans refer to Note 41.

2.6.2   Other disclosures required for related party transactions, including commitments

IAS 24 requires an entity that has had related party transactions during the periods covered by its financial statements to disclose the nature of the related party relationship as well as information about those transactions and outstanding balances, including commitments, necessary for users to understand the potential effect of the relationship on the financial statements. These disclosure requirements are in addition to the requirements for key management personnel compensation discussed above at 2.6.1. *[IAS 24.18]*.

The standard states that, at a minimum, the disclosures must include: *[IAS 24.18]*

(a)   the amount of the transactions;

(b)   the amount of outstanding balances, including commitments, and:

    (i)   their terms and conditions, including whether they are secured, and the nature of the consideration to be provided in settlement; and

    (ii)   details of any guarantees given or received;

(c)   provisions for doubtful debts related to the amount of outstanding balances; and

(d)   the expense recognised during the period for bad or doubtful debts due from related parties.

The standard gives no exemption from disclosure on the grounds of sensitivity or confidentiality. However, since there is no requirement to disclose the name of a related party, this lack of exemption is likely to be less of a concern.

The implication from (b) above is that outstanding balances and commitments should be amalgamated as one balance. However, commitments such as executory contracts do not give rise to outstanding balances. In practice, narrative disclosure of the terms and conditions of material commitments will be necessary.

There is no requirement to disclose individually significant transactions. However, as discussed at 2.6.3 below, there is such a requirement for transactions with government-related entities where a reporting entity has decided to apply the disclosure exemption. One IASB member dissented with the decision not to require all entities to provide information about each individually significant transaction for all related parties. *[IAS 24.DO1]*.

These disclosures are made separately for each of the following categories: *[IAS 24.19]*

(a)   the parent;

(b)   entities with joint control or significant influence over the entity;

(c)   subsidiaries;

(d)   associates;

(e)   joint ventures in which the entity is a venturer;

(f)   key management personnel of the entity or its parent; and

(g)   other related parties.

In our view the reference in (a) and (f) above to 'the parent' should be read as including all parents of the entity, i.e. its immediate parent, any intermediate parent, and the ultimate parent. In the context of the financial statements of an entity within a group, it is insufficient to disclose related party transactions for a single category of 'group companies'. Separate categories are required for parent(s), subsidiaries and 'other related parties'.

Fellow subsidiaries do not have a separate category and would be included within the category 'other related parties'. A preparer might wish to consider separate disclosure of transactions with fellow subsidiaries if it was considered that this provided useful information to users of the financial statements.

The classification of amounts payable to, and receivable from, related parties in the different categories is an extension of the disclosure requirement in IAS 1 for an entity to present information either in the statement of financial position or in the notes. *[IAS 1.78(b)]*. The categories are extended to provide a more comprehensive analysis of related party balances and apply to related party transactions. *[IAS 24.20]*.

IAS 24 discourages an entity from disclosing that transactions are on normal commercial terms or on an arm's length basis, by stating that such disclosures 'are made only if such terms can be substantiated.' *[IAS 24.23]*. This wording implies a rebuttable presumption that related party transactions are not on an arm's length basis unless the reporting entity can demonstrate otherwise. To substantiate that related party transactions are on an arm's length basis an entity would need to be satisfied that a transaction with similar terms and conditions could be obtained from an independent third party.

The company financial statements of J Sainsbury plc provides the following disclosures of related party relationships with subsidiaries and joint ventures.

Extract 37.3: J Sainsbury plc (2011)

Notes to the financial statements [extract]
32   Related party transactions [extract]
Company [extract]
b) Subsidiaries

The company enters into loans with its subsidiaries at both fixed and floating rates of interest on a commercial basis. Hence, the company incurs interest expense and earns interest income on these loans and advances. The Company also received dividend income from its subsidiaries during the financial year..

Transactions with subsidiaries

	2011 £'m	2010 £'m
Loans and advances given to, and dividend income received from subsidiaries		
Loans and advances given	702	310
Loans and advances repaid by subsidiaries	(125)	(103)
Interest income received in respect of interest bearing loans and advances	135	126
Dividend income received	250	268
Loans and advances received from subsidiaries		
Loans and advances received	(321)	(350)
Loans and advances repaid	64	377
Interest expense paid in respect of interest bearing loans and advances	(64)	(69)

Year-end balances arising from transactions with subsidiaries

	2011 £'m	2010 £'m
Receivables		
Loans and advances due from subsidiaries	2,191	1,625
Payables		
Loans and advances due to subsidiaries	(5,282)	(5,267)

(c) Joint ventures

Transactions with joint ventures

For the 52 weeks to 19 March 2011, the Company entered into transactions with joint ventures as set out below.

	2011 £'m	2010 £'m
Services and loans provided to joint ventures		
Interest income received in respect of interest bearing loans	1	1
Dividend income received	1	2

Year-end balances arising from transactions with joint ventures

	2011 £'m	2010 £'m
Receivables		
Loans due from joint ventures		
Floating rate subordinated undated loan capital 1	25	25
Floating rate subordinated dated loan capital 2	30	30
Payables		
Loans due to joint ventures	(5)	(5)

1 The undated subordinated loan capital shall be repaid on such date as the Financial Services Authority shall agree in writing for such repayment and in any event not less than five years and one day from the dates of draw down. In the event of a winding up of Sainsbury's Bank plc, the loan is subordinated to ordinary unsecured liabilities. Interest is payable three months in arrears at LIBOR plus a margin of 1.0 per cent per annum for the duration of the loan.
2 No repayment of dated subordinated debt prior to its stated maturity may be made without the consent of the Financial Services Authority. In the event of a winding up of Sainsbury's Bank plc, the loan is subordinated to ordinary unsecured liabilities. Interest is payable three months in arrears at LIBOR plus a margin of 0.6 per cent per annum for the duration of the loan.

The financial statements of British Sky Broadcasting Group plc illustrates disclosure of transactions with a party controlled by a close family member of key management.

Extract 37.4: British Sky Broadcasting Group plc (2010)
Notes to the consolidated financial statements
Note 30   Transactions with related parties and major shareholders [extract]
c) Other transactions with related parties [extract]

A close family member of one Director of the Company who served during the year has a controlling interest in Shine Limited ('Shine'), in which the Group has a 13% equity shareholding. During fiscal 2009, Shine conducted an equity raising as part of the funding for the acquisition of Metronone Film & television AB. The Group participated in the equity raising, acquiring a further 21,700 shares of the issued share capital of Shine for cash consideration of £19 million. During the year, the Group incurred programming and production costs for television of £6 million (2009: £10 million) from Shine. At 30 June 2010, there were no outstanding balances (2009: nil) due to Shine..

2.6.3 *Disclosures with government-related entities*

The revised version of IAS 24 introduces an exemption from the disclose requirements of paragraph 18, discussed at 2.6.2 above, in relation to related party transactions and outstanding balances, including commitments, with: *[IAS 24.25]*

(a) a government that has control, joint control or significant influence over the reporting entity; and

(b) another entity that is a related party because the same government has control, joint control or significant influence over both the reporting entity and the other entity.

This wording implies that a reporting entity is related to an entity that is significantly influenced by a government that also has significant influence over the reporting entity. However, the definition of a related party does not include entities that are 'related' purely because the same entity has significant influence over both (see 2.2.3 above).

The application of the disclosure exemption is illustrated in the example below, which is based on an illustrative example accompanying IAS 24.

Example 37.8:   Application of the disclosure exemption for government-related entities

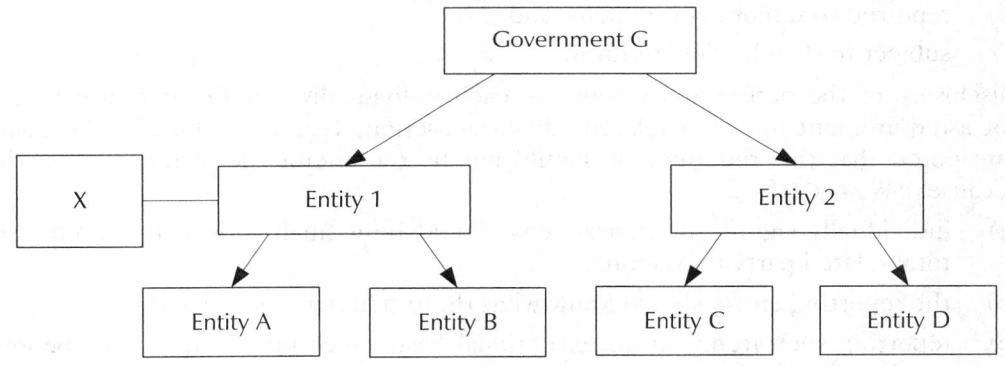

Government G directly or indirectly controls Entities 1 and 2 and Entities A, B, C and D. Person X is a member of the key management personnel of Entity 1.

For Entity A's financial statements the exemption applies to: (a) transactions with Government G which is the government that ultimately controls Entity A; and (b) transactions with Entities 1, 2, B, C and D which are related entities because they are controlled by the same government as A, i.e.: Government G.

The exemption does not apply to transactions with Person X because Person X is not controlled by Government G.

The use of the disclosure exemption is conditional on the reporting entity making the following disclosures about the transactions and related outstanding balances with the government-related entities: *[IAS 24.26]*

(a) the name of the government and the nature of its relationship with the reporting entity (i.e. control, joint control or significant influence);

(b) the following information in sufficient detail to enable users of the entity's financial statements to understand the effect of related party transactions on its financial statements:

   (i) the nature and amount of each individually significant transaction; and

   (ii) for other transactions that are collectively, but not individually, significant, a qualitative or quantitative indication of their extent.

The wording above does not mention 'commitments' when referring to transactions. However, given that IAS 24 describes a commitment as a form of transaction (see 2.5.2 above), we infer that disclosure of individually and collectively significant commitments with government-related entities is required.

In using its judgement to determine the level of detail to be disclosed in accordance with the requirements in (b) above, a reporting entity considers the closeness of the related party relationship and other factors relevant in establishing the level of significance of the transaction such as whether it is: *[IAS 24.27]*

(a)   significant in terms of size;

(b)   carried out on non-market terms;

(c)   outside normal day-to-day business operations, such as the purchase and sale of businesses;

(d)   disclosed to regulatory or supervisory authorities;

(e)   reported to senior management; and

(f)   subject to shareholder approval.

Disclosure of the nature and amount of each individually significant transaction is not a requirement for other related party transactions (see 2.6.2 above). The Board considered that this requirement should not be too onerous for a reporting entity because: *[IAS 24.BC45]*

(a)   individually significant transactions should be a small subset, by number, of total related party transactions;

(b)   the reporting entity should know what these transactions are; and

(c)   reporting such items on an exceptional basis takes into account cost-benefit considerations.

The Board also considered that more disclosure of individually significant transactions would better meet the objective of IAS 24 because this approach focuses on transactions that, through their nature or size, are of more interest to users and are more likely to be affected by the related party relationship. *[IAS 24.BC46]*. In response to concerns about whether a reporting entity would be able to identify whether the counterparty to such transactions was a government-related entity, the Board concluded that 'management will know, or will apply more effort in establishing, who the counterparty to an individually significant transaction is and will have, or be able to obtain, background information on the counterparty'. *[IAS 24.BC47-48]*.

One Board member disagreed with the decision to give a disclosure exemption for government-related parties in IAS 24. That same member also disagreed with the decision not to require all entities to provide information about individually significant transactions with a related party. *[IAS 24.DO1]*.

Lloyds Banking Group plc provides the following disclosure about a material transaction with a government that is a related party:

Extract 37.5: Lloyds Banking Group (2010)

Notes to the consolidated financial statements
Note 53   **Related party transactions** [extract]
HM Treasury [extract]
Credit Guarantee Scheme [extract]

HM Treasury launched the Credit Guarantee Scheme in October 2008 as part of a range of measures announced by the UK government intended to ease the turbulence in the UK banking system. It charges a commercial fee for the guarantee of new short and medium-term debt issuance. The fee payable to HM Treasury on guaranteed issues is based on a per annum rate of 50 basis points plus the median five-year credit default swap rate. At 31 December 2010, the Group had £45,308 million (2009: £49,954 million) of debt issued under the Credit Guarantee Scheme. During 2010, the Group redeemed £4,987 million of bonds. The Group's income statement includes fees of £454 million (2009: £498 million) payable to HM Treasury in respect of guaranteed funding.

The following are other illustrations of the type of disclosures required for transactions with government-related entities based on examples in the standard:

Example 37.9:   *Individually significant transaction carried out on non-market terms*

On 15 January 2010 the company sold a 10 hectare piece of land to an entity controlled by Government G for €5,000,000. On 31 December 2010 a plot of land in a similar location, of similar size and with similar characteristics, was sold for €3,000,000. There had not been any appreciation or depreciation of the land in the intervening period. See Note X for disclosure of government assistance as required by IAS 20.

Example 37.10:   *Individually significant transaction because of size of transaction*

In the year ended 31 December 2010 Government G provided the company with a loan equivalent to 50% of its funding requirement, repayable in quarterly instalments over the next five years. Interest is charged on the loan at a rate of 5% which is comparable to that charged on the company's external bank loans.

Example 37.11:   *Collectively significant transactions*

The company's significant transactions with Government G and other entities controlled, jointly controlled or significantly influenced by Government G are a large portion of its sales of goods and purchases of raw materials [alternately – about 50% of its sales of goods and services and about 35% of its purchases of raw materials].

The company also benefits from guarantees by Government G of the company's bank borrowing. See Note X of the financial statements for disclosure of government assistance as required by IAS 20.

In Example 37.11 above, either a qualitative or a quantitative disclosure is permitted for transactions that are collectively but not individually significant.

3   FUTURE DEVELOPMENTS

As discussed at 2.2.1.D above, the Interpretations Committee requested the IASB to amend the standard as part of its Annual Improvements project so that an entity cannot meet the definition of key management personnel but that any management entity which provides key management personnel services to a reporting entity should be a related party in respect of such services and disclose any service fee. The revised definition would apply to the management entity's parent, subsidiaries and fellow subsidiaries. However, the IASB has expressed concerns about unintended consequences of these proposed amendments and asked the staff to perform further work to ensure consistency of the proposal with the objective of IAS 24 and to bring some examples to the IASB. There have been no further developments on this issue since the October 2010 IASB meeting.

References

1 *IFRIC Update*, IASB, September 2010, p.5.
2 *IASB Update*, IASB, October 2010, p.2.

Chapter 38   Statement of cash flows

Chapter 38

List of examples

Chapter 38

Chapter 38   Statement of cash flows

1   INTRODUCTION

A statement of cash flows provides useful information about an entity's activities in generating cash through operations to repay debt, distribute dividends, or reinvest to maintain or expand operating capacity; about its financing activities, both debt and equity; and about its investing or spending of cash. This information, when combined with information in the rest of the financial statements, is useful in assessing factors that may affect the entity's liquidity, financial flexibility, profitability, and risk.

IAS 7 – *Statement of Cash Flows* – requires disclosures about the historical changes in cash and cash equivalents and the standard's relative flexibility in approach allows it to be applied by all entities, including financial institutions. This flexibility can be seen, for example, in the way entities can determine their own policy for the classification of interest and dividend cash flows, provided they are separately disclosed and this is applied consistently from period to period. It can also accommodate the need of entities to provide additional information specific to their circumstances and indeed encourages additional disclosures.

1.1   Definitions used in IAS 7

The following terms are used in IAS 7 with the meanings specified: *[IAS 7.6]*.

Cash comprises cash on hand and demand deposits.

Cash equivalents are short-term, highly liquid investments that are readily convertible to known amounts of cash and which are subject to an insignificant risk of changes in value.

Cash flows are inflows and outflows of cash and cash equivalents.

Operating activities are the principal revenue-producing activities of the entity and other activities that are not investing or financing activities.

Investing activities are the acquisition and disposal of long-term assets and other investments not included in cash equivalents.

Financing activities are activities that result in changes in the size and composition of the contributed equity and borrowings of the entity.

2   OBJECTIVE AND SCOPE OF IAS 7

2.1   Objective

The objective of IAS 7 is to require entities to provide information about historical changes in cash and cash equivalents in a statement which classifies cash flows during the period from operating, investing and financing activities. In this way the standard aims to give users of financial statements a basis on which to evaluate the entity's ability to generate cash and cash equivalents and its needs to utilise those cash flows. *[IAS 7 Objective]*. The historical cash flow information is often used as an indicator of the amount, timing and certainty of future cash flows and is useful in examining the relationship between profitability and net cash flow and the impact of changing prices. *[IAS 7.5]*.

2.2   Scope

IAS 7 applies to all entities, regardless of size, ownership structure or industry, and therefore includes wholly owned subsidiaries and banks, insurance entities and other financial institutions. There are no exemptions from the standard. Users of an entity's financial statements are interested in how the entity generates and uses cash and cash equivalents regardless of the nature of the entity's activities and irrespective of whether cash can be viewed as the product of the entity, as may be the case with a financial institution. However different their principal revenue-producing activities, all entities need cash to conduct their operations, to pay their obligations, and to provide returns to their investors. Accordingly, all entities are required to present a statement of cash flows. *[IAS 7.3]*. In particular, a parent entity preparing its separate financial statements in accordance with IFRS is required to publish a statement of cash flows, even if the separate financial statements are presented together with consolidated financial statements which include a statement of cash flows.

3   CASH AND CASH EQUIVALENTS

Since the objective of a statement of cash flows is to provide an analysis of changes in cash and cash equivalents, the definitions of cash and cash equivalents at 1.1 above are essential to its presentation. It is also important to understand the reporting entity's cash management policies, especially when considering whether balances should be classified as cash equivalents, as the standard states that cash equivalents are held for the purpose of meeting short-term cash commitments rather than for investment or other purposes. *[IAS 7.7]*. Cash management includes the investment of cash in excess of immediate needs into cash equivalents, *[IAS 7.9]*, such as short-term investments. Provided these investments are highly liquid, are readily convertible into known amounts of cash and are subject to insignificant risk of changes in value, they are in substance equivalent to cash. *[IAS 7.6]*. As such, a statement of cash flows under IAS 7 excludes movements between cash on hand and highly liquid investments classified as cash equivalents because these are components of an entity's cash management, rather than part of its operating, investing and financing activities. *[IAS 7.9]*. However, as will be seen below, the definition of cash equivalents can cause some difficulty in practice.

3.1 Policy for determining components of cash equivalents

Because an entity's cash management policies are an important factor, not all investments that appear to satisfy the definition at 1.1 above are required to be classified as cash equivalents. However, regardless of an entity's policies and practices, an investment can only be classified within cash equivalents if all of the criteria in the definition are satisfied (see 3.2 below).

In view of the variety of cash management practices and banking arrangements around the world, entities are required to disclose the policy adopted in determining the composition of cash and cash equivalents. *[IAS 7.46]*. Changes in that policy, such as a reclassification of financial instruments previously considered as being part of an entity's investment portfolio, should be reported under IAS 8 – *Accounting Policies, Changes in Accounting Estimates and Errors. [IAS 7.47]*. This would require comparatives to be restated and additional disclosures given, including the reasons for the change in policy.

The inclusion or exclusion of a certain type of investment in cash equivalents gives rise to a change in policy, if an entity reclassified investments already held at the beginning of the current period or if it makes a different classification of new investments held for the same purposes as those in the prior period. On the contrary, a new investment in the current period (even in a type of investment previously classified otherwise) which is included in or excluded from cash equivalents according to the reason for holding that investment under the entity's cash management practices, is not considered a change in policy.

VTech Holdings disclosed its policy to include short-term investments and bank overdrafts as components of cash equivalents.

Extract 38.1: VTech Holdings Limited (2008)

Principal Accounting Policies [extract]
P   Cash And Cash Equivalents

For the purpose of the cash flow statement, cash and cash equivalents comprise cash on hand, demand deposits with banks and other financial institutions, short-term highly liquid investments that are readily convertible into known amounts of cash and which are subject to an insignificant risk of changes in value and which have a maturity of three months or less at acquisition. Bank overdrafts that are repayable on demand and form an integral part of the Group's cash management are also included as a component of cash and cash equivalents.

For the purpose of the balance sheet, cash and cash equivalents are cash on hand, deposits with banks and other financial institutions, which are not restricted in its use. Bank overdrafts are included in borrowings in current liabilities.

Lufthansa reconciled the requirement to report cash and cash equivalents (as defined in IAS 7) with the wish to include all the assets used by the entity to manage its liquidity, by adding lines of analysis to the foot of the statement of cash flows.

Chapter 38

Extract 38.2: Deutsche Lufthansa AG (2010)

Consolidated Cash Flow Statement [extract]

The cash flow statement shows how cash and cash equivalents have changed over the reporting period at the Lufthansa Group. In accordance with IAS 7 the cash flows are divided into cash flow from operating activities, from investing activities and from financing activities. The cash and cash equivalents shown in the cash flow statement correspond to the balance sheet item cash and cash equivalents. The amount of liquidity in the broader sense is reached by adding short-term securities.

3.2   Components of cash and cash equivalents

3.2.1   Demand deposits and short-term investments

In defining 'cash', IAS 7 does not explain what is meant by 'demand deposits', perhaps because the term is regarded in common usage to mean amounts that can be withdrawn on demand, without prior notice being required or a penalty being charged. In any event, the distinction is largely irrelevant because amounts not classified as demand deposits may qualify as cash equivalents and end up being treated in the same way. Thus, whether or not an amount meets the definition of a cash equivalent may become the more important determination.

Cash equivalents are held for the purpose of meeting short-term cash commitments rather than for investment or other purposes. For an investment to qualify as a cash equivalent it must be readily convertible to a known amount of cash and be subject to an insignificant risk of changes in value. Normally only an investment with a short maturity of, say, three months or less from the date of acquisition qualifies as a cash equivalent. Equity investments are excluded unless they are cash equivalents in substance. IAS 7 provides an example, being redeemable preference shares acquired within a short period of their maturity and with a specified redemption date. *[IAS 7.7]*.

When the standard refers to a 'known amount of cash' it means that the amount should be known or determinable at the date on which the investment is acquired. Accordingly, traded commodities, such as gold bullion, would not be eligible for inclusion in cash equivalents because the proceeds to be realised from such an investment is determined at the date of disposal rather than being known or determinable when the investment is made.

3.2.2   Money market funds

Entities commonly invest in money market funds (MMF) such as an open-ended mutual fund that invests in certificates of deposit, commercial paper, treasury bills, bankers' acceptances and repurchase agreements and other money market instruments. An investment in a MMF aims to provide investors with low-risk, low-return investment while preserving the value of the assets and maintaining a high level of liquidity. The question then arises as to whether investments in such funds can be classified as cash equivalents.

In most cases, a MMF investment is quoted in an active market and, as such, could be regarded as highly liquid. However, this is not enough to meet the definition of a cash equivalent. The short-term and highly liquid investment must be readily convertible into known amounts of cash which are subject to an insignificant risk of changes in value. *[IAS 7.6]*. The Interpretations Committee considered the issue in July 2009 and confirmed that the amount of cash that will be received must be known at the time of the initial investment. Accordingly, investments in shares or units of money market funds cannot be considered as cash equivalents simply because they are convertible at any time at the then market price in an active market. The Interpretations Committee also confirmed that an entity would have to satisfy itself that any investment was subject to an insignificant risk of change in value for it to be classified as a cash equivalent.[1]

Therefore in assessing whether the change in value of an investment in a money market fund can be regarded as insignificant, an entity has to conclude that the range of possible returns is very small. This evaluation is made at the time of acquiring the investment and will involve consideration of factors such as the maturity of the investment (which should not exceed 90 days); the credit rating of the fund (which should be AAA or an equivalent highest rating); the nature of the investments held by the fund (which should themselves not be subject to volatility); the extent of diversification in the portfolio (which should be very high); and any mechanisms by the fund to guarantee returns (for example by reference to short-term money market interest rates).

Investments are often held for purposes other than to act as a ready store of value that can be quickly converted into cash when needed to meet short-term cash commitments. It is therefore important to understand why the entity invested in a particular money market fund when determining whether classification as a cash equivalent is appropriate. This approach is illustrated by Hunting plc in Extract 38.3 below.

Extract 38.3: Hunting plc (2010)

Notes to the Financial Statements [extract]
25.   Cash and Cash Equivalents [extract]

	Group		Company	
	2010 £m	2009 £m	**2010** £m	2009 £m
Cash at bank and in hand	**86.8**	55.0	4.5	–
Short-term deposits and Money Market Funds	**181.9**	348.6	–	–
	268.7	403.6	**4.5**	–

30.   Financial Risk Factors [extract]

(b) Interest rate risk [extract]

The Group needs to ensure that sufficient liquid funds are available to support its working capital and capital expenditure requirements and to fund acquisitions. During the year, cash was, therefore, invested by the treasury function in AAA rated, instant access Money Market Funds and in fixed-rate bank deposits, with terms of between overnight and four months. As the funds were invested for short periods of time, the interest yield on these was relatively low. However, the preservation of the Group's net cash took priority over earning high interest yields.

3.2.3   Investments with maturities greater than three months

The longer the term of the investment, the greater the risk that a change in market conditions (such as interest rates) can have an effect on its value that is other than insignificant. For this reason, IAS 7 excludes most equity investments from cash equivalents and restricts the inclusion of other investments to those with a short maturity of, say, three months or less from the date of their acquisition by the entity. *[IAS 7.7].*

Similarly, an investment with a term on acquisition of, say, nine months is not reclassified as a cash equivalent from the date on which there is less than three months remaining to its maturity. If such reclassifications were permitted, the statement of cash flows would have to reflect movements between investments and cash equivalents. This would be misleading because no actual cash flows would have occurred.

The criteria explained above are guidelines, not rules, and a degree of common sense should be used in their application. In the final analysis, cash equivalents are held for the purpose of meeting short-term cash commitments and amounts should be included in cash equivalents only if they can be regarded as being nearly as liquid as cash and essentially as free from exposure to changes in value as cash.

For example, an entity might justify including in cash equivalents a fixed deposit with an original term longer than three months if it effectively functions like a demand deposit. Typically, a fixed deposit will carry a penalty charge for withdrawal prior to maturity. A penalty will usually indicate that the investment is held for investment purposes rather than the purpose of meeting short-term cash needs. However, some fixed deposits carry a penalty whereby the entity will forego the higher interest that it would have received if held to maturity, but would still receive interest at a prevailing demand deposit rate. In this case, it may be arguable that there is effectively no significant penalty for early withdrawal, as the entity receives at least the same return that it otherwise would have in a demand deposit arrangement. Where an entity does assert that this type of investment is held for meeting short-term cash needs and classifies the investment as a cash equivalent, the accrual of interest receivable should be on a consistent basis. In this example, the entity should consider accruing interest receivable at the demand deposit rate.

3.2.4   *Bank overdrafts*

Although bank borrowings are generally considered to be financing activities, there are circumstances in which bank overdrafts repayable on demand are included as a component of cash and cash equivalents. This is in cases where the use of short-term overdrafts forms an integral part of an entity's cash management practices. Evidence supporting such an assertion would be that the bank balance often fluctuates from being positive to overdrawn. *[IAS 7.8].*

3.3 Reconciliation with balance sheet items

The amount shown alongside the caption in the balance sheet for 'cash and cash equivalents' will not always be a reliable guide for IAS 7 purposes. Many entities present the components of cash and cash equivalents separately on the face of the balance sheet, such as 'cash and bank balances' and 'short-term bank deposits'. Additionally, some entities may include bank overdrafts in cash and cash equivalents for cash flow purposes, but, if no legal right of set-off exists, will present bank overdrafts separate from cash in the balance sheet as financial liabilities. *[IAS 32.42].*

The standard requires an entity to disclose the components of cash and cash equivalents and to present a reconciliation to the balance sheet, *[IAS 7.45]*, which means that any difference between 'cash and cash equivalents' for IAS 7 purposes and in the balance sheet presentation will be evident in the notes to the financial statements.

Smith & Nephew provides a reconciliation of the components of cash and cash equivalents, which includes overdrafts.

Extract 38.4: Smith & Nephew plc (2010)

Notes to the group accounts [extract]
27.   Cash Flow Statement [extract]
Cash and cash equivalents

For the purposes of the Group Cash Flow Statement, cash and cash equivalents at 31 December comprise cash at bank and in hand net of bank overdrafts.

	2010 $ million	2009 $ million	2008 $ million
Cash at bank and in hand	207	192	145
Bank overdrafts	(12)	(18)	(23)
Cash and cash equivalents	195	174	122

3.4 Restrictions on the use of cash and cash equivalents

The amount of significant cash and cash equivalent balances that is not available for use by the group should be disclosed, together with a commentary by management to explain the circumstances of the restriction. *[IAS 7.48].* Examples include cash and cash equivalents held by a subsidiary operating under exchange controls or other legal restrictions that prevent their general use by the parent or other subsidiaries. *[IAS 7.49].*

Chapter 38

Lloyds TSB discloses balances held by its life fund subsidiaries as restricted cash.

Extract 38.5: Lloyds Banking Group plc (2010)

Notes to the consolidated financial statements [extract]

57   CONSOLIDATED CASH FLOW STATEMENT [extract]

(D)   ANALYSIS OF CASH AND CASH EQUIVALENTS AS SHOWN IN THE BALANCE SHEET

	2010 £m	2009 £m
Cash and balances with central banks	**38,115**	38,994
Less: mandatory reserve deposits[1]	**(1,089)**	(728)
	37,026	38,266
Loans and advances to banks	**30,272**	35,361
Less: amounts with a maturity of three months or more	**(4,998)**	(7,937)
	25,274	27,424
Total cash and cash equivalents	**62,300**	65,690

[1] Mandatory reserve deposits are held with local central banks in accordance with statutory requirements; these deposits are not available to finance the Group's day-to-day operations.

Included within cash and cash equivalents at 31 December 2010 is £14,694 million (2009: £13,323 million) held within the Group's life funds, which is not immediately available for use in the business.

The nature of the restriction must be assessed to determine if the balance is ineligible for inclusion in cash equivalents because the restriction results in the investment ceasing to be highly liquid or readily convertible. For example, where an entity covenants to maintain a minimum level of cash or deposits as security for certain short-term obligations and provided that no amounts are required to be designated for that specific purpose, such balances could still be regarded as cash equivalents, albeit subject to restrictions, as part of a policy of managing resources to meet short-term commitments.

However, an entity may be required to formally set aside cash, for example by way of a deposit into an escrow account, as part of a specific project or transaction, such as the acquisition or construction of a property. In such circumstances, it is necessary to consider the terms and conditions relating to the account and the conditions relating to both the entity's and the counterparty's access to the funds within it to determine whether it is appropriate for the deposit to be classified in cash equivalents.

In Extract 38.5 above, Lloyds TSB excludes from cash and cash equivalents the mandatory reserve deposits held with local central banks, because these amounts are not available to finance the entity's day-to-day operations. Similarly, in the following extract, InterContinental Hotels Group includes certain amounts of restricted cash, which are pledged as collateral to insurance companies for risks retained by the group, in other financial assets rather than cash and cash equivalents.

Extract 38.6: InterContinental Hotels Group PLC (2010)

Notes to the Group financial statements [extract]

15.   Other financial assets [extract]

Other financial assets consist of trade deposits and restricted cash. These amounts have been designated as 'loans and receivables' and are held at amortised cost. Restricted cash of $42 m (2009 $47 m) relates to cash held in bank accounts which is pledged as collateral to insurance companies for risks retained by the Group.

---

4   PRESENTATION OF THE STATEMENT OF CASH FLOWS

The statement of cash flows reports inflows and outflows of cash and cash equivalents during the period classified under:

* operating activities;
* investing activities; and
* financing activities. *[IAS 7.10]*.

This classification is intended to allow users to assess the impact of these three types of activity on the financial position of the entity and the amount of its cash and cash equivalents. Whilst not stated explicitly in the standard, the presentation of operating, investing and financing cash flows usually follows this sequence in practice, and a total net cash flow for each standard heading should be shown. Comparative figures are required for all items in the statement of cash flows and the related notes. *[IAS 1.38]*.

The components of cash flows are classified as operating, investing or financing activities in a manner which is most appropriate to the business of the entity. *[IAS 7.11]*. For example, the purchase of investments would likely be an operating cash flow for a financial institution, but to an investing cash flow for a manufacturer. Additionally, a single transaction may comprise elements of differently classified cash flows. For example, when repayments on a loan include both interest and capital, the interest element may be included in either operating activities or financing activities (see 4.4.1 below); whereas the capital repayment must be classified as a financing cash flow. *[IAS 7.12]*.

The format of the statement of cash flows is illustrated in Extract 38.7. As permitted by the standard, AstraZeneca has included interest paid under operating activities, interest received under investing activities and dividends paid under financing activities.

Extract 38.7: AstraZeneca PLC (2010)

CONSOLIDATED STATEMENT OF CASH FLOWS FOR THE YEAR ENDED 31 DECEMBER

	2010 $m	2009 $m	2008 $m
Cash flows from operating activities			
Profit before tax	10,977	10,807	8,681
Finance income and expense	517	736	463
Depreciation, amortisation and impairment	2,741	2,087	2,620
Decrease/(increase) in trade and other receivables	10	(256)	(1,032)
Decrease in inventories	88	6	185
(Decrease)/increase in trade and other payables and provisions	(16)	1,579	637
Other non-cash movements	(463)	(200)	87
Cash generated from operations	13,854	14,759	11,641
Interest paid	(641)	(639)	(690)
Tax paid	(2,533)	(2,381)	(2,209)
Net cash inflow from operating activities	**10,680**	11,739	8,742
Cash flows from investing activities			
Acquisitions of business operations	(348)	–	–
Movement in short term investments and fixed deposits	(239)	(1,371)	1
Purchase of property, plant and equipment	(791)	(962)	(1,095)
Disposal of property, plant and equipment	83	138	38
Purchase of intangible assets	(1,390)	(624)	(2,944)
Disposal of intangible assets	210	269	–
Purchase of non-current asset investments	(34)	(31)	(40)
Disposal of non-current asset investments	5	3	32
Interest received	174	113	149
Payments made by subsidiaries to minority interests	(10)	(11)	(37)
Net cash outflow from investing activities	**(2,340)**	(2,476)	(3,896)
Net cash inflow before financing activities	**8,340**	9,263	4,846
Cash flows from financing activities			
Proceeds from issue of share capital	494	135	159
Repurchase of shares	(2,604)	–	(610)
Issue of loans	–	–	787
Repayment of loans	(1,741)	(650)	–
Dividends paid	(3,361)	(2,977)	(2,739)
Movement in short term borrowings	(8)	(137)	(3,959)
Net cash outflow from financing activities	**(7,220)**	(3,629)	(6,362)
Net increase/(decrease) in cash and cash equivalents in the period	1,120	5,634	(1,516)
Cash and cash equivalents at beginning of the period	9,828	4,123	5,727
Exchange rate effects	33	71	(88)
Cash and cash equivalents at the end of the period	**10,981**	9,828	4,123

4.1   Cash flows from operating activities

Operating activities are defined as 'the principal revenue-producing activities of the entity and other activities that are not investing or financing activities'. *[IAS 7.6]*. This means that operating is the 'default category', with all cash flows that do not fall within either the investing or financing classifications being automatically deemed to be of an operating nature. The standard states that the value of information on operating cash flows is twofold. It provides a key indicator of the extent to which the entity has generated sufficient cash flows from its operations to repay debt, pay dividends and make investments to maintain and increase its operating capability, without recourse to external sources of financing. Also, information about the components of historical operating cash flows may assist in the process of forecasting future operating cash flows, when used in conjunction with other financial statement information. *[IAS 7.13]*.

Cash flows from operating activities generally result from transactions and other events that enter into the determination of profit or loss. Examples include:

(a) cash receipts from the sale of goods and the rendering of services;

(b) cash receipts from royalties, fees, commissions and other revenue;

(c) cash payments to suppliers for goods and services;

(d) cash payments to and on behalf of employees;

(e) cash receipts and cash payments of an insurance entity for premiums and claims, annuities and other policy benefits;

(f) cash payments or refunds of income taxes unless they can be specifically identified with financing and investing activities; and

(g) cash receipts and payments from contracts held for dealing or trading purposes (see 4.4.6 below regarding allocation of cash flows on derivative contracts). *[IAS 7.14]*.

As discussed at 5.2.1 below, the payment of acquisition-related costs in a business combination that have to be recognised as an expense *[IFRS 3.53]* would also be classified as operating cash flows because there is no related asset that would justify classification as an investing cash flow. *[IAS 7.16]*.

When an entity holds securities and loans for dealing or trading purposes they are similar to inventory acquired specifically for resale. Therefore, any related cash flows are classified as operating activities. Similarly, cash advances and loans made by financial institutions are usually classified as operating activities, since they relate to the main revenue-generating activity of that entity (see 6.1 below). *[IAS 7.15]*.

An example of an item that enters into the determination of profit or loss that is *not* usually an operating cash flow is proceeds from the sale of property, plant and equipment, which are usually included in cash flows from investing activities. *[IAS 7.14]*. However, the proceeds from sales of assets previously held for rental purposes are classified as cash flows from operating activities, if the entity routinely sells such assets in its ordinary course of business. Similarly, cash payments to manufacture or acquire property, plant and equipment held for rental to others, and that are routinely sold in the ordinary course of business after rental, are also classified as cash flows from operating activities (see 4.2.1 below). *[IAS 7.14]*.

Cash flows from operating activities may be reported on a gross or net basis, also known as the direct and indirect methods. *[IAS 7.18]*.

4.1.1   The direct method

Under the direct method, major classes of gross cash receipts and gross cash payments are disclosed. [IAS 7.18]. IAS 7 encourages entities to use the direct method, on the grounds that it provides information which may be useful in estimating future cash flows and which is not available under the indirect method. [IAS 7.19].

Under the direct method, information about major classes of gross cash receipts and payments may be obtained either:

(a)   from the accounting records of the entity (essentially based on an analysis of the cash book); or

(b)   by adjusting sales, cost of sales (interest and similar income and interest expenses and similar charges for a financial institution) and other items recognised in profit or loss for:

    (i)   changes during the period in inventories and operating receivables and payables;

    (ii)   other non-cash items; and

    (iii)   other items for which the cash effects are investing or financing cash flows. [IAS 7.19].

The direct method statement of cash flows should include the same disclosures of gross cash receipts and gross cash payments irrespective of which approach has been used to determine their value. In particular, there is no requirement for entities using the approach described in (b) above to present a reconciliation showing the adjustments made between, for example, revenue in the income statement and cash receipts from customers.

The IASB has contemplated for some time whether it should mandate reporting under the direct method or the indirect method. As part of its joint project with the FASB, the IASB issued a staff draft of an exposure draft *Financial Statement Presentation* in July 2010. The staff draft proposed a requirement for the statement of cash flows to be prepared using the direct method and to be structured based on the following:[2]

(a)   business activities, analysed between

    (i)   operating cash flows; and

    (ii)   investing cash flows;

(b)   financing activities;

(c)   multi-category transactions;

(d)   income taxes; and

(e)   discontinued operations.

At the time of writing, the IASB does not expect to return to this topic until later in 2011 as part of its agenda consultation process.[3]

Portugal Telecom is an example of an entity using the direct method for presenting its cash flows from operating activities, as illustrated in Extract 38.8 below.

Extract 38.8: Portugal Telecom, SGPS, SA (2010)		
CONSOLIDATED STATEMENT OF CASH FLOWS [extract]		
FOR THE YEARS ENDED 31 DECEMBER 2010 AND 2009		EURO
	2010	**2009(restated)**
OPERATING ACTIVITIES		
Collections from clients	4,217,884,234	4,420,355,013
Payments to suppliers	(2,142,344,825)	(2,161,661,096)
Payments to employees	(657,641,753)	(569,386,059)
Payments relating to income taxes	(63,765,524)	(137,817,013)
Payments relating to post retirement benefits	(235,179,099)	(251,165,791)
Payments relating to indirect taxes and other	(215,112,767)	(219,102,436)
Cash flow from operating activities from continuing operations	903,840,266	1,081,222,618
Cash flow from operating activities from discontinued operations	603,033,383	846,239,725
Cash flow from operating activities	**1,506,873,649**	**1,927,462,343**

4.1.2 The indirect method

The indirect method arrives at the same value for net cash flow from operating activities, but does so by working back from amounts reported in the income statement. There are two approaches for presenting the net cash flow from operating activities when using the indirect method. The most common approach adjusts reported profit or loss for the effects of:

(a)   changes during the period in inventories and operating receivables and payables;

(b)   non-cash items such as depreciation, provisions, deferred taxes, unrealised foreign currency gains and losses, and undistributed profits of associates; and

(c)   all other items for which the cash effects are investing or financing cash flows. [IAS 7.20].

InBev has used this adjusted profit approach to present its indirect method statement of cash flows, as illustrated in Extract 38.9 below.

Extract 38.9: InBev NV (2010)		
Consolidated cash flow statement [extract]		
For the year ended 31 December	**2010**	**2009**
Million US dollar		
Operating activities		
Profit	5 762	5 877
Depreciation, amortization and impairment	2 788	2 818
Impairment losses on receivables, inventories and other assets	150	167
Additions/(reversals) in provisions and employee benefits	373	188
Non-recurring finance cost	925	629
Net finance costs	2 811	3 790
Loss/(gain) on sale of property, plant and equipment and intangible assets	(113)	(189)
Loss/(gain) on sale of subsidiaries, associates and assets held for sale	(58)	(1 555)
Equity-settled share-based payment expense	156	208
Income tax expense	1 920	1 786
Other non-cash items included in the profit	72	24
Share of result of associates	(521)	(513)

Chapter 38

Cash flow from operating activities before changes in working capital and provisions	14 265	13 230
Decrease/(increase) in trade and other receivables	(190)	149
Decrease/(increase) in inventories	(134)	301
Increase/(decrease) in trade and other payables	550	337
Pension contribution and use of provisions	(519)	(548)
Cash generated from operations	**13 972**	**13 469**
Interest paid	(2 987)	(2 908)
Interest received	219	132
Dividends received	383	–
Income tax paid	(1 682)	(1 569)
Cash flow from operating activities	**9 905**	**9 124**

Alternatively, the indirect method of presentation can show reported revenues and expenses in the statement of cash flows, with the changes during the period in inventories and operating receivables and payables. *[IAS 7.20]*. An example of this rarely used alternative is given at the end of Appendix A to IAS 7.

When an entity adopts the adjusted profit approach to presenting net cash flows from operating activities under the indirect method, the reconciliation should start either with profit or loss before tax (as in Extract 38.7 above) or profit or loss after tax (as in Extract 38.9 above). Any other basis, such as EBITDA, EBIT, or profit or loss excluding non-controlling interests, does not meet the requirement in IAS 7 for 'adjusting profit or loss', *[IAS 7.20]*, which includes 'all items of income and expense in a period'. *[IAS 1.88]*.

To obtain the information on working capital movements for the indirect method, the balance sheet figures have to be analysed according to the three standard headings of the statement of cash flows. Thus, the reconciliation of profit or loss to cash flow from operating activities will include, not the increase or decrease in all receivables or payables, but only in respect of those elements which relate to operating activities. For example, amounts owed in respect of the acquisition of property, plant and equipment (other than assets held for rental and subsequent sale), intangible assets, or investments will be excluded from the movement in payables included in this reconciliation. Although this may not present practical difficulties in the preparation of a single-entity statement of cash flows, it is important that sufficient information is collected from subsidiaries for preparing the group statement of cash flows.

Furthermore, when a group has made an acquisition of a subsidiary during the year, the change in working capital items will have to be split between the increase due to the acquisition (to the extent that the purchase consideration was settled in cash, this will be shown under investing activities) and the element related to post-acquisition operating activities which will be shown in the reconciliation.

4.2   Cash flows from investing activities

Investing activities are defined as 'the acquisition and disposal of long-term assets and other investments not included in cash equivalents'. *[IAS 7.6]*. This separate category of cash flows allows users of the financial statements to understand the extent to which expenditures have been made for resources intended to generate future income and cash flows. Cash flows arising from investing activities include:

(a)   payments to acquire, and receipts from the sale of, property, plant and equipment, intangibles and other long-term assets (including payments and receipts relating to capitalised development costs and self-constructed property, plant and equipment);

(b)   payments to acquire, and receipts from the sale of, equity or debt instruments of other entiries and interests in jointly controlled entities (other than payments anu receipts for those instruments considered to be cash equivalents or those held for dealing or trading purposes);

(c)   advances and loans made to, and repaid by, other parties (other than advances and loans made by a financial institution); and

(d)   payments for, and receipts from, futures contracts, forward contracts, option contracts and swap contracts, except when the contracts are held for dealing or trading purposes, or the cash flows are classified as financing activities (see 4.4.6 regarding allocation of cash flows on derivative contracts). *[IAS 7.16]*.

Only expenditures that result in a recognised asset in the balance sheet are eligible for classification as investing activities (see 4.2.2 below). *[IAS 7.16]*. Major classes of gross receipts and gross payments arising from investing activities are reported separately, except for those items that IAS 7 permits to be reported on a net basis, as discussed at 4.6 below. *[IAS 7.21]*.

4.2.1   *Property, plant and equipment held for rental*

Payments to acquire and receipts from the sale of, property, plant and equipment are usually included in investing cash flows; however, this is not always the case.

A number of entities sell assets that were previously held for rental, for example, car rental companies that may acquire vehicles with the intention of holding them as rental cars for a limited period and then selling them. IAS 16 – *Property, Plant and Equipment* – requires an entity, that, in its ordinary course of business, routinely sells items of property, plant and equipment that it has held for rental to others, to classify gains on the sale of such property, plant and equipment as revenue. *[IAS 16.68A]*. Accordingly, the proceeds from the sale of such assets are classified as cash flows from operating activities, as are cash payments to manufacture or acquire property, plant and equipment held for rental to others and routinely sold in the ordinary course of business. *[IAS 7.14]*.

The requirement to classify payments for such property, plant and equipment held for rental under operating cash flows is intended to avoid initial expenditure on purchases of assets being classified as investing activities, while inflows from sales are recorded within operating activities. However, this means that management will need to determine, at the time of acquisition or manufacture, which of the assets that it intends to rent out will be ultimately held for sale in the ordinary course of business.

4.2.2   *Cash flows relating to costs intended to generate future income*

As part of its annual improvements process, the IASB amended the definition of investing activities in IAS 7, effective for annual periods beginning on or after 1 January 2010, *[IAS 7.56]*, whereby 'only expenditures that result in a recognised asset in the statement of financial position are eligible for classification as investing activities'. *[IAS 7.16]*. Cash flows relating to costs recognised as an expense can no longer be classified within investing activities. As a result, payments including those for exploration and evaluation activities and for research and development that are recognised as an asset are classified as investing cash flows, while entities that recognise such expenditures as an expense would classify the related payments as operating cash flows.

The IASB believes that this requirement better aligns the classification of investing cash flows with the presentation in the balance sheet; reduces divergence in practice and, therefore, results in financial statements that are easier for users to understand. *[IAS 7.BC7]*. It does not seem unreasonable that recurrent expenditure on the items noted above should be classified as operating cash flows. However, as discussed at 5.2 below, application to other items that do not give rise to an asset in the balance sheet, such as acquisition-related costs and the settlement of contingent consideration in a business combination may prove to be more complicated.

4.2.2.A   *Cash flows for service concession arrangements*

Because a cash flow is only classified in investing activities if it results in a recognised asset in the statement of financial position, a question arises regarding the classification of the cash inflows and outflows of the operator of a service concession arrangement that is within the scope of IFRIC 12 – *Service Concession Arrangements*.

IFRIC 12 features two possible accounting models – the intangible asset model or the financial asset model. Under both models, the service element relating to the construction of the infrastructure asset is accounted for in accordance with IAS 11 – *Construction Contracts*. In the intangible asset model, the revenue recognised gives rise to an intangible asset. Under the financial asset model, a receivable is recognised. Amounts recognised as revenue give rise to a financial asset.

It is unclear whether the cash flows incurred in the construction phase should always be regarded as operating cash flows, because they relate to the provision of construction services; or whether, in the case of an arrangement under the intangible asset model, the related cash flows could be classified in investing activities as relating to the acquisition of an intangible asset. Similarly, when considering the classification of the cash inflows received during the operating phase of the arrangement, there can be divergence in practice. It would seem appropriate to classify in operating activities the cash inflows for arrangements that are accounted for under the intangible asset model. On the other hand, when the financial asset model applies, cash inflows may be reported as inflows from a debt instrument requiring a split to be made between the redemption component, an investing cash inflow, and an interest element that will be an operating or investing cash flow according to the accounting policy of the entity. Since there is no specific guidance relating to the classification of cash flows for service concession arrangements, current practice is mixed. IFRIC 12 is discussed in more detail in Chapter 28.

4.3   Cash flows from financing activities

Financing activities are defined as those 'activities that result in changes in the size and composition of the contributed equity and borrowings of the entity'. *[IAS 7.6].* The standard states that this information is useful in predicting claims on future cash flows by providers of capital to the entity. *[IAS 7.17].* However, it would seem more likely that information on financing cash flows would indicate the extent to which the entity has had recourse to external financing to meet its operating and investing needs in the period. The disclosure of the value and maturity of the entity's financial liabilities would contribute more to predicting future claims on cash flows.

Cash flows arising from financing activities include:

(a)   proceeds from issuing shares or other equity instruments;

(b)   payments to owners to acquire or redeem the entity's shares;

(c)   proceeds from issuing, and outflows to repay, debentures, loans, notes, bonds, mortgages and other short or long-term borrowings; and

(d)   payments by a lessee for the reduction of the outstanding liability relating to a finance lease. *[IAS 7.17].*

In consolidated financial statements, financing cash flows will include those arising from changes in ownership interests in a subsidiary that do not result in a loss of control (see 5.3.2 below). *[IAS 7.42A].*

Major classes of gross receipts and gross payments arising from financing activities should be reported separately, except for those items that can be reported on a net basis, as discussed at 4.6 below. *[IAS 7.21].*

4.4   Allocating items to operating, investing and financing activities

Sometimes it is not clear how cash flows should be classified between operating, investing and financing activities. IAS 7 provides additional guidance on the classification of interest, dividends and income taxes. Other questions are not addressed explicitly in the standard; such as the classification of cash flows for purchase and sales taxes, such as value-added tax (VAT) in the European Union, for receipts and payments arising from the factoring of trade receivables, for the purchase and sale of treasury shares, and for certain derivative contracts, which are also discussed below.

4.4.1   *Interest and dividends*

An entity is required to disclose separately cash flows from interest and dividends received and paid, and their classification as either operating, investing or financing activities should be applied in a consistent manner from period to period. *[IAS 7.31].* For a financial institution, interest paid and interest and dividends received are usually

Chapter 38

classified as operating cash flows. However, IAS 7 notes that there is no consensus on the classification of these cash flows for other entities and suggests that:

- interest paid may be classified under either operating or financing activities; and

- interest received and dividends received may be included in either operating or investing cash flows. *[IAS 7.33].*

The standard allows dividends paid to be classified as a financing cash flow (because they are a cost of obtaining financial resources) or as a component of cash flows from operating activities. *[IAS 7.34].*

In Extract 38.7 at 4 above, AstraZeneca has included interest paid under operating activities, interest received under investing activities and dividends paid under financing activities, as permitted by the standard. A different treatment is adopted by InBev in Extract 38.9 at 4.1.2 above, where interest paid, interest received and dividends received are all disclosed as operating cash flows.

All of these treatments are equally acceptable. Nevertheless, it could be argued that entities which do not include interest or dividends received within revenue should not include interest or dividends in operating cash flows, because cash flows from operating activities are primarily derived from the principal revenue-producing activities of the entity, *[IAS 7.14]*, and the amount of cash flows arising from operating activities is intended to be a key indicator of the extent to which the operations of the entity have generated sufficient cash flows to repay loans, pay dividends and make new investments without recourse to external sources of financing. *[IAS 7.13].* On this basis, interest paid would be a financing cash flow and interest and dividends received classified as investing cash flows. *[IAS 7.33].* Such entities would also treat dividends paid as a financing cash flow, because they are a cost of obtaining financial resources. *[IAS 7.34].* This approach is taken by AstraZeneca (see Extract 38.7 at 4 above).

In addition, the standard requires the total amount of interest paid during the period to be disclosed in the statement of cash flows, whether it has been recognised as an expense or capitalised as part of the cost of an asset in accordance with IAS 23 – *Borrowing Costs.* *[IAS 7.32].*

A literal reading of this requirement might suggest that interest paid should be presented as a single figure under operating or financing activities. However, it would also seem appropriate to include the cash outflow relating to capitalised borrowing costs under investing activities, provided that when this is done, the total amount of interest paid is also disclosed. This apparent inconsistency between IAS 7.16 and IAS 7.32-33 was addressed by the Interpretations Committee in their May 2011 meeting. They recommended that the IASB should amend IAS 7, in the annual improvements project, to clarify that the classification of interest payments capitalised under IAS 23 should be classified in a manner consistent with the classification of the underlying asset to which those payments were capitalised.[4]

Total interest paid could be disclosed either on the face of the statement of cash flows or in the notes.

4.4.2   Taxes on income

Cash flows arising from taxes on income should be separately disclosed within operating cash flows unless they can be specifically identified with investing or financing activities. *[IAS 7.35]*.

Whilst it is possible to match elements of tax expense to transactions for which the cash flows are classified under investing or financing activities; taxes paid are usually classified as cash flows from operating activities, because it is often impracticable to match tax cash flows with specific elements of tax expense. Also, those tax cash flows may arise in a different period from the underlying transaction. *[IAS 7.36]*. This is the presentation adopted by InBev in Extract 38.9 at 4.1.2 above. However, when it is practicable to make this determination, the tax cash flow is identified as an investing or financing activity in accordance with the individual transaction that gives rise to such cash flows. In cases where tax cash flows are allocated over more than one class of activity, the entity should disclose the total amount for taxes paid. *[IAS 7.36]*.

4.4.3   Sales taxes and other non-income tax cash flows

Although it provides guidance on the treatment of taxes on income, IAS 7 does not specifically address the treatment of cash flows relating to other taxes, such as VAT or other sales taxes and duty. The Interpretations Committee has considered whether it should add the question about VAT to its agenda and decided that it was not appropriate to develop an interpretation. Instead, it suggested that the issue of cash flows relating to VAT be considered by the IASB in its review of IAS 7 as part of the project on Financial Statement Presentation.

In explaining why it would not add this question to its agenda, the Interpretations Committee noted that 'IAS 7 does not explicitly address the treatment of VAT' and added that 'while different practices may emerge, they are not expected to be widespread'.[5]

Therefore, it seems that entities can choose to disclose VAT receipts and VAT payments separately in the statement of cash flows or as part of the related cash inflows and outflows. Given the availability of alternative treatments, the Interpretations Committee noted that it would be appropriate in complying with IAS 1 – *Presentation of Financial Statements* – for entities to disclose whether cash flows are presented inclusive or exclusive of related VAT.[6] We believe that the same principles should be applied for other non-income taxes.

4.4.4   Cash flows from factoring of trade receivables

Another question not explicitly addressed in the standard is the classification of cash receipts from the factoring of trade receivables. In these circumstances, an entity uses a factoring structure to provide cash flow from trade receivables more quickly than would arise from normal collection from customers, generally by transferring rights over those receivables to a financial institution. The classification of the cash receipt from the financial institution depends on whether the transfer gives rise to the derecognition of the trade receivable, or to the continued recognition of the trade receivable and the recognition of a financial liability for the consideration received. The characteristics determining which of these accounting treatments would be appropriate are discussed in Chapter 50 at 4.5 and 5.

If the factoring structure results in derecognition of a trade receivable, the cash receipt is included in operating activities. In cases where the trade receivable is not derecognised, we believe that the cash receipt from factoring should be included in financing activities. The later cash inflow from settlement of the trade receivable would be included in operating cash flows and the reduction in the liability to the financial institution would be a financing outflow. Following the same principle in IAS 39 – *Financial Instruments: Recognition and Measurement* – for the disclosure of income and expenditure relating to a transferred asset that continues to be recognised, *[IAS 39.36]*, these two amounts would not be netted off in the statement of cash flows. However, it would be acceptable to disclose the net cash receipts from, and payments to, the financial institution, if it was determined that these relate to advances made for and the repayment of short-term borrowings such as those which have a maturity period of three months or less. *[IAS 7.23]*.

4.4.5 Treasury shares

Treasury shares are an entity's own equity instruments that are acquired and held by the entity, a subsidiary or other members of the consolidated group. The consideration paid or received for treasury shares is recognised directly in equity and not as a movement in investments. *[IAS 32.33]*. As such, it should be clear that payments and receipts to acquire or issue treasury shares should be classified within financing activities. *[IAS 7.17]*. Even where such treasury shares are acquired by the entity as part of an equity-settled share-based payment transaction, the cash outflow should be classified under financing activities. Whilst cash payments to and on behalf of employees are classified under operating activities, *[IAS 7.14]*, the acquisition of treasury shares does not settle a transaction between the entity and its employees. An equity-settled share-based payment transaction is completed when the entity transfers its equity instruments to employees in consideration for the services received.

When a cash payment is made by a subsidiary to its parent or a trust that holds treasury shares as part of an equity-settled share-based payment arrangement, the payment should be accounted for as a deduction from equity, on the grounds that the payment does not settle the transaction with the employees, but is effectively a distribution to the parent or the trust (see Chapter 32 at 12.4.3 and 12.5.3). Having regarded this as a distribution, it follows that the cash flow should be classified as either operating or financing, according to the entity's policy on dividends as discussed at 4.4.1 above.

4.4.6 Cash flows on derivative contracts

Payments and receipts relating to derivative contracts can be classified within operating, investing or financing in different circumstances. Where the contract is held for dealing or trading purposes, the cash flows are classified under operating activities. *[IAS 7.14]*. IAS 7 requires that payments for, and receipts from, futures contracts, forward contracts, option contracts and swap contracts are classified as cash flows from investing activities, except when the contracts are held for dealing or trading purposes, or the cash flows are classified as financing activities. *[IAS 7.16]*.

The standard adds that when a contract is accounted for as a hedge of an identifiable position, the cash flows of the contract are classified under the same heading as the cash flows of the position being hedged. *[IAS 7.16].* An example is an interest rate swap. An entity wishing to convert an existing fixed rate borrowing into a floating rate equivalent could enter into an interest rate swap under which it receives interest at fixed rates and pays at floating rates. All the cash flows under the swap should be reported under the same cash flow heading as interest paid (i.e. as financing activities or operating activities, in accordance with the entity's determined policy, as discussed at 4.4.1 above), because they are equivalent to interest or are hedges of interest payments.

The standard suggests that receipts and payments on contracts might be included in financing cash flows; but, except for the text on contracts accounted for as hedges of an identifiable position, gives no indication of the circumstances under which such a classification would be appropriate. *[IAS 7.16].*

So how should an entity classify the cash flows from a derivative contract that is considered by management as part of a hedging relationship, but for which the entity elects not to apply hedge accounting (taking all movements to profit or loss) or for which hedge accounting is not permitted under IAS 39? Consider the following example.

Example 38.1:   Cash flows from derivatives not qualifying for hedge accounting

Company A has the euro as its functional currency. On 1 January 2011, it sells goods to a US customer for which it charges US$1,000,000. The spot exchange rate on this date is 1:1 and it recognises revenue of €1,000,000. Payment is due to be received on 30 June 2011. A enters into a forward contract to exchange US$1,000,000 for €1,095,000 on 30 June 2011. It does not designate it as a hedge because the effects of movements on the contract and those of retranslating the receivable will already offset in profit or loss. On 30 June 2011 the exchange rate is such that A receives the equivalent of €1,200,000 from its customer and pays €105,000 on the forward contract.

Taken literally, IAS 7 would suggest that the receipt from the customer of €1,200,000 is classified as an operating cash inflow; but, because the forward contract is not held for dealing or trading purposes and is not accounted for as a hedge of an identifiable position, the €105,000 cash outflow on the forward contract cannot be classified under operating activities. As such, the €105,000 would have to appear in investing or possibly financing cash flows. However, had the entity elected to apply hedge accounting, the standard would require the €105,000 to be included in operating cash flows.

This example highlights a current deficiency in IAS 7; its terminology was never updated or refined when IAS 39 was issued. This deficiency is acknowledged by the IASB when it discusses, in the implementation guidance to IAS 39, the classification of cash flows from hedging instruments. *[IAS 39.IG.G.2].* Therefore, in our opinion, since the IASB has not reflected the requirements of IAS 39 in the text of IAS 7, it does not require the treatment of cash flows 'when a contract is accounted for as a hedge of an identifiable position' *[IAS 7.16]* to be restricted only to those hedging relationships that either are designated as hedges under IAS 39 or would otherwise qualify for hedge accounting had they been so designated. Accordingly, in Example 38.1 above, entity A would include the payment on the forward contract in cash flows from operating activities.

Chapter 38

4.5   Exceptional and other material cash flows

The December 2003 revisions to IAS 1 and IAS 8 eliminated the concept of extraordinary items. *[IAS 1.BC61]*. IAS 1 also prohibits the presentation of extraordinary items either on the face of the statement of comprehensive income, the separate income statement (if presented) or in the notes. *[IAS 1.87]*. Consequently, IAS 7 no longer refers to extraordinary items, which previously had to be classified according to their nature as either operating, investing or financing flows and disclosed separately.

IAS 1 requires the nature and amount of material items of income and expense to be disclosed separately, *[IAS 1.97]*. It also requires additional line items, headings and sub-totals to be presented on the face of the balance sheet when this is relevant to an understanding of the entity's financial position. *[IAS 1.55]*. Therefore, although IAS 7 is silent on the matter, it would be appropriate for material cash flows or cash flows relating to material items in the income statement to be presented as separate line items on the face of the statement of cash flows, provided that they remain classified according to their nature as either operating, investing or financing cash flows.

If items are described as 'exceptional' cash flows, the entity's statement of accounting policies should explain the circumstances under which an item would be classified as exceptional and the notes to the financial statements should include an appropriate description of the nature of the amounts so treated.

4.6   Gross or net presentation of cash flows

In general, major classes of gross receipts and gross payments should be reported separately. *[IAS 7.21]*. Operating, investing or financing cash flows can be reported on a net basis if they arise from:

(a)   cash flows that reflect the activities of customers rather than those of the entity and are thereby made on behalf of customers; or

(b)   cash flows that relate to items in which the turnover is quick, the amounts are large, and the maturities are short. *[IAS 7.22]*.

Examples of cash receipts and payments that reflect the activities of customers rather than those of the entity include the acceptance and repayment of demand deposits by a bank, funds held for customers by an investment entity and rents collected on behalf of, and paid over to, the owners of properties. *[IAS 7.23]*. Other transactions where the entity is acting as an agent or collector for another party would be included in this category, such as the treatment of cash receipts and payments relating to concession sales.

Examples of cash receipts and payments in which turnover is quick, the amounts are large and the maturities are short include advances made for and the repayment of:

(a)   principal amounts relating to credit card customers;

(b)   the purchase and sale of investments; and

(c)   other short-term borrowings, such as those with a maturity on draw down of three months or less. *[IAS 7.23]*.

An example noted in IAS 20 – *Accounting for Government Grants and Disclosure of Government Assistance* – where separate presentation is deemed appropriate for major classes of cash flows is the receipt of government grants, which 'are often disclosed as separate items in the statement of cash flows regardless of whether or not the grant is deducted from the related asset for presentation purposes in the statement of financial position'. *[IAS 20.28]*.

4.7 Foreign currency cash flows

IAS 21 excludes from its scope the translation of cash flows of a foreign operation and the presentation of foreign currency cash flows in a statement of cash flows. *[IAS 21.7]*. Nevertheless, IAS 7 requires foreign currency cash flows to be reported in a manner consistent with IAS 21. *[IAS 7.27]*.

Accordingly, cash flows arising from transactions in a foreign currency should be reported in an entity's functional currency in the statement of cash flows by applying the exchange rate in effect at the date of the cash flow. *[IAS 7.25]*. Similarly, the cash flows of a foreign subsidiary should be translated using the exchange rates prevailing at the dates of the cash flows. *[IAS 7.26]*.

For practical reasons, an entity can apply a rate that approximates the actual rate on the date of the cash flow (such as a weighted average for a period), but like IAS 21, translation using the exchange rate as at the end of the reporting period is not permitted. *[IAS 7.27]*. The requirements for entities falling within the scope of IAS 29 – *Financial Reporting in Hyperinflationary Economies* – are discussed in Chapter 18 at 5.3.

Unrealised gains and losses arising from exchange rate movements on foreign currency cash and cash equivalents are not cash flows. However, it is necessary to include these exchange differences in the statement of cash flows in order to reconcile the movement in cash and cash equivalents to the corresponding amounts shown in the balance sheet at the beginning and end of the period. The effect of exchange rate movements on cash and cash equivalents is presented as a single amount at the foot of the statement of cash flows, separately from operating, investing and financing cash flows and includes the differences, if any, had those cash flows been reported at end of period exchange rates. *[IAS 7.28]*. This is illustrated in Extract 38.7 at 4 above.

4.7.1 Entities applying the direct method

When an entity enters into a transaction denominated in a foreign currency, there are no consequences for the statement of cash flows until payments are received or made. The receipts and payments will be recorded in the entity's accounting records at the exchange rate prevailing at the date of payment and these amounts should be reflected in the statement of cash flows. *[IAS 7.25]*.

The consolidated statement of cash flows prepared under the direct method uses the foreign currency financial statements of each foreign subsidiary as the starting point. This means that cash flows are measured first in the functional currency of the subsidiary and then retranslated into the currency in which the consolidated financial statements are presented.

Chapter 38

4.7.2 *Entities applying the indirect method*

Under the indirect method, profit or loss is adjusted for the effects of transactions of a non-cash nature, any deferrals of operating cash receipts or payments and income or expenses associated with investing or financing cash flows. *[IAS 7.18].* Exchange differences will appear in the income statement when the settled amount differs from the amount recorded at the date of the transaction. Alternatively, if the transaction remains unsettled at the balance sheet date, exchange differences will also be taken to the income statement on the retranslation of the unsettled monetary items at closing rates. Entities must determine what adjustments should be made to ensure that foreign currency items are shown in the statement of cash flows at the value as translated on the date of settlement.

4.7.2.A *Foreign currency operating transactions settled in the period*

Where the exchange differences relate to operating items such as sales or purchases of inventory by an entity, no further adjustments need be made when the indirect method of calculating the cash flow from operating activities is used. For example, if a sale transaction and cash settlement take place in the same period, the operating profit will include both the amount recorded at the date of sale and the amount of the exchange difference on settlement, the combination of which gives the amount of the actual cash flow.

4.7.2.B *Unsettled foreign currency operating transactions*

Similarly, where an exchange difference has been recognised on an unsettled balance no reconciling item is needed. This is because the movement in the related receivable or payable included in the reconciliation to operating profit will incorporate the exchange gain or loss. Adjusting profit for the movement on the receivable or payable will eliminate the effect of movements in exchange rates since the date of the transaction.

4.7.2.C *Determining the value of non-operating cash flows*

Any exchange difference arising on a settled transaction relating to non-operating cash flows will give rise to an adjustment between reported profit and the cash flow from operating activities.

For example, the foreign currency purchase of property, plant and equipment would be recorded initially at the rate prevailing on the date of the transaction. The difference on payment of the foreign currency payable would be taken to the income statement as an exchange gain or loss. If left unadjusted in the statement of cash flows, the investing cash flow for the asset purchase would be recorded at the historical rate, rather than at the exchange rate prevailing at the date of settlement. This difference needs to be taken into account in calculating the cash flow to be shown under the relevant classification, in this case investing cash flows, which would otherwise be recorded at the amount shown in the note of the movements in the balance sheet value of property, plant and equipment.

4.7.2.D The indirect method and foreign subsidiaries

Entities should take care when applying the indirect method at the 'more consolidated level' as described at 5.1 below when there are foreign subsidiaries. If the translated financial statements are used, exchange differences will be included in the movements between the opening and closing group balance sheets. For example, an increase in inventories held by a US subsidiary from $240 to $270 during the year will be reported as an unchanged amount of £150 if the opening exchange rate of £1=$1.60 becomes £1=$1.80 by the year-end. In these circumstances an entity should take the functional currency financial statements of the foreign subsidiary as the starting point. The $30 increase in inventories can then be translated at the average exchange rate.

4.8 Non-cash transactions and transactions on deferred terms

Investing and financing transactions that do not involve cash or cash equivalents are excluded from the statement of cash flows. Disclosure is required elsewhere in the financial statements in order to provide all relevant information about these investing and financing activities. *[IAS 7.43].* Examples of such non-cash transactions include the conversion of debt to equity; acquiring assets by assuming directly related liabilities or by means of a finance lease; and issuing equity as consideration for the acquisition of another entity. *[IAS 7.44].* Similarly, asset exchange transactions and the issue of bonus shares out of retained earnings are disclosed as non-cash transactions. Extract 38.10 below shows the disclosures made by Independent News & Media plc.

Extract 38.10: Independent News & Media plc (2010)

29   CASH AND CASH EQUIVALENTS [extract]

Significant non-cash transactions

(i) As part of the Group's refinancing in 2009, 723,200,000 new shares were issued to the Group's Bondholders in settlement of €122.9 m principal and interest outstanding on the Bonds. The remaining principal and interest, of €92.2 m due to the Bondholders was satisfied by a Rights Issue, of which €52.0 m was raised in cash with the remainder being an exchange of shares. The Bondholders received 92,204,958 shares in the Company for underwriting the Rights Issue.

(ii) During 2009, as part of the Group's refinancing, €673 m due under the Group's previous loan facilities was rolled into the Group's new loan facility, which was drawn down in December.

4.8.1 Asset purchases on deferred terms

The purchase of assets on deferred terms can be a complicated area because it may not be clear whether the associated cash flows should be classified under investing activities, as capital expenditure, or within financing activities, as the repayment of borrowings. In the US, FASB ASC Topic 230 – *Statement of Cash Flows* – takes the line that only advance payments, the down payment or other amounts paid at or near to the time of purchase of property, plant and equipment and other productive assets are investing cash flows; and, incurring directly related debt to the seller is a financing transaction with subsequent payments of principal on that debt classified as financing cash flows.[7] This treatment also appears to be implicit in IAS 7.

Where an entity acquires an asset under a finance lease, the acquisition of the asset is clearly a non-cash transaction, [IAS 7.44], and the payments to reduce the outstanding liability relating to a finance lease are clearly financing cash flows. [IAS 7.17]. The amendment to the IAS 7 definition of investing activities resulting from the annual improvements project, discussed above at 4.2.2, further clarifies this treatment, by stating that expenditures can only be classified as investing cash flows if they result in a recognised asset. [IAS 7.16]. As payments of deferred items do not result in recognition of an asset, but rather a reduction of a liability, they would not be treated as investing cash flows.

In our view, this distinction should be applied in all cases where financing is provided by the seller of the asset, with the acquisition and financing being treated as a non-cash transaction and disclosed accordingly. Subsequent payments to the seller are then included in financing cash flows. Nevertheless, if the period between acquisition and payment is not significant, the existence of credit terms should not be interpreted as changing the nature of the cash payment from investing to financing. The period between acquisition and payment would be regarded as significant if it gave rise to the seller recognising imputed interest under IAS 18 – *Revenue* [IAS 18.11] (see Chapter 30 at 3.5). Therefore, the settlement of a short-term payable for the purchase of an asset is an investing cash flow, whereas payments to reduce the liability relating to a finance lease or other finance provided by the seller for the purchase of an asset should be included in financing cash flows.

4.8.2   Asset disposals on deferred terms

By corollary, the disposal of property, plant and equipment under a finance lease or other arrangement determined to be the provision of finance by the vendor would be disclosed as a non-cash transaction. Receipts to reduce the receivable from the purchaser would still be investing cash flows, but described as the repayment of advances and loans rather than the proceeds on sale of property, plant and equipment. [IAS 7.16].

It should be noted that, just as in the case of the factoring of trade receivables (see 4.4.4 above), the proceeds received on disposal of an asset in a sale and leaseback transaction is classified as a financing cash flow if the related asset is not derecognised.

4.9   Voluntary disclosures

IAS 7 encourages the disclosure of additional cash flow related information that may help users better understand the financial position of the entity, including a commentary by management, as follows:

(a)   the amount of undrawn borrowing facilities that may be available for future operating activities and to settle capital commitments, indicating any restrictions on the use of these facilities;

(b)   the aggregate amounts of the cash flows from each of operating, investing and financing activities related to interests in joint ventures reported using proportionate consolidation;

(c)   the aggregate amount of cash flows that represent increases in operating capacity separately from those cash flows that are required to maintain operating capacity (see 4.9.1 below); and

(d)   the amount of the cash flows arising from the operating, investing and financing activities of each reportable segment (as defined in IFRS 8 – *Operating Segments*) (see 4.9.2 below). *[IAS 7.50]*.

4.9.1   Cash flows to increase and maintain operating capacity

IAS 7 does not contain any guidance as to how to distinguish cash flows for expansion from cash flows for maintenance in relation to the voluntary disclosure referred to under (c) above. The standard merely states that this information is useful in helping the user to determine whether the entity is investing adequately in the maintenance of its operating capacity or whether it may be sacrificing future profitability for the sake of current liquidity and distributions to owners. *[IAS 7.51]*.

Hongkong Land Holdings distinguishes renovations expenditure from developments capital expenditure in its analysis of investing cash flows.

Extract 38.11: Hongkong Land Holdings Ltd (2010)

Consolidated Cash Flow Statement [extract]
for the year ended 31st December 2010

	2010 US$m	2009 US$m (restated)
Investing activities		
Major renovations expenditure	(34.6)	(29.5)
Developments capital expenditure	(0.2)	(4.4)
Purchase of a subsidiary	–	(42.0)
Investments in and loans to associates and joint ventures	(17.9)	(305.2)
Purchase of other investments	(2.0)	(37.9)
Cash flows from investing activities	(54.7)	(419.0)

4.9.2   Segment cash flow disclosures

Disclosure is encouraged of segmental cash flows because it reveals the availability and variability of cash flows in each segment and allows users to better understand the relationship between the cash flows of the business as a whole and those of its component parts. *[IAS 7.52]*.

IAS 7 contains an example of the segmental disclosure advocated under (d) above.[8] However, this example simply reports the operating, investing and financing cash flows of its two segments with no reconciliation of the total to the statement of cash flows. In practice it might be difficult to allocate financing cash flows across the entity's reportable segments, given that this is not how treasury functions tend to operate.

A.P. Møller – Mærsk provides an analysis of operating cash flows and capital expenditure (part of its investing cash flows) by reportable segment. The entity does not disclose financing cash flows by reportable segment (comparative information is provided in the financial statements but is not reproduced here).

Chapter 38

Extract 38.12: A.P. Møller – Mærsk A/S (2010)

Notes to the consolidated financial statements [extract]
Amounts in DKK million

3   Segment information [extract]

	Container activities 2010	Oil and gas activities 2010	Terminal activities 2010	Tankers, offshore and other shipping activities 2010	Retail activity 2010	Other businesses 2010	Total reportable segments 2010
Cash flow from operating activities	23,619	22,231	4,749	7,726	2,493	1,078	61,896
Cash flow used for capital expenditure	−5,484	−11,033	−1,694	−5,654	−2,210	451	−25,624

---

5   ADDITIONAL IAS 7 CONSIDERATIONS FOR GROUPS

IAS 7 does not distinguish between single entities and groups, and there are no specific requirements as to how an entity should prepare a consolidated statement of cash flows. In the absence of specific requirements, cash inflows and outflows would be treated in the same way as income and expenses under IAS 27 – *Consolidated and Separate Financial Statements*. Applying these principles, the statement of cash flows presented in consolidated financial statements should reflect only the flows of cash and cash equivalents into and out of the group, i.e. consolidated cash flows are presented as those of a single economic entity. [IAS 27.4]. Cash flows that are internal to the group (such as payments and receipts for intra-group sales, management charges, dividends, interest and financing arrangements) should be eliminated. [IAS 27.20]. However, dividends paid to non-controlling shareholders in subsidiaries represent an outflow of cash from the perspective of the shareholders in the parent entity. They should, accordingly, be included under cash flows from financing activities or operating activities, in accordance with the entity's determined policy for classification of dividend cash flows (see 4.4.1 above). Payments arising from other transactions with non-controlling interests are discussed at 5.3.2 below.

5.1   Preparing a consolidated statement of cash flows

In principle, the group statement of cash flows should be built up from those prepared by individual subsidiaries with intra-group cash flows being eliminated as part of the aggregation process. This would generally be the case for entities presenting operating cash flows under the direct method, where information on gross cash receipts and payments has been obtained from each group entity's accounting records.

In practice, however, it may be possible to prepare a statement of cash flows at a more consolidated level, by starting with the disclosures in the consolidated income statement and balance sheet and then applying the adjustments reflected as part of the financial statements consolidation process, together with information provided on external cash flows by individual subsidiaries. Thus, an entity adopting the direct method could use this information to derive the value of the major classes of gross cash receipts and gross cash payments. *[IAS 7.19].* An entity presenting operating cash flows under the indirect method would use this information to calculate the values for movements in inventories, operating receivables and payables and other non-cash items that appear in the reconciliation of consolidated profit or loss to the group's cash flow from operating activities. *[IAS 7.20].*

Cash flows from investing and financing activities could similarly be derived from a reconciliation of the relevant headings in the consolidated income statement to balance sheet movements. However, for this to be possible, subsidiaries would have to provide supplementary information (as part of internal group reporting) to prevent gross cash flows from being netted off and to ensure that the cash flows are shown under the correct classifications. In particular, detailed information about receivables and payables would be essential to ensure that the movements in operating, investing and financing receivables and payables are identified.

5.2   Acquisitions and disposals

When a subsidiary joins or leaves the group, it should be included in the consolidated statement of cash flows for the same period as its results are reported in the consolidated income statement.

An entity should present separately within investing activities the aggregate cash flows arising from obtaining or losing control of subsidiaries or other businesses. *[IAS 7.39].* For transactions involving obtaining or losing control of subsidiaries or other businesses during the period, disclosure is also required, in aggregate, of each of the following:

(a)   the total consideration paid or received;

(b)   the portion of the consideration consisting of cash and cash equivalents;

(c)   the amount of cash and cash equivalents in the subsidiaries or other businesses over which control is obtained or lost; and

(d)   the amount of the assets and liabilities, other than cash or cash equivalents, in the subsidiaries or other businesses over which control is obtained or lost, summarised by each major category. *[IAS 7.40].*

Cash flows arising from changes in ownership interests in a subsidiary that do not result in a loss of control are classified as financing cash flows (see 5.3.2 below). *[IAS 7.42A].*

The aggregate amount of cash paid or received as consideration is reported in the statement of cash flows net of cash and cash equivalents acquired or disposed of. *[IAS 7.42].* The cash flow effects of losing control are not deducted from those of gaining control. *[IAS 7.41].* This implies that entities should present one analysis for all acquisitions and another for all disposals, such as that presented by Nestlé, shown in Extract 38.13 below.

Extract 38.13: Nestlé S.A. (2010)

Consolidated cash flow statement [extract]
for the year ended 31 December 2010

	2010	2009
Investing activities		
Capital expenditure	(4,576)	(4,641)
Expenditure on intangible assets	(408)	(400)
Sale of property, plant and equipment	113	111
Acquisition of businesses	(5,582)	(796)
Disposal of businesses	27,715	242
Cash flows with associates	254	195
Other investing cash flows	(2,967)	(110)
Cash flow from investing activities[a]	**14,549**	**(5,399)**

[a] Detailed information related to Alcon discontinued operations is disclosed in Note 2. In 2010, even if Alcon's assets and liabilities were classified as held for sale, included lines of the cash flow statement comprise Alcon's movement until disposal.

NOTES [extract]
2   Acquisitions, disposals and discontinued operations [extract]
2.2   Acquisitions of businesses [extract]
In millions of CHF

	2010	2009
Property, plant and equipment	342	54
Intangible assets	2 134	385
Inventories and other assets	292	150
Assets held for sale	845	–
Non-controlling interests	(6)	–
Purchase of non-controlling interests in existing participations	–	3
Financial debt	(18)	(5)
Employee benefits, deferred taxes and provisions	(35)	(90)
Other liabilities	(74)	(48)
Liabilities directly associated with assets held for sale	(177)	–
Fair value of net assets acquired	**3 303**	**449**
Goodwill	2 437	407
Fair value of consideration transferred	**5 740**	**856**
Cash and cash equivalents acquired	(41)	(5)
Consideration payable	(135)	(214)
Payment of consideration payable on prior years acquisition	18	159
Cash outflow on acquisitions	**5 582**	**796**

2.3   Disposal of businesses [extract]:
In millions of CHF

	2010	2009
Property, plant and equipment	4	71
Goodwill and intangible assets	1	64
Other assets	8	52
Non-controlling interests	(4 352)	(12)
Financial debt	–	–
Employee benefits, deferred taxes and provisions	–	(7)
Other liabilities	(31)	(55)
Alcon net assets held for sale disposed of	8 936	–
Net assets and non-controlling interests disposed of	**4 566**	**137**

Cumulative other comprehensive income items, net, reclassified to income statement	899	–
Profit/(loss) on current year disposals	24 472	105
Total disposal consideration	**29 937**	**242**
Cash and cash equivalents disposed of	(2 242)	(2)
Consideration receivable	(2)	(27)
Receipt of consideration receivable on prior years disposals	22	29
Cash inflow on disposals	**27 715**	**242**

5.2.1 Acquisition-related costs

IFRS 3 – *Business Combinations* – requires acquisition-related costs (other than those costs relating to the issue of equity or debt securities) to be recognised as an expense in the period in which the costs are incurred and the services are received. *[IFRS 3.53]*. Considering that acquisition costs can no longer be included in the measure of the cost of a business combination, is it no longer appropriate to classify the related payments in investing activities?

As discussed at 4.2.2 above, the IASB has amended the definition of investing activities in IAS 7, whereby 'only expenditures that result in a recognised asset in the statement of financial position' give rise to investing cash flows. *[IAS 7.16]*. As a result, cash flows relating to acquisition costs recognised as an expense would have to be classified within operating activities.

5.2.2 Deferred and other non-cash consideration

Not all acquisitions or disposals of businesses are satisfied in full by the exchange of cash. The amount to be disclosed on the face of the statement of cash flows for obtaining or losing control of subsidiaries or other business is the aggregate amount of cash paid or received in the transaction, net of cash and cash equivalents acquired or disposed of. *[IAS 7.42]*. Any non-cash consideration, such as shares issued by either party or amounts to be paid or received by the entity at a later date, is not included in the amount presented under investing activities. *[IAS 7.43]*. Instead, the non-cash element of the acquisition or disposal is disclosed; and in acquisitions where the deferred element of the consideration is regarded as the provision of finance by the vendor, its settlement is classified as a financing cash flow. This is explained in more detail at 4.8 above.

5.2.3 Contingent consideration

5.2.3.A Business combinations

When a business combination agreement allows for adjustments to the cost of the combination that are contingent on one or more future events, IFRS 3 requires the acquirer to recognise the acquisition-date fair value of contingent consideration *[IFRS 3.39]* and classify an obligation to pay contingent consideration as a liability or as equity in accordance with the provisions of IAS 32 – *Financial Instruments: Presentation*. *[IFRS 3.40]*. Changes resulting from events after the acquisition date, such as meeting a performance target, are *not* reflected by adjusting the recorded cost of the business combination. Instead, any payment or receipt in excess of the carrying amount of the related liability or asset is recognised in profit or loss or in other comprehensive income. *[IFRS 3.58]*.

As discussed at 4.2.2 above, the IAS 7 definition of investing activities has been amended, whereby only expenditures that result in a recognised asset are eligible for classification as investing activities. *[IAS 7.16]*. This suggests that cash payments for any contingent consideration in excess of the amount recorded on the acquisition date cannot be classified in investing activities, since that incremental amount would not give rise to a recognised asset subsequent to the revision to IFRS 3 discussed above. Accordingly, cash payments in excess of the acquisition-date fair value of the contingent consideration would fall into cash flows from operating activities.

In most circumstances, cash payments up to the amount recognised for the acquisition-date fair value of the contingent consideration would be classified in investing activities, on the basis that these are cash flows arising from obtaining or losing control of subsidiaries. *[IAS 7.39]*. However, to the extent that an element of the contingent consideration payment represents a provision of finance by the seller, it may fall to be included in financing activities (see 4.8.1 above). Judgment is required to determine whether the terms of the arrangement indicate that any of the amount attributed to the acquisition date fair value of the contingent consideration represents the provision of finance by the vendor.

In our view, if the period between acquisition and payment is not significant, it would not be appropriate to regard any of the payment as a financing cash flow. On the other hand, if the period of deferral is significant (to the extent that it would give rise to the vendor recognising imputed interest under IAS 18 *[IAS 18.11]*), payments to reduce this liability could be regarded as financing cash flows. However, the greater the extent to which the actual value of the contingent consideration payable depends on factors other than the time value of money, such as future business performance, the more difficult it would be to identify a financing element.

5.2.3.B   Asset acquisitions outside of business combinations

The purchase price of intangible assets or tangible assets acquired outside of a business combination often includes contingent consideration as well. The appropriate disclosure of the cash payment of that contingent consideration will depend on the facts and circumstances of the transaction. The classification in the statement of cash flow should follow the accounting treatment adopted in the balance sheet and income statement with regard to changes in the fair value of that contingent consideration.

5.2.4   Settlement of amounts owed by the acquired entity

A question that sometimes arises is how to treat a payment made by the acquirer to settle amounts owed by a new subsidiary, either to take over a loan that is owed to the vendor by that subsidiary or to extinguish an external borrowing.

Payments made to acquire debt instruments of other entities are normally included under investing activities. *[IAS 7.16]*. Therefore, the payment to the vendor is classified under the same cash flow heading irrespective of whether it is regarded as being part of the purchase consideration or the acquisition of a debt. This presentation can be contrasted with the repayment of external debt by the new subsidiary, using funds provided by the parent, which is a cash outflow from financing activities. *[IAS 7.17].*

5.2.5   Settlement of intra-group balances on a demerger

A similarly fine distinction might apply on the demerger of subsidiaries. These sometimes involve the repayment of intra-group indebtedness out of the proceeds from external finance raised by the demerged subsidiary. If the external funding is raised immediately prior to the subsidiary leaving the group, it is strictly a financing inflow in the consolidated statement of cash flows, being cash proceeds from issuing short or long-term borrowings. *[IAS 7.17].* If the subsidiary both raises the external funding and repays the intra-group debt after the demerger, the inflow is shown in the consolidated statement of cash flows under investing activities, being a cash receipt from the repayment of advances and loans made to other parties. *[IAS 7.16].*

5.3   Cash flows in subsidiaries, associates and joint ventures

5.3.1   Investments in subsidiaries, associates and joint ventures

Changes in cash and cash equivalents relating to associates or subsidiaries accounted for under the equity or cost method will impact the entity's statement of cash flows only to the extent of the cash flows between the group and the investee. Examples include cash dividends received and loans advanced or repaid. *[IAS 7.37].* This is also the case for jointly controlled entities accounted for under the equity method. *[IAS 7.38].*

Where an interest in a jointly controlled entity is accounted for using proportionate consolidation, the consolidated statement of cash flows will reflect the group's proportionate share of the jointly controlled entity's cash flows on a line-by-line basis. *[IAS 7.38].* Whilst IAS 7 is not explicit in this regard, the same treatment must apply for cash flows arising from an entity's interest in both a jointly controlled operation and jointly controlled assets (see Chapter 13 at 4). This means that the presentation of the statement of cash flows can be materially different depending on whether a jointly controlled entity is accounted for using the equity method or proportionate consolidation. This is certainly an exception to the assertion in the standard that cash flow information eliminates the effects of using different accounting treatments for the same transactions and events. *[IAS 7.4].* If this leads management to question the suitability of the resulting cash flow presentation, it may mean that the decision to adopt either the equity method or proportionate consolidation should be revisited.

5.3.2   Transactions with non-controlling interests

Dividends paid to non-controlling interest holders in subsidiaries are included under cash flows from financing activities or operating activities, in accordance with the entity's determined policy for dividends paid (see 4.4.1 above). Until recently it has not been clear from the standard how other cash flows between a parent or its subsidiary and the non-controlling interest holders in that subsidiary should be classified in the statement of cash flows. However, amendments to IAS 7, consequential to the revision of IAS 27 in 2008, clarify the position.

Chapter 38

For periods beginning on or after 1 July 2009, IAS 27 requires entities to distinguish between transactions that give rise to a change in control and those that do not, because this is consistent with the requirement that non-controlling interests are a separate component of equity. *[IAS 27.BC41-42]*. Since changes in ownership interests in a subsidiary that do not result in a loss of control are accounted for as equity transactions, the resulting cash flows are classified in the same way as other transactions with owners. *[IAS 7.42B]*. Accordingly, IAS 7 requires that cash flows arising from changes in ownership interests in a subsidiary that occur after control is obtained, but do not give rise to a loss of control are classified as cash flows from financing activities. *[IAS 7.42A]*. In cases where there is a loss of control, the proceeds would be disclosed as a cash flow arising from disposals and classified as investing activities. *[IAS 7.16]*.

5.3.3   Group treasury arrangements

Some groups adopt treasury arrangements by which cash resources are held centrally, either by the parent company or by a designated subsidiary company. Any excess cash is transferred to the designated group entity. In some cases a subsidiary might not even have its own bank account, with all receipts and payments being made directly from centrally controlled funds. Subsidiaries record an intercompany receivable when otherwise they would have held cash and bank deposits at each period end. A question that arises is whether or not a statement of cash flows should be presented when preparing the separate financial statements of such a subsidiary given that there is no cash or cash equivalents balance held at each period end. In our view, the preparation of the statement of cash flows should be based upon the actual cash flows during the period regardless of cash and cash equivalents balance held at each period end. The cash and cash equivalents may fluctuate from being positive to overdrawn or nil as the subsidiary needs cash to conduct its operations, to pay its obligations and to provide returns to its investors, or sweeps up excess cash to the designated group entity. This approach is consistent with the requirements in IAS 7 that all entities should prepare a statement of cash flows which forms an integral part of the financial statements. *[IAS 7.1]*.

Where the subsidiary makes net deposits of funds to, or net withdrawals of funds from the designated group entity during the reporting period, a further question arises as to how movements should be presented in the subsidiary's statement of cash flows. Normally these transactions give rise to intercompany balances. Therefore, the net deposits or net withdrawals should be shown as investing activities or financing activities, respectively.

In extremely rare cases the intercompany balances may meet the definition of cash equivalents and be regarded as short-term highly liquid investments that are readily convertible into known amounts of cash and are subject to insignificant risk of changes in value. *[IAS 7.1]*. However, in most cases such funds are transferred to the designated group entity for an indeterminate term and the fact that both the subsidiary and designated group entity are controlled by the parent company makes it difficult to conclude that the subsidiary could demand repayment of amounts deposited independently of the wishes of the parent company.

6 ADDITIONAL IAS 7 CONSIDERATIONS FOR FINANCIAL INSTITUTIONS

IAS 7 applies to banks, insurance entities and other financial institutions. Nevertheless, there are some differences in its application as compared to entities that are not financial institutions. For example, in considering the components of cash and cash equivalents, banks would not usually have borrowings with the characteristics of an overdraft, and cash for their purposes should normally include cash and balances at central banks, together with loans and advances to other banks repayable on demand. Allianz discloses such items as components of its cash and cash equivalents, as shown in Extract 38.14 below.

Extract 38.14: Allianz Group (2010)

Supplementary Information to the Consolidated Balance Sheets [extract]

7 Cash and cash equivalents

As of December 31,	2010	2009
	€ mn	€ mn
Balances with banks payable on demand	5,813	5,243
Balances with central banks	279	198
Cash on hand	169	159
Treasury bills, discounted treasury notes, similar treasury securities, bills of exchange and checks[1]	2,486	489
Total	**8,747**	**6,089**

[1] Includes reclassification of €2,050 mn from loans and advances to banks and customers at the U.S. subsidiaries.

As of December 31, 2010, compulsory deposits on accounts with national central banks under restrictions due to required reserves from the European Central Bank totalled €279 mn (2009: €198 mn).

IAS 7 contains a number of additional provisions affecting the preparation of statements of cash flow by financial institutions. These are covered in broad outline below.

6.1 Operating cash flows

Cash advances and loans made by financial institutions are usually classified as operating activities (and not as investing activities, as they are for other entities) since they relate to a financial institution's main revenue-producing activity. *[IAS 7.15, 16(e)]*. Similarly, receipts from the repayment of loans and advances would be included in operating cash flows. *[IAS 7.16(f)]*.

Interest paid and interest and dividends received are usually classified as operating cash flows for a financial institution. *[IAS 7.33]*.

For an insurance entity, cash receipts and cash payments for premiums and claims, annuities and other policy benefits would be included in its operating cash flows. *[IAS 7.14(e)]*.

Under the direct method of reporting operating cash flows, a financial institution that does not obtain information from its accounting records can derive the disclosures for major classes of gross cash receipts and payments by adjusting interest and similar income and interest expense and similar charges and other items recognised in profit or loss for:

(a)   changes during the period in operating receivables and payables;

(b)   other non-cash items; and

(c)   other items for which the cash effects are investing or financing cash flows. *[IAS 7.19].*

Where an insurance entity presents its operating cash flows using the direct method, it should separately disclose cash flows arising from insurance contracts. *[IFRS 4.37(b)].* Comparative information is required. *[IFRS 4.42].*

6.2   Reporting cash flows on a net basis

Cash flows from each of the following activities of a financial institution may be reported on a net basis:

(a)   cash receipts and payments for the acceptance and repayment of deposits with a fixed maturity date;

(b)   the placement of deposits with and withdrawal of deposits from other financial institutions; and

(c)   cash advances and loans made to customers and the repayment of those advances and loans. *[IAS 7.24].*

6.3   Reporting operating cash flows using the indirect method

Subject to the differences noted at 6.1 above, the principles for a financial institution presenting operating cash flows under the indirect method are the same as those discussed at 4.1.2 above for other entities. An example of presentation by a financial institution using the indirect method is that of UBS AG.

Extract 38.15: UBS AG (2010)

Statement of cash flows

CHF Million	For the year ended		
	31.12.10	31.12.09	31.12.08
Cash flow from/(used in) operating activities			
Net profit	**7,838**	(2,125)	(20,724)
Adjustments to reconcile net profit to cash flow			
from/(used in) operating activities			
Non-cash items included in net profit and other			
adjustments:			
Depreciation of property and equipment	**918**	1,048	1,241
Impairment of goodwill/amortization of intangible			
assets	**117**	1,323	554
Credit loss expense/(recovery)	**66**	1,832	2,996
Share of net profits of associates	**(81)**	(37)	6
Deferred tax expense/(benefit)	**(605)**	(960)	(7,020)
Net loss/(gain) from investing activities	**(531)**	425	(797)
Net loss/(gain) from financing activities	**1,125**	8,355	(47,906)

Net (increase)/decrease in operating assets:			
Net due from/to banks	**9,022**	(41,766)	(41,589)
Reverse repurchase agreements and cash collateral on securities borrowed	**(25,048)**	162,822	236,497
Trading portfolio, net replacement values and financial assets designated at fair value	**21,212**	11,118	350,099
Loans/due to customers	**(3,429)**	(316)	(156,486)
Accrued income, prepaid expenses and other assets	**608**	(4,208)	31,871
Net increase/(decrease) in operating liabilities:			
Repurchase agreements, cash collateral on securities lent	**9,277**	(41,351)	(220,935)
Net cash collateral on derivative instruments	**(988)**	(11,916)	6,316
Accrued expenses, deferred income and other liabilities	**(7,039)**	(29,242)	(56,232)
Income taxes paid, net of refunds	**(498)**	(505)	(887)
Net cash flow from/(used in) operating activities	**11,963**	54,497	77,007
Cash flow from/(used in) investing activities			
Purchase of subsidiaries and associates	**(75)**	(42)	(1,502)
Disposal of subsidiaries and associates	**307**	296	1,686
Purchase of property and equipment	**(541)**	(854)	(1,217)
Disposal of property and equipment	**242**	163	69
Net (investment in)/divestment of financial investments available-for-sale	**(25,631)**	(20,127)	(712)
Net cash flow from/(used in) investing activities	**(25,698)**	(20,563)	(1,676)
Cash flow from/(used in) financing activities			
Net money market paper issued/(repaid)	**4,459**	(60,040)	(40,637)
Net movements in treasury shares and own equity derivative activity	**(1,456)**	673	623
Capital issuance	**(113)**	3,726	23,135
Issuance of long-term debt, including financial liabilities designated at fair value	**78,418**	67,062	103,087
Repayment of long-term debt, including financial liabilities designated at fair value	**(77,497)**	(65,024)	(92,894)
Increase in non-controlling interests [1]	**6**	3	1,661
Dividend paid to/decrease in non-controlling interests	**(2,053)**	(583)	(532)
Net cash flow from/(used in) financing activities	**1,764**	(54,183)	(5,557)
Effects of exchange rate differences	**(12,181)**	5,529	(39,186)
Net increase/(decrease) in cash and cash equivalents	**(24,151)**	(14,721)	30,588
Cash and cash equivalents at the beginning of the year	**164,973**	179,693	149,105
Cash and cash equivalents at the end of the year	**140,822**	164,973	179,693
Cash and cash equivalents comprise:			
Cash and balances with central banks	**26,939**	20,899	32,744
Money market paper [2]	**77,998**	98,432	86,732
Due from banks with original maturity of less than three months [3]	**35,885**	45,642	60,217
Total	**140,822**	164,973	179,693

¹ Includes issuance of preferred securities of CHF 1,617 million for the year ended 31 December 2008.

² Money market papers are included in the balance sheet under Trading portfolio assets, Trading portfolio assets pledged as collateral and Financial investments available-for-sale. CHF 39,768 million, CHF 57,116 million and CHF 19,912 million were pledged at 31 December 2010. 31 December 2009 and 31 December 2008, respectively.

³ Includes positions recognized in the balance sheet under Due from banks and Cash collateral receivables on derivative instruments.

| | For the year ended | | |
CHF Million	**31.12.10**	31.12.09	31.12.08
Additional information			
Cash received as interest	17,344	23,844	68,232
Cash paid as interest	12,606	19,597	62,284
Cash received as dividends on equities (incl. associates)	1,395	1,090	2,779

7   REQUIREMENTS OF OTHER STANDARDS

7.1   Cash flows of discontinued operations

IFRS 5 – *Non-current Assets Held for Sales and Discontinued Operations* – requires an entity to disclose the net cash flows attributable to the operating, investing and financing activities of discontinued operations. These disclosures can be presented either on the face of the statement of cash flows or in the notes. Disclosure is not required for disposal groups that are newly acquired subsidiaries which are classified as held for sale on acquisition in accordance with IFRS 5. *[IFRS 5.33(c)]*. The general presentation requirements of IFRS 5 are dealt with in Chapter 4 at 3.2.

Bayer AG disclosed the net operating cash flows from discontinued operations on the face of the statement of cash flows as part of its indirect method reconciliation from reported profit to cash flows from operating activities. Investing and financing cash flows are shown inclusive of discontinued operations on the face of the statement of cash flows, with the analysis required by IFRS 5 given in the notes. Bayer AG further analysed these cash flows by business segment, as shown below.

Extract 38.16: Bayer AG (2007)

Bayer Group Consolidated Statements of Cash Flows [extract]

€ million	Note	2006	2007
Net cash provided by (used in) operating activities (net cash flow), continuing operations		3.928	4,281
Net cash provided by (used in) operating activities (net cash flow), discontinued operations	[6.3]	275	2
Net cash provided by (used in) operating activities (net cash flow) (total)		4,203	4,283

Notes to the Consolidated Financial Statements of the Bayer Group [extract]
6.3   Divestitures and discontinued operations [extract]
Discontinued operations affected the Group cash flow statements as follows:

€ million	Diagnostics 2006	Diagnostics **2007**	H.C.Stark 2006	H.C.Stark **2007**	Wolff Walsrode 2006	Wolff Walsrode **2007**	Total 2006	Total **2007**
Net cash provided by (used in) operating activities	154	(34)	78	23	43	13	275	2
Net cash provided by (used in) investing activities	(107)	3,292	(55)	927	(17)	429	(179)	4,648
Net cash provided by (used in) financing activities	(47)	(3,258)	(23)	(950)	(26)	(442)	(96)	(4,650)
Change in cash and cash equivalents	**0**	**0**	**0**	**0**	**0**	**0**	**0**	**0**

7.2   Cash flows arising from insurance contracts

IFRS 4 – *Insurance Contracts* – requires that where an insurance entity presents its operating cash flows using the direct method, it should separately disclose cash flows arising from insurance contracts. *[IFRS 4.37(b)]*. Comparative information is required. *[IFRS 4.42]*.

7.3   Cash flows arising from the exploration of mineral resources

In a similar vein, IFRS 6 – *Exploration for and Evaluation of Mineral Resources* – requires that an entity discloses the amounts of operating and investing cash flows arising from the exploration for and evaluation of mineral resources. *[IFRS 6.24(b)]*. The requirements of IFRS 6 are discussed in Chapter 41. The amendment to IAS 7 in respect of investing cash flows, discussed at 4.2.2 above, is also relevant to entities applying IFRS 6.

7.4   Cash flows arising from interests in subsidiaries, joint ventures and associates

IFRS 12 – *Disclosure of Interests in Other Entities* – which is effective for accounting periods beginning on or after 1 January 2013, requires an entity to disclose in its consolidated financial statements summarised financial information about the cash flows for each subsidiary that has non-controlling interests that are material to the entity. *[IFRS 12.B10(b)]*. These amounts are stated before inter-company eliminations. *[IFRS 12.B11]*.

In addition, for each material joint venture and associate an entity is also required to disclose dividends received from the joint venture or associate *[IFRS 12.B12]* and the amount of cash and cash equivalents for the joint venture or associate. *[IFRS 12.B13(a)]*. IFRS 12 is discussed in more detail in Chapter 15.

Chapter 38

References

1 *IFRIC Update*, July 2009.
2 Staff Draft of an Exposure Draft, *Financial Statement Presentation,* IASB and FASB, July 2010.
3 *IASB Work Plan – projected timetable as at 26 July 2011,* IASB.
4 *IFRIC Update*, May 2011, p.4.
5 *IFRIC Update*, August 2005, p.5.
6 *IFRIC Update*, August 2005, p.5.
7 FASB Accounting Standards Codification (ASC) Topic *Statement of Cash Flows,* 230-10-45-13, (Formerly, SFAS 95, *Statement of Cash Flows, FASB, November 1987,* para. 17, footnote.)
8 IAS 7, *Statement of Cash Flows,* IASB, Appendix A, part D. *Segment Information.*

Chapter 39

Interim financial reporting

Chapter 39

Chapter 39

List of examples

Chapter 39   Interim financial reporting

1   INTRODUCTION

The biggest issue in interim financial reporting is whether the interim period is a discrete period, or whether an interim period is an instalment of the full year. Under the first approach, an entity uses the same accounting policies and principles for annual financial statements as for interim periods. Under the second approach, the purpose of the interim report is to give investors, analysts and other users a better guide to the outcome of the full year, which requires modifications to the policies and principles used in annual financial reporting. The former approach is generally referred to as the 'discrete' approach, and the latter as the 'integral' approach.

The integral approach is not clearly defined, but implies allocating inter-period transactions, to match costs more evenly with revenues in the different halves (or quarters) of the year. Critics say that this approach is not matching, but smoothing, which obscures the results of the interim period. On the other hand, proponents say that such modifications prevent distortion; an interim period is a more artificial interval than a financial year, and that to report transactions outside of the context of the annual operating cycle for which they are incurred does not make sense.

In practice, the distinction between discrete and integral approaches is less clear-cut than the description above suggests. IAS 34 – *Interim Financial Reporting* – requires an entity to use a 'year-to-date' approach, *[IAS 34.28]*, which is a hybrid largely based on the requirement to report the entity's financial position as at the interim reporting date, but for which certain estimates and measurements are based on the expected financial position of the entity at year-end. However, the standard does not allow such estimates and measurements to amount to smoothing. For example, the estimate of tax expense for an interim period is based on actual profits earned as at the interim reporting date and not the expected tax expense for the year divided by the number of interim reporting periods, as discussed at 9.5 below.

The extent of disclosures in interim reports raises similar questions as to the purpose. If interim reporting is simply a more frequently published version of annual reporting, then the form and content of the interim reporting should be the same.

However, if interim reporting is only an instalment of a longer period, then a reporting package that highlights changes in circumstances during an interim period makes more sense than an update of all the disclosures in an entity's annual financial statements. IAS 34 allows an entity to include either a complete set of financial statements or a condensed version in the interim report. *[IAS 34.4]*. While some jurisdictions require the complete form and even an audit of the interim report, present practice under IFRS favours the condensed version, although probably more as a practical compromise than as the result of meeting a carefully researched need.

IAS 34 is not mandatory for entities that prepare annual financial statements that contain an explicit and unreserved statement of compliance with IFRS. *[IAS 34.2]*. Historically, interim reporting was the prerogative of capital markets and regulators and IAS 34 leaves governments, securities regulators, stock exchanges and others to determine which entities report interim information, how often and how soon after the reporting period. *[IAS 34.1]*. Accordingly, adherence to local regulatory or legal requirements in interim financial reports is required.

However, governments and regulators are increasingly referring to IFRS as they establish or revise their own requirements for interim financial reporting. For example, the European Union's Council of Economics and Finance Ministers (ECOFIN) issued *Directive 2004/109/EC of the European Parliament and of the Council on the harmonisation of transparency requirements in relation to information about issuers whose securities are admitted to trading on a regulated market and amending Directive 2001/34/EC* (the Transparency Directive) in December 2004. Article 5.3 of that Directive requires half-yearly financial reports that 'where the issuer is required to prepare consolidated accounts, the condensed set of financial statements shall be prepared in accordance with the international accounting standard applicable to the interim financial reporting adopted pursuant to the procedure provided for under Article 6 of Regulation (EC) No. 1606/2002.' Therefore, the half-yearly reports of entities subject to the Transparency Directive in the European Union comply with IAS 34. However, the timing and manner of adoption in member states varies based on local regulations. Other variations arise in interim reports for other periods (e.g. quarterly reporting) because the requirement in the Transparency Directive to apply IAS 34 is limited to half-yearly reports. The differences between full and condensed interim financial statements are discussed at 3 below.

1.1   Definitions

The standard defines an interim period as 'a financial reporting period shorter than a full financial year.' *[IAS 34.4]*.

The term 'interim financial report' means a financial report for an interim period that contains either a complete set of financial statements (as described in IAS 1 – *Presentation of Financial Statements*) or a set of condensed financial statements as described in IAS 34 (see 3.2 below). *[IAS 34.4]*.

2 OBJECTIVE AND SCOPE OF IAS 34

2.1 Objective

The stated objective of the standard is 'to prescribe the minimum content of an interim financial report and to prescribe the principles for recognition and measurement in complete or condensed financial statements for an interim period. Timely and reliable interim financial reporting improves the ability of investors, creditors, and others to understand an entity's capacity to generate earnings and cash flows and its financial condition and liquidity.' *[IAS 34, Objective]*.

2.2 Scope

IAS 34 does not prescribe which entities are required to publish interim financial reports, how often, or how soon after the end of an interim period. The standard notes that governments, securities regulators, stock exchanges, and accountancy bodies often require entities whose debt or equity securities are publicly traded to publish interim financial reports. Therefore, in the absence of any specific regulatory requirement (or obligation of the entity, for example, by covenant), entities are not required to publish interim financial information in a form that complies with IAS 34. Instead, IAS 34 only applies if an entity either elects or is required to publish an interim financial report in accordance with IFRS. *[IAS 34.1]*. Accordingly, if an entity's interim financial report states that it complies with IFRS, then the requirements of IAS 34 must be met in full. *[IAS 34.3]*.

The decision to present interim financial reports in accordance with IFRS operates independently of the annual financial statements. Hence, entities may still prepare annual financial statements conforming to IFRS even if their interim financial statements do not comply with IAS 34. *[IAS 34.2]*.

Nevertheless, the IASB encourages publicly traded entities to issue interim financial reports that conform to the recognition, measurement and disclosure principles set out in IAS 34. Those entities are specifically encouraged: *[IAS 34.1]*

(a)   to provide interim financial reports at least as of the end of the first half of their financial year; and

(b)   to make their interim financial reports available not later than 60 days after the end of the interim period.

However, since an entity can only describe an interim financial report as complying with IFRS if it meets all of the requirements of IAS 34, *[IAS 34.3]*, an entity that applies all IFRS recognition and measurement requirements in its interim financial report, but does not include all the required disclosures may not describe the interim financial report as complying with IFRS.

As shown in the Extract below, before the issuance of the Transparency Directive, British Energy disclosed that its interim financial statements for the period ended 31 December 2006 were not prepared in accordance with IAS 34.

Extract 39.1: British Energy Group plc (Q3, 2006)

Notes to the financial statements [extract]

1.   Basis of Preparation [extract]

In preparing the interim financial statements for the period ended 31 December 2006, the Board of Directors have used the principal accounting policies as set out in the Group's Annual Report and Accounts for the year ended 31 March 2006. The Group has chosen not to adopt IAS 34 – Interim Financial Statements, in preparing these interim financial statements, and therefore this information is not wholly compliant with International Financial Reporting Standards. The preparation of interim financial statements requires management to make judgements, estimates and assumptions that affect the application of policies and reported amounts of assets, liabilities, income and expenses.

---

3   COMPONENTS, FORM AND CONTENT OF AN INTERIM FINANCIAL REPORT UNDER IAS 34

The standard does not prohibit or discourage an entity from: *[IAS 34.7]*

- publishing a complete set of financial statements (as described in IAS 1) in its interim financial report, rather than condensed financial statements and selected explanatory notes; or

- including in condensed interim financial statements more than the minimum line items or selected explanatory notes as set out in IAS 34.

The recognition and measurement guidance in the standard, together with the note disclosures required by the standard, apply to both complete and condensed financial statements presented for an interim period. *[IAS 34.7]*.

3.1   Complete set of interim financial statements

An entity that publishes a complete set of financial statements in its interim financial report should include the following components, as required in IAS 1: *[IAS 34.5]*

(a)   a balance sheet as at the end of the interim period;

(b)   a statement of comprehensive income for the period;

(c)   a statement of changes in equity for the period;

(d)   a statement of cash flows for the period;

(e)   notes, comprising a summary of significant accounting policies and other explanatory information; and

(f)   a balance sheet as at the beginning of the earliest comparative period, if the entity applies a new accounting policy retrospectively, restates prior period financial statements, or reclassifies items in its financial statements.

If an entity publishes a complete set of financial statements in its interim financial report, the form and content of those statements should conform to the requirements of IAS 1. *[IAS 34.9]*. In addition, the entity should disclose the information specifically required by IAS 34 for interim financial reports as well as those required by other IFRSs (particularly those discussed at 4 below). *[IAS 34.7]*.

3.2   Condensed interim financial statements

In the interest of timeliness, cost, and avoiding repetition of previously reported information, an entity might be required or elect to give less information at interim dates as compared with its annual financial statements. *[IAS 34.6]*. The standard defines the minimum content of an interim report, as including condensed financial statements and selected notes, as follows: *[IAS 34.6, 8]*

(a)   condensed balance sheet;

(b)   condensed statement of comprehensive income, presented as either

  (i)   a condensed single statement; or

  (ii)   a condensed separate income statement and a condensed statement of comprehensive income;

(c)   condensed statement of changes in equity;

(d)   condensed statement of cash flows; and

(e)   selected explanatory notes.

The condensed statement of comprehensive income referred to at (b) above should be presented using the same format as the entity's annual financial statements. Accordingly, if an entity presents a separate income statement in its annual financial statements, then it should present a separate condensed income statement in the interim financial report. *[IAS 34.8A]*. Consistent with the standard's requirements for accounting policies, (see 8.1 below) an entity should use the same presentation in its interim financial statements as used in its most recent annual financial statements, adjusted for changes that will be reflected in its next annual financial statements. *[IAS 34.28]*.

As a minimum, the condensed financial statements should include each of the headings and subtotals that were included in the entity's last annual financial statements. *[IAS 34.10]*. However, the primary financial statements do not need to look exactly like the year-end financial statements. This is because the 'headings and subtotals' referred to in IAS 34 are not the same as 'line items' referred to in IAS 1. This is illustrated by the fact that IAS 1 uses all three terms to describe separate components of the balance sheet, statement of comprehensive income and income statement (if presented separately). *[IAS 1.55, 85]*. Therefore, a strict interpretation means that an entity is only required to present non-current assets, current assets, etc., on an interim balance sheet.

On the other hand, one of the purposes of an interim report is to help the users of the financial statements to understand the changes in financial position and performance of the entity since the previous annual reporting period. *[IAS 34.15]*. To that end, IAS 34 also states that additional line items or notes should be included if their omission makes the condensed financial statements misleading. *[IAS 34.10]*. Therefore, judgment is required to determine which line items provide useful information for decision-makers, and are presented, accordingly.

Chapter 39

Inclusion of most of the line items in the annual financial statements is preferable, as this presentation provides the most information to help users of the financial statements understand the changes since the previous year-end. Nonetheless, entities may aggregate line items used in the annual financial statements on a limited basis, if doing so does not make the information misleading or prevent users of the financial statements from performing meaningful trend analysis.

Consideration should also be given to regulatory requirements, for example, where a regulator requires an entity to present certain line items using some form of materiality criteria (e.g. in terms of amount, percentage relative to headings, or percentage change from prior periods). Entities may apply similar measures of materiality as a guide for determining which line items to present separately, even where this is not a regulatory requirement.

The following example illustrates one possible way in which an entity might choose to condense its interim financial statements from the presentation used in the annual financial statements. However, such presentation is at the discretion of management, based on facts and circumstances, including materiality (as noted above), regulatory environment, etc.

Example 39.1:   Sample condensed interim financial statements

Balance sheet	Annual financial statements	Condensed interim financial statements
Assets		
Non-current assets		
Intangible assets	●	●
Property, plant and equipment	●	●
Deferred tax assets	●	●
Investments in associates	○	
Available-for-sale financial assets	○	
Other non-current assets		○
Total non-current assets	●	●
Current assets		
Inventories	○	
Trade and other receivables	●	●
Current income tax assets	○	
Other current assets		○
Cash and cash equivalents	●	●
Total current assets	●	●
Total assets	●	●
Liabilities		
Current liabilities		
Trade and other payables	●	●
Current income tax liabilities	○	
Borrowings	●	●
Provisions for other liabilities	○	
Other current liabilities		○
Total current liabilities	●	●

Non-current liabilities

	Annual financial statements	Condensed interim financial statements
Borrowings	●	●
Pension obligations	●	●
Deferred tax liabilities	●	●
Other non-current liabilities	○	○
Provisions for other liabilities	○	
Total non-current liabilities	●	●
Total liabilities	●	●

	Annual financial statements	*Condensed interim financial statements*
Equity		
Share capital	●	●
Other reserves	●	●
Retained earnings	●	●
Total equity	●	●

● Included same line item in annual and interim financial statements
○ This line item is condensed from the annual to the interim financial statements

Statement of comprehensive income	*Annual financial statements*	*Condensed interim financial statements*
Sale of goods	●	●
Rendering of services	●	●
Total revenue	●	●
Cost of goods	●	●
Cost of services	●	●
Gross profit	●	●
Selling costs	○	
General and administrative costs	○	
Other operating expenses	○	
Total operating expenses	○	○
Operating profit	●	●
Finance costs	●	●
Share of profit of associates	●	●
Profit before tax	●	●
Income tax expense	●	●
Net income	●	●
Translation of foreign operations	○	
Net gain on hedge of net investment	○	
Income tax expense	○	
Total other comprehensive income	○	○
Total comprehensive income	●	●

● Included same line item in annual and interim financial statements
○ This line item is condensed from the annual to the interim financial statements

Chapter 39

Statement of cash flows	Annual financial statements	Condensed interim financial statements
Operating activities		
Net income	●	●
Non-cash adjustments:		
Depreciation and amortisation	○	
Gain on disposal of property	○	

	Annual financial statements	Condensed interim financial statements
Finance cost	○	
Share of net profit of associate	○	
Movements in pensions	○	
Total non-cash adjustments	●	○
Working capital adjustments:		
Trade and other receivables	○	
Inventories	○	
Trade and other payables	○	
Total working capital adjustments	●	○
Net cash flows generated from operations	●	●
Income taxes paid	●	●
Acquisition expenses paid	●	●
Net cash flows from operating activities	●	●
Investing activities		
Interest received	●	●
Proceeds from sale of property	●	●
Purchases of property	●	●
Purchase of intangible assets	●	●
Proceeds from sale of available-for-sale financial assets	●	●
Net cash flows from investing activities	●	●
Financing activities		
Proceeds from borrowings	●	●
Repayment of borrowings	●	●
Interest paid	●	●
Dividends paid	●	●
Net cash flows from financing activities	●	●
Net increase in cash and cash equivalents	●	●
Net foreign exchange difference	●	
Cash and cash equivalents at beginning of year	●	
Cash and cash equivalents at end of year	●	●

● Included same line item in annual and interim financial statements
○ This line item is condensed from the annual to the interim financial statements

Note that this entity did not condense its statement of changes in equity; therefore, it is not presented in this example.

3.3 Requirements for both complete and condensed interim financial information

The general principles for preparing annual financial statements are equally applicable to condensed interim financial statements. These principles include fair presentation, going concern, the accrual basis of accounting, materiality and aggregation, and offsetting. *[IAS 1.4, 15-35].* (see Chapter 3 at 4.1).

Furthermore, the following requirements apply irrespective of whether an entity provides complete or condensed financial statements for an interim period:

- if applicable, basic and diluted earnings per share should be presented on the face of the statement of comprehensive income for an interim period. *[IAS 34.11].* If the entity presents a separate income statement in its annual financial statements, it should present basic and diluted earnings per share on the face of that separate income statement in the interim financial report; *[IAS 34.11A]* and

- if the last annual financial statements were consolidated financial statements, the interim financial report should also be prepared on a consolidated basis. *[IAS 34.14].*

If the entity's last annual financial report included the parent's separate financial statements and consolidated financial statements, IAS 34 neither requires nor prohibits the inclusion of the parent's separate financial statements in the interim financial report. *[IAS 34.14].*

3.4 Management commentary

A management commentary is not explicitly required by IAS 34, but frequently included by entities in their interim financial reports along with the interim financial statements. In most cases the requirement for a narrative review comes from local stock market regulations and the entities should, therefore, follow the relevant guidance issued by those regulators.

4 DISCLOSURES IN CONDENSED FINANCIAL STATEMENTS

4.1 Significant events and transactions

IAS 34 presumes that users of an entity's interim financial report also have access to its most recent annual financial report. *[IAS 34.15A].* On that basis, an interim financial report should explain events and transactions that are significant to an understanding of the changes in financial position and performance of the entity since the previous annual reporting period and provide an update to the relevant information included in the financial statements of the previous year. *[IAS 34.15, 15C].* The inclusion of only selected explanatory notes is consistent with the purpose of an interim financial report, to update the latest complete set of annual financial statements. Accordingly, condensed financial statements avoid duplicating previously reported information and focus on new activities, events, and circumstances. *[IAS 34.6].*

The standard requires disclosure of following events and transactions in interim financial reports, if they are significant: *[IAS 34.15B]*

(a)   write-down of inventories to net realisable value and the reversal of such a write-down;

(b)   recognition of a loss from the impairment of financial assets, property, plant, and equipment, intangible assets, or other assets, and the reversal of such an impairment loss;

(c)   reversal of any provisions for the costs of restructuring;

(d)   acquisitions and disposals of items of property, plant, and equipment;

(e)   commitments for the purchase of property, plant, and equipment;

(f)   litigation settlements;

(g)   corrections of prior period errors;

(h)   changes in the business or economic circumstances that affect the fair value of the entity's financial assets and financial liabilities, whether those assets or liabilities are recognised at fair value or amortised cost;

(i)   any loan default or breach of a loan agreement that is not remedied on or before the end of the reporting period;

(j)   related party transactions;

(k)   transfers between levels of the fair value hierarchy used in measuring the fair value of financial instruments;

(l)   changes in the classification of financial assets as a result of a change in the purpose or use of those assets; and

(m)   changes in contingent liabilities or contingent assets.

The standard specifies that the above list of events and transactions is not exhaustive and the interim financial statements should explain any additional events and transactions that are significant to an understanding of changes in the entity's financial position and performance. *[IAS 34.15, 15B]*. Therefore, when information changes significantly, (for example, the values of assets and liabilities that are marked to market) an entity should disclose information regarding such change, in addition to the requirements listed above; the disclosure should be sufficiently detailed to explain the nature of the change and any changes in estimates. However, the notes to an interim financial report do not need to include insignificant updates to the information presented in the most recent annual report. *[IAS 34.15A]*.

Whilst other standards specify disclosures required in a complete set of financial statements, if an entity's interim financial report includes only condensed financial statements as described in IAS 34, then the disclosures required by those other standards are not mandatory. However, if disclosure is considered to be necessary in the context of an interim report, those other standards provide guidance on the appropriate disclosures for many of these items. *[IAS 34.15C]*.

Thus, there is some tension in determining what disclosures are required when a new accounting pronouncement is issued, and effective for the entity's next annual financial statements, but does not include specific disclosure requirements under

IAS 34. The new disclosures are not specifically required under IAS 34, but may be material to an understanding of the entity. Therefore, judgment is required to determine whether including the disclosures in the interim report will provide the most useful information to users of the financial statements (see 8.1 below).

4.2   Other disclosures

In addition to disclosing significant events and transactions as discussed at 4.1 above, IAS 34 requires an entity to include the following information, in the notes to its interim financial statements if not disclosed elsewhere in the interim financial report: *[IAS 34.16A]*

(a)   a statement that the same accounting policies and methods of computation are followed in the interim financial statements as in the most recent annual financial statements or, if those policies or methods have changed, a description of the nature and effect of the change;

(b)   explanatory comments about the seasonality or cyclicality of interim operations;

(c)   the nature and amount of items affecting assets, liabilities, equity, net income, or cash flows that are unusual because of their nature, size, or incidence;

(d)   the nature and amount of changes in estimates of amounts reported in prior interim periods of the current year or changes in estimates of amounts reported in prior years;

(e)   issues, repurchases, and repayments of debt and equity securities;

(f)   dividends paid (aggregate or per share) separately for ordinary shares and other shares;

(g)   certain segment disclosures required by IFRS 8 – *Operating Segments* – as discussed at 4.4 below;

(h)   events after the interim period that are not reflected in the financial statements for the interim period; and

(i)   the effect of changes in the composition of the entity during the interim period, including business combinations, obtaining or losing control of subsidiaries and long-term investments, restructurings, and discontinued operations. For business combinations, the entity should disclose the information required under IFRS 3 – *Business Combinations* (see Chapter 10 at 16).

IAS 34 defines an 'interim financial report' as 'a financial report containing either a complete set of financial statements... or a set of condensed financial statements... for an interim period.' *[IAS 34.4]*. Therefore, since an interim financial report *contains* the interim financial statements, it is clear that these are two different concepts. Accordingly, an entity is not required to disclose the above information in the interim financial statements themselves (but rather, might include the disclosures in the management commentary), as long as the information is included in the interim financial report.

This information is normally reported on a financial year-to-date basis (see 8 below). *[IAS 34.16A]*. However, the requirement in item (i) above for disclosures of business combinations applies not only for those effected during the current interim period, but also to business combinations after the reporting period but before the interim financial report is authorised for issue. *[IFRS 3.59]*. An entity is not required to provide all of the disclosures for business combinations after the reporting period, if the accounting for the business combination is incomplete as at the date on which the financial statements are authorised for issue. In this case, the entity should state which disclosures cannot be made and the reasons why they cannot be made. *[IFRS 3.B66]*.

For business combinations, the entity should disclose all the information required under IFRS 3 (see Chapter 10 at 16). IFRS 3 requires disclosures in aggregate for business combinations effected during the reporting period that are individually immaterial. *[IFRS 3.B65]*. However, materiality is assessed for the interim period, which implies that IFRS 3 may require more detailed disclosures on business combinations that are material to an interim period even if they could be aggregated for disclosure purposes in the annual financial statements.

If an entity has operations that are discontinued or disposed of during an interim period, these operations should be presented separately in the condensed interim statement of comprehensive income following the principles set out in IFRS 5. In addition if an entity has non-current assets or a disposal group classified as held for sale or distribution at the end of the interim reporting period, then these should be measured in accordance with the requirements of IFRS 5 – *Non-current Assets Held for Sale and Discontinued Operations* – and presented separately from other assets and liabilities in the condensed interim balance sheet.

In summary, the 'minimum' disclosures required in IAS 34 are extensive and more onerous than the previous minimum requirements of many securities markets and regulators. For example, the disclosures are significant for business combinations, segments, and the recognition and reversal of impairments of assets.

4.3   Illustrative examples

The following extracts show examples of disclosures required by IAS 34:

4.3.1   Inventory write-down and reversals

In the extract below, BP disclose write down of its inventories and reversals in current and corresponding periods. *[IAS 34.15B(a)]*.

Extract 39.2: BP p.l.c. (Group results; Second quarter and half year 2010)

Notes [extract]

9.   Inventory valuation [extract]

A provision of $46 million was held at 31 December 2009 to write inventories down to their net realizable value. The net movement in the provision during the second quarter 2010 was an increase of $350 million (first quarter 2010 was a decrease of $22 million and second quarter 2009 was an increase of $92 million). The net movement in the provision in the half year 2010 was an increase of $328 million, compared with a decrease of $1,071 million for the half year 2009.

4.3.2 Impairment

In Extract 39.3 below, Roche discloses the net impairment charge on its intangible assets during the reporting period and provides further breakdown by impairment losses and their reversal. *[IAS 34.15B(b)]*.

Extract 39.3: Roche Group (Half-Year Report, 2010)
Notes to the Roche Group Interim Consolidated Financial Statements [extract]
Note 10.   Intangible assets [extract]
Impairment of intangible assets [extract]

In the Pharmaceuticals operating segment a net impairment charge of 102 million Swiss francs was recorded. An impairment charge of 71 million Swiss francs was recorded, which relates to a decision to stop development of one compound with an alliance partner. The assets concerned, which were not yet being amortised, were fully written down by these charges. A further charge of 47 million Swiss francs was recorded, resulting from a portfolio prioritisation decision on a project acquired as part of a previous business combination. The asset concerned, which was not yet being amortised, was written down to its recoverable value of 95 million Swiss francs. A reversal of previously recorded impairment loss of 16 million Swiss francs was recorded, which follows from the latest clinical data assessment of the project concerned.

4.3.3 Reversal of restructuring provisions

Included in various items, in the below extract, that have impacted net operating income of Statoil, are reversals of restructuring costs. *[IAS 34.15B(c)]*.

Extract 39.4: Statoil (Financial statements and review – 4th quarter 2009)
FINANCIAL REVIEW [extract]
Fourth quarter [extract]

In the fourth quarter of 2009, impairment losses net of reversals (NOK 1.3 billion), other accruals (NOK 0.1 billion) and lower fair value of derivatives (NOK 0.2 billion), negatively impacted net operating income, while overlift (NOK 0.1 billion), higher values of products in operational storage (NOK 0.6 billion) and reversals of restructuring costs related to the NCS(NOK 0.3 billion) had a positive impact on net operating income. Adjusted for these items and the effects of eliminations (NOK 0.3 billion), adjusted earnings were 34.4 billion in the fourth quarter of 2009.

In the fourth quarter of 2008, lower fair value of derivatives (NOK 2.1 billion), impairment charges net of reversals (NOK 1.3 billion), underlift (NOK 1.3 billion), lower values of products in operational storage (NOK 3.6 billion), loss on sale of assets (NOK 0.8 billion) and other accruals (NOK 0.3 billion) all had a negative impact on net operating income. Reversal of restructuring cost accrual (NOK 1.6 billion) had a positive impact on net operating income for the fourth quarter of 2008. Adjusted for these items and the effects of eliminations (NOK 2.2 billion), adjusted earnings were NOK 43.4 billion in the fourth quarter 2008.

4.3.4 Acquisition and disposal of property, plant and equipment

In Extract 39.5 below, Wilmington provides a detailed movement schedule for some of its significant assets. The schedule discloses additions and disposals of items of property, plant and equipment in the interim period. *[IAS 34.15B(d)]*. In addition, Wilmington provides information about movements in the prior interim period and the second half of the comparative financial year, to reconcile to the value shown on the comparative balance sheet.

Chapter 39

Extract 39.5: Wilmington (Interim Report for the six months ended 31 December 2009)

Notes to the Accounts [extract]

12.   Property, plant and equipment, intangible assets and goodwill

	Property, plant and equipment £'000	Intangible assets £'000	Goodwill £'000
Opening net book amount at 1 July 2008	8,263	34,818	67,969
Additions	760	206	–
Acquisitions and sales	(63)	(1,506)	262
Disposals	(92)	–	(103)
Exchange translation differences	7	–	–
Depreciation and amortisation	(902)	(2,595)	–
Movement in offset of provision for future acquisition of minority interests	–	–	43
Closing net book amount at 31 December 2008 (as restated)	7,973	30,923	68,171
Additions	276	352	–
Acquisitions and sales	–	–	(426)
Disposals	(128)	4	–
Exchange translation differences	20	–	–
Depreciation and amortisation	(362)	(2,567)	–
Impairment	–	–	(2,750)
Change in provisions for the future purchase of minority interests	–	–	(2,756)
Movement in offset of provisions for future acquisition of minority interests	–	–	162
Closing net book amount at 30 June 2009	7,779	28,712	62,401
Additions	335	165	–
Acquisitions and sales	–	–	46
Disposals	(1)	(12)	–
Exchange translation differences	103	–	–
Depreciation and amortisation	(797)	(2,458)	–
Movement in offset of provisions for future acquisition of minority interests	–	–	240
Closing net book amount at 31 December 2009	7,419	26,407	62,687

4.3.5   *Capital commitments*

In a brief descriptive note, TESCO discloses its commitments for capital expenditure.
[IAS 34.15B(e)].

Extract 39.6: TESCO PLC (INTERIM RESULTS 2009/10)

Notes to the interim financial information [extract]

NOTE 6   Capital expenditure [extract]

Commitments for capital expenditure contracted for, but not provided, at 29 August 2009 were £1,440m (last interim period – £1,905m).

4.3.6 Litigation settlements

UBS provides chronological details about significant litigations and related settlements in the below extract. *[IAS 34.15B(f)].*

Extract 39.7: UBS AG (Q3, 2008)

Notes to the Financial Statements [extract]
Note 15. **Litigation** [extract]
e) Auction Rate Securities:

UBS was sued by three state regulatory authorities and was the subject of investigations by the US Securities and Exchange Commission ("SEC") and other regulators, including a number of state regulators and the US Attorney for the District of New Hampshire, relating to the marketing and sale of Auction Rate Securities ("ARS") to clients and to UBS's role and participation in ARS auctions. UBS also has been named in several putative class actions and individual civil suits and a large number of individual arbitrations. The regulatory actions and investigations and the class actions followed the disruption in the markets for these securities and related auction failures since mid-February 2008. Plaintiffs and the regulators are generally seeking rescission, i.e. for UBS to purchase their ARS at par value, as well as compensatory damages, disgorgement of profits and in some cases penalties.

In May 2008, UBS entered into a settlement with the Massachusetts Attorney General in which UBS agreed to buy back USD 36 million in auction rate securities that had been sold to general purpose municipal accounts but were impermissible for those accounts. On 8 August 2008, UBS entered into settlements in principle with the SEC, the New York Attorney General ("NYAG") and other state agencies represented by the North American Securities Administrators Association ("NASAA"), including the Massachusetts Securities Division ("MSD"), whereby UBS agreed to offer to buy back ARS from eligible customers within certain time frames, and to pay penalties of USD 150 million (USD 75 million to the NYAG, USD 75 million to the other states).

On 2 October 2008, UBS finalized its settlement with the Massachusetts Securities Division, and is continuing to finalize agreements with the other regulators. UBS's offer to purchase back ARS was done by a registered securities offering effective 7 October 2008. UBS's settlement is largely in line with similar industry regulatory settlements; however, UBS is the only firm of its major competitors that offered to purchase ARS from institutional clients before a date certain. UBS's settlement with the SEC and MSD require UBS to offer to buy eligible ARS from eligible institutional clients by no later than 30 June 2010. Settlements with the other NASAA states will likely follow the same format. The NYAG term sheet (not yet finalized) does not reference a date certain, but contains language similar to other industry settlements requiring that UBS make 'best efforts' to provide liquidity solutions for institutional investors.

The NYAG and SEC continue to investigate individuals affiliated with UBS who traded in ARS or who had responsibility for disclosures. On 7 October 2008, the NYAG announced a settlement with former Investment Bank Global General Counsel relating to his trading of ARS allegedly in violation of New York's Martin Act. The former Investment Bank Global General Counsel neither admitted nor denied the state's allegations, but agreed to certain penalties and sanctions.

4.3.7 Correction of prior period errors

In Extract 39.8 below, UBS provides disclosures around restatement of prior period financial statements due to errors, which they believe are material to the first quarter interim financial statements of 2009 (albeit immaterial to prior period financial statements). *[IAS 34.15B(g)].*

Chapter 39

Extract 39.8: UBS AG (Q1, 2009)

Notes to the Financial Statements [extract]
Note 1.   Basis of accounting [extract]
Restatements made to the financial statements 2008 [extract]

UBS has restated its 2008 financial statements to correct identified accounting errors related to the 2008 financial statements, predominately to the fourth quarter 2008 financial statements. These errors are not material to the annual or quarterly 2008 financial statements, but related corrections would have been material to first quarter 2009 financial statements. The restatement comprises three items in excess of CHF 100 million as follows:

– The fair value of auction rate securities purchase commitments at 31 December 2008, which are recognized as negative replacement values on UBS's balance sheet, was increased by CHF 112 million, resulting in a corresponding charge to net trading income.

– For certain assets reclassified from "held-for-trading" to "loans and receivables" in fourth quarter 2008, recognition of interest income based on the effective interest rate method was reduced by CHF 180 million. Other assets were reduced accordingly as of 31 December 2008.

– The partial disposals of an investment in a consolidated investment fund in 2008 gave rise to the realization of the related foreign currency translation loss deferred in shareholders' equity. This adjustment reduced other income for the year 2008 by CHF 192 million but did not have a net impact on UBS's equity.

In addition to the above mentioned items, a number of misstatements individually below CHF 65 million were adjusted. The aggregate net effect of these items on net profit attributable to UBS shareholders was an increase of net profit attributable to shareholders of CHF 79 million. The total net impact of all restated items on the 2008 results was a reduction of net profit and net profit attributable to UBS shareholders of CHF 405 million, a reduction of equity and equity attributable to UBS shareholders of CHF 269 million, and a reduction of basic and diluted earnings per share by CHF 0.15 and CHF 0.14 respectively. There was no effect on income tax expense. Periods prior to 2008 were not affected by the restatement. 2008 quarterly net profits attributable to UBS shareholders were reduced by the following amounts: CHF 82 million in Q1, CHF 37 million in Q2, CHF 13 million in Q3, and CHF 273 million in Q4.

4.3.8   Changes in circumstances affecting fair values

In their half yearly interim report for 2010, HSBC provides a brief update on the market turmoil and then describes its impact, quantifying financial effect, on fair value of their financial instruments. *[IAS 34.15B(h)]*.

Extract 39.9: HSBC Holdings plc (Interim Report 2010)

Interim Management Report: Impact of Market Turmoil [extract]
Background and disclosure policy [extract]

Following the market turmoil which began in 2007, there was a modest recovery in the risk appetite of investors in 2009. The first quarter of 2010 saw renewed uncertainty regarding the future growth prospects of the global economy, however, and concerns over sovereign credit risk that began in Greece and extended to other obligors, particularly in Southern Europe. As a result, the second quarter of 2010 saw significant falls in the prices of many assets perceived to be of higher risk, although some stability was regained with the announcement of a package of measures by the EU and the International Monetary Fund.

Widespread downgrading of securitised assets continued in the first half of 2010 as rating agencies changed their rating methodologies in response to the new circumstances. Although these downgrades were largely expected and did not affect management's loss estimates, for those institutions subject to the Basel II framework, which ties capital requirements to external credit ratings, the appetite for securitised assets remained limited regardless of the actual level of expected loss on the securities...

...Financial instruments which were most affected by the market turmoil include exposures to direct lending which are held at fair value through profit or loss, or are classified as available for sale and are also held at fair value. Financial instruments included in these categories comprise asset-backed securities ('ABS's), including mortgage-backed securities ('MBS's) and collateralised debt obligations ('CDO's), exposures to and contingent claims on monoline insurers ('monolines') in respect of structured credit activities and leveraged finance transactions originated for distribution...

Financial effect of market turmoil

The write-downs incurred by the Group for the last three half-year periods on ABSs, trading loans held for securitisation, leveraged finance transactions and the movement in fair values on available-for-sale ABSs taken to equity, plus impairment losses on specific exposures to banks, are summarised in the following table. Virtually all of these effects were recorded in Global Banking and Markets. Further analyses of the write-downs taken to the income statement by Global Banking and Markets and the net carrying amounts of the positions that generated these write-downs are shown in the succeeding table:

Financial effect of market turmoil on HSBC

	Half-year to		
	30 June 2010	30 June 2009	31 December 2009
	US$bn	US$bn	US$bn
(Write-downs)/write-backs taken to income statement	0.1	(1.3)	(0.6)
Net movement on available-for-sale reserve on ABSs in the period	4.1	1.2	5.3
Closing balance of available-for-sale reserve relating to ABSs	(8.1)	(17.5)	(12.2)

Global Banking and Markets write-downs/(write-backs) taken to the income statement and carrying amounts

	Write-downs/(write-backs) during half-year to			Carrying amount at		
	30 June 2010	30 June 2009	31 December 2009	30 June 2010	30 June 2009	31 December 2009
	US$m	US$m	US$m	US$m	US$m	US$m
Sub-prime mortgage-related assets						
– loan securitisation	(49)	156	80	478	943	758
– credit trading	(32)	83	17	146	303	282
Other ABSs	(125)	103	(196)	959	1,376	990
Impairments on reclassified assets	(25)	160	3	11,774	16,308	15,612
Derivative exposure to monoclines						
– investment grade counterparts	(6)	25	(78)	828	1,593	897
– Non-investment grade counterparts	(117)	241	45	276	510	408
Leveraged finance loans[4]	(30)	(11)	(120)	154	285	196
Other credit related items	(3)	5	(19)	25	116	61
Available-for-sale impairments and other non-trading related items	256	564	833			
	(131)	1,326	565			

[4] The carrying amount includes funded loans plus the net exposure to unfunded leveraged finance commitments, held within fair value through profit or loss.

4.3.9 Default or breach of loan covenants not remedied before the end of interim period

In Extract 39.10 below, Develica discusses breaches of certain loan covenants. *[IAS 34.15B(i)]*. In view of such defaults that have not been remedied by the end of the reporting period, Develica goes on to explain why the interim financial statements have been prepared on a going concern basis.

Extract 39.10: Develica Deutschland Limited (Interim Report 2009)

Notes to the Consolidated Financial Statements for the period 1 April 2009 to 30 September 2009 [extract]

2   Basis of preparation [extract]

(c)   Fundamental accounting concept [extract]

The current economic climate has resulted in a global trend of declining property values, which results in the Group being exposed to increased risks against covenant breaches set out in the Group's debt facilities.

The 30 September 2009 portfolio valuation indicates that the Loan-to-Value ("LTV") ratio of the loans classified as current liabilities in the consolidated balance sheet would, if tested by the debt providers as set out in the facilities agreement, exceed their respective LTV covenants.

Loan interest and amortisation continues to be well serviced through strong rental income. Due to tenant related difficulties, there is one loan facility of €51.5m in which the Interest Cover Ratio ("ICR") covenant is not being met. The Group is currently in ongoing discussions with the relevant debt provider to remedy the breach. ICR covenants continue to be met on the remaining facilities.

Excluding the amended Citibank International PLC ("Citi") facilities, the Group's borrowing arrangements include covenants that require maintenance of LTV ratios ranging between 85% and 95% with a weighted average of 90.9%.

As reported in the Annual Report, the Group has been notified of two LTV breaches during the six month period relating to €116.1m of the Group's loan facilities. In each case, the lender has requested a valuation entitled under the rights of the respective loan facility agreements. The Group continues to have positive discussions with the lender to seek to remedy these breaches. No further notifications of breach have been served on the Company by its other lenders although we continue in discussion with these lenders regarding the remaining loan facilities.

The strong cash flow generated from a diverse range of quality tenants enables the Group to service these financing obligations. The Group has entered into hedging instruments across the entire portfolio which fix the ongoing interest obligations and also reduce the ongoing debt exposure.

In all cases where an actual or potential breach of any loan has/could arise, the Company has engaged in discussions with the Company's debt providers to work together in reaching a satisfactory conclusion for all parties. The Company has already reached a successful agreement on amending five facilities through Citi and the Directors are hopeful that, through maintaining close links and dialogue with the remaining debt providers, it will be able to implement similar arrangements across the entire portfolio. In the event that a breach occurs resulting in an event of default, and the Group is unable to reach a resolution with the relevant debt provider, then the only recourse available to the debt provider are the assets secured against the given loan at the subsidiary level and not the Group's assets.

As the debt facilities and related interest swaps are ring-fenced and the Company has sufficient cash and other resources, the Directors do not consider that the risk of breaching LTV covenants will impact the ability of the Group to continue to trade as a going concern. Accordingly the financial statements have been prepared on a going concern basis.

4.3.10 Related party transactions

In Extract 39.11 below, Deutsche Bank discloses related party transactions. *[IAS 34.15B(j)]*.

Extract 39.11: Deutsche Bank AG (Interim Report as of June 30, 2010)

Notes to the Consolidated Financial Statements [extract]
Other Financial Information (unaudited) [extract]
Related Party Transactions [extract]

Transactions with related parties are made in the ordinary course of business and on substantially the same terms, including interest rates and collateral, as those prevailing for comparable transactions with other parties.

Transactions with Key Management Personnel

Key management personnel are those persons having authority and responsibility for planning, directing and controlling the activities of Deutsche Bank Group, directly or indirectly. The Group considers the members of the Management Board as currently mandated and the Supervisory Board to constitute key management personnel for purposes of IAS 24. Among the Group's transactions with key management personnel as of June 30, 2010 were loans and commitments of €9 million and deposits of €19 million. As of December 31, 2009, there were loans and commitments of €9 million and deposits of €21 million among the Group's transactions with key management personnel. In addition, the Group provides banking services, such as payment and account services as well as investment advice, to key management personnel and their close family members.

Transactions with Subsidiaries, Joint Ventures and Associates

Transactions between Deutsche Bank AG and its subsidiaries meet the definition of related party transactions. If these transactions are eliminated on consolidation, they are not disclosed as related party transactions. Transactions between the Group and its associated companies and joint ventures also qualify as related party transactions and are disclosed as follows.

Loans

In the six months ended June 30, 2010 and in the year 2009 loans issued and guarantees granted to related parties developed as follows.

in € m.	Associated companies and other related parties	
	Jun 30, 2010	**Dec 31, 2009**
Loans outstanding, beginning of period	965	834
Loans issued during the period	17	366
Loan repayments during the period	100	209
Changes in the group of consolidated companies[1]	(179)	(83)
Exchange rate changes/other	(13)	57
Loans outstanding, end of period[2]	690	965
Other credit risk related transactions:		
Allowance for loan losses	31	4
Provision for loan losses	29	31
Guarantees and commitments[3]	409	135

1 In 2010, some entities were fully consolidated. Therefore, loans issued to these investments were eliminated on consolidation. In 2009, one entity with related party loans, that was accounted for using the equity method, was sold.
2 Loans past due were nil as of June 30, 2010, and totalled €15 million as of December 31, 2009. Loans included loans to joint ventures of €4 million both as of June 30, 2010 and December 31, 2009.
3 Includes financial and performance guarantees, standby letters of credit, indemnity agreements and irrevocable lending-related commitments.

Chapter 39

Deposits

In the six months ended June 30, 2010 and in the year 2009 deposits received from related parties developed as follows.

in € m.	Associated companies and other related parties	
	Jun 30, 2010	**Dec 31, 2009**
Deposits, beginning of period	**367**	**246**
Deposits received during the period	61	287
Deposits repaid during the period	99	161
Changes in the group of consolidated companies[1]	(147)	(6)
Exchange rate changes/other	3	1
Deposits, end of period[2]	**185**	**367**

1 In 2010, some entities were fully consolidated. Therefore, deposits received from these investments were eliminated on consolidation. In 2009, one entity with related party deposits, that was accounted for using the equity method, was sold.

2 The above deposits were made in the ordinary course of business. Deposits included also €0.5 million and €0.4 million deposits from joint ventures as of June 30, 2010 and December 31, 2009, respectively.

As of June 30, 2010, positive and negative market values from derivative financial transactions with associated companies amounted to €5.3 billion and €4.6 billion, respectively. As of December 31, 2009, positive and negative market values of above mentioned transactions amounted to €3.7 billion and €3.0 billion, respectively.

Business Relationships with Deutsche Postbank AG

In 2009, the Group acquired an interest in Deutsche Postbank AG and entered into a cooperation agreement with Deutsche Postbank AG. The cooperation agreement encompasses financing and investment products, business banking and commercial loans as well as customer-oriented services. The agreement also covers sourcing and IT-infrastructure.

Transactions with Pension Plans

The Group has business relationships with a number of its pension plans pursuant to which it provides financial services to these plans, including investment management. Pension funds may hold or trade Deutsche Bank AG shares or securities. As of June 30, 2010, transactions with these plans were not material for the Group.

4.3.11 Transfers between different levels of fair value hierarchy

Detailed reconciliation is provided by HSBC in the below extract relating to fair value measurements in level 3 of the fair value hierarchy. The reconciliation, among other items, includes transfer of items in and out of level 3. *[IAS 34.15B(k)]*. The disclosure indicates that there are no significant transfers between levels 1 and 2 during the reporting period.

Extract 39.12: HSBC Holdings plc (Interim Report 2010)

Interim Management Report: Impact of Market Turmoil [extract]

Reconciliation of fair value measurements in level 3 of the fair value hierarchy [extract]

The following table provides a reconciliation of the movement between opening and closing balances of level 3 financial instruments, measured at fair value using a valuation technique with significant unobservable inputs:

Movement in level 3 financial instruments

	Assets				Liabilities		
	Available for sale US$m	Held for trading US$m	Designated at fair value through profit or loss US$m	Derivatives US$m	Held for trading US$m	Designated at fair value through profit or loss US$m	Derivatives US$m
At 1 January 2010	10,214	6,420	1,224	4,453	8,774	507	5,192
Total gains or losses recognised in profit or loss	112	131	41	199	(245)	(8)	(431)
Total gains or losses recognised in other comprehensive income	198	(181)	(36)	(133)	(325)	(23)	(24)
Purchases	1,428	419	36	–	–	–	–
Issues	–	–	–	–	1,730	–	–
Sales	(960)	(1,044)	(28)	–	–	–	–
Settlements	(173)	18	(6)	(92)	(823)	–	(407)
Transfers out	(4,731)	(339)	(304)	(442)	(1,165)	–	(423)
Transfers in	1,863	218	122	745	494	–	369
At 30 June 2010	**7,951**	**5,642**	**1,049**	**4,730**	**8,440**	**476**	**4,276**
Total gains or losses recognised in profit or loss relating to those assets and liabilities held at the end of the reporting period	70	74	42	720	(246)	(8)	105

...For available-for-sale securities, the greater pricing certainty associated with certain ABSs (particularly related to commercial property and leveraged finance) resulted in assets being transferred out of level 3 during the first half of 2010...

...For derivative assets, transfers into level 3 were driven by certain types of tranched CDS transaction.

For held-for-trading liabilities, issues reflect new structured note issuance, settlements reflect structured note redemptions/maturities and transfers out of level 3 reflect increased observability as the residual maturity of existing notes falls, and also some additional market observability for certain longer-dated equity volatilities...

...During the first half of 2010, there were no significant transfers between levels 1 and 2...

Chapter 39

4.3.12 Changes in classification of financial assets arising from changes in use

Deutsche Bank discloses changes in classification of certain financial assets due to a change in purpose or use, in below extract. *[IAS 34.15B(l)].*

Extract 39.13: Deutsche Bank AG (Interim Report as of June 30, 2009)

Notes to the Consolidated Financial Statements [extract]
Information on the Balance Sheet (unaudited) [extract]
Amendments to IAS 39 and IFRS 7, "Reclassification of Financial Assets" [extract]

During the second half of 2008 and the first quarter of 2009 the Group reclassified certain trading assets and financial assets available for sale to loans and receivables. No reclassifications were made during the second quarter of 2009.

The Group identified assets, eligible under the amendments, for which at the reclassification date it had a clear change of intent and ability to hold for the foreseeable future rather than to exit or trade in the short term. The reclassifications were made at the fair value of the assets at the reclassification date. The disclosures below detail the impact of the reclassifications to the Group.

The following table shows the carrying values and fair values of assets reclassified in 2008 and 2009.

in €m.	Carrying value at reclassification date	June 30, 2009 Carrying value	June 30, 2009 Fair value
Assets reclassified in 2008:			
Trading assets reclassified to loans	23,633	22,501	18,914
Financial assets available for sale reclassified to loans	11,354	10,335	8,245
Total financial assets reclassified to loans[1]	**34,987**	**32,836**	**27,159**
Assets reclassified in 2009:			
Trading assets reclassified to loans	2,961	3,001	2,724
Trading assets reclassified to loans	**2,961**	**3,001**	**2,724**

[1] The decline of the carrying value since reclassification was mainly attributable to repayments, credit loss provisions and foreign exchange movements.

4.3.13 Contingent liabilities

In the Extract below, Skanska discloses changes in its contingent liabilities during the interim period. *[IAS 34.15B(m)]*

Extract 39.14: Skanska (Half-Year Report, 2009)

Skanska Six Month Report, January – June 2009 [extract]
Note, Contingent liabilities [extract]

Contingent liabilities amounted to SEK 14.9 bn on June 30, 2009 (Dec 31, 2008: 7.6). During the period contingent liabilities increased by SEK 7.3 bn. The increase refers mainly to the participation in the consortium for the widening of the M25 orbital road around London.

4.3.14 Accounting policies and methods of computation

In the Extract below, Roche explains how the accounting polices used in the interim report compare to the most recent annual financial statements, and discloses changes in the current period. *[IAS 34.16A(a)]*.

Extract 39.15: Roche Holding Ltd (Half-Year Report 2008)

Notes to the Roche Group Interim Consolidated Financial Statements [extract]

1.   Accounting policies [extract]

Basis of preparation of financial statements [extract]

The Interim Financial Statements have been prepared in accordance with the accounting policies set out in the Annual Financial Statements, except for accounting policy changes made after the date of the Annual Financial Statements. The presentation of the Interim Financial Statements is consistent with the Annual Financial Statements, except where noted below. Where necessary, comparative information has been reclassified or expanded from the previously reported Interim Financial Statements to take into account any presentational changes made in the Annual Financial Statements or in these Interim Financial Statements.

Changes in accounting policies [extract]

In 2007 the Group early adopted IFRS 8 'Operating Segments' and IAS 23 (revised) 'Borrowing Costs' which are required to be implemented from 1 January 2009 at the latest. In 2008 the Group has early adopted the revised versions of IFRS 3 'Business Combinations' and IAS 27 'Consolidated and Separate Financial Statements' that were published in early 2008 and which are required to be implemented from 1 January 2010 at the latest. The Group has also adopted IFRIC interpretation 14 which relates to IAS 19 'Employee benefits'. The Group is currently assessing the potential impacts of the other new and revised standards that will be effective from 1 January 2009, notably the revisions to IFRS 2 'Share-based Payment'.

IFRS 3 (revised): 'Business combinations'. Amongst other matters, the revised standard requires that directly attributable transaction costs are expensed in the current period, rather than being included in the cost of acquisition as previously. The revised standard also requires that contingent consideration arrangements should be included in acquisition accounting at fair value and expands the disclosure requirements for business combinations. The Group has applied the revised standard prospectively for all business combinations since 1 January 2008 and transaction costs totalling 42 million Swiss francs have been expensed in 2008 that would have been included in the cost of acquisition under the previous accounting policy. Business combinations in 2007 and prior periods have not been restated. Had the new accounting policy been applied in 2007, the Group would have expensed an additional 5 million Swiss francs of transaction costs in the interim period of 2007 (15 million Swiss francs in the full year 2007) and goodwill would have been reduced by these amounts in the respective periods. This change has a negative impact of 0.05 Swiss francs on earnings per share and non-voting equity security (basic and diluted) in 2008, and would have had a negative impact of 0.01 Swiss francs in the interim period of 2007 (0.02 Swiss francs in the full year 2007) if the revised standard had been applied retrospectively.

IAS 27 (revised): 'Consolidated and separate financial statements'. Amongst other matters, the revised standard requires that changes in ownership interests in subsidiaries are accounted for as equity transactions if they occur after control has already been obtained and if they do not result in a loss of control. Additionally the revised standard renames 'minority interests' as 'non-controlling interests'. The Group has applied the revised standard retrospectively. There were no transactions in 2007 that required restatement.

IFRIC interpretation 14 to IAS 19: 'Employee benefits'. The interpretation adds to the existing requirements of IAS 19 regarding the interaction between the limits on recognition of assets from defined benefit postemployment plans and any minimum funding requirement of such plans. Some of the Group's plans do have a minimum funding requirement and the application of this interpretation results in an increase in the assets recorded on the Group's balance sheet and a corresponding increase in the Group's equity. The Group has applied the revised standard retrospectively and the impacts on the previously published balance sheet and statement of recognised income and expense are shown in the tables below. The application of the interpretation has no impact on net income and earnings per share.

Chapter 39

Restated balance sheet (selected items) at 31 December 2007 *in millions of CHF*

	As originally published	Application of IFRIC 14	Group restated
Post-employment benefit assets	1,150	182	1,332
Deferred tax liabilities	(1,481)	(46)	(1,527)
		136	
Capital and reserves attributable to Roche shareholders	45,347	136	45,483

Restated statement of recognised income and expense for the six months ended 30 June 2007 *in millions of CHF*

	As originally published	Application of IFRIC 14	Group restated
Available-for-sale investments			
– Valuation gains (losses) taken to equity	23	–	23
– Transferred to income statement on sale or impairment	(111)	–	(111)
Cash flow hedges			
– Gains (losses) taken to equity	8	–	8
– Transferred to income statement	–	–	–
– Transferred to the initial balance sheet carrying value of hedged items	–	–	–
Exchange differences on translation of foreign operations	537	–	537
Defined benefit post-employment plans			
– Actuarial gains (losses)	777	–	777
– Limit on asset recognition	(450)	202	(248)
Income taxes on items taken directly to or transferred from equity	(118)	(50)	(168)
Net income recognised directly in equity	666	152	818
Net income recognised in the income statement	5,862		5,862
Total recognised income and expense	6,528	152	6,528

Presentation of operating results in the income statement: The income statement for the six months ended 30 June 2007 has been restated following the presentational changes adopted in the second half of 2007. The Group has made these presentational changes to more accurately reflect the underlying business, to further improve comparability of its results to those of other healthcare companies and to allow readers to make a more accurate assessment of the sustainable earnings capacity of the Group. Total operating profit is unchanged, and the presentational changes have no effect on the non-operating results, net income and earnings per share. These changes, which have been applied retrospectively, are listed below.

- Intangible assets: Amortisation and impairment of intangible assets are no longer reported as a separate line, but are now reported as part of 'Cost of sales' (for intangibles relating to marketed products) or as part of 'Research and Development' (for intangibles relating to technology and development, and including any impairment on intangibles that are not yet available for use).
- Alliance and royalty expenses: All royalties, alliance and collaboration expenses, including all collaboration profit-sharing arrangements are now reported as part of 'Cost of sales'. Previously some of these were included in 'Marketing and distribution' or 'General and administration' depending upon the terms of the particular agreement. Additionally, royalty expenses payable on royalty income are now reported as part of 'Royalties and other operating' income to more accurately reflect the substance of the underlying transactions. Previously these expenses were included in 'General and administration'.
- Phase IV and similar costs: All such costs, which only arise in the Pharmaceuticals Division, are now reported as part of 'Research and development'. Previously some of these costs were included in 'Marketing and distribution' and 'General and administration' depending on their nature.

Restated income statement for the six months ended 30 June 2007 *in millions of CHF* [extract]

	As originally published	Intangible assets	Alliances/ royalties	Phase IV	Restated
Group					
Sales	22,82	–	–	–	22,827
Royalties and other operating income	1,191	–	(33)	–	1,158
Cost of sales	(5,629)	(456)	(735)	–	(6,820)
Marketing and distribution	(5,552)	–	650	343	(4,559)
Research and development	(3,635)	(32)	–	(350)	(4,017)
General and administration	(1,237)	–	118	7	(1,112)
Amortisation and impairment of intangible assets	(488)	488	–	–	–
Operating profit	7,477	–	–	–	7,477

4.3.15 Seasonality or cyclicality of operations

Extract 39.16 below shows how Lancashire Insurance Holdings discloses the effects of seasonality in its interim report. *[IAS 34.16A(b)].*

Extract 39.16: Lancashire Insurance Holdings (six months ended, 30 June 2009)

Risks and other disclosures [extract]

Seasonality of interim operations [extract]

The Group underwrites worldwide short-tail insurance and reinsurance property risks, including risks exposed to both natural and man-made catastrophes. The Group's exposure in connection with insurance contracts is, in the event of insured losses, whether premium will be sufficient to cover the loss payments and expenses. Insurance and reinsurance markets are cyclical and premium rates and terms and conditions vary by line of business depending on market conditions and the stage of the cycle. Market conditions are impacted by capacity and recent loss events, among other factors. Some of the Group's natural catastrophe portfolio is subject to potential seasonal variation.

A proportion of the Group's business is exposed to large catastrophe losses in North America and Japan as a result of windstorms. The level of windstorm activity, and landfall thereof, during the North American and Japanese wind seasons may materially impact the Group's loss experience. The North American and Japanese wind seasons are typically June to November. The Group also bears exposure to large losses arising from other non-seasonal natural catastrophes, such as earthquakes, from risk losses throughout the year and from war, terrorism and political risk. Given seasonality, the risk of a very large windstorm is higher in the second half of the fiscal year than the first half.

4.3.16 Amounts that are unusual because of their nature, size or incidence

Tomkins discloses the nature and effects of unusual items in Extract 39.17 below by identifying 'restructuring costs' and a 'gain on disposals and on the exit of businesses' not identified as discontinued operations. *[IAS 34.16A(c)].*

Extract 39.17: Tomkins plc (six months ended 28 June 2008)

CONSOLIDATED INCOME STATEMENT UNAUDITED [extract]

	6 months ended 28 June 2008 US$ million	6 months ended 30 June 2007 US$ million	Year ended 29 December 2007 US$ million
Continuing operations			
Sales	**2,927.0**	2,967.9	5,886.1
Cost of sales	**(2,118.4)**	(2,159.1)	(4,284.6)
Gross profit	**808.6**	808.8	1,601.5
Distribution costs	**(313.2)**	(290.3)	(578.4)
Administrative expenses	**(432.1)**	(255.2)	(501.4)
Restructuring costs	**(17.0)**	(3.2)	(27.6)
Gain on disposals and on the exit of businesses	**42.4**	64.3	91.4
Restructuring initiatives	**25.4**	61.1	63.8
Share of profit of associates	**0.5**	0.6	0.8
Operating profit	**89.2**	325.0	586.3

NOTES TO THE CONDENSED FINANCIAL STATEMENTS (UNAUDITED) [extract]

4.   RESTRUCTURING INITIATIVES [extract]

Restructuring costs recognised during the six months ended 28 June 2008 principally related to the rationalisation of production facilities in the Building Products businesses in the United States, the closure of Power Transmission's facility at Moncks Corner, South Carolina and the outsourcing of information technology services.

During the six months ended 28 June 2008, the Group recognised a gain of US$42.4 million on the disposal of Stant Manufacturing, Inc. and Standard-Thomson Corporation.

4.3.17 Changes in estimates

In the Extract below, Telekom Austria Group discloses the nature and amounts of changes in estimates of amounts that resulted in a material effect on the current interim period. *[IAS 34.16A(d)].*

Extract 39.18: Telekom Austria Group (Q1, 2009)

Selected Explanatory Notes to the Consolidated Interim Financial Statement (unaudited) [extract]
Segment Reporting [extract]

In 2009, the Company reduced estimated useful lives of certain technical and office equipment due to the rapid development of technological environment in the relevant areas. The change in estimate resulted in an increase of depreciation by EUR 0.9 million in the Mobile Communication segment.

4.3.18 Issues, repurchases and repayments of debt and equity securities

Extract 39.19 below illustrates the disclosure of material changes in borrowings. *[IAS 34.16A(e)].*

Extract 39.19: Electrolux (Q2, 2009)

Interim report January – June 2009 [extract]
Financial Position [extract]
Net borrowings [extract]

Net borrowings amounted to SEK 2,197m (5,217). The net debt/equity ratio was 0.13 (0.36). The equity/assets ratio was 27.1% (23.8).

During the first half of 2009, SEK 1,632 of new long-term borrowings were raised. Long-term borrowings as of June 30, 2009, excluding long-term borrowings with maturities within 12 months, amounted to SEK 10,702m with average maturities of 4.3 years, compared to SEK 9,963m and 4.7 years by the end of 2008.

During 2009 and 2010, long-term borrowings in the amount of approximately SEK 1,500m will mature. Liquid funds as of June 30, 2009, excluding a committed unused revolving credit facility of EUR 500m, amounted to SEK 12,886m.

4.3.19 Dividends paid for each class of share

In the Extract below, Roche discloses dividends paid during the interim period. *[IAS 34.16A(f)].* In many cases this information may be evident from the disclosure of these amounts in the statement of cash flows.

Extract 39.20: Roche Group Limited (Half-year Report, 2010)

Notes to the Roche Group Interim Consolidated Financial Statements [extract]
Note 13   Equity [extract]
Dividends

On 2 March 2010 the shareholders approved the distribution of a dividend of 6.00 Swiss francs per share and non-voting equity security (2009: 5.00 Swiss francs) in respect of the 2009 business year. The distribution to holders of outstanding shares and non-voting equity securities totalled 5,144 million Swiss francs (2009: 4,300 million Swiss francs) and has been recorded against retained earnings in 2010.

4.3.20 Events after the interim reporting date

Vodafone Group PLC determined in Extract 39.21 below that an additional investment in an associate made after the interim period is a material event requiring disclosure. *[IAS 34.16A(h)].*

Extract 39.21: Vodafone Group PLC (Half-Year Report, 2008)

Notes to the Condensed Consolidated Financial Statements [extract]
11   Other matters [extract]
Events after the balance sheet date [extract]

On 29 October 2008, the Group announced it had agreed to acquire an additional 4.8% stake in Polkomtel S.A. for cash consideration of €176 million (£141 million) plus accrued interest at closing. The acquisition will increase Vodafone's stake in Polkomtel from 19.6% to 24.4% and is expected to close in the fourth quarter of the 2008 calendar year.

Chapter 39

Although not a requirement under IAS 34, it is useful to disclose the date on which the interim financial statements are authorised for issue as it would help the users to better understand the context of any disclosure of events after the interim reporting date.

4.3.21 Changes in the composition of the entity

In the Extract below, BMW discloses changes in the composition of its group during the interim period. *[IAS 34.16A(i)]*.

Extract 39.22: BMW AG (Q2, 2008)

Notes to the Interim Group Financial Statements to 30 June 2008 [extract]

Accounting Principles and Policies [extract]

[2] Consolidated companies

The BMW Group financial statements for the second quarter 2008 include, besides BMW AG, 45 German and 158 foreign subsidiaries. This also includes 17 special purpose securities funds and 24 special purpose trusts, almost all of which are used for asset-backed financing.

SimeLease (Malaysia) Sdn Bhd, Kuala Lumpur, and that entity's subsidiary, SimeCredit (Malaysia) Sdn Bhd, Kuala Lumpur – acquired by BMW Holding B. V., The Hague, on 13 April 2007 following receipt of approval from the relevant local authorities – were consolidated for the first time in the second quarter 2008. The names of these entities were changed to BMW Lease (Malaysia) Sdn Bhd, Kuala Lumpur, and BMW Credit (Malaysia) Sdn Bhd, Kuala Lumpur, immediately after acquisition. [...]

No companies ceased to be consolidated entities during the second quarter 2008.

BMW Roma S. r. l., Rome, BMW de Argentina S. A., Buenos Aires, BMW Lease (Malaysia) Sdn Bhd, Kuala Lumpur, and BMW Credit (Malaysia) Sdn Bhd, Kuala Lumpur, were consolidated for the first time in the first half of 2008.

The companies entory AG, Ettlingen, axentiv AG, Darmstadt, Nexolab GmbH, Munich, and F.A.S.T. Gesellschaft für angewandte Softwaretechnologie mbH, Munich, all ceased to be consolidated companies in the first half of 2008 following their merger with Cirquent GmbH, Munich. Aveling Barford Manufacturing (Pty) Ltd., Cape Town, has also ceased to be a consolidated company.

Compared to the same quarter last year, five subsidiaries, seven special purpose trusts and two special purpose securities funds were consolidated for the first time. In addition, five subsidiaries, two special purpose securities funds and two special purpose trusts ceased to be consolidated companies.

The changes to the composition of the Group do not have a material impact on the earnings performance, financial position or net assets of the Group.

4.4   Segment information in condensed interim financial statements

If an entity is required to disclose segment information in its annual financial statements, certain segment disclosures are required in its interim financial report. IFRS 8 is discussed in more detail in Chapter 34.

An entity applying IFRS 8 in its annual financial statements should include the following information in its interim financial report about its reportable segments: *[IAS 34.16A(g)]*

(a) segment revenues from external customers (if included in the measure of segment profit or loss reviewed by or otherwise regularly provided to the chief operating decision maker);

(b) intersegment revenues (if included in the measure of segment profit or loss reviewed by or otherwise regularly provided to the chief operating decision maker);

(c) a measure of segment profit or loss;

(d) a measure of total assets for a particular reportable segment if such amounts are regularly provided to the chief operating decision maker and if there has been a material change from the amount disclosed in the last annual financial statements for that reportable segment;

(e) a description of differences in the basis of segmentation or in the basis of measurement of segment profit or loss from the last annual financial statements;

(f) a reconciliation of the total profit or loss for reportable segments to the entity's profit or loss before income taxes and discontinued operations. However, if an entity allocates such items as income taxes to arrive at segment profit or loss, the reconciliation can be to the entity's profit or loss after those items. The entity should separately identify and describe all material reconciling items.

Daimler AG adopted IFRS 8 early in its annual financial statements and accordingly disclosed segment revenues and segment profit or loss in its interim financial report for the second quarter of 2008. Presumably, information required by (d) and (e) above is not included because it is not applicable for the periods presented.

Extract 39.23: Daimler AG (Q2, 2008)

Notes to the Unaudited Interim Consolidated Financial Statements [extract]
10. Segment reporting [extract]

	Mercedes-Benz Cars	Daimler Trucks	Daimler Financial Services	Vans, Buses, Other	Total segments	Reconciliation	Consol-idated
Amounts in millions of €							
Three months ended June 30, 2008							
Revenue	12,470	6,848	2,131	3,933	25,382	–	25,382
Intersegment revenue	451	537	100	141	1,229	(1,229)	–
Total revenue	12,921	7,385	2,231	4,074	26,611	(1,229)	25,382
Segment profit (loss) (EBIT)	1,212	608	183	148	2,151	(98)	2,053
	Mercedes-Benz Cars	Daimler Trucks	Daimler Financial Services	Vans, Buses, Other	Total segments	Reconciliation	Consol-idated
Amounts in millions of €							
Three months ended June 30, 2007							
Revenue	12,234	6,386	1,975	3,249	23,844	–	23,844
Intersegment revenue	324	544	120	127	1,115	(1,115)	–
Total revenue	12,558	6,930	2,095	3,376	24,959	(1,115)	23,844
Segment profit (loss) (EBIT)	1,204	601	220	257	2,282	(148)	2,134

Chapter 39

Amounts in millions of €	Mercedes -Benz Cars	Daimler Trucks	Daimler Financial Services	Vans, Buses, Other	Total segments	Reconciliation	Consol -idated
Six months ended June 30, 2008							
Revenue	24,727	12,539	4,282	7,289	48,837	–	48,837
Intersegment revenue	691	1,173	192	233	2,289	(2,289)	–
Total revenue	25,418	13,712	4,474	7,522	51,126	(2,289)	48,837
Segment profit (loss) (EBIT)	2,364	1,011	351	519	4,245	(216)	4,029

Amounts in millions of €	Mercedes -Benz Cars	Daimler Trucks	Daimler Financial Services	Vans, Buses, Other	Total segments	Reconciliation	Consol -idated
Six months ended June 30, 2007							
Revenue	24,003	13,111	4,021	6,079	47,214	–	47,214
Intersegment revenue	625	1,109	226	179	2,139	(2,139)	–
Total revenue	24,628	14,220	4,247	6,258	49,353	(2,139)	47,214
Segment profit (loss) (EBIT)	1,996	1,129	434	2,129	5,688	(262)	5,426

Reconciliation. Reconciliation of the segments' profit (EBIT) to profit before income taxes is as follows:

Amounts in millions of €	Three months ended June 30, 2008	Three months ended June 30, 2007	Six months ended June 30, 2008	Six months ended June 30, 2007
Total segments' profit (EBIT)	**2,151**	2,282	**4,245**	5,688
Corporate items	**(81)**	(157)	**(200)**	(266)
Eliminations	**(17)**	9	**(16)**	4
Group EBIT	**2,053**	2,134	**4,029**	5,426
Interest income (expense), net	**24**	56	**57**	190
Profit Before income taxes	**2,077**	2,190	**4,086**	5,616

The reconciliation of the segments' profit to Group EBIT includes items that by definition are not part of the segments. In addition, the reconciliation includes corporate items that are not allocated, for example items for which headquarters is responsible. Transactions between the segments are eliminated in the reconciliation.

4.5   Disclosure of compliance with IFRS

If an interim financial report complies with the requirements of IAS 34, this fact should be disclosed. Furthermore, an interim financial report should not be described as complying with IFRS unless it complies with all the requirements of International Financial Reporting Standards, [IAS 34.19], a requirement similar to that found in IAS 1. [IAS 1.16]. Therefore, an entity would only provide a statement of compliance with IFRS (as opposed to IAS 34 alone) in its interim report if it prepared a complete set of interim financial statements.

Extract 39.24: BMW AG (Q2, 2008)

Notes to the Interim Group Financial Statements to 30 June 2008 [extract]

Accounting Principles and Policies [extract]

[1] Basis of preparation [extract]

The Group financial statements of BMW AG at 31 December 2007 were drawn up in accordance with International Financial Reporting Standards (IFRSs), as applicable in the EU. The interim Group financial statements (Interim Report) at 30 June 2008, which have been prepared in accordance with International Accounting Standard (IAS) 34 (Interim Financial Reporting), have been drawn up using, in all material respects, the same accounting methods as those employed in the 2007 Group financial statements. All Interpretations of the International Financial Reporting Interpretations Committee (IFRIC) which are mandatory at 30 June 2008, have been applied. The Interim Report also complies with German Accounting Standard No. 6 (GAS 6) – *Interim Financial Reporting* – issued by the German Accounting Standards Committee e.V. (GASC).

When entities either choose or are required by local regulations to meet other requirements in addition to IAS 34, the statement of compliance can be more complicated. In the extract above, BMW simply adds a statement confirming its compliance with the specific German Accounting Standard on interim reporting after the adoption of the Transparency Directive into German law. Additional complexity arises when the entity seeks to meet the requirements of its (IFRS-based) local GAAP as well as IFRS as issued by the IASB. Extract 39.25 below shows how the dual listed BHP Billiton Group disclosed compliance with IFRS, Australian Accounting Standards and the requirements of the Financial Services Authority in the UK.

Extract 39.25: BHP Billiton Group (six months ended 31 December 2007)

Notes to the Half-year Financial Statements [extract]

1   Accounting policies [extract]

This general purpose financial report for the half-year ended 31 December 2007 is unaudited and has been prepared in accordance with IAS 34 'Interim Financial Reporting' as issued by the IASB, IAS 34 'Interim Financial Reporting' as adopted by the EU, AASB 134 'Interim Financial Reporting' and the requirements of the Disclosure and Transparency Rules of the Financial Services Authority in the United Kingdom and the Australian Corporations Act 2001 as applicable to interim financial reporting.

The half-year financial statements have been prepared on the basis of accounting policies consistent with those applied in the 30 June 2007 annual financial statements contained within the Annual Report of the BHP Billiton Group, except for the impact of adopting AASB 2007-4 'Amendments to Australian Accounting Standards Arising from ED 151 and Other Amendments'. AASB 2007-4 reinstates optional accounting treatments permitted by IFRS that were not initially available under Australian Accounting Standards. AASB 2007-4 will be applied in the Group's annual financial statements for the year ending 30 June 2008 and has therefore been applied in these half-year financial statements. The principal impacts of AASB 2007-4 are described below.

The extract above also highlights a compliance issue for adopters of IFRS-based standards, such as entities in Australia and the European Union. Because of the time taken to secure local endorsement of IFRS issued by the IASB, an entity may not be able to state at a particular reporting date that the financial statements comply with both IFRS as issued by the IASB and IFRS as endorsed locally.

Chapter 39

For example, when the Interpretations Committee issues an interpretation that is effective before the end of the interim reporting period, entities may choose not to comply with IAS 34 in their interim financial statements rather than risk applying an interpretation in their full year financial statements that is not yet locally endorsed. Extract 39.1 above shows a disclosure by an entity choosing not to comply with the requirements of IAS 34. Alternatively, an entity may publish interim financial information prepared under locally endorsed IFRS, for example, IFRS as adopted by the European Union. In such cases, the basis of preparation should state that IAS 34 is being applied in this context.

5   PERIODS FOR WHICH INTERIM FINANCIAL STATEMENTS ARE REQUIRED TO BE PRESENTED

Irrespective of whether an entity presents condensed or complete interim financial statements, its interim reports include the following components: *[IAS 34.20]*

(a)   balance sheets as of the end of the current interim period and a comparative balance sheet as of the end of the immediately preceding year;

(b)   statements of comprehensive income for the current interim period and cumulatively for the current year-to-date, with comparative statements of comprehensive income for the comparable interim periods (current and year-to-date) of the immediately preceding year;

(c)   statement of changes in equity cumulatively for the current year-to-date period, with a comparative statement for the comparable year-to-date period of the immediately preceding year; and

(d)   statement of cash flows cumulatively for the current year-to-date, with a comparative statement for the comparable year-to-date period of the immediately preceding year.

Under IAS 1, an interim report may present either a single statement of comprehensive income, or a statement displaying components of profit or loss (a separate income statement) and a second statement beginning with profit or loss and displaying components of other comprehensive income (a statement of comprehensive income) for each period. *[IAS 34.20(b)]*. The condensed statement of comprehensive income referred to at (b) above should be presented in a manner consistent with the entity's annual financial statements. Accordingly, if the entity presents a separate income statement in its annual financial statements, it should present a separate condensed income statement in the interim financial report. *[IAS 34.8A]*.

If an entity's business is highly seasonal, then the standard encourages reporting additional financial information for the twelve months up to the end of the interim period, and comparative information for the prior twelve-month period, in addition to the financial statements for the periods set out above. *[IAS 34.21]*.

The standard does not require an entity to present a balance sheet as at the end of the comparable interim period. However, in practice many entities reporting under IFRS disclose this information, either on a voluntary basis, or due to local regulations. Similarly, many entities also present the income statement for the immediately preceding full year. Such presentation is allowed under IAS 34, but any additional information included in the interim report should be prepared and presented in compliance with the standard.

The examples below illustrate the periods that an entity is required and encouraged to disclose under IAS 34. *[IAS 34.22, Appendix A].* In addition to the requirements set out in these examples and as noted at 3.1 above, an entity presenting a complete set of interim financial statements is required to include a balance sheet as at the beginning of the earliest comparative period if the entity restated prior periods (for example, to change an accounting policy). *[IAS 34.5(f)].*

Example 39.2:   Entity publishes interim financial reports half-yearly

If an entity's financial year ends on 31 December (calendar year), it should present the following financial statements (condensed or complete) in its half-yearly interim financial report as of 30 June 2012:

Half-yearly interim report	End of the current interim period	End of the comparative interim period	Immediately preceding year-end
	30/6/2012	30/6/2011	31/12/2011
Balance sheet	●		●
Statement of comprehensive income (and income statement, where separately presented)			
— Current period and year-to-date (6 months) ending	●	●	
— 12 months ending	○	○	
Statement of changes in equity			
— Year-to date (6 months) ending	●	●	
— 12 months ending	○	○	
Statement of cash flows			
— Year-to-date (6 months) ending	●	●	
— 12 months ending	○	○	

● Required   ○ Disclosure encouraged if the entity's business is highly seasonal

If an entity publishes a separate interim financial report for the final interim period (i.e. second half of its financial year), it presents the following financial statements (condensed or complete) in its second half-yearly interim financial report as of 31 December 2012:

Second half-yearly interim report	End of the current interim period 31/12/2012	End of the comparative interim period 31/12/2011
Balance sheet	●	●
Statement of comprehensive income (and income statement, where separately presented)		
– Current period (6 months) ending	●	●
– Year-to-date (12 months) ending	●	●
Statement of changes in equity		
– Year-to-date (12 months) ending	●	●
Statement of cash flows		
– Year-to-date (12 months) ending	●	●

● Required

Example 39.3:   *Entity publishes interim financial reports quarterly*

If an entity's financial year ends on 31 December (calendar year), it should present the following financial statements (condensed or complete) in its quarterly interim financial reports for 2012:

First quarter interim report	End of the current interim period 31/3/2012	End of the comparative interim period 31/3/2011	Immediately preceding year-end 31/12/2011
Balance sheet	●		●
Statement of comprehensive income (and income statement, where separately presented)			
– Current period and year-to-date (3 months) ending	●	●	
– 12 months ending	○	○	
Statement of changes in equity			
– Year-to-date (3 months) ending	●	●	
– 12 months ending	○	○	
Statement of cash flows			
– Year-to-date (3 months) ending	●	●	
– 12 months ending	○	○	

● Required   ○ Disclosure encouraged if the entity's business is highly seasonal

Second quarter interim report	*End of the current interim period* 30/6/2012	*End of the comparative interim period* 30/6/2011	*Immediately preceding year-end* 31/12/2011
Balance sheet	●		●
Statement of comprehensive income (and income statement, where separately presented)			
– Current period (3 months) ending	●	●	
– Year-to-date (6 months) ending	●	●	
– 12 months ending	○	○	
Statement of changes in equity			
– Year-to-date (6 months) ending	●	●	
– 12 months ending	○	○	
Statement of cash flows			
– Year-to-date (6 months) ending	●	●	
– 12 months ending	○	○	

● Required   ○ Disclosure encouraged if the entity's business is highly seasonal

Third quarter interim report	*End of the current interim period* 30/9/2012	*End of the comparative interim period* 30/9/2011	*Immediately preceding year-end* 31/12/2011
Balance sheet (or statement of financial position)	●		●
Statement of comprehensive income (and income statement, where separately presented)			
– Current period (3 months) ending	●	●	
– Year-to-date (9 months) ending	●	●	
– 12 months ending	○	○	
Statement of changes in equity			
– Year-to-date (9 months) ending	●	●	
– 12 months ending	○	○	
Statement of cash flows			
– Year-to-date (9 months) ending	●	●	
– 12 months ending	○	○	

● Required   ○ Disclosure encouraged if the entity's business is highly seasonal

If an entity publishes a separate interim financial report for the final interim period (i.e. fourth quarter of its financial year), it presents the following financial statements (condensed or complete) in its fourth quarter interim financial report as of 31 December 2012:

Chapter 39

Fourth quarter interim report	*End of the current interim period*	*End of the comparative interim period*
	31/12/2012	31/12/2011
Balance sheet	●	●
Statement of comprehensive income (and income statement, where separately presented)		
– Current period (3 months) ending	●	●
– Year-to-date (12 months) ending	●	●
Statement of changes in equity		
– Year-to-date (12 months) ending	●	●
Statement of cash flows		
– Year-to-date (12 months) ending	●	●
● Required		

5.1   Other comparative information

For entities presenting condensed financial statements under IAS 34, there is no explicit requirement that comparative information be presented in the explanatory notes. Nevertheless, where an explanatory note is required by the standard (such as for inventory write-downs, impairment provisions, segment revenues etc.) or otherwise determined to be needed to provide useful information about changes in the financial position and performance of the entity since the end of the last annual reporting period, *[IAS 34.15]*, it would be appropriate to provide information for each period presented. However, in certain cases it would be unnecessary to provide comparative information where this repeats information that was reported in the notes to the most recent annual financial statements. *[IAS 34.15A]*. For example it would only be necessary to provide information about business combinations in a comparative period when there is a revision of previously disclosed fair values.

For entities presenting complete financial statements, whilst IAS 34 sets out the periods for which components of the interim report are included, it is less clear how these rules interact with IAS 1's requirement to report comparative information for all amounts in the financial statements. *[IAS 1.38]*. In our opinion, a complete set of interim financial statements that contains a statement of compliance under IAS 1 should meet the requirements of IAS 1 in full, irrespective of any apparent contradiction with IAS 34, as shown in the example below.

Example 39.4:   Disclosing movements on non-current assets in a complete set of interim financial statements

An entity preparing complete IFRS financial statements is required to reconcile the carrying amount at the beginning and end of the period showing movements during that period for both intangible assets and property, plant and equipment. *[IAS 38.118, IAS 16.73]*. Therefore, an entity presenting complete IFRS financial statements for the six months ended 30 June 2012 would disclose the movements in intangible assets and in property, plant and equipment between 1 January 2012 and 30 June 2012. In our opinion, the requirement for comparatives in IAS 1 requires the entity to reconcile movements during the comparative interim period, between 1 January 2011 and 30 June 2011, even though the entity is not required to present a balance sheet as at 30 June 2011 (as shown in Example 39.2 above).

In addition to presenting comparative information for the corresponding interim period, it is suggested that entities preparing a complete set of interim financial statements also include information for the previous full year, such as the required comparative information for the current interim period and reconciliations to the previous year-end balance sheet. In Example 39.4 above, this requirement could be achieved by reconciling movements in non-current assets during the second six months of the previous year (between 1 July 2011 and 31 December 2011). This approach is adopted in Extract 39.5 at 4.3.4 above.

If an entity presents complete financial statements and restates comparative information (e.g. following a change in accounting policy, correction of an error, or reclassification) and this restatement is material, then the entity should present a third statement of financial position at the beginning of the earliest comparative period in its interim financial report, as well as the related notes, in accordance with IAS 1. *[IAS 1.10(f)]*. No such requirement applies in the case of an entity preparing a condensed set of interim financial statements, *[IAS 1.BC33]*, however, additional disclosures are required in case of correction of prior period errors, *[IAS 34.15B(g)]* (see 4.3.7 above), or when accounting policies are changed, *[IAS 34.16A(a)]* (see 4.3.14 above).

5.2 Length of interim reporting period

IAS 34 does not limit interim reporting to quarterly or half-yearly periods; an interim period may be any period shorter than a full year. *[IAS 34.4]*. As the extract below illustrates, an entity may present a four-month interim period report under IAS 34.

Extract 39.26: Bossard Holding AG (First four months 2008)

Notes to the Consolidated Financial Statements [extract]

Basis for the Preparation of the Consolidated Financial Statements (2) [extract]

The unaudited, consolidated interim financial statements for the first four months of 2008 were prepared in accordance with the International Financial Reporting Standards (IFRS) "Interim Financial Reporting IAS 34".

The consolidated financial statements of the Bossard Group are based on the financial statements of the individual Group companies at April 30, 2008 prepared in accordance with uniform accounting policies. The consolidated financial statements have been prepared under the historical cost convention except for the revaluation of certain financial assets and liabilities at market value, in accordance with International Financial Reporting Standards (IFRS), including International Accounting Standards (IAS) and interpretations issued by the International Accounting Standards Board (IASB). They are prepared in accordance with Swiss law and the listing rules of the Swiss Exchange SWX.

5.3 Change in financial year-end

A change in an entity's annual financial reporting period-end impacts the periods presented for interim reporting. For example, an entity changing its reporting date from 31 December to 31 March would have to change its half-year reporting date from 30 June to 30 September. As IAS 34 requires comparative information for 'the comparable interim periods (current and year-to-date) of the immediately preceding financial year,' the entity would also have to change the comparative interim periods presented. *[IAS 34.20]*.

Chapter 39

Example 39.5:   Entity changes financial year-end

If an entity changes its financial year-end from 31 December (calendar year) to 31 March, and first reflects the change in its annual financial statements for the period ended 31 March 2012, it should present the following financial statements (condensed or complete) in its half-yearly interim financial reports for 2012:

Half-yearly interim report	End of the current interim period	End of the comparative interim period	Immediately preceding year-end
	30/9/2012	30/9/2011	31/03/2012
Balance sheet	●		●
Statement of comprehensive income (and income statement, where separately presented)			
– Current period and year-to-date (6 months) ending	●	●	
– 12 months ending	○	○	
Statement of changes in equity			
– Year-to date (6 months) ending	●	●	
– 12 months ending	○	○	
Statement of cash flows			
– Year-to-date (6 months) ending	●	●	
– 12 months ending	○	○	

●   Required   ○   Disclosure encouraged if the entity's business is highly seasonal

The entity in the example above should not show information for half-year ended 30 June 2011 as the comparative period, notwithstanding the fact that this period was the reporting date for the last published half-yearly report. If, however, no quarterly information was presented in the previous year, the information for the half-year ended on 30 June 2011 should instead be disclosed as comparative.

6   MATERIALITY

In making judgments on recognition, measurement, classification, or disclosures in interim financial reports, the overriding goal in IAS 34 is to ensure that an interim financial report includes all information relevant to understanding an entity's financial position and performance during the interim period. *[IAS 34.25]*. The standard draws from IAS 1 and IAS 8 – *Accounting Policies, Changes in Accounting Estimates and Errors*, which define an item as material if its omission or misstatement could influence the economic decisions of users of the financial statements but do not contain quantitative guidance on materiality. *[IAS 34.24]*. IAS 34 requires materiality to be assessed based on the interim period financial data. *[IAS 34.23]*.

Therefore, decisions on the recognition and disclosure of unusual items, changes in accounting policies or estimates, and errors are based on materiality in relation to the interim period figures to determine whether non-disclosure is misleading. *[IAS 34.25]*. Neither the previous year's financial statements nor any expectations of the financial position at the current year-end are relevant in assessing materiality for interim reporting. However, the standard adds that interim measurements may rely on estimates to a greater extent than measurements of annual financial data. *[IAS 34.23]*.

7 DISCLOSURE IN ANNUAL FINANCIAL STATEMENTS

An estimate of an amount reported in an interim period can change significantly during the remainder of the year. An entity that does not present a separate interim financial report for its final interim period should disclose the nature and amount of significant changes in estimates in a note to the annual financial statements for that year. *[IAS 34.26]*. This disclosure requirement is intended to be narrow in scope, relating only to the change in estimate, and does not create a requirement to include additional interim period financial information in the annual financial statements. *[IAS 34.27]*.

The requirement to disclose significant changes in estimates since the previous interim reporting date is consistent with IAS 8 and paragraph 16A(d) of IAS 34. These standards require disclosure of the nature and the amount of a change in estimate that has a material effect in the current reporting period or is expected to have a material effect in subsequent periods. IAS 34 cites changes in estimate in the final interim period relating to inventory write-downs, restructurings, or impairment losses recognised in an earlier interim period as examples of items that are required to be disclosed. *[IAS 34.27]*.

8 RECOGNITION AND MEASUREMENT

The recognition and measurement requirements in IAS 34 arise from the hybrid of the discrete and integral methods to interim financial reporting. However, this hybrid creates a tension between IAS 34 and other standards and can cause confusion, especially when IAS 34 seems internally inconsistent.

For the most part, IAS 34 requires the year-to-date to be treated as a discrete period; it prohibits the recognition or deferral of revenues and costs for interim reporting purposes unless such recognition or deferral is appropriate at year-end. At the same time, however, IAS 34 allows estimates and judgements reported in previous interim periods to be revised prospectively, whereas for a set of annual financial statements the requirements in IAS 8, for example, might require prior period adjustment. In addition, IAS 34 allows looking beyond the interim reporting period, for example in estimating the tax rate to be applied on earnings for the period, when a year-to-date approach does not.

Such inconsistencies are due to the age of the standard and its failure to define the overall purpose of interim reporting adequately. IAS 34 was issued in 1998 and its principles, in particular allowing the revision of earlier estimates, sit less comfortably beside subsequent standards that use a balance sheet approach.

The recognition and measurement requirements of IAS 34 are discussed below.

8.1 Same accounting policies as in annual financial statements

The principles for recognising assets, liabilities, income and expenses for interim periods are the same as in the annual financial statements. *[IAS 34.29]*. Accordingly, an entity uses the same accounting policies in its interim financial statements as in its most recent annual financial statements, adjusted for accounting policy changes that will be reflected in the next annual financial statements. However, IAS 34 also states that the frequency of an entity's reporting (annual, half-yearly or quarterly) do not affect the measurement of its annual results. To achieve that objective, measurements for interim reporting purposes are on a year-to-date basis. *[IAS 34.28]*.

8.1.1 Measurement on a year-to-date basis

A purely discrete approach requires measurement as if each interim period stands alone as an independent reporting period and, as such, does not allow later revision unless in correcting an error or in effecting a change in accounting policy. Measurement on a year-to-date basis acknowledges that an interim period is a part of a full year and allows adjustments to estimates of amounts reported in prior interim periods of the current year. *[IAS 34.29]*.

Still, the principles for recognition and the definitions of assets, liabilities, income, and expenses for interim periods are the same as in annual financial statements. *[IAS 34.29, 31]*. Therefore, for assets, the same tests of future economic benefits apply at interim dates as at year-end. Costs that, by their nature, do not qualify as assets at year-end, do not qualify for recognition at interim dates either. Similarly, a liability at the end of an interim reporting period must represent an existing obligation at that date, just as it must at the end of an annual reporting period. *[IAS 34.32]*. Under IAS 34, as under the IASB's *Conceptual Framework*, an essential characteristic of income and expenses is that the related inflows and outflows of assets and liabilities have already occurred. If those inflows or outflows have occurred, the related income and expense are recognised; otherwise they are not recognised. *[IAS 34.33]*.

The standard lists several circumstances that illustrate these principles:

- Inventory write-downs, impairments, or provisions for restructurings are recognised and measured on the same basis as at a year-end. Except for reversals of certain impairments (see 9.2 below), later changes in the original estimate are recognised in the subsequent interim period, either by recognising additional accruals or reversals of the previously recognised amount; *[IAS 34.30(a)]*

- Costs that do not meet the definition of an asset at the end of an interim period are not deferred in the balance sheet, either to await information on whether it meets the definition of an asset, or to smooth earnings over interim periods within a year. *[IAS 34.30(b)]*. For example, costs incurred in acquiring an intangible asset before the recognition criteria are met are expensed under IAS 38 – *Intangible Assets*. Only those costs incurred after the recognition criteria are met can be recognised as an asset; there is no reinstatement as an asset in a later period of costs previously expensed because the recognition criteria were not met at that time; *[IAS 38.71]* and

- Income tax expense is 'recognised in each interim period based on the best estimate of the weighted-average annual income tax rate expected for the full financial year. Amounts accrued for income tax expense in one interim period may have to be adjusted in a subsequent interim period of that financial year if the estimate of the annual income tax rate changes'. *[IAS 34.30(c)]*.

Another example would be acquisition costs incurred in relation to a business combination, even if that business combination had not completed as at the interim reporting date.

The year-to date approach differs from the discrete approach in that the financial position and performance at each reporting date are evaluated not as an isolated period but as part of a cumulative period that builds up to a full year, whose results should not be influenced by interim reporting practices. Amounts reported for previous interim periods are not retrospectively adjusted, and therefore year-to-date measurements may involve changes in estimates of amounts reported in previous interim periods of the current year. As discussed at 4.2 and 7 above, IAS 34 requires disclosure of the nature and amount of material changes in previously reported estimates in the interim financial report and when separate interim financial report is not presented for the final interim period, in the full year financial statements. *[IAS 34.16A(d), 26, 34-36].* However, the principle that the results of the full year should not be influenced by interim reporting practices, has been challenged, as the IASB and Interpretations Committee have identified and tried to resolve certain conflicts between IAS 34 and other standards, as discussed at 9.2 below.

8.1.2 New accounting standards and other changes in accounting policies

As noted above, under IAS 34, an entity uses the same accounting policies in its interim financial statements as in its most recent annual financial statements, adjusted for accounting policy changes that will be in the next annual financial statements, and to determine measurements for interim reporting purposes on a year-to-date basis. *[IAS 34.28].*

Unless transition rules are specified by a new standard or interpretation, IAS 34 requires a change in accounting policy to be reflected by: *[IAS 34.43]*

(a) restating the financial statements of prior interim periods of the current year and the comparable interim periods of any prior financial years that will be restated in the annual financial statements under IAS 8; or

(b) when it is impracticable to determine the cumulative effect at the beginning of the year of applying a new accounting policy to all prior periods, adjusting the financial statements of prior interim periods of the current year, and comparable interim periods of prior years to apply the new accounting policy prospectively from the earliest date practicable.

Therefore, a new accounting policy generally cannot be adopted later than the beginning of the current year. *[IAS 34.44].*

It should be noted that entities preparing condensed interim financial statements in accordance with IAS 34 are not required to include a third statement of financial position when retrospectively applying a change in accounting policy or changing the presentation. *[IAS 1.4, BC33].* However, the requirement to include a third statement of financial position does apply in such cases to entities preparing a complete set of interim financial statements. *[IAS 34.5(f)].*

Chapter 39

8.1.2.A   New standards becoming mandatory during the current year

One objective of the year-to-date approach is to ensure that a single accounting policy is applied to a particular class of transactions throughout a year. *[IAS 34.44]*. To allow accounting policy changes as of an interim date would mean applying different accounting policies to a particular class of transactions within a single year. This would make interim allocation difficult, obscure operating results, and complicate analysis and understandability of the interim period information. *[IAS 34.45]*.

Accordingly, when preparing interim financial information, consideration is given to which new standards and interpretations are mandatory in the next (current year) annual financial statements. The entity generally adopts these standards in all interim periods during that year.

For example, an entity with a 31 December year-end should apply the Amendment to IAS 12 – *Deferred Tax: Recovery of Underlying Assets* – in its half-yearly report for the six months ending 30 June 2012 because this amendment applies for annual periods beginning on or after 1 January 2012. *[IAS 12.98]*.

While IAS 34 generally prohibits an entity from adopting a new accounting policy during an interim period, it makes an exception for standards that specifically require or permit transition during the financial year. *[IAS 34.43]*. For example, IFRIC 18 – *Transfers of Assets from Customers* – is applied prospectively to transfers of assets received from customers *on or after* 1 July 2009, which is a departure from the Interpretations Committee's and IASB's normal practice of issuing standards to be applied for annual periods beginning on or after a certain date. Thus, in this circumstance, an entity may use two different accounting policies during a financial year, if it did not previously have an accounting policy similar to that required by IFRIC 18, which is discussed in more detail in Chapter 20 at 4.1.8.

The disclosure requirements with respect to new standards that are effective for the entity's next annual financial statements, but which do not contain specific disclosure requirements under IAS 34, are not clear. In some cases, it might be determined that an understanding of a new standard is material to an understanding of the entity, in which case the entity discloses this fact, as well as information relevant to assessing the possible impact of the new standard on the entity's financial statements. *[IAS 8.28]*. In other cases, an entity might conclude that the issuance of a new standard is not material to an understanding of its interim financial report, and thus not disclose information about the issuance of the new standard, or its possible impact on the entity.

8.1.2.B   Voluntary changes of accounting policy

An entity can also elect at any time during a year to apply a new standard or interpretation before it becomes mandatory, or otherwise decide to change an accounting policy voluntarily. However, before voluntarily changing an accounting policy, consideration should be given to the interaction of the requirements of IAS 1 and IAS 8, which only permit an entity to change accounting policy if the information results in information that is 'more reliable and more relevant' to the users of the financial statements. *[IAS 8.14(b)]*.

When it is concluded that a voluntary change in accounting policy is permitted and appropriate, its effect is generally reflected in the first interim report the entity presents after the date on which the entity changed its policy. The entity generally restates amounts reported in earlier interim periods, from a date no later than the beginning of the current year. *[IAS 34.44].* An entity is generally not permitted to change an accounting policy from a later date, such as at the start of the most recent interim period. To allow two different accounting policies to be applied to a particular class of transactions within a single year would make interim allocations difficult, obscure operating results, and complicate analysis and understandability of the interim period information. *[IAS 34.45].*

An added complication arises for entities incorporated in the European Union, when the IASB issues a new standard or interpretation that is not yet endorsed as at the end of the interim reporting period. For example, as noted at 4.4 above, an entity applying IFRS 8 should disclose the specified segment information in its interim financial reports. In its interim report for the six months ended 30 June 2007, Deutsche Bank stated its intention to apply IFRS 8 in its first IFRS annual financial statements. However, because the European Union had not yet endorsed the standard as at the end of the interim reporting period, it included the disclosures required by both IFRS 8 and IAS 14 – *Segment Reporting* – as explained in the Extract below.

Extract 39.27: Deutsche Bank AG (H1, 2007)

Basis of Preparation [extract]

The consolidated interim financial statements were prepared in accordance with IFRS issued and effective at December 31, 2006, which were unchanged at 30 June 2007. The segment information presented in this Report is based on IFRS 8, "Operating Segments," with a reconciliation to IAS 14, "Segment Reporting". IFRS 8, whilst approved by the IASB, has yet to be endorsed by the EU. On this basis, the Group presents the accounting policies that are expected to be adopted when the Group prepares its first annual financial statements under IFRS.

One exception to this principle is when an entity changes from the cost model to the revaluation model under IAS 16 – *Property, Plant and Equipment* – or IAS 38. These are not changes in accounting policy that are covered by IAS 8 in the usual manner. *[IAS 8.17].* Rather, IAS 16 and IAS 38 require an entity to account for such changes prospectively from the date on which the decision to change is made and the revaluation is determined. *[IAS 16.31, IAS 38.75].* Therefore, the general requirements of IAS 34 do not over-ride the specific requirements of IAS 16 and IAS 38 to treat such changes prospectively.

However, to avoid using two differing accounting policies for a particular class of assets in a single financial year, consideration should be given to changing from the cost model to the revaluation model at the beginning of the financial year. Otherwise, an entity will end up depreciating based on cost for some interim periods and based on the revalued amounts for later interim periods.

Chapter 39

8.1.3   Change in going concern assumption

Another exception to the general principle under IAS 34, that an entity should use the same accounting policies in its interim financial statements as in its most recent annual financial statements, is when the going concern assumption is no longer appropriate.

Although IAS 34 does not specifically address the issue of going concern, the general requirements of IAS 1 apply to both a complete set and to condensed interim financial statements. *[IAS 1.4]*. IAS 1 states that when preparing financial statements, management assesses an entity's ability to continue as a going concern, and that the financial statements are prepared on a going concern basis unless management either intends to liquidate the entity or cease trading, or has no realistic alternative but to do so. *[IAS 1.25]*. The going concern assessment is discussed in more detail in Chapter 3 at 4.1.2.

Under IAS 1, the assessment is made based on all available information about the future, which at a minimum is twelve months from the *end of the reporting period*. *[IAS 1.26]*. Therefore, with respect to interim reporting under IAS 34, the minimum period for management's assessment is also at least twelve months from the interim reporting date; it is not limited, for example, to one year from the date of the most recent annual financial statements.

Example 39.6:   Going concern assessment

An entity's financial year-end is 31 December (calendar year) and its annual financial statements as of 31 December 2011 are prepared on a going concern basis. In assessing the going concern assumption as at 31 December 2011, management considered all future available information through 31 December 2012.

In preparing its quarterly interim financial statements (condensed or complete) as at 31 March 2012, management should evaluate all future available information to at least 31 March 2013.

If management becomes aware, in making its assessment, of material uncertainties related to events or conditions that may cast significant doubt upon the entity's ability to continue as a going concern, the entity should disclose those uncertainties. If the entity does not prepare financial statements on a going concern basis, it should disclose that fact, together with the basis on which it prepared the financial statements and the reason why the entity is not regarded as a going concern. *[IAS 1.25]*.

8.1.4   Voluntary changes in presentation

In some cases, the presentation of the interim financial statements might be changed from that used in prior interim reporting periods. However, before changing the presentation used in its interim report from that of previous periods, management should consider the interaction of the requirement to apply the same policies as the most recent or the next annual financial report *[IAS 34.28]* and the requirements of IAS 1 as they will relate to those next annual financial statements. IAS 1 states that an entity should retain the presentation and classification of items in the financial statements, unless it is apparent following a significant change in the nature of operations or a review of the financial statements that another presentation is more appropriate, or unless the change is required by IFRS. *[IAS 1.45]*.

If a presentation is changed, the entity should also reclassify comparative amounts for both earlier interim periods of the current financial year and comparable periods in prior years. *[IAS 34.43(a)]*. In such cases, an entity should disclose the nature of the reclassifications, the amount of each item (or class of items) that is reclassified, and the reason for the reclassification. *[IAS 8.29]*.

8.2 Seasonal businesses

Some entities do not earn revenues or incur expenses evenly throughout the year, for example, agricultural businesses, holiday companies, domestic fuel suppliers, or retailers who experience peak demand at Christmas. The financial year-end is often chosen to fit their annual operating cycle, which means that an individual interim period would give little indication of annual performance and financial position.

An extreme application of the integral approach would suggest that they should predict their annual results and contrive to report half of that in the half-year interim financial statements. However, this approach does not portray the reality of their business in individual interim periods, and is, therefore, not permitted under the year-to-date approach adopted in IAS 34. *[IAS 34.28]*.

8.2.1 Revenues received seasonally, cyclically, or occasionally

The standard prohibits the recognition or deferral of revenues that are received seasonally, cyclically, or occasionally at an interim date, if recognition or deferral would not be appropriate at year-end. *[IAS 34.37]*. Examples of such revenues include dividend revenue, royalties, government grants, and seasonal revenues of retailers; such revenues are recognised when they occur. *[IAS 34.38]*.

IAS 34 also requires an entity to explain the seasonality or cyclicality of its business and the effect on interim reporting (see 4.3.15 above). *[IAS 34.16A(b)]*. If businesses are highly seasonal, IAS 34 encourages reporting of additional information for the twelve months up to the end of the interim period and comparatives for the prior twelve-month period (see 5 above). *[IAS 34.21]*.

8.2.2 Costs incurred unevenly during the year

IAS 34 prohibits the recognition or deferral of costs for interim reporting purposes if recognition or deferral of that type of cost is inappropriate at year-end, *[IAS 34.39]*, which is based on the principle that assets and liabilities are recognised and measured using the same criteria as at year-end. *[IAS 34.29, 31]*. This principle prevents smoothing of costs in seasonal businesses, and the recognition of assets or liabilities at the interim date that would not qualify for recognition at the end of an annual reporting period.

For direct costs, this approach has limited consequences, as the timing of recognising these costs and the related revenues is usually similar. However, for indirect costs, the consequences are greater, and depend on which standard an entity follows, as an entity may not recognise or defer such costs under IAS 34 in an interim period if such a policy is not appropriate at year-end.

For example, manufacturing entities that use fixed production overhead absorption rates, should recognise variances and unallocated overheads in the interim period in which they are incurred. *[IAS 2.13]*. In contrast, construction contractors that use the percentage of completion method may recognise as an asset indirect contract costs that are attributable to contract activity in general, if it is probable that they will be recovered. *[IAS 11.27]*. IAS 11 – *Construction Contracts* – does not provide any guidance on how to determine if it is probable that a cost will be recovered when it relates to contract activity in general.

The implications are unclear for professional service companies that recognise revenue under IAS 18 – *Revenue* – using the percentage of completion method. On one hand, IAS 18 refers to IAS 11, *[IAS 18.21]*, implying that such entities can defer costs and the related variances at the end of an interim reporting period, even though they may not be constructing an asset and are therefore not technically within the scope of IAS 11. On the other hand, service providers might also follow the guidance in IAS 2 – *Inventories*, which also gives guidance for the cost of inventories of a service provider, and which results in expensing such costs and variances at the end of the reporting period. *[IAS 2.19]*. However, these are issues that an entity would also face at the end of an annual reporting period. What is clear is that an entity should not diverge from these requirements just because information is being prepared for an interim period.

This application of the discrete approach reflects the reality of that interim period's performance, but also emphasises the limited usefulness of the interim report for a seasonal business, because it shows that the results of that period mean little in isolation. Conversely, allocating costs to interim periods in proportion to the expected levels for the year, which IAS 34 does not allow, might show the results in context, but is subjective and requires forecasting, rather than reporting on the results of the interim period. Probably for this reason, IAS 34 recommends that entities wishing to give the results in context include additional year-to-date disclosures for seasonal businesses, as discussed at 5 above.

9   EXAMPLES OF THE RECOGNITION AND MEASUREMENT PRINCIPLES

In Appendix B, the standard lists several examples that illustrate the recognition and measurement principles in interim financial reports. *[IAS 34.40]*. In addition, the Interpretations Committee addressed one particular conflict between IAS 34 and other standards, in the reversal of impairment losses for goodwill, investments in an equity instruments classified as available-for-sale and financial assets carried at cost.

As discussed below, IAS 34 states that an entity predicts the outcome for the full year for some items to determine the effective rate for the interim period, which appears to be an integral approach. However, it does not mean recognising a proportion of annual revenues and costs in the interim period. The year-to-date approach in IAS 34 requires the estimated effective rate to be applied to transactions and balances as at the end of the interim reporting period. As such, the estimation process is the same as in annual financial statements whenever the base period for measuring a variable amount differs from the financial year. Examples of items mentioned by IAS 34 include taxation, staff bonuses or profit sharing, sales commissions, volume discounts on both purchases and sales, and contingent lease payments.

9.1   Property, plant and equipment and intangible assets

9.1.1   *Depreciation and amortisation*

Depreciation and amortisation for an interim period is based only on assets owned during that interim period and does not consider asset acquisitions or disposals planned for later in the year. *[IAS 34.B24].*

An entity applying a straight-line method of depreciation (amortisation) does not allocate the depreciation (amortisation) charge between interim periods based on the level of activity. However, under IAS 16 and IAS 38 an entity may use a 'unit of production' method of depreciation, which results in a charge based on the expected use or output (see Chapter 20 at 5.6.3). An entity can only apply this method if it most closely reflects the expected pattern of consumption of the future economic benefits embodied in the asset. The chosen method should be applied consistently from period to period unless there is a change in the expected pattern of consumption of those future economic benefits. *[IAS 16.62, IAS 38.98].* Therefore, an entity cannot apply a straight-line method of depreciation in its annual financial statements, while allocating the depreciation charge to interim periods using a 'unit of production' based approach.

9.1.2   *Impairment of assets*

IAS 36 – *Impairment of Assets* – requires an entity to recognise an impairment loss if the recoverable amount of an asset declines below its carrying amount. *[IAS 34.B35].* An entity should apply the same impairment testing, recognition, and reversal criteria at an interim date as it would at year-end. *[IAS 34.B36].*

However, IAS 34 states that an entity is not required to perform a detailed impairment calculation at the end of each interim period. Rather, an entity should perform a review for indications of significant impairment since the most recent year-end to determine whether such a calculation is needed. *[IAS 34.B36].* Nevertheless, the standard does not exempt an entity from performing impairment tests at the end of its interim periods. For example, an entity that recognised an impairment charge in the immediately preceding year, may find that it needs to update its impairment calculations at the end of subsequent interim periods because impairment indicators remain. There is also no exemption under IFRIC 10 – *Interim Financial Reporting and Impairment* – for the assessment of goodwill impairment (see 9.2 below).

9.1.3   *Recognition of intangible assets*

An entity should apply the same IAS 38 definitions and recognition criteria for intangible assets in an interim period as in an annual period. Therefore, costs incurred before the recognition criteria are met should be recognised as an expense. *[IAS 34.B8].* Expenditures on intangibles that are initially expensed under IAS 38 cannot be reinstated and recognised as part of the cost of an intangible asset subsequently (e.g. in a later interim period). *[IAS 38.71].* Furthermore, 'deferring' costs as assets in an interim period in the hope that the recognition criteria will be met later in the year is not permitted. Only costs incurred after the specific point in time at which the criteria are met should be recognised as part of the cost of an intangible asset. *[IAS 34.B8].*

Chapter 39

9.1.4   Capitalisation of borrowing costs

An entity that recognises finance expenses in the cost of a qualifying asset under IAS 23 – *Borrowing Costs* – should determine the amount to be capitalised from the actual finance cost during the period (when funds are specifically borrowed) *[IAS 23.12]* or, when the asset is funded out of general borrowings, by applying a capitalisation rate equal to the weighted-average of the finance costs attributable to actual borrowings outstanding during the period *[IAS 23.14]* (see Chapter 23 at 2.3.2 and 3.3). For interim financial reporting, measurement should be made on a year-to-date basis, *[IAS 34.28]*, even if the entity reports on a quarterly basis. Therefore, the estimated capitalisation rate should be revised in successive quarters during the same year for changes in actual year-to-date borrowings and finance costs. As required in IAS 34, the cumulative effect of changes in the estimated capitalisation rate should be recognised in the current quarter and not retrospectively. *[IAS 34.36]*.

9.2   Reversal of impairment losses recognised in a previous interim period (IFRIC 10)

The two requirements in IAS 34, to apply the same accounting policies in interim financial reports as are applied for the annual financial statements, and to use year-to-date measurements for interim reporting purposes, do not sit easily together when considering the reversal of certain impairments.

As discussed at 9.1.2 above, the requirement to use the same accounting policies means that an entity should apply the same impairment testing, recognition, and reversal criteria at the end of an interim period as it would at year-end. *[IAS 34.B36]*. In applying the same reversal criteria at the end of an interim period, the following requirements are significant: *[IFRIC 10.4-6]*

- IAS 36 prohibits the reversal in a subsequent period of an impairment loss recognised for goodwill; *[IAS 36.124]*

- An impairment loss recognised in profit or loss for an investment in an equity instrument classified under IAS 39 – *Financial Instruments: Recognition and Measurement* – as available for sale cannot be reversed through profit or loss; *[IAS 39.69]*

- IAS 39 also prohibits the reversal of an impairment loss relating to an unquoted equity instrument carried at cost because its fair value cannot be reliably measured, or to a derivative asset that is linked to and must be settled by such an unquoted equity instrument. *[IAS 39.66]*

However, the use of year-to-date measurements implies that the calculation of impairments as at interim reporting dates in the same annual reporting period should be based on conditions as at the end of each interim period and determined independently of assessments at earlier interim dates. Applying this requirement of IAS 34 would lead to reversals of previously reported impairments if conditions change and justify a higher carrying value for the related asset.

In July 2006, IFRIC 10 was issued. Whilst it may be unlikely for the conditions causing an impairment of goodwill at an interim date to reverse before year-end, IFRIC 10 states that the specific requirements of the standards noted above take precedence over the more general statement in IAS 34. *[IFRIC 10.BC9]*. As such, IFRIC 10 prohibits the reversal of an impairment loss recognised in a previous interim period for goodwill or an investment in either an equity instrument or a financial asset carried at cost. *[IFRIC 10.8]*.

Thus, in the albeit unlikely event that the conditions mentioned above do reverse in successive interim periods, there can be situations where two entities facing an identical set of circumstances, yet with different frequency of interim reporting, could end up reporting different annual results. Consider the following example:

Example 39.7: *Impact of IFRIC 10 on results due to differences in frequency of interim financial reporting*

Entity A, reporting quarterly, and entity B, reporting six-monthly, are otherwise identical, having financial years ending on 31 December and holding an investment in equity instruments of Company X. As at 31 March, the fair value of the investment in X has declined significantly below cost. However, the decline has reversed in full before the end of June. In its interim financial statements for the 1st Quarter, entity A recognises an impairment loss on its investment in X based on the significant decline in its fair value below cost. At the end of 2nd Quarter, following the guidance in IFRIC 10, entity A cannot reverse the impairment that it recognised in 1st Quarter to reflect the recovery in the value of the investment.

By contrast, entity B does not recognise any impairment in its investment in entity X in its interim financial statements for half year ended 30 June. Consequently, the entities would report different annual results for the year ended 31 December due to an impairment recognised in an interim period by entity A but not by entity B.

In November 2009, IASB issued IFRS 9 (subsequently amended in October 2010), which inter alia amends IFRIC 10 (see 12.2 below). This amendment should be applied in tandem with the adoption of IFRS 9 and deletes references to equity instruments and financial assets carried at cost. With the adoption of IFRS 9, no financial assets would be carried at cost and therefore, determination of impairment and its reversal would not be relevant for such instruments in this context.

IFRIC 10 should not be applied by analogy to derive a general principle that the specific requirements of a standard take precedence over the year-to-date approach in IAS 34. *[IFRIC 10.9]*. It is unfortunate that the Interpretations Committee did not initiate a wider project to address other similar conflicts.

9.3 Employee benefits

9.3.1 *Employer payroll taxes and insurance contributions*

If employer payroll taxes or contributions to government-sponsored insurance funds are assessed on an annual basis, the employer's related expense should be recognised in interim periods using an estimated average annual effective rate, even if it does not reflect the timing of payments. A common example in Appendix B to IAS 34 is employer payroll tax or insurance contribution subject to a certain maximum level of earnings per employee. Higher income employees reach the maximum income before year-end, and the employer makes no payments for the remainder of the year. *[IAS 34.B1]*.

Chapter 39

9.3.2 Year-end bonuses

The nature of year-end bonuses varies widely. Some bonus schemes only require continued employment whereas others require certain performance criteria to be attained on a monthly, quarterly, or annual basis. Payment of bonuses may be purely discretionary, contractual or based on years of historical precedent. *[IAS 34.B5]*. A bonus is recognised for interim reporting only if: *[IAS 34.B6]*

(a)   the entity has a present legal or constructive obligation to make such payments as a result of past events; and

(b)   a reliable estimate of the obligation can be made.

A present obligation exists only when an entity has no realistic alternative but to make the payments. *[IAS 19.17]*. IAS 19 – *Employee Benefits* – gives guidance on accounting for profit sharing and bonus plans (see Chapter 33 at 6.1.3).

In recognising a bonus at an interim reporting date, an entity should consider the facts and circumstances under which the bonus is payable, and determine an accounting policy that recognises an expense reflecting the obligation on the basis of the services received to date. Several possible accounting policies are illustrated in Example 39.8 below.

Example 39.8:   Measuring interim bonus expense

An entity pays an annual performance bonus if earnings exceed £10 million, under which 5% of any earnings in excess over £10 million will be paid up to a maximum of £500,000. Earnings for the six months ended 30 June 2012 are £7 million, and the entity expects earnings for the full year ended 31 December 2012 to be £16 million.

The following table shows various accounting policies and the expense recognised thereunder in the interim financial statements for the six months ended 30 June 2012.

	Expense (£)
Method 1 – constructive obligation exists when earnings target is met	Nil
Method 2 – assume earnings for remainder of year will be same	200,000
Method 3 – proportionate recognition based on full-year estimate	131,250
Method 4 – one-half recognition based on full-year estimate	150,000

Method 1 is generally not appropriate, as this method attributes the entire bonus to the latter portion of the year, whereas employees provided service during the first six months to towards earning the bonus.

Likewise, method 2 is generally not appropriate, as the expense of £200,000 [(£14 million – £10 million) × 5%] assumes that the employees will continue to provide service in the latter half of the year to achieve the bonus target, but does not attribute any service to that period.

In contrast to Methods 1 and 2, Method 3 illustrates an accounting policy whereby an estimate is made of the full-year expense and attributed to the period based on the proportion of that bonus for which employees have provided service at 30 June 2012. The amount recognised is calculated as (£7 million ÷ £16 million) × [5% × (£16 million – £10 million)].

Similar to Method 3, Method 4 also takes the approach of recognising an expense based on the full year estimate, but allocates that full-year estimate equally to each period (which is similar to the approach used for share-based payment transactions). The amount recognised is calculated as [50% × 5% × (£16 million – £10 million)].

In addition to Methods 3 and 4, which might be appropriate, depending on the facts and circumstances, an entity might determine another basis on which to recognise bonus that considers both the constructive obligation that exists as of 30 June 2012, and the services performed to date, which is also appropriate.

9.3.3 Pensions

Pension costs for an interim period are calculated on a year-to-date basis using the actuarially determined pension cost rate at the end of the prior year, adjusted for significant market fluctuations, curtailments, settlements, or other one-time events. *[IAS 34.B9]*.

In the absence of such significant market fluctuations, curtailments, settlements, or other one-time events, the estimate of the actuarial liabilities is rolled forward in the scheme based on assumptions as at the beginning of the year and adjusted for significant changes in the membership of the scheme. If there are significant changes to pension arrangements during the interim period (such as changes resulting from a material business combination or from a major redundancy programme) consideration should be given to obtaining a new actuarial valuation of scheme liabilities. Similarly, if there are significant market fluctuations, such as those arising from changes in corporate bond markets, the validity of the assumptions in the last actuarial estimate, such as the discount rate applied to scheme liabilities, should be reviewed and revised as appropriate. In normal circumstances, companies would not necessarily go through the full process of measuring pension liabilities at interim reporting dates, but rather would look to establish a process to assess the impact of any changes in underlying parameters (e.g. through extrapolation).

IAS 19 requires entities to measure scheme assets at fair value at the end of the interim reporting period. The effect of revaluing the scheme assets will be more significant for entities that recognise actuarial gains and losses in the period in which they occur, as this movement would be recognised in full at the end of the interim reporting period, albeit through other comprehensive income. Entities applying the 'corridor' approach would only recognise gains or losses (in profit or loss) if the net cumulative unrecognised value exceeded the greater of 10% of the defined benefit obligation and 10% of the fair value of plan assets. *[IAS 19.92-93B]*.

9.3.4 Vacations, holidays, and other short-term compensated absences

IAS 19 distinguishes between accumulating and non-accumulating compensated absences. *[IAS 19.12]*. Accumulating compensated absences are those that are carried forward and can be used in future periods if the current period's entitlement is not used in full. IAS 19 requires an entity to measure the expected cost of and obligation for accumulating compensated absences at the amount the entity expects to pay as a result of the unused entitlement that has accumulated at the end of the reporting period (see Chapter 33 at 6.1.2). IAS 34 requires the same principle to be applied at the end of interim reporting periods. Conversely, an entity should not recognise an expense or liability for non-accumulating compensated absences at the end of an interim reporting period, just as it would not recognise any at the end of an annual reporting period. *[IAS 34.B10]*.

Chapter 39

9.4 Inventories and cost of sales

9.4.1 Inventories

An entity should apply the recognition and measurement requirements of IAS 2 for interim financial reporting in the same way as it does for annual reporting purposes, despite the problems of determining inventory quantities, costs, and net realisable values. However, IAS 34 does comment that to save cost and time, entities often use estimates to measure inventories at interim dates to a greater extent than at annual reporting dates. *[IAS 34.B25].*

Net realisable values are determined using selling prices and costs to complete and dispose at the end of the interim period. A write-down should be reversed in a subsequent interim period only if it would be appropriate to do so at year-end (see Chapter 24 at 3.4). *[IAS 34.B26].*

9.4.2 Contractual or anticipated purchase price changes

Both the payer and the recipient of volume rebates, or discounts and other contractual changes in the prices of raw materials, labour, or other purchased goods and services should anticipate these items in interim periods if it is probable that these have been earned or will take effect. However, discretionary rebates and discounts should not be recognised because the resulting asset or liability would not meet the recognition criteria in the IASB's *Conceptual Framework*. *[IAS 34.B23].*

9.4.3 Interim period manufacturing cost variances

Price, efficiency, spending, and volume variances of a manufacturing entity should be recognised in profit or loss at interim reporting dates to the same extent that those variances are recognised at year-end. It is not appropriate to defer variances expected to be absorbed by year-end, which could result in reporting inventory at the interim date at more or less than its actual cost. *[IAS 34.B28].* See 8.2.2 above for a discussion on this topic as it applies to costs incurred by service providers.

9.5 Taxation

Taxation is one of the most difficult areas of interim financial reporting, primarily because IAS 34 does not adequately distinguish between current income tax and deferred tax, referring only to 'income tax expense.' This causes tension between the approach for determining the expense and the position in the balance sheet. In addition, the standard's provisions combine terminology, suggesting an integral approach with guidance requiring a year-to-date basis to be applied. The integral method is used in determining the effective income tax rate for the whole year, but that rate is applied to year-to-date profit in the interim financial statements. In addition, under a year-to-date basis, the estimated rate is based on tax rates and laws that are enacted or substantively enacted by the end of the interim period. Changes in legislation expected to occur before the end of the current year are not recognised in preparing the interim financial report. The balance sheet position, at least for deferred taxes, are derived solely from a year-to-date approach, but sometimes the requirements of the standard are unclear, as discussed below.

9.5.1 Measuring interim income tax expense

IAS 34 states that income tax expense should be accrued using the tax rate applicable to expected total annual earnings, by applying the estimated weighted-average annual effective income tax rate to pre-tax income for the interim period. *[IAS 34.30(c), B12]*. However, this is not the same as estimating the total tax expense for the year and allocating a proportion of that to the interim period (even though it might sometimes appear that way), as demonstrated in the discussion below.

Because taxes are assessed on an annual basis, using the integral approach to determine the annual effective income tax rate and applying it to year-to-date actual earnings, it is consistent with the basic concept in IAS 34, that the same recognition and measurement principles apply in interim financial reports as in annual financial statements. *[IAS 34.B13]*.

In estimating the weighted-average annual income tax rate, an entity should consider the progressive tax rate structure expected for the full year's earnings, including changes in income tax rates scheduled to take effect later in the year that are enacted or substantively enacted as at the end of the interim period. *[IAS 34.B13]*. This situation is illustrated in Example 39.9 below.

Example 39.9: Measuring interim income tax expense [IAS 34.B15]

An entity reporting quarterly expects to earn 10,000 pre-tax each quarter and operates in a jurisdiction with a tax rate of 20% on the first 20,000 of annual earnings and 30% on all additional earnings. Actual earnings match expectations. The following table shows the income tax expense reported each quarter:

	Pre-tax earnings	Effective tax rate	Tax expense
First quarter	10,000	25%	2,500
Second quarter	10,000	25%	2,500
Third quarter	10,000	25%	2,500
Fourth quarter	10,000	25%	2,500
Annual	40,000		10,000

10,000 of tax is expected to be payable for the full year on 40,000 of pre-tax income (20,000 @ 20% + 20,000 @ 30%), implying an average annual effective income tax rate of 25% (10,000 / 40,000).

In the above example, it might look as if the interim income tax expense is calculated by dividing the total expected tax expense for the year (10,000) by the number of interim reporting periods (4). However, this is only the case in this example because profits are earned evenly over each quarter. The expense is actually calculated by determining the effective annual income tax rate and multiplying that rate to year-to-date earnings, as illustrated in Example 39.10 below.

Example 39.10: Measuring interim income tax expense – quarterly losses [IAS 34.B16]

An entity reports quarterly, earns 15,000 pre-tax profit in the first quarter but expects to incur losses of 5,000 in each of the three remaining quarters (thus having zero income for the year), and operates in a jurisdiction in which its estimated average annual income tax rate is 20%. The following table shows the income tax expense reported each quarter:

	Pre-tax earnings	Effective tax rate	Tax expense
First quarter	15,000	20%	3,000
Second quarter	(5,000)	20%	(1,000)
Third quarter	(5,000)	20%	(1,000)
Fourth quarter	(5,000)	20%	(1,000)
Annual	0		0

The above example shows how an expense is recognised in periods reporting a profit and a credit is recognised when a loss is incurred. This result is very different from allocating a proportion of the expected total income tax expense for the year, which in this case is zero.

If an entity operates in a number of tax jurisdictions, or where different income tax rates apply to different categories of income (such as capital gains or income earned in particular industries), the standard requires that to the extent practicable, an entity: *[IAS 34.B14]*

- estimates the average annual effective income tax rate for each taxing jurisdiction separately and apply it individually to the interim period pre-tax income of each jurisdiction; and

- applies different income tax rates to each individual category of interim period pre-tax income.

This means that the entity should perform the analysis illustrated in Example 39.10 above for each tax jurisdiction and arrive at an interim tax charge by applying the tax rate for each jurisdiction to actual earnings from each jurisdiction in the interim period. However, the standard recognises that, whilst desirable, such a degree of precision may not be achievable in all cases and allows using a weighted-average rate across jurisdictions or across categories of income, if such rate approximates the effect of using rates that are more specific. *[IAS 34.B14].*

Example 39.11:   Measuring interim tax expense – many jurisdictions [IAS 34.B14]

An entity operates in 3 countries, each with its own tax rates and laws. In order to determine the interim tax expense, the entity determines the effective annual income tax rate for each jurisdiction and applies those rates to the actual earnings in each jurisdiction, as follows:

(All values in €)	Country A	Country B	Country C	Total
Expected annual tax rate	25%	40%	20%	
Expected annual earnings	300,000	250,000	200,000	750,000
Expected annual tax expense	75,000	100,000	40,000	215,000
Actual half-year earnings	140,000	80,000	150,000	370,000
Interim tax expense	35,000	32,000	60,000	127,000

By performing a separate analysis for each jurisdiction, the entity determines an interim tax expense of €127,000, giving an effective average tax rate of 34.3% (127,000 ÷ 370,000). Had the entity used a weighted-average rate across jurisdictions, using the expected annual earnings, it would have determined an effective tax rate of 28.7% (215,000 ÷ 750,000), resulting in a tax expense for the interim period of €106,190 (370,000 @ 28.7%). Whether the difference of nearly €21,000 is significant is a matter of judgement.

9.5.2 Changes in the effective tax rate during the year

9.5.2.A Enacted changes for the current year that apply after the interim reporting date

As noted above, the estimated income tax rate applied in the interim financial report should reflect changes that are enacted or substantively enacted as at the end of the interim reporting period, but scheduled to take effect later in the year. *[IAS 34.B13]*. IAS 12 acknowledges that in some jurisdictions, announcements by government have substantively the same effect as enactment. *[IAS 12.48]*. Accordingly, an entity should determine the date on which a change in tax rate or tax law is substantively enacted based on the specific constitutional arrangements of the jurisdiction.

For example, assume that the 30% tax rate (on earnings above 20,000) in Example 39.9 was substantively enacted as at the second quarter reporting date and applicable before year-end. In that case, the estimated income tax rate for interim reporting would be the same as the estimated average annual effective income tax rate computed in that example (i.e. 25%) after considering the higher rate, even though the entity's earnings are not above the required threshold at the half-year.

If legislation is enacted only after the end of the interim reporting period but before the date of authorisation for issue of the interim financial report, its effect is disclosed as a non-adjusting event. *[IAS 10.22(h)]*. Under IAS 10 – *Events after the Reporting Period* – estimates of tax rates and related assets or liabilities are not revised. *[IAS 10.10]*.

9.5.2.B Changes to previously reported estimated income tax rates for the current year

IAS 34 requires an entity to re-estimate at the end of each interim reporting period the estimated average annual income tax rate on a year-to-date basis. *[IAS 34.B13]*. Accordingly, the amounts accrued for income tax expense in one interim period may have to be adjusted in a subsequent interim period if that estimate changes. *[IAS 34.30(c)]*. IAS 34 requires disclosure in interim financial statements of material changes in estimates of amounts reported in an earlier period or, in the annual financial statements, of material changes in estimates of amounts reported in the latest interim financial statements. *[IAS 34.16A(d), 26]*.

Accordingly, just as the integral approach does not necessarily result in a constant tax charge in each interim reporting period, it also does not result in a constant effective tax rate when circumstances change. Coca-Cola HBC describes how its tax rate is estimated in the following interim report.

Extract 39.28: Coca-Cola Hellenic Bottling Company S.A. (Q2, 2008)

Condensed notes to the consolidated financial statements [extract]

5. Tax

The effective tax rate for the Company differs from the 2008 Greek statutory rate of 25% as a consequence of a number of factors, the most significant of which are the non-deductibility of certain expenses and the fact that the tax rates in the countries in which the Company operates differ materially from the Greek statutory tax rate. The statutory tax rates applicable to the country operations of the Company range from 0%-31%.

The effective tax rate for the Company varies on a quarterly basis as a result of the mix of taxable profits and deductible expenses across territories and as a consequence of tax adjustments arising during the year, which do not necessarily refer to the current period's operations.

The effective tax rate (excluding the adjustments to intangible assets) is approximately 17% for the first half of 2008 (2007: 22%). This rate is quoted before any tax credit is recognised for the current recognition of acquired and previously unrecognised accumulated tax benefits.

Example 39.12:   Changes in the effective tax rate during the year

Taking the fact pattern in Example 39.9 above, an entity reporting quarterly expects to earn 10,000 pre-tax each quarter; from the start of the third quarter the higher rate of tax on earnings over 20,000 increases from 30% to 40%. Actual earnings continue to match expectations. The following table shows the income tax expense reported in each quarter:

	Period pre-tax earnings	Pre-tax earnings: year to date	Effective tax rate	Tax expense: year to date	Period tax expense
First quarter †	10,000	10,000	25%	2,500	2,500
Second quarter †	10,000	20,000	25%	5,000	2,500
Third quarter	10,000	30,000	30%	9,000	4,000
Fourth quarter	10,000	40,000	30%	12,000	3,000
Annual	40,000				12,000

† As previously reported from Example 39.9 using an effective tax rate of 25%.

The increase in the tax rate means that 12,000 of tax is expected to be payable for the full year on 40,000 of pre-tax income (20,000 @ 20% + 20,000 @ 40%), implying an average annual effective income tax rate of 30% (12,000 / 40,000). With cumulative pre-tax earnings of 30,000 as at the end of the third quarter, the estimated tax liability is 9,000, requiring a tax expense of 4,000 (9,000 – 2,500 – 2,500) to be recognised during that quarter. In the final quarter, earnings of 10,000 results in a tax charge of 3,000, using the revised effective rate of 30%.

9.5.2.C   Enacted changes applying only to subsequent years

In many jurisdictions, tax legislation is enacted that takes effect not only after the interim reporting date but also after year-end. Such circumstances are not addressed explicitly in the standard. Indeed, the failure of IAS 34 to adequately distinguish between current income tax and deferred tax, combined with the different approaches taken in determining the expense recognised in profit or loss compared to the balance sheet position, can lead to confusion in this situation.

On the one hand, the standard states that the estimated income tax rate for the interim period includes enacted or substantively enacted changes scheduled to take effect later in the year. *[IAS 34.B13]*. Accordingly, the effect of changes that do not take effect in the current year is ignored. On the other hand, IAS 34 also requires that the principles for recognising assets, liabilities, income, and expenses for interim periods are the same as in the annual financial statements. *[IAS 34.29]*. In annual financial statements, deferred tax is measured at the tax rates expected to apply to the period when the asset is realised or the liability is settled, based on tax rates (and tax laws) enacted or substantively enacted by the end of the reporting period, as required by IAS 12. *[IAS 12.47]*. Therefore, an entity should recognise the effect of a change applying to future periods if enacted by the end of the interim reporting period.

These two requirements seem to be mutually incompatible. IAS 34 makes sense only in the context of calculating the effective *current* tax rate on income earned in the period. Once a deferred tax asset or liability is recognised, it should be measured under IAS 12. Therefore, an entity should recognise an enacted change applying to future years in measuring deferred tax assets and liabilities as at the end of the interim reporting period. In our view, the cumulative effect to date of this remeasurement should be recognised in full in the period during which the tax legislation is enacted, in a similar way to the treatment shown in Example 39.12 above, and as illustrated in Example 39.13 below.

Example 39.13:   Enacted changes to tax rates applying after the current year

An entity reporting half-yearly operates in a jurisdiction subject to a tax rate of 30%. Legislation is enacted during the first half of the current year, which reduces the tax rate to 28% on income earned from the beginning of the entity's next financial year. Based on a gross temporary difference of 1,000, the entity reported a deferred tax liability in its most recent annual financial statements of 300 (1,000 @ 30%). Of this temporary difference, 200 is expected to reverse in the second half of the current year and 800 in the next financial year. Assuming that no new temporary differences arise in the current period, what is the deferred tax balance at the interim reporting date?

Whilst the entity uses an effective tax rate of 30% to determine the tax expense relating to income earned in the period, it should use a rate of 28% to measure those temporary differences expected to reverse in the next financial year. Accordingly, the deferred tax liability at the half-year reporting date is 284 (200 @ 30% + 800 @ 28%).

If the effective *current* tax rate is not distinguished from the measurement of deferred tax, it could be argued that IAS 34 allows the reduction in the deferred tax liability of 16 (300 – 284) to be included in the estimate of the effective income tax rate for the year. Approach 2 in Example 39.16 below applies that argument. In our view, it is more appropriate to recognise the reduction in full at the interim reporting date, by a credit to profit and loss or to other comprehensive income, depending on the nature of the temporary difference being remeasured.

9.5.3   Difference in financial year and tax year

If an entity's financial year and the income tax year differ, the income tax expense for the interim periods of that financial year should be measured using separate weighted-average estimated effective tax rates for each of the income tax years applied to the portion of pre-tax income earned in each of those income tax years. *[IAS 34.B17]*. In other words, an entity should compute a weighted-average estimated effective tax rate for each income tax year, rather than for its financial year.

Chapter 39

Example 39.14:   Difference in financial year and tax year [IAS 34.B18]

An entity's financial year ends 30 June and it reports quarterly. Its taxable year ends 31 December. For the financial year that begins 1 July 2011 and ends 30 June 2012, the entity earns 10,000 pre-tax each quarter.

The estimated average annual income tax rate is 30% in the income tax year to 31 December 2011 and 40% in the year to 31 December 2012.

Quarter ending	Pre-tax earnings	Effective tax rate	Tax expense
30 September 2011	10,000	30%	3,000
31 December 2011	10,000	30%	3,000
31 March 2012	10,000	40%	4,000
30 June 2012	10,000	40%	4,000
Annual	40,000		14,000

9.5.4   Tax loss and tax credit carrybacks and carryforwards

Appendix B to IAS 34 repeats the requirement in IAS 12 that for carryforwards of unused tax losses and tax credits, a deferred tax asset should be recognised to the extent that it is probable that future taxable profit will be available against which the unused tax losses and unused tax credits can be utilised. In assessing whether future taxable profit is available, the criteria in IAS 12 are applied at the interim date. If these criteria are met as at the end of the interim period, the effect of the tax loss carryforwards is included in the estimated average annual effective income tax rate. [IAS 34.B21].

Example 39.15:   Tax loss carryforwards expected to be recovered in the current year
[IAS 34.B22]

An entity that reports quarterly has unutilised operating losses of 10,000 for income tax purposes at the start of the current financial year for which a deferred tax asset has not been recognised. The entity earns 10,000 in the first quarter of the current year and expects to earn 10,000 in each of the three remaining quarters. Excluding the effect of utilising losses carried forward, the estimated average annual income tax rate is 40%. Including the carryforward, the estimated average annual income tax rate is 30%. Accordingly, tax expense is determined by applying the 30% rate to earnings each quarter as follows:

	Pre-tax earnings	Effective tax rate	Tax expense
First quarter	10,000	30%	3,000
Second quarter	10,000	30%	3,000
Third quarter	10,000	30%	3,000
Fourth quarter	10,000	30%	3,000
Annual	40,000		12,000

This result is consistent with the general approach for measuring income tax expense in the interim report, in that any entitlement for relief from current tax due to carried forward losses is determined on an annual basis. Accordingly, its effect is included in the estimate of the average annual income tax rate and not, for example, by allocating all of the unutilised losses against the earnings of the first quarter to give an income tax expense of zero in the first quarter and 4,000 thereafter.

In contrast, the year-to-date approach of IAS 34 means that the benefits of a tax loss carryback are recognised in the interim period in which the related tax loss occurs, *[IAS 34.B20]*, and are not included in the assessment of the estimated average annual tax rate, as shown in Example 39.10 above. This approach is consistent with IAS 12, which requires the benefit of a tax loss that can be carried back to recover current tax already incurred in a previous period to be recognised as an asset. *[IAS 12.13]*. Therefore, a corresponding reduction of tax expense or increase of tax income is also recognised. *[IAS 34.B20]*.

Where previously unrecognised tax losses are expected to be utilised in full in the current year, it seems intuitive to recognise the recovery of those carried forward losses in the estimate of the average annual tax rate, as shown in Example 39.14 above. However, where the level of previously unrecognised tax losses exceeds expected taxable profits for the current year, a deferred tax asset should be recognised for the carried forward losses that are now expected to be utilised, albeit in future years.

The examples in IAS 34 do not show how such a deferred tax asset is created in the interim financial report. In our opinion, two approaches are acceptable, as shown in Example 39.16 below.

Example 39.16:   *Tax loss carry forwards in excess of current year expected profits*

An entity that reports half-yearly has unutilised operating losses of 75,000 for income tax purposes at the start of the current financial year for which no deferred tax asset has been recognised. At the end of its first interim period, the entity reports a profit before tax of 25,000 and expects to earn a profit of 20,000 before tax in the second half of the year. The entity reassesses the likelihood of generating sufficient profits to utilise its carried forward tax losses and determines that the IAS 12 recognition criteria for a deferred tax asset are satisfied for the full amount of 75,000. Excluding the effect of utilising losses carried forward, the estimated average annual income tax rate is the same as the enacted or substantially enacted rate of 40%.

As at the end of the current financial year the entity expects to have unutilised losses of 30,000 (75,000 carried forward less current year pre-tax profits of 45,000). Using the enacted rate of 40%, a deferred tax asset of 12,000 is recognised at year-end. How is this deferred tax asset recognised in the interim reporting periods?

Approach 1

Under the first approach, the estimate of the average annual effective tax rate includes only those carried forward losses expected to be utilised in the current financial year and a separate deferred tax asset is recognised for those carried forward losses now expected to be utilised in future annual reporting periods.

In the fact pattern above, using 45,000 of the carried forward tax losses gives an average effective annual tax rate of nil, as follows:

Estimation of the annual effective tax rate – Approach 1

Expected annual tax expense before utilising losses carried forward (45,000 @ 40%)	18,000
Tax benefit of utilising carried forward tax losses (45,000 @ 40%)	(18,000)
Expected annual tax expense before the effect of losses carried forward to future annual periods	0
Expected annual effective tax rate	0%
Effect of tax losses carried forward to future periods (75,000 – 45,000 @ 40%)	(12,000)
Tax income to be recognised in the interim period	(12,000)

The remaining tax losses give rise to a deferred tax asset of 12,000, which is recognised in full at the half-year, to give reported profits after tax as follows:

	First half-year	Second half-year	Annual
Profit before income tax	25,000	20,000	45,000
Income tax (expense)/credit			
– at expected annual effective rate	0	0	0
– recognition of deferred tax asset	12,000	0	12,000
Net profit after tax	37,000	20,000	57,000

Approach 2

Under the second approach, the estimate of the average annual effective tax rate reflects the expected recovery of all the previously unutilised tax losses from the beginning of the period in which the assessment of recoverability changed. In the fact pattern above, recognition of the unutilised tax losses gives an average effective annual tax rate of –26.67%, as follows:

Estimation of the annual effective tax rate – Approach 2

Expected annual tax expense before utilising losses carried forward (45,000 @ 40%)	18,000
Tax benefit of recognising unutilised tax losses (75,000 @ 40%)	(30,000)
Expected annual tax credit after recognising unutilised tax losses	(12,000)
Expected annual effective tax rate (–12,000 ÷ 45,000)	–26.67%

This approach results in reported profits after tax as follows:

	First half-year	Second half-year	Annual
Profit before income tax	25,000	20,000	45,000
Income tax (expense)/credit			
– at expected annual effective rate	6,667	5,333	12,000
Net profit after tax	31,667	25,333	57,000

We believe that Approach 1 is more appropriate, as it results in recognising the full expected deferred tax asset as soon as it becomes 'probable that taxable profit will be available against which the deductible temporary difference can be utilised', as required in IAS 12. *[IAS 12.24]*. However, given that IAS 34 does not specifically address this situation, and is unclear about whether the effective tax rate reflects changes in the assessment of the recoverability of carried forward tax losses, we also believe that Approach 2 is acceptable.

9.5.5 Tax credits

IAS 34 also discusses in more detail the treatment of tax credits, which may for example be based on amounts of capital expenditures, exports, or research and development expenditures. Such benefits are usually granted and calculated on an annual basis under tax laws and regulations and therefore are reflected in the estimated annual effective income tax rate used in the interim report. However, if tax benefits relate to a one-time event, they should be excluded from the estimate of the annual rate and deducted separately from income tax expense in that interim period. Occasionally, some tax credits are more akin to a government grant, which are recognised in the interim period in which they arise. *[IAS 34.B19]*.

In Extract 39.29 below, Tomkins explains the effect of the resolution of an outstanding tax issue in the interim period.

Extract 39.29: Tomkins plc (H1, 2006)

4. OPERATING AND FINANCIAL REVIEW [extract]

Taxation

The tax charge attributable to continuing operations of £35.6 million in the first half (H1 2005: £22.4 million) represents an effective tax rate of 27.0 per cent (H1 2005: 18.2 per cent) applied to profit before tax, which is stated after preference dividends. The tax charge in the first half of 2005 benefited from the reduction in tax provisions of £16.6 million following the resolution of an outstanding tax issue in the United States and adjustments to deferred taxation.

9.6 Foreign currency translation

9.6.1 Foreign currency translation gains and losses

An entity measures foreign currency translation gains and losses for interim financial reporting using the same principles that IAS 21 – *The Effects of Changes in Foreign Exchange Rates* – requires at year-end (see Chapter 17). *[IAS 34.B29]*. An entity should use the actual average and closing foreign exchange rates for the interim period (i.e. it may not anticipate changes in foreign exchange rates for the remainder of the current year in translating at an interim date). *[IAS 34.B30]*. Where IAS 21 requires translation adjustments to be recognised as income or expense in the period in which they arise, the same approach should be used in the interim report. An entity should not defer some foreign currency translation adjustments at an interim date, even if it expects the adjustment to reverse before year-end. *[IAS 34.B31]*.

Chapter 39

9.6.2 Interim financial reporting in hyperinflationary economies

Interim financial reports in hyperinflationary economies are prepared using the same principles as at year-end. [IAS 34.B32]. IAS 29 – *Financial Reporting in Hyperinflationary Economies* – requires that the financial statements of an entity that reports in the currency of a hyperinflationary economy be stated in terms of the measuring unit current at the end of the reporting period, and the gain or loss on the net monetary position be included in net income. In addition, comparative financial data reported for prior periods should be restated to the current measuring unit (see Chapter 18). [IAS 34.B33].

In practice, interim reporting under IAS 34 can be onerous for an entity whose functional currency is that of a hyperinflationary economy. As shown in Examples 39.2 and 39.3 above, IAS 34 requires an interim report to contain many components, which are all restated at every interim reporting date.

The measuring unit used is the same as that as of the end of the interim period, with the resulting gain or loss on the net monetary position included in that period's net income. An entity may not annualise the recognition of gains or losses, nor may it estimate an annual inflation rate in preparing an interim financial report in a hyperinflationary economy. [IAS 34.B34].

IAS 29 applies from the beginning of the reporting period in which an entity identifies the existence of hyperinflation in the country in whose currency it reports. [IAS 29.4]. Accordingly, for interim reporting purposes, IAS 29 should be applied from the beginning of the interim period in which the hyperinflation is identified. The Interpretations Committee clarified that adoption of IAS 29 should be fully retrospective, by applying its requirements as if the economy had always been hyperinflationary (see Chapter 18 at 7.1). [IFRIC 7.3].

It is less obvious though, as to how a parent, which does not operate in a hyperinflationary economy, should account for the restatement of a subsidiary that operates in an economy that becomes hyperinflationary in the current reporting period when incorporating it within its consolidated financial statements.

This issue has been clarified by paragraph 42(b) of IAS 21 which specifically prohibits restatement of comparative figures when the reporting currency is not hyperinflationary. This means that when the financial statements of a hyperinflationary subsidiary are translated into the non-hyperinflationary reporting currency of the parent, the comparative amounts are not adjusted.

Notwithstanding the above, some argue that in interim period reports of the subsequent year, the parent should adjust its comparative information for the corresponding interim periods which are part of the (first) full financial year affected by hyperinflation. This is because comparative interim information had been part of the full year financial statements, which were adjusted for hyperinflation.

In our view, the parent is allowed, but not required, to adjust the comparative interim information that relates to the first full financial year affected by hyperinflation, as illustrated in the example below:

Example 39.17: *Accounting by the parent when a hyperinflationary subsidiary first applies IAS 29*

A parent with 31 December year-end owns a subsidiary, whose functional currency is considered hyperinflationary from 31 July 2011 onwards. In preparing its interim consolidated financial statements for the quarter ended 31 March 2012, the parent consolidates this subsidiary in both the current and comparative interim periods.

In our view the parent is allowed, but not required, to adjust the comparative interim information (for the quarter ended 31 March 2011) in its 31 March 2012 interim financial report.

Whilst IAS 34 and IAS 29 are silent on the matter, a corollary of this approach suggests that when an economy stops being hyperinflationary, the entity should stop applying the requirements of IAS 29 during that interim period. However, in practice, it is difficult to determine when an economy stops being hyperinflationary. The characteristics indicating restored confidence in an economy (such as the population ceasing to store wealth in a more stable foreign currency) change gradually as sufficient time elapses to indicate that the three-year cumulative inflation rate is likely to stay below 100%. When the exit from hyperinflation can reasonably be identified, an entity should stop applying IAS 29 in that interim period. Prior interim periods should not be restated; instead, the entity should treat the amounts expressed in the measuring unit current as at the end of the previous reporting period as the basis for the carrying amounts in its subsequent interim reports *[IAS 29.38]* (see Chapter 18 at 7.2).

9.7 Provisions, contingencies and accruals for other costs

9.7.1 Provisions

IAS 34 requires an entity to apply the same criteria for recognising and measuring a provision at an interim date as it would at year-end. *[IAS 34.B4]*. Hence, an entity should recognise a provision when it has no realistic alternative but to transfer economic benefits because of an event that has created a legal or constructive obligation. *[IAS 34.B3]*. The standard emphasises that the existence or non-existence of an obligation to transfer benefits is a question of fact, and does not depend on the length of the reporting period. *[IAS 34.B4]*.

The obligation is adjusted upward or downward at each interim reporting date, if the entity's best estimate of the amount of the obligation changes. The standard states that any corresponding loss or gain should normally be recognised in profit or loss. *[IAS 34.B3]*. However, an entity applying IFRIC 1 – *Changes in Existing Decommissioning, Restoration and Similar Liabilities* – might instead need to adjust the carrying amount of the corresponding asset rather than recognise a gain or loss.

9.7.2 Other planned but irregularly occurring costs

Many entities budget for costs that they expect to incur irregularly during the year, such as advertising campaigns, employee training and charitable contributions. Even though these costs are planned and expected to recur annually, they tend to be discretionary in nature. Therefore, it is generally not appropriate to recognise an obligation at the end of an interim financial reporting period for such costs that are not yet incurred, as they do not meet the definition of a liability. *[IAS 34.B11]*.

Chapter 39

As discussed at 8.2.2 above, IAS 34 prohibits the recognition or deferral of costs incurred unevenly throughout the year at the interim date if recognition or deferral would be inappropriate at year-end. *[IAS 34.39]*. Accordingly, such costs should be recognised as they are incurred and an entity should not recognise provisions or accruals in the interim report to adjust these costs to their budgeted amount.

Extract 39.30: Coca-Cola Hellenic Bottling Company S.A. (Q2, 2008)

Condensed notes to the consolidated financial statements [extract]
1.   Accounting policies [extract]

The accounting policies used in the preparation of the condensed interim consolidated financial statements of Coca-Cola Hellenic Bottling Company S.A. ('Coca-Cola Hellenic' or the 'Company' or the 'Group') are consistent with those used in the annual financial statements for the year ended 31 December 2007, as described in those annual financial statements.

Operating results for the six months ended 27 June 2008 are not indicative of the results that may be expected for the year ended 31 December 2008 because of business seasonality. Business seasonality results from a combination of higher unit sales of the Company's products in the warmer months of the year and the methods of accounting for fixed costs such as depreciation and interest expense that are not significantly affected by business seasonality.

Costs that are incurred unevenly during the financial year are anticipated or deferred in the interim report only if it would also be appropriate to anticipate or defer such costs at the end of the financial year.

These condensed interim consolidated financial statements have been prepared in accordance with IFRS as issued by the International Accounting Standards Board ('IASB') and IFRS as adopted by the European Union ('EU') applicable to *Interim Financial Reporting* ('IAS 34'). IFRS as adopted by the EU differs in certain respects from IFRS as issued by the IASB. However, the differences have no impact on the Group's condensed interim consolidated financial statements for the periods presented. These condensed interim consolidated financial statements should be read in conjunction with the 2007 annual financial statements, which include a full description of the accounting policies of the Company.

9.7.3   Major planned periodic maintenance or overhaul

The cost of periodic maintenance, a planned major overhaul, or other seasonal expenditures expected to occur after the interim reporting date should not be recognised for interim reporting purposes unless an event before the end of the interim period causes the entity to have a legal or constructive obligation. The mere intention or necessity to incur expenditures in the future is not sufficient to recognise an obligation as at the interim reporting date. *[IAS 34.B2]*. Similarly, an entity may not defer and amortise such costs if they are incurred early in the year, but do not satisfy the criteria for recognition as an asset as at the interim reporting date.

9.7.4   Contingent lease payments

Contingent lease payments can create legal or constructive obligations that are recognised as liabilities. If a lease includes contingent payments based on achieving a certain level of annual sales (or annual use of the asset), an obligation can arise in an interim period before the required level of annual sales (or usage) is achieved. If the entity expects to achieve the required level of annual sales (or usage), it should recognise a liability as it has no realistic alternative but to make the future lease payment. *[IAS 34.B7]*.

9.8 Earnings per share

Earnings per share (EPS) in an interim period is computed in the same way as for annual periods. However, IAS 33 – *Earnings per Share* – does not allow diluted EPS of a prior period to be restated for subsequent changes in the assumptions used in those EPS calculations. *[IAS 33.65]*. This approach might be perceived as inconsistent to the year-to-date approach which should be followed for computing EPS for an interim period. For example, if an entity, reporting quarterly, computes diluted EPS in its first quarter financial statements, it cannot restate the reported EPS subsequently for any changes in the assumptions used. However, following an year-to-date approach, the entity should consider the revised assumptions to compute the diluted EPS for the six months in its second quarter financial statements, which, in this case would not be the sum of its EPS for first quarter and the second quarter.

10 USE OF ESTIMATES

IAS 34 requires that the measurement procedures followed in an interim financial report should be designed to ensure that the resulting information is reliable and that all material financial information that is relevant to an understanding of the financial position or performance of the entity is appropriately disclosed. Whilst estimation is necessary in both interim and annual financial statements, the standard recognises that preparing interim financial reports generally requires greater use of estimates than at year-end. *[IAS 34.41]*. Consequently, the measurement of assets and liabilities at an interim date may involve less use of outside experts in determining amounts for items such as provisions, contingencies, pensions or non-current assets revalued at fair values. Reliable measurement of such amounts may simply involve updating the previously reported year-end position. The procedures may be less rigorous than those at year-end. The example below is based on Appendix C to IAS 34. *[IAS 34.42]*.

Example 39.18: Use of estimates

Inventories	Full stock-taking and valuation procedures may not be required for inventories at interim dates, although it may be done at year-end. It may be sufficient to make estimates at interim dates based on sales margins.
Classifications of current and non-current assets and liabilities	Entities may do a more thorough investigation for classifying assets and liabilities as current or non-current at annual reporting dates than at interim dates.
Provisions	Determining the appropriate provision (such as a provision for warranties, environmental costs, and site restoration costs) may be complex and often costly and time-consuming. Entities sometimes engage outside experts to assist in the annual calculations. Making similar estimates at interim dates often entails updating of the prior annual provision rather than the engaging of outside experts to do a new calculation.

Chapter 39

Pensions	IAS 19 requires that an entity determine the present value of defined benefit obligations and the market value of plan assets at the end of each reporting period and encourages an entity to involve a professionally qualified actuary in measurement of the obligations. As discussed at 9.3.3 above, market values of plan assets as at the interim reporting date should be available without recourse to an actuary, and reliable measurement of defined benefit obligations for interim reporting purposes can often be extrapolated from the latest actuarial valuation.
Income taxes	Entities may calculate income tax expense and deferred income tax liability at annual dates by applying the tax rate for each individual jurisdiction to measures of income for each jurisdiction. Paragraph 14 of Appendix B (see 9.5.1 above) acknowledges that while that degree of precision is desirable at interim reporting dates as well, it may not be achievable in all cases, and a weighted-average of rates across jurisdictions or across categories of income is used if it is a reasonable approximation of the effect of using more specific rates.
Contingencies	The measurement of contingencies may involve the opinions of legal experts or other advisers. Formal reports from independent experts are sometimes obtained for contingencies. Such opinions about litigation, claims, assessments, and other contingencies and uncertainties may or may not also be needed at interim dates.
Revaluations and fair value accounting	IAS 16 allows an entity to choose as its accounting policy the revaluation model whereby items of property, plant and equipment are revalued to fair value. Similarly, IAS 40 requires an entity to determine the fair value of investment property. An entity should revalue at the end of the interim reporting period, but may choose not to rely on professionally qualified valuers to the extent that is required at year-end.
Intercompany reconciliations	Some intercompany balances that are reconciled on a detailed level in preparing consolidated financial statements at year-end might be reconciled at a less detailed level in preparing consolidated financial statements at an interim date.
Specialised industries	Because of complexity, costliness, and time, interim period measurements in specialised industries might be less precise than at year-end. An example is calculation of insurance reserves by insurance companies.

Attention is given to items that are recognised at fair value and that are outside the scope of IAS 36. Although an entity is not required to use professionally qualified valuers at interim reporting dates, and may only update the previous year-end position, the entity is required to recognise impairments in the proper interim period.

11   RESTATEMENT OF PREVIOUSLY REPORTED INTERIM PERIODS

As discussed at 8.1 above, an entity should apply the same accounting policies as applied in the most recent annual financial statements as adjusted for accounting policy changes that are to be reflected in the next annual financial statements. *[IAS 34.28]*. One objective of IAS 34's rules on the adoption of new accounting policies is to ensure that a single accounting policy is applied to a particular class of transactions throughout the year. Another objective is to ensure consistency with IAS 8, under which a change in accounting policy is adopted retrospectively and prior period financial data are restated as far back as practicable. *[IAS 34.44]*.

In the absence of any specified transitional provisions in a new IFRS or interpretation, IAS 34 requires a change in accounting policy to be reflected: *[IAS 34.43]*

(a) by restating the financial statements of prior interim periods of the current year, and the comparable interim periods of any prior years that will be restated in the annual financial statements under IAS 8; or

(b) when it is impracticable to determine the cumulative effect at the beginning of the year of applying a new accounting policy to all prior periods, by:

    (i) adjusting the financial statements of prior interim periods of the current year; and

    (ii) applying the new accounting policy prospectively from the earliest date practicable in comparable interim periods of prior years.

IAS 1 states that application of a requirement is 'impracticable' when the entity cannot apply it after making every reasonable effort to do so. *[IAS 1.7]*.

An entity is generally not permitted to change an accounting policy from a date later than the beginning of the current year, for example, as at the start of the second quarter for an entity reporting quarterly. To do so allows two different accounting policies be applied to a particular class of transactions within a single year and makes interim allocation difficult, obscures operating results, and complicates the analysis and understandability of interim period information. *[IAS 34.45]*. However, as noted in 8.1.2 above, in certain circumstances an entity is allowed or required to adopt an IFRS mid-year in a manner that over-rides the general requirements of IAS 8. If an entity prepares a complete set of financial statements, it should present a third balance sheet and the related notes. *[IAS 34.5(f)]*.

12 EFFECTIVE DATES AND TRANSITIONAL RULES

12.1 First-time presentation of interim reports complying with IAS 34

IAS 34 became effective for financial statements covering periods beginning on or after 1 January 1999; it did not contain any general transitional rules. *[IAS 34.46]*. Therefore, an existing IFRS reporting entity must apply the requirements of IAS 34 in full and without any transitional relief when it first chooses (or is required) to publish an interim financial report prepared under IFRS.

For example, an entity that has already published annual financial statements prepared under IFRS and either chooses (or is required) to prepare interim financial reports in compliance with IAS 34 must present all the information required by the standard for the current interim period, cumulatively for the current year-to-date, and for comparable periods (current and year-to-date) of the preceding year. *[IAS 34.20]*.

Chapter 39

The absence of any transitional provisions requires such entities to restate previously reported interim financial information to comply with IAS 34 and to present information relating to comparative interim periods, such as in respect of segment disclosures or in relation to asset write-downs and reversals thereof, which might not previously have been reported.

12.1.1 Condensed financial statements in the year of incorporation or when an entity converts from its local GAAP to IFRS

The standard defines 'interim period' as a financial reporting period shorter than a full financial year *[IAS 34.4]* and requires the format of condensed financial statements for an interim period to include each of the headings and subtotals that were included in the entity's most recent annual financial statements. *[IAS 34.10]*.

However, IAS 34 provides no guidance for an entity that either is required or chooses to issue interim financial statements before it has prepared a set of IFRS compliant annual financial statements. This situation might arise in the entity's first year of its existence or in the year in which the entity converts from its local GAAP to IFRS. Whilst the standard does not prohibit the entity from preparing a condensed set of interim financial statements, it fails to specify how an entity would interpret the minimum disclosure requirements of IAS 34 when there are no annual financial statements to refer to.

In our opinion, the entity should consider making additional disclosures to recognise that a user of this first set of interim financial statements does not have the access otherwise assumed by the standard to the most recent annual financial report of the entity. Accordingly, the explanation of significant events and transactions and changes in financial position in the period should be more detailed than the update normally expected in IAS 34. *[IAS 34.15]*. In the absence of any specific regulatory requirements to which the entity is subject, the following are examples of additional considerations that would apply:

- Since it is not possible to make a statement that the same accounting policies and methods of computation have been applied, *[IAS 34.16A(a)]*, the entity should disclose all those accounting policies and methods of computation in the same level of detail as it would in a set of annual financial statements. When the entity issues interim reports on a quarterly basis, the first quarter interim report should provide the abovementioned details; subsequent quarterly reports could refer to the details included in the first quarter report;

- Similarly, the disclosure of the nature and amount of changes in estimates of amounts reported in prior periods will have to go into more detail than just the changes normally required to be disclosed; *[IAS 34.16A(d)]*

- Mere disclosure of transfers between levels of the fair value hierarchy used in measuring the fair value of financial instruments, *[IAS 34.15B(k)]*, would not be meaningful unless put in the context of how those fair values are determined (e.g. methods used, any assumptions applied) and providing a detailed classification of all such financial instrument measurements using fair value hierarchy, based on the significance of the inputs used;

- Rather than disclosing changes in the basis of segmentation or in the basis of measurement of segment profit and loss, *[IAS 34.16A(g)(v)]*, a full description will be necessary, as will the disclosure of segment assets *[IAS 34.16A(g)(iv)]*, where such information is required to be disclosed in the annual financial statements *[IAS 34.16A(g)]*;

- More extensive disclosure than simply the changes since the last report date will be required for contingent liabilities and contingent assets; *[IAS 34.15B(m)]* and

- In the absence of a complete set of annual financial statements complying with IFRS, the entity should include each of the headings and subtotals in the condensed financial statements that it would expect to include in its first financial statements prepared under IFRS.

Entities that have converted from local GAAP to IFRS and have not yet published IFRS annual financial statements are subject to additional requirements under IFRS 1 – *First-time Adoption of International Financial Reporting Standards* – when presenting interim reports in accordance with IAS 34. Such requirements are discussed in detail in Chapter 5 at 6.6.

12.2 Consequential amendments to IFRIC 10 when first adopting IFRS 9

As discussed at 9.2 above, the IASB issued IFRS 9 in November 2009 (subsequently expanded and amended in October 2010), which made amendments to IFRIC 10. The amendment deletes references to equity instruments and financial assets carried at cost. With the adoption of IFRS 9, such financial assets would not be carried at cost and as a consequence, the determination of impairment and related reversals would not be relevant for such instruments in this context.

These amendments should be applied concurrently with the adoption of IFRS 9, which is mandatory for annual periods beginning on or after 1 January 2013 *[IFRS 9.7.1.1]*. The transitional arrangements for the adoption of IFRS 9 are discussed in Chapter 47 at 9.

13 FUTURE DEVELOPMENTS

As discussed in more detail at 8 and 9 above, IAS 34 has certain inconsistencies with other standards as well as within the standard itself. Such inconsistencies are due to the age of the standard and its failure to define the overall purpose of interim reporting adequately. IAS 34 was issued in 1998 and its principles, in particular allowing the revision of earlier estimates, sit less comfortably beside subsequent standards that use a balance sheet approach. The IASB plans to reconsider the requirements of IAS 34 after the FASB completes its review of interim reporting in the US.

The FASB deliberations represent the third element, Phase C, of its joint project with the IASB on Financial Statement Presentation. The Joint Project Summary as at 1 July 2009 indicated that Phase C topics include:

Chapter 39

- which financial statements, if any, are presented in an interim financial report;
- whether a condensed interim reporting is allowed, and if so, whether guidance is given on how the information may be condensed; and
- what comparative periods, if any, are required or allowed in interim financial reports and when, if ever, should 12 month-to-date financial statements be required or allowed in interim financial reports.

In November 2010, the IASB and the FASB decided to amend the timetable for projects determined to be 'important but less urgent'. This included the project on Financial Statement Presentation.[1]

In presenting the project for inclusion in its agenda going forward, the IASB states that the main objective is to improve guidance on the organisation and presentation of information in the financial statements, including the development of principles to ensure that an appropriate level of disaggregation of information is presented which at the same time portrays a cohesive picture of the entity's activities.[2]

Furthermore IASB has proposed including in its agenda a separate project on Interim Reporting to consider what improvements should be made to overcome issues that are posed due to the possible tensions between the (underlying) objective of IAS 34 that the frequency of reporting should not affect the measurement of the annual financial statements and the requirement of the standard to apply a 'discrete' approach in the interim financial reports; and to address the associated question of whether full remeasurement of assets and liabilities is required at each interim reporting date.[3]

Should the inclusion of the above projects in the IASB's agenda be confirmed, there will be considerable implications for interim reporting.

References

1 *IASB Work Plan – projected timetable as at 26 July 2011*, IASB.
2 Request for Views *Agenda Consultation 2011*, IASB, July 2011, Appendix C.
3 Request for Views *Agenda Consultation 2011*, IASB, July 2011, Appendix C.

Chapter 40   Agriculture

List of examples

Chapter 40   Agriculture

1   INTRODUCTION

IAS 41 – *Agriculture* – prescribes the accounting treatment for agricultural activity, from the initial recognition of a biological asset to the harvest of agricultural produce.

Practical difficulties arise when determining which assets are within the scope of the standard, particularly for arrangements that involve leases or concessions. However, it is the standard's application of the fair value model that is the most problematic and contentious.

For assets that are in-scope, IAS 41 requires the application of the fair value model to animals and plant life alike, with limited relief. Under this approach, a market price for a part-grown crop is presumed to exist (or is presumed to be accurately determinable if there is no such market price) and the part-grown crop must be valued at this price in the entity's financial statements. The model is also applied to all biological assets regardless of whether they are consumed as part of the agricultural activity (consumable biological assets) or not (bearer biological assets).

During their June 2009 meeting, members of the IFRS Advisory Council observed that bearer biological assets such as rubber trees and vines do not produce offspring, but rather produce a flow of product, be that latex or grapes, in very much the same way as any other piece of plant and equipment. As a result of this discussion the New Zealand and Malaysian national standard setters have been asked to consider further proposals. It is unlikely that these discussions will lead to a complete reconsideration of the principles of IAS 41. However, in their *2011 Agenda Consultation* – Request for views document, the IASB did acknowledge the concerns that had been raised regarding the application of the fair value model to bearer biological assets and noted that a possible future project 'could be a limited-scope improvement to IAS 41 to address bearer biological assets'[1].

2   OBJECTIVE, DEFINITIONS AND SCOPE

2.1   Objective

The stated objective of IAS 41 is to 'prescribe the accounting treatment and disclosures related to agricultural activity'. *[IAS 41 Objective].*

2.2   Definitions

2.2.1   *Agriculture-related definitions*

IAS 41 defines *agricultural activity* as 'the management by an entity of the biological transformation and harvest of biological assets for sale or for conversion into agricultural produce or into additional biological assets'. *[IAS 41.5].*

The standard states that 'agricultural activity' covers a wide range of activities, e.g. 'raising livestock, forestry, annual or perennial cropping, cultivating orchards and plantations, floriculture, and aquaculture (including fish farming)'. *[IAS 41.6].* Nevertheless, these agricultural activities have certain common features:

'(a)   *Capability to change* – Living animals and plants are capable of biological transformation;

(b)   *Management of change* – Management facilitates biological transformation by enhancing, or at least stabilising, conditions necessary for the process to take place (for example, nutrient levels, moisture, temperature, fertility, and light). Such management distinguishes agricultural activity from other activities. For example, harvesting from unmanaged sources (such as ocean fishing and deforestation) is not agricultural activity; and

(c)   *Measurement of change* – The change in quality (for example, genetic merit, density, ripeness, fat cover, protein content, and fibre strength) or quantity (for example, progeny, weight, cubic metres, fibre length or diameter, and number of buds) brought about by biological transformation "or harvest" is measured and monitored as a routine management function.' *[IAS 41.6].*

Biological transformation under IAS 41 'comprises the processes of growth, degeneration, production, and procreation that cause qualitative or quantitative changes in a biological asset'. *[IAS 41.5].* The standard explains that biological transformation results in the following types of outcomes:

'(a)   asset changes through:

(i)   growth (an increase in quantity or improvement in quality of an animal or plant);

(ii)   degeneration (a decrease in the quantity or deterioration in quality of an animal or plant); or

(iii)   procreation (creation of additional living animals or plants); or

(b)   production of agricultural produce such as latex, tea leaf, wool, and milk.' *[IAS 41.7].*

IAS 41 defines the following additional terms that are used throughout the standard: *[IAS 41.5]*

A *biological asset* is a living animal or plant.

A *group of biological assets* is an aggregation of similar living animals or plants.

Agricultural produce is the harvested product of the entity's biological assets.

Harvest is the detachment of produce from a biological asset or the cessation of a biological asset's life processes.

The standard provides the following examples to illustrate the above definitions: *[IAS 41.4]*

Biological assets	Agricultural produce	Products that are the result of processing after harvest
Sheep	Wool	Yarn, carpet
Trees in a plantation forest	Felled trees	Logs, lumber
Plants	Cotton	Thread, clothing
	Harvested cane	Sugar
Dairy cattle	Milk	Cheese
Pigs	Carcass	Sausages, cured hams
Bushes	Leaf	Tea, cured tobacco
Vines	Grapes	Wine
Fruit trees	Picked fruit	Processed fruit

Costs to sell are the incremental costs directly attributable to the disposal of an asset excluding finance costs and income tax.

2.2.2 General definitions

IAS 41 defines the general terms it uses throughout the standard as follows: *[IAS 41.8]*

Carrying amount is the amount at which an asset is recognised in the Statement of Financial Position.

Government grants are as defined in IAS 20 – *Accounting for Government Grants and Disclosure of Government Assistance* (see Chapter 27).

For entities that have adopted IFRS 13 – *Fair Value Measurement* early (see 4.1 below and Chapter 16 for further discussion), the definitions of fair value and active market in that standard apply rather than the definition in IAS 41. Otherwise, IAS 41 defines those terms as follows:

An *active market* is a market where all the following conditions exist:

(a) the items traded within the market are homogeneous;

(b) willing buyers and sellers can normally be found at any time; and

(c) prices are available to the public.

Fair value is the amount for which an asset could be exchanged, or a liability settled, between knowledgeable, willing parties in an arm's length transaction.

The standard requires an entity to take the present location and condition of the biological asset into account in determining its fair value.

2.3   Scope

IAS 41 applies to accounting for biological assets, agricultural produce at the point of harvest and government grants involving biological assets measured at fair value less costs to sell. However to be within the scope of IAS 41, these items must relate to agricultural activity. *[IAS 41.1]*.

IAS 41 explicitly excludes the following assets from its scope: *[IAS 41.2]*

- land related to agricultural activity, which should be accounted for under either IAS 16 – *Property, Plant and Equipment* – or IAS 40 – *Investment Property*; *[IAS 41.B55-B57]*

- intangible assets related to agricultural activity, for instance the costs of developing new disease resistant crops, which should be accounted for under IAS 38 – *Intangible Assets.* *[IAS 41.B58-B60]*.

2.3.1   Biological assets outside the scope of IAS 41

Biological assets may be outside the scope of IAS 41 when they are not used in agricultural activity. For example, animals in a zoo (or game park) that does not have an active breeding programme and rarely sells any animals or animal products would be outside the scope of the standard. Another example is activities in the pharmaceutical industry that involve the culture of bacteria. Such activity would not fall within the scope of IAS 41. While the bacteria may be considered a biological asset, the development of a culture by pharmaceutical company would not constitute agricultural activity.

Biological assets outside the scope of IAS 41 will fall normally within the scope of either IAS 16 or IAS 2 – *Inventories.*

2.3.2   Agricultural produce before and after harvest

IAS 41 only applies to agricultural produce (i.e. harvested crops) at the point of harvest and not prior or subsequent to harvest. Under IAS 41 unharvested agricultural produce is considered to be part of the biological asset from which it will be harvested. Therefore, before harvest, agricultural produce should not be accounted for separately from the biological asset it comes from. Thus, for example, grapes on the vine should be accounted for as part of the vines themselves right up to the point of harvest.

Subsequent to harvest agricultural produce is accounted for under IAS 2. *[IAS 41.3]*. Under that standard the agricultural produce is initially recognised as inventory at its fair value, determined under IAS 41, which becomes its cost for IAS 2 purposes. *[IAS 41.B45]*.

2.3.3   Products that are the result of processing after harvest

IAS 41 does not deal with the processing of agricultural produce after harvest. The standard makes it clear that, even if the processing is considered 'a logical and natural extension of agricultural activity, and the events taking place may bear some similarity to biological transformation, such processing is not included within the definition of agricultural activity'. For example, the processing of grapes into wine – a process in which yeast (a fungus) converts sugars into alcohol – is not deemed to be included within the definition of agricultural activity in the standard. *[IAS 41.3]*. Similarly, cheese production would fall outside the definition of agricultural activity.

2.3.4 Leased assets

Leases involving biological assets are common in many jurisdictions, for example, the leasing of a vineyard, where the lessee rents the vineyard, tends the vines and sells the grapes.

Whether or not a leased biological asset is within the scope of IAS 41 will depend on each arrangement's specific facts and circumstances. A key determinant is the classification of a biological asset lease as either a finance lease or operating lease under IAS 17 – *Leases* (see Chapter 26 for a discussion regarding leases). *[IAS 41.B82(n)]*.

- Finance leases
  - The lessee initially recognises the leased biological asset under IAS 17. Subsequently, the lessee measures and presents it under IAS 41 (for measurement purposes the leased biological asset is outside the scope of IAS 17). The lessee makes disclosures both under IAS 41 and IAS 17. *[IAS 41.B82(n)]*.
  - The lessor accounts for the lease in accordance with IAS 17.
- Operating leases
  - The lessee accounts for the lease in accordance with IAS 17.
  - The lessor measures and presents the leased biological asset under IAS 41 (for measurement purposes the leased biological asset is outside the scope of IAS 17). The lessor makes disclosures both under IAS 41 and IAS 17. *[IAS 41.B82(n)]*.

Biological asset lease arrangements may include the land to which the biological asset is attached. Any leased land would need to be separately accounted for under the relevant standard, for example IAS 16 or IAS 40, as it is explicitly excluded from the scope of IAS 41 (see 2.3 above).

In the example above, where the vines are leased under an operating lease, the arrangement would be within the scope of IAS 41. Therefore, the lessor must account for the leased vines (excluding any related land) under IAS 41 – both upon initial recognition and subsequently – at fair value less costs to sell. It is worth noting that IAS 41.1 requires the standard to be applied to biological assets when they relate to agricultural activity. In this case, the grapes are the agricultural produce and vines are managed, albeit by the lessee and not the lessor. Since IAS 41 does not specify who must do the managing, the definition of agricultural activity is met.

2.3.5 Concessions

A concession typically involves a government, or other controlling authority, granting land to an entity but requiring that the land be used for a specific purpose, for example, growing certain crops for a minimum period of time.

The treatment of each concession will be dependent on the specific facts and circumstances. However, if the concession requires an entity to undertake agricultural activity, the agricultural activity will be within the scope of IAS 41. The grant received (i.e. the land) may also be within the scope of the standard. Section 3.3 below addresses the treatment of government grants related to biological assets.

3   RECOGNITION AND MEASUREMENT PRINCIPLES

3.1   Recognition

An entity shall recognise a biological asset or agricultural produce within the scope of IAS 41 only when: *[IAS 41.10]*

(a)   it controls the asset as a result of past events;

(b)   it is probable that future economic benefits associated with the asset will flow to the entity; and

(c)   the fair value or cost of the asset can be measured reliably.

3.1.1   *Control*

In agricultural activity, an entity may evidence control by, for example, 'legal ownership of cattle and the branding or otherwise marking of the cattle on acquisition, birth, or weaning'. *[IAS 41.11]*.

3.2   Measurement

3.2.1   *Biological assets*

3.2.1.A   *Initial and subsequent measurement*

A biological asset shall be measured on initial recognition and at the end of each reporting period at its fair value less costs to sell, unless the fair value cannot be measured reliably. *[IAS 41.12]*. In the latter case, the entity shall measure the biological assets at historic cost less any accumulated depreciation and any accumulated impairment losses (see 3.2.4 below).

3.2.1.B   *Subsequent expenditure*

IAS 41 does not prescribe how an entity should account for subsequent expenditure in relation to biological assets, because the (then) IASC believed this to be unnecessary with a fair-value-based measurement approach. *[IAS 41.B62]*.

Such expenditure may be expensed as incurred or capitalised as additions to the related biological asset. However, as the biological asset will be re-measured at the end of each reporting period, any amounts capitalised will result in no more than a reallocation between expenses and the fair value gain or loss for the biological asset. Therefore, an entity's policy in relation to subsequent expenditure will have no effect on its equity or net profit or loss, although it will affect:

- the reconciliation of changes in the carrying amount of biological assets;
- the classification of the expenditure in the income statement as either an expense or as part of the net gain or loss on biological assets; and
- the presentation of investments in biological assets in the statement of cash flows.

In our view, an entity should select an accounting policy for subsequent expenditure that is broadly consistent with the principles in other standards, such as IAS 16 and IAS 38. For example, in the case of a vineyard an entity may want to expense maintenance costs such as pruning, while adding capital expenditure such as planting new vines to the carrying value of the asset; though it must be understood that any such additions would be adjusted at each period end when the biological asset concerned was revalued to its new fair value.

3.2.2 Agricultural produce

Agricultural produce harvested from an entity's biological assets should initially 'be measured at its fair value less costs to sell at the point of harvest'. *[IAS 41.13]*. The standard presumes that an entity can always determine this amount and hence does not permit valuation at historical cost on the grounds that the fair value cannot be determined reliably. *[IAS 41.32, B43]*.

The value resulting from initial measurement is subsequently used as cost in applying IAS 2 (if the agricultural produce is to be sold), IAS 16 (if harvested logs are used for the construction of a building) or other applicable International Financial Reporting Standards. *[IAS 41.13, B8]*.

An important reason for requiring agricultural produce at the point of harvest to be measured at fair value was to ensure that the basis of measurement would be consistent with that of biological assets and to avoid inconsistent and distorted reporting of current period performance upon harvest of agricultural produce. *[IAS 41.B42]*.

3.2.3 Gains and losses

IAS 41 requires gains and losses arising on the initial recognition of a biological asset at fair value less costs to sell to be included in profit or loss for the period in which they arise. *[IAS 41.26]*. The standard warns that 'a loss may arise on initial recognition of a biological asset, because costs to sell are deducted in determining fair value less costs to sell of a biological asset.' On the other hand, a gain may arise on the initial recognition of a biological asset (e.g. when a calf is born). *[IAS 41.27]*.

Subsequent to initial recognition, reported gains or losses essentially represent the difference between two fair values. As such, the standard effectively decouples profit recognition from a sales transaction. One consequence of this approach is to anticipate a realised profit, often by a matter of years for long term crops such as trees.

The implications for initial recognition of agricultural produce are similar – an entity may need to recognise a gain or loss on agricultural produce upon harvesting, if the fair value of the harvested produce is different from the pre-harvest valuation. *[IAS 41.29]*. The standard requires that 'a gain or loss arising on initial recognition of agricultural produce at fair value less costs to sell shall be included in profit or loss for the period in which it arises'. *[IAS 41.28]*.

3.2.4   Inability to measure fair value reliably

3.2.4.A   Rebutting the presumption

Under IAS 41, there is a presumption that the fair value of all biological assets can be measured reliably. This presumption can only be rebutted on initial recognition for a biological asset (*not* agricultural produce). To be able to rebut the presumption, an entity must demonstrate:

(a)   Market-determined prices or values for the biological asset are not available; and

(b)   Alternative estimates of fair value for the biological asset are determined to be clearly unreliable. *[IAS 41.30]*.

An entity that previously measured a biological asset at its fair value less costs to sell cannot revert to a cost-based measurement in a later period, even if a fair value can no longer be measured reliably. *[IAS 41.31]*. The standard assumes that reliable estimates of fair value would rarely, if ever, cease to be available. *[IAS 41.B36]*. Section 4.4 below discusses practical problems associated with determining fair value in the absence of a market price more fully.

If it becomes possible at a later date to measure the fair value of a biological asset reliably, the entity shall measure it at fair value less costs to sell. *[IAS 41.30]*. In developing the standard, the (then) IASC noted in this respect that 'in agricultural activity, it is likely that fair value becomes measurable more reliably as biological transformation occurs and that fair value measurement is preferable to cost in those cases'. Therefore, the IASC 'decided to require fair value measurement once fair value becomes reliably measurable'. *[IAS 41.B35]*.

IAS 41 presumes that the fair value of a non-current biological asset that 'meets the criteria to be classified as held for sale (or is included in a disposal group that is classified as held for sale) in accordance with IFRS 5 – *Non-current Assets Held for Sale and Discontinued Operations*' can always be measured reliably. *[IAS 41.30]*.

3.2.4.B   The cost model

If on initial recognition the fair value cannot be measured reliably, the biological asset shall be measured at cost less any accumulated depreciation and any accumulated impairment losses. *[IAS 41.30]*.

In determining cost, accumulated depreciation and accumulated impairment losses the entity needs to consider the requirements of IAS 2, IAS 16 and IAS 36 – *Impairment of Assets*. *[IAS 41.33]*. IAS 41 provides no further guidance on the application of the cost model or the extent to which entities should consider the requirements of these standards.

Both IAS 2 and IAS 16 establish frameworks within which to determine cost. The nature of the biological asset should be taken into consideration when determining which approach to use. Consumable biological assets that are to be harvested as agricultural produce or sold as biological assets, for example livestock to be slaughtered or held for sale, fish in farms or crops to be harvested, may be more consistent with inventories accounted for in accordance with IAS 2. Bearer biological assets, such as dairy cows, grape vines and fruit trees, may be more consistent with plant and equipment accounted for in accordance with IAS 16.

The nature of the biological asset may also be helpful in determining when to commence depreciation and the useful life of the asset. IAS 16.53 requires depreciation to commence when an asset is available for use. Determining when a biological asset is available for use may be more obvious in relation to bearer biological assets. For example, a cow may be considered available for use as soon as it is sufficiently mature to produce milk. However, for consumable biological assets defining when an asset is available for use is less clear. This is because, the period between these assets reaching maturity and being sold or harvested is typically short. It could also be argued that entities do not hold consumable biological assets for use and, as such, applying a depreciation model may be inappropriate.

The last component of the cost model is the assessment of impairment in accordance with IAS 36. Entities that have demonstrated fair value cannot be reliably determined for a biological asset should be careful to apply a consistent approach when determining the asset's recoverable amount. As such, using a value in use approach to determine recoverable amount will be required.

An entity that uses the reliability exception should disclose certain additional information in its financial statements (see 5.2 below). *[IAS 41.B37]*.

3.3 Government grants

Government grants involving biological assets should only be accounted for under IAS 20 if the biological asset is 'measured at its cost less any accumulated depreciation and any accumulated impairment losses' (see Chapter 27 for a discussion of government grants). *[IAS 41.37-38]*. Government grants relating to biological assets accounted for at fair value less costs to sell should be accounted for as follows.

An unconditional government grant related to 'a biological asset measured at its fair value less costs to sell shall be recognised in profit or loss when, and only when, the government grant becomes receivable'. *[IAS 41.34]*. An entity is therefore not permitted under IAS 41 to deduct a government grant from the carrying amount of the related asset. This would be inconsistent with a 'fair value model in which an asset is measured and presented at its fair value' because the entity would recognise even conditional government grants in income immediately. *[IAS 41.B66]*.

Any conditional government grant related to a biological asset measured at its fair value less costs to sell – including government grants that require an entity not to engage in a specified agricultural activity – should be recognised only when the conditions attaching to the grant are met. *[IAS 41.35]*. IAS 41 permits an entity to recognise a government grant as income only to the extent that it (i) has met the terms and conditions of the grant and (ii) has no obligation to return the grant. The following example, which is taken from IAS 41, illustrates how an entity should apply these requirements.

Example 40.1:   Conditional government grants [IAS 41.36]

A government grant requires an entity to farm in a particular location for five years and requires the entity to return the entire government grant if it farms for less than five years. The government grant is not recognised as income until the five years have passed.

A government grant allows part of the government grant to be retained based on the passage of time. The entity recognises the government grant as income on a time proportion basis.

4   DETERMINING FAIR VALUE LESS COSTS TO SELL

4.1   The interaction between IAS 41 and IFRS 13 – Fair Value Measurement

The IASB issued IFRS 13 in May 2011, providing a single source of guidance on how to measure fair value. IFRS 13 must be applied prospectively to annual periods beginning on or after 1 January 2013, but may be adopted early. While IFRS 13 addresses how to measure fair value, it will not change what must be measured at fair value or when a fair value measurement must be performed.

- An entity that elects not to early adopt IFRS 13 continues to apply the existing requirements in IAS 41, until IFRS 13 is mandatorily effective.

- An entity that early adopts IFRS 13, would still look to IAS 41 when assessing what biological assets and agricultural produce to measure at fair value less costs to sell and when to measure (i.e. the measurement date). The entity would then look to IFRS 13 when measuring 'fair value' and IAS 41 when measuring 'costs to sell'. Disclosures in relation to the fair value measurement will need to be prepared in accordance with IFRS 13 and also IAS 41, to the extent that it requires additional agriculture-specific disclosures.

Section 4.4 of this chapter addresses the requirements for determining fair value in accordance with IAS 41 (i.e. for those entities that have not early adopted IFRS 13) and Section 5 addresses IAS 41's existing disclosure requirements. See Chapter 16 for a discussion regarding the requirements of IFRS 13.

4.2   Establishing 'what' to measure

4.2.1   Current condition and location

IAS 41 requires an entity to take the present location and condition of a biological asset into account in determining its fair value. This will have a direct impact on what is being measured. For example, entities measuring partly grown crops may also need to consider the fair value of the land in which it is planted (see 4.2.1.A below). It may also require an entity to consider alternative markets. For example, an entity that rears chickens may have to consider whether there is a market for immature chicks.

It is possible for an active market to exist in one geographical area but not in another area. For example, transportation costs may limit the geographical size of the market for agricultural produce significantly, possibly to the point where a local cooperative or factory is the only buyer. In the latter case, the local market – with one buyer and many sellers – will probably not meet the definition of an active market.

Given the logistical problems and generally high costs of transporting living animals and plants, there will be many different fair values for the same biological assets depending on their location. For example, 'the fair value of cattle at a farm is the price for the cattle in the relevant market less the transport and other costs of getting the cattle to that market'. *[IAS 41.9]*.

4.2.1.A   Biological assets attached to land

The standard observes that 'biological assets are often physically attached to land (for example, trees in a plantation forest).' In many cases there is no separate market for biological assets that are attached to the land, but 'an active market may exist for the combined assets, that is, for the biological assets, raw land, and land improvements, as a package'. An entity can use the information regarding the combined assets to determine the fair value of the biological assets. *[IAS 41.25]*. This suggested method might be difficult to apply in practice as illustrated below.

Example 40.2:   Biological assets attached to land

Entity A acquired a 10-hectare vineyard on 1 January 2011 for $1,200. The purchase price of the vineyard was attributed as follows:

1 January 2011	$
Purchase price	1,200
Land	(780)
Vineyard improvements	(130)
Grape vines	290

At the end of its financial year Entity A needs to determine the fair value of the grape vines in accordance with IAS 41 and invites two equally skilled professional valuers to determine the value of the grape vines.

31 December 2011	Valuer 1 $	Valuer 2 $
Fair value of an average 10-hectare vineyard	1,105	1,100
Adjustment for soil and climatic conditions	135	150
Estimated fair value of Entity A's vineyard	1,240	1,250
Fair value of the land	(830)	(825)
Fair value of vineyard improvements	(135)	(125)
Grape vines	275	300

Valuer 1 and Valuer 2 make a virtually identical assessment of the market values of the vineyard, the land and the vineyard improvements. Nevertheless, because the value of grape vines is calculated by subtracting all the other known elements from the total value of the vineyard, a noticeable difference arises in the valuation of the grape vines. In a similar vein, entities that use only one valuer need to be aware that even small changes in assumptions from period to period could have a significant impact on the valuation of biological assets, and therefore reported profits or losses.

4.2.1.B   Obligation to replant a biological asset after harvest

The Interpretations Committee confirmed in May 2004 its previous decisions that if an entity has an obligation to re-establish a biological asset after harvest, that obligation is attached to the land and does not affect the fair value of the biological assets currently growing on the land.

The problem of how to account for an obligation to replant was considered by the Board in 2007. The difficulty is that IAS 41.22 precludes an entity from including the costs of replanting a biological asset after harvest when using estimated future cash flows to determine the biological asset's fair value less costs to sell. However, circumstances can arise in which an entity is legally obliged to replant a biological asset after harvest. The interaction of the fair value measurement basis of IAS 41, the prohibition on including the replanting costs in determining that fair value and the requirement to recognise a provision for the cost of replanting in accordance with IAS 37 – *Provisions, Contingent Liabilities and Contingent Assets* – when the biological asset is harvested, could lead to a net expense being recognised at the point of harvest. There is concern that this does not appropriately reflect the commercial reality.

The Board made no decision on the matter and asked its staff to develop further possible solutions for later consideration.

4.2.2   *Grouping of assets*

IAS 41 states that 'the determination of fair value for a biological asset or agricultural produce may be facilitated by grouping biological assets or agricultural produce according to significant attributes; for example, by age or quality. An entity selects the attributes corresponding to the attributes used in the market as a basis for pricing'. *[IAS 41.15]*.

For example, when undertaking a forestry valuation, an entity may group trees in the forest based on factors such as species, when and where the trees were planted and the expected yield.

4.3   **Determining costs to sell**

Costs to sell are the incremental costs directly attributable to the disposal of an asset excluding finance costs and income tax. *[IAS 41.5]*.

Costs to sell should include all costs that are necessary for a sale to occur but would otherwise not arise. However, costs already included within the fair value measurement, such as transportation costs, should be excluded. Examples of costs to sell could include brokers' and dealers' commissions, levies by regulatory agencies and commodity exchanges, transfer taxes and duties. *[IAS 41.BC3, B22]*.

4.4   **Determining fair value**

4.4.1   *The fair value hierarchy*

At present the standard provides the following rules on determining the fair value of a biological asset or agricultural produce:

(a)   *an active market exists* – the quoted price in that market is the appropriate basis for determining the fair value of that asset

(b)   *no active market* – if an active market does not exist an entity should use one or more of the following *market-determined prices or values* to estimate fair value *[IAS 41.18]*:

(i)   the most recent market transaction price, provided the economic circumstances have not significantly changed;

(ii) market prices for similar assets with adjustment to reflect differences; and

(iii) sector benchmarks.

(c) *no active market and no market-based information is available* – if an active market does not exist and there is no market-based information available on which to base an estimate of fair value, an entity estimate fair value using a *discounted cash flows* method *[IAS 41.20]. Cost as an approximation of fair value* can only be used in limited circumstances. *[IAS 41.24]*.

Where an active market exists, IAS 41 requires the use of quoted prices in that market (see 4.4.2 below). Where there is no active market, an entity must use 'all available market-determined prices or values since otherwise there is a possibility that entities may opt to use present value of expected net cash flows from the asset even when useful market-determined prices or values are available'. *[IAS 41.B30]*. In other words, an entity is only permitted to use a discounted cash flow model (see 4.4.3.B below) or use cost as an approximation of fair value (see 4.4.3.C below) if there is no market-based information available. There are practical problems in certain industries with the use of market-based valuations where the market price of harvested part-grown produce arguably does not reflect the fair value of not-harvested part-grown produce – see 4.5 below for a discussion of this problem.

The problem of fair value measurement in the absence of a market price was considered by the (then) IASC in the context of IAS 41. It considered setting an explicit hierarchy for fair value measurement in cases where no active market exists. *[IAS 41.B29]*. The IASC concluded that 'a detailed hierarchy would not provide sufficient flexibility to appropriately deal with all the circumstances that may arise and decided not to set a detailed hierarchy in cases where no active market exists'. *[IAS 41.B30]*.

4.4.2   Determining fair value in an active market

If an active market exists for a biological asset or agricultural produce in its present location and condition, the quoted price in that market is the appropriate basis for determining the fair value of that asset.

If the entity has access to different active markets, it should use the quoted price in the most relevant market (i.e. the price in the market that is expected to be used). *[IAS 41.17]*.

The standard does not require an entity to use the most advantageous (highest) price in the accessible markets, *[IAS 41.B31]*, because there may well be sound commercial reasons for not selling in just one geographical market and the most relevant measurement results from using the expected market.

4.4.3   Determining fair value where there is no active market

4.4.3.A   Market-determined prices or values

When determining fair value using market-determined prices or values, the entity should use one or more of the following information sources, when available:

- the most recent market transaction price, provided that there has not been a significant change in economic circumstances between the date of that transaction and the end of the reporting period;
- market prices for similar assets with adjustment to reflect differences; and
- sector benchmarks such as the value of an orchard expressed per export tray, bushel, or hectare, and the value of cattle expressed per kilogram of meat. *[IAS 41.18]*.

If these information sources suggest different conclusions concerning the fair value of a biological asset or agricultural produce, the entity should consider 'the reasons for those differences, in order to arrive at the most reliable estimate of fair value within a relatively narrow range of reasonable estimates'. *[IAS 41.19]*.

4.4.3.B   Discounted cash flows

If market-determined prices or values are not available for a biological asset in its present condition, an entity should use 'the present value of expected net cash flows from the asset discounted at a current market-determined rate in determining fair value'. *[IAS 41.20]*.

The objective of a calculation of the present value of expected net cash flows is to determine the fair value of a biological asset in its present location and condition. An entity should consider this in determining an appropriate discount rate and in estimating expected cash flows.

In determining the present value of expected net cash flows, an entity includes the net cash flows that market participants would expect the asset to generate in its most relevant market. *[IAS 41.21]*. An entity 'incorporates expectations about possible variations in cash flows into either the expected cash flows, or the discount rate, or some combination of the two'. Furthermore, it should ensure that it uses assumptions for determining a discount rate that are consistent with those used in estimating the expected cash flows; this is to avoid double-counting or overlooking risks. *[IAS 41.23]*. In any case, the entity should exclude the cash flows for financing the assets, taxation or re-establishing biological assets after harvest, for example, the cost of replanting trees in a plantation forest after harvest. *[IAS 41.22]*.

In 2009 the Interpretations Committee received a request for guidance on how to determine an appropriate discount rate. The related staff paper made clear that behind the request lay a concern about inappropriate recognition of day 1 profit if too low a discount rate were applied. The Interpretations Committee declined to take this issue onto its agenda. It did however comment that the initial costs in respect of a biological asset may approximate fair value when little biological transformation has taken place. By extension it might be expected that the discount rate selected would produce a fair value which would approximate that cost.[2]

IAS 41 initially specifically excluded any increase in value from additional biological transformation. That prohibition has been removed and replaced it with a requirement that 'in determining the present value of expected net cash flows an entity includes the net cash flows that market participants would expect the asset to generate in its most relevant market'. *[IAS 41.21]*. This change is discussed in more detail at 4.5.

4.4.3.C Cost as an approximation of fair value

Sometimes an entity can use cost as an approximation of fair value, 'particularly when little biological transformation has taken place since initial cost incurrence' or when 'the impact of the biological transformation on price is not expected to be material (for example, for the initial growth in a 30-year pine plantation production cycle)'. *[IAS 41.24].*

4.4.4 Use of external independent valuers

IAS 41 does not require an entity to use an external independent valuer to determine the value of biological assets. In fact, the Board rejected a proposal to require external independent valuations because they are 'not commonly used for certain agricultural activity and it would be burdensome to require an external independent valuation. The Board believes that it is for entities to decide how to determine fair value reliably, including the extent to which independent valuers need to be involved'. *[IAS 41.B33].* Furthermore, the Board even noted that disclosure of the extent to which the carrying amount of biological assets reflects a valuation by an external independent valuer would not be appropriate. *[IAS 41.B81].*

4.4.5 Forward sales contracts

When an entity enters into a contract to sell its biological assets or agricultural produce at a future date, the standard does not permit it to measure those assets at the contracted price, stating that 'the fair value of a biological asset or agricultural produce is not adjusted because of the existence of a contract'. *[IAS 41.16].*

The (then) IASC considered whether it should require sales contracts to be measured at fair value, but concluded that no solution would be practicable without a complete review of the accounting for commodity contracts that are not in the scope of IAS 39 – *Financial Instruments: Recognition and Measurement.* *[IAS 41.B50-B54].*

It follows from this that if an entity engaged in agricultural activity enters into forward sales contracts for its produce it will need to consider whether such contracts are within the scope of IAS 39. IAS 39.5 states 'this standard shall be applied to those contracts to buy or sell a non-financial item that can be settled net in cash or another financial instrument, or by exchanging financial instruments as if the contracts were financial instruments, with the exception of contracts that were entered into and continue to be held for the purpose of receipt or delivery of a non-financial item in accordance with the entity's expected purchase sale or usage requirements'. Accordingly an agricultural commodity sales contract will be accounted for under IAS 39 by an entity which intends to net settle that contract even if it is also a producer of the underlying agricultural produce. Conversely a farmer who intends to settle a forward sales contract for barley by physical delivery would not account for the contract under IAS 39 but would treat it as an executory contract. This issue is discussed further in Chapter 43.

4.4.6   *Onerous contracts*

Although a forward sales contract scoped out of IAS 39 (refer to 4.4.5 above) is treated as an executory contract, IAS 41 notes that if the contracted price is lower than the fair value of the assets, the contract for the sale of a biological asset or agricultural produce may be an onerous contract, as defined in IAS 37, and if so, should be accounted for under that standard *[IAS 41.16]* (the accounting for onerous contracts is dealt with in Chapter 29).

However, IAS 41 provides no further guidance on the subject of when such a contract becomes onerous. The standard is also silent on what this might mean, given the fact that IAS 37 defines an onerous contract as 'a contract in which the unavoidable costs of meeting the obligations under the contract exceed the economic benefits expected to be received under it.' *[IAS 41.B50-B54]*. In other words, a contract that is not loss-making in an historical cost sense, but that has a contract price lower than the fair value of the produce concerned, is not automatically defined as onerous by IAS 37, yet seems to be regarded as onerous under IAS 41.

Nevertheless, it is our view that a contract to sell a biological asset at an amount that is below its fair value less costs to sell (and, therefore, its carrying amount) should be regarded as onerous under IAS 37.

4.5   The problem of measuring fair value for part-grown biological assets

Entities may be required to measure their biological assets part way through the transformation process, particularly when the time to harvest is greater than 12 months. In these circumstances, there may not be an active market for the asset in its current condition and location. As discussed at 4.4.1 above, in the absence of an active market, preparers are required to utilise one of the alternative methods to estimate fair value. In practice, many entities use a discounted cash flow model (see 4.4.3.B above) to estimate fair value.

In these situations, a common question is whether an entity can take into consideration the future biological transformation when estimating a biological asset's fair value.

IAS 41 makes it clear that the fair value of an asset is based on its present location and condition. *[IAS 41.9]*. An entity must consider this objective in determining an appropriate discount rate and estimating its future cash flows, which should be based on what a 'market participant would expect the asset to generate in its most relevant market'. Therefore, if a market participant would consider the potential for future growth, the related cash flows and risks from additional biological transformation should be included in determining the appropriate fair value.

The original version of IAS 41 had caused confusion in this area, as it had required that the estimation of future cash flows 'exclude any increases in value from additional biological transformation and future activities of the entity'. *[IAS 41.21 (2008)]*. This seemed to suggest that the value of immature biological assets should be based on values in their current condition rather than recognising that part of the value must logically lie in their potential, given appropriate husbandry, to grow to full size. The IASB amended IAS 41 to clarify that entities should consider the risks associated with cash flows from additional biological transformation in determining the cash flows, the discount rate or some combination of the two provided a market participant would take the additional biological transformation into consideration.

This clarification is helpful in situations where prices are available in an active market for part-grown biological assets, but that market is not the most relevant. Since an entity can consider the expected cash flows the asset can generate in its most relevant market *[IAS 41.21]*, the entity is not forced to use available prices in other active markets for part-grown biological assets, particularly if a market participant would not consider them. This issue is illustrated by an extract from CESR's database of enforcement decisions published in April 2007 (Decision ref. EECS/0407-11). Norwegian fish farmers had developed a practice of recording live immature fish at cost on the basis that they were unable to value them reliably in accordance with IAS 41.30. The Norwegian regulator took the view that slaughtered fish sold whole and gutted should be considered the same as live salmon under IAS 41.18(b) and that it was possible to value the live immature fish based on the market price for slaughtered fish of the same size. Smaller fish are sold on the market because they are harvested with mature fish, however their value per kilo is significantly below that of mature fish and the Norwegian fish farming entities did not therefore believe that it was appropriate to use their market price as a basis for fair value. The regulators decision was appealed to the Norwegian Ministry of Finance and the database reports the conclusion as follows:

> 'The Ministry of Finance upheld the decision of the enforcer, with some adjustments and additions. Most significantly, the final ruling upholds the enforcer's decision that slaughtered salmon which is sold whole and gutted is in an accounting sense to be considered as a similar asset of live salmon, according to IAS 41.18(b) and that this also applies to so-called immature farmed salmon. Hence, the observable prices of slaughtered salmon shall be used as a basis for determining the fair value of live immature salmon. The key amendment to the decision made by the Ministry of Finance is that it added certain comments relating to how the term "adjustments to reflect differences" in IAS 41.18(b) was to be applied. The adjustments should reflect the differences between the price of an immature salmon and the hypothetical market price in an active market for live immature salmon.'

As a result of this decision, the Norwegian entities were required to record immature salmon at fair value, rather than at cost, by making appropriate adjustments to available market prices for similar sized slaughtered fish, consistent with the requirements of IAS 41.18(b).

5   DISCLOSURE

5.1   General

5.1.1   *Balance sheet*

IAS 1 – *Presentation of Financial Statements* – requires biological assets to be presented separately on the face of an entity's balance sheet (see Chapter 3). *[IAS 1.54]*. Agricultural produce after the point of harvest should be accounted for under IAS 2, which does not require it to be disclosed separately on the face of the balance sheet. The following example, which is taken from the Appendix to IAS 41, illustrates the requirement to disclose biological assets on the balance sheet. *[IAS 41.IE1]*.

Example 40.3:   *Balance sheet presentation of biological assets*

The balance sheet below illustrates how a dairy farming business might present biological assets in its balance sheet.

XYZ Dairy Ltd.
Balance Sheet

ASSETS	31 December 20X1	31 December 20X0
Non-current assets		
Dairy livestock – immature *	52,060	47,730
Dairy livestock – mature *	372,990	411,840
Subtotal – biological assets	425,050	459,570
Property, plant and equipment	1,462,650	1,409,800
Total non-current assets	**1,887,700**	**1,869,370**
Current assets		
Inventories	82,950	70,650
Trade and other receivables	88,000	65,000
Cash	10,000	10,000
Total current assets	**180,950**	**145,650**
Total assets	**2,068,650**	**2,015,020**
EQUITY AND LIABILITIES		
Equity		
Issued capital	1,000,000	1,000,000
Accumulated profits	902,828	865,000
Total equity	**1,902,828**	**1,865,000**
Current liabilities		
Trade and other payables	165,822	150,020
Total current liabilities	**165,822**	**150,020**
Total equity and liabilities	**2,068,650**	**2,015,020**

*   An entity is encouraged, but not required, to provide a quantified description of each group of biological assets, distinguishing between consumable and bearer biological assets or between mature and immature biological assets, as appropriate. An entity discloses the basis for making any such distinctions. (Bearer biological assets are those assets that self-regenerate, e.g. cows that bear calves).

The extract below from the financial statements of the Turners & Growers Group illustrates the proportion of total assets that biological assets can comprise in an agricultural business and that biological assets might be classified as both current and non-current assets. This extract also illustrates some of the other disclosure requirements of the standard discussed at 5.1.4 below.

Extract 40.1: Turners & Growers Limited and Subsidiary Companies (2010)

Balance Sheets

As at 31 December 2010 [extract]

	Notes	Group 2010 $'000	2009 $'000
Current Assets			
Cash and cash equivalents	12	18,414	11,245
Trade and other receivables	13	75,161	62,672
Inventories	14	29,234	32,739
Taxation receivable		6,621	5,546
Biological assets	16	7,026	4,643
Total current assets		136,456	116,845
Non-current Assets			
Trade and other receivables	13	3,550	3,780
Available-for-sale investments	17	329	313
Biological assets	16	13,283	10,568
Property, plant & equipment	18	256,069	257,292
Intangible assets	20	18,386	19,357
Investments in associates	23	19,440	17,202
Total non-current assets		311,057	308,512
Total assets		447,513	425,357

Notes to the Financial Statements year ended 31 December 2010 [extract]

16   Biological Assets [extract]

	Notes	Group 2010 $'000	2009 $'000
Current			
Balance at 1 January		4,643	5,319
Increases due to purchases		29,703	24,722
Changes in fair value less estimated point-of-sale costs attributable to physical changes	6	1,515	357
Changes in fair value less estimated point-of-sale costs attributable to price changes	6	(1,416)	(29)
Decreases due to harvest		(27,419)	(25,726)
Balance at 31 December		7,026	4,643
Non-current			
Balance at 1 January		10,568	7,905
Increases due to purchases		2,656	3,077
Reclassification to/from property, plant & equipment	18	(88)	106
Change in fair value	6	154	(27)
Decreases due to harvest		(7)	(493)
Balance at 31 December		13,283	10,568

At 31 December the biological assets were as follows:

	Hectares planted owned 2010	2009	Hectares planted leased 2010	2009	Production owned 2010	2009	Production leased 2010	2009
Tomatoes	20	20	–	–	8,554,246	8,985,393	–	–
Apples	82	82	–	17	25,007	68,336	–	29,821
Lemons	102	104	–	–	1,666,301	1,708,139	–	–
Kiwifruit	64	64	31	27	344,391	454,193	281,943	217,865
Navels	–	–	19	18	–	–	229,180	171,752
Mandarins	54	54	16	18	747,687	938,368	91,450	130,772

– Tomatoes: kgs
– Apples: export tce (tray carton equivalent)
– Citrus (Lemons, navels and mandarins): kgs for export, tag 1 and tag 2 grades
– Kiwifruit: class 1 trays

The Group's biological assets are stated at valuations completed by management with reference to current or prior years registered valuations prepared for management and are adjusted to reflect the location, plantings, age and varieties of biological assets and productive capacities of the orchards.

5.1.2   Income statement

IAS 1 is silent on the presentation of gains and losses on biological assets and agricultural produce in the income statement. IAS 41 requires that an entity shall disclose 'the aggregate gain or loss arising during the current period on initial recognition of biological assets and agricultural produce and from the change in fair value less costs to sell of biological assets'. *[IAS 41.40]*. The standard only requires disclosure of the aggregate gain or loss; it does not require or encourage disaggregating the gain or loss. *[IAS 41.B78-B79]*. The example in the Appendix to IAS 41 illustrates gains on biological assets and agricultural produce presented near the top of the income statement, although it is not entirely clear from the example whether losses on biological assets should be presented in the same position or elsewhere in the income statement. *[IAS 41.IE1]*.

The extract below from the financial statements of the Mondi group illustrates the presentation of changes in the fair value of biological assets in the notes to the financial statements rather than in the income statement.

Extract 40.2: The Mondi Group (2010)
Notes to the combined and consolidated financial statements [extract]
NOTE 1 Accounting policies [extract]
Owned forestry assets

Owned forestry assets are measured at fair value, calculated by applying the expected selling price, less costs to harvest and deliver, to the estimated volume of timber on hand at each reporting date. The estimated volume of timber on hand is determined based on the maturity profile of the area under afforestation, the species, the geographic location and other environmental considerations and excludes future growth. The product of these is then adjusted to present value by applying a market related pre-tax discount rate.

Changes in fair value are recognised in the combined and consolidated income statement within 'other net operating expenses'.

At point of felling, the carrying value of forestry assets is transferred to inventory.

Directly attributable costs incurred during the year of biological growth and investments in standing timber are capitalised and presented within cash flows from investing activities in the combined and consolidated statement of cash flows.

NOTE 3 Operating profit before special items [extract]

Operating profit before special items for the year has been arrived at after (charging)/crediting:

€ million	2010	2009
Depreciation of property, plant and equipment (see note 12)	(360)	(341)
Amortisation of intangible assets (see note 11)	(13)	(10)
Operating lease charges (see note 2)	(66)	(62)
Research and development expenditure	(11)	(8)
Restructuring/closure costs (excluding special items)	–	(3)
Net foreign currency gains/(losses) (see note 7)	5	(13)
Green energy sales and disposal of emission credits (see note 2)	80	47
Fair value gains on forestry assets (see note 13)	36	28
Felling costs (see note 13)	(65)	(50)
Profit on disposal of tangible and intangible assets	1	4

Total revenue, as defined under IAS 18, 'Revenue', consisting of Group revenue, sale of green energy and disposal of emissions credits, interest income and dividend income, was €6,319 million (2009: €5,313 million).

Other than depreciation and amortisation, and fair value movements on forestry assets which are disclosed above, there are no other significant non-cash items recorded within Group operating profit as stated before operating special items.

NOTE 13 Forestry assets

€ million	2010	2009
At 1 January	251	214
Capitalised expenditure	44	37
Acquisition of assets	2	3
Fair value gains[1]	36	28
Felling costs	(65)	(50)
Reclassification (see note 31)	–	(30)
Currency movements	52	49
At 31 December	**320**	**251**

Note:

1 Forestry assets are revalued to fair value less estimated costs to sell each reporting year in accordance with the accounting policy set out in note 1. The fair value is calculated on the basis of future expected cash flows discounted using a discount rate relevant in the local country, based on a pre tax real yield on long-term bonds over the last five years. All fair value gains/(losses) originate from South Africa.

Forestry assets comprise forests with the maturity profile disclosed in the table below:

€ million	2010	2009
Mature	146	118
Immature	174	133
Total forestry assets	**320**	**251**

Mature forestry assets are those plantations that are harvestable, while immature forestry assets have not yet reached that stage of growth. Plantations are considered harvestable after a specific age depending on the species planted and regional considerations.

IAS 41 is not clear about how gains should be presented in the income statement. IAS 1 prohibits offsetting of income and expenses in the income statement. *[IAS 1.32]*. Therefore, if the sale of biological assets or agricultural produce meets the definition of revenue under IAS 18 – *Revenue*, i.e. it results in a gross inflow of economic benefits during the period arising from the ordinary activities of the entity, it should be presented on a gross basis in the income statement. However, if sales of non-current biological assets are incidental to the main revenue-generating activities of the entity they should be presented on a net basis. *[IAS 1.34]*. However, under IAS 41 the gross margin on agricultural produce sold shortly after harvest may be negligible, as the produce may have been previously carried at a valuation near to its sales price.

5.1.3   Groups of biological assets

The standard requires an entity to provide a narrative or quantitative description of each group of biological assets. *[IAS 41.41-42]*. An entity is encouraged to provide 'a quantified description of each group of biological assets, distinguishing between consumable and bearer biological assets or between mature and immature biological assets, as appropriate'. *[IAS 41.43]*. The standard suggests that an entity may separately disclose the carrying amounts of: *[IAS 41.43-44]*

- consumable biological assets (i.e. assets that are to be harvested as agricultural produce or sold as biological assets); and
- bearer biological assets (i.e. assets that are not consumable but rather are self-regenerating).

The standard continues by suggesting that an entity 'may further divide those carrying amounts between mature and immature assets. These distinctions provide information that may be helpful in assessing the timing of future cash flows'. *[IAS 41.43]*. Mature biological assets are defined by the standard as those assets 'that have attained harvestable specifications (for consumable biological assets) or are able to sustain regular harvests (for bearer biological assets)'. *[IAS 41.45]*. If an entity makes the above distinctions, it should disclose the basis for making the distinction. *[IAS 41.43]*.

5.1.4   Other disclosures

If not disclosed elsewhere in information published with the financial statements, an entity shall describe:

'(a)   the nature of its activities involving each group of biological assets; and

(b)   non-financial measures or estimates of the physical quantities of:

(i)   each group of the entity's biological assets at the end of the period; and

(ii)   output of agricultural produce during the period'. *[IAS 41.46]*.

In addition, an entity shall disclose the following information:

(a)   the methods and significant assumptions applied in determining the fair value of each group of agricultural produce at the point of harvest and each group of biological assets; *[IAS 41.47]*

(b)   the fair value less costs to sell of agricultural produce harvested during the period, determined at the point of harvest; *[IAS 41.48]*

(c)   the existence and carrying amounts of biological assets whose title is restricted, and the carrying amounts of biological assets pledged as security for liabilities; *[IAS 41.49]*

(d)   the amount of commitments for the development or acquisition of biological assets; *[IAS 41.49]*

(e)   financial risk management strategies related to agricultural activity; *[IAS 41.49]*

(f)   a reconciliation of changes in the carrying amount of biological assets between the beginning and the end of the current period, which includes: *[IAS 41.50]*

  (i)   the gain or loss arising from changes in fair value less costs to sell;

  (ii)   increases due to purchases;

  (iii) decreases attributable to sales and biological assets classified as held for sale (or included in a disposal group that is classified as held for sale) in accordance with IFRS 5;

  (iv)   decreases due to harvest;

  (v)   increases resulting from business combinations;

  (vi)   net exchange differences arising on the translation of financial statements into a different presentation currency, and on the translation of a foreign operation into the presentation currency of the reporting entity; and

  (vii) other changes.

The standard encourages an entity 'to disclose, by group or otherwise, the amount of change in fair value less costs to sell included in profit or loss due to physical changes and due to price changes', because this information is 'useful in appraising current period performance and future prospects, particularly when there is a production cycle of more than one year'. *[IAS 41.51, B74-B77]*. IAS 41 notes that physical change itself can be broken down further into growth, degeneration, production and procreation, but the standard does not specifically encourage disclosure of this information. *[IAS 41.52]*. The standard provides the following example that explains how an entity should go about separating the effect of physical changes from those of price changes.

Example 40.4:   Physical change and price change [IAS 41.IE2]

A herd of ten 2-year-old animals was held at 1 January 2011. One animal aged 2½ years was purchased on 1 July 2011 for €108, and one animal was born on 1 July 2011. No animals were sold or disposed of during the period. Per-unit fair values less costs to sell were as follows:

	1/1/2011	1/7/2011	31/12/2011
Newborn animal	–	€70	€72
½ year old animal	–	–	€80
2 year old animal	€100	–	€105
2½ year old animal	–	€108	€111
3 year old animal	–	–	€120

Fair value less costs to sell of herd at 1 January 2011

$$(10 \times \text{€}100) =$$ €1,000

Purchase on 1 July 2011

$$(1 \times \text{€}108) =$$ €108

Increase in fair value less costs to sell due to price change:

$10 \times (\text{€}105 - \text{€}100) =$	€50	
$1 \times (\text{€}111 - \text{€}108) =$	€3	
$1 \times (\text{€}72 - \text{€}70) =$	€2	
		€55

Increase in fair value less costs to sell due to physical change:

$10 \times (\text{€}120 - \text{€}105) =$	€150	
$1 \times (\text{€}120 - \text{€}111) =$	€9	
$1 \times (\text{€}80 - \text{€}72) =$	€8	
$1 \times \text{€}70 =$	€70	
		€237

Fair value less costs to sell of herd at 31 December 2011

$11 \times \text{€}120 =$	€1,320	
$1 \times \text{€}80 =$	€80	
		€1,400

The standard notes that agricultural activity is 'often exposed to climatic, disease and other natural risks. If an event occurs that gives rise to a material item of income or expense, the nature and amount of that item are disclosed in accordance with IAS 1' (see Chapter 3). For example, an entity may need to disclose events such as 'an outbreak of a virulent disease, a flood, a severe drought or frost, and a plague of insects'. *[IAS 41.53]*.

Many of the uncertainties and judgements inherent in the valuations that have to be made under IAS 41 are very clearly explained in the financial statements of Sappi, as shown in the following extract.

Extract 40.3: Sappi Limited (2010)

Notes to the group annual financial statements [extract]
2.3   Critical accounting policies and estimates [extract]
2.3.6 Plantations [extract]

Plantations are stated at fair value less estimated cost to sell at the harvesting stage. In arriving at plantation fair values, the key assumptions are estimated prices less cost of delivery, discount rates, and volume and growth estimations. All changes in fair value are recognised in the period in which they arise.

The impact of changes in estimate prices, discount rates and, volume and growth assumptions may have on the calculated fair value and other key financial information on plantations are disclosed in note 10.

• Estimated prices less cost of delivery

In periods prior to the third quarter of fiscal 2010 the group used unadjusted current market prices to estimate the fair value of timber.

In the third quarter of fiscal 2010, the group revised this methodology for all immature timber and mature timber that is to be felled in more than 12 months from the reporting period to consider a 12 quarter rolling historical average price. This is considered a reasonable period of time taking into consideration the length of the growth cycle of the plantations. The new methodology also takes into consideration expected future price trends and recent market transactions involving comparable plantations.

The group considers the new methodology to be preferable. Current market prices for timber are highly volatile for timber that is expected to be felled in more than 12 months from the reporting period. Therefore, the group considers the use of a rolling historical average price coupled with consideration of expected future price trends and recent market transactions involving comparable plantations to be a preferable methodology.

Mature timber that is expected to be felled within 12 months from the reporting period continues to be valued using unadjusted current market prices. Such timber is expected to be used in the short term and consequently, current market prices are considered an appropriate reflection of fair value.

The fair value is derived by using the prices as explained above reduced by the estimated cost of delivery. Cost of delivery includes all costs associated with getting the harvested plantations to the market, being harvesting, loading, transport and allocated fixed overheads

- Discount rate

The discount rate used is the applicable pre-tax weighted average cost of capital of the business unit.

- Volume and growth estimations and cost assumptions

The group focuses on good husbandry techniques which include ensuring that the rotation of plantations is met with adequate planting activities for future harvesting. The age threshold used for quantifying immature timber is dependent on the rotation period of the specific timber genus which varies from between eight to eighteen years. In the southern African region, softwood less than eight years and hardwood less than five years is classified as immature timber.

Trees are generally felled at the optimum age when ready for intended use. At the time the tree is felled it is taken out of plantations and accounted for under inventory and reported as depletion cost (fellings).

Depletion costs include the fair value of timber felled, which is determined on the average method, plus amounts written off against standing timber to cover loss or damage caused by fire, disease and stunted growth. These costs are accounted for on a cost per metric ton allocation method multiplied by unadjusted current market prices. Tons are calculated using the projected growth to rotation age and are extrapolated to current age on a straight-line basis.

The group has projected growth estimation over a period of eight to 18 years per rotation. In deriving this estimate, the group established a long-term sample plot network which is representative of the species and sites on which trees are grown and the measured data from these permanent sample plots were used as input into the group's growth estimation. Periodic adjustments are made to existing models for new genetic material.

The group directly manages plantations established on land that is either owned or leased from third parties. Indirectly managed plantations represent plantations established on land held by independent commercial farmers where Sappi provides technical advice on the growing and tendering of trees. The associated costs for managing the plantations are recognised as silviculture costs in cost of sales (see note 4.1).

NOTE 10 Plantations [extract]

Sappi manages the establishment, maintenance and harvesting of its plantations on a compartmentalised basis. These plantations are comprised of pulpwood and sawlogs and are managed in such a way so as to ensure that the optimum fibre balance is supplied to its paper and pulping operations in southern Africa.

As Sappi manages its plantations on a rotational basis, the respective increases by means of growth are negated by depletions over the rotation period for the group's own production or sales. Estimated volume changes on a rotational basis amount to approximately five million tons per annum.

We own plantations on land that we own, as well as on land that we lease. We disclose both of these as directly managed plantations. With regard to indirectly managed plantations, Sappi has several different types of agreements with many independent farmers. The agreements depend on the type and specific needs of the farmer and the areas planted. These agreements range in time from one to more than 20 years. In certain circumstances we provide loans to farmers, which are disclosed as accounts receivable in the group balance sheet (these loans are considered immaterial to the group). If Sappi provides seedlings, silviculture and/or technical assistance, the costs are expensed when incurred by the group.

The group is exposed to financial risks arising from climatic changes, disease and other natural risks such as fire, flooding and storms and human-induced losses arising from strikes, civil commotion and malicious damage. These risks are covered by an appropriate level of insurance as determined by management. The plantations have an integrated management system that is certified to ISO 9001, ISO 14001, OHSAS 18001 and FSC standards.

Changes in estimate prices, the discount rate, costs to sell and, volume and growth assumptions applied in the valuation of immature timber may impact the calculated fair value as tabled below:

US$ million	2010	2009
Fair value changes		
1% increase in market prices	2	12
1% decrease in market prices	(2)	(12)
Discount rate (for immature timber)		
1% increase in rate	(5)	(3)
1% decrease in rate	5	3
Volume assumption		
1% increase in estimate of volume	9	6
1% decrease in estimate of volume	(9)	(6)
Costs to sell		
1% increase in costs to sell	(1)	(9)
1% decrease in costs to sell	1	9
Growth assumptions		
1% increase in rate of growth	2	1
1% decrease in rate of growth	(2)	(1)

5.2   Additional disclosures if fair value cannot be measured reliably

If an entity measures biological assets at their cost less any accumulated depreciation and any accumulated impairment losses it shall disclose the following information:

(a)   if the entity holds such assets at the end of the period: [IAS 41.54]

(i)   a description of the biological assets;

(ii)   an explanation of why fair value cannot be measured reliably;

(iii)   if possible, the range of estimates within which fair value is highly likely to lie;

(iv)   the depreciation method used;

(v)   the useful lives or the depreciation rates used; and

(vi)   the gross carrying amount and the accumulated depreciation (aggregated with accumulated impairment losses) at the beginning and end of the period;

(b)   if the entity held such assets at any point during the current period: [IAS 41.55]

(i)   any gain or loss recognised on disposal of such biological assets;

(ii)   the reconciliation required by IAS 41.50 (see 5.1.4 above) shall disclose amounts related to such biological assets separately;

    (iii)   that reconciliation shall include the following amounts included in profit or loss related to those biological assets:

- impairment losses;
- reversals of impairment losses; and
- depreciation;

(c)   if the entity held such assets and their fair value became reliably measurable during the current period: *[IAS 41.56]*

    (i)   a description of the biological assets;

    (ii)   an explanation of why fair value has become reliably measurable; and

    (iii)   the effect of the change.

5.3   Government grants

An entity that has received government grants in relation to biological assets shall disclose the following information:

'(a)   the nature and extent of government grants recognised in the financial statements;

(b)   unfulfilled conditions and other contingencies attaching to government grants; and

(c)   significant decreases expected in the level of government grants.' *[IAS 41.57]*.

References

1 *2011 Agenda Consultation – Request for views*, July 2011, page 21

2 *IFRIC Update*, May 2009

Chapter 41   Extractive industries

Chapter 41

Chapter 41

Chapter 41

List of examples

Chapter 41

Chapter 41 . Extractive industries

1 INTRODUCTION

1.1 Nature of extractive industries

'Extractive industries' were defined in the IASC's Issues Paper – *Extractive Industries* – published in November 2000 as 'those industries involved in finding and removing wasting natural resources located in or near the earth's crust'.[1] However, this chapter adopts a slightly narrower focus and concentrates on the accounting issues that affect mining companies and oil and gas companies.

Many of the financial reporting issues that affect entities that operate in the extractive industries are a result of the environment in which they operate. The financial reports of such entities need to reflect the risks and rewards to which they are exposed. At the same time, however, some of the business arrangements that are aimed at mitigating certain risks give rise to financial reporting complications. The IASC's Issues Paper identified the following characteristics of activities in the extractive industries,[2] which are closely related to the financial reporting issues that are discussed in this chapter:

- *High risks* – In the extractive industries there is a high risk that the amounts spent in finding new mineral reserves will not result in additional commercially recoverable reserves. In financial reporting terms this means that it can remain uncertain for a long period whether or not certain expenditures give rise to an asset. Further risks exist in relation to production (i.e. quantities actually produced may differ considerably from those previously estimated) and price (i.e. commodity prices are often volatile);

- *Little relationship between risks and rewards* – In the extractive industries a small expenditure may result in finding mineral deposits with a value of many times the amount of the expenditure. Conversely, large expenditures can frequently result in little or no future production.[3] This has given rise to different approaches in financial reporting: (1) expense all expenditures as the future benefits are too uncertain, (2) capitalise all expenditures as the cumulative expenditures may be matched to the cumulative benefits, or (3) recognise the mineral reserves found at fair value;

- *Long lag between expenditure and production* – Exploration and/or development may take years to complete. During this period it is often far from certain that economic benefits will be derived from the costs incurred;

- *High costs of individual projects* – The costs of individual projects can be very high (e.g. offshore oil and gas projects and deep mining projects). Exploration expenditures that are carried forward pending the outcome of mineral acquisition and development projects may be highly significant in relation to the equity and the total assets of an entity;[4]

- *Unique cost-sharing arrangements* – High costs and high risks, as discussed above, often lead entities in the extractive industries to enter into risk-sharing arrangements (e.g. joint arrangements, farm-out arrangements, carried interest arrangements and contract mining). These types of arrangements, which are much more common in the extractive industries than elsewhere, often give rise to their own financial reporting issues;

- *Intense government oversight and regulation* – The regulation of the extractive industries ranges from 'outright governmental ownership of some (especially petroleum) or all minerals to unusual tax benefits or penalties, price controls, restrictions on imports and exports, restrictions on production and distribution, environmental and health and safety regulations, and others'.[5] Governments may also seek to charge an economic rent for resources extracted. These types of government involvement give rise to financial reporting issues, particularly when the precise nature of the government involvement is not obvious;

- *Scarce non-replaceable assets* – Mineral reserves are unique and scarce resources that an entity may not be able to replace in any location or in any form; and

- *Economic, technological and political factors* – While these factors are not unique to the extractive industries, the IASC's Issues Paper argues that they tend to have a greater impact on the extractive industries because:

  '(a) fluctuating market prices for minerals (together with floating exchange rates) have a direct impact on the economic viability of reserves and mineral properties. A relatively small percentage change in long-term prices can change decisions on whether or when to explore for, develop, or produce minerals;

  (b) there is a sharp impact from cost changes and technological developments. Changes in costs and, probably more significantly, changes in technology can significantly change the economic viability of particular mineral projects; and

  (c) in almost every country, mineral rights are owned by the state. In those countries where some mineral rights are privately owned, public reliance on adequate sources of minerals for economic and defence purposes often leads to governmental regulations and control. ... At other times, governmental policies may be changed to levy special taxes or impose governmental controls on the extractive industries.'[6]

Whilst it may be the case that the above factors affect the extractive industries more than others, to the extent that they also arise in the pharmaceutical, bio-technology, agricultural and software industries they frequently give rise to similar financial reporting issues. However, those industries are not affected by the combination of these circumstances to the same extent as is the case with the extractive industries.

The following extract from the financial statements of TOTAL illustrates the types of risks frequently faced by entities operating in the extractive industries.

Extract 41.1: TOTAL S.A. (2010)

Other risks [extract]

Risks related to oil and gas exploration and production

Oil and gas exploration and production require high levels of investment and are associated with particular risks and opportunities. These activities are subject to risks related specifically to the difficulties of exploring underground, to the characteristics of hydrocarbons and to the physical characteristics of an oil or gas field. Of risks related to oil and gas exploration, geologic risks are the most important. For example, exploratory wells may not result in the discovery of hydrocarbons, or in amounts that would be insufficient to allow for economic development. Even if an economic analysis of estimated hydrocarbon reserves justifies the development of a discovery, the reserves can prove lower than the estimates during the production process, thus adversely affecting the economic development.

Almost all the exploration and production operations of TOTAL are accompanied by a high level of risk of loss of the invested capital due to the risks related to economic or political factors detailed hereafter. It is impossible to guarantee that new resources of crude oil or of natural gas will be discovered in sufficient amounts to replace the reserves currently being developed, produced and sold to enable TOTAL to recover the capital it has invested.

The development of oil and gas fields, the construction of facilities and the drilling of production or injection wells require advanced technology in order to extract and exploit fossil fuels with complex properties over several decades. The deployment of this technology in such a difficult environment makes cost projections uncertain. TOTAL's operations can be limited, delayed or cancelled as a result of numerous factors, such as administrative delays, particularly in terms of the host states' approval processes for development projects, shortages, late delivery of equipment and weather conditions, including the risk of hurricanes in the Gulf of Mexico. Some of these risks may also affect TOTAL's projects and facilities further down the oil and gas chain.

Risks related to economic or political factors

The oil sector is subject to domestic regulations and the intervention of governments or state-owned companies in such areas as:

- the award of exploration and production interests;
- authorizations by governments or by a state-controlled partner, especially for development projects, annual programs or the selection of contractors or suppliers;
- the imposition of specific drilling obligations;
- environmental protection controls;
- control over the development and abandonment of a field causing restrictions on production;
- calculating the costs that may be recovered from the relevant authority and what expenditures are deductible from taxes; and
- cases of expropriation or reconsideration of contractual rights; and
- cases of nationalization.

The oil industry is also subject to the payment of royalties and taxes, which may be high compared with those imposed with respect to other commercial activities and which may be subject to material modifications by the governments of certain countries.

Substantial portions of TOTAL's oil and gas reserves are located in certain countries that may be considered politically and economically unstable. These reserves and the related operations are subject to certain additional risks, including:

- the establishment of production and export quotas;

- the compulsory renegotiation of contracts;

- the expropriation or nationalization of assets;

- risks relating to changes of local governments or resulting changes in business customs and practices;

- payment delays;

- currency exchange restrictions;

- depreciation of assets due to the devaluation of local currencies or other measures taken by governments that might have a significant impact on the value of activities; and

- losses and decreased activity due to armed conflicts, civil unrest or the actions of terrorist groups.

TOTAL, like other major international oil companies, has a geographically diverse portfolio of reserves and operational sites, which allows it to conduct its business and financial affairs so as to reduce its exposure to such political and economic risks. However, there can be no assurance that such events will not adversely affect the Group.

1.2   Phases in extractive activities

1.2.1   *Upstream and downstream activities*

Upstream activities in the extractive industries are defined as 'exploring for, finding, acquiring, and developing mineral reserves up to the point that the reserves are first capable of being sold or used, even if the enterprise intends to process them further'.[7] *Downstream activities* are 'the refining, processing, marketing, and distributing of petroleum, natural gas, or mined mineral (other than refining or processing that is necessary to make the minerals that have been mined or extracted capable of being sold)'.[8]

Thus, activities that are required to make the product saleable or usable are generally considered to be upstream activities. For example, the removal of water to produce dry gas would be an upstream activity, because otherwise the gas cannot be sold at all. However, refining crude oil is considered to be a downstream activity, because crude oil can be sold.

This chapter focuses on upstream activities in the extractive industries as they are primarily affected by the issues discussed at 1.1 above. However, downstream activities are discussed to the extent that they give rise to issues that are unique to the extractive industries (e.g. provisional pricing clauses) or are subject to the same issues as upstream activities (e.g. production sharing contracts).

1.2.2 Phases in upstream activities

Although there is not a universally accepted classification of upstream activities in the extractive industries, the IASC Issues Paper identified the following eight phases which other authors also commonly identify:[9]

(a) *Prospecting* – Prospecting involves activities undertaken to search for an area of interest, a geologic anomaly or structure that may warrant detailed exploration.[10] Prospecting is undertaken typically before mineral rights in the area have been acquired, and if the prospecting results are negative the area of prospecting generally will be abandoned and no mineral rights acquired.[11] However, sometimes it will be necessary to acquire a prospecting permit as the prospecting activities require access to the land to carry out geological and geophysical tests;[12]

(b) *Acquisition of mineral rights* – The acquisition phase involves the activities related to obtaining legal rights to explore for, develop, and/or produce wasting resources on a mineral property.[13] Legal rights may be acquired in a number of ways as discussed at 5.1 below;

(c) *Exploration* – Exploration is the detailed examination of a geographical area of interest that has shown sufficient mineral-producing potential to merit further exploration, often using techniques that are similar to those used in the prospecting phase.[14] In the mining industry, exploration usually involves taking cores for analysis, sinking exploratory shafts, geological mapping, geochemical analysis, cutting drifts and crosscuts, opening shallow pits, and removing overburden in some areas.[15] In the oil and gas industry, exploration involves techniques such as shooting seismic, core drilling, and ultimately the drilling of an exploratory well to determine whether oil and gas reserves do exist;[16]

(d) *Appraisal or evaluation* – This involves determining the technical feasibility and commercial viability of mineral deposits that have been found through exploration.[17] This phase typically includes:[18]

   (i) detailed engineering studies and drilling of additional wells by oil and gas companies to determine how the reservoir can best be developed to obtain maximum recovery;

   (ii) determination by mining companies of the volume and grade of deposits through drilling of core samples, trenching, and sampling activities in an area known to contain mineral resources;

   (iii) examination and testing by mining companies of extraction methods and metallurgical or treatment processes;

   (iv) surveying transportation and infrastructure requirements;

   (v) conducting market and finance studies; and

   (vi) making detailed economic evaluations to determine whether development of the reserves is commercially justified.

(e) *Development* – Development is the establishment of access to the mineral reserve and other preparations for commercial production. In the mining industry, development includes sinking shafts and underground drifts, making permanent excavations, developing passageways and rooms or galleries, building roads and tunnels, and advance removal of overburden and waste rock.[19] In the oil and gas industry the development phase involves gaining access to, and preparing, well locations for drilling, constructing platforms or preparing drill sites, drilling wells, and installing equipment and facilities;[20]

(f) *Construction* – Construction involves installing facilities, such as buildings, machinery and equipment to extract, treat, and transport minerals;[21]

(g) *Production* – The production phase involves the extraction of the natural resources from the earth and the related processes necessary to make the produced resource marketable or transportable;[22] and

(h) *Closure and decommissioning* – Closure means ceasing production, removing equipment and facilities, restoring the production site to appropriate conditions after operations have ceased and abandoning the site.[23]

The above phases are not necessarily discrete sequential steps. Instead, the phases often overlap or take place simultaneously. Nevertheless, they provide a useful framework for developing accounting policies in the extractive industries. Accounting for expenditures depends very much on the phase during which they are incurred; for example, as discussed further below, costs incurred in the prospecting phase cannot be recognised as assets, whereas most costs incurred in the construction phase should be capitalised.

1.3   Definition of terms

The most important terms and abbreviations used are defined within this chapter when discussed or in the glossary at 7 below. However, alternative or more detailed definitions of financial reporting terms, and of mining and petroleum technical terms and abbreviations, can be found in the following publications:

- *Issues Paper Extractive Industries*, IASC, November 2000;

- *Petroleum Resources Management System*, Society of Petroleum Engineers, 2007; and

- *Accounting for Oil and Gas Exploration, Development, Production and Decommissioning Activities*, Statement of Recommended Practice, UK Oil Industry Accounting Committee, June 2001.

IFRSs currently use the term 'minerals' and 'mineral assets' when referring to the extractive industries as a whole. This is used as a collective term to encompass both mining and oil and gas reserves and resources. In contrast, a distinction between the two industries was introduced in the Extractive Industries Discussion Paper (discussed below at 1.4.2), in that the term 'minerals' has been used to refer to the mining industry and the term 'oil and gas' has been used to refer to the oil and gas industry.

For the purposes of this chapter however, consistency with the current wording in IFRSs will be maintained and therefore, unless stated otherwise, 'minerals' and 'mineral assets' will encompass both mining and oil and gas.

1.4 Development of IFRS guidance

Historically the IASB and its predecessor, the IASC, have avoided dealing with specific accounting issues in the extractive industries by excluding minerals and mineral reserves from the scope of their accounting standards. Currently, minerals and mineral reserves are excluded from the scope of the following standards:

- IAS 2 – *Inventories*; *[IAS 2.3(a), 4]*
- IAS 16 – *Property, Plant and Equipment*; *[IAS 16.3(d)]*
- IAS 17 – *Leases*; *[IAS 17.2(a)]*
- IAS 18 – *Revenue*; *[IAS 18.6(h)]*
- IAS 38 – *Intangible Assets*; *[IAS 38.2(c)]*
- IAS 40 – *Investment Property*; *[IAS 40.4(b)]* and
- IFRIC 4 – *Determining whether an Arrangement contains a Lease. [IFRIC 4.4].*

Although minerals and mineral reserves themselves are excluded from the scope of many standards, assets used for the exploration and extraction of minerals are covered by existing IFRSs.

Nevertheless, many specific accounting issues arise in the extractive industries because of the uncertainties involved in mineral exploration and extraction, the wide range of risk sharing arrangements, and government involvement in the form of mandatory participations and special tax regimes. In many cases, legitimate differences of opinion exist about how an entity should account for these matters.

1.4.1 Development of IFRS 6 – Exploration for and Evaluation of Mineral Resources

Following its replacement of the Board of the IASC in 2001, the IASB recognised the importance of accounting for extractive activities, but decided in September 2002 that 'it was not feasible to complete the detailed analysis required for this project, obtain appropriate input from constituents and undertake the Board's normal due process in time to implement changes before many entities adopted IFRSs in 2005'. *[IFRS 6.IN3].* However, in April 2003, the Board agreed to issue interim guidance 'to clarify the application of IFRSs and the IASB Framework to exploration and evaluation activities and to provide temporary relief from existing IFRSs in some areas'.[24] This led to the publication in January 2004 of ED 6 – *Exploration for and Evaluation of Mineral Resources*. In December 2004, the IASB issued IFRS 6 – *Exploration for and Evaluation of Mineral Resources*. The IASB decided to develop IFRS 6 because: *[IFRS 6.IN1]*

- mineral rights and mineral resources are outside the scope of IAS 16 – *Property, Plant and Equipment* – and IAS 38 – *Intangible Assets*;
- different views existed on how exploration and evaluation expenditures should be accounted for under IFRS;
- accounting practices for exploration and evaluation assets under the requirements of other standard-setting bodies are diverse and often differ from practices in other sectors for expenditures that may be considered analogous;

Chapter 41

- exploration and evaluation expenditures are significant to entities engaged in extractive activities; and

- an increasing number of entities incurring exploration and evaluation expenditures were presenting their financial statements in accordance with IFRSs, and many more were expected to do so from 2005.

One of the IASB's goals in developing IFRS 6 was to avoid unnecessary disruption for both users and preparers. The Board therefore 'proposed to limit the need for entities to change their existing accounting policies for exploration and evaluation assets', as follows: [IFRS 6.BC3]

'(a)   to make limited improvements to accounting practices for exploration and evaluation expenditures, without requiring major changes that might be reversed when the Board undertakes a comprehensive review of accounting practices used by entities engaged in the exploration for and evaluation of mineral resources.

(b)   to specify the circumstances in which entities that recognise exploration and evaluation assets should test such assets for impairment in accordance with IAS 36 *Impairment of Assets*.

(c)   to require entities engaged in the exploration for and evaluation of mineral resources to disclose information about exploration and evaluation assets, the level at which such assets are assessed for impairment and any impairment losses recognised.' [IFRS 6.IN4].

As discussed at 5.4.2 below, the IFRS Interpretations Committee (the Interpretations Committee) (formerly the IFRIC) has noted that the effect of the limited scope of IFRS 6 is to grant relief only to policies in respect of exploration and evaluation (E&E) activities, and that this relief did not extend to activities before or after the E&E phase. The Interpretations Committee confirmed that the scope of IFRS 6 consistently limited the relief from the hierarchy to policies applied to E&E activities only and that there is no basis for interpreting IFRS 6 as granting any additional relief in areas outside its scope.

The detailed requirements of IFRS 6 are discussed at 3 below.

1.4.2   Discussion Paper: Extractive activities

The IASB started work on an extractive activities research project in April 2004. The objective of the project is to develop a standard on accounting for the extractive industries.

On 6 April 2010 the IASB published the staff Discussion Paper – *Extractive Activities* (DP). The DP was developed by a research team comprising members of the Australian, Canadian, Norwegian and South African accounting standard-setters.[25] Preparers, users and regulators were subsequently invited to comment on the DP and submit their responses to the extractive activities project team. The IASB received over 140 responses to the DP. The respondents were predominately from the mining and oil and gas majors, accountancy bodies, regulators and accountancy firms, as well as a number of other bodies interested in one or more of the specific provisions. There appeared to have been little response from the small- and medium-sized extractive industry companies.

A relatively common question raised by the respondents was whether sufficient justification had been provided to support the need for a separate standard for the extractive industries. In addition to this, some of the other more significant concerns, discussed in greater detail in sections 1.4.2.A to 1.4.2.F below, included:

- The proposed asset recognition and measurement model;

- Potentially burdensome disclosure requirements, which included fair value and sensitivity analyses for reserve and resource volumes;

- The inclusion of Publish What You Pay disclosure requirements within the financial statements.

It was evident that there were clear and fundamental differences in operational practices between the mining and oil and gas industries. As a result, there was considerable industry-focused divide between the responses to the DP, particularly as they relate to how the DP's objectives would best be achieved.

Although the IASB has discussed the project team's findings, the Board has yet to develop preliminary views or make any tentative decisions on the DP, and hence the DP only reflects the views of the project team.

In July 2011, the Board launched its public consultation process on the composition of its technical agenda beyond June 2011. Based upon the outcome of this process, in conjunction with the responses to the staff DP, the Board will decide whether to add this project to its active agenda.

The main findings and recommendations included in the DP as well as some of the key themes raised in the comment letters from the respondents to the DP, are discussed at 1.4.2.A to 1.4.2.F below.

1.4.2.A Scope and approach

The aim of the project is to create a single accounting and disclosure model that will only apply to upstream extractive activities in both the minerals and oil and gas industries. This represents a change from IFRS 6, which includes minerals, oil, natural gas and similar non-regenerative resources within its scope. The project team decided against a broader scope in the DP as this would result in the need to develop additional definitions, accounting models and disclosures.[26] The DP addresses financial reporting issues associated with exploring for and finding minerals, oil and natural gas deposits, developing those deposits and extracting the minerals, oil and natural gas. These are collectively referred to as 'extractive activities' or, alternatively, as 'upstream activities'.[27] From a practical perspective, the scope of the issues addressed by the DP is narrower than initially expected. A number of complex issues (such as production sharing arrangements, carried interests, farm-ins/farm-outs and unitisations) that currently present challenges to reporters are not addressed. We support the project team's endeavours in addressing the accounting for extractive activities, but believe that for a final standard to be useful it should address the accounting issues that are unique to both industries.

In the DP, the project team concludes that there are similarities in the main business activities, and the geological and other risks and uncertainties in both the minerals and oil and gas industries.[28] The project team also notes similarities in the definitions of reserves and resources used by the Committee for Mineral Reserves International Reporting Standards (CRIRSCO) and the Society of Petroleum Engineers Oil and Gas Reserves Committee (SPE ORG).[29] Due to these similarities, the project team therefore proposes that there should be a single accounting and disclosure model that applies to all extractive activities (as defined).

As noted above, a significant number of responses from the mining and oil and gas majors, and many from accounting firms and regulators, initially challenged whether sufficient evidence had been provided to justify the need for a separate recognition and measurement standard for extractive activities, particularly as pharmaceuticals and software development industries possess similar technical complexities during the pre-development stage. They asked the IASB to clarify, using a principles-based framework, why such similarities would justify a separate standard.

Instead of a separate standard, these respondents suggested that a preferable approach would be to use the current IFRS conceptual framework and standards for recognition and measurement. They further suggested that industry implementation and/or application guidance should be provided to address industry specific issues. However, there did appear to be general acceptance that there was a need for a separate extractive activities disclosure standard.

Having said this, there were some respondents who did believe that a separate standard would actually be appropriate given that generally accepted practices of the sectors may vary significantly from analogous treatments.

On the basis that a separate standard could be justified, most respondents agreed that targeting upstream operations was appropriate. However, given the integrated nature of many companies, it was highlighted that any such standard should clearly define the scope and boundaries of such upstream activity.

In addition, while it had been generally acknowledged that the issues addressed in the DP were important, a significant number of respondents commented that the current scope did not address many of the more complex accounting issues (which are discussed further in this chapter) where practice was diverse and greater consistency was required.

These issues include:

- The lack of guidance on complex areas such as farm out/ in transactions;
- Accounting for production sharing and royalty agreements;
- The relationship between the proposals and IFRS 6 – *Exploration for and Evaluation of Minerals Resources*; and
- The omission of regenerative activities.

1.4.2.B Definitions of reserves and resources

The DP explores a number of alternatives for defining reserves and resources. As the IASB does not have the required technical expertise to develop and maintain a comprehensive set of reserve and resource definitions, the project team proposes to rely on the following existing definitions of reserves and resources:[30]

- minerals industry – *International Reporting Template for the Public Reporting of Exploration Results, Minerals Resources and Mineral Reserves* (CRIRSCO Template) established by the Committee for Mineral Reserves International Reporting Standards (CRIRSCO); and

- oil and gas industry – *Petroleum Resource Management System* (PRMS) established by the Society of Petroleum Engineers (in conjunction with other industry bodies).

The DP notes that the CRIRSCO Template and the PRMS are widely accepted and are comprehensive classification systems that cover many types of minerals and oil and gas.[31] The project team believes that the nature and extent of the similarities between the CRIRSCO Template and the PRMS reserve and resource definitions indicates that these definitions are capable of providing a platform for setting comparable accounting and disclosure requirements for both minerals and oil and gas assets. Nonetheless, there is some tension between the definition of an asset in the IASB's *Framework* and the assumptions underlying the reserves and resources definitions.[32] There are two points of tension highlighted by the project team. The CRIRSCO Template and the PRMS both make use of entity-specific assumptions that are applied to derive a reserve estimate, whereas IFRSs typically require estimates should make use of economic assumptions that reflect market-based evidence, where available. In addition, the CRIRSCO Template and the PRMS require that certain conditions must exist before a resource can be converted into a reserve. In contrast, management's intentions are not a feature of the Framework's definition of an asset.[33]

While the project team recommends the use of the CRIRSCO Template and PRMS, it also recommends that the alternative option of using the United Nations Framework Classification for Fossil Energy and Mineral Resources (UNFC) should be reconsidered if an extractive activities project is added to the IASB's active agenda.[34]

We believe, however, that making use of the CRIRSCO Template and the PRMS highlights the need for the IASB to establish formal relationships with these bodies. As these definitions would form an integral part of an IFRS, it is imperative for the Board to be appropriately involved in the maintenance of these definitions.

The other respondents also expressed concern that adopting the CRIRSCO and SPE definitions would effectively place reliance on an unregulated third party. Consequently, further guidance would be required to clarify how any changes to the definition of reserves and resources by the CRIRSCO or SPE would be incorporated in a future IFRS. There was also a view that the IASB would have to put in place some form of governance framework to ensure that such definitions continued to be appropriate for financial reporting purposes. Both the CRIRSCO and SPE committed themselves, via their responses, to ongoing maintenance and development (as required) of these definitions and their willingness to work with the IASB to minimise divergence between these definitions and other national reporting codes and standards.

1.4.2.C   Asset recognition

I   Definition

The IASB's *Conceptual Framework* defines an asset as a resource controlled by the entity as a result of past events and from which future economic benefits are expected to flow to the entity. *[Framework.4.4(a)]*.

The DP proposes that legal rights (i.e. exploration rights and extraction rights) should form the basis of a mineral or oil and gas asset. An asset should be recognised when the legal rights are acquired. Associated with these legal rights is information about the (possible) existence of minerals or oil and gas, the extent and characteristics of the deposit, and the economics of their extraction. The project team believes that rights and information associated with minerals or oil and gas properties satisfy the asset recognition criteria. While such information does not represent a separate asset, the project team proposes that information obtained from subsequent exploration and evaluation activities and development works would be treated as enhancements of the asset represented by the legal rights.[35]

However, we (as well as many other respondents) believe that the project team's proposal that subsequent costs incurred are always considered information that enhances the value of that asset needs to be further considered. The current definition of an asset includes a probability criterion in relation to the existence of future economic benefits for recognition purposes. *[Framework.4.4(a)]*. It is difficult to accept, without further analysis to demonstrate the probability that future economic benefits will arise, that all expenditures are enhancements of the minerals or oil and gas property. This would be particularly relevant when considering expenditures that result in negative information. Further, we believe that the project team's proposal is a significant shift away from the 'successful efforts' method, which is well understood by users in both industries. We would therefore suggest that there should be further research on the recognition criteria.

Likewise, while the mining and oil and gas majors agreed that the DP recognition model was conceptually flawed, the two industries did have differing views of what a more appropriate model should look like.

The preferred approach of large oil and gas companies appeared to be the successful efforts method, currently adopted by a large proportion of majors in the industry. See section 5.4.1 below for more information. The DP proposal is more aligned to the full cost method of oil and gas accounting permitted under US GAAP (see section 5.4.2 below), and is more often applied by oil and gas independents and small- to medium-sized companies that focus on exploration projects.

In contrast, major mining companies typically expensed costs early in the project lifecycle. Therefore, their responses reflected their considerable discomfort with the concept of capitalising any expenditure before there was a clear expectation that future economic benefits would be realised from such expenditure. Indeed, several large mining respondents provided examples of the extent of technical and commercial feasibility that would be required to be demonstrated before they would recognise an asset.

These responses suggest that both mining and oil and gas majors would prefer a recognition model that is closer to their own respective industry practices, as they are currently applied. Given the diversity in the nature of the two industries, this will represent a challenge to the project team in finalising a single model applicable to both. In addition, within each of these industries, we expect that companies with exploration as their main business focus would most likely prefer a different model, one that is more akin to full deferral and subject to impairment testing. Typically, such companies would be junior explorers.

Surprisingly, the response rate to the DP from such smaller industry participants was low. The consequence is that their point of view may not be heard. These companies run the risk of future requirements being heavily influenced by those who would prefer alternative and most likely, less attractive, models.

The project team also considered the manner in which mineral or oil and gas information associated with a property should be disclosed in the financial statements to reflect the uncertainties associated with such properties. In conclusion, the project team believes that the most useful approach would be to disclose quantities of minerals or oil and gas as either reserves or resources in accordance with the CRIRSCO Template or the PRMS, the key element being that such disclosure could provide additional certainty about future cash flows. The project team considered it necessary for users to be provided consistently with information that distinguishes properties that have been or will be developed (reserves or extraction rights) and those that may or may not be developed (resources or exploration rights).[36]

II   Unit of account

One of the key issues in the development of accounting standards and in the selection of accounting policies by preparers, is the decision as to the level at which an entity should separately account for assets, i.e. what the 'unit of account' should be (see 4.2 below). The definition of the unit of account has significant accounting consequences – for example it determines whether recognition, measurement and disclosure requirements need to be applied by region, country, contract, geological unit or organisational unit. While the IASB's conceptual framework project has identified the definition of a 'unit of account' as an important issue, this has not yet been addressed.[37]

In the context of extractive activities, the DP proposes that 'the geographical boundary of the unit of account would be defined initially on the basis of the exploration rights held. As exploration, evaluation and development activities take place, the unit of account will contract progressively until it becomes no greater than a single area, or group of contiguous areas, for which the legal rights are held and which is managed separately and would be expected to generate largely independent cash flows. The project team's view is that the components approach in IAS 16 *Property, Plant and Equipment* would determine the items that are accounted for as a single asset'[38]. However, an entity may decide to account for its assets using a smaller unit of account.[39]

Respondents expressed concern over the unit of account concept proposed in the DP. Mining and oil and gas majors alike believed that the concept of a reducing unit of account would be complex to apply in practice and would require significant levels of judgement. Also, in some instances the unit of account may actually increase.

Due to the importance of clearly establishing the unit of account, we and the other respondents believe that additional guidance will be needed in order to implement the concept as recommended by the DP. In particular, the DP should elaborate on the manner in which the unit of account interacts with the components and the cash generating unit concepts and the related impairment considerations.

1.4.2.D   Asset measurement

I   Measurement at historical cost

The DP considers both current value (e.g. fair value) and historical cost as potential measurement bases for minerals and oil and gas assets. As part of the research for the DP, the project team held detailed individual interviews with professional users of financial statements of entities in the extractive industries. The findings from the user interviews were that:[40]

- with some exceptions, historical cost information is not useful because the accumulated costs incurred to find a minerals or oil and gas deposit are not helpful in predicting the future cash flows from that property;

- measurement of minerals or oil and gas properties at fair value in the statement of financial position is not considered useful because there are many significant variables that go into a valuation and there can be substantial subjectivity involved. Users consider it important to apply their own judgement to these factors rather than relying on management's judgement. They would only make use of a fair value provided by the entity if there was extensive disclosure of the assumptions used; and

- current value measurements prepared on the basis of standardised assumptions (e.g. the use of a 10 per cent discount rate and year-end prices and costs) might be less subjective, more consistent between entities and less costly to produce. However, the more the inputs are specified the less likely it is that the valuation will be relevant.

Based on their findings, and taking the views of users and preparers into account, the project team concluded that minerals and oil and gas assets should be measured at historical cost and that detailed disclosures should be provided to enhance the relevance of the financial statements. The project team acknowledges that its choice of historical cost as the measurement basis is based to a large extent on doing the 'least harm'. However, the DP does ask commentators what measurement basis should be used for minerals and oil and gas assets.[41]

An overwhelming majority of respondents to this question indicated their strong support for the historical cost approach. This appeared to be one of the few areas where both mining and oil and gas respondents were broadly in agreement with the proposals set out in the DP.

II Impairment

The IAS 36 impairment testing model is not considered to be feasible for exploration properties for two reasons. Firstly, estimating the recoverable amount for exploration properties each reporting period is likely to involve as much effort as adopting a current value measurement basis. Secondly, it is not possible to limit the number of properties which require an impairment test by using impairment indicators based on adverse changes or new information, because typically there will always be new information available that would be relevant for making judgements about the recoverability of an exploration property's carrying amount.[42]

The project team considers various options and ultimately concludes that exploration properties should only be tested for impairment whenever, in management's judgement, there is evidence that suggests that there is a high likelihood that the carrying amount of an exploration asset will not be recovered in full. This would require management to apply a separate set of indicators to such properties in order to assess whether their continued recognition as assets would be justified. In addition, further disclosures are required in respect of the impairment of exploration properties due to the fact that management may take different views on the exploration properties. These would include separate presentation of exploration properties, the factors that lead to an impairment being recognised, and management's view as to why the remainder are not impaired. This impairment assessment needs to be conducted separately for each exploration property.[43]

1.4.2.E Disclosure

The DP proposes extensive disclosures that are aimed at ensuring that users of financial reports can evaluate:[44]

- the value attributable to an entity's minerals or oil and gas assets
- the contribution of those assets to current period financial performance
- the nature and extent of risks and uncertainties associated with those assets

The DP proposes detailed disclosures about the quantities of reserves and resources, and production revenues and costs. If the assets are measured at historical cost then detailed information should be disclosed about their current value and how it was determined. If, instead, the assets are measured at fair value then detailed information should be disclosed about that fair value and how it was determined.

The project team proposes the following detailed disclosures:[45]

- *reserve quantities by commodity, and further broken down by country or project:*
  - proved reserves and proved and probable reserves;
  - estimation method;
  - main assumptions;
  - sensitivity analysis to main assumptions; and
  - reconciliation of changes in reserve quantities;

- *current value measurement:* if an asset is measured at historical cost, as proposed by the project team, then the following information should be disclosed for each major geographical region:
  - current value information based on either:
    - a range of estimates based on fair value measurement principles; or
    - a standardised measure of proved and probable reserves, which is preferred by the project team;
  - preparation basis;
  - main assumptions; and
  - reconciliation of changes in current value;
- *fair value measurement:* if an asset is measured at fair value then the following information should generally be disclosed for each major geographical region:
  - fair value estimate;
  - main assumptions;
  - sensitivity analysis to main assumptions;
  - reconciliation of changes in reserve values; and
  - other disclosures similar to the proposals in ED/2009/5 *Fair Value Measurements;*
- *production revenues by commodity;*
- *costs:* a five year time series, disaggregated at the same level as the reserves quantity disclosure, of:
  - exploration costs;
  - development cost; and
  - production costs.

Respondents expressed a number of significant concerns related to these proposals, which are discussed further below.

Reserves

While the disclosure of reserves quantities was supported by most, the large oil and gas respondents believed disclosure of probable reserve balances should be optional, not mandatory. The heightened risk and uncertainty associated with probable quantities could lead to heightened litigation risk and would significantly increase compliance costs.

Commercial sensitivity

In addition to the logistical and process challenges associated with collating data and the new disclosure requirements, many large mining respondents expressed concern with the disclosure of key assumptions associated with reserves estimates. While the inclusion of qualitative disclosures regarding reserves measurement was supported, and in fact is already disclosed by many entities, the provision of quantitative disclosures, such as pricing and other assumptions, was not. The disclosure of such information could lead to a loss in competitive advantage and seriously prejudice the position of an entity, for example in merger and acquisition transactions and in certain price negotiations which occur with individual customers, e.g. diamonds and industrial minerals.

Sensitivity analysis and fair value disclosures

Respondents from both industries commented that the inputs into reserve and resource calculations were non-linear, and simply applying sensitivity to one input without re-basing the whole reserves model would produce a result with little meaning or value. Additionally, the complexities and level of judgement involved in producing a value-based asset disclosure would significantly reduce the reliability a user could place on it. It would appear any cost saving created by applying a historical cost measurement basis would be lost through the requirement for such disclosures. Therefore, this would, in effect, mean adopting one of the 'harms' of the fair value measurement basis.

A broader question was raised as to how the IASB could justify fair value disclosures being required only by those entities undertaking extractive activities and not more broadly by other industries. Property, plant and equipment and non-current assets are commonly measured at historical cost across many industries, yet there is currently no similar proposal for related outputs to also be disclosed at fair value. Respondents cannot see a fundamental difference that would sufficiently justify these fair value disclosure requirements.

US GAAP convergence

A number of the proposed disclosures differ from US GAAP. These include disclosures of:

- Key reserve estimate assumptions and sensitivity analysis (not required by US GAAP); and

- Proved and probable reserves (US GAAP only requires proved reserves)

There was broad consensus among the respondents of the need for the IASB to work jointly with the US Financial Accounting Standards Board (FASB), and the various international securities exchange commissions, to produce a single global framework to avoid discrepancies and duplication across reporting jurisdictions. US listed oil and gas respondents also urged the IASB to allow sufficient time to gauge users' reactions to the FASB rule changes for reserve estimation and disclosure that only took effect in 2009, before any changes are made to IFRS. Mining companies commented that US oil and gas filers are used to the more prescriptive and detailed nature of the FASB and SEC guidelines. In light of this, they felt the IASB needed to ensure that they consult with a broad range of companies impacted to determine the most appropriate level of disclosures rather than simply defaulting to the most detailed level of disclosures currently provided as a benchmark.

1.4.2.F   Publish What You Pay proposals

A coalition of non-governmental organisations is promoting a campaign called Publish What You Pay (PWYP), which proposes that entities undertaking extractive activities should be required to disclose, in their financial reports, the payments they make to each host government. PWYP also proposes that disclosures should be provided on a country by country basis for other types of information including minerals and oil and gas reserve quantities, production volumes, production revenues, costs incurred in development and production, and key subsidiaries and properties.[46]

The DP notes that the disclosure of payments made to governments provides information that would be of use to capital providers in making their investment and lending decisions, but notes that providing this information might be difficult and costly for some entities. The project team is seeking to develop an understanding of whether a requirement to disclose this information is justifiable on cost-benefit grounds.[47]

While non-NGO respondents demonstrated their understanding of the positive intent of such requirements, and may provide such information currently under the Extractive Industries Transparency Initiative (EITI), they did question how this would fit within the IASB's conceptual framework.

Putting aside the question of location, broader matters that would still need to be addressed were highlighted, including:

- The definition and scope of governmental payments;
- How the concept of materiality would be applied given the prescriptive PWYP requirement; and
- The value and need for companies to provide such data for countries not signed up to EITI.

Many respondents also believed that significant effort would be required to audit this information, particularly if this information would also be required at a subsidiary level.

2   MINERAL RESERVES AND RESOURCES

2.1   Significance of reserves estimation to financial reporting under IFRS

As noted earlier, IFRSs use the terms 'minerals' and 'mineral assets' as collective terms to encompass both mining and oil and gas reserves and resources. This section discusses in some detail the underlying principles used by entities to estimate the quantity of recoverable mineral reserves that the entity owns or has a right to extract. At the commercial level, these estimates are considered of paramount importance by stakeholders in making investment decisions. Currently IFRS does not require disclosure of reserves, though certain national standards (e.g. US GAAP) and stock exchange regulators (e.g. US Securities and Exchange Commission) do. The importance of estimating reserves is matched by the difficulty in doing so, both technically and methodologically. For example, there is no firm consensus on which commodity prices should be used in determining commercially recoverable reserves (i.e. historical, spot or forward looking).

This section therefore aims to provide an introduction to this subject, and to explain the main methods used to arrive at reserve estimates, including the valuation methods used once quantities of reserves have been estimated. In our view, without a sound grasp of this aspect, it is difficult to make an informed judgement as to how to account for mineral reserves.

Mineral reserves are often the most valuable assets of mining, and oil and gas companies. However, mineral reserves are generally measured under IFRS at their historical cost which, other than by coincidence, will not be their market value.

Even so, mineral reserve estimates are a very important part of the way mining companies and oil and gas companies report to their stakeholders. The IASC Issues Paper listed the following arguments in favour of disclosure of reserve quantity and value information:[48]

(a)   reserves indicate successful performance; costs alone do not;

(b)   mineral reserves are the most valuable asset of most entities in the extractive industries;

(c)   a primary goal of financial reporting is to assist in assessing future cash flows, and the commercial reserves controlled by the entity are the major source of future cash flows from upstream activities;

(d)   reserve information is not generally available elsewhere;

(e)   it is necessary to be able to evaluate how well the entity is replacing reserves as they are produced; and

(f)   reserve data is essential for comparing the financial performance and financial position of two or more entities.

The IASC also identified a number of arguments against detailed disclosure of reserve quantities and values in its Issues Paper:[49]

(a)   reserve estimates are inherently imprecise and subjective, involving numerous assumptions and forecasts;

(b)   value measurements require even more assumptions and forecasts than do quantity measures, making value data even less reliable; and

(c)   data about reserve quantities is proprietary information, and disclosure is anticompetitive.

Even if an entity chooses not to disclose any information about the quantity of the reserves that it holds, detailed reserve estimates are required in order to apply historical cost accounting under IFRS in:

• deciding whether to capitalise exploration and evaluation costs;

• calculating the annual depreciation, depletion and amortisation charge under the units of production method;

• calculating deferred stripping cost adjustments;

• determining impairment charges and reversals under IAS 36;

• determining whether a gain or loss should be recognised on transactions such as asset swaps, carried interest arrangements and farm-in or farm-out arrangements; and

• determining the fair value of acquired mineral reserves when applying the purchase method of accounting under IFRS 3 – *Business Combinations*.

2.2   Reserve estimation and reporting

Reserve reporting in the mining industry and oil and gas industry has been under development since the beginning of the twentieth century. However, reserve estimation techniques in the mining industry and oil and gas industry have developed largely independently as a result of the different nature of the reserves involved. Therefore, the terminology and definitions used in the mining industry and oil and gas industry are discussed separately at 2.2.1 and 2.2.2 below, respectively. The international efforts to harmonise reserve estimation and reporting are discussed at 2.2.3 below.

2.2.1   Petroleum reserve estimation and reporting

2.2.1.A   Standard-setting organisations

The 'SPE/WPC/AAPG/SPEE Petroleum Resources Management System' (SPE-PRMS), which was published in 2007, is the leading framework for the estimation and reporting of petroleum reserves and resources. It was prepared by the Oil and Gas Reserves Committee of the Society of Petroleum Engineers (SPE) and reviewed and sponsored by the World Petroleum Council (WPC), the American Association of Petroleum Geologists (AAPG) and the Society of Petroleum Evaluation Engineers (SPEE). The definitions and guidelines in the SPE-PRMS, which are internationally used within the oil and gas industry, deal with:[50]

- classification and categorisation of resources;
- evaluation and reporting; and
- estimation of recoverable quantities.

International efforts to standardise the definitions and estimations of petroleum resources began in the 1930s. The SPE published definitions for all reserves categories in 1987. In the same year, the WPC, working independently, published Reserves definitions that were strikingly similar. In 1997, the SPE and WPC jointly released a single set of definitions for reserves that could be used worldwide. In 2000, the AAPG, SPE, and WPC jointly developed a classification system for all petroleum resources. This was followed by additional supporting documents: supplemental application evaluation guidelines and a glossary of terms utilised in resources definitions. SPE also published standards for estimating and auditing reserves information (revised 2007).[51] The SPE-PRMS is currently the dominant classification system for petroleum. As noted by the IASB, 'most of the major regulatory agencies have developed disclosure guidelines that impose classification rules similar to, but not directly linked to, the SPE-PRMS. Regulatory agencies typically mandate disclosure of only a subset of the total reserves and resources defined in the SPE-PRMS; for example, the SEC specifies that only Proved Reserves should be disclosed.'[52]

2.2.1.B   Petroleum Resources Management System (SPE-PRMS)

I   Basic principles and definitions

The following diagram summarises the SPE-PRMS resources classification system:[53]

Figure 41.1

The *range of uncertainty* reflects a range of estimated quantities potentially recoverable, while the vertical axis represents the *chance of commerciality*, that is, the chance that the project that will be developed and reach commercial producing status.[54]

The SPE-PRMS defines proved, probable and possible reserves as follows:

- '*Reserves* are those quantities of petroleum anticipated to be commercially recoverable by application of development projects to known accumulations from a given date forward under defined conditions. Reserves must further satisfy four criteria: they must be discovered, recoverable, commercial, and remaining (as of the evaluation date) based on the development project(s) applied. Reserves are further categorized in accordance with the level of certainty associated with the estimates and may be sub-classified based on project maturity and/or characterized by development and production status.'[55]

- '*Proved reserves* are those quantities of petroleum, which, by analysis of geoscience and engineering data, can be estimated with reasonable certainty to be commercially recoverable, from a given date forward, from known reservoirs and under defined economic conditions, operating methods, and government regulations. If deterministic methods are used, the term reasonable certainty is intended to express a high degree of confidence that the quantities will be recovered. If probabilistic methods are used, there should be at least a 90% probability that the quantities actually recovered will equal or exceed the estimate.'[56]

- '*Probable reserves* are those additional Reserves which analysis of geoscience and engineering data indicate are less likely to be recovered than Proved Reserves but more certain to be recovered than Possible Reserves. It is equally likely that actual remaining quantities recovered will be greater than or less than the sum of the estimated Proved plus Probable Reserves (2P). In this context, when probabilistic methods are used, there should be at least a 50% probability that the actual quantities recovered will equal or exceed the 2P estimate.'[57]

- '*Possible reserves* are those additional reserves which analysis of geoscience and engineering data suggest are less likely to be recoverable than Probable Reserves. The total quantities ultimately recovered from the project have a low probability to exceed the sum of Proved plus Probable plus Possible (3P) Reserves, which is equivalent to the high estimate scenario. In this context, when probabilistic methods are used, there should be at least a 10% probability that the actual quantities recovered will equal or exceed the 3P estimate.'[58]

The SPE-PRMS distinguishes between contingent and prospective resources:

- The term *resources* is intended to encompass all quantities of petroleum naturally occurring on or within the Earth's crust, discovered and undiscovered (recoverable and unrecoverable), plus those quantities already produced. Further, it includes all types of petroleum whether currently considered 'conventional' or 'unconventional'.[59]

- '*Contingent resources* are those quantities of petroleum estimated, as of a given date, to be potentially recoverable from known accumulations, but the applied project(s) are not yet considered mature enough for commercial development due to one or more contingencies. Contingent Resources may include, for example, projects for which there are currently no viable markets, or where commercial recovery is dependent on technology under development, or where evaluation of the accumulation is insufficient to clearly assess commerciality. Contingent Resources are further categorized in accordance with the level of certainty associated with the estimates and may be sub-classified based on project maturity and/or characterized by their economic status.'[60]

- '*Prospective resources* are those quantities of petroleum estimated, as of a given date, to be potentially recoverable from undiscovered accumulations by application of future development projects. Prospective Resources have both an associated chance of discovery and a chance of development. Prospective Resources are further subdivided in accordance with the level of certainty associated with recoverable estimates assuming their discovery and development and may be sub-classified based on project maturity.'[61]

Total petroleum initially-in-place is that quantity of petroleum that is estimated to exist originally in naturally occurring accumulations. *Discovered petroleum initially-in-place* is that quantity of petroleum that is estimated, as of a given date, to be contained in known accumulations prior to production. *Undiscovered petroleum initially-in-place* is that quantity of petroleum estimated, as of a given date, to be contained within accumulations yet to be discovered.[62]

Production is the cumulative quantity of petroleum that has been recovered at a given date. *Unrecoverable* is that portion of Discovered or Undiscovered Petroleum Initially-in-Place quantities which is estimated, as of a given date, not to be recoverable by future development projects. A portion of these quantities may become recoverable in the future as commercial circumstances change or technological developments occur; the remaining portion may never be recovered due to physical/chemical constraints represented by subsurface interaction of fluids and reservoir rocks.[63]

II   Classification and categorisation guidelines

The SPE-PRMS provides guidance on classifying resources depending on the relative maturity of the development projects being applied to yield the recoverable quantity estimates, as follows:[64]

Figure 41.2

Project maturity may be indicated qualitatively by allocation to classes and sub-classes and/or quantitatively by associating a project's estimated chance of reaching producing status.

The SPE-PRMS also provides guidance on categorising resources, depending on the associated degrees of uncertainty, into the following cumulative categories:[65]

- proved, probable and possible (1P, 2P and 3P) for reserves;
- low, best and high (1C, 2C and 3C) for contingent resources; and
- low estimate, best estimate and high estimate for prospective resources.

Additionally, guidance is provided on categorisation of reserves and resources related to incremental projects, such as workovers, infill drilling and improved recovery.

III   Evaluation and reporting guidelines

To promote consistency in project evaluations and reporting, the SPE-PRMS provides guidelines on the economic assumptions that are to be used, measurement of production, and resources entitlement and recognition.[66]

IV   Estimating recoverable quantities

Finally, the SPE-PRMS provides guidance on the analytical procedures, and on the deterministic and probabilistic methods to be used.[67]

2.2.2   Mining resource and reserve reporting

2.2.2.A   Standard-setting organisations

The *Australasian Code for Reporting of Exploration Results, Mineral Resources and Ore Reserves* (JORC Code) is prepared by the Joint Ore Reserves Committee (JORC) of the Australasian Institute of Mining and Metallurgy, Australian Institute of Geoscientists and Minerals Council of Australia. The JORC was established 'in 1971 and published several reports containing recommendations on the classification and Public Reporting of Ore Reserves prior to the release of the first edition of the JORC Code in 1989.'[68] The most recent edition of the JORC Code was issued in 2004.

Until the late 1990s, the Australasian JORC Code was the only standard in mineral resource and ore reserve reporting that was recognised internationally, despite the fact that it was linked only to the Australian Stock Exchange for its regulatory controls. The publication of a revised JORC Code in 1999 prompted the development of similar national reporting standards by the following standard-setters:[69]

- Canada: *CIM Definition Standards on Mineral Resources and Mineral Reserves*, Canadian Institute of Mining, Metallurgy and Petroleum (CIM);
- Chile: *Code for the Certification of Exploration Prospects, Mineral Resources and Ore Reserves*, Instituto de Ingenieros de Minas de Chile (IIMCh);
- Pan European Reserves Reporting Committee (PERC) in the United Kingdom, Ireland and Western Europe;
- Peru: *Code for Reporting on Mineral Resources and Ore Reserves*, Joint Committee of the Venture Capital Segment of the Lima Stock Exchange;
- South Africa: *South African Code for Reporting of Mineral Resources and Mineral Reserves*, South African Mineral Resource Committee (SAMREC); and
- United States: *Guide for Reporting Exploration Information, Mineral Resources and Mineral Reserves*, Society for Mining, Metallurgy, and Exploration (SME).[70]

Concurrently with the evolution of the JORC Code, the Combined Reserves International Reporting Standards Committee (CRIRSCO), which was initially a committee of the Council of Mining and Metallurgical Institutions (CMMI), has been working since 1994 to create a set of standard international definitions for reporting mineral resources and mineral ore reserves, modelled on those of the JORC Code.[71] In July 2006 CRIRSCO published a generic International Reporting Template, which reflects best practice national reporting standards but excludes national regulatory requirements. The template serves as a guide to national standard-setters that do not have a reporting standard or who want to revise their existing standard to an internationally acceptable form.[72] 'The system is primarily targeted at establishing international best practice standards for regulatory and public disclosures and combines the basic components of a number of national reporting codes and guidelines that have been adopted in similar forms by all the major agencies [other than] the US Securities and Exchange Commission (SEC). The classification is applied, with small modifications or extensions, by most mining companies for the purpose of internal resource management.'[73]

CRIRSCO has been participating in the activities of the IASB's Discussion Paper – *Extractive Activities* (see 2.2.3.A below).

2.2.2.B   CRIRSCO International Reporting Template

This section describes the main requirements of the CRIRSCO International Reporting Template (CRIRSCO Template) to the extent that they are relevant in financial reporting by mining companies.

I   Scope

The main principles underlying the CRIRSCO Template are transparency, materiality and competence, and are aimed at ensuring that the reader of a public report is provided with:[74]

• sufficient information that is clear and unambiguous,

• a report that contains all information that could reasonably be required to form a reasoned and balanced judgement about the exploration results, mineral resources or mineral reserves being reported, and

• information that is based on work that is the responsibility of suitably qualified and experienced persons who are subject to an enforceable professional code of ethics and rules of conduct.

A *public report* is a report on exploration results, mineral resource or mineral reserves that is prepared for the purpose of informing investors, potential investors and their advisors, or to satisfy regulatory requirements.[75] The CRIRSCO Template is applicable to all solid minerals, including diamonds, other gemstones, industrial minerals, stone and aggregates, and coal.[76] The CRIRSCO Template provides supplementary rules on reporting related to coal, diamonds and industrial minerals, due to the special nature of those types of deposit.

II   Competence and responsibility

A public report should be prepared by a *competent person*, defined in the CRIRSCO Template as a person 'who is a Member or Fellow of a recognised professional body relevant to the activity being undertaken, and who is subject to enforceable Rules of Conduct'.[77]

III   Reporting terminology

The general relationship between exploration results, mineral resources and mineral reserves can be summarised in the following diagram:[78]

Figure 41.3

The terms in the above diagram are defined as follows.

Exploration results include data and information generated by exploration programmes that may be of use to investors. The exploration results may or may not be part of a formal declaration of mineral resources or mineral reserves.[79] The CRIRSCO Template specifically requires that any information relating to exploration results be expressed in such a way that it does not unreasonably imply that potentially economic mineralisation has been discovered.[80]

A *mineral resource* is a concentration or occurrence of material of economic interest in or on the Earth's crust in such form, quality and quantity that there are reasonable prospects for eventual economic extraction. The location, quantity, grade, continuity and other geological characteristics of a mineral resource are known, estimated or interpreted from specific geological evidence, sampling and knowledge. Mineral resources are sub-divided, in order of increasing geological confidence, into inferred, indicated and measured categories:[81]

- 'An *inferred mineral resource* is that part of a Mineral Resource for which tonnage, grade and mineral content can be estimated with a low level of confidence. It is inferred from geological evidence, sampling and assumed but not verified geological and/or grade continuity. It is based on information gathered through appropriate techniques from locations such as outcrops, trenches, pits, workings and drill holes which is limited or of uncertain quality and reliability.'[82]

- 'An *indicated mineral resource* is that part of a Mineral Resource for which tonnage, densities, shape, physical characteristics, grade and mineral content can be estimated with a reasonable level of confidence. It is based on exploration, sampling and testing information gathered through appropriate techniques from locations such as outcrops, trenches, pits, workings and drill holes. The locations are too widely or inappropriately spaced to confirm geological and/or grade continuity but are spaced closely enough for continuity to be assumed.'[83]

- 'A *measured mineral resource* is that part of a Mineral Resource for which tonnage, densities, shape, physical characteristics, grade and mineral content can be estimated with a high level of confidence. It is based on detailed and reliable exploration, sampling and testing information gathered through appropriate techniques from locations such as outcrops, trenches, pits, workings and drill holes. The locations are spaced closely enough to confirm geological and grade continuity.'[84]

A *mineral reserve* is the economically mineable part of a measured and/or indicated mineral resource. It includes diluting materials and allowances for losses, which may occur when the material is mined. Appropriate assessments and studies have been carried out, and include consideration of and modification by realistically assumed mining, metallurgical, economic, marketing, legal, environmental, social and governmental factors. These assessments demonstrate at the time of reporting that extraction could reasonably be justified. Mineral reserves are sub-divided in order of increasing confidence into probable mineral reserves and proved mineral reserves:[85]

- 'A *probable mineral reserve* is the economically mineable part of an Indicated, and in some circumstances, a Measured Mineral Resource. It includes diluting materials and allowances for losses which may occur when the material is mined. Studies to at least Pre-Feasibility level will have been carried out, including consideration of and modification by realistically assumed mining, metallurgical, economic, marketing, legal, environmental, social and governmental factors. The results of the studies demonstrate at the time of reporting that extraction could reasonably be justified.'[86]

- 'A *proved mineral reserve* is the economically mineable part of a Measured Mineral Resource. It includes diluting materials and allowances for losses, which may occur when the material is mined. Studies to at least Pre-Feasibility level will have been carried out, including consideration of, and modification by, realistically assumed mining, metallurgical, economic, marketing, legal, environmental, social and governmental factors. These studies demonstrate at the time of reporting that extraction is justified.'[87]

Chapter 41

The CRIRSCO Template contains more detailed guidance on how a competent person should decide on mineral resource and mineral reserve classification and contains a checklist and guideline for the preparation of public reports.

2.2.3   International harmonisation of reserve reporting

2.2.3.A   IASB Discussion Paper – Extractive Activities

Following a request from the IASB, the SPE (see 2.2.1 above) and CRIRSCO (see 2.2.2 above) agreed 'to review their definitions of reserves and resources to identify opportunities for refining the industry-based definitions to potentially improve their suitability for application in financial reporting as well as remaining suitable for other industry-based uses'.[88] The SPE and CRIRSCO participated in the activities of the IASB Extractive Activities Research Project designed to investigate the need for, and practicalities of, an IFRS for the extractive industries.

During the educational sessions on the extractive activities research project (see 1.4.2 above), several IASB board members indicated an interest in an extractive industries standard under which reserves and resources would be recognised in the statement of financial position at fair value. This focused attention on what the SPE and CRIRSCO definitions actually mean in accounting terms. The approach of the SPE and CRIRSCO was 'to leave the respective definitions intact, but aim to provide "convergence" of terminology where possible and modify the accompanying guidelines where appropriate to accommodate financial reporting requirements. Many questions remain to be resolved; for example when does a body of hydrocarbons or mineralisation first become an asset as defined in accounting terms? What rules should be applied for depreciating assets over the life of a mineral reserve? And perhaps most fundamentally, what reliance can be placed on numbers that are derived from estimates? What exactly do we mean by low, reasonable and high levels of confidence?'[89]

In June 2007, the Extractive Activities Research Project team (the project team) presented their conclusion that 'there is a high degree of compatibility in the classification logic that petroleum and minerals evaluators apply in determining quantities of their respective materials that reside in a field or a deposit'.[90] In the March 2008 IASB Board meeting, representatives from SPE and CRIRSCO presented 'the findings of a review, which was undertaken at the request of the Board, to compare their respective oil & gas and minerals reserve and resource definitions and classification systems. The review concluded that there is a high degree of compatibility in the classification logic that petroleum and minerals evaluators apply in determining quantities of their respective minerals that reside in a field or a deposit and can be extracted and marketed. The review findings are presented in a report prepared by SPE and CRIRSCO that "maps" the oil & gas and minerals reserve and resource definitions to illustrate the extent of comparability between the respective definitions.'[91]

The Board believed that 'this mapping report would be useful for developing accounting and disclosure models for reserves and resources that are comparable across minerals and oil & gas. ... In addition, the Board expressed the view that the research project's discussion paper should identify the SPE and CRIRSCO definition and classification systems as representing the preferred sets of definitions for use in supporting accounting and disclosure requirements for minerals and oil & gas reserves and resources.'[92] At the same meeting the Board asked the project team to continue to monitor the SEC's decisions in relation to its Concept Release, which is discussed below.

As discussed at 1.4.2.B, the project team concluded in the Discussion Paper – *Extractive Activities* – that the nature and extent of the similarities that exist between the CRIRSCO Template and the PRMS reserve and resource definitions indicates that these definitions are capable of providing a platform for setting comparable accounting and disclosure requirements for both minerals and oil and gas properties. Therefore they recommended that the CRIRSCO template and the PRMS definitions of reserves and resources are suitable to use in a future IFRS for Extractive Activities. Nonetheless, there is some tension between the definition of an asset in the IASB's *Framework* and the assumptions underlying the reserves and resources definitions.[93] While the project team recommends the use of the CRIRSCO Template and PRMS, it also recommends that the alternative option of using the *United Nations Framework Classification for Fossil Energy and Mineral Resources* (UNFC) should be reconsidered if an extractive activities project is added to the IASB's active agenda.[94]

2.2.3.B SEC final rule – Modernization of Oil and Gas Reporting

In December 2007, the SEC issued a Concept Release on *Possible Revisions to the Disclosure Requirements Relating to Oil and Gas Reserves* in order to obtain information about the extent and nature of the public's interest in revising oil and gas reserves disclosure requirements which the SEC adopted between 1978 and 1982.[95] The SEC noted that 'in the decades that have passed since the adoption of these rules, there have been significant changes in the oil and gas industry. Some commentators have expressed concern that the Commission's rules have not adapted to current practices and may not provide investors with the most useful picture of oil and gas reserves public companies hold'.[96]

Almost all who commented on the Concept Release supported 'some form of revision to the current oil and gas disclosure requirements, particularly given the length of time that has elapsed since the requirements were initially adopted'.[97] Consequently, in January 2009, the SEC published a final rule – *Modernization of Oil and Gas Reporting (Release No. 33-8995)* – to revise its oil and gas reserves estimation and disclosure requirements. The primary objectives of the revisions are to increase the transparency and information value of reserve disclosures and improve comparability among oil and gas companies – including comparability between domestic registrants and foreign private issuers. The rule became effective for registration statements filed on or after 1 January 2010, and for annual reports for fiscal years ending on or after 31 December 2009. The final rule, among other things:[98]

- expanded the definition of oil and gas producing activities to include reserves from non-traditional sources such as oil sands, shale and coalbeds;

- defined the term 'reasonable certainty,' as used in the existing definition of proved oil and gas reserves, as 'high degree of confidence';

- added a definition of the term 'reliable technology' to clarify the types of technology that can be used to establish reasonable certainty of the economic producibility of estimated reserves and requires general disclosure surrounding the technologies used to estimate reserves;

- permitted the optional disclosure of probable and possible reserves;

- modified the prices used to estimate reserves for SEC disclosure purposes to a 12-month average price instead of a single-day, period-end price;

- revised the full-cost method of accounting and depletion accounting to clarify that 'current prices' are to be a 12-month average price. The FASB has amended ASC 932 – *Extractive Activities – Oil and Gas* – to align with the SEC's final rule;

- permitted companies to disclose reserves using an optional price sensitivity analysis;

- required narrative disclosure of proved undeveloped reserves, including a description of why individual fields or countries have remained undeveloped for five years or more;

- updated and codified Industry Guide 2, with minimal revisions, into Regulation S-K;

- required companies to disclose the internal controls used 'to assure objectivity in the reserves estimation process,' including disclosure of the qualifications of the technical person (whether an employee or third party) primarily responsible for overseeing the preparation of the reserves estimates. If the company discloses that an audit of the reserves was performed, similar disclosures are required of the third party that performed the audit;

- required filing a report of the third party as an exhibit if the company represents that a third party prepared or audited reserves estimates or performed a process review;

- amended the definition of geographic area and established percentage thresholds for purposes of presenting disaggregated reserves and production disclosures; and

- amended the instructions to Form 20-F such that the same disclosures are required of domestic registrants and foreign private issuers – although it is worth noting that domestic registrants have some additional specific disclosures required under ASC 932 which do not apply to foreign private issuers.

2.2.3.C   Mining resource and reserve reporting

I   Convergence with the United States

In the United States, public disclosures of mineral resources and mineral reserves are regulated by the SEC, which does not recognise the CRIRSCO guidelines. Unsurprisingly, some of the SEC requirements (Industry Guide 7) for public release of information are materially different from those applicable in other countries.[99]

Therefore, in 2004, an Industry Working Group was formed under the auspices of the US Society for Mining, Metallurgy and Exploration (SME) to formulate a response to fundamental reporting issues, such as:[100]

- that fact that the SEC does not allow the term 'resources' to be used in reports;

- the SEC requirement that final feasibility studies need to be completed before new greenfield reserves can be declared; and

- the SEC requirement to use historical (currently three year trailing average) rather than forward looking commodity prices in reserve estimation. (NOTE – as a result of the modernized oil and gas reporting requirements (see 2.2.3.B above), oil and gas entities are now required to use a 12-month average price instead of a year-end price in estimating reserves.)

The Industry Working Group presented its conclusions to the SEC in April 2005. However, no progress has been made in achieving convergence between the CRIRSCO guidelines and the SEC requirements. In February 2008, both the CRIRSCO and the SME provided comments on the SEC's Concept Release (see 2.2.3.B above). In its comment letter, CRIRSCO called for the SEC to consider 'concurrent revisions to disclosure requirements relating to minerals exploration and mining as well as oil and gas',[101] while SME noted that 'given the increasing overlap between oil and gas, and mining in such areas as tar sands and oil shales, the need for convergence should not be ignored when reviewing oil and gas rules.'[102] However, so far no progress has been made in achieving convergence in these areas.

2.3   Disclosure of mineral reserves and resources

As discussed at 2.1 above, mineral reserves are a significant element in communications by mining companies and oil and gas companies to their stakeholders. IFRS requires an entity to provide 'additional disclosures when compliance with the specific requirements in IFRSs is insufficient to enable users to understand the impact of particular transactions, other events and conditions on the entity's financial position and financial performance'. *[IAS 1.17(c)]*. Therefore, although IFRS does not specifically require this, disclosures regarding mineral resources and reserves will generally be necessary under IFRS to provide users with the information that they need to understand the entity's financial position and performance. In the absence of specific guidance, entities should develop a method for communicating reserves that is consistent with the overall IFRS conceptual framework. As previously discussed, entities have to calculate reserves data for a number of accounting purposes and the methodology should be consistent with the definitions within the IFRS conceptual framework for asset recognition. We believe that users of the financial statements need to be able to identify the methodology used to estimate reserves in order to understand an entity's financial statements. Hence if management uses proven reserves for investment appraisal, and uses these same reserves for depreciation and impairment calculations, this should be clearly identified in the reserves disclosure. Conversely, if management uses different reserves definitions for different purposes, that should be made clear in the financial statements.

As mentioned above, there is currently no guidance under IFRS dealing with the disclosure of information about mineral reserves and resources. Entities not subject to the requirements of a national regulator may therefore wish to use the disclosure requirements of other standard-setters as a starting point in developing their own policies. The section below discusses the disclosure requirements of several standard-setters concerning mineral reserve and resource quantities (see 2.3.1 below) and reserve values (see 2.3.2 below).

2.3.1   Disclosure of proved/proven, probable and possible reserves

As discussed at 2.1 above, while disclosure of information about mineral reserves is clearly very useful, users of financial statements should be aware that many differences exist between different jurisdictions or even within those jurisdictions. Therefore, comparisons between entities may be difficult or even impossible. In particular, the following points of definition are important:

- *Proven and probable reserves* – The definition of reserves can vary greatly, e.g. the UK Oil Industry Accounting Committee's Statement of Recommended Practice (OIAC SORP) permits disclosure of either 'proven and probable' or 'proved developed and undeveloped' reserves (see 2.3.1.A I below), whereas Accounting Standards Codification (ASC) Topic 932-235-50 – *Extractive Activities – Oil and Gas – Notes to Financial Statements – Disclosure* (pre-codification FAS 69 – *Disclosures about Oil and Gas Producing Activities*) requires disclosure of 'proved reserves and proved developed reserves'[103] (see 2.3.1.A II below);

- *Commodity price* – The quantity of economically recoverable reserves may depend to a large extent on the price assumptions that an entity uses. Differences often arise because the entity:

  - uses its own long-term price assumption which, for example, is permitted under the OIAC SORP;

  - was required to use year-end prices (this was required by the SEC in the oil and gas industry until 2009 (see Extract 41.2 below) – oil and gas entities are now required to use 12-month average prices – see 2.2.3.B above); or

  - is required to use 12-month average prices, which is required by the SEC Release No. 33-8995 in the oil and gas industry (see 2.2.3.B above); or

  - is required to use a three year trailing average, which is required under the SEC's Industry Guide 7 in the mining industry (see 2.2.3.C I above);

- *Royalties* – Royalties payable in-kind to the government or legal owner of the mineral rights may or may not be included within reserves;

- *Non-controlling interests* – Generally 'reserves' include all reserves held by the parent and its consolidated subsidiaries. While in many jurisdictions mining companies and oil and gas companies are required to disclose the reserves attributable to significant non-controlling interests, this is not always required;

- *Associates and other investments* – An entity may have economic ownership of reserves through investments in associates and joint ventures, equity interests or royalty yielding contracts (see 5.2 below). Such reserves are generally not included within consolidated reserves, but may need to be disclosed separately; and

- *Production sharing contracts and risk service contracts* (see 5.1 below) – Frequently the mining company or oil and gas company does not legally own the mineral reserves in the ground, i.e. the government retains legal ownership. A significant amount of judgement concerning the nature of the rights and economic interests of the entity may be required to determine whether the entity is the economic owner of any reserves. Depending on the reserve reporting framework that the entity is subject to, such 'economic' reserves may or may not be included within reserves.

Undoubtedly there are other differences between the disclosures of reserves required in different jurisdictions of which users of IFRS financial statements should be aware. As illustrated in the extract below from BP's 2006 financial statements, such differences in reserve definition may also affect IFRS financial reporting directly.

Extract 41.2: BP plc (2006)

Notes on financial statements [extract]

3 Oil and natural gas reserves estimates

At the end of 2006, BP adopted the US Securities and Exchange Commission (SEC) rules for estimating oil and natural gas reserves for all accounting and reporting purposes instead of the UK accounting rules contained in the Statement of Recommended Practice 'Accounting for Oil and Gas Exploration, Development, Production and Decommissioning Activities' (UK SORP). The main differences relate to the SEC requirement to use year-end prices, the application of SEC interpretations of SEC regulations relating to the use of technology (mainly seismic) to estimate reserves in the reservoir away from wellbores and the reporting of fuel gas (i.e. gas used for fuel in operations) within proved reserves. Consequently, reserves quantities under SEC rules differ from those that would be reported under application of the UK SORP.

The change to SEC reserves represents a simplification of the group's reserves reporting, as in the future only one set of reserves estimates will be disclosed. In addition, the use of SEC reserves for accounting purposes will bring our IFRS and US GAAP reporting into closer alignment, as well as making our results more comparable with those of our major competitors.

This change in accounting estimate has a direct impact on the amount of depreciation, depletion and amortization (DD&A) charged in the income statement in respect of oil and natural gas properties which are depreciated on a unit-of-production basis as described in Note 1. The change in estimate is applied prospectively, with no restatement of prior periods' results. The group's actual DD&A charge for the year is $9,128 million, whereas the charge based on UK SORP reserves would have been $9,057 million, i.e. an increase of $71 million due to the change in reserves estimates which was used to calculate DD&A for the last three months of the year. Over the life of a field this change would have no overall effect on DD&A but the estimated effect for 2007 is expected to be an increase of approximately $400 million to $500 million for the group.

2.3.1.A   Oil and gas industry

Many oil and gas companies are required to disclose information about reserve quantities in accordance with the rules and requirements of the stock exchange on which they are listed. However, those oil and gas companies that are not subject to the specific disclosure requirements of a stock exchange or other local regulator may wish to consider disclosing the information required under the UK Oil Industry Accounting Committee's Statement of Recommended Practice (OIAC SORP) (see I below) or ASC 932-235-50 – *Extractive Activities – Oil and Gas – Notes to Financial Statements – Disclosure* (see II below).

i   OIAC SORP disclosure of commercial reserve quantities

The OIAC SORP requires disclosure, in a separate unaudited statement, of the net quantities of an entity's interest in 'commercial reserves of crude oil (including condensate and natural gas liquids) and natural gas ... as at the beginning and end of each accounting period in total and by geographical area'.[104] Under the OIAC SORP, an entity should adopt one of the following definitions for its 'commercial reserves':

(a)   proven and probable oil and gas reserves; or

(b)   proved developed and undeveloped oil and gas reserves.

There should be a 50% probability that the actual quantity of recoverable reserves will be more than the amount estimated as proved and probable and a 50% probability that it will be less. The equivalent statistical probabilities for the proven component of proved and probable reserves are 90% and 10% respectively.[105] Furthermore, the OIAC SORP specifies regarding commercial reserves that:[106]

- net quantities of reserves include those relating to the entity's operating and non-operating interests in properties;

- net quantities should not include reserves relating to interests of others in properties owned by the entity, nor quantities available under long-term supply agreements;

- net quantities should only include amounts that may be taken by governments as royalties-in-kind where it is the entity's policy to record as turnover the value of production taken as royalty-in-kind;

- if the company issues consolidated accounts, 100% of the net reserve quantities attributable to the parent company and 100% of the net reserve quantities attributable to its consolidated subsidiaries should be included, whether they are wholly-owned or not; and

- if the company's consolidated accounts include investments that are accounted for by the equity method, the net oil and gas reserves of those investments should not be included in the disclosures of the entity's reserves.

The OIAC SORP requires changes in the net quantities of commercial reserves during each accounting period to be disclosed as illustrated in Example 41.1 below.[107]

Example 41.1:   Net commercial oil and gas reserve quantities

Net Commercial Oil and Gas Reserve Quantities for the year ended 31 December xxxx

	Total		Area A		Area B	
	Oil	**Gas**	**Oil**	**Gas**	**Oil**	**Gas**
Net commercial reserves, beginning of year:						
– commercial developed reserves	×	×	×	×	×	×
– commercial undeveloped reserves	×	×	×	×	×	×
	×	×	×	×	×	×
Changes during the year:						
– revisions of previous estimates	×	×	×	×	×	×
– purchases of reserves-in-place	×	×	×	×	×	×
– extensions, discoveries & other additions	×	×	×	×	×	×
– sales of reserves-in-place	(×)	(×)	(×)	(×)	(×)	(×)
– production	(×)	(×)	(×)	(×)	(×)	(×)
	×	×	×	×	×	×
Net commercial reserves, end of year:						
– commercial developed reserves	×	×	×	×	×	×
– commercial undeveloped reserves	×	×	×	×	×	×
	×	×	×	×	×	×
Company's share of net commercial reserves of associates and joint ventures at end of year *)	×	×	×	×	×	×

Of total net commercial oil and gas reserves at 31 December xxxx, × barrels of oil and y cubic feet of gas are attributable to non-controlling shareholders of certain subsidiaries.

*)   The definitions of associates and joint ventures under UK GAAP are, however, different from those under IFRS.

The OIAC SORP requires the following additional information to be disclosed:

- the source of the estimates, together with a description of the basis used to arrive at net quantities;[108]

- a supporting narrative explanation that describes the effect of significant unusual events (e.g. redeterminations of equity interests in unitised fields) which would be included within 'purchases of reserves-in-place' or 'sales of reserves-in-place';[109]

- if a significant portion of the reserve quantities of the parent and its consolidated subsidiaries at the end of the year is attributable to consolidated subsidiaries in which there is a significant non-controlling interest, that fact and the approximate portion should be disclosed;[110]

- if the entity's consolidated accounts include investments that are accounted for by the equity method, the entity's share of those investments' net commercial reserve quantities as at the end of the year should be shown separately;[111] and

- reserves of oil and natural gas liquids should be stated in barrels and gas reserves in cubic feet.[112]

II   ASC 932-235-50 (pre-codification FAS 69) disclosure of reserves

All entities engaged in significant oil and gas producing activities that report under US GAAP are required by ASC 932-235-50 (pre-codification FAS 69) to disclose supplementary information about proved oil and gas reserve quantities as follows:

'50-4   Net quantities of an entity's interests in proved oil and gas reserves, proved developed oil and gas reserves, and proved undeveloped oil and gas reserves of each of the following shall be disclosed as of the beginning and the end of the year:

a.   Crude oil, including condensate and natural gas liquids. (If significant, the reserve quantity information shall be disclosed separately for natural gas liquids)

b.   Natural gas

c.   Synthetic oil

d.   Synthetic gas

e.   Other non-renewable natural resources that are intended to be upgraded into synthetic oil and gas

Net quantities of reserves include those relating to the entity's operating and nonoperating interests in properties. Quantities of reserves relating to royalty interests owned shall be included in net quantities if the necessary information is available to the entity; if reserves relating to royalty interests owned are not included because the information is unavailable, that fact and the entity's share of oil and gas produced for those royalty interests shall be disclosed for the year. Net quantities shall not include reserves relating to interests of others in properties owned by the entity.

50-5   Changes in the net quantities of an entity's proved reserves of oil and of gas during the year shall be disclosed. Changes resulting from all of the following shall be shown separately with appropriate explanation of significant changes:

a.   Revisions of previous estimates. Revisions represent changes in previous estimates of proved reserves, either upward or downward, resulting from new information (except for an increase in proved acreage) normally obtained from development drilling and production history or resulting from a change in economic factors.

b.   Improved recovery. Changes in reserve estimates resulting from application of improved recovery techniques shall be shown separately, if significant. If not significant, such changes shall be included in revisions of previous estimates.

c.   Purchases of minerals in place.

d.   Extensions and discoveries. Additions to proved reserves that result from either of the following:

1.   Extension of the proved acreage of previously discovered (old) reservoirs through additional drilling in periods subsequent to discovery

2.   Discovery of new fields with proved reserves or of new reservoirs of proved reserves in old fields.

e.   Production.

f.   Sales of minerals in place.

50-6   The disclosures of net quantities of proved reserves of oil and of gas and changes in them required by paragraphs 932-235-50-4 through 50-5 shall be presented in the aggregate and separately by geographic area (see the following paragraph) in which significant reserves (see paragraph 932-235-50-6B) are located. If an entity's proved reserves of oil and of gas are located entirely within its home country, that fact shall be disclosed.

50-6A   Any one of the following may constitute a geographic area, as appropriate for meaningful disclosure in the circumstances:

a.   An individual country

b.   A group of countries within a continent

c.   A continent.

50-6B   In determining whether reserves are significant:

a.   An entity shall consider all facts and circumstances and not solely the quantity of reserves.

b.   At a minimum, net quantities of reserves shall be presented in the aggregate and separately by geographic area and for each country containing 15 percent or more of an entity's proved reserves, expressed on an oil-equivalent-barrels basis.

Reserves shall include an entity's proportionate share of reserves of equity method investees

50-7   Net quantities disclosed in conformity with paragraphs 932-235-50-4 through 50-6B shall not include oil or gas subject to purchase under long-term supply, purchase, or similar agreements and contracts, including such agreements with governments or authorities. However, quantities of oil or gas subject to such agreements with governments or authorities as of the end of the year, and the net quantity of oil or gas received under the agreements during the year, shall be separately disclosed if the entity participates in the operation of the properties in which the oil or gas is located or otherwise serves as the producer of those reserves, as opposed, for example, to being an independent purchaser, broker, dealer, or importer.

50-8   In determining the reserve quantities to be disclosed in conformity with paragraphs 932-235-50-4 through 50-7:

a.   If the entity issues consolidated financial statements, 100 percent of the net reserve quantities attributable to the parent and 100 percent of the net reserve quantities attributable to its consolidated subsidiaries (whether or not wholly owned) shall be included. If a significant portion of those reserve quantities at the end of the year is attributable to a consolidated subsidiary or subsidiaries in which there is a significant noncontrolling interest, that fact and the approximate portion shall be disclosed.

Chapter 41

b. If the entity's financial statements include investments that are proportionately consolidated, the entity's reserve quantities shall include its proportionate share of the investees' net oil and gas reserves.

c. If the entity's financial statements include investments that are accounted for by the equity method, the entity shall separately disclose the net reserve quantities required by paragraphs 932-235-50-4 through 50-7 for both of the following:

1. Consolidated entities

2. The entity's share of equity method investees.

The entity may, in addition to separate disclosure, disclose a combined total for items (1) and (2) for each of the quantities required to be disclosed by this paragraph.

50-9 In reporting reserve quantities and changes in them, oil reserves and synthetic oil reserves and natural gas liquids reserves shall be stated in barrels, and gas and synthetic reserves in cubic feet.

50-10 If important economic factors or significant uncertainties affect particular components of an entity's proved reserves, explanation shall be provided. Examples include unusually high expected development or lifting costs, the necessity to build a major pipeline or other major facilities before production of the reserves can begin, and contractual obligations to produce and sell a significant portion of reserves at prices that are substantially below those at which the oil or gas could otherwise be sold in the absence of the contractual obligation.

50-11 An entity need not disclose the proved reserves in either of the following circumstances:

a. The government of a country containing reserves prohibits disclosing reserves in that country.

b. The government of a country containing reserves prohibits disclosing a particular field, and disclosing reserves in that country would have the effect of disclosing reserves in particular fields

50-11A If a country's government prohibits disclosing the reserves in that country but does not prohibit including those reserves as part of a more aggregated total quantity of reserves (for example, the quantity of reserves disclosed for a group of countries within a continent or a continent), the entity shall include the reserves located in that country in total reserves disclosed for the most disaggregated geographic area that does not violate specific government prohibitions.

50-11B If a government restricts the disclosure of estimated reserves for properties under its authority, or of amounts under long-term supply, purchase, or similar agreements or contracts, or if the government requires the disclosure of reserves other than proved, the entity shall indicate that the disclosed reserve estimates or amounts do not include figures for the named country or that reserve estimates include reserves other than proved.'[113]

Example 41.2 below illustrates an extract from the disclosures required under ASC 932-235-55 (pre-codification FAS 69).[114]

Example 41.2: *ASC 932-235-55-2 reserve disclosures (extract)*

Reserve quantity information (a)
For the year ended December 31, 20X0

	Total	Total – by product		Continent A		Continent B – Country A		Other Countries in Continent B	
	All products	Oil	Syn Oil*	Oil	Syn Oil*	Oil	Syn Oil*	Oil	Syn Oil*
Proved developed and undeveloped reserves (consolidated entities only) Beginning of year	×	×	×	×	×	×	×	×
Revisions of previous estimates	×	×	×	×	×	×	×	×
Improved recovery	×	×	×	×	×	×	×	×
Purchases of minerals in place	×	×	×	×	×	×	×	×
Extensions and discoveries	×	×	×	×	×	×	×	×
Production	(×)	(×)	(×)	(×)	(×)	(×)	(×)	(×)
Sales of minerals in place	(×)	(×)	(×)	(×)	(×)	(×)	(×)	(×)
End of year	×(b)	×	×	×	×	×	×	×
Entity's share of proved developed and undeveloped reserves of investees accounted for by the equity method Beginning of year	×	×	×	×	×	×	×	×
Revisions of previous estimates	×	×	×	×	×	×	×	×
Improved recovery	×	×	×	×	×	×	×	×
Purchases of minerals in place	×	×	×	×	×	×	×	×
Extensions and discoveries	×	×	×	×	×	×	×	×
Production	(×)	(×)	(×)	(×)	(×)	(×)	(×)	(×)
Sales of minerals in place	(×)	(×)	(×)	(×)	(×)	(×)	(×)	(×)
Entity's share of reserves of investees accounted for by the equity method – end of year	×	×	×	×	×	×	×	×
Total consolidated and equity interests in reserves – end of year	×	×	×	×	×	×	×	×

Note: Total consolidated and equity interests in reserves – end of year is permitted, but is not required (see paragraph 932-235-50-8(c))

	Total	Total – by product		Continent A		Continent B – Country A		Other Countries in Continent B	
	All products	Oil	Syn Oil*	Oil	Syn Oil*	Oil	Syn Oil*	Oil	Syn Oil*

Proved developed reserves (consolidated entities only):

Beginning of year		×	×	×	×	×	×	×	×
End of year		×	×	×	×	×	×	×	×

Proved undeveloped reserves (consolidated entities only):

Beginning of year		×	×	×	×	×	×	×	×
End of year		×	×	×	×	×	×	×	×

Oil and gas subject to long-term supply, purchase, or other similar agreements with governments or authorities in which the entity participates in the operation of the properties where the oil and gas is located or otherwise serves as the producer of these reserves (consolidated entities only)

Total under contract (quantity subject to agreement) – end of year		×	×			×	×		
Received during the year		×	×			×	×		

*   Synthetic Oil

(a)   Oil and synthetic oil reserves stated in barrels

(b)   Includes reserves of X barrels attributable to a consolidated subsidiary in which there is an X percent noncontrolling interest.

Notes:

If applicable, reserve quantity information is required for gas and synthetic gas reserves, and other products by paragraph 932-235-50-4.

The table above discloses quantities of proved developed and undeveloped reserves, and oil and gas subject to long-term supply, purchase, or similar agreements with governments or authorities in which the entity participates in the operation of the properties where the oil and gas is located or otherwise serves as the producer of those reserves, attributable to consolidated entities (see paragraph 932-235-50-4 and 932-235-50-7). The entity shall disclose the same information for the entity's share of reserves of investees accounted for by the equity method, if applicable (see paragraph 932-235-50-8).

The table above discloses information for the total quantity of reserves for all products, in addition to disclosing the information by product. This disclosure is permitted, but is not required (see paragraph 932-235-50-4).

2.3.1.B   Mining industry

Many mining companies are required to disclose information about reserve quantities in accordance with the rules and requirements of the stock exchange on which they are listed. However, those mining companies that are not subject to the specific disclosure requirements of a stock exchange or other local regulator may wish to consider disclosing the information required under the US Securities and Exchange Commission's Industry Guide 7 – *Description of Property by Issuers Engaged or to Be Engaged in Significant Mining Operations.*

It should be noted, though, that mining companies that are subject to the SEC rules and regulations need to understand not only the content of Industry Guide 7, as described below, but also the current interpretation of this content by the SEC's staff. While many of the definitions may seem familiar, the SEC staff's interpretations may differ considerably from that of regulators in other countries.[115]

I   SEC Industry Guide 7 definitions

Industry Guide 7 applies to all SEC registrants that are engaged or to be engaged in significant mining operations.[116] As discussed at 2.2.3.C I, some of the requirements of Industry Guide 7 for public release of information are materially different from those applicable in other countries. Under Industry Guide 7, the following definitions apply to registrants engaged or to be engaged in significant mining operations:

'(1)   *Reserve.* That part of a mineral deposit which could be economically and legally extracted or produced at the time of the reserve determination. Note. Reserves are customarily stated in terms of "ore" when dealing with metalliferous minerals; when other materials such as coal, oil, shale, tar, sands, limestone, etc. are involved, an appropriate term such as "recoverable coal" may be substituted.

'(2)   *Proven (Measured) Reserves.* Reserves for which (a) quantity is computed from dimensions revealed in outcrops, trenches, workings or drill holes; grade and/or quality are computed from the results of detailed sampling and (b) the sites for inspection, sampling and measurement are spaced so closely and the geologic character is so well defined that size, shape, depth and mineral content of reserves are well-established.

'(3)   *Probable (Indicated) Reserves.* Reserves for which quantity and grade and/or quality are computed from information similar to that used for proven (measure) reserves, but the sites for inspection, sampling, and measurement are farther apart or are otherwise less adequately spaced. The degree of assurance, although lower than that for proven (measured) reserves, is high enough to assume continuity between points of observation.

'(4)   (i)   *Exploration Stage* – includes all issuers engaged in the search for mineral deposits (reserves) which are not in either the development or production stage.

(ii)   *Development Stage* – includes all issuers engaged in the preparation of an established commercially minable deposit (reserves) for its extraction which are not in the production stage.

(iii)   *Production Stage* – includes all issuers engaged in the exploitation of a mineral deposit (reserve).'[117]

It is worth noting that, in accordance with Industry Guide 7, mining companies in the exploration stage should not refer to themselves as development stage companies in the financial statements, even though such companies should comply with ASC 915 – *Development Stage Entities* (pre-codification FAS 7 – *Accounting and Reporting by Development Stage Enterprises*), if applicable.

II   SEC Industry Guide 7 mining operations disclosures

Under Industry Guide 7, mining companies should furnish the following information as to each of the mines, plants and other significant properties owned or operated, or presently intended to be owned or operated, by the registrant:

'(1)   The location and means of access to the property;

'(2)   A brief description of the title, claim, lease or option under which the registrant and its subsidiaries have or will have the right to hold or operate the property, indicating any conditions which the registrant must meet in order to obtain or retain the property. If held by leases or options, the expiration dates of such leases or options should be stated. Appropriate maps may be used to portray the locations of significant properties;

'(3)   A brief history of previous operations, including the names of previous operators, insofar as known;

'(4)   (i)   A brief description of the present condition of the property, the work completed by the registrant on the property, the registrant's proposed program of exploration and development, and the current state of exploration and/or development of the property. Mines should be identified as either open-pit or underground. If the property is without known reserves and the proposed program is exploratory in nature, a statement to that effect shall be made;

        (ii)   The age, details as to modernization and physical condition of the plant and equipment, including subsurface improvements and equipment. Further, the total cost for each property and its associated plant and equipment should be stated. The source of power utilized with respect to each property should also be disclosed.

'(5)   A brief description of the rock formations and mineralization of existing or potential economic significance on the property, including the identity of the principal metallic or other constituents, insofar as known. If proven (measured) or probable (indicated) reserves have been established, state (i) the estimated tonnages and grades (or quality, where appropriate) of such classes of reserves, and (ii) the name of the person making the estimates and the nature of his relationship to the registrant.

'(6)   If technical terms relating to geology, mining or related matters whose definition cannot readily be found in conventional dictionaries (as opposed to technical dictionaries or glossaries) are used, an appropriate glossary should be included in this report.

'(7)   Detailed geographic maps and reports, feasibility studies and other highly technical data should not be included in the report but should be, to the degree appropriate and necessary for the Commission's understanding of the registrant's presentation of business and property matters, furnished as supplemental information.'[118]

In respect of the information required under (5) above, a mining company is required to comply with the following:

'1.   It should be stated whether the reserve estimate is of in-place material or of recoverable material. Any in-place estimate should be qualified to show the anticipated losses resulting from mining methods and beneficiation or preparation.

'2.   The summation of proven (measured) and probable (indicated) ore reserves is acceptable if the difference in degree of assurance between the two classes of reserves cannot be readily defined.

'3.   Estimates other than proved (measured) or probable (indicated) reserves, and any estimated values of such reserves shall not be disclosed unless such information is required to be disclosed by foreign or state law; provided, however, that where such estimates previously have been provided to a person (or any of its affiliates) that is offering to acquire, merge, or consolidate with, the registrant or otherwise to acquire the registrant's securities, such estimates may be included.'[119]

III   *SEC Industry Guide 7 supplemental information*

Under Industry Guide 7, mining companies should provide the following supplemental information:

'(c)(1) If an estimate of proven (measured) or probable (indicated) reserves is set forth in the report, furnish:

(i)   maps drawn to scale showing any mine workings and the outlines of the reserve blocks involved together with the pertinent sample-assay thereon.

(ii)   all pertinent drill data and related maps.

(iii)   the calculations whereby the basic sample-assay or drill data were translated into the estimates made of the grade and tonnage of reserves in each block and in the complete reserve estimate.

Instructions to paragraph (c)(1).

1.   Maps and drawings submitted to the staff should include:

(a)   A legend or explanation showing, by means of pattern or symbol, every pattern or symbol used on the map or drawing; the use of the symbols used by the U.S. Geological Survey is encouraged;

(b)   A graphical bar scale should be included; additional representations of scale such as "one inch equals one mile" may be utilized provided the original scale of the map has not been altered;

(c)   A north arrow on the maps;

(d)   An index map showing where the property is situated in relationship to the state or province, etc., in which it was located;

(e)   A title of the map or drawing and the date on which it was drawn;

> *(f)   In the event interpretive data is submitted in conjunction with any map, the identity of the geologist or engineer that prepared such data; and*
>
> *(g)   Any drawing should be simple enough or of sufficiently large scale to clearly show all features on the drawing.*

'(c)(2) Furnish a complete copy of every material engineering, geological or metallurgical report concerning the registrant's property, including governmental reports, which are known and available to the registrant. Every such report should include the name of its author and the date of its preparation, if known to the registrant.

Instruction to paragraph (c)(2).

1.   Any of the above-required reports as to which the staff has access need not be submitted. In this regard, issuers should consult with the staff prior to filing the report. Any reports not submitted should be identified in a list furnished to the staff. This list should also identify any known governmental reports concerning the registrant's property.

'(c)(3) Furnish copies of all documents such as title documents, operating permits and easements needed to support representations made in the report.

For purposes of the above table, short-term outstandings are trade credits and interbank deposits (and similar items) which, at the time they were extended, had maturities of one year or less. This table should be supplemented with the amounts of (short-term outstandings that are included in the end-of-period aggregate amounts reported for each country.'[120]

2.3.2   Disclosure of the value of reserves

Many of the same arguments in favour of disclosure of reserve quantities (see 2.3.1 above) also apply to disclosure of reserve values. However, the arguments against disclosure of reserves values are much stronger as 'value measurements require even more assumptions and forecasts than do quantity measures, making value data even less reliable'.[121]

2.3.2.A   Discussion Paper – Extractive activities

As part of its work on the Discussion Paper, the IASB staff is currently considering whether a disclosure-focused approach might be appropriate in an extractive industries financial reporting standard. It is in this context that the project team noted that:

> 'Focusing on disclosures goes against the view that disclosure is not a substitute for recognition and measurement. The project team does not disagree that appropriate accounting for transactions so that they are faithfully represented in the income statement, balance sheet and cash flow statement, in general, makes financial statements more useful than including the information in footnote disclosures. However, the research project team believes that this is subject to being able to develop an accounting approach for transactions concerning pre-production costs that results in relevant

information in the income statement, balance sheet and cash flow statement. It may be that no such accounting approach can be developed. If this is so, then the only alternative may be to focus on the disclosures. Given the near unanimity of the feedback from users on the lack of relevance of either historical cost or current value accounting for reserves and resources, the research project team believes a disclosure-focused approach needs to be considered as one alternative in the discussion paper.'[122]

One of the key issues to consider before developing a disclosure-focused approach will be whether or not disclosure of the value of mineral reserves should be a requirement. A secondary issue is whether the mineral reserves should be disclosed at their fair value or at a standardised measure of value, similar to the requirement under ASC 932-235-50 – *Extractive Activities – Oil and Gas – Notes to Financial Statements – Disclosure* (pre-codification FAS 69) (see 2.3.2.B below). This disclosure requirement in ASC 932-235-50 is not uncontroversial, as the 'standardized measure of oil and gas' (often abbreviated to SMOG) does not represent the market value of an entity's proved reserves. As illustrated in Extract 41.3, some companies caution against over-reliance on these disclosures.

Extract 41.3: BP plc (2010)

Supplementary information on oil and natural gas [extract]

Standardized measure of discounted future net cash flows and changes therein relating to proved oil and gas reserves [extract]

The following tables set out the standardized measures of discounted future net cash flows, and changes therein, relating to crude oil and natural gas production from the group's estimated proved reserves. This information is prepared in compliance with FASB Oil and Gas Disclosures requirements.

Future net cash flows have been prepared on the basis of certain assumptions which may or may not be realized. These include the timing of future production, the estimation of crude oil and natural gas reserves and the application of average crude oil and natural gas prices and exchange rates from the previous 12 months. Furthermore, both proved reserves estimates and production forecasts are subject to revision as further technical information becomes available and economic conditions change. BP cautions against relying on the information presented because of the highly arbitrary nature of the assumptions on which it is based and its lack of comparability with the historical cost information presented in the financial statements.

As discussed at 2.3.2.B below, the standardised measure of the value of oil and gas reserves required by ASC 932-235-50 (pre-codification FAS 69) greatly reduces the impact of managements' opinion about future development on the value calculated (e.g. the method prescribes the discount rate and commodity price to be used). Whilst this may not take into account relevant insights that management may have, the advantage is that comparability of the disclosures between entities is increased. The IASB's project team found that:

'The FAS 69 standardised measure and the disclosure of "net future revenue" required in Canada by National Instrument 51-101 *Standards of Disclosure for Oil and Gas Activities* are examples of current value estimates. Some oil and gas analysts noted that the FAS 69 standardised measure provides some insight into, among other things, future development and operating costs and the impact of commodity price changes on the value of reserves. The general view among these oil & gas analysts seemed to be that the standardised measure should be treated with caution and is a long way from being perfect, but nevertheless it is referred to because that information may not be provided elsewhere. As one analyst suggested, it is not the measure itself which is useful, but the changes – and the reconciliation of those changes – that is useful. This view seems to be consistent with the comments in the FAS 69 Basis for Conclusions, which notes that the standardised measure is not intended to be representative of value, but rather its objectives are to provide users with information that can be used for their own valuation and to allow for a reasonable comparison of reserves.'[123]

It is clear from the above that getting agreement as to what constitutes useful and relevant disclosures about the value of mineral reserves is neither straightforward nor uncontroversial. Still, in September 2008, the Board indicated support for the Discussion Paper to propose the disclosure of 'a current value measurement, such as a standardised measure of discounted cash flows, and the key assumptions necessary for a user to make use of that measurement. This would not be disclosed if the minerals or oil & gas assets are measured on the statement of financial position at fair value or some other current value measurement. In that case, an entity would provide disclosures similar to those required in the US by ASC 820-10-50-1,2,3 – *Fair Value Measurements and Disclosures* (pre-codification SFAS 157.32 – *Fair Value Measurements*).'[124] Accordingly, as discussed at 1.4.2.E above, the project team concluded in the DP – *Extractive Activities* – that:

- if the assets are measured at historical cost then detailed information should be disclosed about their current value (either fair value or standardised measure) and how it was determined;

- if, instead, the assets are measured at fair value then detailed information should be disclosed about that fair value and how it was determined.

2.3.2.B   ASC 932-235-50 (pre-codification FAS 69) – disclosure of standardised measure of oil and gas

All entities engaged in significant oil and gas producing activities that report under US GAAP are required by ASC 932-235-50 (pre-codification FAS 69) to disclose a standardised measure of discounted future net cash flows relating to proved oil and gas reserve quantities as follows:

'50-30 A standardized measure of discounted future net cash flows relating to an entity's interests in both of the following shall be disclosed as of the end of the year:

    a.   Proved oil and gas reserves (see paragraphs 932-235-50-3 through 50-11B)

    b.   Oil and gas subject to purchase under long-term supply, purchase, or similar agreements and contracts in which the entity participates in the operation of the properties on which the oil or gas is located or otherwise serves as the producer of those reserves (see paragraph 932-235-50-7).

The standardized measure of discounted future net cash flows relating to those two types of interests in reserves may be combined for reporting purposes.

50-31 All of the following information shall be disclosed in the aggregate and for each geographic area for which reserve quantities are disclosed in accordance with paragraphs 932-235-50-3 through 50-11B:

    a.   Future cash inflows. These shall be computed by applying prices used in estimating the entity's proved oil and gas reserves to the year-end quantities of those reserves. Future price changes shall be considered only to the extent provided by contractual arrangements in existence at year-end.

    b.   Future development and production costs. These costs shall be computed by estimating the expenditures to be incurred in developing and producing the proved oil and gas reserves at the end of the year, based on year-end costs and assuming continuation of existing economic conditions. If estimated development expenditures are significant, they shall be presented separately from estimated production costs.

    c.   Future income tax expenses. These expenses shall be computed by applying the appropriate year-end statutory tax rates, with consideration of future tax rates already legislated, to the future pretax net cash flows relating to the entity's proved oil and gas reserves, less the tax basis of the properties involved. The future income tax expenses shall give effect to tax deductions and tax credits and allowances relating to the entity's proved oil and gas reserves.

    d.   Future net cash flows. These amounts are the result of subtracting future development and production costs and future income tax expenses from future cash inflows.

    e.   Discount. This amount shall be derived from using a discount rate of 10 percent a year to reflect the timing of the future net cash flows relating to proved oil and gas reserves.

    f.   Standardized measure of discounted future net cash flows. This amount is the future net cash flows less the computed discount.

50-32 If a significant portion of the economic interest in the consolidated standardized measure of discounted future net cash flows reported is attributable to a consolidated subsidiary or subsidiaries in which there is a significant noncontrolling interest, that fact and the approximate portion shall be disclosed.

50-33 If the financial statements include investments that are accounted for by the equity method, the entity shall separately disclose the amounts required by paragraphs 932-235-50-30 through 50-32 for both of the following:

a. Consolidated entities

b. The entity's share of equity method investees.

The entity may, in addition to separate disclosure, disclose a combined total for items (a) and (b) for each of the amounts required to be disclosed by this paragraph.

...

50-35 The aggregate change in the standardized measure of discounted future net cash flows shall be disclosed for the year. If individually significant, all of the following sources of change shall be presented separately:

a. Net change in sales and transfer prices and in production (lifting) costs related to future production

b. Changes in estimated future development costs

c. Sales and transfers of oil and gas produced during the period

d. Net change due to extensions, discoveries, and improved recovery

e. Net change due to purchases and sales of minerals in place

f. Net change due to revisions in quantity estimates

g. Previously estimated development costs incurred during the period

h. Accretion of discount

i. Other–unspecified

j. Net change in income taxes.

In computing the amounts under each of the above categories, the effects of changes in prices and costs shall be computed before the effects of changes in quantities. As a result, changes in quantities shall be stated at prices used in estimating proved oil and gas reserves and year-end and costs. The change in computed income taxes shall reflect the effect of income taxes incurred during the period as well as the change in future income tax expenses. Therefore, all changes except income taxes shall be reported pretax.

50-35A If the financial statements include investments that are accounted for by the equity method, the entity shall separately disclose the amounts required by the preceding paragraph for both of the following:

a. Consolidated entities

b. The entity's share of equity method investees.

The entity may, in addition to separate disclosure, disclose a combined total for items (a) and (b) for each of the amounts required to be disclosed by this paragraph.

50-36 Additional information necessary to prevent the disclosure of the standardized measure of discounted future net cash flows and changes therein from being misleading also shall be provided.'[125]

The extract below from the financial statements of TOTAL illustrates the disclosures under ASC 932-235-50 relating to the standardised measure of discounted future net cash flows relating to proved oil and gas reserve quantities.

Extract 41.4: TOTAL S.A. (2010)

Appendix 2 – Supplemental oil and gas information (unaudited) [extract]

Standardized measure of discounted future net cash flow

The standardized measure of discounted future net cash flows relating to proved oil and gas reserve quantities was developed as follows:

- Estimates of proved reserves and the corresponding production profiles are based on existing technical and economic conditions;

- The estimated future cash flows are determined based on prices used in estimating the Group's proved oil and gas reserves;

- The future cash flows incorporate estimated production costs (including production taxes), future development costs and asset retirement costs. All cost estimates are based on year-end technical and economic conditions;

- Future income taxes are computed by applying the year-end statutory tax rate to future net cash flows after consideration of permanent differences and future income tax credits; and

- Future net cash flows are discounted at a standard discount rate of 10 percent.

These principles applied are those required by ASC 932 and do not reflect the expectations of real revenues from these reserves, nor their present value; hence, they do not constitute criteria for investment decisions. An estimate of the fair value of reserves should also take into account, among other things, the recovery of reserves not presently classified as proved, anticipated future changes in prices and costs and a discount factor more representative of the time value of money and the risks inherent in reserves estimates.

(in million euros)	Consolidated subsidiaries					
As of December 31, 2008	**Europe**	**Africa**	**Americas**	**Middle East**	**Asia**	**Total**
Future cash inflows	42,749	67,761	7,963	7,047	19,745	145,265
Future production costs	(8,593)	(15,372)	(4,040)	(1,942)	(5,224)	(35,171)
Future development costs	(10,423)	(21,594)	(1,863)	(733)	(7,497)	(42,110)
Future income taxes	(15,651)	(14,571)	(367)	(1,577)	(2,545)	(34,711)
Future net cash flows, after income taxes	8,082	16,224	1,693	2,795	4,479	33,273
Discount at 10%	(3,645)	(8,144)	(715)	(1,333)	(3,450)	(17,287)
Standardized measure of discounted future net cash flows	**4,437**	**8,080**	**978**	**1,462**	**1,029**	**15,986**

As of December 31, 2009

Future cash inflows	50,580	107,679	18,804	9,013	32,004	218,080
Future production costs	(11,373)	(23,253)	(8,286)	(2,831)	(6,996)	(52,739)
Future development costs	(12,795)	(21,375)	(5,728)	(698)	(6,572)	(47,168)
Future income taxes	(17,126)	(36,286)	(1,293)	(2,041)	(5,325)	(62,071)
Future net cash flows, after income taxes	9,286	26,765	3,497	3,443	13,111	56,102
Discount at 10%	(3,939)	(13,882)	(2,696)	(1,558)	(8,225)	(30,300)
Standardized measure of discounted future net cash flows	**5,347**	**12,883**	**801**	**1,885**	**4,886**	**25,802**

As of December 31, 2010

Future cash inflows	65,644	142,085	42,378	14,777	41,075	305,959
Future production costs	(16,143)	(29,479)	(19,477)	(4,110)	(6,476)	(75,685)
Future development costs	(18,744)	(25,587)	(8,317)	(3,788)	(8,334)	(64,770)
Future income taxes	(20,571)	(51,390)	(3,217)	(2,541)	(7,281)	(85,000)
Future net cash flows, after income taxes	10,186	35,629	11,367	4,338	18,984	80,504
Discount at 10%	(5,182)	(16,722)	(8,667)	(2,106)	(11,794)	(44,471)
Standardized measure of discounted future net cash flows	**5,004**	**18,907**	**2,700**	**2,232**	**7,190**	**36,033**

Minority interests in future net cash flows as of						
December 31, 2008	217	(50)	–	–	–	167
December 31, 2009	212	60	–	–	–	272
Year ended December 31, 2010	**273**	**344**	**–**	**–**	**–**	**617**

(in million euros)	Equity affiliates					
Group's share of future net cash flows as of	Europe	Africa	Americas	Middle East	Asia	Total
As of December 31, 2008	–	418	608	4,275	–	5,301

As of December 31, 2009

Future cash inflows	–	1,432	16,750	48,486	–	66,668
Future production costs	–	(624)	(6,993)	(30,739)	–	(38,356)
Future development costs	–	(26)	(1,924)	(3,891)	–	(5,841)
Future income taxes	–	(245)	(3,650)	(1,843)	–	(5,738)
Future net cash flows, after income taxes	–	537	4,183	12,013	–	16,733
Discount at 10%	–	(239)	(2,816)	(6,383)	–	(9,438)
Standardized measure of discounted future net cash flows	**–**	**298**	**1,367**	**5,630**	**–**	**7,295**

As of December 31, 2010

Future cash inflows	–	1,814	22,293	59,472	–	83,579
Future production costs	–	(765)	(8,666)	(40,085)	–	(49,516)
Future development costs	–	(26)	(2,020)	(3,006)	–	(5,052)
Future income taxes	–	(349)	(5,503)	(2,390)	–	(8,242)
Future net cash flows, after income taxes	–	674	6,104	13,991	–	20,769
Discount at 10%	–	(203)	(3,946)	(7,386)	–	(11,535)
Standardized measure of discounted future net cash flows	**–**	**471**	**2,158**	**6,605**	**–**	**9,234**

Changes in the standardized measure of discounted future net cash flows

Consolidated subsidiaries (in million euros)	2010	2009	2008
Beginning of year	25,802	15,986	48,464
Sales and transfers, net of production costs	(22,297)	(17,266)	(26,109)
Net change in sales and transfer prices and in production costs and other expenses	30,390	35,738	(81,358)
Extensions, discoveries and improved recovery	716	(267)	556
Changes in estimated future development costs	(7,245)	(4,847)	(2,227)
Previously estimated development costs incurred during the year	7,896	7,552	6,960
Revisions of previous quantity estimates	5,523	164	2,693
Accretion of discount	2,580	1,599	4,846
Net change in income taxes	(6,773)	(12,455)	63,611
Purchases of reserves in place	442	230	50
Sales of reserves in place	(1,001)	(632)	(1,500)
End of year	36,033	25,802	15,986

Equity affiliates (in million euros)	2010	2009
Beginning of year	7,295	5,301
Sales and transfers, net of production costs	(1,583)	(987)
Net change in sales and transfer prices and in production costs and other expenses	2,366	2,789
Extensions, discoveries and improved recovery	–	407
Changes in estimated future development costs	195	(88)
Previously estimated development costs incurred during the year	651	854
Revisions of previous quantity estimates	308	(790)
Accretion of discount	730	530
Net change in income taxes	(728)	(721)
Purchases of reserves in place	–	–
Sales of reserves in place	–	–
End of year	9,234	7,295

3 IFRS 6 – EXPLORATION FOR AND EVALUATION OF MINERAL RESOURCES

3.1 Objective and scope

Although the IASB recognised the importance of accounting for the extractive industries, it concluded in September 2002 that, given the limited agenda time available, it would not be possible to 'complete the detailed analysis required for this project, obtain appropriate input from constituents and undertake the Board's normal due process in time to implement changes before many entities adopted IFRSs in 2005'. *[IFRS 6.IN3]*. As discussed at 1.4.1 above, the IASB's objectives in developing IFRS 6 were restricted to making limited improvements to existing accounting practices for 'exploration and evaluation expenditures' (E&E expenditures), specifying when entities need to assess E&E assets for impairment in accordance with IAS 36 – *Impairment of Assets* – and requiring certain disclosures. E&E expenditures are 'expenditures incurred by an entity in connection with the exploration for and evaluation of mineral resources before the technical feasibility and commercial viability of extracting a mineral resource are demonstrable', while E&E assets are 'exploration and evaluation expenditures recognised as assets in accordance with the entity's accounting policy'. *[IFRS 6 Appendix A]*.

The objective of IFRS 6 is limited to specifying the financial reporting for the 'exploration for and evaluation of mineral resources', *[IFRS 6.1]*, which the standard defines as 'the search for mineral resources, including minerals, oil, natural gas and similar non-regenerative resources after the entity has obtained legal rights to explore in a specific area, as well as the determination of the technical feasibility and commercial viability of extracting the mineral resource'. *[IFRS 6 Appendix A]*.

The scope of the standard is specifically limited to accounting for E&E expenditures and it does not 'address other aspects of accounting by entities engaged in the exploration for and evaluation of mineral resources'. *[IFRS 6.3-4]*. Therefore, an entity should not apply IFRS 6 to expenditures incurred before the exploration for and evaluation of mineral resources (e.g. expenditures incurred before the entity has obtained the legal rights to explore a specific area) or after the technical feasibility and commercial viability of extracting a mineral resource are demonstrable. *[IFRS 6.5]*.

In other words, IFRS 6 does not deal with the phases of upstream operations that take place before (e.g. prospecting and acquisition of mineral rights) or after (e.g. development, construction, production and closure) exploration and evaluation. Furthermore, the standard deals only with E&E expenditures and it does not provide guidance on other industry specific issues that may arise during the E&E phase.

The IASB deliberately decided not to expand the scope of the standard as 'it did not want to prejudge the comprehensive review of the accounting for such activities' and it concluded 'that an appropriate accounting policy for pre-exploration activities could be developed from an application of existing IFRSs' or the *Framework*. *[IFRS 6.BC7, BC10]*. A further, far more practical, reason for not expanding the scope of IFRS 6 was that this would have required additional due process and possibly another exposure draft; consequently, in view of 'the many entities engaged in extractive activities that would be required to apply IFRSs from 1 January 2005, the Board decided that it should not delay issuing guidance by expanding the scope of the IFRS beyond the exploration for and evaluation of mineral resources'. *[IFRS 6.BC8]*.

3.1.1 Scope exclusions in other standards relating to the extractive industries

In the Basis for Conclusions on IFRS 6 the IASB confirmed that 'even though no IFRS has addressed extractive activities directly, all IFRSs (including International Accounting Standards and Interpretations) are applicable to entities engaged in the exploration for and evaluation of mineral resources that make an unreserved statement of compliance with IFRSs in accordance with IAS 1'. *[IFRS 6.BC6]*. However, certain aspects of the extractive industries' activities that fall outside the scope of IFRS 6 are sometimes excluded from the scope of other standards.

Various standards exclude 'minerals' from their scope, but the exact wording of the scope exclusions differs from standard to standard. Therefore, it would be incorrect to conclude that the same aspects of the extractive industries' activities are excluded from the scope of these standards:

- IAS 2 – *Inventories* – does not apply to the measurement of 'minerals and mineral products, to the extent that they are measured at net realisable value in accordance with well-established practices in those industries'. *[IAS 2.3(a), 4]*. The practice of measuring minerals and mineral products inventories at net realisable value is, in reality, relatively rare in many extractive industry sectors;

- IAS 16 – *Property, Plant and Equipment* – does not apply to 'mineral rights and mineral reserves such as oil, natural gas and similar non-regenerative resources'. *[IAS 16.3(d)]*. In addition, the standard does not apply to 'the recognition and measurement of exploration and evaluation assets'. *[IAS 16.3(c)]*. Equipment used in extracting reserves is within the scope of IAS 16;

- IAS 17 – *Leases* – does not apply to 'leases to explore for or use minerals, oil, natural gas and similar non-regenerative resources'. *[IAS 17.2(a)]*. However, leases of assets used in such exploration are within the scope of IAS 17;

- IAS 18 – *Revenue* – does not deal with revenue arising from 'the extraction of mineral ores'; *[IAS 18.6(h)]*

- IAS 38 – *Intangible Assets* – does not apply to 'expenditure on the exploration for, or development and extraction of, minerals, oil, natural gas and similar non-regenerative resources' or to the recognition and measurement of E&E assets; *[IAS 38.2(c)-(d)]*

- IAS 40 – *Investment Property* – does not apply to 'mineral rights and mineral reserves such as oil, natural gas and similar non-regenerative resources'; *[IAS 40.4(b)]* and

- IFRIC 4 – *Determining whether an Arrangement contains a Lease* – does not apply to arrangements that are, or contain, leases excluded from the scope of IAS 17. *[IFRIC 4.4]*.

3.2   Recognition of exploration and evaluation assets

3.2.1   Temporary exemption from IAS 8

Entities active in the extractive industries follow a large variety of accounting practices, which range 'from deferring on the balance sheet nearly all exploration and evaluation expenditure to recognising all such expenditure in profit or loss as incurred'. *[IFRS 6.BC17]*. IFRS 6 requires that an entity recognising E&E assets should apply paragraph 10 of IAS 8 – *Accounting Policies, Changes in Accounting Estimates and Errors* – in developing its accounting policies. *[IFRS 6.6, BC19]*. Hence management should use its judgement in developing and applying an accounting policy that results in information that is relevant and reliable. *[IAS 8.10]*.

In the light of its objective to require limited improvements to existing accounting practices and its desire to minimise disruption for first-time adopters, the IASB decided to provide an exemption from paragraphs 11 and 12 of IAS 8, *[IFRS 6.BC17]*, which 'specify sources of authoritative requirements and guidance that management is required to consider in developing an accounting policy for an item if no IFRS applies specifically to that item' (the so-called 'GAAP hierarchy', see Chapter 3 at 4.3). *[IFRS 6.7]*. The Basis for Conclusions to IFRS 6 seems to suggest that the standard 'grandfathers' all existing practices by stating that 'the Board decided that an entity could continue to follow the accounting policies that it was using when it first applied the IFRS's requirements, provided they satisfy the requirements of paragraph 10 of IAS 8 and with some exceptions noted below'. *[IFRS 6.BC22]*. These exceptions in IFRS 6 have a rather more profound impact than may be obvious at first sight and, in fact, impose a number of significant constraints on an entity's choice of accounting policy because:

- an entity needs to specify which expenditures are recognised as E&E assets and apply that accounting policy consistently (see 3.3.2 below); *[IFRS 6.9]*

- expenditures related to the development of mineral resources should not be recognised as E&E assets (see 3.3.2 below); *[IFRS 6.10]* and

- the requirement to apply IAS 16, IAS 38 and IAS 36 after the E&E phase affects the choice of accounting policies during the E&E phase. In January 2006, the IFRIC clarified that 'it was clear that the scope of IFRS 6 consistently limited the relief from the hierarchy to policies applied to E&E activities and that there was no basis for interpreting IFRS 6 as granting any additional relief in areas outside its scope'.[126] For example, an entity may be able to apply the full cost method of accounting (see 5.4.2 below) during the E&E phase, but it will not be able to apply that policy after the E&E phase.

The IASB believed that waiving these requirements in IFRS 6 would 'detract from the relevance and reliability of an entity's financial statements to an unacceptable degree'. *[IFRS 6.BC23]*. Therefore, instead of allowing previous national GAAP accounting policies, IFRS 6 effectively prohibits many national GAAP practices.

The extract below from Xstrata illustrates a typical accounting policy for E&E assets for a mining company.

Extract 41.5: Xstrata plc (2010)

Notes to the financial statements [extract]

6. Principal accounting policies [extract]

Exploration and evaluation expenditure

Exploration and evaluation expenditure relates to costs incurred on the exploration and evaluation of potential mineral reserves and resources and includes costs such as exploratory drilling and sample testing and the costs of pre-feasibility studies. Exploration and evaluation expenditure for each area of interest, other than that acquired from the purchase of another mining company, is carried forward as an asset provided that one of the following conditions is met:

- such costs are expected to be recouped in full through successful development and exploration of the area of interest or alternatively, by its sale; or

- exploration and evaluation activities in the area of interest have not yet reached a stage that permits a reasonable assessment of the existence or otherwise of economically recoverable reserves, and active and significant operations in relation to the area are continuing, or planned for the future.

Purchased exploration and evaluation assets are recognised as assets at their cost of acquisition or at fair value if purchased as part of a business combination.

An impairment review is performed, either individually or at the cash-generating unit level, when there are indicators that the carrying amount of the assets may exceed their recoverable amounts. To the extent that this occurs, the excess is fully provided against, in the financial year in which this is determined. Exploration and evaluation assets are reassessed on a regular basis and these costs are carried forward provided that at least one of the conditions outlined above is met.

Expenditure is transferred to mine development assets or capital work in progress once the work completed to date supports the future development of the property and such development receives appropriate approvals.

Mineral properties and mine development expenditure

The cost of acquiring mineral reserves and mineral resources is capitalised on the balance sheet as incurred. Capitalised costs (development expenditure) include costs associated with a start-up period where the asset is available for use but incapable of operating at normal levels without a commissioning period.

Mineral reserves and capitalised mine development expenditure are, upon commencement of production, depreciated using a unit of production method based on the estimated economically recoverable reserves to which they relate or are written off if the property is abandoned. The net carrying amounts of mineral reserves and resources and capitalised mine development expenditure at each mine property are reviewed for impairment either individually or at the cash-generating unit level when events and changes in circumstances indicate that the carrying amount may not be recoverable. To the extent that these values exceed their recoverable amounts, that excess is fully provided against in the financial year in which this is determined.

The extract below from BP illustrates an accounting policy for E&E assets for an oil and gas company.

Extract 41.6: BP plc (2010)

Notes on financial statements [extract]

1. Significant accounting policies [extract]

Oil and natural gas exploration, appraisal and development expenditure

Oil and natural gas exploration, appraisal and development expenditure is accounted for using the principles of the successful efforts method of accounting.

Licence and property acquisition costs

Exploration licence and leasehold property acquisition costs are capitalized within intangible assets and are reviewed at each reporting date to confirm that there is no indication that the carrying amount exceeds the recoverable amount. This review includes confirming that exploration drilling is still under way or firmly planned or that it has been determined, or work is under way to determine, that the discovery is economically viable based on a range of technical and commercial considerations and sufficient progress is being made on establishing development plans and timing. If no future activity is planned, the remaining balance of the licence and property acquisition costs is written off. Lower value licences are pooled and amortized on a straight-line basis over the estimated period of exploration. Upon recognition of proved reserves and internal approval for development, the relevant expenditure is transferred to property, plant and equipment.

Exploration and appraisal expenditure

Geological and geophysical exploration costs are charged against income as incurred. Costs directly associated with an exploration well are initially capitalized as an intangible asset until the drilling of the well is complete and the results have been evaluated. These costs include employee remuneration, materials and fuel used, rig costs and payments made to contractors. If potentially commercial quantities of hydrocarbons are not found, the exploration expenditure is written off as a dry hole. If hydrocarbons are found and, subject to further appraisal activity, are likely to be capable of commercial development, the costs continue to be carried as an asset.

Costs directly associated with appraisal activity, undertaken to determine the size, characteristics and commercial potential of a reservoir following the initial discovery of hydrocarbons, including the costs of appraisal wells where hydrocarbons were not found, are initially capitalized as an intangible asset.

All such carried costs are subject to technical, commercial and management review at least once a year to confirm the continued intent to develop or otherwise extract value from the discovery. When this is no longer the case, the costs are written off. When proved reserves of oil and natural gas are determined and development is approved by management, the relevant expenditure is transferred to property, plant and equipment.

Development expenditure

Expenditure on the construction, installation and completion of infrastructure facilities such as platforms, pipelines and the drilling of development wells, including service and unsuccessful development or delineation wells, is capitalized within property, plant and equipment and is depreciated from the commencement of production as described below in the accounting policy for property, plant and equipment.

3.2.2   Changes in accounting policies

The standard permits a change in an entity's accounting policies for E&E expenditures only if 'the change makes the financial statements more relevant to the economic decision-making needs of users and no less reliable, or more reliable and no less relevant to those needs'. *[IFRS 6.13, BC49]*. In making such a change, an entity should judge the relevance and reliability using the criteria in IAS 8. The entity should justify the change by demonstrating that the change 'brings its financial statements closer to meeting the criteria in IAS 8, but the change need not achieve full compliance with those criteria'. *[IFRS 6.14]*.

3.3   Measurement of exploration and evaluation assets

3.3.1   Measurement at recognition

IFRS 6 draws a distinction between measurement at recognition (i.e. the initial recognition of an E&E asset on acquisition) and measurement after recognition (i.e. the subsequent treatment of the E&E asset). Measurement after recognition is discussed at 3.3.3 below.

The standard requires that upon initial recognition E&E assets should be measured at cost, *[IFRS 6.8]*, which is the same as the initial recognition requirements found in IAS 16, *[IAS 16.15]*, and IAS 38. *[IAS 38.24]*. Therefore the question arises as to what may be included in the cost of an item, and the standard contains considerable guidance on this matter, under the heading 'Elements of cost of exploration and evaluation assets'.

3.3.2 *Elements of cost of exploration and evaluation assets*

The standard requires an entity to determine an accounting policy specifying which expenditures are recognised as E&E assets and apply the policy consistently. Such accounting policy should take into account the degree to which the expenditure can be associated with finding specific mineral resources. The standard gives a non-exhaustive list of examples of types of expenditure that may be included in cost at initial recognition:

'(a)   acquisition of rights to explore;

(b)   topographical, geological, geochemical and geophysical studies;

(c)   exploratory drilling;

(d)   trenching;

(e)   sampling; and

(f)   activities in relation to evaluating the technical feasibility and commercial viability of extracting a mineral resource.' *[IFRS 6.9].*

It is worth noting that (b) above includes geological and geophysical costs (G&G costs) as an example of costs that may be included in the initial measurement of E&E assets. IFRS 6 is different in this respect from ASC 932 – *Extractive Activities – Oil and Gas* (pre-codification FAS 19 – *Financial Accounting and Reporting by Oil and Gas Producing Companies)* – under US GAAP, which does not permit capitalisation of G&G costs,[127] and may differ from the requirements under other national standards as well.

In the exposure draft that led to the standard, the IASB proposed that administration and other general overhead costs should be excluded from the initial measurement of E&E assets. However, in the light of inconsistencies between IAS 16 (which does not allow such costs to be capitalised) and IAS 2 and IAS 38 (which do permit capitalisation of such costs), the IASB decided that 'the treatment of such expenditures would be an accounting policy choice; the chosen policy should be consistent with one of the treatments available under IFRSs.' *[IFRS 6.BC28].*

IFRS 6 does not apply to activities after the E&E phase and, therefore, expenditures related to the 'development of mineral resources' should not be recognised as E&E assets. Instead the IASB's *Conceptual Framework* and IAS 38 should be applied in developing guidance on accounting for such assets. *[IFRS 6.10].* The Board did not define 'development of mineral resources', but noted that 'development of a mineral resource once the technical feasibility and commercial viability of extracting the mineral resource had been determined was an example of the development phase of an internal project'. *[IFRS 6.BC27].* While this is not a full definition, it confirms that the IASB intended to restrict the scope IFRS 6 to E&E activities and does not allow the application by analogy. In practice this means that until a feasibility study is complete and a development is approved, accumulated costs are considered E&E assets and are accounted for under IFRS 6.

The standard specifically requires application of IAS 37 – *Provisions, Contingent Liabilities and Contingent Assets* – to any obligations for 'removal and restoration that are incurred during a particular period as a consequence of having undertaken the exploration for and evaluation of mineral resources'. *[IFRS 6.11]*. Although IFRS 6 did not make a corresponding amendment to the scope of IFRIC 1 – *Changes in Existing Decommissioning, Restoration and Similar Liabilities*, which applies to such liabilities when they are recognised in property, plant and equipment under IAS 16, we believe that the interpretation should also be applied in relation to E&E assets.

3.3.3   *Measurement after recognition*

IFRS 6 allows either of two alternatives to be chosen as the accounting policy for E&E assets after initial recognition. Still, whichever policy an entity chooses, it must be applied consistently to all E&E assets. The first alternative is the 'cost model' whereby the item is carried at cost less impairment. The standard does not provide any guidance on whether and, if so, how an entity should account for depreciation, depletion or amortisation of E&E assets. *[IFRS 6.12]*. Entities that apply the 'cost model' should therefore develop an accounting policy within the constraints of IFRS 6 (see 3.2.1 above). As a result an entity can (1) develop an accounting policy that requires E&E costs to be written off as incurred, or (2) develop an accounting policy – based on the successful efforts method or area-of-interest method (see 5.4.1 and 5.4.3 below) – that requires capitalisation of E&E costs pending evaluation. The other alternative is the 'revaluation model', which is not defined in IFRS 6 itself. Instead, the standard requires an entity to classify E&E assets as tangible or intangible assets (see 3.4.1 below) and apply the IAS 16 revaluation model to the tangible assets and the IAS 38 revaluation model to the intangible assets (see Chapter 20 at 6 and Chapter 19 at 10.2). *[IFRS 6.12]*. In practice this means that E&E intangible assets may not be revalued, since the IAS 38 revaluation model may only be applied to homogeneous intangible assets that are traded in an active market. *[IAS 38.8, 72, 75, IFRS 6.BC29-BC30]*.

3.3.4   *Capitalisation of borrowing costs*

IAS 23 – *Borrowing Costs* – requires capitalisation of borrowing costs that are directly attributable to the acquisition, construction or production of a 'qualifying asset' as part of the cost of that asset. *[IAS 23.8]*. An E&E asset will generally meet the definition of a qualifying asset as it 'necessarily takes a substantial period of time to get ready for its intended use or sale'. *[IAS 23.5]*. However, IAS 23 requires capitalisation of borrowing costs only when it is probable that they will result in future economic benefits to the entity and the costs can be measured reliably. *[IAS 23.9]*. Unlike IAS 23, IFRS 6 permits capitalisation of E&E assets even when it is not probable that they will result in future economic benefits. Unless an entity's E&E project has resulted in the classification of mineral resources as proven or probable, it is unlikely that future economic benefits from that project can be considered probable. Therefore, it is entirely consistent with the requirements of IFRS 6 and IAS 23 to capitalise an E&E asset but not capitalise borrowing costs in respect of it.

3.4 Presentation

3.4.1 Classification of E&E assets

E&E assets should be classified consistently as either tangible or intangible assets in accordance with the nature of the assets acquired. *[IFRS 6.15]*. For example, drilling rights should be presented as intangible assets, whereas vehicles and drilling rigs are tangible assets. A tangible asset that is used in developing an intangible asset should still be presented as a tangible asset. However, to the 'extent that a tangible asset is consumed in developing an intangible asset, the amount reflecting that consumption is part of the cost of the intangible asset'. For example, the depreciation of a drilling rig would be capitalised as part of the intangible E&E asset that represents the costs incurred on active exploration projects. *[IFRS 6.16, BC33]*.

3.4.2 Reclassification of E&E assets

E&E assets should no longer be classified as such when 'technical feasibility and commercial viability of extracting a mineral resource are demonstrable'. *[IFRS 6.17]*. Before reclassification, however, E&E assets should be assessed for impairment individually or as part of a cash-generating unit and any impairment loss should be recognised.

3.5 Impairment

When it was developing IFRS 6, the IASB initially wanted entities to apply the normal impairment testing guidance under IAS 36 to E&E assets. *[IFRS 6.BC35]*. Feedback to the Board pointed out that in many cases E&E assets 'do not generate cash flows and there is insufficient information about the mineral resources in a specific area for an entity to make reasonable estimates of E&E assets' recoverable amount ... Without such information, it is not possible to estimate either fair value less costs to sell or value in use, the two measures of recoverable amount in IAS 36. Respondents noted that this would lead to an immediate write off of exploration assets in many cases.' *[IFRS 6.BC36]*. The IASB therefore decided that under IFRS 6 the 'assessment of impairment should be triggered by changes in facts and circumstances. However, it also confirmed that, once an entity had determined that an E&E asset was impaired, IAS 36 should be used to measure, present and disclose that impairment in the financial statements, subject to special requirements with respect to the level at which impairment is assessed.' *[IFRS 6.BC37]*.

3.5.1 Recognition and measurement of impairment

Although the impairment test of E&E assets should be performed in accordance with IAS 36 and any impairment loss should be measured, presented and disclosed as an expense in accordance with that standard, IFRS 6 makes two important modifications: *[IFRS 6.18-20]*

- it defines separate impairment testing 'triggers' for E&E assets; and
- it allows groups of cash-generating units to be used in impairment testing.

3.5.1.A   Impairment testing 'triggers'

E&E assets should be assessed for impairment 'when facts and circumstances suggest that the carrying amount of an E&E asset may exceed its recoverable amount'. *[IFRS 6.18]*. Under IFRS 6 one or more of the following facts and circumstances may 'indicate that an entity should test E&E assets for impairment (the list is not exhaustive):

(a)   the period for which the entity has the right to explore in the specific area has expired during the period or will expire in the near future, and is not expected to be renewed.

(b)   substantive expenditure on further exploration for and evaluation of mineral resources in the specific area is neither budgeted nor planned.

(c)   exploration for and evaluation of mineral resources in the specific area have not led to the discovery of commercially viable quantities of mineral resources and the entity has decided to discontinue such activities in the specific area.

(d)   sufficient data exist to indicate that, although a development in the specific area is likely to proceed, the carrying amount of the E&E asset is unlikely to be recovered in full from successful development or by sale.' *[IFRS 6.20]*.

The above list does not mention, as an impairment indicator, finding that an exploratory or development well does not contain oil or gas in commercial quantities (i.e. finding a 'dry hole'). Nevertheless, if finding a 'dry hole' marks the end of budgeted or planned exploration activity, indicator (b) above would require impairment testing under IAS 36. Additionally, indicator (d) requires an entity to do an impairment test if it is unlikely that it will recover the E&E costs from successful development or sale.

3.5.1.B   Specifying the level at which E&E assets are assessed for impairment

The IASB's original proposals in ED 6 – *Exploration for and Evaluation of Mineral Resources* – regarding the level at which E&E assets should be assessed for impairment attracted considerable comment. Consequently, the Board decided that, rather than introduce a special cash-generating unit for E&E assets as it had proposed, it would allow cash-generating units to be aggregated in a way consistent with the approach to goodwill in IAS 36. *[IFRS 6.BC40-BC47]*. Therefore, an entity should determine an accounting policy for allocating E&E assets to cash-generating units or to groups of cash-generating units for the purpose of assessing such assets for impairment. *[IFRS 6.21]*. IFRS 6 requires that each cash-generating unit or group of units to which an E&E asset is allocated should not be larger than an operating segment (which is smaller than a reportable segment) determined in accordance with IFRS 8 – *Operating Segments*. *[IFRS 6.21]*.

Hence, the level identified by an entity for the purposes of testing E&E assets for impairment may be comprised of one or more cash-generating units. *[IFRS 6.22]*.

3.5.1.C   Cash-generating units comprising successful and unsuccessful E&E projects

Although IFRS 6 does not specifically address the question of whether successful and unsuccessful E&E projects can be combined in a single cash-generating unit (which will occur under full cost accounting and may occur under area of interest accounting), there are a couple of issues to consider before doing this:

- when the technical feasibility and commercial viability of extracting a mineral resource are demonstrable, IFRS 6 requires the E&E assets to be tested for impairment before reclassification, regardless of whether there is an impairment trigger (see 3.5 above). *[IFRS 6.17]*. That means that the successful conclusion of a small E&E project would result in an impairment test of a much larger cash-generating unit and possible recognition of an impairment loss on that larger cash-generating unit; and

- successful E&E projects should be reclassified as tangible or intangible assets under IAS 16 and IAS 38, respectively. *[IFRS 6.15]*. Therefore, a cash-generating unit comprising both successful and unsuccessful E&E projects would be subject to the impairment triggers in both paragraph 20 of IFRS 6 *and* paragraphs 8 to 17 of IAS 36. This would significantly increase the frequency of impairment testing.

Finally, an entity should carefully consider the consequences of including several E&E projects in a cash-generating unit, because under paragraph 20 of IFRS 6 the unsuccessful conclusion of one project would usually trigger an impairment test of the entire cash-generating unit.

3.5.1.D Order of impairment testing

Cash-generating units often contain not only E&E assets but also other assets. ED 6 specifically stated that such other assets should be tested for impairment in accordance with IAS 36 before testing for impairment the cash-generating unit for E&E assets.[128] IFRS 6 is silent on this topic and hence it appears that an entity can choose, as a matter of accounting policy, in which order to test E&E assets and other assets for impairment.

3.5.2 Reversal of impairment losses

Any impairment loss on an E&E asset that has been recognised in accordance with IFRS 6 needs to be reversed when the requirements specified in paragraphs 109 to 123 of IAS 36 have been met (see Chapter 22 at 6). *[IFRS 6.BC48]*.

In some circumstances when an entity recognises an impairment of an E&E asset, it also needs to decide whether or not to derecognise the asset because no future economic benefits are expected, as illustrated in Example 41.3 below.

Example 41.3:   Reversal of impairment losses on E&E assets

Entity A's exploration activity in a specific area does not discover oil and/or gas reserves. Therefore, A recognises an impairment of the cash-generating unit and derecognises the related E&E assets.

Entity B's exploration activity in a specific area leads to the discovery of a significant quantity of reserves, but these are located in a complex reservoir. Therefore, at present the costs of extraction of the discovered reserves do not justify the construction of the required infrastructure. Nevertheless, B's management believes that the surrounding area has strong potential to yield other discoveries on other geological structures and it is considered possible that the required infrastructure will be constructed in the future, although at this stage management has no plans to undertake further exploration activity. Entity B recognises an impairment of the E&E assets, but since it expects future economic benefits the related E&E assets are not derecognised.

If an entity concludes that production is not technically feasible or commercially viable, that provides evidence that the related E&E asset needs to be tested for impairment. Based on such evidence an entity may conclude that no future economic benefits are expected. Although IFRS 6 does not specifically deal with derecognition of E&E assets, the entity should derecognise the E&E asset because (1) the asset is no longer in the exploration and evaluation phase and hence outside the scope of IFRS 6, and (2) other asset standards such IAS 16 and IAS 38 would require derecognition under those circumstances. Subsequent to derecognition, the costs of an E&E asset that have been written off cannot be re-recognised as part of a new E&E asset.

3.6   Disclosure

To identify and explain 'the amounts recognised in its financial statements arising from the exploration for and evaluation of mineral resources' an entity should disclose: *[IFRS 6.23]*

'(a)   its accounting policies for exploration and evaluation expenditures including the recognition of exploration and evaluation assets.

(b)   the amounts of assets, liabilities, income and expense and operating and investing cash flows arising from the exploration for and evaluation of mineral resources.' *[IFRS 6.24]*.

The extract below from Tullow Oil's 2010 financial statements illustrates the disclosures required by IFRS 6:

Extract 41.7: Tullow Oil plc (2010)

Group income statement [extract]
Year ended 31 December 2010

	Notes	2010 $m	2009 $m
Sales revenue	2	1,089.8	915.9
Cost of sales		(611.4)	(625.5)
Gross Profit		**478.4**	290.4
Administrative expenses		(89.6)	(77.6)
Profit on disposal of subsidiaries	25	–	16.0
Profit on disposal of oil and gas assets		0.5	4.9
Exploration costs written off	9	(154.7)	(82.7)
Operating profit	3	**234.6**	151.0

Group balance sheet [extract]
As at 31 December 2010

	Notes	2010 $m	2009 $m
ASSETS			
Non-current assets			
Intangible exploration and evaluation assets	9	4,001.2	2,121.6
Property, plant and equipment	10	2,974.4	2,199.8
Investments	11	1.0	1.0
Deferred tax assets	20	110.7	50.4
Derivative financial instruments	18	–	–
		7,087.3	4,372.8

Group cash flow statement [extract]
Year ended 31 December 2010

	Notes	2008 £'000	2007 £'000
Cash flows from investing activities			
Disposal of subsidiaries	25	–	5.1
Disposal of oil and gas assets		6.7	12.3
Purchase of intangible exploration and evaluation assets		(2,006.1)	(668.4)
Purchase of property, plant and equipment		(625.6)	(520.9)
Advances to contractors		(172.4)	–
Finance revenue		5.4	1.2
Net cash used in investing activities		(2,792.0)	(1,170.7)

Accounting policies [extract]
(j)   Exploration, evaluation and production assets

The Group adopts the successful efforts method of accounting for exploration and appraisal costs. All licence acquisition, exploration and evaluation costs and directly attributable administration costs are initially capitalised in cost centres by well, field or exploration area, as appropriate. Interest payable is capitalised insofar as it relates to specific development activities. Pre-licence costs are expensed in the period in which they are incurred.

These costs are then written off as exploration costs in the income statement unless commercial reserves have been established or the determination process has not been completed and there are no indications of impairment.

All field development costs are capitalised as property, plant and equipment. Property, plant and equipment related to production activities are amortised in accordance with the Group's depletion and amortisation accounting policy.

Note 9   Intangible exploration and evaluation assets [extract]

	2010 $m	2009 $m
At 1 January	2,121.6	2,052.8
Additions	2,047.7	684.7
Disposals	(6.2)	–
Amounts written off	(154.7)	(82.7)
Transfer (to) /from property, plant and equipment (note 10)	(7.0)	(542.1)
Currency translation adjustments	(0.2)	8.9
At 31 December	**4,001.2**	**2,121.6**

The amounts for intangible exploration and evaluation assets represent active exploration projects. These amounts will be written off to the income statement as exploration costs unless commercial reserves are established or the determination process is not completed and there are no indications of impairment. The outcome of ongoing exploration, and therefore whether the carrying value of exploration and evaluation assets will ultimately be recovered, is inherently uncertain.

Additions include $1,450 million in relation to the acquisition of a 50% stake in Blocks 1 and 3A in Uganda (2009: $nil, 2008: $nil) and capitalised interest of $30.7 million (2009: $17.5 million, 2008: $nil million). The Group only capitalises interest in respect of intangible exploration and evaluation assets where it is considered that development is highly likely and advanced appraisal and development is ongoing.

In 2008 amounts written off included an impairment charge calculated in accordance with IAS 36 – *Impairment of Assets* – of $111.5 million, determined by estimating value in use. The impairment resulted from lower reserves estimates following a change in the most likely development plans and lower assumed oil prices following the fall in oil prices in the second half of 2008. In calculating this impairment, management used a range of assumptions, including a long-term oil price of $80 per barrel and a 15% pre-tax discount rate.

An entity should treat E&E assets as a separate class of assets and make the disclosures required by IAS 16 and IAS 38 for tangible E&E assets and intangible E&E assets, respectively. [IFRS 6.25, BC53].

3.6.1   Statement of cash flows

Paragraph 16 of IAS 7 – *Statement of Cash Flows* – was amended (for annual periods beginning on or after 1 January 2010) to state that 'only expenditures that result in a recognised asset in the statement of financial position are eligible for classification as investing activities'. [IAS 7.16]. The IASB specifically notes that 'the exemption in IFRS 6 applies only to recognition and measurement of exploration and evaluation assets, not to the classification of related expenditures in the statement of cash flows'. [IFRS 6.BC23B].

3.7   Effective date and transitional provisions

IFRS 6 has been applicable for annual periods beginning on or after 1 January 2006. [IFRS 6.26]. IFRS 6 does not contain special transitional rules and should be applied fully retrospectively.

4   PRACTICAL ISSUES IN THE EXTRACTIVE INDUSTRIES

4.1   Guidance under national accounting standards

Entities complying with IFRS do not have a free hand in selecting accounting policies – indeed the very purpose of a body of accounting literature is to restrict such choices. To this end, IAS 8 – *Accounting Policies, Changes in Accounting Estimates and Errors* – makes it clear that when a standard or an interpretation specifically applies to a transaction, other event or condition, the accounting policy or policies applied to that item should be determined by applying the standard or interpretation and considering any relevant implementation guidance issued by the IASB for the standard or interpretation. [IAS 8.7].

However, in the extractive industries there are many circumstances where a particular event, transaction or other condition is *not* specifically addressed by IFRS. When this is the case, IAS 8 sets out a hierarchy of guidance to be considered in the selection of an accounting policy (see Chapter 3 at 4.3).

The primary requirement of the standard is that management should use its judgement in developing and applying an accounting policy that results in information that is both relevant and reliable. [IAS 8.10].

In making the judgement, management *should* refer to, and consider the applicability of, the following sources in descending order: [IAS 8.11]

(a)   the requirements in standards and interpretations dealing with similar and related issues; and

(b)   the definitions, recognition criteria and measurement concepts for assets, liabilities, income and expenses in the Conceptual Framework.

Management may also take into account 'the most recent pronouncements of other standard setting bodies that use a similar conceptual framework to develop accounting standards, other accounting literature and accepted industry practices', to the extent that these do not conflict with the sources in (a) and (b) above. *[IAS 8.12].*

4.1.1 Other standard-setting bodies

The stock exchanges in Australia, Canada, South Africa, the United Kingdom and the United States have historically been home to the majority of the listed mining companies and oil and gas companies. Consequently it is organisations from those countries that have been the most active in developing both reserves measurement standards and accounting standards specifically for the extractive industries. In developing an accounting policy for an issue that is not specifically dealt with in IFRS, an entity operating in an extractive industry may find it useful to consider accounting standards developed in these countries. It should be noted, however, that the requirements in such guidance was developed under national accounting standards and may contradict specific requirements and guidance in IFRS that deals with similar and related issues, or may not all be consistent.

4.2 Unit of account

4.2.1 What is the unit of account?

One of the key issues in the development of accounting standards and in the selection of accounting policies by preparers, is the decision about the level at which an entity should separately account for assets, i.e. what the 'unit of account' should be. The definition of the unit of account has significant accounting consequences, as can be seen in the example below.

Example 41.4: Dry well

An oil and gas company concludes, based on a number of exploration wells, that oil and gas reserves are present. However, it needs to drill a number of delineation wells to determine the amount of reserves present in the field. The first delineation well that is drilled is a dry hole, i.e. no reserves are found.

There are two ways of looking at the cost of drilling the dry hole:

- the dry hole provides important information about the extent of the oil and gas reserves present in the oil field and should therefore be capitalised as part of the oil field; or
- the dry hole will not produce oil in the future and in the absence of future economic benefits the costs should be expensed immediately.

The above example suggests that assets or actions that have no value or meaning at one level, may actually be valuable and necessary at another level. For example, the time a construction worker spends reading a blueprint prior to installing an electrical system will not result in a separately identifiable asset, but it is obvious that the cost of the worker's time should be included in the total amount capitalised as the cost of the building.

In 2002, the IASB and the Interpretations Committee discussed the issue of 'linkage' (i.e. whether the accounting treatment for two or more transactions or contracts differs depending on whether the contracts are accounted for separately or together) without reaching any conclusions.[129] More recently, the IASB has been using the phrase 'unit of account' in its meetings to describe similar issues in accounting for assets. Still, IFRS does not provide comprehensive guidance on either 'unit of account' or 'linkage'. However, some standards give guidance about the choice of a unit of account in certain limited circumstances:

- IAS 16 – *Property, Plant and Equipment* – requires an entity to identify the major parts of an item of property, plant and equipment and depreciate each part over its economic life. *[IAS 16.43]*. Furthermore, the standard requires derecognition of those parts of an item of property, plant and equipment that are replaced during repairs and maintenance; *[IAS 16.13]*

- IAS 38 – *Intangible Assets* – requires software that is not an integral part of the related hardware to be accounted for separately; *[IAS 38.4]*

- IAS 23 – *Borrowing Costs* – requires cessation of the capitalisation of borrowing costs when the construction of a part of a qualifying asset is completed and that part is capable of being used while construction continues on other parts; *[IAS 23.24]*

- IAS 11 – *Construction Contracts* – and IAS 18 – *Revenue* – provide guidance on the circumstances under which the substance of a transaction requires individual contracts to be combined or to be segmented; *[IAS 11.7-10, IAS 18.13]*

- impairments under IAS 36 – *Impairment of Assets* – should be determined at the level of individual assets or cash-generating units, but may, in the case of goodwill and E&E assets, be determined for groups of cash generating units that are not larger than an operating segment under IFRS 8. *[IAS 36.59, 66, 80, 102]*. Moreover, cash-generating units can comprise both assets and liabilities and corporate assets may be allocated on a reasonable and consistent basis;

- IAS 32 – *Financial Instruments: Presentation* – requires an entity to evaluate the terms of financial instruments issued by it to determine whether they contain both a liability and an equity component. The individually identified components should be classified separately as financial liabilities, financial assets or equity instruments in accordance with the standard; *[IAS 32.28]*

- IAS 37 – *Provisions, Contingent Liabilities and Contingent Assets* – defines 'an onerous contract as a contract in which the unavoidable costs of meeting the obligations under the contract exceed the economic benefits expected to be received under it'. *[IAS 37.68]*. In determining whether a contract is onerous, an entity is required not to look at the contract in isolation but to assess whether the unit of account, of which the contract is part of, is loss-making because of it;

- IAS 39 – *Financial Instruments: Recognition and Measurement* – and IFRS 9 – *Financial Instruments* – consider the published price quotation in an active market to be the best estimate of fair value. *[IAS 39.AG71, IFRS 9.5.4.2, B5.4.3]*. Large holdings of shares are not treated as a single unit of account and should, instead, be valued at the published price quotation, thereby ignoring the fact that a large holding may attract either a control premium or a liquidity discount; *[IAS 39.E.2.2, IFRS 9.B5.4.4]*

- IAS 39 and IFRS 9 require certain embedded derivatives to be separated from their host contracts and requires those derivatives to be accounted for separately; *[IAS 39.11, IFRS 9.4.3]*

- IFRIC 1 – *Changes in Existing Decommissioning, Restoration and Similar Liabilities* – considers the asset to which a decommissioning liability relates as the unit of account; *[IFRIC 1.BC11]* and

- IFRIC 4 requires an entity to determine whether an arrangement is, or contains, a lease as defined in IAS 17. *[IFRIC 4.5]*.

The unit of account therefore plays a significant role in (1) recognition and derecognition of assets, (2) determining the rate of depreciation or amortisation, (3) deciding whether or not certain costs should be capitalised, (4) undertaking impairment testing, (5) determining the substance of transactions, (6) application of the measurement model subsequent to recognition of the asset, and (7) determining the level of detail of the disclosures required. While the IASB has not developed any principles for determining the appropriate unit of account in any given circumstance, guidance can be derived from the above examples, as follows:

(a) *Cost/benefit* – While it is possible, in theory, to account for the smallest possible component of each asset, the IASB considers the balance between benefit and cost to be a pervasive constraint rather than a qualitative characteristic. Thus the benefits derived from information should exceed the cost of providing it. *[Framework.QC39]*. For instance, an entity would not be expected to account separately for the engine in each of its trucks;

(b) *Materiality* – Under the IASB's *Conceptual Framework*, information is 'material if omitting it or misstating it could influence decisions that users make on the basis of financial information about a specific reporting entity'. *[Framework.QC11]*. For instance, a mining company would normally not consider each individual handheld drill to be material and account for it separately;

(c) *Capable of being used separately* – Assets or parts of assets that are capable of being used separately should be accounted for separately. For instance, individual cars in a fleet would generally be accounted for separately, even if they are not individually material;

(d) *Useful economic life* – Assets or parts of assets should be accounted for separately when:

(i) they have significantly different economic lives; or

(ii) parts of assets are replaced several times over the life of the entire asset they form part of, in which case the replaced part should be derecognised and the replacement part recognised (e.g. the lining of a blast furnace might be treated as a separate part of an asset);

(e) *Inseparability of economic benefits* – If economic benefits from a group of assets cannot be attributed to individual assets within that group then, subject to the other principles listed here, those assets are typically accounted for together as one asset. For instance, a drilling rig would be considered a single asset for the purposes of impairment testing rather than as collection individual components;

(f) *Nature and understanding* – Parts of an asset that are significantly different in nature from the asset as a whole should be accounted for separately when this enhances the understandability and relevance of the financial information. For instance, land and buildings are typically accounted for separately as they have fundamentally different economic characteristics. Similarly, a host contract may contain embedded elements that are quite different in nature. For example, if the price of electricity in a copper mine's electricity supply contract is based on that of copper, then the commodity-based pricing feature is accounted for separately as an embedded derivative;

(g)   *Substance of the transaction* – Frequently the commercial intent of a decision is achieved through a number of steps that, considered individually, do not reflect the commercial reality achieved. Therefore, it may be necessary to combine contracts for the purchase or sale of assets in order to reflect the substance of the management decision. Conversely, it may be necessary to segment a contract for the purchase or sale of an asset in order to reflect the substance of the matter. For example, if an entity provides a non-recourse loan to an employee for the purchase of shares in the entity, then this is generally considered to be a share-based payment rather than a separate loan and issuance of shares; and

(h)   *Industry practice* – To some degree the choice of the unit of account will depend on practice, as illustrated in Example 41.5 below.

The above criteria do not provide definitive guidance or a strict hierarchy of principles in identifying the unit of account, but they can help in determining an appropriate one under IFRS.

Example 41.5:   Unit of account

An entity purchases the following items:

(1)   asphalt and drainage pipes, which it has used to construct a car park;

(2)   twelve trucks; and

(3)   an aircraft.

In each of the above cases the entity needs to decide what the asset is that it will recognise in its books. Practical considerations will generally lead entities to conclude that in (1) above they should account for one asset being the car park. Assuming that the individual components have the same economic lives and can only be used together as one asset, this conclusion is not controversial. However, there is nothing in IFRS that would prohibit an entity from accounting for either (a) the asphalt and drainage pipes separately or (b) 120 individual parking bays.

Example (2) above, again, is not very controversial and most entities would account for the individual trucks separately. Although in theory it would be possible to account for the tyres and engine separately, because they have shorter economic lives, in practice this is not what most entities would do. However, it would generally be considered inappropriate to account for the twelve trucks as if they were one asset, because the trucks can be used separately.

In example (3) most entities would account for the main components of an aircraft separately, e.g. they would account for the engines, airframe and interior separately. The reason for separating the individual components is that they have different economic lives and maintenance requirements and they are individually significant in relation to the total cost of the aircraft or the financial statements as a whole.

Indicators (a), (b), (e), (g) and (h) tend to reduce the level of detail at which assets are accounted for, while indicators (c), (d) and (f) will increase the level of detail. It should be noted, however, that one asset may be part of different units of account for the purposes of different standards as illustrated in the example below.

Example 41.6: Office building and multi-storey car park

At the beginning of 2010, entity A is constructing an office building and an adjacent multi-storey car park. The construction of the office building is completed on 15 July 2010, while the car park is completed on 15 September 2010. Entity A then leases both assets to a single tenant under a 10-year operating lease. For accounting purposes entity A identifies the following units of account:

- For the purpose of capitalising borrowing costs under IAS 23, the office building and car park are treated as separate units of account;

- In applying IAS 16, entity A separately recognises within both the office building and the car park smaller units of account such as the structure, lifts, fittings and roof; and

- In applying IAS 36, entity A treats the office building and the car park as one cash-generating unit because both are leased to the same tenant.

In Example 41.4 above, an individual dry hole might not be considered a separate asset because (1) individual wells are typically not capable of being used separately; (2) their economic benefits are inseparable; (3) the wells are similar in nature and (4) the substance of the matter can only be understood at the level of the project as a whole. In such a scenario, the costs of dry holes will typically be capitalised as the individual well is not considered to be a separate unit of account.

4.2.2 Unit of account in the extractive industries

In the extractive industries the definition of the unit of account is particularly important in: deciding whether or not certain costs may be capitalised; determining the rate of depreciation; and impairment testing. Historically entities in the extractive industries have accounted for preproduction costs using methods such as the:

- successful efforts method;
- area-of-interest method; and
- full cost method.

A key issue under each of these models is determining the appropriate unit of account, which is referred to in the industry as the 'cost centre' or 'pool'. In practice, entities would define their cost centres along geographical, political or legal boundaries or align them to the operating units in their organisation. The IASC's Issues Paper listed the following, commonly used, cost centres:[130]

(a) the world;

(b) each country or group of countries in which the entity operates;

(c) each contractual or legal mineral acquisition unit, such as a lease or production sharing contract;

(d) each area of interest (geological feature, such as a mine or field, that lends itself to a unified exploration and development effort);

(e) geological units other than areas of interest (such as a basin or a geologic province); or

(f) the entity's organisational units.

IFRS does not provide industry specific guidance on determining appropriate units of account for the extractive industries. Nevertheless, we believe that in determining the unit of account an entity should take the legal rights (see (c) above) as its starting point and apply the criteria discussed at 4.2.1 above to assess whether the unit of account should be larger or smaller. The other cost centres listed above might result in a unit of account that is unjustifiably large when viewed in the light of the criteria set out at 4.2.1 above.

As discussed at 1.4.2.C II above, the IASB is considering the definition of 'unit of account' in its Discussion Paper – *Extractive Activities*. While the DP would not need to be considered in the context of the IAS 8 hierarchy, it does draw attention to the fact that the selection of an appropriate unit of account might need to take into account the stage of the underlying activities. In particular, the DP proposes that '...the geographical boundary of the unit of account would be defined initially on the basis of the exploration rights held. As exploration, evaluation and development activities take place, the unit of account would contract progressively until it becomes no greater than a single area, or group of contiguous areas, for which the legal rights are held and which is managed separately and would be expected to generate largely independent cash flows'. The project team's view is that the components approach in IAS 16 – *Property, Plant and Equipment* – would apply to determine the items that should be accounted for as a single asset. However, the DP suggests that an entity may decide to account for its assets using a smaller unit of account.

The thinking underlying the above proposal in the DP would be relevant in the following types of situations:

• certain transactions in the extractive industries (e.g. carried interests arrangements) result in the creation of new legal rights out of existing legal rights. Whenever this is the case, an entity needs to assess whether such transactions give rise to new units of account. If so, the accounting policies should be applied to those new units of account rather than the previous unit/s of account; and

• when an entity acquires a business that owns reserves and resources, it needs to consider whether it should define the unit of account at the level of (1) the license or (2) separate ore zones or reservoirs within the license. Application of the criteria (a) to (h), as discussed at 4.2.1 above, may well result in units of account that are smaller than the license.

Determining the unit of account is an area that requires a significant amount of judgement, which may need to be disclosed under IAS 1 – *Presentation of Financial Statements* – together with other judgements '...that management has made in the process of applying the entity's accounting policies and that have the most significant effect on the amounts recognised in the financial statements'. [IAS 1.122].

4.3   Investments in the extractive industries

Extractive industries are characterised by the high risks associated with the exploration for and development of mineral reserves. To mitigate those risks, industry participants use a variety of ownership structures that are aimed at sharing risks, such as joint investments through subsidiaries, joint ventures, associates or equity interests. IFRS defines each of these as follows:

- *subsidiaries* – entities controlled by the reporting entity (see 4.3.1 below);

- *joint ventures* – contractual arrangements whereby two or more parties undertake an economic activity that is subject to joint control (see 4.3.2 below). (This is the current definition in IAS 31 – *Interests in Joint Ventures*. With the issuance of IFRS 11 – *Joint Arrangements* – this definition has changed – see 4.3.3 and 4.3.4 below);

- *associates* – entities that, while not controlled or jointly controlled by the reporting entity, are subject to significant influence by it (see 4.3.5 below);

- *equity interests* – entities over which the reporting entity cannot exercise any control, joint control or significant influence (see 4.3.6 below); and

- *undivided interests* – participations in projects which entitle the reporting entity only to a share of the production or use of an asset, and do not of themselves give the entity any form of control, joint control or significant influence (see 4.3.7 below).

4.3.1   Investments in subsidiaries

In the extractive industries it is common to find that a parent company is not exposed to all the risks and rewards from its investments in subsidiaries. Instead, there are often significant non-controlling shareholders that share in the risks and rewards. Accounting for non-controlling interests is discussed in detail in Chapter 8 at 4. Furthermore, there sometimes exist put and/or call options over non-controlling interests that transfer some of the risks between the parent company shareholders and the non-controlling shareholders. This issue is discussed in detail in Chapter 8 at 5.

4.3.2   Investments in joint ventures – IAS 31

Joint ventures have always been, and continue to be, a common structure in the extractive industries. Such arrangements are used to bring in partners to source new projects, combine adjacent mineral licences, improve utilisation of expensive infrastructure, attract investors and help manage technical or political risk or comply with local regulations. The majority of entities operating in the extractive industries are party to at least one joint venture arrangement. However, not all arrangements that are casually described as 'joint ventures' meet the definition of a joint venture under IFRS.

IAS 31 defines a joint venture as a contractual arrangement whereby two or more parties undertake an economic activity that is subject to joint control. *[IAS 31.3]*. Joint control is defined as 'the contractually agreed sharing of control over an economic activity, and exists only when the strategic financial and operating decisions relating to the activity require the unanimous consent of the parties sharing control (the venturers)'. *[IAS 31.3]*. Although joint ventures take many different forms and structures, IAS 31 identifies three broad types:

- jointly controlled operations (see 4.3.2.A below);
- jointly controlled assets (see 4.3.2.B below); and
- jointly controlled entities (see 4.3.2.C below).

IAS 31 emphasises that it is the existence of a contractual arrangement that distinguishes interests that involve joint control from investments in associates in which the investor has 'significant influence', *[IAS 31.9]*, meaning the power to participate in the financial and operating policy decisions of the investee but not amounting to control or joint control over those policies. *[IAS 31.3]*.

Activities that have no contractual arrangement to establish joint control are not joint ventures for the purposes of IAS 31. *[IAS 31.9]*. In other words, if two entities A and B set up a third entity C in which A and B each hold 50% of the equity, C will not, by virtue of the relative shareholdings *alone*, be a joint venture of A and B for the purposes of IAS 31. There needs to be an agreement (implicit or explicit) for unanimous decision making on key matters – although this might automatically flow from the general provisions of corporate law in the jurisdiction concerned. The requirements of IAS 31 in respect of joint venture agreements are discussed in detail in Chapter 13 at 2.2.2.A.

In the absence of a contractual arrangement to establish joint control, an investment in an entity cannot be a joint venture and should be accounted for either as a subsidiary under IAS 27 – *Consolidated and Separate Financial Statements*, a special purpose entity under SIC-12 – *Consolidation – Special Purpose Entities*, an associate under IAS 28 – *Investments in Associates* (see 4.3.5 below) or as a financial asset under IAS 39 or IFRS 9 (see 4.3.6 below).

The accounting for jointly controlled operations, jointly controlled assets and jointly controlled entities is discussed in detail in Chapter 13 at 3, 4 and 5, respectively. These accounting requirements are summarised at 4.3.2.A, 4.3.2.B and 4.3.2.C below.

IFRS 11 – *Joint Arrangements*, issued in May 2011, which will replace IAS 31 and SIC-13, is discussed at 4.3.3 and 4.3.4 below.

4.3.2.A   Jointly controlled operations

A jointly controlled operation (JCO) is a joint venture that involves the use of assets and other resources of the venturers, rather than the establishment of a corporation, partnership or other legal entity, or a financial structure, separate from the venturers themselves. Each venturer uses its own property, plant and equipment and carries its own inventories. It also incurs its own expenses and liabilities, raises its own finance, and is responsible for its own obligations only. Activities may be carried out by the venturer's employees alongside similar activities of the other venturer. The JCO agreement usually provides the basis for sharing among the venturers the revenue from the joint product, and any common expenses incurred. *[IAS 31.13]*.

In respect of its interest in a jointly controlled operation, IAS 31 requires a venturer to recognise in its financial statements:

- the assets that it controls and the liabilities that it incurs; and
- the expenses that it incurs and its share of the income that it earns from the sale of goods or services by the joint venture. *[IAS 31.15]*.

The extract below shows a typical accounting policy for jointly controlled operations.

Extract 41.8: Xstrata plc (2010)

Notes to the financial statements [extract]

6. Principal accounting policies [extract]

Jointly controlled operations

A jointly controlled operation involves the use of assets and other resources of the Group and other venturers rather than the establishment of a corporation, partnership or other entity.

The Group accounts for the assets it controls and the liabilities it incurs, the expenses it incurs and the share of income that it earns from the sale of goods or services by the joint venture.

4.3.2.B   Jointly controlled assets and undivided interests

Jointly controlled assets (JCAs) are the most common form of joint venture in the extractive industries. They involve the joint control, and often joint ownership, of one or more assets contributed to, or acquired for, and dedicated to the purposes of, the joint venture. The assets are used to obtain benefits for the venturers, who may each take a share of the output from the assets and bear an agreed share of the expenses incurred. Such ventures do not involve the establishment of an entity or financial structure separate from the venturers themselves, so that each venturer has control over its share of future economic benefits through its share in the jointly controlled asset. *[IAS 31.18-19]*.

IAS 31 notes that joint ventures of this type are particularly common in the extractive industries. For example, a number of oil companies may jointly control and operate an oil pipeline. Each venturer uses the pipeline to transport its own product in return for which it bears an agreed proportion of the operating expenses of the pipeline.

A JCA is similar to an 'undivided interest', which is 'a fractional ownership interest in the entire area of the property. For example, if an entity owning 100 per cent of the working interest in a property sells a 50 per cent undivided interest to another party, the purchaser owns 50 per cent of the entire property, and the seller owns 50 per cent of the same property.'[131] This is called an 'undivided' interest because neither party owns a physically identifiable half of the property concerned. However, as discussed at 4.3.7 below, it is possible for an undivided interest not to be subject to joint control.

In respect of its interest in jointly controlled assets, IAS 31 requires a venturer to recognise in its financial statements: *[IAS 31.21-22]*

- its share of the jointly controlled assets, classified according to the nature of the assets (i.e. a share in a jointly controlled pipeline should be shown within property, plant and equipment rather than as an investment);
- any liabilities that it has incurred;
- its share of any liabilities incurred jointly with the other venturers;
- any income from the sale or use of its share of the output of the joint venture;
- its share of any expenses incurred by the joint venture; and
- any expenses which it has incurred in respect of its interest in the joint venture (e.g. those relating to financing the venturer's interest in the assets and selling its share of the output).

The IASB believes that this treatment reflects the substance and economic reality and, usually, the legal form of the joint venture. *[IAS 31.23]*. However, it should be noted that, as Example 13.4 in Chapter 13 at 5.1 illustrates, the classification of a joint venture as either a jointly controlled asset or a jointly controlled entity is, currently, largely form driven.

The extract below shows a typical accounting policy for jointly controlled assets.

Extract 41.9: Xstrata plc (2010)

Notes to the financial statements [extract]

6. Principal accounting policies [extract]

Jointly controlled assets

A jointly controlled asset involves joint control and ownership by the Group and other venturers of assets contributed to or acquired for the purpose of the joint venture, without the formation of a corporation, partnership or other entity.

The Group accounts for its share of the jointly controlled assets, any liabilities it has incurred, its share of any liabilities jointly incurred with other venturers, income from the sale or use of its share of the joint venture's output, together with its share of the expenses incurred by the joint venture, and any expenses it incurs in relation to its interest in the joint venture.

4.3.2.C   Jointly controlled entities

In contrast to a jointly controlled operation or jointly controlled asset, a jointly controlled entity (or JCE) is a joint venture that involves the establishment of a corporation, partnership or other entity in which each venturer has an interest. The entity operates in the same way as any other entity, except that a contractual arrangement between the venturers establishes joint control over the economic activity of the entity. *[IAS 31.24]*.

IAS 31 maintains that many jointly controlled entities are similar in substance to jointly controlled operations or jointly controlled assets. For example, the venturers may transfer a jointly controlled asset, such as an oil pipeline, into a jointly controlled entity for tax or other reasons. Similarly, the venturers may contribute assets into a jointly controlled entity which will be operated jointly. Some jointly controlled operations also involve the establishment of a jointly controlled entity to deal with particular aspects of the activity, for example, the design, marketing, distribution or after-sales service of the product. *[IAS 31.27]*.

This emphasises the fact that, whilst the economic substance of a jointly controlled asset and a jointly controlled entity may in fact be similar, the difference in form does matter in determining the accounting treatment. Under IAS 31, the substance of a joint venture is determined by its legal form and it follows that, once a joint venture takes the form of a separate legal entity, it becomes a jointly controlled entity under IAS 31. Therefore a contractual arrangement that involves the establishment of a legal entity under joint control would be a jointly controlled entity, even if the entity does not carry on a trade or business of its own and merely owns a group of assets.

IAS 31 currently permits two methods of accounting for jointly controlled entities:

- proportionate consolidation (see Chapter 13 at 5.3), using one of two permitted formats; and
- the equity method (see Chapter 13 at 5.4). *[IAS 31.30, 38].*

Proportionate consolidation of jointly controlled entities remains popular under IFRS in those countries whose previous national GAAP permitted or required some form of proportionate consolidation. In countries whose national GAAP never permitted proportionate consolidation the equity method remains prevalent. On balance, however, neither method is dominant within the extractive industries. An entity would therefore have a free choice in selecting its accounting policy, but may wish to consider the policy adopted by its peer group and the more subtle differences between the two methods, as discussed in Chapter 13 at 5.2.1. Also, once a policy is selected it must be applied consistently to all JCEs. Any decision to change between proportionate consolidation and equity accounting would require the application of the provisions of IAS 8 relating to changes in accounting policy.

The extract below shows a typical proportionate consolidation accounting policy for jointly controlled entities.

Extract 41.10: Xstrata plc (2010)

Notes to the financial statements [extract]

6. Principal accounting policies [extract]

Jointly controlled entities

A jointly controlled entity involves the establishment of a corporation, partnership or other legal entity in which the Group has an interest along with other venturers.

The Group recognises its interest in jointly controlled entities using the proportionate method of consolidation, whereby the Group's share of each of the assets, liabilities, income and expenses of the joint venture are combined with the similar items, line by line, in its consolidated financial statements.

When the Group contributes or sells assets to a joint venture, any gain or loss from the transaction is recognised based on the substance of the transaction. When the Group has transferred the risk and rewards of ownership to the joint venture, the Group only recognises the portion of the gain or loss attributable to the other venturers, unless the loss is reflective of an impairment, in which case the loss is recognised in full. When the Group purchases assets from the joint venture, it does not recognise its share of the profits of the joint venture from the transaction until it resells the assets to an independent party. Losses are accounted for in a similar manner unless they represent an impairment loss, in which case they are recognised immediately.

Joint ventures are accounted for in the manner outlined above, until the date on which the Group ceases to have joint control over the joint venture.

The extract below shows how AngloGold Ashanti applies equity accounting to its investments in jointly controlled entities.

Extract 41.11: AngloGold Ashanti Limited (2010)

Notes to the financial statements [extract]

1 Accounting Policies [extract]

1.3 Summary of significant accounting policies [extract]

Joint ventures

A joint venture is an entity in which the group holds a long-term interest and which the group and one or more other venturers jointly control under a contractual arrangement, that provides for strategic, financial and operating policy decisions relating to the activities requiring unanimous consent of the parties sharing control. The group's interests in jointly controlled entities are accounted for using the equity method.

Profits and losses realised in connection with transactions between the group and jointly controlled entities are eliminated in proportion to share ownership. Such profits and losses are deducted from the group's equity and related statement of financial position amount and released in the group accounts when the assets are effectively realised outside the group.

Joint ventures are accounted for at cost and are adjusted for impairments where appropriate in the company financial statements.

4.3.3   Investments in joint arrangements – IFRS 11: Overview

Since 2002, the IASB had frequently discussed whether or not it should remove the option of proportionate consolidation for jointly controlled entities under IAS 31. The reasons for wishing to abolish proportionate consolidation included the concern that the approach was not conceptually justifiable, the belief that accounting standards should not allow alternative accounting treatments and the IASB's desire to pursue US GAAP convergence.

In May 2011 the IASB issued IFRS 11 – *Joint Arrangements*, which will replace IAS 31 and SIC-13.

IFRS 11 prescribes the accounting for a 'joint arrangement', which is defined as a contractual arrangement over which two or more parties have joint control. Despite a perceived increase in scope implied by the change in the title of the standard (i.e. from 'joint ventures' to 'joint arrangements'), the scope of IFRS 11 is not intended to be broader than IAS 31. It still only applies to joint arrangements where there is joint control. However, the definition of joint control has changed and is based upon the new definition of control in the newly issued IFRS 10 – *Consolidated Financial Statements* (see Chapter 7 at 3). Therefore it is possible that the assessment of, and conclusions relating to the existence of, joint control may change, which would impact which arrangements are determined to be within scope.

In addition, some of the terminology has changed – which has created some confusion. For example, what many in the extractive industries would refer to as 'joint ventures' are now collectively referred to as 'joint arrangements'; the term 'joint venture' is now narrowly defined in IFRS 11.

Likewise, the term 'proportionate consolidation' has been (and still is) casually used to describe all methods of joint venture accounting where an entity recognises its share of the assets and liabilities of the joint venture. However, from an accounting perspective, this term means something quite specific and is not reflective of the accounting treatment that currently applies to jointly controlled assets (JCAs) and jointly controlled operations (JCOs) under IAS 31, and that which will apply to joint operations under IFRS 11.

The principal change to IAS 31 is that proportionate consolidation of jointly controlled entities which are classified as joint ventures under IFRS 11 will no longer be allowed.

Under IFRS 11, joint arrangements are to be classified into two types (i.e. joint operations and joint ventures) based on the rights and obligations that arise from the contractual arrangement:

'Joint operation'

• A joint operation is defined in IFRS 11 as 'a joint arrangement whereby the parties that have joint control of the arrangement have rights to the assets, and obligations for the liabilities, relating to the arrangement.' *[IFRS 11 Appendix A]*.

• This term will effectively replace the terms 'jointly controlled operation' (JCO) and 'jointly controlled asset' (JCA) used in IAS 31. JCOs and JCAs are discussed above at 4.3.2.A and 4.3.2.B, respectively.

• An entity with joint control over a joint operation will be referred to as a 'joint operator'. *[IFRS 11 Appendix A]*.

• The joint operator shall recognise in relation to its interest in a joint operation:

    (a)   its assets, including its share of any assets held jointly;

    (b)   its liabilities, including its share of any liabilities incurred jointly;

    (c)   its revenue from the sale of its share of the output arising from the joint operation;

    (d)   its share of the revenue from the sale of the output by the joint operation; and

    (e)   its expenses, including its share of any expenses incurred jointly. *[IFRS 11.20]*.

For more information on accounting for joint operations under IFRS 11 refer Chapter 14 at 6.

'Joint venture'

• A joint venture is defined in IFRS 11 as 'a joint arrangement whereby the parties that have joint control of the arrangement have rights to the net assets of the arrangement.' *[IFRS 11 Appendix A]*.

• Arrangements currently referred to a 'jointly controlled entities' (JCEs) (see 4.3.2.C above) under IAS 31 could either be joint operations or joint ventures under IFRS 11. This will depend upon the assessment of the rights and obligations of the arrangement.

Chapter 41

- An entity with joint control over a joint venture will be referred to as a 'joint venturer'. *[IFRS 11 Appendix A]*.

- A joint venturer recognises its interest in a joint venture as an investment and shall account for that investment using the equity method in accordance with IAS 28 (as amended in 2011) – *Investments in Associates and Joint Ventures* – unless the entity is exempted from applying the equity method as specified in that standard. *[IFRS 11.24]*.

For more information on accounting for joint ventures under IFRS 11 refer Chapter 14 at 7.

IFRS 11 establishes a core principle that an entity that is party to a joint arrangement is to determine the type of joint arrangement in which it is involved by assessing its rights and obligations and to account for those rights and obligations in accordance with that type of joint arrangement. *[IFRS 11.2]*. The objective of this broad principle is to shift the focus from how the form of a joint arrangement dictates the accounting to focus more on the contractual rights and obligations within the arrangement. Therefore, the legal structure of the arrangement is only one element in assessing these rights and obligations. This is a change from the present position under IAS 31, where the treatment of a joint venture is determined by its legal form, and once a joint venture is set up in a separate legal entity (being a corporation, partnership or other entity), it becomes a jointly controlled entity under the standard.

Given that the rights and obligations provided to a party to a joint arrangement will drive the accounting, an entity will need to have a detailed understanding of the specific rights and obligations of each of its arrangements to be able to determine the impact of this new standard.

Further details of IFRS 11 and its requirements are set out in Chapter 14.

4.3.4   Investments in joint arrangements – IFRS 11: Impact on the extractive industries

Given the prevalence of joint arrangements in the extractive industries, careful analysis of IFRS 11 (in conjunction with the requirements of IFRS 10 and IFRS 12 – *Disclosure of Interests in Other Entities* (see Chapter 15) will be required. Some specific areas to consider are as follows:

4.3.4.A   New definition of joint control

As noted above, joint control is defined as '...the contractually agreed sharing of control of an arrangement which exists only when the decisions about the relevant activities require the unanimous consent of the parties sharing control'. *[IFRS 11.7, Appendix A]*. IFRS 11 describes the key aspects of joint control as follows:

- *Contractually agreed* – contractual arrangements are usually, but not always, written, and set out the terms of the arrangements *[IFRS 11.5(a), B2]*.

- *Control and relevant activities* – IFRS 10 describes how to assess whether a party has control, and how to identify the relevant activities *[IFRS 11.8, B5]*.

- *Unanimous consent* – exists when the parties to an arrangement have collective control over the arrangement, but no single party has control *[IFRS 11.9, B6]*.

The new requirements within this new definition of joint control relate to the assessment of control and relevant activities. The requirement for there to be unanimous consent is not new, however, additional guidance has been added to clarify when it exists.

I   Determination of control – impact of changes to the consolidation standard

It is common in the extractive industries for one of the parties to be appointed as the operator or manager of the joint arrangement ('the operator'), to whom some of the decision-making powers might be delegated. Currently, many consider that the operator does not control a joint arrangement, but simply carries out the decisions of the parties under the joint venture (or operating) agreement (JOA), i.e. acts as an agent. This view is based on the way in which these roles are generally established and referred to / perceived, in the sector. Under the new standards, it may be possible to conclude that the operator actually controls the arrangement. This is because when decision-making rights have been delegated, IFRS 10 now provides new requirements on how to assess whether an entity is acting as principal or agent, which is then used to determine which party has control.

Careful consideration will be required to assess whether an operator acts as a principal (and, therefore, may potentially control the arrangement) or as an agent. In the former situation, the impact of determining that an operator controls an arrangement will depend upon the rights and obligations conveyed by the arrangement (see 4.3.4.A I-1 below for further discussion on this issue). In the latter situation, as an agent, the operator would always only recognise its own interests in the joint arrangement (the accounting for which will depend upon whether it is a joint operation or joint venture) and its operator/management fee.

The factors to be considered in making this assessment include:

- Scope of the operator's decision-making authority;
- Rights held by others (e.g. protective, removal rights);
- Exposure to variability in returns through the remuneration of the operator; and
- Variable returns held through other interests (e.g. direct investments by the operator in the joint arrangement).

The following factors may be particularly relevant.

Rights held by others – If a non-operator party has a right to remove the operator that is substantive (e.g. it can be exercised without cause), then the operator would be an agent. However, if the exercise of that removal right requires agreement by more than one of the non-operator parties, then it is not conclusive as to whether the operator is a principal or an agent.

Variable returns held through other interests – When an operator holds other interests in a joint arrangement over and above the remuneration it receives for being the operator, this may indicate it is not an agent. It is common in the extractive industries for an operator to also have a direct financial interest in the joint arrangement. By virtue of holding this other interest, the standard indicates that decisions made by the operator may differ from those it would have made if it did not hold the other interest, and potentially may indicate the operator is acting as principal.

Chapter 41

It is important to note that assessing whether an entity is a principal or an agent will require consideration of all factors collectively. See Chapter 7 at 6.1 for more details regarding the new principal versus agent requirements.

I-1   Implications of control

The impact of controlling an arrangement depends on a number of factors.

The most important of these will be identifying and assessing the rights and obligations the contractual arrangement provides the parties, as well as assessing whether the arrangement is a business.

a) Identifying and assessing rights and obligations

- *Rights to the underlying assets and obligations for the underlying liabilities of the arrangement:* While the principal / agent assessment may lead to a conclusion that an operator has control, the fact that each party has specific rights to, and obligations for, the underlying assets and liabilities of the arrangement, means the operator does not control anything over and above its own direct interest in those assets and liabilities. Therefore, it still only recognises its interest in those assets and liabilities conveyed to it by the contractual arrangement.

This accounting applies regardless of whether the arrangement is in a separate vehicle or not, as the contractual terms are the primary determinant of the accounting. NOTE: IFRS 11 defines a separate vehicle as 'A separately identifiable financial structure, including separate legal entities or entities recognised by statute, regardless of whether those entities have a legal personality.' *[IFRS 11 Appendix A].*

To explain this further, it is worth considering the two types of joint arrangements contemplated by IFRS 11 – one that is not structured through a separate vehicle (e.g. a contract alone) and one that is structured through a separate vehicle.

No separate vehicle: The IASB acknowledged that while it is possible that the contractual terms of a joint arrangement not structured through a separate vehicle might give the parties rights only to the net assets of the arrangement, they expected this would be rare. *[IFRS 11.BC27].* Instead, they considered it would be more common for the parties to have rights to, and obligations for, the underlying assets and obligations of the arrangement.

So in such a situation, even if the operator 'controlled' the arrangement, there is really nothing for it to control. This is because each party would continue to account for its rights and obligations arising from the contract e.g. it would apply IAS 16 to account for its rights to any tangible assets, IAS 38 to account for its rights to any intangible assets or IAS 39 to account for its obligations for any financial liabilities etc. Additionally, an entity cannot consolidate a contract, as the requirements of IFRS 10 only apply to entities and in most circumstances, a contract does not create an entity.

Separate vehicle: Some may initially conclude that if an operator controls an arrangement structured through a separate vehicle e.g. a company, it would automatically look to IFRS 10 and consolidate the arrangement and account for the interests of the other parties as non-controlling interests. However, in such situations, a contract still exists which gives the parties to the arrangement rights to, and obligations for, the underlying assets and liabilities of that arrangement. These rights and obligations should be accounted for first. That is, each party to the arrangement would recognise its respective share of the assets and liabilities (applying each IFRS as appropriate e.g. IAS 16, IAS 38, IAS 39 etc.).

From the perspective of the separate vehicle, what this means is that the rights to, and obligations for, its assets and liabilities have been contracted out to other parties (i.e. the parties to the contractual arrangement) and therefore there are no assets or liabilities left within the separate vehicle.

Consequently, from the perspective of the operator, who may be considered to control the separate vehicle, it would initially account for its rights and obligations arising from the contract, and then when it looks to consolidate the separate vehicle, there is nothing left to consolidate, as the separate vehicle is empty.

The above analysis demonstrates that where parties to an arrangement genuinely have rights to, and obligations for, the underlying assets and liabilities of the arrangement, concluding that an operator controls the arrangement does not change the accounting for either the operator nor the non-operator parties.

- *Rights to the net assets of the arrangement:* As noted above, the IASB acknowledged that it would be rare for an arrangement not structured through a separate vehicle to provide the parties with rights to the net assets. Therefore it is considered that rights to the net assets of an arrangement would be more likely to only arise where the arrangement is structured through a separate vehicle. In this instance, the operator would consolidate the separate vehicle and recognise any non-controlling interest/s.

b)   Is the arrangement a business?

The other relevant factor is whether the arrangement is a business, as this determines whether, upon obtaining control, the requirements of IFRS 3 – *Business Combinations* – apply. All of the requirements of IFRS 3 apply if the entity controls the arrangement where it has rights to the net assets, and that arrangement is a business. However, if that controlled arrangement is not a business, the entity identifies and recognises the individual assets acquired and liabilities assumed based on their relative fair value, and does not recognise any goodwill.

For arrangements where there are rights to the assets and obligations for the liabilities, it is not clear whether IFRS 3 applies and whether goodwill could / should be recognised. This issue has recently been referred to the Interpretations Committee. This is discussed further in 4.3.4.B below.

I-2   What are relevant activities?

Relevant activities are those activities of the arrangement which significantly affect the returns of the arrangement. Determining what these are for each arrangement will require significant judgement.

Examples of decisions about relevant activities include, but are not limited to:

* Establishing operating and capital decisions of the arrangement including budgets – for example, for a mining and metals arrangement, approving the capital expenditure programme for the next year

* Appointing and remunerating a joint arrangement's key management personnel or service providers and terminating their services or employment – for example, appointing a contract miner to undertake mining operations.

For more information on identifying relevant activities, see Chapter 14 at 4.1.

I-3   Meaning of unanimous consent

While the requirement for unanimous consent is not new, IFRS 11 does provide additional guidance that clarifies when unanimous consent exists, and over which activities it is required. Unanimous consent means that any party with joint control can prevent any of the other parties, or a group of parties, from making unilateral decisions about relevant activities.

Sometimes the decision-making process agreed between the parties in the JOA implicitly leads to joint control. For example, in a 50% / 50% joint arrangement, the JOA specifies that at least 51% of the voting rights are required to make a decision about relevant activities. Therefore, the parties have implicitly agreed that they have joint control because decisions about relevant activities cannot be made without both parties agreeing.

However, in other instances, the JOA may require a minimum proportion of the voting rights to make decisions. Unless it is obvious how this minimum must be achieved, or the JOA specifies which parties are required to unanimously agree, then there would not be joint control.

For further discussion on unanimous consent, see Chapter 14 at 4.3.

In some extractive industries operations, decision-making may vary over the life of the project e.g. during the exploration and evaluation phase, the development phase and / or the production phase. For example, it may be agreed at the time of initially entering the contractual arrangement that during the exploration and evaluation phase, one party to the arrangement may be able to make all of the decisions, whereas once the project enters the development phase, decisions may then require unanimous consent. To determine whether the arrangement is jointly controlled, it will be necessary to decide (at the point of initially entering the contractual arrangement, and subsequently, should facts and circumstances change) which of these activities e.g. exploration and evaluation and/or development, most significantly affect the returns of the arrangement. This is because the arrangement will only be considered to be a joint arrangement if those activities which require unanimous consent are the ones that most significantly affect the returns. This will be a highly judgemental assessment.

This view is supported by the application guidance to IFRS 10. It states that when two or more investors have the current ability to direct relevant activities and those activities occur at different times, the investors shall determine which investor is able to direct the activities that most significantly affect those returns consistently with the treatment of concurrent decision-making rights, to determine who controls the arrangement. The investors shall reconsider this assessment over time if relevant facts or circumstances change. *[IFRS 10.B13]*.

For further information on the impact of different decision-making arrangements over various activities, see Chapter 14 at 4.1.

4.3.4.B Differences between joint ventures and joint operations

Once it has been established that there is joint control, joint arrangements are then classified as either joint operations or joint ventures. For more information on the requirements for classifying a joint arrangement as a joint operation or joint venture, see Chapter 14 at 5.

Does IFRS 3 apply to joint operations?

One area where there is currently a lack of clarity when accounting for acquisitions of interests in JCAs and JCOs, and unless resolved, will present similar issues for joint operations, is whether IFRS 3 applies.

- One view is that IFRS 3 does not apply. This is on the basis that even though the activity of the JCA / JCO or joint operation may constitute a business, the venturer/joint operator does not control that business – it only has joint control.

- The other view is that IFRS 3 is applicable. This is on the basis that the unit of account for assessing control is the venturer's/joint operator's own interest in the business of the JCA/JCO or joint operation, and the entity controls this. If IFRS 3 were to apply, the acquisition method of accounting would need to be applied – that is: goodwill or a bargain purchase may be recognised; assets acquired and liabilities assumed would be measured at fair value; transaction costs would have to be expensed; deferred tax would have to be recognised; and contingent consideration would have to be measured at fair value at date of acquisition, with subsequent movements either going to profit or loss or equity (depending upon the nature of the contingent consideration). See 4.4.1.C below for more details.

This lack of clarity has led to diversity in practice. This issue was referred to the Interpretations Committee and considered at their July and September 2011 meetings. See Chapter 14 at 8.3.1 for more information.

I What is proportionate consolidation?

As mentioned earlier, there is some misunderstanding as to what proportionate consolidation is under IFRS, and how this compares to JCA/JCO accounting under IAS 31, and the accounting for joint operations under IFRS 11. This confusion is partly due to the two approaches being technically different, from an accounting perspective, and also partly due to the way the term 'proportionate consolidation' is used under US GAAP. Under US GAAP, proportionate consolidation is used to describe a method of accounting that would be the equivalent of IFRS's JCA/JCO (and now joint operation) accounting.

As a consequence, there is some unwarranted concern that all interests in joint arrangements will require equity accounting – which is not the case. And for JCEs that are classified as joint operations under IFRS 11, it may not be clear whether the adoption of IFRS 11 will impact the financial statements.

To illustrate this:

- Where a joint operator has rights to a specified percentage of all assets (e.g. 50%) and obligations for the same specified percentage (50%) of all liabilities, there would likely be no difference between the accounting for a joint operation and proportionate consolidation.

- However, where the joint operator has differing rights to various assets, and/or differing obligations for various liabilities, the financial statements would look different when accounting for those individual rights and obligations, as compared with proportionately consolidating the same percentage of all assets and liabilities. *[IFRS 11.BC38].*

See Chapter 14 at 6.1 for further discussion about the differences between proportionate consolidation and JCA/JCO and joint operation accounting.

4.3.4.C   Gross versus net – what should be recognised?

It is clear that a participant in a joint operation is required to recognise its rights to the assets, and its obligations for the liabilities (or share thereof), of the joint arrangement. Therefore it is important that an entity fully understands what these rights and obligations are and how these may differ between the parties.

I   Operators of joint arrangements

Operators of joint arrangements may have a direct legal liability in respect of the entire balance of certain obligations arising from transactions related to the joint arrangement. These may include, but are not limited to, third party creditors, leases, employee liabilities, etc. They may also have a right of reimbursement (by virtue of the JOA) from the non-operator parties. The operator would be required to recognise 100% of such liabilities and would recognise a receivable from the non-operator parties for their share of such liabilities. IFRS prohibits the offsetting of these liabilities against these receivables in the statement of financial position. However, there is no effect on profit or loss if these costs are being incurred on behalf of the non-operator parties, i.e. the operator is acting as agent, and such costs are directly recharged. This is because these recharges are considered to be a reimbursement which can be offset against the related expense.

While, in most circumstances, the ability / willingness of the non-operator parties to pay their share of the costs incurred by the operator will not be in doubt, particularly where cash calls are paid in advance, there may be instances where they are unable to pay. Here the operator might not be able to recognise a corresponding receivable and reimbursement, and consequently, this would negatively impact its financial statements.

II   Non-operators

Non-operators would recognise an amount payable to the operator, which would be recognised as a financial instrument under IAS 32 – *Financial Instruments: Presentation* / IAS 39 – *Financial Instruments: Recognition and Measurement* – or IFRS 9 – *Financial Instruments* – or potentially a provision under IAS 37 – *Provisions, Contingent Liabilities and Contingent Assets* – and not under the standard which relates to the type of cost being reimbursed. For example, the non-operator's share of employee entitlements relating to the operator's employees who work on the joint project would not be recognised as an employee benefit under IAS 19 – *Employee Benefits*. In addition, the related disclosure requirements of IAS 19 would not apply, instead the disclosure requirements of other standards, e.g. IFRS 7 – *Financial Instruments: Disclosures,* would apply.

III   Joint and several liability

It is also possible that there may be liabilities in the arrangement where the obligation is joint and several. That is, an entity is not only responsible for its proportionate share, but it is also liable for the other party's / parties' share/s should it/they be unable or unwilling to pay. A common example of this in the extractives industries is rehabilitation / decommissioning obligations.

In these instances, each party not only takes up its proportionate share of the rehabilitation obligation, it is also required to assess the likelihood that the other party/ies will not be able or willing to meet their share. The facts and circumstances would need to be assessed in each case, and any additional liability and/or disclosures would be accounted for, and disclosed, in accordance with IAS 37 – *Provisions, Contingent Liabilities and Contingent Assets.*

Any increase in the provision would be accounted for under IFRIC 1, if it related to a rehabilitation / decommissioning liability that had both been included as part of an asset measured in accordance with IAS 16 and measured as a liability in accordance with IAS 37 (see 4.8.2 for more details). Such an addition to the asset would require an entity to consider whether this is an indication of impairment of the asset as a whole, and if so, would need to test for impairment in accordance with IAS 36. Increases that do not meet the requirements of IFRIC would be recognised in profit or loss.

4.3.4.D   An entity does not have joint control or control?

The accounting treatment of an interest in a contractual arrangement that does not give rise to joint control or control depends on a number of factors most importantly the rights and obligations arising under the contractual arrangement.

I   Identifying and assessing the rights and obligations
- *Rights to the underlying assets and obligations for the underlying liabilities of the arrangement:* Despite not having joint control (or control) the party still has rights to, and obligations for, the underlying assets and obligations. Therefore, it would continue to recognise its interest in those assets and liabilities.

This accounting would apply regardless of whether the arrangement is in a separate vehicle or not, as the contractual terms are the primary determinant of the accounting.

To explain this further, it is worth considering the two types of joint arrangements contemplated by IFRS 11 – one that is not structured through a separate vehicle (e.g. a contract alone) and one that is structured through a separate vehicle.

No separate vehicle: As explained at 4.3.4.A I-1 above, an arrangement not structured through a separate vehicle is considered to give the parties to the arrangement rights to, and obligations for, the underlying assets and obligations of the arrangement. Therefore, each party would continue to account for its rights and obligations arising from the contract e.g. it would apply IAS 16 to account for its rights to any tangible assets, IAS 38 to account for its rights to any intangible assets or IAS 39 to account for its obligations for any financial liabilities etc. The requirements of IAS 28 (as amended in 2011) would not apply as an associate is defined as an 'entity over which the investor has significant influence' *[IAS 28.3 (2011)]*. and in most circumstances, a contract does not create an entity.

Separate vehicle: Some may initially consider that if an entity concludes it does not have control or joint control over an arrangement within a separate vehicle, that IAS 28 (as amended in 2011) may apply (assuming that their percentage interest in the arrangement provided them with significant influence). However, similar to the situation discussed above regarding control, in such situations, a contract still exists which gives the parties to the arrangement rights to, and obligations for, the underlying assets and liabilities of that arrangement. These rights and obligations should be accounted for first. That is, each party to the arrangement would recognise its respective share of the assets and liabilities (applying each IFRS as appropriate e.g. IAS 16, IAS 38, IAS 39 etc.).

The above analysis demonstrates that where parties to an arrangement genuinely have rights to, and obligations for, the underlying assets and liabilities of the arrangement, concluding that an operator has neither control nor joint control over the arrangement does not change the accounting for that party.

- *Rights to the net assets of the arrangement:* Again, as noted above, the IASB acknowledged that rights to the net assets of an arrangement would be more likely to only arise where the arrangement is structured through a separate vehicle. In this instance, if the party is considered to have significant influence over the arrangement, it accounts for its interest in accordance with IAS 28 – *Investments in Associates and Joint Ventures* (as amended in 2011) – equity accounting; otherwise it accounts for its interest under IAS 32/IAS 39/IFRS 9 – fair value through profit or loss or other comprehensive income (unless the investment was held for trading).

4.3.4.E Summary

Given the unique nature of the various arrangements that currently exist, and are emerging, in the extractive industries, an entity will need to individually analyse each contract to be able to complete this assessment. The difficulty of this task will be impacted by the number and complexity of the arrangements an entity has. Robust systems and processes will need to be developed, not only to complete the initial assessment, but also to enable the ongoing assessment of current arrangements (should facts and circumstances change) and the assessment of new arrangements.

4.3.5 Investments in associates

An investor should apply the equity method in accounting for investments in associates, which are entities over which the investor can exercise significant influence (i.e. the investor has the power to participate in the financial and operating policy decisions of the investee but it does not have control or joint control over those policies). *[IAS 28.2]*. Significant influence is deemed to exist under IFRS when an investor holds between 20% and 50% of the voting rights in an investee. However, significant influence may also exist in limited circumstances when the investor holds an interest of less than 20% or more than 50% (see Chapter 12 at 2.2.1.B and 2.2.1.C). Finally, some arrangements that are aimed at establishing joint control over an entity do not always meet the definition of a joint venture under IAS 31. Those types of arrangement will, however, often give rise to significant influence and, therefore, the requirement to account for the investment as an associate.

4.3.6 Investments in financial assets

Small investments in the equity instruments of an entity over which the investor cannot exercise control, joint control or significant influence meet the definition of a financial asset under IAS 32. If the investor is not only exposed to credit risk, such investments do not meet the definition of 'loans and receivables' under IAS 39 and should, instead, be classified as either 'at fair value through profit or loss' or 'available for sale' *[IAS 39.9]*. or 'fair value' under IFRS 9. *[IFRS 9.4.1.1]*.

4.3.7 Investments in undivided interests

Undivided interests are usually subject to joint control (see Chapter 13 at 2.2) and can, therefore, be accounted for as jointly controlled assets. However, some joint operating agreements (JOAs) do not establish joint control but are, instead, based on some form of supermajority voting whereby a qualified majority (e.g. 75%) of the venturers can approve decisions. This situation usually arises when the group of venturers is too large for joint control to be practical or when the main investor wants to retain a certain level of influence.

Such undivided interests cannot be accounted for as jointly controlled assets in the absence of joint control. The appropriate accounting treatment depends on the nature of the arrangement:

- If the investor is entitled to use the underlying asset then the arrangement should be accounted for as a tangible or intangible asset under IAS 16 or IAS 38, respectively. The investor's proportionate share of the operating costs of the asset (e.g. repairs and maintenance) should be accounted for in the same way as the operating costs of wholly owned assets; or

- If the investor is entitled only to a proportion of the cash flows generated by the asset then its investment will generally meet the definition of a financial asset under IAS 32. As the investor is not exposed only to credit risk, such investments do not meet the definition of 'loans and receivables' under IAS 39 and should, instead, be classified as either 'at fair value through profit or loss' or 'available for sale' *[IAS 39.9]*. or 'fair value' under IFRS 9. *[IFRS 9.4.1.1]*.

4.3.8   Operators of joint ventures

A joint venture agreement may identify one venturer as the operator or manager of the joint venture. An operator does not control the joint venture but acts within the financial and operating policies agreed by the venturers in accordance with the contractual arrangement and delegated to the operator. However, if an entity described as an 'operator' has the power to govern (i.e. not merely to execute) the financial and operating policies of the economic activity then it controls the venture and it should consolidate the venture as a subsidiary. *[IAS 31.12]*.

See also 4.3.3 and 4.3.4 for discussion of the impact of IFRS 11, the new joint arrangements standard.

4.3.8.A   Reimbursements of costs

An operator often carries out activities on behalf of the joint venture on a no gain / no loss basis. Generally these activities can be identified separately and are carried out by the operator in its capacity as an agent for the joint venture, which is the principal in those transactions. The operator receives reimbursement of direct costs recharged to the joint venture. Such recharges are reimbursements of costs that the operator incurred as an agent for the joint venture and therefore have no effect on profit or loss in the statement of comprehensive income (or income statement).

In many cases an operator also incurs certain general overhead expenses in carrying out activities on behalf of the joint venture. As these costs can often not be specifically identified, many joint venture agreements allow the operator to recover the general overhead expenses incurred by charging an overhead fee that is based on a fixed percentage of the total costs incurred for the year. Although the purpose of this recharge is very similar to the reimbursement of direct costs, the operator is not acting as an agent in this case. Therefore, the operator should recognise the general overhead expenses and the overhead fee in profit or loss in its statement of comprehensive income (or income statement) as an expense and income, respectively.

4.3.8.B   Direct legal liability

The operator of a joint venture may have a direct legal liability to third party creditors in respect of the entire balance arising from transactions related to the joint venture.[132] IFRS prohibits offsetting of such liabilities against the amounts recoverable from the other joint venturers. *[IAS 1.32, IAS 32.42]*. The operator may therefore need to disclose, for example, some of the leases that it has entered into on behalf of the joint venture, if entered into in its own name.

4.4   Acquisitions

4.4.1   Business combinations versus asset acquisitions

When an entity acquires an asset or a group of assets, careful analysis is required to identify whether what is acquired constitutes a business or represents only an asset or group of assets (see 4.4.1.A below). The accounting for purchases of assets is discussed at 4.4.1.B below, while the main differences between accounting for an asset purchase and a business combination are discussed at 4.4.1.C below. Accounting for business combinations is discussed in detail in Chapter 10.

4.4.1.A   Definition of a 'business'

A business is defined in IFRS 3 – *Business Combinations* – as 'an integrated set of activities and assets that is capable of being conducted and managed for the purpose of providing a return in the form of dividends, lower costs or other economic benefits directly to investors or other owners, members or participants.' *[IFRS 3 Appendix A]*. The main modifications compared to the IFRS 3 (2007) are that IFRS 3: *[IFRS 3.BC18]*

- requires the integrated set of activities and assets to be 'capable' of being conducted and managed for the purpose of providing a return in the form of dividends, lower costs or other economic benefits directly to investors or other owners, members or participants. The focus on the capability to achieve the purposes of the business helps avoid the unduly restrictive interpretations that existed under the former guidance;

- clarifies the meanings of the terms 'inputs', 'processes' and 'outputs', which helps eliminate the need for extensive detailed guidance and the misinterpretations that sometimes stem from such guidance;

- clarifies that inputs and processes applied to those inputs are essential and that although the resulting outputs are normally present, they need not be present; and

- clarifies that a business need not include all of the inputs or processes that the seller used in operating that business if a market participant is capable of continuing to produce outputs, which helps avoid the need for extensive detailed guidance and assessments about whether a missing input or process is minor.

In summary, the definition of a business in IFRS 3 may include 'integrated sets of activities' that were previously not considered to be businesses. The definition of a business under IFRS 3 is discussed in more detail in Chapter 10 at 3.2.

Determining whether a particular set of integrated activities and assets is a business will often require a significant amount of judgement as illustrated in Example 41.7 below.

Example 41.7:   Definition of a business under IFRS 3

Oil and gas company C acquires a single oil exploration area where oil has been found but implementation of the development plan has not yet commenced.

This may be a business under IFRS 3 if a market participant is capable of producing outputs by integrating that input with its own inputs and processes.

Mining company D acquires a development stage mine, including all inputs (i.e. employees, mineral reserve and property, plant and equipment) and processes (i.e. exploration and evaluation processes e.g. active drilling programmes etc.,) that are required to generate output.

This meets the definition of a business under IFRS 3 because it includes inputs, processes and outputs.

Oil and gas company E acquires a group of pipelines (or a fleet of oil or gas tankers) used for transporting gas on behalf of customers and the employees responsible for operational, maintenance and administrative tasks transfer to the buyer.

This meets the definition of a business under IFRS 3 because it includes inputs, processes and outputs.

Mining company F acquires a mine that was abandoned 10 years ago. It plans to perform new geological and geophysical survey to determine whether sufficient economic reserves are present.

The abandoned mine does not meet the definition of a business because there are no processes associated with the assets purchased.

Oil and gas company G acquires a producing oil field, but the seller's on-site staff will *not* transfer to the buyer. Instead, oil and gas company G will enter into maintenance and oil field services contracts with different contractors.

A business need not include all of the inputs or processes that the seller used in operating that business if market participants are capable of continuing to produce outputs. If market participants can easily outsource processes to contractors then the oil field would be a business under IFRS 3.

The definition of a business under IFRS 3 is broader than under IFRS 3 (2007) because an integrated set of activities and assets:

- only needs to be 'capable' of being run as a business,
- is not required to have any outputs, and
- does not need all of the inputs and processes that the seller used,

in order to qualify as a business.

4.4.1.B   Asset purchase transactions

The acquisition of an asset, group of assets or an entity that does not constitute a business is not a business combination. In such cases the acquirer should identify and recognise the individual identifiable assets acquired and liabilities assumed. The cost of the acquisition should be allocated to the individual identifiable assets and liabilities on the basis of their relative fair values at the date of purchase. Such a transaction or event does not give rise to goodwill. *[IFRS 3.2(b)].*

Any difference between the carrying amount of the assets and liabilities thus recognised and their tax base would not give rise to a recognised deferred tax asset or liability under IAS 12 – *Income Taxes* – as it would fall within the initial recognition exemption under that standard (see Chapter 31 at 7.2). *[IAS 12.15, 24].*

4.4.1.C   Differences between asset purchase transactions and business combinations

The main differences between accounting for an asset purchase and a business combination can be summarised as follows:

- goodwill or a bargain purchase (previously referred to as negative goodwill) only arises in business combinations;

- assets and liabilities are accounted for at fair value in a business combination, while they are assigned a carrying amount based on their relative fair values in an asset purchase transaction;

- transaction costs should be recognised as an expense under IFRS 3, but can be capitalised on an asset acquisition; and

- in an asset purchase transaction no deferred tax will arise in relation to acquired assets and assumed liabilities as the initial recognition exemption for deferred tax under IAS 12 applies.

4.4.1.D   Acquisition of an interest in a jointly controlled entity that constitutes a business

There are divergent views as to manner in which to account for the acquisition of an interest in a jointly controlled entity (JCE) that represents a business. IFRS 3 specifically excludes the formation of a joint venture from the scope of the standard. *[IFRS 3.2(a)].*

The issue is not specifically addressed in IFRS, and the following considerations have been proposed to deal with the issue:

- IFRS 3 considers the acquisition of a business, and hence should be applied by analogy to the acquisition of an interest in a JCE, where such a joint venture constitutes a business. Such an accounting policy would need to be developed by applying the hierarchy in IAS 8. *[IFRS 8.10)].* However, IFRS 3 only applies to situations where control is exerted over a business – when in the case of a JCE, only joint control is achieved. Albeit that control is not obtained, IAS 28 does include the principles of the acquisition method for the purposes of equity accounting an investment in an associate (i.e. only when significant influence is achieved). *[IAS 28.23].*

- IAS 31 provides some guidance regarding the contribution of assets to a JCE *[IAS 31.48],* but this guidance is open to interpretation and deals with contributions rather than acquisitions.

- SIC-13, which is specifically applicable to contributions of non-monetary assets to JCE, does provide some analogous guidance but again, is not directly applicable to such an acquisition.

Chapter 13 at 5.6.2 considers the issue of whether the acquisition of an interest in a JCE, when applying proportionate consolidation, should be aligned to the principles of IFRS 3. For the reasons provided in Chapter 13, we believe that it would be more appropriate to apply the 'fair value' principles in IFRS 3 when acquiring such a jointly controlled interest in a business.

4.4.1.E   Acquisition of an interest in a jointly controlled asset or jointly controlled operation (IAS 31), or joint operation (IFRS 11) that constitutes a business

One area where there is currently a lack of clarity when accounting for acquisitions of interests in jointly controlled assets (JCAs) and jointly controlled operations (JCOs), and which, unless resolved, will present similar issues for joint operations under IFRS 11, is whether IFRS 3 applies. See 4.3.4.B above for further discussion on this.

4.4.2   Business combinations

4.4.2.A   Goodwill in business combinations

Traditionally, many mining companies and oil and gas companies assumed that the entire consideration paid for upstream assets should be allocated to the identifiable net assets acquired, i.e. any excess over the fair value would be included within mineral reserves acquired. However, goodwill could arise as a result of synergies, overpayment by the acquirer, or when IFRS requires that acquired assets and/or liabilities are measured at an amount that is not fair value (e.g. deferred taxation). Therefore it is not appropriate for mining companies or oil and gas companies to simply assume that, under IFRS, goodwill never arises in a business combination. Instead, mineral reserves acquired should be valued separately and any excess consideration over and above the value of the identifiable net assets (which include mineral reserves), should be allocated to goodwill.

Under IFRS, an entity is required to provide for deferred taxation on the temporary differences relating to all identifiable net assets acquired (including mineral reserves), but not on temporary differences related to goodwill. Therefore, if the excess of the consideration transferred over the fair value of the identifiable assets were to be classified within mineral reserves, IAS 12 would give rise to a deferred tax liability on the temporary difference. In principle, that would result in an iterative calculation in which the deferred tax liability recognised would increase the amount attributed to mineral reserves, which would in turn give rise to an increase in the deferred tax liability (see Chapter 31 at 7.2.2). Given the very high marginal tax rates to which extractive activities are often subject (i.e. tax rates of 60 to 80% are not uncommon) the mineral reserves might end up being grossed up by a factor of 2.5 to 5 (i.e. $1/(1 - 60\%) = 2.5$). This issue would not arise if the recognition of the deferred tax liability were offset by the recognition of goodwill.

The extract below from Xstrata illustrates a typical accounting policy for business combinations in which excess consideration transferred is treated as goodwill.

Extract 41.12: Xstrata plc (2010)

Notes to the financial statements [extract]

6. Principal accounting policies [extract]

Business combinations

On the acquisition of a subsidiary, the acquisition method of accounting is used, whereby the purchase consideration is allocated to the identifiable assets, liabilities and contingent liabilities (identifiable net assets) on the basis of fair value at the date of acquisition. Those mining rights, mineral reserves and resources that are able to be reliably valued are recognised in the assessment of fair values on acquisition. Other potential reserves, resources and mineral rights, for which in the Directors' opinion values cannot be reliably determined, are not recognised. Acquisition costs are expensed.

When the cost of acquisition exceeds the fair values attributable to the Group's share of the identifiable net assets, the difference is treated as purchased goodwill, which is not amortised but is reviewed for impairment annually or where there is an indication of impairment. If the fair value attributable to the Group's share of the identifiable net assets exceeds the cost of acquisition, the difference is immediately recognised in the income statement.

Non-controlling interests represent the portion of profit or loss and net assets in subsidiaries that are not held by the Group and are presented in equity in the consolidated balance sheet, separately from the parent's shareholders' equity.

[...]

Similar procedures are applied in accounting for the purchases of interests in associates. Any goodwill arising on such purchases is included within the carrying amount of the investment in the associates, but not thereafter amortised. Any excess of the Group's share of the net fair value of the associate's identifiable assets, liabilities and contingent liabilities over the cost of the investment is included in income in the period of the purchase.

4.4.2.B Impairment of assets and goodwill recognised on acquisition

There are a number of circumstances in which the fair value of assets or goodwill acquired as part of a business combination and as recorded in the consolidated accounts, may be measured at a higher amount through recognition of deferred tax or notional tax benefits. Application of IAS 36 to goodwill which arises upon recognition of deferred tax liabilities in a business combination is discussed in Chapter 22 at 5.4.1.

4.4.2.C Value beyond proven and probable reserves (VBPP)

In the mining industry, the value beyond proven and probable reserves (VBPP) is the economic value of the estimated cash flows of a mining asset beyond that asset's proven and probable reserves. IFRS 3 requires that an acquirer recognises the identifiable assets acquired and liabilities assumed that meet the definitions of assets and liabilities at the acquisition date. *[IFRS 3.11]*.

While the legal or contractual rights that allow an entity to extract minerals are not themselves tangible assets, the mineral reserves concerned clearly are. Under IFRS, mineral reserves are to be treated as tangible assets. The legal or contractual rights – that allow an entity to extract mineral reserves – acquired in business combinations should be recognised, without exception, at fair value.

There are various situations in which mineralisation and mineral resources might not be classified as proven or probable:

- prior to the quantification of a resource, a mining company may identify mineralisation following exploration activities. However, it may be too early to assess if the geology and grade is sufficiently expansive to meet the definition of a resource;

- Acquired Exploration Potential (AEP) represents the legal right to explore for minerals in a particular property, occurring in the same geological area of interest;

- carrying out the required assessments and studies to obtain classification of mineral reserves can be very costly. Consequently, these activities are often deferred until they become necessary for the planning of future operations. Significant mineral resources are often awaiting the initiation of this process; and

- if an entity acquires a mining company at a time when commodity prices are particularly low, the mineral resources owned by the acquiree may not meet the definition of proven or probable reserves because extraction might not be commercially viable.

While the above types of mineralisation and mineral resources cannot be classified as proven or probable, they will often be valuable because of the future potential that they represent (i.e. reserves may be proven in the future and commodity prices may make extraction commercially feasible).

An entity that acquires mineral reserves and resources that cannot be classified as proven or probable, should account for the VBPP as part of the value allocated to mining assets, to the extent that a market participant would include VBPP in determining the fair value of the asset, under IFRS rather than as goodwill.[133] Acquired exploration potential, however, would often be indistinguishable from the value of the mineral license to which it relates and would, therefore, need to be accounted for as an intangible asset.

Determining the fair value of VBPP requires a considerable amount of expertise. An entity should not only take account of commodity spot prices but also consider the effects of anticipated fluctuations in the future price of minerals, in a manner that is consistent with the expectations of a market participant. Generally, an entity should consider all available information including current prices, historical averages, and forward pricing curves. Those market participant assumptions typically should be consistent with the acquiring entity's operating plans for developing and producing minerals. The potential upside associated with mineral resources that are not classified as reserves can be much larger than the downward risk. A valuation model that only takes account of a single factor, such as the spot price, historical average or a single long-term price, without considering other information that a market participant would consider, would generally not be able to reflect the upward potential that determines much of the value of VBPP. Consequently, an entity may need to apply option valuation techniques in measuring VBPP.

The CRIRSCO reporting standards consider the geological definition of mineral resources that have not yet been tested for economic viability. Valuation techniques used include:

- Probability weighted discounted-cash flows
- Resource reserve conversion adjustment
- Comparable transactions
- Option valuation.

In relation to early mineralisation, while it may represent a discovery, its true value will be determined by further appraisal activities to confirm whether a resource exists. This stage of VBPP is often grouped with the next stage (even though it has a higher intrinsic value) and is valued using:

- Cost based methods
- Budgeted expenditure methods
- Comparable sales
- Farm in/out values
- Sophisticated option pricing.

In relation to AEP, which is the final category of VBPP, the basis for valuing it varies from studying historic cost to the use of sophisticated option valuation techniques.

As VBPP does not provide current economic benefits, there is no need to allocate its cost against current revenue and hence no need for amortisation or depreciation. However, VBPP would need to be tested for impairment under IAS 36 if there is, depending the classification of VBPP, an indicator of impairment under that standard or IFRS 6. The VBPP may ultimately be impaired because it may never be converted into proven or probable reserves, but impairment may not be confirmed until the entity is satisfied that the project will not continue.

An impairment of VBPP should be recognised if its book value exceeds the higher of: (1) fair value less cost to sell and (2) value in use. In practice, there may not be a convenient method to determine the value in use. Hence, impairment testing will often need to rely on a fair value based approach.

Extract 41.13 below illustrates that AngloGold Ashanti does not include the 'value beyond proven and probable reserves' within goodwill.

Chapter 41

Extract 41.13: AngloGold Ashanti Limited (2010)

Notes to the financial statements [extract]

1 Accounting Policies [extract]

1.3 Summary of significant accounting policies [extract]

Intangible assets [extract]

Acquisition and goodwill arising thereon

Where an investment in a subsidiary, joint venture or an associate is made, any excess of the consideration transferred over the fair value of the attributable Mineral Resource including value beyond proved and probable, exploration properties and net assets is recognised as goodwill. Goodwill in respect of subsidiaries is disclosed as goodwill. Goodwill relating to equity accounted joint ventures and associates is included within the carrying value of the investment and tested for impairment when indicators exist.

4.4.3   Asset acquisitions

4.4.3.A   Conditional purchase consideration

IFRS defines cost as 'the amount of cash or cash equivalents paid or the fair value of the other consideration given to acquire an asset at the time of its acquisition or construction or, where applicable, the amount attributed to that asset when initially recognised in accordance with the specific requirements of other IFRSs, e.g. IFRS 2 *Share-based Payment*'. *[IAS 16.6, IAS 38.8, IAS 40.5]*. In other words, under IFRS cost does not include the subsequent revision of the purchase price of an asset or group of assets.

These requirements sometimes give rise to issues in situations where the purchase price is conditional upon certain events or facts. These issues can best be illustrated by an example.

Example 41.8:   Asset acquisitions with a conditional purchase price

Scenario 1

Entity A agrees to buy a group of assets from entity B for a total purchase price of $15 million. However, the purchase contract provides a formula for adjusting the purchase price upward or downward based on the report of a surveyor on the existence and quality of the assets listed in the contract.

Scenario 2

Entity C agrees to buy an exploration license and several related assets from entity D for a total purchase price of $35 million. However, Entity C would only be allowed to extract minerals in excess of 20 million barrels (or tonnes), upon payment of an additional consideration transferred of $12 million.

In scenario 1, entity A would be required to account for the fair value of the consideration transferred as determined at the date of acquisition. In contrast to the treatment under IFRS 3, there is no purchase price allocation or measurement period under IAS 16. However, suppose that three weeks after the initial accounting the surveyor reports that at the date of acquisition a number of assets listed in the contract were not present or were of inferior quality, the purchase price is therefore adjusted downward to $14.5 million. Rather than recognising a profit arising from this adjustment, the entity should adjust the cost of the asset as the surveyor's report provides evidence of conditions that existed at the date of acquisition. *[IAS 10.3(a)]*.

In scenario 2 above, entity C pays an additional $12 million in exchange for the right to extract minerals in excess of 20 million barrels (or tonnes) agreed upon in the initial transaction. At the date that entity C purchases the additional rights it accounts for an additional asset acquisition. In more complicated scenarios it might be necessary, though, to assess whether the first and second acquisition should be accounted for together.

It is clear from the above two scenarios that changes in the facts and circumstances can have a significant effect on the accounting for conditional purchase consideration.

The issue of conditional purchase consideration in relation to the acquisition of property, plant and equipment was recently referred to the Interpretations Committee. It was considered that there was considerable divergence in practice. However, the Committee decided to defer further work on this project until the IASB concludes its discussions on the accounting for the liability for variable payments as part of the leases project.

4.5   Depreciation, depletion and amortisation (DD&A)

4.5.1   *Requirements under IFRS*

The main types of depreciable assets of mining companies and oil and gas companies are property, plant and equipment, intangible assets and mineral reserves, although the exact titles given to these types of assets may vary. The different accounting standards that apply to each of these types of assets are discussed below.

4.5.1.A   *Property, plant and equipment*

Property, plant and equipment (PP&E) used in the extraction of mineral reserves fall within the scope of IAS 16. *[IAS 16.2, 3].* Various descriptions are used for such assets as well as PP&E, e.g. producing mines, mine assets, oil and gas assets, producing properties. Whatever the description given, IAS 16 requires depreciation of an item of property, plant and equipment over its useful life, which it defines as '(a) the period over which an asset is expected to be available for use by an entity; or (b) the number of production or similar units expected to be obtained from the asset by an entity'. *[IAS 16.6].* The depreciation method used should reflect the pattern in which the asset's future economic benefits are expected to be consumed by the entity. *[IAS 16.60].* IAS 16 permits a variety of depreciation methods, such as the straight-line method, the diminishing balance method and the units of production method. *[IAS 16.62].* An entity is required to review the depreciation method 'at least at each financial year-end and, if there has been a significant change in the expected pattern of consumption of the future economic benefits embodied in the asset, the method shall be changed to reflect the changed pattern'. *[IAS 16.61].* It is most common for assets with a life shorter than the expiration of reserves to be depreciated over the period they are available for use. All other assets are usually depreciated using the units of production method to a residual value expected at the conclusion of production.

4.5.1.B   *Intangible assets*

While 'mineral rights and expenditure on the exploration for, or development and extraction of, minerals, oil, natural gas and similar non-regenerative resources' are outside the scope of IAS 38, any other intangible assets that are used in the extraction of mineral reserves should be accounted for under IAS 38. *[IAS 38.2]*. That standard requires amortisation of an intangible asset over its useful life, which it defines as '(a) the period over which an asset is expected to be available for use by an entity; or (b) the number of production or similar units expected to be obtained from the asset by an entity'. *[IAS 38.8]*. The amortisation method used should reflect the pattern in which the asset's future economic benefits are expected to be consumed by the entity. *[IAS 38.97]*. An entity is required to review the depreciation method 'at least at each financial year-end. If there has been a change in the expected pattern of consumption of the future economic benefits embodied in the asset, the amortisation method shall be changed to reflect the changed pattern.' *[IAS 38.104]*.

IAS 38 permits a variety of amortisation methods, such as the straight-line method, the diminishing balance method and the unit-of-production method, but requires an entity to select the method on the basis of the expected pattern of consumption of the expected future economic benefits embodied in the asset. *[IAS 38.98]*. In May 2008, the final sentence of paragraph 98 of IAS 38 (2007) was deleted; this had stated that 'there is rarely, if ever, persuasive evidence to support an amortisation method for intangible assets with finite useful lives that results in a lower amount of accumulated amortisation than under the straight-line method'. The Board considered that 'using the straight-line method could be inconsistent with the general requirement of paragraph 38 that the amortisation method should reflect the expected pattern of consumption of the expected future economic benefits embodied in an intangible asset'. *[IAS 38.98, BC72A]*.

4.5.1.C   *Mineral reserves*

As discussed at 4.5.1.A and 4.5.1.B above, mineral reserves are outside the scope of IAS 16 and IAS 38. In the absence of a standard or an interpretation specifically applicable to mineral reserves, management needs to develop an accounting policy for mineral reserves in accordance with the hierarchy in IAS 8, taking into account '(a) the requirements and guidance in Standards and Interpretations dealing with similar and related issues; and (b) the definitions, recognition criteria and measurement concepts for assets, liabilities, income and expenses in the Framework'. *[IAS 8.11]*. In practice, an entity will therefore develop an accounting policy that is based on the principles underlying IAS 16 and IAS 38, which deal with similar and related issues. The units of production method is the most common method applied for producing assets.

4.5.1.D   *Unit of account*

As discussed at 4.2 above, an entity needs to exercise judgement in selecting the unit of account that is to be used for the purposes of calculating depreciation, depletion and amortisation (DD&A). Under IAS 16, an entity should calculate depreciation separately for each part of an item of property, plant and equipment with a cost that is significant in relation to the total cost of the item, unless the item can be grouped with other items of property, plant and equipment that have the same useful life and depreciation method. *[IAS 16.43, 45]*. The remainder of an asset that has not been separately identified into parts may consist of other parts that are individually not significant and the entity may need to use approximation techniques to calculate an appropriate depreciation method for all of these parts. *[IAS 16.46]*.

Although the above guidance from IAS 16 does not apply directly to intangible assets or mineral rights, we believe that entities should take the underlying principles into account in determining the appropriate unit of account for those types of assets as well. Furthermore, we would expect an entity to take into account the general principles for determining an appropriate unit of account that are outlined at 4.2.1 above.

4.5.1.E   Practical issues

There are a number of practical issues that arise in selecting and applying an accounting policy for the DD&A of property, plant and equipment, mineral reserves and intangible assets, respectively, which are discussed at 4.5.2 and 4.5.3 below.

4.5.2   Straight-line method

The straight-line method of depreciation is generally preferred in accounting for the depreciation of property, plant and equipment. The main practical advantages of the straight-line method are considered to be its simplicity and the fact that its results are often not materially different from the units of production method if annual production is relatively constant.[134] In general the straight-line method is considered to be preferable for:

- assets whose loss in value is more closely linked to the passage of time than to the quantities of minerals produced (e.g. front-end loaders that are used in stripping overburden and production of minerals);

- assets that are unrelated to production and that are separable from the field or mine (e.g. office buildings);

- assets with a useful life that is either much longer (e.g. offshore platforms) or much shorter (e.g. drill jumbos) than that of the field or mine in which they are used;

- assets used in fields or mines whose annual production is relatively constant. However, if assets are used in fields or mines that are expected to suffer extended outages, due to weather conditions or periodic repairs and maintenance, then the straight-line method may be less appropriate; and

- assets that are used in more than one field or mine (e.g. service trucks).

Finally, if the production of a field or mine drops significantly towards the end of its productive life, then straight-line method may result in a relatively high depreciation charge per units of production. In those cases, an entity may need to perform an impairment test on the assets involved.

The extract below indicates the assets to which BHP Billiton applies the straight-line method.

Chapter 41

Extract 41.14: BHP Billiton Group (2010)

NOTES TO FINANCIAL STATEMENTS [extract]

1 Accounting policies [extract]

Depreciation of property, plant and equipment

The carrying amounts of property, plant and equipment (including initial and any subsequent capital expenditure) are depreciated to their estimated residual value over the estimated useful lives of the specific assets concerned, or the estimated life of the associated mine, field or lease, if shorter. Estimates of residual values and useful lives are reassessed annually and any change in estimate is taken into account in the determination of remaining depreciation charges. Depreciation commences on the date of commissioning. The major categories of property, plant and equipment are depreciated on a unit of production and/or straight-line basis using estimated lives indicated below. However, where assets are dedicated to a mine, field or lease and are not readily transferable, the below useful lives are subject to the lesser of the asset category's useful life and the life of the mine, field or lease:

- Buildings   – 25 to 50 years
- Land   – not depreciated
- Plant and equipment   – 3 to 30 years straight-line
- Mineral rights and petroleum   – based on reserves on a unit of production basis
  interests
- Capitalised exploration, evaluation   – based on reserves on a unit of production basis
  and development expenditure

4.5.3 *Units of production method*

'The underlying principle of the units of production method is that capitalised costs associated with a cost centre are incurred to find and develop the commercially producible reserves in that cost centre, so that each unit produced from the centre is assigned an equal amount of cost.'[135] The units of production method thereby effectively allocates an equal amount of depreciation to each unit produced, rather than an equal amount to each year as the straight-line method does.

When the level of production varies considerably over the life of a project (e.g. the production of oil fields is much higher in the periods just after the start of production than in the final periods of production), depreciation based on a units of production method will produce a more equal cost per unit from year to year than straight-line methods. Under the straight-line method the depreciation charge per unit in the early years of production could be 'much less than the depreciation per unit in later years. That factor, coupled with the fact that typically production costs per unit increase in later years, means that the profitability of operations would be distorted if the straight-line method is used, showing larger profits in early years and lower profits in later years of the mineral resource's life. The higher cost per unit in later years is, in part, due to fewer units being produced while many production costs remain fixed and, in part, a result of many variable costs per unit increasing over time because reserves may be harder to extract, there may be greater equipment repairs, and similar other factors.'[136] Nevertheless, it should be noted that even under the units of production method, profitability often drops significantly towards the end of the productive life of a field or mine. When this happens an entity will need to carry out an impairment test and may need to recognise an impairment charge (see 6.4.1 below).

In general the units of production method is considered to be preferable for:

- assets used in fields or mines whose annual production may vary considerably over their useful economic life;

- assets whose loss in value is more closely linked to the quantities of minerals produced than to the passage of time (e.g. draglines used in the extraction of mineral ore);

- assets that are used in production or that are inseparable from the field or mine (e.g. wells and well heads);

- assets with a useful life that is the same as that of the field or mine in which they are used; and

- assets that are used in only one field or mine (e.g. overland conveyor belts).

Extract 41.14 above and Extract 41.15 below indicate the classes of asset to which BHP Billiton and Lonmin, respectively, apply the units of production method.

Extract 41.15: Lonmin Plc (2010)

1 Statement on accounting policies [extract]

Intangible assets

Intangible assets, other than goodwill, acquired by the Group have finite useful lives and are measured at cost less accumulated amortisation and accumulated impairment losses. Where amortisation is charged on these assets, the expense is taken to the income statement through operating costs.

Amortisation of mineral rights is provided on a units of production basis over the remaining life of mine to residual value (20 to 40 years).

All other intangible assets are amortised over their useful economic lives subject to a maximum of 20 years and are tested for impairment at each reporting date when there is an indication of a possible impairment.

Property, plant and equipment

Recognition

Property, plant and equipment is included in the balance sheet at cost and subsequently less accumulated depreciation and any accumulated impairment losses.

Costs include expenditure that is directly attributable to the acquisition of the asset. The cost of self-constructed assets includes the cost of materials and direct labour, any other costs directly attributable to bringing the asset to a working condition for its intended use, and any other costs of dismantling and removing the items and restoring the site on which they are located. Cost may also include transfers from equity of any gain or loss on qualifying cash flow hedges of foreign currency purchases of property, plant and equipment. Borrowing costs incurred on the acquisition or construction of qualifying assets are capitalised to the cost of the asset.

Gains and losses on disposals of an item of property, plant and equipment are determined by comparing the proceeds on disposal with the carrying value of property, plant and equipment and are recognised net in the income statement.

Componentisation

When significant parts of an item of property, plant and equipment have different useful lives, they are accounted for as separate items (major components) of property, plant and equipment.

The cost of replacing part of an item of property, plant and equipment is recognised in the carrying amount of the item if it is probable that the future economic benefits embodied within the part will flow to the Group and its cost can be measured reliably. The carrying amount of the replaced part is derecognised upon replacement. The costs of the day-to-day servicing of property, plant and equipment are recognised in the income statement as incurred.

Chapter 41

Capital work in progress

Development costs are capitalised and transferred to the appropriate category of property, plant and equipment when available for use. Capitalised development costs include expenditure incurred to develop new operations and to expand existing capacity. Costs include interest capitalised during the period up to the level that the qualifying assets permit.

Depreciation

Depreciation is provided on a straight-line or units of production basis as appropriate over their expected useful lives or the remaining life of mine, if shorter, to residual value. The life of mine is based on proven and probable reserves. The expected useful lives of the major categories of property, plant and equipment are as follows:

	Method	Rate	
Shafts and underground	Units of production	2.5%-5.0% per annum	(20-40 years)
Metallurgical	Straight line	2.5%-7.1% per annum	(14-40 years)
Infrastructure	Straight line	2.5%-2.9% per annum	(35-40 years)
Other plant and equipment	Straight line	2.5%-50.0% per annum	(2-40 years)

No depreciation is provided on surface mining land which has a continuing value and capital work in progress.

Residual values and useful lives are re-assessed annually and if necessary changes are accounted for prospectively.

Rehabilitation costs

Rehabilitation costs are provided in full based on estimates of the future costs to be incurred, calculated on a discounted basis. As the provision is recognised, it is either capitalised as part of the cost of the related mine or written off to the income statement if utilised within one year. Where costs are capitalised the impact of such costs on the income statement is spread over the life of mine through the accretion of the discount of the provision and the depreciation over a units of production basis of the increased costs of the mining assets.

The practical application of the units of production method gives rise to the following issues that require entities to exercise a considerable degree of judgement in determining the:

(a)   units of production formula (see 4.5.3.A below);

(b)   reserves base (see 4.5.3.B below);

(c)   unit of measure (see 4.5.3.C below); and

(d)   joint and by-products (see 4.5.3.D below).

As discussed at 4.5.3.B I and II below, the asset base that is subject to depreciation should be consistent with the reserves base that is used, which may require an entity to exclude certain costs from (or include future investments in) the depreciation pool.

4.5.3.A   Units of production formula

There are a number of different ways in which an entity could calculate a depreciation charge under the units of production method. The most obvious of these is probably the following formula:

$$\text{Depreciation charge for the period} = \text{Current period's production} \times \frac{\text{Cost of the asset at the beginning of the period} - \text{Cumulative depreciation and impairment at the beginning of the period}}{\text{Opening reserves estimated at the beginning of the period}}$$

The reserve estimate used in the above formula is the best estimate of the reserves at the beginning of the period, but by the end of the period a revised and more accurate estimate is often available. It could therefore be argued that in order to take into account the most recent information, the opening reserves should be calculated by adding the 'closing reserves estimated at the end of the period' to the 'current period's production'. However, reserve estimates might change for a number of reasons:

(a)   more detailed knowledge about existing reserves (e.g. detailed engineering studies or drilling of additional wells);

(b)   new events that affect the physical quantity of reserves (e.g. major fire in a mine); and

(c)   changes in economic assumptions (e.g. higher commodity prices).

It is generally not appropriate to take account of these events retrospectively. For example, changes in reserves estimates that result from events that took place after the end of the reporting period (such as those under (b) and (c) at 4.5.3 above) are non-adjusting events that should be accounted for prospectively in accordance with IFRS. *[IAS 8.32-38, IAS 10.3].* Changes in reserve estimates that result from 'new information or new developments' which do not offer greater clarity concerning the conditions that existed at the end of the reporting period (such as those under (a) at 4.5.3 above) are not considered to be corrections of errors; *[IAS 8.5]* instead they are changes in accounting estimates that should be accounted for prospectively under IFRS. *[IAS 8.32-38].*

In practice, many mining and oil and gas companies take new information and new developments into account from the beginning of their current reporting period (e.g. the beginning of the current quarter for quarterly reporters or the beginning of the year for those who report only annually). However, if the reporting period is sufficiently short or the change in mineral reserves is relatively insignificant then the impact of retrospective application from the beginning of the reporting period is unlikely to be material. Determining whether these events should be treated as adjusting or non-adjusting events will depend upon the specific facts and circumstances and may require significant judgement.

Usually an entity will continue to invest during the year in assets in the depreciation pool (see 4.5.3.B below for a discussion of 'depreciation pools') that are used to extract minerals. This raises the question whether or not assets that were used for only part of the production during the period should be depreciated on a different basis. Under the straight-line method, an entity will generally calculate the depreciation of assets acquired during the period based on the assumption that they were acquired (1) at the beginning of the period, (2) in the middle of the period or (3) at the end of the period. While method (2) is often the best approximation, methods (1) and (3) are generally not materially different when the accounting period is rather short (e.g. monthly or quarterly reporting) or when the level of acquired assets is relatively low compared to the asset base.

The above considerations explain why the units of production formula that is commonly used in the extractive industries is slightly more complicated than the formula given above:

$$
\begin{array}{c}
\text{Depreciation} \\
\text{charge for} \\
\text{the period}
\end{array}
=
\begin{array}{c}
\text{Current} \\
\text{period's} \\
\text{production}
\end{array}
\times
\dfrac{
\begin{array}{c}
\text{Cost of the asset at the} \\
\text{end of the period}
\end{array}
-
\begin{array}{c}
\text{Cumulative depreciation and impairment} \\
\text{at the beginning of the period}
\end{array}
}{
\begin{array}{c}
\text{Closing reserves estimated} \\
\text{at the end of the period}
\end{array}
+
\begin{array}{c}
\text{Current period's} \\
\text{production}
\end{array}
}
$$

This units of production formula is widely used in the oil and gas industry by entities that apply US GAAP or the OIAC SORP. In the mining industry, however, both the first and the second units of production formulae are used in practice.

4.5.3.B   Reserves base

An important decision in applying the units of production method is selecting the reserves base that will be used. The following reserves bases could in theory be used:

(a)   proved developed reserves (see I below);

(b)   proved developed and undeveloped reserves (see II below);

(c)   proved and probable reserves (see III below); and

(d)   proved, probable and possible reserves.

The term 'possible reserves', which is used in the oil and gas industry, is associated with a probability of only 10% (see 2.2.1.B I above). Therefore, it is not considered acceptable to include possible reserves within the reserves base in applying the units of production method.

It is important that whatever reserves base is chosen the costs applicable to that category of reserves are included in the depreciable amount to achieve a proper matching of costs and production.[137] For example, 'if the cost centre is not fully developed ... there may be costs that do not apply, in total or in part, to proved developed reserves, which may create difficulties in matching costs and reserves. In addition, some reserve categories will require future costs to bring them to the point where production may begin.'[138]

IFRS does not provide any guidance on the selection of an appropriate reserves base or cost centre (i.e. unit of account) for the application of the units of production method. At I to III below, the relative merits for the use of each of the reserves bases listed under (a) to (c) above are discussed in detail.

I   Proved developed reserves

Under some national GAAPs that have accounting standards for the extractive industries, an entity is required to use proved developed reserves as its reserves base. An entity would therefore calculate its depreciation charge on the basis of actual costs that have been incurred to date. However, the problem often exists that the cost centre includes capitalised costs that relate to undeveloped reserves. To calculate the depreciation charge correctly, it will be necessary to exclude a portion of the capitalised costs from the depreciation calculation. Example 41.9 below, which is taken from the IASC's Issues Paper, illustrates how this might work.

Example 41.9:   Exclusion of capitalised costs relating to undeveloped reserves[139]

In an offshore oil and gas field a platform may be constructed from which 20 development wells will be drilled. The platform's cost has been capitalised as a part of the total cost of the cost centre. If only 5 of the 20 wells have been drilled, it would be inappropriate to depreciate that portion of platform costs, as well as that portion of all other capitalised costs, that are deemed to be applicable to the 15 wells not yet drilled. Only 5/20ths of the platform costs would be subject to depreciation in the current year, while 15/20ths of the platform costs (those applicable to the 15 undrilled wells) would be withheld from the depreciable amount. The costs withheld would be transferred to the depreciable amount as the additional wells are drilled. In lieu of basing the exclusion from depreciation on the number of wells, the exclusion (and subsequent transfer to depreciable amount) could be based on the quantity of reserves developed by individual wells compared with the estimated total quantity of reserves to be developed.

Similarly, to the extent that 'prospecting costs, mineral acquisition costs, exploration costs, appraisal costs, and future dismantlement, removal, and restoration costs have been capitalised, an appropriate portion of those costs, should be withheld from the depreciation calculation if proved developed reserves are used as the reserves base and if undeveloped reserves exist in the cost pool'.[140]

By withholding some of the costs from the depreciation pool, an entity is able to achieve matching of the costs incurred with the benefits of production. This is particularly important in respect of predevelopment costs, which provide future economic benefits in relation to reserves that are not yet classified as 'proved developed'.

This form of matching, which relies on selecting the appropriate 'unit of account' (see 4.2 above) for the calculation of the depreciation charge, is permitted under the IASB's *Conceptual Framework* as it does not result in the recognition of items in the statement of financial position that do not meet the definition of assets or liabilities. *[Framework.4.50].*

However, it should be noted that excluding costs from the depreciation pool may not be appropriate if (1) it is not possible to determine reliably the portion of costs to be excluded or (2) if the reserves that are not 'proved developed' are highly uncertain. Finally, it may not be necessary to exclude any costs from the depreciation pool if those costs are immaterial, which is sometimes the case in mining operations.

As illustrated in Extract 41.16, Royal Dutch Shell, in reporting under IFRS, applies the units of production method based on proved developed reserves.

Extract 41.16: Royal Dutch Shell plc (2010)

NOTES TO THE CONSOLIDATED FINANCIAL STATEMENTS [extract]

2 ACCOUNTING POLICIES [extract]

PROPERTY, PLANT AND EQUIPMENT AND INTANGIBLE ASSETS [extract]

[B] Depreciation, depletion and amortisation

Property, plant and equipment related to hydrocarbon production activities are depreciated on a unit-of-production basis over the proved developed reserves of the field concerned, except in the case of assets whose useful life differs from the lifetime of the field, in which case the straight-line method is applied. Rights and concessions are depleted on the unit-of-production basis over the total proved reserves of the relevant area. Where individually insignificant, unproved properties may be grouped and amortised based on factors such as the average concession term and past experience of recognising proved reserves.

Other property, plant and equipment are depreciated on a straight-line basis over their estimated useful lives, which is generally 30 years for upgraders, 20 years for refineries and chemical plants and 15 years for retail service station facilities. Major inspection costs are amortised over the estimated period before the next planned major inspection (three to five years). Property, plant and equipment held under finance leases are depreciated over the lease term.

Goodwill is not amortised.. Other intangible assets are amortised on a straight-line basis over their estimated useful lives which is generally five years for software and up to 40 years for other assets. Estimates of the useful lives and residual values of property, plant and equipment and intangible assets are reviewed annually and adjusted if appropriate.

II   Proved developed and undeveloped reserves

The IASC's Issues Paper noted that it could be argued that 'the choice is either to use (a) both developed and undeveloped proved reserves and add to the depreciable costs already incurred estimated future development costs applicable to proved undeveloped reserves or (b) to use proved developed reserves only and withhold from the depreciation computation those development costs applicable to reserves whose remaining development will occur in the future', but that 'it is often difficult to allocate costs that have already been incurred between developed and undeveloped reserves'.[141]

Therefore, another approach that is common under IFRS is to use 'proved developed and undeveloped reserves' as the reserves base for the application of the units of production method. This approach has the advantage that it effectively straight-lines the depreciation charge per units of production across the different phases of a project. For example, if the depreciation cost in phase 1 of the development is $24/barrel and the depreciation cost in phase 2 of the development could be $18/barrel, an entity that uses proved developed and undeveloped reserves as its reserves base might recognise depreciation of, say, $22/barrel during phase 1 and phase 2.

Application of this approach is complicated by the fact that phase 1 of the project will start production before phase 2 is completed. To apply the units of production method on the basis of proved developed and undeveloped reserves, the entity would need to forecast the remaining investment related to phase 2. The approach does not appear unreasonable at first sight, given that the proved reserves are reasonably certain to exist and 'the costs of developing the proved undeveloped reserves will be incurred in the near future in most situations, the total depreciable costs can also be estimated with a high degree of reliability'.[142] Nevertheless, the entity would therefore define its cost pool (i.e. unit of account) as including both assets that it currently owns and certain future investments. Although there is no precedent within IFRS for using such a widely defined unit of account, such an approach is not prohibited, while in practice it has gained a broad measure of acceptance within the extractive industries.

III   Proved and probable reserves

The arguments in favour of using 'proved and probable reserves' as the reserves base in applying the units of production method are similar to those discussed at II above. The IASC's Issues Paper summarised the arguments in favour of this approach as follows:

'Proponents of [using "proved and probable reserves" as the reserve base] use the same arguments given for including proved undeveloped reserves and related future costs in calculating depreciation. They point out that in a cost centre in which development has only begun a large part of capitalised prospecting, mineral acquisition, exploration, and appraisal costs may apply to probable reserves. Often in this situation there are large quantities of probable reserves, lacking only relatively minor additional exploration and/or appraisal work to be reclassified as proved reserves. They argue that, in calculating depreciation, it would be possible to defer all costs relating to the probable reserves if either proved developed reserves only, or all proved reserves, were to be used as the quantity on which depreciation is based. They contend that using probable and proved reserves in the reserve base and including in the depreciable costs any additional costs anticipated to explore and develop those reserves provides more relevant and reliable information.'[143]

The main drawbacks of this approach are that (1) estimates of probable reserves are almost certainly different from actual reserves that will ultimately be developed and (2) estimates of the costs to complete the development are likely to be incorrect because of the potentially long time scales involved.[144] Nevertheless, this approach has also found a considerable degree of acceptance under IFRS among mining companies and oil and gas companies that were permitted to apply the approach under their national GAAP before (e.g. UK GAAP). Both Tullow Oil and Anglo American apply this approach, as illustrated in Extracts 41.17 and 41.18 below.

Extract 41.17: Tullow Oil plc (2010)

Accounting policies [extract]

(k) Commercial reserves

Commercial reserves are proven and probable oil and gas reserves, which are defined as the estimated quantities of crude oil, natural gas and natural gas liquids which geological, geophysical and engineering data demonstrate with a specified degree of certainty to be recoverable in future years from known reservoirs and which are considered commercially producible. There should be a 50 per cent statistical probability that the actual quantity of recoverable reserves will be more than the amount estimated as proven and probable reserves and a 50 per cent statistical probability that it will be less.

(l) Depletion and amortisation – discovery fields [extract]

All expenditure carried within each field is amortised from the commencement of production on a unit of production basis, which is the ratio of oil and gas production in the period to the estimated quantities of commercial reserves at the end of the period plus the production in the period, generally on a field-by-field basis. Costs used in the unit of production calculation comprise the net book value of capitalised costs plus the estimated future field development costs. Changes in the estimates of commercial reserves or future field development costs are dealt with prospectively.

> **Extract 41.18: Anglo American plc (2010)**
>
> **Notes to the financial statements** [extract]
>
> **1. ACCOUNTING POLICIES** [extract]
>
> **Property, plant and equipment** [extract]
>
> Mining properties and leases include the cost of acquiring and developing mining properties and mineral rights.
>
> Mining properties are depreciated to their residual values using the unit of production method based on proven and probable ore reserves and, in certain limited circumstances, other mineral resources. Mineral resources are included in depreciation calculations where there is a high degree of confidence that they will be extracted in an economic manner. Depreciation is charged on new mining ventures from the date that the mining property is capable of commercial production. When there is little likelihood of a mineral right being exploited, or the value of the exploitable mineral right has diminished below cost, an impairment loss is recognised in the income statement.

IV   Conclusion

An entity preparing its financial statements under IFRS will need to choose between using 'proved developed reserves', 'proved developed and undeveloped reserves' and 'proved and probable reserves' as its reserves base. Each of these approaches is acceptable under IFRS. Preparers of financial statements should be aware of the difficulties that exist in ensuring that the reserves base and the costs that are being depreciated correspond. Users of financial statements need to understand that comparability between entities reporting under IFRS may sometimes be limited and need to be aware of the impact that each of the approaches has on the depreciation charge that is reported.

4.5.3.C   Unit of measure

Under the units of production method, an entity assigns an equal amount of cost to each unit produced. Determining the appropriate unit by which to measure production requires a significant amount of judgement. An entity could measure the units of production by reference to physical units or, when different minerals are produced in a common process, cost could be allocated between the different minerals on the basis of their relative sales prices.

I   Physical units of production method

If an entity uses the physical units of production method, each physical unit of reserves (such as barrels, tonnes, ounces, gallons, and cubic metres) produced is assigned a pro rata portion of undepreciated costs less residual value.

Example 41.10:   Physical units of production method[145]

If an entity produces 100 units during the current period and the estimated remaining commercial reserves at the end of the period are 1,900 units, the units available would be 2,000. The fractional part of the depreciable basis to be charged to depreciation expense would be 100/2,000. Therefore, if the depreciable basis was 5,000 monetary units, the depreciation for the period would be 250 monetary units.

In applying the physical units of production method a mining company needs to decide whether to use either (1) the quantity of ore produced or (2) the quantity of mineral contained in the ore as the unit of measure.[146] Similarly, an oil and gas company needs to decide whether to use either (1) the volume of hydrocarbons or

(2) the volume of hydrocarbons plus gas, water and other materials. When mining different grades of ore, a mining company's gross margin on the subsequent sale of minerals will fluctuate far less when it uses the quantity of minerals as its unit of measure. While a large part of the wear and tear of equipment used in mining is closely related to the quantity of ore produced, the economic benefits are more closely related to the quantity of mineral contained in the ore. Therefore, both approaches are currently considered to be acceptable under IFRS.

II   Revenue-based units of production method

Another approach in applying the units of production method is to measure the units produced based on the gross selling price of mineral.[147] Under the gross revenue approach the depreciation charge would be calculated by multiplying the depreciable cost base by:[148]

(a)   the gross revenues from sale during the period, divided by

(b)   the total of the gross revenues for the period plus the estimated future gross revenues to be derived from sale of the reserves remaining at the end of the period.

If an entity bases its forecast of future gross revenues on the average sales price for the current period, the depreciation charge calculated will be the same as that calculated using a physical unit of measure. Nevertheless, given the substantial uncertainties that surround future commodity prices, application of a revenue based units of production method will rarely be acceptable.

It is also worth noting that for similar reasons, a sales value approach was also rejected in finalising the Interpretation on accounting for the removal of waste in the production phase of a surface mine (IFRIC 20), to allocate waste removal costs between inventory and the stripping activity asset. Specifically, applying such a basis would involve practical difficulties, such as identifying a sales price for ore that will be mined in the future, particularly given the volatility of market prices for many minerals. Further complexities would also arise when more than one mineral as present (whether by-products or joint products) when the ore was extracted. See 6.2.2 for more information.

4.5.3.D   Joint and by-products

In the extractive industries it is common for more than one product to be extracted from the same reserves (e.g. copper mines often produce gold and silver, and many oil fields produce both oil and gas). When the ratio between the joint products or between the main product and the by-products is stable, this does not pose any complications. Also, if the value of the by-products is immaterial then it will often be acceptable to base the depreciation charge on the main product. In other cases, however, it will be necessary to define a unit of measure that takes into account all minerals produced. The IASC's Issues Paper listed the following approaches in defining conversion factors for calculating such a unit of measure:[149]

Chapter 41

'(a)   physical characteristics:

    (i)   based on volume: such as barrels, litres, gallons, thousand cubic feet or cubic metres;

    (ii)   based on weight: such as tonnes, pounds, and kilograms; or

    (iii)   based on energy content (British thermal units) of oil and gas;

(b)   gross revenues for the period in relation to estimated total gross revenues of the current period and future periods (more commonly seen in the mining industry); and

(c)   net revenues for the period in relation to total net revenues of the current and future periods'.

Calculation of a conversion factor based on volume or weight has the benefit of being easy to apply and can lead to satisfactory results if the relative value of the products is fairly stable. For example, some mining companies that produce both gold and silver from the same mines express their production in millions of ounces of silver equivalent, which are calculated as the sum of the ounces of silver produced plus 60 times the ounces of gold produced.

Calculation of a conversion factor based on other physical characteristics is quite common in the oil and gas industry. Typically production and reserves in oil fields are expressed in millions of barrels of oil equivalent (mmboe), which is calculated by dividing the quantity of gas expressed in thousands of cubic feet by 6 and adding that to the quantity of oil expressed in barrels. This conversion is based on the fact that one barrel of oil contains as much energy as 6,000 cubic feet of gas. While this approach is commonly used, it is important to recognise two limiting factors: (1) the actual energy conversion factor will not always be 1:6 but may vary between 1:5½ to 1:6½ and (2) the market price of gas per unit of energy (typically BTU) is often lower than that of oil because of government price controls and the need for expensive infrastructure to deliver gas to end users.

An approach that is commonly used (more so in the mining industry than the oil and gas industry) in calculating a conversion factor when joint products are extracted, is to base it on gross revenues. As discussed at 4.5.3.C above, the main drawback of this method is that it requires an entity to forecast future commodity prices. Despite this drawback, there will be situations where no other viable alternative exists for calculating an appropriate conversion factor.

Finally, it is possible to calculate a conversion factor based on net revenue after deducting certain direct processing costs. An argument in favour of this method is that gross revenues do not necessarily measure the economic benefits from an asset. However, taken to an extreme this argument would lead down a path where no depreciation is charged in unprofitable years, which is clearly not an acceptable practice.

Accounting for the sale of joint products and by-products is addressed at 6.5.3 below.

4.6 Impairment of assets

The following issues require additional attention when a mining company or oil and gas company applies the impairment testing rules under IFRS:

- impairment indicators (see 4.6.1 below);
- future capital expenditure (see 4.6.2 below);
- identifying cash-generating units (see 4.6.3 below);
- projections of cash flows (see 4.6.4 below);
- mineral reserves and resources (see 4.6.5 below);
- risk-adjusted discount rates (see 4.6.6 below);
- foreign currency cash flows (see 4.6.7 below); and
- commodity price assumptions (see 4.6.8 below).

The general requirements of IAS 36 are covered in Chapter 22.

4.6.1 Impairment indicators

As discussed at 3.5.1.A above, IFRS 6 describes a number of situations in which an entity should test E&E assets for impairment, while an entity should apply the impairment indicators in IAS 36 to assets other than E&E assets. However, the lists of impairment indicators in IFRS 6 and IAS 36 are not exhaustive. Therefore, entities operating in the extractive industries may also consider carrying out an impairment test in the following situations:[150]

- declines in prices of products or increases in production costs;
- governmental actions, such as new environmental regulations, imposition of price controls and tax increases;
- actual production levels from the cost centre or cost pool are below forecast and/or there is a downward revision in production forecasts;
- serious operational problems and accidents;
- capitalisation of large amounts of unsuccessful preproduction costs in the cost centre;
- decreases in reserve estimates;
- increases in the anticipated period over which reserves will be produced;
- substantial cost overruns during the development and construction phases of a field or mine; and
- adverse drilling results.

The extract below shows BHP Billiton's accounting policy for impairment testing.

Extract 41.19: BHP Billiton Group (2010)

NOTES TO FINANCIAL STATEMENTS [extract]

1. Accounting policies [extract]
Exploration and evaluation expenditure [extract]

Capitalised exploration and evaluation expenditure considered to be tangible is recorded as a component of property, plant and equipment at cost less impairment charges. Otherwise, it is recorded as an intangible asset (such as licences). As the asset is not available for use, it is not depreciated. All capitalised exploration and evaluation expenditure is monitored for indications of impairment. Where a potential impairment is indicated, assessment is performed for each area of interest in conjunction with the group of operating assets (representing a cash generating unit) to which the exploration is attributed. Exploration areas at which reserves have been discovered but that require major capital expenditure before production can begin are continually evaluated to ensure that commercial quantities of reserves exist or to ensure that additional exploration work is under way or planned. To the extent that capitalised expenditure is not expected to be recovered it is charged to the income statement.

Impairment of non-current assets

Formal impairment tests are carried out annually for goodwill. Formal impairment tests for all other assets are performed when there is an indication of impairment. The Group conducts annually an internal review of asset values which is used as a source of information to assess for any indications of impairment. External factors, such as changes in expected future prices, costs and other market factors are also monitored to assess for indications of impairment. If any such indication exists an estimate of the asset's recoverable amount is calculated, being the higher of fair value less direct costs to sell and the asset's value in use.

If the carrying amount of the asset exceeds its recoverable amount, the asset is impaired and an impairment loss is charged to the income statement so as to reduce the carrying amount in the balance sheet to its recoverable amount.

Fair value is determined as the amount that would be obtained from the sale of the asset in an arm's length transaction between knowledgeable and willing parties. Fair value for mineral assets is generally determined as the present value of the estimated future cash flows expected to arise from the continued use of the asset, including any expansion prospects, and its eventual disposal, using assumptions that an independent market participant may take into account. These cash flows are discounted by an appropriate discount rate to arrive at a net present value of the asset.

Value in use is determined as the present value of the estimated future cash flows expected to arise from the continued use of the asset in its present form and its eventual disposal. Value in use is determined by applying assumptions specific to the Group's continued use and cannot take into account future development. These assumptions are different to those used in calculating fair value and consequently the value in use calculation is likely to give a different result (usually lower) to a fair value calculation.

In testing for indications of impairment and performing impairment calculations, assets are considered as collective groups and referred to as cash generating units. Cash generating units are the smallest identifiable group of assets, liabilities and associated goodwill that generate cash inflows that are largely independent of the cash inflows from other assets or groups of assets.

The impairment assessments are based on a range of estimates and assumptions, including:

Estimates/assumptions:	Basis:
Future production	Proved and probable reserves, resource estimates and, in certain cases, expansion projects
Commodity prices	Forward market and contract prices, and longer-term price protocol estimates
Exchange rates	Current (forward) market exchange rates
Discount rates	Cost of capital risk-adjusted appropriate to the resource

4.6.2   Future capital expenditure

IAS 36 defines recoverable amount as the higher of 'value in use' and 'fair value less costs to sell'. Value in use is determined using a discounted cash flow method. Although the standard permits an entity to take account of cash outflows required to make an asset ready for use, *[IAS 36.42]*, it does not allow inclusion of cash outflows relating to future enhancements of an asset's performance or capacity to which an entity is not committed. *[IAS 36.44]*. This may have a significant impact on relatively new assets and on fields or mines that will be developed over time. There are no such restrictions when determining fair value provided that it can be demonstrated that a potential buyer would be willing to attribute some value to the future enhancement. Therefore, many entities calculate the fair value of their assets using a discounted cash flow approach, as illustrated in Extract 41.19 above. The treatment of future capital expenditure is discussed in more detail in Chapter 22 at 4.3.1.

4.6.3   Identifying cash-generating units

An entity is required under IAS 36 to test individual assets for impairment. However, if it is not possible to estimate the recoverable amount of an individual asset then an entity should determine the recoverable amount of the cash-generating unit to which the asset belongs. *[IAS 36.66]*. A cash-generating unit is defined by the standard as the smallest identifiable group of assets that generates cash inflows that are largely independent of the cash inflows from other assets or groups of assets. *[IAS 36.6]*. In determining appropriate cash-generating units an entity will need to consider the following issues in particular:

(a)   is there an active market for intermediate products;

(b)   are there external users of the processing assets;

(c)   are there fields or mines that are operated as one 'complex' though the use of shared infrastructure; and

(d)   are there stand-alone fields or mines that operate on a portfolio basis.

These issues are discussed at 4.6.3.A to 4.6.3.D below.

4.6.3.A   Markets for intermediate products

In vertically integrated mining operations the successive stages of the mining and production process are often considered to be one cash-generating unit, as it is not possible to allocate net cash inflows to individual stages of the process. However, if there exists an active market for intermediate commodities (e.g. bauxite, alumina and aluminium) then a vertically integrated mining company needs to consider whether its smelting and refining operations are part of the same cash-generating unit as its mining operations, because under IAS 36: 'even if part or all of the output produced by an asset or a group of assets is used by other units of the entity (for example, products at an intermediate stage of a production process), this asset or group of assets forms a separate cash-generating unit if the entity could sell the output on an active market. This is because the asset or group of assets could generate cash inflows that would be largely independent of the cash inflows from other assets or groups of assets.' *[IAS 36.71, IE Example 1B]*.

4.6.3.B   External users of processing assets

When an entity is able to derive cash inflows from its processing assets (e.g. smelting or refining facilities) under tolling arrangements (see 6.6 below), this will raise the question as to whether or not those processing assets are a separate cash-generating unit. If an entity's processing assets generate significant cash inflows from arrangements with third parties then those assets are likely to be a separate cash-generating unit.

4.6.3.C   Shared infrastructure

When several fields or mines share infrastructure (e.g. pipelines, railways, ports or refining and smelting facilities) the question arises whether the fields or mines and the shared infrastructure should be treated as a single cash-generating unit. Treating the fields or mines and the shared infrastructure together is not appropriate under the following circumstances:

(a)   if the shared infrastructure is relatively insignificant it would generally not be appropriate to treat the different fields or mines as part of the same cash-generating unit;

(b)   if the fields or mines are capable of selling their product without making use of the shared infrastructure that again would indicate that they are not part of the same cash-generating unit; and

(c)   if the shared infrastructure is classified as a corporate asset, which is defined under IAS 36 as 'assets other than goodwill that contribute to the future cash flows of both the cash-generating unit under review and other cash-generating units'. *[IAS 36.6]*. In that case, the entity should apply the requirements in IAS 36 regarding corporate assets, which are discussed in Chapter 22 at 4.2.2.

However, if the conditions under (a) to (c) above do not apply then it may be appropriate to treat the fields or mines and the shared infrastructure as one cash-generating unit.

4.6.3.D   Fields or mines operated on a portfolio basis

Mining companies and oil and gas companies sometimes operate a 'portfolio' of similar fields or mines, which are completely independent from an operational point of view. However, IAS 36 includes the following illustrative example.

Example 41.11:   Single product entity [IAS 36 IE Example 1C]

Entity M produces a single product and owns plants A, B and C. Each plant is located in a different continent. A produces a component that is assembled in either B or C. The combined capacity of B and C is not fully utilised. M's products are sold worldwide from either B or C. For example, B's production can be sold in C's continent if the products can be delivered faster from B than from C. Utilisation levels of B and C depend on the allocation of sales between the two sites.

Although there is an active market for the products assembled by B and C, cash inflows for B and C depend on the allocation of production across the two sites. It is unlikely that the future cash inflows for B and C can be determined individually. Therefore, it is likely that B and C together are the smallest identifiable group of assets that generates cash inflows that are largely independent.

The same rationale could also be applied by a mining company that, for example, operates two coal mines on a portfolio basis. However, judgement needs to be exercised before concluding that it is appropriate to treat separate fields or mines as one cash-generating unit. This is particularly the case when the production costs of fields or mines differ considerably, as it may not be appropriate to combine them into one cash-generating unit, thereby avoiding recognition of an impairment charge on the higher cost fields or mines.

4.6.4 Projections of cash flows

IAS 36 requires that in calculating 'value in use' an entity base its cash flow projection on 'the most recent financial budgets/forecasts approved by management, but exclude any estimated future cash inflows or outflows expected to arise from future restructurings or from improving or enhancing the asset's performance. Projections based on these budgets/forecasts shall cover a maximum period of five years, unless a longer period can be justified.' *[IAS 36.33(b)]*. However, an entity 'may use cash flow projections based on financial budgets/forecasts over a period longer than five years if it is confident that these projections are reliable and it can demonstrate its ability, based on past experience, to forecast cash flows accurately over that longer period'. *[IAS 36.35]*.

In practice, most production or mining plans will cover a period of more than five years and hence management will typically make financial forecasts for a corresponding period. The use of such longer term forecasts, while permitted, is restricted by the requirement that an entity has shown in the past that it can forecast cash flows accurately. This restriction is more onerous than it might seem, as it implicitly requires management to demonstrate its ability to forecast commodity prices accurately – which is a rare ability indeed.

The recoverable amount of an asset or a cash-generating unit is the higher of its fair value less costs to sell and its value in use. *[IAS 36.6]*. As IAS 36 does not impose any restrictions on how an entity determines the 'fair value less cost to sell' of an asset, many entities therefore calculate the fair value using a discounted cash flow method using assumptions that a market participant could take into account. As market participants would not restrict themselves to a five-year projection horizon, it is possible to take into account cash flow forecasts exceeding five-year periods in determining the 'fair value less cost to sell' of assets. Moreover, market participants would also take into account future capital expenditures related to subsequent phases in the development of a property. As illustrated in Extract 41.19 at 4.6.1 above, BHP Billiton uses this approach in determining the fair value less cost to sell of its mineral assets.

4.6.5 Mineral reserves and resources

As discussed at 2.2.2 above, a significant amount of work is required before an entity can conclude that its mineral resources should be classified as mineral reserves. In practice, an entity may not have formally completed all of the detailed work that is required in order to designate mineral resources as mineral reserves. IAS 36 requires the cash flow projection used in calculating the 'value in use' of assets to be based on 'reasonable and supportable assumptions that represent management's best estimate of the range of economic conditions that will exist over the remaining useful life of the asset'. *[IAS 36.33(a)]*. Therefore, it may sometimes be appropriate under IAS 36 to take into account mineral resources that have not formally been designated as mineral reserves. As discussed at 4.6.6 below, an entity would need to adjust the discount rate it uses in its 'value in use' calculation for the additional risks associated with mineral resources for which the future cash flow estimates have not been adjusted. *[IAS 36.55]*.

4.6.6   Risk-adjusted discount rates

When the future cash flows have been estimated and allocated to different periods, the present value of these cash flows should then be calculated by discounting them. IAS 36 expresses this as follows:

> 'The discount rate (rates) shall be a pre-tax rate (rates) that reflect(s) current market assessments of:
>
> (a)   the time value of money; and
>
> (b)   the risks specific to the asset for which the future cash flow estimates have not been adjusted.' *[IAS 36.55]*.

This means the discount rate to be applied should be an estimate of the rate that the market would expect on an equally risky investment. The standard states:

> 'A rate that reflects current market assessments of the time value of money and the risks specific to the asset is the return that investors would require if they were to choose an investment that would generate cash flows of amounts, timing and risk profile equivalent to those that the entity expects to derive from the asset.' *[IAS 36.56]*.

The requirements of IAS 36 for determining an appropriate discount rate are discussed in detail in Chapter 22 at 4.4, while the practical issues that this gives rise to, are discussed in the following sections of Chapter 22:

- discount rates and the weighted average cost of capital (see Chapter 22 at 4.4.1);
- pre-and post-tax discount rates (see Chapter 22 at 4.4.2 and 4.4.3);
- determining pre-tax rates taking account of tax losses (see Chapter 22 at 4.4.6);
- entity-specific WACCs and different project risks within the entity (see Chapter 22 at 4.4.7);
- entity-specific WACCs and capital structure (see Chapter 22 at 4.4.8); and
- use of discount rates other than the WACC (see Chapter 22 at 4.4.9).

4.6.7   Foreign currency cash flows

An entity in the extractive industries will often sell its product in a currency that is different from the one in which it incurs its production costs (e.g. silver production may be sold in US dollars while production costs are incurred in pesos). Impairment testing under IAS 36 requires in such cases that the foreign currency cash flows should first be estimated in the currency in which they will be generated and then discounted using a discount rate appropriate for that currency. An entity should translate the present value calculated in the foreign currency using the spot exchange rate at the date of the value in use calculation. *[IAS 36.54]*. This is to avoid the problems inherent in using forward exchange rates, which are based on differential interest rates. Using such a rate would result in double-counting the time value of money, first in the discount rate and then in the forward rate. *[IAS 36.BCZ49].* However, the method requires an entity to perform, in effect, separate impairment tests for cash flows generated in different currencies but make them consistent with one another so that the combined effect is meaningful, an extremely difficult exercise. Many different factors need to be taken into account including relative inflation rates and relative interest rates as well as appropriate discount rates for the currencies in question. Because of this, the possibility for error is great and the greatest danger is understating the present value of cash outflows by using too high a discount rate. In practice, valuers may assist entities to obtain a good enough result by assuming that cash flows are generated in a single currency even though they may be received or paid in another.

4.6.8 Commodity price assumptions

Forecasting commodity prices is never straightforward, because it is not usually possible to know whether recent changes in commodity prices are a temporary aberration or the beginning of a longer-term trend. Given the long life of most mines and oil fields, an entity should not just consider price levels in, say, the past three or four years. Instead, it should consider historical price levels for longer periods and assess how these prices are influenced by changes in underlying supply and demand levels. This requires an understanding of the industry marginal cost curves to determine at which price levels competitors are forced to reduce production as this will determine long-term minimum price levels in the industry. It will also require an understanding of whether or not new low cost producers are about to enter the market. Finally, the commodity assumptions need to match the profile of the life of the mine or oil field. Spot and forward curve prices are more relevant for short-lived mines and oil fields, while long-term price assumptions are more relevant for longer life mines and oil fields.

The commodity price is a key assumption in calculating the value in use and the fair value less cost to sell of any mine or oil field. Only in the context of impairment testing of goodwill and intangible assets does IAS 36 require disclosure of:

'(i)   a description of each key assumption on which management has based its cash flow projections for the period covered by the most recent budgets/forecasts. Key assumptions are those to which the unit's (group of units') recoverable amount is most sensitive.

(ii)   a description of management's approach to determining the value(s) assigned to each key assumption, whether those value(s) reflect past experience or, if appropriate, are consistent with external sources of information, and, if not, how and why they differ from past experience or external sources of information.'[151]

In practice, considerable differences may exist between entities in their estimates of future commodity prices. Therefore, we recommend disclosure of the actual commodity prices used in calculating the value in use and the fair value less cost to sell of any mine or oil field, even though this is not specifically required by IAS 36. A possible approach to such disclosures is illustrated in the following extract from the financial statements of BP.

> **Extract 41.20: BP plc (2010)**
>
> **Notes on financial statements** [extract]
>
> **Critical accounting policies – Recoverability of asset carrying values** [extract]
>
> For oil and natural gas properties, the expected future cash flows are estimated using management's best estimate of future oil and natural gas prices and reserves volumes. Prices for oil and natural gas used for future cash flow calculations are based on market prices for the first five years and the group's long-term planning assumptions thereafter. As at 31 December 2010, the group's long-term planning assumptions were $75 per barrel for Brent and $6.50/mmBtu for Henry Hub (2009 $75 per barrel and $7.50/mmBtu). These long-term planning assumptions are subject to periodic review and modification. The estimated future level of production is based on assumptions about future commodity prices, production and development costs, field decline rates, current fiscal regimes and other factors.

The extract below illustrates a similar type of disclosure by Randgold Resources, in this case as part of the disclosures on critical accounting estimates and judgements.

> **Extract 41.21: Randgold Resources Limited (2010)**
>
> **Notes to the consolidated financial statements** [extract]
>
> **3 CRITICAL ACCOUNTING ESTIMATES AND JUDGEMENTS** [extract]
>
> **Gold price assumptions**
>
> The following gold prices were used in the mineral reserves optimisation calculations:
>
> | US$000 | 2010 | 2009 |
> |---|---|---|
> | Morila | 800 | 700 |
> | Loulo: open pit | 800 | 700 |
> | Loulo: underground | 800 | 700 |
> | Tongon | 800 | 700 |
> | Kibali | 800 | 700 |
> | Massawa | 800 | 700 |
> | Gounkoto | 800 | 700 |
>
> Changes in the gold price used could result in changes in the mineral reserve optimisation calculations. Mine modelling is a complex process and hence is it not feasible to perform sensitivities on gold price assumptions.

4.7   Events after the reporting period

4.7.1   Reserves proven after the reporting period

IAS 10 – *Events after the Reporting Period* – distinguishes between two types of events:

'(a)   those that provide evidence of conditions that existed at the end of the reporting period (adjusting events after the reporting period); and

(b)   those that are indicative of conditions that arose after the reporting period (non adjusting events after the reporting period).' *[IAS 10.3].*

This raises the question as to how an entity should deal with information regarding mineral reserves that it obtains after the end of its reporting period, but before its financial statements are authorised for issue i.e. finalised. For example, suppose that an entity concludes after the year-end that its remaining mineral reserves at that date were not 10 million barrels (or tonnes) but only 8 million barrels (or tonnes). As discussed at 4.5.3.A above, it may not always be entirely clear under IFRS whether such a change in mineral reserves should be treated as an adjusting event in accordance with IAS 10 (i.e. the new estimate provides evidence of conditions that existed previously) or as a change in estimate in accordance with IAS 8 (i.e. the new estimate resulted from new information or new developments).

If an entity believes that the change in the estimate of mineral reserves resulted from new information or new developments (see 4.5.3.A above) then it should account for that change prospectively from the date the new information becomes available. However, if such a change in mineral reserves is considered to be an adjusting event, only then should the entity base its depreciation, depletion and amortisation calculations under the units of production method on the most recent insight and base the calculation on the assumption that the remaining reserves at the end of the year were 8 million barrels (or tonnes). This assessment will depend upon the specific facts and circumstances associated with each individual event that occurs after the reporting period. Regardless of the approach it takes, an entity would need to consider whether the revision of the reserves estimate constitutes an impairment indicator.

4.7.2 Application of the acquisition method

If the initial accounting for a business combination can be determined only provisionally by the end of the period in which the combination is effected – because either the fair values to be assigned to the acquiree's identifiable assets, liabilities or contingent liabilities or the fair value of the combination can be determined only provisionally – the acquirer should account for the combination using those provisional values. Where, as a result of completing the initial accounting within twelve months from the acquisition date, adjustments to the provisional values have been found to be necessary, IFRS 3 requires them to be recognised from the acquisition date. *[IFRS 3.46].* This raises the question of how an entity should account for new information that it receives regarding an acquiree's reserves before it has finalised its acquisition accounting.

Example 41.12: Acquisition of an entity that owns mineral reserves

Entity A acquires entity B for €27 million at 31 October 2010. At the time it assigned the following fair values to the acquired net assets:

	€ million
Mineral reserves (assuming reserves of 10 million barrels)	10
Other net assets acquired	5
Goodwill	12
Consideration transferred	27

At 30 June 2011, after conducting a drilling programme, entity A determines that the mineral reserves at the date of acquisition were not 10 million barrels, as previously thought, but were only 8 million barrels.

Can entity A revise its initial acquisition accounting to reflect the fact that the mineral reserves are only 8 million barrels, rather than 10 million?

The answer to this question is not straightforward. To use another example, if entity A had sold the mineral reserves four months after acquisition for €18 million this would – in the absence of a significant increase in oil prices or other change in circumstances –

suggest that the provisional fair value assigned to the mineral reserves was in error. In that case, it would be necessary to review the provisional acquisition accounting and adjust goodwill as appropriate. Keeping this in mind, there would seem to be an intuitive logic to treating the new information about the mineral reserves in Example 41.12 above in the same way, i.e. as an adjustment to goodwill. However, this would be incorrect, because IFRS 3 requires the acquired mineral reserves to be accounted for at fair value at the date of acquisition. IFRS 3 defines fair value as: the amount for which an asset could be exchanged, or a liability settled, between knowledgeable, willing parties in an arm's length transaction. Therefore, entity A should not be valuing the acquired mineral reserves retrospectively on the assumption that there are 8 million barrels. Instead, it should be valuing the mineral reserves on the basis that a knowledgeable, willing party *would* have used in an arm's length transaction at 31 October 2010 – even if those assumptions subsequently proved to be incorrect. Hence, it would not be appropriate for entity A to adjust goodwill, unless it was obvious that the initial assessment of 10 million barrels was clearly made in error (i.e. entity A had not taken into account all information at the date of acquisition that was available or could reasonably be expected to have been obtained).

Similarly, if entity A had concluded at 30 June 2011 that its internal long-term oil price assumption was $80/barrel instead of $60/barrel that would not have any effect on the acquisition accounting. Also in that case entity A should be valuing the mineral reserves on the basis that a knowledgeable, willing party *would* have used in an arm's length transaction at 31 October 2010 (i.e. it is entirely possible that such a market participant would not have used $80 or $60 in valuing the mineral reserves).

4.7.3   Completion of E&E activity after the reporting period

As discussed at 3.5.1.A above, IFRS 6 requires E&E assets to be tested for impairment when 'exploration for and evaluation of mineral resources in the specific area have not led to the discovery of commercially viable quantities of mineral resources and the entity has decided to discontinue such activities in the specific area'. *[IFRS 6.20]*. An entity that concludes, after its reporting period, that an exploration and evaluation project is unsuccessful, should account for this conclusion as:

- a *non-adjusting event* if the conclusion is indicative of conditions that arose after the reporting period, for example new information or new developments that did not offer greater clarity concerning the conditions that existed at the end of the reporting period (one possible example may be drilling that only commenced after reporting date). The new information or new developments are considered to be changes in accounting estimates under IAS 8. Also, based on the information that existed at the reporting period, the fair value less cost to sell of the underlying E&E asset might well have been in excess of its carrying amount; *[IAS 8.5]*

- an *adjusting event* if the decision not to sanction the project for development was based on information that existed at the reporting date. Failure to use, or misuse of, reliable information that was available when financial statements for those periods were authorised for issue and could reasonably be expected to have been obtained and taken into account in the preparation and presentation of those financial statements, would constitute an error under IAS 8. *[IAS 8.5]*.

4.8 Decommissioning

4.8.1 *Recognition and measurement issues*

4.8.1.A *Initial recognition*

Initial recognition of a decommissioning provision only upon commencement of commercial production is generally not appropriate under IFRS, because the obligation to remove facilities and to restore the environment typically arises during the construction of the facilities, with some further obligations arising during the production phase. Therefore, a decommissioning provision should be recognised during the development or construction phase (see 1.2.2 above) of the project, i.e. before any production takes place. It may also be necessary to recognise a further decommissioning provision during the production phase (see 4.8.1.D below). While the damage caused in the exploration phase is generally immaterial, an entity should recognise a restoration provision where the damage is material and the entity will be required to carry out remediation. Finally, even if decommissioning and restoration were planned to take place in the foreseeable future (for example because the related assets are continually renewed and replaced), IAS 37 would still require a decommissioning or restoration provision to be recognised. However, in these cases the discounted value of the obligation may be comparatively insignificant.

4.8.1.B *Measurement of the liability*

As illustrated in Extract 41.22 below, measurement of a decommissioning provision requires a significant amount of judgement because:

- the amount of remedial work required will depend on the scale of the operations. In the mining industry the environmental damage may vary considerably depending on the development of the mine;

- the amount of remedial work further depends on environmental standards imposed by local regulators, which may vary over time;

- detailed decommissioning and remedial work plans will often not be developed until fairly shortly before closure of the operations;

- it may not always be clear which costs are directly attributable to decommissioning (e.g. security costs, maintenance cost, ongoing environmental monitoring and employee termination costs);

- the value of materials recovered during decommissioning may depend on commodity prices (e.g. gold recovered in processing a tailings pond);

- the timing of the decommissioning depends on when the fields or mines cease to produce at economically viable rates, which depends upon future commodity prices; and

- the actual decommissioning work will often be carried out by specialised contractors, the cost of which will depend on future market prices for the necessary remedial work.

Many of the uncertainties above can only be resolved towards the end of the production phase, shortly before decommissioning and remediation are to take place. A significant increase in the decommissioning provision resulting from revised estimates could result in recognition of an additional decommissioning asset that is immediately impaired.

Therefore, a significant increase in a decommissioning provision close to the end of the production phase is a trigger for impairment testing. Conversely, a decrease in the decommissioning provision could exceed the carrying amount of the related asset, in which case the excess should be recognised as a gain in profit or loss.

Accounting for decommissioning costs is discussed in more detail in Chapter 20 at 4.3.

4.8.1.C   Discount rate

IAS 37 requires that where the effect of the time value of money is material, the amount of a provision should be the present value of the expenditures expected to be required to settle the obligation. *[IAS 37.45]*. The discount rate (or rates) to be used in arriving at the present value should be 'a pre-tax rate (or rates) that reflect(s) current market assessments of the time value of money and the risks specific to the liability. The discount rate(s) shall not reflect risks for which the future cash flow estimates have been adjusted.' *[IAS 37.47]*. There are a number of complications in applying these requirements that are discussed in Chapter 29:

- real discount rate or a nominal discount rate (see Chapter 29 at 4.3.1);
- adjusting cash flow estimates and discount rates for risk (see Chapter 29 at 4.3.2); and
- determining the pre-tax discount rate (see Chapter 29 at 4.3.4).

Although IAS 37 provides an entity the option of reflecting risk either in the discount rate or in the cash flow estimates, entities generally use a risk free discount rate and reflect the risks in the cash flow estimates. Finally, the discount rate of a provision should be *reduced* to reflect an increase in risk (i.e. only a lower discount will result in a higher provision).

4.8.1.D   Decommissioning costs incurred in the production phase

IAS 16 considers 'the initial estimate of the costs of dismantling and removing the item and restoring the site on which it is located' to be part of the cost of an item of property, plant and equipment. *[IAS 16.16(c)]*. However, an entity should apply IAS 2 to 'the costs of obligations for dismantling, removing and restoring the site on which an item is located that are incurred during a particular period as a consequence of having used the item to produce inventories during that period'. *[IAS 16.18]*. That means that such additional decommissioning costs resulting from production activities should be included in the cost of inventories, *[IAS 2.10]*, while decommissioning costs resulting from the construction of assets should be accounted for as discussed at 4.8.1.A above. An entity that incurs abnormal amounts of costs (e.g. costs of remediation of soil contamination from oil spills or overflowing of a tailings pond) should not treat these as part of the cost of inventories under IAS 2, but expense them immediately. *[IAS 2.16]*.

4.8.2   Accounting for changes in decommissioning and restoration costs

IAS 16 is unclear about the extent to which an item's carrying amount should be affected by changes in the estimated amount of dismantling and site restoration costs that occur *after* the estimate made upon initial measurement. This issue is the subject of IFRIC 1 – *Changes in Existing Decommissioning, Restoration and Similar Liabilities* – issued in May 2004.

IFRIC 1 applies to any decommissioning or similar liability that has both been included as part of an asset measured in accordance with IAS 16 and measured as a liability in accordance with IAS 37. *[IFRIC 1.2].* It deals with the impact of events that change the measurement of an existing liability. Such events include a change in the estimated cash flows, the discount rate and the unwinding of the discount. *[IFRIC 1.3].*

IFRIC 1 differentiates between the treatment required depending upon whether the items of PP&E concerned are valued under the cost or under the revaluation model of IAS 16. If the asset is carried at cost, changes in the liability are added to, or deducted from, the cost of the asset. Any deduction may not exceed the carrying amount of the asset and any excess over the carrying value is taken immediately to profit or loss. If the change in estimate results in an addition to the carrying value, the entity is required to consider whether this is an indication of impairment of the asset as a whole and test for impairment in accordance with IAS 36 (see Chapter 22). *[IFRIC 1.5].*

Where a reduction in a decommissioning / restoration obligation is to be deducted from the cost of the asset, the cost of the asset is the written down carrying value of the whole asset (comprising its construction costs and decommissioning / restoration cost). It is not just the value of the decommissioning / restoration asset originally recognised. Accordingly, we believe that it would not be appropriate to recognise any gain until the carrying value of the whole asset is extinguished. See Chapter 29 at 5.5.1 for more details.

If the related asset is carried at a revalued amount and changes in the estimated liability alter the revaluation surplus (i.e. the re-estimation takes place independently of the revaluation of the asset), then a decrease in the liability is credited directly to the revaluation surplus in equity, unless it reverses a revaluation deficit on the asset that was previously recognised in profit or loss, in which case it should be taken to profit or loss. Similarly, an increase in the liability is taken straight to profit or loss, unless there is a revaluation surplus existing in respect of that asset. *[IFRIC 1.6].*

If the liability decreases and the deduction exceeds the amount that the asset would have been carried at under the cost model (e.g. its depreciated cost), the amount by which the asset is reduced is capped at this amount. Any excess is taken immediately to profit or loss. *[IFRIC 1.7].* This means that the maximum amount by which an asset can be reduced is the same whether it is carried at cost or valuation.

Any change in the revalued amount must conform to the requirements of IAS 16 concerning revalued assets, particularly the requirement that they must be carried at an amount that does not differ materially from fair value (see Chapter 20 at 6 for the standard's rules regarding revaluations of assets). Such an adjustment is an indication that the carrying amount may differ from fair value and the asset may have to be revalued. Any such revaluation must, of course, take account of the adjustment to the estimated liability. If a revaluation is necessary, all assets of the same class must be revalued. *[IFRIC 1.7].*

Any changes in estimate taken to equity must be disclosed on the face of the statement of changes in equity in accordance with IAS 1 (see Chapter 3). *[IFRIC 1.6].* Depreciation of the 'decommissioning asset' and any changes thereto are covered in

Chapter 41

Chapter 20 at 4.3. The unwinding of the discount must be recognised in profit or loss as a finance cost as it occurs. The allowed alternative treatment of capitalisation under IAS 23 is not permitted. *[IFRIC 1.8]*.

The extract below from Tullow Oil illustrates a typical accounting policy for decommissioning costs and the disclosure of decommissioning costs.

Extract 41.22: Tullow Oil plc (2010)

Accounting policies [extract]

(m) Decommissioning [extract]

Provision for decommissioning is recognised in full when the related facilities are installed. A corresponding amount equivalent to the provision is also recognised as part of the cost of the related property, plant and equipment. The amount recognised is the estimated cost of decommissioning, discounted to its net present value, and is reassessed each year in accordance with local conditions and requirements. Changes in the estimated timing of decommissioning or decommissioning cost estimates are dealt with prospectively by recording an adjustment to the provision, and a corresponding adjustment to property, plant and equipment. The unwinding of the discount on the decommissioning provision is included as a finance cost.

Note 20. Provisions [extract]

(i) Decommissioning costs

	2010 $m	2009 $m
At 1 January	223.5	194.0
New provisions and changes in estimates	55.5	6.6
Disposal of subsidiaries (note 26)	–	(2.2)
Decommissioning payments	(10.3)	(2.0)
Unwinding of discount (note 5)	13.3	14.7
Currency translation adjustment	(3.4)	12.4
At 31 December	**278.6**	**223.5**

The decommissioning provision represents the present value of decommissioning costs relating to the UK, African and Asian oil and gas interests, which are expected to be incurred up to 2035. During 2010 a review of all decommissioning estimates was undertaken by an independent specialist and the 2010 financial statements now include estimates in accordance with this study.

Assumptions, based on the current economic environment, have been made which management believe are a reasonable basis upon which to estimate the future liability. These estimates are reviewed regularly to take into account any material changes to the assumptions. However, actual decommissioning costs will ultimately depend upon future market prices for the necessary decommissioning works required which will reflect market conditions at the relevant time. Furthermore, the timing of decommissioning is likely to depend on when the fields cease to produce at economically viable rates. This in turn will depend upon future oil and gas prices, which are inherently uncertain.

One matter that IFRIC 1 does not specifically address is the treatment of obligations arising after the asset has been constructed, for example as a result of a change in legislation. *[IFRIC 1.BC23]*. Nevertheless, in our opinion, the cost of the related asset should be measured in accordance with the principles set out in IFRIC 1 regardless of whether the obligation exists at the time of constructing the asset or arises later in its life. For further discussion on this matter see Chapter 29 at 5.5.2.

4.8.3   Treatment of exchange differences

In most cases it will be appropriate for the exchange differences arising on provisions to be taken to profit or loss in the period they arise. However, it may be that an entity has recognised a decommissioning provision under IAS 37 – *Provisions, Contingent Liabilities and Contingent Assets*. One practical difficulty with such a provision is that due to the long period over which the actual cash outflows will arise, an entity may not know the currency in which the transaction will actually be settled. Nevertheless if it is determined that it is expected to be settled in a foreign currency it will be a monetary item. The main issue then is what should happen to any exchange differences. As discussed in Chapter 29 at 5.5, IFRIC 1 – *Changes in Existing Decommissioning, Restoration and Similar Liabilities* – applies to any decommissioning or similar liability that has been both included as part of an asset measured as a liability in accordance with IAS 37. IFRIC 1 requires, *inter alia*, that any adjustment to such a provision resulting from changes in the estimated outflow of resources embodying economic benefits (e.g. cash flows) required to settle the obligation should not be taken to profit or loss as it occurs, but should be added to or deducted from the cost of the asset to which it relates. Therefore, the requirement of IAS 21 – *The Effects of Changes in Foreign Exchange Rates* – to take the exchange differences arising on the provision to profit or loss in the period in which they arise conflicts with this requirement in IFRIC 1. It is our view that IFRIC 1 is the more relevant pronouncement for decommissioning purposes, therefore we consider that this type of exchange difference should not to be taken to profit or loss, but dealt with in accordance with IFRIC 1.

4.8.4   Deferred tax on decommissioning obligations

The exception in IAS 12 from recognising the deferred tax effects of certain temporary differences arising on the initial recognition of some assets and liabilities is generally referred to as the 'initial recognition exemption'. The initial recognition exemption can give strange results in accounting for decommissioning obligations, which involve the initial recognition of an equal and opposite asset and liability which subsequently unwind on different bases. A strict interpretation of IAS 12 would be to argue that upon initial recognition, the tax base of both the decommissioning liability and the decommissioning part of the asset are nil. Therefore, no deferred taxation should be recognised relating to the deductible temporary difference on the decommissioning liability or the taxable temporary difference on the decommissioning part of the asset. However, the unrecognised deductible and taxable temporary differences will unwind at a different rate, which can result in significant fluctuations in the effective tax rate (see Example 27.18 in Chapter 31).

That leads some to argue, given that the asset and liability recognised on establishment of a decommissioning provision are the result of a single transaction, that they should be regarded as effectively giving rise to a single (net) temporary difference of zero. This means that, as and when (net) temporary differences emerge after initial recognition, deferred tax may be recognised on those temporary differences, with the effect that the effective tax rate in profit or loss reflects the statutory rate actually applicable to the transaction as a whole.

Those who take this view might also argue that it is consistent with the implied, if not explicit, intention of the initial recognition exemption that deferred tax should always be recognised unless it creates a 'day one' tax charge or credit in profit or loss. In this case a 'day one' profit or loss is avoided by establishing an equal and opposite deferred tax asset and liability.

Others argue that this approach is not acceptable. The financial statements present a clearly separate asset and liability which do not meet any offset criteria. The 'initial recognition exemption' should therefore be applied to the asset and liability separately and not as if the two comprised some form of single net asset or liability.

The Interpretations Committee considered this issue on two occasions in 2005. The *IFRIC Update* for April 2005 appeared to support the latter view:

> 'The IFRIC noted that initial recognition exemption applies to each separate recognised element in the balance sheet, and no deferred tax asset or liability should be recognised on the temporary difference existing on the initial recognition of assets and liabilities arising from finance leases or subsequently.'

However, only two months later, the Interpretations Committee added:

> 'The IFRIC considered the treatment of deferred tax relating to assets and liabilities arising from finance leases.
>
> While noting that there is diversity in practice in applying the requirements of IAS 12 to assets and liabilities arising from finance leases, the IFRIC agreed not to develop any guidance because the issue falls directly within the scope of the Board's short-term convergence project on income taxes with the FASB.'

It would therefore seem that, whilst the Interpretations Committee regards the analysis that the asset and liability must be considered separately as consistent with a literal reading of IAS 12, it accepts the alternative approach.

4.8.5   Indefinite life assets

While the economic lives of oil fields and mines are finite, certain infrastructure assets (e.g. pipelines and refineries) are continually being repaired, replaced and upgraded. While individual parts of such assets may not have an indefinite economic life, these assets may occupy a particular site for an indefinite period.

IAS 37 requires a decommissioning provision to be recognised when:

'(a)   an entity has a present obligation (legal or constructive) as a result of a past event;

(b)   it is probable that an outflow of resources embodying economic benefits will be required to settle the obligation; and

(c)   a reliable estimate can be made of the amount of the obligation.' *[IAS 37.14].*

Regardless of whether or not the related asset has an indefinite life, the decommissioning provision will normally meet the criteria under (a) and (b) above. While it might seem that a reliable estimate of the decommissioning provision cannot be made if the underlying asset has an indefinite life, IAS 37 presumes that:

> 'Except in extremely rare cases, an entity will be able to determine a range of possible outcomes and can therefore make an estimate of the obligation that is sufficiently reliable to use in recognising a provision.' *[IAS 37.25].*

Therefore, it should be extremely rare for an entity to conclude that it cannot make a reliable estimate of the amount of the obligation. Even if an entity did conclude in an extremely rare case that no reliable estimate could be made, a contingent liability would still exist and the following disclosures would be required: *[IAS 37.26, 86]*.

- a brief description of the nature of the contingent liability; and
- where practicable:
  - an estimate of its financial effect, measured under paragraphs 36-52 of IAS 37;
  - an indication of the uncertainties relating to the amount or timing of any outflow; and
  - the possibility of any reimbursement.

Finally, it should be noted that the discounted value of decommissioning costs that will only be incurred far into the future may be relatively insignificant.

4.8.6   Funds established / put aside to meet a decommissioning / rehabilitation obligation

Some entities may participate in a decommissioning, restoration or environmental rehabilitation fund, the purpose of which is to segregate assets to fund some or all of the costs of decommissioning. IFRIC 5 – *Rights to Interests arising from Decommissioning, Restoration and Environmental Rehabilitation Funds* – was issued in December 2004 to address this issue. See Chapter 29 at 5.5.3 for more information.

Entities may also set aside cash, for example in an escrow account, for the purpose of meeting future decommissioning, rehabilitation or restoration obligations.

A common question raised is whether the decommissioning / rehabilitation fund asset or cash held in escrow can be offset against the rehabilitation / restoration provision. For decommissioning / rehabilitation fund assets, IFRIC 5 requires the contributor to a fund to recognise its obligations to pay decommissioning / rehabilitation costs as a liability and recognise its interest in the fund separately, unless the contributor is not liable to pay decommissioning / rehabilitation costs even if the fund fails to pay. *[IFRIC 5.7]*. Accordingly, in most cases it would not be appropriate to offset the decommissioning / rehabilitation liability and the interest in the fund. See Chapter 29 at 5.5.3.C for more information as to why they should be presented gross.

In relation to cash held in escrow, similar considerations would apply. While funds have been set aside to meet the obligation at some point in the future, they have not yet been applied to extinguish the decommissioning obligation. Therefore, the entity remains liable for the decommissioning costs and hence should continue to recognise the decommissioning / rehabilitation provision.

4.9   Revenue recognition

4.9.1   Revenue in the development phase: Incidental revenue

Under IAS 16, the cost of an item of property, plant and equipment includes any costs directly attributable to bringing the asset to the location and condition necessary for it to be capable of operating in the manner intended by management. *[IAS 16.16(b)]*.

However, during the construction of an asset, an entity may enter into incidental operations that are not, in themselves, necessary to bring the asset itself into the location and condition necessary for it to be capable of operating in the manner intended by management. The standard gives the example of income earned by using a building site as a car park prior to starting construction. Because incidental operations such as these are not necessary to bring an item to the location and condition necessary for it to be capable of operating in the manner intended by management, the income and related expenses of incidental operations are recognised in profit or loss and included in their respective classifications of income and expense. *[IAS 16.21]*. Such incidental income is not offset against the cost of the asset.

If, however, some income is generated wholly and necessarily as a result of the process of bringing the asset into the location and condition for its intended use, for example from the sale of samples produced when testing the equipment concerned, then the income should be credited to the cost of the asset (see 4.9.2 below).

On the other hand, if the asset is *already in* the location and condition necessary for it to be capable of being used in the manner intended by management, then IAS 16 requires capitalisation to cease and depreciation to start. *[IAS 16.20]*. In these circumstances, all income earned from using the asset must be recognised as revenue in profit or loss and the related costs of the activity should include an element of depreciation of the asset.

4.9.2   Revenue in the development phase: Integral to development

Under IAS 16, the directly attributable costs of an item of property, plant and equipment include the costs of testing whether the asset is functioning properly, after deducting the net proceeds from selling any items produced while bringing the asset to that location and condition. *[IAS 16.17(e)]*. The standard gives the example of samples produced when testing equipment.

There are other situations in which income may be earned whilst bringing the asset to the intended location and condition. For example, the mining industry is highly capital intensive – particularly so in the case of deep level mining – and a mining operation may extract some saleable 'product' during the phase of its operation to sink mine shafts to the depth where the main ore-bearing rock is located. During the evaluation and construction phases, income can be earned by an entity in various ways. For example, during the evaluation phase – i.e. when the technical feasibility and commercial viability are being determined – an entity may 'trial mine', to determine which method would be the most profitable and efficient in the circumstances, and which metallurgical process is the most efficient. Ore mined through trial mining may be processed and sold during the evaluation phase. At the other end of the spectrum, income may be earned from the sale of product from 'ramping up' the mine to full production at commercial levels.

It will be a matter of significant judgement as to what is incidental revenue, as well as when the asset is in the location and condition intended by management, but capitalisation (including the recording of income as a credit to the cost of the mine) ceases when the asset is fully operational, regardless of whether or not it is achieving its targeted levels of production or profitability, or even operating at all.

4.9.3   *Exchanges of inventories*

Under IAS 18, when goods or services are exchanged or swapped for goods or services that are of a similar nature and value, the exchange is not regarded as a transaction that generates revenue. This is often the case with commodities like oil, where suppliers exchange or swap inventories in various locations to fulfil demand on a timely basis in a particular location. However, when goods are sold in exchange for dissimilar goods, the exchange is regarded as a transaction that generates revenue. *[IAS 18.12]*.

Accounting for exchanges of inventories requires a degree of judgement particularly:

• when the inventories exchanged are not identical (e.g. swaps of slightly different oil products, possibly with an adjustment for the difference in quality); or

• there is some past practice of settling net in cash.

Furthermore, any receivable or payable balance does not entirely meet the definition of inventory in IAS 2 but is instead a non-monetary receivable or payable. The product receivable (payable) is normally recorded at cost within current assets (liabilities).

Extract 41.23: TOTAL S.A. (2010)

Notes to the Consolidated Financial Statements [extract]

1) Accounting policies [extract]

D. Sales and revenues from sales [extract]

Exchanges of crude oil and petroleum products within normal trading activities do not generate any income and therefore these flows are shown at their net value in both the statement of income and the balance sheet.

4.10   Long-term contracts and leases

4.10.1 *Embedded leases*

IFRIC 4 – *Determining whether an Arrangement contains a Lease* – notes that there are arrangements that do not take the legal form of a lease but that convey rights to use items for agreed periods of time in return for a payment or series of payments. *[IFRIC 4.1]*. However, the Interpretation addresses not only this type of arrangement but also the more traditional forms of arrangement that are also within its scope.

The Interpretation focuses on the accounting implications of the following, in all of which an entity (the supplier) conveys a right to use an asset to another entity (the purchaser), together with related services or outputs:

• outsourcing arrangements, including outsourcing of the data processing functions of an entity;

• arrangements in the telecommunications industry, where suppliers of network capacity enter into contracts to provide purchasers with rights to capacity; and

• take-or-pay and similar contracts, in which purchasers must make specified payments regardless of whether they take delivery of the contracted products or services (e.g. where purchasers are committed to acquiring substantially all of the output of a supplier's power generator). *[IFRIC 4.1]*.

The Interpretation does not apply to service concession arrangements, which are the subject of IFRIC 12 – *Service Concession Arrangements* (see Chapter 28 at 2.2).

The Interpretations Committee concluded that an arrangement of one of these types could be within the scope of IAS 17 if it met the definition of a lease, e.g. if it conveyed to the lessee the right to use an asset for an agreed period of time in return for a payment or series of payments. *[IFRIC 4.BC2]*. IAS 17 applies to the lease element of the arrangement notwithstanding the related services or outputs because IAS 17 applies to 'agreements that transfer the right to use assets even though substantial services by the lessor may be called for in connection with the operation or maintenance of such assets.' *[IAS 17.3]*. This is regardless of the fact that the arrangement is not described as a lease and is likely to grant rights that are significantly different from those in a formal lease agreement. The Interpretations Committee therefore concluded that it should provide guidance to assist in determining whether an arrangement is, or contains, a lease. *[IFRIC 4.BC2]*.

The detailed requirements of IFRIC 4 are discussed in Chapter 26 at 2.1.

4.10.2 Take-or-pay contracts

A 'take-or-pay' contract is an agreement between a buyer and seller in which the buyer will still pay a specified amount even if the product or service is not provided. Take-or-pay contracts for the supply of gas are particularly common, because entities developing gas fields need to make very significant investments in infrastructure such as pipelines, liquefaction plants and shipping terminals, to make transport of gas to the end-consumer economically viable. In order to raise the funds to finance such investments, it is crucial to know that there is a profitable market for the gas, as it cannot easily be diverted and sold in an alternative market or to an alternative customer.

While take-or-pay contracts perhaps most commonly involve the supply of gas, they can also include other arrangements such as contracts for pipeline capacity or LNG regasification facilities. Take-or-pay contracts also are used in the mining industry, though less frequently than in the oil and gas industry. Typically, in the mining industry take-or-pay contracts permit the purchaser to recover payments for quantities not taken, by allowing the purchaser to take more than the minimum in later years and to apply the previously paid-for undertake amount towards the cost of product taken in the later years.[152]

Extract 41.24 below from the financial statements of GDF SUEZ gives an overview of some of the important terms and conditions that exist in take-or-pay contracts.

Extract 41.24: GDF SUEZ (2010)

5 RISK FACTORS [extract]

5.3 BUSINESS MODEL LIMITATIONS [extract]

5.3.1 SHORT- AND LONG-TERM ENERGY PURCHASES [extract]

5.3.1.1 Long-term take-or-pay gas procurement contracts with minimum volume commitments [extract]

The gas business in Europe operates largely on the basis of long-term "take-or-pay" contracts. According to these contracts, the seller agrees to serve the buyer on a long-term basis, in exchange for a commitment on the behalf of the buyer to pay for minimum quantities, whether or not they are delivered. These minimum amounts may vary only partially depending on weather contingencies. These commitments are subject to protective (force majeure) and flexibility conditions.

To guarantee availability of the quantities of gas required to supply its customers in future years, a major proportion of the Group's contracts are "take-or-pay" contracts. Regular price revision mechanisms included in the long-term contracts guarantee competitive gas prices to the buyer on the final market. If the purchased gas loses its price competitiveness, GDF SUEZ would only be exposed to the "take-or-pay" risk on the quantities purchased prior to the next price revision.

Most long-term procurement contracts are indexed on oil products price indices. However, with the emergence of short-term gas markets, gas prices are increasingly changing independently of oil prices, which are creating a conflict between short-term and long-term gas prices. A situation where the gas price remains constantly below the price of oil indexed contracts could have a significant impact on the Group's revenues, in particular if the Group fails to renegotiate its long-term gas procurement contracts satisfactorily against the backdrop of a prolonged mismatch between gas and oil prices.

2 PRESENTATION OF ACTIVITIES [extract]

2.1 ORGANIZATION OF ACTIVITIES AND DESCRIPTION OF BUSINESS LINES [extract]

2.1.3.7 GDF SUEZ Gas Supplies [extract]

Gas purchases [extract]

GDF SUEZ Gas Supplies brings to the Group one of the largest and most diversified contract portfolios in Europe and its flexibility is a real competitive edge in the natural gas market in Europe.

It consists largely of long term contracts with a term of some 20 years. As of December 31, 2010, the average residual term of these long-term contracts (weighted by volume) was 14.9 years. This portfolio is balanced through purchases in short-term markets through Gaselys. Through this, [GDF SUEZ] adjusts its supply to the group's needs by optimizing its purchasing costs. Close cooperation between the GDF SUEZ Gas Supplies and Gaselys allows that the portfolio can be finely balanced from day to day.

According to market practice, the long-term purchase contracts include take-or-pay clauses, according to which the buyer agrees to pay for minimum gas volumes each year, whether or not delivery occurs (except in the event of supplier default or force majeure). Most contracts also stipulate flexibility clauses. These are compensation mechanisms that allow volumes already paid for but not taken to be carried over to a subsequent period (make-up) or limited volumes to be deducted from the take-or-pay obligation, when the volumes taken over the course of previous years exceeds the minimum volumes applicable to these years (carry forward).

The price of natural gas under these contracts is indexed to the market price of energy products with which gas is directly or indirectly substitutable (mainly oil products). In addition, these contracts provide for periodic (two to four year) revisions of price and indexing formulae to account for market changes. Finally, most contracts provide for the possibility of adjusting prices (jokers' rights) in exceptional circumstances, over and above the periodic reviews.

In certain cases, it is possible to change other contractual provisions in response to exceptional events affecting their economic balance (hardship clause). The parties are then required to negotiate in good faith and can, in the event of disagreement, revert to arbitration.

Supply contracts stipulate one or more delivery points. The delivery points of gas delivered by pipeline are spread across the entire European transport system and, in the case of LNG, are mainly sited at vessel loading docks at suppliers' liquefaction plants.

GDF SUEZ Gas Supplies constantly seeks to match its portfolio to the market situation. This is materialized by drawing up new contracts and by price reviews. In a context marked by the decoupling of oil prices, to which the long-term contracts are indexed, from those of the gas sold in the market place, GDF SUEZ Gas Supplies started negotiations with all its main suppliers in 2009.

20.2 NOTES TO THE CONSOLIDATED FINANCIAL STATEMENTS [extract]

NOTE 1 SUMMARY OF SIGNIFICANT ACCOUNTING POLICIES [extract]

1.4 Significant accounting policies [extract]

1.4.9 Leases [extract]

1.4.9.3 Accounting for arrangements that contain a lease

IFRIC 4 deals with the identification of services and take-or-pay sales or purchasing contracts that do not take the legal form of a lease but convey rights to customers/suppliers to use an asset or a group of assets in return for a payment or a series of fixed payments. Contracts meeting these criteria should be identified as either operating leases or finance leases. In the latter case, a finance receivable should be recognized to reflect the financing deemed to be granted by the Group where it is considered as acting as lessor and its customers as lessees.

The Group is concerned by this interpretation mainly with respect to:

● some energy purchase and sale contracts, particularly where the contract conveys to the purchaser of the energy an exclusive right to use a production asset;

● certain contracts with industrial customers relating to assets held by the Group.

The following issues need to be considered in accounting for take-or-pay contracts:

● *Special purpose entities* – If a take-or-pay contract transfers the majority of the risks and rewards from the development of a gas field to the customer, it is necessary to consider whether the entity developing the gas field has, in effect, become a special purpose entity of that customer (see Chapter 6 at 2.2); NOTE: SIC-12, which currently deals with the accounting for special purpose entities, is being replaced by IFRS 10 – *Consolidated Financial Statements* (see Chapter 7 at 4.4.1) and the term special purpose entities is being replaced with the term 'structured entities'.

● *Embedded leases* – Take-or-pay contracts are often for a very significant portion of the output of the gas field that it relates to. Therefore, as illustrated in Extract 41.24 above, the operator and customer need to consider whether the take-or-pay contract contains a lease of the related assets (see 4.10.1 above);

● *Embedded derivatives* – As illustrated in Extract 41.24 above, the price of gas sold under take-or-pay contracts is often based on a 'basket' of fuel prices and/or inflation price indices. If there is an active market for gas then this often means that an embedded derivative needs to be separated from the underlying host take-or-pay contract (see 4.12.2 below);

- *Guarantees* – Lenders are often willing to provide funding for the development of a gas field only if the operator can present a solid business case, which includes a 'guaranteed' stream of revenue from a reputable customer. In such cases, the take-or-pay contract acts as a form of credit enhancement or possibly as a guarantee. The operator and customer may need to consider whether the take-or-pay arrangement includes a guarantee that should be accounted for such under IAS 39 (see Chapter 43 at 3.4);

- *Makeup product and undertake* – A customer that fails to take the specified volume during the period specified must nevertheless pay for the agreed-volume. However, a take-or-pay contract sometimes permits the customer to take an equivalent amount of production (makeup product) at a later date after the payment for the guaranteed amount has been made (see 4.10.2.A below).

4.10.2.A Makeup product and undertake

A customer who is required to pay for gas not taken will often have no right of future recovery. The customer should recognise an expense equal to the payment made, while the operator recognises the same amount as revenue. However, if the substance of the relationship between the operator and customer is such that a renegotiation of the arrangement is probable then it may be more appropriate for the operator to recognise the penalty payment as deferred revenue. The customer, however, should still recognise an expense in this case as it does not have a legal right to receive reimbursement or makeup product.[153]

The accounting is different when a customer that is required to pay for gas not taken has a right to take makeup product in the future. In that case the operator of the gas field would recognise deferred revenue equal to the amount paid for the 'undertake' as it represents an obligation to provide gas in the future. The operator only recognises revenue in accordance with IAS 18 once the makeup gas has been taken by the customer. *[IAS 18.14(a)]*. Only once the makeup period has expired or it is clear that the purchaser has become unable to take the gas, would the liability be eliminated and revenue recognised.[154] The customer would normally recognise a prepaid amount representing the makeup gas that it is entitled to receive in the future. However, if the customer is entitled to more makeup gas than it can sell, it may need to recognise an impairment charge.

Extract 41.25 below illustrates how Tullow Oil as an operator accounts for undertakes.

Extract 41.25: Tullow Oil plc (2010)

Accounting policies [extract]

(f) Revenue [extract]

Sales revenue represents the sales value, net of VAT and overriding royalties, of the Group's share of liftings in the year together with tariff income. Revenue is recognised when goods are delivered and title has passed.

Revenues received under take-or-pay sales contracts in respect of undelivered volumes are accounted for as deferred income.

4.11   Taxation

4.11.1 Determining the nature of the taxation

As mentioned at 1.1 above, one of the characteristics of the extractive industries is the intense government involvement in their activities, which ranges from 'outright governmental ownership of some (especially petroleum) or all minerals to unusual tax benefits or penalties, price controls, restrictions on imports and exports, restrictions on production and distribution, environmental and health and safety regulations, and others'.[155]

Consequently, mining companies and oil and gas companies typically need to make payments to governments in their capacity as:

*   owner of the mineral resources;
*   co-owner or joint venture partner in the projects;
*   regulator of, among other things, environmental matters and health and safety matters; and
*   tax authority.

The total payment to a government is often described as the 'government take'. This includes fixed payments or variable payments that are based on production, revenue, or a net profit figure; and which may take the form of fees, bonuses, royalties or taxes. Determining whether a payment to the government meets the definition of income tax is therefore not straightforward.

IAS 12 should be applied in accounting for income taxes, defined as including:

(a)   all domestic and foreign taxes which are based on taxable profits; and

(b)   taxes, such as withholding taxes, which are payable by a subsidiary, associate or joint venture on distributions to the reporting entity. *[IAS 12.1-2]*.

As discussed in Chapter 31 at 4.1, it is not altogether clear what an income tax actually is. In the extractive industries the main problem with the definition in IAS 12 occurs when:

(a)   a government raises 'taxes' on sub-components of net profit (e.g. net profit before financing costs or revenue minus allowed costs); or

(b)   there is a mandatory government participation in certain projects that entitle the government to a share of profits as defined in a joint venture agreement.

A considerable amount of judgement is required to determine whether a particular arrangement falls within the definition of 'income tax' under IAS 12 or whether it is another form of government take. From a commercial perspective the overall share of the economic benefits that the government takes is much more important than the distinction between its different forms. In practice, most governments receive benefits from extractive activities in several different ways (see 4.11.2 below). Governments can choose any of these methods to increase or decrease their share of the benefits. However, under IFRS the distinction is crucial given the considerable differences in the accounting policies that apply to income taxes, other taxes, fees and government participations.

4.11.2 *Excise duties, production taxes and severance taxes*

Excise duties, production taxes and severance taxes result in payments that are due upon production (or severance) of minerals from the earth. Depending on the jurisdiction and the type of mineral involved, they are calculated:

(a) as a fixed amount per unit produced;

(b) as a percentage of the value of the minerals produced; or

(c) based on revenue minus certain allowable costs.

4.11.2.A *Production-based taxation*

If the tax is based on a fixed amount per unit produced or as a percentage of the value of the minerals produced, then it will not meet the definition of an income tax under IAS 12. In these cases the normal principles of liability recognition under IAS 37 apply in recognising the tax charge.

Another issue that arises is whether the tax should be presented as a cost of production or whether it should be deducted in arriving at revenue. Given that excise duties, production taxes and severance taxes are aimed at taxing the production of minerals rather than the sale of minerals, they are a tax on extractive activities rather than a tax collected by a mining company or oil and gas company on behalf of the government. Based on this argument the tax should be presented as a production cost. It should be noted though that revenue from the extraction of mineral ores is outside the scope of IAS 18. *[IAS 18.6]*.

However, it could also be argued, particularly when the excise duty, production tax or severance tax is payable in kind, that the mining company or oil and gas company never receives any of the benefits associated with the production of the associated minerals. Hence, it would only be appropriate to present revenue net of the production or severance tax as it is in substance the same as royalty payment. For this reason, revenue is generally presented net of excise duties, as illustrated by Extract 41.26 below from the accounts of Royal Dutch Shell.

Extract 41.26: Royal Dutch Shell plc (2010)

NOTES TO THE CONSOLIDATED FINANCIAL STATEMENTS [extract]

2 ACCOUNTING POLICIES [extract]

REVENUE RECOGNITION

Revenue from sales of oil, natural gas, chemicals and all other products is recognised at the fair value of consideration received or receivable, after deducting sales taxes, excise duties and similar levies, when the significant risks and rewards of ownership have been transferred, which is when title passes to the customer. For sales by Upstream operations, this generally occurs when product is physically transferred into a vessel, pipe or other delivery mechanism. For sales by refining operations, it is either when product is placed onboard a vessel or offloaded from the vessel, depending on the contractually agreed terms. For wholesale sales of oil products and chemicals it is either at the point of delivery or the point of receipt, depending on contractual conditions.

> Revenue resulting from the production of oil and natural gas properties in which Shell has an interest with other producers is recognised on the basis of Shell's working interest (entitlement method). Gains and losses on derivative contracts and the revenue and costs associated with other contracts that are classified as held for trading purposes are reported on a net basis in the Consolidated Statement of Income. Purchases and sales of hydrocarbons under exchange contracts that are necessary to obtain or reposition feedstock for Shell's refinery operations are presented net in the Consolidated Statement of Income.

4.11.2.B   Petroleum revenue tax (or resource rent tax)

Determining whether a petroleum revenue tax (or resource rent tax) is a production- or profit-based tax is often not straightforward. Example 41.13 describes the petroleum revenue tax in the United Kingdom.

Example 41.13:   Petroleum revenue tax[156]

Petroleum revenue tax (PRT) is a special tax that seeks to tax a high proportion of the economic rent (super-profits) from the exploitation of the UK's oil and gas. PRT is a cash-based tax that is levied on a field-by-field basis: in general, the costs of developing and running a field can only be set against the profits generated by that field. Any losses, e.g. arising from unused expenditure relief, can be carried back or forward within the field indefinitely. There is also a range of reliefs, including:

* oil allowance – a PRT-free slice of production;
* supplement – a proxy for interest and other financing costs;
* Tariff Receipts Allowance (TRA) – participators owning assets, for example pipelines, relating to one field will sometimes allow participators from other fields to share the use of the asset in return for the payment of tariffs, and TRA relieves some of the tariffs received from PRT;
* exemption from PRT for gas sold to British Gas under a pre-July 1975 contract; and
* cross-field relief for research expenditure.

PRT is currently charged at 50% on profits after these allowances. For a limited period, safeguard relief then applies to ensure that PRT does not reduce the annual return in the early years of production of a field to below 15% of the historic capital expenditure on the field.

PRT was abolished on 16 March 1993 for all fields given development consent on or after that date. This was part of a package of PRT reforms which also included the reduction of the rate of PRT from 75 per cent to 50 per cent and the abolition of PRT relief for Exploration and Appraisal (E&A) expenditure.

The petroleum revenue tax is similar to an income tax in that the tax is a percentage of revenue minus certain costs. However, there are also a number of other features that are not commonly found in income taxes nor in some other resource rent taxes:

* the oil allowance is a physical quantity of oil that is PRT exempt in each field, subject to a cumulative maximum over the life of the field; and
* the tax is levied on individual oil fields rather than the entity owning the oil field as a whole.

There are many different types of petroleum revenue taxes (or resource rent taxes) around the world, some of which are clearly not income taxes, while others have some of the characteristics of an income tax. In determining whether a particular production tax meets the definition of an income tax under IAS 12, an entity will need to assess whether or not the tax is based on (or closely enough linked to) net profit for the period. If it does not meet the definition of an income tax, an entity should develop an accounting policy under the hierarchy in IAS 8.

Practice is mixed, which means that while some entities may treat a particular petroleum revenue tax (or resource rent tax) as an income tax under IAS 12 (see Extract 41.27 below), others may consider the same tax to be outside the scope of IAS 12.

Extract 41.27: Woodside Petroleum (2010)

1. Summary of significant accounting policies [extract]

z) Tax – Petroleum Resource Rent Tax

PRRT is considered, for accounting purposes, to be a tax based on income. Accordingly, current and deferred PRRT expense is measured and disclosed on the same basis as income tax.

As illustrated in Extract 41.28 below, BHP Billiton assesses resource rent taxes and royalties individually to determine whether they meet the definition of an income tax or not.

Extract 41.28: BHP Billiton Group (2010)

Notes to Financial Statements [extract]

1 Accounting policies [extract]

Taxation [extract]

Royalties and resource rent taxes are treated as taxation arrangements when they have the characteristics of a tax. This is considered to be the case when they are imposed under government authority and the amount payable is calculated by reference to revenue derived (net of any allowable deductions) after adjustment for items comprising temporary differences. For such arrangements, current and deferred tax is provided on the same basis as described above for other forms of taxation. Obligations arising from royalty arrangements that do not satisfy these criteria are recognised as current provisions and included in expenses.

4.11.3 Grossing up of notional quantities withheld

Many production sharing contracts provide that the income tax to which the contractor is subject is deemed to have been paid to the government as part of the payment of profit oil (see 5.1.2 below). This raises the question as to whether an entity should be presenting current and deferred taxation arising from such 'notional' income tax, which is only deemed to have been paid, on a net or a gross basis.

Example 41.14:   Grossing up of notional quantities withheld

Entity A is the operator of an oil field that produces 10 million barrels of oil per year. Under the production sharing contract between entity A and the national government, entity A and the government are entitled to 4,000,000 and 6,000,000 barrels of oil, respectively. The production sharing contract includes the following clause:

> 'The share of the profit petroleum to which the government is entitled in any calendar year in accordance with the production sharing contract shall be deemed to include a portion representing the corporate income tax imposed upon and due by entity A, and which will be paid directly by the government on behalf of entity A to the appropriate tax authorities.'

Assuming the following facts, how should entity A account for the income tax that it is deemed to have paid in 2011:

- the normal corporate income tax rate in the country in which entity A operates is 40%;
- entity A made a net profit of USD 30 million in 2011; and
- the average oil price during the year was USD 50/barrel.

Gross presentation

Entity A's profit after 40% corporate income tax was USD 30 million. Therefore, its profit before tax would have been USD 50 million (i.e. USD 30 million ÷ (100% − 40%)). In other words, the government is deemed to have paid corporate income tax of USD 20 million on behalf of entity A. Therefore, the government is deemed to have taken 400,000 barrels (i.e. USD 20 million ÷ USD 50/barrel) out of entity A's share of the production. Hence, entity A's share of production before corporate income tax was 4,400,000 barrels (i.e. 4,000,000 barrels + 400,000 barrels).

Net presentation

Under the net presentation approach, entity A ignores the corporate income tax that was deemed to have been paid by the government because it is not a transaction that entity A was party to *or* because the deemed transaction did not actually take place.

The disadvantage of presenting such tax on a gross basis is that the combined production attributed to the entity and that attributable to the government exceeds the total quantity of oil that is actually produced (i.e. in the above example the government and entity A would report a combined production of 10.4 million barrels). Similarly, if the reserves were to be expressed on the same basis as revenues, the reserves reported by the entity would include oil reserves that it would not actually be entitled to.

On the other hand, if (1) the host country has a well established income tax regime that falls under the authority of the ministry of finance and (2) the production sharing contract requires an income tax return to be filed, then the entity would have a legal liability to pay the tax until the date on which the national oil company or the ministry responsible for extractive activities (e.g. the ministry of mines, industry and energy) pays the tax on its behalf. In such cases it may be appropriate to present revenue and income tax on a gross basis.

4.12   Financial instruments

4.12.1 Normal purchase and sales exemption

4.12.1.A   Requirements of IAS 32 and IAS 39

Contracts to buy or sell non-financial items do not meet the definition of a financial instrument because the contractual right of one party to receive a non-financial asset or service and the corresponding obligation of the other party do not establish a present right or obligation of either party to receive, deliver or exchange a financial asset. For example, contracts that provide for settlement only by the receipt or delivery of non-financial items (e.g. forward purchase of oil or a forward purchase of copper) are not financial instruments. However, some of these contracts are traded in a standardised form on organised markets in the same way as derivative financial instruments. The ability to buy or sell a commodity contract for cash does not alter the characteristics of the contract and make it into a financial instrument. *[IAS 32.AG20]*. Nevertheless, IAS 32 and IAS 39 should be 'applied to those contracts to buy or sell a non-financial item that can be settled net in cash or another financial instrument, or by exchanging financial instruments, as if the contracts were financial instruments, with the exception of contracts that were entered into and continue to be held for the purpose of the receipt or delivery of a non-financial item in accordance with the entity's expected purchase, sale or usage requirements'. *[IAS 32.8, IAS 39.5]*. Contracts that fall within this exemption, which is known as the 'normal purchase or sale exemption', 'executory contract exemption' or 'own-use exemption', are accounted for as executory contracts. An entity recognises such contracts in its statement of financial position only when one of the parties meets its obligation under the contract to deliver either cash or a non-financial asset. *[Framework.4.46]*.

There are various ways in which a contract to buy or sell a non-financial item can be settled net, including when:

(a)   the terms of the contract permit either party to settle it net;

(b)   the ability to settle the contract net is not explicit in its terms, but the entity has a practice of settling similar contracts net (whether with the counterparty, by entering into offsetting contracts or by selling the contract before its exercise or lapse);

(c)   for similar contracts, the entity has a practice of taking delivery of the underlying and selling it within a short period after delivery for the purpose of generating a profit from short-term fluctuations in price or dealer's margin; and

(d)   the non-financial item that is the subject of the contract is readily convertible to cash.

The IASB views the practice of settling net or taking delivery of the underlying and selling it within a short period after delivery as an indication that the contracts are not normal purchases or sales. Therefore, contracts to which (b) or (c) apply cannot be subject to the normal purchase or sale exception. Other contracts that can be settled net are evaluated to determine whether this exception can actually apply *[IAS 32.9, IAS 39.6, BC24]*.

A written option to buy or sell a non-financial item that can be settled net in cash or another financial instrument, or by exchanging financial instruments, in accordance with (a) or (d) should be accounted for under IAS 39 and does not qualify for use of the normal purchase or sale exemption. *[IAS 39.7]*.

4.12.1.B   Application of the normal purchase or sale exemption in the extractive industries

The conditions attached to use of the normal purchase or sale exemption often pose problems for mining companies and oil and gas companies because, historically, they have settled many purchase and sales contracts on a net basis.

A further problem may arise when a mining company or oil and gas company holds a written option for the purpose of the receipt or delivery of a non-financial item in accordance with the entity's expected purchase, sale or usage requirements – because IAS 39 would require such contracts to be accounted for as derivative financial instruments.

Finally, mining companies and oil and gas companies that need to settle contracts for the sale of commodities on a net basis because of operational problems would need to treat those contracts and similar contracts as derivative financial instruments under IAS 39. The extract below from AngloGold Ashanti's 2008 financial statements illustrates how this could affect an entity's reported financial position.

(NOTE: In October 2010, AngloGold Ashanti removed the last of its gold hedging instruments and long-term sales contracts.)

Extract 41.29: *AngloGold Ashanti Limited (2008)*

Risk management and internal controls [extract]

Risks related to AngloGold Ashanti's operations [extract]

AngloGold Ashanti uses gold hedging instruments and has entered into long-term sales contracts, which may prevent the company from realising potential gains resulting from subsequent commodity price increases in the future. AngloGold Ashanti's reported financial condition could be adversely affected as a result of the need to fair value all of its hedge contracts.

AngloGold Ashanti has used gold hedging instruments to protect and fix the selling price of some of its anticipated production. The use of such instruments prevents full participation in subsequent increases in the market price for the commodity with respect to covered production. Since 2001, AngloGold Ashanti has been reducing its hedge commitments through hedge buy-backs (limited to non-hedge derivatives), deliveries into contracts and restructuring in order to provide greater participation in a rising gold price environment. As a result of these measures, AngloGold Ashanti has, and expects to continue to have, substantially less protection against declines in the market price of gold as compared with previous years.

AngloGold Ashanti continues to use gold hedging instruments to fix the selling price of a portion of its anticipated gold production and to protect revenues against unfavourable gold price and exchange rate movements. While the use of these instruments may protect against a drop in gold prices and exchange rate movements, it will do so for only a limited period of time and only to the extent that the hedge remains in place. The use of these instruments may also prevent AngloGold Ashanti from fully realising the positive impact on income from any subsequent favourable increase in the price of gold on the portion of production covered by the hedge and of any subsequent favourable exchange rate movements.

In 2008, AngloGold Ashanti used part of the proceeds from its $1.7 billion rights offer to undertake a major restructuring of the hedge book. This hedge restructuring resulted in hedge commitments reducing by 5.29 million ounces (or 47%) from 11.28 million ounces as at 31 December 2007 to 5.99 million ounces as at 31 December 2008. Although this hedge restructuring has significantly reduced the exposure to the hedge book, a rising gold price may result in a gap between the spot price and AngloGold Ashanti's received price of gold for ounces still hedged, and this may continue as AngloGold Ashanti closes out its existing hedge positions by delivering into contracts.

A significant number of AngloGold Ashanti's forward sales contracts are not treated as derivatives and fair valued on the financial statements as they fall under the normal purchase sales exemption. Should AngloGold Ashanti fail to settle these contracts by physical delivery, then it may be required to account for the fair value of a portion, or potentially all of, the existing contracts in the financial statements. This could adversely affect AngloGold Ashanti's reported financial condition.

As the global financial crisis continues, some of AngloGold Ashanti's hedge counterparties may either be unable to perform their obligations under the applicable derivative instrument or in certain cases elect to terminate their contracts early in 2010, which may result in the company being called upon to immediately meet any obligation under the hedge contracts with such hedge counterparties. This could adversely affect AngloGold Ashanti's financial condition.

4.12.2 Embedded derivatives

4.12.2.A Separating embedded derivatives

Even if a contract qualifies for the normal purchase and sale exemption, it still needs to be assessed for the existence of embedded derivatives. An embedded derivative is a component of a hybrid or combined instrument that also includes a non-derivative host contract; it has the effect that some of the cash flows of the combined instrument vary in a similar way to a stand-alone derivative. In other words, it causes some or all of the cash flows that otherwise would be required by the contract to be modified according to a specified interest rate, financial instrument price, commodity price, foreign exchange rate, index of prices or rates, credit rating or credit index, or other underlying variable (provided in the case of a non-financial variable that the variable is not specific to a party to the contract). *[IAS 39.10, IFRS 9 Appendix A]*.

The detailed rules and requirements regarding the separation of embedded derivatives, and the interpretation and application of those requirements, are discussed in Chapter 44. A number of issues related to embedded derivatives that are of particular importance to the extractive industries are discussed at 4.12.2.B to 4.12.2.E below.

4.12.2.B Foreign currency embedded derivatives

The most common embedded derivatives in the extractive industries are probably foreign currency embedded derivatives which arise when a producer of minerals sells these in a currency that is not (1) the functional currency of any substantial party to the contract, (2) the currency in which the price of the related commodity is routinely denominated in commercial transactions around the world or (3) a currency that is commonly used in contracts to purchase or sell non-financial items in the economic environment in which the transaction takes place. *[IAS 39.AG33(d), IFRS 9.B4.3.7(d)]*. A more detailed analysis of these requirements can be found in Chapter 44 at 5.2.1.

4.12.2.C Provisionally priced contracts

As discussed at 6.3.1 below, the sales contracts for certain commodities (e.g. copper and oil) generally provide for provisional pricing at the time of shipment, with final pricing based on the average market price for a future period. In those cases, the non-financial contract for the sale or purchase of the mineral concentrate at a future date would be treated as the host contract, while the exposure to the price movements from the date of sale to the end of the quotational period would be treated as an embedded derivative.

4.12.2.D Long-term supply contracts

Long-term supply contracts sometimes contain embedded derivatives because of a desire to shift certain risks between contracting parties or as a consequence of existing market practices. The fair value of embedded derivatives increases as a function of the duration of the contract. Hence the fair value of embedded derivatives in long-term supply contracts is often highly material to the entities involved.

As can be seen in the following extract from BHP Billiton's 2007 financial statements, the pricing terms of embedded derivatives in purchase (sales) contracts often match those of the product that the entity sells (purchases).

Extract 41.30: BHP Billiton Group (2007)

Notes to Financial Statements [extract]

28 Financial instruments [extract]

Embedded derivatives

Derivatives embedded in host contracts are accounted for as separate derivatives when their risks and characteristics are not closely related to those of the host contracts or have intrinsic value at inception and the host contracts are not carried at fair value. These embedded derivatives are measured at fair value with gains or losses arising from changes in fair value recognised in the income statement.

Contracts are assessed for embedded derivatives when the Group becomes a party to them, including at the date of a business combination. Host contracts which incorporate embedded derivatives are entered into during the normal course of operations and are standard business practices in the industries in which the Group operate.

The following table provides information about the principal embedded derivatives contracts:

	Maturity date 2007	2006	Volume 2007	2006		Exposure price
Commodity Price Swaps						
Electricity purchase arrangement (a)	31 Dec 2024	31 Dec 2024	240,000	240,000	MWh	Aluminium
Electricity purchase arrangement (a)	30 June 2020	30 June 2020	576,000	576,000	MWh	Aluminium
Gas sales (b)	31 Dec 2013	31 Dec 2013	1,195,572	1,428,070	'000 therms	Electricity
Commodity Price Options						
Finance lease of plant and equipment (b)	31 Dec 2018	30 Dec 2018	38.5	39.5	mmboe	Crude Oil
Copper concentrate purchases and sales (b)	31 Dec 2007	31 Dec 2006	52	41	'000 tonnes	Copper
Lead concentrate purchases and sales (b)	31 Dec 2007	1 January 2007	11	67	'000 tonnes	Lead
Zinc concentrate purchases and sales (b)	31 Dec 2007	2 January 2007	51	6	'000 tonnes	Zinc
Silver concentrate sales (b)	31 Dec 2007	–	4,604	–	'000 ounces	Silver

(a)   The volumes shown in these contracts indicate a megawatt volume per hour for each hour of the contract.

(b)   The volumes shown in these contracts indicate the total volumes for the contract.

As illustrated above, in the mining industry electricity purchase contracts sometimes contain price conditions based on the commodity that is being sold, which provides an economic hedge for the mining company. Whereas in the oil and gas industry, as illustrated above, the sales price of gas is at times based on that of electricity, which provides an economic hedge for the utility company that purchases the gas.

4.12.2.E   Development of gas markets

Prior to the development of an active local market in gas, market participants often entered into long-term contracts that were priced on the basis of a basket of underlying factors, such as oil prices, electricity prices and inflation indices. In the absence of an active market in gas, such price clauses are not considered to give rise to embedded derivatives because there is no accepted benchmark price for gas that could have been used instead.

An entity is required under IFRIC 9 – *Reassessment of Embedded Derivatives* – to assess whether an embedded derivative is required to be separated from the host contract and accounted for as a derivative when the entity first becomes a party to the contract and subsequent reassessment is generally prohibited (see Chapter 44 at 7). *[IFRIC 9.7].* Therefore, when subsequently an active gas market develops, an entity is not permitted to separate embedded derivatives from existing gas contracts, unless there is a change in the terms of the contract that significantly modifies the cash flows that otherwise would be required under the contract. However, if the entity enters into a new gas contract with exactly the same terms and conditions, it would be required to separate embedded derivatives from the new gas contract.

Judgement is required in determining (1) whether an active gas market exists in a particular geographic region and (2) the relevant geographic market for any type of commodity.

The extract below from BP shows that the fair value of embedded derivatives in long-term gas contracts can be quite significant.

Extract 41.31: BP plc (2010)

Notes on financial statements [extract]

34 Derivative financial instruments [extract]

Embedded derivatives [extract]

Prior to the development of an active gas trading market, UK gas contracts were priced using a basket of available price indices, primarily relating to oil products, power and inflation. After the development of an active UK gas market, certain contracts were entered into or renegotiated using pricing formulae not directly related to gas prices, for example, oil product and power prices. In these circumstances, pricing formulae have been determined to be derivatives, embedded within the overall contractual arrangements that are not clearly and closely related to the underlying commodity. The resulting fair value relating to these contracts is recognized on the balance sheet with gains or losses recognized in the income statement.

All the embedded derivatives relate to commodity prices, are categorized in level 3 of the fair value hierarchy and are valued using inputs that include price curves for each of the different products that are built up from active market pricing data. Where necessary, these are extrapolated to the expiry of the contracts (the last of which is in 2018) using all available external pricing information. Additionally, where limited data exists for certain products, prices are interpolated using historic and long-term pricing relationships.

The following table shows the changes during the year in the net fair value of embedded derivatives, within level 3 of the fair value hierarchy.

	$ million	
	2010	2009
	Commodity price	Commodity price
Net fair value of contracts at 1 January	**(1,331)**	(1,892)
Settlements	**37**	221
Gains (losses) recognized in the income statement (a)	**(350)**	535
Exchange adjustments	**37**	(195)
Net fair value of contracts at 31 December	**(1,607)**	(1,331)

(a) The amount for gains (losses) recognized in the income statement for 2009 includes a loss of $224 million arising as a result of refinements in the modelling and valuation methods used for these contracts.

4.12.3 Volume flexibility in supply contracts

It is not uncommon for other sales contracts, such as those with large industrial customers, to contain volume flexibility features. For example, a supplier might enter into a contract requiring it to deliver, say, 100,000 units at a given price as well as giving the counterparty the option to purchase a further 20,000 units at the same price. Very often such a supply contract is readily convertible to cash as parties to the contract can settle the contract on a net basis (see 4.12.1 above). For example, precious metals or base metals quoted on the London Metal Exchange are considered to be readily convertible to cash, whereas bulk materials without spot prices (e.g. coal and iron) are generally not considered to be readily convertible to cash.

If the customer has access to markets for the non-financial item and, following the guidance of the Interpretations Committee (see Chapter 43 at 4.2), the supplier might consider such a contract to be within the scope of IAS 39 as it contains a written option. However, some would say that the supplier could split the contract into two separate components for accounting purposes: a forward contract to supply 100,000 units (which may qualify as a normal sale) and a written option to supply 20,000 units (which would not). Arguments put forward include:

- the parties could easily have entered into two separate contracts, a forward contract and a written option; and

- it is appropriate to analogise to the requirements for embedded derivatives and separate a written option from the normal forward sale or purchase contract because it is not closely related.

Although these arguments are not universally accepted, we believe that there is merit in them.

This issue is discussed in more detail in Chapter 43 at 4.2.4 and 4.2.5.

5　PRACTICAL ISSUES IN THE OIL AND GAS INDUSTRY

5.1　Legal rights to explore for, develop and produce mineral properties

An entity can acquire legal rights to explore for, develop and produce wasting resources on a mineral property by:[157]

(a)　purchasing of minerals (i.e. outright ownership);

(b)　obtaining a lease or concession (see 5.1.1 below);

(c)　entering into a production-sharing contract or production-sharing agreement (see 5.1.2 below);

(d)　entering into a pure-service contract (see 5.1.3 below);

(e)　entering into a service contract (also called a service agreement or risk service contract) (see 5.1.4 below); and

(f)　entering into a joint operating agreement (see 5.1.5 below).

The IASC issues paper noted that 'in the mining industry, rights to explore for, develop, and produce minerals are often acquired by purchase of either the mineral rights alone (which does not include ownership of the land surface) or by purchase of both mineral rights and surface rights. In other cases, they are acquired through a right to mine contract, which grants the enterprise the rights to develop and mine the property and may call for a payment at the time the contract becomes effective and subsequent periodic payments. In the mining industry, rights to explore, develop, and produce minerals may also be acquired by mineral leases from private owners or from the government.'[158]

In the oil and gas industry entities usually obtain the rights to explore for, develop, and produce oil and gas through mineral leases, concession agreements, production-sharing contracts, or service contracts.[159] The type of legal arrangement used depends to a large extent on the legal framework of the country and market practice. The main features of each of these legal rights to access mineral reserves, except for the outright ownership of minerals, are discussed below.

The extract below from the financial statements of TOTAL illustrates the different types of legal arrangements that an oil and gas company may enter into to secure access to mineral reserves.

Extract 41.32: TOTAL S.A. (2010)

Risk factors [extract]

Other risks [extract]

Legal aspects of exploration and production activities

TOTAL's exploration and production activities are conducted in many different countries and are therefore subject to an extremely broad range of regulations. These cover virtually all aspects of exploration and production activities, including matters such as leasehold rights, production rates, royalties, environmental protection, exports, taxes and foreign exchange rates. The terms of the concessions, licenses, permits and contracts governing the Group's ownership of oil and gas interests vary from country to country. These concessions, licenses, permits and contracts are generally granted by or entered into with a government entity or a state-owned company and are sometimes entered into with private owners. These arrangements usually take the form of concessions or production sharing agreements.

The oil concession agreement remains the traditional model for agreements entered into with States: the oil company owns the assets and the facilities and is entitled to the entire production. In exchange, the operating risks, costs and investments are the oil company's responsibility and it agrees to remit to the relevant State, usually the owner of the subsoil resources, a production-based royalty, income tax, and possibly other taxes that may apply under local tax legislation.

The production sharing contract (PSC) involves a more complex legal framework than the concession agreement: it defines the terms and conditions of production sharing and sets the rules governing the cooperation between the company or consortium in possession of the license and the host State, which is generally represented by a state-owned company. The latter can thus be involved in operating decisions, cost accounting and production allocation.

The consortium agrees to undertake and finance all exploration, development and production activities at its own risk. In exchange, it is entitled to a portion of the production, known as "cost oil", the sale of which should cover all of these expenses (investments and operating costs). The balance of production, known as "profit oil", is then shared in varying proportions, between the company or consortium, on the one hand, and with the State or the state-owned company, on the other hand.

In some instances, concession agreements and PSCs coexist, sometimes in the same country. Even though other contractual structures still exist, TOTAL's license portfolio is comprised mainly of concession agreements. In all countries, the authorities of the host State, often assisted by international accounting firms, perform joint venture and PSC cost audits and ensure the observance of contractual obligations.

In some countries, TOTAL has also signed contracts called "risked service contracts" which are similar to production sharing contracts. However, the profit oil is replaced by risked monetary remuneration, agreed by contract, which depends notably on the field performance. Thus, the remuneration under the Iraqi contract is based on an amount calculated per barrel produced.

Hydrocarbon exploration and production activities are subject to public authorities (permits), which can be different for each of these activities. These permits are granted for limited periods of time and include an obligation to return a large portion, in case of failure the entire portion, of the permit area at the end of the exploration period.

TOTAL is required to pay tax on income generated from its oil and gas production and sales activities under its concessions, production sharing contracts and risked service contracts, as provided for by local regulations. In addition, depending on the country, TOTAL's production and sale activities may be subject to a range of other taxes, fees and withholdings, including special petroleum taxes and fees. The taxes imposed on oil and gas production and sale activities may be substantially higher than those imposed on other businesses.

The legal framework of TOTAL's exploration and production activities, established through concessions, licenses, permits and contracts granted by or entered into with a government entity, a state-owned company or, sometimes, private owners, is subject to certain risks which in certain cases can diminish or challenge the protections offered by this legal framework.

5.1.1 *Mineral leases and concession agreements*

In most countries the government owns all mineral rights, but in the United States and some other countries mineral rights are directly owned by individuals. In the United States it is common for oil and gas companies to enter into a mineral lease agreement with the legal owner of the mineral rights. While these contracts are negotiated individually, and may therefore each be different, they typically share a large number of features, which are discussed below:

(a)   the *owner/lessor* of the mineral rights retains a *royalty interest*, which entitles it to a specified percentage of the mineral produced. The lessor is normally only required to pay for its share of the severance taxes and the costs of getting the production into a marketable state, but not for any exploration and development costs. The *royalty* is either payable in cash or payable in-kind. Although the lessor is normally not interested in receiving its royalty in kind, the option of receiving the royalty in kind is often included for tax purposes;

(b)   the lessee obtains a *working interest* under the mineral lease, which entitles it to explore for, develop, and produce oil and gas from the property as its cost. The working interest can be held by more than one party, in which case a *joint operating agreement* needs to be executed (see 5.1.5 below);

(c)   upon signing of the mineral lease agreement the lessee typically pays the lessor a *lease bonus* or *signature bonus*, which is a one-off upfront payment in exchange for the lessor's signing of the mineral lease agreement;

(d)   it is in the lessor's interest for the lessee to explore the property as quickly as possible. To ensure that the lessee does not delay exploration and development unnecessarily, the following terms are typically included:

- • most mineral leases define a *primary term* during which the lessee is required to commence drilling;

- • normally the lessee has a *drill obligation* that must be met within a certain period. However, by paying *delay rentals* the lessee can defer commencement of drilling; and

- • the mineral lease will remain in force once the obligatory drilling programme has been completed successfully and production commences, but the lease will be cancelled if activities are suspended for a prolonged period;

(e)   most mineral leases provide that the lessee and the lessor have the right to assign their interest without approval to another party. This means that both the lessee and the lessor can create new rights out of existing rights (see 5.2 below);

(f)   under many lease contracts the lessee can be required to pay *shut-in royalties* when a successful well capable of commercial production has been completed, but production has not commenced within a specified time; and

(g)   the lessor is typically not entitled to royalties on oil and gas consumed in producing further oil and gas from a property.

5.1.1.A   Concessionary agreements (concessions)

Concessionary agreements or concessions are mineral leases 'under which the government owning mineral rights grants the concessionaire the right to explore, develop, and produce the minerals'.[160] However, unlike a production sharing contract (see 5.1.2 below), under a concessionary agreement the oil and gas company retains title to the assets constructed during the term of the concession. Furthermore, the oil and gas company bears all the risks and there is no profit sharing arrangement with the government. Rather, the government is entitled to a royalty computed in much the same way as a royalty under lease contracts.[161] In addition, depending on the country's fiscal policies, the government will typically also collect taxes such as duties, severance or production taxes, and income taxes.

In some jurisdictions the government may retain the option to participate in the project as a working interest owner in the property. In this case, the oil and gas company initially holds 100% of the working interest. If the project is successful and reserves are found, the national oil company becomes a working interest owner and will pay for its proportionate share of the investment.

5.1.2   Production sharing contracts

A production sharing contract (PSC) or production sharing arrangement (PSA) is a contract between a national oil company (NOC) or the government of a host country and a contracting entity (contractor) to carry out oil and gas exploration and production activities in accordance with the terms of the contract, with the two parties sharing mineral output.[162] In such countries the ownership of the mineral reserves in the ground does not pass to the contractor. Instead, the contractor is permitted to recover its costs and share in the profits from the exploration and production activities. Although the precise form and content of a PSC may vary, the following features are likely to be encountered:[163]

(a)   the government retains ownership of the reserves and grants the contractor the right to explore for, develop, and produce the reserves;

(b)   the government is often directly involved in the operation of the property, either (1) by way of an *operating committee* that comprises representatives of the contractor and the government or NOC, or (2) by requiring the contractor to submit its annual work programme and corresponding annual budget to the government or NOC for approval. The contractor is responsible to the NOC for carrying out operations in accordance with contract terms;

(c)   upon signing of the PSC the contractor pays the government a *signature bonus*, which is a one-off upfront payment in exchange for the government's signing of the PSC;

(d)   the contractor pays the government a *production bonus* upon commencement of production and when the average production over a given period first exceeds a threshold level;

(e)   the government is entitled to a *royalty payment* that is calculated as a percentage of the net production (i.e. net of petroleum lost, flared or re-injected) and which is payable in kind or in money at the option of the government. The royalty rate applicable is not necessarily a fixed percentage, but may depend on the production volume or destination of the production (e.g. different rates may apply to crude oil and gas that is exported);

(f)   the contractor provides all financing and technology necessary to carry out operations and pays all of the costs specified;

(g)   the contractor is typically required to bear all of the risks related to exploration and, perhaps, to development (i.e. the government does not have a working interest during exploration and development phases);

(h)   the contractor is frequently required to provide infrastructure, such as streets, electricity, water systems, roads, hospitals, schools, and other items during various phases of activities. Additionally, the contract customarily requires the contractor to provide specified training of personnel. Infrastructure and training costs may or may not be recoverable from future production by the contractor;[164]

(i)   the contractor may have a *domestic market obligation* that requires them to meet, as a priority, the needs of domestic oil and/or gas consumption in the host country. Alternatively, the contractor may be required to sell oil and/or gas to the NOC at the official oil or gas price;

(j)   the contractor is normally committed to completing a *minimum work programme* in each of the phases of the project, which generally needs to be completed within a specified period. If the work is not performed, the contract may require the unspent amount to be paid in cash to the government;

(k)   a production sharing contract normally requires *relinquishment* of a certain percentage of the original contract area by the end of the initial term of the exploration period. A further reduction is typically required by the end of the exploration period. The government can negotiate a new contract with another party for the continued exploration of the surrendered acreage. Any data and information relating to the surrendered area often becomes the exclusive property of the government;

(l) equipment that is acquired for the development and production activities normally becomes the property of the government or NOC;

(m) operating costs and specified exploration and development costs are recoverable out of *cost recovery oil*, which is a specified percentage of production revenues after the royalty payment each year. The production sharing contract specifies whether particular types of cost are recoverable or non-recoverable. Recoverable costs not recovered by the contractor in the current period can be carried forward to the following reporting period for recovery purposes;

(n) revenues remaining after royalty and cost recovery are called *profit oil*. Profit oil is split between the government and the contractor on a predetermined basis;

(o) many production sharing contracts provide that the income tax to which the contractor is subject is deemed to have been paid to the government as part of the payment of profit oil (see 4.11.3 above); and

(p) some production sharing contracts give the contractor the right to set up a decommissioning reserve fund which enables the contractor to recover the costs associated with future decommissioning and site restoration. In cases where the PSC terminates before the end of the life of the field, the government is typically responsible for decommissioning and site restoration.

Even in situations where the provisions of a PSC are fairly straightforward at first sight, it may be rather complicated to calculate the entitlement of each of the parties involved as is illustrated in the example below.

Example 41.15: Production sharing contract

An oil and gas company (contractor) entered into a PSC that includes the following terms:

- the oil and gas company pays for all exploration costs;
- the government is entitled to:
  - 15% royalty on the production;
  - severance tax of USD 2.50 per barrel;
  - USD 5 million when average production first exceeds 25,000 barrels per day; and
  - 10% of the profit oil;
- operating expenses are recoverable before exploration costs;
- development costs are recoverable after exploration costs;
- cost recovery oil is capped at 45% of the annual production; and
- the national oil company (NOC) and the contractor have a 51% and 49% working interest, respectively.

How should the production be allocated between parties, assuming the following for 2012:

- annual production in 2012 is 10 million barrels;
- recoverable operating costs in 2012 are USD 25 million;
- the average oil price in 2012 is USD 100/barrel;
- during 2012 average production exceeded 25,000 barrels per day for the first time;
- unrecovered exploration costs at the beginning of 2012 were USD 180 million; and
- unrecovered development costs at the beginning of 2012 were USD 275 million.

Chapter 41

		Barrels	Contractor (49%)	NOC (51%)	Government
Production in 2012	a	10,000,000			
Royalty 15% of 10,000,000 =	b	1,500,000			1,500,000
Severance tax 10,000,000 × $2.50 ÷ $100 =	c	250,000			250,000
Cost oil Operating costs $25,000,000 ÷ $100 =	d	250,000	122,500	127,500	
Exploration cost $180,000,000 ÷ $100 =	e	1,800,000	1,800,000		
Development cost $275,000,000 ÷ $100, but capped at 2,450,000	f	2,450,000	1,200,500	1,249,500	
Total cost oil 45% of 10,000,000 =	g	4,500,000			
Production bonus $5,000,000 ÷ $100 =	h	50,000			50,000
Profit oil: a − b − c − g − h =	i	3,750,000			
Government profit oil 10% of 3,750,000 =	j	375,000			375,000
Working interest in profit oil 3,375,000 − 375,000 =	k	3,375,000	1,653,750	1,721,250	
Total		10,000,000	4,776,750	3,098,250	2,175,000
Unrecovered development costs $275,000,000 − 2,450,000 × $100 =		$30,000,000	$14,700,000	$15,300,000	

The above example illustrates not only that calculating an entity's share in the production of the current period requires a detailed knowledge of the PSC's provisions, but also that calculating the contractor's share of the remaining reserves requires a number of assumptions.

The reserves and production that the parties are entitled to varies depending on the oil price. Had the average oil price in 2012 been $50/barrel the parties' entitlements would have been as follows: Contractor 5,540,400 barrels, NOC 2,019,600 barrels and Government 2,440,000 barrels. The quantity of reserves and production attributable to each of the parties often reacts to changes in oil prices in ways that, at first, might seem counterintuitive.

It is also worth noting that the type and nature of contracts emerging continue to evolve. As a consequence, new contracts are emerging that, while they have some aspects of a PSC, do differ from the traditional PSC. Therefore, determining the accounting implications of these contracts is becoming more complex. This not only impacts the accounting for such contracts but also impacts whether, and the extent to which, the contractor entity is able to recognise reserves.

Reserves recognition involves a considerable amount of judgement. Each contractual arrangement needs to be analysed carefully to determine whether reserves recognition is appropriate. Such an analysis would include, at a minimum:

- The extent of risk to which the contractor party is exposed, including exploration and / or development risk;
- The structure of the contractor's reimbursement arrangements and whether it is subject to performance / reservoir risk or price risk;
- The ability for the contractor to take product in-kind, rather than a cash reimbursement only.

Other facts and circumstances may also be relevant in reaching the final assessment. Given the varying terms and conditions that exist within these contracts and the fact that they are continuing to change / evolve, each contract will need to be individually analysed and assessed in detail.

5.1.3 Pure-service contracts

'A pure-service contract is an agreement between a contractor and a host government that typically covers a defined technical service to be provided or completed during a specific period of time. The service company investment is typically limited to the value of equipment, tools, and personnel used to perform the service. In most cases, the service contractor's reimbursement is fixed by the terms of the contract with little exposure to either project performance or market factors. Payment for services is normally based on daily or hourly rates, a fixed turnkey rate, or some other specified amount. Payments may be made at specified intervals or at the completion of the service. Payments, in some cases, may be tied to the field performance, operating cost reductions, or other important metrics.

The risks of the service company under this type of contract are usually limited to non-recoverable cost overruns, losses owing to client breach of contract, default, or contractual dispute. These agreements generally do not have exposure to production volume or market price; consequently, reserves are not usually recognized under this type of agreement.'[165] Such a contract is considered to be a management contract that gives rise to revenue from rendering services and not income from the production of mineral. Therefore, the minerals produced are not included in the normal reserve disclosures of the contractor,[166] and the contractor bears no risk if reserves are not found.

5.1.4 Risk service contracts

Unlike pure-service contracts, under a risk service contract (also called risked service agreement or at-risk service contract) a fee is not certain: an entity (contractor) agrees to explore for, develop, and produce minerals on behalf of a host government, but the contractor is at risk for the amount spent on exploration and development costs. That is, if no minerals are found in commercial quantities, no fee is paid.[167] Although a risk service contract (RSC) does not result in the contractor's ownership of the minerals in place, the contractor may be at risk for the costs of exploration and may have economic interest in those minerals. The IASC Issues Paper noted that in the case of risk service contracts:[168]

- the fee may be payable in cash or in minerals produced;

- the contract may call for the contractor to bear all or part of the costs of exploration that are usually recoverable, in whole or in part, from production. If there is no production, there is no recovery; and

- the contract may also give the contractor the right to purchase part of the minerals produced.

As noted in Extract 41.32 above from TOTAL's financial statements, risk service contracts are similar to production sharing contracts in a number of respects. Although the precise form and content a risk service contract may vary, the following features are common:

(a)   the repayment of expenses and the compensation for services are established on a monetary basis;

(b)   an RSC is for a limited period, after which the government or national oil company will take over operations;

(c)   under an RSC the contractor does not obtain ownership of the mineral reserves or production;

(d)   the contractor is normally required to carry out a minimum amount of work in providing the contracted services;

(e)   the fee that is payable to the contractor covers its capital expenditure, operating costs and an agreed-upon profit margin; and

(f)   ownership of the assets used under the contract passes to the government when the contractor has been reimbursed for its costs.

The SPE's *Guidelines for the Evaluation of Petroleum Reserves and Resources* notes in connection with risk service contracts that 'under the existing regulations, it may be more difficult for the contractor to justify reserves recognition, and special care must be taken in drafting the agreement. If regulations are satisfied, reserves equivalent to the value of the cost-recovery-plus-revenue-profit split are normally reported by the contractor.'[169]

As noted above, similar to PSCs, the nature and terms and conditions of these risk services contracts continue to evolve. Therefore each contract will need to be analysed in detail to determine how it should be accounted for.

5.1.5   Joint operating agreements

When several entities are involved in a joint arrangement (e.g. joint ownership of a property, production sharing contract or concession) they will need to enter into some form of joint operating agreement (JOA). A JOA is a contract between two or more parties to a joint arrangement that sets out the rights and obligations to operate the property. Typically, a JOA designates one of the working interest owners as the operator and it governs the operations and sharing of costs between parties. A JOA does not override, but instead builds upon, the contracts that are already in place (such as production sharing contracts). In fact, many production sharing contracts require the execution of a JOA between the parties. Often a JOA will give rise to a joint venture under IAS 31 (see 4.3.2 above) and may potentially give rise to a joint arrangement under IFRS 11 (see 4.3.3 and 4.3.4 above).

5.2 Different types of royalty interests

5.2.1 *Working interest and basic royalties*

As discussed at 5.1.1 above, under a mineral lease the owner/lessor of the mineral rights retains a *basic royalty* interest (or non-operating interest), which entitles it to a specified percentage of the mineral produced, while the lessee obtains a *working interest* (or operating interest) under the mineral lease, which entitles it to explore for, develop, and produce oil and gas from the property.

If the owner of a working interest cannot fund or does not wish to bear the risk of the exploration, development or production of oil and gas from the property, it may be able – if this is permitted by the underlying lease – to sell the working interest or to create new types of interest out of its existing working interest. By creating new types of non-operating interests, the working interest owner is able to raise financing and spread the risk of the development. The original working interest holder may either:

- retain the new non-operating interest and transfer the working interest (i.e. the rights and obligations for exploring, developing and operating the property); or
- carve out and transfer a new non-operating interest to another party, while retaining the working interest.

The following non-operating interests are commonly created in practice:[170]

- overriding royalties (see 5.2.2 below);
- production payment royalties (see 5.2.3 below); and
- net profits interests (see 5.2.4 below).

5.2.2 *Overriding royalties*

An *overriding royalty* is very similar to a basic royalty, except that the former is created out of the operating interest and if the operating interest expires, the overriding royalty also expires.[171] An overriding royalty owner bears only its share of production taxes and sometimes of the costs incurred to get the oil or gas into a saleable condition.

5.2.3 *Production payment royalties*

A *production payment royalty* is the right to recover (1) a specified amount of cash or (2) a specified quantity of minerals, out of the working interest's share of gross production. For example, the working interest holder may assign a production payment royalty to another party for USD 12 million, in exchange for a repayment of USD 15 million plus 12% interest out of the first 65% of the working interest holder's share of production. Production payments that are specified as a quantity of minerals are often called volume production payments or VPPs.

5.2.4 *Net profits interests*

A *net profits interest* is similar to an overriding royalty. However, the amount to be received by the royalty owner is a share of the net proceeds from production (as defined in the contract) that is paid solely from the working interest owner's share. The owner of a net profit interest is not liable for any expenses.

5.3   Risk-sharing arrangements

As discussed at 1.1 above, the high costs and high risks in the extractive industries often lead entities to enter into risk-sharing arrangements. The following types of risk-sharing arrangements are discussed in this chapter:

- carried interests (see 5.3.1 below);
- farm-ins and farm-outs (see 5.3.2 below);
- asset swaps (see 5.3.3 below);
- unitisations (see 5.3.4 below);
- investments in subsidiaries, joint ventures and associates (see 4.3 above);
- production sharing contracts (see 5.1.2 above), which result in a degree of risk sharing with local governments; and
- risk service contracts (see 5.1.4 above).

5.3.1   Carried interests

Carried interests often arise when a party in an arrangement is either unable to bear the risk of exploration or is unable to fund its share of the cost of exploration or development. A carried interest is an agreement under which one party (the carrying party) agrees to pay for a portion or all of the pre-production costs of another party (the carried party) on a licence in which both own a portion of the working interest.[172] In effect, commercially, the carried party is trading a share of any production to which it is entitled in exchange for the carrying party funding one or more phases of the project. In other words, the parties create a new interest out of an existing working interest. If the project is unsuccessful then the carrying party will not be reimbursed for the costs that it has incurred on behalf of the carried party. If the project is successful then the carrying party will be reimbursed 'either (a) in cash out of proceeds of the share of production attributable to the carried party, or (b) by receiving a disproportionately high share of the production until the carried costs have been recovered'.[173]

5.3.1.A   Types of carried interest arrangements

Carried interest arrangements tend to fall into one of the following two categories:

- *Financing-type arrangements* – The carrying party provides funding to the carried party and receives a lender's return on the funds provided, while the right to additional production acts as a security that underpins the arrangement; or
- *Purchase/sale-type arrangement* – The carried party effectively sells an interest or a partial interest in a project to the carrying party. The carrying party will be required to fund the project in exchange for an increased share of any proceeds if the project succeeds, while the carried party retains a much reduced share of any proceeds.

In practice, however, it is not always easy to determine in which category a particular carried interest arrangement falls, as is illustrated in the example below.

Example 41.16:   Carried interests (1)

Scenario 1

The carrying party has proposed a $10 million project, which has a very high chance of succeeding. The carried party, which is unable to fund its share of the project, agrees that the carrying party is entitled to recover its cost plus 7% interest by giving it a disproportionately high share of the production. If the production from this project is insufficient to repay the initial investment, the carried party should reimburse the carrying party out of its share of production from other fields within the same licence.

Scenario 2

The carrying party has proposed a project that may cost up to $6 million, the outcome of which is uncertain. The carried party, which is unwilling to participate in the project, agrees that the carrying party is entitled to all production from the project until it has recovered three times its initial investment.

Scenario 3

The carrying party has proposed a project that may cost up to $5 million, which has a good chance of succeeding. The carrying party has a 60% interest in the licence and the carried party holds the remaining 40%. The carried party, which is unable to fund its share of the project, agrees that the carrying party is entitled to an additional 25% of the production until the carrying party has recovered its costs plus a 20% return.

Some of the indicators that a carried interest arrangement should be accounted for as a financing-type arrangement are that:

- the carried party is unable to fund its share of the project;

- the risks associated with the development are not significant, i.e. financing-type arrangements will be more common in the development stage; and

- the carrying party receives a return that is comparable to a lender's rate of return.

On the other hand, indicators that a carried interest arrangement should be treated as a purchase/sale-type arrangement include:

- the carrying party and carried party have genuinely different opinions about the chances of success of the project, and the carried party could fund its share of the project if it wanted to;

- there are significant uncertainties about the outcome of the project. Purchase/sale-type arrangements are therefore be more common in the E&E phase;

- the arrangement gives the carrying party voting rights in the project;

- there are significant uncertainties about the costs of the project, perhaps because it involves use of a new technology or approach;

- the carrying party could lose all of its investment or possibly earn a return significantly in excess of a lender's rate of return; and

- the carrying party can only recover its investment from the project that is subject to the arrangement and there is no recourse to other assets or interests of the carried party.

In Example 41.16 above, scenario 1 has the characteristics of a financing-type arrangement, while scenario 2 has those of a purchase/sale-type arrangement. However, when an arrangement (such as scenario 3) has financing-type and purchase/sale-type characteristics (e.g. as a result of the relative bargaining strength of the parties), an entity will need to analyse the arrangement carefully and exercise judgement in developing an appropriate accounting policy.

The following types of carried interest arrangements are discussed below:

- carried interest arrangements in the E&E phase (see 5.3.1.B below);
- financing-type carried interest arrangements in the development phase (see 5.3.1.C below); and
- purchase/sale-type carried interest arrangements in the development phase (see 5.3.1.D below).

5.3.1.B   Carried interest arrangements in the E&E phase

While IFRS 6 should be applied to accounting for E&E expenditures, the standard does not 'address other aspects of accounting by entities engaged in the exploration for and evaluation of mineral resources'. *[IFRS 6.4]*. That leaves somewhat unanswered the question of whether carried interest arrangements can ever fall within the scope of IFRS 6. In the case of a purchase/sale-type carried interest arrangement the transaction, at least in economic terms, leads to the acquisition of an E&E asset by the carrying party and a disposal by the carried party. Therefore, we believe that purchase/sale-type carried interest arrangements would fall within the scope of IFRS 6. Hence an entity has two options: either to develop an accounting policy under IAS 8 as discussed under 5.3.1.C below, or to develop an accounting policy under IFRS 6 that is based on its previous national GAAP. In practice this usually means that:

- the carrying party accounts for its expenditures under a carried interest arrangement in the same way as directly incurred E&E expenditure (see 3.2 and 3.3 above); and
- the carried party may need to recognise a loss when the terms of the transaction indicate that the asset is impaired. However, to the extent that an arrangement is favourable, the carried party would – depending on its accounting policy – recognise the gain either (1) in profit or loss or (2) as a reduction in the carrying amount of the E&E asset.

On the other hand, a finance-type carried interest arrangement that has no significant impact on the risks and rewards that an entity derives from the underlying E&E working interest, may be more akin to a funding arrangement. As IFRS 6 deals only with accounting for E&E expenditures and assets, it is a matter of judgement whether or not the accounting for finance-type carried interest arrangements is considered to be outside the scope of the standard. If an arrangement is considered to be outside the scope of IFRS 6, it might be sensible to account for it in the same way as finance-type carried interest arrangements that relate to projects that are not in the E&E phase (see 5.3.1.C below).

5.3.1.C   Financing-type carried interest arrangements in the development phase

As financing-type carried interest arrangements do not result in the transfer of the economic risks and rewards of the underlying working interest between parties, such arrangements are not accounted for as a sale (purchase) by the carried party (carrying party). Instead such arrangements are in effect secured borrowings in which the underlying asset is used as collateral that provides an identifiable stream of cash flows.

Such arrangements are most appropriately accounted for as giving rise to a financial asset for the carrying party and a financial liability for the carried party.

The carried party therefore recognises an investment in an asset, representing its full share of the working interest prior to the execution of the carried interest arrangement, and a corresponding financial liability for the amount that it is expected to reimburse to the carrying party, irrespective of whether it is a non-recourse arrangement or not. The liability is accounted for as a loan at amortised cost under IAS 39, which means that the carried party should accrete interest on the liability and reduce the loan to the extent the carrying party recovers its costs. It should be noted, however, that the application of the effective interest rate method under IAS 39 requires adjustment of the carrying amount when the entity revises its estimates of the payments to be made. *[IAS 39.AG8]*.

Conversely the carrying party should recognise a financial asset for the amount that it expects to recover as a reimbursement. Classification of such a financial asset as a loan or receivable under IAS 39 is only possible when the carrying party expects to recover substantially its entire investment, *[IAS 39.9]*, or a financial asset at amortised cost under IFRS 9 if both of the following conditions are met:

- The asset is held within a business model whose objective is to hold assets in order to collect contractual cash flows, and

- The contractual terms of the financial asset give rise on specified dates to cash flows that are solely payments of principal and interest on the principal amount outstanding *[IFRS 9.4.1.2]*.

which should normally be the case in financing-type carried interest arrangements.

The above approach to accounting for carried interest arrangements would not be appropriate if there were more than an insignificant transfer of risk (without necessarily resulting in a purchase/sale-type carried interest arrangement), because the transfer of risk would suggest that:

- the carried party should recognise a provision under IAS 37 rather than a liability under IAS 39;

- the carrying party should account for its right to receive reimbursement as an available-for-sale investment under IAS 39 / financial asset measured at fair value under IFRS 9 or a reimbursement right under IAS 37.

5.3.1.D *Purchase/sale-type carried interest arrangements in the development phase*

The accounting suggested here for the carried party is the same as that required by paragraph 155 of the OIAC SORP in UK GAAP, which states that the disposal should be accounted for in accordance with the entity's normal accounting policy.

Historically, some entities have accounted for these types of transactions on a cash basis, i.e. the carried party does nothing and the carrying party accounts for its actual cash outlays. It is hard to see how this can be justified under IFRS.

In purchase/sale-type carried interest arrangements, the carried party effectively sells part of its interest in a project to the carrying party. For example, the carried party may sell part of its interest in the mineral reserves to the carrying party which, in exchange, is obliged to fund the remaining costs of developing the field. Consequently, the arrangement has two elements, the purchase/sale of mineral reserves and the funding of developments costs, which should be accounted for in accordance with their substance. Therefore, the carried party should:

- derecognise the part of the asset that it has sold to the carrying party in accordance with the requirements of IAS 16 or IAS 38. Determining the amount to be recognised may require a considerable amount of judgement depending on how the interest sold is defined; *[IAS 16.67, IAS 38.112]*

- recognise the consideration received or receivable from the carrying party;

- recognise a gain or loss on the transaction for the difference between the net disposal proceeds and the carrying amount of the asset disposed of. *[IAS 16.71, IAS 38.113]*. Recognition of a gain would be appropriate only when the value of the consideration can be determined reliably. If not, then the carried party should account for the consideration received as a reduction in the carrying amount of the underlying assets; and

- test the retained interest for impairment if the terms of the arrangement indicate that the retained interest may be impaired.

In accounting for its purchase the carrying party should:

- recognise an asset that represents the underlying (partially) undeveloped interest acquired at cost in accordance with IAS 16 or IAS 38. *[IAS 16.15, IAS 38.21]*. Cost is defined in these standards as 'the amount of cash or cash equivalents paid or the fair value of the other consideration given to acquire an asset at the time of its acquisition or construction or, where applicable, the amount attributed to that asset when initially recognised in accordance with the specific requirements of other IFRSs'; *[IAS 16.6, IAS 38.8]* and

- recognise a liability for the obligation to make defined payments on behalf of the carried party, which relate to the carried party's share of future investments.

The application of this approach is illustrated in Example 41.17 below.

Example 41.17:   Carried interests (2)

An oil and gas company is developing an oil field in the North Sea. Assume that the company did not capitalise any E&E costs in relation to the field, but that by 1 January 2011 it had capitalised $250 million of costs in relation to the construction of property, plant and equipment. To complete the development of the oil field and bring it to production a further investment in property, plant and equipment of $350 million is required in the first half of 2011.

At 1 January 2011, the oil and gas company (the carried party) enters into a purchase/sale-type carried interest arrangement with a carrying party, which will fund the entire $350 million required for the further development of the field. Upon entering into the carried interest arrangement the carried party's entitlement to oil is expected to be reduced from 15,000,000 barrels of oil to 9,000,000 barrels of oil, i.e. its interest in the oil field and the related property, plant and equipment has been reduced to (9,000,000 ÷ 15,000,000 =) 60%. In practice, calculating the portion of the interest sold may require a considerable amount of judgement (e.g. in scenario 2 in Example 41.16 above it would not be straightforward to calculate the portion of the interest sold).

Both parties believe that the fair value of the oil field and related property, plant and equipment will be $1 billion once the remaining investment of $350 million has been made. Consequently, the fair value of the oil field and related property, plant and equipment at 1 January 2011 is ($1 billion − $350 million =) $650 million.

The fair value of the interest acquired (which comprises a portion of the oil field and a portion of the related property, plant and equipment) by the carrying party is (40% × $650 million =) $260 million. In exchange for its interest, the carrying party will pay $50 million in cash and undertakes to pay the remaining investments related to the carried party's interest.

The carried party accounts for the transaction as follows:

	$	$
Cash received from the carrying party	50	
Capital calls to be paid by the carrying party (60% × $350 million =) †	210	
Property, plant and equipment (40% × $250 million =)		100
Gain on sale (40% × ($650 million – $250 million) =)		160

† *The carried party has obtained the commitment from the carrying party to make certain payments on its behalf.*

If the carried party had recognised a loss on the interest sold, it would need to perform an impairment test on the interest retained.

The carrying party accounts for the transaction as follows:

	$	$
Assets acquired ($50 million + $210 million =) †	260	
Cash paid to the carried party		50
Capital calls payable on behalf of the carried party (60% × $350 million =) ‡		210

† *As discussed above, the cost of property, plant and equipment is defined as the fair value of the consideration. In an arm's length transaction the fair value of property, plant and equipment acquired is normally equal to the fair value of the consideration paid. The fair value of the portion of the oil field and the portion of the related property, plant and equipment acquired is (40% × $650 million =) $260 million.*

‡ *The carrying party has assumed a liability to make these payments on behalf of the carried party. The carrying party will also be required to pay (40% × $350 million =) $140 million for its own share of the future investments, but that amount is only recognised as a liability upon recognition of the related property, plant and equipment.*

The receivable recognised by the carried party and the corresponding liability recognised by the carrying party are reduced over the course of the construction of the assets to which they relate. The carrying party reduces the liability as it funds the carried party's share of the investment and the carried party recognises its share of the assets being constructed while reducing the balance of the receivable. The carrying party should recognise a provision under IAS 37 if the timing and amount of the liability are uncertain. *[IAS 37.10]*. However, if the carried interest arrangement requires payment of a fixed monetary amount then it could be argued that the liability meets the definition of a financial liability under IAS 32 that should be accounted for in accordance with IAS 39. *[IAS 32.11]*.

5.3.1.E   Government as the carried party

The IASC's Issues Paper observed that 'production sharing contracts (PSCs) may be viewed as a sharing arrangement. Some consider production sharing contracts to be a form of carried interest because many of the terms of a production sharing contract are very similar to those found in carried interests.'[174] Nevertheless, production sharing contracts typically contain a number of features not commonly found in carried interest arrangements and are discussed at 5.1.2 above.

5.3.2   *Farm-ins and farm-outs*

A farm-out (from the viewpoint of the transferor) or a farm-in (from the viewpoint of the transferee) is defined in the OIAC SORP as 'the transfer of part of an oil and gas interest in consideration for an agreement by the transferee ("farmee") to meet, absolutely, certain expenditure which would otherwise have to be undertaken by the owner ("farmor").'[175] Farm-in transactions generally occur in the exploration or development phase and are characterised by the transferor (i.e. farmor) giving up future economic benefits, in the form of reserves, in exchange for a reduction in future funding obligations.

Under a carried interest arrangement the carried party transfers a *portion* of the risks and rewards of a property, in exchange for a funding commitment from the carrying party. While under a farm-in arrangement the farmor transfers all the risks and rewards of a *proportion* (i.e. a straight percentage) of a property, in exchange for a commitment from the farmee to fund certain expenditures. Therefore, a farm-out represents the complete disposal of a *proportion* of a property and is similar to purchase/sale-type carried interest arrangements as discussed at 5.3.1.D above.

The following types of farm-in arrangements are separately discussed below:

- farm-in arrangements in the E&E phase (see 5.3.2.A below); and
- farm-in arrangements outside the E&E phase (see 5.3.2.B below).

5.3.2.A   *Farm-in arrangements in the E&E phase*

IFRS 6 deals with accounting for E&E expenditures and does not 'address other aspects of accounting by entities engaged in the exploration for and evaluation of mineral resources'. *[IFRS 6.4]*. That leaves open the question whether farm-in arrangements can ever fall within the scope of IFRS 6. However, as a farm-in arrangement leads to the acquisition of an E&E asset by the farmee and a disposal by the farmor, we believe that a farm-in arrangement would fall within the scope of IFRS 6. Hence an entity has two options: either to develop an accounting policy under IAS 8 as discussed under 5.3.2.B below; or to develop an accounting policy under IFRS 6. In practice many entities use the second option and apply an accounting policy to farm-in arrangements that is based on their previous national GAAP.

Accounting policies for farm-in arrangements in the E&E phase that are based on an entity's previous national GAAP will often require that:

- the farmee recognises its expenditure under the arrangement in respect of its own interest and that retained by the farmor, as and when the costs are incurred. The farmee accounts for its expenditures under a farm-in arrangement in the same way as directly incurred E&E expenditure; and
- the farmor accounts for the farm-out arrangement as follows:

- the farmor does not record any expenditure made by the farmee on its behalf;

- the farmor does not recognise a gain or loss on the farm-out arrangement, but rather redesignates any costs previously capitalised in relation to the whole interest as relating to the partial interest retained; and

- any cash consideration received is credited against costs previously capitalised in relation to the whole interest with any excess accounted for by the farmor as a gain on disposal.

If an entity applies its previous GAAP accounting policy in respect of farm-in arrangements, we would expect the entity also to make the farm-in disclosures required by its previous GAAP.

Extract 41.35 below shows Revus Energy's historical cost based accounting policy, under which no gain or loss is recognised, for farm-in transactions in the exploration phase.

5.3.2.B   Farm-in arrangements outside the E&E phase

I   Farmee

As discussed at 5.3.2 above, a farm-in represents the complete acquisition of a *proportion* of a property. Therefore, the farmee should:

- recognise an asset that represents the underlying (partially) undeveloped interest acquired at cost in accordance with IAS 16 or IAS 38; *[IAS 16.15, IAS 38.21]* and

- recognise a liability that reflects the obligation to fund the farmor's share of the future investment from which the farmee itself will not derive any future economic benefits.

As illustrated below in the extract from Star Energy's 2006 UK GAAP financial statements, farm-in arrangements can be structured in numerous ways, some requiring payment of a fixed monetary amount while others are more flexible and state, for example, that capital expenditures over the next five years will be paid for by the farmee regardless of what those amounts may be. In the latter scenario, the farmee should recognise a provision under IAS 37 as the timing and amount of the liability are uncertain. *[IAS 37.10].* However, in the former scenario it could be argued that the liability meets the definition of a financial liability under IAS 32 that should be accounted for in accordance with IAS 39. *[IAS 32.11].*

Extract 41.33: Star Energy Group plc (2006)

Notes to the Financial Statements [extract]

26. Contingent liabilities [extract]

In relation to a farm-out agreement farmed into during the year with Virgo Energy Limited, the Group will undertake a feasibility study and in addition contribute up to £1,000,000 towards the cost of a 3D seismic survey on the Forbes field, a licence in which it has acquired a 25% interest. In addition to this 25% interest, the Group has an option to acquire a further 25% in return for undertaking and funding a Front End Engineering & Design study for the development of the Forbes field as a gas storage facility. As at 31 December 2006, the feasibility study had not commenced and no amounts had been paid to Virgo Energy Limited.

II   Farmor

In accounting for a farm-in arrangement the farmor should:

- derecognise the proportion of the asset that it has sold to the farmee in accordance with the requirements of IAS 16 or IAS 38; *[IAS 16.67, IAS 38.112]*

- recognise the consideration received or receivable from the farmee, which represents the farmee's obligation to fund the capital expenditure in relation to the interest retained by the farmor;

- recognise a gain or loss on the transaction for the difference between the net disposal proceeds and the carrying amount of the asset disposed of. *[IAS 16.71, IAS 38.113]*. Recognition of a gain would be appropriate only when the value of the consideration can be determined reliably. If not, then the carried party should account for the consideration received as a reduction in the carrying amount of the underlying assets; and

- test the retained interests for impairment if the terms of the arrangement indicate that the retained interest may be impaired.

Under IAS 16 and IAS 38, the consideration receivable on disposal of an item of property, plant and equipment or an intangible asset is recognised initially at its fair value by the farmor. However, if 'payment for the item is deferred, the consideration received is recognised initially at the cash price equivalent. The difference between the nominal amount of the consideration and the cash price equivalent is recognised as interest revenue in accordance with IAS 18 reflecting the effective yield on the receivable.' *[IAS 16.72, IAS 38.116]*. However, any part of the consideration that is receivable in the form of cash will meet the definition of a financial asset under IAS 32 and should be accounted for in accordance with IAS 39 / IFRS 9, *[IAS 32.11]*; either at amortised cost or fair value depending on how the farmor designates the receivable.

The extract below describes the farm-in transactions of Roxi Petroleum.

Extract 41.34: Roxi Petroleum Plc (2008 and 2010)

2008 farm-ins

Notes to the Financial Statements [extract]

30 Post balance sheet events [extract]

30.1 Ravninnoe farm-in

On 14 November 2008 the Company, Kuat Oraziman, Ravninnoe BV, Vertom International BV and Canamens Energy BV signed an SPA to farm out part of Ravninnoe Oil LLP ("Ravninnoe").

Under the SPA the initial consideration of $5,000,000 was payable by Canamens Energy BV (the purchaser) to Kuat Oraziman in exchange for 10 per cent of the equity of Ravninnoe (stage 1) and $1,750,000 of the Company's loans to Ravninnoe (being 10% of the total loans from the Company, Ravninnoe BV and Vertom International BV to Ravninnoe). Additionally the purchaser has the option to purchase an additional 22.5% of the equity and loans from Ravninnoe BV and Kuat Oraziman for a cash consideration of $8.5m (stage 2), that would be required to be lent to Ravninnoe for the purposes of drilling a well. This would leave the Company with an interest of 30% in Ravninnoe. Subject to taking up the option for stage 2, the purchaser has the option to fund the drilling of a further well in the amount of $8,500,000.

If prior to 30 June 2010 the flow rates from the well funded by stage 2 are above 900 barrels of oil per day for 45 consecutive days and the oil price is above US$100 per barrel for the same period, then a further US$5,000,000 is payable by the purchaser to Ravninnoe BV.

As the required waivers for the transfer of the interests to Canamens were not received until June 2009, no stages of this SPA have yet completed.

In December 2008 Canamens advanced the initial payment of US$5,000,000 for the purchase of a 10% interest from Kuat Oraziman, which was lent by Kuat Oraziman to the Company (note 29.3(b)).

On 27 April 2009 this advance of US$5,000,000 was formalised as a prepayment from Canamens to Kuat Oraziman and the Company. This amount bears interest at LIBOR plus 0.5%, is secured on Kuat Oraziman's stake of 12.5% in Ravninnoe and is repayable prior to 30 July 2009.

In January 2009 Canamens placed the US$8,500,000 required for stage 2 into escrow, of which US$500,000 has since been received by the Group under a second prepayment agreement date dated 29 April 2009, which allows up to US$1,500,000 to be advances from escrow for the purpose of fulfilling the 2009 work program for Ravninnoe.

Amounts advances under the second prepayment agreement bear interest at LIBOR plus 0.5%, is secured on 100% of the shares of Ravninnoe BV and is repayable prior to 30 July 2009.

30.2 BNG farm-in

On 15 January 2009 the Company, Eragon Petroleum Limited, BNG Energy BV and Lifecare Hungary Holdings BV (part of the Canamens group) signed an SPA to farm out part of BNG Ltd LLP ("BNG"). This agreement was amended on 6 April 2009.

Under the amended SPA the initial consideration of $7,999,999 is payable by Lifecare Hungary Holdings BV (the purchaser) to BNG Energy BV in exchange for 6 per cent of the equity in BNG and 6% of the loans due from BNG to Roxi Petroleum Plc and BNG Energy BV (stage 1). Additionally the purchaser has the option to purchase an additional 17% of the equity and loans for a cash consideration of $24,000,000 (stage 2), that would be required to be lent to BNG for the work program. Subject to taking up the option for stage 2, the purchaser has the option to acquire a further 12% of the equity and loans for $23,000,000.

The completion of this SPA is subject to shareholder approval and obtaining the relevant waivers from the Kazakh authorities.

Following the year end BNG Energy BV has received as prepayments amounts totalling US$7,999,000 from Lifecare Hungary Holdings BV. These amounts are secured on BNG and repayable prior to 30 June 2009.

30.3 Galaz SPAs

During the year, KazRosMunai LLP entered a farm-in arrangement with the Company to earn an interest of up to 32.5 per cent of Galaz & Company LLP in return for KZT2,040,000,000 (US$17,000,000). Further to these arrangements, on 13 November 2008, Galaz Energy BV (a wholly owned subsidiary or Eragon) and KazRosMunai LLP signed an SPA for the sale of 32.5% of Galaz and Company LLP for a total consideration of KZT2,040,000,000 (US$17,000,000 at an exchange rate of KZT120:US$1). The consideration has not been received and accordingly the SPA has not completed.

KazRosGeophysics LLP has drilled four wells during the year, at a cost of KZT7,330,000,000 (approximately $6,000,000).

The Company is in discussions with KazRosMunai LLP and KazRosGeophysics LLP over the possibility of an equity stake in Galaz and Company LLP being transferred in exchange for these services. Additionally on 13 November 2008 Galaz Energy BV signed another SPA for the sale of 1.5% of Galaz and Company LLP for a total consideration of KZT60,000,000 (approximately US$500,000). The consideration has been received however the SPA has not been completed.

2010 farm-ins

32 Events after the reporting period [extract]

32.2 Galaz SPA

a) LGI farm-in

On 27 April 2010 Galaz Energy BV entered into a SPA with LG International Corp ("LGI") for the sale of 40% of the equity in Galaz and Company LLP for US$15.6 million.

As part of this transaction LGI agreed to provide a loan of US$34.4 million to Galaz and Company LLP. Under the terms of the loan agreement the first tranche of US$20 million was applied as follows:

(i) US$8.5 million for the repayment of historical debt associated with drilling wells in the North West Konys field;

(ii) US$8.4 million for the partial refinancing of loans due to the Company and general corporate purposes, and

(iii) US$3.1 million for financing the ongoing operational costs.

The second tranche of the loan is to be used for investment for ongoing development costs under the current work programme.

On 12 May 2010 the first tranche of US$20 million under the loan agreement was received as an advance by Galaz and Company LLP.

The sale of 40% of the equity in Galaz and Company LLP was finalised on 20 January 2011.

The extract below from Revus Energy's 2007 financial statements shows the different accounting policies that it applies to farm-in transactions in the exploration phase and development phase.

Extract 41.35: Revus Energy ASA (2007)

Accounting principles [extract]

Acquisitions and divestments [extract]

Farm-ins generally occur in the exploration or development phase and are characterised by the transferor giving up future economic benefits, in the form of reserves, in exchange for reduced future funding obligations. In the exploration phase the Group accounts for farm-ins on a historical cost basis. As such no gain or loss is recognised. In the development phase, the Group accounts for farm-ins as an acquisition at fair value when the Group is the transferee and a disposal at fair value when the Group is the transferor of a part of an oil and gas property. The fair value is determined by the costs that have been agreed as being borne by the transferee.

5.3.3   Asset swaps

Asset exchanges are transactions that have challenged standard-setters for a number of years. For example, an entity might swap certain intangible assets that it does not require or is no longer allowed to use for those of a counterparty that has other surplus assets. It is not uncommon for entities to exchange assets as part of their portfolio and risk management activities or simply to meet demands of competition authorities. The key accounting issues that need to be addressed are:

• whether such an exchange should give rise to a profit when the fair value of the asset received is greater than the carrying value of the asset given up; and

• whether the exchange of similar assets should be recognised.

In the extractive industries an exchange of assets could involve property, plant and equipment (PP&E), intangible assets, investment property or E&E assets, which are in the scope of IAS 16, IAS 38, IAS 40 and IFRS 6, respectively. Hence there are three possible types of exchanges (which will be discussed below), those involving:

(a)   only E&E assets;

(b)   only PP&E, intangible assets and investment property; and

(c)   a combination of E&E assets, PP&E, intangible assets and investment property.

5.3.3.A E&E assets

Accounting for E&E assets, and therefore also accounting for swaps involving only E&E assets, falls within the scope of IFRS 6. *[IFRS 6.3].* As that standard does not directly address accounting for asset swaps, it is necessary to consider its hierarchy of guidance in the selection of an accounting policy. IFRS 6 does not require an entity to look at other standards and interpretations that deal with similar issues, or the guidance in the IASB's *Conceptual Framework. [IFRS 6.7].* Instead, it allows entities to develop their own accounting policies, or use the guidance issued by other standard-setters, thereby effectively allowing entities to continue using accounting policies that they applied under their previous national GAAP. Therefore, many entities, especially those which consider that they can never determine the fair value of E&E assets reliably, have selected an accounting policy under which they account for E&E assets obtained in a swap transaction at the carrying amount of the asset given up. An alternative approach, which is also permitted under IFRS 6, would be to apply an accounting policy that is based on the guidance in other standards as discussed under 5.3.3.B below.

5.3.3.B PP&E, intangible assets and investment property

I Measurement of assets exchanged

Three separate international accounting standards contain virtually identical guidance on accounting for exchanges of assets: IAS 16 (see Chapter 20 at 4.4), IAS 38 (see Chapter 19 at 7) and IAS 40 (see Chapter 21 at 4.7). These standards require the acquisition of PP&E, intangible assets or investment property, as the case may be, in exchange for non-monetary assets (or a combination of monetary and non-monetary assets) to be measured at fair value. The cost of the acquired asset is measured at fair value unless: *[IAS 16.24, IAS 38.45, IAS 40.27].*

(a)   the exchange transaction lacks 'commercial substance' (see II below); or

(b)   the fair value of neither the asset received nor the asset given up is reliably measurable.

The acquired asset is measured in this way even if an entity cannot immediately derecognise the asset given up. If an entity is able to determine reliably the fair value of either the asset received or the asset given up, then the fair value of the asset given up is used to measure cost unless the fair value of the asset received is more clearly evident. *[IAS 16.26, IAS 38.47, IAS 40.29].* If the fair value of neither the asset given up, nor the asset received can be measured reliably the cost is measured at the carrying amount of the asset given up. *[IAS 16.24, IAS 38.47, IAS 40.27].*

II Commercial substance

The commercial substance of an exchange is to be determined by forecasting and comparing the future cash flows budgeted to be generated by the incoming and outgoing assets. For commercial substance to be present there must be a significant difference between the two forecasts:

'(a)   the configuration (i.e. risk, timing and amount) of the cash flows of the asset received differs from the configuration of the cash flows of the asset transferred; or

(b)   the entity-specific value of the portion of the entity's operations affected by the transaction changes as a result of the exchange; and

(c)   the difference in (a) or (b) is significant relative to the fair value of the assets exchanged.' *[IAS 16.25, IAS 38.46, IAS 40.28].*

The standards state that the fair value of an asset 'for which comparable market transactions do not exist is reliably measurable if (a) the variability in the range of reasonable fair value estimates is not significant for that asset or (b) the probabilities of the various estimates within the range can be reasonably assessed and used in estimating fair value.' *[IAS 16.26, IAS 38.47, IAS 40.29].* The standards allow an entity to forego the effort of performing these detailed calculations when the outcome would be clear in advance *[IAS 16.25, IAS 38.46, IAS 40.28]* – perhaps if it is obvious that there is no 'commercial substance' in this very restricted sense.

5.3.3.C   Exchanges of E&E assets for other types of assets

An entity that exchanges E&E assets for PP&E, intangible assets or investment property needs to apply an accounting treatment that meets the requirements of IFRS 6 and those of IAS 16, IAS 38 or IAS 40. As discussed at 5.3.3.B above, exchanges involving PP&E, intangible assets and investment property that have commercial substance should be accounted for at fair value. Since this treatment is also allowed under IFRS 6, an entity that exchanges E&E assets for assets within the scope of IAS 16, IAS 38 or IAS 40 should apply an accounting policy that complies with the guidance in those standards.

5.3.4   Unitisations and redeterminations

5.3.4.A   Unitisations

A unitisation arrangement is 'an agreement between two parties each of which owns an interest in one or more mineral properties in an area to cross-assign to one another a share of the interest in the mineral properties that each owns in the area; from that point forward they share, as agreed, in further costs and revenues related to the properties'.[176] The parties 'pool their individual interests in return for an interest in the overall unit, which is then operated jointly to increase efficiency'.[177] Once an area is subject to a unitisation arrangement, the parties 'will share costs and production in accordance with their percentages established under the unit agreement. Costs and production associated with non-unitised areas within the original licences will continue to fall to the original licensees.'[178]

The example below, which is taken from the IASC's Issues Paper, illustrates how a unitisation transaction might work in practice.

Example 41.18:   Unitisation[179]

Entities E and F have carried out exploration programs on separate properties owned by each in a remote area near the Antarctic Circle. Both entities have discovered petroleum reserves on their properties and have begun development of the properties. Because of the high operating costs and the need to construct support facilities, such as pipelines, dock facilities, transportation systems, and warehouses, the entities decide to unitise the properties, which means that they have agreed to combine their properties into a single property. A joint operating agreement is signed and entity F is chosen as operator of the combined properties. Relevant data about each entity's properties and costs are given as follows:

Party E

Prospecting costs incurred prior to property acquisition	€8,000,000
Mineral acquisition costs	€42,000,000
Geological and geophysical exploration costs (G&G)	€12,000,000
Exploratory drilling costs:	
Successful	€16,000,000
Unsuccessful	€7,000,000
Development costs incurred	€23,000,000
Estimated reserves, agreed between parties (in barrels)	30,000,000

Party F

Prospecting costs incurred prior to property acquisition	€3,000,000
Mineral acquisition costs	€31,000,000
Geological and geophysical exploration costs (G&G)	€17,000,000
Exploratory drilling costs	
Successful	€24,000,000
Unsuccessful	€4,000,000
Development costs incurred	€36,000,000
Estimated reserves, agreed between parties (in barrels)	70,000,000

Ownership ratio in the venture is to be based on the relative quantity of agreed-upon reserves contributed by each party (30% to E and 70% to F). The parties agree that there should be an equalisation between them for the value of pre-unitisation exploration and development costs that directly benefit the unit, but not for other exploration and development costs. That is, there will be a cash settlement between the parties for the value of assets (other than mineral rights) or services that each party contributes to the unitisation. This is done so that the net value contributed by each party for the specified expenditures will equal that venturer's share of the total value of such expenditures at the time unitisation is consummated. Thus, the party contributing a value less than that party's share of ownership in the total value of those costs contributed by all the parties will make a cash payment to the other party so that each party's net contribution will equal that party's share of total value. The agreed amounts of costs to be equalised that are contributed by E and F are:

Expenditures made by:	E	F	Total
	€	€	€
Successful exploratory drilling	12,000,000	12,000,000	24,000,000
Development costs	18,000,000	30,000,000	48,000,000
Geological and geophysical exploration	4,000,000	14,000,000	18,000,000
Total expenditure	34,000,000	56,000,000	90,000,000

As a result of this agreement, F is obliged to pay E the net amount of €7,000,000 to equalise exploration and development costs. This is made up of the following components:

(a) €4,800,000 excess of value of exploratory drilling received by F (€16,800,000 = 70% × €24,000,000) in excess of value for successful exploratory drilling contributed (€12,000,000); plus

(b) €3,600,000 excess of value of development costs received by F in the unit (€33,600,000 = 70% × €48,000,000) in excess of the value of development costs contributed by F (€30,000,000); and less

(c) €1,400,000 excess of value of G&G costs contributed by F (€14,000,000) over the value of the share of G & G costs owned by F after unitisation (€12,600,000 = 70% × €18,000,000).

IFRS does not specifically address accounting for a unitisation arrangement. Therefore, the accounting for such an arrangement depends on the type of asset that is subject to the arrangement. If the assets subject to the arrangement were E&E assets, then the transaction would fall within the scope of IFRS 6, which provides a temporary exemption from IAS 8 (see 3.2.1 above). An entity would be permitted to develop an accounting policy for unitisation arrangements involving E&E assets that is not based on IFRS. However, unitisations are unlikely to occur in the E&E phase when technical feasibility and commercial viability of extracting a mineral resource are not yet demonstrable.

The first step in developing an accounting policy for unitisations is setting criteria for determining which assets are included within the transaction. Particularly important is the assessment whether the unitisation includes the mineral reserves themselves or not. The main reason for not including the mineral reserves derives from the fact that they are subject to redetermination (see 5.3.4.B below). Although the reserves are unitised in the physical sense (i.e. each party will end up selling oil or gas that physically came out of the reserves of the other party), in volume terms the parties remain entitled to a quantity of reserves that is equal to that which they contributed. However, the timing of production and the costs to produce the reserves may be impacted by the unitisation agreement. The example below explains this in more detail.

Example 41.19:   Reserves contributed in a unitisation

Entities A and B enter into a unitisation agreement and contribute Licenses A and B, respectively. The table below shows the initial determination, redetermination and final determination of the reserves in each of the fields.

	Initial determination		Redetermination		Final determination	
	mboe		mboe		mboe	
License A	20	40.0%	19	37.3%	21	38.9%
License B	30	60.0%	32	62.7%	33	61.1%
	50	100.0%	51	100.0%	54	100.0%

Although Licenses A and B were unitised, ultimately Entity A will be entitled to 21 mboe and Entity B will be entitled to 33 mboe, which is exactly the same quantity that they would have been entitled to had there been no unitisation.

To the extent that the unitisation of the mineral reserves themselves lacks commercial substance (see 5.3.3.B II above), it may be appropriate to exclude the mineral reserves in accounting for a unitisation. However, it should be noted that where the unitisation significantly affects the risk and timing of the cash flows or the type of product (e.g. a unitisation could lead to an exchange of, say, gas reserves for oil reserves) there is likely to be substance to the unitisation of the reserves.

If the assets subject to the unitisation arrangement are not E&E assets, or not only E&E assets, then it is necessary to develop an accounting policy in accordance with the requirements of IAS 8. Unitisation arrangements generally give rise to joint control over the underlying assets or entities:

(a)   if the unitisation arrangement results in joint control over an underlying entity then the parties should apply SIC-13 – *Jointly Controlled Entities – Non-monetary Contributions by Venturers* – to the formation of the joint venture (see Chapter 13 at 6.3). In addition, each of the parties would need to disclose the information required by IAS 31 (see Chapter 13 at 10). SIC-13 and IAS 31 are being replaced with IFRS 11 (see Chapter 14) and the relevant disclosure requirements are to be contained in IFRS 12 (see Chapter 15); or

(b)   if the unitisation arrangement gives rise to jointly controlled assets or results in a swap of assets that are not jointly controlled, then each of the parties should account for the arrangement as an asset swap (see 5.3.3 above).

Under both (a) and (b) above, a party to a unitisation agreement would report a gain (or loss) depending on whether the fair value of the interest received is higher (or lower) than the carrying amount of the interest given up.

5.3.4.B   Redeterminations

The percentage interests in a unitisation arrangement are based on estimates of the relative quantities of reserves contributed by each of the parties. As field life progresses and production experience is gained, many unitisation agreements require the reserves to be redetermined, which often leads the parties to conclude that the recoverable reserves in one or perhaps both of the original properties are not as previously estimated. Unitisation agreements typically require one or more 'redeterminations' of percentage interests once better reservoir information becomes available. In most cases, the revised percentage interests are deemed to be effective from the date of the original unitisation agreement, which means that adjustments are required between the parties in respect of their relative entitlements to cumulative production and their shares of cumulative costs.[180]

Unitisation agreements normally set out when redeterminations need to take place and the way in which adjustments to the percentage interests should be effected:[181]

'(a)   Adjustments in respect of cumulative "capital" costs are usually made immediately following the redetermination by means of a lump sum reimbursement, sometimes including an "interest" or uplift element to reflect related financing costs.

(b)   Adjustments to shares of cumulative production are generally effected prospectively. Participants with an increased share are entitled to additional "make-up" production until the cumulative liftings are rebalanced. During this period adjusted percentage interests are applied to both production entitlement and operating costs. Once equity is achieved the effective percentage interests revert to those established by the redetermination.'[182]

An adjustment to an entity's percentage interest due to a redetermination does not meet the definition of a prior period error under IFRS. This is because the adjustment did not result from 'a failure to use, or misuse of, reliable information that: (a) was available when financial statements for those periods were authorised for issue; and (b) could reasonably be expected to have been obtained and taken into account in the preparation and presentation of those financial statements'. *[IAS 8.5]*. Accordingly, we believe that a redetermination should not be accounted for as a correction of an error and therefore should not result in a fully retrospective adjustment. Instead, the redetermination results from new information or new developments and therefore should be treated as a change in an accounting estimate.

I   Capital reimbursements

Redeterminations give rise to some further accounting issues, which are illustrated in the example below.

Example 41.20:   Redetermination (1)

Entities A and B have a 10% and 90% percentage interest in a unitised property, respectively. On 1 January 2012, after three years of operations, their interests in the property are redetermined. The relevant data about each entity's interest in the property are as follows:

	A	B	Total
Percentage interest after initial determination	10%	90%	100%
Percentage interest after redetermination	8%	92%	100%
Initial reserves in 2009 (million barrels of oil equivalent)	100 mboe	900 mboe	1000 mboe
Total production from 2009 to 2011	30 mboe	270 mboe	300 mboe
Remaining reserves at 31/12/2011 before redetermination	70 mboe	630 mboe	700 mboe
Reserves after redetermination at 1/1/2012	56 mboe	644 mboe	700 mboe
'Make-up' oil: 300 mboe × (10% − 8%) =	−6 mboe	6 mboe	–
Total entitlement at 1/1/2012	50 mboe	650 mboe	700 mboe
	$	$	$
Exploration and development asset at 1/1/2009	400	3,600	4,000
Units of production depreciation:			
$400 ÷ 100 mboe × 30 mboe =	120		120
$3,600 ÷ 900 mboe × 270 mboe =		1,080	1,080
Exploration and development asset at 31/12/2011 before redetermination	280	2,520	2,800

	A	B	Total
Total investment based on 'initial determination':			
A: 10% of $4,000 = $400 and B: 90% of $4,000 = $3,600	400	3,600	4,000
Total investment based on redetermination:			
A: 8% of $4,000 = $320 and B: 92% of $4,000 = $3,680	320	3,680	4,000
Reimbursement of exploration and development costs	80	−80	–
Decommissioning asset at 1/1/2009	100	900	1,000
Units of production depreciation:			
$100 ÷ 100 mboe × 30 mboe =	30		30
$900 ÷ 900 mboe × 270 mboe =		270	270
Decommissioning asset at 31/12/2011 before redetermination	70	630	700

Decommissioning provision at 1/1/2009	100	900	1,000
Accreted interest from 1/1/2009 to 31/12/2011	20	180	200
Decommissioning provision at 31/12/2011 before redetermination	120	1,080	1,200
Reimbursement of decommissioning costs	–24	24	–
Decommissioning provision at 1/1/2012: A: 8% of $1,200 = $96 and B: 92% of $1,200 = $1,104	96	1,104	1,200

The redetermination gives rise to a number of questions, for example, how should A and B account for:

• the reimbursement of cumulative capital costs;

• the adjustment of their share in the remaining reserves;

• the 'make-up' oil obligation (see II below); and

• their revised shares in the decommissioning liabilities (see III below).

There are different ways in which an entity might interpret the effect of a redetermination on the exploration and development asset:

(a) Reimbursement of capital expenditure; or

(b) Sale/purchase of a partial interest.

Reimbursement of capital expenditure

Under this approach, the redetermination is treated as a reimbursement of capital expenditure and the 'make-up' oil is accounted for prospectively. This would lead entity A to make the following journal entries:

	$	$
Dr Cash	80	
Cr Exploration and development asset		80

The reimbursement of exploration and development costs is accounted for as a reduction in the exploration and development asset.

The overall impact on the statement of financial position of both entities A and B is summarised in the table below:

	A $	B $	Total $
Exploration and development asset at 31/12/2011 before redetermination	280	2,520	2,800
Reimbursement of exploration and development costs	–80	80	–
Exploration and development asset at 1/1/2012 after redetermination	200	2,600	2,800

Before the redetermination both A and B would record a depreciation of exploration and development asset of $4/barrel (i.e. A: $400 ÷ 100 mboe = $4/barrel and B: $3,600 ÷ 900 mboe = $4/barrel). After the redetermination the depreciation of exploration and development asset is still $4/barrel for both A and B (i.e. A: $200 ÷ 50 mboe = $4/barrel and B: $2,600 ÷ 650 mboe = $4/barrel).

Sale/purchase of a partial interest

The second approach, which is sometimes advocated, is to treat the redetermination as the equivalent of a sale or purchase of part of an interest.

		$		$
Dr Cash		80		
Cr Exploration and development asset:				56
$(8\% - 10\%) \div 10\% \times \$280 =$				
Cr Gain on disposal of exploration and development asset				24

The reimbursement of exploration and development costs is accounted for as a partial disposal of the exploration and development asset.

However, entity B will treat its entire payment of $80 to entity A as the cost of the additional 2% interest that it 'acquired' in the redetermination. The overall impact on the statement of financial position of both entities A and B is summarised in the table below:

	A $	B $	Total $
Exploration and development asset at 31/12/2011 before redetermination	280	2,520	2,800
Reimbursement of exploration and development costs	−56	80	–
Exploration and development asset at 1/1/2012 after redetermination	224	2,600	2,824

After the redetermination the depreciation of exploration and development asset for entity A is ($224 ÷ 50 mboe =) $4.48/barrel and for entity B is ($2,600 ÷ 650 mboe =) $4/barrel.

Under many national GAAPs redeterminations are accounted for as reimbursement of capital expenditure rather than as sales/purchases of a partial interest. Given that this second approach could result in the recognition of a gain upon redetermination, followed by a higher depreciation charge per barrel, we believe that redeterminations should be accounted for as reimbursements of capital expenditure under IFRS.

II   'Make-up' oil

As indicated in Example 41.20 above, entity B would be entitled to 6 mboe of 'make-up' oil out of entity A's share of the production. This raises the question whether entity A should recognise a liability for the 'make-up' oil and whether entity B should recognise an asset for the 'make-up' oil that it is entitled to.

'Make-up' oil is in many ways comparable to an over- or underlift of oil, because after the redetermination it appears that entity A is effectively in an overlift position (i.e. it has sold more product than its proportionate share of production) while entity B is in an underlift position (i.e. it has sold less product than its proportionate share of production).

IFRS does not directly address accounting for underlifts and overlifts (as discussed at 5.6.2 below) or accounting for 'make-up' oil following a redetermination. Consequently, an entity that is entitled to receive or is obliged to pay 'make-up' oil will need to apply the hierarchy in IAS 8 to develop an accounting policy. Therefore, an entity might develop either an accounting policy that is:

(a)   similar to the 'entitlements method' (see 5.6.2.B below) and account for a 'make-up' oil asset or liability that is similar to an underlift asset or and overlift liability; or

(b)   based on the accounting standards of another standard-setter with a similar conceptual framework, such as US GAAP or UK GAAP, in which case the entity would recognise an asset or liability and account for the 'make-up' oil prospectively.

Under many unitisation agreements, entities are required to give up oil only to the extent that there is production from the underlying field. Proponents of method (b) therefore argue that in the absence of future production, entity A would have no obligation to deliver oil or make another form of payment to the other parties under the unitisation agreement. In those cases, the 'make-up' oil obligation would not meet the definition of financial liability under IAS 32 or that of a provision under IAS 37. They would also argue that entity B cannot recognise an asset, because its right to 'make-up' oil only arises because of a future event (i.e. the future production of oil).

III   Decommissioning provisions

Another effect of a redetermination is that it may increase or decrease an entity's share of the decommissioning liability in relation to the project, as illustrated in the example below.

Example 41.21:   Redetermination (2)

Assuming the same facts as in Example 41.20 above, how should entities A and B account for the change in the decommissioning provision?

Under IFRIC 1 – *Changes in Existing Decommissioning, Restoration and Similar Liabilities* – the change in a decommissioning provision should be added to, or deducted from, the cost of the related asset in the current period. However, if a decrease in the liability exceeds the carrying amount of the asset, the excess should be recognised immediately in profit or loss. *[IFRIC 1.5].*

This would lead entities A and B to make the following journal entries:

	$	$
Entity A		
Dr Decommissioning provision	24	
Cr Decommissioning asset		24
Entity B		
Dr Decommissioning asset	24	
Cr Decommissioning provision		24

The decommission asset is adjusted in accordance with IFRIC 1 for the change in the decommissioning provision.

If entity A had recognised a gain of $24 upon the reduction of the decommissioning liability, this would have resulted in an increase in the depreciation of the decommissioning asset from ($100 ÷ 100 mboe =) $1/barrel to ($70 ÷ 50 mboe =) $1.40/barrel. The IFRIC 1 approach avoids this although it increases the depreciation of the decommissioning asset slightly to ($56 ÷ 50mboe =) $1.12/barrel, as the decommissioning provision is also affected by the accretion of interest. Nevertheless, the approach required by IFRIC 1 is largely consistent with the treatment of a redetermination as a reimbursement of capital expenditure in Example 41.20 above.

5.4   Exploration and evaluation costs

5.4.1   Successful efforts method

The successful efforts methods that have been developed by different accounting standard-setters are based on the successful efforts concept, under which 'generally only those costs that lead directly to the discovery, acquisition, or development of specific, discrete mineral reserves are capitalised and become part of the capitalised costs of the cost centre. Costs that are known at the time of incurrence to fail to meet this criterion are generally charged to expense in the period they are incurred, although some interpretations of the successful efforts concept would capitalise the cost of unsuccessful development wells.'[183]

Under the successful efforts method an entity will generally consider each individual mineral lease, concession, or production sharing contract as a cost centre.

When an entity applies the successful efforts method under IFRS, it will need to account for prospecting costs incurred before the E&E phase under IAS 16 or IAS 38. As economic benefits are highly uncertain at this stage of a project, prospecting costs will typically be expensed as incurred. Costs incurred to acquire undeveloped mineral rights, however, should be capitalised under IFRS if an entity expects an inflow of future economic benefits.

To the extent that costs are incurred within the E&E phase of a project, IFRS 6 does not prescribe any recognition and measurement rules. Therefore, it would be acceptable for such costs (1) to be recorded as assets and written off when it is determined that the costs will not lead to economic benefits or, (2) to be expensed as incurred if the outcome is uncertain. 'The deferred costs of an undeveloped mineral right may be depreciated over some determinable period, they may be subject to an impairment test each period with the amount of impairment charged to expense, or the costs may be kept intact until it is determined whether the property contains mineral reserves.'[184] However, E&E assets should no longer be classified as such when the technical feasibility and commercial viability of extracting mineral resources are demonstrable. *[IFRS 6.17]*. At such time the asset should be tested for impairment under IAS 36, reclassified in the statement of financial position and accounted for under IAS 16 or IAS 38. If it is determined that no commercial reserves are present then the costs capitalised should be expensed. Costs incurred after the E&E phase should be accounted for in accordance with IFRS (i.e. IAS 16 and IAS 38).

While some elements of the successful efforts method as applied under certain national GAAPs are prohibited, IFRS only requires relatively minor modifications to the method and the essence of the approach – that costs are capitalised pending evaluation – can be retained under IFRS.

The following extract from the financial statements of Premier Oil illustrates a typical successful efforts method accounting policy applied under IFRS.

Extract 41.36: Premier Oil plc (2010)

Accounting policies [extract]

Oil and gas assets [extract]

The company applies the successful efforts method of accounting for exploration and evaluation (E&E) costs, having regard to the requirements of IFRS 6 – 'Exploration for and Evaluation of Mineral Resources'.

(a) Exploration and evaluation assets

Under the successful efforts method of accounting, all licence acquisition, exploration and appraisal costs are initially capitalised in well, field or specific exploration cost centres as appropriate, pending determination. Expenditure incurred during the various exploration and appraisal phases is then written off unless commercial reserves have been established or the determination process has not been completed.

Pre-licence costs

Costs incurred prior to having obtained the legal rights to explore an area are expensed directly to the income statement as they are incurred.

Exploration and evaluation costs

Costs of E&E are initially capitalised as E&E assets. Payments to acquire the legal right to explore, costs of technical services and studies, seismic acquisition, exploratory drilling and testing are capitalised as intangible E&E assets.

Tangible assets used in E&E activities (such as the group's vehicles, drilling rigs, seismic equipment and other property, plant and equipment used by the company's exploration function) are classified as property, plant and equipment. However, to the extent that such a tangible asset is consumed in developing an intangible E&E asset, the amount reflecting that consumption is recorded as part of the cost of the intangible asset. Such intangible costs include directly attributable overhead, including the depreciation of property, plant and equipment utilised in E&E activities, together with the cost of other materials consumed during the exploration and evaluation phases.

E&E costs are not amortised prior to the conclusion of appraisal activities.

Treatment of E&E assets at conclusion of appraisal activities

Intangible E&E assets related to each exploration licence/prospect are carried forward, until the existence (or otherwise) of commercial reserves has been determined subject to certain limitations including review for indications of impairment. If commercial reserves have been discovered, the carrying value, after any impairment loss, of the relevant E&E assets, is then reclassified as development and production assets. If, however, commercial reserves have not been found, the capitalised costs are charged to expense after conclusion of appraisal activities.

(b) Development and production assets

Development and production assets are accumulated generally on a field-by-field basis and represent the cost of developing the commercial reserves discovered and bringing them into production, together with the E&E expenditures incurred in finding commercial reserves transferred from intangible E&E assets, as outlined in accounting policy (a) above.

The cost of development and production assets also includes the cost of acquisitions and purchases of such assets, directly attributable overheads, finance costs capitalised, and the cost of recognising provisions for future restoration and decommissioning.

Depreciation of producing assets

The net book values of producing assets are depreciated generally on a field-by-field basis using the unit-of-production method by reference to the ratio of production in the year and the related commercial reserves of the field, taking into account future development expenditures necessary to bring those reserves into production.

Producing assets are generally grouped with other assets that are dedicated to serving the same reserves for depreciation purposes, but are depreciated separately from producing assets that serve other reserves.

Pipelines are depreciated on a unit-of-throughput basis.

5.4.2 Full cost method

The full cost method under most national GAAPs requires that 'all costs incurred in prospecting, acquiring mineral interests, exploration, appraisal, development, and construction are accumulated in large cost centres ... For example, costs may be accumulated for each individual country, for groups of countries, or for the entire world'.[185] However, IFRS 6 does not permit application of the full cost method outside the E&E phase. The Interpretations Committee was asked to clarify the effect of the limited scope of IFRS 6 on E&E activities:

'The IFRIC was asked if this limited scope (a) reflected the Board's intention to impose limits on current national GAAP practices only in respect of activities conducted in the E&E phase, while permitting industry practices in other

Chapter 41

extractive industry areas (e.g. development and exploitation) to continue unchanged, or (b) whether the IASB focused only on E&E activities because it was the only area for which the IASB was willing to grant some relief from the hierarchy for selection of accounting policies in IAS 8. Under the latter view, the IAS 8 hierarchy would apply fully to an entity's selection of IFRS accounting policies for activities outside of the E&E phase. The submission identified some inconsistencies between current extractive industry full-cost accounting practices in respect of development and exploitation activities but questioned whether the IASB intended to require change from current practices in these areas in advance of a comprehensive extractive industry project.

'The IFRIC noted that the effect of the limited scope of IFRS 6 was to grant relief only to policies in respect of E&E activities, and that this relief did not extend to activities before or after the E&E phase. The Basis for Conclusions on IFRS 6 includes the Board's intention of limiting the need for entities to change their existing accounting policies for E&E activities. The IFRIC believed it was clear that the scope of IFRS 6 consistently limited the relief from the hierarchy to policies applied to E&E activities and that there was no basis for interpreting IFRS 6 as granting any additional relief in areas outside its scope. Therefore, the IFRIC believed that diversity in practice should not become established and decided not to add the issue to its agenda.'[186]

There are several other areas in which application of the full cost method under IFRS is restricted because:

- while the full cost method under most national GAAPs requires application of some form of 'ceiling test', IFRS 6 requires – when impairment indicators are present – an impairment test is to be performed in accordance with IAS 36;
- IFRS 6 requires E&E assets to be classified as tangible or intangible assets according to the nature of the assets. [IFRS 6.15]. In other words, even when an entity accounts for E&E costs in relatively large pools, it will still need to distinguish between tangible and intangible assets; and
- once the technical feasibility and commercial viability of extracting mineral resources are demonstrable, IFRS 6 requires E&E assets to be tested for impairment under IAS 36, reclassified in the statement of financial position and accounted for under IAS 16 or IAS 38. [IFRS 6.17]. That means that it is not possible to account for successful and unsuccessful projects within one cost centre or pool.

For these reasons it is not possible to apply the full cost method of accounting under IFRS without making very significant modifications in the application of the method. An entity might want to use the full cost method as its starting point in developing its accounting policy for E&E assets under IFRS. However, it will rarely be appropriate to describe the resulting accounting policy as a 'full cost method' because key elements of the full cost method are not permitted under IFRS.

In July 2009, the IASB published an amendment to IFRS 1 – *Additional Exemptions for First-time Adopters* (Amendments to IFRS 1), which introduces a first-time adoption exemption for first-time adopters that accounted under their previous GAAP for 'exploration and development costs for oil and gas properties in the development or production phases ... in cost centres that include all properties in a large geographical area' (i.e. the full cost method).[187] Under the exemption, a first-time adopter may elect to measure oil and gas assets at the date of transition to IFRSs on a deemed cost basis (see Chapter 5 at 5.5.4), but does not permit continued application of the previous GAAP accounting policy.

Cairn Energy, which had originally wanted to apply the full cost method of accounting under IFRS, decided after the Interpretations Committee clarification in January 2006 to apply the successful efforts method.

Extract 41.37: Cairn Energy PLC (2006)

Restatement of 2004 Results from UK GAAP to IFRS

Updated 28 February 2006 [extract]

Introduction [extract]

Cairn originally released restated IFRS results for prior periods on 8 September 2005 and its interim 2005 results under IFRS on 20 September 2005. Both sets of results were prepared on the basis of the Group's continued application of its full cost accounting policy for oil and gas assets to both the exploration and appraisal activity phase and to those in the development and production phase. When these results were authorised for issue, the Board were aware that, owing to a lack of clarity in the authoritative literature, no consensus had been reached amongst the UK oil industry and the accounting profession on the status of full cost accounting policies under IFRS beyond the exploration and appraisal phase. As noted in the restatement document, this point was referred to the Agenda Committee of the International Financial Reporting Interpretations Committee ("IFRIC") to request clarification. The Agenda Committee subsequently issued guidance that the scope of IFRS 6 "Exploration for and Evaluation of Mineral Resources" is limited to exploration and appraisal activities and that accounting policies for development and production activities are to be based on the provisions of other existing IFRS.

Following this clarification from the IFRIC Agenda Committee, Cairn has reviewed its oil and gas accounting policy for both exploration and appraisal and development/producing assets. Cairn has decided to adopt a successful efforts based accounting policy for the Group's 2005 Annual Report and Accounts and has updated its restatement of prior periods to reflect this change in policy. The revised accounting policy is detailed in Note 1.

The key implications for Cairn's financial statements on adopting this policy are as follows:

* Costs of unsuccessful wells initially capitalised within exploration assets are expensed in the Income Statement in the period in which they are determined unsuccessful;

* depletion of development/producing assets is now performed on a field by field basis although fields within development areas can be combined where appropriate; and

* impairment testing for development/producing assets is now performed on each cash generating unit – this is usually, but not always, the development area.

5.4.3   Area-of-interest method

The area-of-interest method is an accounting concept by which 'costs incurred for individual geological or geographical areas that have characteristics conducive to containing a mineral reserve are deferred as assets pending determination of whether commercial reserves are found. If the area of interest is found to contain commercial reserves, the accumulated costs are capitalised. If the area is found to contain no commercial reserves, the accumulated costs are charged to expense.'[188]

Some consider the area-of-interest method to be a version of the successful efforts method that uses an area-of-interest, rather than an individual licence, as its unit of account (see 4.2 above). Others believe that the area-of-interest method is more akin to the full cost method applied on an area-of-interest basis.[189] 'Under the area-of-interest concept, all costs identified with an area of interest would be deferred and capitalised if commercial reserves are later determined to exist in the area. However, costs incurred up to the point that an area of interest is identified (prospecting costs) are often charged to expense by those who consider that they are applying the area-of-interest concept. ... Costs of individual unsuccessful activities incurred on a specific area of interest, such as drilling an exploratory well that finds no reserves, are accumulated as part of the total cost of the area of interest.'[190]

While IFRS 6 will often not permit all aspects of an area-of-interest method defined by a national GAAP, an entity that uses relatively small areas of interest may be able to implement the method in a meaningful way under IFRS. The area-of-interest method is more common in the mining industry than in the oil and gas industry. Still, there are some entities that apply the method to oil and gas activities.

Extract 41.38: BHP Billiton Group (2010)

Notes to Financial Statements [extract]
1. Accounting policies [extract]
Exploration and evaluation expenditure [extract]

Exploration and evaluation activity involves the search for mineral and petroleum resources, the determination of technical feasibility and the assessment of commercial viability of an identified resource. Exploration and evaluation activity includes:

- researching and analysing historical exploration data
- gathering exploration data through topographical, geochemical and geophysical studies
- exploratory drilling, trenching and sampling
- determining and examining the volume and grade of the resource
- surveying transportation and infrastructure requirements
- conducting market and finance studies

Administration costs that are not directly attributable to a specific exploration area are charged to the income statement. Licence costs paid in connection with a right to explore in an existing exploration area are capitalised and amortised over the term of the permit.

Exploration and evaluation expenditure (including amortisation of capitalised licence costs) is charged to the income statement as incurred except in the following circumstances, in which case the expenditure may be capitalised:

- In respect of minerals activities:
    - the exploration and evaluation activity is within an area of interest which was previously acquired in a business combination and measured at fair value on acquisition, or
    - the existence of a commercially viable mineral deposit has been established.
- In respect of petroleum activities:
    - the exploration and evaluation activity is within an area of interest for which it is expected that the expenditure will be recouped by future exploitation or sale; or
    - exploration and evaluation activity has not reached a stage which permits a reasonable assessment of the existence of commercially recoverable reserves.

Capitalised exploration and evaluation expenditure considered to be tangible is recorded as a component of property, plant and equipment at cost less impairment charges. Otherwise, it is recorded as an intangible asset (such as licences). As the asset is not available for use, it is not depreciated. All capitalised exploration and evaluation expenditure is monitored for indications of impairment. Where a potential impairment is indicated, assessment is performed for each area of interest in conjunction with the group of operating assets (representing a cash generating unit) to which the exploration is attributed. Exploration areas at which reserves have been discovered but that require major capital expenditure before production can begin are continually evaluated to ensure that commercial quantities of reserves exist or to ensure that additional exploration work is under way or planned. To the extent that capitalised expenditure is not expected to be recovered it is charged to the income statement.

Application of critical accounting policies and estimates [extract]

Exploration and evaluation expenditure

The Group's accounting policy for exploration and evaluation expenditure results in certain items of expenditure being capitalised for an area of interest where it is considered likely to be recoverable by future exploitation or sale or where the activities have not reached a stage which permits a reasonable assessment of the existence of reserves. This policy requires management to make certain estimates and assumptions as to future events and circumstances, in particular whether an economically viable extraction operation can be established. Any such estimates and assumptions may change as new information becomes available. If, after having capitalised the expenditure under the policy, a judgement is made that recovery of the expenditure is unlikely, the relevant capitalised amount will be written off to the income statement.

5.5 Capitalisation of costs

5.5.1 *Major maintenance and turnarounds*

Some assets (e.g. refineries and oil rigs) require major maintenance at regular intervals, which is often described as an overhaul or turnaround. IAS 16 requires the cost of an item of property, plant and equipment to be recognised when future economic benefits are probable and the cost of the item can be measured reliably. *[IAS 16.7]*. When an entity subsequently incurs further costs in relation to such an item of property, plant and equipment it needs to determine the nature of such costs:

(a)   if the costs relate to the replacement of a part of the entire asset then the entity derecognises the carrying amount of the part that is replaced and recognises the cost of the replacement part; *[IAS 16.13]*

(b)   costs of day-to-day servicing costs (e.g. costs of labour and consumables, and possibly the cost of small parts) should be expensed as incurred; *[IAS 16.12]* and

(c)   'when each major inspection is performed, its cost is recognised in the carrying amount of the item of property, plant and equipment as a replacement if the recognition criteria are satisfied. Any remaining carrying amount of the cost of the previous inspection (as distinct from physical parts) is derecognised. This occurs regardless of whether the cost of the previous inspection was identified in the transaction in which the item was acquired or constructed.' *[IAS 16.14]*.

Subsequent costs that meet the recognition criteria under (a) or (c) above should therefore be capitalised even if the costs incurred merely restore the assets to their original standard of performance. However, under IAS 37 an entity cannot provide for the costs of planned future maintenance (e.g. refinery turnarounds) as is illustrated by Example 41.22 from the standard.

Example 41.22:   Refurbishment costs – no legislative requirement [IAS 37 Appendix C,
                        Example 11A]

A furnace has a lining that needs to be replaced every five years for technical reasons. At the end of the reporting period, the lining has been in use for three years.

Under IAS 37 no provision should be recognised as there is no present obligation. The cost of replacing the lining is not recognised because, at the end of the reporting period, no obligation to replace the lining exists independently of the company's future actions – even the intention to incur the expenditure depends on the company deciding to continue operating the furnace or to replace the lining. Instead of a provision being recognised, the depreciation of the lining takes account of its consumption, i.e. it is depreciated over five years. The re-lining costs then incurred are capitalised with the consumption of each new lining shown by depreciation over the subsequent five years.

Even a legal requirement to refurbish does not make the costs of a turnaround a liability under IAS 37, because no obligation exists independently of the entity's future actions – the entity could avoid the future overhaul expenditure by its future actions, for example by selling the refinery. *[IAS 37 Appendix C, Example 11B].*

The extract below from BP illustrates a typical accounting policy for repairs, maintenance and inspection costs under IFRS.

Extract 41.39: BP plc (2010)

Notes on financial statements [extract]

1. Significant accounting policies [extract]

Property, plant and equipment [extract]

Expenditure on major maintenance refits or repairs comprises the cost of replacement assets or parts of assets, inspection costs and overhaul costs. Where an asset or part of an asset that was separately depreciated is replaced and it is probable that future economic benefits associated with the item will flow to the group, the expenditure is capitalized and the carrying amount of the replaced asset is derecognized. Inspection costs associated with major maintenance programmes are capitalized and amortized over the period to the next inspection. Overhaul costs for major maintenance programmes, and all other maintenance costs are expensed as incurred.

Refinery turnarounds can have a considerable impact on financial performance because of additional costs incurred and lower revenues. Therefore, many oil and gas companies disclose fairly detailed information about turnaround costs incurred in the past and turnarounds planned in the future.

Extract 41.40: TOTAL S.A. (2010)

Business segment reporting [extract]

Downstream results [extract]

2010 vs. 2009 [extract]

For the full year 2010, the refinery utilization rate based on crude throughput was 73% (77% for crude and other feedstock) compared to 78% in 2009 (83% for crude and other feedstock), reflecting essentially the shutdown of the Dunkirk refinery and a distillation unit at the Normandy refinery as well as impacts from strikes in France. In 2010, the level of scheduled turnarounds for refinery maintenance was low, with turnaround activity expected to increase notably in 2011.

2009 vs. 2008 [extract]

For the full year 2009, the refinery utilization rate based on crude throughput was 78% (83% for crude and other feedstock) compared to 88% in 2008 (91% for crude and other feedstock), reflecting the voluntary throughput reductions in the Group's refineries. Five refineries had scheduled turnarounds for maintenance in 2009 compared to six in 2008.

Liquidity and capital resources [extract]

In the Downstream segment, about 70% of capital expenditures are related to refining activities (essentially 40% for existing units including maintenance and major turnarounds and 60% for new construction), the balance being used in marketing/retail activities and for information systems.

5.5.2 Well workovers and recompletions

Well workovers or recompletions often are required when the producing oil sands become clogged and production declines, or other physical or mechanical problems arise.[191] Workover costs that relate to the day-to-day servicing of the wells (i.e. primarily the costs of labour and consumables, and possibly the cost of small parts) should be expensed as incurred. However, as discussed at 5.5.1 above, costs incurred to restore a well to its former level of production should be capitalised under IFRS, but an entity should derecognise any relevant previously capitalised well completion costs. However, to the extent that an entity can forecast future well workovers, it will need to depreciate the original well completion costs over a shorter economic life. Conversely, if an entity unexpectedly incurs well workover costs, it may need to consider whether those additional costs result in the need to perform an impairment test.

5.6 Revenue recognition

5.6.1 Royalties

Many mineral leases, concession agreements and production sharing contracts require the payment of a royalty to the original owner of the mineral reserves or the government. Under IAS 18 it is not entirely clear whether revenue should be presented net of royalty payments or not. Historically, many oil and gas companies have presented revenue net of those royalties that are paid in kind as they never received any inflow of economic benefits. *[IAS 18.8]*. However, an entity that is required to sell the oil or gas in the market and remit the net proceeds (after deduction of certain costs incurred) to the royalty holder, may be exposed to risks and rewards of ownership to such an extent that it is appropriate to present revenue on a gross basis and include the royalty payment within cost of sales.

Extract 41.41 below, from the financial statements of Premier Oil, illustrates a typical accounting policy for royalties under IFRS.

Extract 41.41: Premier Oil plc (2010)

Accounting policies [extract]

Royalties

Royalties are charged as production costs to the income statement in the year in which the related production is recognised as income.

Extract 41.42 below, from the financial statements of StatoilHydro, illustrates some of the complications that may arise in determining revenue when an entity sells product on behalf of the government.

Extract 41.42: StatoilHydro ASA (2010)

8.1 Notes to the Consolidated Financial Statements [extract]

8.1.2 Significant accounting policies [extract]

Transactions with the Norwegian State [extract]

Statoil markets and sells the Norwegian State's share of oil and gas production from the Norwegian Continental Shelf (NCS). The Norwegian State's participation in petroleum activities is organised through the State's direct financial interest (SDFI). All purchases and sales of the SDFI oil production are classified as purchases [net of inventory variation] and revenue, respectively. Statoil ASA sells, in its own name, but for the Norwegian State's account and risk, the State's production of natural gas. This sale and related expenditures refunded by the State, are presented net in Statoil's financial statements. Sales made by Statoil subsidiaries in their own name, and related expenditure, are however presented gross in Statoil's financial statements where the applicable subsidiary is considered the principal when selling natural gas on behalf of the Norwegian State. In accounting for these sales activities, the State's share of profit or loss is reflected in Statoil's Selling, general and administrative expenses as expenses or reduction of expenses, respectively.

The SPE-PRMS notes that 'royalty volumes should be deducted from the lessee's entitlement to resources. In some agreements, royalties owned by the host government are actually treated as taxes to be paid in cash. In such cases, the equivalent royalty volumes are controlled by the contractor who may (subject to regulatory guidance) elect to report these volumes as reserves and/or contingent resources with appropriate offsets (increase in operating expense) to recognize the financial liability of the royalty obligation.'[192]

5.6.2   Overlift and underlift

In jointly owned operations it is often not practical for each participant to take in kind or to sell its exact share of production during a period. In most periods some participants in the jointly owned operations will be in an overlift position (i.e. they have taken more product than their proportionate entitlement) while other participants may be in an underlift position (i.e. they have taken less product than their proportionate entitlement). Such lifting imbalances are usually settled in one of three ways:[193]

- In future periods the owner in an underlift position may sell or take product in excess of the entitled amounts, while the owner in an overlift position will sell or take less product than the normal entitlement.

- Cash balancing may be used, whereby the overlift party will make a cash payment to the underlift party for the value of the imbalance volume.

- If the co-owners have joint ownership interests in other properties, they may agree to offset balances in the two properties to the extent possible.

The two methods of accounting for underlifts and overlifts that are commonly used in the oil and gas industry are (a) the sales method and (b) the entitlements method.[194]

5.6.2.A   Sales method

Under the *sales method*, revenue is the value of what a participant sells or the value of all product that has been transferred to its downstream activity.[195] The sales method is similar to the revenue recognition approach in IAS 18 as revenue is only recognised when an entity has transferred ownership of the goods and the amount of revenue can be measured reliably. However, it should be noted here that revenue arising from the extraction of mineral ores is outside the scope of IAS 18. *[IAS 18.6(h)].*

A drawback of the sales method is that when an imbalance occurs it gives rise to a mismatch between expenses and revenue. This mismatch arises because the participants' share of expenses for the period is often equal to its ownership percentage, while its revenues are based on actual sales. There are two approaches to dealing with the effects of such mismatches:

(a) *Accrue or defer expenses* – It has been argued that an overlift participant should accrue for future expenses that are not matched by corresponding future revenues. Conversely, an underlift participant should defer expenses and match them against future catch-up production. Therefore, an overlift liability would be accounted for as accrued production costs, while an underlift asset would be accounted for as a prepaid cost at the lower of the amount of accrued production costs or net realisable value. However, as IFRS does not require matching of revenue and expenses, it seems that accrued (deferred) expenses would not meet the definition of a liability (asset) under the IASB's *Conceptual Framework*;

(b) *No adjustment* – Not accounting for the effects of imbalances has been justified on the grounds that (1) the amounts involved are immaterial, or (2) operating costs for the period should be expensed as incurred because they relate to the period's production activity and not to the revenues recognised.[196]

5.6.2.B   Entitlements method

Under the *entitlements method*, net revenue reflects the participant's share of production regardless of which participant has actually made the sale and invoiced the production. This is achieved by applying one of the following approaches in dealing with imbalances between actual sales and entitlements:[197]

(a) *Adjusting revenue* – The excess of (1) product sold during the period over (2) the participant's ownership share of production from the property is recognised by the overlift party as a liability and not as revenue.[198] Conversely, the underlift party would recognise an underlift asset and report corresponding revenue. As the participants' share of expenses for the period is generally equal to its ownership percentage, there is no need to make any further adjustments;[199] or

(b) *Adjusting cost of sales* – This version of the entitlements method, which is the recommended approach under the UK OIAC SORP, requires the cost of sales to be adjusted to take account of an asset or liability that reflects the lifting imbalance. If the adjustments are recorded at the market value of the product then it results in recognition of gross profit on an entitlements basis, while at the same time permitting revenues to be shown at the actual invoiced amount.

It is important for an entity to define clearly the measurement point for determining its 'share of production' and to apply that definition consistently. While it is possible to measure production at the well head, in practice production is often measured at the point where product is transferred (1) into a pipeline or (2) from a floating production, storage and offloading (FPSO) vessel into a ship.

I   Cash balancing

If participants have the right to settle imbalances on a cash basis then an underlift asset (overlift liability) clearly meets the definition of a financial asset (financial liability) under IFRS and should be accounted for under IAS 39/IFRS 9. Depending on the designation of the financial asset or financial liability, it should be measured either at amortised cost or at fair value. The fair value in such cases would equal the cash settlement amount that participants are entitled to or required to pay.

II   Physical settlement

If settlement of imbalances takes place physically by adjusting future liftings or providing a quantity of product from another source, it is not immediately obvious at what value the asset or liability should be recognised.

An overlift liability generally meets the definition of a provision under IAS 37 as the timing and amount of the settlement are uncertain. Applying IAS 37 the amount recognised as a provision should be 'the best estimate of the expenditure required to settle the present obligation at the end of the reporting period', *[IAS 37.36]*, which is 'the amount that an entity would rationally pay to settle the obligation at the end of the reporting period'. *[IAS 37.37]*.

An underlift asset that gives an entity the right to receive a quantity of product from another party is equivalent to a prepaid commodity purchase (and also similar to product borrowing). Therefore, it is reasonable to account for such underlift assets in the same way and apply the guidance in IAS 2 by analogy. Therefore, an underlift asset can be measured either (1) at the lower of cost or net realisable value, or (2) at net realisable value in accordance with well-established industry practice. *[IAS 2.3(a), IAS 2.9]*.

5.6.2.C   Overlift and underlift in practice

IFRS does not address accounting for underlifts and overlifts directly; hence an entity that applied the hierarchy in IAS 8 could consider guidance from a number of sources: *[IAS 8.12]*

- Under US GAAP, ASC 932-10-S99-5 – *Extractive Activities – Oil and Gas – Overall – SEC Materials – General* (pre-codification EITF 90-22 – *Accounting for Gas-Balancing Arrangements*) – does not express a preference for the sales method or the entitlements method. In practice, it seems that of those companies that apply the sales method under US GAAP a large majority do not make adjustments for operating expenses related to imbalances;[200] and

- The OIAC SORP under UK GAAP recommended that entities apply the entitlements method and adjust cost of sales for the effect of underlifts and overlifts.

As illustrated in the extracts below, in practice both the entitlements method and the sales method are used under IFRS.

Extract 41.43: BG Group plc (2010)

Principal accounting policies [extract]

Revenue recognition [extract]

Revenue associated with exploration and production sales (of natural gas, crude oil and petroleum products) is recorded when title passes to the customer. Revenue from the production of natural gas and oil in which BG Group has an interest with other producers is recognised based on the Group's working interest and the terms of the relevant production sharing contracts (entitlement method). Differences between production sold and the Group's share of production are not significant.

Extract 41.44: StatoilHydro ASA (2010)

8.1 Notes to the Consolidated Financial Statements [extract]

8.1.2 Significant accounting policies [extract]

Revenue recognition

Revenues associated with sale and transportation of crude oil, natural gas, petroleum and chemical products and other merchandise are recognised when title and risk pass to the customer, which is normally at the point of delivery of the goods based on the contractual terms of the agreements.

Revenues from the production of oil and gas properties in which Statoil has an interest with other companies are recognised on the basis of volumes lifted and sold to customers during the period (the sales method). Where Statoil has lifted and sold more than the ownership interest, an accrual is recognised for the cost of the overlift. Where Statoil has lifted and sold less than the ownership interest, costs are deferred for the underlift.

Revenue is presented net of customs, excise taxes and royalties paid in-kind on petroleum products.

Sales and purchases of physical commodities, which are not settled net, are presented on a gross basis as revenue and cost of goods sold in the statement of income. Activities related to trading and commodity-based derivative instruments are reported on a net basis, with the margin included in revenue.

5.6.2.D   Facility imbalances

Imbalances that are similar to overlifts and underlifts can also arise on facilities such as pipelines when a venturer delivers more or less product into a pipeline than it takes out in the same period. The resulting accounting issues arising are similar to those concerning overlifts and underlifts.

5.6.3   Trading activities

Many oil and gas companies engage in oil and gas trading (e.g. crude oil cargos) and they may either take delivery of the product or resell it without taking delivery. Even when an entity takes physical delivery and becomes the legal owner of a crude oil cargo or contents of a storage tank, it may still only be as part of its trading activities. Such transactions do not fall within the normal purchase and sales exemption (see 4.12.1 above) when 'the entity has a practice of taking delivery of the underlying and selling it within a short period after delivery for the purpose of generating a profit from short-term fluctuations in price or dealer's margin'. *[IAS 32.9(c), IAS 39.6(c)].* In that case, the purchase and sales contracts should be accounted for as derivatives within the scope of IAS 39.

The extract below from BP illustrates an accounting policy that an entity can apply in accounting for trading activities.

Extract 41.45: BP plc (2010)

Notes on financial statements [extract]

1. Significant accounting policies [extract]

Revenue [extract]

Revenue arising from the sale of goods is recognized when the significant risks and rewards of ownership have passed to the buyer and it can be reliably measured.

Revenue is measured at the fair value of the consideration received or receivable and represents amounts receivable for goods provided in the normal course of business, net of discounts, customs duties and sales taxes.

Revenues associated with the sale of oil, natural gas, natural gas liquids, liquefied natural gas, petroleum and petrochemicals products and all other items are recognized when the title passes to the customer. Physical exchanges are reported net, as are sales and purchases made with a common counterparty, as part of an arrangement similar to a physical exchange. Similarly, where the group acts as agent on behalf of a third party to procure or market energy commodities, any associated fee income is recognized but no purchase or sale is recorded. Additionally, where forward sale and purchase contracts for oil, natural gas or power have been determined to be for trading purposes, the associated sales and purchases are reported net within sales and other operating revenues whether or not physical delivery has occurred.

5.6.4   Inventories

5.6.4.A   Pipeline fill and cushion gas

In certain industries, for example the petrochemical industry, certain processes or storage arrangements require a core of inventory to be present in the system at all times. For example in order for a crude oil refining process to take place, the plant must contain a certain minimum quantity of oil. This can only be taken out once the plant is abandoned and could then only be sold as sludge. Similarly, underground gas storage caves are filled with gas; but a substantial part (25%) of that gas can never be sold as its function is to pressurise the cave, thereby allowing the remaining 75% to be extracted. Even though the gas will be turned around on a continuing basis, at any one time 25% of it will never be available to sell and cannot be recouped from the cave. Finally, long distance pipelines contain a significant volume of gas that keeps them operational.

It is our view that if an item of inventory is not held for sale or consumed in a production process, but is necessary to the operation of a facility during more than one operating cycle, and its cost cannot be recouped through sale (or is significantly impaired), this item of inventory should be accounted for as an item of property, plant and equipment under IAS 16. This applies even if the part of inventory that is deemed to be an item of property, plant and equipment (PP&E) cannot be separated physically from the rest of inventory.

These matters will always involve the exercise of judgement, however, in the above instances, we consider that:

- the deemed PP&E items do not meet the definition of inventories;

- although it is not possible to physically separate the chemicals involved into inventory and PP&E categories, there is no accounting reason why one cannot distinguish between identical assets with different uses and therefore account for them differently. Indeed, IAS 2 does envisage such a possibility in paragraph 25 when discussing different cost formulas;

- the deemed PP&E items are necessary to bring another item of PP&E to the condition necessary for it to be capable of operating in the manner intended by management. This meets the definition of the costs of PP&E in paragraph 16(b) of IAS 16 upon initial recognition; and

- recognising these items as inventories would lead to an immediate loss because these items cannot be sold or consumed in a production process, or during the process of rendering services. This does not properly reflect the fact that the items are necessary to operate another asset over more than one operating cycle.

By contrast, core inventory that is not necessary to operate the asset and that is recoverable (e.g. gas in a pipeline) is considered to be held for sale or to be consumed in the production process or process of rendering services. Therefore such gas is accounted for as inventory.

The extract below from the financial statements of Gaz de France shows how cushion gas is accounted for as a tangible asset that is depreciated over its economic life.

Extract 41.46: Gaz de France, S.A. (2010)

20.2 NOTES TO THE CONSOLIDATED FINANCIAL STATEMENTS [extract]

NOTE 1 SUMMARY OF SIGNIFICANT ACCOUNTING POLICIES [extract]

1.4 Significant accounting policies [extract]

1.4.5 Property, plant and equipment [extract]

1.4.5.1 Initial recognition and subsequent measurement [extract]

Cushion gas

"Cushion" gas injected into underground storage facilities is essential for ensuring that reservoirs can be operated effectively, and is therefore inseparable from these reservoirs. Unlike "working" gas which is included in inventories, cushion gas is reported in property, plant and equipment. It is measured at average purchase price, plus regasification, transportation and injection costs.

1.4.10 Inventories [extract]

Gas inventories

Gas injected into underground storage facilities includes working gas which can be withdrawn without adversely affecting the operation of the reservoir, and cushion gas which is inseparable from the reservoirs and essential for their operation (see the section on property, plant and equipment).

Working gas is classified in inventory and measured at weighted average purchase cost upon entering the transportation network regardless of its source, including any regasification costs.

Group inventory outflows are valued using the weighted average unit cost method.

An impairment loss is recognized when the net realizable value of inventories is lower than their weighted average cost.

5.6.4.B   Carried at fair value

Inventories should be measured at the lower of cost and net realisable value under IAS 2. However, IAS 2 does not apply to the measurement of inventories held by:

'(a)   producers of agricultural and forest products, agricultural produce after harvest, and minerals and mineral products, to the extent that they are measured at net realisable value in accordance with well established practices in those industries. When such inventories are measured at net realisable value, changes in that value are recognised in profit or loss in the period of the change. *[IAS 2.3(a)].*

(b)   commodity broker traders who measure their inventories at fair value less costs to sell. When such inventories are measured at fair value less costs to sell, changes in fair value less costs to sell are recognised in profit or loss in the period of the change.' *[IAS 2.3(b)].*

Both these scope exemptions are relevant to the oil and gas industry. An oil and gas company that wishes to use the exemption under (a) above needs to confirm that valuation at net realisable value is a 'well-established' practice in its industry.

The exemption under (b) above is commonly used by oil and gas companies that engage in oil and gas trading. The extract below from BP illustrates a typical accounting policy for an oil and gas company that makes use of this exemption.

Extract 41.47: BP plc (2010)

Notes on financial statements [extract]

1. Significant accounting policies [extract]

Inventories

Inventories, other than inventory held for trading purposes, are stated at the lower of cost and net realizable value. Cost is determined by the first-in first-out method and comprises direct purchase costs, cost of production, transportation and manufacturing expenses. Net realizable value is determined by reference to prices existing at the balance sheet date.

Inventories held for trading purposes are stated at fair value less costs to sell and any changes in net realizable value are recognized in the income statement.

Supplies are valued at cost to the group mainly using the average method or net realizable value, whichever is the lower.

5.6.4.C   Recognition

Under IFRS an asset should be recognised 'in the balance sheet when it is probable that the future economic benefits will flow to the entity and the asset has a cost or value that can be measured reliably'. *[Framework.4.44].* Oil and gas companies often do not separately report work in progress inventories of either oil or gas. As is noted in the IASC Issues Paper 'the main reason is that, at the point of their removal from the earth, oil and gas frequently do not require processing and they may be sold or may be transferred to the enterprise's downstream operations in the form existing at the time of removal, that is, they are immediately recognised as finished goods. Even if the oil and gas removed from the earth require additional processing to make them saleable or transportable, the time required for processing is typically minimal and the amount of raw products involved in the processing at any one time is likely to be immaterial.'[201] However, if more than an insignificant quantity of product is undergoing processing at any given point in time then an entity may need to disclose work in progress under IAS 2. *[IAS 2.8, 37].*

6   PRACTICAL ISSUES IN THE MINING INDUSTRY

6.1   Functional currency of mining companies

6.1.1   *Determining the functional currency*

Many mining businesses have found that determining the functional currency of their operations is complicated. Determining the functional currency correctly is important because it will, for example, (1) affect volatility of revenue and operating profit resulting from exchange rate movements, (2) determine whether transactions can be hedged or not, (3) influence the identification of embedded currency derivatives, and (4) may give rise to temporary differences that affect profit or loss. *[IAS 12.41].* While under IAS 21 an entity can select any presentation currency, it does not have a free choice in determining its functional currency. Instead, IAS 21 requires an entity to consider the following factors in determining its functional currency (see Chapter 17 at 4): *[IAS 21.9]*

(a)   the currency that mainly influences sales prices for goods and services (this will often be the currency in which sales prices for its goods and services are denominated and settled);

(b)   the currency of the country whose competitive forces and regulations mainly determine the sales prices of its goods and services; and

(c)   the currency that mainly influences labour, material and other costs of providing goods or services (this will often be the currency in which such costs are denominated and settled).

While the currency referred to under (a) above will often be the currency in which sales prices for its goods and services are denominated and settled, this is not always the case. In the mining industry the US dollar is often used as the contract or settlement currency in transactions (e.g. iron ore), but the pricing of transactions is often driven by factors completely unrelated to the US dollar (e.g. demand from China). When this is the case, management may need to conclude that the US dollar is not the currency that mainly influences the sales price.

In the mining industry, which is international in nature, it is often difficult to determine the currency of the country whose competitive forces and regulations mainly determine the sales prices of its goods and services. Therefore, factor (b) above will often prove to be inconclusive when a particular mineral is mined in many different countries.

It will generally be fairly straightforward to identify the currency that mainly influences an entity's key inputs (i.e. factor (c) above). In developing countries an entity will often need to import a significant proportion of its key inputs (e.g. fuel, equipment and expatriate workers) and even local inputs in an economy with a high inflation rate will often be linked to the US dollar. In such a case, the local currency is less likely to be the main currency that influences an entity's key inputs. In most developed countries, however, the inputs tend to be denominated in the local currency, although some inputs (e.g. mining equipment) may be denominated in another currency. As the mining industry is capital intensive, the cost of equipment often far exceeds the operating expenses incurred. Given that equipment is often purchased in US dollars, even in developed countries there is a general bias towards the US dollar as the functional currency.

Although local statutory and tax requirements should be ignored in determining the functional currency, there may be a requirement to keep two sets of accounting records when an entity concludes that its local currency is not its functional currency.

When the factors (a) to (c) above are mixed, as they often are in practice, and the functional currency is not obvious, management should use 'its judgement to determine the functional currency that most faithfully represents the economic effects of the underlying transactions, events and conditions'. *[IAS 21.12]*. If the above factors are inconclusive then an entity should also consider the following secondary factors: *[IAS 21.10, 11]*

- the currency in which funds from financing activities (i.e. issuing debt and equity instruments) are generated;
- the currency in which receipts from operating activities are usually retained; and
- the functional currency of the reporting entity that has the foreign operation as its subsidiary, branch, associate or joint venture.

Even after considering both the primary and secondary factors the functional currency of a mining entity may not be obvious because, for example, its revenue is denominated in US dollars while virtually all expenses are denominated in its local currency. Nevertheless, even in that situation management may conclude that revenue, while denominated in US dollars, is in fact influenced by a basket of currencies. It is therefore possible that mining companies operating in a similar environment can reach different conclusions about their functional currency. From observation, it appears that about half of the mining companies outside the United States have concluded that the US dollar is their functional currency.

Finally, IAS 21 requires an entity to determine separately the functional currency of each entity in a consolidated group. There is no concept as the functional currency of the group, only a presentation currency. Therefore, the functional currency of an operating subsidiary will often differ from that of the group's parent and/or foreign sales company to which it sells its production.

The extract below from Rio Tinto illustrates a typical currency translation accounting policy of a mining company.

Extract 41.48: Rio Tinto Group (2010)

Notes to the 2010 financial statements [extract]

1 Principal accounting policies [extract]

(d) Currency translation

The functional currency for each entity in the Group, and for jointly controlled entities and associates, is the currency of the primary economic environment in which it operates. For many entities, this is the currency of the country in which they operate. Transactions denominated in other currencies are converted to the functional currency at the exchange rate ruling at the date of the transaction unless hedge accounting applies, in which case the contract rate is used. Generally, this applies when derivatives or embedded derivatives are designated as cash flow hedges of the Group's sales. The Group's accounting policies for derivative financial instruments and hedge accounting are explained in more detail in note 1(p) (iii). Monetary assets and liabilities denominated in foreign currencies are retranslated at year end exchange rates.

The US dollar is the currency in which the Group's Financial statements are presented, as it most reliably reflects the global business performance of the Group as a whole. On consolidation, income statement items are translated from the functional currency into US dollars at average rates of exchange. Statement of financial position items are translated into US dollars at year end exchange rates. Exchange differences on the translation of the net assets of entities with functional currencies other than the US dollar, and any offsetting exchange differences on net debt hedging those net assets, are recognised directly in the foreign currency translation reserve via the statement of comprehensive income (with the exception of translation adjustments relating to Rio Tinto Limited's share capital which are shown in the Group statement of changes in equity).

Exchange gains and losses which arise on balances between Group entities are taken to the foreign currency translation reserve where the intragroup balance is, in substance, part of the Group's net investment in the entity.

The balance of the foreign currency translation reserve relating to an operation that is disposed of is transferred to the income statement at the time of the disposal.

The Group finances its operations primarily in US dollars but part of the Group's US dollar debt is located in subsidiaries having functional currencies other than the US dollar. Except as noted above, exchange gains and losses relating to such US dollar debt are charged or credited to the Group's income statement in the year in which they arise. This means that the impact of financing in US dollars on the Group's income statement is dependent on the functional currency of the particular subsidiary where the debt is located.

Exchange differences arising on closure provisions are capitalised at operating mines. Except as noted above, or in note 1 (p) relating to derivative contracts, all other exchange differences are charged or credited to the income statement in the year in which they arise.

6.1.2   Changes in functional currency

IAS 21 requires management to use its judgement to determine the entity's functional currency such that it most faithfully represents the economic effects of the underlying transactions, events and conditions that are relevant to the entity. In this context it is important to note that IAS 21 requires the functional currency to be determined by reference to factors that exist *during* the reporting period. Therefore, an entity should ignore future developments in its business, no matter how likely those developments are. For example, even if an entity is absolutely convinced that in three years time it will have US dollar sales revenue, this is not a factor to be considered in determining its functional currency today. Consequently, a mining company may conclude that during the development phase of the mine the local currency is its functional currency, but that once production and sales commence the US dollar will become its functional currency. This is illustrated in the extract below from Hochschild Mining's 2008 financial statements.

> **Extract 41.49: Hochschild Mining plc (2008)**
>
> **Notes to the consolidated financial statements continued**
>
> **For the year ended 31 December 2008** [extract]
>
> **36 Financial risk management** [extract]
>
> **(a) Foreign currency risk** [extract]
>
> 1   Minera Santa Cruz, one of the Group's subsidiaries which is the legal owner of the San José mine, had debts denominated in US dollars. As Minera Santa Cruz's functional currency was the peso during 2007, the translation of this loan into Pesos created a loss. Following the commencement of operations the Group was required to change the functional currency in Minera Santa Cruz to US dollars and as a result, these loans were no longer being exposed to foreign currency risk.

Once the functional currency is determined, the standard allows it to be changed only if there is a change in those underlying transactions, events and conditions. For example, a change in the currency that mainly influences the sales prices of goods and services may lead to a change in an entity's functional currency. *[IAS 21.36].* The extract below, from Angel Mining plc's financial statements, provides an example of a change in conditions that resulted in a change in functional currency. Accounting for a change in functional currency is discussed in Chapter 17 at 5.5.

> **Extract 41.50: Angel Mining plc (2010)**
>
> **Notes to the financial statements**
>
> **Year ended 28 February 2010** [extract]
>
> **1a. Basis of preparation – Change in functional currency**
>
> Previously, the directors considered the functional currency of the Company to be Sterling. In light of developments within the Company's operations and the nature of its funding, the directors have reassessed the functional currency of the Company and concluded that the currency of the primary economic environment in which Angel Mining operates is now the US dollar. The date of change from Sterling to US dollars has been taken as 1 March 2009. The key factors influencing this decision include the following:
>
> (i)   During the year, the Company acquired the Nalunaq license and mining assets. This will be the first producing mine for the Company. The consideration for these assets was paid in US dollars;
>
> (ii)   During the year, the Company sourced plant, machinery and employees with technical skills on a global basis. A significant proportion of these costs were based in US dollars. In prior years, the Company's costs had been incurred primarily in Sterling;
>
> (iii) The Company's primary form of finance during the period was the long term and short term debt facilities provided by FBC. These facilities are all based in US dollars. During prior periods, the Company had been more heavily dependent upon equity finance which was denominated in Sterling;
>
> (iv)   The vast majority of the forms of finance which the Company has been pursuing and is likely to pursue going forward are US dollar based;
>
> (v)   Commencing during the year, one of the largest consumables used by the Company in its operations in Greenland was diesel fuel. Although the Company pays for its diesel in Danish Kroner, the price of diesel is determined globally and priced in US dollars; and
>
> (vi)   The resources that the Company is working to exploit are global commodities which are always priced in US dollars. When the Company begins producing, all its revenues will be dollar based.
>
> The change in the Company's functional currency has been accounted for prospectively from 1 March 2009 in accordance with IAS 21. This change constituted a prospective change in accounting policy. The financial statements for 2009 have been prepared using Sterling as the functional currency and US dollars as the presentational currency.

> The change in the presentational currency from Sterling to US dollar is and therefore is applied retrospectively in accordance with IAS 8 'Accounting Policies, Changes in Accounting Estimates and Errors' and therefore require comparative information to be restated and consequently, a third balance sheet is required to be presented in the financial statements.
>
> The impact of this change in presentational currency for 2009, is as follows:
>
> (i) The assets and liabilities for both the Group and the Company at 28 February 2009 have been translated using the closing rate for the same date of \$1.426/£;
>
> (ii) The consolidated income statement for 2009 has been translated using the average rate for the year ended 28 February 2009 of \$1.771/£ on the basis that this average rate approximates the exchange rates on the dates of transactions; and
>
> The resulting gain on retranslation from average to closing rate has been recognised in the consolidated statement of comprehensive income.

6.2 Stripping costs and overburden

In surface mining operations it is necessary to remove overburden and other waste materials to gain access to ore from which minerals can be extracted. It is generally accepted that the costs of removal (also known as stripping) of overburden and waste materials during the development of a mine, i.e. before production commences, should be capitalised as part of the investment in the construction of the mine. For these purposes the 'mine' is considered to be an asset that is separate from the 'mineral rights and mineral reserves', which are outside the scope of IAS 16. *[IAS 16.3(d)]*.

Until the guidance provided by IFRIC 20 (expected to be issued by the Interpretations Committee in October 2011 (see 6.2.2 below)) there was no consensus regarding the treatment of stripping costs that were incurred during the production phase. IFRS was not clear on whether stripping costs were to be treated as costs of inventory under IAS 2 or as a period cost. In practice the following three approaches were used, which are discussed below:

• expensing of production stripping costs as incurred (see 6.2.1.A below);

• capitalising production stripping costs as cost of inventory (see 6.2.1.B below); and

• deferral of production stripping costs (see 6.2.1.C below).

Entities will be able to continue to use one of these methods until IFRIC 20 becomes effective – which is expected to be for annual reporting periods commencing on or after 1 January 2013, unless an entity decides to early adopt.

Until then, irrespective of the method applied, we believe that users would still benefit from disclosure of the following information:

(a) accounting policy applied to stripping costs;

(b) amount of deferred stripping costs, if any;

(c) statement of financial position caption in which deferred stripping costs are recognised; and

(d) how the entity defines a mine.

The definition of a 'mine' is of importance in determining whether stripping costs incurred in creating an additional pit or access point to an ore body, are development stripping costs or production stripping costs. Additionally, the definition of a 'mine' is also important in applying the average strip ratio approach as discussed at 6.2.1.C II below. For the purposes of IFRIC 20, it is our understanding that the determination of 'component of the ore body' will be critical. In defining a 'mine', an entity may want to apply the guidance on selecting the appropriate 'unit of account' at 4.2 above.

6.2.1   Current practice

6.2.1.A   Expensing of production stripping costs as incurred

In some mining operations the stripping ratio, which is the ratio between waste and mineral ore extracted, is expected to be relatively consistent over the life of the mine because of the physical characteristics of the mineral deposit. In particular, when an entity uses an extraction method such as open cast (strip) mining, which only requires removal of overburden shortly before the mineral ore is extracted, there will be little advance stripping and the period-to-period fluctuations of stripping costs will be insignificant. In such cases it is generally considered acceptable to expense stripping costs as a production cost when incurred. The extract below illustrates the application of this approach by BHP Billiton.

> *Extract 41.51: BHP Billiton Group (2010)*
>
> **Notes to financial statements** [extract]
>
> **1. Accounting policies** [extract]
>
> **Overburden removal costs** [extract]
>
> Production stripping commences at the time that saleable materials begin to be extracted from the mine and normally continues throughout the life of a mine. The costs of production stripping are charged to the income statement as operating costs when the ratio of waste material to ore extracted for an area of interest is expected to be constant throughout its estimated life. ...

6.2.1.B   Capitalising production stripping costs as cost of inventory: US GAAP

Application of ASC 930-330-25-1 *Extractive Activities – Mining – Inventory – Recognition – General* (pre-codification EITF 04-6 *Accounting for Stripping Costs Incurred during Production in the Mining Industry*), a US GAAP pronouncement, adoption of which is permitted under the hierarchy in IAS 8, [IAS 8.12], has found some acceptance by companies reporting under IFRS, in particular those that also report financial information under US GAAP. ASC 930-330-25-1 states that 'stripping costs incurred during the production phase of a mine are variable production costs that should be included in the costs of the inventory produced (that is, extracted) during the period that the stripping costs are incurred'.[202]

The US GAAP approach can lead to earnings volatility when accounting for stripping costs in mines that experience material fluctuations in the ratio of overburden to mineral ore mined. Proponents of the approach argue that such earnings volatility only reflects the actual volatility of operational results. However, others note that stripping costs incurred in one period are not necessarily related to the production of mineral ore in that period. For example, there are often good operational reasons for stripping overburden well ahead of the period in which production will occur.

As illustrated in the extract below from Randgold's 2007 financial statements, some companies did adopt the principles of EITF 04-6 in their financial statements under IFRS.

Extract 41.52: Randgold Resources Limited (2007)

Notes to the consolidated financial statements [extract]

2 Significant accounting policies [extract]

STRIPPING COSTS

All stripping costs incurred during the production phase of a mine are treated as variable production costs and as a result are included in the cost of inventory produced during the period that the stripping costs are incurred. Refer to note 6.

6 CHANGES IN ACCOUNTING POLICY [extract]

The company changed its accounting policy on stripping costs, under both IFRS and US GAAP, in 2006. Previously, costs of production stage waste stripping in excess of the expected pit life average stripping ratio were deferred and then charged to production when the actual stripping ratio was below the expected pit life average stripping ratio. Under the revised accounting policy, all stripping costs incurred during the production phase of a mine are treated as variable production costs and as a result are included in the cost of the inventory produced during the period that the stripping costs are incurred.

Under US GAAP, EITF 04-06 'Accounting for Stripping Costs Incurred during Production in the Mining Industry' is effective for reporting periods beginning after 15 December 2005. The consensus does not permit the deferral of any waste stripping costs during the production phase of a mine, but requires instead that they should be treated as variable production costs. The directors have decided to adopt the same treatment under IFRS which will ensure that the accounting policies applied under IFRS and US GAAP remain in line.

With regard to the conclusions reached by the EITF, the directors believe the revised policy will mean that the financial statements provide reliable and more relevant information about the group's financial position and its financial performance. In accordance with the requirements of IAS 8 'Accounting Policies, Changes in Accounting Estimates and Errors', the change in the IFRS policy was applied retrospectively and hence the 2005 figures were restated.

6.2.1.C   Deferral of production stripping costs to match future production identification

In some mining operations, the stripping costs will vary significantly from period to period because of variations in the thickness of the layer of overburden, the physical properties of the ore body and operational requirements that determine when overburden can be removed. When stripping costs fluctuate significantly between periods, entities generally defer and capitalise excess stripping costs (i.e. costs that do not relate to production in the current period) and allocate those costs to the production derived in later years. In theory, two approaches can be applied in determining which portion of the stripping costs should be deferred.

I   Specific identification approach

Under the specific identification approach the costs for each stripping campaign are allocated to the quantity of mineral ore that becomes accessible. The costs of each stripping campaign are then capitalised and amortised when the related mineral ore is extracted. Although support for this approach can be found in both IAS 2 and IAS 16, the approach is often considered too cumbersome for record keeping and has not been popular in practice under IFRS – although this is the approach adopted previously under Canadian GAAP.

II   *Average strip ratio approach*

The average strip ratio approach requires the current period ratio of 'overburden to mineral ore extracted' to be compared to the expected average over the life of the mine in accordance with the mine plan. Excess stripping costs are deferred when the strip ratio exceeds the average strip ratio costs. Deferred stripping costs are expensed in the opposite situation. Whether application of the average strip ratio approach is appropriate depends on the circumstances:

• *Gradually increasing strip ratio* – The average strip ratio approach is not appropriate in this case as it would result in the recognition of a stripping cost liability. In the absence of a legal or constructive obligation to continue to mine the deposit an entity should not recognise a liability. If this is the case, one of the other methods discussed above will be more appropriate;

• *Gradually decreasing strip ratio* – Although this situation is unlikely to occur in practice (i.e. typically mining operations will start at the point where the stripping ratio is most favourable), the average strip ratio approach might be considered appropriate; and

• *Substantially constant or stable strip ratio* – In this case the average strip ratio approach is considered acceptable, but the results of the approach will approximate those of the other methods discussed above.

A final scenario, which combines elements of the above scenarios, would be one in which the strip ratio fluctuates over time, e.g. because the depth of the mineral deposit varies. In such cases an entity needs to exercise judgement in developing an appropriate accounting policy. An entity that applies the average strip ratio approach should regularly reassess whether the approach is still appropriate. For example, the mining of an unexpected fault or dyke should not be spread out over future production but should be recognised as a period cost instead.

While the average strip ratio approach is imperfect, many entities in the mining industry consider that it provides more reliable and relevant information about their financial position and financial performance than the alternative and therefore has been commonly adopted in practice.

Extract 41.53: Rio Tinto Group (2010)

Notes to the 2010 financial statements [extract]

1 Principal accounting policies [extract]

(h) Deferred stripping

As noted above, stripping costs incurred in the development of a mine (or pit) before production commences are capitalised as part of the cost of constructing the mine (or pit) and subsequently amortised over the life of the mine (or pit) on a units of production basis.

Where a mine operates several open pits that are regarded as separate operations for the purpose of mine planning, stripping costs are accounted for separately by reference to the ore from each separate pit. If, however, the pits are highly integrated for the purpose of mine planning, the second and subsequent pits are regarded as extensions of the first pit in accounting for stripping costs. In such cases, the initial stripping (i.e. overburden and other waste removal) of the second and subsequent pits is considered to be production phase stripping relating to the combined operation.

The Group's determination of whether multiple pit mines are considered separate or integrated operations depends on each mine's specific circumstances. The following factors would point towards the stripping costs for the individual pits being accounted for separately:

- If mining of the second and subsequent pits is conducted consecutively with that of the first pit, rather than concurrently.

- If separate investment decisions are made to develop each pit, rather than a single investment decision being made at the outset.

- If the pits are operated as separate units in terms of mine planning and the sequencing of overburden and ore mining, rather than as an integrated unit.

- If expenditures for additional infrastructure to support the second and subsequent pits are relatively large.

- If the pits extract ore from separate and distinct orebodies, rather than from a single orebody.

This additional factor would point to an integrated operation in accounting for stripping costs:

- If the designs of the second and subsequent pits are significantly influenced by opportunities to optimise output from the several pits combined, including the co-treatment or blending of the output from the pits.

The relative importance of each of the above factors is considered in each case to determine whether, on balance, the stripping costs should be attributed to the individual pit or to the combined output from the several pits.

The Group defers stripping costs incurred subsequently, during the production stage of its operations, for those operations where this is the most appropriate basis for matching the costs against the related economic benefits and the effect is material. This is generally the case where there are fluctuations in stripping costs over the life of the mine (or pit). The amount of stripping costs deferred is based on the ratio ('Ratio') obtained by dividing the tonnage of waste mined either by the quantity of ore mined or by the quantity of minerals contained in the ore. In some operations, the quantity of ore is a more practical basis for matching costs with the related economic benefits where there are important co-products or where the grade of the ore is relatively stable from year to year. Stripping costs incurred in the period are deferred to the extent that the current period Ratio exceeds the life of mine (or pit) Ratio. Such deferred costs are then charged against reported profits to the extent that, in subsequent periods, the current period Ratio falls short of the life of mine (or pit) Ratio.

The life of mine (or pit) Ratio is based on proved and probable reserves of the mine (or pit). The life of mine (or pit) waste-to-ore ratio is a function of the pit design(s) and therefore changes to that design will generally result in changes to the Ratio. Changes in other technical or economic parameters that impact on reserves will also have an impact on the life of mine (or pit) Ratio even if they do not affect the pit design(s). Changes to the life of mine (or pit) Ratio are accounted for prospectively.

In the production stage of some mines (or pits), further development of the mine (or pit) requires a phase of unusually high overburden removal activity that is similar in nature to pre-production mine development. The costs of such unusually high overburden removal activity are deferred and charged against reported profits in subsequent periods on a units of production basis. This accounting treatment is consistent with that for stripping costs incurred during the development phase of a mine (or pit), before production commences.

Deferred stripping costs are included in 'Mining properties and leases' within property, plant and equipment or in 'Investments in equity accounted units', as appropriate. These form part of the total investment in the relevant cash generating unit, which is reviewed for impairment if events or changes in circumstances indicate that the carrying value may not be recoverable. Amortisation of deferred stripping costs is included in net operating costs or in the Group's share of the results of its equity accounted units, as appropriate.

6.2.1.D Presentation of deferred stripping costs

IFRS does not currently prescribe where in the statement of financial position an entity should present deferred stripping costs. In practice, many large mining companies recognise preproduction deferred stripping costs within property, plant and equipment. Mining companies normally report production deferred stripping costs in the costs of the inventory produced or within 'other assets' or 'prepaid amounts'. Given the diversity of practice we recommend that an entity discloses the presentation it has adopted.

It should be noted that IFRIC 20 (see 6.2.2 below) will specify that any stripping activity asset would be considered an addition to, enhancement of, the mine asset, although it will not specify whether such a mine asset is a tangible or intangible asset. Either way, once the Interpretation is effective, any capitalised stripping costs will now form part of a non-current asset (tangible or intangible) in the statement of financial position. Therefore, if an entity presented such costs elsewhere, such amounts will now need to be reclassified.

6.2.2   IFRIC 20 – Stripping Costs in the Production Phase of a Surface Mine

In November 2009, the IFRS Interpretations Committee (Interpretations Committee) started discussions on a new interpretation on how to account for stripping (waste removal) costs.[203] This project culminated in IFRIC Interpretation 20 – *Stripping Costs in the Production Phase of a Surface Mine* – which was ratified by the IASB in September 2011 and is expected to be issued in October 2011.

IFRIC 20 considers the different types of stripping costs encountered in a surface mining operation. These costs are separated into those incurred in the development phase of the mine (i.e. pre-production) and those that are incurred in the production phase. Generally those costs that are incurred in the development phase of the mine would be capitalised as part of the depreciable cost of building, developing and constructing the mine, under the principles of IAS 16. Ultimately these capitalised costs are depreciated or amortised on a systematic basis, usually by using the units of production, once production commences. The stripping costs incurred in the development phase of a mine are not considered by the Interpretation. The Interpretations Committee considered that there was little divergence in practice when accounting for these costs.

Despite the importance of the term 'production phase', this is not defined in the Interpretation, or elsewhere in IFRS. The determination of the commencement of the production phase not only affects stripping costs, but also impacts many other accounting issues in the extractives industries. These include the cessation of the capitalisation of other costs, including borrowing costs, the commencement of depreciation/amortisation, and the treatment of certain pre-production revenues.

6.2.2.A   Scope

The Interpretation will apply to all waste removal (stripping) costs that are incurred in surface mining activity, during the production phase of the mine (production stripping costs). In addition, the Interpretation limits its scope to only surface mining activity, excluding oil and natural gas extraction, including the question of whether oil sands extraction was a surface mining activity, and underground mining activities.

The Interpretation then acknowledges that stripping activity undertaken during the production phase may create two benefits – the first being the extraction of ore (inventory) in the current period and the second being improved access to the ore body to be mined in a future period. Where the benefits are realised in the form of inventory produced, the production stripping costs are to be accounted for in accordance with IAS 2 – *Inventories.* Where the benefit is improved access to ore to be mined in the future, these costs are to be recognised as a non-current asset, if the required criteria are met (see 6.2.2.B below). The Interpretation refers to this non-current asset as the 'stripping activity asset'.

6.2.2.B   Recognition criteria – stripping activity asset

IFRIC 20 states that an entity must recognise a stripping activity asset if, and only if, all of the following criteria are satisfied:

(a)   it is probable that the future economic benefit (improved access to the ore body) associated with the stripping activity will flow to the entity;

(b)   the entity can identify the component of the ore body for which access has been improved; and

(c)   the costs relating to the stripping activity associated with that component can be measured reliably.

Instead of being a separate asset, the stripping activity asset is to be accounted for as an addition to, or as an enhancement of, an existing asset. This means that the stripping activity asset will be accounted for as part of an existing asset. IFRIC 20 will not specify whether the stripping activity asset will be a tangible or intangible asset. Instead it simply states that it should be classified as tangible or intangible according to the nature of the existing asset of which it is part – so it will depend upon whether an entity classifies its mine assets as tangible or intangible.

The Interpretation considers that the stripping activity asset might add to or improve a variety of existing assets, such as, the mine property (land), the mineral deposit itself, an intangible right to extract the ore or an asset that originated in the mine development phase. In most instances, entities classify their producing mine assets as tangible assets; therefore it is likely that the stripping activity assets will also be classified as tangible assets.

Given this, as noted above at 6.2.1.D, for entities that currently present their capitalised stripping costs as an asset separate from their mine assets or mining rights, for example, if they present these as part of other current or non-current assets, upon adoption of IFRIC 20, such amounts will need to be presented as part of the mining related assets (either tangible or intangible), which will be presented within non-current assets.

6.2.2.C   Initial recognition

The stripping activity asset is to be initially measured at cost. This will be the accumulation of costs directly incurred to perform the stripping activity that benefits the identified component of ore, plus an allocation of directly attributable overhead costs. In the Basis for Conclusions to IFRIC 20, examples of the types of costs that the Interpretations Committee would expect to be included as directly attributable overhead costs would be items such as salary costs of the mine supervisor overseeing that component of the mine, and an allocation of rental costs of any equipment which was hired specifically to perform the stripping activity.

The Interpretation acknowledges that some incidental operations may take place at the same time as the production stripping activity, but which are not necessary for the production stripping activity to continue as planned. The costs associated with these incidental operations are not to be included in the cost of the stripping activity asset. An example provided in the interpretation is the building of an access ramp in the area in which the production stripping activity is taking place. These ancillary costs shall be recognised as assets or expensed in accordance with other IFRSs.

Allocating costs between inventory and the stripping activity asset

The Interpretation acknowledges that when inventory is produced at the same time as access to the ore body is improved, it may be difficult in practice, to separately identify the costs of the inventory produced and the stripping activity asset. Given this, the Interpretation permits an entity to use an allocation approach that is based on a relevant production measure. The Interpretations Committee decided to use an allocation approach based on a relevant production measure, because a production measure was considered to be a good indicator of the nature of benefits that are generated for the activity taking place in the mine.

The production measure is calculated for the identified component of the ore body. It effectively involves a comparison of the expected level of activity for that component of the ore body, with the actual level of activity, to identify when additional activity may be creating a future benefit. Activity incurred at the expected level and the associated costs of such, would form part of the cost of inventory produced. Any excess of actual activity over the expected level (and the associated cost) would then need to be considered to determine whether it represents a stripping activity asset.

In determining an appropriate allocation basis, the Interpretation provides a (non-exhaustive) list of some of the possible metrics that could be used. These include:

- cost of inventory produced compared with expected cost;
- volume of waste extracted compared with expected volume, for a given volume of ore production; and
- mineral content of the ore extracted compared with expected mineral content to be extracted, for a given quantity of ore produced.

While this list is non-exhaustive, the Interpretations Committee made it clear that an allocation basis which uses sales value or relative sales value is not acceptable.

It is worth noting that while the allocation approaches set out in the Interpretation are similar to the life-of-mine average strip ratio approach used by many entities today, there are differences.

The key difference is that the level at which the expected level of activity is determined may not be the entire ore body – instead it is required to be determined for each component of the ore body. See below for further discussion on determining components of the ore body.

The other difference relates to the way in which any stripping activity asset is recognised in profit or loss. Under the life-of-mine average stripping ratio approach, a portion of the deferred stripping asset is recognised in profit or loss when the actual stripping ratio falls below the expected average life of mine stripping ratio. Under IFRIC 20 however, the stripping activity asset is to be depreciated or amortised over the useful life of the identified component of the ore body that becomes more accessible. The units of production (UOP) method is to be used unless another method is more appropriate. See below at 6.2.2.D for further discussion regarding subsequent measurement.

Identifying the component of the ore body

One of the critical steps an entity will need to undertake when applying this new Interpretation is identifying the various components of the ore body. This will be necessary for several reasons:

(a)   production stripping costs can only be capitalised as an asset if the component of the ore body for which access has been improved, can be identified;

(b)   to allocate stripping activity costs between inventory and the stripping activity asset, an entity will need to determine the expected level of activity for each component of the mine; and

(c)   the stripping activity asset is required to be depreciated or amortised on a systematic basis, over the expected useful life of the identified component of the ore body that becomes more accessible as a result of the stripping activity.

Despite the importance of identifying the various components, limited guidance is provided within the Interpretation, although it does appear evident that the Interpretations Committee expected a component to be a subset of the whole ore body. This view is supported in several sections of IFRIC 20.

• The Basis for Consensus explains that: 'component' refers to the specific volume of the ore body that is made more accessible by the stripping activity; the identified component of the ore body would typically be a subset of the total ore body of the mine; and a mine may have several components, which are identified during the mine planning stage.

• The depreciation or amortisation requirements state that the expected useful life of the identified component of the ore body that is used to depreciate or amortise the stripping activity asset will differ from the expected useful life that is used to depreciate or amortise the mine itself and the related life-of-mine assets, unless the stripping activity provides improved access to the whole of the ore body.

Identification of the various components of an ore body will require significant management judgement. While the Interpretations Committee considered that an entity's mine plan would provide the information required to allow these judgements to be made with reasonable consistency, this may not be a straightforward exercise, and it will be particularly challenging for the more complex mines.

6.2.2.D   Subsequent measurement

IFRIC 20 requires that after initial recognition, the stripping activity asset must be carried at its cost or revalued amount less depreciation or amortisation and less impairment losses, in the same way as the existing asset of which it is a part. The stripping activity asset is to be depreciated or amortised on a systematic basis, over the expected useful life of the identified component of the ore body that becomes more accessible as a result of the stripping activity.

The Interpretation effectively requires that the units of production method is to be applied unless another method is more appropriate. As noted earlier, the Interpretations Committee noted that the expected useful life of the identified component that is used to depreciate or amortise the stripping activity asset will differ from the expected useful life that is used to depreciate or amortise the mine itself and the related life-of-mine assets, unless the stripping activity provides improved access to the whole of the ore body.

6.2.2.E   Effective date and transition

Once issued (expected to be in October 2011), IFRIC 20 is expected to be effective for annual periods beginning on or after 1 January 2013. Earlier application is permitted. If an entity applies this Interpretation for an earlier period, it shall disclose that fact.

The Interpretation is to be applied prospectively to production stripping costs incurred on or after the beginning of the earliest period presented.

If an entity has any existing stripping related asset balances as at the beginning of the earliest period presented that arose due to stripping activity undertaken during the production phase, it shall reclassify this asset as part of an existing asset to which the stripping activity related, to the extent there remains an identifiable component of the ore body with which the stripping activity asset can be associated. Such balances shall be depreciated or amortised over the remaining expected useful life of the identified component of the ore body to which each existing asset balance relates.

Where an entity cannot identify the component of the ore body to which that existing asset balance relates, the asset shall be recognised in opening retained earnings at the beginning of the earliest period presented.

6.2.2.F   Disclosures

There are no specific disclosure requirements within IFRIC 20 other than the requirement to disclose if an entity early adopts the Interpretation. However, the general disclosure requirements of IAS 1 would be relevant. For example, the requirements to disclose significant accounting policies *[IAS 1.117]*. and also any significant judgements, estimates and assumptions. *[IAS 1.125]*. For many entities, it is likely that the accounting policy for stripping costs would be considered a significant accounting policy which would therefore warrant disclosure, as would the judgements, estimates and assumptions they make when applying this policy.

6.3   Revenue recognition

6.3.1   Provisionally priced contracts

Sales contracts for certain commodities (e.g. copper) often provide for provisional pricing at the time of shipment of metal concentrate with final pricing based on the average market price for a particular future period. This type of arrangement is particularly common when an entity produces a mineral concentrate that is sold to a smelter or refiner, which will produce the fully refined metal that is then sold into the market. The final sales price is often (1) based on the average market prices during a subsequent period (the 'quotational period'), (2) the price on a fixed date after delivery or (3) the amount subsequently realised by the smelter or refiner, net of tolling charges.

Price adjustment features contained in non-cancellable contracts that are based on quoted market prices for a date subsequent to the date of shipment or delivery (e.g. the spot price three weeks after shipment or the average spot price for the month of shipment) are considered to be embedded derivatives that require separation under IAS 39/IFRS 9, because the forward price at which the contract is to be settled is not closely related to the spot price. *[IAS 39.11, AG30(e), IFRS 9.4.3]*. The non-financial contract for the sale or purchase of the mineral concentrate at a future date would be treated as the host contract, while the exposure to the price movements from the date of sale to the end of the quotational period would be treated as an embedded derivative.

If the contract is cancellable without penalty before delivery, the price adjustment feature does not meet the definition of a derivative because there is no contractual obligation until delivery takes place.

If the contract is not cancellable, there will be a contractual obligation, but until delivery, the embedded derivative would be considered to be closely related to the host commodity contract and does not need to be recorded separately.

When the embedded derivative is separated from the host contract, the host contract will normally meet the revenue recognition criteria – in particular the requirement that revenue can be measured reliably – at the date that the mineral concentrate is delivered. *[IAS 18.14]*.

Changes in the fair value of the embedded derivative should be recognised in profit or loss for the period. While gains or losses from embedded derivatives should normally be presented together with those from other derivatives, many mining companies include adjustments of provisional prices within revenue, presumably on the grounds of materiality or as a matter of industry practice.

Antofagasta is an example of a mining company that discloses the effects of provisional pricing in its financial statements in considerable detail, including the quantities of minerals that are subject to provisional prices.

Extract 41.54: Antofagasta plc (2010)

Notes to the Financial Statements [extract]

2 Principal Accounting Policies [extract]

d) Revenue recognition [extract]

Revenue represents the value of goods and services supplied to third parties during the year. Revenue is measured at the fair value of consideration received or receivable, and excludes any applicable sales tax.

A sale is recognised when the significant risks and rewards of ownership have passed. This is generally when title and any insurance risk has passed to the customer, and the goods have been delivered to a contractually agreed location or when any services have been provided.

Revenue from mining activities is recorded at the invoiced amounts with an adjustment for provisional pricing at each reporting date, as explained below. For copper and molybdenum concentrates, which are sold to smelters and roasting plants for further processing, the invoiced amount is the market value of the metal payable by the customer, net of deductions for tolling charges. Revenue includes revenues from the sale of by-products.

Copper and molybdenum concentrate sale agreements and copper cathode sale agreements generally provide for provisional pricing of sales at the time of shipment, with final pricing based on the monthly average London Metal Exchange ("LME") copper price or the monthly average market molybdenum price for specified future periods. This normally ranges from 30 to 120 days after delivery to the customer. Such a provisional sale contains an embedded derivative which is required to be separated from the host contract. The host contract is the sale of metals contained in the concentrate or cathode at the provisional invoice price less tolling charges deducted, and the embedded derivative is the forward contract for which the provisional sale is subsequently adjusted. At each reporting date, the provisionally priced metal sales together with any related tolling charges are marked-to-market, with adjustments (both gains and losses) being recorded in revenue in the consolidated income statement and in trade debtors in the balance sheet. Forward prices at the period end are used for copper concentrate and cathode sales, while period-end average prices are used for molybdenum concentrate sales due to the absence of a futures market.

25 Financial Instruments and Financial Risk Management [extract]

d) Embedded derivatives – provisionally priced sales [extract]

Copper and molybdenum concentrate sale agreements and copper cathode sale agreements generally provide for provisional pricing of sales at the time or month of shipment, with final pricing being based on the monthly average London Metal Exchange copper price or monthly average molybdenum price for specified future periods. This normally ranges from 30 to 120 days after delivery to the customer.

Under IFRS, both gains and losses from the marking-to-market of open sales are recognised through adjustments to revenue in the income statement and to trade debtors in the balance sheet. The Group determines mark-to-market prices using forward prices at each period end for copper concentrate and cathode sales, and period-end monthly average prices for molybdenum concentrate sales due to the absence of a futures market for that commodity.

...

(i) Copper sales

...

i) Copper concentrate

At 31 December 2010 and 31 December 2009 copper concentrate sales at Los Pelambres had an average settlement period of approximately three months after shipment date.

At 31 December 2010 sales totalling 101,900 tonnes remained open as to price, with an average mark-to-market price of 436.7 cents per pound compared with an average provisional invoice price of 381.3 cents per pound. At 31 December 2009 sales totalling 73,700 tonnes remained open as to price, with an average mark-to-market price of 334.0 cents per pound compared with an average provisional invoice price of 295.8 cents per pound.

Tolling charges include a mark-to-market gain for copper concentrate sales open as to price at 31 December 2010 of less than US$0.1 million (2009 – mark-to-market loss of US$5.1 million).

ii) Copper cathodes

At 31 December 2010 and 31 December 2009 copper cathode sales at El Tesoro and Michilla had an average settlement period of approximately one month after shipment date.

At 31 December 2010, sales totalling 12,700 tonnes remained open as to price, with an average mark-to-market price of 437.3 cents per pound compared with an average provisional invoice price of 417.9 cents per pound. At 31 December 2009, sales totalling 10,400 tonnes remained open as to price, with an average mark-to-market price of 333.5 cents per pound compared with an average provisional invoice price of 322.9 cents per pound.

(ii) Molybdenum sales

	Los Pelambres Molybdenum concentrate 2010 US$m	Los Pelambres Molybdenum concentrate 2009 US$m
Provisionally invoiced gross sales	318.0	189.2
Effects of pricing adjustments to previous year invoices		
Reversal of mark-to-market adjustments at the end of the previous year	1.1	13.3
Settlement of molybdenum sales invoiced in the previous year	8.1	(15.5)
Total effect of adjustments to previous year invoices in the current year	9.2	(2.2)
Effects of pricing adjustments to current year invoices		
Settlement of molybdenum sales invoiced in the current year	(10.9)	6.4
Mark-to-market adjustments at the end of the current year	0.3	(1.1)
Total effects of adjustments to current year invoices	(10.6)	5.3
Total pricing adjustments	(1.4)	3.1
Revenue before deducting tolling charges	316.6	192.3
Tolling charges	(13.1)	(12.2)
Revenue net of tolling charges	303.5	180.1

At 31 December 2010, molybdenum concentrate sales at Los Pelambres had an average settlement period of approximately two months after shipment date. Sales totalling 1,300 tonnes remained open as to price, with an average mark-to-market price of US$16.1 per pound compared with an average provisional invoice price of US$16.0 per pound.

At 31 December 2009, molybdenum concentrate sales at Los Pelambres had an average settlement period of approximately two months after shipment date. Sales totalling 1,400 tonnes remained open as to price, with an average mark-to-market price of US$11.3 per pound compared with an average provisional invoice price of US$11.6 per pound.

6.3.2 The recognition of revenue at the completion of production

Under some circumstances, mining companies can recognise revenue once the production of the commodity has been completed.

Clearly, the uncertainty surrounding the cost of production is removed when the product is completed; it is therefore necessary to evaluate the remaining uncertainties in order to determine whether or not completion of production can be used as the critical event for revenue recognition. Where the entity has entered into a firm contract for the production and delivery of a product, the sales price will have been determined and the selling costs will have already been incurred. Consequently, provided that both the delivery expenses and the bad debt risk can satisfactorily be assessed, it may be appropriate to report revenue on this basis. One application of this practice is the completed contract method of recognising revenue on construction contracts, under which revenue is recognised only when the contract is completed or substantially completed.

It has also become accepted practice in a limited number of industries to recognise revenue at the completion of production, even though a sales contract may not have been entered into. This practice has been adopted, for example, in the case of the production of certain minerals and mineral products, provided that the following criteria are met: *[IAS 2.3(a), 4]*

(a)   the minerals have been extracted;

(b)   sale is assured under a forward contract or a government guarantee or an active market exists and there is a negligible risk of failure to sell; and

(c)   the market price is determinable and stable.

The historical cost principles of IAS 2 – *Inventories* – do not apply mandatorily to inventories held by 'producers of agricultural and forest products, agricultural produce after harvest, and minerals and mineral products, to the extent that they are measured at net realisable value in accordance with well-established practices in those industries.' *[IAS 2.3(a)]*. However, in order to be able to apply this scope exemption, changes in net realisable value must be recognised in profit or loss in the period of the change. *[IAS 2.3(a)]*. Net realisable value is defined in IAS 2 as 'the estimated selling price in the ordinary course of business less the estimated costs of completion and the estimated costs necessary to make the sale'. *[IAS 2.6]*. It is important to note also that the valuation of inventory at net realisable value under these circumstances is permitted only if this approach is adopted in accordance with 'well-established' industry practice.

The US FASB's Concepts Statement 5 – *Recognition and Measurement in Financial Statements of Business Enterprises* – refers to such assets as being 'readily realisable' (since they are saleable at readily determinable prices without significant effort), and acknowledges that revenue may be recognised on the completion of production of such assets, provided that they consist of interchangeable units and quoted prices are available in an active market that can rapidly absorb the quantity held by the entity without significantly affecting the price.[204] The accounting treatment for this basis would be to value closing stock of items such as minerals and mineral products at net realisable value (i.e. sales price less estimated selling costs), and to write off the related production costs.

6.4   Impairment of assets

6.4.1   *Low mine profitability near end of life*

Most mining plans aim to maximise the net present value of mineral reserves by first extracting the highest grade ore with the lowest production costs. Consequently, in most mining operations the grade of the ore mined steadily declines over the life of the mine which results in a declining annual production, while the production costs gradually increases as it becomes more difficult to extract the reserves. From an economic perspective, a mining company will continue to mine as long as the cash inflows from the sale of minerals exceed the cash cost of production. Therefore, a mining company with a positive net cash flow will continue to mine even if it does not fully recover the depreciation of its property, plant and equipment and mineral reserves, as is likely to occur towards the end of the life of a mine. In part this is the result of the deprecation methods applied:

• the straight-line method of depreciation allocates a relatively high depreciation charge to periods with a low annual production;

• a units of production method based on the quantity of ore extracted allocates a relatively high depreciation charge to production of lower grade ore; and

• a units of production method based on the quantity of minerals produced allocates a relatively high depreciation charge to production of minerals that are difficult to recover.

Each of these situations is most likely to occur towards the end of the life of a mine. It could be argued that the methods of depreciation most commonly used in the mining industry do not allocate a sufficiently high depreciation charge to the early life of a mine when production is generally most profitable. An entity should therefore be mindful of the fact that relatively small changes in facts and circumstances can lead to an impairment of mining assets.

6.4.2 *Impairment testing assumptions*

In carrying out an impairment test on a value in use basis under IAS 36 an entity is required to 'base cash flow projections on the most recent financial budgets/forecasts approved by management'. *[IAS 36.33(b)].* When commodity prices are high, management of many mining companies will often base their budgets on the assumption that forward commodity prices will revert to a lower trend. In many cases, the futures market will be in backwardation (i.e. the price of a commodity for future delivery is lower than its spot price).

In this situation an impairment test will reveal the early years in the life of a mine to be profitable (i.e. the mine is not impaired) while the same exercise in later years may show accounting losses as a result of a relatively high depreciation charge. Where this is the case, we recommend that an entity discloses that fact together with the reasons for not recognising an impairment at the end of the earlier reporting period. See 4.6 for more information.

6.5 Inventories

6.5.1 *Recognition*

Under IFRS an asset should be recognised in the statement of financial position 'when it is probable that the future economic benefits will flow to the entity and the asset has a cost or value that can be measured reliably'. *[Framework.4.44].* It has become accepted practice in the mining industry to recognise work in progress at the point at which ore is broken and the entity can make a reasonably assessment of quantity, recovery and cost.[205]

Extract 41.55 from the financial statement of Harmony Gold Mining illustrates the need for judgement in determining when work in progress can be recognised.

Extract 41.55: Harmony Gold Mining Company Limited (2010)

Notes to the group financial statements [extract]

2 Accounting policies [extract]

2.10 Inventories

Inventories which include bullion on hand, gold in process, gold in lock-up, ore stockpiles and stores and materials, are measured at the lower of cost and net realisable value after appropriate allowances for redundant and slow moving items. Cost of bullion, gold in process and gold in lock-up is determined by reference to production cost, including amortisation and depreciation at the relevant stage of production.

Ore stockpiles are valued at average production cost. Stockpiles and gold in lock-up are classified as a non current asset where the stockpile exceeds current processing capacity and where a portion of static gold in lock-up is expected to be recovered more than 12 months after balance sheet date.

Stores and materials consist of consumable stores and are valued at weighted average cost.

Net realisable value is the estimated selling price in the ordinary course of business less the estimated cost of completion and the estimated cost necessary to perform the sale.

Gold in process inventories represent materials that are currently in the process of being converted to a saleable product. Conversion processes vary depending on the nature of the ore and the specific mining operation, but include mill in-circuit, leach in-circuit, flotation and column cells, and carbon in-pulp inventories. In-process material is measured based on assays of the material fed to process and the projected recoveries at the respective plants. In-process inventories are valued at the average cost of the material fed to process attributable to the source material coming from the mine, stockpile or leach pad plus the in-process conversion costs, including the applicable depreciation relating to the process facility, incurred to that point in the process. Gold in process includes gold in lock-up which is generally measured from the plants onwards. Gold in lock-up is estimated as described under the section dealing with critical accounting estimates and judgements (refer to note 3). It is expected to be extracted when plants are demolished at the end of their useful lives, which is largely dependant on the estimated useful life of the operations feeding the plants. Where mechanised mining is used in underground operations, in-progress material is accounted for at the earliest stage of production when reliable estimates of quantities and costs are capable of being made. Given the varying nature of the Group's open pit operations, gold in process represents either production in broken ore form or production from the time of placement on heap leach pads.

Determining the quantities of work in progress may require a significant degree of estimation, as is illustrated in Extract 41.56 below from the financial statements of Anglo Platinum.

Extract 41.56: Anglo Platinum Limited (2010)

PRINCIPAL ACCOUNTING POLICIES [extract]

Critical accounting estimates [extract]

Metal inventory

Work-in-progress metal inventory is valued at the lower of net realisable value and the average cost of production or purchase less net revenue from sales of other metals, in the ratio of the contribution of these metals to gross sales revenue. Production costs are allocated to platinum, palladium, rhodium and nickel (joint products) by dividing the mine output into total mine production costs, determined on a 12-month rolling average basis. The quantity of ounces of joint products in work-in-progress is calculated based on the following factors:

- The theoretical inventory at that point in time which is calculated by adding the inputs to the previous physical inventory and then deducting the outputs for the inventory period.
- The inputs and outputs include estimates due to the delay in finalising analytical values.
- The estimates are subsequently trued up to the final metal accounting quantities when available.
- The theoretical inventory is then converted to a refined equivalent inventory by applying appropriate recoveries depending on where the material is within the pipeline. The recoveries are based on actual results as determined by the inventory count and are in line with industry standards.

Other than at the precious metal refinery, an annual physical count of work-in-progress is done, usually around February of each year. The precious metal refinery is subject to a physical count every two years. The annual physical count is limited to once per annum due to the dislocation of production required to perform the physical inventory count and the in-process inventories being contained in tanks, pipes and other vessels. Once the results of the physical count are finalised, the variance between the theoretical count and actual count is investigated and recorded. Thereafter the physical quantity forms the opening balance for the theoretical inventory calculation. Consequently the estimates are refined based on actual results over time. The nature of the process inherently limits the ability to precisely measure recoverability levels. As a result, the metallurgical balancing process is constantly monitored and the variables used in the process are refined based on actual results over time.

6.5.2 *Stockpiles of low grade ore*

Mining companies often stockpile low grade ore that cannot be economically processed at current market prices or to give priority to the processing of higher grade ore. Low grade ore stockpiles may not be processed for many years until market prices or technology have improved or until no higher grade ore remains available. Extract 41.57 below from AngloGold Ashanti illustrates that stockpiles of low grade ore may be held for many years.

The IASB's *Conceptual Framework* defines an asset as 'a resource controlled by the entity as a result of past events and from which future economic benefits are expected to flow to the entity'. *[Framework.4.4(a)]*. Mineralised waste that is stockpiled in the hope, but without the expectation, that it may become economical to process in the future should be accounted in the same way as overburden and other waste materials (see 6.2 above). Low grade ore that is stockpiled with the expectation that is will be processed in the future should be accounted for in the same way as high grade ore. However, if the cost of the low grade ore exceeds its net realisable value, an entity should recognise an impairment charge that it might need to reverse if commodity prices were to increase.

If and when processing of low grade ore becomes economically viable and management intend to process the stockpile in the future, the ore should be accounted for as non-current inventory under IAS 2 – *Inventories*. Such stockpiles should be measured at the lower of cost and net realisable value. *[IAS 2.9, 30]*. In allocating production costs to the low grade ore stockpile an entity should be mindful that:

(1) the commodity price at the end of the reporting period date may not be representative of the price that can realistically be expected to prevail when the ore is expected to be processed,

(2) the costs of processing may change in the future because of inflation, technological changes and new environmental regulations and

(3) the time value of money reduces the net realisable value.

The extract below shows how AngloGold Ashanti accounts for ore stockpiles.

Extract 41.57: AngloGold Ashanti Limited (2010)

Notes to the financial statements [extract]
1 Accounting policies [extract]
1.2 Significant accounting judgements and estimates [extract]
Stockpiles, metal in process and ore on leach pad

Costs that are incurred in or benefit the production process are accumulated as stockpiles, metals in process and ore on leach pads. Net realisable value tests are performed at least annually and represent the estimated future sales price of the product, based on prevailing and long-term metals prices, less estimated costs to complete production and bring the product to sale.

Stockpiles and underground metals in process are measured by estimating the number of tonnes added and removed from the stockpile and from underground, the number of contained gold ounces based on assay data, and the estimated recovery percentage based on the expected processing method. Stockpile and underground ore tonnages are verified by periodic surveys.

Estimates of the recoverable gold on the leach pads are calculated from the quantities of ore placed on the pads based on measured tonnes added to the leach pads, the grade of ore placed on the leach pads based on assay data and a recovery percentage based on metallurgical testing and ore type.

Although the quantities of recoverable metal are reconciled by comparing the grades of ore to the quantities of gold actually recovered (metallurgical balancing), the nature of the process inherently limits the ability to precisely monitor recoverability levels. As a result, the metallurgical balancing process is constantly monitored and engineering estimates are refined based on actual results over time.

Variations between actual and estimated quantities resulting from changes in assumptions and estimates that do not result in write-downs to net realisable value are accounted for on a prospective basis.

The carrying amount of inventories (excluding finished goods and mine operating supplies) for the group at 31 December 2010 was $860m, R5,651m (2009: $661m, R4,919m).

1.3 Summary of significant accounting policies [extract]

Inventories [extract]

Inventories are valued at the lower of cost and net realisable value after appropriate allowances for redundant and slow moving items. Cost is determined on the following bases:

...

- ore stockpiles are valued at the average moving cost of mining and stockpiling the ore. Stockpiles are classified as a non-current asset where the stockpile exceeds current processing capacity;

The extract below illustrates the disclosure of an impairment of stockpiled ore (in 2008) and then disclosures relating to the reversal of impairment of stockpiled ore.

Extract 41.58: Kazakhmys PLC (2008 and 2010)

Notes to the consolidated financial statements [extract]

7. IMPAIRMENT LOSSES – 2008 [extract]

(d) Kazakhmys Copper and MKM inventories

Impairment of inventories include an amount of $73 million and $15 million in respect of Kazakhmys Copper and MKM, respectively. For Kazakhmys Copper, the impairment primarily relates to the impairment of stockpiled ore which is not going to be processed in the foreseeable future as its processing is uneconomic at current commodity price levels. Within MKM, a provision has been recognised to record inventory at the lower of cost and net realisable value. This primarily relates to finished goods held in stock at the end of the year which have been written down reflecting the fall in copper price in December.

---

8. IMPAIRMENT LOSSES – 2010 [extract]

(b) Kazakhmys Copper inventories

Included within the provisions against inventories is an impairment loss of $15 million relating to general slow moving inventory, and a reversal of a previous impairment against certain stockpiled ore of $18 million. In 2008, it was envisaged that the stockpiled ore would not be processed in the future as this would have been uneconomic at the prevailing commodity prices. However, during 2010 certain of these stockpiles were processed and the previous impairment reversed.

6.5.3   Sale of by-products and joint products

6.5.3.A   By-products

In the extractive industries it is common for more than one product to be extracted from the same reserves, e.g. copper is often found together with gold and silver. In most cases where more than one product is produced there is a clear distinction between the main product and the by-products. IAS 2 prescribes the following accounting for by-products:

> '...When the costs of conversion of each product are not separately identifiable, they are allocated between the products on a rational and consistent basis. The allocation may be based, for example, on the relative sales value of each product either at the stage in the production process when the products become separately identifiable, or at the completion of production. Most by-products, by their nature, are immaterial. When this is the case, they are often measured at net realisable value and this value is deducted from the cost of the main product. As a result, the carrying amount of the main product is not materially different from its cost.' *[IAS 2.14]*.

By-products that are significant in value should be accounted for as joint products as discussed at 6.5.3.B below.

The extract from AngloGold Ashanti's accounts illustrates how insignificant by-products are deducted from costs of sales and how significant by-products are accounted for separately within inventories.

Extract 41.59: AngloGold Ashanti Limited (2010)

Notes to the financial statements [extract]

1 Accounting policies [extract]

1.3 Summary of significant accounting policies [extract]

Inventories [extract]

Inventories are valued at the lower of cost and net realisable value after appropriate allowances for redundant and slow moving items. Cost is determined on the following bases:

...

- by-products, which include uranium oxide and sulphuric acid, are valued on an average total production cost method. By-products are classified as a non-current asset where the by-products on hand exceed current processing capacity;

Revenue recognition [extract]

Revenue is recognised at the fair value of the consideration received or receivable to the extent that it is probable that economic benefits will flow to the group and revenue can be reliably measured. The following criteria must also be present:

...

● where a by-product is not regarded as significant, revenue is credited against cost of sales, when the significant risks and rewards of ownership of the products are transferred to the buyer.

Although IAS 2 does not require extensive disclosures in respect of by-products, if amounts are material, disclosure of the following information, which many mining companies provide on a voluntary basis, will greatly assist users:

● accounting policies applied to by-products;
● line items in the primary financial statements in which revenues and carried amounts have been disclosed;
● quantities of by-products sold; and
● average prices of by-products sold.

6.5.3.B   Joint products

In the case of joint products a common production process results in a number of products, each of which has a significant relative value. Joint products are very common in both the oil and gas industry (e.g. crude oil when run through a refinery produces a variety of products) and the mining industry.

Joint products, by definition, are all significant in value and require that an entity allocate on a rational and consistent basis the costs of conversion that are not separately identifiable for each product. The IASC Issues Paper outlined two approaches that have found acceptance in practice:[206]

(a)   *allocation on the basis of physical characteristics* – In the oil and gas industry, entities often combine quantities of oil and gas based on their relative energy content (i.e. 6,000 cubic feet of gas is roughly equal in energy to one barrel of oil). This method, however, does not take account of the fact that, for example, gas is cheaper per unit of energy than oil because it is more difficult to transport; and

(b)   *allocation on the basis of relative values* – This approach is more common in the mining industry where often it is not possible to identify a relevant physical characteristic that can be used to combined quantities of different products. The drawback of this method is that it results in very similar profit margins for each of the joint products, which may not be reflective of the underlying economic reality (i.e. one of the joint products, if mined in isolation, might have a completely different profit margin).

Although it should be kept in mind that neither method is perfect, both approaches are currently permitted under IFRS. It is true also that whichever method is selected, it is unlikely to have a material effect on reported profit overall. The extract below illustrates the application of approach (b) by Anglo American.

Extract 41.60: Anglo American plc (2010)

Notes to the financial statements [extract]
1. ACCOUNTING POLICIES [extract]
Inventory

Inventory and work in progress are measured at the lower of cost and net realisable value. The production cost of inventory includes an appropriate proportion of depreciation and production overheads. Cost is determined on the following bases:

- Raw materials and consumables are measured at cost on a first in, first out (FIFO) basis.
- Finished products are measured at raw material cost, labour cost and a proportion of manufacturing overhead expenses.
- Metal and coal stocks are included within finished products and are measured at average cost.

At precious metals operations that produce 'joint products', cost is allocated amongst products according to the ratio of contribution of these metals to gross sales revenues.

6.5.4 Heap leaching

Heap leaching is a process used for the recovery of metals from low grade ore. The crushed ore is laid on a slightly sloping, impermeable pad and leached by uniformly trickling a chemical solution through the heaps to be collected in ponds. The metals are subsequently extracted from the pregnant solution. Although heap leaching is one of the lowest cost methods of processing, recovery rates are relatively low.

An entity that develops an accounting policy for heap leaching needs to consider the following:

- recovery of metal is relatively low and will depend on the metallurgical characteristics of the material on the heap leach pad. An entity will therefore need to estimate the quantity of recoverable metal on each of its heap leach pads, based on laboratory test work or historical ore performance;

- the assayed head grade of ore put on the heap;

- the ore stockpiles on heap leach pads are accounted for as inventories that are measured at cost under IAS 2. As the valuable metal content is leached from these ore stockpiles, the cost basis is depleted based upon expected grades and recovery rates. The depletion charge should be accounted as the cost of production of work in progress or finished goods; and

- ore stockpiles on heap leach pads from which metals are expected to be recovered in a period longer than 12 months are classified as non-current assets.

The extracts below from the financial statements of AngloGold Ashanti and from the 2008 financial statements of KazakhGold Group (now known as Polyus Gold International Ltd) illustrate the issues that an entity will need to consider in developing an accounting policy for heap leaching.

Extract 41.61: AngloGold Ashanti Limited (2010)

Notes to the financial statements [extract]
1 Accounting policies [extract]
1.3 Summary of significant accounting policies [extract]
Inventories [extract]

Inventories are valued at the lower of cost and net realisable value after appropriate allowances for redundant and slow moving items. Cost is determined on the following bases:

...

- heap leach pad materials are measured on an average total production cost basis. The cost of materials on the leach pad from which gold is expected to be recovered in a period longer than 12 months is classified as a non-current asset.

Extract 41.62: KazakhGold Group Limited (2008) (now known as Polyus Gold International Ltd)

Notes forming part of the financial statements for the year ended 31 December 2008 [extract]
2 Basis of preparation and accounting policies [extract]
n. Inventories [extract]

Long-term inventories comprise ore stockpiles being treated on heap leach pads. These stockpiles are depleted based upon expected grades and recovery rates. As product is extracted a charge is made to cost of production of finished goods for the relevant proportion of costs.

6.6   Tolling arrangements

In the mining industry it is common for entities to provide raw material to a smelter or refiner for further processing. If the raw material is sold to the smelter or refiner, the mining company recognises revenue in accordance with IAS 18. However, under a 'tolling' arrangement a mining company supplies, without transferring ownership, raw material to a smelter or refiner which processes it for a fee and then returns the finished product to the customer. Alternatively, the mining company may sell the raw material to the smelter or refiner, but is required to repurchase the finished product. In the latter two situations, no revenue should be recognised when the raw material is shipped to the smelter or refiner as there has not been a transfer of the risks and rewards. An entity should carefully assess the terms and conditions of its tolling arrangements to determine:

- when it is appropriate to recognise revenue;
- whether those arrangements contain embedded leases that require separation under IFRIC 4 (see 4.10.1 above);
- whether the tolling arrangement is part of a series of transactions with a joint venture; and
- whether the toll processing entity is a special purpose entity that requires consolidation under SIC-12 – *Consolidation – Special Purpose Entities*. NOTE: SIC-12 is to be replaced by IFRS 10 – *Consolidated Financial Statements* (see Chapter 7 at 4.4.1 for more information).

The extract below describes a tolling arrangement between Norsk Hydro and one of its joint ventures.

Extract 41.63: Norsk Hydro ASA (2010)

NOTE 26 – Investments in jointly controlled entities [extract]

Aluminium Norf GmbH (Alunorf) is the world's largest rolling mill and is located in Germany. Alunorf is jointly owned by Hydro and Hindalco Industries (50 percent each). Through a tolling arrangement each partner supplies Alunorf with raw material which is transformed to flat rolled coils and delivered to the partners. Sales from Alunorf to Hydro amounted to NOK 1,423 million in 2010 and NOK 1,378 million in 2009. The tolling fee is based on cost recovery, in which each partner bears its share of cost. Hydro's capital and financing commitments are regulated in the Joint Venture agreement. Alunorf has investment commitments amounting to NOK 235 million as of 31 December 2010. Hydro's financing commitment based on its interest is NOK 109 million as of 31 December 2010. Alunorf is part of Rolled Products.

6.7 Hedging sales of metal concentrate

In the mining industry metals are often sold in the form of a polymetalic concentrate that comprises various metals and impurities. The metal content of concentrate varies depending on the mine and grade of ore being mined. Therefore, the sales price of concentrate is typically determined by calculating the fair value of each of the metals contained (i.e. the quantity of each metal contained in the concentrate is multiplied by its market price) minus a refining, processing charge and impurity penalties. Each of the metals contained in a concentrate is therefore sold at its market price, which is determined independently from the price of any other metal in the concentrate. As noted in Chapter 30 at 3.6, identifying multiple elements in sales transactions is an acceptable practice under IFRS. Hence, the sale of each metal – in a multiple element transaction that does not require a subjective allocation of the total sales price – can therefore be accounted for separately. Consequently, the sale of each individual metal can be hedged separately because each metal is a separate non-financial asset for the purposes of hedge accounting under IAS 39. The terms and conditions of each sales contract will need to be considered carefully in determining whether individual metals or only the metal content as a whole can be designated as a hedged item.

Under the above approach paragraph 82 of IAS 39 requires that a non-financial asset should be 'designated as a hedged item (a) for foreign currency risks, or (b) in its entirety for all risks, because of the difficulty of isolating and measuring the appropriate portion of the cash flows or fair value changes attributable to specific risks other than foreign currency risks'.

This approach is conceptually no different from hedging the contents of a box that contains a number of non-financial assets, each of which is priced at fair value and itemised separately on the invoice. However, the approach clearly differs from hedging jet fuel with crude oil based derivatives because in that case the underlying of the hedging instruments contains substances that are not present in the hedged item. In addition, prices of components of crude oil cannot be determined independently.

Chapter 41

6.8   Block caving – depreciation, depletion and amortisation

Given the nature of mining operations, determining the appropriate unit of account has always been a matter requiring considerable judgement for mining entities. See 4.5.1.D above for further discussion. This issue is particularly relevant when assessing how to account for new mining techniques. For example, block cave mining is one such mining technique that is being increasingly proposed / used for a number of deposits worldwide.

Block cave mining is a mass mining method that allows for the bulk mining of large, relatively lower grade, ore bodies for which the grade is consistently distributed throughout. The word 'block' refers to the layout of the mine – which effectively divides the ore body into large sections, with areas that can be several thousand square metres in size. This approach adopts a mine design and process which involves the creation of an undercut by fracturing the rock section underneath the block through the use of blasting. This blasting destroys the rock's ability to support the block above. Caving of the rock mass then occurs under the natural forces of gravity (which can be in the order of millions of tonnes), when a sufficient amount of rock has been removed underneath the block. The broken ore is then removed from the base of the block. This mine activity occurs without the need for drilling and blasting, as the ore above continues to fall while the broken ore beneath is removed. Broken ore is removed from the area at the extraction level through the use of a grid of draw points. These effectively funnel the broken ore down to a particular point so that it can be collected and removed for further processing.

Block caving has been applied to large scale extraction of various metals and minerals, sometimes in thick beds of ore but more usually in steep to vertical masses. Examples of block caving operations include Northparkes (Australia), Palabora (South Africa), Questa Mine (New Mexico) and Freeport (Indonesia).[207]

Block cave mining does require substantial upfront development costs, as initial underground access followed by large excavations (undercutting), must be completed to gain access and then initially 'undermine' the block that is to cave. In addition, large underground, and above ground, haulage and milling infrastructure must be established to extract and then process the ore tonnages that a successful cave will generate.

One of the key issues to be addressed is how these substantial upfront development costs, in addition to the ongoing development costs associated with each block (i.e. to extend the undercutting beneath each new block and construct the draw points for each block) should be treated for depreciation or amortisation.

Generally these costs are depreciated or amortised on a units of production basis – therefore in determining useful life, it is necessary to determine what the appropriate reserves base should be for each of these costs. For example, in relation to the costs associated with initially going underground and constructing the main haulage tunnel which will be used to access and extract the reserves from the entire ore body, the useful life associated with such assets may be the reserves of the entire ore body.

In relation to the costs associated in constructing the milling infrastructure, it is possible that such assets may be used to process ore from multiple ore bodies. Therefore, the useful life of such assets may be the reserves of multiple ore bodies. However, this will depend upon the specific facts and circumstances of the particular development.

For those costs associated with each individual block e.g. the undercutting costs directly attributable to each block and the costs associated in constructing the draw points for that block, the appropriate reserves base may potentially only be those to be extracted from that particular block, which may only be a component of the entire ore body.

The approach adopted by each entity will be determined by the specific facts and circumstances of each mine development, such as the nature of the block cave mining technique employed and how the associated assets will be used. Such an assessment will require entities to exercise considerable judgement.

7 GLOSSARY

The glossary below defines some of the terms and abbreviations commonly used in the extractive industries.[208]

Abandon	To discontinue attempts to produce oil or gas from a well or lease, plug the reservoir in accordance with regulatory requirements and recover equipment.
Area-of-interest method	An accounting concept by which costs incurred for individual geological or geographical areas that have characteristics conducive to containing a mineral reserve are deferred as assets pending determination of whether commercial reserves are found. If the area of interest is found to contain commercial reserves, the accumulated costs are capitalised. If the area is found to contain no commercial reserves, the accumulated costs are charged to expense.
Barrels of oil equivalent (BOE)	Using prices or heating content, units of sulphur, condensate, natural gas and by products are converted to and expressed in equivalent barrels of oil for standard measurement purposes.
British Thermal Unit (BTU)	A measure of the amount of heat required to raise the temperature of one pound of water one degree Fahrenheit at the temperature at which water has its greatest density (39 degrees Fahrenheit).
Bullion	Metal in bars, ingots or other uncoined form.

Carried interest	An agreement by which an entity that contracts to operate a mineral property and, therefore, agrees to incur exploration or development costs (the carrying party) is entitled to recover the costs incurred (and usually an amount in addition to actual costs incurred) before the entity that originally owned the mineral interest (the carried party) is entitled to share in revenues from production.
Carried party	The party for whom funds are advances in a carried interest arrangement.
Carrying party	The party advancing funds in a carried interest agreement.
Concession	A contract, similar to a mineral lease, under which the government owning mineral rights grants the concessionaire the right to explore, develop, and produce the minerals.
Cost recovery oil	Oil revenue paid to an operating entity to enable that entity to recover its operating costs and specified exploration and development costs from a specified percentage of oil revenues remaining after the royalty payment to the property owner.
Customer smelter	A smelter which processes concentrates from independent mines. Concentrates may be purchased or the smelter may be contracted to do the processing for the independent company.
Delay rental	Annual payments by the lessee of a mineral property to the lessor until drilling has begun.
Delineation well	A well to define, or delineate, the boundaries of a reservoir.
Development well	A well drilled to gain access to oil or gas classified as proved reserves.
Downstream Activities	The refining, processing, marketing, and distributing of petroleum, natural gas, or mined mineral (other than refining or processing that is necessary to make the minerals that have been mined or extracted capable of being sold).
Dry gas	Natural gas composed of vapours without liquids and which tends not to liquefy.

Chapter 41

Dry hole	An exploratory or development well that does not contain oil or gas in commercial quantities.
Entitlements method	A method of revenue recognition by which a joint venturer records revenue based on the share of production for the period to which that venturer is entitled.
Exploratory well	A well drilled to find and produce oil or gas in an unproved area, to find a new reservoir in a field previously found to be productive of oil or gas in another reservoir, or to extend a known reservoir.
Farm out and farm in	An agreement by which the owner of operating rights in a mineral property (the farmor) transfers a part of that interest to a second party (the farmee) in return for the latter's paying all of the costs, or only specified costs, to explore the property and perhaps to carry out part or all of the development of the property if reserves are found.
Full cost method	An accounting concept by which all costs incurred in searching for, acquiring, and developing mineral reserves in a cost centre are capitalised, even though a specific cost clearly resulted from an effort that was a failure
Geological and geophysical costs (G&G)	Costs of topographical, geological, geochemical, and geophysical studies.
Infill drilling	Technical and commercial analyses may support drilling additional producing wells to reduce the spacing beyond that utilised within the initial development plan. Infill drilling may have the combined effect of increasing recovery efficiency and accelerating production.
Joint Operating Agreement (JOA)	A contract between two parties to a sharing arrangement that sets out the rights and obligations to operate the property, if operating interests are owned by both parties after a sharing arrangement.
Overlift or underlift	Overlift is the excess of the amount of production that a participant in a joint venture has taken as compared to that participant's proportionate share of ownership in total production. Underlift is the shortfall in the amount of production that a participant in a joint venture has taken as compared to that participant's proportionate share of ownership in total production.

Production sharing contract (PSC)	A contract between a national oil company or the government of a host country and a contracting entity (contractor) to carry out oil and gas exploration and production activities in accordance with the terms of the contract, with the two parties sharing mineral output.
Profit oil	Revenue in excess of cost recovery oil and royalties.
Recompletion	The process of re-entering a previously completed well to install new equipment or to perform such services necessary to restore production.
Redetermination	A retroactive adjustment to the relative percentage interests of the participants in a field that is subject to a unitisation agreement.
Risk service contract	A contract by which an entity agrees to explore for develop, and produce minerals on behalf of a host government in return for a fee paid by the host government.
Royalty	A portion of the proceeds from production, usually before deducting operating expenses, payable to a party having an interest in a lease.
Sales method	A method of revenue recognition by which a joint venturer records revenue based on the actual amount of product it has sold (or transferred downstream) during the period. No receivable or other asset is recorded for undertaken production (underlift) and no liability is recorded for overtaken production (overlift).
Stripping ratio	The ratio of tonnes removed as waste relative to the number of tonnes of ore removed from an open pit mine.
Successful efforts method	An accounting concept that capitalises only those upstream costs that lead directly to finding, acquiring and developing mineral reserves, while those costs that do not lead directly to finding, acquiring and developing mineral reserves are charged to expense.
Take-or-pay contracts	An agreement between a buyer and seller in which the buyer will still pay some amount even if the product or service is not provided. If the purchaser does not take the minimum quantity, payment is required for that minimum quantity at the contract price. Normally, deficiency amounts can be made up in future years if purchases are in excess of minimum amounts.

Unitisation	An agreement between two parties each of which owns an interest in one or more mineral properties in an area to cross-assign to one another a share of the interest in the mineral properties that each owns in the area; from that point forward they share, as agreed, in further costs and revenues related to the properties.
Upstream activities	Exploring for, finding, acquiring, and developing mineral reserves up to the point that the reserves are first capable of being sold or used, even if the entity intends to process them further.
Workovers	Major repairs, generally of oil and gas wells.

Chapter 41

References

1 IASC Issues Paper, *Issues Paper Extractive Industries*, IASC, November 2000, 1.5.
2 IASC Issues Paper, 1.19-1.29.
3 IASC Issues Paper, 1.23.
4 IASC Issues Paper, 1.25.
5 IASC Issues Paper, 1.27.
6 IASC Issues Paper, 1.29.
7 IASC Issues Paper, 1.16.
8 IASC Issues Paper, 1.18.
9 IASC Issues Paper, 2.3.
10 IASC Issues Paper, 2.5.
11 IASC Issues Paper, 2.6.
12 IASC Issues Paper, 2.10.
13 IASC Issues Paper, 2.12.
14 IASC Issues Paper, 2.24.
15 IASC Issues Paper, 2.26.
16 IASC Issues Paper, 2.27.
17 IASC Issues Paper, 2.29.
18 IASC Issues Paper, 2.29, 2.30.
19 IASC Issues Paper, 2.32.
20 IASC Issues Paper, 2.34.
21 IASC Issues Paper, 2.36.
22 IASC Issues Paper, 2.38.
23 IASC Issues Paper, 2.42.
24 *IASB Update*, April 2003, p. 3-4 and *IASB Update*, September 2003, p. 4-5.
25 Discussion Paper DP/2010/1, *Extractive Activities*, IASB, April 2010, P6.
26 DP/2010/1, P1.4-1.5.
27 DP/2010/1, 1.1.
28 DP/2010/1, 1.9.
29 DP/2010/1, 1.10.
30 DP/2010/1, 2.67.
31 DP/2010/1, 2.15-2.17.
32 DP/2010/1, 2.47.
33 DP/2010/1, 2.48.
34 DP/2010/1, 2.23.
35 DP/2010/1, 3.18-3.21.
36 DP/2010/1, 3.38.
37 DP/2010/1, 3.40.
38 DP/2010/1, Question 5.
39 DP/2010/1, 3.68.
40 DP/2010/1, 1.23, 4.23-4.26.
41 DP/2010/1, 4.85.
42 DP/2010/1, 4.59.
43 DP/2010/1, 4.73-4.76.
44 DP/2010/1, Question 8.
45 DP/2010/1, Table 5.1 and Question 9.
46 DP/2010/1, 6.1, 6.5.
47 DP/2010/1, Question 10.
48 IASC Issues Paper, 14.13.
49 IASC Issues Paper, 14.14.
50 SPE-PRMS, *Petroleum Resources Management Systems*, Society of Petroleum Engineers, 2007.
51 SPE-PRMS, p. 1.
52 IASB Agenda Paper 13A, *Comparison of Petroleum and Minerals Reserves and Resource Classification Systems*, IASB, 22 June 2007, p. 3-4.
53 IASB Agenda Paper 13A, p.8 and SPE-PRMS, Figure 1-1.
54 SPE-PRMS, p. 2-3.
55 SPE-PRMS, p. 2-3.
56 SPE-PRMS, p.10-11.
57 SPE-PRMS, p.10-11.
58 SPE-PRMS, p.10-11.

59 SPE-PRMS, p. 2-3.
60 SPE-PRMS, p. 2-3.
61 SPE-PRMS, p. 2-3.
62 SPE-PRMS, p. 2-3.
63 SPE-PRMS, p. 2-3.
64 SPE-PRMS, p. 6-9.
65 SPE-PRMS, p. 9-13.
66 SPE-PRMS, p. 13-19.
67 SPE-PRMS, p. 19-29.
68 JORC Code, Australasian Code for Reporting of Exploration Results, Mineral Resources and Ore Reserves, Joint Ore Reserves Committee of the Australasian Institute of Mining and Metallurgy, Australian Institute of Geoscientists and Minerals Council of Australia (JORC), 2004, para. 1.
69 Niall Weatherstone, The present and future of international resource and reserve reporting, Committee for Mineral Reserves International Reporting Standards (CRIRSCO), 2007, p. 1, 3 and 29.
70 The standards issued by the Society for Mining, Metallurgy, and Exploration in the United States are not recognised by the Securities and Exchange Commission (SEC).
71 JORC Code para. 1.
72 Weatherstone, p. 5.
73 IASB Agenda Paper 13A, p. 3.
74 CRIRSCO Template, *International Reporting Template for the public reporting of exploration results, mineral resources and mineral reserves*, CRIRSCO, July 2006, 3.
75 CRIRSCO Template, 4.
76 CRIRSCO Template, 5.
77 CRIRSCO Template, 10.
78 CRIRSCO Template, Figure 1.
79 CRIRSCO Template, 16.
80 CRIRSCO Template, 18.
81 CRIRSCO Template, 19.
82 CRIRSCO Template, 20.
83 CRIRSCO Template, 21.
84 CRIRSCO Template, 22.
85 CRIRSCO Template, 28.
86 CRIRSCO Template, 29.
87 CRIRSCO Template, 30.
88 IASB Agenda Paper 13, *Education session – status report on review of convergence opportunities between minerals and oil & gas reserve and resource definitions*, IASB, 22 June 2007, para. 12.
89 Weatherstone, p. 7.
90 IASB Agenda Paper 13A, p. 11.
91 *IASB Update*, March 2008, p. 4.
92 *IASB Update*, March 2008, p. 4.
93 Discussion Paper DP/2010/1, para. 2.48.
94 Discussion Paper DP/2010/1, para. 2.23.
95 Concept Release No. 33-8870, *Possible Revisions to the Disclosure Requirements Relating to Oil and Gas Reserves*, Securities and Exchange Commission (SEC), 12 December 2007.
96 Concept Release No. 33-8870.
97 Release No. 33-8935, *Modernization of the Oil and Gas Reporting Requirements*, Securities and Exchange Commission (SEC), 26 June 2008, p. 8.
98 Release No. 33-8995, *Modernization of Oil and Gas Reporting*, Securities and Exchange Commission (SEC), 14 January 2009.
99 J. M. Rendu, *Reporting Mineral Resources and Mineral Reserves in the United States of America – Technical and Regulatory Issues*, 20-25 August 2006, p. 2.
100 Weatherstone, p. 8.
101 *Comments on SEC File No. S7-29-07 'Concept Release on Possible Revisions to the Disclosure Requirements Relating to Oil and Gas Reserves'*, The Committee for Mineral Reserves International Reporting Standards, 12 February 2008, p. 1.
102 *Comments on SEC File No. S7-29-07 'Concept Release on Possible Revisions to the Disclosure Requirements Relating to Oil and Gas Reserves'*, The Society for Mining, Metallurgy, and Exploration, Inc., 4 February 2008. p. 1-2.
103 Pre codification FAS 69, *Disclosures about Oil and Gas Producing Activities an amendment of FASB Statements 19, 25, 33, and 39*, FASB, November 1982, para. 10.
104 OIAC SORP, *Statement of Recommended Practice – Accounting for Oil and Gas Exploration, Development, Production and Decommissioning Activities*, UK Oil Industry Accounting Committee (OIAC), 7 June 2001, para. 246.
105 OIAC SORP 12.
106 OIAC SORP, 247, 250.
107 OIAC SORP, Appendix 4.
108 OIAC SORP 248.
109 OIAC SORP 249.
110 OIAC SORP 250.
111 OIAC SORP 250.
112 OIAC SORP 251.
113 ASC 932-235-50, *Extractive Activities – Oil and Gas – Notes to Financial Statements – Disclosure*, 50-4 to 50-11B.
114 ASC 932-235-55-2, *Extractive Activities – Oil and Gas – Notes to Financial*

Statements – Implementation Guidance and Illustrations.
115 Rendu, p. 9 and 10.
116 Industry Guide 7, *Description of Property by Issuers Engaged or to be Engaged in Significant Mining Operations*, Securities and Exchange Commission, Securities Act Release No. 33-6949, effective 13 August 1992.
117 Industry Guide 7, (a).
118 Industry Guide 7, (b).
119 Industry Guide 7, (b)(5) Instructions.
120 Industry Guide 7, (c).
121 IASC Issues Paper, 14.14.
122 IASB Agenda Paper 15C, *Possible principles for a historical cost accounting model that accompanies decision-useful disclosures of minerals and oil & gas reserves and resources*, IASB, 22 June 2007, 6.
123 IASB Agenda Paper 15A, *Findings from user survey*, IASB, 22 June 2007, 39.
124 *IASB Update*, September 2008, p. 3.
125 ASC 932-235, *Extractive Activities – Oil and Gas – Notes to Financial Statements – Disclosure*, 50-30 to 50-33, 50-35 to 50-36.
126 *IFRIC Update*, January 2006, p. 3.
127 ASC 932-720-25-1, *Extractive Activities – Oil and Gas – Other Expenses – Recognition*. (pre-codification FAS 19, *Financial Accounting and Reporting by Oil and Gas Producing Companies*, FASB, December 1977, 13).
128 ED 6, *Exploration for and Evaluation of Mineral Resources*, IASB, January 2004, 14.
129 *IASB Update*, October 2002, p. 3, *IFRIC Update*, April 2002, p. 2 and *IFRIC Update*, July 2002, p. 1.
130 IASC Issues Paper, 6.3.
131 IASC Issues Paper, 13.21.
132 OIAC SORP para 144.
133 ASC 930-805-30-1 *Extractive Activities – Mining – Business Combinations – Initial Measurement* (pre-codification EITF 04-3, *Mining Assets: Impairment and Business Combinations*, EITF, March 2004).
134 IASC Issues Paper, 7.13.
135 IASC Issues Paper, 7.19.
136 IASC Issues Paper, 7.20.
137 IASC Issues Paper, 7.36.
138 IASC Issues Paper, 7.39.
139 IASC Issues Paper, 7.41.
140 IASC Issues Paper, 7.42.
141 IASC Issues Paper, 7.47.
142 IASC Issues Paper, 7.46.
143 IASC Issues Paper, 7.49.
144 IASC Issues Paper, 7.50.
145 IASC Issues Paper, 7.23.
146 IASC Issues Paper, 7.24.
147 IASC Issues Paper, 7.25.
148 IASC Issues Paper, 7.26.
149 IASC Issues Paper, 7.61.
150 IASC Issues Paper, 9.26.
151 IAS 36, 134(d)(i)-(ii), 134(e)(i)-(ii).
152 IASC Issues Paper, 10.26.
153 IASC Issues Paper, 10.23.
154 IASC Issues Paper, 10.24.
155 IASC Issues Paper, 1.27.
156 HM Revenue & Customs website, www.hmrc.gov.uk, *International – Taxation of UK oil production*.
157 IASC Issues Paper, 2.12.
158 IASC Issues Paper, 2.13.
159 IASC Issues Paper, 2.14.
160 IASC Issues Paper, 2.21.
161 IASC Issues Paper, 2.21.
162 IASC Issues Paper, Glossary.
163 IASC Issues Paper, 2.19.
164 IASC Issues Paper, 12.12(b).
165 *Guidelines for the Evaluation of Petroleum Reserves and Resources – A Supplement to the SPE/WPC Petroleum Reserves Definitions and the SPE/WPC/AAPG Petroleum Resources Definitions*, Society of Petroleum Engineers, 2001, p. 120.
166 IASC Issues Paper, 12.68.
167 IASC Issues Paper, 12.69.
168 IASC Issues Paper, 2.23.
169 *Guidelines for the Evaluation of Petroleum Reserves and Resources – A Supplement to the SPE/WPC Petroleum Reserves Definitions and the SPE/WPC/AAPG Petroleum Resources Definitions*, Society of Petroleum Engineers, 2001, p. 120.
170 D. R. Jennings, J. B. Feiten and H. R. Brock, *Petroleum Accounting, Principles, Procedures, & Issues*, 5th edition, Professional Development Institute, Denton (Texas), p. 165-169.
171 IASC Issues Paper, 12.9.
172 OIAC SORP 149.
173 OIAC SORP 150.
174 IASC Issues Paper, 12.11.
175 OIAC SORP 16.
176 IASC Issues Paper, 12.14.
177 OIAC SORP 175.
178 OIAC SORP 176.
179 IASC Issues Paper, 12.14.
180 OIAC SORP 177-178.
181 OIAC SORP 179.
182 OIAC SORP 180.
183 IASC Issues Paper 4.18.
184 IASC Issues Paper 4.20.
185 IASC Issues Paper 4.45.

Chapter 41

186 *IFRIC Update*, January 2006, p. 3.
187 Amendments to IFRS 1, *Additional Exemptions for First-time Adopters*, IASB, July 2009, D8A.
188 IASC Issues Paper 4.16(b).
189 IASC Issues Paper 4.36.
190 IASC Issues Paper 4.39.
191 IASC Issues Paper 6.64.
192 SPE-PRMS, p. 18.
193 IASC Issues Paper 10.27.
194 IASC Issues Paper 10.29, 10.32. OIAC SORP 114-121.
195 IASC Issues Paper 10.29.
196 IASC Issues Paper 10.29.
197 IASC Issues Paper 10.32.
198 IASC Issues Paper 10.32.
199 IASC Issues Paper 10.32.
200 IASC Issues Paper 10.29.
201 IASC Issues Paper 11.17.
202 ASC 930-330-25-1 *Extractive Activities – Mining – Inventory – Recognition – General* (pre-codification EITF 04-6, *Accounting for Stripping Costs Incurred during Production in the Mining Industry*, EITF, June 2005).
203 *IFRIC Update*, November 2009.
204 SFAC No. 5, *Recognition and Measurement in Financial Statements of Business Enterprises*, FASB, December 1984, paras. 83-84.
205 IASC Issues Paper 11.9-11.16.
206 IASC Issues Paper 7.61-7.68.
207 Global infomine www.technology.infomine.com / reviews – "Block caving".
208 IASC Issues Paper, Glossary of Terms.

Index of extracts from financial statements

Index of standards

IFRS 5

IFRS 6

IFRS 7

IFRS 8

IFRS 10

IFRS 11

IAS 2

IAS 7

IAS 8

IAS 12

IAS 19 (2011)

IAS 20

IAS 23

IAS 24

IAS 27 (2011)

IAS 27

IAS 28 (2011)

IAS 28

IAS 29

IAS 31

IAS 32

IAS 33

IAS 34

IAS 37

IAS 39

IAS 40

IAS 41

Index

Notes

Notes

Also available online

We value feedback from our customers to ensure our product meet the highest expectations and requirements.

To provide your feedback and enter our free prize draw to win £250 worth of Wiley books, please complete our online survey

www.wiley.com/go/igaapsurvey

Quality In Everything We Do

Now you know.

wiley.com